PENGUIN HANDBOOKS

THE PENGUIN GUIDE TO COMPACT DISCS YEARBOOK 1997/8

EDWARD GREENFIELD, until his retirement in 1993, was for forty years on the staff of the *Guardian*, succeeding Neville Cardus as Music Critic in 1975. He still contributes regularly to the record column which he founded in 1954. At the end of 1960 he joined the reviewing panel of *Gramophone*, specializing in operatic and orchestral issues. He is a regular broadcaster on music and records for the BBC, not just on Radios 3 and 4 but also on BBC World Service, latterly with his weekly programme, 'The Greenfield Collection'. In 1958 he published a monograph on the operas of Puccini. More recently he has written studies on the recorded work of Joan Sutherland and André Previn. He has been a regular juror on International Record awards and has appeared with such artists as Dame Elisabeth Schwarzkopf, Dame Joan Sutherland and Sir Georg Solti in public interviews. In October 1993 he was given a *Gramophone* Award for Special Achievement and in June 1994 received the OBE for services to music and journalism.

ROBERT LAYTON studied at Oxford with Edmund Rubbra for composition and with Egon Wellesz for the history of music. He spent two years in Sweden at the universities of Uppsala and Stockholm. He joined the BBC Music Division in 1959 and has been responsible for such programmes as *Interpretations on Record*. He has contributed a 'Quarterly Retrospect' to *Gramophone* for a number of years, and he has written books on Berwald and Sibelius and has specialized in Scandinavian music. He has written a monograph on the Dvořák symphonies and concertos for the BBC Music Guides, of which he was General Editor for many years. His translation of the first two volumes of Erik Tawastsjerna's definitive study of Sibelius was awarded the 1984 Finnish State Literary Prize. In 1987 he was awarded the Sibelius Medal and in the following year was made a Knight of the Order of the White Rose of Finland for his services to Finnish music.

IVAN MARCH is a former professional musician. He studied at Trinity College of Music, London, and at the Royal Manchester College. After service in the Central Band of the RAF, he played the horn professionally for the BBC and travelled with the Carl Rosa and D'Oyly Carte opera companies. Now director of the Long Playing Record Library, the largest commercial lending library for classical music on compact discs in the British Isles, he is a well-known lecturer, journalist and personality in the world of recorded music. As a journalist, he contributes to a number of record-reviewing magazines, including *Gramophone*, where his regular monthly 'Collector's Corner' deals particularly with important reissues.

The Penguin Guide to Compact Discs Yearbook 1997/8

Ivan March, Edward Greenfield and Robert Layton

Edited by Ivan March

PENGUIN BOOKS

PENGUIN BOOKS

Published by the Penguin Group
Penguin Books Ltd, 27 Wrights Lane, London W8 5TZ, England
Penguin Books USA Inc., 375 Hudson Street, New York, New York 10014, USA
Penguin Books Australia Ltd, Ringwood, Victoria, Australia
Penguin Books Canada Ltd, 10 Alcorn Avenue, Toronto, Ontario, Canada M4V 3B2
Penguin Books (NZ) Ltd, 182–190 Wairau Road, Auckland 10, New Zealand

Penguin Books Ltd, Registered Offices: Harmondsworth, Middlesex, England

First published 1997
10 9 8 7 6 5 4 3 2 1

Set in 8/9.5pt PostScript Monotype Times New Roman
Typeset, from material supplied, by Rowland Phototypesetting Ltd, Bury St Edmunds, Suffolk
Made and printed in Great Britain by Clays Ltd, St Ives plc

Contents

Preface

The present *Penguin Guide to Compact Discs Yearbook 1997/8* is as much an extension of the 1996 main volume as it is an interim yearbook. For the continuing expansion of recorded repertoire outside the 'standard classics' has now brought about a situation in which, even if we include only the very finest versions of major works available, we no longer have room within a single book adequately to cover the periphery of the repertoire.

The 1,600 pages of our companion volume – the 1996 *Penguin Guide* – represents the maximum number of pages which it is feasible to bind securely in paperback format; but this is still not big enough for our needs! At that time we *just* managed to find room for all our composer entries, but the greater part of the Collections and Recitals had to be carried forward to the present volume – especially the growing number of special editions celebrating the achievement of a single performer or artistic group.

Since then CDs have continued to pour in on us from all sides in such numbers as to make even the initial selection (which recordings should be included) a formidable task. The centenary of Brahms's death and the bicentenary of Schubert's birth have brought their own individual torrents of CDs to be considered; but the past year has also seen a further remarkable cascade of reissues featuring virtually all the major composers. There are, as always, many fascinating new discoveries from less famous names, and it would be easy to build a pretty impressive collection (or to fill out a larger one) just from the cream of the current year's releases which are discussed within these pages.

Ideally, the present volume should be used in conjunction with the 1996 *Guide*. But in order that it can also exist as an independent survey, over 500 key recordings have been carefully selected by the Editor from the 1996 volume (together with their abbreviated reviews) and re-listed within these pages. In this way new readers are provided with a comprehensive series of 'best buys', taking into account both the newer releases and the older, existing repertoire – wherein many of the top choices are still to be found. We have thought it useful to indicate these special recommendations, brought forward from the 1996 edition, by using the symbol **500♪** placed immediately before the evaluation, catalogue number and performance details.

The special rewards of compact discs hardly need restating: ease of access, great presence and clarity of the sound-image, with background noise either obliterated (as in a digital master) or greatly minimized and made unobtrusive by modern technology. To this must be added the extraordinary expertise which is developing in the transfer of older recordings from the mono LP era and of even earlier, shellac, 78-r.p.m. discs. In a growing number of cases the sound-quality of the CD transfers has greatly improved on what the ear would have expected from the originals, even if using the finest reproducing equipment of the time.

Ivan March (Editor)

Introduction

As in previous editions, the object of the current *Penguin Guide to Compact Discs Yearbook* is to give the serious collector a comprehensive survey of the finest recordings of permanent music on CD. As most records are issued almost simultaneously on both sides of the Atlantic and use identical international catalogue numbers, this *Yearbook* should be found to be equally useful in Great Britain and the USA. The internationalization of repertoire and numbers now applies to almost all CDs issued by the major international companies and by many smaller ones too, while most of the smaller European labels are imported in their original formats into both Britain and the USA.

It is sad that the tape cassette has now been all but superseded by the bargain-price CD. Few recordings are available on musicassettes, but honourable exceptions are provided by the analogue bargain Sony 'Essential Classics' series and the resuscitated Decca Eclipse bargain label – in which the repertoire is now exclusively digital. All issues in both series have cassette equivalents and we have included the tape catalogue number in each instance.

The sheer number of records of artistic merit now available causes considerable problems in any assessment of overall and individual excellence. While in the case of a single popular repertoire work it might be ideal for the discussion to be conducted by a single reviewer, it has not always been possible for one person to have access to every version, and division of reviewing responsibility becomes inevitable. Also there are certain works and certain recorded performances for which one or another of our team has a special affinity. Such a personal identification can often carry with it a special perception too. We feel that it is a strength of our basic style to let such conveyed pleasure or admiration for the merits of an individual recording come over directly to the reader, even if this produces a certain ambivalence in the matter of choice between competing recordings. Where disagreement is more positive (and this has rarely happened), readers will find an indication of this difference in the text.

We have considered (and rejected) the use of initials against individual reviews, since this is essentially a team project. The occasions for disagreement generally concern matters of aesthetics, for instance in the manner of recording-balance, where a contrived effect may trouble some ears more than others, or in the matter of style, where the difference between robustness and refinement of approach appeals differently to listening sensibilities, rather than involving a question of artistic integrity. But over the years our views seem to grow closer together rather than to diverge; perhaps we are getting mellower, but we are seldom ready to offer strong disagreement following the enthusiastic reception by one of the team of a controversial recording, if the results are creatively stimulating. Our perceptions of the advantages and disadvantages of performances of early music on original (as against modern) instruments seem fairly evenly balanced; again, any strong feelings are indicated in the text.

EVALUATION

Most recordings issued today by the major companies are of a high technical standard and offer performances of a quality at least as high as is experienced in the concert hall. In adopting a starring system for the evaluation of records, we have decided to make use of from one to three stars. Brackets round one or more of the stars indicate some reservations about its inclusion, and readers are advised to refer to the text. Brackets round all the stars usually indicate a basic qualification: for instance, a mono recording of a performance of artistic interest, where considerable allowances have to be made for the sound-quality, even though the recording may have been digitally remastered.

Our evaluation system may be summarized as follows:

*** An outstanding performance and recording in every way.

** A good performance and recording of today's normal high standard.

* A fair performance, reasonably well or well recorded.

Our evaluation is normally applied to the record as a whole, unless there are two main works or groups of works, and by different composers. In this case, each is dealt with separately in its appropriate place. In the case of a collection of shorter works we feel that there is little point in giving a separate starring to each item, even if their merits are uneven, since the record has to be purchased as a complete programme.

ROSETTES

To a very few records we have awarded a Rosette: ❁.

Unlike our general evaluations, in which we have tried to be consistent, a Rosette is a quite arbitrary compliment by a member of the reviewing team to a recorded performance which, he finds, shows special illumination, magic, or a spiritual quality, or even outstanding production values, that places it in a very special class. Occasionally a Rosette has been awarded for an issue that seems to us to offer extraordinary value for money, but that presupposes that the performance or performances are outstanding too. The choice is essentially a personal one (although often it represents a shared view) and in some cases it is applied to an issue where certain reservations must also be mentioned in the text of the review. The Rosette symbol is placed before the usual evaluation and the record number. It is quite small – we do not mean to imply an 'Academy Award' but a personal token of appreciation for something uniquely valuable. We hope that, once the reader has discovered and perhaps acquired a 'rosetted' CD, its special qualities will soon become apparent.

DIGITAL RECORDINGS

Nearly all new compact discs are recorded digitally, but an increasingly large number of digitally remastered, reissued analogue recordings are now appearing, and we think it important to include a clear indication of the difference:

Dig. This indicates that the master recording was digitally encoded.

BARGAIN AND SUPER-BARGAIN ISSUES

Since the publication of our last main volume we are seeing a continuing expansion of the mid- and bargain-price labels from all the major companies. These are usually standard-repertoire works in excellent analogue recordings, digitally remastered. Often these reissue CDs are generous in playing time, increasing their value to the collector. There are also even cheaper classical CDs at super-bargain price, usually featuring performances by artists whose names are not internationally familiar, notably on the now rightly famous Naxos label. While many of these recordings derive from Eastern Europe, where recording costs have in the past been much lower than in the West, now this enterprising company is spreading its wings to embrace major orchestras and ensembles from Great Britain, Ireland and elsewhere.

The major companies have responded vigorously to this competition, not only by issuing further bargain and super-bargain issues of their own (as on the DG Classikon, Decca Eclipse and Polygram Belart logos) but also by the introduction of Duos, Doubles, Dyads and the RCA Twofers: two CDs packaged back-to-back in a single jewel-case, generously filled with top-line repertoire and offered for the cost of a single premium-price CD. More recently EMI have introduced their even less expensive Seraphim duos, which offer two discs for the cost of a single *mid-priced* CD. Thus the collector has plenty of scope in deciding how much to pay for a recorded performance, with a CD range from just under £5 up to three times that amount.

Our listing of each recording first indicates if it is not in fact in the premium-price category, as follows:

(M) Medium-priced label
(B) Bargain-priced label
(BB) Super-bargain label

See below for price structures for CDs and cassettes in the UK and the USA.

LAYOUT OF TEXT

We have aimed to make our style as simple as possible, even though the catalogue numbers of recordings are no longer as straightforward as they once were. So, immediately after the evaluation and before the catalogue number, the record make is given, often in abbreviated form. In the case of a set of two or more CDs, the number of units involved is given in brackets after the catalogue number. Cassette numbers, if they exist, are still denoted by being given in italic type.

AMERICAN CATALOGUE NUMBERS

The numbers which follow in square brackets are US catalogue numbers, while the abbreviation [id.] indicates that the American number is identical to the European, which is increasingly becoming the case. Even RCA has recently moved over to completely identical numbers, although earlier issues have an alphabetical prefix in the UK which is not used by the *Schwann* catalogue in the USA.

There are certain other small differences to be remembered by American readers. For instance, a CBS/Sony number could have a completely different catalogue number on either side of the Atlantic, or it could use the same digits with different alphabetical prefixes, although this now seldom occurs. Both will be clearly indicated. EMI/Angel use extra digits for their British compact discs; thus the US number CDC 47001 becomes CDC7 47001-2 in Britain (the -2 is the European indication that this is a compact disc). We have taken care to check catalogue information as far as is possible, but as all the editorial work has been done in England there is always the possibility of error; American readers are therefore invited, when ordering records locally, to take the precaution of giving their dealer the fullest information about the music and recordings they want.

The indications (M), (B) and (BB) immediately before the starring of a disc refer only to the British record, as pricing systems are not always identical on both sides of the Atlantic. Where CDs on the smaller labels are imported into the USA, they are often in the premium-price range.

Where no American catalogue number is given, this does not necessarily mean that a record is not available in the USA; the transatlantic issue may not have been made at the time of the publication of this *Guide*. Readers are advised to check the current *Schwann* catalogue and to consult their local record store.

ABBREVIATIONS

To save space we have adopted a number of standard abbreviations in listing orchestras and performing groups (a list is provided below), and the titles of works are often shortened, especially where they are listed several times. Artists' forenames are sometimes omitted if they are not absolutely necessary for identification purposes. Also we have not usually listed the contents of operatic highlights and collections; these can sometimes be found in *Classical Catalogue*, published by RED Publishing Ltd (Paulton House, 8 Shepherdess Walk, London N1 7LD).

We have followed common practice in the use of the original language for titles where it seems sensible. In most cases, English is used for orchestral and instrumental music and the original language for vocal music and opera. There are exceptions, however; for instance, the Johann Strauss discography uses the German language in the interests of consistency.

ORDER OF MUSIC

The order of music under each composer's name broadly follows that adopted by *Classical Catalogue*: orchestral music, including concertos and symphonies; chamber music; solo instrumental music (in some cases with keyboard and organ music separated); vocal and choral music; opera; vocal collections; miscellaneous collections.

Classical Catalogue now usually includes stage works alongside opera; in the main we have not followed this practice, preferring to list, say, ballet music and incidental music (where no vocal items are involved) in the general orchestral group. Within each group our listing follows an alphabetical sequence, and couplings within a single composer's output are *usually* discussed together instead of separately with cross-references. Occasionally and inevitably because of this alphabetical approach, different recordings of a given work can become separated when a record is listed and discussed under the first work of its alphabetical sequence. The editor feels that alphabetical consistency is essential if the reader is to learn to find his or her way about.

CATALOGUE NUMBERS

Enormous care has gone into the checking of CD catalogue numbers and contents to ensure that all details are correct, but the editor and publishers cannot be held responsible for any mistakes that may have crept in despite all our zealous checking. When ordering CDs, readers are urged to provide their record-dealer with full details of the music and performers, as well as the catalogue number.

DELETIONS

Compact discs, especially earlier, full-priced issues not too generous in musical content, are now steadily succumbing to the deletions axe, and more are likely to disappear during the lifetime of this book. Sometimes copies may still be found in specialist shops, and there remains the compensatory fact that most really important and desirable recordings are eventually reissued, usually costing less!

Readers will have noted that EMI's new Special UK Import Service, which began in August 1995, means that the whole EMI international catalogue will be available to UK customers. EMI suggest that dealers should be able to obtain these special import discs quite quickly, and such records will probably cost about £1 more than those in the UK catalogue.

Polygram have now followed suit with their own import service, and we hope that this will provide a more stable supply situation for British collectors, even if, again, the cost is slightly higher.

COVERAGE

As the output of major and minor labels continues to expand, it will obviously be impossible for us to mention *every* CD that is available, within the covers of a single book; this is recognized as a practical limitation if we are to update our survey regularly. We have to be carefully selective in choosing the discs to be included (although on rare occasions a recording has been omitted simply because a review copy was not available); anything which eludes us can always be included next time. However, we do welcome suggestions from readers about such omissions if they seem to be of special interest, and particularly if they are inexpensive. But borderline music on specialist labels that are not readily and reliably obtainable on both sides of the Atlantic cannot be given any kind of priority.

ACKNOWLEDGEMENTS

Our thanks, as ever, are due to Roger Wells, our copy editor, who has worked closely alongside us throughout the preparation of this book and, as a keen CD collector himself, also frequently made valuable creative suggestions.

Kathleen March once again zealously checked the proofs for errors and reminded us when the text proved ambiguous, clumsily repetitive in its descriptive terminology, or just plain contradictory, occasionally removing reviews that had somehow appeared twice!

Barbara Menard and Roy Randle contributed to the titling – never an easy task, and especially complicated in the many boxed anthologies involving a bouquet of different performers. Alan Livesey also cast an eagle eye over the proofs, in particular looking for mistakes in the musical listings; he also helped with both titling and retrieval of earlier material (connected with reissues) in the hectic period immediately before we sent off our final copy. Our team of Penguin proofreaders are also indispensable.

Grateful thanks also go to all those readers who write to us to point out factual errors and to remind us of important recordings which have escaped our notice.

To American Readers

From your many letters and from visiting record stores in the USA, we know that our *Penguin Guide* is read, enjoyed and used as a tool by collectors on both sides of the Atlantic. We also know that some of you feel that our reviews are too frequently orientated towards European and British recordings and performances.

In concentrating on records which have common parlance in both Europe and the USA, we obviously give preference to the output of international companies, and in assessing both performers and performances we are concerned with only one factor: musical excellence. In a 400-year-old musical culture centred in Europe, it is not surprising that a great number of the finest interpreters should have been Europeans, and many of them have enjoyed recording in London, where there are four first-class symphony orchestras and many smaller groups at their disposal, supported by recording producers and engineers of the highest calibre. However, the continued reissue of earlier recordings by major American recording orchestras and artists is slowly redressing the balance

Our performance coverage in the present volume – helped by the huge proportion of reissued older records – certainly reflects the American achievement, past and present; with the current phenomenal improvements in transferring technology we hope that more of the early recordings made by the great names from America's musical past will enjoy the attention of the wider public.

Price Differences in the UK and USA

Compact discs and cassettes in all price ranges are more expensive in Britain and Europe than they are in the USA but, fortunately, in most cases the various premium-price, mid-price, bargain and super-bargain categories are fairly consistent on both sides of the Atlantic. However, where records are imported in either direction, this can affect their domestic cost. For instance, (British) EMI's Classics for Pleasure and Eminence labels are both in the mid-price range in the USA, whereas CfP is a bargain series in the UK. Similarly Naxos, a super-bargain digital label in the UK, is a bargain label in the USA. Dutton Lab. transfers from early recordings, too, are more expensive in the USA.

Of course retail prices are not fixed in either country, and various stores may offer even better deals at times, so our price structure must be taken as a guideline only. One major difference in the USA is that almost all companies make a dollar surcharge (per disc) for mid-priced opera sets (to cover the cost of librettos) and Angel apply this levy to all their boxed sets. The Carlton compact disc series appears to be available only as a special import in the USA. The Vanguard CD label (except for the 8000 Series, which retails at around $15) is upper-mid-price in the USA but lower-mid-price in the UK. In *listing* records we have not often used the major record companies' additional label subdivisions (like Decca/London's Ovation, DG's Galleria, EMI's Studio and Références, Philips's Concert Classics, Sony's Essential Classics, and so on) in order to avoid further confusion, although these designations are sometimes referred to in the text of reviews.

Comparable Prices in the UK and USA

Premium-priced CDs (although they cost less west of the Atlantic) are top-price repertoire the world over. Here are comparative details of the other price ranges:

(M) MID-PRICED SERIES (sets are multiples of these prices)
Includes: Chandos (Collect); Decca/London; DG; EMI/Angel (Studio and Références; Eminence); Erato/Warner (UK), Erato/WEA (USA); DHM; Mercury; Philips; RCA Gold Seal; Saga; Sony; Teldec/Warner (UK), Teldec/WEA (USA); Unicorn (UK only).

UK
CDs: under £10; more usually £8–£9
Cassettes: around £5 – but few are available
USA
CDs: under $12
Cassettes: $5–$6.50 – but very few are available

(B) DUOS – two CDs for the cost of one premium-priced CD, which results in an 'upper' bargain price per disc but compensates by offering exceptionally generous playing time.
Includes: Erato Bonsai Duos; Decca/London and DG Doubles; Philips Duos; EMI Rouge et Noir (CZS) and Hyperion Dyads. (The EMI forte series is available only in Europe; Angel have decided to call their equivalent series double forte and it will feature a mixture of American and European recordings.)
BARGAIN-PRICED SERIES (sets are multiples of these prices)
Includes: CfP (UK only); Decca Eclipse/London; Discover; Harmonia Mundi Musique d'Abord; Philips; Sony VoxBoxes and Turnabout. Also includes EMI Seraphim – two CDs for the cost of one mid-priced CD.

UK
CDs: £5–£7.50
Cassettes: around £4
USA
CDs: under $7
Cassettes: around $4

SPECIAL SETS: Decca, DG, Nimbus and Philips (as indicated); EMI CZS multiple sets are also within the bargain range in the UK but may cost rather more in the USA.

(BB) SUPER-BARGAIN SERIES – CDs
Includes: ASV Quicksilva (UK only); DG Classikon; Naxos; Polygram Belart; RCA Navigator (UK only).

UK

CDs: under £5; some (including Navigator) cost even less

USA

CDs: under $5–$6

(In some cases, equivalent cassettes are available, usually costing slightly less than bargain cassettes.)

An International Mail-order Source for Recordings in the UK

Readers are urged to support a local dealer if he is prepared and able to give a proper service, and to remember that obtaining many CDs involves expertise and perseverance. However, because of the recession many specialist sources have disappeared and, for that reason, if any difficulty is experienced in obtaining the CDs you want, we suggest the following mail-order alternative, which offers competitive discount, operates world-wide and is under the direction of the Editor of *The Penguin Guide to Compact Discs*, whose advice on choice of recordings is always readily available to mail-order customers:

Squires Gate Music Centre (PG Dept)
Rear 13 St Andrew's Road South
St Annes on Sea
Lancashire FY8 1SX
England
Tel.: 01253 782588; Fax: 01253 782985

This organization patiently extends compact disc orders until they finally come to hand. A full guarantee of safe delivery is made on any order undertaken. Please write for further details, or make a trial credit card order, by fax or telephone.

❁THE ROSETTE SERVICE

Squires Gate also offers a try-before-you-buy weekly loan service (within the UK only) so that customers can try out at home rosetted recordings, plus a hand-picked group of recommended key repertoire works, for a small charge, without any obligation to purchase. If a CD is subsequently purchased, it will be discounted and the trial charge waived. Full details sent on request.

Squires Gate Music Centre also offers a simple bi-monthly mailing, listing a hand-picked selection of current new and reissued CDs, chosen by the Editor of the *Penguin Guide*, Ivan March. Regular customers of Squires Gate Music Centre, both domestic and overseas, receive the bulletin as available, and it is sent automatically with their purchases.

An International Mail-order Source for Recordings in the USA

American readers seeking a domestic mail-order source may write to the following address, where a comparably expert and caring supply service is in operation (for both American and imported European labels). Please write for further details (enclosing a stamped, self-addressed envelope if within the USA) or make a trial order by letter, fax or phone to:

Serenade Records (PG Dept)
1800 M St, N.W.
Washington DC 20036
USA
Tel.: (202) 638-5580; Fax: (202) 783-0372
Tel.: (for US orders only) **1-800-237-2930**
e-mail address: NREVAH @ SERENADE-MUSIC.com
Internet We Page address: HTTP://WWW.SERENADE-MUSIC.com

Regular customers of Serenade Records, both domestic and overseas, can also on request receive the mailing, with a hand-picked selection of current new and reissued CDs chosen by the Editor of the *Penguin Guide*, Ivan March.

Abbreviations

AAM	Academy of Ancient Music	LAPO	Los Angeles Philharmonic Orchestra
Ac.	Academy, Academic	LCO	London Chamber Orchestra
Amb. S.	Ambrosian Singers	LMP	London Mozart Players
Ang.	Angel	LOP	Lamoureux Orchestra of Paris
Ara.	Arabesque	LPO	London Philharmonic Orchestra
arr.	arranged, arrangement	LSO	London Symphony Orchestra
ASMF	Academy of St Martin-in-the-Fields	(M)	mid-price CD
(B)	bargain-price CD	Mer.	Meridian
(BB)	super-bargain-price CD	Met.	Metropolitan
Bar.	Baroque	MoC	Ministry of Culture
Bav.	Bavarian	movt	movement
BBC	British Broadcasting Corporation	N.	North, Northern
		nar.	narrated
BPO	Berlin Philharmonic Orchestra	Nat.	National
Cal.	Calliope	NY	New York
Cap.	Caprice	O	Orchestra, Orchestre
CBSO	City of Birmingham Symphony Orchestra	OAE	Orchestra of the Age of Enlightenment
CfP	Classics for Pleasure	O-L	Oiseau-Lyre
Ch.	Choir; Chorale; Chorus	Op.	Opera (in performance listings); opus (in music titles)
CO	Chamber Orchestra		
COE	Chamber Orchestra of Europe	orch.	orchestrated
Col. Mus. Ant.	Musica Antiqua, Cologne	ORR	Orchestre Révolutionnaire et Romantique
Coll.	Collegium		
Coll. Aur.	Collegium Aureum	ORTF	L'Orchestre de la radio et télévision française
Coll. Mus.	Collegium Musicum		
Concg. O	Royal Concertgebouw Orchestra of Amsterdam	Ph.	Philips
		Phd.	Philadelphia
cond.	conductor, conducted	Philh.	Philharmonia
Cons.	Consort	PO	Philharmonic Orchestra
DG	Deutsche Grammophon	Qt	Quartet
DHM	Deutsche Harmonia Mundi	R.	Radio
Dig.	digital recording	RLPO	Royal Liverpool Philharmonic Orchestra
E.	England, English		
ECCO	European Community Chamber Orchestra	ROHCG	Royal Opera House, Covent Garden
ECO	English Chamber Orchestra	RPO	Royal Philharmonic Orchestra
ENO	English National Opera Company	RSNO	Royal Scottish National Orchestra
Ens.	Ensemble	RSO	Radio Symphony Orchestra
ESO	English Symphony Orchestra	RTE	Radio Television Eireann
Fr.	French	S.	South
GO	Gewandhaus Orchestra	SCO	Scottish Chamber Orchestra
HM	Harmonia Mundi France	Sinf.	Sinfonietta
Hung.	Hungaroton	SO	Symphony Orchestra
[id.]	same record number for US and European versions	Soc.	Society
		Sol. Ven.	I Solisti Veneti
L.	London	SRO	Suisse Romande Orchestra

Sup.	Supraphon	VPO	Vienna Philharmonic Orchestra
trans.	transcription, transcribed	VSO	Vienna Symphony Orchestra
V.	Vienna	W.	West
Van.	Vanguard	WNO	Welsh National Opera Company
VCM	Vienna Concentus Musicus		

500♪ 'Best Buy'

Adam, Adolphe (1803–56)

Giselle (older European score; complete).
(M) **(*) Mercury 434 365-2 (2) [id.]. LSO, Fistoulari – OFFENBACH: *Gaîté parisienne;* Johann STRAUSS: *Graduation ball.* *

Giselle (ballet): abridged version.
500♪ (M) *** Sony Dig. SMK 42450 [id.]. LSO, Michael Tilson Thomas.

Mercury's complete recording of *Giselle*, like Mogrelia's on Naxos, draws on the score which was in general use before the war and which incorporates music that is not by Adam at all. Fair enough, but this means that with Fistoulari there are some eighteen minutes of the score to take over to a second CD. Fistoulari was a great ballet conductor and the LSO play superbly for him: there is drama in plenty, while in the gentle lyrical music his magical touch consistently beguiles the ear. Moreover, in its CD format the early stereo sounds remarkably modern, and the over-resonant bass response which disfigured the LPs has been tamed, so that the sound-picture is resonantly full without an exaggerated imbalance. The snag is that the quite logical fill-ups of the Offenbach/Rosenthal *Gaîté parisienne* and the Offenbach/Dorati *Graduation ball* were among Mercury's least successful Minneapolis recordings, dry and lustreless, greatly detracting from the appeal of this reissue. We hope that Mercury will decide to recouple *Giselle*. Michael Tilson Thomas's generous (77-minute) single-CD selection with the LSO on Sony, which offers all the important music and which was recorded in the Henry Wood Hall, is a first choice, now that it is offered at mid-price, for the LSO playing is beautifully polished.

Adams, John (born 1947)

Harmonium.
*** Telarc Dig. CD 80363 [id.]. Atlanta Ch. & SO, Robert Shaw – RACHMANINOV: *The Bells.* ***

Harmonium is a setting of three poems. John Donne's curiously oblique 'Negative love' opens the piece, with the orchestra lapping evocatively round the chorus. The other two poems are by Emily Dickinson. Robert Shaw's performance is very impressive and the Telarc recording is suitably atmospheric and spectacular in its spaciousness and amplitude in the closing *Wild nights*. Coupled with Rachmaninov, this easily displaces the earlier, San Francisco version under Edo de Waart (ECM 821 465-2) which had no coupling at all.

Alain, Jehan (1911–40)

Prière pour nous autres charnels.
*** Chandos Dig. CHAN 9504 [id.]. Martyn Hill, Neal Davies, BBC PO, Yan Pascal Tortelier – DUTILLEUX: *Violin concerto etc.* ***

Jehan Alain was a highly original composer whose life was cut short by the Second World War; he was killed during the defence of Saumur. He composed this short but beautiful setting of a prayer by Péguy for two soloists and organ only months before his death, and Dutilleux's transcription of it serves to ensure its wider dissemination. It is a moving piece, modal yet rich in its musical language, and it makes an admirable makeweight to the Dutilleux works.

Albéniz, Isaac (1860–1909)

GUITAR MUSIC

Cantos de España: Córdoba, Op. 232/4; Mallorca (Barcarola), Op. 202. Suite española: Cataluña; Granada; Sevilla; Cádiz, Op.47/1–4.
500♪ ❁ (BB) *** RCA Navigator Dig. 74321 17903-2. Julian Bream (guitar) – GRANADOS: *Collection;* RODRIGO: *3 Piezas españolas.* *** ❁

Julian Bream is in superb form in this splendid recital. The playing itself has wonderfully communicative rhythmic feeling, great subtlety of colour, and its spontaneity increases the impression that one is experiencing a 'live' recital. This is perhaps the finest single recital of Spanish guitar music in the catalogue and, at its new price, a bargain of bargains.

Iberia; Navarra; Suite española.
500♪ ✽ *** Decca Dig. 417 887-2 [id.]. Alicia de Larrocha.

Alicia de Larrocha brings an altogether beguiling charm and character to these rewarding miniature tone-poems and makes light of their sometimes fiendish technical difficulties. The recording is among the most successful of piano sounds Decca has achieved.

Albinoni, Tommaso (1671–1750)

Double oboe and string concertos, Volume 1: (i) *Double oboe concertos: Op. 7/2 & 5; Op. 9/3 & 6. String concertos: Op. 7/1 & 4; Op. 9/1 & 4; Sinfonia for strings in G min.*
**(*) Chandos Dig. CHAN 0602 [id.]. Coll. Mus. 90, Simon Standage; (i) with Anthony Robson, Catherine Latham.

Chandos are beginning a new series of Albinoni concertos, interweaving works for oboes and strings and mixing up Op. 7 and Op. 9. Except for those who are tidy-minded and prefer their concertos in sets (as they were published), this seems a good way of offering greater variety. Anthony Robson and Catherine Latham are stylish soloists, and Collegium Musicum 90 (as can be guessed from the name of their director) is a period-instrument group, but one which here plays in good and lively style without excesses of plangent timbre or bulging phrases, so important in Albinoni with his smooth lines and sunny invention. However, the warmth which, for instance, I Musici bring to their performances of this repertoire is less obvious here. The players clearly all respond to the music (and the timbre of the baroque oboes is particularly ripe), but there is a slight air of reserve here, although authenticists will probably expect this. The recording, however, cannot be faulted. We continue to recommend Holliger and Bourgue, with I Musici, in their complete sets of Op. 7 (Ph. 432 115-2), and Op. 9 (Ph. 426 080-2 and 434 157-2).

Alfvén, Hugo (1872–1960)

(i) *En Bygdesaga* (suite), *Op. 53;* (ii) *Synnöve Solbakken* (suite), *Op. 50.*
** Sterling CDS 1012-2 [id.]. (i) Helsingborg SO, Hans-Peter Frank; (ii) Norrköping SO, Harry Damgaard.

This disc collects the suites Alfvén made from his two film-scores: *Synnöve Solbakken*, a Swedish-Norwegian collaboration from 1934 based on Bjørnson's novel, and making extensive use of Norwegian folk music, and *Mans Kvinna*, an adaptation from 1945 by Vilhelm Moberg of his novel of that name. If neither score finds Alfvén at his most inspired, both give much pleasure, particularly in these committed and dedicated performances. The recordings are both analogue, coming from 1973 and 1982, and are beautifully balanced, spacious and natural. It is, however, unrealistically priced, particularly in view of the fact that the music runs to no more than 45 minutes.

Alwyn, William (1905–85)

(i) *Autumn legend* (for cor anglais and string orchestra); (ii) *Lyra Angelica* (concerto for harp and string orchestra); (iii) *Pastoral fantasia* (for viola and string orchestra); *Tragic interlude.*
500♪ *** Chandos Dig. CHAN 9065 [id.]. (i) Nicholas Daniel; (ii) Rachel Masters; (iii) Stephen Tees; City of L. Sinfonia, Richard Hickox.

The highlight of the disc is the *Lyra Angelica*, a radiantly beautiful, extended piece (just over half an hour in length), inspired by the metaphysical poet, Giles Fletcher's, '*Christ's victorie and triumph*'. The performance here is very moving and the recording has great richness of string-tone, and Rachel Masters's contribution is distinguished. This is the record to start with for those beginning to explore the music of this highly rewarding composer.

Anderson, Leroy (1908–75)

(i) *Carol suite:* excerpts. *A Christmas festival. Goldilocks: Pirate dance.* (ii) *Irish suite. Bugler's holiday; Forgotten dreams; Penny-whistle song; Sandpaper ballet; Trumpeter's lullaby.*
(M) *** Mercury 434 376-2 [id.]. (i) London Pops O; (ii) Eastman-Rochester Pops O, Frederick Fennell – COATES: *Four ways; London suites.* **(*)

Here Mercury complete their reissues of the vintage Fennell recordings of Leroy Anderson, including the *Irish suite*. Commissioned by the Boston Eire Society in 1947, this is one of Anderson's more ambitious enterprises. Some very familiar Irish tunes are used and the composer's orchestral treatment impresses his personality firmly on the music without spoiling the freshness of the melodic ideas. '*The wearing of the green*' with its alternating pizzicato and brass sonorities is very effective, but the highlight is a clever arrangement of *The Minstrel boy* in the form of a haunting little funeral march, advancing and retreating. The half-dozen orchestral lollipops include several favourites, notably *Bugler's holiday* and *Forgotten dreams*. Fennell also includes some arrangements of notable Christmas carols, and the vintage, rather dry and studio-ish recording suits the bright precision of the playing. (The companion collection is still available on Mercury 432 013-2 – see our main volume.)

Antheil, George (1900–1959)

Symphony No. 4, '1942'.

(*) Everest EVC 9039 [id.]. LSO, Sir Eugene Goossens – COPLAND: *Statements for orchestra.* *

The American composer, George Antheil was born in Trenton, New Jersey, of Polish and German ancestry. There are influences of his East European background in this symphony, which is probably his best. It was composed at the beginning of the First World War. It is immediately approachable music, the four movements linked by the introductory fanfare-like idea with which the brass introduce the first movement. This is based on a little Shostakovichian march theme. The second and third movements reflect the composer's alarmed response to European events; the Scherzo is ironic, the finale more optimistic with a further brassy flavour of Shostakovich. The performance, from a famous advocate of contemporary music, could not be more convincing, and the Everest stereo (from 1959) entirely belies its age. This music is not deep but it readily communicates, and one's only real complaint is that this excellently remastered reissue should have been offered less expensively – the disc plays for only 49 minutes.

Arensky, Anton (1861–1906)

Violin concerto in A min., Op. 54.

*** Chandos Dig. CHAN 9528 [id.]. Alexander Trostiansky, I Musici de Montréal, Yuli Turovsky – GLAZUNOV: *Concerto ballata* etc. ***

Overshadowed by his mentor, Tchaikovsky, and his pupil, Rachmaninov – understandably so, for no one would claim that he is their peer – Arensky is still a composer to reckon with, and his neglect is our loss. The *Violin concerto in A minor* is a delightful piece that deserves to be every bit as popular as, say, the Glazunov. It has generosity of spirit and is brimming over with lyrical invention and memorable ideas. The concerto is beautifully played by Alexander Trostiansky, now in his early- to mid-twenties. He is not a larger-than-life showman who plays like a machine but a talented young artist from Novosibirsk, and he has refinement, musicianship and impeccable taste. He is perhaps balanced rather too reticently, but the case for this concerto, which is not generously represented in the present catalogue, is made very persuasively by orchestra and engineers alike.

Variations on a theme of Tchaikovsky, Op. 35a.

(B) *** EMI forte CZS5 69361 (2). LSO, Barbirolli – RIMSKY-KORSAKOV: *Scheherazade* **; GLAZUNOV: *The Seasons; Concert waltzes.* ***

Rimsky-Korsakov, whose pupil he was, may have been unduly harsh in dismissing Arensky, whose talent he had seen dissipated in drink and gambling. These delightful variations, arguably his best-known work, originally formed the slow movement of the *Second String quartet in A minor*, composed in 1894, a year after Tchaikovsky's death, and subsequently arranged for full strings. The theme itself comes from the *Sixteen Songs for children*, Op. 54 (1883), and is entitled 'When Jesus Christ was but a child'. (Tchaikovksy himself made an orchestral transcription of it in 1884.) Sir John Barbirolli's recording, made in the Kingsway Hall in 1965 and first published in harness with the Tchaikovsky *Serenade for strings*, is warm and spacious. There is affection too, of course, and a splendid flexibility of phrasing and dynamic. Thus the slow variation, which obviously is modelled on the famous *Andante cantabile* from Tchaikovsky's *D major String quartet*, is wonderfully gentle. The playing of the LSO under this endearing conductor is suitably affectionate. It comes as part of a quite attractive two-CD Russian music package, let down a little by Svetlanov's rather idiosyncratic *Scheherazade*.

CHAMBER MUSIC

Piano trio in D min., Op. 32.
**(*) MDG Dig MDGL 3247 [id.]. Trio Parnassus – SMETANA: *Piano trio in G min.* **(*)

An above-average account of this delightful *Trio* comes from the Parnassus Trio, paired with the Smetana. It is very well recorded, albeit rather forwardly; although these players incline to a very romantic approach and are not afraid of portamenti – authentic and in period, surely – they can hold their own with all but the most distinguished rivals. This is surely the way Arensky might have expected the work to be performed in his own time.

Arnell, Richard (born 1917)

Punch and the child (ballet), *Op. 49.*
(B) (***) Sony mono SBK 62748; *SBT 62748* [id.]. RPO, Beecham – BERNERS: *Triumph of Neptune;* DELIUS: *Paris.* (***)

Richard Arnell enjoyed something of a vogue immediately after the war. His *Fourth Symphony* scored some success at the Cheltenham Festival in the late 1940s and his imaginative and inventive ballet, *Punch and the child*, was mounted by the New York City Ballet. Yet his present representation in the catalogue is meagre in the extreme and by no means commensurate with his gifts. Sir Thomas Beecham recorded the *Punch and the child suite* on five 78-r.p.m. sides in 1950. Its musical inspiration is as fresh, individual and memorable as its neglect is unaccountable. We have relished this score over the years, and its attractions remain as strong as ever in this well-transferred set. The sound is amazingly good for 1950 – but then it was pretty much state-of-the-art at that time – and this is very attractive indeed at bargain price.

Arnold, Malcolm (born 1921)

(i) *Clarinet concerto No. 1, Op. 20;* (ii) *Flute concertos Nos. 1, Op. 45; 2, Op. 111;* (iii) *Horn concerto No. 2, Op. 58;* (iv) *Oboe concerto, Op. 39;* (v) *Trumpet concerto, Op. 125.*
(M) *** EMI Eminence Dig./Analogue CD-EMX 2271. (i) Hilton; (ii) Adeney; (iii) Civil; (iv) Hunt; (v) Wallace; Bournemouth Sinf.; (i; iii–v) Del Mar; (ii) Thomas.

This is a compilation of superb concerto performances, made towards the end of the LP era, with the two *Flute concertos* added to the original LP package, here superbly played by the dedicatee. All of them demonstrate Arnold's mastery in writing both for woodwind and for brass instruments, each crisply conceived within a compact frame, with each bringing out Arnold's gifts of surprise and ready lyricism.

Having been a trumpeter himself, he writes with uncommon skill for the instrument, and the same brilliance characterizes John Wallace's dazzling playing. Like so much of his music, it has a broad appeal but touches a richer vein of imagination in the slow movement. The *Oboe concerto*, written for Leon Goossens, is played with quite superb panache and virtuosity by Gordon Hunt, who is surely second to none among the later generation of players; Janet Hilton in the *First Clarinet concerto* and Alan Civil in the *Second Horn concerto* are hardly less brilliant. It is appropriate to have included here the *First Flute concerto* in a winningly light-hearted performance by its dedicatee, Richard Adeney, alongside the second, written two decades later. This is a deeper, subtler and more melancholy work, which Adeney plays with complete understanding, especially the wistfully memorable *Andante grazioso*. All this music is well crafted and readily tuneful in Arnold's most spontaneous manner, and the composer's admirers will find much to delight them in these performances, which are very well recorded. All but the *Flute concertos* are digital and were recorded in the composer's presence in 1984; the two concertos for flute are analogue and date from five years earlier.

(i) *Flute concertos Nos. 1–2;* (ii) *Serenade for small orchestra;* (iii) *5 Pieces for violin and piano;* (iv) *Children's suite.*
*** Koch Dig. 3-7607-2 [id.]. (i) Alexa Still, New Zealand CO, Nicholas Braithwaite; (ii) San Diego CO, Donald Barra; (iii) St Clair Trio (members); (iv) Benjamin Frith.

Koch seem to be offering collectors a choice in their Malcolm Arnold series, for the delightful performance of the *Serenade*, (both witty and ironic) by Donald Barra and the San Diego Chamber Orchestra is also available on another disc (Koch 3-7134-2), where it is accompanied by the pair of *Sinfoniettas* and the *Double violin concerto*. As the account of the latter isn't entirely successful, the present collection must be the preferable recommendation, since the *Serenade* is not otherwise available on CD. Alexa Still gives memorable accounts of the two *Flute concertos*, full of dazzling virtuosity, while the central soliloquy of

No. 1 is utterly haunting. If she doesn't turn the corner of the magical blues theme of the finale of the *Second* quite as seductively as its dedicatee, Richard Adeney, this is still a highly recommendable alternative. The five diverse vignettes for violin and piano, with their remarkably wide range of styles, are also available in Koch's instrumental anthology (see below), while Benjamin Frith's sympathetic account of the *Children's suite* comes from his comprehensive coverage of the piano repertoire (Koch 3-7162-2), which is no less distinguished and is discussed in our main volume. But for a sampler of this ever-stimulating composer, writing with equal skill in four different formats, the present collection is hard to beat.

(i; ii) *Concerto for 2 pianos, three hands;* (iii; iv) *Horn concerto No. 2, Op. 58;* (v; vi) *Viola concerto, Op. 108;* (vii; viii) *Double violin concerto, Op. 77;* (viii) *4 Cornish dances, Op. 91;* (ii) *Fair field overture, Op. 110; Peterloo overture;* (iv) *Sinfonietta, Op. 1;* (ix) *Fantasy for solo harp, Op. 117;* (x) *5 Blake songs, Op. 66;* (xi; iv) *Song of Simeon* (Nativity masque), *Op. 69*.
(B) *** BBC Radio Classics 15656 91817 (2). (i) Cyril Smith, Phyllis Sellick; (ii) BBC SO; (iii) Alan Civil; (iv) ECO; (v) Roger Best; (vi) N. Sinfonia; (vii) Alan Loveday & Frances Mason; (viii) LPO; (ix) Osian Ellis; (x) Pamela Bowden, BBC N. O; (xi) Ann Dowdall, Christopher Keyte, Forbes Robinson, Jean Allister, Ursula Connors, Ian Partridge, Simon Hutton, Amb. S.; all cond. composer.

There could hardly be a more winning collection of Arnold works to celebrate his 75th birthday, exuberantly performed under the composer's baton. These are radio recordings drawn from different sources, all well engineered, and with the Prom recordings – of the *Peterloo overture*, the *Two-piano concerto (three hands)*, the *Double violin concerto* and the *Cornish dances* – vividly capturing the flavour of special occasions at the Royal Albert Hall. *Peterloo* opens the programme, even more warmly communicative than the composer's studio recording with the CBSO. Like the *Fair field overture*, which starts the second disc, it is an attractively old-fashioned example of illustrative programme music. The *Cornish dances* too have a joyful wildness in this Prom version which sets them apart from studio performances.

The *Three-handed Piano concerto*, which Arnold wrote for Cyril Smith and Phyllis Sellick after Smith tragically lost the use of his left arm, follows *Peterloo* on the first disc, with a performance not just vigorous but most moving, with an unforgettable finale. The slow movement brings a masterly example of Arnold's unique gift for writing a hauntingly distinctive tune. The slow movements of the other three concertos in the collection similarly reveal the composer's genius as a tunesmith, notably that of the *Double violin concerto*, originally written for Yehudi Menuhin and Alberto Lysy, and here beautifully played by Alan Loveday and Frances Mason, an even warmer performance than we remember on disc before.

In a generous and well-planned layout, each of the two discs has an overture, two concertos, a popular orchestral piece (the *Sinfonietta No. 1* on the second disc balancing the *Cornish dances* on the first) and, most importantly, rare vocal works which have been inexplicably neglected. Both of them are masterpieces in their different ways. The exuberant and colourful nativity masque, *A Song for Simeon*, on the first disc was originally written in 1960 for a fund-raising event. In its original form, as recorded here in 1967, it extravagantly requires extra brass and percussion, as well as a choir, half a dozen singing soloists and a boy taking a speaking role. It is a piece, half an hour long, full of colourful ideas, with many good tunes, such as a galumphing song in the style of music-hall for the three shepherds. It all leads up to a setting of the *Nunc dimittis*, Simeon's song, most movingly sung by Ian Partridge. Just why the *Five Blake songs* for mezzo and strings have also been so neglected is even more incomprehensible, for these are engagingly direct and lyrical settings of early, relatively little-known poems which, in their simplicity, are most moving and fit Pamela Bowden's warm mezzo perfectly, well caught in the mono recording, the only one in the collection. The sole item not conducted by Arnold himself is the *Harp fantasy* in five brief and brilliant movements, written for Osian Ellis and here recorded from the first broadcast performance in 1977. Besides Piers Burton-Page's note and a range of delightful portraits (including Hoffnung's witty caricature on the front), the booklet has a page of Arnold anecdotes, delightfully told with telegraphic brevity by Stan Hibbert. Not to be missed!

4 Cornish dances, Op. 91; 8 English dances, Set 1, Op. 27; Set 2, Op. 33; 4 Irish dances, Op. 126; 4 Scottish dances, Op. 59; 4 Welsh dances, Op. 138.
(B) *** Naxos Dig. 8.553526 [id.]. Queensland SO, Andrew Penny.

The advantage this Naxos disc has over its competitors – to say nothing of its price – is the inclusion of the four *Welsh dances*, the last to be written and closer in mood to the *Cornish* and *Irish dances* than to the cheerful ebullience of the masterly *English dances* of 1950–51. They remain perennial favourites, and Andrew Penny and the Queensland Orchestra present them with their colours gleaming. The Scottish set goes particularly well too, notably the third dance with its glorious lyrical evocation of the Scottish lakes and mountains, while the closing Highland fling, with echoes of *Tam o'Shanter* on an inebriated Glaswegian Saturday night, are wittily and lustily caught. Then Arnold's optimism became more sporadic and he includes a sadly reflective picture of the deserted copper mines in his Cornish set, while the two central *Irish dances* are curiously disconsolate, although there is an Irish jig to liven things up. But the *Welsh dances* continue that element of Celtic melancholy which Penny captures admirably. These performances have the composer's *imprimatur* (he was present at the recording sessions) and can be cordially recommended. Only Arnold's own Lyrita recordings surpass them, and then only marginally. The Naxos sound might be thought a shade over-resonant, but it does not lack brilliance.

(i) *8 English dances, sets 1–2, Opp. 27 & 33; Homage to the Queen* (ballet), *Op. 42; 4 Scottish dances, Op. 59*. (ii) *The Sound Barrier* (rhapsody), *Op. 38*.
(M) (***) EMI mono/stereo CDM5 66120-2. (i) Philh. O, Robert Irving; (ii) RPO, composer.

It was a pity to sandwich *Homage to the Queen* (written for the Coronation celebrations) in between the *English* and *Scottish dances*, for their unceasing melodic fecundity serves only to emphasize the relative lack of similarly memorable ideas in the stage work. Dame Ninette de Valois is reported as describing Arnold as 'the finest ballet composer since Tchaikovsky' and what she obviously meant was that he provided a series of very danceable musical vignettes, vividly scored. For Arnold, like Tchaikovsky, worked closely to the detailed demands of his choreographer Frederick Ashton, to create appropriate music for the four sections, *Earth*, *Water*, *Fire* and *Air*.

The ballet opens with a regal, fanfare-style march after the style of Walton and Bliss, but without a *nobilmente* tune. Then the evocative opening of *Earth*, with its bird-calls, develops a string line which becomes lyrically skittish (the effect rather like Hérold's *La Fille mal gardée*). But the most translucent scoring comes in *Water*, with its delicate *Pas de trois*, producing a fragile Waltz, and, for the first 'Man's variation', an aural impression of swimming through swirling waters. The *Fire* section is pungently, exuberantly aggressive, but *Air* brings aural relief and the writing here often recalls Arnold's flight simulation for *The Sound Barrier* (see below). But it is not until the final *Pas de deux* that the listener's attention is caught and held by a really striking melodic flow.

Both the ballet and the *Dances* are very well played indeed by the Philharmonia under Robert Irving, but, in spite of the Kingsway Hall ambience, one sadly misses the spaciousness and warmth of stereo. In the Scottish group (which are stereo), Irving gives a particularly beautiful account of the lovely lyrical third number.

The programme opens with Arnold himself conducting the orchestral rhapsody he fashioned out of his score for the David Lean film, *The Sound Barrier*, and anyone who remembers the visual imagery will find it is readily recalled by the music.

Symphonies Nos. (i) *2, Op. 40;* (ii) *5, Op. 74;* (i) *Peterloo overture, Op. 97*.
(M) *** EMI CDM5 66324-2 [id.]. (i) Bournemouth SO, Groves; (ii) CBSO, composer.

The recoupling of two of Arnold's most impressive symphonies can be warmly welcomed. Both recordings date from the 1970s. The composer secures an outstanding response from the Birmingham orchestra; in many ways his performance has not been surpassed, particularly in the expressive power of the slow movement. Groves, too, in Bournemouth is equally dedicated, and this is one of his finest recordings. The CD transfer is outstandingly successful, and the overture makes a highly effective encore. Splendid value at mid-price.

Symphonies Nos. 3, Op. 63; 4, Op. 71.
*** Conifer Dig. 75605 51258-2 [id.]. RLPO, Vernon Handley.

As the Royal Liverpool Philharmonic Society commissioned the *Third Symphony* and the Liverpool orchestra gave its première, it is not surprising that they should play it with such sympathy, with most engagingly sensitive woodwind contributions to the opening movement and the strings at their most eloquent in the Mahlerian *Lento*. Handley's performances of both works are second to none – every bit the equal of the competing Chandos pairing from Hickox and the LSO. The sinuously seductive treatment of the swinging Arnoldian tune in the first movement of the *Fourth* is very winning indeed and the rumbustious finale of this work, with its grotesque pastiche of a Sousa march, has irresistible vigour and impulse. The Conifer recording is in the demonstration class, spacious and vivid, with a most convincing hall ambience.

(i) *Symphony No. 9;* (i; ii) *Concertino for oboe and strings* (orch. Steptoe); (ii) *Fantasia for oboe solo, Op. 90*.
*** Conifer Classics Dig. 75605 51273-2. (i) Bournemouth SO, Handley; (ii) Nicholas Daniel.

Hard on the heels of the first recording of this culminating work in Sir Malcolm Arnold's cycle of symphonies by the National Symphony Orchestra of Ireland under Andrew Penny comes this rival Handley version, providing a different slant, equally valid, on what, for all its simplicity of texture, is an enigmatic work. With a unique coupling of two oboe pieces, superbly played by Nicholas Daniel, it makes a formidable alternative, even though one has to remember that the earlier, Naxos issue (8.553540) comes at budget price. The contrast of recording quality, with the Conifer issue presenting the orchestra much closer, with textures made warmer and beefier, matches the broad contrast of interpretation. Where the slight distancing of sound on the Naxos issue keeps the music at one remove, the weight of sound which Handley draws from the Bournemouth Symphony in his fuller-bodied recording goes with a rather more expressive style, so that unison string melodies, as in the Trio of the third-movement Scherzo or throughout the long, slow finale, sound more obviously Mahlerian. The result is that the Handley version is less desolate in its presentation of that extended slow finale, almost all of it in two parts only, with the two main contrasting themes hypnotically repeated. There is much to be said for Penny's balder, chillier treatment in music which, as the composer himself has explained, reflects a period when he had 'been through hell'. However thin the argument may look on the page, this is a masterly conclusion to Arnold's unique, keenly original symphony cycle.

The fill-up is most welcome. The *Oboe concertino*, not to be confused with Arnold's *Oboe concerto*, has been arranged by Roger Steptoe from the charming *Oboe sonatina*, written for Leon Goossens in 1951, with a flowingly lyrical first movement followed by a deeply melancholy slow movement and a jig finale. The *Fantasy* for oboe solo, written for a wind competition, makes one marvel at a solo oboe offering such variety over such a brief span.

CHAMBER MUSIC

Brass quintet.
*** Collins Dig. 1489-2 [id.]. Center City Brass Quintet (with Concert: *Brass quintets* ***).

Arnold's *Brass quintet* dates from the early, exuberant period in his career, not too long after his huge public success with the film score for *The Bridge on the River Kwai*. The highly animated opening theme, with its contrasting chorale, reminds one superficially of Britten's fugue in his Purcell variations and the sombre central 'Chaconne' is darkly affecting. Then the irreverent finale brings a characteristic fizzing bouquet of mixed influences, including jazzy syncopations, and of course there is a quirky Arnoldian tune to match. The performance from a virtuoso group of American orchestral principals is superlative – they are especially happy with the jazzy inflexions – and the recording is in the demonstration bracket. The rest of the concert, too, proves highly stimulating.

Hobson's Choice (suite from the film score, arr. for piano trio by Leslie Hogan); *Fantasy for solo cello, Op. 130; Piano trio, Op. 54; 5 Pieces for violin and piano, Op. 130; Homage to the Queen* (ballet suite, arr. for piano by the composer).
*** Koch Dig. 3-7266-2 [id.]. St Clair Trio.

The highlight here must be Leslie Hogan's apt arrangement for piano trio of some of the more delightful ideas from Arnold's score for David Lean's Lancashire movie, *Hobson's Choice*. Charles Laughton is pictured on the front of the booklet on his way to the local, but one could equally imagine him repairing to the Grand Hotel to sort things out with his daughter, Maggie, while the Palm Court Trio is playing this engaging music in the background. The quality of the ensemble of the St Clair Trio is far more sophisticated than such an image would imply, and they clearly relish the winning charm of Arnold's light-hearted invention. The *Five Pieces for violin and piano* were written in 1984 for Yehudi Menuhin to use as encores, and they are by no means just lightweight trivia. Each has its own atmosphere, although the closing *Moto perpetuo* is meant to dazzle jazzily, as it does here. The terse *Piano trio* (an early work from 1954) is austere by Arnoldian standards, although with its overlapping, imitative part-writing it is essentially lyrical, and its arguments are not difficult to follow. The central *Andante* is very touching and the toccata-like finale brilliant but surprisingly unoptimistic for its period. Written for Julian Lloyd Webber, the *Cello fantasy* (1987) is a late work, improvisational in feeling, laid out in seven succinct movements, beginning and ending with a searching *Andantino* and yet also including two further melancholy *Lento* sections which invite – and here receive – a darkly tender response from the soloist. The other movements are lighter in feeling, and the engaging fifth-movement *Allegretto* turns the cello momentarily into a guitar. The piano suite arranged from the ballet, *Homage to the Queen*, is played with charm and a free choreographic feeling. The music is not out of Arnold's top drawer, but both the *Pas de deux* and (especially) the *Water waltz* are seductive in the hands of Pauline Martin. The recording is excellent throughout.

Auber, Daniel (1782–1871)

Overtures: The Bronze horse; Fra Diavolo; Masaniello.
500♪ ❁ (M) *** Mercury 434 309-2 [id.]. Detroit SO, Paray – SUPPE: *Overtures.* ***

Dazzling performances, full of verve and style, which will surely never be surpassed. The present recordings, made in the suitably resonant acoustic of Detroit's Old Orchestra Hall, shows Mercury engineering (1959 vintage) at its very finest.

Bach, Carl Philipp Emanuel (1714–88)

see also in Vocal Recitals, below, under 'Codex'

Cello concerto in A, Wq.172.
(M) *** Virgin/EMI Ultraviolet Dig. CUV5 61320-2. Caroline Dale, Scottish Ens., Rees – J. S. BACH: *Violin concertos.* ***

Caroline Dale at a spacious *Largo* plays the slow movement of the splendid *A major Cello concerto* with full expressiveness. With vigorous outer movements, this is a valuable work to have as makeweight for three of J. S. B.'s most popular violin concertos.

Complete harpsichord concertos

Harpsichord concertos Nos. 1 in A min.; 2 in E flat; 3 in G, Wq.1–3 (H.403–5).
**(*) BIS Dig. CD 707 [id.]. Miklós Spányi (harpsichord), Concerto Armonico, Péter Szüts.

This is the first CD of an ongoing project in which Miklós Spányi is planning to record all 52 keyboard concertos which Carl Philipp Emanuel wrote between 1733 and 1788, most of which date from the early years of his musical life at the court of Frederick the Great in Berlin. From the very beginning his style moves away from the baroque concerto principles of Vivaldi and Handel to a more clearly defined and always engaging dialogue between the soloist and ensemble, making a direct path to the piano concertos of Mozart.

The first concerto was written in Leipzig in 1733, the second in 1734; the third followed in 1737 (although all three were revised a decade later in Berlin). The early works are simply scored for strings and, although not without surprises, are free from the idiosyncrasies which the composer subsequently developed; instead they concentrate on display – the soloist has frequent bravura running passages, if sometimes a bit rambling – and charm. Both these qualities they possess; lyrical lines often faintly pre-echo early Mozart, while allegros radiate energy. This is immediately striking in the bustling finale of the *A minor Concerto*, which is otherwise fairly conventionally *galant*, though with an appealing central *Andante* in which the responses between soloist and accompanying group are already becoming a cultivated conversation. The *Second Concerto* follows the same pattern, although in the tender *Largo* the dotted orchestral interruptions confirm that Bach's imagination is consistently preventing any routine responses. The finale is again rhythmically energetic, as indeed is the opening movement of the *G major Concerto*, which nevertheless also has plenty of light and shade. Miklós Spányi has chosen to play the early concertos on a harpsichord with a strong personality: a modern copy by Michael Walker of a 1734 Haas whose original maker lived in Hamburg. It is very well balanced with a period-instrument string-group (6;2;1;1), which is probably larger than the ensemble the composer would have expected, and the resonance of the recording (made in a Budapest church) also militates against a really intimate effect. But the playing has animation and elegance, and the soloist effectively improvises his own cadenzas at the recording sessions, which increases the sense of spontaneity. So, with spirited and sympathetic accompaniments one can readily warm to music-making which is polished and always alive, if not perhaps in the last resort distinctive.

Harpsichord concertos Nos. 4 in G ; 7 in A; 12 in F, Wq.4, 7 & 12 (H.406, 410 & 415).
**(*) BIS Dig. CD 708 [id.]. Miklós Spányi (harpsichord), Concerto Armonico, Péter Szüts.

The three concertos on the second disc all date from Carl Philipp's early years in Berlin, yet each has its own individuality. Indeed the *G major Concerto* (1738) marks a remarkable change of manner, with its Italianate grace and with the soloist avoiding bravura for its own sake. The *Adagio* is even more gracious and the finale gambols elegantly. The composer's mood changes again for the lively opening of the *A major* (1740), which is punctuated by orchestral sforzandos, while the solo part is wholly individual; the slow movement makes a proper expressive contrast, but the finale again proceeds with elegant poise rather than scurrying. The *F major Concerto* (1744) opens gruffly, but the soloist takes a much more lyrical stance and refuses to be chastised by the strong orchestral chords. The *Largo e sostenuto* continues with the participants not wholly reconciled, but they join together to share the joyously vigorous finale; the orchestral comments remain strong, but more genially so. A wholly original and remarkable work, and one of the very best performances in the series so far. Indeed all three works here are strongly characterized.

Harpsichord concertos Nos. 6 in G min.; 8 in A; 18 in D, Wq.6, 8 & 18 (H.409, 411 & 421).
**(*) BIS Dig. CD 767 [id.]. Miklós Spányi (harpsichord), Concerto Armonico, Péter Szüts.

On the third disc both the *G minor* (1740) and *A major* (1741) *Concertos* are among the more remarkable of the composer's early works: in the former the lively dialogue between orchestra and keyboard, each independent though sharing ideas, has great individuality, and the following serene *Largo* is quietly memorable, followed by a robust *Allegro molto* of the strongest character. The slow movement of the *A major* (here played just a little heavily) is very beguiling with its muted strings; though the invention in the *D major* (1745) is probably more consistent in quality, its roving *Andante* is less appealing as presented here. The pert closing *Allegro di molti* is, however, nicely enunciated. Excellent, if resonant, sound.

Harpsichord concertos Nos. 9 in G; 13 in D; 17 in D min., Wq.9, 13 & 17 (H.412, 416 & 420).
**(*) BIS Dig. CD 768 [id.]. Miklós Spányi (harpsichord or fortepiano), Concerto Armonico, Péter Szüts.

In the first movements of both the *G major* and *D major Concertos*, Wq. 9 and 13, Bach establishes a pioneering principle of sonata form. The closing section of the opening movement of the *G major* (1742) repeats the material of the opening section but moving from the dominant key to which the first section has modulated, back to the tonic. There is even a cadenza (improvised by the soloist) before the final statement. In the *D major Concerto* (1744) there is a similar move back from the relative minor to present the movement's close in the home key. The ruminative dialogue of the *Adagio* of the *G major* work is also forward-looking, as is the pensive *un poco Adagio* of the *D minor*, where the theme on the violins floats over a gentle stalking bass (reminding one momentarily of Mozart's *Concerto*, K.467), but with characteristic interrupting flourishes from the lower strings, before the soloist makes a wistful entry. The structure of the opening movement of this work is also inventively individual, opening boldly in the orchestra; the soloist then enters with a new theme which bears only a slight relationship with the tutti. Both ideas are interwoven in the free fantasia which follows, and the work closes with a partnership centred on the home key. Spányi introduces a highly suitable fortepiano (built by Hemel after a 1749 Freiburg) for the *D major Concerto*, Wq. 13, which works especially well in the *un poco Andante* and offers contrast of colour and dynamic in the finale, where the string tuttis are so vigorously forthright. All these performances are impressive, and it is only in the opening of the *G major Concerto* that the resonance blurs the focus of the bold hustling ritornellos.

(i) *Double concerto in E flat for harpsichord & fortepiano, Wq.47;* (ii) *Double concerto in F, for 2 harpsichords, Wq.46;*(i) *Sonatina for 2 harpsichords & orchestra in D, Wq.109.*
500♪ (B) *** DHM 05472 77410-2 [id.]. (i) Eric Lynn Kelley, Jos van Immersel (fortepiano or harpsichord); (ii) Alan Curtis, Gustav Leonhardt; Coll. Aur., Maier.

The spirited and delightful *E flat Concerto for harpsichord and fortepiano* has a chirpily inviting opening theme and is given a wholly persuasive account here, with the solo instruments naturally balanced and a warm acoustic assisting a lively (but painless) authentic accompaniment. It is very well played and, at its very economical price, this is a reissue not to be missed.

CHAMBER MUSIC

Duo for flute and violin in E min., Wq.140; 12 Short pieces for 2 flutes, 2 violins & continuo, Wq.81; Sonata for flute & continuo in G (Hamburg Sonata), Wq.133; Trios for flute, violin & continuo: in B min., Wq.143; in C, Wq.147; (i) Cantata: *Phyllis and Thirsis, Wq.232.*
(B) *** DHM Analogue/Dig. 05472 77435-2 [77188-2]. Soloists, Les Adieux, Schola Cantorum Basiliensis.

A wholly engaging anthology. The dozen pieces for two flutes, two violins and continuo deftly vary textures and the result is most attractive when the authentic timbres are so fresh. The following *Hamburg Flute sonata* needs to be played separately because there is a pitch change as it begins; but it is the *Trio sonatas* which form the kernel of the concert, and they each have touchingly nostalgic *Adagios* to contrast with their bright outer movements. The programme ends with a miniature (7-minute) pastoral cantata, *Phyllis and Thirsis*, obviously selected because it includes obbligatos for two flutes. Although designed as a solo soprano work, it is even more effective in dialogue between tenor and soprano, and especially so when both soloists (Nigel Rogers and Rosmarie Hofmann) rise to the occasion as they do here. Excellent recording – a real bargain.

Flute sonatas: in C, Wq.73; in D, Wq.83; in E, Wq.84; in G, Wq.85; in G, Wq.86.
(BB) **(*) ASV Quicksilva Dig. CDQS 6205 [id.]. Christopher Hyde-Smith, Jane Dodd (harpsichord).

This collection is preferable to its Naxos competitor (8.550513 – see our main volume). The ASV performances have plenty of life and feeling and, though again the recording is resonant and with the flute close-miked, the effect is very spirited. The collection includes one of the least predictable of these works, Wq.73 (*in C major*), written in 1745, with its striking *Allegro di molto* opening movement, alongside Wq. 84 (*in E major*) of four years later, which has an equally remarkable central *Adagio di molto.*

Flute sonatas: in G, Wq.86; in C, Wq.87; in E min., Wq.124; in D, Wq.129; (Solo) *Flute sonata in A min., Wq.132;* (i) *12 2- and 3-part kleine Stücke for 2 flutes, Wq.82.*
*** ASV Gaudeamus Dig. CDGAU 161 [id.]. Nancy Hadden, Lucy Carolan; Erin Headly; (i) Elizabeth Walker.

The most striking work here is the unaccompanied *Flute sonata in A minor*, written in 1747, with its remarkable opening *Adagio*, an improvisatory work of characteristic originality written for Frederick the Great, who, Bach said, 'could not play it'. Nancy Hadden certainly can (using a copy of a mid-eighteenth-century Dresden transverse flute). The twelve *Little pieces* (1770) alternate trio and duo format and are very jolly and entertaining until the expressively wilting closing *Andante*. Bach favoured the clavichord rather than the harpsichord as appropriate in duo sonatas and, while the early *E minor* and the obviously more mature (1740) *D major Sonatas* feature a harpsichord as part of the continuo, both the *G major*, Wq. 86 (1755), and the *C major*, Wq.87, with its winning finale use the clavichord, and how beautifully balanced it is. But whichever keyboard instrument she is using, Lucy Carolan proves a fine partner, and the balance is equally well judged in the works with additional viola da gamba. This is all most engaging music, and it is admirably presented here in a concert running for 74 minutes.

Organ sonatas Nos. 1–6, Wq.70/1–6.
**(*) Erato/Warner Dig. 0630 14777-2 [id.]. Marie-Claire Alain (organ).
(M) **(*) Teldec/Warner 0630 17431-2 [id.]. Herbert Tachezi.

In the past these works have been mistakenly thought to be for harpsichord or fortepiano rather than organ as there is no pedal part. But it seems very probable that they were written for Princess Anna Amalia, for she had a two-manual chamber organ especially built for her, but she confessed that she could not cope with the pedal. The special interest of this Erato recording is that they are played on the very instrument for which they were composed, which has great character and which is now installed in the Karlshorst-Kirche in Berlin. Carl Philipp Emanuel's six works are simply written (especially the slow movements), often featuring imitative passages. They are all agreeable but not distinctive, reflecting the fact that the Princess did not claim to be a virtuoso. The *F major*, Op. 70/3, and *A minor*, Op. 70/4, are perhaps the most interesting, though the finales of the *D major* and *G minor* (the last two) are both made striking by attractive registration. Marie-Claire Alain is a stylish and lively advocate and the organ is beautifully recorded, but there are no masterpieces here.

Herbert Tachezi plays a restored eighteenth-century instrument at Castle Matzen in the Austrian Tyrol which is reputed to have some affinity with the original. The playing is good throughout. Tachezi is sometimes a trifle mannered, but he is generally true to the spirit of the music. The recording is excellent.

Bach, Johann Christian (1735–82)

Clavier concertos, Op. 1/1–6; Op. 7/1–6.
(B) *** Ph. Duo 438 712-2 (2) [id.]. Ingrid Haebler (fortepiano), V. Capella Ac., Melkus.

(i) *Clavier concertos, Op. 13/1–6;* (ii) *6 Sinfonias, Op. 3.*
(B) *** Ph. Duo 456 064-2 (2) [id.]. (i) Ingrid Haebler (fortepiano), V. Capella Ac., Melkus; (ii) ASMF, Marriner.

J. C. Bach composed three sets of *Clavier concertos*, each comprising six works. All the concertos here are in major keys and are attractive, well-wrought compositions. It would be difficult to find a more suitable or persuasive advocate than Ingrid Haebler, who is excellently accompanied and most truthfully recorded. There is some delightful invention here and it is difficult to imagine it being better presented.

The *Sinfonias* are beguilingly played by the Academy of St Martin-in-the-Fields under Sir Neville Marriner, and beautifully recorded. None of this can be called great music but it has an easy-going and fluent charm. Erik Smith, who has edited them, describes them as 'in essence Italian overtures, though with an unusual wealth of singing melody'.

Bach, Johann Sebastian (1685–1750)

Ton Koopman Edition

Ton Koopman Edition, Part 1: *Brandenburg Concertos; Harpsichord concertos; Violin concertos.*
(M) *(*) Erato/Warner Dig. 0630 16162-2 (6) [id.]. Soloists, Amsterdam Bar. O, Koopman.

This is not a set to recommend as a whole, as the *Brandenburg Concertos* are the only Koopman performances which can claim an unqualified recommendation.

Brandenburg concertos Nos. 1–3, BWV 1046–8; (i) *Triple concerto for flute, violin and harpsichord in A min., BWV 1044.*
(M) *** Erato/Warner Dig. 0630 16163-2 [id.]. (i) Hazelzet, Manze, Koopman; Amsterdam Bar. O, Koopman.

Brandenburg concertos Nos. 4–6, BWV 1049–51; (i) *Organ concerto in D min., BWV 1059.*
(M) *** Erato/Warner Dig. 0630 16164-2 [id.]. (i) Koopman; Amsterdam Bar. O, Koopman.

Relaxed and intimate, Koopman's account makes a highly recommendable mid-price alternative to Pinnock for those who prefer expressive contrasts to be less sharply marked. Like Pinnock, Koopman is not afraid to read *Affettuoso* on the slow movement of No. 5 as genuinely expressive and warm, though without sentimentality. As with Pinnock, players are one to a part, with excellent British soloists included in the band. In the *Third Concerto*, Koopman effectively interpolates the *Toccata in G*, BWV 916, as a harpsichord link between the two movements. The sound on CD is immediate, but not aggressively so. The *Triple concerto* is quite successful as a performance but, like the keyboard concertos discussed below, the resonant recording clouds inner detail. However, the little *Organ concerto* (reconstructed from music in Bach's Cantata No. 35) sounds attractively intimate.

Harpsichord concertos Nos. 1–2, BWV 1052–3; Nos. 5–6, BWV 1056–7.
(M) ** Erato/Warner Dig. 0630 16166-2 [id.]. Koopman; Amsterdam Bar. O, Koopman.

The solo *Harpsichord concertos* are more successful in Koopman's hands than the multiple works, the effect neat and intimate if short of being rhythmically buoyant. But the keyboard profile is too slight to balance satisfactorily with the full orchestral sound, and inner detail is often made opaque by the resonance.

Harpsichord concertos Nos. 3–4, BWV 1054–5; 7 in G min., BWV 1058; (i) *Triple harpsichord concertos No. 1 in D min.; 2 in C, BWV 1063–4.*
(M) *(*) Erato/Warner Dig. 0630 16167-2 [id.]. Koopman, (i) with Mathot, Marisaldi; Amsterdam Bar. O, Koopman.

Double harpsichord concertos Nos. 1–3, BWV 1060–62; (i) *Quadruple harpsichord concerto in A min., BWV 1065.*
(M) *(*) Erato/Warner Dig. 0630 16168-2 [id.]. Koopman, Mathot, (i) with Mustonen, Marisaldi; Amsterdam Bar. O, Koopman.

Koopman is a fine player, but his set of the multiple *Harpsichord concertos* cannot be recommended with any confidence, for the performances and recording are disappointing. The harpsichords are made to sound jangly, with mechanical noises intruding, while the orchestra seems too heavy, lacking the transparency of period performances and with Koopman often failing to lift rhythms.

Violin concertos Nos. 1 in E; 2 in A min.; (i) *Double violin concerto in D min., BWV 1041–3.*
(M) * Erato/Warner Dig. 0630 16165-2 [id.]. Monica Huggett, (i) with Alison Bury; Amsterdam Bar. O, Koopman.

Here allegros are reasonably lively, but slow movements are uninspiring in the two solo concertos, and the justly famous solo interplay in the *Double concerto* only just falls short of dullness – a remarkable achievement when the music itself is so inspired.

Ton Koopman Edition, Part 2: Keyboard works.
(M) **(*) Erato/Warner Dig. 0630 16169-2 (8) [id.] (details below).

The Art of fugue, BWV 1080 (version for two harpsichords).
(M) *** Erato/Warner Dig. 0630 16173-2 [id.]. Ton Koopman, Tini Mathot (harpsichords).

Koopman chooses a pair of instruments made by Willem Kroesbergen of Utrecht, himself leading with a copy of a Rückers, while his colleague, Tini Mathot, uses another modern copy, but of a Couchet. The partnership works well: pacing is well judged and and contrapuntal detail is clear, yet within a not too dry acoustic. The approach is didactic, but by no means rigid.

Chromatic fantasia and fugue in D min., BWV 903; French suite No. 5 in G, BWV 816; Italian concerto in F, BWV 971; Musical offering, BWV 1079: Ricercar; Toccata in G, BWV 916.
(M) *** Erato/Warner Dig. 0630 16171-2 [id.]. Ton Koopman (harpsichord).

Koopman is at his liveliest here, particularly in the brilliant *Chromatic fantasia*. The *French suite*, bright and brisk except for the thoughtful *Loure*, has plenty of character, and the *Italian Concerto* comes off equally vividly, helped by the clean projection of the Dutch harpsichord, built by Willem Kroesbergen of Utrecht, which Koopman is using for his Bach series.

French suites Nos. 1–6, BWV 812–17.
(M) *** Erato/Warner Dig. 0630 16172-2 [id.]. Ton Koopman (harpsichord).

Ton Koopman fits all six *French suites* on to a single 70-minute CD. He uses a copy of a Rückers to admirable effect and these performances are stimulatingly rhythmic, exciting and thoughtful by turns. The best-known *Fifth suite* is especially spontaneous. The effect of the recording – not too closely balanced – is vivid and realistic. Ornaments are nicely handled and there is not a trace of pedantry here. A first choice for those not wanting the extra suites offered by Hogwood.

Goldberg Variations, BWV 988.
(M) **(*) Erato/Warner Dig. 0630 16170-2 [id.]. Ton Koopman (harpsichord).

Koopman opens by taking the *Aria* very slowly and deliberately, so that the brilliance of the first variation makes a striking contrast. His survey produces plenty of vitality, articulation is clean, ornamentation is crisp and rhythms have plenty of lift. He does not play all the repeats (the playing time is 62 minutes), but the result flows convincingly and one has a sense of ongoing spontaneity. The recording is bright and realistic and the Kroesbergen harpsichord is an instrument of real character. Not an out-and-out first choice, but distinctly enjoyable and well worth considering at mid-price.

The Well-tempered Clavier, Book I, Preludes and fugues Nos. 1–24, BWV 846–69.
(B) ** Erato/Warner Duo Dig. 0630 16174-2 (2) [id.]. Ton Koopman (harpsichord).

The Well-tempered Clavier, Book II, Preludes and fugues Nos. 25–48, BWV 870–93.
(B) ** Erato/Warner Duo Dig. 0630 16175-2 (2) [id.]. Ton Koopman (harpsichord).

Ton Koopman uses a fine copy of a Rückers harpsichord and plays with consistent vitality and often with obvious thoughtfulness. But his speeds are often brisk, and at times there is a feeling that the forward momentum is pursued somewhat relentlessly. This is more striking in the first book than in the second. He is well recorded, and this set is inexpensive, being offered on two Bonsai Duo issues with each of the two CDs offered for the price of one. However, the non-existent documentation and inadequate titling is characteristic of this poorly produced bargain series.

Choral works: *Mass in B min., BWV 232; St Matthew Passion, BWV 244; St John Passion, BWV 245.*
(M) **(*) Erato/Warner Dig. 0630 16176-2 (7) [id.]. Schlick, Wessel, Guy de Mey, Türk, Kooy, Prégardien, Mertens, Amsterdam Bar. Ch., Netherlands Bach Soc. Ch., Breda Sacramentskoor, Amsterdam Bar. O, Ton Koopman.

Koopman's collection of the three major Bach oratorios makes a fair mid-priced recommendation for those wanting period performances; each work is also available separately at premium price. Excellent, stylish soloists contribute to all three sets. Koopman's account of the *B minor Mass* is purposeful, consistently persuasive. The keenly responsive choral singing – rather soft-grained as recorded – is warmer than with most period performances, but it lacks something in brightness and bite. The soloists are at their finest in the *St John Passion*, and here the chorus has a much more dramatic profile (see below). In the *St Matthew Passion* Koopman is comparatively relaxed, avoiding speeds as controversially fast as Gardiner's, and again the choral sound lacks bite.

ORCHESTRAL MUSIC

Brandenburg concertos Nos. 1–6, BWV 1046–51.
(B) *** Hyperion Dyad Dig. CDD 22001 (2) [id.]. Brandenburg Consort, Roy Goodman.
(B) (*) Millennium MCD 80075 (*Nos. 1–3*); MCD 80121 (*Nos. 4–6*) [MCA MCAD2 9831]. V. State Op. O, Herman Scherchen.

The excellent Hyperion set of the *Brandenburgs* now re-emerges on a Dyad, with the two discs offered for the price of one. Roy Goodman not only directs but also acts as a string soloist. The stylish, lively playing is another attractive example of authenticism, lacking something in polish (notably from the horns in No. 1) but not in spirit, with the last three concertos especially fresh. There is also fine trumpet-playing from Stephen Keavy in No. 2. Characterization is strong and slow movements are often appealingly expressive, especially the delicately managed *Affettuoso* of No. 5 which, like No. 4, gains from the fine flute contribution of Rachel Brown. Tempi of outer movements are generally very brisk, but often bringing the lightest rhythmic touch. Very good sound, making this a strong competitor for Pinnock's DG set, which costs twice as much (410 500/501-2 – see our main volume).

Scherchen's Viennese *Brandenburgs* (from 1959), in spite of their warmth, are a non-starter. Of curiosity value only, they are obviously under-rehearsed: there is poor ensemble in No. 1, and the solo trumpet does not sound quite comfortable in the first movement of No. 2. Scherchen's tempi are very leisurely indeed, incredibly so in the first movement of No. 3, and they are funereal in No.5.

Brandenburg concertos Nos. 1–6, BWV 1046–51; Brandenburg concerto No. 5 (early version), *BWV 1050a; Triple concerto in A min. for flute, violin and harpsichord, BWV 1044.*
(M) *** Virgin/EMI VCD5 45255-2 (2). La Stravaganza, Hamburg, Siegbert Rampe.

The new set of *Brandenburgs* from La Stravaganza is immensely vigorous and stimulating: indeed it is very difficult to resist and, although it is not perhaps an obvious first choice, it is very enjoyable indeed; at mid-price it can be recommended alongside Goodman. Overall, the tempi must be among the fastest on record (disconcertingly so upon first hearing) and the throaty hand-horn playing in the outer movements of No. 1 brings the most extraordinary virtuosity – while the intonation is remarkably accurate. Not to be outdone, the strings in No. 3 (which follows) play with enormous zest, particularly in the finale, where the light buoyancy of rhythm and crispness of attack and ensemble are a joy. The opening movement of No. 6 which comes next is hardly less vital and in the slow movement (even more than in the *Adagio* of No. 1) there is the warmest expressive feeling: this is period-instrument playing with a smile of pleasure thrown in. The finale is joyously buoyant, as are the outer movements of No. 2, with the solo trumpet (Hans-Martin Kothe) admirably balanced with the baroque oboe (Alfredo Barnardini); the flute comes into its own in the engaging interplay of the *Andante*. No. 5 is offered not only in the 1719 version we know so well, but also in an earlier chamber version, probably written in Carlsbad a year earlier, when Bach only had five players at his disposal. It is refreshingly light-textured, with engaging interchanges between flute (Michael Schmidt-Casdorff) and violin (Gesinne Hildebrandt). Siegbert Rampe (his virtuosity ever impressive) directs from the harpsichord and plays as felicitously and involvingly here as he does throughout, in this instance using a smaller instrument to match what the composer himself had available, but which nevertheless comes through the texture quite admirably. The *Triple concerto* is played with comparable spirit, and the harpsichord is balanced more forwardly to dominate the outer movements, while the flute and violin gently ravish the ear in the *Adagio*. With outstandingly realistic recording, this is highly recommendable in its way, even if it is difficult to believe that Bach's own players could have generated this kind of virtuosity, or that their chosen tempi would have been so swift.

Brandenburg concertos Nos. 1–6, BWV 1046–51; Orchestral suites Nos. 1–4, BWV 1066–9; Chorale: Jesu, joy of man's desiring.
(BB) ** RCA Navigator 74321 30364-2 (3). Augmented Lucerne Festival Strings, Baumgartner.

Rudolf Baumgartner's recordings were made in 1977–8 and offer full, pleasingly natural sound, not sharply defined but not clouded either. Tempi are appreciably less brisk in the *Brandenburgs* than we would expect today, but the playing remains stylish in its way and certainly alive, while Baumgartner's warm *espressivo* in slow movements is undoubtedly appealing. In the *Suites* there is less difference in pacing, but the style is still more relaxed and dance movements are elegant. Aurèle Nicolet's flute contribution to No. 2 is a highlight and the famous *Badinerie* is most winning. Some will undoubtedly find Baumgartner too leisured in his manner, but what comes over here is the breadth of Bach's music, and the glorious *Air* from the *Third Suite* is very beautiful when the violin textures are rich and the phrasing has a restrained depth of feeling.

Harpsichord concertos Nos. 1 in D min.; 2 in E; 3 in D; 4 in A; 5 in F min.; 6 in F; 7 in G min., BWV 1052–8; (i) *Double harpsichord concertos: Nos. 1 in C min.; 2 in C; 3 in C min., BWV 1060–62;* (i; ii) *Triple harpsichord concertos Nos. 1 in D min.; 2 in C, BWV 1063–4;* (i–iii) *Quadruple harpsichord concerto in A min., BWV 1065.*
500♪ (B) *** DG Analogue/Dig. 447 709-2 (3) [id.]. Pinnock with (i) Gilbert; (ii) Mortensen; (iii) Kraemer; E. Concert.

Pinnock's performances of the Bach *Harpsichord concertos* first appeared in 1981, and they have dominated the catalogue ever since. In the solo concertos he plays with real panache, his scholarship tempered with excellent musicianship. Pacing is brisk, but to today's ears, used to period performances, the effect is convincing when the playing is so spontaneous and the analogue sound bright and clean.

Harpsichord concertos Nos. 1–7, BWV 1052–8; Double harpsichord concertos Nos. 1–3, BWV 1060–62.
(B) *** Ph. Duo Analogue/Dig. 454 268-2 (2) [id.]. Raymond Leppard, Andrew Davis, Philip Ledger, ECO, Leppard.

Anyone wanting the solo and double harpsichord concertos accompanied on modern instruments will find it hard to better this Philips Duo set. Leppard, Davis and Ledger play with skill and flair; the ECO shows plenty of life and, if the performances overall are less incisive than the English Concert versions with Pinnock, they have resilience and communicate such joy in the music that criticism is disarmed. The Philips sound is very realistic, the harpsichords life-size and not too forward; one does reflect that modern strings, however refined, create a body of tone which tends slightly to outweigh the more slender keyboard timbres. However, in the works for two or more harpsichords there is a pleasing absence of jangle. Excellent value.

Clavier concertos Nos. 1 in D min.; 2 in E; 3 in D, 4 in A; 5 in F; 6 in F; 7 in G min., BWV 1052–8.
500♪ *** Decca Dig. 425 676-2 (2) [id.]. András Schiff (piano), COE.

As in his solo Bach records, Schiff's control of colour and articulation never seeks to present merely a harpsichord imitation, and his shaping of Bach's lovely slow movements brings fine sustained lines and a subtle variety of touch. This makes a clear first choice for those who, like us, enjoy Bach on the piano.

Clavier concerto No. 1 in D min., BWV 1052.
(M) **(*) Decca 448 598-2 [id.]. Vladimir Ashkenazy (piano), LSO, Zinman – CHOPIN: *Piano Concerto No. 2* ***; MOZART: *Piano concerto No. 6.* **(*)

This is no imitation of a plucked string instrument but the piano on its own terms, with a wide variety of colour in the first movement and gentle half-tones in the *Adagio*. In the finale there are some surprisingly pianistic figurations. David Zinman's accompaniment is most stylish, buoyantly rhythmic in the allegros; textures are fuller than we would expect today, but the effect is never heavy. Excellent (1965) recording, but this seems a curious coupling for a fine Chopin reissue in Decca's Classic Sound series.

Violin concertos Nos. (i) *1–2;* (ii) *Double violin concerto, BWV 1041–3;* (iii) *Double concerto for violin & oboe in C min., BWV 1060.*
500♪ ✿ (M) *** Ph. 420 700-2. Grumiaux; (ii) Krebbers, (iii) Holliger; (i–ii) Les Solistes Romandes, Arpad Gerecz; (iii) New Philh. O, Edo de Waart.
(M) *** Nimbus Dig. NI 7031 [id.]. Oscar Shumsky, Scottish CO; with (ii) John Tunnell; (iii) Robin Miller.

Arthur Grumiaux is joined in the *Double concerto* by Hermann Krebbers and the result is an outstanding success. The way Grumiaux responds to the challenge of working with another great artist comes over equally clearly in the concerto with oboe, reconstructed from the *Double harpsichord concerto in C minor*. Grumiaux's performances of the two solo concertos are equally satisfying.

One has only to sample the simple beauty of Shumsky's playing in the *Andante* of the *A minor Violin concerto* to be won over to his dedicated Bach style, which is not quite as pure as Grumiaux's but is seductive in its simplicity of line and tonal beauty. John Tunnell makes highly musical exchanges with him in the *Double violin concerto* and Robin Miller is a no less appealing partner in the work for violin and oboe, and his line in the slow movement is beautifully echoed by Shumsky. Shumsky directs the orchestra from the bow and, although the sound is full in the way of modern-instrument performances, rhythms are resilient and there is no excess weightiness in the bass. The recording is warm to match. A most enjoyable collection for those looking for (fairly) modern (1984) digital recordings of these works at mid-price.

Violin concertos Nos. 1 in A min.; 2 in E, BWV 1041–2; in G min. (from *BWV 1056*); (i) *Double concerto for violin and oboe, BWV 1056.*
** Ph. Dig. 446 675-2 [id.]. Viktoria Mullova, (i) with François Leleux; Mullova Ensemble.

Viktoria Mullova's performances use modern instruments, but the transparent string textures, with one instrument to a part, are agreeable, and there is light, chimerical solo playing in allegros, with a nice buoyancy in the accompaniments. She phrases the famous cantabile melody in the *Largo* of BWV 1056 (an arrangement of the *F minor Harpsichord concerto*) simply and pleasingly, although in the *Adagio* of the work for violin and oboe, in which she is joined by François Leleux, the line is rather less imaginatively flexible. An enjoyable and well-recorded but not a distinctive collection and, with a playing time of only 52 minutes, there would have been plenty of room for the *Double violin concerto*, BWV 1043.

Violin concertos Nos. 1 in A min.; 2 in E; (i) *Double violin concerto in D min., BWV 1041–3;* (i; ii) *Triple violin concerto in D* (arr. from BWV 1064).
**(*) Chandos Dig. CHAN 0594 [id.]. Simon Standage with (i) Micaela Comberti; (ii) Miles Golding; Coll. Mus. 90.

Simon Standage's collection is strictly for authenticists. The performances are impeccable, with allegros brisk and vital, but the astringent solo playing is only just short of a vinegary vintage and, for all the impeccable purity of the melodic lines, most listeners will want to be coaxed a little more in slow movements. The opening of the *Triple concerto*, arranged by Standage from the concerto for three harpsichords, sounds distinctly thin. However, the excellently balanced recording projects the music-making within a pleasing acoustic.

(i) *Violin concertos Nos. 1 in A min.; 2 in D min., BWV 1041–2; Double violin concerto in D min., BWV 1043.* (Unaccompanied) *Violin partita No. 2 in D min., BWV 1004.*
(M) *(*) Ph. Dig./Analogue 454 128-2 [id.]. Gidon Kremer; (i) with ASMF.

Kremer adopts (by electronic means) both solo roles in the *Double concerto* and thus the interplay of human personality is lost in this most human of works. Kremer also directs the accompanying ensemble, so these interpretations cannot be accused of any kind of artistic inconsistency – indeed they have the forward thrust of a determined advocate, in slow movements as well as allegros, which are extremely vigorous. The same comment might be applied to his recording of the solo *Partita*, which includes the famous *Chaconne*. There is no doubting the facility of his playing but he conveys little sense of musical enjoyment. The end effect is relentless and, despite vivid recording (the concertos are digital), these performances offer only limited rewards.

Violin concertos Nos. 1 in A min.; 2 in E; Double violin concerto in D min., BWV 1041–3; Sonata in E min., BWV 1023 (arr. Respighi for violin and strings); *Suite No. 3, BWV 1068: Air.*
(BB) **(*) Naxos Dig. 8.550194 [id.]. Nishizaki, Jablokov, Capella Istropolitana, Oliver Dohnányi.

The first thing about the Naxos recording that strikes the ear is the attractively bright, gleaming sound of the orchestral string-group, who play with fine resilience. Neither soloist is a strong personality and the espressivo in the *Adagio* of the *E major* solo *Concerto* and in the famous lyrical dialogue of the slow movement of the *Double concerto* brings rather deliberate phrasing. Yet these players are certainly musical, and there is a sense of style here and plenty of vitality in allegros. The Respighi arrangement is effective enough, and the concert ends with Bach's most famous string tune, played simply and eloquently.

Violin concerto No. 2 in E, BWV 1042; in G min. (from *BWV 1056*); (i) *Double violin concerto in D min., BWV 1043.*
(M) *** Virgin/EMI Ultraviolet CUV5 61320-2. Jonathan Rees, (i) with Jane Murdoch, Scottish Ens., Jonathan Rees – C. P. E. BACH: *Cello concerto.* ***

With forward and bright sound, well detailed, Jonathan Rees directs the Scottish Ensemble in warm, buoyant recordings of three of Bach's violin concertos. Allegros are infectiously sprung, while slow movements are allowed full expressiveness without sentimentality. This is a reissue of a CD which first appeared on the super-bargain Virgo label, and the absence of the *A minor solo Violin concerto* must be counted a drawback. Nevertheless these are more enjoyably characterful performances than those on the competing Mullova disc and, with its excellent C. P. E. Bach coupling, this collection is worth considering.

A Musical offering, BWV 1079.
(M) ** Teldec/Warner 0630 13563-2 [id.]. VCM, Harnoncourt.

Harnoncourt's recording dates from 1970. It is musically sound, somewhat plain-spun and a little lacking in imaginative vitality; but it is well recorded and is offered at mid-price. Short measure at 46 minutes.

Orchestral suites Nos. 1–4; Violin concerto movement in D, BWV 1045; Sinfonias from Cantatas Nos. 29; 42; 209.
(B) *** Hyperion Dyad Dig. CDD 22002 (2) [id.]. Brandenburg Consort, Roy Goodman.

Orchestral suites Nos. 1–4; Concerto movement from Cantata No. 152; March from Cantata 207; Sinfonias from Cantatas Nos. 18 & 31 & from Easter oratorio.
**(*) O-L Dig. 452 000-2 (2) [id.]. New L. Cons., Philip Pickett.

Roy Goodman directs brisk and stylish readings of the four Bach *Orchestral Suites*, which are aptly supplemented by four *Sinfonias*, each following a suite in the same key. Though in the *Suites* Goodman in his eagerness occasionally chooses too breathless a tempo for fast movements, the lightness of rhythm and the crispness of ensemble are consistently persuasive, with textures cleanly caught in excellent, full-bodied sound. These are among the finest versions on a long list, with Rachel Brown an exceptionally warm-toned flautist in No. 2. Goodman observes all repeats, making the opening overtures longer than usual. As indicated above, the discs are available either separately or in a box.

Pickett's opening for the *Overture* of the *First Suite* is surprisingly leisurely, and generally his tempi are unconventional and sometimes unexpected: the attractively lively pacing for the closing *Gigue* of *Suite No. 3* and the sprightly, beautifully pointed *Polonaise* in the *Suite No. 2*. Indeed this *B minor Suite for flute and strings* is given a refreshing new look, and No. 4, which can sometimes seem the least interesting of the group, is full of interest. While not missing the imposing qualities of the grander movements, these performances are distinctly more lightweight than usual; the relaxed feeling is attractive and the full colours of the period instruments emerge pleasingly blended. Like Goodman before him, Pickett chooses instrumental excerpts from cantatas as fillers (though not the same ones), and they are presented most enjoyably. The *Marcia* from the *Cantata*, BWV 207, makes a buoyant close for the concert. The recording is first class.

CHAMBER MUSIC

(Unaccompanied) *Cello suites Nos. 1–6, BWV 1007–12.*
500♪ ❁ *** EMI Dig. CDS5 55363-2 (2) [id.]. Mstislav Rostropovich.
(M) *** DG 449 711-2 (2) [id.]. Pierre Fournier.

Rostropovich, the most intrepid of cellists, ever eager to tackle concertos by the score, has nevertheless approached these supreme masterpieces of the solo cello repertory with caution. He played them all in his teens but, until the 1990s, refrained from recording them as a complete cycle. The result is revelatory, in many ways the most powerful recording of all, positive and personal, full of individual perceptions.

Fournier's richly phrased and warm-toned performances carry an impressive musical conviction. Fournier can be profound and he can lift rhythms infectiously in dance movements, but above all he conveys the feeling that this is music to be enjoyed. This recording has been remastered splendidly for reissue in DG's 'Legendary Recordings' series and now has even greater presence and realism.

Flute sonatas Nos. 1 in B min., BWV 1030; (i) *4 in C* (with continuo), *BWV 1033; 6 in E, BWV 1035* (with continuo). *Sonata in G min., BWV 1020* (now attrib. C. P. E. Bach); (i) *Trio sonata in G, BWV 1039.*
(BB) ** Naxos Dig. 8.553755 [id.]. Petri Alanko, Anssi Mattila (harpsichord); (i) with Jukka Rautasalo.

(i–ii) *Flute sonatas Nos. 2 in E flat, BWV 1031; 3 in A, BWV 1032;* (i–iii) *5 in E min.* (with continuo), *BWV 1034.* (i) *Partita for solo flute in A min., BWV 1013.*
(BB) ** Naxos Dig. 8.553754 [id.]. (i) Alanko; (ii) Mattila (harpsichord); (iiii) with Rautasalo.

These two Naxos CDs inexpensively cover all Bach's major *Flute sonatas*, including one now thought to be by his son, Carl Philipp Emanuel. They are played very musically and in good style. However, the ASV Quicksilva super-bargain disc (CDQS 6108) includes the six main works, played with even more character by the illustrious William Bennett and George Malcolm, with Michael Evans providing the necessary viola da gamba part in BWV 1033–5, and this remains a more obvious choice unless the collector finds the other works essential.

Lute suites transcribed for guitar

Lute suites Nos. 1–4, BWV 995–7 and 1006a.
(M) *** DG Dig. 445 563-2 [id.]. Göran Söllscher.

Lute suites (arranged for guitar) *Nos. 1–3, BWV 995–7. Prelude in C min.; Fugue in G min., BWV 999–1000.*
(B) *** Sony SBK 62972; *SBT 62972* [id.]. John Williams (guitar).

John Williams shows a natural response to Bach; the flair of his playing, with its rhythmic vitality and sense of colour, is always telling. He does not here give us the *E major Suite*, BWV 1006a, which is a transcription of the *Partita in E major for unaccompanied violin* (BWV 1006); instead he offers a *Prelude in C minor*, BWV 999, followed by the *Fugue in G minor*, BWV 1000, which originates in the (unaccompanied) *Violin sonata*, BWV 1001. The guitar is closely balanced, but when the volume is turned down a bit the guitar image has a believable presence, and background noise is not a problem.

Göran Söllscher's performances of the four *Lute suites*, recorded between 1981 and 1984, bring an advantage over his chief competitor, John Williams, in that the recording is digital and a silent background is a great advantage in such repertoire. Söllscher is a highly musical player, well attuned to Bach. His style is fluent and there is a judicious use of light and shade. The playing is technically immaculate, as is the recorded sound, which is suitably intimate, though not to be reproduced at too high a volume level. With the four works together on a single mid-priced CD, this is highly recommendable, although John

Williams's analogue set with its rhythmic vitality and sense of colour remains very highly recommendable.

6 (organ) *Trio sonatas: Nos. 1 in B flat; 2 in E min.; 3 in G min.; 4 in E min.; 5 in F; 6 in C, BWV 525–30.*
*** Virgin Veritas/EMI Dig. VC5 45192-2. Musica Pacifica.

Musica Pacifica is an excellent period-instrument group which is part of the San Francisco Early Music Society. Like the Palladian Ensemble on Linn (see our main volume), their arrangements of Bach's organ *Trio sonatas* necessitate transcriptions in order to place the upper voices in a suitable range for the recorder, partnered by the violin, with the cello given the upper bass lines and the harpsichord filling in the continuo. The effect here is admirably fresh; Judith Linsenberg, the recorder player who leads the ensemble, plays with fine spirit, while the liveliness of the allegros is matched by striking, often melancholic expressive feeling in slow movements. The recording is first class, and this ranks as a fine alternative to the (differently scored) King's versions on Hyperion (CDA 66843).

Viola da gamba sonatas Nos. 1–3, BWV 1027–9.
*** Virgin Veritas/EMI VER5 61291-2 [EMI CDM 61291]. Jordi Savall (viola da gamba), Ton Koopman (harpsichord).

Though the modern-instrument performances of these fine works on the cello by Ma (Sony MK 37794) and Maisky (DG 415 471-2) will probably be a preferable choice for most listeners, it is good to have an outstanding version on period instruments. While the timbre of the viola da gamba may perhaps be an acquired taste, Jordi Savall certainly makes his instrument sing in slow movements, and Ton Koopman is an excellent partner. With allegros as lively as you could wish the added advantage here is the transparency of the contrapuntal lines, when the two instruments are so well and naturally balanced. Recommended alongside Kuijken and Leonhardt (DHM GD 77044), also at mid-price.

Viola da gamba sonatas Nos. 1–3, BWV 1027–9; (i) *Trio sonata in G for 2 flutes and continuo, BWV 1039.*
(M) ** Teldec/Warner 0630 13583-2 [id.]. Nikolaus Harnoncourt, Herbert Tachezi; (i) with Bruggen, Stastny.

The three sonatas for viola da gamba and harpsichord come from Bach's Cöthen period, and the *G minor*, BWV 1029, is arguably the highest peak in this particular literature. Harnoncourt is brisk and full-blooded in the opening of the *G major* (he is twice as fast as most of his competitors). Immediate comparison betrays the age of the recording (1969) though, taken in its own right, it is eminently acceptable. This gives a bonus in the form of the *G major Sonata* (in which Harnoncourt changes over to the cello and joins the continuo) and, of course, it enjoys a price advantage over the newer versions.

(Unaccompanied) *Violin sonatas Nos. 1–3, BWV 1001, 1003 & 1005; Violin partitas Nos. 1–3, BWV 1002, 1004 & 1005.*
*** Testament SBT 2090 (2) [id.]. Ida Haendel.
(B) *** DG Double 453 004-2 (2) [id.]. Henryk Szeryng.
(M) (***) Sony mono MP2K 46721 (2) [id.]. Henryk Szeryng.
(B) ** Hyperion Dyad Dig. CDD 22009 (2) [id.]. Elizabeth Wallfisch (baroque violin).

Ida Haendel, too long neglected by the record companies, remains among the most powerful violinists we have; here, thanks to the enterprise of the Testament label (mainly devoted to historic reissues), we have a completely new recording, one of the most distinctive yet of Bach's solo violin music. Though Haendel's speeds are exceptionally broad, her playing is magnetic, making one welcome her decision to observe all repeats. She takes a full 18 minutes over the great *Chaconne* of the *D minor Partita*, but the strong, steady pacing means that the build-up is all the more powerful, with counterpoint clearly defined, helped by vividly immediate recording.

When they were first issued in 1968, Henryk Szeryng's performances came under the shadow of the much-praised Grumiaux set, recorded at the beginning of the 1960s. They now emerge on CD with astonishing presence and vividness, aided by DG's 'original-image bit-processing'. Szeryng's tone has never been caught before on record with such leonine fullness and beauty. The technical mastery and polish are quite remarkable, his intonation flawless. His opening attack on the *G minor Sonata* is very compelling, as is the positive, bold style – he plays every note as if he means it! Yet these performances are rhythmically free and full of subtle touches of baroque light and shade; there is a thoughtful, improvisatory feeling too. The resilient *Preludio*, delicately expressive *Loure*, and the joyful *Gavotte en Rondeau* of the *E major Partita* are among the most persuasive on record, so full of character, while the improvisational feeling which permeates this music-making is heard at its most impressive in Szeryng's imaginative and never predictable progress through the famous *Chaconne* which climaxes BWV 1004.

We are grateful to a *Gramophone* reader for drawing our attention to Szeryng's earlier set, recorded in mono in the mid-1960s. The recording is equally real and present and the performances are just as fresh, never identical but following the same general pattern of interpretation. In the *First Sonata*, for instance, the opening *Adagio* is actually slightly faster in the earlier, Sony performance but, because Szeryng's style is slightly less deliberate, the DG version *seems* faster. The closing *Presto* of the same work again brings fascinating minor differences. One certainly would not say that generally one performance is finer than the other, both having much refreshment to offer, yet when one comes to the famous *Chaconne* of the *D minor Partita* there is no question that the earlier account is seemingly more spontaneous.

Elizabeth Wallfisch uses a baroque instrument and bow. Her playing is technically secure and extremely fluent, sometimes quite dazzling – witness the spiccato playing of the *Double* in the *B minor Partita*, taken incredibly fast. The *Tempo di borea* in the same work is strikingly characterful. The famous *Chaconne* has plenty of leonine character too, even if it is not very prepossessing. But it is difficult to warm to her angular lyrical style, and the bold-edged timbre gets tiresome after a while. Was this really the way Bach would have imagined this music? This set is for dedicated 'authenticists' only, for all its detailed imaginative touches.

Violin and harpsichord sonatas Nos. 1–6, BWV 1014–19; 1019a; Sonatas for violin and continuo, BWV 1020–24.

500♪ ❁ (B) *** Ph. Duo 454 011-2 (2) [id.]. Arthur Grumiaux, Christiane Jaccottet, Philippe Mermoud (in *BWV 1021 & 1023*).

Violin and harpsichord sonatas Nos. 1–6, BWV 1014–19; Alternative movements, *BWV 1019a;* (i) *Sonatas for violin and continuo, BWV 1021 & BWV 1023.*

*** Chandos Dig. CHAN 0603 (2) [id.]. Catherine Mackintosh, Maggie Cole; (i) with Jennifer Ward Clarke.

The Bach *Sonatas for violin and harpsichord* and for *violin and continuo* are marvellously played, with all the beauty of tone and line for which Grumiaux is renowned. There is endless treasure to be discovered here, particularly when the music-making is so serenely communicative.

However, it is good to welcome a superb modern recording of these consistently refreshing and melodically appealing works, authentically balanced and beautifully played on period instruments. Hitherto we have favoured Siegfried Kuijken and Gustav Leonhardt, and their analogue set remains highly recommendable at mid-price (RCA GD 77170). But these Chandos versions are even more attractive. Catherine Mackintosh uses a baroque violin, but her timbre is full, her lyrical line flows with an affecting sensitivity and she brings fine musicianship to her phrasing and much subtlety in the matter of light and shade. Articulation in allegros is exhilaratingly crisp and clean, and both players express their joy in the music. Maggie Cole's persuasive contribution is well in the picture, and the balance between violin and double-manual harpsichord could hardly be managed more adroitly, with the players set slightly back within a pleasingly resonant – but not too resonant – ambience. The first disc opens with one of Bach's two *Sonatas for violin and continuo* (BWV 1021), in which Jennifer Ward Clarke's cello contribution adds to the interest and sonority of the music. Our special allegiance to the Grumiaux performances of the same music on modern instruments remains undiminished, and their Philips Duo costs half as much as the Chandos set. But these new interpretations are very stimulating.

KEYBOARD MUSIC

'Bach and Tureck at home' (A birthday offering): (i) *Adagio in G, BWV 968; Aria and 10 variations in the Italian style, BWV 989; Capriccio on the departure of a beloved brother, BWV 992; Chromatic fantasia and fugue, BWV 903; Fantasia, adagio and fugue in D, BWV 912; The Well-tempered clavier, Book 1: Prelude & fugue in B flat, BWV 866.* (ii) *English suite No. 3 in G min., BWV 808; Italian concerto, BWV 971; Sonata in D min., BWV 964* (trans. from Unaccompanied *Violin sonata No. 2 in A min., BWV 1003*); *Well-tempered clavier, Book 1: Preludes & fugues: in C min; in C, BWV 847–8; Book 2: Preludes & fugues in C sharp, BWV 872; in G, BWV 884.* (iii) *Goldberg variations, BWV 988;* (iv) *Partitas Nos. 1 in B flat, BWV 825; 2 in C min., BWV 826; 6 in E min., BWV 830.*

500♪ ❁ *** (i) VAIA 1041; (ii) VAIA 1051; (iii) VAIA 1029; (iv) VAIA 1040 (available separately). Rosalyn Tureck (piano).

Rosalyn Tureck's Bach playing is legendary, and the performances here show that her keyboard command and fluent sense of Bach style are as remarkable as ever. Miss Tureck uses a wide dynamic and expressive range with consummate artistry, her decoration always adds to the musical effect, and she makes us feel that Bach's keyboard music could be played in no other way than this – the hallmark of a great artist.

Chorale preludes: Ich ruf' zu dir, BWV 639; Nun komm' der Heiden Heiland, BWV 659 (both arr. Busoni); *Chromatic fantasia and fugue in D min., BWV 903; Fantasia and fugue in A min., BWV 904; Italian concerto in F, BWV 971; Fantasia in A min., BWV 922.*
(M) *** Ph. 454 409-2 [id.]. Alfred Brendel (piano).

Brendel's fine Bach recital originally appeared in 1978; it has been digitally remastered for the CD format and now appears for the first time at mid-price. The performances are of the old school, with no attempt to strive after harpsichord effects, and with every piece creating a sound-world of its own. The *Italian concerto* is particularly imposing, with a finely sustained sense of line and beautifully articulated rhythms. The recording is in every way truthful and present, bringing the grand piano very much into the living-room before one's very eyes. Masterly.

Chorales: *Ich ruf' zu dir, Herr Jesu Christ, BWV 639; Jesu, joy of man's desiring,* from *BWV 147; Partita No. 1 in B flat, BWV 825; Prelude and fugue No. 8 in B flat min., BWV 853; Sicilienne* from *Flute sonata, BWV 1031; Toccata, BWV 914.*
(B) **(*) Cal. Approche CAL 6203. Inger Södergren (piano) – BERG: *Sonata.* **(*)

Södergren opens with the famous chorale, *Jesu, joy of man's desiring*, and its gentle outline sets the mood for this recital, relaxed and thoughtful pianism of deep musicality. The *Partita* might be found not crisp enough for those favouring the Bach style of Rosalyn Tureck, and the *Toccata* is not forceful either. But this is appealing in a less assertive way, with slightly muted keyboard colours. Playing which is very persuasive in its intimacy, while the piano-image is warm and glowing.

Chromatic fantasia and fugue, BWV 903; 4 Duets, BWV 802–5; English suites Nos. 1–6, BWV 806–11; Goldberg variations, BWV 988; 2- & 3-Part Inventions, BWV 772a–786; French suites Nos. 1–6, BWV 812–17; Partitas Nos. 1–6 BWV 825–30; Partita in B min., BWV 831; Well-tempered Clavier, Books I–II, Preludes and fugues Nos. 1–48, BWV 846–93.
(M) *** Decca Dig. 452 269-2 (12). András Schiff (piano).

András Schiff recorded Bach's major keyboard works for Decca over a decade between 1982 and 1991, and it is perhaps remarkable that, during an era when original instruments are all the rage, he has made such a convincing case for recording this music on the piano. Moreover he makes no apologies for the range of dynamic and colour that the modern keyboard can command and of which Bach can have had no inkling. Yet Schiff's playing is so stylish, his expressive phrasing and rubato so natural, the presentation so spontaneous, that the critical listener is disarmed and is encouraged to sit back and simply enjoy the music. Most of these recordings are available separately; only in the *Inventions* is there a suspicion that Schiff's expressive freedom approaches the outer boundaries of what is permissible, and even here the musical flow remains convincing. The Decca recording, natural and not too resonant, is surely ideal for such repertoire.

Chromatic fantasia and fugue in D min., BWV 903; Italian concerto, BWV 971; French suites Nos. 1 in D min., BWV 812; 2 in C min., BWV 813.
(BB) ** Naxos Dig. 8.550709 [id.]. Wolfgang Rübsam (piano).

French suites Nos. 3 in B min., BWV 814; 4 in E flat, BWV 815; 5 in G, BWV 816; 6 in E, BWV 817.
(BB) ** Naxos Dig. 8.550710 [id.]. Wolfgang Rübsam (piano).

Partitas Nos. 1 in B flat, BWV 825; 2 in C min., BWV 826; Capriccio on the departure of a beloved brother, BWV 992; Prelude and fuguetta in G, BWV 902.
(BB) ** Naxos Dig. 8.550692 [id.]. Wolfgang Rübsam (piano).

Partitas Nos. 3 in A min., BWV 827; 4 in D, BWV 828.
(BB) ** Naxos Dig. 8.550693 [id.]. Wolfgang Rübsam (piano).

Partitas Nos. 5 in G, BWV 829; 6 in E min., BWV 830.
(BB) ** Naxos Dig. 8.550694 [id.]. Wolfgang Rübsam (piano).

Toccatas Nos. 1 in F sharp min.; 2 in C min.; 3 in D; 4 in D min.; 5 in E min.; 6 in G min.; 7 in G, BWV 910/916.
(BB) ** Naxos Dig. 8.550708 [id.]. Wolfgang Rübsam (piano).

Wolfgang Rübsam is embarking on a complete survey of Bach's keyboard music on the piano for Naxos. His manner is simple and thoughtful, never inflexible, always sensing the flow of the musical line. Ornamentation is unfussy, and the only cavil is that his expressive playing brings little hesitations, which are very much part of his style and to which one adjusts, although this may trouble some listeners. Nothing here is metronomic and tempi are never pushed too hard. The *Chromatic fantasia*, brilliantly articulated as it is, is not treated as a chance for virtuoso display for its own sake and some might feel that the *Toccatas* are not flamboyant enough, but Rübsam sees them as being like sinfonias, beginning with a flourish and with the music satisfyingly brought together in the closing sections. The recording is clear and truthful.

Chromatic fantasia and fugue, BWV 903; Italian concerto, BWV 971; Well-tempered Clavier, Book I: Preludes and fugues: in D, BWV 850; in F sharp, BWV 858; in B flat, BWV 866; in C sharp, BWV 848. Book II: Preludes and fugues: in C min., BWV 871; in C sharp, BWV 872; in G, BWV 884; in G min., BWV 885; in A min., BWV 903. Encore: Goldberg variations: Variation No. 29.
*** VAI Audio VAIA 1139 [id.]. Rosalyn Tureck (harpsichord).

Those collectors who have dipped into Rosalyn Tureck's ever-stimulating Bach performances on the piano, which received a Rosette in our main volume (see above), will surely also want this superb harpsichord recital, recorded live in 1981 at the Metropolitan Museum of Art, New York. The balance is very close, but the sharp focus of the instrument suits Tureck's amazingly clean articulation. She opens with direct, considered performances of five *Preludes and fugues* from Book II of the *Well-tempered Clavier*; then, after a dazzling account of the *Chromatic fantasia* and a reflective fugue, she moves back to give us four *Preludes and fugues* from Book I, of which the opening *D major* brings the most remarkable bravura articulation, echoed in the equally sparkling *B flat major*; the fugues, however, unfold precisely. Then comes a buoyant *Italian concerto* with a touchingly thoughtful central *Andante*; her encore brings a final burst of virtuosity in the twenty-ninth variation from the *Goldberg variations*, but Tureck's brilliance is always at Bach's service rather than being displayed for its own sake. Not to be missed: the ear soon adjusts to the dry, close, slighty tinkly harpsichord image.

English suites Nos. 1–6; French suites Nos. 1–6.
(M) **(*) Teldec/Warner 0630 13582-2 (3) [id.]. Alan Curtis (harpsichord).

Anyone wanting both the *English* and *French suites* played on a fine period harpsichord will find Alan Curtis's 1970 Teldec set excellent value: by putting them together (with the first *English suite* followed by the first *French suite*, and so on), the twelve works have fitted neatly on to three discs. Curtis uses a harpsichord made by Christian Zell of Hamburg in 1928. The sound is a fraction over-resonant but, provided a not-too-high volume level is set, the result is pleasing to the ear. This is lively, thoughtful playing in excellent style. Slow movements go particularly well and there is no feeling of didacticism. Not quite a first choice, but well worth considering.

(i) *French suites Nos. 1–6, BWV 812–17;* (ii) *English suite No. 3 in G min., BWV 808; Italian concerto in F, BWV 971.*
(B) **(*) EMI forte Dig. CZS5 69479-2 (2). (i) Andrei Gavrilov (piano); (ii) Stanislav Bunin (piano).

Gavrilov's 1984 set of the *French suites* is full of interesting things, and there is some sophisticated, not to say masterly, pianism. The part-writing is keenly alive and the playing full of subtle touches. He draws a wide range of tone-colour from the keyboard and employs a wider dynamic range than might be expected. There is an element of the self-conscious here and a measure of exaggeration in some of the *Gigues*, but there is much that is felicitous, too. To fill up the pair of discs, Stanislav Bunin's performances of the *Third English suite* and the *Italian concerto*, recorded six years later, have been added. His style is bold and direct, less flexible than Gavrilov's approach but totally unselfconscious. The slow movement of the *Italian concerto* is pleasingly thoughtful. Both artists receive excellent recording.

French suite No. 5 in G, BWV 816; Fugue in 3 parts, BWV 953; Fughetta, BWV 961; Italian concerto; 3 Minuets, BWV 841–3; 2 Minuets, BWV anh. 114–15; Partita No. 1 in B flat, BWV 825; 6 Little Preludes, BWV 939–43 & BWV 999; 6 Preludes, BWV 924–8 & BWV 930.
(B) ** EMI Debut CDZ5 69700-2 [id.]. Richard Egarr (harpsichord).

Richard Egarr is a pupil of Gustav Leonhardt and he makes his first recording on a modern Katzman copy of a 1638 Rückers. He is intimately recorded and here combines miniatures (some of these pieces come from the *Clavier-Büchlein*, intended to instruct the young Wilhelm Friedemann Bach) with one or two major works. He plays very musically, but not all will take to his little nudges of rubato which thoughtfully prevent the melodic line from being austere but which do not always sound entirely spontaneous. A promising début, nevertheless.

Goldberg variations, BWV 988.
500♪ *** O-L Dig. 444 866-2 [id.]. Christophe Rousset (harpsichord).
500♪ ✿ *** VAI Audio VAIA 1029 [id.]. Rosalyn Tureck (piano).
(B) *** HM Dig. HMT 7901240 [HMC 901240]. Kenneth Gilbert (harpsichord).

Christophe Rousset takes his place fairly easily at the top of the list. He plays a 1751 Hemsch, which is superbly recorded within a generous but not too resonant acoustic, so that the harpsichord is very real and believable.

While this work should properly be heard on the harpsichord, Rosalyn Tureck's recording is very special indeed – there is no other record of Bach played on the piano quite as compelling as this, and for I. M. it would be a desert island disc.

Kenneth Gilbert gives a refreshingly natural performance of the *Goldberg*. He uses a recent copy of a Rückers–Taskin, and it makes a very pleasing sound. His is an aristocratic reading; he avoids excessive display and there is a quiet, cultured quality to his playing that is very persuasive. His is an essentially introspective account, recorded in a rather less lively acoustic than is Pinnock on Archiv, and Gilbert is a thoughtful and thought-provoking player. His approach to repeats is discussed in the accompanying notes and seems eminently sensible. This can be strongly recommended alongside Maggie Cole (on Virgin), but the Harmonia Mundi reissue has a distinct price advantage (in the UK only).

15 2-Part Inventions, BWV 772–86; 15 3-Part Inventions, BWV 787–801; Ornamented versions: *2-Part Invention No. 1 in C, BWV 772a* (ornamented in triplets); *3-Part Inventions Nos. 4, 5, 7, 9, 11 & 13, BWV 790–91, 793, 795, 797 & 799.*
*** Astrée Audivis Dig. E 8603 [id.]. Blandine Verlet (harpsichord).

Blandine Verlet uses a 1624 Rückers which seems quite ideal for this repertoire, and it sounds very real when one achieves the right volume-control setting. She plays with great spirit and the imitation between the parts is admirably clear. Her passage-work is never inflexible and, when the writing is comparatively expressive, her minor hesitations in the flow prevent any sense of rigidity; this is more striking in the *Three-part* pieces. Having played through both sets, she then offers a selection with judicious ornamentation, strikingly effective in the very first of the *Two-part Inventions*. This can be recommended alongside – though not in preference to – Koopman whose approach is rather less free but still seemingly spontaneous.

Partitas Nos. 1–6, BWV 825–30.
(M) *** Virgin Veritas/EMI Dig. VED5 61292-2 (2) [ZDMB 61292]. Gustav Leonhardt (harpsichord).
*** Hyperion Dig. CDA 67191/2 [id.]. Angela Hewitt (piano).

Partitas Nos. 1–4, BWV 825–8.
**(*) Ongaku Records Dig. 024-108 [id.]. Sergey Schepkin (piano).

Partitas Nos. 5–7, BWV 829–31; 4 Duets, BWV 802–5.
**(*) Ongaku Records Dig. 024-109 [id.]. Sergey Schepkin (piano).

Gustav Leonhardt's set was recorded (in 1986) on a Dowd (modelled on an eighteenth-century German instrument by Michael Mietke) in the excellent acoustic of the Doopsgezinde Gemeente Kerk in Haarlem. In terms of sheer sound it is among the most satisfactory available versions, and in terms of style it combines elegance, spontaneity and authority. There is nothing didactic about this playing, but it is never less than thought-provoking. In many respects it is musically the most satisfying of current sets, save for the fact that Leonhardt observes no repeats. This will undoubtedly diminish its appeal – which is a great pity, since both illumination and pleasure are to be had from this set. It is offered at medium price, but the first disc plays for only 40 minutes 36 seconds and the second for 54 minutes 36 seconds.

Angela Hewitt's is a most impressive and enjoyable set of *Partitas*. Her pacing is admirable, her style is simple, direct and flexible, with a natural use of light and shade. In faster movements, like the Scherzo of the *A minor Suite*, her articulation is a delight, and the preceding *Burlesca* has great charm. Slow movements are expressive, and the whole effect is spontaneous. She is beautifully recorded: this sounds like a piano but without exaggerated sonority.

Sergey Schepkin really keeps the music moving. His tempi are much faster than Miss Hewitt's. His *Correntes* are crisp and brilliant and he fairly rattles through the *Capriccio* which ends the *Second Partita*. The earlier *Allegro* which precedes the *Allemande* is very impulsive. Yet the *Sarabande* of the same suite is beautifully judged, and this is playing of strong personality. The G major work, BWV 829, which opens the second disc, is exceptionally fine. Schepkin is very well (if forwardly) recorded, and these performances are certainly stimulating. The last three movements of the *A minor Suite* are pressed on a little too strongly. He needs to gain a shade more poise; nevertheless altogether this is most enjoyable.

Partitas Nos. 1–7, BWV 825–31; 4 Duets, BWV 802–5; Italian Concerto, BWV 971.
(B) ** Ph. Dig. Duo 456 068-2 (2) [id.]. Jean-Louis Steuerman (piano).

Eminently straightforward and unfussy playing from Steuerman which some collectors may prefer to the more purely 'pianistic' version like Schiff's. Steuerman has a well-developed sense of style, as one might expect from a prizewinner at the Leipzig Bach Competition, and he does not cultivate beauty of sound for its own sake. At times he is a little inhibited – as if he mistrusts spontaneity – and there are others when he is a little prosaic and literal. He is also somewhat inconsistent about repeats. Nevertheless he remains a generally sound guide to the *Partitas* and he is certainly well recorded. For this inexpensive reissue he adds some worthwhile bonuses, for his *Italian Concerto* has infectious buoyancy in the outer movements, while the *Andante*, like the serene *Sarabande* in the *B minor Partita*, BWV 831, (now added to the set) has a simple beauty which is affecting. The *Duets* (which derive from the so-called *Organ Mass* in the third volume of the *Clavierübung*) are engagingly fresh, the rhythmic articulation consistently deft. Not a first choice for the *Partitas*, but excellent value.

The Well-tempered Clavier (48 Preludes and fugues), BWV 846–93.
(B) *** HM Musique d'Abord HMA 1901285/8 [id.]. Davitt Moroney (harpsichord).

The Well-tempered Clavier, Book I, Preludes and fugues Nos. 1–24, BWV 846–69.
500♪ ❁ *** Decca Dig. 414 388-2 (2) [id.]. András Schiff (piano).
*** ECM Dig. 835246-2 (2) [id.]. Keith Jarrett (piano).

The Well-tempered Clavier, Book II, Preludes and fugues Nos. 25–48, BWV 870–93.
500♪ ❁ *** Decca Dig. 417 236-2 (2) [id.]. András Schiff (piano).
*** ECM Dig. 847936-2 (2) [id.]. Keith Jarrett (harpsichord).

Schiff often takes a very individual view of particular preludes and fugues, but his unexpected readings regularly win one over long before the end. Consistently he translates this music into pianistic terms, rarely if ever imitating the harpsichord, and though his very choice of the piano will rule him out with those seeking authenticity, his voyage of discovery through this supreme keyboard collection is the more riveting, when the piano is an easier instrument to listen to over long periods. First-rate sound.

Keith Jarrett has recorded Book I on a modern piano, and we like it very much for its dedication, simplicity and integrity. In its way it is quite the equal of Schiff's recording. There is no attempt at any excessive indulgence in keyboard colour and the recording is very satisfying in its natural sonority. On the face of it, it seems a rather odd idea to revert to the harpsichord for Book II and, if his reasoning does not completely persuade us, his qualities of musicianship do. He is a highly intelligent and musical player whose readings and precise articulation can hold their own against the current competition.

Davitt Moroney uses a modern harpsichord (built in 1980) which has a full-bodied yet cleanly focused image but which is rather too closely balanced. Yet the effect is certainly tangible and realistic, the perspective more convincing than with Leonhardt. His thoughtful, considered approach is satisfying in its way, stylistically impeccable, although the playing is less concentrated than with Gilbert, the result less exuberantly spontaneous than with Van Asperen (see our main volume). But it will suit those who like a thoughtful, unostentatious approach to Bach, yet one which does not lack rhythmic resilience. Moreover, with full documentation it is a very real bargain on Harmonia Mundi's Musique d'Abord budget label.

ORGAN MUSIC

Complete organ music

Wolfgang Rübsam Complete Philips series

Volume I, Disc 1: *Fantasia, BWV 572; Preludes and fugues, BWV 531–2; 535, 541, 544–5, 549–50; Toccata and fugue in D min., BWV 565* (438 172-2).

Disc 2: *Fugues, BWV 577–8; Fugue on a theme of Corelli, BWV 579; Prelude, BWV 568; Preludes and fugues, BWV 533–4; 536; 543; 546–7; Toccata and fugue in D min. (Dorian), BWV 538* (438 173-2).

Disc 3: *Canzona in D min., BWV 588; Preludes and fugues, BWV 537, 539–40, 542, 548; Prelude, Adagio-trio; Fantasia and fugue* (without BWV No.) (438 174-2).

Disc 4: *Allabreve in D, BWV 589; Fantasias: in C min.* (without BWV No.); *in C min., BWV 562; Fugues, BWV 575, 581; Passacaglia in C min., BWV 582; Pedal-Exercitium, BWV 598; Toccata, BWV 564; Toccata and fugue in E, BWV 566; Trios, BWV 583, 586, 1027a* (438 175-2).

Disc 5: *Fantasia in G, BWV 571; Trio sonatas for 2 keyboards and pedal, BWV 525–9* (438 177-2).

Disc 6: *Trio sonata No. 6, BWV 530; Chorales, BWV 691a, 717, 725; Chorale partitas, BWV 766–7; 770; Chorale preludes, 745, 747* (438 178-2).

Disc 7: *Canonic variations on 'Vom Himmel hoch', BWV 768; Chorale partita on 'Sei gegrüsset, Jesu gütig', BWV 768; Chorale variations on 'Allein Gott in der Höh' sei Ehr'', BWV 771; Chorale: 'Wie schön leuch't uns der Morgenstern', BWV 739; Fugue in C min. (Theme Legrenzianum, elaboratum cum subjecto pedaliter), BWV 574; Pastorale in D, BWV 590* (438 179-2).

Disc 8: *Orgelbüchlein: Chorales, BWV 599–644* (438 180-2).

Volume II, Disc 9: *Chorales, BWV 653b; O Lamm Gottes unschuldig* (without BWV No.); *Chorale preludes, BWV 748–50, 754, 756, 759; Fuga sopra il Magnificat, BWV 733; 6 Schübler chorales, BWV 645–50; Clavier-Ubung, Part 3: German organ Mass* (beginning): *Prelude in E flat, BWV 552, & Chorale preludes, BWV 669–74* (438 182-2).

Disc 10: *Clavier-Ubung, Part 3: German organ Mass* (cont.); *Chorale preludes, BWV 675–89; Fugue in E flat, BWV 552; Duets 1–4, BWV 802–5* (438 183-2).

Disc 11: *6 Concertos after various composers, BWV 592–7; Leipzig chorales Nos. 1–3, BWV 651–3* (438 184-2).

Disc 12: *18 Leipzig chorales, Nos.4–18* (438 185-2).

Disc 13: *Chorales and Chorale preludes, BWV 690, 692–4, 700, 703, 710, 715, 719, 722, 724, 729, 732, 734, 738, 746, 751, 755, 757–8, 763; Chorale fugues and fuguettas, BWV 699, 701–2, 716; Fantasia super 'Valet will ich dir geben', BWV 735; Fantasia in C, BWV 570; Fugues, BWV 570 & BWV 576; Kleines harmonisches Labyrinth, BWV 591; Prelude in C, BWV 567; Prelude and fugue in A min., BWV 551; Trio in G min., BWV 584* (438 187-2).

Disc 14: *Chorales and Chorale preludes, BWV 691, 695, 705–9, 711–12, 714, 718, 720, 723, 726, 730, 740–44, 752, 765; Chorale fantasia, BWV 713; Chorale fuguettas, BWV 696–8, 704* (438 188-2).

Disc 15: *Aria in F, BWV 587; Chorales and Chorale preludes, BWV 721, 760–62, 727–8, 731, 736–7; Fantasia con imitazione, BWV 563; Fantasia and fugue in A min., BWV 561; Fugue in D, BWV 580; Prelude in A min., BWV 569; Trio in C min., BWV 585; The Art of Fugue, BWV 1080* (beginning): *Contrapunctus 1–5* (438 189-2).

Disc 16: *The Art of Fugue* (conclusion): *Contrapunctus 6–11; Canon all'Ottava; Fua a 3 soggetti. Chorale: 'Wenn wir in Höchsten Nöten sein', BWV 668a* (438 190-2).
(B) *** Ph. 456 080-2 (16). Wolfgang Rübsam (organs of Frauenfeld & Freiburg).

As can be seen, Wolfgang Rübsam's magnificent survey of Bach's organ music, made at the beginning of the 1970s, has been re-ordered and reissued, still on 16 CDs and with excellent documentation, but now in two boxes of 8 discs, contained within a sturdy slip-case. The bulk of the music was recorded on the fine instrument at St Nikolaus in Frauenfeld, Switzerland; for the chorale preludes and a few miscellaneous works, Rübsam turned to the Belgian Hockhois organ at Freiburg Münster. Sonically the results are highly stimulating, offering the widest range of colour, a rich overall blend without clouding of detail, and plenty of support from the pedals. The *Trio sonatas* are especially attractive and compare well with Simon Preston's set (DG 437 835-2) in both their luminous palette and their liveliness. The six solo *Concertos*, based on music of others, principally Ernst and Vivaldi, are comparably successful, although here Rübsam adopts extreme tempi, with adagios very measured against sprightly allegros.

But the key to the success of any Bach survey must lie with the way the performer approaches the large-scale concert pieces, notably the *Preludes and fugues* and *Toccatas and fugues*, and these are nearly all in the first volume. Certainly in these works Rübsam is consistently vital, and his registration often tickles the ear. The famous *Toccata, adagio and fugue*, BWV 564, is very well judged, a work that can easily become ponderous, while the *Passacaglia in C minor*, BWV 582, has a convincing forward momentum and plenty of imaginative detail.

The so-called *German organ Mass* is split between CDs, which should not have been necessary, and the *Art of Fugue* has now been placed at the end; a suitable postlude is provided with a complete version of the *Chorale*, BWV 668a. There are many special insights here and, with such a spontaneous approach, Rübsam's distinguished and consistently enjoyable survey may readily be placed alongside that of Peter Hurford on Decca, while the newly remastered Philips analogue recording is of comparable demonstration quality – a very major achievement.

Canonic variations on 'Vom Himmel hoch', BWV 769; Fantasia in G, BWV 572; Fantasia and fugue in G min., BWV 542; Passacaglia in C min., BWV 582; Preludes and fugues: in D, BWV 532; in E flat, BWV 552; 6 Schübler chorale preludes, BWV 645–50; Toccatas and fugues: in D min., BWV 536 (Dorian) & 565; in F, BWV 540; Trio sonata No. 3 in D min. BWV 527.

(B) ** DG Double 453 064-2 (2) [id.]. Helmut Walcha (organs of St-Pierre-le-Jeune, Strasbourg, St Laurenskerk, Alkmaar).

It is good to be inexpensively reminded of the German tradition of playing in this repertoire, as represented by its most distinguished exponent, Helmut Walcha. The *Canonic variations* and *Schübler chorales* (recorded in Strasbourg, and part of his complete survey, made at the beginning of the 1970s) show him at his most didactic. The playing is calm and assured and certainly authoritative. Its control is never in doubt, but the famous chorales are rather straitlaced and entirely lacking in charm. Most of the rest of the programme was recorded at St Laurenskerk in 1963–4. The remastered recordings sound extremely well, the reedy brightness supported by an underlying depth, and there is a sense of perspective too, particularly in the interplay of the famous *D minor Fugue*, which was the first piece to be recorded (in 1959) and which shows Walcha at his more extrovert. The other performances are usually registered effectively, notably the first movement of the *Trio sonata*, but Walcha's pulse remains steady. Structures are well controlled and detail is lucid, but at times there is a feeling of ponderousness, which one does not experience with players like Peter Hurford, Kevin Bowyer and Christopher Herrick.

(i) *Concertos in D min., BWV 596; in A min., BWV 593* (after Vivaldi); (ii) *Passacaglia and fugue in C min., BWV 582; Toccata, adagio and fugue in C, BWV 564; Toccata and fugue in D min., BWV 565.*

(B) ** EMI forte CZS5 69328-2 (2). Fernando Germani (organ of (i) Selby Abbey, Yorkshire; (ii) Royal Festival Hall, London) – FRANCK: *Chorales Nos. 1–3* etc. *(*); WIDOR: *Toccata.* **(*)

The Festival Hall with its dry acoustics, where BWV 564, 565 and 582 were recorded in 1959, proves a fascinatingly different way of hearing Bach. Germani plays the *Toccatas* brilliantly enough but presents the fugues in a very relaxed fashion, and especially so the *C minor Passacaglia*, and while the listener can hear every detail of the registration in crystal clarity, he lets the tension build itself slowly to its climax. Each of these performances becomes aurally quite a *tour de force* – if also a somewhat didactic experience. For the *Concertos* we are transferred to the warmer ambience of Selby Abbey. These works are much more Vivaldi than Bach, although it is surprising how much of Bach's personality is superimposed by Germani on that of the Italian composer. This is emphasized in the *D minor Concerto* by a certain heaviness of style in the playing; whereas in the *A minor* Germani finds slightly more Italianate jauntiness in the writing of the outer movements and a pealing-bell effect for the finale. He sets the mood of the *Adagio*, which he plays very slowly indeed, as a serene contrast. The recordings are superb, but the Abbey organ is not ideally chosen for the concertos, which need more sonic brilliance.

VOCAL MUSIC

Cantata Nos. (i) *11: Lobet Gott in seinen Reichen (Ascension oratorio);* (ii) *50: Chorus: Nun ist das Heil und die Kraft.*

(M) **(*) Virgin Veritas/EMI Dig. VM5 61340-2. (i) Kirkby, Tubb, Cable, Jochens, Charlesworth; (ii) Van Evera, Cable, Crook, Grant, Tubb, Trevor, Jochens, Charlesworth; Taverner Players, Parrott – *Magnificat.* **(*)

Bach's cantata, BWV 11, is also known as the 'Ascension oratorio' as it was written for Ascension Day (19 May) 1735, with the biblical events narrated by the Evangelist. The first alto aria, *Ach, bleibe doch, mein liebstes Leben*, was later taken by its composer to form the *Agnus Dei* in the *Mass in B minor*. It is impressively sung here by Margaret Cable, and the other soloists do not disappoint either. As in the coupled *Magnificat*, the five soloists also economically provide the choruses, one voice to a part, and eight singers pit themselves antiphonally against Bach's spectacular orchestration (including three trumpets) for the chorus from the companion cantata, used as an encore. Some might feel that a larger group would have been more effective here, although the vocal detail is fairly clear. Parrott's performances are certainly refreshingly different and very well recorded.

Cantatas Nos. 12: Weinen, Klagen, Sorgen, Zagen; 54: Widerstehe doch der Sünde; 162: Ach! ich sehe, jetzt, da ich zur Hochzeit gehe; 182: Himmelskönig, sei willkommen.

*** BIS Dig. CD 791 [id.]. Yumiko Kurisu, Yoshikazu Mera, Makoro Sakurada, Peter Kooy, Bach Coll. Japan, Suzuki.

We commented with enthusiasm in our main volume on the first issue of the BIS series of Bach cantatas (Nos. 4, *Christ lag in Todesbanden*, 150, *Nach dir, Herr verlanget mich* and 196, *Der Herr denket an uns*) with the Bach Collegium Japan under Masaaki Suzuki. The present issues are the next in what BIS plan as a complete Bach cantata series from Japanese artists with period instruments. A pupil of Ton Koopman, Suzuki has directed the Bach Collegium Japan since 1990, and in some ways one feels that the results he achieves are as good as – and at times even finer than – those of the master. As with the earlier issue, these performances radiate a sheer joy in music-making that is inspiriting. The strings have none of the sense of inhibition, of excessive awareness of the constraints of period performance and self-consciousness that mar some of their European colleagues. Even more striking is the quality of the diction, not an easy matter for most Japanese – only Peter Kooy is non-Japanese. Suzuki uses a higher pitch (A = 465) with its concomitant brighter sound, as does Koopman, and female voices rather than boys.

At almost 80 minutes, the second issue in the series offers splendid value for money and its artistic excellence is again not in dispute. Readers will recognize the opening of No. 12, *Weinen, Klagen, Sorgen, Zagen*, as a model for the *Crucifixus* of the *B minor Mass* and Suzuki gives it with feeling and gravitas, while his characterization elsewhere, both in No. 54, *Widerstehe doch der Sünde*, and in 162, *Ach! ich sehe, jetzt, da ich zur Hochzeit gehe*, inspires confidence. No grumbles about the quality of the singing, the instrumental response or the present and pleasing sound, which is in the best traditions of the house.

Cantatas Nos. 22: Jesus nahm zu sich die Zwölfe; 23: Du wahrer Gott und Davids Sohn; 54: Widerstehe doch der Sünde; 63: Christen, ätzet diesen Tag; 155: Mein Gott, wie lang, ache lange; 161: Komm, du süsse Todenstunde; 162: Ach! ich sehe, jetzt, da ich zur Hochzeit gehe; 163: Nur jedem das Seine; 165: O heilgese Geist- und Wasserbad; 208: Was mir behagt, ist nur die muntre Jagd.

**(*) Erato/Warner 14336-2 (3) [id.]. Barbara Schlick, Caroline Stam, Ruth Holton, Els Bongers, Elisabeth von Magnus, Andreas Scholl, Paul Agnew, Klaus Mertens; Amsterdam Bar. Ch. & O, Ton Koopman.

We welcomed the first two sets of Ton Koopman's new complete cycle in our main volume without being able to make a choice between the newcomer and the long-established Leonhardt–Harnoncourt survey (Teldec). Unlike them, Koopman opts for female soloists rather than boys, as would have been the case in Bach's day, and he favours mixed rather than solely male choirs, which will be a plus point for many collectors. Koopman goes for a higher than normal pitch – a semitone above that used now, which is what Bach would have known in Mühlhausen and Weimar, and which brightens the sonority quite a lot. He continues now his survey (which is proceeding on largely chronological lines) with ten more cantatas, one of them – the delightful No. 208, *Was mir behagt, ist nur die muntre Jagd*, which includes '*Sheep may safely graze*' – secular. All come from Bach's Weimar years. For the most part the singing here is of a high order of accomplishment – in particular Andreas Scholl and Elisabeth von Magnus, and the instrumental playing is certainly more finished than is often the case in the Teldec set, though here it is by no means always as fresh or secure as on the Japanese series now underway from BIS, where cantatas overlap. In No. 54, *Widerstehe doch der Sünde*, the pupil (Suzuki studied with Koopman at the Sweelinck Conservatoire in Amsterdam in the late 1980s) surpasses the master in expressive power, and even when he doesn't (in No. 63, *Christen, ätzet diesen Tag*) the string playing yields in vigour and polish to the Japanese. The Dutch players sound uncharacteristically wanting in sonority both here and elsewhere in the set. In this same cantata, and in No. 162, *Ach! ich sehe, jetzt, da ich zur Hochzeit gehe*, Koopman offers alternative versions, giving him an undoubted advantage over the opposition. One cannot suppress the thought that it would be good if some enterprising company were to record an artist like Raymond Leppard, whose musicianship rules his scholarship, in a modern-instrument cycle, with the richer sonorities and less meagre palette that authentic ensembles provide.

Cantatas Nos. (i; ii) *32: Liebster Jesu mein Verlangen;* (i) *51: Jauchzet Gott in allen Landen;* (iii) *56: Ich will den Kreuzstab gerne tragen;* (i; ii) *57: Selig ist der Mann;* (iv–vii) *74: Wer mich liebet, der wird mein Wort halten;* (iii) *82: Ich habe genug;* (v; vi; ii) *128: Auf Christi Himmelfahrt allein;* (v–vi) *134: Ein Herz, das seinen Jesum lebend weiss;* (iv–vii) *147: Herz und Mund und Tat und Leben;* (viii) *151: Süsser Trost, mein Jesus kömmt;* (iv; v; vi; ii) *173: Erhöhtes Fleisch und Blutt;* (iv–vi) *191: Gloria in excelsis Deo;* (i) *199: Mein Herze schwimmt im Blut. Sinfonias from Cantatas Nos. 4; 29; 31 (Sonata); 49; 106 (Sonatina in B flat); 52; 142 & 146 (Concertos); 150; 169; 174; 196; 207 (March); 221; Cantata No. 65:* Chorale: *Die Kön'ge aus Saba; Cantata No. 147: Jesu, joy of man's desiring. Christmas oratorio: Sinfonia;* Chorale: *Ach, mein Herzliebes Jesuslein.* (ix) (Organ) *Chorale & Choral prelude: In dulci jubilo, BWV 729 & BWV 368; Chorale variations on 'Vom Himmel hoch', BWV 738.*

(B) ** Ph. 454 346-2 (5) [id.]. (i) Ameling; (ii) Prey; (iii) Souzay; (iv) Cotrubas; (v) Hamari; (vi) Equiluz; (vii) Reimer; (viii) Giebel, Finnilä, Ellenbeck; Ch. of German Bach Soloists; or Kantorei Barmen Gemarke; or Netherlands Vocal Ens.; or Berlin Capella; German Bach Soloists & O, Helmut Winschermann; (ix) Schönstedt (organ).

The thirteen cantatas performed here by Winschermann and his German Bach Soloists, apart from being among Bach's finest, seem to have no special linking factor except that many of them were composed for feast days. They were recorded in the late 1960s and early 1970s, and the sound is very musically balanced, especially in the matter of solo voices and solo wind and brass instruments, although the chorus could be better defined. This is immediately noticeable in the first cantata offered here, *Gloria in excelsis Deo* (No. 191) written for Christmas Day in 1745. *Liebster Jesu* (No. 32), however, is a solo cantata (the chorus sings only in the final chorale). Written for the first Sunday after Epiphany, it is one of the highlights of the set and receives eloquent treatment. Elly Ameling sings most beautifully and the oboe obbligato (Saschko Gawriloff) calls for special mention too. Hermann Prey is no less impressive. Winschermann is a very sympathetic accompanist but (as elsewhere) he alternates between harpsichord and organ in the accompaniment (there should be no harpsichord) and some listeners will find this eccentric. The companion cantata for the same forces (No. 57: *Selig ist der Mann*) is another of Bach's most deeply felt sacred works, and here Winschermann is less searching than he might be. Both these works are very well recorded.

Elly Ameling follows the example of the opening trumpet (Maurice André) when she begins *Jauchzet Gott* (No. 51) and her voice has an appropriate clarion ring to it. The accompaniment is admirably done. The problem of the alternation of harpsichord and organ continuo arises again in the two solo cantatas (Nos. 56 and 82 – *Ich habe genug*) sung with great simplicity of feeling by Gérard Souzay; these are both very recommendable performances. The Netherlands Vocal Ensemble opens No. 74 strongly, and here they are well caught by the engineers. The contributions from all four soloists are dramatically managed, with the tenor (Kurt Equiluz) both commanding and lyrical in his aria, *Kommt, eilet*. Winschermann directs with spirit. No. 128 is notable for its fine opening chorus (with excellent horn-playing), its bass solo (Prey) with a splendid trumpet obbligato (Maurice André), and a fine tenor/alto duet (Equiluz and Hamari) with Helmut Winschermann himself contributing a delicate oboe d'amore obbligato; No. 134, too, is notable for another extended tenor/alto duet by the same soloists, and Kurt Equiluz's contribution also stands out in No. 173 (the cantata for Whit Monday). The instrumental playing in this cantata is most pleasing, as is the closing chorale.

The extended opening chorus of No. 147 (*Herz und Mund und Tat und Leben*) is very well sung by the Netherlands group against a vivid accompaniment, and it is a pity that the choral sound is not more cleanly focused. But all the soloists are impressive (so is the obbligato playing) and the famous final chorale (better known as *Jesu, joy of man's desiring*) is beautifully sung. Winschermann's performance is far better than Richter's old Archiv account, with the continuo here varied very effectively, using harpsichord to provide contrast with organ when appropriate. No. 151 is even more appealing with its lovely pastoral soprano aria, *Süsser Trost, mein Jesus kömmt* (Agnes Giebel intertwining with a flute obbligato), and later offering an equally beautiful contribution from the contralto (Birgit Finnilä, with oboe d'amore). Elly Ameling returns to open her solo cantata, *Mein Herze schwimmt in Blut* (No. 199), strongly and dramatically, and the intensity of her words comes over with commitment. With much sensitive playing and singing, this is very enjoyable indeed, and if Ameling does not always convey the aching depth of feeling in the way a singer like Janet Baker can, her singing has a freshness and eloquence that tells in a quite different way. The recording too is of Philips's very best, full and natural, and makes one reflect how beautiful Bach cantatas can sound using modern string instruments. The final disc looks like a miscellaneous hotch-potch but turns out to be an attractive collection of sinfonias (some in the form of 'concertos' or 'sonatas', two of them quoting from the *Brandenburg Concertos*) to demonstrate the variety of Bach's instrumentation, plus some famous vocal chorales, and with a couple of organ solos thrown in for good measure. They are very well played and sung, although the recording is at times a bit resonant.

Cantatas Nos. 54: Widerstehe doch der Sünde; 82: Ich habe genug; 170: Vergnütge Ruh', beliebte Seelenlust.

*(*) RCA Dig. 09026 62655-2 [id.]. Nathalie Stutzmann, Hanover Band, Roy Goodman.

The three cantatas here afford an admirable vehicle for the artistry of Nathalie Stutzmann, and her wide circle of admirers will welcome its appearance. Most people will associate *Ich habe genug* with such incomparable singers as Hans Hotter, Dietrich Fischer-Dieskau and Gérard Souzay (see Winschermann's Philips box above), but Bach himself made transcriptions for both the soprano and mezzo ranges. Stutzmann sings with suitable expressive restraint, though some may find her voice just a little too matronly in this repertoire. Roy Goodman gives her attentive support, but there is some incongruity between the rich sonority of the soloist and the carefully controlled, even inhibited sound the strings produce. Not a wholly successful marriage of sound-worlds, and from the players an often limited expressive and emotional range. There are more convincing accounts of both Nos. 54, *Widerstehe doch der Sünde*, and 170, *Vergnütge Ruh', beliebte Seelenlust*, on the market. Recommendable primarily for Stutzmann fans.

Cantatas Nos. (i) *63: Christen, ätzet diesen Tag;* (ii) *65: Sie werden aus Saba alle kommen;* (iii) *Magnificat, BWV 243.*
(B) ** DG 439 489-2 [id.]. (i) Mathis, Reynolds, Schreier; (ii) Adam; (ii; iii) Haefliger; (iii) Stader, Töpper; (i; iii) Fischer-Dieskau; Munich Bach Ch. & O, Karl Richter.

In Bach's *Magnificat* Richter is a bit heavy-handed at times, but there is plenty of vigour and the chorus responds well to his direction. The soloists are very good, except for Hertha Töpper who lacks refinement in some of the florid writing. Sonically this sounds its age – it dates from the early 1960s – but the remastering is quite acceptable on CD, though the opening chorus could do with greater freshness, even if its vitality is in no doubt. Both cantatas are fine works – No. 63 joyfully celebrates Christmas Day with gleaming trumpets, and the Epiphany cantata is hardly less festive. In the former, Edith Mathis's soprano aria is beautifully sung, but in the two duets these very individual voices match less comfortably; however, Ernst Haefliger and Theo Adam both make fine contributions to the following work. Again the sound is good rather than outstanding.

Cantatas Nos. 71: Gott ist mein König; 106: Gottes Zeit ist die allerbeste Zeit; 131: Aus der Tiefe rufe ich, Herr, zu dir.
*** BIS Dig. CD 781 [id.]. Midori Suzuki, Aki Yanagisawa, Yoshikazu Mera, Gerd Türk, Peter Kooy, Bach Coll. Japan, Suzuki.

The present disc collects some of the earliest in the canon from Bach's time at Mühlhausen. Some may feel that Suzuki's slow tempo at the opening of No. 106, the *Actus Tragicus* or *Gottes Zeit ist die allerbeste Zeit*, is a little too much of a good thing, but others (this listener included) may well be convinced by the breadth and space he brings to it. The singing is of a high standard throughout, and Midori Suzuki gives particular pleasure in No. 71, *Gott ist mein König*, with her freshness and expressiveness – as for that matter do Aki Yanagisawa and Gerd Türk. Freshness is what characterizes the chorus and instrumentalists too and what communicates a greater intensity of feeling than many rivals. The BIS sound is first class, in terms of both clarity and ambience.

Cantatas Nos. (i; ii) *82: Ich habe genug;* (i; iii; iv) *159: Sehet, wir gehn hinauf gen Jerusalem;* (iii) *170: Vergnügte Ruh', beliebte Seelenlust.*
500♪ ❁ (M) *** Decca 430 260-2 [id.]. (i) Shirley-Quirk; (ii) Lord; (iii) J. Baker; (iv) Tear, St Anthony Singers; ASMF, Marriner.

John Shirley-Quirk's performance of *Ich habe genug* is much to be admired, not only for the sensitive solo singing but also for the lovely oboe obbligato of Roger Lord. But this reissue is to be prized even more for the other two cantatas. Both Dame Janet Baker and Shirley-Quirk are in marvellous voice, and *Vergnügte Ruh'* makes a worthy companion. This is among the half-dozen or so cantata records that ought to be in every collection.

Cantatas Nos. (i) *131: Aus der Tiefen rufe ich;* (ii) *198: Lass Fürstin lass noch einen Strahl (Trauerode).*
(B) ** Sony SB2K 62656 (2) [id.]. (i) Driscoll, Oliver; (ii) Nixon, Bonazzi, Castel, Binder; (i–ii) American Concert Ch., Margaret Hillis, Columbia SO, Craft – MONTEVERDI: *Vespro della Beata Vergine.* **

Cool and intimate – if not distinctive – performances from Craft, but with good choral singing and excellent accompaniments from a well-balanced chamber orchestra who produce excellent wind soloists for the obbligatos. Marni Nixon was an interesting choice as soprano soloist for the *Trauerode* and she sings simply and freshly, as do her colleagues. The tenor and bass are quite effective in the companion work, and the bass aria with chorus (*So du willst . . . Erbarm dich*) works well. The early stereo is remarkably convincing.

Christmas oratorio, BWV 248.
*** Erato/Warner Dig. 0630 14775-2 (2) [id.]. Larsson, Von Magnus, Prégardien, Mertens, Amsterdam Bar. Ch. & O, Ton Koopman.
(B) *** EMI forte CZS5 69503-2 (2). Elly Ameling, Janet Baker, Robert Tear, Dietrich Fischer-Dieskau, King's College, Cambridge, Ch., ASMF, Philip Ledger.

Koopman with his superb choir and orchestra directs a relaxed and genial account of the *Christmas oratorio*, not as sharply focused as Gardiner's even more polished version on DG Archiv (423 232-2), currently our prime recommendation. It is partly a question of the Erato recording-balance, which favours instruments over voices, but most compellingly so, on a relatively intimate scale. The four soloists also sing the arias, and that includes the Evangelist, Christoph Prégardien, with his sweetly tuned tenor, who translates with no sense of strain from one role to the other. The others may not be as distinctive, but each voice is fresh and clear, well caught in the recording.

With generally brisk tempi (controversially so in Dame Janet's cradle-song, *Schlafe mein Liebster*, in

Part II) Philip Ledger's 1976 King's performance anticipates more recent 'authentic' practice. The result is an intensely refreshing account which grows more winning the more one hears it. It was Ledger who played the harpsichord continuo in many of Benjamin Britten's performances of this work, and some of Britten's imagination comes through here, helped by four outstanding and stylish soloists. The King's acoustic gives a warm background to the nicely styled performance of choir and orchestra and, although in the CD transfer the choral focus is not absolutely clean, the sound overall is attractively balanced – certainly the timpani at the very start sound spectacularly impressive. On EMI's two-for-the-price-of-one forte label, this makes an obvious choice for those wanting a recommendable lower-priced version.

Magnificat in D, BWV 243.

(M) **(*) Virgin Veritas/EMI Dig. VM5 61340-2. Van Evera, Tubb, Trevor, Crook, Grant, Taverner Cons. & Players, Parrott – *Cantata No. 11* etc. **(*)

(M) * Teldec/Warner Dig. 0630 13573-2 [id.]. Heichele, Gardow, Esswood, Equiluz, Holl, V. Boys' Ch., Ch. Viennensis, VCM, Harnoncourt – HANDEL: *Utrecht Te Deum.* *(*)

Parrott favours a chorus with one voice to each part, using women (rather than boys) to sing the soprano and alto parts, which gives the performance a lightweight, almost chamber-like character, helped by brisk tempi. The singers are impressive individually and they also make a good team, and the music-making is extremely lively – the opening chorus fizzes. Although not all will respond to Parrott's briskness, the music-making is characteristically fresh, with a fine, authentic instrumental contribution (especially the woodwind obbligati) from the Taverner group, and this well-balanced recording certainly has its place in the catalogue.

Harnoncourt's 1984 version now resurfaces at mid-price. It is generously coupled with a major Handel piece, but the squareness of rhythm, with repeated quavers chugging instead of lifting, makes the result pedestrian despite some excellent solo singing. The chorus is far less imaginative, pedestrian like the playing. The sound is clear but on the dry side, not at all atmospheric.

Mass in B min., BWV 232.

500♪ *** DG Dig. 415 514-2 [id.]. Argenta, Dawson, Fairfield, Knibbs, Kwella, Hall, Nichols, Chance, Collin, Stafford, Evans, Milner, Murgatroyd, Lloyd-Morgan, Varcoe, Monteverdi Ch., E. Bar. Soloists, Gardiner.

*** Hyperion Dig. CDA 67201/2 (2) [id.]. Fritter, Mrasek, Schloderer, Fraas, Rolfe Johnson, George, Tölz Boys' Ch., King's Consort Ch., King's Consort, Robert King.

(M) *** Virgin Veritas/EMI Dig. VMD5 61337-2 (2) [ZDCB 47292]. Kirkby, Van Evera, Iconomou, Immler, Kilian, Covey-Crump, David Thomas, Soloists from Tölz Boys' Ch., Taverner Cons. & Players, Parrott.

John Eliot Gardiner gives a magnificent account of the *B minor Mass*, one which attempts to keep within an authentic scale but which also triumphantly encompasses the work's grandeur. The regular solo numbers are taken by choir members, making a cohesive whole. The recording is warmly atmospheric but not cloudy.

What distinguishes Robert King's vigorous and alert reading of the *B minor Mass* is the use of boy trebles not just for the upper parts of the choruses but as soloists too, both soprano and alto. With the distinctive continental tone of the Tölzer Boys, very different from their English counterparts, the performance has extra freshness, with 24 boys set brightly against 12 of the King's Consort tenors and basses. The individual finesse of the boy singers is impressively demonstrated in the solos. The interplay is charming between the treble of Matthias Ritter and the tenor of Anthony Rolfe Johnson in *Domine Deus*, and the direct, careful manner of Matthias Schloderer in the penultimate number, *Agnus Dei*, taken slowly, is most moving in its simplicity. With such a choir it is inevitable that ensemble is not always quite as crisp as in such a version as Gardiner's on DG Archiv, but this is a reading which consistently brings out the joy of Bach's inspiration, not least in the great celestial outbursts of the *Sanctus* or the final *Dona nobis pacem*. Warm, atmospheric recording.

Parrott, hoping to re-create even more closely the conditions Bach would have expected in Leipzig, adds to the soloists a ripieno group of five singers from the Taverner Consort for the choruses. The instrumental group is similarly augmented with the keenest discretion. Speeds are generally fast, with rhythms sprung to reflect the inspiration of dance; however, the inner darkness of the *Crucifixus*, for example, is conveyed intensely in its hushed tones, while the *Et resurrexit* promptly erupts with a power to compensate for any lack of traditional weight. Soloists are excellent, with reduction of vibrato still allowing sweetness as well as purity. If you want a performance on a reduced scale, the recording, made in St John's, Smith Square, is both realistic and atmospheric.

Mass in B min. BWV 232; Magnificat in D, BWV 243.
(M) *** Erato/Warner 0630 13732-2 (2) [id.]. (i) Rachel Yakar, Jennifer Smith, Birgit Finnilä, Anthony Rolfe Johnson, Philippe Huttenlocher, José van Dam, Lausanne Vocal and Instrumental Ens., Corboz.

Corboz offers the *Mass in B minor* and the *Magnificat* together on a pair of mid-priced Erato discs, and they make a splendid bargain. The two works were recorded in Switzerland in 1979, and the analogue sound is first class in every way, very well balanced in a warm acoustic, yet the chorus has both body and clarity. The professional singers of the Lausanne choir are admirable in both works. In the *B minor Mass* the *Kyrie* is sung at a comparatively spacious tempo, but Corboz's performance has underlying concentration and the *Cum sancto spiritus* is splendidly incisive; like a live performance, as the work proceeds the music-making steadily increases in concentration and power. The *Sanctus*, brightened with trumpets, is splendid. The *Magnificat* has comparable life and spontaneity, and in both works the soloists make an excellent team. If the soprano solos are particularly fine, Anthony Rolfe Johnson's *Benedictus* in the *Mass* is memorable and Birgit Finnilä rises eloquently to the *Agnus Dei*. If there are more urgent original-instrument versions of both works available at premium price, notably from Gardiner, this dedicated and inexpensive set should give great satisfaction, particularly as the coupling is so generous and the sound so pleasing.

Motets: *Singet dem Herrn ein Neues Lied; Der Geist hilft unser Schwachheit auf; Jesu, meine Freude; Fürchte dich nicht, ich bin bei dir; Komm, Jesu, komm!; Lobet den Herrn alle Heiden, BWV 225–30.*
(M) *** Teldec/Warner Dig. 0630 17430-2 [id.]. Stockholm Bach Ch., VCM, Harnoncourt.

To Bach's motets, which include some of the greatest music he ever wrote for chorus, went the honour of being the first of his vocal music to be issued digitally in 1980. The recording is very successful indeed, beautifully fresh and clear, the acoustic attractively resonant without clouding detail, and the accompanying instrumental group giving discreet yet telling support. The vigour and joy of the singing come over splendidly in *Singet dem Herrn* which opens the collection, while the expressive feeling of *Jesu, meine Freude* is matched by a sense of drama. This is one of Harnoncourt's most impressive Bach records, and the conductor's timing and use of pauses are finely judged, while the Stockholm chorus show stamina as well as sympathy; the spontaneity of their performance is impressive. At mid-price this must now be the prime recommendation for these six works.

St John Passion.
*** Erato/Warner Dig. 4509-94675-2 (2) [id.]. Barbara Schlick, Kai Wessel, Guy de Mey, Gerd Türk, Peter Kooy, Klaus Mertens, Netherlands Bach Soc. Ch., Amsterdam Bar. O, Koopman.
*** Columns Dig. 290241 (2). John Mark Ainsley, Catherine Bott, Paul Agnew, Michael Chance, King's College, Cambridge, Ch., Brandenburg Consort, Stephen Cleobury.
*** Hänssler Dig. CD 98.170 [id.]. Juliane Banse, Ingelborg Danz, Michael Schade, James Taylor, Matthias Goerne, Andreas Schmidt, Helmuth Rilling, Stuttgart Gächinger Kantorei & Bach-Collegium, Rilling.

Bach's *St John Passion* is exceptionally well represented on CD at present for, apart from Gardiner's exhilarating version (DG 419 324-2), one must not forget Britten's inspired (1971) set, sung in English, which is superbly recorded and available inexpensively on a Decca Double (see below).

The great glory of the Koopman version is the vividly dramatic singing of the choir, very much a protagonist in the drama of the Passion, both in the virtuoso rendering of the turba choruses (one can really imagine an angry mob) and also in the meditative commentary of the big choruses and in the freshness of the chorales. The soprano, Barbara Schlick, is pure and silvery, setting the pattern for clear, fresh voices. The other soloists complete a fine team, with Guy de Mey an expressive Evangelist, well contrasted with the solo tenor in the arias, Gerd Türk, and with the Jesus of Peter Kooy contrasted against Klaus Mertens in the arias and incidental roles, though not everyone will like the hooty counter-tenor of Kai Wessel. This is a keen contender even against the Gardiner version, though the Erato recording is not as bright and clear, with the chorus set a little behind the orchestra.

Stephen Cleobury conducts a lively, well-paced reading using period instruments, with an excellent team of characterful soloists and with the fresh-toned choir of King's College Choir, including boy-trebles, adding dramatic bite. What specially distinguishes this set is that the alternative numbers which Bach wrote for the revival in 1725 are given in an appendix, including the chorale fantasy which he wrote in place of the opening chorus and the chorale postlude he wrote in place of the final chorale, as well a bass aria and two tenor arias. They are fitted on to the second disc, a generous fill-up, and even though none of those numbers takes priority over those in the regular text it is good to be able to programme them into a domestic performance, if desired. John Mark Ainsley is a warmly expressive tenor Evangelist, nicely contrasted with the lighter-toned Paul Agnew, who sings the tenor arias. Among the others, Catherine

Bott is warmer and more tenderly expressive than almost any latterday rival, very different from the usual light, bright sopranos used in most period performances; and the counter-tenor, Michael Chance, sounds in fuller, warmer voice here than in Gardiner's DG Archiv version, a question of recording-balance, with the Cleobury performance setting the soloists close so as to counteract the reverberant acoustic of King's College Chapel. Most enjoyable.

The Rilling version on Hänssler uses rather larger forces than on most period versions and, paradoxically, modern instruments are used in period style, using today's higher pitch. Speeds in recitative tend to be broader in a relatively traditional way, but that allows the soloists, notably the superb Evangelist, Michael Schade, to bring out the meaning of the words most vividly, with an electrifying sense of drama, most important in this work. The other soloists are outstanding too, all of them young singers with firm, characterful voices, and they sound particularly well on record. The third disc comes as a (free) appendix, giving not just the five alternative numbers which Bach wrote for the 1725 revival but also detailed changes in various numbers, setting fragments from the original against the amended versions. These are explained in a spoken commentary between items, so that it is vital for English-speaking listeners to get the English-language version, instead of Hänssler's main German issue, which also has a single-language booklet of notes.

St John Passion, BWV 245 (sung in English).

500♪ ❁ (B) *** Decca Double 443 859-2 (2) [id.]. Peter Pears, Heather Harper, Alfreda Hodgson, Robert Tear, Gwynne Howell, John Shirley-Quirk, Wandsworth School Boys' Ch., ECO, Britten.

Britten characteristically refuses to follow any set tradition, whether baroque, Victorian or whatever; and, with greater extremes of tempo than is common (often strikingly fast), the result makes one listen afresh. The soloists are all excellent, Heather Harper radiant, and the Wandsworth School Boys' Choir reinforces the freshness of the interpretation. A superb bargain.

St Matthew Passion, BWV 244.

500♪ *** DG Dig. 427 648-2 (3) [id.]. Rolfe Johnson, Schmidt, Bonney, Monoyios, Von Otter, Chance, Crook, Bär, Hauptmann, Monteverdi Ch., E. Bar. Soloists, Gardiner.

Gardiner's version of the *St Matthew Passion* brings an intense, dramatic reading which now makes a clear first choice, not just for period-performance devotees but for anyone not firmly set against the new authenticity.

Transcriptions

Chaconne (from *Partita No. 2 in D min., BWV 1004*) (arr. Busoni).

(M) *** Nimbus Dig. NI 8810 [id.]. Ferruccio Busoni (piano) – CHOPIN: *Preludes* **; LISZT: *Etudes d'exécution transcendante* etc. ***

This is the nearest we shall ever come to hearing Busoni play and, as nearly always, the impression with a first-class modern recording taken from a piano-roll gives an uncanny feeling of the artist's presence. His famous transcription of the Bach *Chaconne* is almost as much Busoni as it is Bach, but it is none the less compelling for that. The prodigious account of it by its arranger projects powerfully in this splendid digital recording, in the Nimbus Duo-Art Grand Piano series. The recording dates from 1925, but the reproduction makes it sound as if it were made yesterday.

Arrangements: Bach–Stokowski

Chorale prelude: Wir glauben all' an einen Gott ('Giant fugue'), BWV 680; Easter cantata, BWV 4: Chorale; Geistliches Lied No. 51: Mein Jesu, BWV 487; Passacaglia and fugue in C min., BWV 582; Toccata and fugue in D min., BWV 565; Well-tempered Clavier, Book 1: Prelude No. 8 in E flat min., BWV 853 (all orch. Stokowski).

(M) *** Decca Phase Four 448 946-2 [id.]. Czech PO, Stokowski (with Concert of miscellaneous orchestral transcriptions – see under LSO ***).

Stokowski's flamboyant arrangements of Bach organ works inspired some of the Philadelphia Orchestra's ripest records in the old days of 78-r.p.m. records. Here with spectacular, closely balanced but truthful Phase Four sound to match, big, bold and reverberant, the results are massively satisfying for anyone prepared to put his purist conscience to one side for a moment. Stokowski, over ninety at the time, challenges his players in expansive tempi, but the results are passionate in concentration. The famous *D minor Toccata and fugue* (for which Disney's animators provided extraordinarily imaginative visual imagery in *Fantasia*) is perhaps a shade less vital here than in Stokowski's earlier, mono version with the Philadelphia Orchestra (RCA GD 60922 – see our main volume), but the stereo sumptuousness is ample compensation. Most remarkable of all is the mighty *Passacaglia and fugue in C minor*, highly romantic in its decorative detail, but moving steadily to an overwhelming climax.

Balakirev, Mily (1837–1910)

Overture on three Russian tunes.
*(*) Finlandia/Warner Dig. 0630 14910-2 [id.]. Norwegian R. O, Ari Rasilainen – BORODIN: *Symphony No. 1 in E flat;* RIMSKY-KORSAKOV: *Sinfonietta on Russian themes.* *(*)

Balakirev's overture is disconcerting for the experienced listener, as the second of the folksongs he chooses is also featured by Tchaikovsky (far more effectively) as the jolly second subject of the Finale of his *Fourth Symphony.* Here the same tune seems a little lukewarm, but perhaps that is partly because the polished, amiable performance lacks something in robust excitement, and the recording lacks real vividness.

Symphonies Nos. (i) *1 in C;* (ii) *2 in D min.*
(M) *** Revelation RV 10038 [id.]. (i) USSR State SO, Svetlanov; (ii) Grand SO of R. & TV, Rozhdestvensky.

Rescued from the Soviet radio archive, these performances of the early 1970s have a passion and urgency, a natural feeling for idiomatic phrasing and rhythm, which make you forget any slight shortcoming in the recorded sound. This Russian performance from Svetlanov of No. 1 is altogether tauter and more urgent than the version he recorded in London for Hyperion. Rarely if ever has there been such a radiant account on disc of the lovely slow movement, surging warmly forward, with resonant strings and with a prominent harp, superbly played, adding flair. Though as a rule the *Second Symphony* seems rather pale after the powerful inspiration of No. 1, Rozhdestvensky convinces one that it is a worthy successor, rich and passionate in the dance rhythms of the first movement, furious and swaggering in the Scherzo, electrically alert in the slow movement and Polacca finale. An ideal coupling, strongly recommended.

Islamey (oriental fantasy).
500♪ ❀ *** Teldec/Warner Dig. 4509 96516-2 [id.]. Boris Berezovsky (with LIADOV: *Preludes, Opp. 39/4; 40/2; 57/1;* MEDTNER: *Fairy tales, Opp. 20/1; 34/2–3; 51/1;* RACHMANINOV: *Etudes-tableaux, Op. 39/3–4, 7 & 9* ***) MUSSORGSKY: *Night on a bare mountain.* *** ❀

An amazing account of *Islamey* from Boris Berezovsky. One is tempted to hail it as the best *Islamey* ever Stunning, effortless virtuosity. Berezovsky makes an ideal Rachmaninov interpreter too, and it would be difficult to flaw these fine accounts of four of the Op. 39 set of *Etudes-tableaux*. Berezovsky is also a champion of Medtner. He has all the subtlety, poetic feeling and keyboard mastery that this music calls for. The Liadov *Preludes* too are played impeccably. This is in every respect an outstanding recital.

Barber, Samuel (1910–81)

Adagio for strings, Op. 11.
500♪ *** Argo 417 818-2 [id.]. ASMF, Marriner – COPLAND: *Quiet city;* COWELL: *Hymn;* CRESTON: *Rumor;* IVES: *Symphony No. 3.* ***

Marriner's 1976 performance of Barber's justly famous *Adagio* is arguably the most satisfying version we have had since the war, although Bernstein's alternative has the advantage of digital recording. The quality of sound on the remastered Argo CD retains most of the richness and body of the analogue LP, but at the climax the brighter lighting brings a slightly sparer violin texture than on the original LP. There is, however, a comparably outstanding performance from Slatkin and the St Louis Symphony Orchestra, with a glorious violin-timbre, in a collection entitled '*Encore*' (RCA 09026 68511-2 – see the Concerts section, below).

Violin concerto.
500♪ ❀ *** DG Dig. 439 886-2 [id.]. Gil Shaham, LSO, Previn – KORNGOLD: *Violin concerto* etc. *** ❀
**(*) Revelation RV 10058 [id.]. Kogan, Ukrainian SO, Pavel Kogan – BARSUKOV: *Violin concerto No. 2;* BUNIN: *Violin concerto.* **

Gil Shaham's performance of the Barber has great virtuosity and is a reading of strong profile, with every moment of dramatic intensity properly characterized. The effect is warm and ripe, with the sound close and immediate, bringing out above all the work's bolder side. This really *is* good and is to be preferred to the richly extrovert Perlman account.

Leonid Kogan in this 1981 recording proves a passionately committed interpreter of this romantic American concerto, giving one of the most persuasive performances yet, with the Ukrainian orchestra matching his ardour with some brilliant playing. The balance seriously favours the soloist, though ample orchestral detail comes through. The two Soviet violin concertos, equally romantic in style, make an unexpected but attractive coupling.

PIANO MUSIC

Ballade, Op. 46; 4 Excursions, Op. 20; Interlude, Op. posth.; Nocturne (Homage to John Field), Op. 33; Sonata, Op. 26; Souvenirs, Op. 28.
*** Virgin/EMI Dig. VC5 45270-2 [id.]. Leon McCawley.

This CD accommodates Barber's entire output for the piano – including the *Souvenirs*, which date from 1952 and which exist both as an orchestral (ballet) score and in alternative piano versions for two and four hands. Leon McCawley manages excellently with just two, even in the prodigiously difficult *Sonata*, written for Horowitz. McCawley's account is highly convincing, breathtakingly so in the dazzling Scherzo and the formidable closing *Fuga*, while his freely spontaneous approach suits the opening movement especially well. The *Souvenirs*, too, are brilliantly played; if the *Tango* seems a bit heavy-going, he makes a great deal of the *Pas de deux*. The posthumous *Interlude* is also well worth having; and this well-recorded survey displaces Angela Brownridge's Hyperion disc, which omits the latter piece as well as the *Souvenirs*.

Barsukov, Sergei (born 1912)

Violin concerto No. 2.
** Revelation RV 10058 [id.]. Kogan, Grand R. & TV SO, Rozhdestvensky – BARBER: *Violin concerto* **(*); BUNIN: *Violin concerto.* **

The Soviet composer, Sergei Barsukov, is here influenced more by the exotic world of Scriabin than by any Soviet model, and Kogan in this 1969 recording gives a warmly persuasive reading, rather better balanced in sound than the much later recording of the Barber.

Bartók, Béla (1881–1945)

Concerto for orchestra; Music for strings, percussion and celesta.
500♪ *** DG Dig. 429 747-2 [id.]. Chicago SO, Levine.

James Levine gives larger-than-life performances of both these favourite Bartók works. The results are thrillingly magnetic in the thrust and drama of the performances, and the recording, far finer than most from this source, adds to the impact, immediate and resonant and with the widest colour range.

Piano concertos Nos. 1–3.
*** Teldec/Warner Dig. 0630 13158-2 [id.]. Schiff, Budapest Festival O, Fischer.
(M) *** Decca Dig./Analogue 448 125-2 [id.]. Ashkenazy, LPO, Solti.

András Schiff has become so magnetic an interpreter of the central classics that his Hungarian roots are easily forgotten, yet his colourful, winning performances of Bartók's three piano concertos are totally idiomatic, brilliantly and warmly accompanied by the fine Budapest orchestra. Above all, Schiff gives the lie to the idea of Bartók as a mainly violent composer, bringing out point and sparkle even in aggressive music like the first movements of both No. 1 and No. 2. Equally his depth of meditation in the slow movements matches that which equally he brings to Bach or Schubert, while the *Third Concerto* has rarely sounded so exuberant in its outer movements. This now takes precedence as a prime recommendation for these three works, marginally preferable to Kocsis (Philips 446 366-2) or Donohoe (EMI CDC7 54871-2), although Géza Anda's partnership with Fricsay shows a special feeling for the music's inner world (DG 447 399-2 – see our main volume). But the partnership of Ashkenazy and Solti, combined with vintage Decca sound, also makes this Ovation mid-price reissue a strong competitor. The *Second* and *Third Concertos* were recorded first in 1978–9 and both performances spark off the kind of energy and dash one would usually expect only at a live performance. With the Slavonic bite of the soloist beautifully matched by the Hungarian fire of the conductor, the readings of both works are wonderfully urgent and incisive. The tempi tend to be fast, but the focus of the playing is superbly clear. The *First Concerto* came last, recorded digitally in 1981; the performance is even tougher, urgent and biting, with the widest range of dynamics, never relaxing in the outer movements. The sound is slightly sharper but the Kingsway Hall aura remains, and the slow movements in all three works bring a hushed inner concentration, beautifully captured in warmly refined recording. With red-blooded Hungarian qualities underlined, these three works from three different periods of Bartók's career seem more closely akin than usual, with the *First* – especially the brilliant finale – marginally the most aggressive, the *Third* somewhat mellower.

Violin concerto No. 2 in B min.

(M) *** EMI CDM5 66060-2 [id.]. Perlman, LSO, Previn – CONUS: *Violin concerto;* SINDING: *Suite.* ***

Perlman's is a superb performance, totally committed and full of youthful urgency, with the sense of spontaneity that comes more readily when performers have already worked together on the music in the concert hall. The contrasts are fearlessly achieved by both soloist and orchestra, with everyone relishing virtuosity in the outer movements. The slow movement is deliberately understated by the soloist, with the fragmentation of the theme lightly touched in, but even there the orchestra has its passionate comments. The 1973 recording is full and gains much from the Kingsway Hall acoustics for, though Perlman is balanced characteristically forward and the CD transfer has brightened the orchestral tuttis, the sound has plenty of depth and ambient warmth. With its interesting new couplings, this is one of the most stimulating reissues taken from EMI's 'Perlman Collection'.

The Miraculous Mandarin (ballet): suite.

(M) **(*) EMI CDM5 65922-2 [id.]. Philh. O, Irving – KABALEVSKY: *The Comedians* (suite); KHACHATURIAN: *Gayaneh; Masquerade:* suites; SHOSTAKOVICH: *Age of Gold.* **(*)

Irving had already conducted Bartók's ballet at Covent Garden before he recorded the suite in 1960, one of the first in stereo. He transmits his own confidence to the orchestra, and even if the punches are not as shattering as some later versions, with such superb playing from the Philharmonia the evocation is most compelling, especially in the sexily sinuous *Dance of the Young Girl.* The Kingsway Hall recording is remarkably full and richly coloured.

Music for strings, percussion and celesta.

(M) (***) Mercury mono 434 378-2 [id.]. Chicago SO, Rafael Kubelik – MUSSORGSKY: *Pictures at an exhibition.* (***)

This was the second LP Mercury made in Chicago in 1951, following the coupled *Pictures at an exhibition*, and if the sound is not as spectacular as the Mussorgsky/Ravel score, that is partly because in those early LP days the timbre of the upper strings still remained somewhat illusive to the available microphones. But the balance is excellent, and the warmth and intensity at the work's opening are maintained throughout, and especially in the evocation of the *Adagio*, with subtly concentrated string-playing. The rhythmic freedom and energy of the second and fourth movements combine to make Kubelik's performance highly compelling overall.

String quartets Nos. 1–6.

500♪ (M) *** DG 445 241-2 (3). Tokyo Qt.

(M) *** Audivis Astrée V 4809 (3) [id.]. Végh Qt.

(B) ** Hyperion Dyad Dig. CDD 22003 (2) [id.]. New Budapest Qt.

The DG performances by the Tokyo Quartet bring an almost ideal combination of fire and energy with detailed point and refinement. The readings are consistently satisfying. Though the polish is high, the sense of commitment and seeming spontaneity are greater too. The layout is on three discs, but they are offered at mid-price and the splendid recording is admirably transferred to CD.

The analogue Végh recordings date from 1972, but the CD transfers are splendidly managed: there is a fine sense of presence, but also the ambient fullness one associates with the best analogue recordings, and there is bite without edginess on top. The Végh players sometimes respond with more expressive warmth than some would expect to be applied to Bartók; but others (including I.M.) will find this the very quality in their music-making which prevents the music from becoming too aggressive. On the whole they give very perceptive performances. They are not flawless technically but they understand what this music is about and, above all, they produce an effect of seeming spontaneity. They were last reviewed by us in 1988 (then at full price). Welcome back.

Like the Novák Quartet on a Philips Duo (442 284-2), the New Budapest Quartet enjoy an advantage in accommodating all six *Quartets* on two discs (odd numbers on the first CD and even numbers on its companion). The performances are generally very good, though they are not as imaginative or as compelling as the Tokyo, Lindsay or Alban Berg quartets. Nor does the recording have the tonal richness and bloom of the Alban Berg or Tokyo Quartet on DG. But if you need an economically priced set of these works, the Novák is the one to go for; there are no complaints about the Philips sound either.

Bluebeard's Castle.

*** EMI Dig. CDC5 65162-2 [id.]. Tomlinson, Von Otter, Sandor Elès (nar.), BPO, Haitink.

Never before has Bartók's darkly intense one-acter been given such a beautiful performance on disc, intense and concentrated, as by Bernard Haitink in EMI's live recording of a concert performance with the Berlin Philharmonic. Rival versions by such Hungarian-born conductors as Solti, Kertész and Dorati may bite more sharply, but, guided by Haitink, Anne-Sofie von Otter conveys new tenderness in Judith, with John Tomlinson magisterially Wagnerian as the implacable Bluebeard, both singing superbly, naturally balanced, not spotlit. Most impressive of all, Haitink builds the performance to a terrifying climax, when Judith is consigned to darkness with her predecessors.

Bax, Arnold (1883–1953)

3 Pieces for small orchestra: Evening piece; Irish landscape; Dance in the sunlight.
(M) **(*) EMI Dig. CDM7 64200-2 [id.]. ECO, Jeffrey Tate – BRIDGE: *There is a willow;* BUTTERWORTH: *Banks of green willow;* MOERAN: *2 Pieces.* **(*)

The three Bax *Pieces* as attractive rarities make a welcome appearance in Tate's English recital. The first two are characteristically evocative, while the third is in Bax's brightest, most extrovert vein. Refined performances, warmly recorded, with the CD bringing good detail and presence without loss of atmosphere.

Symphonies 1–7.
500♪ (M) *** Chandos Dig. CHAN 8906/10 [id.]. LPO or Ulster O, Bryden Thomson.

Chandos have repackaged the cycle of seven symphonies and it makes better sense for those primarily interested in these richly imaginative symphonies to pay for five rather than seven CDs. The recordings continue to make a strong impression and are all available separately (see our main volume).

VOCAL MUSIC

I sing of a maiden; Mater ora filium; This world's joie.
(M) *** EMI Dig. CDM5 65595-2 [id.]. King's College, Cambridge, Ch., Cleobury – FINZI: *Choral music;* VAUGHAN WILLIAMS: *Mass.* ***

Bax's ambitious setting of a medieval carol, *Mater ora filium*, is one of the most difficult *a cappella* pieces in the choral repertory. Here under Stephen Cleobury the King's College choir gives it a virtuoso performance, with trebles performing wonders in the taxingly high passages. Perhaps the composer anticipated, when he wrote this piece, that trebles would one day be able to cope with such writing, but the timbre of boys' voices adds to the poignancy of the piece. It is particularly apt too, when the original inspiration for the piece came from his hearing Byrd's *Mass in five voices*. The other two Bax pieces, also setting medieval texts, are also done most beautifully, with the unaccompanied voices vividly recorded against the spacious acoustic of King's Chapel. Besides the original Finzi coupling, the reissue includes a splendid analogue performance of Vaughan Williams's beautiful *Mass in G minor*.

Beach, Amy (1867–1944)

Piano concerto in C sharp min., Op. 45.
(B) ** Carlton/Turnabout 30371 00282 [in VoxBox CDX 5069]. Boehm, Westphalian SO, Siegfried Landau – MASON: *Prelude and fugue* etc. **

The more one hears of the music of Amy Beach, the more impressed one becomes, and her *Piano concerto* is a very considerable piece whose main theme in the first movement has a surprising resemblance to a dominating tune from Dvořák's *New World Symphony*. It also has a delectably frothy Scherzo, recalling Saint-Saëns, a short but expressive *Largo* and a shimmeringly seductive Spanish finale. That may sound like a curious mix, but it hangs together uncommonly well. Mary Louise Boehm is a fine soloist but her orchestral accompaniment is only just adequate, with thin violin-timbre. However, this is still enjoyable, and the cost is modest.

PIANO MUSIC

Ballad in D flat, Op. 6; Hermit thrush at eve; at morn, Op. 91/1–2; Nocturne, Op. 107; Prelude and fugue, Op. 81; 4 Sketches, Op. 15; (i) *Suite for 2 pianos on Irish melodies, Op. 104.*
*** Koch Dig. 3-7254-2 [id.]. Virginia Erskin, (i) with Kathleen Supove.

Amy Beach continues to surprise as we discover more of her music. Her piano writing has a number of eclectic influences, but they are all well absorbed. Her invention is always pleasing, and sometimes an apparently trivial piece becomes more than that – witness the *Valse caprice*. The *Four Sketches* (*In Autumn*; *Phantoms*; *Dreaming*; *Fireflies*) are charmingly evocative, as are the two pictures of the *Hermit thrush*, yet her imposing *Prelude and fugue* is impressively worked out. Virginia Erskin is thoroughly sympathetic, never undervaluing a piece, and Kathleen Supove makes a fine partner in the demanding but by no means predictable *Suite for two pianos on Irish melodies*.

Beethoven, Ludwig van (1770–1827)

Piano concertos Nos. 1–5.

500♪ *** Sony S3K 44575 (3) [id.]. Perahia, Concg. O, Haitink.

(M) ** Ph. Dig. 456 045-2 (3) [id.]. Alfred Brendel, Chicago SO, James Levine.

Perahia brings us as close to the heart of this music as any. These are masterly performances and the sound is full and well balanced. This set has now reverted to full price, but it has to be said that it is still worth it.

Brendel's Chicago version was intended to prove how much more effective live recording is than studio performance, but the results – recorded at Orchestra Hall, Chicago – belie that. Anything Brendel does has mastery and distinction but, compared with his earlier studio recordings of the concertos on Turnabout and with Haitink and the Concertgebouw, this sounds self-conscious, less rather than more spontaneous-sounding. He did after all know that the tape was running, and that in itself must have affected the performances. The recorded sound gives a good sense of presence but is badly balanced, and loud applause at the end of each concerto is most intrusive.

Piano concertos Nos. 1–5; (i) *Choral Fantasia, Op. 80.*

(B) **(*) Carlton VoxBox CDX3 3502 (3) [id]. Alfred Brendel; Stuttgart PO, Boettcher (*No. 1*); V. Volksoper O (*No. 2*); VSO (*Nos. 3–4*); Wallberg (*Nos. 2, 3 & 4*); V. Pro Musica O, Mehta (*No. 5*); (i) Stuttgart Lehrergesangverein, Stuttgart PO, Boettcher.

There are many who hold that Brendel never again quite matched the early Beethoven recordings which he made for Vox in the 1950s and 1960s, and certainly the *Piano concertos* are very special, in spite of the thin sound of the orchestral strings. Indeed this is one of the most satisfying readings of the *First Concerto* available at any price. Brendel's tempi for the outer movements are measured, but such is his rhythmic point (particularly in the dactylic rhythms of the finale), and such his concentration, that the result is never heavy. Similarly in the slow movement his tempo is rather slow for *Largo*, but the natural weight of expression has the immediacy of a live performance. The long cadenza in the first movement is interestingly confected from two of the cadenzas the composer himself wrote. The snag lies in the playing and the recording of the orchestra, with violin timbre that often sounds seedy. Similarly in No. 2, Brendel's concentration makes up for indifferently played accompaniments, thinly recorded. Fortunately the quality of the piano recording is far higher, so that Brendel's contribution at least can be appreciated to the full. Wallberg's conducting is lively and sympathetic.

The recordings of Nos. 3, 4 and 5 were much earlier (1959) and the orchestral sound again leaves much to be desired, although once again the piano-image is convincing and the pleasing ambient effect throughout means that the listener can easily adjust. The interpretations of Nos. 3 and 4 are deeply satisfying, with the most delicate tonal and rhythmic control married to intellectual strength. The slow movement of No. 3, again very spaciously conceived, combines depth with poetry, and the finale is engagingly jaunty. In No. 4 the orchestral accompaniment is unimaginative: the first-movement tutti, for example, is rhythmically stodgy; but Brendel's control of phrase and colour is such that his reading rides over this impediment and the contrasts of the slow movement are made strongly and poetically. It is noteworthy that he uses the second of the cadenzas written for this work, one not generally heard. The reading of the *Emperor* is splendidly bold and vigorous, and Brendel is well supported by the young Zubin Mehta with the Vienna Pro Musica Orchestra; although here the thin body of string-tone is more disadvantageous than in the early concertos, the performance generates a spontaneity which is less apparent in Brendel's later versions for Philips. It may be a reading without idiosyncrasy, but it is strong in style, and the slow movement is movingly sustained. The beginning of the finale is then prepared beautifully, and the main rondo theme emerges vividly and with great character. As a coupling we are given the *Choral Fantasia*, recorded in the mid-1960s. Boettcher again takes over and proves unimaginative in a work that is unusually difficult to hold together. However, as many collectors will recall, Brendel's commanding opening cadenza is in every way memorable, and he compensates for others' weakness. The chorus sings well, but the brief vocal solos are poorly done. But the warm acoustic means that this still makes enjoyable listening. The booklet includes an attractive photo of Brendel taken at the time he made the recordings, and the notes include a good (true) story about the Viennese première of the *Choral Fantasia* with the composer at the piano.

(i) *Piano concertos Nos. 1–5;* (ii) *Violin concerto, Op. 61.*
(BB) ** RCA Navigator Dig./Analogue 74321 30366-2 (3). (i) Ax, RPO, Previn; (ii) Ughi, LSO, Sawallisch.

This three-disc super-bargain set offers exceptionally generous measure. These are thoughtful, unassertive performances, which in the first two concertos clearly relate the music to Mozart. Previn gives his very musical soloist good support, particularly in the slow movements, which are gentle and touching. Finales are enjoyably brisk and sparkling. The *Third Concerto* is given rather more weight, without ever being forceful: here the finale is more relaxed and measured – pleasingly lyrical in feeling. The warmly lyrical account of the *Fourth Concerto* shows these artists at their best (although the central dialogue could be more dramatic), but the relaxed playing in the *Emperor* makes this a less bitingly compelling version than it can be, with the finale less weighty than usual. Excellent, natural, 1985–6 digital recording, warmly resonant but clear. Ughi's 1981 account of the *Violin concerto* also has realistic and well-balanced sound. His performance is in every way recommendable, fresh and unaffected, marked by consistent purity of tone in every register. If the last degree of imagination of the kind which creates special magic is missing in all these performances, their freshness makes them well worth considering for those with limited budgets.

Piano concertos Nos. 1 in C, Op. 15; 2 in B flat, Op. 19.
(M) ** EMI CDM5 66090-2 [id.]. Weissenberg, BPO, Karajan.

Piano concertos Nos. 3 in C min., Op. 37; 5 in E flat (Emperor), Op. 73.
(M) ** EMI CDM5 66091-2 [id.]. Weissenberg, BPO, Karajan.

(i) *Piano concerto No. 4 in G, Op. 58;* (ii) *Triple concerto for violin, cello and piano in C, Op. 56.*
(M) ** EMI CDM5 66092-2 [id.]. (i) Weissenberg; (ii) David Oistrakh, Rostropovich, Richter; (i–ii) BPO, Karajan.

Alexis Weissenberg's playing in the set of piano concertos, reissued as part of EMI's Karajan Edition, sounds rather run-of-the-mill, although there are individual felicities and Karajan and the Berlin Philharmonic create a strong impression in the beautifully played accompaniments. There are no complaints on sonic grounds (the recordings are full and well balanced and date from the mid- to late 1970s). The *Triple concerto* is treated with apt opulence by the star soloists, with Beethoven's priorities among them well preserved in the extra dominance of Rostropovich over his colleagues. This is warm, expansive music-making. The 1969 recording is rather too reverberant and orchestral climaxes could be smoother, but the sound is better focused here than on LP, and the balance between the soloists and the orchestra is well managed.

Piano concertos Nos. 1 in C, Op. 15; 2 in B flat, Op. 19; 3 in C min., Op. 37; 4 in G, Op. 58.
(B) *** EMI forte CZS5 69506-2 (2). Gilels, Cleveland O, Szell.

Gilels is an incomparable Beethoven player. He is unfailingly illuminating and poetic and his playing is consistently a matter for marvel. It goes without saying that Szell has tremendous grip and that the playing of the Cleveland Orchestra is beyond reproach, with a rhythmical point that has an exhilarating lift. The recordings, made in Severance Hall in 1968, are dry and clear rather than expansive, but certainly do not lack atmosphere. A treasurable set.

Piano concertos Nos. 1 in C, Op. 15; 2 in B flat, Op. 19.
(B) *** Decca Eclipse Dig. 448 982-2; *448 982-4* [id.]. Alicia de Larrocha, Berlin RSO, Chailly (with SCHUBERT: *Moment musical No. 6 in A flat, D.780* ***).
**(*) Sony Dig. SK 68250 [id.]. Jos van Immerseel, Tafelmusik, Bruno Weil.

Alicia de Larrocha recorded all five of the Beethoven concertos in the early 1980s with the Berlin Radio Symphony Orchestra playing freshly under Chailly. The set was rather uneven, but the first two concertos were given delightful performances, lightly pointed, on a Mozartian scale, but with beautifully poised accounts of both slow movements. Full, vivid recording, made in Jesus-Christus-Kirche. The Schubert *Impromptu* also is played with simplicity but with much poetic feeling.

These are lively and stylish performances on Sony, but Jos van Immerseel does not emerge as a strongly individual interpreter here and his fortepiano convinces less readily than the instrument played by Melvyn Tan, whose coupling of these two concertos has both more sparkle and a warmer expressive feeling (Virgin Veritas VER5 61295-2).

Piano concertos Nos. 1–2; Piano concerto No. 1 (2nd performance, with cadenzas by Glenn Gould).
*** EMI Dig. CDC5 56266-2 [id.]. Lars Vogt, CBSO, Rattle.

The curiosity of this superb EMI issue is that it comes with a bonus disc containing a repeat performance of the *First Concerto* using Glenn Gould's weirdly atonal cadenzas instead of Beethoven's. That is more than a gimmick, for the young German pianist, Lars Vogt, combines magnetism with keen imagination, so that one quickly starts comparing him with the great Beethovenians of the past. Broadly, one might say that where his crisp, clean articulation and preference for transparent textures (matched by Rattle's work with the orchestra) reminds one of Wilhelm Kempff, his speeds – with allegros very fast and slow movements unusually slow and concentrated – reflects the practice of Artur Schnabel. The parallel with Kempff is the closer, and Rattle at the very start of each first movement tutti establishes (as he does in Haydn) his debt to period performance in lightly articulated string-playing with little vibrato. Not that either pianist or conductor is at all rigid, and their use of rubato and agogic hesitation, naturally expressive, never sounds self-conscious. Excellent, transparent sound to match. A most stimulating issue.

Piano concertos Nos. 2 in B flat, Op. 19; 3 in C min., Op. 37.
(BB) *** Tring Dig. TRP 076 [id.]. Michael Roll, RPO, Howard Shelley.

Michael Roll, winner of the very first Leeds International Piano Competition in 1963, when he was still in his teens, has been shockingly neglected by the record companies. This excellent super-bargain disc, offering bright, fresh, spontaneous-sounding performances of Nos. 2 and 3, recorded in full and warm digital sound, is most welcome. There is a touch of clatter in the piano-tone at the top, but the natural expressiveness and the magnetic urgency of the playing, with beautifully even passage-work, firm left hand and the crispest of trills makes one's ears adjust very quickly, and the orchestral playing under a fine pianist-turned-conductor is equally compelling.

Piano concerto No. 5 (Emperor); Grosse Fuge in B flat, Op. 133.
500♪ ❀ (M) *** EMI Dig. CD-EMX 2184. Stephen Kovacevich, Australian CO.

Kovacevich is unsurpassed today as an interpreter of this most magnificent of concertos. His superb account, with the soloist directing from the keyboard, is a first choice for this much-recorded work, even with no allowance for price (although the older Gilels/Szell version should not be forgotten – see below). For fill-up, Kovacevich conducts a comparably electrifying account of the *Grosse Fuge*.

(i) *Piano concerto No. 5 in E flat (Emperor). Overtures: Coriolan, Op. 62; Creatures of Prometheus, Op. 43; Leonora No. 3.*
(M) *** Chandos Dig. CHAN 7028 [id.]. (i) John Lill; CBSO, Walter Weller.

John Lill has recorded all the Beethoven concertos for Chandos with considerable success, but the *Emperor* suits his bold, authoritative Beethoven style especially well. The breadth and majesty of the opening movement is arresting, the slow movement is coolly serene and the finale vigorously joyful. So are Walter Weller's performances of the three overtures, which come first on the disc and are splendidly alive. The CBSO is on top form throughout, and the full, resonant sound is of best Chandos vintage. A good alternative mid-priced choice for those who fancy the programme, and John Lill's admirers certainly won't be disappointed.

(i) *Piano concerto No. 5 (Emperor). Piano sonata No. 7 in D, Op. 10/3.*
(M) (***) EMI mono CDH7 61005-2 [id.]. Edwin Fischer, (i) with Philh. O, Furtwängler.

Edwin Fischer's 1951 recording with Furtwängler and the Philharmonia Orchestra is one of the classics of the gramophone, one of the most imperious and imperial of *Emperors*. It did not receive its full due when it first came out on LP, though this was due partly to the inferior quality of the EMI pressing; but its remastered form does it much greater justice. The *D major Sonata* was recorded in 1954, Fischer's last recording session, and within a year both soloist and conductor had died.

(i) *Piano concerto No. 5 in E flat (Emperor), Op. 73. 32 Variations on an original theme in C min., WoO 80; 12 Variations on a Russian dance from 'Das Waldmädchen' (Wranitzky), WoO 71; 6 Variations on a Turkish march from 'The Ruins of Athens', Op. 76.*
(B) *** EMI forte CZS5 69509-2 (2). Emil Gilels; (i) Cleveland O, Szell – DVORAK: *Symphony No. 8.* **(*)

Of the many versions of the *Emperor Concerto* available, few are more superb than Gilels's. Here strength is matched with poetry in no small measure, with Szell offering the strongest backing. The Severance Hall recording is bright in regard to violin tone but has plenty of supporting ambience. The *C minor Variations* are marvellously done, and the other two sets bring the strongest characterization and contrasting moments of poetry and charm. Gilels's playing is masterly throughout and the piano is truthfully caught; the pianism implies a wide dynamic range, even if the engineers reduce it somewhat by the close balance. Not to be missed.

(i) *Piano concerto No. 5 (Emperor). 15 Variations and fugue in E flat (Eroica variations), Op. 35.*
(M) *(**) Decca 452 302-2 [id.]. Clifford Curzon, (i) VPO, Knappertsbusch.

Curzon's is a refined and thoughtful reading of the *Emperor*. His playing in the slow movement is beautifully controlled and brings out the poetry gently and movingly. The finale is the only movement where one feels that his restraint shifts the viewpoint back almost to Mozart; there is a restraint about this essentially rumbustious movement which seems almost to be too much of a good thing. Yet the keen intelligence of the playing and the inner concentration working throughout the reading are by no means to be dismissed. The Vienna Philharmonic plays strongly and authoritatively under Knappertsbusch, but the 1957 recording seems hardly worthy of reissue in Decca's Classic Sound series, for the string tutti are fierce and there is a degree of roughness in orchestral tuttis, although the piano timbre is convincing enough. The *Eroica variations* are transferred at a higher level and the piano is much more forward, so one needs to be prepared to adjust the volume control; moreover something curious happens on the bold opening chord: it seems to fluctuate and there is a beat in the tuning. Otherwise the sound is fuller than in the concerto and Curzon's fine performance holds the variations together splendidly.

Piano concerto No. 5 (Emperor); (i) *Choral Fantasia, Op. 80.*
**(*) DG Dig. 447 771-2; *447 771-4* [id.]. Robert Levin (fortepiano), ORR, Gardiner; (i) with Monteverdi Ch.

Gardiner here follows up his Beethoven symphony cycle with the first of a Beethoven concerto series, with Robert Levin as soloist, the fortepianist who earlier recorded Mozart concertos with Christopher Hogwood for Oiseau-Lyre. As in other versions of the *Emperor* on period instruments, the sense of struggle which we expect at the very start between the orchestra's E flat chords and the pianist's bravura flourishes is here muted, yet the rewards are as great as in other period performances, once one listens in a historical context. When Gardiner's orchestra is fuller-bodied than those on rival versions, the discrepancy is underlined, and the 1812 instrument chosen is disconcertingly twangy at the top, though one quickly appreciates the fine, positive qualities of a reading in which the soloist, matching Gardiner himself, takes a more freely expressive view than Melvyn Tan or Steven Lubin, playing with a greater element of bravura. Speeds are midway between Tan (faster) and Lubin (slower), with the finale given an exhilarating performance. The performance of the *Choral Fantasy* too has great panache, treating the variations on the little song, *Gegenliebe*, with a winning degree of wit, even flippancy. Gardiner crowns the piece with a superb choral section, in which soloists and full chorus are cleanly contrasted, with an exciting stringendo in the lead-up to the final Presto. As a supplement, Levin offers on separate tracks two alternative improvisations of his own, easily interchangeable with the one Beethoven published years after the first performance.

Violin concerto in D, Op. 61.
500♪ ❁ (M) *** DG 447 403-2 [id.]. Schneiderhan, BPO, Jochum – MOZART: *Violin concerto No. 5.* ***
(***) APR Signature mono APR 5506 [id.]. Bronislaw Huberman, VPO, Szell – LALO: *Symphonie espagnole.* (**(*))
(**(*)) Testament mono SBT 1083. Ida Haendel, Philh. O, Kubelik – BRUCH: *Violin concerto No. 1.* (**(*))
(BB) *** Belart 461 355-2. Campoli, LPO, Krips – MENDELSSOHN: *Violin concerto.* ***

Violin concerto in D; Romances Nos. 1–2, Opp. 40 & 50.
500♪ ❁ *** Teldec/Warner Dig. 9031 74881-2 [id.]. Kremer, COE, Harnoncourt.
** Sony Dig. SK 53287 [id.]. Salvatore Accardo, La Scala PO, Giulini.

Gidon Kremer's Teldec account of Beethoven's *Violin concerto* was taken from performances with Nikolaus Harnoncourt and the COE in Graz in July 1992, and offers one of his most commanding recordings, both polished and full of flair, magnetically spontaneous from first to last, with tone ravishingly pure. Altogether one of the most refreshing versions of the concerto ever put on disc, backed up by crisp, unsentimental readings of the two *Romances*, with the first of the two flowing faster and more freshly than we are used to.

Wolfgang Schneiderhan's stereo version of the *Violin concerto* is among the greatest recordings of this work: the serene spiritual beauty of the slow movement, and the playing of the second subject in particular, have never been surpassed on record; the orchestra under Jochum provides a background tapestry of breadth and dignity.

Huberman's 1934 performance is another classic version, raptly intense – as in a magical opening to the first-movement coda – but taken at speeds that flow easily, far faster overall than is now the rule. The APR transfer is first rate, with the violin astonishingly immediate and full of presence, even if the timpani is rather boomy. The Lalo (minus its central intermezzo), recorded with the same conductor and orchestra, makes an apt coupling.

Campoli was to re-record the concerto later for HMV, but this early stereo Decca version has an appealing, freshly spontaneous lyricism, and the slow movement has depth and a simple poetry. Krips is in obvious sympathy with his soloist, and the orchestra displays a pleasingly light touch in the finale. The age of the recording hardly comes through, though it was very good in its day. But this Belart reissue is even more notable for the captivating Mendelssohn coupling, a work Campoli was born to play. A splendid bargain.

Ida Haendel's 1951 recording originally appeared on 11 sides of short-playing 78-r.p.m. discs and was never issued on LP in Britain. Though, in a comment quoted in Alan Sanders's excellent note, the violinist points out that this is no longer the way she interprets the work, this is an exceptionally powerful reading, commanding and concentrated even at spacious speeds. In a transfer of Testament's highest standard, it makes a welcome reissue, particularly in coupling with an outstanding account of the Bruch concerto. However, this reissue is priced unrealistically.

The Sony version with Accardo and Giulini offers very good sound. Accardo brings his usual purity of tone and dedication to bear on this score, and there is a naturalness of utterance and poetic feeling that resonate in the mind. Giulini is inclined, however, to be very leisurely and there are moments when one feels that the distinguished soloist is impatient to push things along. Aristocratic and well groomed, but ultimately somewhat too measured.

Triple concerto for violin, cello and piano in C, Op. 56.

500♪ (B) *** EMI forte CZS5 69331-2 (2) [id.]. David Oistrakh, Lev Oborin, Sviatoslav Knushevitzky, Philh. O, Sargent – BRAHMS: *Double concerto;* MOZART: *Violin concerto No. 3;* PROKOFIEV: *Violin concerto No. 2.* ***

The early EMI recording, featuring distinguished Russian soloists, dates from the early days of stereo, yet the sound is excellent for its period and the balance (with Walter Legge producing) perhaps the most successful this concerto has received in the recording studio.

SYMPHONIES

Symphonies Nos. 1–9; 10 (realized and completed Barry Cooper).

(M) *** Chan. Dig. CHAN 7042 (5) [id.]. CBSO, Walter Weller (with Barstow, Finnie, Rendall, Tomlinson, CBSO Ch. in *No. 9*).

Symphonies Nos. 1–9.

500♪ (B) *** RCA Dig. 74321 20277-2 (5). N. German RSO, Günter Wand (with Wiens, Hartwig, Lewis, Hermann, combined Ch. from Hamburg State Op. and N. German R. in *No. 9*).

(BB) ** RCA Navigator 74321 30365-2 (5). Boston SO, Erich Leinsdorf (with Jane Marsh, Josephine Veasey, Plácido Domingo, Sherrill Milnes, Pro Musica Ch., New England Conservatory Ch. in *No. 9*).

Symphonies Nos. 1-9; Overtures: Coriolan; Egmont.

(B) **(*) O-L Dig. 452 551-2 (5) [id.]. AAM, Hogwood (with Augér, Robbin, Rolfe Johnson, Reinhardt, London Symphony Ch. in *No. 9*).

Wand's digital set with the North German Radio Orchestra, recorded between 1985 and 1988, makes a first-class bargain choice, and indeed is thoroughly recommendable irrespective of cost, offering performances without idiosyncrasy yet full of character that are consistently satisfying to live with. There is a directness about Wand's approach to Beethoven, both early and mature, which is the opposite of dull or stuffy. Throughout the orchestral playing is of the highest quality and the recording is superb, both clean and atmospheric, and admirably transparent.

The reissued Chandos Weller set arrived just as our main volume went to press, and it seems sensible to repeat here our original 1990 review. The set remains by far Weller's finest achievement on record. Although this is the City of Birmingham Symphony Orchestra, there is a warm, refined, Viennese quality in the playing and interpretation, to remind you that this conductor started his career as concertmaster of the Vienna Philharmonic. The Chandos sound is full and glowing to match, by far the finest to date given to any conductor in a collected Beethoven cycle. Broadly speaking, one might categorize Weller as a Beethovenian whose sympathies centre on the even-numbered symphonies, rather than on the odd-numbered works with their cataclysmic symphonic statements. Not that the great odd-numbered symphonies lose freshness or bite under Weller; but these are all friendly performances which, in their continuing alertness and the feeling of live communication, give consistent pleasure. There is an exuberance and a sense of joyful adventure running through all of them, so that even the first movement of the *Eroica* (with exposition repeat observed) is presented in happy optimism rather than epic grandeur. (The *Seventh* and the *Pastoral*, incidentally, are the only two symphonies in which Weller omits exposition repeats.) These are not the most monumental readings you will find, but they are the most companionable; and that applies too to the final culmination, the *Ninth*. Now, conveniently fitted on to five discs and including Dr Barry Cooper's re-creation of the first movement of No. 10, this cycle must move very near the top of the list of recommendations, especially for those who seek outstanding sound-quality.

Hogwood's set with the Academy of Ancient Music now reappears in a five-disc bargain box and thus, in terms of economy, upstages Norrington, whose competing recordings have been reissued separately at mid-price. While Gardiner remains the prime recommendation for a Beethoven cycle on period instruments, Hogwood's set makes the safest recommendation in the lower price category. It is the most vividly recorded, with the keenest sense of presence and, above all, the sound adds appropriate weight to the *Ninth*, with the London Symphony Chorus fuller and more vivid than rival choirs for Norrington and Goodman. Hogwood also has the finest quartet of soloists, though in the first movement he is too rigid. Like his rivals, Hogwood has taken note of Beethoven's metronome markings, but he applies them rather less consistently. His pointing of rhythms is not always as alert or imaginative as that of his direct rivals; as a whole, the cycle may lack something in individual moments of insight but, with clean and generally well-disciplined playing, it is consistently satisfying.

Erich Leinsdorf recorded his cycle of Beethoven symphonies between 1962 and 1969. The first disc, coupling the *First* and *Seventh Symphonies*, immediately demonstrates his interpretative style. The *First Symphony* hardly ever smiles, but its vigour and strength clearly look forward to the *Eroica*. The *Seventh* brings relatively measured but rhythmically strong outer movements which, like the *Allegretto*, generate considerable tension; its conclusion is powerfully positive and really lifts off in the coda. There is no doubting the polish and commitment of the Boston orchestra's playing, but the hard-driven first-movement allegros of Nos. 1, 2 and 4, though generating a high voltage, also bring fierceness and a very literal rhythmic feeling, without a compensating sense of relaxation and warmth in slow movements. Indeed, in the *Fourth* Leinsdorf gives a curiously pedantic impression in the first movement, as though he is conducting the quavers, and the stodgy accompaniment to the slow movement's great melody is unappealing. The opening movement of the *Eroica* is strong but heavy, and the first movement of the *Fifth* is bold but square, even if the finale erupts powerfully. The *Pastoral Symphony* is beautifully played (like the slow movement of the *Fifth*) but lacks charm, and the *Eighth* is without geniality. The *Choral Symphony* epitomizes Leinsdorf's approach to the cycle overall: the opening two movements are powerful and sharply articulated, the rhythmic drive compelling if unrelenting. The atmosphere of the *Adagio* brings repose but remains cool. The introduction of the finale then erupts very dramatically and Leinsdorf presses on forcefully. He has a well-matched and distinguished team of soloists – Jane Marsh, Josephine Veasey, Plácido Domingo and Sherrill Milnes – who blend well even under pressure. The soprano's big moment is managed confidently. The combined Pro Musica and New England Conservatory Chorus (recorded with fine clarity) respond with great vigour to the conductor's energetic drive. The close of the symphony is pressed onwards to the point of frenzy, and no one could fail to be excited by the coda. Overall, Leinsdorf's lack of poise and humanity means that his readings have one dimension missing, but the orchestra consistently plays superbly. The Boston acoustic adds weight and resonance to the sound which, in these excellent CD transfers, remains both clear and full.

Symphonies Nos. 1 in C, Op. 21; 2 in D, Op. 36.
500♪ *** DG Dig. 447 049-2 [id.]. ORR, Gardiner.

Rather than treating the two early symphonies as Mozartian in the way most period performers do, John Eliot Gardiner uses his sonorous but clean-textured forces to bring out the power and revolutionary bite of the young Beethoven, as ever opting for speeds on the fast side. Vivid, immediate sound in both the live recording of No. 1 and the studio one of No. 2.

Symphonies Nos. 1–2 (trans. Liszt).
(M) ** Teldec/Warner Dig. 4509 97952-2 [id.]. Cyprien Katsaris (piano).

Although this is less remarkable than Katsaris's recordings of the Liszt transcriptions of the later symphonies, the clarity of the playing illuminates the detail of both works and the performances have plenty of vitality.

Symphonies Nos. 1 in C, Op. 21; 3 (Eroica), Op. 55.
500♪ *** EMI Dig. CDC7 54501-2 [id.]. Concg. O, Sawallisch.
(M) *** EMI Eminence Dig. CD-EMX 2246; *TC-EMX 2246*. RLPO, Mackerras.
(M) **(*) Virgin Veritas/EMI Dig. VM5 61374-2 [id.]. L. Classical Players, Norrington.
(M) ** Ph. Dig. 454 132-2 [id.]. Concg. O, Haitink.

The *First Symphony* sounds fresh and vibrant in Sawallisch's hands and the textures are clean and transparent in this splendidly engineered EMI recording. However, it is the *Eroica* for which collectors will buy this disc. It is a performance of some stature and has breadth and dignity; the orchestral playing is a joy in itself.

Sir Charles Mackerras, as in his other Beethoven readings on the Eminence label, consciously seeks to reconcile the new doctrines of period performance with traditional ones; as he says himself, with the collaboration of an orchestra willing to modify tone and technique he succeeds remarkably well, with fast speeds so subtly controlled that there is no sense of haste. The *First* is fresh and alert in a Haydnesque way, while the *Eroica* has ample power, with heightened dynamic contrasts and with the flowing speed for the *Funeral march* still conveying dedication. The horns in the trio of the Scherzo are superb, helped by first-rate recording.

Norrington's Beethoven cycle now reappears on the Virgin label at mid-price, in this case with a new pairing. No. 1 lacks the lively energy of the best of the series, but the *Eroica* is one of the most successful performances. It is consistently even faster than his closest period-performance rivals, yet one quickly forgets any feeling of haste when rhythms are so crisp and supple in their spring, and the great *Funeral march* has natural gravity.

Haitink gives strong and straightforward, if not distinctive, readings of both symphonies, beautifully played; but the digital recording, though warm and pleasing, is disconcertingly opaque by modern Concertgebouw standards.

Symphonies Nos. 1 in C, Op. 21; 6 in F (Pastoral), Op. 28.
(BB) **(*) Naxos Dig. 8.553474 [id.]. Nicolaus Esterházy Sinfonia, Béla Drahos.

In his projected Beethoven cycle on the Naxos label Drahos offers fresh, spontaneous-sounding performances, beautifully played by a chamber-sized group from Budapest, with recording outstandingly vivid. Plainer and less subtle than the finest versions, these lively, well-sprung performances make excellent bargains.

Symphonies Nos. 2; 8 in F, Op. 93.
500♪ *** EMI Dig. CDC7 54502-2 [id.]. Concg. O, Sawallisch.
(M) *** Virgin Veritas/EMI Dig. VM5 61375-2 [id.]. L. Classical Players, Norrington.

A lovely, alert account of both symphonies from Sawallisch that gives much pleasure. The *Second Symphony* in particular sounds beautifully fresh; the orchestral playing is of the high standard one expects from this great orchestra and Sawallisch has a fine sense of proportion.

The coupling of Nos. 2 and 8 was the first of Norrington's Beethoven series and showed the London Classical Players as an authentic group with a distinctive sound, sweeter and truer in the string section than most, generally easier on non-specialist ears. In following Beethoven's own metronome markings for both symphonies the results are exhilarating, never merely breathless, bringing far more than proof of an academic theory.

Symphonies Nos. 3 in E flat (Eroica), Op. 55; 8 in F, Op. 93.
(BB) **(*) Naxos Dig. 8.553475 [id.]. Nicolaus Esterházy Sinfonia, Béla Drahos.

Drahos's performances on Naxos with his excellent chamber orchestra from Budapest benefit greatly from the superb sound, clearer and with more vivid presence than on many other recent discs. The performances have the same qualities of freshness and spontaneity that mark the other initial disc in the series, making a good bargain, even if there are more searching readings of the *Eroica*.

Symphonies Nos. 4 in B flat, Op. 60; 6 in F (Pastoral).
500♪ ❁ (M) *** Bruno Walter Edition: Sony SMK 64462 [id.]. Columbia SO, Walter.
(M) *** EMI Eminence Dig. CD-EMX 2245; *TC-EMX 2245*. RLPO, Mackerras.

Bruno Walter's coupling of the *Fourth* and *Sixth Symphonies* is the one to go for. Walter's reading of the *Fourth* is splendid, the finest achievement of his whole cycle. There is intensity and a feeling of natural vigour which makes itself felt in every bar. The pairing with the *Pastoral* is apt. It is an affectionate and completely integrated performance from a master who thought and lived the work all his life. The sound is beautifully balanced, with sweet strings and clear, glowing woodwind, and the bass response is firm and full.

Following the pattern of his other Eminence recordings of Beethoven with this orchestra, Sir Charles Mackerras adopts consistently fast speeds in both symphonies, except in the slow introduction to No. 4. Crisp, light articulation allows for superb definition from the strings in the outer movements of No. 4, with resilient rhythms, and Mackerras's rubato in such a passage as the opening of the *Pastoral* demonstrates how subtly he avoids any feeling of rigidity. With hard sticks used by the timpanist, the Storm has rarely sounded so thrilling, resolving on an ecstatic, slowing finale.

Symphonies Nos. 4 in B flat; 7 in A, Op. 92.
(M) *** Virgin Veritas/EMI Dig. VM5 61376-2 [id.]. L. Classical Players, Norrington.
(BB) *** Naxos Dig. 8.553477 [id.]. Nicolaus Esterházy Sinfonia, Béla Drahos.

The coupling of Nos. 4 and 7 is one of the most successful of the Drahos Naxos series so far. No. 4 has a pervading joyful vitality, while in No. 7 Drahos keeps a spring in the rhythms without forcing the pace, lifting the finale with bouncing accents, leading to a thrilling coda. The orchestral playing is first class and the recording outstanding in its combination of vivid clarity and atmospheric warmth: there is certainly no lack of weight in either symphony. This disc would be recommendable if it cost far more.

The coupling of Nos. 4 and 7 also shows Norrington at his finest. In both symphonies he adopts fast speeds and in the *Seventh* sforzandos are sharply accented and rhythms lightly sprung. He follows Beethoven's metronome markings – as in the brisk second-movement Allegretto – but finds time for detail and fine moulding of phrase. The recording is warm, but not ideally clear on detail.

Symphony No. 5 in C min., Op. 67.
500♪ (M) *** DG Dig. 445 502-2 [id.]. LAPO, Giulini (with SCHUMANN: *Symphony No. 3 (Rhenish)* ***).

Giulini's 1982 Los Angeles recording of Beethoven's *Fifth* is among the finest performances this symphony has ever received on record. The performance possesses majesty in abundance and conveys the power and vision of this inexhaustible work. The slow movement is glorious and the finale almost overwhelming in its force and grandeur.

Symphonies Nos. 5 in C min.; 6 in F (Pastoral).
(M) **(*) Virgin Veritas/EMI Dig. VM5 61377-2 [id.]. L. Classical Players, Norrington.

No. 5 shows Norrington at his most exciting and inspired, relishing his fast speeds, while the finale has an infectious swagger. No. 6, however, fails to live up to expectations. The EMI sound leaves something to be desired in refinement and clarity, and Norrington is at times surprisingly fussy in his treatment. The *Scene by the brook*, for example, fails to flow when the phrasing is so short-winded, and there is not quite the same flow of energy that makes the *Fourth* so refreshing.

Symphonies Nos. 5 in C min., Op. 67; 7 in A, Op. 92.
500♪ ❁ (M) *** DG 447 400-2 [id.]. VPO, Carlos Kleiber.
*** DG Dig. 449 981-2 [id.]. Philh. O, Christian Thielemann.

If ever there was a legendary recording, it is Carlos Kleiber's version of the *Fifth* from the mid-1970s. In Kleiber's hands the first movement is electrifying but still has a hushed intensity. The slow movement is tender and delicate, with dynamic contrasts underlined but not exaggerated; the finale releases the music into pure daylight.

Still in his thirties, Christian Thielemann is an exceptionally positive interpreter, daring in these two Beethoven warhorses to fly boldly in the face of current fashion, opting for broad speeds and resonant textures to remind one of the weighty Klemperer with this same orchestra, yet with speeds fluctuating in a manner far nearer to Furtwängler. The results are magnetic rather than mannered or self-conscious so that, with outstanding playing from the Philharmonia (the strings in lustrous form) and vivid digital recording, this is an excellent recommendation for anyone wanting a traditional view with modern sound.

Symphony No. 6 in F (Pastoral), Op. 68; Overtures: Egmont; Leonora No. 3.
(B) *** Decca Eclipse Dig. 448 986-2; *448 986-4* [id.]. Philh. O, Ashkenazy.

Ashkenazy's performance has a beguiling warmth and it communicates readily. With generally spacious tempi, the feeling of lyrical ease and repose is most captivating, thanks to the response of the Philharmonia players and the richness of the recording, made in the Kingsway Hall. The two overtures make a thoroughly satisfactory makeweight, and this is a clear front runner in the bargain range.

Symphony No. 7 in A, Op. 92.
500♪ ❁ (B) *** EMI forte CZS5 69364-2 (2) [id.]. RPO, Sir Colin Davis – SCHUBERT: *Symphony No. 9* ***; ROSSINI: *Overtures.* **(*)

Sir Colin Davis's early (1961) *Seventh* is a great performance that can be spoken of in the same breath as Carlos Kleiber's *Fifth*. Here is an ideal illustration of the difference between a studio run-through and an interpretation that genuinely takes one forward compellingly from bar to bar. The finale, taken very fast indeed, barely allows one to breathe for excitement.

Symphony No. 9 in D min. (Choral), Op. 125.
500♪ (M) *** DG 415 832-2 [id.]. Tomowa-Sintow, Baltsa, Schreier, Van Dam, V. Singverein, BPO, Karajan.
*** Sony Dig. SK 62634 [id.]. Jane Eaglen, Waltraud Meier, Ben Heppner, Bryn Terfel, Swedish R. Ch., Ericson Chamber Ch., BPO, Abbado.
*** DG Dig. 453 423-2 [id.]. Solveig Kringelborn, Felicity Palmer, Thomas Moser, Alan Titus, Dresden State Op. Ch., Dresden State O, Sinopoli.

(M) **(*) Virgin Veritas/EMI Dig. VM5 61378-2 [id.]. Kenny, Walker, Power, Salomaa, Schütz Ch., L. Classical Players, Norrington.

*(*) EMI Dig. CDC7 54505-2 [id.]. Margaret Price, Marjana Lipovšek, Peter Seiffert, Jan-Hendrik Rootering, Concg. O, Sawallisch.

(i) *Symphony No. 9 in D min. (Choral). Overture Egmont, Op. 84.*

(M) *** Decca Phase Four 452 487-2 [id.]. (i) Harper, Watts, Young, McIntyre, L. Symphony Ch.; LSO, Stokowski.

(M) ** Ph. Dig. 442 644-2 [id.]. (i) Janet Price, Birgit Finnilä, Horst Laubenthal, Marius Rintzler, Concg. Ch.; Concg. O, Haitink.

Of the three stereo recordings Karajan has made of the *Ninth*, his 1977 account is the most inspired in its insight, above all in the *Adagio*, where he conveys spiritual intensity at a slower tempo than in his earlier, 1962 version. In the finale, the concluding eruption has an animal excitement rarely heard from this highly controlled conductor. The soloists make an excellent team, with contralto, tenor and bass all finer than their predecessors. The sound has tingling projection and drama.

Just ten years after Claudio Abbado recorded Beethoven's *Ninth Symphony* with the Vienna Philharmonic, he has returned to it in a recording made at the 1996 Salzburg Easter Festival, this time as Artistic Director of the Berlin Philharmonic, Karajan's successor. The contrasts are astonishing, notably over speeds (consistently faster) and performing style (lighter and crisper in articulation). So the opening with its string tremolos is fresh and clear rather than ominous. Abbado, like other conductors, has been influenced by the period-performance movement, rejecting heavyweight manners built up during the late nineteenth century, with string-tone less honeyed, more athletic. The slow movement this time flows so freely that it lasts a full three minutes less than before, and the difference in overall timing for the whole work is no less than six and a half minutes, an amazing degree of change. What is important is that, though both recordings were made live in concert, this one captures the electricity of a great occasion far more clearly. Above all, the finale with a superb quartet of soloists and fine Swedish choirs brings the feeling of climax too often missing in recordings of the *Ninth*. Highly recommended.

Sinopoli's powerful version was recorded live in 1996 at the annual Palm Sunday performance of the *Ninth* in Dresden, an important event in the city which here gives the performance a magnetic sense of occasion. The venue was the relatively small Semper Opera House, with the sound full and immediate, conveying a vivid sense of presence. Where in romantic music Sinopoli generally favours a moulded, flexible style, here in Beethoven he takes a rugged view, warmly sympathetic but largely without mannerism. So the first movement is sharply dramatic in its pointing of high contrasts, pressing ahead in urgency. The Scherzo is tough and forceful too, but well sprung, and the slow movement, at speeds on the broad side, has a songful intensity, with the two variation themes well contrasted, and with dynamic contrasts again sharply underlined, as in the climactic fanfare passage and sweet resolution. Sinopoli takes a broad view of the finale too, with the opening bringing an element of wildness and with the recitatives very emphatic. The weight of the chorus is splendidly caught, again with high dynamic contrasts and with the soloists an undistractingly well-matched team.

Stokowski's 1967 version, recorded in the Kingsway Hall, makes another very impressive mid-priced choice for the *Ninth*, although first choice probably rests with Mackerras (an exceptional, inspired account) on EMI Eminence (CD-EMX 2186) or Karajan's 1977 version, both in the same price-range. The Phase Four recording has been vividly remastered and retains its fullness, both vocally and orchestrally. The soloists are closely balanced and when they combine with the chorus, who sing with great ardour, the result is sonically thrilling. Indeed there is the sort of tension about this recorded performance which one expects from a great conductor in the concert hall, and that compulsion carries one over all Stokowski's idiosyncrasies, including a fair amount of retouching in the orchestration. The first movement is strong and dramatic, taken at a Toscanini pace; the Scherzo is light and pointed, with timpani cutting through; the slow movement has great depth and *Innigkeit* – and that, perhaps more than anything, confirms the greatness of the performance, for the finale, with some strangely slow tempi, is uneven, despite fine singing, yet ends resplendently. The *Egmont Overture*, recorded just over five years later, is a strong, exciting performance without idiosyncrasy. The sound here is full but slightly fierce on top.

Much of the sharp intensity and exhilaration of Norrington's reading of the *Ninth* comes over on his record, with many of his contentions over observing Beethoven's fast metronome markings validated in the success of the performance. What has to remain controversial is the slow movement which, at tempi far swifter than we are used to, becomes a sweet interlude rather than a meditation, far shorter than the other movements. A more serious snag is the contribution of the male soloists. Petteri Salomaa's tremulous, aspirated singing on the command '*Nicht diese Töne*' is painful, while Patrick Power's plaintive tenor timbre goes with a very slow pace for the drum-and-fife march passage. Nevertheless the impact of the whole performance is considerable, with reverberant recording still allowing the bite of timpani and valveless horns to cut through the texture. In no sense, except in the number of performers involved, is this a small-scale performance, rather an intensely refreshing view of a supreme masterpiece.

Haitink's digital *Ninth* was made at a live concert in the Concertgebouw, but one would hardly know that: there are few if any signs of an audience and – disappointingly – the performance rather fails to convey the feeling of an occasion, lacking a little in tension even in comparison with Haitink's earlier, studio version with the LPO. The reading, as in his earlier, analogue account, is satisfyingly unidiosyncratic, direct and honest, but with this work one needs more.

Sawallisch's version with the Concertgebouw is a disappointment. This is a reading which fails to convey the electric tensions of the work, well played but in a routine way at uncontroversial speeds. Nor is the sound sharply focused enough.

Wellington's victory (Battle symphony), Op. 91.

500♪ ✿ (M) *** Mercury 434 360-2 [id.]. Cannon & musket fire directed Gerard C. Stowe, LSO, Dorati (with separate descriptive commentary by Deems Taylor) – TCHAIKOVSKY: *1812; Capriccio italien.* *** ✿

This most famous of all Mercury records sounds far more convincing than it ever did in its vinyl format – indeed its sense of spectacle is quite extraordinary, an astonishing fusillade of fire, in which no one could complain at the use of period cannon and muskets or the engaging way the firing peters out as the battle comes to an end. This is surely an account which is unlikely to be bettered or realistically simulated in a live performance, and it is good to hear the endearing voice of Deems Taylor (famous for his commentary in Walt Disney's *Fantasia*) explaining how it was all done.

CHAMBER MUSIC

(i) *Cello sonatas Nos. 1–5;* (ii) *7 Variations on 'Bei Männern, welche Liebe fühlen'* (from Mozart's *Die Zauberflöte*), *WoO 46; 12 Variations on 'Ein Mädchen oder Weibchen'* (from Mozart's *Die Zauberflöte*), *Op. 66; 12 Variations on 'See the conqu'ring hero comes'* (from Handel's *Judas Maccabaeus*), *WoO 45.*

500♪ (B) *** Ph. Duo 442 565-2 (2) [id.]. (i) Mstislav Rostropovich, Sviatoslav Richter; (ii) Maurice Gendron, Jean Françaix.

(B) *** DG Double 453 013-2 (2) [id.]. Pierre Fournier, Wilhelm Kempff.

(B) **(*) Hyperion Dyad Dig. CDD 22004 (2) [id.]. Anthony Pleeth, Melvyn Tan (fortepiano).

Made in the early 1960s, the classic Philips performances by Mstislav Rostropovich and Sviatoslav Richter, two of the instrumental giants of the day, have withstood the test of time astonishingly well and sound remarkably fresh in this transfer. The performances of the *Variations* by Maurice Gendron and Jean Françaix have an engagingly light touch and are beautifully recorded.

Fournier and Kempff recorded their cycle of the sonatas at live festival performances, but the Paris audience is relatively unintrusive and these artists were inspired by the occasion to produce unexaggeratedly expressive playing and to give performances which are marked by their light, clear textures and rippling scale-work, even in the slow introductions which are taken relatively fast. Clearly Kempff is the leading personality here, and if some of the weight is missing such a stylish spontaneity is irresistible. Admirers of both artists will find this set a fine bargain as a DG Double, the sound enhanced by the current remastering, beautifully clear, with the cello timbre somewhat dry.

Though the cello is balanced rather forwardly in relation to the fortepiano, the Hyperion collection of Beethoven's music for cello and piano – not just the five *Sonatas* but the three sets of variations too – makes an attractive issue for anyone wanting period versions. Tan recorded these performances with Pleeth in 1987, not long before he began his Beethoven series for EMI, and his imagination is comparably keen here. Anthony Pleeth is a responsive enough partner but, although his phrasing does not lack warmth, his tone is comparatively wan and despite the balance it is Tan who easily dominates the set and makes the allegros sparkle. The *Variations* are particularly enjoyable in this respect.

Clarinet trio in B flat, Op. 11.

*** Sony Dig SK 57499 [id.]. Stoltzman, Ax, Ma – BRAHMS: *Clarinet trio* ***; MOZART: *Clarinet trio (Kegelstatt).* **

The early *Clarinet trio*, Op. 11, comes off well on Sony and is accorded excellent sound. Stoltzman plays with great sensitivity and Yo-Yo Ma with almost too much! All the same, this is well worth investigating, and Emanuel Ax is his spirited and vibrant self.

Octet for wind, Op. 103; (i) *Piano and wind quintet in E flat, Op. 16. Symphony No. 7 in A* (arr. Netherlands Wind Ens.).
** Chandos Dig. CHAN 9470 [id.] (i) Peter Donohoe; Netherlands Wind Ens.

No quarrels with any of the performances here. The early *Octet in E flat* is crisply played and splendidly recorded, and the Op. 16 *Piano and wind quintet*, usually coupled with the Mozart *Quintet* in the same key, on which it is modelled, comes off well. Murray Perahia with members of the ECO wind are neither eclipsed nor even challenged by the newcomer, though the present performance has plenty of spirit. It is good to hear the transcription of the *Seventh Symphony*, even if it is an unnecessary addition to the catalogue. It is marvellously played and recorded, though it is difficult to imagine many listeners returning to it very often.

Piano trios Nos 1–9; 10 (Variations on an original theme in E flat), Op. 44; 11 (Variations on 'Ich bin der Schneider Kakadu'), Op. 121a; Allegretto in E flat, Hess 48.
500♪ *** EMI Dig. CDS7 47455-8 (4) [Ang. CDCD 47455]. Ashkenazy, Perlman, Harrell.

Ashkenazy, Perlman and Harrell lead the field in this repertoire. The playing is unfailingly perceptive and full of those musical insights that make one want to return to the set. The *Archduke*, coupled with *No. 9 in B flat*, is available separately on CDC7 47010-2.

Piano trios Nos. 5 in D (Ghost); 6 in E flat, Op. 70/1–2; 7 (Archduke); 11 (Variations on 'Ich bin der Schneider Kakadu'); 12 (Allegretto in E flat).
500♪ (B) *** Carlton Double Dig. 30366 00107 (2). Solomon Trio.

Piano trios Nos. 5 in D (Ghost), Op. 70/1; 7 in B flat (Archduke), Op. 97.
(M) ** Ph. Dig./Analogue 454 129-2 [id.]. Beaux Arts Trio.

Three of Beethoven's greatest trios played with fine dedication and intelligence by Yonty Solomon, Rodney Friend and Timothy Hugh in lively but not over-bright acoustics that do justice to their music-making. The *Kakadu variations* are also done splendidly and the brief *Allegretto in E flat* makes a fresh bonus.

On Philips, the Beaux Arts Trio offer a popular coupling and they are realistically recorded. The *Archduke* was made in 1979 at La Chaux-de-Fonds in Switzerland, and the *Ghost* was recorded digitally, two years later, in London. The *Ghost Trio* comes off marvellously and sounds very fresh, but the *Archduke* is not as spontaneous as their earlier (mid-1960s) version, even if the ensemble remains excellent. The first movement, at a very slow tempo, sounds self-conscious and mannered; the Scherzo fails to maintain its spring and so does the finale. The slow variations have little sense of flow. For this coupling readers would do better to stay with Istomin, Stern and Rose (Sony SBK 53514) or the excellent Solomon Trio.

Piano trio No. 7 in B flat (Archduke), Op. 97.
(B) *** EMI forte CZS5 69367-2 (2). David Oistrakh, Sviatoslav Knushevitzky, Lev Oborin – BRAHMS: *Violin sonatas Nos. 1–2* **(*); SCHUBERT: *Piano trio 1* *** (with: KODALY: *Three Hungarian folksongs;* SUK: *Love song;* WIENIAWSKI: *Légende;* YSAYE: *Extase* ***).
** Ph. Dig. 442 123-2 [id.]. Viktoria Mullova, Heinrich Schiff, André Previn – BRAHMS: *Piano trio No. 1.* **

Piano trios Nos. 7 in B flat (Archduke), Op. 97; 4 in B flat (arr. of *Trio for piano, clarinet and cello*), *Op. 11.*
*** EMI Dig. CDC5 55187-2 [id.]. Chung Trio.

From the Chungs an *Archduke* to rank among the best. The Chungs cannot find time to meet and relax with chamber music very often, but they sound as if they do. This is very natural playing and, though Myung-Wha Chung's cello is often just a little on the reticent side, this does not worry us here. Both the *Archduke* and the Op. 11 can hold their own against all comers for sheer dedication and spirit. The EMI recording is exemplary.

On EMI forte a well-rounded, well-groomed yet thoroughly alive performance by three eminent soloists who are nevertheless experienced enough as chamber-music players to allow the necessary blend of personalities, the give-and-take that is essential for a great performance. They are rugged and assured in the first movement, brilliant in the last, and only a shade less compelling in the intervening movements. The Abbey Road recording is equally impressive; even though it was made in 1958, it hardly sounds dated, smooth on top with a good balance, a tribute to Walter Legge's skill in the early days of stereo; and the Schubert coupling is equally impressive. The encores derive from a concurrent recital disc. Oistrakh is placed rather near the microphones, but his tone is pure and exceptionally rich, yet he is capable of bringing off astonishing changes of tone-colour – listen to the little-known but seductive Ysaÿe work and the *Hungarian folksongs* by Kodály. Yampolski provides supportive accompaniments and the balance remains very good.

A good, very well-recorded performance from Mullova, Schiff and Previn that is full of life. As often with Mullova, there is a certain *froideur* about the approach; one feels that she is not as wholly involved in the proceedings as her partners, though there is no question that she is supremely accomplished. There are other more searching *Archdukes* on the scene, though none that is better recorded.

Piano and wind quintet in E flat, Op. 16.
500♪ (M) *** Sony Dig. SMK 42099 [id.]. Perahia, ECO (members) – MOZART: *Quintet.* ***
✿ (***) Testament mono STB 1091 [id.]. Gieseking, Philh. Wind Ens. – MOZART: *Quintet* etc. (***) ✿

First choice for Beethoven's *Piano and wind quintet* remains with Perahia's CBS version, recorded at The Maltings. Perahia's playing is wonderfully poetic. With the recording most realistically balanced, this issue can be recommended with all enthusiasm, especially as it is now offered at mid-price.

But chamber music-making doesn't come much finer than this earlier version by Walter Gieseking and members of the Philharmonia Wind (Dennis Brain, Sidney Sutcliffe, Bernard Walton and Cecil James). They recorded this performance in 1955 and, in terms of tonal blend and perfection of balance and ensemble, it has few rivals. Only Perahia and the ECO have equalled it. The mono sound comes up wonderfully fresh in this Testament transfer. This is a full-price reissue and worth every penny of the asking price.

Septet in E flat, Op. 20.
500♪ (B) *** Decca Eclipse Dig. 448 232-2; *448 232-4* [id.]. Vienna Octet (members) (with MOZART: *Clarinet quintet* ***).

Over the years the Vienna Octet have been justly famous for their recordings of Beethoven's *Septet* for Decca, and this newest version is no disappointment. Brio and good humour mark the performance. The recording is wonderfully warm and real; it was made as recently as 1991.

(i) *Serenade in D for flute, violin and viola, Op. 25;* (ii) *Serenade in D* (arr. of *Op. 25) for flute and piano, Op. 41; Flute sonata in B flat* (attrib.); *6 National airs with variations, Op. 105; 10 National airs with variations, Op. 105* (both sets for piano with flute obbligato).
(B) ** Ph. Duo 454 247-2 (2) [id.]. (i) Larrieu, Grumiaux, Janzer; (ii) Gazzelloni, Canino.

This set claims to garner Beethoven's 'complete music for flute', but the *Sonata in B flat* is of very dubious provenance: it sounds too simplistic even for very early Beethoven, although it is nimbly played. Easily the finest work here is the thoroughly engaging *Serenade in D*; but we are offered this twice, both in its original version for flute, violin and viola and in an arrangement for flute and piano, probably made by Franz Xaver Kleinheinz, but 'improved' by the composer. The sets of *Variations on National airs* were commissioned by the Scottish publisher, George Thomson, and were based on folksong settings which Beethoven had previously supplied and which are musically far superior. The composer's instructions were to 'write the variations in a familiar and easy and perhaps rather brilliant style so that the largest number of our young ladies can play and enjoy them'. The result is quite pleasing but highly ingenuous, although performances and recording are impeccable.

String quartets

String quartets Nos. 1–6, Op. 18/1–6; 10 in E flat (Harp), Op. 74; 11 in F min., Op. 95.
500♪ (M) *** ASV CDDDCS 305 (3) [id.]. Lindsay Qt.

String quartets Nos. 7 in F; 8 in E min.; 9 in C (Rasumovsky), Op. 59/1–3.
500♪ (M) *** ASV Dig. CDDCS 207 (2) [id.]. Lindsay Qt.

String quartets Nos. 12–16; Grosse Fuge in B flat, Op. 133.
500♪ (M) *** ASV Dig. CDDCS 403 (4) [id.]. Lindsay Qt.

String quartets Nos. 1–16; Grosse Fuge, Op. 133.
(B) *** Ph. 454 062-2 (10) [id.]. Italian Qt.
* DG Dig. 447 075-2 (7) [id.]. Emerson Qt.

The great merit of the Lindsay Quartet in Beethoven lies in the natural expressiveness of their playing, most strikingly of all in slow movements, which bring a hushed inner quality too rarely caught on record. They are performances of real stature and, though they are not unrivalled in some of their insights, among modern recordings they are not often surpassed. The Lindsays get far closer to the essence of this great music than most of their rivals. They have the benefit of very well-balanced recording; the sound of the ASV set is admirably present. Taken overall, these are among the very finest versions to have been made in recent years.

The Italian performances, which are in superb style, now return in a bargain box to offer almost unbeatable value. The Végh versions are in some ways even finer, but they are at mid-price; however, as they are on eight discs instead of ten, the difference in cost is relatively marginal (Valois V 4000). But the current Philips remastering is very impressive indeed: the sound is much smoother than hitherto, and very naturally balanced. The recordings were made in reverse order, starting with Op. 132 in 1967 and moving backwards to Op. 18, recorded between 1973 and 1975, with Op. 59/1 in the middle (1974), but the quality is remarkably consistent and the sonority they produce is beautifully blended and splendidly focused. In Op. 18 the only reservations concern Nos. 2 and 4: the latter is perhaps a little wanting in forward movement, while the conventional exchanges at the opening of No. 2 seem a shade too deliberate. But in general their superiority in terms of sheer quartet playing is still striking: purity of intonation and superb ensemble and attack. In the *Rasumovsky Quartets* in particular their tempi are perfectly judged and every phrase is sensitively shaped; in the later quartets their searching and thoughtful interpretations will ultimately prove most satisfying.

The Emerson Quartet recordings were made at the American Academy and Institute of Arts and Letters in New York in 1994–5. It is difficult to accord them a star-rating since, in one sense, their playing is quite in a class of its own. As we noted when discussing individual issues in the series, no other quartet now before the public can match the Emersons' sheer perfection of ensemble, polish, power of attack and refinement of tonal shading. Their technical finish is incredible, amazing – indeed awesome. It goes without saying that their cycle offers many incidental beauties: it is immaculate in its precision, dazzling in its unanimity. But the sheer thrust of this playing is less appropriate in music composed before the discovery of electricity, let alone the jet-engine. Those who want high-powered, gleaming Beethoven will find much to please them, but others will find that the Emersons make contact with this great music only intermittently, particularly in the late quartets. This is 'Beethoven on Madison Avenue': glamorized, fashionably attired and well manicured, with sparkling white teeth and vitaminized hair – in other words, it concentrates on virtuosity and presentation rather than on substance. Of course there are insights during the course of the cycle, and the DG recording is marvellous, but for the most part the playing is brilliant but shallow. For a really satisfying Beethoven *Quartet* cycle, readers should look elsewhere.

String quartets Nos. 7 in F; 8 in E min.; 9 in C, Op. 59/1–3; 10 in E flat (Harp), Op. 74.
(M) ** Berlin Classics 0091 622 BC (2) [id.]. Suske Qt.

The Suske Quartet was formed in the mid 1960s by members of the Berlin Staatskapelle, but the division of Germany at that time prevented them from making much of a reputation outside the Eastern bloc. The sleeve-notes mention that they shared second prize with the Melos Quartet of Stuttgart at the Geneva Competition in 1966. These performances were recorded in the late 1960s and, in the case of the *Harp Quartet*, leave no doubt of their credentials. Theirs are thoughtful, serious readings that would undoubtedly have been competitive at the time. The recordings are slightly forward but perfectly acceptable, but overall they do not displace any of our existing recommendations.

String quartets Nos. 12–16; Grosse Fuge.
(**(*)) Testament mono SBT 3082 (3) [id.]. Hollywood Qt.

String quartets Nos. 12 in E flat, Op. 127; 13 in B flat, Op. 130; 16 in F, Op. 135; Grosse Fuge in B flat, Op. 133.
(B) *** Ph. Duo 454 711-2 (2) [id.]. Italian Qt.

String quartets Nos. 14 in C sharp min., Op. 131; 15 in A min., Op. 132.
(B) **(*) Ph. Duo 454 712-2 (2) [id.]. Italian Qt.

As we have suggested above in considering their complete set, the merits of the Italian Quartet's performances are very considerable and their separate reissue on a pair of Philips Duos is very competitive, even if the second of the two sets seems short measure at only 90 minutes. The remastered sound is very satisfying.

It has been some years since the renowned (1957) Hollywood set of the late Beethoven *Quartets* appeared. They did not resurface on LP until the early 1980s and their reappearance on CD is a question of 'better late than never'. This is one of the classic sets and – *pace* the Budapest and Hungarian sets which appeared in the 1950s – ranks as the finest after the Busch. Technically, the Hollywood players are superior to the latter (though the Busch have the deeper musical insights), and their virtuosity in the *Grosse Fuge* has to be heard to be believed. But there is no playing to the gallery at any time: this is Beethoven perfectly played without any thought to display. The recordings are mono but have plenty of presence. They are accommodated on three CDs, not available separately, and some collectors will find them overpriced considering that they are on a premium label. Playing like this is, however, very special.

String trios Nos. 1 in E flat, Op. 3; Serenade in D, Op. 8.
(M) *** Unicorn Kanchana Dig. UKCD 2082 [id.]. Cummings Trio.

String trios Nos. 2 in G; 3 in D; 4 in C min., Op. 9/1–3.
(M) *** Unicorn Kanchana Dig. UKCD 2081 [id.]. Cummings Trio.

Alas, in our main volume we got the catalogue numbers reversed for this pair of highly recommendable mid-priced reissues. The playing of the Cummings Trio is cultured but not over-civilized; there is an unforced naturalness about it all. These players let Beethoven speak for himself, and in quieter moments there is a winning sense of repose; in short, this is real chamber-music-making, with excellent recording – in the demonstration class. Now at mid-price, it will be difficult to surpass this set.

Violin sonatas

Violin sonatas Nos. 1–10 (complete).
500♪ (M) *** Decca 421 453-2 (4); 436 892-2 (*Nos. 1–3*), 436 893-2 (*Nos. 4–5*), 436 894-2 (*Nos. 6–8*), 436 895-2 (*Nos. 9–10*). Itzhak Perlman, Vladimir Ashkenazy.
(M) *** Sony Stern Edition IV Dig./Analogue SM3K 64524 (3) [id.]. Isaac Stern, Eugene Istomin.

Perlman and Ashkenazy's set of the *Violin sonatas* will be difficult to surpass. These performances offer a blend of classical purity and spontaneous vitality that it is hard to resist; moreover the realism and presence of the recording in its CD format are very striking. They are also now available on four separate mid-priced CDs.

The performances by Stern and Istomin have striking rhythmic strengths as well as lyrical appeal: how delightfully the lilting opening theme of *No. 2 in A major* dances along, and how superbly the great *Adagio* of the *C minor*, Op. 30/2, is sustained. This and the very first sonata are analogue and were recorded in 1969; the remainder are digital and date from 1982–3. The *Spring Sonata* is more intense than some versions, but in the most involving way; the *C minor*, Op. 30/2, has similar electricity and the *Kreutzer* is splendid. The recording has great presence – some might feel the balance is too close but it suits this highly projected style of music-making; Istomin has a strong artistic personality and keeps well in the picture.

Violin sonatas Nos. 2 in A, Op. 12/2; 4 in A min., Op. 23; 5 in F (Spring), Op. 24; 8 in G, Op. 30/3.
(M) **(*) Ph. 442 651-2 [id.]. Arthur Grumiaux, Claudio Arrau.

This CD combines two pairs of performances recorded in the mid-1970s. *No. 2 in A* is particularly fresh; one can sense these artists enjoying their rapport; *No. 4 in A minor*, if fractionally less spontaneous, also comes off well. But in the *Spring Sonata* and the *G major*, although the readings are sensitive, understatement and lack of tension go together to undermine a feeling of live performance. The recording is fairly closely balanced but warmly refined and truthful; by the side of Perlman and Ashkenazy, however, these readings lack the last degree of character, although by any standards they are still distinguished.

Violin sonatas Nos. 5 in F (Spring), Op. 24; 9 in A (Kreutzer), Op. 47.
(BB) *** Tring Dig. TRP 082 [id.]. Jonathan Carney, Ronan O'Hora.

Couplings of the *Spring* and *Kreutzer Sonatas* are legion, but the stimulating partnership of Jonathan Carney (leader of, first, the RPO and currrently of the Bournemouth Symphony Orchestra) and Ronan O'Hora need not fear comparison with the finest. These highly dramatic performances have great concentration and spontaneity. After the well-sustained *Variations*, the finale of the *Kreutzer* bursts with joy. The recording is resonant, but the balance excellent: O'Hora makes the strongest contribution, with his colleague leading from the front.

SOLO PIANO MUSIC

Piano sonatas Nos. 1–32 (complete).
500♪ *** Elektra Nonesuch/Warner Dig. 7559 79328-2 (10). Richard Goode.
500♪ ✽ (B) (***) DG mono 447 966-2 (8) [id.]. Wilhelm Kempff.

It is not just the power of Goode's playing that singles him out, but the beauty, when he has such subtle control over a formidably wide tonal and dynamic range. Even at its weightiest, the sound is never clangorous. Particularly in the early sonatas Goode brings out the wit and parody, while slow movements regularly draw sensuously velvety legato. Above all, Goode has a natural gravity which compels attention. One has to go back to the pre-digital era to find a Beethoven cycle of comparable command and intensity – to the jewelled clarity of Wilhelm Kempff. We feel this is now a clear first choice for those wanting a modern digital cycle.

Kempff's qualities are even more intensely conveyed in his mono set, recorded between 1951 and

1956. The interpretations are the more personal, the more individual, at times the more wilful; but for any listener who responds to Kempff's visionary concentration, it is a magical series of interpretations. No other set of the sonatas so clearly gives the impression of new discovery, of fresh inspiration in the composer as a pianist. A ninth disc comes free, celebrating Kempff's achievement in words and music, on the organ in Bach, on the piano in Brahms, Chopin and Beethoven (a masterly pre-war recording of the *Pathétique sonata*) and accompanying Fischer-Dieskau in four of his own songs.

Piano sonatas Nos. 1 in F min.; 2 in A; 3 in C, Op. 2/1–3.
500♪ *** Sony Dig. SK 64397 [id.]. Murray Perahia.
*** Ph. Dig. 442 124-2 [id.]. Alfred Brendel.

Perahia's are commanding accounts of the greatest elegance and freshness. The *C major Sonata* recalls the classic Solomon account and, along with the Gilels on DG, is arguably the best we have had since the days of Kempff.

Brendel's third Beethoven cycle has been under way for some time. These recordings were made early in 1994 at The Maltings, Snape, and, unlike earlier cycles, he couples the first three together, eminently different in character as they are. This is distinguished, highly characterful playing which evinces superb control. Too controlled, some might say, for one sometimes feels the need, not so much for the unexpected, since Brendel is full of surprises, but for the volatile, bad-tempered quality that one remembers from Schnabel's records. Vividly alive recording.

Piano sonatas Nos. 1 in F min., Op. 2/1; 5 in C min.; 6 in F, Op. 10/1–2; 9 in E; 10 in G, Op. 14/1–2; 13 in E flat; 14 in C sharp min. (Moonlight), Op. 27/1–2; 15 in D (Pastoral), Op. 28.
(B) **(*) Carlton VoxBox CDX 5056 (2) [id.]. Alfred Brendel.

From the very start of the little F minor work which opens the greatest of all sonata cycles, Brendel makes clear the weight and seriousness of his approach. This is no mere Haydnesque reading, but a determined attempt to present the work as revolutionary, in the way it must have struck its first listeners. Yet the music flows spontaneously and the *Adagio* is poised and serene. Equally, in the two shorter sonatas from Op. 10, Brendel's clear, direct style suits the pithiness of the argument; although the *Adagio* of the *C minor Sonata* seems a little deliberate, the *Allegretto* of the F major work has plenty of colour. It is a pity, however, that the layout of the VoxBox prevents the usual arrangement of having all three Op. 10 sonatas together. The less ambitious but closely argued sonatas of Op. 14 are both fine works, despite their associations with piano lessons. Except perhaps in the great D minor slow movement, Brendel's strong, direct manner is consistently satisfying. For the first and less famous of the two Op. 27 *'Fantasy' Sonatas*, his concentration makes for satisfying results. Though fantasy in a strict sense is not one of his strongest suits, the work's opening is full of atmosphere. The *Moonlight* is hushed and gentle in its cool stillness, with veiled tone (a straight style helping, though there is no mystery). The finale, at a relaxed tempo, is beautifully pointed but does not seek extrovert excitement. The *Pastoral* is enjoyable in its relaxed simplicity. Brendel consistently holds the attention with his unforced and straightforward manner but by his very reticence misses some of the charm which a pianist like Barenboim in his more idiosyncratic way uses to heighten the music's effect. However, Brendel is at his finest in the elusive *G major Sonata*, Op. 79, which also offers good sound. The recordings, made between 1962 and 1964, have been excellently remastered: the piano-image is bright, bold and resonant with fine presence, the somewhat clattery quality of the original LPs now better controlled within the ambience, and no lack of sonority. Good notes.

Piano sonatas Nos. 2 in A; 3 in C, Op. 2/2–3; 7 in D, Op. 10/3; 8 in C min. (Pathétique); 11 in B flat, Op. 22; 12 in A flat, Op. 26; 24 in F sharp, Op. 78.
(B) **(*) Carlton VoxBox CDX 5060 (2) [id.]. Alfred Brendel.

Brendel opens here with No. 7, the third of the Op. 10 set, the most expansive of the early sonatas, with its orchestral texture in the first movement and its genuine depth in the *D minor* slow movement. Except perhaps in that movement, Brendel's strong, direct manner is consistently satisfying, yet in Op. 2/2 which follows Brendel does find a deeper imaginative vein, and in Op. 2/3 his concentration once again underlines the strength of the writing. The *Pathétique*, however, is one of the more disappointing of his series. There is little spark in the allegros and the slow movement is relatively inexpressive. Op. 26, too, provides a comparatively pedestrian reading. *No. 11 in B flat*, one of Beethoven's imaginative 'in-between' sonatas which give a clear foretaste of his middle period, fires Brendel to give a clean, concentrated performance which is commanding, and the little *F sharp major Sonata*, Op. 18, rounds off the set neatly. As in the first box, the piano-tone seems considerably improved over the old LPs, bright and clean and with plenty of supporting sonority, plus a distinct sense of presence.

Piano sonata Nos. 4 in E flat, Op. 7; 15 in D (Pastoral), Op. 28; 20 in G, Op. 49/2.
*** Ph. Dig. 446 624-2 [id.]. Alfred Brendel.

Spacious and majestic are the words that spring to mind when the *E flat Sonata*, Op. 7, gets under way, and Brendel takes a magisterial view of the whole sonata. The *Pastoral* is now more inward-looking and has more gravitas than the VoxBox account or the earlier Philips cycle, and some may find it less congenial. Few, however, will find it less than thought-provoking.

Piano sonatas Nos. 7 in D, Op. 10/3; 14 in C sharp min. (Moonlight), Op. 27/2; 28 in A, Op. 101.
(**(*)) Testament mono SBT 1070 [id.]. Géza Anda.

These recordings come from 1955 (the *Moonlight*) and 1958 (Opp. 10/3 and 101) during the heyday of Géza Anda's years as a Columbia (EMI) artist when he produced some 14 or so LPs of generally exceptional quality. The outstanding performance on the disc is the other-worldly account of the *A major Sonata*, Op. 101. As Bryce Morrison puts it in his liner-note, 'I doubt whether it has often been more intimately or beguilingly confided than by Anda, its outline haloed, as it were, by his unmistakable sonority'. Only Arrau and Gilels could command a sound-world that was as distinctive, and only Gilels and Solomon have made this sound as ethereal. Anda studied in Budapest with Dohnányi and inherited some of the latter's aristocratic poise as well as an immaculate technical prowess. All three sonatas are played with a vibrant sense of line and impeccable taste, and the recordings, though never state of the art, are very serviceable and clean. Music-making of some stature. However, the one drawback is that this is reissued at full price.

Piano sonatas Nos. 8 (Pathétique), Op. 13; 14 (Moonlight), Op. 27/2; 15 (Pastoral), Op. 28; 17 (Tempest), Op. 31/2; 21 (Waldstein), Op. 53; 23 (Appassionata), Op. 57; 26 (Les Adieux), Op. 81a.
500♪ (B) *** Ph. Duo 438 730-2 [id.]. Alfred Brendel.

In offering seven of Beethoven's most popular named sonatas, this Duo set – two discs for the price of one – is in every way an outstanding bargain, well worth having even if duplication is involved. All the performances are undeniably impressive and the recording consistently excellent. While Brendel's earlier *Waldstein* (on Vox/Turnabout) has claims to be considered among the very finest on record, this is only marginally less impressive and is certainly much better recorded.

Piano sonatas Nos. 8 in C min. (Pathétique), Op. 13; 14 in C sharp min. (Moonlight), Op. 27/2; 23 in F min. (Appassionata), Op. 57.
(B) **(*) Carlton Turnabout 30371 00292. Walter Klien.

Anyone familiar with Walter Klien's recordings of the Mozart *Sonatas* will not be surprised to find that his Beethoven has a comparable integrity. These are highly musical, admirably paced readings, strong yet flexible. The opening of the *Moonlight Sonata* (altogether a very fine performance) has a touching simplicity, matched by the slow movements of the other two works. The recording is fully acceptable, not unlike the sound Vox provide for Brendel. The CD is delightfully adorned by three classical ladies who look very like the three Graces, each of whom is presumably allotted to one of these works.

Piano sonatas Nos. 8 in C min. (Pathétique); 21 in C (Waldstein); 23 in F min. (Appassionata).
500♪ ✿ (M) *** Beethoven Edition DG Analogue/Dig. 447 914-2 [id.]. Emil Gilels.
(M) **(*) Ph. Dig. 454 686-2 [id.]. Claudio Arrau.

Gilels's account of the *Appassionata* has previously been hailed by us as among the finest ever made, and much the same must be said of the *Waldstein*. It has a technical perfection denied even to Schnabel and, though in the slow movement Schnabel found special depths, Gilels is hardly less searching and profound. If the *Pathétique* does not quite rank among his very best, such are the strengths of his playing that the reading still leaves a profound impression.

Arrau's performances are magnificently recorded. They were made at different times (1984–7) and in different places (Switzerland and New York), but the digital piano sonority is full and satisfying, the image bold and realistic. This helps to make Arrau's *Appassionata* very commanding indeed, with gloriously rich timbre in the central *Andante*. It is a distinguished performance, powerful and commanding in the same way as his *Emperor concerto*. The *Waldstein* is impressive too, though not as incandescent as Kempff's. The *Pathétique* (recorded in 1986 when Arrau was eighty-three) is just a little wanting in colour and vitality, and some listeners may feel that the *Adagio cantabile* is too measured. However, the playing throughout this record is impressive and, for all the individual mannerisms, the interpretations are authoritative and convincing.

Piano sonatas Nos. 12 in A flat, Op. 26; 19 in G min., Op. 49/1; 20 in G, Op. 49/2; 30 in E, Op. 109.
(*) EMI Dig. CDC5 56148-2 [id.]. Stephen Kovacevich.

Stephen Kovacevich's credentials as a Beethoven interpreter are well known; anyone who heard his 1970s Philips recording of Opp. 110 and 111 or who has had the good fortune to hear his Op. 109 in the concert hall will know that in this work he is second to none. The recording quality of the present issue has prompted criticism in some quarters. *Gramophone* magazine's Richard Osborne went so far as to call it 'ugly – thin, metallic, discoloured'. Systems differ, but trying this on a variety of equipment has not produced very satisfactory results. For a few bars into Op. 109 one is lured into believing that the sound will be serviceable but, once the dynamic level rises to *forte* or *fortissimo*, the sound becomes shallow and wiry. The sound remains unpleasant even after filtering or other adjustment of the tone controls. The playing itself is distinguished, but the sound-quality calls for more tolerance than most listeners will be willing to extend.

Piano sonatas Nos. 13 in E flat; 14 in C sharp min. (Moonlight), Op. 27/1–2; 15 in D (Pastoral), Op. 28; 26 in E flat (Les Adieux), Op. 81a.
(M) *** DG Dig. 445 593-2 [id.]. Daniel Barenboim.

Spontaneity and electricity, extremes of expression in dynamic, tempo and phrasing, as well as mood, mark Barenboim's performances. The lyrical flow in the *Pastoral* is as evident as the spontaneity of the music-making. The plainness in the first movement of the *Moonlight* is the one disappointment, with little veiled tone; however, the *Andante espressivo* of *Les Adieux* is played touchingly. The recordings are firm and the acoustic spacious.

Piano sonatas Nos. 14 in C sharp min. (Moonlight), Op. 27/2; 15 in D (Pastoral), Op. 28; 17 in D min. (Tempest), Op. 31/2; 21 in C (Waldstein), Op. 53; 22 in F, Op. 54; 23 in F min. (Appassionata), Op. 57; 24 in F sharp, Op. 78; 32 in C min., Op. 111.
(B) ** Decca Double 443 012-2 (2) [id.]. Friedrich Gulda.

This series of Beethoven sonatas was recorded in the late 1950s and Gulda proves a thoroughly reliable Beethovenian. The recording quality is good, and the directness of manner characteristic of this pianist is naturally projected. Gulda's view of Op. 101 is thoughtful and unforced, and so in its way is the *Waldstein*, though some may find too little weight. His view of the *Appassionata* is purposeful and direct, lacking something in fantasy, but satisfying on its own terms. The reading of Op. 111 is penetrating, even if it rarely rises to the supreme heights of the greatest interpretations. At Double Decca price, this is acceptable value, but Brendel's pair of Duos (Philips 438 730-2 and 438 374-2) cover this repertoire and much else besides, and offer a far better investment.

Piano sonatas Nos. 16 in G; 17 in D min. (Tempest); 18 in E flat, Op. 31/1–3.
500♪ *** EMI Dig. CDC5 55226-2 [id.]. Stephen Kovacevich.

Even in this highly competitive field Stephen Kovacevich brings some extra distinction which makes this set special. This is playing of insight and of unfailing artistry that illumines and delights the listener.

Piano sonata No. 17 in D min., Op. 31/2.
❀ (B) *** EMI forte CZS5 69340-2 (2). Sviatoslav Richter – HANDEL: *Suites Nos. 9–16.* *** ❀

Richter's classic 1961 account of the so-called *Tempest Sonata* returns to circulation as a fill-up to the sublime set of Handel suites he recorded with Andrei Gavrilov at the Château de Marcilly-sur-Maulne during the 1979 Tours Festival. It previously appeared coupled with the Dvořák *Piano Concerto in G minor* that Richter recorded with Carlos Kleiber and, as far as we can hear, the new transfer does not differ to any marked degree from its predecessor. Richter makes the most of possibilities of contrast. He plays the opening extremely slowly, and then when the allegro comes he takes it unusually fast. Far from being odd, this effect is actually breathtaking. Richter observes the repeats in both the first and last movements, and this last (the *Allegretto*) he plays at a perfectly controlled tempo, never giving way to nervous virtuosity. Excellent Abbey Road sound. Not to be missed.

Piano sonatas Nos. 21 (Waldstein); 24 in F sharp, Op. 78; 31 in A flat, Op. 110.
500♪ *** EMI Dig. CDC7 54896-2 [id.]. Stephen Kovacevich.

This second disc in Stephen Kovacevich's projected Beethoven cycle for EMI brings revelatory performances from one of the deepest thinkers among Beethoven pianists. Compared with Richard Goode, Kovacevich allows himself a degree more expressive freedom, giving foretastes of romantic music to come. The *Waldstein* as well as Op. 110 has a visionary quality.

Piano sonatas Nos. 27 in E min., Op. 90; 28 in A, Op. 101; 29 in B flat (Hammerklavier), Op. 106; 30 in E, Op. 109; 31 in A flat, Op. 110; 32 in C min., Op. 111.
❁ (B) *** DG Double 453 010-2 (2) [id.]. Wilhelm Kempff.
❁ (M) (***) EMI mono CHS7 64708-2 (2) [id.]. Solomon.

Kempff has never been more inspirationally revealing than in these performances of the last six Beethoven sonatas. The first movement of Op. 90 is treated very like a romantic improvisation, with strength and lyricism contrasted, while the second movement, flowing fairly fast, is almost Schubertian. Op. 101 begins with a fastish, carefree account of the visionary first movement, essentially rhapsodic in feeling. The Scherzo has all the sharpness of edge that it needs. By contrast the brief slow movement is extrovert, and the final fugue is magnificent. The *Hammerklavier* brings a preference for measured allegros and fastish *Andantes*, giving a weighting to movements that is different from the usual, but there is a thoughtfulness of utterance which brings profundity. The reading of Op. 109 then sets the style for Kempff's performances of the last three sonatas, intense in its control of structure but with a feeling of rhapsodic freedom too, of new visions emerging. The second movement of Op. 110 is not as fast as it might be, but the result is the cleaner for that and, in typical Kempff style, the great *Arietta* of Op. 111 is taken at a flowing tempo, not nearly as slowly as with many a recorded rival. These are all great performances, and the remastered recordings have been enhanced to an extraordinary degree to give an uncannily realistic piano-image, helped by the immediacy of Kempff's communication.

EMI have been slow to reissue Solomon's classic performances of the late Beethoven *Sonatas*. His stroke prevented the great pianist from completing the cycle, but he did at least give us the last six. This is Beethoven pure and unadulterated; this music-making comes as near to the truth as any in the catalogue. They have something of the depth of Schnabel, the tonal beauty of Arrau, the selflessness and integrity of Kempff and the perfect pianism of Pollini on DG or the magisterial, early Brendel set. While Solomon has been ignored in the UK, his reputation in Germany has remained high, thanks to the advocacy of such authorities as Joachim Kayser. The *Hammerklavier sonata* is one of the greatest recordings of the work ever made (this is one of the few weaknesses in Schnabel's complete set) and few have matched – let alone surpassed – it. Opp. 109 and 111 were recorded in 1951, the *Hammerklavier* a year later; Opp. 90 and 110 in 1956, not long before he was struck down. The engineers have done wonders with the transfers. The sound emerges in startling freshness and fullness. Magisterial, thoughtful, deeply lyrical and commanding performances that make so many later versions sound quite shallow.

Piano sonatas Nos. 27 in E min., Op. 90; 28 in A, Op. 101; 32 in C min., Op. 111.
500♪ *** EMI Dig. CDC7 54599-2 [id.]. Stephen Kovacevich.

Stephen Kovacevich's Op. 90 is among the finest in the catalogue and the *A major*, Op. 101, is among the most serene since the eloquent account by Gilels on a beautifully recorded DG LP. The *C minor*, Op. 111, is a performance of stature, free from any attempt to beautify. The recording is excellent.

Piano sonatas Nos. 28 in A, Op. 101; 29 in B flat (Hammerklavier), Op. 106; 30 in E, Op. 109; 31 in A flat, Op. 110; 32 in C min., Op. 111.
(B) *** Decca Double Analogue/Dig. 452 176-2 (2) [id.]. Vladimir Ashkenazy.
(M) **(*) DG Originals 449 740-2 (2) [id.]. Maurizio Pollini.

Distinguished performances on Decca, as one would expect, and an impressive sense of repose in the slow movement of Op. 109, while the account of No. 28 is searching and masterly. This was Ashkenazy's second recording of the *Hammerklavier*, the performance fresher, more spontaneous than the earlier version, but the total experience is less than monumental. The last two sonatas, however, are played with a depth and spontaneity which put them among the finest available. In the slow movement of Op. 111 Ashkenazy matches the concentration of the slowest possible speed which marks out the reading of his friend Barenboim, but there is an extra detachment. If anything, the interpretation of Op. 110 is even more remarkable, consistently revealing. The analogue recordings date from between 1971 and 1980, and the remastering is very successful. The *Hammerklavier* is a digital recording and has a touch of hardness on top. Highly recommendable at Double Decca price.

Pollini's recordings of the late *Sonatas* (which on LP originally included No. 27) won the 1977 *Gramophone* Critics' award for instrumental music, and they contain playing of the highest order of mastery. Joan Chissell spoke of the 'noble purity' of these performances, and that telling phrase aptly sums them up, if also hinting perhaps at a missing dimension, which the CD transfer seems to emphasize. The sound has great presence, but on the first disc there is hardness to the timbre in Opus 101 which becomes almost brittle in the fortissimos of the *Hammerklavier* with an adverse effect on the music-making. Pollini's *Hammerklavier* is undoubtedly eloquent, and so is Op. 111, which has a peerless authority and power. However, the slow movement of Op. 110 may be a trifle fast for some tastes, and in the A major work Gilels has greater poetry and humanity. The second disc brings a close balance to Opp. 109 and 110 but the recordings seem fractionally mellower, although a touch of hardness comes back in Op. 111. The current remastering for reissue as a DG 'Original' seems to have afforded no marked improvement, but the two discs are now packaged like a DG Double and are offered at a special price.

Piano sonatas Nos. 30 in E min., Op. 109; 31 in A flat, Op. 110; 32 in C min., Op. 111.
*** Ph. Dig. 446 701-2 [id.]. Alfred Brendel.

We have not heard all of the latest Brendel Beethoven cycle but, if the others are as illuminating as these, we have something to look forward to. These performances can best be described as searching and concentrated. They draw one into Beethoven's world immediately; they possess an eloquence that is all the more potent for being selfless. The recordings, made at Henry Wood Hall and at The Maltings, Snape, are of the highest quality in terms of realism and presence.

Miscellaneous piano music

Allegretto in C min., WoO 53; 6 Ecossaises, WoO 83; 6 Easy variations on a Swiss air in F; Für Elise; Polonaise in C, Op. 89; Rondo in G, Op. 51/2; Piano sonatas Nos. 4 in E flat, Op. 7; 20 in G, Op. 49/2; 5 Variations on 'Rule Britannia' in D, WoO 79; 6 Variations on an original theme in F, Op. 34; 6 Variations on a theme from The Ruins of Athens, Op. 76; 6 Variations on an original theme, in G, WoO 77; 7 Variations on 'God save the King' in D; 8 Variations on Grétry's air 'Une fièvre brûlante' in C; 9 Variations on Paisiello's Air 'Quant è più bello' in A, WoO 69; 12 Variations on a Russian dance from Wranitsky's ballet 'Das Waldmädchen' in A; 15 Variations and a fugue on a theme from Prometheus in E flat (Eroica variations), Op. 35.
(B) ** Carlton VoxBox CDX3 3017 (2) [id.]. Alfred Brendel.

It is good to have Brendel's Vox recordings of the variations back in the catalogue, even if the recording is too close and rather hard. As in his early set of the Beethoven sonatas on the same label, his manner is strong and purposeful. Sometimes the toughness may seem too keen for these miniature pieces, but Brendel's naturally spontaneous manner brings out many felicities and the playing is never matter-of-fact. The well-known set of variations on the *Prometheus* theme is done with directness and brilliance and muscular fingerwork, and the inclusion of the other incidental pieces is also valuable. Brendel throws off the *Ecossaises* splendidly, and the *Polonaise* (not in the least characteristic) is given a flexible rubato. The variations on the two famous British national airs also come off splendidly. Of the two sonatas included as makeweights, Op. 7 comes off the better. Brendel's concentration underlines the strength, and in the orchestral textures of the first movement his directness is particularly impressive. He is less persuasive in the 'little' *G major Sonata*, which lacks charm, not helped by the unglamorous sound.

Andante favori in F, WoO 57; 7 Bagatelles, Op. 33; 11 Bagatelles, Op. 119; 6 Bagatelles, Op. 126; Rondo in C, Op. 51/1; Rondo a capriccio in G ('Rage over a lost penny'), Op. 129; 33 Variations on a waltz by Diabelli, Op. 120; Zemlich Lebhaft in B flat, WoO 60.
(B) **(*) Carlton VoxBox CDX 5112 (2) [id.]. Alfred Brendel.

Most of the familiar *Bagatelles* (including one or two that we might have tried to play ourselves) are in the first set, Op. 33. These date from the very beginning of the new century, whereas Op. 119 spans the period between 1800 and 1825, when the third set was published. But if the listener expects the same kind of development in the writing that can be found in the composer's major output, he or she will be disappointed. These are chippings from the workshop and the finish on some of the earlier pieces is as polished as in the later ones. Indeed the first four of Op. 119, which follow immediately after the *Diabelli variations*, are among the most attractive of all. Brendel treats them as miniatures and he shapes them with care and precision. His taste can never be faulted, and he is supported by mainly excellent recording. The treble is sometimes a bit bright, but the brittleness noticeable on the LPs has been much mitigated and the focus is very good. The *Diabelli variations* open the first CD. As one would expect, Brendel gives a powerful, commanding performance of what is almost certainly Beethoven's most taxing piano work. As in his live performances, he builds up the variations unerringly, but it is surprising to find to what degree he indulges in little accelerandos in each half of those variations which involve crescendos. Broadly his approach is romantic with the adagio variation, No. 29, made into a moving lament. Few if any performances of this work on record convey its continuity so convincingly. The recording is faithful enough but not really adequately soft. The other pieces are placed on the second disc before and after the Op. 33 *Bagatelles*. The *Rondo a capriccio* comes first and is suitably impulsive, Brendel marginally less clean-fingered than usual here; but the two closing encores, the charming *Andante favori* and the *Zemlich lebhaft Klavierstück* (written, like *Für Elise*, for a young lady) bring a gentle romanticism.

6 Bagatelles, Op. 126; 6 Easy variations on an original theme, WoO 77; 6 Ecossaisen, WoO 83; Klavierstücke in B min., WoO 61; 7 Ländler, WoO 11; Minuet in E flat, WoO 82; Rondo in C, Op. 51/1; 6 Variations on national airs: The cottage maid (Wales); Of noble race was Shenkin (Scotland); A Schüsserl und a Reindl (Austria); The last rose of summer; Chiling O'Guiry; Paddy Whack (Ireland). 12 Variations on a minuet à la Viganò from Haibel's 'Le nozze disturbate', WoO 68.
*** Decca 452 206-2 [id.]. Olli Mustonen.

Olli Mustonen plays the Op. 126 *Bagatelles* and the *Klavierstücke* with appealing simplicity and he finds a surprising depth in their lyrical inspiration. By their side, most of the other music, although skilfully crafted, stops only just short of triviality, but in Mustonen's hands the programme becomes a string of jewelled miniatures of great charm. His deliciously pointed articulation is a joy, particularly in the *Ländler*, while the *Easy variations*, WoO 77, are captivating, and the *Ecossaisen* hop and gallop along. The recording is most natural and believable. An outstanding collection in every respect, but one to be dipped into, and certainly not to be taken all at once.

33 Variations on a waltz by Diabelli, Op. 120.
500♪ *** Hyperion Dig. CDA 66763 [id.]. William Kinderman.

The *Diabelli* is the greatest set of variations ever written. William Kinderman's version on Hyperion is really in a class of its own, remarkably fresh and well thought out, and it is almost worth buying the present disc for the sake of his illuminating liner-notes. He is very well recorded, too. The most outstanding *Diabelli variations* to have appeared for ages.

VOCAL MUSIC

Adelaide; Der Kuss; Resignation; Zärtliche Liebe.
(M) *** DG Originals 449 747-2 [id.]. Fritz Wunderlich, Hubert Giesen – SCHUBERT: *Lieder;* SCHUMANN: *Dichterliebe.* ***

Wunderlich was thirty-five when he recorded these songs, and the unique bloom of the lovely voice is beautifully caught. Though the accompanist is too metrical at times, we see no reason to withhold a third star, for the freshness of Wunderlich's singing makes one grieve again over his untimely death.

(i–iv) *Cantata on the death of Emperor Joseph II, WoO 87;* (ii–v) *Cantata on the accession of Emperor Leopold II, WoO 88. Meerestille und glückliche Fahrt, Op. 112;* (ii) *Opferlied.*
✿ *** Hyperion Dig. CDA 66880 [id]. (i) Janice Watson; (ii) Jean Rigby; (iii) John Mark Ainsley; (iv) José van Dam; (v) Judith Howarth; Corydon Singers & O, Matthew Best.

Beethoven was only nineteen when in Bonn in 1790 he was commissioned to write his 40-minute cantata on the Emperor's death. It was never performed, the musicians claiming it was too difficult, and remained buried for almost a century. Arguably Beethoven's first major masterpiece, it was one of his few early unpublished works of which he approved: when he came to write *Fidelio* he used the soaring theme from the first of the cantata's soprano arias for Leonore's sublime moment in the finale, *O Gott! Welch ein Augenblick.* The aria is radiantly sung here by Janice Watson. The tragic C minor power of the choruses framing the work is equally memorable, with dramatic tension kept taut through all seven sections. Matthew Best conducts a superb performance, at once fresh and incisive and deeply moving, with excellent soloists as well as a fine chorus. The second cantata, much shorter, written soon after, brings fascinating anticipations of the *Fifth Symphony* and of the choral finale of the *Ninth*, while the two shorter pieces – with Jean Rigby as soloist in the *Opferlied* – make a generous fill-up, equally well performed. With plenty of air round the chorus, the recording combines weight and transparency.

Egmont (incidental music), *Op. 84:* complete recording, with narration based on the text by Grillparzer, and melodrama from the play by Goethe.
(M) **(*) Decca 448 593-2 [id.]. Pilar Lorengar, Wussow (narrator), VPO, Szell.

The problem with performing Beethoven's incidental music for Goethe's *Egmont* within the original dramatic context is at least partially solved by using a text by the Austrian poet, Franz Grillparzer. The music is interspersed at the appropriate points, including dramatic drum-rolls in Egmont's final peroration, this last scene being from Goethe's original. The Decca presentation, with Klaus-Jürgen Wussow the admirably committed narrator, is dramatic in the extreme. Szell's conducting is superb, the music marvellously characterized, the tension lightened in certain places with subtlety, and the whole given a flowing dramatic impact. The songs are movingly sung by Pilar Lorengar. This has, appropriately enough, been reissued in Decca's Classic Sound series, and the CD transfer is immensely vivid. The snag is that, though a full translation is included, there are no separating bands for the spoken narrative, so that it is impossible to programme the CD to listen only to the music.

Readers will note that our main volume lists an even more complete bargain version, and if this Belgian performance is not as electrifying as Szell's, Alexander Rahbari still directs the proceedings with plenty of drama and Miriam Gauci is a warm-toned soloist (Discover DICD 920114).

Missa solemnis, Op. 123.

500♪ *** DG Dig. 435 770-2 (2) [id.]. Studer, Norman, Domingo, Moll, Leipzig R. Ch., Swedish R. Ch., VPO, Levine.

500♪ *** DG Dig. 429 779-2; *429 779-4* [id.]. Margiono, Robbin, Kendall, Miles, Monteverdi Ch., E. Bar. Soloists, Gardiner.

(B) *** DG Double 453 016-2 (2). Janowitz, Ludwig, Wunderlich, Berry, V. Singverein, BPO, Karajan – MOZART: *Coronation Mass.* **(*)

(M) (**) DG Originals 449 737-2 (2) [id.]. Stader, Radev, Dermota, Greindl, St Hedwig's Cathedral Ch., BPO, Boehm – REGER: *Variations and fugue on a theme by Mozart.* (**)

This performance of Beethoven's *Missa solemnis* conducted by James Levine brings an incandescence that conveys the atmosphere of a great occasion, as this work should. This version has no rival, and the DG engineers have obtained the richest, weightiest sound yet on any recording made in the tricky Salzburg venue, not least from the massed choruses. The two-disc format may be extravagant, but for such an intense visionary experience, defying the conventional view of Levine, this is a version not to be missed.

Gardiner's inspired reading matches even the greatest of traditional performances on record in dramatic weight and spiritual depth, while bringing out the white heat of Beethoven's inspiration with new intensity. The Monteverdi Choir sings with bright, luminous tone, and the four soloists are excellent. The recording is vivid too. Even those who normally resist period performance will find this very compelling.

On Karajan's earlier (1966) analogue recording, made in the Jesus-Christus-Kirche, both the chorus and, even more strikingly, the superbly matched quartet of soloists, never surpassed as a team in this work, convey the intensity and cohesion of Beethoven's deeply personal response to the liturgy. Gundula Janowitz is even more meltingly beautiful here than in her later, EMI recording for Karajan. Christa Ludwig, as there, is a firm and characterful mezzo, while Walter Berry is a warmly expressive bass. Best of all is the ill-fated Fritz Wunderlich whose lovely, heroic but unstrained tenor adds supremely to the radiance of the performance, one of his great recordings. The balance between soloists, chorus and orchestra is far clearer and more precise than in most recent recordings, and the clarity of detail is exemplary. Now on a DG Double, coupled with Mozart's *Coronation Mass*, the attractions of this performance are undoubtedly enhanced.

Boehm's *Missa solemnis* was recorded in the Berlin Jesus-Christus-Kirche in 1955 and must have been one of the last major mono recordings to be made there. It has a fine team of soloists and the sound is vivid, full and well balanced, but both those soloists and the chorus emerge intertwined with little or no difference of dynamic. If it were an electrically charged affair, like some of the recordings made by Fricsay in this period, this would not matter very much, but it is just a strong, brightly paced account which affords musical satisfaction but could hardly be counted preferable to the best mid-priced stereo versions.

OPERA

Fidelio (complete).

500♪ ❁*** EMI CDS5 55170-2 (2). Ludwig, Vickers, Frick, Berry, Crass, Philh. Ch. & O, Klemperer.

Klemperer's great set of *Fidelio* has been superbly remastered. The result is a technical triumph to match the unique incandescence and spiritual strength of the performance, with wonderful contributions from all concerned and a final scene in which, more than in any other recording, the parallel with the finale of the *Choral Symphony* is underlined.

Bellini, Vincenzo (1801–35)

Norma (complete).

500♪ (M) *** Decca 425 488-2 (3) [id.]. Sutherland, Horne, Alexander, Cross, Minton, Ward, London Symphony Ch., LSO, Bonynge.

(***) EMI mono CDS5 56271-2 (3). Callas, Stignani, Filippeschi, Rossi-Lemeni, La Scala, Milan, Ch. and O, Serafin.

In her first, mid-1960s recording of *Norma*, Sutherland was joined by an Adalgisa in Marilyn Horne whose control of florid singing is just as remarkable as Sutherland's own, and who sometimes even outshines the heroine in musical imagination. Overall this is a most compelling performance.

In Callas's earlier, mono set, though the flatness of the 1954 recording is emphasized by the precision of CD, the sense of presence gives wonderful intensity to one of the diva's most powerful performances, recorded at the very peak of her powers, before the upper register acquired its distracting wobble. Balance of soloists is close, and the chorus could hardly be dimmer, but, as a perfect re-creation of a classic, irreplaceable recording, this is one of the jewels of the CD catalogue. With Callas in much fresher, firmer voice with electric intensity in every phrase, the casting of the veteran, Ebe Stignani, as Adalgisa gives Callas a worthily characterful partner in the sisters' duets. Filippeschi is disappointing by comparison, thin-toned and at times strained, and Rossi-Lemeni is not well treated by the microphone either.

Norma: highlights.
(M) ** EMI CDM5 66047-2 [id.] (from complete recording, with Callas, Corelli, Ludwig, Zaccaria; La Scala Ch. & O, cond. Serafin).

The selection from the (1960) Callas set is not particularly generous (barely 64 minutes). However, the key items which Callas fans will need are included and there is a synopsis, placing each aria in context. This is probably a better buy than the complete set (CDS5 56271-2).

I Puritani (complete).
500♪ *** Decca 417 588-2 (3). Sutherland, Pavarotti, Ghiaurov, Luccardi, Caminada, Cappuccilli, ROHCG Ch. & O, Bonynge.
(M) ** Decca 448 969-2 (2). Sutherland, Duval, Capecchi, Flagello, Elkins, De Palma, Maggio Musicale Fiorentino Ch. & O, Bonynge.
(***) EMI mono CDS5 56275-2 (2). Callas, Di Stefano, Panerai, Rossi-Lemeni, La Scala, Milan, Ch. & O, Serafin.

Sutherland's singing is fresh and bright. Pavarotti shows himself a remarkable Bellini stylist, Ghiaurov and Cappuccilli make up an impressive cast. Vivid, atmospheric recording.

As in the recording of *La Sonnambula*, made a year earlier, Joan Sutherland slides about too freely in *portamento*, but the beauty and freshness of the sound, as well as the phenomenal agility, are what matter above all. The final *Ah, non giunge* is dazzling. Pierre Duval generally controls his ringing tenor well, powerful at the top, though he is far less stylish than Nicola Monti, the tenor on the *Sonnambula* set. Renato Capecchi is a strong Riccardo, if not always well enough focused. Though Bonynge conducts most sympathetically, controlling ensembles well, what confirms this as less recommendable than Sutherland's later set is that the text is far less complete, while Pavarotti in the 1973 performance is a far more characterful Riccardo.

Those who complain that this opera represents Bellini at his dramatically least compelling should certainly hear Callas. In 1953, when she made the recording, her voice was already afflicted by hardness on top with some unsteadiness, and for sheer beauty of sound Sutherland is consistently preferable. But Callas, once heard, is unforgettable, uniquely compelling. None of the other soloists is ideally stylish, though most of the singing is acceptable. As can be heard at the very opening, the upper range of the sound is restricted, though later the recording opens up and the solo voices project vividly. As with other EMI/Callas recordings, this one has currently been remastered and handsomely redocumented.

La Sonnambula (complete).
500♪ *** Decca Dig. 417 424-2 (2) [id.]. Sutherland, Pavarotti, Della Jones, Ghiaurov, L. Op. Ch., Nat. PO, Bonynge.
(M) **(*) Decca 448 966-2 (2) [id.]. Sutherland, Monti, Elkins, Stalman, Corena, Maggio Musicale Fiorentino Ch. & O, Bonynge.
(***) EMI mono CDS5 56278-2 (2). Callas, Monti, Cossotto, Zaccaria, Ratti, La Scala, Milan, Ch. and O, Votto.

La Sonnambula was the first Bellini opera that Sutherland recorded complete, in 1962, and this earlier version, now reissued at mid-price in Decca's Grand Opera series, proves even more beautiful than her remake of 1980 when the voice was weightier but less even. Though her use of *portamento* is often excessive, the freshness of the voice is a constant delight, Bonynge's direction is outstanding, and the casting is first rate too, with Nicola Monti as stylish a Bellini tenor as Italy could produce at the time. Both Sylvia Stahlman as Lisa and Margareta Elkins as Teresa sing most beautifully and with keen accuracy. Even Fernando Corena's rather coarse, *buffo*-style Rodolfo has an attractive vitality. It is a pity, however, that Bonynge could not persuade Monti and Corena to decorate their reprises, as Sutherland and Stahlman do most beautifully. The recording has come up marvellously on CD, with both pin-point clarity and immediacy of atmosphere within a warm acoustic that one had come to expect from Decca in those vintage early years of analogue stereo. Sutherland's later set with Pavarotti (Decca 417 424-2) is still preferable, more affecting and more stylish, but this first version, when the voice was still pristine in its freshness, is still well worth hearing.

Substantially cut, the Callas version was recorded in mono in 1957, yet it gives a vivid picture of the diva at the peak of her powers. Nicola Monti makes a strong rather than a subtle contribution but blends well with Callas in the duets; and Fiorenza Cossotto is a good Teresa.

Scenes and arias from: *Bianca e Fernando; Norma* (including *Casta diva*); *Il Pirata*.
**(*) Sony Dig. SK 62032 [id.]. Jane Eaglen, OAE, Elder – WAGNER: Excerpts from: *Götterdämmerung* etc. **(*)

It shows the formidable merits of Jane Eaglen, a singer who has both Brünnhilde and Norma in her stage repertory, that she dares to couple Bellini and Wagner. With such a massive voice it is amazing in Bellini cabalettas that she can tackle coloratura divisions with such agility, even if the results can be rather ungainly. The legato in Bellini's soaring melodies is not as seamless as it might be, and the steadiness of pace brings a lack of thrust; but this is a magnificent voice, used with wonderfully clean attack on even the most exposed top notes. The period instruments of the Orchestra of the Age of Enlightenment add attractive colour.

Benjamin, Arthur (1893–1960)

Concertino for piano and orchestra; Concerto quasi una fantasia for piano and orchestra.
** Everest EVC 9029 [id.]. Lamar Crowson, LSO, composer.

Benjamin's *Concertino* dates from 1929 and was inspired directly by Gershwin's *Rhapsody in blue*. The jazz influence is mainly rhythmic and is felt at its strongest in the work's closing pages. The piece has an attractive spontaneity; the writing is fluent, the style eclectic. In fact the atmosphere is not so very different from that of the *Concerto quasi una fantasia* of 1949, and the scherzando sections of both works have much in common. Lamar Crowson gives spirited accounts of them here and is well, if not impeccably, accompanied by the LSO under the composer's direction. The recording was made in 1959 in Walthamstow Assembly Hall, but the microphones must have been fairly close, for the sound is crisp and clear and a little dry for the strong lyrical impulse which both works readily show. An entertaining if not distinctive disc which would be more attractive at a lower price.

Symphony No. 1; Ballad for string orchestra.
**(*) Marco Polo Dig. 8.223764 [id.]. Queensland SO, Christopher Lyndon-Gee.

Anyone familiar with Arthur Benjamin's inconsequentially tuneful *Jamaican rumba* will find his symphony very different. The composer had served in each World War, and when it was written, in 1944–5, he was surely reflecting his personal experience in both conflicts. The opening of the first movement with its violent drum-beats immediately creates a darkness of mood which is seldom to lift throughout the work, although there is a chorale-like tune on the strings to offer a more positive feeling, and the movement soon develops into a kind of restless march. Benjamin's style of writing is rhapsodic and at times is rather like film music. The Scherzo is orchestrally the most effective movement with its delicate string-textures and almost pointillist woodwind colouring, even if the vehement brass soon harshens the texture. The tragic string cantilena of the *Adagio appassionato* develops an agonized intensity, and the finale resumes a martial tread; at its climax, the opening of the first movement is powerfully recalled to provide a certain organic cohesion. The *Ballad* is hardly less disconsolate in feeling, again expressing its melancholy through an ongoing string cantilena, with passionate bursts of near desperation. Here the Queensland strings are especially impressive, and Christopher Lyndon-Gee always responds convincingly to the emotional intensity which all this music carries. The recording is good, spacious but just a little two-dimensional.

Bennett, Richard Rodney (born 1936)

(i) *Violin concerto. Diversions; Symphony No. 3.*
*** Koch Dig. 3-7431-2 [id.]. (i) Vadim Gluzman; Monte Carlo PO, DePreist.

With non-British performers Koch here fills an important gap in the catalogue, offering excellent performances of three of Bennett's later works, written between 1975 and 1990 and recorded in very full, well-balanced sound. The earliest of the three, the *Violin concerto* of 1975, was written when he was bringing his idiom closer to that of his highly successful film music, embracing tonality more firmly. For all the heartfelt warmth of the melodic writing, it does not stick in the memory, but the tautness of Bennett's argument is never in doubt. Though the two substantial movements are marked *Allegro* and *Andante lento*, the mood is predominantly contemplative in both, with the Ukrainian-born soloist, Vadim Gluzman, playing superbly, a young artist (born 1973) whose expressive warmth, technical command and flawless intonation have one wanting to hear much more from him on disc. James DePreist is also most persuasive, both in the *Concerto* and in the other two works, drawing well-drilled, strongly committed playing from the Monte Carlo Philharmonic. The *Symphony*, dating from 1987, is in three compact movements, marked *Andante*, *Allegretto* and *Adagio*, and here too the feeling is of a predominantly reflective work, bleaker than before. After these two works, the energy and directness of the *Diversions* of 1990 is all the more attractive, for here you have a set of variations lasting 19 minutes, brilliantly scored, based on a sort of Irish jig theme which Bennett varies in ever more inventive ways, sustaining the length well.

Berg, Alban (1885–1935)

Violin concerto.

500♪ (M) *** DG 447 445-2 [id.]. Itzhak Perlman, Boston SO, Ozawa (with RAVEL: *Tzigane;* STRAVINSKY: *Concerto* ***).

(M) *** Decca Dig 452 696-2 [id.]. Kyung Wha Chung, Chicago SO, Solti – ELGAR: *Violin concerto.* ***

Perlman's performance is totally commanding. The Boston orchestra accompanies superbly and, though the balance favours the soloist, the recording is excellent. This is an obvious candidate for DG's series of 'Originals' and is the more welcome at mid-price with the added bonus of the Ravel *Tzigane*.

Perlman may be tougher, more purposeful in his performance of the Berg *Concerto*, but he does not excel Chung in tenderness and poetry. Played like this, it makes an excellent coupling for the Elgar, another twentieth-century concerto but of a wholly different character. The violin is placed well in front of the orchestra, but not aggressively so. The recording is brilliant in the Chicago manner, but more spacious than some from this source.

Piano sonata, Op. 1.

(B) **(*) Calliope Approche CAL 6203. Inger Södergren – J. S. BACH: *Keyboard collection.* **(*)

Inger Södergren's performance of Berg's *Sonata* has real character, but she certainly softens its angst. Those attracted to her enjoyably relaxed Bach coupling may well be converted to enjoying her Berg too. Others may feel that the music's profile is a little blunted. The recording is pleasingly full and unpercussive, and with plenty of keyboard colour.

Lulu (with orchestration of Act III completed by Friedrich Cerha).

500♪ *** DG 415 489-2 (3) [id.]. Stratas, Minton, Schwarz, Mazura, Blankenheim, Riegel, Tear, Paris Op. O, Boulez.

The full three-act structure of Berg's *Lulu*, with Yvonne Minton singing the Countess Geschwitz's lament, is most moving, though Lulu remains to the last a repulsive heroine. Teresa Stratas's bright, clear soprano is well recorded. Altogether this is an intensely involving performance of a work which in some ways is more lyrically approachable than *Wozzeck*.

Wozzeck (complete).

*** Decca Dig. 417 348-2 (2) [id.]. Waechter, Silja, Winkler, Laubenthal, Jahn, Malta, Sramek, VPO, Dohnányi (with SCHOENBERG: *Erwartung* ***).

**(*) Teldec/Warner Dig. 0630 14108-2 (2) [id.]. Grundheber, Meier, Baker, Wottrich, Clark, Von Kannen, German Opera, Berlin, Ch. & Children's Ch., Berlin State O, Barenboim.

Barenboim's Teldec version of *Wozzeck*, recorded live at the Deutsche Staatsoper in Berlin in 1994, is a counterpart of the Abbado version of 1987 from DG, also recorded live and with Franz Grundheber in the title-role. Here too he is superb, characterizing vividly, with the voice focusing cleanly, never woolly. The big contrast between the sets is that where on DG the voices are set behind the orchestra, the voices here are well to the fore, at times even masking the orchestra, which in instrumental sound lacks the bite and intensity of the earlier recording. Not that balances are always consistent, with some incidental voices set back.

Though the playing of the Berlin orchestra is not as refined as that of its Viennese counterpart, Barenboim leads a warmly expressive performance and the cast is an outstanding one, with such characterful singers as Graham Clark (Captain) in incidental roles. Less successful is Waltraud Meier as Marie, with an uneven, grainy quality in the voice which is exaggerated by the recording, acceptable if you see harshness as one of Marie's prime qualities. The 1979 Decca digital version with Dohnányi and the Vienna Philharmonic and with Eberhard Waechter as Wozzeck and Anja Silja an outstanding Marie remains a first choice, beautifully balanced in a studio recording which is more vivid than any. It also comes with a generous coupling in Schoenberg's *Erwartung*, where again Silja is at her most passionately committed.

Berkeley, Lennox (1903–89)

Violin concerto, Op. 59.
(M) *** EMI CDM5 66121. Menuhin, Menuhin Festival O, Boult – PANUFNIK: *Concerto;* WILLIAMSON: *Concerto.* ***

The Berkeley *Concerto* dates from 1961. It is scored for a small orchestra, horns, oboes and strings, and is slightly baroque in feeling. Its inspiration at times suggests something of Berkeley's keen admiration for Stravinsky, and its craftsmanship is as polished as one would expect from this composer. Although it is not one of his strongest works, it has a movingly austere slow movement and is well worth investigating. It is beautifully played by Yehudi Menuhin and the Menuhin Festival Orchestra under Sir Adrian Boult, and is excellently recorded (at Abbey Road in 1971).

(i) *Music for piano four hands: Sonatina, Op. 39; Theme and variations, Op. 73; Palm Court waltz, Op. 81/2.* (Solo piano music): *5 Short pieces, Op. 4; 6 Preludes, Op. 23; Sonata, Op. 20.*
*** British Music Society Dig. BMS 416CD. Raphael Terroni, (i) with Norman Beedie.

Christopher Headington has already introduced us to the cultivated and tuneful piano music of Lennox Berkeley, and it is a pity that this specially recorded recital, sponsored by the British Music Society, has duplicated the estimable *Sonata* with its sensuously coloured *Adagio*, the often witty *Preludes* and the five charming *Short pieces*, which often have a whiff of Poulenc, while also remaining very English. Raphael Terroni is an accomplished and sympathetic exponent, and this latest CD has the advantage of including some four-handed piano music in which Norman Beedie proves an admirable partner. The *Sonatina* has another elegantly individual slow movement; this and the debonair character of the finale remind us again that the composer – during his twenties – spent seven years in Paris studying under Nadia Boulanger. The *Theme and variations* is more complex, but rewarding, and the *Palm Court waltz* has an engaging insouciance. The piano recording is most natural. The CD is available direct from the British Music Society, 7 Tudor Gardens, Upminster, Essex.

Berlioz, Hector (1803–69)

Harold in Italy, Op. 16.
(M) (*) Revelation RV 10051 [id.]. Mikhail Tolpygo, USSR SO, David Oistrakh – BRUCH: *Scottish Fantasy.* **(*)

The rough sound on this 1972 recording completely rules it out of court, despite an inspired account of the Bruch which comes as coupling. The performance has plenty of fire and conviction, though one feels that these musicians are not approaching *Harold* as if they are used to playing it every day of the week. It is a pity that more could not have been done to refine the recorded sound. Mikhail Tolpygo is a fine viola player, firm and true, but he is balanced far too close, with the orchestra only half heard in the background. Those who can tolerate the coarseness of the climaxes, which come close to distortion, should hear him.

(i) *Harold in Italy, Op. 16;* (ii) *Rêverie et caprice for violin and orchestra, Op. 8; Overture Les Francs-juges, Op. 3.*
(BB) ** Naxos Dig. 8.553034 [id.]. (i) Rivka Golani; (ii) Igor Gruppman; San Diego SO, Yoav Talmi.

Talmi conducts a refined and warmly expressive performance of *Harold in Italy*, making this a welcome bargain at Naxos price. Sadly, the distancing of sound, set in an over-reverberant acoustic, means that the impact and bite of the performance are undermined, and that also affects the viola soloist, Rivka Golani, in one of her most warmly sympathetic performances. The San Diego Symphony is an excellent orchestra, as one can appreciate more readily in the fill-ups, where the sound has rather more body. *Les Francs-juges* is given a light and refined reading, with a chamber quality in some of the string playing, but it is the performance of the *Reverie and Caprice* with the San Diego concertmaster as soloist which proves the most magnetic on the disc.

(i) *Harold in Italy, Op. 16. Overtures: Benvenuto Cellini; Le Carnaval romain; Le Corsaire.*
*** DG Dig. 447 102-2 [id.]. (i) Laurent Verney; O de l'Opéra Bastille, Myung-Whun Chung.

A good and thoroughly idiomatic performance of Berlioz's ardent score, with plenty of warmth, from Myung-Whun Chung on DG, and this can be numbered among the best now before the public. It certainly makes a good alternative to the Imai–Eliot Gardiner account on Philips and is in some ways superior to it. Chung has already shown himself to be a born Berliozian in the *Symphonie fantastique*, and both *Harold* and the overtures reaffirm his credentials.

Overtures: *Béatrice et Bénédict; Benvenuto Cellini; Le Carnaval romain; Le Corsaire. Roméo et Juliette: Queen Mab scherzo. Les Troyens: Royal hunt and storm.*
500♪ ❁ (M) *** RCA 9026 61400-2 [id.]. Boston SO, Munch (with SAINT-SAENS: *Le rouet d'Omphale* ***).

Dazzlingly brilliant performances of four favourite overtures – the virtuosity of the Boston players, especially the violins in *Béatrice et Bénédict* and *Le Corsaire* – is breathtaking. But it is for the wonderfully poetic and thrilling account of the *Royal hunt and storm* from *Les Troyens* that this CD earns its Rosette. The horn solo is ravishing and the brass produce a riveting climax as the storm reaches its peak. The early stereo (1957/9) is remarkable: one really feels the hall ambience, and John Pfeiffer's remastering is expert.

Symphonie fantastique, Op. 14.
500♪ *** DG Dig. 445 878-2 [id.]. Paris Opéra-Bastille O, Myung-Whun Chung (with DUTILLEUX: *Métaboles* ***).
(M) **(*) Virgin Veritas/EMI VM5 61379-2 [id.]. L. Classical Players, Norrington (with *Les Francs-juges*).
(M) ** Decca 452 305-2 [id.]. Paris Conservatoire O, Ataufo Argenta (with LISZT: *Les Préludes* *).

Symphonie fantastique; Les Troyens: Royal hunt and storm.
** Denon Dig. CO-78902 [id.] O Nat. de Lyon, Krivine.

(i) *Symphonie fantastique;* (ii) *La damnation de Faust: Danse des sylphes.*
(M) *** Decca Phase Four 448 955-2 [id.]. New Philh. O; (ii) LSO; Stokowski (with DVORAK: *Slavonic dance No. 10 in E min., Op. 72/2:* Czech PO ***).

Myung-Whun Chung and the Bastille Orchestra convey to a rare degree the nervously impulsive inspiration of a young composer. With the hints of hysteria and overtones of nightmare in Berlioz's programme freshly brought out, the result is volatile rather than symphonically foursquare, and the originality of the inspiration seems all the greater. Speeds tend to be extreme in both directions, but tension is superbly sustained.

There is no more spectacular recording than Stokowski's, made in Phase Four in the Kingsway Hall in 1968 and multi-miked so that detail can be highlighted, and the brass is given satanic impact in the *Marche au Supplice* and finale (where the bells also toll plangently). As might be expected, the performance is as idiosyncratic as it is charismatic and it is certainly thrilling, by some Stokowskian magic conveying complete, warm-hearted conviction. Stokowski's warmth of phrasing is aptly romantic, but generally the surprising thing is his meticulous concern for markings. The hairpin dynamics are even exaggerated but, unlike many less flamboyant conductors, he refuses to whip up the coda for the finale, yet it does not affect the adrenalin flow. The close of the symphony is followed by two totally contrasted encores. First an exquisite *bonne bouche*, affectionately introducing Berlioz's sylphs from *La Damnation de Faust*. They enter slowly but with exquisite, sensuous grace, the effect more Stokowski than Berlioz perhaps, but delicious in its way. Then comes a seductive account of the *E minor Slavonic dance*, just as beautifully played by the Czech Philharmonic Orchestra.

Norrington does his utmost to observe the composer's metronome markings; but where his Beethoven is consistently fast, some of these speeds are more relaxed than we are used to – as in the *March to the scaffold* and the *Ronde du sabbat*. As usual, his lifting of rhythms prevents the music from dragging, at the same time giving new transparency; *Les Francs-juges* Overture is, however, disappointingly low-key.

The new transfer of Argenta's highly regarded early stereo (1957) version with the Paris Conservatoire Orchestra is a disappointment, not for the performance but because the thin violin-timbre is hardly worthy of inclusion in Decca's Classic Sound series. The orchestral playing is impressive and the French brass is full of character. The reading is individual and distinguished, with the balance between reflection and neurosis remarkably well judged. Argenta observes the repeat in the *March to the scaffold* – for the first time on disc – and the finale is strong on atmosphere as well as drive. *Les Préludes*, recorded two years later, is no great asset either. The sound is better, the account is lively enough, but the orchestral playing is undistinguished.

In the late 1980s Denon produced a spectacular recording of the *Symphonie fantastique* from Eliahu Inbal which reproduced this endlessly fascinating score with unparalleled clarity and realism. Now they have done it again in Lyon, and collectors interested in demonstration-quality sound should try it out. Alas, the recommendation must be qualified for, although the quality of the orchestral playing is not in question, Emmanuel Krivine – whose work we have admired in other contexts – is always musical but too wayward in the first movement and in the second is wanting in charm. There is no lack of excitement, however, in the *Marche au supplice*. Allegiance to Davis (LSO) and the recent Myung-Whun Chung from DG is unchallenged.

VOCAL MUSIC

La damnation de Faust (complete).

*** Decca Dig. 444 812-2 [id.]. Pollet, Leech, Cachemaille, Philippe, Montreal Ch. & SO, Charles Dutoit.

(B) **(*) DG Double 453 019-2 (2) [id.]. Mathis, Burrows, McIntyre, Paul, Tanglewood Festival Ch., Boston Boys' Ch. & SO, Ozawa.

** Erato/Warner Dig. 0630 10692-2 (2) [id.]. Moser, Graham, Van Dam, Canton, Lyon Opéra Ch. & O, Kent Nagano.

(i) *La damnation de Faust, Op. 24;* (ii) *La mort de Cléopâtre.*

(B) **(*) EMI forte CZS5 68583-2 (2). Janet Baker; (i) Gedda, Bacquier, Thau, Paris Opera Ch., O de Paris, Prêtre; (ii) LSO, Gibson.

Dutoit follows up his epic recording of *Les Troyens* with an account of this unique work which brings out its fully operatic qualities. So the chorus, a key element, sings with biting dramatic point to heighten the plot, rather than singing with oratorio discipline as a commentary. The choice of mainly French-speaking soloists – with Richard Leech also very much at home singing in French – equally intensifies the storytelling element, with singers balanced so as to allow words to be heard, and with the atmospheric warmth of the Montreal sound adding to the illusion of a stage picture. Dutoit, more than his brilliant Decca rival in this work, Solti, brings out the light and shade of such a showpiece as the *Hungarian march*. Leech is not the most characterful Faust but, unlike many, he sings clearly and without strain. Françoise Pollet is a warm, expressive Marguerite, tenderly affecting in her two big solos, and Gilles Cachemaille, though not the most powerful Mephistopheles, is brilliant at pointing words and bringing out the wry humour.

The best part of the EMI *Damnation de Faust* is Dame Janet Baker's Marguerite. This affecting music is sung most beautifully and has fine focus of tone. Prêtre is not always as perceptive as he might be and, though there are many dramatic touches in his reading of this inspired score, in general the set does not compete with either Markevitch or Ozawa in this price-range. Needless to say, Berlioz's early scena on the death of a famous classical heroine, *La mort de Cléopâtre*, is beautifully performed.

Now offered, economically priced, on a DG Double (with translation and full documentation included), Ozawa's performance provides an alternative, in a much more moulded style. The relative softness of focus is underlined by the reverberant Boston acoustics; with superb playing and generally fine singing, however, the results are seductively enjoyable. The digital remastering has improved definition without losing the effect of the hall ambience.

Nagano with his Lyon Opéra forces has the benefit of stage experience in this work – though, unlike Gardiner on Philips, also with Lyon forces, his version was not recorded live. Nagano's dramatic pacing is most persuasive, with the chorus and orchestra responding superbly, but the closeness of the sound, though adding to the excitement in display passages, reduces the element of light and shade. Susan Graham's beautiful voice sounds uncharacteristically hard, lacking a pianissimo, and the unevenness in Thomas Moser's tenor is also exaggerated, particularly on top. The dry acoustic also makes this less atmospheric than most other versions. The big bonus is the magnificent portrayal of Mephistopheles by José van Dam, even more expressive and idiomatic here than he is for Solti in his Chicago version.

L'enfance du Christ, Op. 25.

500♪ *** Hyperion Dig. CDA 66991/2 [id.]. Rigby, Miles, Finley, Aler, Howell, Corydon Singers & O, Best.

Vividly recorded in beautifully balanced digital sound, immediate yet warm, Matthew Best's version offers a keenly dramatic view of the story of the Flight into Egypt, consistent vocally to make an ideal choice for those who want a relatively intimate view, and a superb modern recording with vivid presence.

'Chant d'amour': La Mort d'Ophélie; Zaïde.

*** Decca Dig. 452 667-2; *452 667-4* [id.]. Cecilia Bartoli, Myung-Whun Chung – BIZET; DELIBES; RAVEL: *Mélodies.* ***

Cecilia Bartoli's collection of French songs is one of the most ravishing of her records yet, and these Berlioz items are among the highlights. Chung's contribution is both imaginative and supportive (see below under Recitals).

(i) *Les nuits d'été* (song-cycle), *Op. 7;* (ii) *La mort de Cléopâtre.*

(M) *** DG Dig. 445 594-2 [id.]. O de Paris, Barenboim, with (i) Kiri Te Kanawa; (ii) Jessye Norman.

(i) *Les nuits d'été* (song-cycle), *Op. 7;* (ii) *La mort de Cléopâtre* (lyric scena); (ii; iii) *Les Troyens, Act V, Scenes ii & iii.*

500♪ ❁ (M) *** EMI CDM7 69544-2. Dame Janet Baker, (i) New Philh. O, Barbirolli; (ii) LSO, Gibson; (iii) with Greevy, Erwen, Howell & Amb. Op. Ch.

The collaboration of Dame Janet Baker at the peak of her powers and Sir John Barbirolli in what is probably the most beautiful of all orchestral song-cycles produces unforgettable results.

The coupling of Jessye Norman in the scena and Dame Kiri Te Kanawa in the song-cycle makes for one of the most ravishing of Berlioz records, with each singer at her very finest. Norman has natural nobility and command as the Egyptian queen in this dramatic scena, while Te Kanawa encompasses the challenge of different moods and register in *Les nuits d'été* more completely and affectingly than any singer on record in recent years.

(i) *Requiem Mass (Grande Messe des Morts), Op. 5.* (ii) *Symphonie fantastique.*

(B) *** EMI forte Dig./Analogue CZS5 69512-2 (2). (i) Robert Tear, LPO Ch., LPO; (ii) LSO; Previn.

Previn's 1980 Walthamstow recording of Berlioz's great choral work is still the most impressive so far put on disc. Spectacular digital sound allows the registration of the extremes of dynamic in this extraordinary work for massed forces. The gradations of pianissimo against total pianissimo are breathtakingly caught, making the great outbursts of the *Dies irae* and the *Tuba mirum* the more telling. The acoustic is admirably chosen and there is a fine bloom on the voices, while the separation of sound gives a feeling of reality to the massed brass and multiple timpani. No doubt one day we shall have (from Gardiner perhaps) the full expansive glory experienced in a great cathedral, but meanwhile this inexpensive forte reissue will more than suffice. Previn's view is direct and incisive (like that of Sir Colin Davis on his long-established Philips version), not underlining expressiveness but concentrating on rhythmic qualities. So the *Rex tremendae* is given superb buoyancy, and even if Previn misses some of the animal excitement captured by other conductors, such as Bernstein, the contrasts of the closing *Agnus Dei* are movingly brought off. Robert Tear is a sensitive soloist, though the voice is balanced rather close.

Fortunately the coupled performance of the *Symphonie fantastique* does not disappoint (as it did when RCA issued the marvellous old Munch *Requiem* on CD, similarly paired), for Previn's reading is not only compelling but highly individual. He manages the dash off into the first-movement allegro very spontaneously, yet he presents the work above all as a symphonic structure. The pastoral serenity of the slow movement is beautifully sustained. Some may find him not volatile enough in the last two movements, which are without the rhythmic impetus of some versions. Nevertheless the *Marche au supplice* makes a very powerful impact and the finale certainly does not lack satanic force with the brass so telling. On its own direct terms this is a highly involving reading which almost completely avoids vulgarity; moreover it is a performance which gains from repeated hearing. The 1976 recording (made partly at Abbey Road and partly in Kingsway Hall) again represents EMI's finest standards of balance and truthfulness: the violins sound particularly rich.

(i) *Requiem Mass (Grande Messe des morts).* (ii) *Symphonie funèbre et triomphale.* (iii) Choral music: *Tantum ergo; Le temple universel; Veni creator.*

(B) ** Decca Double Analogue/Dig. 452 262-2 [id.]. (i) Kenneth Riegel, Cleveland Ch. & O, Maazel; (ii) Montreal Ch. & SO, Dutoit; (iii) Soloists, Heinrich Schütz Ch. & Chorale, Norrington.

Especially by the side of Dutoit's exhilarating 1985 digital account of the *Symphonie funèbre*, Maazel's version of the *Requiem*, with the choir set at a distance, is relatively uninvolving. The recording offers clean, truthful 1978 Decca analogue sound. The *Tuba mirum*, with its spectacular brass, is certainly physically impressive, and here the chorus is boldly focused. But overall Maazel's reading is comparatively unimaginative and no match for Previn's version. The *Symphonie funèbre* is also available at full price, coupled with Dutoit's *Roméo et Juliette*, a far better investment (417 302-2 – see our main volume). The rare choral items, however, add much to the interest of the present set, showing Berlioz in an unfamiliar and rewarding light, particularly when two out of the three works have a piquant harmonium accompaniment. The *Tantum ergo* and *Veni creator* are late works and both contrast the choir with solo voices, the latter almost like the slow movement of a vocal concerto grosso, while *Le temple universel* is for double choir. It was inspired by the visit of a huge French choir to London's Crystal Palace in 1860. At the close, 4,000 French singers sang *God save the Queen*, and the audience rose to its feet and responded with the *Marseillaise*. Berlioz intended that the two choirs should sing the same words in English and French, but here Norrington manages with rather smaller forces and has both groups singing in French. The effect is undoubtedly stirring, for there is much of the spirit of the French national anthem, and the (originally Argo) recording from the late 1960s is first rate.

Roméo et Juliette, Op. 17.
❀ *** Ph. Dig. 442 134-2 [id.]. Borodina, Moser, Miles, Bav. R. Ch., VPO, Sir Colin Davis.

For those old enough to remember its first appearance, Colin Davis's first recording of *Roméo et Juliette* is now almost 30 years old – although this is hard to believe! It long reigned supreme in the catalogue, and now its successor is likely to do the same for another thirty. Doubtless Philips will undermine the newcomer in the curious way gramophone companies often do, by reissuing the old LSO version at a rock-bottom price, but do not succumb to the temptation of economy. In this Vienna performance Sir Colin's interpretative approach remains basically unchanged – yet, like a vintage wine that has matured, it offers greater depth, colour and body. He has the advantage of fine soloists, and Olga Borodina has the full measure of the Berlioz style. Thomas Moser is no less ardent and idiomatic, and Alastair Miles is a more than acceptable Friar Laurence. Apart from its all-round artistic excellence, this scores over all comers in the sheer quality of the sound, which reproduces the whole range of Berlioz's fantastic score in all its subtle colourings in remarkable detail and naturalness. The perspective is natural and the orchestral texture astonishing in its transparency. It is no surprise to discover that the sound-picture is the work of Volker Strauss.

OPERA

Béatrice et Bénédict (complete).
(M) ** DG 449 577-2 (2) [id.]. Minton, Domingo, Cotrubas, Fischer-Dieskau, Ch. & O de Paris, Barenboim.

Although it opens well with an exciting account of the overture, Barenboim's 1982 version of *Béatrice et Bénédict* is seriously marred by the spoken dialogue (in French) which links the numbers of this off-beat adaptation of Shakespeare. It is done by Geneviève Page in the over-intimate manner of a French film. With the transfer to CD the cueing means that the listener can programme it out at will, but even then the musical performance lacks the last degree of freshness and style, though it is good to hear Bénédict's part sung with such ringing tone by Plácido Domingo. Yvonne Minton is less warm and less characterful than Dame Janet Baker for Davis, and Dietrich Fischer-Dieskau is miscast as Somarone (the comic role added by Berlioz to replace Dogberry and Verges). The beauty of the score is caught, rather than its point and wit. Apart from the discrepancy between the narration and the rest, the recorded quality is first rate, as is the CD transfer.

Les Troyens, Parts 1 & 2 (complete).
500♪ *** Ph. 416 432-2 (4) [id.]. Veasey, Vickers, Lindholm, Glossop, Soyer, Partridge, Wandsworth School Boys' Ch., ROHCG Ch. & O, C. Davis.

Throughout this long and apparently disjointed score Davis compels the listener to concentrate, to appreciate its epic logic. Only in the great love scene of *O nuit d'ivresse* would one have welcomed the more expansive hand of a Beecham. Veasey on any count, even next to Dame Janet Baker, makes a splendid Dido, singing always with fine heroic strength, with Vickers a ringing Aeneas. The Covent Garden Chorus and Orchestra excel themselves in virtuoso singing and playing, while CD brings out the superb quality of sound all the more vividly.

Berners, Lord (1883–1950)

Luna Park; March; (i) *A Wedding bouquet.*
** Marco Polo Dig. 8.223716 [id.]. (i) RTE Chamber Ch.; RTE Sinf., Kenneth Alwyn.

Lord Berners does not figure in our 1995–6 *Yearbook* or in our latest main volume, though he was well represented in earlier editions, in which both the Beecham and the recent account by Barry Wordsworth of his best-known ballet, *The Triumph of Neptune*, were discussed. Stravinsky spoke of him as 'droll and delightful . . . an amateur, but in the best – literal – sense'. Apart from Constant Lambert, he was the only English composer taken up by Diaghilev; as well as *The Triumph of Neptune* he wrote four other ballets. *A Wedding bouquet* (1936), a choral ballet to words of Gertrude Stein, is the most rewarding of them. There are touches of *Les Noces* (Stravinsky and Casella had encouraged him in his youth). *Luna Park* (1930) was written for a C. B. Cochran revue, but with choreography by Balanchine. Although a couple of excerpts have been recorded *A Wedding bouquet* has never been done in its entirety since it was choreographed by Frederick Ashton and mounted at Sadler's Wells in 1937 with décor and costumes as well as music by Berners. This is good light music. Performances are decent, as are the recordings, but the acoustic does not permit tutti to open out.

Les Sirènes (ballet; complete); *Caprice péruvien; Cupid and Psyche* (ballet suite).
** Marco Polo Dig. 8.223780 [id.]. Miriam Blennerhassett, RTE Sinf., David Lloyd-Jones.

Les Sirènes was the first ballet Ashton mounted in 1946, when the Sadler's Wells Ballet took up residence at Covent Garden. It was not a great success, and it must be said that the music, despite some bright moments, does not sustain a high level of invention. The *Caprice péruvien* derives from Berners's one and only opera, *Le Carrosse du Saint-Sacrement*, a one-acter which shared a triple-bill with Stravinsky and Sauguet at the Théâtre des Champs-Elysées in 1924. The *Caprice* itself was expertly put together by Constant Lambert with Berners's help. The ballet *Cupid and Psyche* was another Ashton work, which was mounted in 1939 but which folded after four performances. Good performances, that could perhaps do with a bit more polish. Again the recordings, made at a different venue from the companion disc listed above, are wanting in bloom. *The Triumph of Neptune* shows Berners at his most characteristically witty and inventive, and by its side these works do not make a strong impression.

The Triumph of Neptune (ballet suite): excerpts.
(B) (***) Sony mono SBK 62748; *SBT 62748* [id.]. Phd. O, Beecham – ARNELL: *Punch and the child* (ballet); DELIUS: *Paris*. (***)

The Triumph of Neptune was a rare example of music by an English composer being commissioned and performed by Diaghilev's Ballets Russes. The composer has often been called the English Satie, and Satie's love of circus music was echoed by Berners's taste for the music hall.

Sir Thomas recorded the nine excerpts with the Philadelphia Orchestra in 1952. Two items (the charming *Cloudland* and the delicately haunting evocation of *The frozen forest*) were not included on his earlier (1937) recording of the suite for EMI (currently unavailable). On Sony, Robert Grooter is the intoxicated sailor who makes a brave shot at singing 'The last rose of summer'. The Philadelphia Orchestra respond to this music in a brilliant if rather bemused fashion – what must they have thought of the vocal contributions they were required to add to the *Schottische*! However, they obviously enjoy the music, and Sir Thomas ensures that there is no lack of suave polish and wit. The recording is remarkably good, and this disc is also a 'must' for the sake of the couplings.

Bernstein, Leonard (1918–90)

(i) *Arias and Barcarolles* (orch. Coughlin). *A Quiet place: suite; West Side Story: symphonic dances*.
*** DG Dig. 439 926-2 [id.]. (i) Von Stade, Hampson; LSO, Tilson Thomas.

It was Michael Tilson Thomas who joined Leonard Bernstein himself at two pianos for the first performance of the original chamber version of *Arias and Barcarolles*, one of Bernstein's very last works. With colourful orchestration by Bruce Coughlin, Tilson Thomas here fully justifies the expansion, intensifying the impact of this wayward sequence of settings of texts, each glorifying the family in ways very personal to Bernstein. What is completely avoided here, a danger in this work, is the coyness which these texts can suggest; and that also has much to do with the superb singing of Frederica von Stade (not least in the baby-talk fairy story attributed to Bernstein's mother) and of Thomas Hampson. The result is both beautiful and moving, not least the fifth-movement *Greeting* from Bernstein to his new-born son and the final humming duet. Similarly, the suite drawn from Bernstein's big 1983 opera, *A Quiet place*, offers a symphonic synthesis which both brings out the freshness and power of this late inspiration, and intensifies the emotions of an opera which tends to sprawl dramatically. Brilliant and heartfelt playing from the LSO, both in those two works and in the *Symphonic dances* from *West Side Story*, here vividly recorded to pack even greater punch than the composer's own last recording.

(i) *Candide* (final, revised version); (ii) *West Side Story:* complete recording.
500♪ ❀ *** DG Dig. 447 958-2 (3) [id.]. (i) Hadley, Anderson, Green, Ludwig, Gedda, Della Jones, Ollmann, London Symphony Ch., LSO; (ii) Te Kanawa, Carreras, Troyanos, Horne, Ollmann, Ch. and O; composer.

The composer's complete recordings of *Candide* and *West Side Story* have been coupled together on three mid-priced discs for the Bernstein Edition to make an irresistible bargain for those who have not already acquired one or the other of these inspired scores. The result is a triumph, both in the studio recording (which Bernstein made immediately after the concert performances) and in the video recording of the actual concert at the Barbican. It confirms *Candide* as a classic, bringing out not just the vigour, the wit and the tunefulness of the piece more than ever before, but also an extra emotional intensity, something beyond the cynical Voltaire original. It was an inspired choice to have Adolph Green, lyric writer for Broadway musicals as well as cabaret performer, for the dual role of Dr Pangloss and Martin. What is missing in the CD set is the witty narration, prepared by John Wells and spoken by Adolph Green and

Kurt Ollmann in the Barbican performance. As included on the video of the live concert (Laser disc DG 072 423-1; VHS DG 072 423-3), those links leaven the entertainment delightfully. Even those with the CDs should investigate the video version, which also includes Bernstein's own moving speeches of introduction before each Act.

Bernstein's recording of the complete score of *West Side Story* takes a frankly operatic approach in its casting, but the result is highly successful, for the great vocal melodies are worthy of voices of the highest calibre. Tatiana Troyanos, herself brought up on the West Side, spans the stylistic dichotomy to perfection in a superb portrayal of Anita. The clever production makes the best of both musical worlds, with Bernstein's son and daughter speaking the dialogue most affectingly.

Berwald, Franz (1796–1868)

Symphonies Nos. 1 in G min. (Sérieuse); 2 in D (Capricieuse); 3 in C (Singulière); No. 4 in E flat; (i) *Konzertstück for bassoon and orchestra.*

*** BIS Dig. CD 795/6 [id.]. (i) Christian Davidsson; Malmö SO, Sixten Ehrling.

As collectors who recall his 1968 account for Decca of the *Sinfonie singulière* and the *E flat Symphony* with the LSO (or, for that matter, of the *Sinfonie sérieuse* with the Swedish Radio Orchestra, made two years later), Sixten Ehrling has a natural feeling for the classic Swedish symphonist. Tempi are all well judged and there is an admirable lightness of touch. There is plenty of breadth in the *Sérieuse* and no want of sparkle in the *E flat Symphony*. The *Konzertstück*, composed in 1827 (the year before the *Septet*), is a charming piece much in its manner. This could well be regarded as a first choice in this repertoire. Järvi's Gothenberg DG set (445 581-2) costs much less but has no coupling.

Grand septet in B flat.

(M) *** EMI CDM5 65995-2 [id.]. Gervase de Peyer, Melos Ens. – SPOHR: *Double quartet* **; WEBER: *Clarinet quintet.* **(*)

The *Septet* is an earlier work than any of Berwald's four symphonies. It dates from 1828, though how far it embodies material from an earlier work for the same combination is a matter for conjecture. Like the symphonies, it has a freshness and grace that should earn wide appeal, and the Melos Ensemble give an immaculately polished account of it. It is vividly recorded and well balanced.

Piano quintet No. 1 in C min.; Piano trio No. 4 in C; Duo in D for violin and piano.

**(*) Hyperion Dig. CDA 66835 [id.]. Susan Tomes, Gaudier Ens.

Unlike the earlier issue in this series, which spanned Berwald's output from 1819 to 1851, this concentrates on his music from the 1850s. The *Piano quintet* (1853) comes off marvellously and compares favourably with any performance on record, past or present. Susan Tomes is both sensitive and expert, and the Gaudier Ensemble are hardly less distinguished. No quarrels with Tomes in the *Piano trio No. 4*, composed the same year, or in the less inventive *D major Duo*, written in the latter half of the decade, but the balance does allow her too dominant a role in the aural picture. True, the *Duo* is for piano and violin – not the other way round – but the violinist, Marieke Blankenstijn, an impeccable artist, sounds far too pale and reticent. In every other respect this attractive music is well served.

String quartets Nos. 1 in G min.; 2 in A min.; 3 in E flat.

*** BIS Dig. CD 759 [id.]. Yggdrasil Qt.

First-rate performances by this young Swedish ensemble of their great compatriot's output in this medium. The *G minor Quartet* was one of two that Berwald composed in 1818 (the second, in B flat, was lost). It is a remarkable piece, forward-looking for its time and full of modulatory audacities. The Trio section of the Scherzo almost suggests Schubert – whom Berwald could not possibly have known. The two remaining *Quartets* were both composed in 1849, four years after the completion of the *Sinfonie singulière* and are both original and rewarding. This gifted ensemble play them very well indeed and are splendidly recorded. Anyone who enjoys the Mendelssohn or Schumann *Quartets* should not delay in investigating this music.

Bizet, Georges (1838–75)

L'Arlésienne: suites Nos. 1–2; Carmen: suites Nos. 1–2.

500♪ *** Decca Dig. 417 839-2 [id.]. Montreal SO, Dutoit.

With playing that is both elegant and vivid, and with superb, demonstration-worthy sound, Dutoit's polished yet affectionate coupling of the *L'Arlésienne* and *Carmen* suites makes a clear first choice.

Symphony in C; La jolie fille de Perth: suite; Overture, La Patrie.
*(**) Decca Dig. 452 102-2 [id]. Montreal SO, Charles Dutoit.

Dutoit and the Montreal orchestra last recorded the Bizet *Symphony* in 1988, but this time the coupling is different. The orchestral playing is of decent quality, very animated and spirited, and the recording (as one would expect after Decca's long and successful experience in this venue) transparent and well detailed. There is some of the sparkle and allure that this music must have, but not really enough to make these performances in any way memorable. This does not glow with the charm which Beecham brought to it – nor, for that matter, Martinon. Of course charm, like beauty, is in the eye of the beholder and others may respond with greater enthusiasm to these accounts. The recording is worth three stars, the performance barely rates two.

'Chant d'amour': Mélodies: *Adieux de l'hôtesse arabe; Chant d'amour; La Coccinelle; Ouvre ton coeur; Tarantelle.*
*** Decca Dig. 452 667-2; *452 667-4* [id.]. Cecilia Bartoli, Myung-Whun Chung – BERLIOZ; DELIBES; RAVEL: *Mélodies.* ***

These delightful Bizet songs come as part of an outstanding recital of French repertoire, readily demonstrating the versatility of Bartoli who is so sympathetically accompanied by Chung. One of the highlights is *La coccinelle* ('The Ladybird'), a witty fast waltz. Both voice and piano are recorded beautifully. The collection is considered more fully in our Recitals section below.

Carmen (complete).
(M) *** RCA 74321 39495-2 (3) [6199-2-RG]. Leontyne Price, Corelli, Merrill, Freni, Linval, V. State Op. Ch., VPO, Karajan.
** EMI CDS 56281-2 (3). Callas, Gedda, Guiot, Massard, René Duclos Ch., Children's Ch., Paris Nat. Op. O, Prêtre.

With Karajan's RCA version, made in Vienna in 1964, much depends on the listener's reaction to the conductor's tempi and to Leontyne Price's smoky-toned Carmen. Corelli has moments of coarseness, but his is still a heroic performance. Robert Merrill sings with gloriously firm tone, while Mirella Freni is, as ever, enchanting as Micaëla. With spectacular recording, full of atmosphere, and attractively re-packaged at mid-price in RCA's UK Opera Treasury series, this is a very strong contender, even if Karajan's later, premium-priced set, with Carreras and Baltsa a vibrant, vividly compelling Carmen, remains our primary recommendation (DG 410 088-2).

Though in so many ways the vibrant, flashing-eyed personality of Maria Callas was ideally suited to the role of Carmen, her complete recording – unlike two separate aria recordings she made earlier – is disappointing. One principal trouble is that the performance, apart from her, lacks a taut dramatic rein, with slack ensemble from singers and orchestra alike. The moment the heroine enters, the tension rises; but by Callas standards this is a performance rough-hewn, strong and characterful but lacking the full imaginative detail of her finest work. 'Callas is Carmen', said EMI's original advertisements, but in fact very clearly Callas remains Callas. The CD transfer clarifies textures but brings out the limitations of the Paris recording. The set has been remastered and a new booklet prepared for this reissue.

(i) *Les pêcheurs de perles* (complete); (ii) *Ivan IV:* highlights.
(M) ** EMI CMS5 66020-2 [CDMB 66020] (2). (i; ii) Micheau; (i) Gedda, Blanc; (ii) Roux, Legay, Sénéchal, Noguera, Savignol; (i) Paris Opéra-Comique O, Dervaux; (ii) French R. Ch. & O, Tzipine.

Paul Dervaux is a no more than efficient conductor, failing to draw out the relaxed charm of this exotic score with its soaringly lyrical set numbers. The lack of affection infects the principals, who are all stylish artists but who here sing below their best, even the dependable Nicolai Gedda. On two mid-price CDs, the set might still be worth considering, however, when it also includes selections from the opera which Bizet wrote immediately after *Pearlfishers*, *Ivan IV*. There is a fine scena for the heroine, beautifully sung by Janine Micheau; and the heady-toned tenor, Henri Legay, an outstanding artist, sings superbly in his vengeance aria. It is also good to hear the fine bass, Pierre Savignol. In the newly reissued set, full and clearly printed translations are provided for both operas. The CD transfers hardly betray the age of the recordings.

Blacher, Boris (1903–75)

Variations on a theme of Paganini Op. 26.
*** Decca Dig. 452 853-2 [id.]. VPO, Solti – ELGAR: *Enigma variations;* KODALY: *Peacock variations.* ***

Attractively coupled with comparable sets by Elgar and Kodály, the Blacher *Paganini variations* make a delightful fill-up, a brilliant quarter-hour work not nearly as well known outside Germany as it should be. The performance is infectious in its pointing of rhythm. Jazzy syncopations are consistently interpreted with a sense of fun, and the element of fantasy in Blacher's sequence of 16 free variations is regularly brought out, ending with a breathtaking account of the final *moto perpetuo*. The Decca engineers have done wonders in capturing the unique acoustic of the Musikverein splendidly, with plenty of air round the sound.

Bliss, Arthur (1891–1975)

Adam Zero (ballet; complete); *A Colour Symphony*.
(BB) *** Naxos Dig. 8.553460 [id.]. N. Philh. O, David Lloyd-Jones.

Naxos here offer the first of a planned series of Sir Arthur Bliss's music, including his best-known major work, the *Colour Symphony* of 1922. Full of striking ideas and effects to illustrate four heraldic colours, the symphony here receives a refined and idiomatic reading, marked by superb wind-playing. More valuable still is the first complete recording of the ballet, *Adam Zero*, in which the process of creating a ballet is presented as an allegory for the ongoing life-cycle. Lloyd-Jones directs a dramatically paced performance, amply confirming this as one of Bliss's most inventive, strongly co-ordinated scores, shamefully neglected. Full, well-balanced sound.

(i) *Cello concerto. Hymn to Apollo;* (ii) *The Enchantress*.
*** Chandos Dig. CHAN 8818 [id.]. (i) Raphael Wallfisch; (ii) Linda Finnie; Ulster O, Vernon Handley.

Raphael Wallfisch is a powerful soloist in the *Cello concerto* which Bliss wrote for Rostropovich in 1970, launching into the piece with a bite and attack which are instantly compelling. This is a reading which brings out the red-blooded warmth of the writing, with the soloist strongly supported by the Ulster Orchestra under Handley. They are equally persuasive accompanying Linda Finnie in the extended scena which Bliss wrote for Kathleen Ferrier nearly 20 years earlier, when he had just completed his opera, *The Olympians*. There, similarly, Bliss was inspired by the individual artistry of a great musician, even though, as he himself said, he found it hard to reconcile the goodness of Ferrier with the character of Simaetha, the central figure in the passage of Theocritus which he chose to set. The *Hymn to Apollo*, dating from much earlier and less demanding, is the attractive makeweight. Excellent, full-ranging sound.

(i) *Cello concerto. Music for strings; 2 Studies, Op. 16*.
(BB) ** Naxos Dig. 8.553383 [id.]. Tim Hugh, E. N. Philh., David Lloyd-Jones.

This second issue in the Naxos Bliss series couples one of Bliss's most successful works, the *Music for strings*, commissioned for the 1935 Salzburg Festival, with the *Cello concerto*, given in a reading far more reflective, less boldly extrovert, than the rival version on Chandos. The recording is partly responsible, not as full and forward as usual from this source, with the solo cello rather backwardly placed. Poetry rather than power is the keynote, centring on the *Larghetto* slow movement. The *Music for strings* also lacks a little in bite and definition, but this is a useful and enjoyable coupling, well supplemented by the two early *Studies*, a pastoral piece and a vigorous piece with a nautical flavour.

(i) *Meditations on a theme by John Blow;* (ii) *Metamorphic variations*.
(B) **(*) BBC Radio Classics 15656 91682 [id.]. (i) RLPO, Groves; (ii) BBC SO, Handley.

This is a valuable and generous coupling of two of the most ambitious of Bliss's later orchestral works, both in BBC radio recordings. Bliss was at his most effective in such sectional works as these, each of them providing an original slant on variation form. Dating from the early 1950s, the eight sections of the *Meditations on a theme of John Blow* each illustrate a verse from Psalm 23, taking a theme from a string sinfonia by John Blow, written as an introduction to Psalm 23. The result is one of Bliss's most thoughtful and poetic works, though the recording here, made at the 1975 Cheltenham Festival, is not as full or clear as it might be. The later *Metamorphic variations*, dating from 1972, come in an exceptionally fine studio recording, made in 1975 in the presence of the composer, a work on an even larger scale, which, as Bliss explained, is based on three themes or 'elements', heard at the start, which 'undergo a greater transformation during the 40 minutes than the simple word ''variation'' implies'. Handley is an inspired interpreter, drawing the 14 contrasted sections tautly together.

Morning heroes (A choral symphony conceived as a Requiem for the victims of the First World War).
(B) *** BBC Radio Classics 15656 91992 [id.]. Richard Baker (nar.), BBC SO Ch. & O, Sir Charles Groves.

Inspired by the death of his younger brother in the First World War, and dedicated to all the victims of that conflict, *Morning heroes* is one of the most warmly emotional of all Bliss's works, a choral symphony with spoken narration in five movements, lasting over an hour. It may not be quite as distinctive as comparable works by Britten or Vaughan Williams, but in this live broadcast performance of 1982 Sir Charles Groves conveys far more of the thrust of emotion than he did in his earlier, studio recording. Richard Baker is an authoritative narrator and the chorus sings passionately, to cancel out any flaws of ensemble. First-rate radio sound.

Bloch, Ernest (1880–1959)

Schelomo (Hebraic Rhapsody) for cello and orchestra.
(B) **(*) DG 447 349-2 (2) [id.]. Fournier, BPO, Wallenstein – BRUCH: *Kol Nidrei* **; DVORAK: *Cello concerto*. *** (See also under Concerts.)

In spite of the fervent advocacy of Fournier, the recording lets down his account of *Schelomo*. Fournier is closely balanced and the orchestral detail is not fully revealed. Even so, the sound is otherwise impressive, and this performance is easy to enjoy.

Blow, John (1649–1708)

Venus and Adonis.
*** O-L Dig. 440 220-2 [id.]. Bott, George, Crabtree, Gooding, King, Grant, Robson, Agnew, Westminster Abbey School Choristers, New L. Consort, Pickett.

Venus and Adonis is already well represented on CD, at both mid- and bargain price, but Pickett has a pair of trump cards to play: Catherine Bott's imaginative, enticing Venus and Michael George's strongly characterized Adonis. The result is that this simple drama springs to life with unexpected vividness. The supporting cast is excellent, and so is the recording, and we are made to realize that this is a far finer and deeper work than hitherto suspected.

Boccherini, Luigi (1743–1805)

Cello concertos Nos. 4 in C, G.477; 6 in D, G.479; 7 in G, G.480; 8 in C, G.481.
(B) *** Teldec/Warner 4509 97991-2 [id.]. Anner Bylsma, Concerto Amsterdam, Schröder.

These concertos were originally published as Nos. 1–4 but are numbered as above in the Gérard catalogue. They are scored for strings with the addition of simple horn parts in Nos. 4 and 8, and they are agreeable works which sit easily between the *galant* and classical styles. There are few moments of routine in the writing, and it is always elegant and pleasing. *No. 6 in D major* is a particularly fine work, while the finale of No. 8 is very jolly. Anner Bylsma is a fine player and seems eminently suited to this repertoire, while Schröder's accompaniments are most stylish and full of vitality. Charm, too, is an important element and it is not missing here, while the sombre *Adagio* of No. 7 has undoubted eloquence and is ideally paced to contrast with the sprightly and tuneful finale. The 1965 recording is first class and, like so many of Teldec's *Das alte Werk* series, the immaculate CD transfer makes the very most of the sound. This is even more attractive at bargain price.

Symphonies: in D, G.490; in D min. (La casa del diavolo), Op. 12/4; in A; in F, Op. 35/3–4.
(B) **(*) HM Dig. Musique d'Abord HMA 190121 [id.]. Ensemble 415, Chiara Banchini.

Boccherini could write sunny, three-movement symphonies with winning *Andantes*, like the attractive A major work here, Op. 35/3, in which the central movement is a serenade. The F major work, Op. 35/4, has an assertive opening movement but is most notable for its agreeable finale, which has a central Minuet. But Boccherini could also be both innovative and dramatic, as in the *D minor Symphony*, subtitled *La casa del diavolo*. Here he quotes from Gluck in the energetic finale, introduces the fast movements with a recitativo declamation, and provides an individual central *Andantino*. This moves forward in an elegant *moto perpetuo* on the violins, with comments from two solo cellos. It is presented most delicately, while allegros are alert and bustling. Indeed, these period-instrument performances by the excellent Ensemble 415, led by Chiara Banchini, are very enjoyable. The slight drawback is the resonance of the recording which tends to cloud the busier fortissimos.

Symphonies, Op. 12, Nos. 1 in D; 2 in E flat; 3 in C; 4 in D min.; 5 in B flat; 6 in A.
(B) *** Ph. Duo 456 067-2 (2) [id.]. New Philh. O, Leppard.

Boccherini's Op. 12 was published in 1776. The scoring is for the normal classical orchestra, including two flutes or oboes and horns; but the composer's individuality emerges in his writing for the strings – with divided cellos – which are always predominant in the main argument. Even so, there are many pleasing touches of woodwind colour. The *E flat Symphony* (No. 2) is a remarkably fine work, virtually a sinfonia concertante with important bravura duets, first for two violins, then for a pair of cellos (the composer's own instrument); there is even a cadenza. The other symphonies are all of comparable interest, with Boccherini's silken melancholy strongly featured in the lyrical writing. The composer's craftsmanship is as ever deft, although perhaps his attempt at cyclic construction brings a too easy solution in *No. 6 in A major* when, after the *Grave* introduction to the finale, he simply repeats the latter part of the first movement, starting at the central double bar! In short, this set of six attractive symphonies is well worth exploring, particularly as Leppard consistently secures playing from the highly alert New Philharmonia Orchestra that is polished, elegant and never superficial. The Philips 1971 recording is excellent and so is the CD transfer, losing nothing of the bloom but firming up the overall focus admirably.

Piano quintets: in A min., Op. 56/2, G.412; in E flat, Op. 56/3, G.410; in E min., Op. 57/3, G.415; in C, Op. 57/6, G.418.
(B) *** DHM 05472 77448-2 [id.]. Les Adieux.

This a particularly attractive group of Boccherini works, and it is made the more so by its reissue on the bargain Baroque Esprit label. The lovely *E minor* (Op. 57/3) which starts the disc and the *A minor* (Op. 56/2) both have those hints of beguiling, almost sultry melancholy that makes this composer's musical language so distinctive. This accomplished period-instrument group turn in performances of great finesse and charm, though the recording-balance places the listener very much in the front row of the salon.

String quintet in E, Op. 13/5.
**(*) Sony Dig. SK 53983 [id.]. Stern, Lin, Laredo, Ma, Robinson – SCHUBERT: *String quintet in C.* **

Stern and his illustrious colleagues create a much more intimate effect in Boccherini than they do in the Schubert coupling. This is the quintet with the famous 'Boccherini Minuet' and it is exquisitely played. An enjoyable if not distinctive account overall, and the recording balance seems less upfront than the coupling.

String quintets: in E, Op. 13/5; A min., Op. 47/1.
(B) ** Carlton/Turnabout 30371 00032. Günter Kehr Quintet.

The famous Minuet is played here with delicacy and restraint, and one feels it deserves its fame. But the work as a whole is attractive, particularly the opening movement which is harmonically rich to remind the listener almost of Mozart. It is played here with warmth and gives pleasure. Only in the finale does one feel that the players miscalculate, but this is partly Boccherini's fault for writing yet another *galant* movement instead of a rondo with more fire to it. The tendency to blandness is felt throughout the A minor work, which is pleasant but less distinguished. But here the players could have helped with more bite to the outer movements. The recording is warm-toned but with the microphones very close to the players, which exaggerates their reluctance to make contrasts of both style and dynamic. The CD plays for only 40 minutes and one feels a makeweight could have been provided.

3 String quintets (with double bass), Op. 39/1–3 (G.337–9); String quartet in G (La Tiranna), Op. 44/4 (G 223).
(B) *** HM Dig. HMT 7901334. Ensemble 415.

Boccherini wrote only three (out of a total of 125) quintets using a double-bass to (lightly) carry the bottom line of the harmony. They date from 1787 and the device seems very effective, with the careful balance of Ensemble 415 ensuring that Boccherini's scheme works extremely well. All three works are very attractive and none is predictable. The first opens with an elegant and rather touching *Andante lento*, with the following two movements chimerically changing mood and tempo; the second has a gentle *Adagio* with pizzicato accompaniment, the third brings a delicate central *Pastorale*, and all three quintets have contrasting bursts of good-humoured energy in outer movements. The programme is completed with a two-movement *Quartet*, the first of which is based on a Spanish dance of the time, hence its sobriquet. The performances here are first class, refined and sensitive, and using period instruments always to bring aural pleasure. The recording is excellent too. A highly recommendable bargain reissue.

KEYBOARD MUSIC

6 Quartets, Op. 26; Fandango (from *Quintettino, Op. 40/2*) (arr. for two harpsichords).
(B) **(*) HM Dig. HMT 7901233. William Christie, Christophe Rousset (harpsichords).

It is not known who made this arrangement for two harpsichords of Boccherini's six *Quartets*, published in 1781 as Op. 32, but in the hands of William Christie and Christophe Rousset – who are obviously enjoying themselves – the music is robustly jolly and communicative and made to sound as if written for the keyboard, especially the imitative opening of No. 3. Each sonata is in two movements, with the second a minuet. The *Larghetto* which begins No. 2 has its moments of quirkiness, while the *Andante appassionato* opening movement of the last sonata sounds almost like that of a transcribed Haydn *Sturm und Drang* symphony. The *Fandango* from Op. 40/2 is, not surprisingly, the most striking movement of all; but there is plenty of verve throughout, even if the close balance of the two harpsichords means that the dynamic range is limited.

Boëllmann, Léon (1862–97)

Cello sonata in A min., Op. 40; 2 Pieces for cello and piano, Op. 31.
*** Hyperion Dig. CDA 66888 [id.]. Lidström, Forsberg – GODARD: *Cello sonata in D min.* etc. ***

Neither Léon Boëllmann nor Benjamin Godard were blessed with long lives. Boëllmann was one of 14 children and he left his native Alsace after the Franco-Prussian war to study in Paris, where he made a considerable name for himself as a teacher and organist. He is indeed best known for his organ music and in particular the *Suite gothique*, whose final Toccata is a familiar *cheval de bataille*. His *Variations symphoniques* for cello and orchestra were widely played during his lifetime. The *A minor Sonata* reveals him to be a cultured and imaginative musician, more individual in style than Godard, but no less a craftsman. As in the Godard, Mats Lidström and Bengt Forsberg play with such passion and conviction that they almost persuade you that this piece is worthy to rank alongside the Brahms *Sonatas*. The recording is just a trifle close but produces more than acceptable results. Strongly recommended.

Boismortier, Joseph Bodin de (1689–1755)

Bassoon concerto in D.
(B) ** Carlton/Turnabout 30371 0004-2 [id.]. George Zukerman, Württemberg CO, Heilbronn, Faerber – CORRETTE: *Le Phénix;* F. COUPERIN: *Double bassoon concerto in G;* DEVIENNE: *Quartet in C.* **

As part of an intriguing collection of bassoon repertoire, the excellent George Zukerman, who has already given us fine accounts of concertos by Mozart and Weber, turns his attention to this mini-concerto of Boismortier. It is not great music perhaps, but it is very pleasant withal. Zukerman is a persuasive soloist and he is accompanied by the reliable Faerber. His attractively 'woody' timbre is well caught by the recording.

(i) *Suites for solo flute Nos. 3, 5 & 6;* (ii) *Harpsichord suites Nos. 1–4.*
(B) *** Calliope Approche Analogue/Dig. CAL 6865 [id.]. (i) Luc Urbain; (ii) Mireille Lagacé.

These four *Harpsichord suites* were Boismortier's only works for harpsichord, published as a set in Paris in 1731. They are very much in the style of the *Pièces de clavecin* of Rameau, and Boismortier follows his practice in giving each movement a colourful sobriquet. *La Cavernesque*, which begins the *First Suite*, is aptly titled. The invention is attractive, if perhaps not as individual as with Rameau, although the finale of the last suite shows Boismortier writing a very characterful set of variations. Mireille Lagacé is an excellent advocate and she uses a restored Hemsch, which is truthfully recorded and suits the repertoire admirably. Interleaved with the harpsichord works are three suites for unaccompanied flute, also made up with dance movements but each with an introductory *Prelude* which has an improvisatory feeling about it. Again the playing is highly responsive, and altogether this makes a rewarding concert and brings yet another name out of the musical history books.

Boito, Arrigo (1842–1918)

Mefistofele (complete).
** RCA Dig. 09026 68284-2 (2) [id.]. Ramey, La Scola, Crider, La Scala, Milan, Ch. & O, Muti.

If any opera demands brilliant recording, this is it, with its visions of heaven and a witches' sabbath. Sadly, the Muti version, for all its many merits, suffers from being recorded live at La Scala. Though the RCA engineers put more air round the sound than usual in that house, the results are not focused sharply enough, lacking detail and presence. The bonus is that Muti's direction has something of the high-voltage electricity which made Toscanini's classic recording of the *Prologue* so memorable, and a live performance adds to the intensity. The casting is flawed. Samuel Ramey sings richly and powerfully in the title-role, but this is in no way an evil-sounding voice, lacking the bite and edge such a singer as Ghiaurov gives.

Vincenzo La Scola sings with more style than he does in the Naxos recording of *L'elisir d'amore*, obviously drilled by Muti, but he is far from ideal. Michele Crider has so vibrant a voice that it spreads uncomfortably under pressure, not least in the big aria, *L'altra notte*. It is also disappointing that she takes the role of Helen of Troy in the *Walpurgisnacht* Act, as well as that of Margherita. First choice remains with the modern, digital set on Decca, conducted by Fabritiis, with Ghiaurov, Pavarotti and Freni (410 175-2 – see our main volume).

Bononcini, Giovanni (1670–1755)

Griselda (highlights).

(M) *** Decca 448 977-2 (2) [id.]. Elms, Sutherland, M. Sinclair, Elkins, Malas, Amb. S., LPO, Bonynge – GRAUN: *Montezuma*. ***

Bononcini is remembered well enough as Handel's rival as an opera composer, but how rarely one has the chance to study his theatrical music. All credit to Richard Bonynge for resurrecting what by all accounts is his most impressive work, and providing a sample of a score of numbers. By no stretch of the imagination does this music match Handel's in inspiration, but the numbers are nicely varied, with several lovely arias for the patient Griselda (sung by Lauris Elms), several simpler pastoral airs and a couple of jolly bass arias. Joan Sutherland's contribution in the castrato role of Ernesto is limited to four arias and a duet but, with bright, lively conducting from Richard Bonynge the whole performance is most enjoyable. Excellent (1966) Kingsway Hall recording and a full translation provided. It was perhaps a pity that this reissue had to come in harness with Graun's *Montezuma*, but that too is well worth having on CD.

Borodin, Alexander (1833–87)

'The World of Borodin': (i) *In the Steppes of Central Asia; Prince Igor:* (ii) *Overture;* (ii–iii) *Polovtsian dances;* (iv) *Symphony No. 2 in B min.;* (v) *String quartet No. 2: Nocturne;* (vi) *Scherzo in A flat;* (vii, viii) *Far from the shores of your native land;* (vii, ix) *Prince Igor: Galitzky's aria.*

500♪ (M) *** Decca Analogue/Dig. 444 389-2; *444 389-4*. (i) SRO, Ansermet; (ii) LSO, Solti; (iii) with London Symphony Ch., (iv) LSO, Martinon, (v) Borodin Qt, (vi) Ashkenazy, (vii) Nicolai Ghiaurov, (viii) Zlatina Ghiaurov; (ix) London Symphony Ch. and LSO, Downes.

An extraordinarily successful disc that will provide for many collectors an inexpensive summation of the art of Borodin. There can be few if any other collections of this kind that sum up a composer's achievement so succinctly or that make such a rewarding and enjoyable 76-minute concert. Solti's *Prince Igor overture* is unexpectedly romantic, and very exciting too; there is no finer account in the current catalogue, and the same can be said for the *Polovtsian dances*, with splendid choral singing. Martinon's unsurpassed 1960 LSO performance of the *B minor Symphony* is notable for its fast tempo for the famous opening theme. The strong rhythmic thrust suits the music admirably, the Scherzo has vibrant colouring and the slow movement, with a beautifully played horn solo, is most satisfying. The sound has remarkable presence and sparkle.

(i) *Symphonies Nos. 1–3; Prince Igor:* (i; ii) *Overture and Polovtsian dances;* (iii) *In the Steppes of central Asia;* (iv) *String quartet No. 2: Notturno* (arr. for orchestra).

(B) ** Sony SB2K 62406 (2) [id.]. (i) Toronto SO, Andrew Davis; (ii) with Ch.; (iii) NYPO, Bernstein; (iv) St Petersburg Camerata, Sondeckis.

At bargain price in Sony's Essential Classics series, this makes a fairly recommendable compilation, with Andrew Davis's readings of the three symphonies and of the *Prince Igor* items bluff and bouncy, supplemented by two favourite bonus items. With the extra brightness of the CD transfer the amiable qualities of Davis's readings consistently come out. There is no neurasthenia in his view of Borodin here, consistently strong, purposeful and well sprung, with the warmly lyrical folk flavour of the themes regularly brought out. The Sony (originally CBS) recording may be too upfront and may lack a genuine pianissimo, but that matches the rugged quality of the performances, which yet bring some fine playing from the Toronto wind and brass principals. The two encores are new to the present bargain reissue, and neither is outstanding. The *Nocturne* from the *Second String quartet* is described as being 'arranged for violin and string orchestra by Rimsky-Korsakov', but proves to have no soloist, and to be scored for a fuller orchestra, including woodwind. The performance is warm, but its sentience is rather too sultry and lethargic. Similarly, and more surprisingly, Bernstein's *In the Steppes of central Asia* is heavily expressive and fails to spring fully to life and be truly evocative; moreover, its first climax is rather square. Both these pieces are much better recorded than the three symphonies. Good value, if the sound quality is acceptable.

Symphony No. 1 in E flat.

*(*) Finlandia/Warner Dig. 0630 14910-2 [id.]. Norwegian R. O, Ari Rasilainen – BALAKIREV: *Overture on three Russian tunes;* RIMSKY-KORSAKOV: *Sinfonietta on Russian themes.* *(*)

By far the finest movement of Borodin's *First Symphony* is the Scherzo, and that is played here with an elegantly light touch. There are some highly sensitive woodwind solos too, in the *Andante*, but overall this performance lacks a robustly extrovert Russian quality. The recording, although naturally balanced, also lacks vividness and real sparkle.

Prince Igor: overture.

(M) ** Mercury 434 373-2 [id.]. LSO, Dorati – TCHAIKOVSKY: *Symphony No. 4.* **

Prince Igor: Overture and Polovtsian dances.

(BB) *** Belart 450 017-2. LSO, Solti – GLINKA: *Ruslan and Ludmilla: overture* *** ❀; MUSSORGSKY: *Khovanshchina Prelude; Night.* ***

Solti's performances are among the finest ever recorded, with very good choral singing – even if the chorus takes a little while to warm up, the closing dance generates much adrenalin. The *Overture*, too, cuts a fine dash but is also warmly romantic, with a gloriously played horn solo.

Dorati's account of the *Prince Igor Overture* is bold and dramatic, its excitement very Slavonic in feeling. The recording is bright and vivid to match but is not out of Mercury's top drawer.

Petite suite.

** Chandos Dig. CHAN 9309 [id.]. Luba Edlina – TCHAIKOVSKY: *The Seasons.* *(*)

Borodin's charming suite is not so generously represented on CD in its piano form, though both Rozhdestvensky and Järvi have recorded it in the Glazunov orchestration. Luba Edlina gives a good account of the piece, which she characterizes with greater insight than she brings to Tchaikovsky's *The Seasons*, with which it is coupled.

Prince Igor (complete).

500♪ *** Ph. Dig. 442 537-2 (3) [id.]. Kit, Gorchakova, Ognovienko, Minjelkiev, Borodina, Grigorian, Kirov Ch. & O, St Petersburg, Gergiev.

(M) ** BMG/Melodiya 74321 29346-2 (3) [id.]. Petrov, Tugarinova, Eisen, Atlantov, Vedernikov, Obraztsova, Bolshoi Theatre, Moscow, Ch. & O, Mark Ermler.

Gergiev has been an inspired musical director of the Kirov company in St Petersburg, and this electrifying account of Borodin's epic opera reflects not only his own magnetic qualities as a conductor but also the way he has welded his principal singers as well as the chorus and orchestra into a powerful team. Of the solo casting, the two principal women here, not just Gorchakova but Olga Borodina too as Konchak's daughter, Konchakovna, are both magnificent. Yet in the end the overall control of this massive score is what matters, and there Gergiev, with a finer and more polished orchestra, clearly takes the palm.

Recorded in Moscow in 1969, the BMG/Melodiya set offers at mid-price a lusty, red-blooded performance of the traditional text, presented in close, vivid sound. The male cast could hardly be bettered, with Ivan Petrov most impressive as Igor and Artur Eisen as Galitsky equally firm and dark, and with Alexander Vedernikov a resonant, powerful Konchak. Vladimir Atlantov was unmatched at the time among Russian tenors, clear and unstrained, while Yelena Obraztsova as Konchakova was also in her prime with her firm, ripe chest-register. Though Tatyana Tugarinova has some squally moments as Yaroslavna, it is a firm voice, aptly Slavonic in timbre. The snag is the relative coarseness of the sound, underlining the hard-driven quality in Ermler's powerful treatment of the score. In the big set-numbers like the *Polovtsian dances*, one needs more subtlety, warmly committed as the results are.

Bortkiewicz, Sergei (1877–1952)

Piano concerto No. 1 in B flat, Op. 16.

(B) ** Millennium MCD 80116. Marjorie Mitchell, N. German RSO, Strickland – BUSONI: *Indian fantasy;* BRITTEN: *Piano concerto.* **

Sergei Bortkiewicz was born in St Petersburg, where he studied law as well as the piano. He studied and taught in Berlin before the First World War, when he settled in Turkey. While he was not a good enough pianist to make an international career, he was respected as a composer for the instrument. In the first of his three piano concertos, Russian and Lisztian influences mingle and there are some attractive ideas. Stephen Coombs's fine Hyperion recording, with the Arensky *F minor Concerto* as coupling, is the only current alternative and can be strongly recommended; it is uncut (CDA 66624 – see our main volume). The present recording was first published in the UK in 1964, though the sleeve gives no indication of its provenance. It attributes the orchestral contribution to the Nord Deutscher Rundfunk Orchestra, whereas the original Brunswick issue spoke of the Vienna State Opera Orchestra. It brings as coupling the only current account of Busoni's *Indian fantasy*.

Börtz, Daniel (born 1943)

Sinfonias Nos. 1; 7; Parados; Strindberg suite.
*** Chandos Dig. CHAN 9473 [id.]. Stockholm PO, Rozhdestvensky.

Daniel Börtz is a Swedish composer of the middle generation. A pupil first of Hilding Rosenberg then of Karl-Birger Blomdahl and Ingvar Lidholm, he also studied electronic music at Utrecht. He made his name with two church operas, then came to wider notice in 1991 with his opera, *The Bacchantes*, to a libretto by Ingmar Bergman. However you may react to his music, you will not find it boring, though his limited range of expressive devices may deter listeners from hearing all these pieces straight off! However, Börtz does possess real imagination and a refined sense of orchestral colour. There is, however, little or no sense of movement: the music is static, and there is extensive use of chord-clusters and strong dynamic contrasts. Both the *First* and *Seventh Symphonies* have powerful atmospheres and – for the most part – hold the listener's attention. The playing of the Stockholm orchestra is altogether superb and the Chandos recording is of demonstration standard: marvellously present, well balanced and realistic.

Bowen, York (1884–1961)

PIANO MUSIC

Ballade No. 2, Op. 87; Berceuse, Op. 83; Moto perpetuo from Op. 39; Preludes, Op. 102, Nos. 1 in C; 2 in C min.; 6 in D min.; 7 in E flat; 8 in E flat min.; 10 in E min.; 15 in G; 16 in G min.; 18 in G sharp min.; 19 in A; 20 in A min.; 21 in B flat; 22 in B flat min. Romances Nos. 1, Op. 35/1; 2, Op. 45; Sonata No. 5 in F min., Op. 72. Toccata, Op. 155.
❀ *** Hyperion Dig. CDA 66838 [id.]. Stephen Hough.

Few new discs of piano music match this for sheer magic: magnetic performances that come as a revelation, demonstrating that this long-neglected composer was a master of keyboard writing. Hough, always compelling on disc, not only technically brilliant but spontaneously expressive, was drawn to this composer on hearing a performance by Philip Fowke. Hough's love for Bowen's music which then developed brims out in every item, starting with 13 of the 24 *Preludes*. He puts them in his own, very effective order, bringing out the contrasted qualities of jewelled miniatures, reflecting Rachmaninov on the one hand, Ireland and Bax on the other, but with a flavour of their own. The most powerful, most ambitious work is the *Sonata No. 5*, with two weighty, wide-ranging movements separated by an *Andante* interlude; but such easily lyrical pieces as the two *Romances*, rounding off the sequence, in Hough's hands have rare, heart-easing depth. Vivid piano sound and illuminating notes by Francis Pott and Hough himself.

Boyce, William (1710–79)

Symphonies Nos. 1–8, Op. 2.
(BB) ** Arte Nova Dig. 74321 34032-2. L. Festival O, Ross Pople.
(B) ** Carlton/Turnabout 30371 00052. Württemberg CO, Joerg Faerber.
(M) ** Carlton Dig. 30367 01722. Serenata of London, Barry Wilde.

Pleasing performances on Arte Nova of Boyce's eight symphonies written in either the three-part French or Italian overture styles and neatly scored, using flutes and oboes for added colour. They are nicely turned, and this is music that is easy to enjoy on modern instruments. The recording is truthful, well balanced if a little studio bound and somewhat less characterful than Pople's companion CD of Handel's *Water music*. Good value.

At the very opening of the Carlton digital disc, the ear notices that the sound is slightly abrasive: Barry Wilde, although using modern instruments, is clearly seeking a 'period-instrument' manner. The performances are lively and clean, enjoyably fresh, if not distinctive, and first choice at mid-price for these enjoyable works still rests with Marriner (Decca 444 523-2), who directs exhilarating accounts in which the rhythmic subtleties in both fast and slow music are guaranteed to enchant. For those wanting authenticity, Christopher Hogwood and the Academy of Ancient Music turn in performances that are comparably lively and well shaped, although this (digital) version is at premium price (O-L 436 761-2).

Faerber made one of the most successful pioneering recordings of the eight Boyce *Symphonies* and his performances are alive and spirited, while the vigour and weight of the Württemberg approach are in keeping with a sense of symphonic style. The Turnabout recording is vivid and clear, and this disc gives pleasure and relatively little cause for criticism, even if more recent versions are considerably more refined.

Brahms, Johannes (1833–97)

CENTENARY COLLECTIONS

DG Complete Brahms Edition: Volume 1: Orchestral works: (i; ii) *Symphonies Nos. 1–4;* (i; iii) *Academic festival overture;* (iii; iv) *Hungarian dances Nos. 1–21;* (i; iii) *Serenades Nos. 1–2;* (i; ii) *Tragic overture; Variations on a theme of Haydn.*
(M) ** DG Dig./Analogue 449 601-2 (5) [id.]. (i) BPO; (ii) Karajan; (iii) Abbado; (iv) VPO.

Sampler: *Hungarian dances Nos. 1–21.*
(B) *** DG Dig. 449 655 [id.]. VPO, Abbado.

With variably focused recording, Karajan's last digital cycle (1986–8) of the Brahms *Symphonies* is not his finest, but he remained a natural Brahmsian to the last. The sound is full and weighty but tends to be thick and generalized in tuttis. Characteristically Karajan does not observe the first-movement exposition repeats. He draws a typically powerful and dramatic performance of the *First Symphony*, but his reading does not have the grip of his earlier account, made in the 1960s. The *Second Symphony* is far more impressive, suffering less from the thick, undifferentiated recording, when textures in this later work tend to be lighter. As a performance, it is the highlight of the cycle, a highly satisfying reading, at times warmer and more glowing than his previous versions, with consistently fine playing from the orchestra. The opening of the *Third Symphony* makes a massively bold impression, but again the ill-defined textures are a drawback, and here the omission of the exposition repeat may be counted much more serious. The *Fourth Symphony* sounds fresher, with the slow movement expansively lyrical, but the very purposeful finale is again heavily weighted. Overall this series lacks the spontaneous inspiration of Karajan's earlier recordings.

Abbado's performance of the *First Serenade* is vital, imaginative and sensitive, but the digital recording (1981) is rather dry and lacking in bloom, though clear enough. The *Second Serenade* was recorded much earlier (1967) and the sound is greatly to be preferred, with plenty of analogue bloom; the performance is very persuasive and marvellously held together, with dynamic nuances nicely observed. Again the Berlin Philharmonic play superbly both here and in the *Academic festival overture*, made at the same time. Karajan's *Tragic overture* is impressively done and, though one may criticize the recording balance, the result is powerful and immediate; he also gives an appealing performance of the *Haydn variations*. Abbado's account of the *Hungarian dances* has great sparkle and lightness, and this CD is additionally offered as a bargain sampler for the whole edition.

Volume 2: Concertos: *Piano concertos Nos.* (i; ii) *1 in D min., Op. 15;* (i; iii) *2 in B flat, Op. 83;* (iv) *Violin concerto in D, Op. 77;* (iv–v) *Double concerto for violin, cello and orchestra in A min., Op. 102.*
(M) ** DG Analogue/Dig. 449 607-2 (3) [id.]. (i) Pollini, VPO; (ii) Boehm; (iii) Abbado; (iv) Mutter, BPO, Karajan; (v) with Meneses.

Piano concertos Nos. 1–2; Tragic overture, Op. 81; Variations on a theme of Haydn, Op. 56a.
(B) *** DG Double 453 067 (2) [id.]. Pollini, VPO, Boehm (*No. 1*) or Abbado (*No. 2*).

Although Pollini and the Vienna Philharmonic under Karl Boehm are given finely detailed recording, in the *First Piano concerto* other versions (notably Gilels) provide greater wisdom and humanity. Not that Pollini is wanting in keyboard command, but he is a little short on tenderness and poetry. All too often here he seems to have switched on the automatic pilot and, although the *B flat Concerto* under Abbado is much fresher and offers some masterly pianism, there are warmer and more spontaneous accounts to be had. (Admirers of Pollini will note that his accounts of the two piano concertos are also available – less expensively – on a DG Double.) Anne-Sophie Mutter's strikingly fresh version of the *Violin concerto* (available separately, coupled with the Mendelssohn *Concerto* – DG 445 515-2) can hold its own with the best, and the *Double concerto*, too, is particularly successful. With two young soloists Karajan conducts an outstandingly spacious and strong performance. Mutter conveys a natural authority comparable to Karajan's own, and the precision and clarity of Meneses's cello as recorded make an excellent match. The central slow movement in its spacious way has a wonderfully Brahmsian glow.

Volume 3: Chamber music: (i) *Cello sonatas Nos. 1–2;* (ii; iii) *Clarinet quintet, Op. 115;* (ii; iv) *Clarinet sonatas Nos. 1–2;* (ii; v; vi) *Clarinet trio, Op. 114;* (v; vii; viii) *Horn trio, Op. 40;* (v; vi; viii; ix) *Piano quartets Nos. 1–3;* (x) *Piano quintet, Op. 34;* (v; vi; viii) *Piano trios Nos. 1–3;* (xi) *String quartets Nos. 1–3;* (iii; xii) *String quintets Nos. 1–2;* (iii; xii; xiii) *String sextets Nos. 1–2;* (xiv) *Violin sonatas Nos. 1–3; F.A.E. Sonata: Scherzo.*

(M) **(*) DG Dig./Analogue 449 611-2 (11) [id.]. (i) Rostropovich, Rudolf Serkin; (ii) Leister; (iii) Amadeus Qt; (iv) Demus; (v) Vásáry; (vi) Borwitzky; (vii) Hauptmann; (viii) Brandis; (ix) Christ; (x) Pollini, Italian Qt; (xi) LaSalle Qt; (xii) with Aronowitz; (xiii) Pleeth; (xiv) Zukerman, Barenboim.

The Rostropovich/Serkin partnership in the *Cello sonatas* proved an outstanding success and these performances, recorded digitally in 1982, are self-recommending. The *Piano quintet* also brings some very commanding playing from Pollini, and the Italian Quartet is eloquent too. The balance, however, is very much in the pianist's favour; he dominates the texture rather more than is desirable and occasionally masks the lower strings. There are also minor agogic exaggerations. However, neither these nor the other reservations need necessarily put off the prospective listener, even if at fortissimo levels the piano and strings in the 1979 recording could ideally be better separated. Karl Leister is a fine soloist in the *Clarinet sonatas* and his 1968 analogue recording is more convincingly balanced. The *Clarinet* and *Horn trios* date from much later (1981) and, like the *Piano quartets*, are digital. The *Clarinet trio* again brings excellent playing, although Leister's individuality comes over less strongly here than in the *Clarinet quintet* and the forward balance is less flattering. Norbert Hauptmann shines in the *Horn trio*, an enjoyably lively and warmly persuasive performance which is convincingly projected. The *Piano trios* also date from 1981 and, like the *Piano quartets* from 1982, are undoubtedly commanding. Tamás Vásáry is very impressive throughout, and the string playing from the three principals of the Berlin Philharmonic is hardly less magnificent. The *Piano quartets* are particularly successful. These artists have a thorough grasp of these unfailingly rich and inventive scores and penetrate their character completely; but again there is a problem with the recording balance, made in the Berlin Jesus-Christus-Kirche. The microphones have been placed very close and the effect is artificial: the players are very forward and it is as if one were listening to them in the confines of an enclosed space, without room for the sound to expand. The bright, forward timbre of the strings is achieved at the expense of a natural tonal bloom. The LaSalle Quartet give efficient, streamlined accounts of the *String quartets*, but their expressive style lacks tenderness. There is no question as to the polish and expertise of their ensemble, but these are not performances that bring one closer to the music. The 1978–9 analogue recording is bright and immediate. The Amadeus performances of the *String quintets* and *Sextets* were recorded a decade earlier in 1967–8, yet the sound is remarkably full and pleasingly balanced, while the music-making has plenty of life and warmth. Here the element of suaveness which at times enters the Amadeus ethos seems minimized by the immediacy. The playing is consistently polished, and tempi are well chosen. Karl Leister plays with considerable sensitivity in the *Clarinet quintet*, and there is much to enjoy here. Zukerman and Barenboim take an expansive view of the *Violin sonatas*, producing songful, spontaneous-sounding performances that catch the inspiration of the moment. Their 1974 recording is basically ripe and warm, but the CD transfer does not entirely flatter the upper partials of the violin timbre.

Volume 4: Keyboard works: Piano duet: (i) *Hungarian dances Nos. 1–21; Sonata in F min., Op. 34b; Souvenir de la Russie; Variations on a theme of Haydn, Op. 56b; Variations on a theme of Schumann, Op. 23; 16 Waltzes, Op. 39;* (ii) *4 Ballades, Op. 10; Fantasias, Op. 116; 3 Intermezzi, Op. 117;* (iii) *Pieces, Op. 76;* (ii) *Pieces, Op. 118–19; 2 Rhapsodies, Op. 79; Scherzo, Op. 4;* (iv) *Sonatas Nos. 1–3;* (v) *Theme and variations in D min.* (from 2nd movement of *String sextet, Op. 18*); (iii) *Variations on an original theme, Op. 21/1; Variations on a Hungarian song, Op. 21/2;* (v) *Variations and fugue on a theme of Handel, Op. 24;* (iii) *Variations on a theme of Paganini, Op. 35;* (v) *Variations on a theme of Schumann, Op. 9;* (iv) Arr. of BACH: *Chaconne from Partita, BWV 1004* (for left hand). Organ: (vi) *11 Chorale preludes, Op. 122; Chorale prelude and fugue in A min.; Fugue in A flat min.; Preludes and fugues in A min., G min.*

(M) *(*) DG Analogue/Dig. 449 623-2 (9) [id.]. (i) Alfons and Aloys Kontarsky; (ii) Wilhelm Kempff; (iii) Tamás Vásáry; (iv) Anatol Ugorski; (v) Daniel Barenboim; (vi) Peter Planyavsky.

The Kontarskys' four-handed set of the *Hungarian dances* is available separately (see below) and is vivaciously recommendable, but the *Schumann variations* and the *Waltzes* are a little short on charm. The *Double piano sonata* began as a string quintet before migrating to the keyboard and then ending life as the *Piano quintet*. The Kontarskys make heavy weather of much of it and are too prone to point-making and to interrupting the rhythmic flow of the music to be wholly recommendable. The opening theme is treated in an extremely mannered fashion and, generally speaking, one feels the lack of a true inner tension. Much the same applies to the *Haydn variations*. The *Souvenir de la Russie* is very lightweight and Brahms did not publish it under his own name. In Kempff's hands the four *Ballades* emerge very much as a young man's music and, like Opp. 116–19, these are highly individual performances with the Kempff magic most striking in the *Intermezzi*, Op. 117, and the *Pieces* of Op. 119. The Op. 79 *Rhapsodies* perhaps suit his temperament less obviously, but he plays them with conviction. He is more than acceptably recorded. Barenboim is allotted the *Theme and variations in D minor*, transcribed from the *Sextet*, Op. 18, plus the *Schumann variations*, Op. 9, and the *Variations and fugue on a theme of Handel*, Op. 24, and he shows himself in inspirational form. Both the latter sets have received more cohesive performances on record, but Barenboim has a magical way of making the listener's attention perk up at the start of each variation, and he shares his own sense of discovery with you. He is afforded first-class sound. To Vásáry, alongside the eight *Pieces*, Op. 76, go the *Variations on an original theme*, the *Variations on a Hungarian song* and the *Paganini variations*, Op. 35, which sound marvellously fresh and sparkling. His virtuosity is effortless and unostentatious and, generally speaking, he is well recorded too. The three *Sonatas* are brand-new recordings and one wonders why DG did not choose to use Zimerman's highly concentrated accounts. Ugorsky is infinitely more wayward, impulsive and self-aware, and in the first two *Sonatas* he fails to hold the architecture together convincingly. The first movement of the *F minor Sonata* is then pulled about unmercifully, and this performance is so eccentrically wilful that it cannot be taken seriously. Ugorsky is also very free in his handling of Brahms's transcription of Bach's *D minor Chaconne* for the left hand, which is more austere than the familiar Busoni arrangement, but it does not sound so here. The recording is excellent. Overall, this set is too flawed for a general recommendation.

Volume 5: Lieder: *Gesäng, Opp. 3; 6; 7; 43; 69–72;* (i) *91; Gedich, Op. 19; Lieder. Opp. 46–9; 85–6; 94–7; 105–7; WoO post. 23; Lieder und Gesänge, Opp. 32; 57–9; 63; Lieder und Romanzen, Op. 14; Ophelia-Lieder, WoO post. 23; Romanzen und Lieder. Op. 84; Die schöne Magelone (Romanzen), Op. 33; Vier ernste Gesänge (4 Serious songs), Op. 121; Zigeunerlieder, Op. 103.*

(M) *** DG Analogue/Dig. 449 633-2 (7) [id.]. Jessye Norman, Dietrich Fischer-Dieskau, Daniel Barenboim; (i) with Wolfgang Christ.

Song-writing for Brahms was as natural as breathing, and this glorious collection, spanning the fullest breadth of his career, consistently bears witness to his unique genius, more as an exuberant songsmith than as a practitioner of the German Lied. For him melody lay at the very heart of song-writing and, even more than Schubert, his songs go straight to the heart of the German folksong. Through most of his career he was more concerned with the immediate musical challenge of a poem rather than its literary merit, but this magnificent collection, recorded with love and understanding and with not a suspicion of routine, effectively establishes that the Brahmsian approach to the world of Lieder provides a valid and important addition to that of ostensibly subtler Lieder-composers such as his friend, Schumann, or Hugo Wolf. Fischer-Dieskau's 1972 recording of the culminating *Four Serious songs* provides a superb conclusion, but the rest of the recordings were made between 1978 and 1982. Jessye Norman, full and golden of tone, consistently reveals her art at its most persuasive, in most ways matching even the imagination of Fischer-Dieskau, who is in equally ravishing voice. Not the least important element is the playing of Barenboim who, in accompanying Lieder, gives an impression almost of improvisation, of natural fluidity and pianistic sparkle to match every turn of the singer's expression. Beautiful, faithful recording, admirable transfers and first-class documentation.

Volume 6: Vocal ensembles: *Ballads and Romances, Op. 75; 14 Children's folksongs; 49 Deutsche Volkslieder; Duets, Opp. 20; 28; 61; 66; Liebeslieder, Op. 52; Neue Liebeslieder, Op. 65; Quartets, Opp. 31; 64; 92; 112; Zigeunerlieder, Op. 103.*

(M) *** DG Dig./Analogue 449 641-2 (4) [id.]. Edith Mathis, Brigitte Fassbaender, Peter Schreier, Dietrich Fischer-Dieskau; Karl Engel, Wolfgang Sawallisch, Gernot Kahl; N. German R. Ch., Günter Jena.

This box includes all Brahms's vocal ensembles for solo voices with piano, and they receive fresh, brightly affectionate performances from an almost ideally chosen quartet of distinguished singers, accompanied by excellent, imaginative pianists. The writing here represents Brahms at his most engagingly domestic, though – as in the famous set of *Liebeslieder waltzes* – his imagination quickly took him beyond the normal capabilities of an amateur musical household. The result is seductive but surprisingly difficult. On the other hand, you find an essentially domestic delight in the lovely folksong settings of the *Deutsche Volkslieder* and *Volks-Kinderlieder*, originally devised for the family of Robert and Clara Schumann. There is treasure to be found throughout these four discs, recorded with a nice balance between intimacy and immediacy.

Volume 7: Choral works: Female chorus: *Ave Maria, Op. 12; 13 Canons, Op. 113; Psalm 13, Op. 27; 3 Geistliche Chöre, Op. 37; 4 Songs, Op. 17; 12 Songs and Romances, Op. 44*. Male chorus: *7 Canons; Little wedding cantata; Songs, Op. 41; 23 German folksongs*. Mixed chorus: *Begräbnisgesang, Op.13; 3 Fest- und Gedenksprüche, Op. 109; Marienlieder, Op. 22; Motets, Opp. 29; 74; 110; Geistliches Lied, Op. 30; Songs, Opp. 42; 62; 104; Songs and Romances, Op. 93a; Tafellied Dank der Damen, Op. 93b*.
(M) *** DG Dig. 449 646-2 (4) [id.]. Mathis, Murray, Julia Raines Hahn, Gerhard Dickel, Gernot Kahl, Martin-Albrecht Rohde, Jan Schroeder, Hans-Ulrich Winkler; N. German R. Ch., Günter Jena.

This four-disc collection of Brahms's unaccompanied choral music ranges wide, representing all periods of his career in intimate, warmly characterful writing, whether in motets, part-songs, canons or folksong settings. Even more than other boxes in the DG Brahms Edition, it contains much buried treasure, not least the fine *Motets for double chorus*, Opp. 109 and 110, which open the second disc. These settings, particularly the *Fest- und Gedenksprüche*, Op. 109, using biblical texts, find Brahms using that elaborate medium in joyful complexity and understanding. The same CD includes the *Songs*, Op. 17, for women's voices, two horns and harp, ravishing pieces. The Hamburg choir gives radiant performances, beautifully recorded with no hint of routine: the recording is both clear and pleasingly atmospheric. Highly recommended.

Volume 8: Choral works with orchestra: (i; ii) *Alto rhapsody, Op. 53;* (iii) *German requiem, Op. 45; Nänie, Op. 82;* (ii; iv) *Rinaldo, Op. 50;* (ii) *Song of destiny (Schicksalslied), Op. 54; Song of the Fates, Op. 89;* (ii; v) *Song of triumph, Op. 55*.
(M) **(*) DG Dig. 449 651-2 (3) [id.]. (i) Fassbaender; (ii) Prague Philharmonic Ch., Czech PO, Sinopoli; (iii) Bonney, Schmidt, V. Op. Ch., VPO, Giulini; (iv) Kollo; (v) W. Brendel.

When this box was originally issued on LP, all the music was conducted by Sinopoli; now Giulini's performance of the *German Requiem* has been substituted for Sinopoli's version, not altogether an advantage. Giulini's account is deeply dedicated but one which at spacious speeds lacks rhythmic bite. Meditation is a necessary part of Brahms's scheme, but here, with phrasing smoothed over and the choral sound rather opaque, there is too little contrast. With Sinopoli the effect was more consistently positive. The rest of the programme brings performances both challenging and controversial which – particularly in the rarer works – are a revelation. Fassbaender makes a strong, noble soloist in the *Alto rhapsody*, but it is the other works which command first attention in such a collection, not least the one generally dismissed as mere occasional music, the *Triumphlied* of 1870 which, Elgar-like, had Brahms doing his patriotic bit. Sinopoli, helped by incandescent singing from the Czech choir, gives it Handelian exhilaration. There is freshness and excitement too in the other rare works, with Sinopoli lightening the rhythms and textures. In *Rinaldo*, for example – the nearest that Brahms came to writing an opera – Sinopoli moulds the sequence of numbers very dramatically. René Kollo is the near-operatic soloist. The recordings, made in Prague, bring sound which is warm and sympathetic, with the orchestra incisively close and the chorus atmospherically behind, if sometimes a little confusingly so.

Decca '*Masterworks*'
(B) **(*) Decca Analogue/Dig. 452 328-2 (12) [id.].

Decca have celebrated the Brahms centenary more modestly than DG with a bargain set of 12 CDs in a slipcase, but also issued separately in pairs – as Decca Doubles at bargain price – and, while there is comparatively little to disappoint here, many collectors will prefer to make their own choice within this comprehensive anthology.

Volume I: *Symphonies Nos. 1–2; Academic festival overture; Variations on a theme of Haydn, Op. 56a; Tragic overture*.
(B) **(*) Decca Double 452 329-2 (2) [id.]. Chicago SO, Solti.

Volume II: (i) *Symphonies Nos. 3–4;* (ii) *Hungarian dances Nos. 1–21*.
(B) *** Decca Double Analogue/Dig. 452 332-2 (2) [id.]. (i) Chicago SO, Solti; (ii) RPO, Weller.

Sir Georg Solti came to the Brahms symphonies at the end of the 1970s, after a quarter-century of experience in the recording studio, having deliberately left them aside over the years. His study was intensely serious, and that is reflected in his often measured but always forceful renderings. Those who think of Solti as a conductor who always whips up excitement may be surprised at the sobriety of the approach, but in a way his Brahms performances are the counterparts of those he recorded of the Beethoven symphonies: important and thoughtful statements, lacking only a degree of the fantasy and idiosyncrasy which make fine performances great. The *Variations* are also very successful, and there is a splendidly committed account of the *Tragic overture*. However, it is the second of the two Doubles which offers the two finest performances: Solti's big-scale view of the *Third Symphony* is most compelling, and the *Fourth* shows him at his most vibrantly individual, with the *Andante moderato* second movement treated more like an Adagio, unfailingly pure and eloquent. This second box also includes Walter Weller's splendid, complete, digital set of the *Hungarian dances*. Here the RPO play with wonderful spirit as if they were enjoying every moment – and, indeed, as if their very lives depended on it. Weller secures excellent playing from every department of the orchestra. The recording is lively and bright, eminently truthful in timbre and with good, natural perspective.

Volume III: *Piano concertos Nos.* (i) *1;* (ii) *2;* (iii) *Violin concerto.*
(B) **(*) Decca Double Analogue/Dig. 452 335-2 (2) [id.]. (i) Lupu, LPO, de Waart; (ii) Ashkenazy, LSO, Mehta; (iii) Belkin, LSO, Fischer.

Radu Lupu's approach to the *First Piano concerto* is that of the time when the piano was not the leonine monster it was to become later on in the century. His is a deeply reflective and intelligent performance, full of masterly touches and an affecting poetry which falls short of the thrusting combative power of a Serkin or Curzon. De Waart provides sensitive support and matches Lupu's approach admirably. Decca produce a particularly truthful sound-picture. This could be recommended enthusiastically to those who want a second, alternative view. However, Ashkenazy's account of the *Second Piano concerto* is less successful, its chief shortcoming being a lack of tension. With much beautiful detail and some wonderfully poetic playing, the performance still fails to come alive as it should. Naturally Ashkenazy is most successful in the lighter moments, but one is continually left uninvolved. On the other hand, Boris Belkin's performance of the *Violin concerto* is direct and spontaneous, a spaciously warm reading that makes a strong impression. No complaints about the recorded sound.

Volume IV: *4 Ballades, Op. 10; Intermezzo, Op. 117/2; 6 Piano pieces, Op. 118; Piano sonata No. 3, Op. 5; 2 Rhapsodies, Op. 79; Variations and fugue on a theme by Handel, Op. 24; Variations on a theme by Paganini, Op. 35.*
(B) **(*) Decca Double 452 338-2 (2) [id.]. Julius Katchen.

Julius Katchen's style in Brahms is distinctive; it sometimes has a slightly unyielding quality that suits some works better than others. In general the bigger, tougher pieces come off better than, for example, the gentle *Intermezzo*. But such pieces as the two *Rhapsodies* are splendidly done, and so are the *Ballades*. The *Sonata* receives a commanding performance. However, the two sets of *Variations*, for all their sheer pyrotechnical display, are rather less compelling.

Volume V: (i; ii) *Cello sonata No. 2 in F, Op. 99;* (iii) *Clarinet quintet in B min., Op. 115;* (iv) *Horn trio in E flat, Op. 40;* (i; ii; v) *Piano trio No. 1 in B, Op. 8;* (ii; v) *Violin sonata No. 3 in D min., Op. 108.*
(B) *** Decca Double 452 341-2 (2) [id.]. (i) Starker; (ii) Katchen; (iii) Brymer & Allegri Qt; (iv) Tuckwell, Perlman, Ashkenazy; (v) Suk.

The recordings of the *Piano trio* and the *Cello sonata* represent the results of Julius Katchen's last recording sessions before his untimely death. They were held at The Maltings, and the results have much warmth. Katchen and his team judge the tempi of the Op. 8 *Piano trio* admirably and they resist the temptation to dwell too lovingly on detail. The *Cello sonata* is given a strong and characterful performance, while Jack Brymer gives a masterly and finely poised account of the *Clarinet quintet*, which in terms of polish and finesse can hold its own with the very best. Apart from Brymer's well-characterized playing, the Allegri Quartet are also in excellent shape, and they are given the benefit of eminently truthful recording; but it must be conceded that something of the nostalgia and the melancholy of this score eludes them. The highlight of this set is the superbly passionate performance of Brahms's marvellous *Horn trio* from Tuckwell, Perlman and Ashkenazy. By contrast, Josef Suk's personal blend of romanticism and the classical tradition in the *Violin sonata* is warmly attractive but small in scale. An intimate performance, then, but most enjoyable and well recorded. All in all, this Double Decca is well worth investigating.

Volume VI: (i; ii) *Alto rhapsody, Op. 53;* (iii) *German Requiem, Op. 45;* (iv) *Song of destiny (Schicksalslied), Op. 54;* (v) *Geistliches Lied, Op. 30;* (vi) *Vier ernste Gesänge (4 Serious songs), Op. 121;* (i; vii) *2 songs with viola, Op. 91.*
(B) **(*) Decca Double Analogue/Dig. 452 344-2 (2) [id.]. (i) Watts; (ii) SRO, Ansermet; (iii) Te Kanawa, Weikl, Chicago Ch. & SO, Solti; (iv) Amb. Ch., New Philh. O, Abbado; (v) King's College, Cambridge, Ch., Cleobury; (vi) Holl, Schiff; (vii) Parsons, Aronowitz.

Even more strikingly than in his set of the Brahms *Symphonies*, Solti favours very expansive tempi, smooth lines and refined textures in the *Requiem*. There is much that is beautiful, even if the result overall is not as involving as it might be. Dame Kiri Te Kanawa sings radiantly, but Bernd Weikl with his rather gritty baritone is not ideal. Fine recording, glowing and clear. Helen Watts gives a sensitive account of the *Alto Rhapsody*, while the *Song of destiny* brings a refined contribution from the Ambrosian Chorus with Abbado directing strongly. Helen Watts, too, is in good form in her sensitive performances of the two songs with viola as well as piano accompaniment. Cecil Aronowitz plays his obbligato with great finesse, and the combination of voice, viola and piano is particularly effective in *Gestillte Sehnsucht*, where the poet Rückert is in his most elegantly Petrarchan mood, telling of the soft evening sunlight on the woods, and the desire and longing of the solitary lover. The contributions of Robert Holl, accompanied by András Schiff, are slightly marred by the slow tempi chosen but are well sung, with due note taken of the texts.

ORCHESTRAL MUSIC

(i) *Piano concertos Nos. 1–2. Fantasias, Op. 116.*
500♪ (M) *** DG 447 446-2 (2) [id.]. Gilels; (i) BPO, Jochum.

The Gilels performances can still hold their own against virtually all the competition; the present set is offered at a reduced price and the remastered recording is quite outstanding.

(i) *Piano concerto No. 1;* (ii) *2 Songs, Op. 91.*
500♪ ✿ *** EMI Dig. CDC7 54578-2. (i) Stephen Kovacevich, LPO, Sawallisch; (ii) Ann Murray, Nobuko Imai.

Noble and dedicated, Stephen Kovacevich's account of the Brahms *D minor Concerto* is a performance of stature which belongs in the most exalted company. It can be recommended alongside such classic accounts as the Gilels/Jochum (DG 439 979-2); indeed, it must now take precedence. There is a welcome fill-up in the form of the two Op. 91 *Songs* with viola, admirably presented by Ann Murray and Nobuko Imai.

(i) *Piano concerto No. 2 in B flat, Op. 83. Variations on a theme of Haydn, Op. 56a.*
(M) * EMI CDM5 66093-2 [id.]. BPO, Karajan, (i) with Hans Richter-Haaser.

This reissue appears as part of EMI's Karajan Edition, and whether you like the Karajan/Richter-Haaser (Karajan's name is advisedly put first) interpretation as a whole depends on whether you respond to Karajan's super-subjective way of handling the tempo as if it were a rubber band. A romantic score it may be, and deserving of a warm and human touch; but the liberties taken with the speed of the first movement alone would be enough to put one off rubato for the rest of one's life. Richter-Haaser was a capable and artistic player, but he is here so obviously a pawn of the conductor that nothing can be done. Even though the recording of both piano and orchestra is of good, late-1950s vintage and it has been impressively remastered, it would be a risk to buy this version and try and live with it. There are no complaints about the performance of the *Variations*; it is very well played indeed.

Violin concerto in D, Op. 77.
500♪ *** Decca Dig. 444 811-2 [id.]. Joshua Bell, Cleveland O, Christoph von Dohnányi – SCHUMANN: *Violin concerto.* ***
(B) *** Decca Eclipse Dig. 448 988-2; *448 988-4* [id.]. Boris Belkin, LSO, Ivan Fischer – R. STRAUSS: *Violin concerto.* **(*)
** Hänssler Dig. 98 934. Sitkovetsky, ASMF, Marriner – MENDELSSOHN: *Violin concerto.* **
(B) *(*) EMI forte CZS5 69334-2 (2). Gidon Kremer, BPO, Karajan – SCHUMANN: *Concerto* **(*); SIBELIUS: *Concerto* ** (with Andrei Gavrilov: HINDEMITH: *Sonata;* SCHNITTKE: *Quasi una sonata;* WEBER: *Grand duo concertant* **(*)).
(M) *(*) EMI CDM5 66101-2 [id.]. Gidon Kremer, BPO, Karajan – MOZART: *Sinfonia concertante, K.297b.* **
(BB) * Naxos Dig. 8.550195 [id.]. Nishizaki, Slovak PO, Gunzenhauser – BRUCH: *Concerto No. 1.* *(*)

Joshua Bell's commanding performance of the Brahms *Concerto* will surely confirm his reputation as a major recording artist. The playing is full of flair, demonstrating not only his love of bravura display, but also his ready gift for turning a phrase individually in a way that catches the ear, always sounding spontaneous. Regularly one registers moments of new magic, not least when, in the most delicate half-tones, pianissimos seem to convey an inner communion. Full, atmospheric recording and a no less outstanding coupling put this among the very finest versions.

Those looking for a bargain digital recording should be well pleased with Boris Belkin's 1983 Decca Eclipse reissue, particularly as it is now generously recoupled with the engaging Mendelssohnian violin concerto of Richard Strauss. The performance is deeply felt, direct and spontaneous and makes a strong impression. The tempo of the first movement is measured and spacious, but this is far more than a routine performance and, with excellent sound and a good balance, it is very competitive.

Sounding more passionately involved than he sometimes has done on disc, Sitkovetsky gives a sweetly expressive account of the Brahms, as he does of the Mendelssohn coupling. He is helped by vivid recording and crisply responsive playing from the Academy under Marriner. Even with the first movement on the broad side, Sitkovetsky slows markedly for the second subject, naturally with a sense of spontaneity. Even so, this is not as compelling or individual a reading as the finest available.

Gidon Kremer came well recommended as a pupil of David Oistrakh, and the Brahms *Concerto* was one of his first major recordings, made in 1976. He proved an impressive violinist and he phrases very lyrically, but he established his artistic personality in a reading which at times is a little too inward-looking, with moments of self-indulgence, particularly in the first movement. From the opening bars Karajan provides an imposing accompaniment, and the recording, which is well balanced, opens out spaciously, but is not out of the ordinary. The forte set, for all its diversity and economy, does not constitute a challenge to the premier recommendations for the three major concertos. Although the sonata recital with Gavrilov is much more successful, this hardly alters the basic appeal of this collection.

Takako Nishizaki seems somehow not quite comfortable in this concerto, as if straining to make a bigger, more ardent reading than is natural to her. Some of the upper tessitura, so pressured, is not very sweet, and she makes Kreisler's first-movement cadenza sound laboured. The coupled Bruch suits her better, but this is not one of her recommendable records.

Violin concerto in D, Op. 77; (i) *Double concerto for violin and cello in A min., Op. 102.*
(M) ** DG Dig. 445 595-2 [id.]. Gidon Kremer; (i) with Mischa Maisky; VPO, Bernstein.

Kremer's version of the *Violin concerto* is powerful in attack, but he favours consistently fast speeds: his second movement is hardly a true *Adagio*. Bernstein, who accompanies him with the VPO, is much broader than the soloist, who tries to move things on; ultimately Kremer is too narcissistic and idiosyncratic to carry a firm recommendation. The *Double concerto* was recorded at concerts in the Vienna Musikvereinsaal in 1981–2. Mischa Maisky is a superb player with wonderful tonal finesse, but some of the dynamic extremes are self-conscious, while Kremer's playing is often posturing and, again, narcissistic. The playing of the VPO for Bernstein is marvellous and the reading is expansive and warm. The excellence of the recording is not in question: there is plenty of concert-hall ambience and a wide dynamic range with real body and presence. There is an admirable breadth about much of it, but this is outweighed in the first two movements by a want of real momentum.

Double concerto for violin, cello and orchestra in A min., Op. 102.
500♪ (B) *** EMI forte CZS5 69331-2 (2). David Oistrakh, Pierre Fournier, Philh. O, Galliera – BEETHOVEN: *Triple concerto;* MOZART: *Violin concerto No. 3;* PROKOFIEV: *Violin concerto No. 2.* ***

David Oistrakh's first stereo account with Fournier dates from 1959, but the recording was balanced by Walter Legge and the sound is remarkably satisfying. The performance is distinguished, strong and lyrical – the slow movement particularly fine – and, with Galliera and the Philharmonia providing excellent support, this version, coupled with three other outstanding concerto recordings, makes an ideal choice for bargain-hunters.

Hungarian dances Nos. 1–21 (complete).
500♪ ❁ (BB) *** Naxos Dig. 8.550110; *4550110 (Nos. 1–2; 4–21)*. Budapest SO, István Bogár.

The Budapest recording of the Brahms *Hungarian dances* is sheer delight from beginning to end. The playing has warmth and sparkle, and the natural way the music unfolds brings a refreshing feeling of rhythmic freedom. This is an outright winner among the available versions.

Tragic Overture, Op. 81.
(M) *** EMI CMS5 66109-2 (2) [id.]. BPO, Karajan – BRUCKNER: *Symphony No. 8;* HINDEMITH: *Mathis der Maler* (symphony). ***

A strong and impulsive, yet highly sympathetic performance from Karajan, showing him at his most charismatic. It is very well played and excellently recorded in the Berlin Jesus-Christus-Kirche in 1970. This set is a highlight of EMI's Karajan Edition, for the couplings are equally fine.

Symphonies Nos. 1–4.
(B) *** RCA Dig. 74321 20283-2 (2) [60085-2-RG (3)]. N. German RSO, Günter Wand.
(M) **(*) Mercury 434 380-2 (2) [id.]. LSO, or (*No. 2*) Minneapolis SO, Antal Dorati.
(M) (**(*)) DG mono 449 715-2 (2) [id.]. BPO, Eugen Jochum.

Symphonies Nos. 1–4; Academic festival overture; Tragic overture; Variations on a theme of Haydn; (i) *Alto rhapsody. Op. 54.*
(M) *(*) Virgin/EMI Dig. VBQ5 61360-2 (4). Houston SO, Christoph Eschenbach; (i) with Dunja Vejzovic & Houston Symphony Male Ch.

Symphonies Nos. 1–4; Academic festival overture; Tragic overture; Variations on a theme of Haydn, Op. 56a; (i) *Alto rhapsody, Op. 53; Fragment from Goethe's Harz Journey in Winter;* (ii) *Gesang der Parzen (Song of the Fates), Op. 89; Nänie, Op. 82; Schicksalslied, Op. 54.*
*** DG Dig. 435 683-2 (4) [id.]. BPO, Abbado; (i) with Marjana Lipovšek, Ernest Senf Ch.; (ii) Berlin R. Ch.

Symphonies Nos. 1–4; Tragic overture; Variations on a theme by Haydn.
(BB) *** RCA Navigator 74321 30367-2 (3) [Eurodisc 69220-2-RV]. Dresden State O, Kurt Sanderling.

Symphonies Nos. 1–4; Tragic overture; (i) *Alto rhapsody, Op. 53.*
**(*) DG Dig. 449 829-2 (3) [id.]. VPO, James Levine; (i) with Anne Sofie von Otter, Arnold Schoenberg Ch.

Sanderling's 1971–2 Dresden recordings of the four Brahms symphonies make a clear first choice in the budget range. They originally appeared on the Eurodisc label and enjoyed a brief life in the LP catalogues. They have a warmth and humanity that stand out from the general run of Brahms cycles, with the Dresden orchestra responding to Sanderling's direction with playing of an unaffected and natural eloquence, so that the performances can stand comparison with any in the catalogue at any price. The magnificence of the Dresden orchestra is immediately displayed in the *First Symphony*, and Sanderling's reading has such a natural warmth and is so strongly characterized that it has the keenest claims on the collector. Everyone plays as if they meant every note and this sense of conviction gives the performance a rare eloquence. The Dresden performance of No. 3 is marvellously rich: the slow movement is particularly warm-hearted and generous in feeling, as is the autumnal *Poco allegretto*, and here the horn soloist has a slight vibrato to show that this is an East German orchestra. This is a deeply experienced reading and yet spontaneous. The *Fourth* balances fire with lyrical feeling; the symphony is beautifully played and fluently shaped. It has a sense of enjoyment that makes it very rewarding indeed, and the *Variations* are also very successful. In the passages we sampled alongside the LPs, the present transfers have remained faithful to the original without brightening the upper strings or adding the kind of glare one encounters in so many modern digital recordings. These were for R.L. the touchstone of Brahms symphony records for many years during the 1970s and early 1980s, and their return to circulation is a cause for celebration; with the three discs offered at about the same cost as that of a premium-priced CD, this is a bargain *par excellence*. Strongly recommended.

While not an obvious first choice, Dorati's set of the Brahms symphonies, made between 1957 and 1963, is a competitive proposition, always vital and interesting. From the very opening bar of the *First Symphony* he presses onward with no lingering whatsoever and, if anything, the first movement of the *Third* (which overall is a splendid version, for the music suits his Hungarian spirit especially well) thrusts forward even more vehemently. Yet inner movements have plenty of warmth (if not quite as much as Jochum on DG) as well as lyrical ardour, while the *Andante* of the *Fourth* opens as a gentle idyll. Finales are consistently gripping: the great horn tune in the finale of the *First*, for instance, has seldom been played with greater breadth and power, and the closing movements of both the *Second* and *Third Symphonies* have exhilarating impetus and weight. The playing of the LSO is extremely brilliant and they back Dorati's wilful surging with enormous conviction. The Minneapolis orchestra also plays very well in the *Second Symphony*, where Dorati warms to Brahms's pastoral feeling at the opening of the first movement, yet takes hold of the onward flow as soon as the allegro gets under way, while the *Adagio* expands passionately. The recording throughout is brightly lit in the Mercury manner, a bit fierce at times, but there is supporting body (Watford Town Hall was the venue). No listener could fail to be stimulated by this musicianly, strongly involved and involving music-making.

Levine's new set of the Brahms *Symphonies* brings a certain lack of unanimity of view. For E.G. the special chemistry between Levine and the Vienna Philharmonic has rarely worked as tellingly as in these big and bold readings. The influence of Toscanini is immediately apparent in the keen tension and fastish speed for the introduction to the *First Symphony*, and Levine's control of tension never falters. These are interpretations, conceived on a large scale, which yet are full of refinement and detailed subtleties, with speeds generally on the fast side, but never with any hint of breathlessness, well illustrated in the powerful accounts of the outer movements of No. 4. The performances are made the more magnetic, when (except for the *Tragic overture*) they were recorded live in Vienna at the Musikverein between 1992 and 1995 with warm, well-focused sound that has plenty of air round it. The *Alto rhapsody* is a delight too, with the soloist, Anne Sofie von Otter, warm and intense. The *First Symphony* is coupled with the *Alto rhapsody*; the *Second* with the *Tragic Overture* and the *Third* and *Fourth* are together on the last CD.

R.L. is impressed by the playing of the Vienna Philharmonic, which undoubtedly has great finish, but while he agrees that Levine's interpretations are free from undue eccentricity he also finds them pretty hard-driven and not making as positive an impression as, say, either of the recently reissued (and undoubtedly more wayward) Jochum sets on bargain label or, above all, as Sanderling's on RCA. Of course they have the benefit of modern, digital recording but, even so, that is less than transparent in detail or ideally balanced.

As a modern digital cycle, Levine's undoubtedly impressive performances vie with those in the rather broader, glowing but less forwardly recorded Abbado Berlin cycle, which receives the Editor's casting vote. In most respects this still remains a clear first choice. With playing from the Berlin Philharmonic that is at once polished and intense, Abbado proves a passionate and romantic advocate, presenting the warmth of Brahms in full strength, and his set gains from having a generous collection of imaginatively chosen couplings.

One must not forget, however, that on two bargain discs from RCA one can get a set of spontaneously compelling readings from Günter Wand which are also very well played. Wand's is a consistently direct view of Brahms, yet the reading of each symphony has its own individuality. In the *First* the unity is clear, even though Wand does not observe the exposition repeat. If No. 2 is the pick of the series, a sunny, characteristically glowing reading, the *Third* (this time with exposition repeat included) just as readily shows Wand's wise way with Brahms, strong and easy and steadily paced, bringing out the autumnal moods. If the *Fourth* at first seems a shade understated, with the first movement, taken at a fastish speed, sounding melancholy rather than tragic, it is still a strong reading and provides a generally satisfying conclusion. The early (1982–3) digital recording, however, although giving plenty of bloom to the *Second Symphony*, brings a degree of fierceness on string-tone elsewhere, which verges on shrillness in No. 3. However, for E.G. these readings are even more inspired than Sanderling's, and the sound does not lack weight and body.

Jochum's mono DG recordings of the Brahms *Symphonies* are characteristically wayward and could hardly be regarded as a primary recommendation, even though the concentration of the playing generally holds the readings together. The *First Symphony* opens strongly and, for all the flexibility of tempi, there is underlying tension which creates a sense of ongoing momentum. Although the opening seems recessed (only partly the fault of the recording), the *Second* soon springs vividly to life. It is a characteristically warm, romantic performance in the German tradition, the contrasts between lyrical and dramatic in the first movement brought out confidently with no shame about speed-changes, and this applies consistently throughout, helped by the remarkably wide dynamic range of the recording. The finale has great vitality and moves to a thrilling close. The *Third Symphony* opens massively rather than exuberantly, and Jochum's spacious approach reminds one of the *First Piano concerto*. The effect overall is warm but mannered, although the central movements have a simple lyricism, and the close of the finale is tenderly elegiac. Again in the *Fourth*, which opens simply and delicately, there are wilful speed-changes which some listeners will resist, yet they follow the lyrical flow. The second movement is for the most part gently idyllic and lacks something in momentum. On balance, Jochum is more sympathetic and exciting in the last two movements, especially the finale, which (as with the *Second Symphony*) moves strongly to a zestful close. The Berlin Philharmonic playing is splendid throughout, and the mono recordings, made between 1951 and 1956, are amazingly good, full and clear, far more detailed and vivid than the original LPs. Jochum aficionados will certainly want this set, which is priced comparably to a Polygram Double.

With their extravagant layout on four discs (partly caused by the inclusion of the first-movement exposition repeats in the first three symphonies) Eschenbach's set could compete only if the Houston performances were truly outstanding, which they are not. They are beautifully played and very well balanced and recorded. But Eschenbach, highly musical Brahmsian as he is, has not yet entirely mastered the art of bringing a performance fully to life in the recording studio. No. 1 is singularly lacking in a strong profile, for here the conductor's easy, lyrical style works least well: the effect is more like a final rehearsal than a vivid consummation. In spite of a fine introductory horn solo, the finale hangs fire and really comes together only in the coda. The conductor's recessive manner may in theory be more suitable for the pastoral No. 2, but again there is simply not enough tension to hold each movement together, until the performance suddenly springs to life in the finale. No. 3 is much more impressive: the first movement immediately generates a stronger electrical charge. It sails off heftily, and there is plenty of momentum in the finale too, with impressive brass playing and the closing pages movingly autumnal. The inner movements, however, tend to sag just a little before the end, although the playing is affectionate and warm. Easily the finest Houston performance is of the *Fourth Symphony*, where the tension is consistently maintained and Eschenbach's steady lyrical flow, often impassioned, reminds one of Karl Boehm – and there can be no higher compliment. The *Academic festival overture* and *Haydn variations* are comparatively subdued, while the *Tragic overture*, which is coupled with the *Fourth Symphony*, is equally impressive. One of the highlights of the set is the moving account of the *Alto rhapsody*. Dunja Vejzovic is in glorious voice and the choral entry is a moment of serene magic, with the Houston Chorus beautifully balanced with the solo voice. But as a general recommendation this Virgin set is a non-starter.

Symphonies Nos. 1–3; Academic festival overture; Tragic overture.
❀ (B) *** EMI forte CZS5 69515-2 (2). LPO, Eugen Jochum.

Jochum's EMI stereo versions of the Brahms symphonies were made in the Kingsway Hall in 1976; the analogue recordings, produced by Christopher Bishop, are outstandingly full and vivid, with a rich Brahmsian ambience which means that the strings are brilliant, without edge, the bass is ample yet clean, and the overall balance is very convincing indeed. These remastered discs indeed sound better than almost any of their mid- or bargain-priced competitors (they are smoother on top than Wand's RCA set, and the violin timbre is much more distinguished than with Sanderling). The DG engineers secured a remarkably fine mono balance with Jochum's earlier, DG set (which is admired by R.L.) and the playing of the BPO is rather more polished and sleekly integrated than the LPO. But the LPO playing is excellent too, the greater spontaneity of its performances carrying the listener along on a wave of inspiration, and this also applies to the exuberant *Academic festival overture* and the hardly less vibrant *Tragic overture*. Moreover the first-movement exposition repeats are included in the first three symphonies and in every case are made to seem essential to the structure. The high drama of the *First Symphony* immediately shows Jochum at his most persuasive, giving the feeling of live communication in the ebb and flow of tension and natural flexibility. He is not as free as Furtwängler was – a specially revered master with him – but the warmth and lyricism go with comparable inner fire. Equally, No. 2 is a warmly lyrical reading, expansive in the first movement – helped by the richness of the recording of the middle and lower strings, allowing extremes of expression – fast and exciting in the finale. The inner movements are beautifully played and the natural fervour of the orchestral response is most compelling, justifying the natural flexibility. The *Third Symphony* represents the peak of Jochum's cycle, and this is among the most rewarding versions of this work, irrespective of price. He conveys the full weight and warmth of the work with generally spacious speeds, finely moulded. The first movement is magnificent, leading to a passionate coda, and in the central movements there is an engaging autumnal feeling, while in the finale, starting from hushed expectancy in the opening pianissimo, he builds powerfully and exuberantly and then creates a feeling of elegy in the closing pages. For I.M. these performances are unsurpassed; at its very reasonable price, this forte reissue is an almost obligatory purchase for any dedicated Brahmsian.

Symphony No. 1 in C min., Op. 68.
500♪ (M) *** DG 447 408-2 [id.]. BPO, Karajan – SCHUMANN: *Symphony No. 1.* ***

Symphony No. 1 in C min., Op. 68; Tragic overture, Op. 81.
*(*) Teldec/Warner Dig. 4509 90883-2 [id.]. NYPO, Kurt Masur.

Symphony No. 1; Tragic overture; Variations on a theme of Haydn, Op. 56a.
(M) **(*) Ph. 454 133-2 [id.]. Concg. O, Haitink.

Karajan's 1964 recording of Brahms's *First Symphony* seems by general consensus to be regarded as his finest, and the result is very powerful. The remastering has restored the original full, well-balanced, analogue sound, with plenty of weight in the bass (as is obvious at the timpani-dominated opening), yet detail is firmer.

As an interpretation, Haitink's performance with the Concertegebouw Orchestra from the early 1970s stands up well. It is a strong, well-argued reading of considerable power, supported by first-class orchestral playing. Haitink does not observe the first-movement exposition repeat, but not everyone will object to that. The lively and well-shaped *Variations* and the excitingly volatile *Tragic overture* are an asset, and the recording is spacious and well balanced, if now somewhat sounding its age. This would have been more competitive on a bargain label.

Kurt Masur, who has secured some fine performances from the orchestra of which he is music director, is here surprisingly slack, with fast movements lacking in dramatic tension. Only the beautifully moulded slow movement reveals his usual mastery, and even that is not as hushed as it might be.

Symphony No. 2 in D, Op. 73; Academic festival overture.
*(*) Teldec/Warner Dig. 9031 77291-2 [id.]. NYPO, Kurt Masur.

Symphony No. 2; Tragic overture, Op. 81.
(M) *** Carlton Dig. 30367 00982-2 [id.]. Hallé O, Skrowaczewski.

This completes the Carlton reissue of Skrowaczewski's Hallé performances of the four Brahms symphonies, undoubtedly his finest recording achievement during his not altogether successful Manchester era. The others, equally recommendable, are available on PCD 2014 (No. 1 and *Academic festival overture*); PCD 2039 (No. 3 and the *Variations on a theme of Haydn*); and 30367 00272 (No. 4 and the *Hungarian dances Nos. 1, 3* and *10*). With beautifully open and transparent sound, Skrowaczewski and the Hallé Orchestra give a measured and restrained reading of the *Second Symphony*, unsensational, fresh and thoughtful. The opening may seem sleepy, but Skrowaczewski's broad speeds and patient manner build up increasingly as the work progresses. With exposition repeat observed and a generous fill-up, plus excellent digital recording, luminous to match the performance, it is a good bargain-priced recommendation.

Masur is better attuned to the lyrical *Second Symphony* than to No. 1, but despite some first-rate playing from the New York orchestra the result sounds too easy, again lacking in tension until the finale.

Symphonies Nos. 2–3.
500♪ (M) *** Bruno Walter Edition Sony SMK 64471 [id.]. Columbia SO, Walter.

The new Bruno Walter coupling of the *Second and Third Symphonies* is very recommendable indeed. Walter's performance of the *Second* is wonderfully sympathetic, with an inevitability, a rightness which makes it hard to concentrate on the interpretation as such, so cogent is the musical argument. Walter's pacing of the *Third* is admirable and the vigour and sense of joy which imbues the opening of the first movement (exposition repeat included) dominates throughout. The finale goes splendidly, the secondary theme given characteristic breadth and dignity, and the softening of mood for the coda sounding structurally inevitable.

Symphony No. 3 in F, Op. 90; Tragic Overture; (i) *Alto rhapsody, Op. 53.*
**(*) DG Dig. 439 887-2 [id.]. (i) Anne Sofie von Otter, Arnold Schoenberg Ch.; VPO, Levine.

Where in Levine's complete cycle the *Symphony No. 3* is coupled with No. 4, this separate issue comes with the two fill-ups, equally warm and sympathetic. Levine's treatment of the first movement is strong and urgent, warmly expressive without lingering. It is characteristic that in the hushed opening of the finale he does not start slowly, as many conductors do, but sets the tempo he means to adopt for the whole movement, instantly establishing a mood of expectancy. Glowing sound in live recording, not perfectly balanced but capturing the atmosphere of the Musikverein.

Symphony No. 3 in F, Op. 90; Variations on a theme by Haydn.
** Teldec/Warner Dig. 4509 90862-2 [id.]. NYPO, Kurt Masur.

Masur is more sympathetic in this symphony than in the others, but it is still a reading which is rather smoothed over, lacking detail and some of the bite that is really needed.

Symphonies Nos. 3 in F, Op. 90; 4 in E min., Op. 98.
500♪ (M) *** DG 437 645-2 [id.]. BPO, Karajan.
** EMI Dig. CDC5 56118-2 [id.]. LCP, Norrington.

In his 1978 recording Karajan gives superb grandeur to the opening of the *Third Symphony*. Comparing this reading with Karajan's earlier, 1964 version, one finds him more direct and strikingly more dynamic and compelling. In the *Fourth Symphony* Karajan's easy, lyrical style is fresh and unaffected and highly persuasive. The Scherzo, fierce and strong, leads to a clean, weighty account of the finale.

Using period instruments in an orchestra of the modest size that Brahms expected, Roger Norrington conducts performances which have extra lightness and clarity. Unlike his readings of Beethoven, these employ speeds no faster than we would expect today in modern-instrument performances, with results that are always clean and fresh, with string-tone sweet and clear rather than rich. Natural horns cut through the texture in such movements as the finale of No. 3 and the slow movement of No. 4, and so does the dry-toned timpani. Interpretative manners are plain and direct, even metrical, with speeds held steady, making one question whether this was indeed the way Brahms expected to hear these symphonies when there is ample evidence that nineteenth-century performances involved flexible speeds.

Symphony No. 4; Academic festival overture.
500♪ *** Erato/Warner 4509 95194-2 [id.]. Chicago SO, Barenboim.

Barenboim's Chicago reading is grippingly compulsive. He opens the first movement gently and affectionately, but the performance soon develops a compulsive lyrical power. There is a tremendous burst of energy in the coda to make the *Passacaglia*'s final apotheosis very gripping indeed. The *Academic festival overture* is unusually expansive, bringing superb playing from the Chicago brass.

(i) *Symphony No. 4;* (ii) *German Requiem, Op. 45;* (iii) *Schicksalslied, Op. 54.*
(B) **(*) EMI forte Analogue/Dig. CZS5 69518-2 (2). (i) LPO, Jochum; (ii) Jessye Norman, Jorma Hynninen; (ii–iii) BBC Symphony Ch., LPO Ch., LPO, Tennstedt.

In the *Fourth Symphony*, Jochum's very opening phrase establishes the reading as warmly affectionate and, as in Bruckner, he combines a high degree of expressive flexibility with a rapt concentration, which holds the symphonic structure strongly together. Though the orchestra is British and the LPO is in fine form, this represents the German tradition at its most communicative; more than that, however, it demonstrates Jochum's passionate feeling for Brahms, with its spirit of soaring lyricism and – in the finale especially – a strong, even irresistible forward momentum. Although the performance has its idiosyncrasies of tempo, it is highly compelling in every bar, and it is a great pity that the appeal of this inexpensive reissue is somewhat diluted by the performance of the coupling, which may not be to all tastes.

Tennstedt's is an unusually spacious view of the *Requiem*, with speeds slower than on any rival version. His dedication generally sustains them well, with a reverential manner always alert, never becoming merely monumental, though the choir's ensemble is not always perfect. Jorma Hynninen proves an excellent soloist. What does sound monumental rather than moving is Jessye Norman's solo, *Ihr habt nun Traurigkeit*, though the golden tone is glorious. The *Schicksalslied* is also given a spacious, strong performance, with the London Philharmonic Choir singing dedicatedly, and the 1984–5 digital recording is spacious to match.

Symphony No. 4; (i) *Schicksalslied, Op. 54.*
** Teldec/Warner Dig. 0630 13965-2 [id.]. NYPO, Kurt Masur; (i) with Westminster Symphonic Ch.

Masur takes a broad view of the outer movements of No. 4; like his accounts of the earlier symphonies, the performance is not really tense enough, often smoothed over. The *Schicksalslied*, with the Westminster Choir a little distant, makes an attractive coupling; but the Abbado cycle offers a whole sequence of rare and valuable couplings performed more magnetically than here.

Complete chamber music

(i; ii) *Cello sonatas Nos. 1–2;* (iii; iv) *Clarinet quintet in B min., Op. 115;* (v; vi) *Clarinet sonatas Nos. 1–2;* (v; vii) *Clarinet trio in A min., Op. 114;* (ii; viii; ix) *Horn trio in E flat, Op. 40;* (x; xi) *Piano quartets Nos. 1–3;* (iv; xii) *Piano quintet in F min., Op. 34;* (x) *Piano trios Nos. 1–4;* (xiii) *String quartets Nos. 1–3;* (iv) *String quintets Nos. 1–2; String sextets Nos. 1–2;* (ii; ix) *Violin sonatas Nos. 1–3.*
(B) *** Ph. 454 073-2 (11) [id.]. (i) Starker; (ii) Sebók; (iii) Stähr; (iv) BPO Octet (members); (v) Pieterson; (vi) H. Menuhin; (vii) Pressler, Greenhouse; (viii) Orval; (ix) Grumiaux; (x) Beaux Arts Trio; (xi) Trampler (viola); (xii) Haas; (xiii) Quartetto Italiano.

This Philips bargain box of Brahms's chamber music happily combines a series of warmly appealing recordings made in Germany with other distinguished contributions from the Beaux Arts Trio and the Quartetto Italiano. Grumiaux and Starker lead the instrumental duos with slightly less success, but Starker and Sebók compensate by their passionate and subtle response to the *Cello sonatas* (this is a Mercury recording and is discussed separately below). The Berlin performance of the *Clarinet quintet* (led by Herbert Stähr) is exceptionally beautiful, and it is faithful to Brahms's intentions, an outstanding version in every way. It is an autumnal reading, and is recorded with comparable refinement. In the *Clarinet trio* George Pieterson is the soloist, another first-rate artist, and this account with members of the Beaux Arts group offers masterly playing from all three participants, and a very well-integrated recording. The balance in the *Horn trio* is managed even more adroitly, among the most successful on record. The fine horn player, Francis Orval, seeks not to dominate but to be one of the group, and he achieves this without any loss of personality in his playing (note the richness of his contribution to the Trio of the Scherzo). The performance is warmly lyrical and completely spontaneous, with a racy finale to round off a particularly satisfying reading, never forced but deeply felt. Arthur Grumiaux's contribution is a constant pleasure, and the pianist, György Sebók, is hardly less admirable. The Beaux Arts set of *Piano trios* includes the *A major Trio*, which may or may not be authentic but which is certainly rewarding. The performances are splendid, with strongly paced, dramatic allegros, consistently alert, and with thoughtful, sensitive playing in slow movements. Characterization is positive (yet not over-forceful), and structural considerations are well judged: each reading has its own special individuality. The sound is first class. Their recording of the *Piano quartets* is bold and full-bloodedly Brahmsian in outer movements, which have splendid impetus. Thoughtful, sensitive playing in slow movements, lively tempi in allegros, characteristic musicianship plus spontaneity combine to make this set highly recommendable throughout. Not surprisingly, the *String quartets* are marvellously played by the Italian Quartet, with detail sensitively observed. The two Op. 51 *Quartets* are especially fine, with a searching and penetrating reading of the first revealing depths that elude many other performers. The Berlin Philharmonic group return for the *String quintets* and their playing is searching and artistically satisfying, combining freshness with polish, warmth with well-integrated detail. The sound, though not entirely transparent, is full, warm and well balanced. In the *Piano quintet* they are joined by the excellent Werner Haas, and this is another performance which is strongly felt, with the *Andante* combining warmth with an imaginative use of colour and dynamic contrast. They then respond readily to the glories of the *Second Sextet*, playing with warmth and eloquence. The *First* is slightly less committed but still shows a great degree of feeling. The sound has a touch of shrillness. The *Violin sonatas* bring highly musical if rather mellifluous playing from Arthur Grumiaux, expertly partnered by György

Sebók, and the overall effect is perhaps a shade bland. But this is still enjoyable, and the recording is eminently acceptable.

Cello sonatas Nos. 1 in E min., Op. 38; 2 in F, Op. 99.
500♪ *** DG Dig. 410 510-2 [id.]. Mstislav Rostropovich, Rudolf Serkin.
(M) *** Mercury 434 377-2 [id.]. Starker, Sebók – MENDELSSOHN: *Cello sonata No. 2.* ***

The partnership of the wild, inspirational Russian cellist and the veteran Brahmsian pianist on DG is a challenging one. It proves an outstanding success, with inspiration mutually enhanced, whether in the lyricism of Op. 38 or the heroic energy of Op. 99. Good if close recording.

Starker was on his finest form when he made his Mercury recordings, and he had a splendid and understanding partner in György Sebók. These highly spontaneous performances rank alongside those by Rostropovich and Serkin: they have ardour and subtlety and an impressive sense of line. The 1964 recording is very well balanced, the acoustic is warm, yet the focus is admirably clear. With an equally fine account of the Mendelssohn *D major Sonata*, the measure is greater than with most competitors, and this CD comes at mid-price.

Clarinet quintet in B min., Op. 115.
500♪ (M) *** Carlton Dig. 3036 70097-2 [id.]. Keith Puddy, Delmé Qt – DVORAK: *Quartet No. 12.* ***

Keith Puddy's warm tone is well suited to Brahms and, with spacious speeds in all four movements, this is a consistently sympathetic reading; the Carlton digital recording is equally fine, vivid and full. Excellent value.

(i) *Clarinet quintet in B min., Op. 115;* (ii) *Piano quintet in F min., Op. 34; String quintets Nos. 1 in F, Op. 88; 2 in G, Op. 111.*
500♪ (B) *** Ph. Duo 446 172-2 (2) [id.]. (i) Herbert Stähr; (ii) Werner Haas; Berlin Philharmonic Octet (members).

The Berlin performance of the *Clarinet quintet* is both beautiful and faithful to Brahms's instructions, an outstanding version in every way. The two *String quintets* are also admirably served. The performances are searching and artistically satisfying, combining freshness and polish, warmth with well-integrated detail. For the *Piano quintet* Werner Haas joins the group, and they give a strongly motivated, spontaneous account of this splendid work that is in every way satisfying. The recordings come from the early 1970s and the sound is remarkably full and warm. This is among the finest bargains in the Philips Duo list.

(i) *Clarinet quintet in B min., Op. 115. String quartet No. 2 in A min., Op. 51/2.*
*** MDG Dig. 307 079-2 [id.]. Karl Leister; Leipzig Qt.

These performances from the Leipzig Quartet, with Karl Leister in the *Clarinet quintet*, are second to none. The quartet and its distinguished soloist produce impressive results in what is surely Brahms's most serene utterance, and the *A minor Quartet* also receives an authoritative and musical performance. For those wanting this particular coupling, this disc can certainly be recommended.

Clarinet trio in A min., Op. 114.
*** Sony Dig SK 57499 [id.]. Stoltzman, Ax, Ma – BEETHOVEN: *Clarinet trio* ***; MOZART: *Clarinet trio (Kegelstatt).* **

With Stolzman, Ax and Ma, the *Clarinet trio* comes off well and finds this team in excellent form. This is now one of the most recommendable of current versions, with Stoltzman playing with great sensitivity.

Horn trio in E flat, Op. 40.
500♪ (M) *** Decca 452 887-2 [id.]. Tuckwell, Perlman, Ashkenazy (with FRANCK: *Violin sonata* ***).

A superb performance of Brahms's marvellous *Horn trio* from Tuckwell, Perlman and Ashkenazy. They realize to the full the music's passionate impulse, and the performance moves forward from the gentle opening, through the sparkling scherzo and the more introspective but still outgiving *Adagio*, to the gay and spirited finale.

(i) *Piano quartets Nos. 1 in G min., Op. 25; 2 in A, Op. 26; 3 in C min., Op. 60. Piano trio in A, Op. posth.*
500♪ (B) *** Ph. Duo 454 017-2 (2) [id.]. Beaux Arts Trio, (i) with Walter Trampler.

The Beaux Arts set of *Piano quartets* is self-recommending at Duo price, with the *A major Piano trio* thrown in as a bonus. The recording is bold and full-bloodedly Brahmsian in outer movements, which have splendid impetus. Thoughtful, sensitive playing in slow movements, lively tempi in allegros, characteristic musicianship plus spontaneity combine to make these recordings highly recommendable throughout.

Piano trios Nos. 1 in B, Op. 8; 2 in C, Op. 87; 3 in C min., Op. 101; 4 in A, Op. posth.
500♪ *** Teldec/Warner Dig. 9031 76036-2 (2) [id.]. Trio Fontenay.

Powerful, spontaneous playing with a real Brahmsian spirit, given excellent, modern recording, puts these admirable performances by the Trio Fontenay at the top of the list.

Piano trio No. 1 in B, Op. 8.
(M) (***) RCA mono 09026 61763-2 [id.]. Heifetz, Feuermann, Rubinstein – DOHNANYI: *Serenade in C;* R. STRAUSS: *Violin sonata.* (***)

A commanding performance of the *B major Trio* comes from the legendary partnership of Heifetz, Feuermann and Rubinstein. Recorded in 1941, the sound calls for considerable tolerance on the part of the listener but this is well worth extending, given the quality of the playing.

(i-ii) *Piano trios Nos. 1 in B; 2 in G; 3 in C min.;* (i) *Cello sonata No. 2 in F;* (ii) *F.A.E. Sonata: Scherzo.*
(B) *** Decca Double 448 092-2 (2) [id.]. Julius Katchen, with (i) János Starker; (ii) Josef Suk.

The Katchen/Suk/Starker recordings of the *Piano trios* and *Cello sonata* were made in The Maltings in July 1968; the *Scherzo* from the *F.A.E. Sonata* comes from the previous year and was recorded in the Kingsway Hall. The performances of the first two *Piano trios* are warm, strong and characterful, while the tough *C minor Trio* and the epic, thrustful *Cello sonata* bring a comparably spontaneous response. The *Scherzo* from the composite *F.A.E. Sonata* (written in conjunction with Schumann and Albert Dietrich as a tribute to Joachim) makes a lively end to the programme. The richness of the acoustics adds to the Brahmsian glow, and the results have a warmth that did not always characterize Katchen's recordings of Brahms. If the sound of the CD transfers is a little limited in the upper range, the ear is grateful that no artificial brightening has been applied, for it provides a real Brahmsian amplitude which is very satisfying. Highly recommended

String quartets Nos. 1 in C min.; 2 in A min., Op. 51/1–2; 3 in B flat, Op. 67.
500♪ *** EMI Dig. CDS7 54829-2 (2) [id.]. Alban Berg Qt.

On EMI, the outer quartets, the *C minor*, Op. 51/1, and the *B flat*, Op. 67, were recorded in Switzerland (in a church) and are accommodated on the first CD; the *A minor*, Op. 51/2, is from a live performance given at the Palais Yusopov in St Petersburg and is on the second CD – rather short measure these days for a full-price CD. All the same there is nothing short-measured about the performances, which have all the finesse and attack one expects from the Alban Berg Quartet along with impeccable technical address.

String quintets Nos. 1 in F, Op. 88; 2 in G, Op. 111.
*** DG Dig. 453 420-2 [id.]. Hagen Qt, Gérard Caussée.

The Hagen Quartet and Gérard Caussée give highly enjoyable accounts of the two *Quintets* and the DG engineers give them good recorded sound. No need to say more than that it can rank alongside the Raphael Ensemble on Hyperion (CDA 66804 – see our main volume) as a primary recommendation.

String quintet No. 2 in G, Op. 111.
*** Nimbus Dig. NI 5488 [id.]. Brandis Qt, with Brett Dean – BRUCKNER: *String quintet.* ***

Eminently good value. This Brandis version of the *G major Quintet* offers good value in being coupled with Bruckner's *F major Quintet* and, although it might well not be a first choice in the present work, it remains a very good performance. The Brandis are a fine quartet and they give a warm and sympathetic account of this lovely work; the Nimbus recording is natural and lifelike.

String sextets Nos. 1 in B flat, Op. 18; 2 in G, Op. 36.
** Sony Dig. SK 68252 [id.]. L'Archibudelli.

The boundaries of period-instrument performance are now being extended all the way into the late nineteenth century. Indeed we have had ensembles aping the glissandi of Elgar's orchestras in recent years. L'Archibudelli use gut strings, thus producing a translucent texture but at the expense of depth of sonority. They are scrupulously attentive to dynamic shading and phrasing generally, and are agreeably straightforward without ever losing personality. Those who want to try this approach can rest assured that these are accomplished performances. They are decently recorded too. All the same, this does not represent a challenge to the three-star recordings by the Raphael Ensemble (Hyperion CDA 66276), the Academy of St Martin-in-the-Fields (Chandos CHAN 9151) or Isaac Stern, Cho-Liang Lin, Laredo, Yo Yo Ma *et al.*, also on Sony (S2K 45820) – see our main volume.

Viola sonatas Nos. 1 in F min.; 2 in E flat, Op. 120/1–2.
500♪❀ *** Virgin/EMI Dig. VC7 59309-2 [id.]. Lars Anders Tomter, Leif Ove Andsnes (with SCHUMANN: *Märchenbilder* ***).

This young Norwegian partnership gives us the best account of these sonatas in their viola form now on CD. Theirs is playing of great sensitivity and imagination. Altogether rather special.

Viola sonatas Nos. 1 in F min.; 2 in E flat, Op. 120/1–2; (i) *2 Songs for contralto, viola and piano, Op. 91.*
*(*) DG Dig. 453 421-2 [id.]. Veronika Hagen, Paul Gulda, (i) with Iris Vermilion.

No doubts here as to the artistry of Veronika Hagen, the violist of the eponymous quartet, but her partner can sound pretty thunderous at times. The recording balance does not help matters. She is a thoughtful player and he is far from insensitive in the reflective, inward-looking moments. No challenge to Lars Anders Tomter and Leif Ove Andsnes on Virgin (VC7 59309-2), which is a first recommendation. The DG issue offers the *Two Songs*, Op. 91, instead of the Schumann *Märchenbilder* that the two Norwegian artists give us.

Violin sonatas Nos. 1 in G, Op. 78; 2 in A, Op. 100.
(B) **(*) EMI forte CZS5 69367-2 (2). Igor Oistrakh, Ginzburg – BEETHOVEN: *Archduke trio;* SCHUBERT: *Piano trio No. 1.* ***

Igor Oistrakh finds a rich tone and a fine lyrical line for two essentially lyrical works, and he is accompanied sympathetically by Anton Ginzburg. The recording of both instruments is beautiful, but the piano is backwardly balanced in a resonant acoustic and the violin is well forward. This is not disastrous, but it may irritate those who rightly consider that these are works for violin *and* piano.

Violin sonatas Nos. 1 in G, Op. 78; 2 in A, Op. 100; 3 in D min., Op. 108.
*(*) Ph. Dig. 446 709-2 [id.]. Viktoria Mullova, Piotr Anderszewski.

While no one wants to revert to the up-front violin and distant piano balance favoured in the 1970s, Piotr Anderszewski looms larger in the aural picture than Viktoria Mullova. Her playing has elegance and sweetness of tone, though by comparison with such partnerships as Krysia Osostowicz and Susan Tomes (Hyperion CDA 66465, our first choice for this coupling) there is a certain coolness. Mullova sounds both unengaged and unengaging.

PIANO MUSIC

Piano music, 4 hands: *Hungarian dances Nos. 1–21* (complete); *Liebeslieder waltzes, Op. 52; Waltzes, Op. 39.*
(B) ** EMI forte CZS5 69311-2 (2). Michel Béroff and Jean-Philippe Collard – DVORAK: *Slavonic dances.* **

Béroff and Collard are crisp and unlingering in a characteristically French way: these are sparkling performances which are freshly convincing rather than charming. Some Brahmsians may prefer a more relaxed approach, but the urgency of these brilliant, young-at-the-time French pianists is infectious. The 1973–4 recording of the *Hungarian dances* is bright and clearly chiselled, rather hard, but there is warmth of timbre too. The recordings of the two sets of *Waltzes* date from six years later but are disappointingly clangorous, much more clattery on top, though the recording venue is the same.

Hungarian dances Nos. 1, 2, 5 & 17; Liebeslieder waltzes, Op. 52a; Neue Liebeslieder waltzes, Op. 75a; 16 Waltzes, Op. 39.
(B) ** Cal. Approche Dig. CAL 6219 [id.]. Inger Södergren, Fernanda Soares.

A generous bargain selection of Brahms's four-handed piano music, including the *Liebeslieder waltzes*, which are often coaxed quite seductively. The *Hungarian dances* and *Waltzes* also go well and certainly are not without sparkle, even if they are not perhaps really distinctive. The digital recording is bright and faithful.

Solo piano music

7 Fantasias, Op. 116; 3 Intermezzi, Op. 117; 8 Piano pieces, Op. 76; 6 Piano pieces, Op. 118; 4 Piano pieces, Op. 119
(B) *** EMI forte CZS5 69521-2 (2). Alexeev – SCHUMANN: *Etudes symphoniques.* ***

Dmitri Alexeev enjoys the advantage of really first-class piano-sound, full-bodied and totally natural and truthful. The piano timbre is rich, slightly bass-orientated, but eminently suitable for Brahms. Alexeev's playing has authority and he produces an ideally weighted sonority with the correct blend of colour. He brings the right kind of tenderness and insight to the quieter pieces. His mastery of rubato is consummate, and these performances generally hold their own with any now before the public. With its excellent Schumann coupling this is very highly recommendable.

3 Intermezzi, Op. 117; 6 Pieces, Op. 118; 2 Rhapsodies, Op. 79.
(B) **(*) Cal. Approche CAL 6679 [id.]. Inger Södergren.

Inger Södergren's Brahms is imaginative and poetic: her performances of the three *Intermezzi* are enticingly intimate, while there is a commanding volatility and passion in the *Rhapsodies*. She brings out all the colour of the Op. 118 *Pieces* and captures their variety of mood and atmosphere. The analogue recording is truthful but with a touch of hardness at fortissimo levels.

Piano sonatas Nos. 1 in C, Op. 1; 2 in F sharp min., Op. 2; 3 in F min., Op. 5; Variations and fugue on a theme of Handel, Op. 24; Bach: Chaconne in D min., transcribed for the left hand.
* DG Dig. 449 182-2 [id.]. Anatol Ugorski.

When DG were recompiling their Brahms Edition, they replaced Krystian Zimerman's admirable accounts of the *Piano sonatas* with these new recordings by the Russian pianist, Anatol Ugorski. Neither his virtuosity nor his mastery of keyboard colour can be questioned but, as in his account of Beethoven's Op. 111 *Sonata*, he is prone to self-conscious agogic eccentricity. This rules the *F minor Sonata* out of court, where he really does linger and languish too long. The piano is in absolutely first-class condition (which is not always the case on record), though the DG sound is at times less ideal in focus and a trace clangorous. Our recommendation for the first two *Sonatas* remains with Sviatoslav Richter (DG 436 457-2), and Clifford Curzon is hard to beat in the *F minor* (Decca 448 578-2, admirably coupled with Schubert's masterly final *Sonata in B flat major*).

Piano sonata No. 3; Intermezzi: in E flat, Op. 117/1; in C, Op. 119/3.
500♪ (M) *** Decca 448 578-2 [id.]. Clifford Curzon – SCHUBERT: *Piano sonata No. 21.* ***

Piano sonata No. 3 in F min., Op. 5; Theme and variations in D min. (from *String sextet, Op. 18*).
(M) *** Decca 448 129-2 [id.]. Radu Lupu – SCHUBERT: *Sonata No. 5* etc. ***

Curzon's account of the *F minor Sonata* is special. His approach is both perceptive and humane, and his playing has great intensity and freshness. Curzon was at his peak, powerful and sensitive and, above all, spontaneous-sounding, both in the *Sonata* and in the two *Intermezzi* which act as encores.

Noble, dignified and spacious are the adjectives that spring to mind when listening to Lupu's Op. 5. If he does not have the youthful ardour of a Kocsis, there is a reflective feeling that more than makes up for this, especially in the memorable account of the *Andante*. Lupu's view is inward, ruminative and always beautifully rounded. The arrangement of the slow-movement theme and variations from the *B flat major String sextet* was made by the composer and presented to Clara Schumann as a forty-first birthday present in 1860. In Lupu's hands the transcription seems tailor-made for the piano. The 1981 digital recording is most realistic, the piano set slightly back, the timbre fully coloured and the focus natural.

VOCAL MUSIC

(i–ii) *Alto Rhapsody, Op. 53;* (ii) *Begrabnisgesang, Op. 13; Gesang der Parzen, Op. 89;* (iii) *Geistlicheslied, Op. 30;* (iv) *2 Motets, Op. 29;* (iii) *2 Motets, Op. 74; 3 Motets, Op. 110;* (ii) *Nänie, Op. 82;* (v) *Rinaldo, Op. 50;* (ii) *Song of Destiny (Schicksalslied), Op. 54.*
(B) *** Decca Double Dig./Analogue 452 582-2 (2) [id.]. (i) Jard van Nes; (ii) San Francisco Ch. and SO, Blomstedt; (iii) New English Singers, Preston; (iv) King's College, Cambridge, Ch., Cleobury; (v) James King, Ambrosian Ch., New Philh. O, Abbado.

The recordings of the five key choral works here, the *Alto Rhapsody*, *Begrabnisgesang* (Funeral hymn), *Gesang der Parzen* (*Song of the Fates*), *Nänie* and the *Song of Destiny* (*Schicksalslied*), come from an outstanding 1989 collection using the Davis Symphony Hall, San Francisco, where the Decca team have made many outstanding records. This is no exception and, with inspired singing from the splendid San Francisco Choir, darkly intense in the rare and memorable *Funeral hymn*, exultant at the opening of *Nänie* and reaching a glorious climax. The *Song of the Fates* invites a more subtle approach, especially in the matter of light and shade, but is also very dramatically expansive, and Blomstedt and his choristers are not found wanting. The programme is capped by Jard van Nes's superbly eloquent and moving account of the *Alto rhapsody*, which can stand alongside the famous versions from Dame Janet Baker and Kathleen Ferrier, although it is different from either; again the choral contribution is splendid. Throughout, the glowing support from the orchestra, especially the lower strings, adds to the character of these performances and there is no finer collection of Brahms's shorter choral works in the catalogue. The King's College Choir under Cleobury then follows on with the two lovely *a cappella* five-part Motets of Op. 29, the second of which, *Schaffe in mir, Gott, ein rein Herz* ('Create in me a clean heart, O God'), is a partial setting of Psalm 51. Both these earlier (1860) Brahms settings pay tribute to the Bach tradition, whereas the later motets of Op. 74 (1877) and especially the three of Op. 110 (1889) look forward as well as backward in style. The first of Op. 74 with its questioning *Warum?* ('Wherefore is light given?') is the most ambitious of all, the second a set of choral variations on an Advent hymn. The final set here, Op. 110, is scored for double chorus. Here the second of the three is the most traditional; the third brings vigorous interchanges between the two groups. The *Geistliches Lied* is given a serene organ accompaniment; it is in fact a double canon, but the listener is hardly aware of its underlying structural mastery, so simply do the parts flow and interweave, with an exultant outpouring on the final 'Amen'. The final item on the second disc is the most substantial and the least satisfactory. James King's rather coarse Heldentenor approach to the 40-minute cantata *Rinaldo* is less than ideal for music that is much more easily lyrical than Wagner. However, again this is rare repertoire, and there is excellent singing from the Ambrosian Chorus, and Abbado ensures that the performance overall is fairly convincing. In any case the rest of the content of this set is more than worth its asking price.

German Requiem, Op. 45.

500♪ ❁ *** Ph. Dig. 432 140-2 [id.]. Margiono, Gilfry, Monteverdi Ch., ORR, Gardiner.

** HM Dig. HMC 901608 [id.]. Oelze, Finley, Chapelle Royale, Ghent Coll. Vocale, O des Champs Elysées, Herreweghe.

Gardiner's 'revolutionary' account of the *German Requiem* brings a range of choral sound even more thrilling than in the concert hall. Charlotte Margiono makes an ethereal soprano soloist, while Rodney Gilfry, despite a rapid vibrato, is aptly fresh and young-sounding. One could not ask for a more complete renovation of a masterpiece often made to sound stodgy and square.

In a live recording from Montreux, with two excellent young soloists, using his exceptionally sweet-sounding period orchestra and with a modest-sized choir, Herreweghe conducts a performance which avoids extremes. More than his period-style rivals he adopts traditional speeds and a conventional approach, while finding extra lightness of texture. Anyone fancying such an approach will not be disappointed, but this is a performance, live as it is, which rather lacks fervour, as for example in the choral cries of *mit Freuden* ('with joy') in the opening number. And even the soprano Christiane Oelze, with her lovely silvery tone, sounds more detached than she usually does. Good, atmospheric sound, though both soloists are set less forwardly than usual in a slightly reverberant acoustic.

Braunfels, Walter (1882–1954)

Die Vögel (complete).

*** Decca Dig. 448 679-2 (2) [id.]. Kwon, Wottrich, Kraus, Holzmair, Görne, Berlin R. Ch., German SO, Berlin, Lothar Zagrosek.

In contrast with most issues in Decca's 'Entartete Musik' series, this charming opera, based on Aristophanes' *The Birds*, brings warm, uncomplicated music, setting no problems. The idiom is from the late nineteenth century rather than the twentieth, yet the innocence of the writing and the clarity of the composer's own libretto avoid any feeling of sentimentality. Bruno Walter, who conducted the first performance in Munich in 1920, remembered it many years later as a work which had 'given value to life', and with its richness and beauty that sums it up. It had phenomenal success in the early 1920s but, with Braunfels condemned by the Nazis, it was totally neglected from the 1930s and was never revived until the 1990s, 40 years after the composer's death.

The very opening magically introduces the Nightingale, a coloratura role sung at the first performance by Maria Ivogun. Another ravishing sequence is the long duet, which opens Act II, between the Nightingale and Good Hope, a tenor role beautifully sung by Endrik Wottrich. Helen Kwon as the Nightingale sings not just brilliantly but with sensuous beauty and a formidable range of tone. The rest of the cast could hardly be bettered, with such outstanding singers as Wolfgang Holzmair and Matthias Görne in smaller roles. Zagrosek conducts a glowing performance, superbly played and recorded.

Bridge, Frank (1879–1941)

(i) *Enter spring* (rhapsody); (ii) *Summer* (tone-poem).

(B) ** BBC Radio Classics 15656 91752 [id.]. (i) BBC SO, Groves; (ii) BBC Concert O, Ashley Lawrence – BRITTEN: *Spring Symphony.* **

These two orchestral pieces, among the finest that Bridge ever wrote, make an apt coupling for Rozhdestvensky's Prom performance of Britten's *Spring Symphony*, even though the recording quality is variable.

2 Poems for orchestra.
(B) ** BBC Radio Classics BBCRD 9129. BBC N. SO, Del Mar – BRITTEN: *Sinfonia da Requiem* etc. **

These two orchestral pieces 'after Richard Jeffries' find Frank Bridge at his most imaginative and inspired. They alone are worth the modest price of the disc. There is no alternative version, and Norman Del Mar gives excellent accounts of them. The recording, made in 1977, suffers from the unflattering acoustic of the then BBC Manchester studios, but is fully acceptable.

There is a willow grows aslant a brook.
(M) **(*) EMI Dig. CDM7 64200-2 [id.]. ECO, Jeffrey Tate – BAX: *3 Pieces;* BUTTERWORTH: *Banks of green willow; Idylls;* MOERAN: *2 Pieces.* **(*)

Bridge's 'Impression for small orchestra', *There is a willow grows aslant a brook*, is a masterpiece of evocation that yet completely avoids English cliché, bringing many indications of the composer's later development. It makes a welcome item in Tate's English collection, beautifully if not quite magically done in warm and refined sound.

String quartets Nos. 2 in G min.; 3.
*** Mer. Dig. CDE 843111 [id.]. Bridge Qt.

As more of Bridge's music comes to be recorded, so his stature seems to grow greater. His series of four quartets may one day come to be seen as a landmark of English chamber music. No. 2, written in 1915, immediately captures the listener's attention and brings together a sequence of movements thematically linked, each of which has a wide range of moods and tempi, phantasy-style. The central Scherzo represents the work's kernel. There is no slow movement as such, but the result is beautifully balanced and well worked out, with really memorable ideas, to produce a satisfying and original structure, yet music which is immediately communicative. The *Third Quartet*, written a decade after the *Second*, marks a radical change in Bridge's compositional style. It was at exactly this period that Benjamin Britten as a boy became his pupil and benefited enormously from his master's concentration on self-discipline, which is shown so readily in the highly organized and at times densely textured first movement. The writing, without being strictly atonal, shows affinities with the Second Viennese School, yet, after the intensity of the argument and a haunting central *Andante*, the work has a valedictory close. The two quartets are superbly played by this eponymous group, who are right inside the music and present it with an almost improvisational spontaneity. The recording is first class, with fine body to the sound as well as a convincing interplay of detail.

Britten, Benjamin (1913–76)

An American overture; Canadian carnival, Op. 19; Sinfonia da Requiem, Op. 20; Suite on English folksongs (A time there was . . .), Op. 90; The Young person's guide to the orchestra (Variations and fugue on a theme of Purcell), Op. 34.
*** EMI Dig. CDC5 55394-2 [id.]. CBSO, Rattle.

Although concentrating on early works, this collection spans Britten's composing career. Both the *Sinfonia da Requiem* (1940) and the *American overture* (1941) with its attractive whiff of Copland belong to the composer's wartime residency in the USA. The *Suite on English folksongs* was not completed until 1974, although one movement, the quirky *Hankin Booby* (for wind and drums), dates from 1966, a commission for the opening of the Queen Elizabeth Hall in London. While the most ambitious piece is the *Sinfonia da Requiem*, written after the death of Britten's parents, the *Folksongs suite* is a good deal more diverse in mood than one might expect, with the eloquent last movement, *Lord Melbourne*, with its beautiful cor anglais evocation, the longest and most memorable. The whole programme is splendidly played by the City of Birmingham orchestra under Simon Rattle. His passionate view of the *Sinfonia da Requiem* is unashamedly extrovert, yet it finds subtle detail too. All these recordings come from the 1980s, but *The Young person's guide to the orchestra* is a brand-new (1995) recording, and the performance has the freshness of new discovery – a performance to match and even surpass the composer's own Decca version. The ravishingly played oboe variation is matched by the elegiac eloquence of the violas while the violins dance engagingly and the harp creates a magical evocation. The closing fugue has fine impetus and, as Purcell's tune re-emerges majestically, Rattle ensures that the contrapuntal texture is not overwhelmed. The recording is admirably vivid throughout.

An American overture; (i) *King Arthur suite* (arr. Hindmarsh); (i–ii) *The World of the Spirit* (cantata).
*** Chandos Dig. CHAN 9487 [id.]. BBC PO, Hickox, with (i) Britten Singers; (ii) Hannah Gordon, Cormac Rigby, Donald Mitchell, Philip Reed.

Since Britten died, a whole range of his music has been brought out of the cupboard, mostly written in the 1930s. The two main works here both derive from music written for radio productions, an epic dramatization of the *King Arthur* story by D. G. Bridson in 1937 and the religious cantata, *The World of the Spirit*, in 1938, using a sequence of texts prepared by R. Ellis Roberts. Though the mature Britten style is identifiable only occasionally, the invention and imagination are characteristic from first to last, for these are the inspirations of a prolific young composer rising to early challenges. The fanfares which open the *King Arthur* music – here assembled into four self-contained movements by Paul Hindmarsh – have the flavour of the film music of the period, but with a clear, Britten-like slant, and each of the four movements is equally strongly characterized. The religious cantata, *The World of the Spirit*, follows the pattern of *The Company of Heaven* of the previous year, but the wide range of texts prompts Britten to use an astonishing range of techniques, starting with plainsong (*Veni creator spiritus*) set in a diatonic frame and even continuing with a Bach-like chorale. The result is a fascinating mosaic of contrasting elements, culminating at the end of the second of the three parts in an open imitation of Walton's *Belshazzar's Feast*, a work which Britten admired on hearing the first performance in 1931. The repeated brass notes and the *Alleluias* could not be closer to that model. The dozen or so spoken links, beautifully delivered by Hannah Gordon and Cormac Rigby, are drawn from wide-ranging and often unexpected sources. Full texts are given; but just as useful is the sharply perceptive musical commentary of Donald Mitchell and Philip Reed. *An American overture* – written during the composer's exile in the USA in 1941 and more typical of the mature Britten – was rediscovered in his lifetime but was not performed until 1983, a good companion-piece to the radio-inspired works. First-rate singing from soloists and choir alike in the cantata, helped by full and rich recording.

Piano concerto in D, Op. 13.
(B) ** Millennium MCD 80116. Marjorie Mitchell, N. German RSO, Strickland – BORTKIEWICZ: *Piano concerto No. 1;* BUSONI: *Indian fantasy*. **

A good performance of the *Piano concerto*, which must have been recorded in the late 1950s or early 1960s. The sleeve is unforthcoming as to its actual provenance. It is decently recorded but is far from a first choice, given the modestly priced account available from Richter and Britten on Decca (417 308-2, an admirable recommendation if you also want the *Violin concerto*) and the quality of the premium-priced alternatives listed in our main volume, of which the finest comes from Joanna MacGregor (on Collins 1102-2). Some collectors may want the present disc for the Busoni; as a bonus item the Britten is perfectly acceptable.

Violin concerto, Op. 15 (original version).
(M) (**) EMI mono CDM5 66053-2 [id.]. Theo Olof, Hallé O, Barbirolli – HEMING: *Threnody;* RUBBRA: *Symphony No. 5; Improvisations*. (***)

Allowances have to be made for the quality of this première recording, made by the young Dutch virtuoso, Theo Olof, and the Hallé Orchestra under Barbirolli in 1948, which makes its first appearance on CD. Perhaps knowing that he was at work on a revised version of the score, Britten never sanctioned its release, though he can surely have entertained no doubts as to the virtuosity and dedication of the soloist or of Sir John, who had championed the piece in his New York days. Certainly worth hearing, but not a prime recommendation – the quality of sound is a handicap.

(i) *Violin concerto, Op. 15. Canadian carnival overture, Op. 19; Mont Juic* (written with Lennox Berkeley).
500♪ ❀ *** Collins Dig. 1123-2 [id.]. (i) Lorraine McAslan, ECO, Steuart Bedford.

Lorraine McAslan's virtuosity is effortless and always subservient to musical ends; her artistic insights are unusually keen and she brings to the *Concerto* a subtle imagination and great emotional intensity. Steuart Bedford gets first-class playing from the English Chamber Orchestra and emphasizes the pain and poignancy underlying much of this music. *Mont Juic* and the *Canadian carnival overture* are eminently well served by these splendid musicians and the engineers.

(i) *Diversions for piano (left hand) and orchestra, Op. 21;* (ii) *Sinfonia da Requiem, Op. 20;* (iii) *The Young person's guide to the orchestra, Op. 34.*
(B) **(*) Sony SBK 62746; *SBT 62746* [id.]. (i) Leon Fleisher, Boston SO, Ozawa; (ii) St Louis SO, Previn; (iii) LSO, Andrew Davis.

The *Diversions* is a wartime work, highly inventive and resourceful, whose neglect over the years is puzzling. Fleisher lost the use of his right hand at the height of his career, so Britten's *Diversions* is custom-made for him. He gives a sensitive and intelligent account with great sympathy and skill. His playing has strong character and he receives more than decent support from Ozawa and the Boston orchestra, and eminently truthful recording. Previn's coupling is also worth having at bargain price. It is obviously deeply felt; if not quite a match for the composer's own, it has a well-detailed (1963) recording. To complete the disc, Andrew Davis directs an account of *The Young person's guide to the orchestra* that is bright and workmanlike rather than one with any special flair or brilliance. But it is enjoyable enough and the (1975) Abbey Road recording sounds well on CD.

(i; ii) *Lachrymae (Reflections on a song by Dowland);* (i) *Prelude and fugue, Op. 29; Simple Symphony, Op. 4; Variations on a theme of Frank Bridge, Op. 10;* (ii) *Elegy for solo viola.*
500♪ ❁ *** Virgin/EMI Dig. VC5 45121-2. (i) Norwegian CO, Iona Brown; (ii) Lars Anders Tomter.

Iona Brown gives performances of the *Simple Symphony* and the *Frank Bridge variations* to match and almost surpass the composer's own. The *Simple Symphony* fizzes with youthful energy and the poignant *Sentimental sarabande* elevates Britten's writing far beyond any suggestion of juvenilia. The *Playful pizzicato* has a splendid bounce. The *Frank Bridge variations* have never sounded more emotionally powerful on record and, after the opening flourish, the raptly quiet playing of the solo strings draws a parallel with the Vaughan Williams *Tallis fantasia*. The starkness of the *Funeral march* compares with the famous Karajan/Philharmonia version in its intensity, and in the following *Chant* the Norwegian players show they understand all about icy landscapes. In the *Lachrymae* Lars Anders Tomter is an outstanding soloist. He follows with an ardent account of the solo *Elegy*. The recording is in the demonstration bracket.

The Prince of the Pagodas (complete).
500♪ ❁ *** Virgin/EMI Dig. VCD7 59578-2 (2). L. Sinf., Knussen.

The multicoloured instrumentation – much influenced by Britten's visit to Bali – is caught with glorious richness in Oliver Knussen's really complete version. Most importantly he opens out more than 40 cuts, most of them small, which Britten sanctioned to fit his own recording on to four LP sides. The performance is outstanding and so is the recording.

Sinfonia da Requiem; Gloriana: symphonic suite; Peter Grimes: 4 Sea interludes and Passacaglia.
500♪ *** Collins Dig. 1019 2 [id.]. LSO, Bedford.

(i) *Sinfonia da Requiem, Op. 20;* (ii) *Gloriana: suite;* (i) *Peter Grimes: Passacaglia.*
(B) ** BBC Radio Classics BBCRD 9129. (i) BBC SO, Rozhdestvensky; (ii) BBC N. SO, Del Mar (with PART: *Cantus in memory of Benjamin Britten*) – BRIDGE: *2 Poems for orchestra.* **

In his Britten series for Collins, Steuart Bedford conducts strong, idiomatic performances of these works, helped by exceptionally vivid recording. The atmosphere of the *Peter Grimes Interludes* is caught superbly, and the *Sinfonia da Requiem*, treated expansively, culminates in a radiant account of the final *Requiem aeternam*.

Rozhdestvensky's account of the *Sinfonia da Requiem* was recorded while the BBC Symphony Orchestra were on tour in 1981, the only version of the work to be recorded in Japan, 'its onlie beggetter', as it were, the country which commissioned it! It is very good without in any way upstaging existing recommendations listed in our main volume, notably the composer's Decca disc (425 100-2), Rattle's very passionate view (EMI CDC7 64870-2) or Steuart Bedford's fine disc with the LSO. Rozhdestvensky's *Passacaglia* from *Peter Grimes* emanates from a concert in London's Royal Festival Hall in 1978, and is also eminently well played. The *Gloriana* suite was recorded in the BBC's Manchester studios the preceding year. All are satisfactory performances and well-balanced recordings and are worth the asking price. A small pendant is Arvo Pärt's *Cantus in memory of Benjamin Britten*, heard at its first performance in a 1979 Prom and eloquently done.

Variations and fugue on a theme by Frank Bridge; Young person's guide to the orchestra; Peter Grimes: 4 Sea interludes & Passacaglia.
500♪ *** Teldec/Warner Dig. 9031 73126 [id.]. BBC SO, Andrew Davis.

Andrew Davis gives full weight as well as brilliance to these masterpieces from early in Britten's career, making a particularly attractive triptych. The *Frank Bridge variations*, set here against the more popular Purcell set, gain particularly from large-scale treatment, with each variation strongly characterized. Excellent recording.

The Young person's guide to the orchestra (Variations and fugue on a theme of Purcell), Op 34.
(M) **(*) Decca Phase Four 444 104-2 [id.]. Sean Connery (nar.), RPO, Dorati – PROKOFIEV: *Peter and the wolf* etc. **(*)

** Cala Dig. CACD 1022 [id.]. Ben Kingsley (nar.), LSO, Mackerras – DUKAS: *L'apprenti sorcier;* PROKOFIEV: *Peter and the wolf.* **

Sean Connery's voice is very familiar and his easy style is attractive. His narration should go down well with young people, even if some of the points are made rather heavily. The orchestral playing is first rate and the vivid, forwardly balanced recording – with a Decca Phase Four source – is effective enough in this context. The performance has plenty of colour and vitality.

Alongside Connery, Ben Kingsley's exposition of the character of the orchestral instruments sounds very matter-of-fact, almost like a kindly professor lecturing his students; although the LSO provide admirable instrumental illustrations, it is only at the end, when Mackerras gives them their head in the brilliant closing fugue, that the performance really fires up.

CHAMBER MUSIC

Cello suites (Suites for unaccompanied cello) Nos. 1, Op. 72; 2, Op. 80; 3, Op. 87.
*** Decca Dig. 444 181-2 [id.]. Robert Cohen.
**(*) Hyperion Dig CDA 66274 [id.]. Tim Hugh.
(BB) ** Naxos Dig. 8.553663 [id.]. Tim Hugh.

The *Cello suites* were all written for Rostropovich, and his recording has special claims on the collector. He offers inspired accounts of the first two *Suites*, coupled with the *Cello sonata* (Decca 421 859-2). Among later versions, the fine Swedish cellist, Torleif Thedéen (on BIS CD 446), also demands attention. Robert Cohen is a commanding performer and his version of all three *Suites* is satisfyingly musical and thoughtful. He has the advantage of superbly natural recorded sound, with plenty of air round the instrument and the balance not too close.

Tim Hugh earlier recorded the three Britten *Suites* for Hyperion, but since then (1987) his view of them seems to have changed radically. His Naxos version is no less than nine minutes shorter overall, with speeds faster both in allegros and andantes. The manner is also more clearly dramatic, strong and positive, though the meditative depth of the earlier account is largely missing. The result is taut and tough – as if he is keen to de-gentrify Britten's muse. At times he is in just a little bit too much of a hurry, but there is plenty of spirit and fire. However, the Hyperion sound is fuller and better focused than the slightly reverberant Naxos, which is otherwise good value.

(i) *Lachrymae, Op. 48a. Movement for wind sextet*; (ii) *Night Mail* (end sequence). *Sinfonietta; The Sword in the Stone* (concert suite for wind and percussion); (iii) *Phaedra, Op. 93.*
*** Hyperion Dig. CDA 66845 [id.]. (i) Roger Chase; (ii) Nigel Hawthorne; (iii) Jean Rigby; Nash Ens, Lionel Friend.

Using different groupings for each work, the Nash Ensemble here offers a fascinating collection of neglected Britten works, mostly from the 1930s but starting with his last piece for solo voice, the scena *Phaedra*, which he wrote for Dame Janet Baker. Jean Rigby sings beautifully but lacks the biting intensity which Dame Janet brought to this vividly dramatic piece. *Lachrymae*, for viola with string accompaniment, also dates from Britten's very last years, an adaptation of a piece written in 1950 for William Primrose, played here with the beauty intensified, thanks to the firm, true playing of Roger Chase. Both the *Sinfonietta* of 1932 (with hints of Schoenbergian influence) and the *Wind sextet* movement of 1930 are astonishingly accomplished for a teenage composer, but they reflect the mature Britten style only occasionally, while the concert suite for wind and percussion was drawn from music for a radio production of T. H. White's ironic Arthurian piece, *The Sword in the Stone*, and brings some delightful Wagner parodies. It is also good to have the final sequence from Britten's music for the GPO film documentary, *Night Mail*, with Auden's rattling verse spoken by Nigel Hawthorne, the music so much more vivid here than on the original soundtrack. Excellent playing from the Nash Ensemble, and first-rate recording.

(i) *String quartets Nos. 1 in D, Op. 25; 2 in C, Op. 36; 3, Op. 94; String quartet in D; Quartettino; Alla marcia; 3 Divertimenti; Rhapsody* (all for string quartet); (ii) *Elegy for solo viola;* (i; iii) *Phantasy for oboe and string trio, Op. 2;* (i; iv) *Phantasy in F min. for string quintet.*
500♪ (M) *** EMI Dig. CMS5 65115-2. (i) Endellion Qt; (ii) Garfield Jackson; (iii) Douglas Boyd; (iv) Nicholas Logie.

In addition to the three mature *Quartets* which are familiar to collectors, this set brings a number of early works, many of which are completely new (although some have appeared in alternative versions since this EMI compilation first appeared in 1987). The *Phantasy quintet* for strings comes from 1932, the same year as the eloquent *Oboe Phantasy quartet*; one is taken aback by the sheer fertility of its invention and the abundance of his imagination. The playing throughout is as responsive and intelligent as one could wish for. In the three published *Quartets* both performances and recordings are exemplary.

String quartet No. 3, Op. 94.
❀ *** Koch Dig. 3-6436-2 [id.]. Medici Qt – JANACEK: *Quartet No. 1;* RAVEL: *Quartet;* SHOSTAKOVICH: *Quartet No. 8;* SMETANA: *Quartet No. 1.* *** ❀

The Medici Quartet, in inspired form, are totally involved in Britten's valedictory utterance in this medium, with its rarefied atmosphere and ethereal slow movement, where Paul Robertson's *Solo* creates a haunted atmosphere, at once austere and powerfully communicative. The *Burlesque* is splendidly robust and the long final *Passacaglia* is sustained with complete concentration. The recording, like the playing, gives the impression of live music-making at the end of the listener's room.

VOCAL MUSIC

A Ceremony of carols; Deus in adjutorium meum; Hymn of St Columba; Hymn to the Virgin; Jubilate Deo in E flat; Missa brevis, Op. 63.
500♪ *** Hyperion Dig. CDA 66220 [id.]. Westminster Cathedral Ch., David Hill; (i) with S. Williams; J. O'Donnell (organ).

Particularly impressive here is the boys' singing in the *Ceremony of carols*, where the ensemble is superb, the solo work amazingly mature, and the range of tonal colouring a delight. Along with the other, rarer pieces, this is an outstanding collection, beautifully and atmospherically recorded.

A Ceremony of carols; Festival Te Deum; Jubilate Deo!; A Hymn of Saint Columba; Hymn to Saint Peter; Hymn to the Virgin; Missa brevis in D; A New Year carol; A Shepherd's carol; Sweet was the sound.
500♪ *** Collins Dig. 1370-2 [id.]. The Sixteen, Harry Christophers.

With bright-toned sopranos taking the place of boy trebles, Harry Christophers directs superbly incisive, refreshingly dramatic performances of all these works, giving extra bite even to so well-known a piece as the *Ceremony of carols*. The delightful *Missa brevis* has never been more telling, and the shorter pieces all confirm Britten's mastery in choral writing. Excellent sound, both warm and well detailed.

(i) *A ceremony of carols;* (ii) *Shepherd's carol; A Boy was born; Jesus, as Thou art our Saviour.*
(M) *** ASV CDWHL 2097 [id.]. Christ Church Cathedral Ch., Francis Grier; (i) with Frances Kelly; (ii) Harry Bicket (with Collection: *'Carols from Christ Church'* ***).

A first-class account of Britten's *Ceremony of carols*, attractively vigorous, full of the right sort of rhythmic energy. There is an earthy quality which reflects the composer's own rejection of over-refined choirboy tone, yet the two treble solos, the delicate *That yongë child* (Andrew Olleson) and *Balulalow* (Edward Harris), are both delicate, and the latter soloist is radiantly assured, as he is in *Jesus, as Thou art our Saviour*. The dialogue *Shepherd's carol* is also sung most effectively. The reissue is combined with a dozen other carols by various composers, mostly English, making for a very enticing Christmas CD.

The Holy Sonnets of John Donne, Op. 35; 7 Sonnets of Michelangelo, Op. 22; Winter words, Op. 52; The children and Sir Nameless; If it's ever spring again.
*** Collins Dig. 1468-2 [id.]. Philip Langridge, Steuart Bedford.

Following up his inspired portrayals in the principal tenor roles in the Britten operas – not least as Peter Grimes and as Aschenbach in *Death in Venice* – Philip Langridge here gives intense and dramatic performances of the three most important Britten song-cycles with piano, also originally written with Peter Pears in mind. With Steuart Bedford, Britten's long-time collaborator, as accompanist, this reading of the Donne sonnet-cycle is marked by high contrasts of dynamic and tone, so that one hears echoes of Grimes's music. In the other two cycles Langridge is just as expressive but is generally lighter in manner, certainly than Pears in his recordings. Valuably, Langridge adds two more Hardy settings, originally intended for *Winter words* but which neither fit the main pattern nor quite match the rest in imagination. Well-balanced sound.

(i) *Les Illuminations* (song-cycle), *Op. 18;* (ii) *Nocturne;* (iii) *Serenade for tenor, horn and strings, Op. 31.*
500♪ (M) *** Decca 436 395-2 [id.]. (i–iii) Peter Pears; (i) ECO; (ii) wind soloists; (ii; iii) LSO strings, composer; (iii) with Barry Tuckwell.

With dedicated accompaniments under the composer's direction, these Pears versions of *Les Illuminations* and the *Serenade* (with its horn obbligato superbly played by Barry Tuckwell) make a perfect coupling. For the CD release Decca have added the recording of the *Nocturne* from 1960. It is a work full – as is so much of Britten's output – of memorable moments. Pears, as always, is the ideal interpreter, the composer a most efficient conductor, and the fiendishly difficult obbligato parts are played superbly.

Spring Symphony.
(M) **(*) Revelation RV 10010 [id.]. Yakovenko, Postavnicheva, Mahov, Ch. & Grand USSR State SO, Rozhdestvensky – WALTON: *Viola concerto*. *
(B) ** BBC Radio Classics 15656 91752 [id.]. Harrhy, Finnie, Tear, L. Voices, Southend Boys' Ch., BBC SO & Ch., Rozhdestvensky – BRIDGE: *Enter spring; Summer*. **

(i; ii) *Spring Symphony, Op. 44;* (ii) *5 Flower songs* (for mixed chorus), *Op. 47;* (ii; iii) *Hymn to St Cecilia, Op. 27*.
*** DG Dig. 453 433-2 [id.]. (i) Alison Hagley, Catherine Robbin, John Mark Ainsley, Boy and Girl Choristers of Salisbury Cathedral, Philh. O; (ii) Monteverdi Ch.; (iii) with Preston-Dunlop, Ross, Vickers, Mitchell, Savage; Philh. O, Gardiner.

In his version of the *Spring Symphony* John Eliot Gardiner provides a striking contrast with Britten himself in what used to be counted a definitive reading. Never before on disc has there been a performance of this colourful anthology-work that so clarifies the complex textures at speeds generally flowing more briskly than usual. With Gardiner's Monteverdi Choir achieving wonders of precision both in ensemble and in shading of dynamic, this reading is far more refined than those on rival discs, including Britten's. With Gardiner drawing equally refined playing from the Philharmonia, one is made to appreciate afresh how often Britten marked pianissimos in the score; though the result is less wild and rustic-sounding in numbers like the bluff final chorus, with trebles singing 'Sumer is icumen in', the sharpness of focus and clarity, combined with clean attack, make the result intensely refreshing.

The soloists equally are fresh-toned, and the refined orchestral textures allow the words to be heard far more clearly than usual, not least in Catherine Robbin's moving account of the biggest song, the setting of Auden's 'Out on the lawn I lie in bed'. The two fill-ups also demonstrate the Monteverdi Choir's astonishing virtuosity, with the syncopated rhythms of another Auden setting, the *Hymn to St Cecilia*, superbly sprung, and with the rare *Flower Songs* sounding just as fresh.

Rozhdestvensky's Russian version of the *Spring Symphony* comes from the long-hidden archives of Moscow Radio, and it is fascinating to hear the work in Russian in a live recording made in 1963, not long after the composer's own version, for this is an invigoratingly fresh, high-voltage performance. Soloists and choirs are presented in sharp focus with no Slavonic wobbles. The boys' choir is wonderfully earthy but, sadly, is drowned by the horns in the final *Sumer is icumen in*. Though the Walton concerto suffers badly from having the viola far too close, it makes an interesting coupling, with a superstar viola player, Yuri Bashmet.

Rozhdestvensky's later version from the BBC Radio archive was recorded live at a Prom performance in 1980, and though he is again a persuasive advocate, helped by an excellent trio of soloists, with some good choral singing, the performance is much slacker, with speeds far broader. Nor is the recording as clear or well focused as the Russian one. Only worth considering if you fancy the coupling of works by Britten's teacher, Frank Bridge.

War Requiem.
(BB) ** Naxos Dig. 8.553558/9 [id.]. Russell, Randle, Volle, Scottish Festival Ch., St Mary's Episcopal Cathedral, Edinburgh, Ch., BBC Scottish SO, Brabbins (with Boddice).

(i) *War Requiem;* (ii) *Ballad of heroes, Op. 14; Sinfonia da requiem, Op. 20*.
500♪ *** Chandos Dig. CHAN 8983/4 [id.]. (i) Harper, Langridge, Shirley-Quirk, (ii) Hill; St Paul's Cathedral Choristers, London Symphony Ch., LSO & CO, Richard Hickox.

Richard Hickox's Chandos version rivals even the composer's own definitive account in its passion and perception, and must be now regarded as a first choice. Hickox thrusts home the big dramatic moments with unrivalled force, helped by the weight of the Chandos sound. Heather Harper is as golden-toned as she was at the very first Coventry performance, fearless in attack. Philip Langridge has never sung more sensitively on disc, and both he and John Shirley-Quirk bring many subtleties to their interpretations. Adding to the attractions of the set come two substantial choral works, also in outstanding performances.

The first glory of the Naxos version, on two bargain discs, is the sound, with spatial contrasts caught thrillingly and atmospherically, thanks to the recording venue. Surprisingly, Naxos chose the former engine-shed of the Harland & Wolff shipyard, now converted into a media centre. With the benefit of a cathedral-like acoustic, it was able to cope with very large forces better than any available church, and the boys' choir in particular is beautifully caught, clear but at a distance, exactly the effect the composer had in mind. The choral singing generally is excellent, vivid and immediate in the big climaxes of such sections as *Dies irae*. Under Martyn Brabbins for the full orchestral sections, and under Nigel Boddice for the chamber orchestra settings of Wilfred Owen poems, the BBC Scottish Symphony Orchestra plays with fine point and precision, underlining the drama of the piece.

The power of the whole is not in doubt, but the solo singing is less impressive, notably that of Thomas Randle who, as recorded, sounds strained and fluttery, failing to bring out the tragic intensity of the words. It is apt that a German baritone was chosen as the other male soloist, reflecting Britten's debt to Dietrich Fischer-Dieskau as the original inspiration for that role. Michael Volle has a firm, clear, if not specially distinctive baritone and, though one can hardly complain of slight mispronunciations (as in bugel for 'bugle'), he too fails to plumb the depths of the poems. Nor is the soprano, Lynda Russell, ideal for, though it is a dramatic performance, the fruity voice too often has an edge and unevenness to it.

OPERA

Albert Herring.

*** Collins Dig. 7042-2 (3) [id.]. Gillett, Barstow, Palmer, Della Jones, Taylor, Finley, Lloyd, Savidge, N. Sinfonia, Bedford.

Britten's own 33-year-old Decca recording of the comic opera, *Albert Herring*, has long seemed as definitive as could be, but here Steuart Bedford – whom Britten chose to follow him in conducting operas at Aldeburgh – presents a brilliant new recording. Not only is it fuller and more immediate in sound than the still vivid Decca original, but it also offers a performance which regularly brings out the fun of the piece even more infectiously than Britten himself did. It consistently gives the illusion of a stage comedy rather than a studio recording. Bedford has long made a speciality of conducting this opera in the theatre, a very English piece which yet amazingly has been among the most widely appreciated of Britten operas throughout the world. Bedford's practical experience makes it second nature for him to time humorous lines with delectable point. So the passage at the end of the village fête scene, where the inebriated Albert as May King gets the hiccoughs, is far funnier here with Christopher Gillett in the title-role than with Peter Pears, for whom the role was written. It helps that Gillett has a clear, youthful-sounding tenor, whereas Pears, recording in his mid-fifties, 17 years after the first performance, inevitably sounds rather old for the role of the gawky hero, however inspired his vocal acting. As Lady Billows, Josephine Barstow, with rasp in the voice, is every bit as formidable as Sylvia Fisher was before, and Felicity Palmer is wonderfully characterful as her prim housekeeper, Florence Pike. The other village worthies are also strongly cast, including Robert Lloyd as the pompous Superintendent Budd and Peter Savidge as the Vicar. The lower orders in this class-conscious story, Albert's Mum (Della Jones), Sid the butcher's boy (Gerald Finley) and Nancy (Ann Taylor), are earthier and lustier than their predecessors, with Sid and Nancy's love duets tenderly touched in. What seals the set's success is the way that in the ensembles – whether the fast chattering ones or the great Threnody when they think that Albert is dead – Bedford secures such crisp ensemble, lifting rhythms even more wittily than Britten, regularly making the music swagger.

A Midsummer Night's Dream (complete).

** Ph. Dig. 454 122-2 (2) [id.]. McNair, Asawa, Lloyd, Bostridge, Janice Watson, John Mark Ainsley, LSO, Sir Colin Davis.

Following on a brilliantly successful concert performance at the Barbican, Sir Colin Davis made his recording of *A Midsummer Night's Dream* in the same venue. The cast is a strong one, with the lovers aptly taken by generally younger, if sometimes less characterful, singers than in rival sets. The LSO play brilliantly but, thanks to a rather dry acoustic, there is little of the atmospheric magic which makes both Hickox's Virgin set and the composer's own original so compelling. Davis is also a more metrical, more literal, less freely expressive interpreter of Britten than Hickox, which does not help. In the casting there are incidental points of advantage, as in the choice of Sylvia McNair as Tytania with her pure, silver tone, and Ian Bostridge masterly in the tenor role of Flute. As Bottom it is fascinating to have the dark-toned Robert Lloyd responding strongly, with fine feeling for words, even though it is only in the Verdi parody of the play scene at the end that his timbre sounds totally apt. A serious snag is the choice of the counter-tenor, Brian Asawa, as Oberon, not nearly as characterful as James Bowman or Alfred Deller, with a marked vibrato which makes him sound not sinister but too womanly. First choice remains with the composer's own recording (Decca 425 663-2 – see our main volume).

Peter Grimes (complete).

500♪ ❁ *** Decca 414 577-2 (3) [id.]. Pears, Claire Watson, Pease, Jean Watson, Nilsson, Brannigan, Evans, Ch. and O of ROHCG, composer.

The Decca recording of *Peter Grimes* was one of the first great achievements of the stereo era. Few opera recordings can claim to be so definitive, with Peter Pears, for whom it was written, in the name-part, Owen Brannigan (another member of the original team) and a first-rate cast. Britten conducts superbly and secures splendidly incisive playing, with the whole orchestra on its toes throughout. The recording, superbly atmospheric, has so many felicities that it would be hard to enumerate them, and the Decca engineers have done wonders in making up aurally for the lack of visual effects.

Bruch, Max (1838–1920)

Double concerto in E min., for clarinet, viola and orchestra, Op. 88.
(B) *** Hyperion Dyad Dig. CDD 22017 (2) [id.]. Thea King, Nobuko Imai, LSO, Francis (with Concert – see below ***).

Bruch's *Double concerto* is a delightful work with genuinely memorable inspiration in its first two lyrical movements and a roistering finale making a fine contrast. Clarinet and viola are blended beautifully, with the more penetrating wind instrument dominating naturally and with melting phrasing from Thea King. The recording is excellent. This is part of an excellent two-disc set including other attractive concertante works by Mendelssohn, Crusell, Spohr and other less familar names.

Violin concerto No. 1 in G min., Op. 26.
(**(*)) Testament mono SBT 1083. Haendel, Philh. O, Kubelik – BEETHOVEN: *Violin concerto.* (**(*))
(BB) *(*) Naxos Dig. 8.550195 [id.]. Nishizaki, Slovak PO, Gunzenhauser – BRAHMS: *Concerto.* *

It is good to have some of Ida Haendel's magnificent violin recordings restored to the catalogue, when – being in mono – they had an unfairly short life in the regular catalogue. Her 1948 reading of the Bruch, rather like her accounts of the Brahms and Tchaikovsky, reissued earlier by Testament, combines power and great warmth, with the first movement strong and purposeful, the second passionate in its lyricism and the third brilliant and sparkling. Excellent transfer, but it is a pity this is offered at full price.

Takako Nishizaki plays the slow movement gently and sweetly, and the first movement goes quite well. But the finale lacks sparkle, and altogether this is not one of her recommendable couplings.

Violin concerto No. 2 in D min., Op. 44.
500♪ ✿ *** Delos Dig. DE 3156 [id.]. Nai-Yan Hu, Seattle SO, Schwarz – GOLDMARK: *Violin concerto.* *** ✿

As with the Goldmark coupling, Nai-Yan Hu is ideally balanced and Schwarz and the Seattle orchestra provide a highly supportive accompaniment. The composer could not understand why this very tuneful concerto was so dwarfed by the earlier, G minor work, and Hu's soaring lyrical lines underline its warmth and consistent melodic inspiration. Though Perlman strikes a high profile in his EMI version, the sympathetic warmth of this Hu/Schwarz partnership and the concert-hall fullness of the Delos recording is altogether preferable.

Kol Nidrei, Op. 47.
*** EMI Dig. CDC5 56126-2 [id.]. Han-Na Chang, LSO, Rostropovich – FAURE: *Elégie* ***; SAINT-SAENS: *Cello concerto No. 1* ***; TCHAIKOVSKY: *Rococo variations.* *** ✿
(B) ** DG 447 349-2 (2) [id.]. Fournier, LOP, Martinon – DVORAK: *Cello concerto* ***; BLOCH: *Schelomo.* **(*) (See also under Concerts.)

The phenomenally gifted thirteen-year-old Korean-born cellist, Han-Na Chang, catches the intense, somewhat plangent atmosphere of Bruch's Hebrew melody with a natural sensitivity, and her use of dynamic contrast seems instinctive. Rostropovich has said, 'I did not play as well as her at that age,' and indeed the extraordinary poise and assurance of this playing, matched by her ability to touch the listener, reminds one of the young Yehudi Menuhin. Her mentor accompanies her with great sympathy and the Abbey Road recording is beautifully balanced. The other items in this recital are equally appealing, and her account of Tchaikovsky's *Rococo variations* is unsurpassed among modern versions. A collection not to be missed.

Pierre Fournier's performance, while not without feeling, is slightly lacking in romantic urgency. The recording is acceptable.

Scottish fantasy (for violin and orchestra), *Op. 46.*
(M) *** EMI Eminence Dig. CD-EMX 2277 [id.]. Tasmin Little, Royal SNO, Vernon Handley – LALO: *Symphonie espagnole.* ***
(B) **(*) Revelation RV 10051 [id.]. David Oistrakh, USSR State SO, Rozhdestvensky – BERLIOZ: *Harold in Italy.* (*)

It is an excellent idea to couple Bruch's evocation of Scotland with Lalo's of Spain, both works in unconventional, five-movement, concertante form. Tasmin Little takes a riper, more robust and passionate view of both works than her direct rival on disc, the poetic Anne Akiko Meyers on RCA (RD 60942), projecting them more strongly, as she would in the concert hall. Little's speeds are a degree broader than those of Meyers, which gives her more freedom to point rhythms infectiously, to play with an extra degree of individuality in her phrasing, using portamentos or agogic hesitations daringly in a way that adds to the character of the reading. In this she is greatly helped by the splendid, keenly polished playing of the Scottish orchestra under Vernon Handley, a most sympathetic partner. The recording is superb, with brass in particular vividly caught. Unlike Meyers on RCA, Little plays the Guerriero finale absolutely complete. At mid-price on the Eminence label, this is an issue to recommend to anyone wanting either work.

It is sad that as inspired a version as David Oistrakh's of the Bruch *Scottish fantasy* should be coupled on Revelation with so seriously flawed a recording of *Harold in Italy*. The irony is that where the sound for the Bruch, dating from 1960, is full-bodied and generally well balanced, if limited in range, the 1974 recording of the Berlioz is very dim. With Rozhdestvensky drawing fine playing from the orchestra, Oistrakh gives the fast movements a rare sparkle, always spontaneous in his expressiveness, and in the *Andante* he builds from heartfelt meditation to the most passionate climax.

Bruckner, Anton (1824–96)

Symphonies Nos. '0'; 1–9; in F min.

(B) ** Teldec/Warner Dig. 0630 14192-2 (11) [id.]. Frankfurt RSO, Eliahu Inbal.

Eliahu Inbal has strong Brucknerian instincts and his survey of the first versions of all the Bruckner *Symphonies*, which includes the fascinating early *Study Symphony*, is of permanent interest to Brucknerians, especially as Nos. 3, 4 and 8 had never been recorded before in their original versions. Although the Frankfurt Radio Orchestra is not thought of as being in the very first rank, it responds well to Inbal's advocacy, always producing more than acceptable results and sometimes offering playing of considerable concentration and power. The recordings too, if not in the demonstration bracket, are spacious, bold and clear. The 11 discs are offered in a slip-case at bargain price, and the set could be recommended with little reservation, had the documentation been adequate. But each CD contains only a folded insert leaflet which documents the date of the edition used and the date and location of the recording. When one considers how different some of these first versions are from what is normally presented in the concert hall, this seems an unforgivable omission and, as there is no additional covering booklet, collectors would be better advised to choose from the individual issues, which are also in the budget price range.

Symphonies Nos. '0'; 1–9.

(B) **(*) Decca Dig. 448 910-2 (10) [id.]. Chicago SO, Solti.

Solti had previously recorded the *Eighth* with the VPO for John Culshaw in the Sofiensaal as early as 1966 (see below). With the Chicago Symphony Orchestra he began with the *Sixth* (1979), following with the *Fifth* (1980) and *Fourth* (1981). Then there was a gap of four years before the *Ninth* (1985) and *Seventh* (1986) and another before the *Eighth*, recorded in Russia (1990), the *Second* (1991) and the *Third* (1992).

The two early symphonies are discussed below and the *Second*, where he follows Nowak and which is similarly successful, appeared in our main volume. Alas, the *Third* is the one failure. Despite excellent Decca engineering, the result is pretty crude and coarse, with little of the refinement of sonority which distinguishes the rest of the series.

In the *Fourth*, where he again chooses Nowak, Solti can hardly be faulted, selecting admirable tempi, keeping concentration taut through the longest paragraphs and presenting the architecture of the work in total clarity. Raptness is there too, and only the relative lack of Brucknerian idiosyncrasy, especially when compared with his readings of the earliest symphonies, will disappoint those who prefer a more affectionate and personal approach. This aspect of the interpretation is not helped by the slightly artificial brightness of the early digital sound-picture. This comment might also be applied to the *Fifth*, where the clarity and brilliance of the digital sound underlines Solti's precise control of the dramatic contrasts. The slow movement finds the necessary warmth, with Solti in what might for him be counted an Elgarian mood.

However, in the *Sixth* it is the slow movement which is less persuasive than usual, failing to flow quite as it might so that the expressiveness does not sound truly spontaneous. It comes within a reading that is strong and rhetorical, powerfully convincing in the outer movements. Here the analogue recording emerges vividly enough in its CD format.

The *Seventh* is a disappointment. Solti takes an extraordinarily spacious view and, while the Chicago orchestra respond to his affectionate care over detail with playing of great refinement and produce climaxes of great weight and power, this very relaxed approach means that the outer movements are lacking in ultimate grip and the Scherzo is comparatively lightweight. The *Adagio* is drawn out to an inordinate length and, in spite of the great beauty of the orchestral textures, many listeners will find Solti's indulgence verging on lassitude.

The *Eighth* rights the balance, with an inspired reading, opening with powerful gravitas. (Solti, as before in Vienna, uses the 1890 version edited by Nowak.) The expansive *Adagio* is magnificently sustained by the most magical response from the orchestra over its long eventful progress. Without ever seeming over-intense, Solti achieves an extraordinary grip over the movement as a whole, and notably so in the extended, quietly elegiac string cantilena in the closing pages which is tenderly moving. The ambitiously extended finale then erupts boisterously and caps the performance with a finely judged balance between glowing lyricism and weighty splendour, especially in the exultant coda. The recording, made in the Great Hall of the St Petersburg Philharmonia, is superb in every respect.

The *Ninth* is a similarly spacious and large-scale reading. Again there is no question of Solti rushing the argument. He gives the music full time to breathe, but here the tension is unrelenting, making the big climaxes thrillingly powerful, as in the outbursts of the long last movement. Other performances may be more deeply meditative – Walter for one – but the power of Solti and the brilliance of the playing and the digital recording are formidable.

Symphonies Nos. (i) *'0' in D min.* (ed. Wöss): *Scherzo* (only); *1 in C min.* (ed. Schalk): *Scherzo* (only); *2 in C min.* (ed. Herbeck): *Scherzo* (only); (ii) *3 in D min.* (ed. Schalk): *Scherzo* (only); (iii) *4 in E flat* (ed. Löwe and Schalk): *Scherzo* (only); (iv) *4 in E flat* (complete; ed. Haas); *5 in B flat* (complete; ed. Haas); *7 in E* (complete; ed. Löwe).

(M) (**) EMI mono CHS6 66206 (3) [CDHC 66206]. (i) Berlin State Op. O, Fritz Zaun; (ii) VSO, Anton Konrath; (iii) Saxon State O, Karl Boehm.

Symphonies Nos. (i) *6 in A* (ed. Haas): *Adagio, Scherzo & Finale* (only); (ii) *7 in E* (ed. Löwe); (i) *8 in C min.* (ed. Haas); (iii) *9 in D min.* (ed. Orel).

(M) (***) EMI mono CHS5 66210 (3) [CDHC 66210]. (i) BPO, Furtwängler; (ii–iii) Munich PO; (ii) Oswald Kabasta; (iii) Siegmond von Hausegger.

These two three-CD sets of historic Bruckner symphonies cover all the material in the pre-war HMV and Electrola catalogues, together with some wartime and post-war off-air recordings. The scherzo movements of *Die Nullte* (No. 0) and Nos. 1–4 come from 1928–34, but the first time EMI Electrola recorded a complete Bruckner symphony was in 1936, though this was not the very first recording: Oscar Fried and Jascha Horenstein had recorded Bruckner symphonies in the 1920s, and Ormandy's RCA account of the *Seventh* was also earlier. By 1936 the International Anton Bruckner Gesellschaft had published its authoritative edition of the 1878–80 score of the *Fourth Symphony* by Robert Haas, which Karl Boehm used; and it was, incidentally, to the same edition that he turned in 1937 for his recording of the *Fifth*. Incredible though it may seem to the younger collector, the early LP catalogues were meagre in their Bruckner offerings, and the first Bruckner symphony recorded by a British orchestra was the *Fourth*, played by the Philharmonia with Lovro von Matačić in 1955: the first under a British conductor is yet to appear (though Sir Henry Wood had recorded the *Overture in G minor* before the war).

It is the combination of childlike vision and awesome majesty that makes the Bruckner symphonies unique in music and which, on the face of it, makes the LP with its continuity (and in particular the stereo LP with its wider dynamic range and sense of space), a more congenial medium than shellac. Yet returning to these pre-war performances serves as a reminder that they possess that freshness of discovery and atmosphere which première recordings always seem to have. Boehm's *Fifth* was superseded by Jochum's, 20 years later, in the 1950s. The *Seventh* under Furtwängler comes from a 1949 broadcast. (Furtwängler made only one commercial recording of Bruckner, the slow movement of No. 7 in 1942, though there are four different surviving accounts of the whole work from his baton.)

Brucknerians will want both of these sets, but those whose funds will not stretch to both should go for the second volume. Furtwängler conducted the *Sixth Symphony* only once, in 1943, and three movements of that performance have come down to us. The *Adagio* is particularly elevated in feeling. His *Eighth*, again from a 1949 broadcast, has the ardour and intensity he brought to all his music-making. Special interest focuses on Oswald Kabasta's passionate and full-blooded wartime account of the *Seventh Symphony* and Siegmund von Hausegger's pioneering account of the *Ninth*, both with the Munich Philharmonic. This remains one of the most atmospheric of all *Ninths* and has a wonderful sense of mystery and vision which leaves you feeling that this is how this awesome music must have sounded to Bruckner in his own mind's ears. Excellent transfers.

Symphonies Nos. 1–9.

500♪ (M) *** DG 429 648-2 (9) [id.]. BPO, Karajan.

We have sung the praises of these Karajan recordings loud and long, and in their new format they are outstanding value.

Symphony No. '00' in F min. (Study Symphony).
(B) *** Teldec/Warner Dig. 0630 14193-2 [id.]. Frankfurt RSO, Inbal.

Bruckner's *Study Symphony*, a student work, was written in 1863. The composer, a late starter, was just turning forty and at the very beginning of his composing career. The surprise is the way the music has distinct pre-echoes of what was to come, especially the *Andante*, a remarkable piece of writing with brief tuttis stabbing into the lyrical flow. (This is particularly well brought off here.) The Scherzo, too, is entirely typical and with a delightful, flowing trio on the woodwind. The finale, however, is Schumannesque, with lyrical influences from Wagner – but none the worse for that – and its waywardness again has Brucknerian fingerprints. Inbal and his orchestra are in excellent form and they approach the music with total freshness as if it were a mature work; at times they almost convince the listener that it is. They are very well recorded, and this is well worth considering at budget price.

Symphony No. '0' in D min.
(B) *** Teldec/Warner Dig. 0630 14194-2 [id.]. Frankfurt RSO, Inbal.
*(**) Decca Dig. 452 160-2 [id.]. Chicago SO, Solti.

Die Nullte is a work of striking quality that at times portends the greatness to come. Although it may not be ideally proportioned, some of its ideas have all the innocence and purity of utterance that distinguishes the finest early Bruckner.

Inbal and his Frankfurt orchestra are again in impressive form here, giving a performance of undoubted spontaneity. The character of the first movement is immediately caught at the atmospheric opening with its neatly delineated little march theme, and the first climax expands naturally. This is not an easy movement to hold together, but Inbal succeeds both in retaining tension and in creating a natural forward flow. The hushed opening of the *Andante* is well sustained, and with warmly responsive playing the listener is held throughout. The Scherzo, too, is nicely pointed in the strings and woodwind to offer a light-hearted counterpart to the bombast from the heavy brass, and the contrasts in the powerful and exciting finale are handled equally convincingly. All in all, this is one of the most impressive of Inbal's series and is well worth its modest price.

Solti's version was the last of his cycle to be recorded (in 1995) and one of the most successful. His affection shows immediately at the jaunty opening and his pacing is admirable throughout: he keeps a fine momentum without pressing too hard (unlike Barenboim with the same orchestra who is too often inclined to linger by the wayside). With Solti the concentration is never in doubt: his warmth in the slow movement communicates readily and there is some wonderfully relaxed pianissimo playing from the Chicago violins. Indeed the orchestra plays very beautifully throughout. The Scherzo has plenty of gruff energy, helped by superbly clear articulation, but lightens winningly to sound almost Mahlerian in the central section. In the finale Solti convincingly knits together Bruckner's bold, sudden brass tuttis with moments of lyrical Schubertian delicacy. With first-class recording, full-bodied but not too massive, this would have made a clear first choice for an elusive work. Decca's planners, however, should have known better than to issue this without any fill-up. Who these days will want to pay premium price for 38 minutes? The *Overture in G minor*, admittedly not a work of comparable quality, would have been a worthwhile addition to the catalogue.

Symphony No. 1 in C min. (original, Linz version).
*** Decca Dig. 448 898-2 [id.]. Chicago SO, Solti.
(B) ** Teldec/Warner Dig. 0630 14195-2 [id.]. Frankfurt RSO, Inbal.

Bruckner's *First* is a somewhat intractable symphony. Although the mood is basically amiable, the composer's restless alternations of heavy tuttis, energetic passages more lightly scored, and lyrical blossoming are less well knit together than in his mature works. But Solti, on top form, as in the '*Nullte*', again creates a sweeping forward momentum, especially in the finale, which disguises the weaknesses. Repeating his approach to the '*Nullte*', he opens with a sprightly momentum and a debonair rhythmic lift, and is warmly tender in the movement's gentler lyrical side. The Scherzo has splendid rumbustious vigour, while the very beautiful *Adagio* opens with a hushed, rapt pianissimo, and the superb Chicago string playing sustains Solti's spacious tempo with compelling concentration and the widest range of dynamic. There is much subtle delicacy of nuance from the whole orchestra and the long Wagnerian approach to the climax is superbly sustained. The excellent recording is atmospheric, clear in inner detail, yet does not lack ripeness and body, with tuttis firm and uncongealing.

Inbal's direct, comparatively brisk approach – he handles the tempo changes in the first movement convincingly enough – makes quite a good case for Bruckner's earlier (1866) Linz version of No. 1, although the lack of opulence in the recording adds to the impression that the end result is lightweight. The *Adagio* does not lack tension, and the finale is held together dramatically, even if there is not the breadth or the kind of added dimension one has with Jochum or Karajan. But, unlike some of the other early versions of Bruckner symphonies in Inbal's valuable survey, the Linz edition of No. 1 is favoured in most other recordings, notably Solti's, which makes a much stronger impression.

Symphony No. 1 in C min.
** DG Dig. 453 415-2 [id.]. VPO, Claudio Abbado.

Abbado offers a very cool survey of the Brucknerian landscape. It is difficult to flaw, but one comes to wonder why it is that the performance is not drawing you into Bruckner's world in a way that such conductors as Karajan, Wand and Jochum succeed in doing. Every phrase is well shaped and nicely tailored, but somehow it does not add up. The DG recording is very good and the Vienna Philharmonic play beautifully, but the overall impression is curiously uninvolving.

Symphony No. 2 in C min. (original, Haas (1872) version).
(B) ** Teldec/Warner Dig. 0630 14196-2 [id.]. Frankfurt RSO, Inbal.

In his Frankfurt performance, Inbal, so the label tells us, offers the revised version of 1877; but what we get is something much closer to the 1872 Haas version. This retains the Scherzo and trio with all its repeats and uses the original horn instead of the clarinet, substituted by Herbeck in 1876, at the end of the slow movement. Incidentally, the closing string chords are missing here, which brings one up with a start. For the most part the playing is good without being outstanding, and the recording, made at the Frankfurt Opera, is very good.

Symphony No. 3 in D min. (original, 1873 version).
(B) *** Teldec/Warner Dig. 0630 14197-2 [id.]. Frankfurt RSO, Inbal.
** EMI Dig. CDC5 56167-2 [id.]. LCP, Norrington.

There are in all three versions of the *Third Symphony*: the first, completed on the last day of 1873; a second, which Bruckner undertook immediately after completion of the *Fifth Symphony* in 1877; and then, after this second version proved unsuccessful, a third which he completed in 1889. The 1873 version is by far the longest, running to nearly 66 minutes (the first movement alone lasts 24 minutes), and for those who have either of the others it will make far more than a fascinating appendix. The playing of the Frankfurt Radio Orchestra under Eliahu Inbal is very respectable indeed, with a sensitive feeling for atmosphere and refined dynamic contrasts; the recording is most acceptable without being top-drawer.

From ur-text Bruckner symphonies the next step is ur-instrumentation. Inbal's version of the original (1873) score now has an effective challenger. Roger Norrington offers Bruckner's *Third* in what is the very first reading to use period instruments. The balance of the texture is, of course, much altered – as is much else besides. Bracing tempi tend to rob the symphony of its atmosphere and breadth. It is all very well to 'humanize' them and divest them of being 'religious tracts', as Norrington puts it in his stimulating notes; but many would argue that religious feeling and Bruckner are indivisible. It goes without saying that there are many points to make you think, but tempi are far too brisk to make this an unqualified recommendation. Inbal does not dawdle, but Norrington takes some eight minutes less overall. (His first movement alone is five minutes faster.) Splendid playing from the London Classical Players and no lack of thought from the conductor, but the wrong kind of feeling. The Inbal version is the one to go for, and it is very economically priced.

Symphony No. 3 in D min. (1877 version).
*** Ph. Dig. 422 411-2 [id.]. VPO, Bernard Haitink.
** Teldec/Warner Dig. 0630 13160-2 [id.]. BPO, Barenboim.
(BB) * Discovery Dig. DICD 920319 [id.]. Belgian R. & TV PO, Rahbari.

Haitink gives us the 1877 version, favoured by many Bruckner scholars. Questions of edition apart, this is a performance of enormous breadth and majesty, and Philips give it a recording to match. The playing of the Vienna Philharmonic is glorious throughout, and even collectors who have alternative versions should acquire this magnificent issue.

Daniel Barenboim gets impressive results and draws opulent sound from the Berlin Philharmonic, and the recorded sound does them justice. (After listening to Norrington and the London Classical Players, the sound is positively sumptuous and full-bodied.) There is considerable passion and musical conviction, and the performance and recording would not disgrace any collector's library. However, it does not have the same blend of natural eloquence and architectural strength as the Haitink Vienna account, nor is it quite as beautifully recorded.

Alexander Rahbari's performance with Belgian Radio forces has the merit of economy, though it is not otherwise as competitive in terms of the distinction of the orchestral playing or the excellence of the recorded sound. Bargain versions of this symphony are relatively thin on the ground; but it would make better sense to get, say, the Boehm version – which, admittedly, is the later (1889) revision – coupled with the *Fourth* on a Double Decca (448 098-2 – see our main volume). Both performances have genuine stature.

Symphony No. 4 in E flat (Romantic) (original, 1874 version).
(B) **(*) Teldec/Warner Dig. 0630 14198-2 [id.]. Frankfurt RSO, Inbal.

Like the *Third*, there are three versions of the *Romantic Symphony*, and no one has recorded the original before. The differences are most obvious in the Scherzo, a completely different and more fiery movement; but the opening of the finale is also totally different. Inbal's performance is more than adequate – indeed he has a genuine feeling for the Bruckner idiom and pays scrupulous attention to dynamic refinements. The recording is well detailed, though the climaxes almost (but not quite) reach congestion. An indispensable and fascinating issue.

Symphony No. 4 in E flat (Romantic).
(M) *** DG 449 718-2 [id.]. BPO, Eugen Jochum (with SIBELIUS: *Night ride and sunrise, Op. 55* with Bav. RSO (***)).
(M) (***) Dutton Lab. mono CDEA 5007 [id.]. Dresden State O, Karl Boehm (with R. STRAUSS: *Don Juan* (***)).
(M) **(*) EMI CDM5 66094-2 [id.]. BPO, Karajan.

Jochum's way with Bruckner is unique. So gentle is his hand that the opening of each movement or even the beginning of each theme emerges into the consciousness rather than starting normally. The purist may object that, in order to do this, Jochum reduces the speed far below what is marked, but Jochum is for the listener who wants above all to love Bruckner. The recording has undoubtedly been further enhanced in this reissue in DG's 'Originals' series, and a fascinating mono recording of Sibelius's *Night ride and sunrise* has been added. Jochum was not thought of as a Sibelian, but this performance is undoubtedly impressive and well worth having.

Karl Boehm made the very first commercial recording of the *Fourth Symphony* in 1936, and the performance has a simplicity and directness of utterance that have not since been surpassed. Moreover the *Andante quasi Allegretto* (like the early Mahler of Bruno Walter) has a seamless flow which makes it difficult to believe that it was recorded in four-minute chunks. We remember well that purchasers of the 78-r.p.m. shellac set were instructed to replay the record side containing the Scherzo, with its exuberant hunting horns (which is unchanged at its reprise), after listening to the Trio. It works excellently when the sides are edited together on Mike Dutton's CD transfer, just as it did in those days of constant side-changing which was part of the pre-LP ritual of listening to recorded music. Boehm had a special relationship with the Dresden orchestra which he felt displayed 'a certain brilliancy and splendour'. He also suggested that 'the Dresden strings had a very special sound – partly due to the old Italian instruments which are communally owned by the orchestra, but mainly . . . attributable to the proximity of Czechoslovakia, which seems to me the spiritual home of good string players'. Boehm's account of Richard Strauss's *Don Juan* is full of passion at the climax, but during the seduction scene it does not emphasize the sexuality in the way some contemporary performances manage to do. The recordings were made in the Semper Opera House in Dresden, so tuttis are not as resonantly expansive as they might be, but the glowing Dresden sound is particularly well caught in the slow movement, and the Scherzo is remarkably brilliant. The Dutton transfer, as ever, re-creates the original 78 sound with the utmost faithfulness – and, indeed, improves on it.

Karajan's 1970 recording for EMI, made in the Berlin Jesus-Christus-Kirche and now reissued in the Karajan Edition, had undoubted electricity and combines simplicity and strength. The playing of the Berlin Philharmonic is very fine. The resonance means that there is a touch of harshness on the considerable fortissimos, while pianissimos are relatively diffuse. However, at mid-price this remains well worth considering.

Symphonies Nos. 4 in E flat; 7 in E; 9 in D min.
(BB) ** RCA Navigator 74321 30368-2 (3). Leipzig GO, Masur.

Three favourite Bruckner symphonies are here offered very inexpensively on RCA's super-budget label, very well played by the Leipzig orchestra, directed by Kurt Masur, who is obviously a sound guide in this repertoire (no pun intended). The recording is resonant but full-blooded. No. 4 comes off the most successfully, opening poetically and with individual movements shaped spaciously and convincingly: the *Andante* has a gentle concentration and genuine atmosphere. No. 7 again brings fine playing and the sound is spacious, but this very expansive reading lacks the grip of real concentration and (whichever edition is used) the absence of cymbals at the climax of the slow movement is a great drawback. Masur's reading of the *Ninth* is again leisured, but there is rather more tension. The Leipzig orchestra certainly understands

Bruckner's expansive paragraphs, and again the recording is warm and spacious. Altogether a fair recommendation in the super-bargain range.

Symphony No. 5 in B flat (original version).
(B) *(*) Teldec/Warner Dig. 0630 14199-2 [id.]. Frankfurt RSO, Inbal.

Eliahu Inbal makes a promising start to the *Fifth Symphony* and gets reasonably good playing from the Frankfurt Radio forces. Unfortunately his slow movement is far too brisk to be remotely convincing: he gets through it in 14 minutes, as against Jochum's 19 and Karajan's 21. Rather unsatisfactory.

Symphony No. 5 in B flat.
500♪ *** Decca Dig. 433 819-2 [id.]. Concg. O, Chailly.
*** RCA Dig. 09026 68503-2 [id.]. BPO, Günter Wand.
(M) (***) EMI mono CDH5 56750-2 [id.]. VPO, Furtwängler.
** DG Dig. 445 879-2 [id.]. VPO, Claudio Abbado.

Chailly gave us an outstanding Bruckner *Seventh* with the Berlin Radio Symphony Orchestra in the early days of CD which still ranks high among all the competition (see below). This new version of the *Fifth* is, if anything, even finer. The Royal Concertgebouw Orchestra play with sumptuous magnificence, and Chailly's overall control of a work that is notable for its diversive episodes is unerring, moving towards an overwhelming final apotheosis. The *Adagio* is very beautiful and never sounds hurried. The Decca recording is superb, very much in the demonstration bracket, with the brass attacking brilliantly, yet producing the fullest sonority, and the strings equally expansive. An easy first choice.

The latest contender is from Günter Wand, who forsakes the Cologne and Hamburg orchestras (with which he made his earlier recordings) in favour of the Berlin Philharmonic. The present disc was put together from three concert performances given in January 1996, so it has not taken as long to reach us as the Abbado. It will probably be difficult to persuade those who have invested in either of the earlier discs to acquire the newcomer in spite of the magnificence of the orchestral playing and the nobility of the reading. Wand is an experienced and selfless interpreter, and no one coming to it afresh will be greatly disappointed.

Furtwängler's account of the *Fifth Symphony* comes from the invaluable Salzburg Archives and was recorded at the 1951 Salzburg Festival. (The remainder of the concert included Mendelssohn's *Fingal's Cave* and Mahler's *Lieder eines fahrenden Gesellen* with the 26-year-old Fischer-Dieskau.) Considering its age, the sound is remarkably good; the EMI engineers have done wonders in restoring its colours, and the performance has that blend of warmth, majesty and radiance which distinguishes the best Furtwängler.

Like his *First* (see above), Abbado's account of the *Fifth* is curiously wanting in atmosphere, as indeed is the recording. The performance comes from a concert at the Musikverein in October 1993. It is what one might call a well-bred, carefully manicured but cool account, which finds the great Viennese orchestra sounding less than their sumptuous best. Judging from this and the *First* and *Seventh* symphonies, Abbado does not seem to have that natural affinity with Bruckner that distinguishes Jochum, Karajan or Wand in any of his three recordings – or, of course, Furtwängler – see below.

Symphony No. 6 in A.
** Decca Dig. 436 152-2 [id.]. Cleveland O, Christoph von Dohnányi (with BACH/WEBERN: *Musical Offering: Fuga ricercata a 6 voci* **).
** RCA Dig 09026 68452-2 [id.]. N. German RSO, Hamburg, Günter Wand.
(B) ** Teldec/Warner Dig. 0630 14200-2 [id.]. Frankfurt RSO, Inbal.

Dohnányi fails to get a real grip on this symphony, and the necessary ebb-and-flow of tempi eludes him, particularly in the outer movements, although the *Adagio* is undoubtedly affecting. The Cleveland Orchestra responds to his demands with their customary virtuosity, but the burnished Decca sound seems a shade too brightly lit in fortissimos. Webern's highly individual scoring of the *Ricercar* from Bach's *Musical offering* makes an unusual if curiously cool coupling. Blomstedt's version of the symphony is the one to go for, and it is more appropriately coupled with Wagner's *Siegfried idyll* (Decca 436 129-2).

Günter Wand and the same orchestra, producer and engineer recorded this symphony in the same venue only five years earlier, and it is difficult to see why they should repeat the operation. This newcomer is not always as successful as the 1989 version, though improvements or differences are pretty marginal. In any case, there are more impressive accounts of this symphony to be had.

Again Inbal secures good playing from the Frankfurt Radio Orchestra, and he is well served by the engineers. The recording is full-bodied and spacious and has a dramatically wide dynamic range. Nevertheless the performance, even taking into account some fine string playing in the slow movement (the best part of the performance), is a little short on personality and is ultimately bland. After the *Fifth*, the *Sixth* is probably the least well-served of Inbal's cycle.

Symphony No. 7 in E (original version).
(B) ** Teldec/Warner Dig. 0630 14201-2 [id.]. Frankfurt RSO, Inbal.

In terms of excellence of orchestral playing and vividness of recording, Inbal's *Seventh* is well up to the standard of his Bruckner series, using the original scores; but the performance itself, although it does not lack an overall structural grip, is without the full flow of adrenalin that can make this symphony so compulsive, and the orgasmic climax of the slow movement is much less telling without those two famous cymbal-crashes.

Symphony No. 7 in E.
500♪ (B) *** Decca Eclipse Dig. 448 710-2; *448 710-4* [id.]. Berlin RSO, Chailly (with MAHLER: *Des Knaben Wunderhorn: Des Antonius von Padua Fischpredigt; Das irdische Leben* – with Brigitte Fassbaender ***).
(M) *** EMI CDM5 66095-2 [id.]. BPO, Karajan.

Chailly's account, with its superb Decca digital recording, ranks among the best available and makes an obvious first choice, a committed and very moving performance. He has a considerable command of the work's architecture and controls its sonorities expertly. The recording, made in the Jesus-Christus-Kirche, Berlin, is outstanding in every way. Reissued on Eclipse with the bonus of two delightful songs from Mahler's *Des Knaben Wunderhorn* sung by Brigitte Fassbaender, this is an unbeatable bargain.

Karajan's outstanding EMI version (recorded in the Berlin Jesus-Christus-Kirche in 1970–71) also shows a superb feeling for the work's architecture and the playing of the Berlin Philharmonic is gorgeous. The recording has striking resonance and amplitude. This EMI reading, generally preferable to his later, digital recording for DG, has a sense of mystery that is really rather special. The new transfer for the Karajan Edition enhances the quality, and this recording has never sounded better.

Symphonies Nos. 7 in E; 9 in D min.
(B) (**(*)) DG Double mono 445 418-2 (2). BPO, Furtwangler.

These are both historic accounts, conveniently packaged as a Double; but the *Seventh Symphony*, recorded when the Berlin Philharmonic were on tour in Cairo in 1951, offers less appealing sound than the *Ninth*, which emanates from the closing months of the war, October 1944, not long before Furtwängler fled from the Nazis. The terrible times through which Europe was passing lent a special intensity to music-making, and this is a performance of real vision. The *Seventh* is not quite so special; but the set is well worth acquiring, given the price, for the sake of the *Ninth*.

Symphony No. 8 in C min. (original, 1887 version).
(B) **(*) Teldec/Warner Dig. 0630 14202-2 [id.]. Frankfurt RSO, Inbal.

Eliahu Inbal continues his stimulating series with a generally impressive and well-played first version of No. 8. There are considerable divergences here from the versions we know, and readers will undoubtedly derive much satisfaction from comparing them. The recording is very good.

Symphony No. 8 in C min. (1890 version, ed. Nowak).
*** DG Dig. 447 744-2 [id.]. Dresden State O, Sinopoli – STRAUSS: *Metamorphosen*. ***
(M) ** Decca 448 124-2 [id.]. VPO, Solti.

In the *Seventh Symphony* (see our main volume) we welcomed Sinopoli's straightforward approach to Bruckner. He confounded expectations, for at times he tends to underline and italicize, in order to draw our attention to some expressive detail or other, and at others he takes us by the lapels to make sure we haven't missed some incidental beauty. His *Eighth Symphony* is refreshingly straightforward and is likewise untouched by any suggestion of exaggeration. The playing of the Staatskapelle, Dresden, has an expressive power and beauty that are greatly enhanced by sumptuous recorded sound. The DG engineers have produced outstanding quality. Readers who have come to mistrust Sinopoli can confidently put their misgivings to one side. In this performance one might speak of him as 'coming of age', for his approach is shorn of the affectation that disfigures his Mahler.

Splendidly recorded in the Sofiensaal in 1966, Solti's earlier, VPO version of the *Eighth* is no match for his later, Chicago recording, at present available only within his complete cycle. Again he uses the Nowak edition, and the Vienna Philharmonic responds to his direction with great fervour and incisiveness. But the account of the long slow movement lacks the inspired spontaneous feeling of his later reading, and the result seems mannered.

Symphony No. 8 in C min.
500♪ ✿ *** DG Dig. 427 611-2 [id.]. VPO, Karajan.
(M) *** EMI CMS5 66109-2 (2) [id.]. BPO, Karajan – BRAHMS: *Tragic Overture;* HINDEMITH: *Mathis der Maler* (symphony). ***

*** Ph. Dig 446 659-2 [id.]. VPO, Haitink.

Karajan's last version of the *Eighth Symphony* is with the Vienna Philharmonic Orchestra and is the most impressive of them all. The sheer beauty of sound and opulence of texture is awe-inspiring but never draws attention to itself: this is a performance in which beauty and truth go hand in hand. The recording is superior to either of its predecessors in terms of naturalness of detail and depth of perspective. This is quite an experience!

The 1957 sound of Karajan's Berlin Bruckner *Eighth* is impressively spacious and, if the sonorities are not quite as sumptuous as we would expect today, the strings do not lack body and the brass makes a thrilling impact. The slow movement is very fine indeed, conveying dark and tragic feelings, and the finale makes a fine apotheosis. With its excellent couplings this set is among the highlights of EMI's Karajan Edition.

Bernard Haitink and the Vienna Philharmonic are a formidable combination; add to them the doyen of Philips engineers, Volker Strauss, and the results are outstanding. Too late for the Bruckner year – though, had Philips got their act together, they could have had it out in good time, as the recording was made in January 1995. The performance is magnificent in its breadth and nobility, and Haitink has the full measure of its majesty and grandeur. Not only does it possess great dramatic sweep, its slow movement has a greater depth than his earlier reading. The Vienna Philharmonic play with great fervour and warmth, and the recorded sound is sumptuous. This does not displace the magisterial account Karajan made with this orchestra for DG (or his earlier, Berlin version) but it can be recommended alongside it.

Symphony No. 9 in D min. (original version – with finale reconstructed Samale/Mazzuca).
(B) **(*) Teldec/Warner Dig. 0630 14203-2 [id.]. Frankfurt RSO, Inbal.

Eliahu Inbal's reading of the *Ninth* with the Frankfurt Radio Orchestra is far from negligible, even though it may not be a performance of the highest stature. The playing is often very fine, and Inbal is scrupulously attentive to detail; however, there is not the sense of scale that is to be found in the finest of his rivals. In 1934, Alfred Orel published the fragmentary sketches of the finale of the symphony without attempting to impose any sequence on them. They have fascinated many scholars: Hans Redlich and Robert Simpson prepared a keyboard edition, and the present reconstruction has been made by two Italian scholars, Nicola Samale and Giuseppe Mazzuca. It is, in the very nature of things, highly conjectural and is, of course, interesting to hear once.

Symphony No. 9 in D min.
500♪ ✿ (M) *** Sony Bruno Walter Edition SMK 64483 [id.]. Columbia SO, Walter.
** BMG/RCA Dig. 09026 62650-2 [id.]. N. German RSO, Günter Wand.

Bruno Walter's 1959 account of Bruckner's *Ninth Symphony* represents the peak of his achievement during his Indian summer in the CBS recording studios just before he died. Walter's mellow, persuasive reading leads one on through the leisurely paragraphs so that the logic and coherence seem obvious where other performances can sound aimless.

Given the extraordinary competition now on the market, even as distinguished a Brucknerian as Günter Wand has to yield pride of place to rivals. This version of the *Ninth Symphony*, recorded at a concert performance in Hamburg in 1993, is his third; there are earlier accounts from 1979 (Cologne) and 1988 (Lübeck). This is less impressive than either of its predecessors, and rather confirms the doubts we voiced about his recent *Sixth* – that there is no need for a re-make. It is well recorded, but the playing of the Hamburg orchestra is by no means as spontaneous – or, for that matter, as impeccable – as such rivals as the Berlin and Vienna orchestras for Karajan (analogue, at mid-price – DG 429 904-2) or Giulini (DG Dig. 437 345-2).

String quintet in F.
*** Nimbus NI 5488 [id.] Brandis Qt, with Brett Dean – BRAHMS: *String quintet No. 2*. ***

Eminently good value. This Brandis version of the *Quintet* offers a splendid coupling in Brahms's *G major Quintet*, Op. 111, and their playing stands up well alongside the current competition. They are well recorded and have a natural feeling for the space and pacing of this piece. For those attracted by the coupling, this could well be a first choice.

Masses Nos. (i) *1 in D min.* (for soloists, chorus and orchestra); *2 in E min.* (for 8-part chorus and wind ensemble); (ii) *3 in F min.* (for soloists, chorus and orchestra).
500♪ ✿ (M) *** DG 447 409-2 (2) [id.]. (i) Mathis, Schiml, Ochman, Ridderbusch; (ii) Stader, Hellman, Haefliger, Borg; Bav. R. Ch. & O, Jochum.

Masses Nos. 1 in D min.; 2 in E min.; 3 in F min. Aequalis Nos. 1 & 2. Motets: Afferentur regi virgines; Ave Maria; Christus factus est; Ecce sacardos magnus; Inveni David; Locus iste; Os justi; Pange lingua; Tota pulchra es, Maria; Vexilla regis; Virga Jesse; Libera me; Psalm 150; Te Deum.
*** Hyperion Dig. CDS 4407 (3) [id.]. Soloists, Corydon Singers and O; ECO Wind Ens., Matthew Best; T. Trotter (organ).

Bruckner composed his three *Masses* between 1864 and 1868, although all three works were revised two decades later. Each contains magnificent music; Eugen Jochum is surely an ideal interpreter, finding their mystery as well as their eloquence, breadth and humanity. Throughout all three works the scale and drama of Bruckner's inspiration are fully conveyed. A remarkable achievement and a splendid choice for DG's 'Original' series of Legendary Recordings.

It makes good sense to assemble all of the Bruckner choral music that the Corydon Singers and Matthew Best have done during the last few years in one three-CD set. They are very fine indeed and make a splendid modern alternative to the Jochum; their eloquence and naturalness – as well as the excellence of the recorded sound – make them a perfectly viable one artistically. Best's direction is imaginative and he achieves a wide tonal range.

Te Deum.
(B) **(*) DG Double 453 091-2 (2) [id.]. Tomowa-Sintow, Baltsa, Schreier, Van Dam, V. Singverein, VPO, Karajan – VERDI: *Requiem Mass.* **(*)

Karajan's analogue account of the *Te Deum* is spacious and strong, bringing out the score's breadth and drama. This is very satisfying and, if the Verdi coupling is acceptable, this is self-recommending.

Bunin, Revol Samuilovich (1924–76)

Violin concerto.
(B) ** Revelation RV 10058 [id.]. Kogan, USSR State Academic SO, Lazarev – BARBER: *Violin concerto* **(*); BARSUKOV: *Violin concerto No. 2.* **

Like the other concertos on this disc, Bunin's is an unashamedly romantic work, in places reflecting the idiom of his teacher, Shostakovich, but generally following a more conservative style. In a committed performance like Leonid Kogan's, it makes an attractive novelty, coupled with the Barber as well as the Barsukov. Curiously, the disc fails to insert tracks between the movements in this long, 32-minute work, and the live recording is marred by audience noise.

Burgon, Geoffrey (born 1941)

Acquainted with night; Cançiones del Alma; Lunar beauty; Nunc dimittis; This ean night; Worldës blissë.
(M) *** EMI Dig. CDM5 66527-2 [id.]. James Bowman, Charles Brett, City of L. Sinf., Hickox.

This collection of Geoffrey Burgon's music for counter-tenor makes a hauntingly unusual record. Appropriately, it has at the centre his most celebrated piece, the setting of the *Nunc dimittis* used as theme-music in the television adaptation of John Le Carré's *Tinker, Tailor, Soldier, Spy*, originally for treble but well within counter-tenor range. Some of the other works are just as striking. In his three settings of St John of the Cross, *Cançiones del Alma*, Burgon was consciously seeking to get away from Anglican church-choir associations of the counter-tenor voice, and some of the bell-like effects are most beautiful. *Worldës blissë*, another religious inspiration, was prompted by a dream of a counter-tenor and oboe in duet; while in *This ean night* he dared to set the same text as Britten in the *Serenade* and Stravinsky in the *Cantata*, the *Lyke-Wake Dirge*, producing – despite obvious echoes of Britten – distinctive results in the tangy duetting of counter-tenors. The performances are strongly committed, with James Bowman taking the lion's share of solos. The recording gives an aptly ecclesiastical glow to the sound while keeping essential clarity.

Busoni, Ferruccio (1866–1924)

Indian fantasy for piano and orchestra, Op. 44.
(B) ** Millennium MCD 80116. Marjorie Mitchell, N. German RSO, Strickland – BORTKIEVITCH; BRITTEN: *Piano concertos.* **

There is no alternative version of Busoni's *Indian fantasy* (1913) currently available in the UK catalogue. This recording was first published in the UK in 1964, though the sleeve gives no indication of its provenance. It attributes the orchestral contribution to the Nord Deutscher Rundfunk Orchestra, whereas the original Brunswick issue spoke of the Vienna State Opera Orchestra. Nothing that Busoni composed is uninteresting, and the *Indian fantasy* is no exception; though it is uneven, its atmosphere is exploratory and forward-looking. The CD transfer is an improvement on the original, though there is a slight halo of reverberation round the excellent soloist.

An die Jugend: Giga bolero e variazione. Elegies: All'Italia; Berceuse; Turandots Frauengemach. Exeunt omnes; Fantasia nach J. S. Bach; Indianisches Tagebuch (Red Indian Diary), Book I; Sonatinas Nos. 2; 6 (Kammerfantasie on Carmen); Toccata. Transcription of Bach: *Prelude and fugue in D, BWV 532.*
*** Chandos Dig. CHAN 9394 [id.]. Geoffrey Tozer.

Elegies Nos. 1 (Nach der Wendung); 7 (Elegy); Fantasia in modo antico, Op. 33b/4; Macchiette medioevali; Sonatinas Nos. 4 (In diem navitatis Christi MCMXVII); 6 (Kammerfantasie on Bizet's Carmen); Suite campestre. arr. of BACH: *Choral preludes: Ich ruf' zu dir Herr Jesu Christ; Non komm, der Heiden Heiland.*
*** Olympia Dig. OCD 461 [id.]. William Stephenson.

Both these collections are thoroughly worthwhile and they overlap very little. William Stephenson is possibly the more natural Busoni interpreter, and his programme is very stimulating. Yet the Chandos disc assembles nearly 80 minutes of Busoni's piano music and makes an admirable and well-chosen introduction to it. Most pieces come off very well indeed, and often brilliantly, from the *Exeunt omnes* and the *Elegien* to the *Indianisches Tagebuch* and the attractive *Turandots Frauengemach*. This is an excellent CD, very well recorded and thoroughly recommendable, but not in preference to the Olympia selection, if one has to make an outright choice between them.

Doktor Faust: Symphonic intermezzo.
(M) ** DG 439 488-2 [id.]. Bav. RSO, Ferdinand Leitner – HINDEMITH: *Mathis Symphony* **; PFITZNER: *Palestrina: 3 Preludes* **; WEILL: *Kleine Dreigroschenmusik.* ***

The symphonic intermezzo is the *Sarabande* in the form in which it occurs in the opera between scenes one and two. Leitner's account comes from the 'complete' opera that he recorded in 1969 with Dietrich Fischer-Dieskau in the title-rôle but which was marked by numerous small cuts. Decent playing and recording.

Butterworth, George (1885–1916)

The banks of green willow; 2 English idylls.
(M) **(*) EMI Dig. CDM7 64200-2 [id.]. ECO, Jeffrey Tate – BAX: *3 Pieces;* BRIDGE: *There is a willow;* MOERAN: *2 Pieces.* **(*)

The banks of green willow and the two *English idylls* make attractive items in Tate's recital of English pieces, but it is a pity that *A Shropshire Lad* was not also included. The playing is refined and sensitive but lacks something in magic, with slow speeds for the *Idylls* making them sound a little unspontaneous. The 1985 Abbey Road sound is outstanding, warm, full and atmospheric.

Buxtehude, Diderik (*c.* 1637–1707)

Canzonetta in G, BuxWV 171; Ciaconas: in C min., BuxWV 159; in E min., BuxWV 160. Chorales: *Ach, Herr, mich armen Sünder, BuxWV 178; Der Tag der ist so freudenreich, BuxWV 182; Durch Adams Fall ist ganz verderbt, BuxWV 183; In dulci jubilo, BuxWV 197; Komm, heiliger Geist, Herr Gott, BuxWV 199; Nimm von uns, BuxWV 207; Nun komm der Heiden Heiland, BuxWV 211; Wie schön leuchtet der Morgenstern, BuxWV 223. Fugue in C, BuxWV 174; Magnificat primi toni, BuxWV 203; Passacaglia in D min., BuxWV 161; Preludes: in A min., BuxWv 153; in C, BuxWV 137; in D, BuxWV 139; in D min., BuxWV 140; E min., BuxWV 142; F, BuxWV 145; F sharp min., BuxWV 146; G min., BuxWV 149. Te Deum laudamus, BuxWV 218; Toccatas: in D min., BuxWV 155; in F, BuxWV 156.*
500♪ (M) *** Erato/Warner Dig. 0630 12979-2 (2). Marie-Claire Alain (Schnitger-Ahrend organ, Groningen).

Marie-Claire Alain's admirable mid-priced, two-disc set on Erato currently seems just about the best buy for those wanting a comprehensive survey of Buxtehude's splendid organ music. The complex *Magnificat primi toni* and the large-scale chorale fantasia on the *Te Deum* make one understand why Bach so admired this music. The arresting *Toccata in D minor*, with its dramatic pauses, undoubtedly influenced Bach's most famous organ work in the same key. Superb playing throughout, and demonstration-standard recording.

Byrd, William (1543–1623)

Music for viols: *Browning; 2 Fantasias a 3 in C; Fantasias a 4 in D and G; Prelude and voluntary;* (i) *Prelude (Pavana, Gagliarda Ph. Tregian); Ut re mi fa sol la* (for harpsichord); (ii; iii) *Delight is dead;* (ii) *Farewell false love;* (iii) *My mistress had a little dog; Rejoice unto the Lord;* (ii; iii) *Who made thee, Hob, forsake the plough?* (ii) *Ye sacred muses.*
*** Lyrichord Dig. LEMS 8015 [id.]. (i) Louis Bagger; (ii) Tamara Crout; (iii) Lawrence Lipnik; NY Cons. of Viols.

Those who know only Byrd's church music – and in particular the Latin Masses – will find this concert a refreshing experience. The New York Consort of Viols create a particularly attractive blend of timbre, and everything they play is thoroughly alive. The harpsichordist, Louis Bagger, isn't a show-off and he plays with character, and with considerable bravura when *Ut re mi fa sol* becomes more and more florid as it proceeds. The two vocal soloists work well together, especially in the rustic dialogue song, *Who made thee, Hob, forsake the plough?* Tamara Crout sings with great charm in her solo numbers – with the lightest touch in the charming song about the 'murdered' pet dog, and very expressively in *Rejoice unto the Lord* and the touching *Ye sacred muses*. In every way this is a most rewarding programme, excellently balanced and recorded.

My Ladye Nevells Booke, 1591 (42 keyboard pieces).
500♪ ❁ *** O-L 430 484-2 (3). Christopher Hogwood (virginal, harpsichord, chamber organ).

This collection of Byrd's music was compiled by John Baldwin of Windsor and must be reckoned the finest collection in Europe of keyboard writing of the sixteenth century. Christopher Hogwood rings the changes by using a variety of instruments: a virginal, two harpsichords (one Flemish and the other Italian) and a fine chamber organ, all of which he plays with sympathy and vitality. Hogwood's scholarly gifts are shown in the fine notes that accompany the set, but, more importantly, his masterly keyboard technique and artistic sensitivity are sustained throughout the three discs. The recording is exemplary, very real and in excellent perspective. A landmark in records of early keyboard music.

Mass for 3 voices; Mass for 4 voices; Mass for 5 voices.
500♪ ❁ (M) *** Decca 433 675-2 [id.]. King's College, Cambridge, Ch., Willcocks.

Masses for 3, 4 and 5 voices; Ave verum corpus; Magnificat; Nunc dimittis.
(B) *** Decca Double 452 170-2 (2) [id.]. King's College, Cambridge, Ch., Willcocks – TAVERNER: *Western Wynde Mass.* ***

Although later versions of the *Mass for 5 voices* have produced singing that is more dramatic and more ardent, the performances of the *Masses for 3* and *4 voices*, dating from 1963, remain classics of the gramophone. Under Willcocks there is an inevitability of phrasing and effortless control of sonority and dynamic that completely capture the music's spiritual and emotional feeling. On Double Decca the 1959 recordings of the *Ave verum, Magnificat* and *Nunc dimittis* have been added, representing a more reticent, less forceful style than some might expect. But the singing is still affectingly beautiful and the sound comparably spacious, and the coupled Taverner programme shows the choir on top form.

Mass for 5 voices with the Propers for the Feast of All Saints; Motets: *Ad Dominum cum tribularer; Diliges Dominum.*
**(*) Virgin Veritas/EMI Dig. VER5 61297-2. The Sixteen, Harry Christophers.

The *Mass for 5 voices* comes here in its ecclesiastical context together with the *Propers for the Feast of All Saints*, which are from the *Gradualia* of 1605. The disc also includes a pair of eight-part motets, *Ad Dominum cum tribularer*, notable for its rich-textured, poignant false relations, and the shorter *Diliges Dominum* (another early work). The latter is a remarkable eight-part canon in which the voices are paired and at the half-way point each then performs the music first sung by its partner – backwards! Yet the effect is above all expressively serene. The singing is very impressive, the recording excellently focused and the acoustic appropriately spacious; but this reissue now seems rather short measure at 55 minutes 32 seconds.

Caldara, Antonio (*c*. 1670–1736)

Christmas cantata (Vaticini di Pace); Sinfonias Nos. 5 & 6.
(BB) *** Naxos 8.553772 [id.]. Mary Enid Haines, Linda Dayiantis-Straub, Jennifer Lane, David Arnot, Aradia Baroque Ens., Kevin Mallon.

Caldara, an Italian contemporary of Bach and Handel, wrote this rare and delightful cantata for the

Christmas celebrations in Rome in 1712. Preceded by an overture, it is a free-running sequence of 14 arias for the allegorical characters of Peace, Human Heart and Divine Love, with Justice initially representing Old Testament values. Peace, in the longest and most beautiful of the arias, a siciliano, then woos Justice to mercy through a vision of the Infant Christ. This Canadian performance is fresh and lively, with four excellent soloists (notably Mary Enid Haines as Peace) and a good period-instrument ensemble. A rarity made doubly enticing at Naxos super-bargain price.

Maddalena ai piedi di Cristo (oratorio; complete).
*** HM Dig. HMC 905221/22 (2) [id.]. Kiehr, Dominguez, Fink, Scholl, Messthaler, Türk, Schola Cantorum Basiliensis O, René Jacobs.

This oratorio about Mary Magdalene at the feet of Christ, an early work dating from around 1700, inspired Caldara to an astonishing sequence of *da capo* arias, full of striking invention, plus one duet which ends the first of the two parts. There are 28 arias in all, most of them brief, but with several longer ones given to Maddalena herself, notably the heartfelt *Pompo inutile*, inspiring Maria Cristina Kiehr to warm, golden tone, or the agonized *In lagrime stemprato*, depicting falling tears. In contrasting characterization, her sister Marta has such jolly numbers as *Vattene, corri, vola*, with Rosa Dominguez bright and agile. The role of Christ is given to a tenor, but neither of his two arias is reflective, and the biggest proportion of arias go to the counterpart characters of Earthly Love (a mezzo, Bernarda Fink) and Heavenly Love (a counter-tenor, Andreas Scholl), both of them singing superbly, subtly contrasted in tone. René Jacobs draws fresh and alert playing from the Schola Basiliensis Orchestra, with the instruments, including varied continuo, set in a warm acoustic slightly behind the singers.

Campra, André (1660–1744)

OPERA

Idomenée: highlights.
(B) *** HM Dig. HMX 290844/46 (3) [id.] (from complete recording, with Delétré, Piau, Zanetti, Fouchécourt, Les Arts Florissants; cond. Christie) – LULLY: *Atys:* highlights; RAMEAU: *Castor et Pollux:* highlights. ***

This is one of Harmonia Mundi's enterprising 'Trios', compiling three discs of operatic highlights at bargain price with full documentation, including translations. *Idomenée* is a fascinating work vividly recorded (on HMC 901396/8,) and this 70-minute selection, with items well balanced to include the Overture, a brief reminder of the Prologue and excerpts from all five Acts, if taken in harness with its companions costs but a fraction of the price of the three-disc complete set. It will be interesting to see if this marketing experiment is a success.

Canteloube, Marie-Joseph (1879–1957)

Chants d'Auvergne: L'Antouèno; Baïlèro; 3 Bourrées; Lou Boussu; Brezairola; Lou coucut; Chut, chut; La Déläissádo; Lo Fïolairé; Jou l'pount d'o Mirabel; Malurous qu'o uno fenno; Passo pel prat; Pastourelle; Postouro, sé tu m'aymo; Tè, l'co, tè.
500♪ ❁ (M) *** EMI Dig. CD-EMX 9500; *TC-EMX 2075* [Ang. CDM 62010]. Jill Gomez, RLPO, Handley.

Jill Gomez's selection of these increasingly popular songs, attractively presented on a mid-price label, makes for a memorably characterful record which, as well as bringing out the sensuous beauty of Canteloube's arrangements, keeps reminding us, in the echoes of rustic band music, of the genuine folk base. An ideal purchase for the collector who wants just a selection.

Caplet, André (1878–1925)

La Masque de la mort rouge (Conte fantastique); Divertissements for harp; (i) *Les prières*, for soprano, harp & string quartet; (ii) *2 Sonnets*, for soprano & harp; (i–iii) *Septet à cordes vocales et instrumentales.*
(B́) *** HM Musique d'Abord Dig. HMA 1901417 [id.]. Laurence Cabel, Ens. Musique Oblique; with (i) Sharon Coste; (ii) Sandrine Piau; (iii) Sylvie Deguy.

André Caplet's best-known work is the *Conte fantastique* for harp and strings, based on Edgar Allen Poe's *Masque of the Red Death*, a work strong on evocative menace. This bargain-priced Harmonia Mundi reissue is highly recommendable. It offers the more intimate, chamber version of the score, and the rest of the programme is admirably chosen and serves to flesh out a portrait of Caplet himself. In the other three major works, female voices are richly integrated with the string quartet, and the composer makes a great success of this combination of voices and strings, especially in the *Septet*, using a trio of two sopranos and a mezzo. Beautiful singing, sensitive playing and warmly atmospheric sound add to the listener's aural pleasure. Two solo *Divertissements* for harp make an agreeable central interlude.

Cardoso, Frei Manuel (*c.* 1566–1650)

Missa Miserere mihi Domine; Magnificat seccundi toni.
*** HM Dig. HMC 901543 [id.]. European Vocal Ens., Philippe Herreweghe.

Once again in the *Missa Miserere mihi Domine* we are aware of the extraordinary individuality of Cardoso's polyphony and its powerful and sumptuous expressive content. The *Et incarnatus* of the *Credo* and the *Hosanna* of the *Sanctus* are moments of special potency. The composer's forward-looking use of harmonic relationships is also a striking feature of the *Magnificat*, a shorter but no less impressive work. The performers here really sound as if they believe both in the music and in the words they are singing, and the recording, made in L'Abbaye aux Dames de Saintes, is fully worthy of their richly sonorous blend of tone.

Cartellieri, Casimir Anton (1772–1807)

Clarinet concertos Nos. 1 in B flat; 2 – Adagio pastorale; 3 in E flat.
*** Chandos/MDG Dig. MDG 301 0527-2 [id.]. Dieter Klöcker, Prague CO.

Hardly a household name, Casimir Anton Cartellieri was born in Danzig and eventually found his way to Vienna, where he probably studied with Salieri and certainly became a pupil of Albrechtsberger. He came to the attention of Beethoven's patron, Prince Lobkowitz, whose service he entered. In his three *Clarinet concertos* (only the slow movement of the second survives) he could call on the advice of Mozart's Anton Stadler, and it is hardly surprising that they are expertly laid out for the instrument. While they are not searching or profound, they are astonishingly inventive and full of both charm and wit. Dieter Klöcker and the Prague Chamber Orchestra give thoroughly committed accounts of these delightful pieces, and the MDG recording is immaculate.

Carwithen, Doreen (born 1922)

(i) *Concerto for piano and strings. Overtures: ODTAA, ('One damn thing after another'); Bishop Rock; Suffolk suite.*
*** Chandos Dig. CHAN 9524 [id.]. (i) Howard Shelley; LSO, Hickox.

Having virtually given up her composing career for many decades, acting instead as amanuensis to her composer husband, William Alwyn, Doreen Carwithen here emerges as a warmly communicative composer in her own right, owing rather more to Walton's style than to her husband's, but always writing purposefully with strong rhythms (often syncopated in jazzy Waltonian style) and stirring melodies, all enhanced with brilliant and inventive orchestration. In the years after the Second World War she was successful in the world of films, writing some 30 scores, and the two overtures in their vigour and atmospheric colour relate readily to film music, the one inspired by John Masefield's novel, *ODTAA*, the other inspired by the rock in the Atlantic that marks the last contact with the British Isles, stormy in places, gently sinister in others. The four compact movements of the charming *Suffolk suite* use melodies originally written for a film on East Anglia, with music so warm and colourful that you would never realize that this was originally designed for schoolchildren to play. Much the most ambitious work is the *Concerto for piano and strings*, with powerful virtuoso writing for the piano set against rich-textured strings. A deeply melancholy slow movement – in which the piano is joined by solo violin – leads to a strong finale which in places echoes the Ireland *Piano concerto*. Howard Shelley is the persuasive soloist, with Richard Hickox and the LSO equally convincing in their advocacy of all four works. Warm, atmospheric sound.

Chabrier, Emmanuel (1841–94)

Bourrée fantasque; España (rhapsody); *Joyeuse marche; Menuet pompeux; Prélude pastorale; Suite pastorale; Le Roi malgré lui: Danse slave; Fête polonaise.*
500♪ *** EMI Dig. CDC7 49652-2. Capitole Toulouse O, Plasson.

Chabrier is Beecham territory and he calls for playing of elegance and charm. Michel Plasson and his excellent Toulouse forces bring just the right note of exuberance and *joie de vivre* to this delightful music. The recording is eminently satisfactory, though it lacks the last ounce of transparency. Even so, the effect suits the music, and the elegant performance of the delightful *Suite pastorale* ensures a strong recommendation for this CD.

España; Fête polonaise; Gwendoline overture; Habanera; (i) *Larghetto for horn and orchestra. Marche joyeuse; Prélude pastorale; Suite pastorale.*
*(**) DG Dig. 447 751-2 [id.]. (i) Janezic; VPO, Gardiner.

This collection has received much praise in other quarters, but we find it disappointing. The fortissimos bring coarseness into the music-making and readily become tiring to listen to. Easily the most attractive and refined playing comes in the charming *Suite pastorale*, with the rustling leaves in *Sous-bois* delicately caught. Elsewhere the recording (made in the Grosse Saal of the Vienna Musikverein) is determinedly spectacular, and will no doubt appeal to hi-fi fans, but the reverberation and the heaviness at the bottom end introduce an element of crudeness. The performances certainly do not lack vigour but are hardly subtle in rhythmic feeling. Clearly the VPO are not at home in this repertoire and, for all the brilliance of Gardiner's approach, *España* becomes heavy-going, with its over-enthusiastic bass drum, while the orchestra is not very seductive either in nudging the rhythms of the *Habanera*. Both the *Marche joyeuse* (which is certainly roisterous) and the *Fête polonaise* (where the lilting rubato is clumsily managed) make a bold impact but almost overwhelm the listener. The climax of the charming *Prélude pastorale* is similarly larger-than-life, and the *Gwendoline overture*, for all its energy, is over-dramatized.

(i) Piano music, four hands: *Cortège burlesque; Joyeuse marche; Souvenirs de Munich* (*Quadrille* on themes from Wagner's *Tristan und Isolde*); *3 Valses romantiques*. (Piano): *Air de ballet; Bourrée fantasque; Capriccio* (finished by Maurice le Boucher); *Habanera; Impromptu; Marche des Cipayes; 5 Pièces (Ballabile; Feuillet d'album; Aubade; Caprice; Ronde champêtre); 10 Pièces pittoresques; Suite de valses.*
(B) ** Carlton VoxBox/Turnabout 30371 0014-2 (2). Rena Kyriakou; (i) with Walter Klien.

Rena Kyriakou is spontaneous enough, but she is also a highly impulsive player. There is temperament in excess, and she tends to get carried away by the music instead of staying in firm rhythmic control. In the music for four hands she is joined by Walter Klien (although he is not credited) and the playing has splendid panache, especially in the *Cortège burlesque* and of course the highly disrespectful *Souvenirs de Munich*. This VoxBox may tempt some readers by its very inexpensiveness and it should not be written off, though music of this kind needs poise.

Gwendoline (complete).
*(**) HM Dig. ED 13059 (2) [id.]. Kohutková, Henry, Garino, Brno Philharmonic Ch., Slovak PO, Penin.

Like the unfinished *Briseis*, recorded by Hyperion, *Gwendoline* is a high romantic opera written in the shadow of Wagner. In the story – with the same librettist as *Briseis*, Catulle Mendes – there are echoes of both *Tristan* and the *Ring*. Set in England in the dark ages (in the eighth century, not the eighteenth, as stated in the booklet) the story tells of Harald, a marauding Dane, who falls in love with Gwendoline, the daughter of the Saxon chief, Armel, whom he has defeated. Armel arranges for Gwendoline to murder Harald on her wedding night, but she falls passionately in love with her betrothed, refusing to kill him. At the wedding feast, Armel stabs Harald instead. In grief Gwendoline kills herself, leaving time for them both to enjoy a substantial Liebestod duet, with a vision of flying to Valhalla, home of heroes, as they die.

With few direct echoes of Wagner, the score is yet vigorously red-blooded to match the story's blood and thunder, with many sensuous sequences, not just the love-duets but such evocative choral passages as the *Epithalamium*. The final love-death brings more echoes of the final trio of Gounod's *Faust* than it does of Wagner, with the idiom identifiably French throughout. This live recording, made in Bratislava in January 1996, offers a performance flawed vocally but with Jean-Paul Penin drawing playing that is both sensitive and passionate from the Slovak Philharmonic. In the title-role Adriana Kohutková sings sympathetically but with bright tone that leads to shrillness on top. Didier Henry's grainy baritone grows rough under pressure, hardly heroic-sounding, and Gérard Garino's fine, clear tenor sounds far too youthful for the aged Armel. Nevertheless, a very enjoyable first recording, with first-rate sound.

Chaminade, Cécile (1857–1944)

Piano trios Nos. 1 in G min., Op. 11; 2 in A min., Op. 34; Pastorale enfantine, Op. 12; Ritournelle; Serenade, Op. 29 (all 3 arr. Marcus); *Serenade espagnole* (arr. Kreisler).
*** ASV Dig. CDDCA 965 [id.]. Tzigane Piano Trio.

With warmly expressive performances from the Tzigane Piano Trio, well recorded, this is another attractive addition to ASV's growing collection of rare romantic chamber works. Cécile Chaminade, once popular for her salon pieces, was more ambitious early in her career. In these two *Piano trios* she confidently controls larger forms, building on a fund of melody. The two central movements of the *Piano trio No. 1* are charming, a passionately lyrical *Andante* and a sparkling, Mendelssohnian Scherzo. The *Piano trio No. 2*, in three movements, without a Scherzo, is weightier, almost Brahmsian, with themes rather more positive. Three of the four miniatures which come as fill-ups have been arranged for trio by the Tzigane's pianist, Elizabeth Marcus.

PIANO MUSIC

Album des enfants, Op. 123/4, 5, 9 & 10; Op. 126/1, 2, 9 & 10; Arabesque, Op. 61; Cortège, Op. 143; Inquiétude, Op. 87/3; Le Passé; Prelude in D min., Op. 84/3; Rigaudon, Op. 55/6; Sérénade espagnole; Sonata in C min., Op. 21; Les Sylvains, Op. 60; Valse-ballet, Op. 112; Valse brillante No. 3, Op. 80; Valse No. 4, Op. 91.
*** Hyperion Dig. CDA 66846 [id.]. Peter Jacobs.

In his ongoing survey of the Chaminade piano music Peter Jacobs continues to show his stylish sympathy for a composer who, while not probing the depths, was never dull. He makes one feel there is more to this composer than one had suspected. The opening *Prelude in D minor* shows the pianistic range of the writing, *Les Sylvains* and the *Valse-ballet* its ready charm. But the highlight of this recital is the set of excerpts from the *Album des enfants*, beautifully written pieces to entice any young player, notably the engaging *Idylle*, and *Gavotte* and certainly the rhythmically catchy *Rondeau* (quite a lollipop). The *Troisième Valse brillante* and the *Tarantelle* (both sparklingly presented) give Jacobs a fine chance to display his light-hearted bravura. The *Sonata* is no mean achievement, essentially romantic with its songful *Andante*, but with an unexpected contrapuntal line emerging in the first movement. First rate recording.

Arlequine, Op. 53; Au pays dévasté, Op. 155; Chanson Brétonne; Divertissement, Op. 105; Etudes de concert, Op. 35: Impromptu; Tarantella. Etude symphonique, Op. 28; Feuillets d'album, Op. 98: Elégie. Gigue in D, Op. 43; Libellules, Op. 24; Pastorale, Op. 114; Pièces humoristiques Op. 87: Sous bois; Consolation. Nocturne, Op. 165; Passacaille in E, Op. 130; Poème romantique, Op. 7; Tristesse, Op. 104; Valse tendre, Op. 119; Scherzo-valse, Op. 148.
*** Hyperion Dig. CDA 66706 [id.]. Peter Jacobs.

Again there is plenty to enjoy here, from the fluent *Poème romantique* to the delightful *Consolation*. The characteristic pieces are full of colour and nicely flavoured by this very sympathetic pianism, so spontaneous and readily conveying the player's appreciation and enjoyment. Excellent sound.

Charpentier, Marc-Antoine (1634–1704)

VOCAL MUSIC

(i) *Canticum in honorem Sancti Ludovici Regis Galliae; Laudate Dominum; 3rd Magnificat;* (ii) *Te Deum.*
(M) *** Erato/Warner Analogue/Dig. 0630 13724-2 [id.]. Bernadette Degelin, Jean Nirouët, Jean Caals, Kurt Widmer; with (i) Dominique Mols, David James; (i–ii) Lieve Jansen; Gents Madrigaalkoor, Cantabile Gent, Musica Polyphonica, Devos.

The *Canticum in honorem Sancti Ludovici* dates from the last years of Charpentier's life as Master at Sainte-Chapelle. It is richly scored, and this lends force to the view that it was written for the visit of the King and Queen of England in 1698. It is a splendid piece and a typical Grand motet of the period, full of variety. Most readers will know the *Te Deum* from the European fanfare. It has been recorded a number of times, but this account from Louis Devos is as good as any and better than most of its predecessors. The two companion pieces, the setting of Psalm 116 (*Laudate Dominum*) and the present setting of the *Magnificat* (one of many) are also from the mid-1690s and are comparative rarities. The performances are very good indeed and the standard of singing excellent. The digital recording balances the team of soloists rather forwardly, but overall this is a rewarding and inexpensive CD with which to fill out a Charpentier collection.

Méditations pour le Carême; Le reniement de St Pierre.
(B) *** HM Dig. HMC 1905151 [id.]. Les Arts Florissants, William Christie.

Le reniement de Saint Pierre is one of Charpentier's most inspired and expressive works and its text draws on the account in all four Gospels of St Peter's denial of Christ. The *Méditations pour le Carême* are a sequence of three-voice motets for Lent with continuo accompaniment (organ, theorbo and bass viol) that may not have quite the same imaginative or expressive resource but which are full of nobility and interest. The performances maintain the high standards of this ensemble, and the same compliment can be paid to the recording. Now reissued on Harmonia Mundi's bargain Musique d'abord label, this is now doubly attractive.

Médée (complete).
500♪ ❁ *** Erato/Warner Dig. 4509 96558-2 (3) [id.]. Hunt, Padmore, Delétré, Zanetti, Salzmann, Les Arts Florissants, William Christie.

Christie's performance easily surpasses his previous one in its extra brightness and vigour, with consistently crisper and more alert ensembles, often at brisker speeds, with the drama more clearly established. It is a powerful and moving piece, readily matching the finest of the exploratory operas of Charpentier's predecessor, Lully. Lorraine Hunt is outstanding in the tragic title-role. Her soprano has satisfying weight and richness, as well as the purity and precision needed in such classical opera; and Mark Padmore's clear, high tenor copes superbly with the role of Jason.

Chausson, Ernest (1855–99)

Poème for violin and orchestra, Op. 25.
(M) *** Decca 448 128-2 [id.]. Kyung Wha Chung, RPO, Dutoit – SAINT-SAENS: *Violin concertos Nos. 1 & 3;* VIEUXTEMPS: *Violin concerto No. 5.* ***

Chung's performance of Chausson's beautiful *Poème* is deeply emotional; some may prefer a more restrained approach but, with committed accompaniment from the RPO and excellent 1977 recording, this makes an admirable postlude, following the concertos of Saint-Saëns and Vieuxtemps.

Chávez, Carlos (1899–1978)

Sinfonia de Antigona (Symphony No. 1); Sinfonia India (Symphony No. 2); Sinfonia Romantica (Symphony No. 4).
**(*) Everest EVC 9041 [id.]. New York Stadium SO, composer.

These Everest performances carry the authority of the composer's direction and include the best known, *Sinfonia India*, which is based on true Indian melodies. It has a savage, primitive character which is very attractive. The 1958 recording is detailed and bright, if not absolutely sharp in focus because of the resonance, and is somewhat wanting in real depth and weight. Nevertheless this is a valuable reissue, and it is a pity that it is not offered in a lower price range.

Cherubini, Luigi (1760–1842)

OPERA

Medea (complete).
(B) ** Decca Double 452 611-2 (2) [id.]. Gwyneth Jones, Prevedi, Lorengar, Diaz, Cossotto, Accademia di Santa Cecilia, Rome, Ch. and O, Gardelli.

Cherubini's original score of 1797 is here modified – as in virtually all modern revivals – by the work of the German composer, Franz Lachner, half a century later. The result brings its stylistic clashes, for Lachner's recitatives have their post-Weberian touches and even a touch or two of Wagner. But his work certainly helps to maintain the dramatic tension of the piece and to underline the fiery character of the heroine. This version gives only an imperfect idea of the work's power. Gwyneth Jones, for all her achievements thus far, was not ready to record this taxing part, particularly not in Italian, in which she was not really fluent. There are too many uncontrolled notes and, though she throws herself into the drama and Bruno Prevedi as Jason provides some stylish tenor singing, the set is only a partial success, although it is very well recorded and certainly inexpensive. The Callas recording completely outshines any rival in this opera (EMI CMS7 63625-2 – see our main volume).

Chopin, Frédéric (1810–49)

Piano concertos Nos. 1 in E min., Op. 11; 2 in F min., Op. 21.
500♪ *** DG 415 970-2 [id.]. Zimerman, LAPO, Giulini.
(M) *** Mercury 434 374-2 [id.]. Gina Bachauer, LSO, Dorati.

The CD coupling of Zimerman's performances of the two Chopin concertos with Giulini is hard to beat. Elegant, aristocratic, sparkling, it has youthful spontaneity and at the same time a magisterial authority, combining sensibility with effortless pianism. Both recordings are cleanly detailed.

The orchestral accompaniments for the two Chopin *Concertos* can surely never have been presented with such a strong profile as under Dorati, tuttis strong and expansive and with every detail coming through – the bassoon and oboe solos really catch the ear. And how beautifully he prepares for the first piano entry in the *E minor Concerto*. Gina Bachauer obviously sees these as full-bloodedly romantic concertos and Dorati gives her every support. Yet her passage-work scintillates and her phrasing and rubato have fine sensitivity. Both slow movements bring appealing delicacy, and finales have a lilting panache, while the central episode of the *Larghetto* of the *F minor* work can seldom have sounded more dramatic. With Mercury's spaciously realistic Watford Town Hall recording of orchestra and piano alike, and an excellent balance, this is very enjoyable indeed, perhaps not an out-and-out first choice but offering a genuine mid-priced alternative to Zimerman, Perahia (Sony SK 44922) and the twelve-year-old Kissin (RCA 09026 68378-2).

Piano concerto No. 1 in E min., Op. 11.
(M) *** DG 449 719-2 [id.]. Argerich, LSO, Abbado – LISZT: *Piano concerto No. 1.* ***

Martha Argerich's recording dates from 1968 and helped to establish her international reputation. The distinction of this partnership is immediately apparent in the opening orchestral ritornello with Abbado's flexible approach. Argerich follows his lead and her affectionate phrasing provides some lovely playing, especially in the slow movement. Perhaps in the passage-work she is rather too intense, but this is far preferable to the rambling style we are sometimes offered. This version is now reissued as one of DG's 'Originals' in a coupling with an equally individual and charismatic account of Liszt's *First Concerto*, and great trouble has been taken by the DG engineers to add lustre to a recording which was originally of very high quality and which now sounds even fresher.

Piano concerto No. 1 in E min., Op. 11; Andante spianato & Grande polonaise brillante in E flat, Op. 22; Variations on 'Là ci darem la mano', Op. 2.
*(*) Decca Dig. 448 238-2 [id.]. Nebolsin, Deutsches SO, Berlin, Vladimir Ashkenazy.

The youthful Eldar Nebolsin proves something of a disappointment here. He has no lack of technical fluency and polish, but his readings are what one might call professional and little else. They are conspicuously lacking in the freshness and ardour one expects from a young artist, and one with such an abundance of gifts. Indeed they are curiously low in voltage and are rather short on poetic feeling. They are well accompanied and recorded, but the interpretations hardly rise above the routine.

Piano concerto No. 2 in F min., Op. 21.
(M) *** Decca 448 598-2 [id.]. Vladimir Ashkenazy, LSO, Zinman – BACH: *Clavier concerto No. 1;* MOZART: *Piano concerto No. 6.* **(*)

Ashkenazy's 1965 recording is a distinguished performance: his sophisticated use of light and shade in the opening movement and the subtlety of phrasing and rubato are a constant source of pleasure. The recitativo section in the *Larghetto*, which can often sound merely rhetorical, is here shaped with mastery, and there is a delectable lightness of touch in the finale. David Zinman and the LSO are obviously in full rapport with their soloist and the vintage recording has been remastered most satisfactorily. This is now reissued in Decca's Classic Sound series with new couplings, which are perhaps less than ideally chosen, although enjoyable enough.

Les Sylphides (ballet; orch. Douglas).
500♪ ❀ (B) *** DG Double 437 404-2 (2) [id.]. BPO, Karajan (with DELIBES: *Coppélia suite* ***; GOUNOD: *Faust: ballet music and Waltz* **(*); OFFENBACH: *Gaîté parisienne;* RAVEL: *Boléro* ***; TCHAIKOVSKY: *Sleeping Beauty* (suite) **(*)).
(B) **(*) Decca Eclipse Dig. 448 984-2; *448 984-4* [id.]. Nat. PO, Bonynge (with MASSENET: *Thaïs: Méditation* with Nigel Kennedy) – ROSSINI/RESPIGHI: *La Boutique fantasque.* **(*)

Karajan conjures consistently beautiful playing with the Berlin Philharmonic Orchestra, and he evokes a delicacy of texture which consistently delights the ear. The woodwind solos are played gently and lovingly, and one can feel the conductor's touch on the phrasing; the recording is full and atmospheric. Within a two-disc Double DG set, it is now coupled not only with the *Coppélia suite* (no longer truncated) but also with ballet music by Offenbach, Gounod and Tchaikovsky.

Bonynge's performance shows a strong feeling for the dance rhythms of the ballet, and the orchestral playing is polished and lively. Bonynge also has the advantage of excellent (1982) digital recording, made in the Kingsway Hall. Nigel Kennedy plays very appealingly in the Massenet lollipop which acts as an encore. Even so, Karajan remains unsurpassed in this beautiful score.

Cello sonata in G min., Op. 65; Grand duo concertante in E on themes from Meyerbeer's 'Robert le Diable'; Nocturne in C sharp min., Op. posth (arr. Piatigorsky); *Etudes: in E min., Op. 25/7; D min., Op. 10/6* (arr. Glazunov; ed. Feuermann); *Waltz in A min., Op. 34/3* (arr. Ginsburg).
(BB) *** Naxos 8.553259 [id.]. Maria Kliegel, Bernd Glemser.

Fresh and ardent performances of the *Sonata* and the remaining two pieces that comprise Chopin's complete output for cello and piano. The Naxos collection also throws in some cello arrangements for good measure. These gifted and accomplished young artists are also very well recorded indeed and, at the price, this is a bargain.

SOLO PIANO MUSIC

Ballades Nos. 1–4; Etudes: in E; C sharp min., Op. 10/3–4; Mazurkas: in F min., Op. 7/4; in A min., Op. 17/4; in D, Op. 33/2; Nocturne in F, Op. 15/1; Waltzes: in E flat (Grande valse brillante), Op. 18; in A flat, Op. 42.
500♪ ❀ *** Sony Dig. SK 64399 [id.]. Murray Perahia.

Chopin playing does not come better than this. Perahia's set of the *Ballades* is unlikely to be surpassed, and the *Waltzes* prompt one's thoughts to turn to the classic post-war Lipatti set, although comparison does not find Perahia less poetic. Moreover the Sony engineers do him justice. In every respect a masterly recital that is in a class of its own and which readers should not miss.

(i) *Ballades Nos. 1–4;* (ii) *Scherzi Nos. 1–4.*
(M) ** Ph. 454 135-2 [id.]. (i) Bella Davidovich; (ii) Rafael Orozco.

Bella Davidovich plays the *Ballades* with unaffected sensibility; these are considerable performances, and the digital recording is most realistic. However, in the *Scherzi* Rafael Orozco is as impetuous as Davidovich is considered. The famous *B flat minor* comes off well enough with its volatile display, but in the opening *B minor*, Orozco almost gets carried away in a headlong rush of bravura, while the *C sharp minor* and *E major* are hardly less reckless, although technically impressive. Good, clear recording.

Mazurkas Nos. 1–59, Op. 6/1–4; Op. 7/1–5; Op. 17/1–4; Op. 24/1–4; Op. 30/1–4; Op. 33/1–4; Op. 41/1–4; Op. 50/1–3; Op. 56/1–3; Op. 59/1–3; Op. 63/1–3; Op. 67/1–4; Op. 68/1–4; & Op. 68/4 (revised version); *Nos. 60–68, Op. posth.*
500♪ (B) *** Decca Double Dig./Analogue 448 086-2 (2) [id.]. Vladimir Ashkenazy.

As can be seen, Ashkenazy's survey of Chopin's *Mazurkas* is the most comprehensive available and as such must take pride of place over Rubinstein's set (irrespective of its extremely modest cost).

Nocturnes Nos. 1–19.
500♪ *** RCA RD 89563 (2) [RCA 5613-2-RC]. Artur Rubinstein.

Nocturnes Nos. 1–21 (complete).
*** DG Dig. 447 096-2 (2). Maria João Pires.

Rubinstein in Chopin is a magician in matters of colour; his unerring sense of nuance and the seeming inevitability of his rubato demonstrate a very special musical imagination in this repertoire. The recordings were the best he received in his Chopin series for RCA.

However, from Pires comes quite the best set of *Nocturnes* we have had from any pianist for some years. She gives performances of great character, her playing often bold as well as meltingly romantic (as in the beautifully nuanced *D flat major Nocturne*, Op. 27/2). She brings the right poetic feel to this music. Hers is the art that conceals art, and that serves the composer to perfection. She uses the widest dynamic range and is recorded with a brilliant presence as well as a basically warm sonority. However, as we go to press Ashkenazy's highly poetical complete set of *Nocturnes* is reissued on a Double Decca (452 579-2); which also includes the four *Ballades*.

Polonaises Nos. 1–16, Op. 26/1–2; Op. 40/1–2; Op. 44; Op. 53; Polonaise-Fantaisie, Op. 61; Op. 71/1–3; Op. Posth./1–6. Albumblatt in E; Allegro de concert, Op. 46; Barcarolle in F sharp, Op. 60; Berceuse in D flat, Op. 57; 2 Bourrées; 3 Nouvelles Etudes; Fugue in A min.; Galop marquis; Tarantelle in A flat, Op. 43; Wiosna (arr. from *Op. 74/2*).
(B) *** Decca Double Analogue/Dig. 452 167-2 (2) [id.]. Vladimir Ashkenazy.

We listed Ashkenazy's highly recommendable Double Decca set of the *Polonaises* in our main volume (p. 333) and commented (on p. 329) that the set was due to appear at about the same time as we went to print. What Decca failed to tell us was that the second CD would also contain a great deal more music. Some of the items are quite short (the piano transcription of Chopin's song *Wiosna* lasts for barely a minute, but it is very fetching). But there are substantial works too: the *Barcarolle* and *Berceuse*, the latter meltingly done, and the *Allegro de Concert* and *Nouvelles Etudes* also show Ashkenazy at his finest. The recordings are excellent.

Polonaises Nos. 1 in C sharp min.; 2 in E flat min., Op. 26/1–2; 3 in A; 4 in C min., Op. 40/1–2; 5 in F sharp min., Op. 44; 6 in A flat, Op. 53; 7 in A flat, 'Polonaise-fantaisie', Op. 61.
* Teldec/Warner 4509-96532-2 [id.]. Elisabeth Leonskaja.

Elisabeth Leonskaja brings abundant technical address to these marvellous pieces, but her approach tends to be heavy-handed and wanting in natural poetic feeling. She is very well recorded, but there is no real challenge to Ashkenazy.

24 Preludes, Op. 28; Ballades Nos. 2 in F, Op. 38; 4 in F min., Op. 53; Fantaisie in F min., Op. 49.
(B) **(*) Decca Eclipse Dig. 448 985-2; *448 985-4* [id.]. Jorge Bolet.

There is some lovely playing from Bolet in this recital, especially in the two *Ballades*. He is happiest when he is at his most reflective and contemplative, less so when the music calls for abandon. He brings keen musical insights to the *Preludes* and his characterization is never wanting in the individuality that avoids any feeling of routine. But there is a certain want of fire by the side of the youngest keyboard lions on record, and he does not quite command the effortless virtuosity that distinguished his earlier Liszt recordings: he is best in the more inward-looking *Preludes*. He enjoys the benefit of first-class recording, particularly beautiful in the *Ballades*, but does not displace Ashkenazy or indeed Argerich in Op. 28.

Preludes, Op. 28, Nos. 1–11; 14–16; 20 & 23.
(M) ** Nimbus Dig. NI 8810 [id.]. Ferruccio Busoni (piano) BACH: *Chaconne;* LISZT: *Etudes d'exécution transcendante* etc. ***

There is no reason to believe that Busoni's Duo-Art piano-roll recordings (from 1923) do not project his Chopin manner truthfully, and he proves no stylist in this music. Indeed much of his playing, if strong in character, is heavy going. The opening *C major Etude* is gabbled, and the famous *E minor* is quite wilful, while *No. 9 in E major*, played sombrely, hardly sounds like Chopin at all. *No. 7 in A* bounces along, and in the *D flat major* (No. 15) the control of rubato is unconvincing. *No. 20 in C minor* opens very stolidly indeed, but the closing *F major* (No. 23), recorded four years after the rest of the sequence, brings a much lighter touch. Excellent sound.

Piano sonatas Nos. 1 in C min., Op. 4; 2 in B flat min. (Funeral march), Op. 35; 3 in B min., Op. 58.
(M) *** Decca 448 123-2 [id.]. Vladimir Ashkenazy.
(M) *(*) Revelation RV 10032 [id.]. Vera Gornosteyova.

Piano sonatas Nos. 1–3; Etudes, Op. 10/6; Op. 25/3, 4, 10 & 11; Mazurkas, Op. 17/1–4.
500♪ (B) *** Virgin/EMI Dig. VCD5 45187-2 (2) [ZDMB 61317]. Leif Ove Andsnes.

The young Norwegian pianist has the advantage of state-of-the-art piano-sound and his recital comes in a slim, two-for-the-price-of-one CD pack. As such it is splendid value. Andsnes proves as idiomatic an interpreter of Chopin as he has done of Grieg.

The *C minor Sonata*, Op. 4, is a comparative rarity; it comes from 1827 and is not deeply characteristic; it is of greater interest to students of Chopin's style and budding pianists than to the wider musical public. But the distance Chopin covered between this and the *B flat minor Sonata* is very striking, as Ashkenazy's 1981 performance readily demonstrates. Indeed the first movement in particular seems more concentrated in feeling and the finale is very exciting indeed. In this repertoire one cannot speak of the finest performance, for this is terrain that has been conquered by Rubinstein (RCA RD 89812), Pollini (DG 415 346-2) and Perahia (Sony SK 76242) and others, but it would be surprising if Ashkenazy's account does not (like the finest of its rivals) enjoy classic status, and it is certainly the best recorded, with very vivid sound. The *Third (B minor) Sonata* is almost as distinguished and is certainly memorable. Some might not like the accelerando treatment of the finale, but it is undoubtedly exciting. The recording throughout is well up to the high standard set by this series.

Vera Gornosteyova studied with Heinrich Neuhaus, among whose pupils were numbered Gilels and Richter, and she is obviously an artist of quality. Her reputation did not extend beyond the borders of the old Soviet Union, as she was considered politically unreliable, but she was a widely respected teacher at the Moscow Conservatoire. The present recording comes from a recital given on 25 February 1986 and would warrant consideration as it offers all three sonatas on one disc at mid-price. However, the sound is far from distinguished (a bit close and shallow) and the performances do not achieve the distinction one had hoped to encounter. Ashkenazy provides the obvious answer at mid-price.

Piano sonata No. 2 in B flat min., Op. 35.
(***) Testament mono STB 1089 [id.]. Emil Gilels – MOZART: *Sonata No. 17;* SHOSTAKOVICH: *Preludes and fugues Nos. 1, 5 & 24.* (***)

The *B flat minor Sonata* was recorded in New York and previously appeared in 1984 in a three-LP EMI box called 'The Art of Emil Gilels'. Testament have reissued other recordings from this collection, including the Saint-Saëns *G minor* and Rachmaninov *Third Concertos* conducted by André Cluytens, and the present issue is more than welcome. The passage of time has not dimmed its classic status or its poetic intensity and, although some allowances have to be made for the recorded sound, they are few. Performances of this stature are rare indeed.

Piano sonata No. 3 in B min., Op. 58.
(B) ** EMI forte CZS5 69527-2 (2). Anievas – LISZT: *Sonata* ***; RACHMANINOV: *24 Preludes* etc. **(*)

Agustin Anievas gives a strong if not absolutely distinctive performance of the lesser-known *B minor Sonata*. However, the slow movement has the same thoughtfulness and sensitivity that distinguish his performance of the Liszt *Sonata*, and the bravura of the finale is striking. Good recording. If the couplings are suitable, this is worth considering.

19 Waltzes; Polonaise No. 6 in A flat, Op. 53.
* Decca Dig. 448 645-2 [id.]. Peter Jablonski.

Waltzes Nos. 1–14; Barcarolle, Op. 60; Mazurka in C sharp min., Op. 50/3; Nocturne in D flat, Op. 27/2.
500♪ ❁ (M) (***) EMI CDH7 69802-2. Dinu Lipatti.

Lipatti's classic performances were recorded by Walter Legge in the rather dry acoustic of a Swiss Radio studio at Geneva in the last year of Lipatti's short life, and with each LP reincarnation they seem to have grown in wisdom and subtlety. The reputation of these meticulous performances is fully deserved.

Peter Jablonski, the talented young Swedish pianist whom Decca added to their roster a year or two ago, disappoints in this set of the *Waltzes*. Decca give him an eminently lifelike recording, but – to be frank – there is nothing particularly special about his Chopin and, unfortunately, much that approaches the routine and pedestrian.

Recital collections

Andante spianato & Grande polonaise brillante, Op. 22; Ballade No. 3 in A flat, Op. 47; Fantaisie in F min., Op. 49; Polonaise-fantaisie in A flat, Op. 81; Sonata No. 3 in B min., Op. 58.
(M) ** Decca 452 308-2 [id.]. Wilhelm Kempff.

Barcarolle in F sharp, Op. 60; Berceuse in D flat, Op. 57; Impromptus Nos. 1 in A flat, Op. 29; 2 in F sharp, Op. 26; 3 in G flat, Op. 51; Fantaisie-impromptu in C sharp min., Op. 66; Nocturne in B, Op. 9/3; Scherzo No. 3 in C sharp min., Op. 39; Sonata No. 2 in B flat min. (Funeral march), Op. 35.
(M) Decca ** 452 307-2 [id.]. Wilhelm Kempff.

Reissued in Decca's Classic Sound series, these Kempff recordings from February 1958 were among the last he made for Decca before switching back to the DG label. He was 62 at that time and was virtually unknown on the London musical scene, although already his mono DG records of the Beethoven sonatas had established his European reputation. His readings of Chopin are very personal and individual. In Chopin performances we have come to expect a technical brilliance that in all honesty Kempff could no longer provide, although his musical fluency tends to cover up the technical smudges. He is at his finest in the two sonatas, and it is a pity that Decca chose not to couple them together as on the original LP, for somehow the very scale of these works seems to inspire him to the sort of concentration that invariably marks his Beethoven performances. The first theme of the first movement of the *Funeral march Sonata*, for example, has great delicacy and clarity, but this does not make for a small, prettified effect, for underneath one can clearly feel the urgency of the playing. Then in the second subject Kempff plays with great romantic warmth but, unlike so many pianists, does not lose the pulse of the movement. In the funeral march itself his speed is rather faster than usual, but again this makes for a feeling of purpose in the insistent pulse. Only in the finale of the *Third Sonata* does he sound a little less than happy but, all told, these are wonderfully poetic readings, just such performances, one feels, as Clara Schumann might have given to her circle of intimate friends. Of the other pieces included in the first recital (452 307-2) it is the *Berceuse*, *Barcarolle* and *B major Nocturne* which stand out, where Kempff shows a natural feeling for the shading of a phrase, so that it sounds not like an 'interpretation' in inverted commas, but an inevitable part of the music. On the companion disc (the *B minor Sonata* apart), while there are some truly poetic moments – the *Andante spianato*, the opening of the *A flat Ballade* and the *F minor Fantaisie* – there are otherwise passages when the pianist seems unable to surmount the technical difficulties, and there is somehow not the sense of control which he provides in the sonatas. In the opening of the *Grande polonaise brillante* there is far too little brilliance and too much labouring, and in the *Fantaisie* the comparative absence of bravura is a drawback. But whatever Kempff does, he cannot fail to be interestingly individual: for this reason all these performances are refreshing and will provide enjoyment far longer than many a more immaculate recording.

Vanguard 'Alfred Brendel collection', Volume 2: *Andante spianato et Grande polonaise brillante, Op. 22; Polonaises Nos. 4 in C min., Op. 40/2; 5 in F sharp min., Op. 44; 6 in A flat, Op. 53; 7 (Polonaise-fantaisie), Op. 61.*
(M) ** Van. 08 9163 72. Brendel – LISZT: *Hungarian rhapsodies.* ***

Although not possessing a natural affinity for Chopin – the least effective piece here is the *Andante spianato* – nothing Brendel does is unstimulating, and these rather Schumannesque performances certainly have their interest. They were very well recorded (in 1968), and the natural piano-timbre, with a full resonant bass, has been expertly transferred to CD.

Ballade No. 1 in G min.; Fantasy impromptu, Op. 66; Mazurkas: in B flat, Op. 7/1; in D, Op. 33/2; Nocturnes: in B flat min.; in E flat, Op. 9/1–2; in C min., Op. 48/1; Polonaises: in A, Op. 40/1; in F sharp min., Op. 44; Waltzes: in E min; in E flat, Op. 18.
(B) ** Tring Dig. TRP 087 [id.]. Ronan O'Hora.

The most commanding performance here is the *Ballade in G minor*, its romantic impulse finely judged. The *B flat minor Nocturne*, too, is beautifully played, and the *Waltzes* and *Mazurkas* show that Ronan O'Hora has a nice feeling for Chopinesque rhythmic nuance. However, in the *C minor* and (especially) the famous *E flat Nocturnes*, his hesitant rubato seems over-thoughtful and not completely spontaneous. The *Polonaises* are played without barnstorming and could effectively be more extrovert, although the *A major* is quite strong and certainly enjoyably robust. Good recording.

'Favourite piano works': Ballades Nos. 1 in G min., Op. 23; 3 in A flat, Op. 47; Barcarolle, Op. 60; Etudes: in E; in G flat (Black keys); in C min. (Revolutionary), Op. 10/3, 5 & 12; in A min. (Winter wind), Op. 25/11; Fantaisie-impromptu, Op. 66; Mazurkas: in B flat, Op. 7/1; in D, Op. 33/1; Nocturnes: in E flat, Op. 9/2; in F sharp min., Op. 15/2; in B, Op. 32/1; in F min., Op. 55/1; Polonaises: in A (Military), Op. 40/1; in A flat, Op. 53; Preludes: in D flat (Raindrop), Op. 28/15; in C sharp min., Op. 45; Scherzos Nos. 1 in B flat min., Op. 31; 3 in C sharp min., Op. 39; Waltzes: in E flat (Grande valse brillante), Op. 18; in A min., Op. 34/2; in D flat (Minute); in C sharp min., Op. 64/1-2; in A flat, Op. 69/1; in B min., Op. 69/2; in G flat, Op. 70/1.
500♪ (B) *** Decca Double 444 830-2 (2) [id.]. Vladimir Ashkenazy.

Most music-lovers would count themselves lucky to attend a recital offering the above programme, as effectively laid out as it is on these two discs (offered for the price of one) and with a total playing time of 130 minutes.

Ballade No. 2 in F, Op. 38; Barcarolle in F sharp, Op. 60; Boléro, Op. 19; Mazurkas: Nos. 20 in D flat; 25 in B min., Op. 33/3–4; 33 in B; 34 in C; 35 in C min., Op. 56/1–3; F min., Op. 68/4; Nocturnes, Op. 62/1–2; Scherzo No. 4 in E, Op. 80.
** BIS CD 673 [id.]. Roland Pöntinen.

Roland Pöntinen is a gifted all-round musician, an excellent chamber-music player, and he is blessed with a secure and effortless technical prowess. He brings special insights to such composers as Scriabin, and his artistry is heard to good effect in this generous Chopin recital, which runs to no less than 78 minutes. Not everything comes off equally well. He is generally at his best in the *Mazurkas*, but he can be unimaginative too. Many details in the *E minor Scherzo* are cavalier. He is very well recorded, and followers of this young artist can invest in this recital with some confidence. But put alongside the likes of Perahia or, among his own peers, Kissin, this does not register as great Chopin playing.

Ballade No. 3 in A flat, Op. 47; Barcarolle in F sharp min., Op. 60; Etudes: in E (Tristesse), Op. 10/3; in G flat (Black key), Op. 10/5; in C min. (Revolutionary), Op. 10/12; in A min. (Winter wind), Op. 25/11; Nocturne in F min., Op. 55/1; Polonaise in A, Op. 40/1; Scherzo No. 3 in C sharp min., Op. 39; Preludes: in D flat (Raindrop), Op. 28/15; in C sharp min., Op. 45; Waltzes: in D flat (Minute); in C sharp min., Op. 64/1–2.
(M) **(*) Decca 452 623-2; *452 623-4* [id.]. Vladimir Ashkenazy.

This is an admirable collection in many ways, and the performances are self-recommending. But with only 57 minutes' playing time, readers might be better advised to choose the Double Decca set, above, which costs not much more and contains a great deal more music.

Fantaisie in F min., Op. 49; Nocturnes in C sharp min., Op. 27/1; in D flat, Op. 27/2; in A flat, Op. 32/2; Polonaise in F sharp min., Op. 44; Scherzo No. 2 in B flat min., Op. 31; Waltzes: in A flat, Op. 34/1; in A min., Op. 34/2; in A flat, Op. 42.
500♪ ❁ *** RCA Dig. 09026 60445-2 [id.]. Evgeni Kissin.

Evgeni Kissin's Chopin anthology comes from a Carnegie Hall recital given early in 1993 when he was still only twenty-one. His virtuosity and brilliance are always harnessed to musical ends and there is total dedication to Chopin.

Coates, Eric (1886–1958)

Four ways suite: Northwards; Eastwards. London suite.
(M) **(*) Mercury 434 376-2 [id.]. London Pops O, Frederick Fennell – Leroy ANDERSON: *Collection.* ***

Polished, spirited and sympathetic performances from Fennell of Coates's best-known suite, including what was once the most popular march of all (*Knightsbridge*), though perhaps these days it is upstaged by *The Dambusters*. The novelty is the inclusion of the two engaging excerpts from the *Four ways suite*, winningly played, with pleasing rhythmic character. The dry, close, studio-ish recording is most effective here.

Coleridge-Taylor, Samuel (1875–1912)

(i) *Hiawatha's wedding feast. The Bamboula* (rhapsodic dance).
(M) *** EMI Eminence Dig. CD-EMX 2276. (i) Rolfe Johnson, Bournemouth Ch.; Bournemouth SO, Alwyn.

In its day *Hiawatha's wedding feast* blew a fresh breeze through a turgid British Victorian choral tradition; since then, the work has been kept alive in fairly frequent performances by amateur choral societies. This reissue is first class in every way, and Kenneth Alwyn secures a vigorous and committed contribution from his Bournemouth forces, with Anthony Rolfe Johnson an excellent soloist in the famous *Onaway! Awake, beloved!* The music throughout is delightfully melodious and extremely well written for the voices. *The Bamboula* makes an agreeable if inconsequential encore.

Conus, Julius (1869–1942)

Violin concerto.
(M) *** EMI CDM5 66060-2 [id.]. Perlman, Pittsburgh O, Previn – BARTOK: *Violin concerto No. 2;* SINDING: *Suite.* ***

Julius Conus, of French extraction from a family of musicians, wrote his *Violin concerto* in Moscow in 1896–7, a ripely romantic piece in one continuous movement with only a few memorable ideas but with luscious violin writing, while the lyrical theme of the opening movement blossoms persuasively. It was a favourite of Heifetz's and needs a powerful, persuasive advocate to sound anything more than trivial. Here the opening is very commanding and Perlman's first entry quite magical; he shows his supreme mastery in giving the piece new intensity, helped by fine playing from Previn and the Pittsburgh orchestra. The 1979 recording is vivid and, if the violin is very close, Perlman's tone is honeyed; the Pittsburgh hall ensures orchestral weight and provides an attractive background warmth.

Copland, Aaron (1900–1990)

(i) *An outdoor overture;* (ii) *Fanfare for the common man;* (ii; iii) *Lincoln portrait;* (iv) *The Red Pony* (film score): suite; (i) *Rodeo: 3 dance episodes.*
(B) ** Sony SBK 62401; *SBT 62401* [id.]. (i) Cleveland Pops O, Louis Lane; (ii) Phd. O, Ormandy; (iii) with Adlai Stevenson; (iv) St Louis SO, Previn.

An attractive if not distinctive permutation of Copland works, including the underrated *Red Pony* film-score, in which Previn is very persuasive. Louis Lane and the Cleveland Pops give ebullient accounts of *An outdoor overture* and *Rodeo*, but Adlai Stevenson is a rather laid-back narrator for the *Lincoln portrait*. The recordings are forwardly balanced and resonantly larger than life.

Appalachian spring (ballet): *suite; Billy the Kid* (ballet): *suite; Rodeo: 4 dance episodes; Symphony No. 3: Fanfare for the common man.*
500♪ ❁ (M) *** Sony SMK 47543 [id.]. NYPO, Leonard Bernstein.
(BB) **(*) Naxos Dig. 8.550282 [id.]. Slovak RSO (Bratislava), Gunzenhauser.

Bernstein recorded these ballet scores in the early 1960s when he was at the peak of his creative tenure with the NYPO, and we are fortunate that the recordings are so good, vivid, spacious and atmospheric. No one – not even the composer – has approached these performances for racy rhythmic exuberance or for the tenderness and depth of nostalgia in the lyrical music, and the amazing precision of ensemble from the New York players, whose adrenalin is obviously running at unprecedented levels. The *Fanfare for the common man* is not the original, commissioned in 1942 by Eugene Goossens for the Cincinnati Orchestra, but the composer's reworking, when he introduced it as a springboard for the finale of his *Third Symphony*.

One does not expect a Czech orchestra, excellent as the Bratislava players are, to achieve quite the exhilarating rhythmic precision that Bernstein and the NYPO bring to this music, but they play with such spontaneous enjoyment in *Rodeo* and *Billy the Kid* that one cannot help but respond. Gunzenhauser, a fine conductor of Czech music, is equally at home in Copland's folksy cowboy idiom, and all this music has plenty of colour and atmosphere. If some of the detail in *Appalachian spring* is less sharply etched than with Dorati, the closing pages are tenderly responsive. The recording is admirably colourful and vivid with a fine hall ambience, and the spectacle of the *Fanfare for the common man* is worth anybody's money. A bargain.

Appalachian spring (ballet) *suite;* (i) *Piano concerto. Symphonic ode.*
**(*) Delos Dig. DE 3154 [id.]. (i) Lorin Hollander; Seattle SO, Gerard Schwarz.

The glowing acoustics of the Seattle Opera House smooth some of the abrasiveness away from Lorin Hollander's impressive account of Copland's *Piano concerto* and also filter out some of the glitter from the jazzy piano-writing. Similarly, *Appalachian spring* loses some of the bite in the dance rhythms, although the glowing woodwind detail and the richly expansive closing variations on *A gift to be simple* are more than compensation. The exultantly monumental close of the pungently flamboyant *Symphonic ode* is given similar weight and breadth. The Seattle orchestra plays splendidly throughout and Schwarz is a master of all this repertoire.

Billy the Kid (complete ballet); *Danzón Cubano; El salón Mexico; Rodeo* (4 dance episodes).
** Argo Dig. 440 639-2 [id.]. Baltimore SO, David Zinman.

A disappointment. The Baltimore orchestra is an impressive ensemble and they play Copland's atmospheric, open-air music in these cowboy ballets with fine evocative warmth. They also manage the sleazy rhythm of the indelible main theme of *El Salón México* very seductively. But Zinman fails to catch the sharp rhythmic bite of the livelier numbers of *Billy the Kid* and *Rodeo*, and his performances pale by the side of Bernstein's irrepressibly energetic versions (Sony SMK 47543), which remain unsurpassed.

Dance Symphony.
(B) ** Carlton Turnabout 30371 00112 [id.]. MIT SO, David Epstein – IVES: *Holidays Symphony.* **

The *Dance Symphony* dates from 1929. It is short and full of originality and is tautly constructed. It is a rewarding score, though the listener approaching it for the first time may feel that the influence of Stravinsky has not yet been fully assimilated. It would be idle to pretend that the orchestra from the Massachusetts Institute of Technology is a virtuoso body (there is some less-than-perfect intonation) nor is the Turnabout recording first class: the strings sound thin. But what the playing here lacks in polish it makes up for in vitality, and the music is well projected. It is a pity that Carlton have abandoned the splendid original coupling – Piston's *Incredible Flutist* ballet – but the new one, Ives's *Holidays Symphony*, is well worth having, and the recording is distinctly serviceable,

Statements for orchestra.
*** Everest EVC 9039 [id.]. LSO, Sir Eugene Goossens – ANTHEIL: *Symphony No. 4.* **(*)

Statements for orchestra (1934–5), as the bald title suggests, is one of Copland's less expansive works, but its six vignettes, *Militant*, *Cryptic* (hauntingly scored for brass and flute alone), *Dogmatic* (but disconsolate), *Subjective* (an elegiac soliloquy for strings), the witty *Jingo* and the thoughtfully *Prophetic* conclusion, reveal a compression of material and sharpness of ideas that are most stimulating. Goossens's performance is first rate in every way; so is the LSO playing, and the atmospheric (1959) recording sounds hardly dated at all.

Symphony No. 3.
*(*) Chandos Dig. CHAN 9474 [id.]. Detroit SO, Järvi – HARRIS: *Symphony No. 3.* *

Neeme Järvi's account of Copland's epic *Third Symphony* sounds curiously underpowered. This is Copland at low voltage without the vital current that this score must have. Good recording, but readers should stick with Copland's own account or wait until DG reissue, as they surely will, the Bernstein version of the same coupling.

Symphony No. 3; Billy the Kid (ballet): *suite.*
** Everest EVC 9040 [id.]. LSO, Copland.

Dating from 1959, the composer's first recordings of these two key works (made at Walthamstow) are presented in stereo of sharp clarity with inner detail remarkable clear; the violins, however, are distinctly thin, which makes fortissimos sharp-edged, in spite of the basically warm ambience. The LSO are obviously coming fresh to *Billy the Kid*, and clearly they are enjoying the music's colour, playing with plenty of rhythmic bite. However, they were to re-record this music (alongside *Appalachian spring*), under Dorati in 1961 for Mercury with even more electrifying results (434 301-2). They give a far less virtuoso performance of the *Symphony*, which is convincing as an expression of emotion in the opening movement and the *Andantino*, but less than perfect in the playing of the brilliant Scherzo.

Corelli, Arcangelo (1653–1713)

Concerti grossi, Op. 6/1–12.
*** RCA Dig. RD 60071 (2) [09026 60071-2]. Guildhall Ens., Robert Salter.
*** HM Dig. HMC901406/7 [id.]. Ensemble 415, Banchini.
(B) *** Hyperion Dyad Dig. CDD 22011 (2) [id.]. Brandenburg Consort, Roy Goodman.
(BB) *** Naxos Dig. 8.550402/3 [id.]. Capella Istropolitana, Jaroslav Krček.

Concerti grossi, Op. 6/1–6.
*** HM Opus 111 Dig. OPS 30-147 [id.]. Europa Galante, Fabio Biondi.

Concerti grossi, Op. 6/7–12.
*** HM Opus 111 Dig. OPS 30-155 [id.]. Europa Galante, Fabio Biondi.

Corelli's glorious set of *Concerti grossi*, Op. 6, is now very well represented in the catalogue in all price-ranges. In fact one cannot go wrong with any of the three-star listings here. The Guildhall Ensemble and Robert Salter, for example, are very fine indeed and will be a first choice for those who enjoy modern instruments. They have the benefit of really excellent recording: immediate and present without being too forward, full-bodied and transparent in detail. The playing is really vital and imaginative and has plenty of warmth and imagination. It exudes a generosity of spirit less obvious with Goodman or indeed the old ASMF/Marriner set (now available on a Double Decca: 443 862-2) which, though lively and expertly played, at times brings a hint of blandness.

For those who prefer period performances there is plenty of choice and, with the Goodman set now available as a two-for-the-price-of-one Hyperion Dyad, Pinnock's full-priced DG set (423 626-2), for all its very considerable merits, including a strikingly fresh concertino group, seems marginally upstaged, although Kuijken's mid-priced DHM set (GD 77007) continues to hold its own. However, although a clear-cut recommendation is difficult, the balance of advantage in authenticity seems to lie between Goodman and Banchini. One can invest in either with confidence. Roy Goodman and the Brandenburg Consort use the smaller forces (17 string players) plus harpsichord continuo, archlute and organ; Harmonia Mundi's Ensemble 415, with Chiara Banchini and Jesper Christensen, number 32 strings and a comparably larger continuo section with several archlutes, chitarrone, harpsichords and organ. The richer bass and altogether fuller sonority may cause some readers to prefer it (and we would incline towards it for its greater splendour and imaginative use of continuo instruments, whereas at times Goodman's textures sound just a little meagre). However, there is a sense of style and a freshness of approach in the Goodman version that is very persuasive. In both instances the recorded sound is first class. Choice will largely rest on whether you want a more chamber-like approach, as on Hyperion, or the richer sonority the Harmonia Mundi set offers.

At super-bargain price, the Naxos set by the Capella Istropolitana under Jaroslav Krеček represents very good value indeed. The players are drawn from the Slovak Philharmonic and have great vitality and, when necessary, virtuosity to commend them. The digital recording is clean and well lit, but not over-bright, and makes their version strongly competitive.

The newest set, from the appropriately named Europa Galante, is as fine as any. The chamber-sized ripieno of period instruments (2,2,2,1,1) offers crisp detail yet no feeling of any lack of sonority, and the elegant playing is alert and vital yet smiles pleasingly: these musicians are obviously enjoying the music and so do we. The soloists are excellent, as is the recording.

At the time of going to print, the second disc, which is available separately, is accompanied by a free sampler CD, with excerpts from other recordings on this label, ranging widely and temptingly from vocal music of Marcello and Scarlatti to Shostakovich's *14th Symphony* and liturgical music and '*Songs of old Russia*'.

Concerti grossi, Op. 6/1, 3, 7–9 & 11.
(B) *(**) DHM 054472 77445-2 [7908-2-RC]. Tafelmusik, Jean Lamon.

This is one of Tafelmusik's earlier period performances, dating from 1989. They play Corelli's allegros with characteristic bright vitality. The recording is a bit up-front and there is a degree of abrasiveness, though no lack of ambient atmosphere; but it is the plangent quality of the lyrical music that will not suit all ears, and the famous *Pastorale* from the *Christmas concerto*, which ends the concert, surely needs more of a feeling of repose.

Corigliano, John (born 1938)

(i) *Piano concerto. Elegy; Fantasia on an ostinato; Tournaments.*
*** RCA Dig. 09026 68100-2. (i) Barry Douglas; St Louis SO, Slatkin.

Corigliano's *Piano concerto* is a powerful and ambitious work in four sharply contrasted movements. Dating from 1968, long before his Aids-inspired *Symphony No. 1* and the brilliantly successful Met. opera, *The Ghosts of Versailles*, it communicates with similar immediacy. The substantial opening Allegro, much the longest movement, is in modified sonata form, with a jazzy first subject prompting heavyweight virtuoso writing for the soloist, quickly leading to a broadly lyrical, meditative second theme. If Corigliano unashamedly uses a freely eclectic style, his writing is consistently positive and energetic, never merely conventional. This version, unlike the previous one, has the advantage of an all-Corigliano coupling. The *Elegy* and the showpiece, *Tournaments*, both date from even earlier, his first full orchestral works – the one developed from the love scene in incidental music Corigliano wrote for a play about Helen of Troy, the other a virtuoso piece, substantially monothematic, that tests the orchestra to the limit in its three clearly defined sections, fast–slow–fast. Slatkin draws outstanding playing from the St Louis orchestra, and Barry Douglas proves the most powerful advocate, using a daringly wide dynamic range and tonal palette. Adopting slightly broader speeds in all four movements, the earlier version from Alain Lefevre (on Koch 3-7250-2) may not be quite so commanding, but it is often more warmly expressive (see our main volume).

Symphony No. 1; Of rage and remembrance (Chaconne).
*** RCA Dig. 09026 68450-2 [id.]. Choral Arts and Oratorio Soc. of Washington Ch., Nat SO, Slatkin.

John Corigliano's *Symphony No. 1*, first heard in 1990, is an elegy in memory of the composer's friends who have died of Aids – deeply felt, vitally communicative, directly challenging the listener to respond in an openly emotive way. The first three large-scale movements all commemorate particular musician friends, poignantly using material which Corigliano associates with each of them, as for example Albéniz's *Tango* heard from afar. The result is made the more intense by those specific references, venturing, Tchaikovsky-like, to the very verge of sentimentality. This superb new recording outshines Barenboim's previous Chicago one (Erato 2292 45601-2) not only in its brilliant, clean-focused sound, but also in having as supplement the choral piece which reworks the symphony's beautiful slow movement, restoring the words which provided the original inspiration.

Cornelius, Peter (1824–74)

6 Weihnachtslieder, Op. 8: Christbaum; Die Hirten; Die Könige; Simeon; Christus der Kinderfreud; Christkind.

❁ *** EMI Dig. CDC5 56204-2 [id.]. Bär, Deutsch (with Recital: *'Christmas Lieder'* *** ❁).

Peter Cornelius was born on Christmas Eve, so perhaps it is not surprising that his set of *Weihnachtslieder* so readily captures the seasonal mood with such charm and spontaneity. The opening description of the *Christmas tree* within its family setting is followed by a pastoral evocation of the *Shepherds in the fields*; then the *Three kings* arrive, but without ostentation, followed by the devout Simeon who prophetically takes the Child in his arms. Cornelius's setting of this and the following *Christus der Kinderfreud* have a winningly tender simplicity, and the final *Christkind* turns the mood into light-hearted happiness. Olaf Bär sings with a natural beauty of line and phrase and much affection, and his accompanist, Helmut Deutsch, is wonderfully supportive.

Corrette, Michel (1709–95)

Le Phénix (for four bassoons and continuo).

(B) ** Carlton/Turnabout 30371 0004-2 [id.]. Zukerman, Gode, Wolken, Steinbrecher, Galling – BOISMORTIER: *Bassoon concerto in D;* F. COUPERIN: *Double Bassoon concerto in G;* DEVIENNE: *Quartet in C.* **

This is something of a lollipop, a jolly three-movement piece for four bassoons and harpsichord (the excellent Martin Galling) which does not outstay its welcome.

Couperin, Armand-Louis (1725–1789)

Pièces de clavecin, Books I–II: excerpts.

** CPO Dig. CPO 999 312-2 [id.]. Harald Hoeren (harpsichord).

Armand-Louis Couperin is a name new to the catalogue. He was distantly related to both François and Louis. His *Pièces de clavecin* were published in 1751 in two books, and here we are offered a good selection of 19 pieces – about 74 minutes of music. Some of the music is unadventurous but he could write a good Minuet. *La Chéron* is a tribute to an admired organist and is rather touching, while *L'Affligée* is also suitably expressive. *L'Enjouyée*, *La Fouchet* and *La Semillant ou la Joly* have striking rhythmic character. *L'Arlequin* is quite engagingly spirited and *Le Blanchet* with its further flurry of scales gives the soloist another chance to display his confident bravura. The closing piece, *Les tendres sentiments*, has a pleasingly ingenuous melodic line. In short this is not great music but it is very much of its period. Harald Hoeren plays expertly, he does not over-decorate and is obviously sympathetic. He plays a German copy of a Flemish harpsichord which has plenty of character and is well caught, if just a shade close.

Couperin, François (1668–1733)

L'Art de toucher le clavecin; Harpsichord suites, Books 1–4, Ordres 1–27 (complete); (i) *L'apothéose de Lulli. La Paix du Parnasse; Le Parnasse ou l'Apothéose de Corelli; Pièces de clavecin: 9e Ordre: Allemand à deux. 14e Ordre: La Julliet. 15e Ordere: Musète de Choisi; Musète de Taverni; 16e Ordre: La Létiville.*

(B) *** HM Dig. HMX 901442–52 (& HMC 901269) (12) [id.]. Christophe Rousset (harpsichord); (i) with William Christie; with Blandine Rannou (in Book 3); with Kaori Uemura (in Book 4).

Rousset's distinguished series of the *Pièces de clavecin* includes *L'Art de toucher le clavecin*, using appropriate instruments. Apart from his inherent sense of style and feeling for decoration, Rousset well understands terms like *gracieusement*, *gayement*, *très tendrement* and *agréable, sans lenteur*, which he realizes to perfection. The *Concerts royaux* were of course written for a small chamber group, but the composer also encouraged their performance on the keyboard alone. In Book 2, Rousset is joined in certain pieces (the *Allemande* which opens Ordre No. 9 is for two harpsichords) by the estimable William Christie. In Book 3, he is joined in a very few items by Blandine Rannou on a second harpsichord; and in *La Croûilli ou la Couperinète*, from Book 4, Ordre 20, Kaori Uemura provides a vigorous basso continuo for the closing section. One could carp here and there about choice of tempi and so on, but Couperin wanted his music to be played creatively and flexibly, and that is what Christophe Rousset does – and with total spontaneity, too. He is beautifully recorded within an open but not too resonant acoustic, and this series can be welcomed very cordially indeed. This whole set now comes as a special offer at bargain price and throws in as a bonus the extra disc in which Rousset is joined by William Christie and which includes *L'apothéose de Lulli* and *Le Parnasse ou l'apothéose de Corelli* among other pieces. Couperin's preface explains that he himself played these works on two harpsichords with members of his family and pupils; and William Christie has chosen to follow his example. Surprisingly, they sound rather more exciting in this form than in the more familiar instrumental versions, largely perhaps because of the sheer sparkle and vitality of these performers. This collection and the four *Suites* are also still available separately at premium price, but the lover of this repertoire will surely want to opt for the whole series when this bargain offer is so tempting.

Concerto in G for two solo bassoons (arr. from *Concerts Royaux*).

(B) ** Carlton/Turnabout 30371 0004-2 [id.]. Zukerman, Gode – BOISMORTIER: *Bassoon concerto in D;* CORRETTE: *'Le Phénix'; *DEVIENNE: *Quartet in C.* **

François Couperin did not compose a 'double bassoon concerto' (with continuo) and we have guessed at the source of this five-movement suite. Its provenance and arranger remain undisclosed by the documentation here, which also fails to reveal who is responsible for the simple accompaniment. Suffice it to say that the result is pleasing and nicely played – not surprising when the lead bassoonist is George Zukerman.

ORGAN MUSIC

Messe à l'usage ordinaire des Paroisses; Messe propre pour les Couvents de religieux et religieuses (reconstructed by Jean Saint-Arromen to include Plainchant and Motets: *Domine salvum fac Regem* (2 versions); *Quid retribuam tibi dominum*).

(M) *** Virgin Veritas/EMI Dig. VED5 61298-2 (2). Jean-Patrice Brosse (organ of Saint-Bertrand, Saint-Bertrand de Comminges), with Isabel Poulenard, Jacques des Longchamps, François Le Roux, Val-de-Grâce Gregorian Ch.

Couperin was only 21 when he wrote his pair of organ Masses in 1690; yet these works, far more than conventional commentaries on the theme of the Mass, are among the finest of all his instrumental compositions. The *Mass for Parishes* is the grander, but the *Mass for convents*, basically simpler, has its contrapuntal complexities and is not without moments of flamboyance. There have been a number of fine solo recordings of the organ scores in the past, but until now none has given us these pieces with the plainsong framework in which they were intended to be heard and which dictates the degree of flamboyance needed from the organ to achieve convincing performances. Jean-Patrice Brosse has the full measure of this music and the Saint-Bertrand organ brings the necessary plangent French timbre: indeed the opening *Plein chant du premier Kyrie en taille* which introduces the *Kyrie eleison* of the *Mass for Parishes* has a convincingly throaty vocal tang. In this work the plainsong interpolations are mostly brief and always simple, although the *Credo* is an obvious exception. Indeed one can imagine how the worshipping congregation of the time must have been thrilled by the organ spectacularly framing this declaration of faith with the elaborately registered *Dialogue sur les grands jeux* and the *Offertoire sur les grands jeux*. Brosse faithfully follows the composer's indicated registrations, and there are many piquant sounds throughout both works, using solo stops or combinations featuring the cromorne, voix-humaine, cornet or tierce, the striking pedal trompette and the beguiling jeux doux (soft flutes). In the *Mass for convents*, the organ versets are usually based on the cantus firmus of the plainchant (rather like Bach's chorale preludes only less elaborate). In reconstructing his conjectural performances, Jean Saint-Arromen has added short motets within the Elévation for the *Benedictus* and *Agnus Dei*, and these are sung effectively enough by Jacques des Longchamps (alto) and François Le Roux (baritone); although to have a vocal ending for each Mass does bring something of an anticlimax after the organ's final *Deo gratias, petit plein jeu*, it emphasizes the dedicated spiritual nature of Couperin's overall conception. These beautifully recorded performances give a splendid illusion of being in the cathedral and participating in an occasion which is alternately solemn and lively, evocative and vividly colourful.

Cowell, Henry (1897–1965)

Hymn and fuguing tune No. 10 for oboe and strings.

500♪ *** Argo 417 818-2 [id.]. Nicklin, ASMF, Marriner – BARBER: *Adagio;* COPLAND: *Quiet city;* CRESTON: *Rumor;* IVES: *Symphony No. 3.* ***

This likeable *Hymn and fuguing tune*, by a composer otherwise little known, is well worth having and is expertly played and recorded here. The digital remastering has slightly clarified an already excellent recording.

Creston, Paul (born 1906)

A Rumor.

500♪ *** Argo 417 818-2 [id.]. ASMF, Marriner – BARBER: *Adagio;* COPLAND: *Quiet city;* COWELL: *Hymn;* IVES: *Symphony No. 3.* ***

A Rumor is a witty and engaging piece and is played here with plenty of character by the Academy under Sir Neville Marriner. It completes a thoroughly rewarding and approachable disc of twentieth-century American music that deserves the widest currency. The sound is first class.

Crusell, Bernhard (1775–1838)

Clarinet concertos Nos. 1 in E flat, Op. 1; 2 in F min., Op. 5; 3 in E flat, Op. 11.

500♪ ❀ *** ASV Dig. CDDCA 784 [id.]. Emma Johnson, RPO/ECO, Herbig; Groves; or Schwarz.

No one brings out the fun in the writing quite as infectiously as Emma Johnson, and this generous recoupling (74 minutes) bringing all three concertos together is a delight. With well-structured first movements, sensuous slow movements and exuberant finales, Johnson establishes her disc as a first choice above all others.

Introduction and variations on a Swedish air (for clarinet and orchestra), *Op. 12.*

(B) *** Hyperion Dyad Dig. CDD 22017 (2) [id.]. Thea King, LSO, Francis (with Concert – see below ***).

The Weberian Crusell *Variations* show Thea King's bravura at its most sparkling. It is far from being an empty piece; its twists and turns are consistently inventive. This is part of an excellent two-disc set including other attractive concertante works by Max Bruch, Mendelssohn, Spohr and other less familiar names.

Da Crema, Giovanni Maria (died *c.* 1550)

Con lagrime e sospiri (Philippe Verdelot); De vous servir (Claudin de Sermisy); Lasciar il velo (Jacques Arcadelt); O felici occhi mieie (Arcadelt); Pass'e mezo ala bolognesa; Ricercars quinto, sexto, decimoquarto, decimoquinto, duodecimo, tredecimo; Saltarello ditto Bel fior; Saltarello ditto El Giorgio; Saltarello ditto El Maton.

(BB) *** Naxos Dig. 8.550778 [id.]. Christopher Wilson (lute) – DALL'AQUILA – *Lute pieces.* ***

Even less is known about Giovanni Maria Da Crema than his contemporary, Dall'Aquila. The pieces here are taken from a First Lute Book which he published in 1546. Some of the music is adapted from or offers simple variants on the music of others. The inclusion of the dance movements alongside reflective pieces like *Con lagrime e sospiri* gives variety to an attractive programme, and the *Pass'e mezo ala bolognesa* is rather catchy. The performances are of the highest order, and Christopher Wilson is recorded most naturally. Well worth exploring, especially at such a modest cost.

Dall'Aquila, Marco (*c.* 1480–1538)

Amy souffrez (Pierre Moulu); La cara cosa; Priambolo; Ricercars Nos. 15, 16, 18, 19, 22, 24, 28, 33, 70, 101; 3 Ricercar/Fantasias; La Traditora.

(BB) *** Naxos Dig. 8.550778 [id.]. Christopher Wilson (lute) – DA CREMA – *Lute pieces.* ***

Marco dall'Aquila was a much-admired lutenist in his day, but little is known of his background. Born in Aquila, he settled in Venice as musician and publisher. These are relatively simple lute pieces, rhythmically active but with chordal textures. They are often dolorous. The two pieces which are more individually identified, *Amy souffrez* and *La cara cosa*, are among the more striking, but the *Ricercars* can be haunting too, and there is considerable variety of style and mood. They are beautifully played by Christopher Wilson and the recording is admirably balanced: the lute is not too close and is heard within a pleasing ambience.

Danzi, Franz (1763–1826)

Cello concerto in E min.

(B) **(*) Carlton/Turnabout 30371 0023-2 [id.]. Thomas Blees, Berlin SO, Carl-August Bünte – STAMITZ: *Cello concerto in A;* WEBER: *Grand Potpourri.* **(*)

Franz Danzi, born near Mannheim, was an almost exact contemporary of Beethoven; unlike that master, however, he stayed happily within the proper court circles of the lesser German princes during his whole working career. He wrote an opera based on Gozzi's *Turandot*, but generally he is too often dismissed as a rather insignificant follower of the late Mannheim School of symphonists. The *Cello concerto*, vividly played by Thomas Blees (a fine artist), suggests there is much more to discover. Danzi himself was a cellist, leaving the Mannheim orchestra to become a conductor and court composer. His concerto exploits the potentiality of the instrument far more than was common at the time. Bünte provides a more than adequate accompaniment and the Turnabout recording is better than average. A valuable addition to the catalogue.

Horn concerto in E.
(M) **(*) Teldec/Warner 0630 12324-2 [id.]. Hermann Baumann, Concerto Amsterdam, Jaap Schröder – HAYDN: *Horn concerto in D;* ROSETTI: *Horn concerto in D min.* **(*)

Danzi's *Horn concerto* is a straightforward affair. The opening of the first movement is elegant, with flutes decorating the simple orchestration; the *Romance* is smoothly contoured, but the amiable closing Rondo is the most attractive section. Baumann plays the piece sympathetically and he is well accompanied. The remastered 1969 recording gives him an open rather than an opulent timbre, and the violins are projected clearly rather than warmly.

Bassoon quartets Nos. 1 in C; 2 in D min.; 3 in B flat.
*** CRD Dig. CRD 3503 [id.]. Robert Thompson, Coull Qt.

Danzi was known as a good-humoured man, a friend of Spohr and Weber, and although his output was prodigious in many fields he was particularly famous for his works featuring wind instruments. These three charming *Quartets* have a *galant* innocence and a gentle lyrical feeling which has something in common with Mozart, whom the composer greatly admired, especially in his sensitive writing for the strings. Danzi seeks primarily to capture the bassoon's doleful, lyrical character; its lighter side is not dismissed, but he never becomes too jocular. In short, these are slight but appealing works, and they are presented here with affectionate warmth and spirit, and they are beautifully recorded. The finale of No. 2 is especially endearing, and the whole of the third work shows the composer at his most genially inventive.

Debussy, Claude (1862–1918)

(i) *Berceuse héroïque;* (ii; iii) *Danses sacrée et profane* (for harp and strings); (ii) *Images; Jeux; Marche écossaise; La Mer;* (ii; iv) *Nocturnes;* (ii) *Prélude à l'après-midi d'un faune;* (ii; v) *Première rapsodie for clarinet and orchestra.*
500♪ ❀ (B) *** Ph. Duo 438 742-2 (2) [id.]. Concg. O, (i) Eduard van Beinum; (ii) Bernard Haitink; with (iii) Vera Badings; (iv) women's Ch. of Coll. Mus.; (v) George Pieterson.

This must now rank as the finest Debussy collection in the CD catalogue and one of the greatest bargains that the gramophone has to offer at present – all for the cost of a single premium-priced CD. Although the programme as a whole is directed by Haitink, it is good that his distinguished predecessor, Eduard van Beinum, is remembered by the opening *Berceuse héroïque*, played with great delicacy. For the *Danses sacrée et profane* Haitink takes over, with elegant playing from the harpist, Vera Badings. Haitink's reading of *Images* is second to none, and this applies equally to *Jeux*, where Haitink's reading is wonderfully expansive and sensitive to atmosphere and easily matches any recent rivals. *La Mer* is comparable with Karajan's 1964 recording. The Philips recording is truthful and natural, with beautiful perspectives and realistic colour, a marvellously refined sound.

Fantaisie for piano and orchestra.
*** Ph. Dig. 446 713-2 [id.]. Zoltán Kocsis, Budapest Festival O, Iván Fischer – RAVEL: *Concertos.* **

Zoltán Kocsis's credentials as a Debussy interpreter scarcely need asserting. His earlier, solo Debussy record for Philips was superb in every respect and was accorded a Rosette in our main edition (422 404-2). His account of the *Fantaisie* is no less lucid and delicate and can be recommended with confidence. This would be a clear first choice, but the two Ravel concertos with which it is coupled are not.

Images; Le Martyre de Saint Sébastien (symphonic fragments).
(M) *** Ph. 442 595-2 [id.]. LSO, Monteux.

The restoration of Monteux's classic coupling to the catalogue is most welcome, and it makes a splendid addition to the Debussy discography, particularly as the remastered CD has fine immediacy and detail. Indeed, one would hardly suspect that the recording dates from 1963, for the woodwind colouring is translucent and there is a fine sheen of sensuousness to the string-tone (especially in *Les parfums de la nuit*). Monteux's performance of the *Images* was notable for its freshness and impetus (although this is achieved by the electricity of the playing rather than fast tempi). There is a vivid yet refined feeling for colour which is carried through into the orchestral sections from *Le Martyre* (in its fuller form a cantata written to a text by D'Annunzio). The delicacy of texture of Debussy's exquisite scoring is marvellously balanced by Monteux and he never lets the music become static. There is very little background noise, and our only real reservation is that this might have had some more music added. The playing time is just under 58 minutes.

Images: Ibéria.
500♪ ❁ (M) *** RCA GD 60179 [60179-2-RG]. Chicago SO, Fritz Reiner – RAVEL: *Alborada* etc. *** ❁

This marvellously evocative performance, and the Ravel with which it is coupled, should not be overlooked, for the recorded sound with its natural concert-hall balance is greatly improved in terms of body and definition. It is amazingly realistic even without considering its vintage.

La Mer.
500♪ (M) *** RCA 09026 68079-2 [id.]. Chicago SO, Fritz Reiner – RESPIGHI: *Fountains & Pines of Rome*. *** ❁

La Mer; Prélude à l'après-midi d'un faune.
500♪ (M) *** DG 427 250-2. BPO, Karajan (with RAVEL: *Boléro; Daphnis et Chloé* ***).

After three decades, Karajan's 1964 account of *La Mer*, now reissued in DG's Legendary Recordings series of 'Originals', is still very much in a class of its own. So strong is its evocative power that one feels one can almost see and smell the ocean. It is still available with an equally distinguished coupling of the *Prélude à l'après-midi d'un faune* and Ravel's *Daphnis et Chloé*.

Reiner's 1960 recording has all the warmth and atmosphere that make his version of *Ibéria*, recorded at about the same time (see above), so unforgettable.

CHAMBER MUSIC

Cello sonata; Sonata for flute, viola and harp; Violin sonata; Syrinx for solo flute; Prélude à l'après-midi d'un faune (arr. Sachs for 2 violins, viola, cello, double-bass, flute, oboe, clarinet, antique cymbals, piano & harmonium).
(M) **(*) DG 449 549-2 [id.]. Boston Symphony Chamber Players.

During the early years of the First World War Debussy planned to compose a set of six sonatas for various combinations of instruments, but he died before he could complete the project. However, the three that he did write are all masterpieces, particularly the exquisite *Sonata for flute, viola and harp*. It is a logical idea to assemble them on one disc and, though the performances do not wholly dislodge others from one's affections – Rostropovich's Decca account of the *Cello sonata* (417 833-2) and Kyung Wha Chung's version of the *Violin sonata* with Radu Lupu (see below) – they are very nearly as fine. As a bonus, Doriot Anthony Dwyer plays the *Syrinx* for solo flute most beautifully; but the most intriguing item, which opens the concert, is the familiar *Prélude à l'après-midi d'un faune*, heard in a very clever arrangement for chamber ensemble by Benno Sachs, a pupil of Schoenberg. Berg apparently took part at its première in 1920. Debussy's harp parts are transferred to the pianist and the harmonium gently fills in the sustained harmony. Although one misses a fuller body of violins at the central climax, the result remains remarkably transparent. The Boston musicians (who include Joseph Silverstein as violinist and Michael Tilson Thomas as an elegant pianist in the *Violin sonata*) do not disappoint in any of these pieces; but the reverberation of the Boston acoustic, although it suits the *Prélude*, very slightly clouds the textural subtleties of the *Trio*. Nevertheless this remains an attractive collection.

String quartet in G min.
(B) **(*) Sony SBK 62413; *SBT 62413* [id.]. Tokyo Qt – RAVEL: *Quartet* **(*); FAURE: *Piano trio*. (*)

As in their more recent recording for RCA (09026 62552-2), the Tokyo Quartet play with ardour and finesse. In the slow movement their blend of timbres is very beautiful. But the outer movements are very volatile indeed and, although they are of one mind, the result at times seems too restless. The 1977 recording is close but otherwise very good.

(i) *String quartet in G min.;* (ii) *Cello sonata;* (iii; iv); *Sonata for flute, viola and harp;* (v) *Violin sonata in G min.;* (iii) *Syrinx*.
(M) *** Ph. 442 655-2 [id.]. (i) Italian Qt; (ii) Gendron, Françaix; (iii) Bourdin; (iv) Lequien, Challan; (v) Grumiaux, Hajdu.

These excellent sonata performances from the mid-1960s do not wholly dislodge others from one's affections, for example Rostropovich's account of the *Cello sonata* or the Chung version (also on Decca) of the *Violin sonata*, but they are nearly as fine. Gendron's version of the *Cello sonata* is most eloquent and, with the estimable Italian performance of the *Quartet* added for good measure, this very naturally recorded 72-minute collection can be given a warm welcome

Violin sonata in G min.
*** Sony Dig. SK66839 [id.]. Cho-Liang Lin, Paul Crossley – POULENC: *Violin sonata;* RAVEL: *Sonatas; Tzigane.* ***

(i) *Violin sonata in G min.;* (ii) *Sonata for flute, viola and harp.*
500♪ ❀ (M) *** Decca 421 154-2. (i) Kyung Wha Chung, Radu Lupu; (ii) Melos Ens. (members) – FRANCK: *Violin sonata;* RAVEL: *Introduction and allegro.* *** ❀

Kyung Wha Chung plays with marvellous character and penetration, and her partnership with Radu Lupu could hardly be more fruitful. Nothing is pushed to extremes, and everything is in perfect perspective. The *Sonata for flute, viola and harp* and the Ravel *Introduction and allegro* are wonderfully sensitive and the music's ethereal atmosphere well caught. The recording sounds admirably real.

Cho-Liang Lin and Paul Crossley give a vibrant, well-argued account of the Debussy *Sonata* to which Sony accord excellent recording. Of course, we are spoilt for choice (see our main volume), but the strength of the present issue, apart from the quality of the playing and the exemplary recorded sound, is the generous programme on offer. In addition to the Ravel *G major Sonata* (1922), they include the poignant and touching earlier essay Ravel made in this medium.

PIANO MUSIC

2 Arabesques; Ballade; Danse bohémienne; Danse (Tarantelle styrienne); Images (1894); *Nocturne; Pour le piano; Rêverie; Suite bergamasque; Valse romantique.*
(M) *(**) Carlton Dig. 30367 01012 [id.]. Martin Tirimo.

Tirimo's playing is distinguished and there is never any doubt as to his Debussian credentials. He plays only the two outer movements of the 1894 *Images*, arguing quite reasonably that the differences between the two versions of the *Sarabande* are very slight. But the balance is very close and the microphone even picks up the pedal mechanism (try the opening of the *Danse* on track 8) to an almost unacceptable extent. The acoustic of Rosslyn Hill Chapel, Hampstead, does permit the sound to expand – but some slight background noise from the environs (probably what was posing problems for the engineer) would be better than putting the listener virtually on the piano stool.

2 Arabesques; Danse bohémienne; D'un cahier d'esquisses; Estampes; Images oubliées; L'isle joyeuse; Morceau de concours; Nocturne; Pour le piano; Préludes, Books 1–2 (complete); *Masques; Rêverie.*
500♪ *** Decca Dig. 452 022-2 (2) [id.]. Jean-Yves Thibaudet.

Beautifully recorded, Thibaudet's new survey of Debussy's piano music (this is Volume I of an ongoing series) looks set to take first place in a competitive field. Thibaudet's wide range of tone and dynamic is used with great imagination, and his playing often suggests an improvisatory quality. The *Préludes* are among the finest on record.

(i) *2 Arabesques; Danse; L'isle joyeuse; Masque; La plus que lente; Pour le piano;* (ii) *Préludes, Books I–II* (complete); (i) *Suite bergamasque.*
(B) *** DG 453 070-2 (2) [id.]. (i) Tamás Vásáry; (ii) Dino Ciani.

Vásáry is at his finest in the *Suite bergamasque*, and *Clair de lune* is beautifully played, as are the *Arabesques*. Diano Ciani has a fine technique (witness *Feux d'artifice*) and plays both Books of *Préludes* with intelligence and taste. Both artists are very well recorded indeed. There is a good deal of Debussy's best-known piano music here, offered inexpensively, and this is a very satisfying pair of discs in its own right.

Etudes, Books 1–2.
500♪ ❀ *** Ph. Dig. 422 412-2 [id.]. Mitsuko Uchida.

Mitsuko Uchida's remarkable account of the *Etudes* on Philips is not only one of the best Debussy piano records in the catalogue and arguably her finest recording, but also one of the best ever recordings of the instrument.

Images: Poissons d'or. Préludes: La fille aux cheveux de lin; Général Lavine – eccentric; Feux d'artifice. La Plus que lente; Rêverie.
(M) (***) EMI mono CDM5 66069-2 [id.]. Rudolf Firkušny – SMETANA: *Polkas & dances.* (***)

This record is of special interest for the sparkling Smetana items which are Firkušny's special province. But his Debussy is also distinguished and, if the sound is limited, it is perfectly acceptable.

Préludes, Books 1–2 (complete).
500♪ ❁ (M) *** EMI mono CDH7 61004-2 [id.]. Walter Gieseking.

Gieseking penetrates the atmosphere of the *Préludes* more deeply than almost any other artist. This is playing of rare distinction and great evocative quality. However, the documentation is concerned solely with the artist and gives no information about the music save the titles and the cues.

VOCAL MUSIC

Mélodies: *Beau soir; 3 Chansons de Bilitis; 3 Chansons de France; Les cloches; Fêtes galantes* (2nd group); *Mandoline.*
(M) *** Unicorn-Kanchana Dig. UKCD 2078 [id.]. Sarah Walker, Roger Vignoles – ENESCU: *Chansons* ***; ROUSSEL: *Mélodies.* **(*)

Sarah Walker's Debussy collection makes an outstandingly fine disc of French songs. With deeply sympathetic accompaniment from Roger Vignoles, Sarah Walker's positive and characterful personality comes over vividly, well tuned to the often elusive idiom. Excellent recording in a warm acoustic.

OPERA

Pelléas et Mélisande (complete).
500♪ *** DG Dig. 435 344-2 (2) [id.]. Ewing, Le Roux, Van Dam, Courtis, Ludwig, Pace, Mazzola, Vienna Konzertvereingung, VPO, Abbado.
(B) *** Naxos 8.660047-9 (3) [id.]. Mireille Delusch, Gérard Theruel, Armand Arapian, Gabriel Bacquier, Hélène Jessoud, Ch. Regional Nord/Pas de Calais, O Nat. de Lille, Jean-Claude Casadesus.

Abbado's outstanding version broadly resolves the problem of a first recommendation in this opera, which has always been lucky on record. If among modern versions the choice has been hard to make between Karajan's sumptuously romantic account, almost Wagnerian, and Dutoit's clean-cut, direct one, Abbado satisfyingly presents a performance more sharply focused than the one and more freely flexible than the other, altogether more urgently dramatic. The casting is excellent, with no weak link.

Enterprisingly, Naxos went to Lille to record stage performances by the excellent opera company there, and though the spaciousness of Casadesus's sensitive and poetic reading means that the set stretches to three discs rather than two the result is most compelling, with fresh, young voices helping to make the drama more involving. Mireille Delusch is a bright and girlish Mélisande, well matched against the high baritone of Gérard Theruel as a boyish Pelléas. Their dreamy wonder at meeting each other is touchingly conveyed, and it provides a convincing slant on the story that the young and virile Golaud of Armand Arapian is a more credible lover-figure than is usually presented, not just a jealous villain but a puzzled and frustrated elder brother. The others are first rate too, including the veteran, Gabriel Bacquier, aptly sounding old as Arkel. The voices are to the fore in the recording, with every word made clear, though the staging occasionally brings a discrepancy of balance. The orchestra, with a modest band of strings, adds to the chamber-scale intimacy. The libretto comes in French only, but with good notes and a synopsis in English – though it would have made it easier for the non-French speaker to follow, had there been more than a minimal number of cue-points provided. An outstanding bargain nevertheless.

De la Rue, Pierre (*c.* 1460–1518)

Missa l'homme armé; Missa pro defunctis (Requiem).
(B) *** HM Dig. HMT 7901296. Clement Janequin Ens., Dominique Visse.

Pierre de la Rue was a Flemish composer who entered into the service of Margaret of Austria, Governess of the Netherlands, whose favourite he was – and no wonder. His music is extraordinarily expressive, his flowing polyphony procures the richest harmonies and vivid colouring. His *Mass*, based on the chanson *L'homme armé*, exploits that famous tune with great resourcefulness: the music is outgoing and affirmative in spirit and full of imagination. He composed his *Requiem* before its liturgical sequence was fixed, and its format is: *Introitus* (*Requiem*); a brief *Kyrie*; *Psalmus* (No. 41); *Offertorium*; *Sanctus et Benedictus*; *Agnus Dei* and *Communio*. The lyrical melancholy of its lines is most affecting, with the harmony often resting sonorously on its firm bass. The *Sanctus* and *Bendictus* is simple yet remarkably diverse and powerful, the *Qui tollis* haunting. The closing *Communio* is compressed (*Lux aeterna . . . Cum sanctis . . . Requiem aeternam . . . Et lux perpetua luceat eis*) but none the less telling for that. Marvellous music, beautifully sung and recorded. A real find.

Delibes, Léo (1836–91)

Coppélia (ballet) extended excerpts: Act I, Nos. 1–2, 6–8, 10; Act II, Nos. 12, 14, 15–20, 22; Act III, Nos. 23–8, 30, 32, 34–6.
500♪ *** Erato/Warner 4509 96368-2 [id.]. Lyon Opéra O, Kent Nagano.

A very comprehensive selection from our top recommendation for Delibes's delightful score for *Coppélia*, which Tchaikovsky admired so much. The whole set on two CDs (4509 91730-2) plays for only 99 minutes and here are 74 minutes 35 seconds of them. Every bar of the music-making is of the highest quality, and the recording, with its nicely judged acoustic, is as attractive as the playing. Self-recommending.

Les filles de Cadiz.
*** Decca Dig. 452 667-2; *452 667-4* [id.]. Cecilia Bartoli, Myung-Whun Chung (with VIARDOT: *Les filles de Cadiz; Hai Luli!; Havanaise*) – BIZET; BERLIOZ; RAVEL: *Mélodies*. ***

Cecilia Bartoli could hardly be more seductive or more Carmen-like than she is here in Delibes's most famous song, *Les filles de Cadiz*; here, within a delectable recital of French songs, it is placed alongside the setting of the same poem made by the great prima donna, Pauline Viardot, giving a refreshingly different view. The other Viardot items too are highly engaging in this memorable collection of French mélodies.

Delius, Frederick (1862–1934)

(i) *Appalachia;* (ii) *Song of the high hills. Over the hills and far away.*
**(*) Decca Dig. 443 171-2 [id.]. (i) Daniel Washington; (ii) Rebecca Evans, Peter Hoare; Welsh Nat. Op. Ch. & O, Mackerras.

Partly because of the somewhat intractable acoustics of Brangwyn Hall, Swansea, which has meant that the microphones convey a not entirely natural impression, this collection is only a partial success. The soloists are good and the chorus sings with fervour; indeed the wide dynamic range means that fortissimos are sonically almost overwhelming. Mackerras shapes everything positively and directly, with less subtlety than we would expect from Beecham, and less lovingly affectionate than with Barbirolli. The recording reveals vivid detail but could be more evocative, especially in the ardent account of *A Song of the high hills*.

Brigg Fair; Dance rhapsody No. 2; Fennimore and Gerda: Intermezzo. Florida suite; Irmelin: Prelude. Marche-caprice; On hearing the first cuckoo in spring; Over the hills and far away; Sleigh ride; Song before sunrise; Summer evening; Summer night on the river; (i) *Songs of sunset.*
500♪ ❁ *** EMI CDS7 47509-8 (2) [CDCB 45709]. RPO, Beecham; (i) with Forrester, Cameron, Beecham Ch. Soc.

The remastering of the complete stereo orchestral recordings of Delius's music, plus the choral *Songs of sunset*, is something of a technological miracle. Beecham's fine-spun magic, his ability to lift a phrase, is apparent throughout. In the *Songs of sunset* the choral focus is soft-grained, but the words are surprisingly audible, and the backward balance of the soloists is made to sound natural against the rich orchestral textures. The gramophone here offers music-making which is every bit as rewarding as the finest live performances.

Brigg Fair; Dance rhapsody No. 2; On hearing the first cuckoo in spring; In a summer garden.
(B) *** Sony SBK 62645; *SBT 62645* [id.]. Phd. O, Ormandy – VAUGHAN WILLIAMS: *Fantasias* etc. ***

Ormandy and his great orchestra, on peak form in the early 1960s, give warm, stirring and highly romantic performances of these four masterpieces. *Brigg Fair* – without loss of refinement of detail – expands gloriously at the appearance of the great string-tune, echoed by the horn, while the *Dance rhapsody* is particularly successful in its spontaneous vitality. Ormandy and his engineers do not seek the fragility, the evanescence of Delius's visions; for that one can turn to Beecham. But this music responds well to a riper approach and there is no danger here of Delius sounding faded. The sound is remarkably full and expansive, far more convincing than the original LP. With its equally involving coupling, this is a true bargain.

Cello concerto.
*** EMI Dig. CDC5 55529-2 [id.]. Jacqueline du Pré, RPO, Sir Malcolm Sargent – Recital. ***

The newly revamped version of the Delius (du Pré's first concerto recording) offers more body and warmth in the cello sound. The recital is a transfer of the material, mainly from her very first EMI sessions in 1962 which gave such clear promise of glories to come. Most recommendable, although readers will note that it remains at full price.

(i–ii) *Dance rhapsody No. 1* (ed. Beecham); (i; iii) *Dance rhapsody No. 2; Fantastic dance;* (iv) (Piano) *Preludes Nos. 1–3; Zum carnival* (polka); (v; i; iii) *Song of the high hills.*
500♪ ❁ (M) *** Unicorn Dig. UKCD 2071 [id.]. (i) RPO; (ii) Del Mar; (iii) Fenby; (iv) Parkin; (v) Amb. S.

Norman Del Mar, a natural Delian, gives a spontaneously volatile performance of the *Dance rhapsody No. 1.* Fenby's performance of the *Dance rhapsody No. 2* is both fluid and crisply sprung. Eric Parkin also breathes Delian air naturally. But the highlight of this well-planned programme is the *Song of the high hills*, written in 1911. Fenby, the composer's life-long advocate, draws a richly atmospheric performance from Beecham's old orchestra in what proves to be one of the most ravishingly beautiful of Delius's choral works, here finely balanced within an evocative sound-picture, ideally warm yet with the most delicate pianissimo detail.

Eventyr; North country sketches; Over the hills and far away; (i) *Koanga: Closing scene.*
(B) (***) Sony SBK 62747; *SBT 62747* [id.]. RPO, Beecham; (i) with RPO Ch. (members).

A particularly valuable bargain reissue offering very successful transfers of Beecham recordings which have not been available for some time and which have never seemed as firm and realistic as this. The orchestral playing is memorably fine, with some superbly romantic horn playing in *Over the hills and far away*. But it is the *North country sketches* that are especially valuable, with translucent sounds from the high violins in *Winter landscape* that are almost Sibelian in feeling. The woodwind shine in the closing *March of spring* and also in the capricious *Eventyr* (*Once upon a time*), where Beecham handles the rhapsodic changes of impetus and dynamic with characteristic passion and subtlety. The closing scene from *Koanga*, full of evocative feeling, makes a fascinating coda with its brief solo and choral sequence. No apologies need be made for the mono recordings – made in 1950–51 – for Beecham was a master of orchestral balance.

Paris (The song of a great city).
(B) (***) Sony mono SBK 62748; *SBT 62748* [id.]. RPO, Beecham – ARNELL: *Punch and the child;* BERNERS: *Triumph of Neptune.* (***)

Many Delius connoisseurs prefer Sir Thomas's 1934 account of *Paris*, but to our ears there is nothing much wrong and a lot right about this 1955 version. There is plenty of atmosphere and the old Beecham magic still casts a strong spell. Music-making of stature, and an indispensable acquisition for admirers of both conductor and composer. The new transfer is really very good, clear and well balanced, if lacking amplitude at the climax.

(i) *An Arabesque;* (ii) *Hassan* (incidental music); (iii) *Sea drift.*
(B) (**(*)) Sony mono SBK 62752; *SBT 62752* [id.]. (i) Einar Nørby; (ii) Lesley Fry; (iii) Bruce Boyce; (i–iii) BBC Ch., RPO, Beecham.

It is sad that these three Delius recordings, though made between December 1954 and February 1958 (after the advent of stereo), were done in mono only. Once that is said, the results are persuasive in a way unsurpassed by any rival Delius interpreter, with the lyrical line of each passage, central to the argument, lovingly drawn out. The transfers are clear but have some roughness from the original recording.

Florida suite; Idylle de printemps; Over the hills and far away; La Quadroone; Scherzo; (i) *Koanga: closing scene.*
(BB) *** Naxos Dig. 8.553535 [id.]. E. N. Philh. O, Lloyd-Jones; (i) with Susannah Glanville, Susan Lees, Irene Evans, Sandra Francis, Sue Peerce, Shirley Thomas.

This collection of early Delius works, most of them directly inspired by his years in Florida, makes a richly enjoyable first disc in Naxos's planned new Delius series, seductively played and beautifully recorded in full and atmospheric sound. Several of the works are new to disc, including the *Idylle de printemps*, fresh and charming, leading to an ecstatic climax. *La Quadroone* and *Scherzo* were originally planned as movements in a suite, the first inspired by the sort of dances Delius came upon in Florida. Lloyd-Jones has clearly learnt from Beecham's example in his glowing and intense readings of the other three works, with the orchestra's woodwind soloists excelling themselves in delicate pointing, not least in the haunting *La Calinda*, included in the *Florida suite*. *Over the hills and far away*, raptly done, is richly evocative too, and the epilogue to the opera, *Koanga*, rounds off a generously filled disc with music both sensuous and passionate, featuring six female vocal soloists from Opera North, three sopranos and three mezzos.

(i) *A Mass of Life* (sung in German); (ii) *Requiem*.
*** Chandos CHAN 9515 (2) [id.]. (i) Joan Rodgers, Jean Rigby, Nigel Robson; (ii) Rebecca Evans; (i–ii) Peter Coleman-Wright; Waynflete Singers, Bournemouth Ch. & SO, Hickox.

In the whole of Delius there are few passages to match the first part of the *Mass of Life* for sheer exhilaration, generally urgent and energetic rather than meditative. Hickox here follows up his earlier outstanding Delius recordings with a glowing account of this ambitious setting of a German text drawn from Nietzsche's *Also sprach Zarathustra*. Hickox's concentration is then sustained over the more expansive, generally reflective second part of the work, where one can readily miss the earlier thrust. He is helped by excellent singing and playing from his Bournemouth forces, and by fine solo singing, notably from the soprano, Joan Rodgers. The full and atmospheric Chandos recording confirms the primacy of this version even over the excellent previous recordings. The *Requiem*, half an hour long, makes the ideal coupling. Completed in 1916 at the height of the First World War, it was described by the composer as his 'Pagan Requiem', again setting Nietzsche, but also quoting passages from Ecclesiastes. The text was criticized when it was first performed in 1923, and after that it was totally neglected for many decades. It now emerges as a fine example of Delius's later work, not as distinctive in its material as the *Mass*, but with an element of bleakness tempering the lushness of the choral writing. Here too – with Rebecca Evans this time as soprano soloist – Hickox conducts a most persuasive performance, ripely recorded.

(i) *Sea drift; Songs of farewell;* (i; ii) *Songs of sunset*.
500♪ *** Chandos Dig. CHAN 9214 [id.]. (i) Bryn Terfel; (ii) Sally Burgess; Bournemouth Symphony Ch., Waynflete Singers, Southern Voices, Bournemouth SO, Hickox.

Hickox in this second recording of *Sea drift* finds even more magic, again taking a spacious view – which keeps the flow of the music going magnetically. Bryn Terfel adds to the glory of the performance, the finest since Beecham, as he does in the *Songs of sunset*, with Sally Burgess the other characterful soloist. The *Songs of farewell*, helped by incandescent choral singing, complete an ideal triptych, presented in full and rich Chandos sound.

OPERA

Fennimore and Gerda (complete).
(M) ** EMI CDM5 66314-2. Söderström, Tear, Rayner Cook, Danish R. Ch. & SO, Meredith Davies.

Question: which opera includes in its libretto the line: 'Here is a telegram'? Not anything by Kurt Weill, or Menotti – let alone anyone more recent – but Frederick Delius who, with Philip Heseltine (Peter Warlock), wrote his own libretto for this adaptation of a novel by the Danish author, Jens Peter Jacobsen. It was Delius's last opera, full of the yearning mood-painting which is characteristic of him. It needs above all a musical persuader of the calibre of Beecham before it can really rivet the attention, and Meredith Davies falls short of that in his sympathetic but rather straight and unmagical direction. Though Elisabeth Söderström is not ideally cast, it is good to hear a singer so sensitive to the Delian vocal line. Good singing, too, from the rest of the team and excellent (1976) recording (made in Denmark), well transferred – happily on a single CD as against the original pair of LPs. Good notes, a synopsis and a full libretto are provided, so this reissue is excellent value and worth the attention of Delians.

Devienne, François (1759–1803)

Quartet in C for bassoon and string trio, Op. 73/1.
(B) ** Carlton/Turnabout 30371 0004-2 [id.]. Zukerman, Lautenbacher, Beyer, Blees – BOISMORTIER: *Bassoon concerto in D;* CORRETTE: *'Le Phénix';* F. COUPERIN: *Concerto in G for two bassoons*. **

Devienne, a contemporary of Mozart, provides a genuine novelty here: a *Quartet* for bassoon and strings which curiously evokes the latter's *Clarinet quintet*. Yet it is a most attractive three-movement work, and it is persuasively presented by the inimitable George Zukerman, with an excellent supporting group.

Diamond, David (born 1915)

(i) *Concert piece for flute and harp. Concert piece for orchestra.* (i) *Elegy in memory of Ravel. Rounds for string orchestra; Symphony No. 11: Adagio.*
*** Delos Dig. DE 3189 [id.]. Seattle SO, Gerard Schwarz, (i) with Glorian Duo.

The *Rounds for string orchestra* (1944) is a masterpiece and ought to be part of the international repertoire. It is a deceptively simple construction in three movements with a poignant central *Adagio*, remarkably still and serene, yet warm in expressive feeling. It conjures up the vastness of the American continent but suggests also the presence of humanity, while the vigorous closing movement encapsulates barn-dance energy within a neo-classical structure, with a really memorable secondary idea. The *Concert piece for orchestra* is also snappily rhythmic, more jagged, with a cool, elegiac counterpart and a sudden resolution. The *Elegy for Ravel* is unexpectedly troubled and dissonant, a student work admired by Elliott Carter as 'the most original and daring new piece'. The delicately evoked *Concert piece for flute and harp* is far closer to Ravel's world; indeed, its transparent textures are quite French in feeling, the slow movement especially so. The eloquent *Adagio* from the *Eleventh Symphony* has been described as Brucknerian, although Bruckner would not have acknowledged the degree of dissonance at its somewhat inflated climax. All this music is played superbly by the fine Seattle orchestra and the disc is worth considering for the *Rounds* alone.

Dittersdorf, Carl Ditters von (1739–99)

(i) *Harp concerto in A;* (ii) *Double-bass concerto in E;* (ii–iii) *Sinfonia concertante for double-bass, viola and orchestra in D.*
(B) ** Carlton Turnabout 30371 0006-2 [id.]. (i) Helga Storck; (ii) George Hörtnagel; (iii) Günter Lemmen; Württemberg CO, Heilbronn, Jörg Faerber – STAMITZ: *Bassoon concerto in F.* **

The virtuosity of George Hörtnagel is in no doubt, but in almost every bar his solo double-bass concerto sounds like a cello concerto being played an octave too low! At this level a lyrical baroque line makes a minimum effect, and even when Hörtnagel is joined by the viola, in the *Sinfonia concertante*, the naïveté of the writing detracts from any continued listening pleasure, except out of curiosity. The *Harp concerto* is a different matter: it is delectable in texture and is certainly enjoyable here in its winsome way. Throughout the disc, playing and recording are excellent.

Dohnányi, Ernö (1877–1960)

Symphony No. 2, Op. 40; Symphonic minutes, Op. 36.
*** Chandos Dig. CHAN 9455 [id.]. BBC PO, Bamert.

At one time Dohnányi's *Symphonic minutes*, composed in the early 1930s, featured regularly in concert and radio programmes. They were a favourite of Sir Malcolm Sargent's and are richly inventive and have enormous charm. Oddly enough, neither they nor the enchanting *Suite in F sharp minor* are currently represented in the catalogues except by historic recordings, the former by Sir Henry Wood and the other by Frederick Stock. Those who do not know them will find them close in idiom to Richard Strauss, Kodály and Rachmaninov. It will probably be news to many collectors that Dohnányi composed one symphony, let alone two! The *Second Symphony* was composed in 1944 during the Nazi occupation of Budapest and was revised during the 1950s after Dohnányi had settled in Florida. It is a generally well-argued and finely crafted piece which betrays none of the trauma of its genesis. It is well worth getting to know, even if (at nearly 50 minutes) it rather outstays its welcome. The playing of the BBC Philharmonic under Mathias Bamert is vital and sensitive, and the Chandos recording in the best traditions of the house.

Variations on a nursery tune, Op. 25.
(M) *** Decca 448 604-2 [id.]. Julius Katchen, LPO, Boult – RACHMANINOV: *Piano concerto No. 2* etc. ***

500♪ (M) (***) Dutton mono CDLXT 2504 [id.]. Julius Katchen, LPO, Boult – RACHMANINOV: *Piano concerto No. 2* etc. (***)

It is surprising that the *Nursery variations*, once a regular repertory work, have fallen into relative neglect both on disc and in the concert hall. Katchen's 1954 mono recording with Boult has never been surpassed: there is a sense of new discovery, and the humour is all the more delightful for not being overplayed. The waltz variation is given the most delectable Viennese lilt, and the final pay-off after the fugue is charmingly pointed. This vivid Dutton transfer offers full and firm piano-sound with fine presence, though there is a degree of edge on the thin, exposed high violins.

Katchen's 1959 remake of the *Nursery variations* has the advantage of Decca's finest vintage stereo and it has never sounded better than in this CD reissue, fully worthy of inclusion in Decca's Classic Sound series. The Wagnerian introduction is richly portentous, and from it grows a performance that is both perceptive and spontaneous, as full of wit as it is of lilt and flair. While the earlier account of 1954 by the same artists remains a dazzling example of Decca's mono recording at its most electrifying, collectors should not miss this more modern version which is otherwise unsurpassed and very beautifully balanced and recorded – indeed, in the demonstration bracket for its period. The generous couplings are hardly less recommendable.

Piano quintets Nos. 1 in C min., Op. 1; 2 in E flat min., Op. 26; Serenade in C, Op. 10.
*** Hyperion Dig. CDA 66786 [id.]. Schubert Ens. of London.

Choice here can be left to whatever couplings may appeal. The *First Piano quintet* of 1895, an astonishing achievement for an eighteen-year-old, has been receiving belated attention in recent years. András Schiff and the Takács Quartet recorded it in the late 1980s for Decca, and this will surely be returned to circulation in due course. There are two current versions, by Wolfgang Manz and the Gabrielis (coupled with the *Second String quartet*) on Chandos, and by Martin Roscoe and the Vanbrugh Quartet on ASV, partnered by the darker and more imaginative *Second Piano quintet* of 1914, and these are discussed in our main edition. Both can be counted upon to give real musical satisfaction. Roscoe also offers the *Suite in olden style* for piano, and the Schubert Ensemble give us the *Serenade for string trio*. Good though this newcomer is, both artistically and in terms of recording, readers should not forget the amazing 1941 set with Heifetz, Primrose and Feuermann, which is now back in circulation after many years (see below). Still, a clear three-star recommendation to the Hyperion disc and their excellent pianist, William Howard, which can be recommended alongside (or perhaps even in preference to) the Roscoe version and ahead of the Manz on Chandos.

Serenade in C for string trio, Op. 10.
(M) (***) RCA mono 09026 61763-2 [id.]. Heifetz, Primrose, Feuermann – BRAHMS: *Piano trio No. 1;* R. STRAUSS: *Violin sonata.* (***)

Quite sublime playing from Heifetz, Primrose and Feuermann, recorded in 1941. This performance has never been surpassed, though the recorded sound has! However, its deficiences do not diminish the artistic impact of the performance.

Sextet in C for piano, clarinet, horn, violin, viola and cello, Op. 37.
*** ASV Dig. CDDCA 943 [id.]. Endymion Ens. – FIBICH: *Piano quintet.* ***

Although this version of Dohnányi's fine *Sextet* does not quite banish memories of the one which Schiff, Berkes, Vlatkovič and the Takács Quartet recorded for Decca (now withdrawn) and about which we waxed lyrical in an earlier edition, there is not much to choose between them. The Endymions play with great feeling and panache, they are splendidly recorded and can be strongly recommended.

Donizetti, Gaetano (1797–1848)

Don Pasquale (complete).
500♪ *** RCA Dig. 09026 61924-2 (2) [id.]. Bruson, Mei, Allen, Lopardo, Bav. R. Ch., Munich R. O, Roberto Abbado.

Roberto Abbado's Munich set for RCA is on balance the finest modern version of Donizetti's sparkling comedy. The cast has no weak link. Renato Bruson may accentuate Pasquale's comic lines with little explosions of underlining, but that helps to distinguish him sharply as a *buffo* character from his opposite number, Malatesta, here sung with rare style and beauty by Thomas Allen, as well as with a nicely timed feeling for the comedy. Frank Lopardo as Ernesto shades his clear tenor most sensitively. Eva Mei sings the role of Norina with an apt brightness and precision.

L'elisir d'amore (complete).
(M) *** Erato/Warner Dig. 0630 17787-2 (2) [id.]. Devia, Alagna, Spagnoli, Praticò, Tallis Chamber Ch., ECO, Viotti.
(B) ** Naxos Dig. 8.66045/6 [id.]. La Scola, Ruffini, Alaimo, Frontali, Hungarian State Op. Ch. & O, Pier Morandi.

When this Erato set was first issued it presented no really familiar names, but since then Roberto Alagna's star has risen high in the heavens, and it seems an opportune moment for Erato to reissue his recording at mid-price. It presents an exceptionally winning performance, in many ways the finest of all on record, with no weak leak. Marcello Viotti proves an inspired Donizetti conductor, drawing playing from the ECO that sparkles consistently, with witty pointing of phrase and rhythm, subtle in rubato and finely polished. Consistently too, his timing helps the singers. This is a light, generally brisk account of the score that provides an ideal modern alternative to Richard Bonynge's version with Joan Sutherland as Adina and with the young Pavarotti (Decca, full price – 414 461-2). On Erato, Mariella Devia cannot match Sutherland for beauty of tone in the warmly lyrical solos, but she sparkles more, bringing out what a minx of a heroine this is.

At the time of making this recording Roberto Alagna's tenor timbre was not unlike Pavarotti's, lighter if not quite so firm, and, like Devia, he delectably brings out the lightness of the writing. His performance culminates in a winningly hushed and inner account of the soaring aria, *Una furtiva lagrima*. Rounding off an excellent cast, Pietro Spagnoli is a fresh, virile Belcore, and Bruno Praticò a clear, characterful Dr Dulcamara, an excellent *buffo* baritone, making the very most of a voice on the light side. The sound is first rate, if not as forwardly focused as the analogue Decca.

Naxos offers a sparkling performance of this enchanting comic opera, very well played and warmly – if reverberantly – recorded, which is sadly flawed by the choice of tenor to sing Nemorino. Vincenzo La Scola is far too strenuous in his delivery for this bel canto role, underlining too heavily. The great legato test-piece, *Una furtiva lagrima*, finds him less coarse, but this is a knowing, not an innocent, Nemorino. The others are better chosen, with Alessandra Ruffini bright-toned and vivacious as Adina, Simone Alaimo an excellent Dulcamara and Roberto Frontali agile and characterful as Belcore, both of them getting into their stride as the opera progresses.

La Favorita (complete).

(B) ** Decca Double 452 469-2 (2) [id.]. Simionato, Poggi, Bastianini, Maggio Musicale Fiorentino Ch. & O, Erede.

La Favorita has at least three outstandingly memorable numbers – *Spirito gentil*, *O mio Fernando* and *Per tanto amore* – as well as some characteristically brisk ensembles; but on the whole it falls short of the most famous Donizetti operas. The story of the young man who falls in love with his father's mistress has its dramatic point, but this was the sort of situation that Verdi was to develop much further. Donizetti's setting is not without its red-blooded moments, but this performance is not ingratiating enough to make one forget the weaknesses, for Gianni Poggi is a coarse tenor and neither Simionato nor Bastianini is in top form, for one detects the stiffness of new learning. Nor is Erede's conducting very dramatic, and the orchestra is not very vividly projected. But with very acceptable early stereo (1955) the voices and the chorus are well caught, and at Double Decca price any Donizettian could readily find this set worth while, especially as its only real competitor (also from Decca, with Cossotto and Pavarotti under Bonynge – 414 520-2) costs twice as much. There is, however, no translation, only an uncued synopsis.

Lucia di Lammermoor (complete).

500♪ *** Decca 410 193-2 (2) [id.]. Sutherland, Pavarotti, Milnes, Ghiaurov, Ryland Davies, Tourangeau, ROHCG Ch. & O, Bonynge.

**(*) EMI CDS5 56284-2 (2). Callas, Tagliavini, Cappuccilli, Ladysz, Philh. Ch. & O, Serafin.

Though some of the girlish freshness of voice which marked the 1961 recording disappeared in the 1971 set, Sutherland's detailed understanding was intensified. Power is there as well as delicacy, and the rest of the cast is first rate. Pavarotti, through much of the opera not as sensitive as he can be, proves magnificent in his final scene. The sound-quality is superb on CD. In this set, unlike the earlier one, the text is absolutely complete.

The Callas stereo version was recorded in Kingsway Hall in 1959, at the very same time that Serafin was conducting this opera at Covent Garden for the newly emergent Joan Sutherland. The sound is very good for its period and comes over the more freshly on CD, with Callas's edgy top notes cleanly caught. Her flashing-eyed interpretation of the role of Lucia remains unique, though the voice has its unsteady moments. One instance is at the end of the Act I duet with Edgardo, where Callas on the final phrase moves sharpwards and Tagliavini – here past his best – flatwards. Serafin's conducting is ideal, though the score, as in Callas's other recordings, still has the cuts which used to be conventional in the theatre.

Dowland, John (1563–1626)

LUTE MUSIC

Complete lute works, Volume 1: *Almain, P 49; Dr Cases Pauen; A Dream (Lady Leighton's paven); A Fancy, P 5; Farwell; Frogg galliard; Galliards, P 27; P 30; P 35; P 104; Go from my windowe; The Lady Laitons Almone; Mellancoly galliard; M. Giles Hobies galliard; Mistris Whittes thinge; Mr Knights galliard; Mrs whites nothing; Mrs Winters jumpp; My Ladie Riches galyerd; My lord willobies wellcome home; Orlando sleepeth; Pavan P 18; Pavana (Mylius 1622); Piece without a title, P 51; What if a day.*
*** HM Dig. HMU 907160 [id.]. Paul O'Dette (lute and orpharion).

Dowland wrote about 100 lute solos, using every musical form familiar at the time. Many of his pieces celebrate famous persons or events, but others have no identification other than their form, and these are often among the more interesting or memorable items. He was a master of the division (or variation) format and it must be remembered that these decorations were not always written down. The same applies to ornamentation: quite often it was left to the performer, but in the later pieces it is written out in detail. Where either divisions or ornaments are obviously missing, Paul O'Dette has supplied his own – and very convincing they are. The music on this first disc is particularly rich in ideas: the opening *Piece without a title* is immediately inviting: it has a striking melody, and O'Dette in his excellent notes suggests that it may be a song arrangement. The elaborate *Pavana* which follows is quite splendid in its divisions, yet never obscuring the lyrical flow. The *Frogg galliard* is justly well known, heard here in two versions: the first simple, the second elaborately varied. *Orlando sleepeth* is a hauntingly delicate miniature and it is played, like *Mrs Winters Jumpp* and *Go from my window*, on the orpharion, a wire-strung instrument very like the lute but with a softer focus in sound because 'the fingers must be easily drawn over the strings, and not sharply gripped or stroken, as the lute is'. This is very striking when O'Dette returns to the lute for the cheerful *Almain* which immediately follows the latter piece. The first programme ends appropriately with *Farwell*, another highly original piece, full of atmosphere and contrapuntally ingenious, even including quotations from two of the composer's songs. Paul O'Dette is an acknowledged master of this repertoire: his playing, which can be robust or with the most subtle nuance, is permeated with a natural and unexaggerated expressive feeling and is seemingly totally spontaneous. The recording is quite perfectly judged – not too close – with the lute placed within a very pleasing ambience.

Complete lute works, Volume 2: *Aloe; As I went to Walsingham; Can she excuse; Captain Candishe his galyard; Captain Digorie Piper his galliard; A coye joye; Dowlands first galliard; Dowland's galliard; Farwell (An 'In nomine'); Fantasia; Lachrimae; Mayster Pypers pavyn; Mignarda; Mounsieur's almaine; Mrs Brigide fleetwoods paven alias Solus sine sola; Mrs vauxes galliarde; Mrs vauxes gigge; My lady hunnsdons puffe; Sir Henry Guilforde his almaine; Sir John Smith his almain; Sir John Souche his galliard; Solus cum sola; Suzanna galliard; Sweet Robyne.*
*** HM Dig. HMU 907161 [id.]. Paul O'Dette (lute).

Dowland's use of other composers' music is very prevalent in this programme, and several of the works are not certainly his but are of such a quality that the attribution is just. What is perhaps the most famous of all his pieces, the *Lachrimae* (heard here in an early and very beautiful version in A minor, and played most affectingly), is surely a highlight, but there is a good deal of melancholy music here; even the *Mignarda* is doleful and so, perhaps less expectedly, is the *Galliard* named after *Captain Digorie Piper*. The *Farwell* here is based on the '*In nomine*' theme used by other of Dowland's contemporaries, but rarely heard as a lute solo. Of course there is robust writing too. The opening *My lady hunnsdons puffe* is very catchy, as is *Can she excuse* with its sharp cross-rhythms, while *Sir John Smith's Almain* is distinctly perky – another very good tune, neatly ornamented. Once again Paul O'Dette constantly beguiles the ear, with his feeling for the special mood and colour of Dowland's writing, and the recording is impeccable.

Complete lute works, Volume 3: *Dowlands adew for Master Oliver Cromwell; A Fancy, P 7; Forlorne hope fancye; Fortune my foe; Lord Strangs march; Mistresse Nichols almand; The most high and mightie Christianus, the fourth King of Denmark, his galliard; The most Sacred Queene Elizabeth, her galliard; Mr Dowlands midnight; Mr Langtons galliard; Mrs Cliftons allmaine; A Pavan, P 16; The Queenes galliard; The Right Honourable Ferdinando Earle of Darby, his galliard; The Right Honourable the Lady Cliftons spirit; Semper Dowland semper dolens; Sir John Langton, his pavin; Tarletones riserrectione; Tarletons Willy; Wallsingham & A galliard on Wallsingham.*
*** HM Dig. HMU 907162 [id.]. Paul O'Dette.

Dowland was never satisfied with his music; he was always revising and rethinking earlier works. The exotic *King of Denmark's galliard*, the opening item here, was originally called the 'Battle galliard' because of its bugle-calls, so engagingly portrayed on the lute. *Queen Elizabeth's* not dissimilar *galliard* was originally written for someone else, but Dowland was angling for a court position. As a professed Catholic, Dowland didn't make it; indeed, the basis for his depression was his failure to obtain a court post. Nevertheless, it is an excellent, characterful piece, lively as a galliard should be. *The Queenes galliard* (an earlier work) is less optimistic. *Lady Clifton's galliard* is another (brilliantly complex) decorated version of an earlier piece. *A Pavane* (P 16) is also quite ambitious (five minutes long); touchingly it opens with the *Lachrimae* theme but then introduces other contrasting inventions. *Walsingham* is used as a basis for typically subtle and imaginative divisions, and is more like a set of variations from a later period; the following galliard, based on the same theme, makes a good coda. Generally the third volume of this excellent series has more extrovert music, but there are still interludes of melancholy. *Fortune my foe* is very pensive and *Mr Dowlands midnight* is a comparably disconsolate piece. The closing *Semper Dowland semper dolens* (extended to seven minutes) speaks for itself. All this music comes evocatively to life here, with Paul O'Dette's standard of playing and presentation as high as ever, and the recording is absolutely real.

Complete lute works, Volume 4: *Almand, P 96; Awake sweet love – Galliard; Come away; Coranto, P 100; Fancy, P 6; Fantasia, P 71; Frog Galliard; Galliard, P 82; Galliard on a galliard by Daniel Bachelar; Galliard to Lachrimae; Lachrimae, P 15; The Lady Russells pavane; La mia Barbara; Loth to depart; My Lord Wilobies welcome home; Pavana; Preludium; The Right Honourable the Lord Viscount Lisle, his galliard; The Right Honourable Robert, Earl of Essex, his galliard; The shoemaker's wife – A Toy.*
**(*) HM Dig. HMU 907163 [id.]. Paul O'Dette.

For his fourth volume, Paul O'Dette uses two different lutes as appropriate, an 8-course and a 10-course, both after Hans Frei. He dedicates his programme to the memory of the pioneering Dowland scholar, Diana Poulton (1903–95), and he seems affected by his dedication: for the most part this is a low-key programme, very much in the '*semper dolens*' mood. Of course there are highlights, like the famous *Fantasia*, P 71, and the mood perks up for the galliard written for the Earl of Essex, while the galliard after Daniel Bachelar is also very striking and the *Frog Galliard* is delightful. Towards the end, the tension increases and the penultimate piece, *La mia Barbara*, is very charmingly presented. But overall this is not one of the more memorable of the O'Dette collections.

Music for lute and (i) orpharion: (i) *Can she excuse me; A Dream. Fancies, P 6 & P 73; Fantasie, P 1a; Farwell; Frog galliard; Lachrimae, P 15; Lady Hunsdon's puffe; Melancholy galliard; Mignarda; The most high and mightie Christianus, the fourth King of Denmark, his galliard; Mr Knights galliard; Mrs Brigide Fleetwood's pavan alias Solus sine sola; Mrs Vaux Jig;* (i) *Mrs Winters jump; My Lord Willoughby's welcome home;* (i) *Orlando sleepeth; Resolution; The Right Honourable The Lord Viscount Lisle, his galliard; Semper Dowland semper dolens; The Shoemaker's wife; Sir John Smith his almain; Tarleton's riserrection; Walsingham.*
*** BIS Dig CD 824 [id.]. Jacob Lindberg (lute), or (i) orpharion.

Those not collecting Paul O'Dette's complete series will find this BIS CD offers a cross-section of many of the finest of Dowland's lute pieces. The programme is generous (75 minutes) and Jacob Lindberg is no less at home in this repertoire than his colleague on Harmonia Mundi. If anything, his lute image is a little bolder as recorded, although there is little enough in it. After opening with an appealingly characterful performance of the *Frog galliard*, Lindberg shows himself an equal master of the Dowland melancholy in the following *Lachrimae*. He is particularly successful in the more striking numbers: for instance the lively (battle) galliard written for the King of Denmark is full of personality, as is the gentle piece called *Resolution*. The orpharion is used to atmospheric effect in the four works for which it was intended. *Semper Dowland, semper dolens* is most eloquently presented, as is the remarkable *Farwell*; and the divisions on *Walsingham* are played with a nice flow and an unexaggerated bravura. The recording is first class.

Lute songs: *Can she excuse my wrongs?; Come again! Sweet love doth now invite; Far from triumphing court; Flow so fast, ye fountain; In darkness let me dwell; I saw my lady weep; Lady, if you so spite me; Thou almighty God; Shall I sue?; Weep you no more, sad fountains.* Lute solos: *Lachrimae antiquae pavane; Semper Dowland, sempre dolens.*
*** Lyrichord LEMS 8011 [id.]. Russell Oberlin, Joseph Iadone (lute).

One can hardly believe this recital was recorded in 1958, so fresh and vivid is the sound. Russell Oberlin's very special counter-tenor timbre is beautifully caught. The very free rhythmic style of *Can she excuse my wrongs?* is confidently handled and *Shall I sue?* also brings a lively element into what is essentially a melancholy selection. *I saw my lady weep* is most moving, while *Flow my tears* soars; but most touching of all is the closing *In darkness let me dwell*. Joseph Iadone contributes two of Dowland's most famous instrumental pieces. He affects a very mellow style which is believed to be authentic. The only drawback to this disc is the comparatively short playing-time of 48 minutes.

Du Fay, Guillaume (*c.* 1400–1474)

Chanson and Mass: *Se la face ay pale;* Motet: *Gloria ad modum tubae.*
(M) *** Virgin Veritas/EMI VER5 61283-2 [CDM 61283]. Early Music Cons. of L., David Munrow.

David Munrow's pioneering recording of Du Fay's Mass was first issued on LP to mark the quincentenary of the composer's death in 1974 and the first-class recording, immaculately transferred to CD, sounds as fresh as on the day it first appeared. The performance of this austere yet moving work is superb in every way. The Mass itself is prefaced by the chanson on which it is based, first in its original three-part version, then in two keyboard versions from the Buxheimer Organ Book, and finally in a four-part instrumental version scored for alto cornett, alto shawm and alto and tenor sackbutts, attributed to the great Burgundian master himself. The performance is accompanied by instruments, tenor and bass viols in the solo sections of the *Gloria* and *Credo*, cornetts and sackbutts in the full sections. The soloists are all distinguished (they include James Bowman), and David Munrow himself plays the alto shawm. As a curtain-raiser before the Mass, we are offered the catchy motet, *Gloria ad modum tubae*, written in a lively canonic form, with the effect of a round. An indispensable reissue. It calls for and rewards concentrated and repeated listening.

Missa Santi Anthoni de Padua. Hymnus: *Veni creator spiritus*.
*** DG Dig. 447 772-2 [id.]. Pomerium, Alexander Blachly.

Missa Santi Anthoni de Padua. Motet: *O proles Hispaniae/O sidus Hispaniae*.
*** Hyperion Dig. CDA 66854 [id.]. Binchois Cons., Andrew Kirkman.

It was long thought that Du Fay's *Mass for St Anthony of Padua* was lost but, at the beginning of the 1980s, the British musicologist, Dr David Fallows, produced evidence to suggest that two separate groups of manuscripts held at Trent, Italy, the first with the Mass Ordinary movements (*Kyrie*, *Gloria*, *Credo*, *Sanctus* and *Agnus Dei*), the second with the Proper movements dedicated specifically to the saint, could convincingly be linked to make a whole, and that is what is recorded here. Moreover we have a choice of style of performance for this beautiful music. The Binchois Consort is a small, intimate, all-male group, while Alexander Blachly's Pomerium is a much larger choir, drawing on four sopranos, three altos, four tenors and four basses, although the whole ensemble is used only in the Ordinary movements. This makes for greater dynamic contrast; moreover the two recording acoustics are different, the DG Archiv recording being made in the richly resonant Grotto Church of Notre Dame in New York, whereas the Hyperion ambience is drier and the inner detail emerges with much greater clarity. The effect is undoubtedly more austere, though full of character. If you relish polyphonic detail, choose Andrew Kirkman; if you want to enjoy the flowing melismas in a more glowingly sensuous way, then Alexander Blachly is your man. Pomerium offer as a bonus Du Fay's setting of the hymn, *Veni creator spiritus*, while the Binchois Consort performs a motet with two texts also associated with St Anthony. Both recordings are first class.

Dukas, Paul (1856–1937)

L'apprenti sorcier (The sorcerer's apprentice).
500♪ *** DG Dig. 419 617-2 [id.]. BPO, Levine (with SAINT-SAENS: *Symphony No. 3* ***).
** Cala Dig. CACD 1022 [id.]. LSO, Mackerras – BRITTEN: *Young person's guide;* PROKOFIEV: *Peter and the wolf.* **

L'apprenti sorcier; La péri (with *Fanfare*); *Polyeucte: overture.*
❀ (M) *** Ph. 454 127-2 [id.]. Rotterdam PO, David Zinman – D'INDY: *Symphonie sur un chant montagnard.* **

Levine chooses a fast basic tempo, though not as fast as Toscanini (who managed with only two 78 sides), but achieves a deft, light and rhythmic touch to make this a real orchestral scherzo. Yet the climax is thrilling, helped by superb playing from the Berlin Philharmonic. The CD has an amplitude and sparkle which are especially telling.

Dukas's *La péri* was written for Diaghilev in 1912. It is based on a tale from ancient Persian mythology. King Iskander discovers the Péri asleep and steals her lotus-blossom with its power of immortal youth. The Péri awakens and stimulates the King's desire with an erotic dance. The King succumbs and returns the flower, whereupon the object of his passion promptly vanishes, leaving him to reflect that he has been caught out by the oldest trick of all. Those who cherish rosy memories of the pre-war set of *La péri* by

Philippe Gaubert and the Paris Conservatoire Orchestra will not be disappointed by this CD reissue of David Zinman's 1978 recording, which is every bit as haunting and atmospheric. In fact the Rotterdam Philharmonic give us here what is arguably the finest account of Dukas's colourful score ever to have been put on record. Here is a conductor acutely sensitive to the most delicate colourings and the hushed atmosphere of this evocative score, with its colours drawn as much from Rimsky-Korsakov as from Debussian impressionism. Zinman captures the fairy-tale spirit better than any of his rivals and more magically than the recently reissued Boulez version. The well-balanced recording creates a warm, misty web of sound with wide-ranging dynamics and a truthful perspective, very reminiscent of Haitink's analogue Concertgebouw recordings of Debussy's *Images*, *Jeux* and *Nocturnes*, if less sharply defined. Only in the introductory *Fanfare* could some ears crave more sonic brilliance, and that comment might also be applied to *L'apprenti sorcier*, in which the same atmospheric translucence is equally evocative at the opening before the apprentice sets off on his watery task with jaunty insouciance. Certainly no one should be disappointed with either the climax or the tale's rueful dénouement. The *Polyeucte overture* is not dissimilar in style to *La péri* but has less interesting material; it is presented equally effectively.

A brilliantly played account from Mackerras and the LSO, but the work is treated primarily as a display piece and its ironic subtleties are glossed over.

Piano sonata in E flat min.

(M) *** EMI CDM5 65996-2 [id.]. John Ogdon – DUTILLEUX: *Sonata;* Florent SCHMITT: *Deux mirages.* ***

This performance of the Dukas *Sonata* was originally issued in the early 1970s in an enterprising five-LP box called 'Musical Philosophies', which included a number of challenging pieces. Unless our memory deceives us, none was ever reissued separately. This is one of the best performances in that set, and one of the finest – save for the Busoni *Piano concerto* – John Ogdon ever committed to disc. Some of his admirers, including the late lamented Christopher Headington, maintained that Ogdon's playing could often sound like brilliant sight-reading – that the music had not fully become part of his musical bloodstream. This is not the case here. This is a powerful, totally committed performance of a work which was much admired by Debussy and which enjoys scant exposure in the catalogue. There is an excellent account by Margaret Fingerhut on Chandos, but this EMI version is as good, is less expensive and has the advantage of even more appealing couplings than hers.

Dunstable, John (d. 1453)

Missa Rex seculorum. Motets: *Albanus roseo rutilat – Quoque ferundus eras – Albanus domini Laudus; Ave maris stella; Descendi in ortum meum; Gloria in canon; Preco preheminence – Precursor premittur – textless – Inter natos mulierum; Salve regina mater mire; Specialis Virgo; Speciosa facta es; Sub tuam protectionem; Veni sancte spiritus – Veni creator spiritus*.

*** Metronome Dig. METCD 1009 [id.]. Orlando Con.

The Orlando Consort are an impressive new vocal group, specializing in early vocal repertoire, and they present their generous, 74-minute survey with an impressive combination of direct, impassioned feeling and style. Some of this fine music was discovered only recently and the splendid *Missa Rex seculorum* is of doubtful attribution. But every piece here, motets and antiphons alike, is clearly by a major composer with a highly individual voice. The recording is excellent in every way, and this CD, which won the *Gramophone*'s Early Music Award in 1996, offers the collector an admirable and highly rewarding entry into this composer's sound-world.

Motets: *Agnus Dei; Alma redemptoris Mater; Credo super; Da gaudiorum premia; Gaude virgo salutata; Preco preheminenciae; Quam pulcra es; Salve regina misericordiae; Salve sceme sanctitatis; Veni creator; Veni sancte spiritus*.

*** Virgin Veritas/EMI Dig. VER5 61342-2 [id.]. Hilliard Ens., Hillier.

In the time of Henry V, John Dunstable (or Dunstaple, which is historically more correct) was not only the leading English composer of his day but also one of the most influential figures in Europe. His music has not always been well served by the gramophone, but this reissued record by the Hilliard Ensemble of nine motets and Mass movements makes a major contribution to his discography. These motets give a very good idea of his range, and they are sung with impeccable style. The Hilliard Ensemble has perfectly blended tone and impeccable intonation, and their musicianship is of the highest order. Some collectors may find the unrelieved absence of vibrato a little tiring on the ear when taken in large doses, but most readers will find this a small price to pay for music-making of such excellence, so well recorded.

Duparc, Henri (1848–1933)

Mélodies (complete): *Au pays où se fait la guerre; Chanson triste; Elégie; Extase; La fuite (duet); Le galop; L'invitation au voyage; Lamento; Le Manoir de Rosamonde; Phidylé; Romance de Mignon; Sérénade; Sérénade florentine; Soupir; Testament; La vague et la cloche; La vie antérieure.*
500♪ *** Hyperion Dig. CDA 66323 [id.]. Sarah Walker, Thomas Allen, Roger Vignoles.

The Hyperion issue is as near an ideal Duparc record as could be. Here are not only the thirteen recognized songs but also four early works – three songs and a duet – which have been rescued from the composer's own unwarranted suppression. Roger Vignoles is the ever-sensitive accompanist; and the recording captures voices and piano beautifully, bringing out the tang and occasional rasp of Walker's mezzo and the glorious tonal range of Allen's baritone.

Duruflé, Maurice (born 1902)

Requiem, Op. 9.
500♪ *** Teldec/Warner Dig. 4509 90879-2 [id.]. Jennifer Larmore, Thomas Hampson, Amb. S., Philh. O, Legrand – FAURE: *Requiem.* ***

Michel Legrand uses the full orchestral version and makes the most of the passionate orchestral eruptions in the *Sanctus* and *Libera me*. He strikes a perfect balance between these sudden outbursts of agitation and the work's mysticism and warmth. The Ambrosian Choir sing ardently yet find a treble-like purity for the *Agnus Dei* and *In Paradisum*, while Jennifer Larmore gives the *Pie Jesu* more plangent feeling than its counterpart in the Fauré *Requiem*. The recording, made in Watford Town Hall, is spacious and most realistically balanced. A clear first choice.

Dutilleux, Henri (born 1916)

(i) *Cello concerto (Tout un monde lointain);* (ii) *Violin concerto (L'arbre des songes).*
500♪ *** Decca Dig. 444 398-2 [id.]. (i) Harrell; (ii) Amoyal; Fr. Nat. O, Dutoit.

Both concertos have been recorded before and are listed here, but they have not been coupled together, so this remains in many respects an obvious choice for the serious collector. Both Pierre Amoyal and Lynn Harrell are first class and withstand the exalted comparisons they confront. The Decca recording is finer than that of rivals, clean, well detailed and with great presence and refinement. What imaginative music this is.

(i) *Violin concerto (L'arbre des songes); Timbres, espaces, mouvement;* (ii) *2 Sonnets de Jean Cassou.*
*** Chandos Dig. CHAN 9504 [id.]. (i) Olivier Charlier; (ii) Neal Davies; BBC PO, Yan Pascal Tortelier – ALAIN: *Prière.* ***

For long marginalized by Boulez's clique in Paris, Dutilleux has at long last taken his rightful place on the French musical map, which is more central than the periphery to which musical history will consign them. The *Violin concerto*, written for Isaac Stern, who recorded it with Lorin Maazel on Sony (now available at mid-price coupled with the Bernstein *Serenade for violin, strings, harp and percussion*) is now engaging wider attention. Pierre Amoyal and Charles Dutoit couple it more logically with the *Cello concerto* (*Tout un monde lointain*); now Olivier Charlier has recorded it with the BBC Philharmonic in Manchester, with Yan Pascal Tortelier conducting. It makes a useful follow-up to Tortelier's account of the two *Symphonies* on Chandos (see below) and it can be recommended with similar enthusiasm. In terms of artistry and musicianship Charlier yields nothing to either of his rivals, and Tortelier gives us the *Timbres, espaces, mouvement* (*La nuit étoilée*) from 1979 as a makeweight. This is its fourth recording (Baudo, Rostropovich and Bychkov have already committed it to disc), and suffice it to say that this newcomer can hold its own alongside them even in terms of recorded quality – except perhaps in the case of the Bychkov on Philips, which is stunning. The *Deux Sonnets de Jean Cassou* come in Dutilleux's own orchestral transcription, in which Martyn Hill and Neal Davies are effective soloists.

Symphonies Nos. 1–2.
500♪ ❁ *** Chandos Dig. CHAN 9194 [id.]. BBC PO, Tortelier.

Marvellously resourceful and inventive scores which are given vivid and persuasive performances by Tortelier and the BBC Philharmonic Orchestra. The engineers give us a splendidly detailed and refined portrayal of these complex textures – the sound is really state-of-the-art. This issue supersedes Serge

Baudo's version with the Orchestre National de Lyon of the *First Symphony*, coupled with *Timbres, espace, mouvement*.

Piano sonata.

(M) *** EMI CDM5 65996-2 [id.]. John Ogdon – DUKAS: *Sonata;* Florent SCHMITT: *Deux mirages*. ***

An enterprising release of a totally idiomatic and thoroughly convincing account of a brilliant twentieth-century work that does not enjoy the exposure it deserves. This can take its place alongside the current recommendation by Geneviève Joy in an excellent three-CD set devoted to Dutilleux.

Dvořák, Antonín (1841–1904)

(i) *American suite in A, Op. 98b;* (ii) *Serenade for strings in E, Op. 22; Serenade for wind in D min., Op. 44.*

(B) *** Decca Eclipse Dig. 448 981-2; *448 981-4* [id.]. (i) RPO, Dorati; (ii) LPO, Hogwood.

Dvořák's *American suite*, which has clear influences from the New World, was written first as a piano version (1894) but was turned into an orchestral piece the following year. Dorati has its measure and the RPO are very responsive, while the Kingsway Hall recording-balance seems to suit the scoring rather well. It is slight but charming music and makes a good coupling for the two *Serenades*. These receive fresh, bright, spring-like accounts from Hogwood and the LPO in clean, slightly recessed sound. Textually this version of the *String serenade* is unique on record when it uses the original score, newly published, in which two sections (one of 34 bars in the Scherzo and the other of 79 bars in the finale), missing in the normal printed edition, are now included. Though these performances are not quite as winning or as rhythmically subtle as those of Schneider or Marriner, they are still very enjoyable, and the inclusion of the extra material brings added interest.

Cello concerto in B min., Op. 104.

500♪ ✿ (M) *** DG 447 413-2 [id.]. Rostropovich, BPO, Karajan – TCHAIKOVSKY: *Variations on a rococo theme*. *** ✿

(B) *** DG 447 349-2 (2) [id.]. Fournier, BPO, Szell – BLOCH: *Schelomo* **(*); BRUCH: *Kol Nidrei* ** (with Concert – see below under Fournier ***).

(BB) ** Naxos Dig. 8.550503 [id.]. Maria Kliegel, RPO, Halasz – ELGAR: *Cello concerto*. **

(i) *Cello concerto in B min., Op. 104;* (ii) *Symphony No. 8 in G, Op. 88.*

(B) *** DG 439 484-2 [id.]. (i) Fournier; (i–ii) BPO; (i) Szell; (ii) Kubelik.

There have been a number of distinguished recordings of both the Dvořák *Concerto* and its equally seductive Tchaikovsky coupling over the two and a half decades since Rostropovich's DG record was made, but none to match it for intensity of lyrical feeling and the spontaneity of the partnership between Karajan and Rostropovich. The orchestral playing is glorious.

Pierre Fournier's reading of the *Cello concerto* has a sweep of conception and a richness of tone and phrasing which carry the melodic lines along with exactly that mixture of nobility and tension the work demands. The phrasing in the slow movement is ravishing, and the interpretation as a whole balances beautifully. DG's recording, dating from 1962, is forward and vivid, with a broad, warm tone for the soloist. Kubelik's *Eighth* is appealingly direct and the polished, responsive playing of the Berlin Philharmonic adds to the joy and refinement of the performance. The 1966 sound is bright and clear, if a little dry. It has been splendidly remastered, and altogether this is a highly recommendable bargain coupling. Fournier's performance of the *Cello concerto* is also available in an attractive anthology entirely centred on this artist – see Concerts section below.

On the Naxos bargain label it makes a generous coupling having the two greatest of all cello concertos. Maria Kliegel is a warmly expressive soloist, generally persuasive, whose tone is yet not ideally opulent, and whose expansive manner – as in the second subject of the first movement – runs to extremes. If the orchestral accompaniment was tauter, the results would be even more convincing. As it is, the reading runs the risk of self-indulgence. Yet with good, modern, digital sound and so generous a coupling, it makes a fair bargain in the lowest price range.

(i) *Cello concerto;* (ii) *Rondo in G min., Op. 94;* (iii) *Silent woods, Op. 68/5.*

**(*) Channel Classics Dig. CCS 8695 [id.]. Pieter Wispelwey; (i) Netherlands PO, Lawrence Renes; (ii–iii) Paulo Giacometti (piano or harmonium) (with: ARENSKY: *Chant triste, Op. 56/3;* DAVIDOV: *Am Springbrunnen, Op. 20/2;* TCHAIKOVSKY: *Andante cantabile, from Op. 11* **(*)).

The Dutch cellist, Pieter Wispelwey, equally at home in period or modern style, here gives a more intimate reading than most on disc, using a relatively narrow dynamic range, with rather more *portamento* than usual, bringing out autumnal tone-colours, as he does in the shorter pieces which come as fill-up. The contrast between soloist and the orchestra in tuttis, incisively played, is the more extreme. The performance may be less bitingly dramatic than most, but the concentration and expressive warmth make it extremely compelling. Three of the shorter pieces – in all of which Wispelwey uses gut strings – have harmonium accompaniment. That is most effective in the Tchaikovsky and the Arensky (which sounds as though it is about to turn into Tchaikovsky's song, *None but the lonely heart*), but then sounds muddled in Dvořák's *Silent woods*. Happily the *Rondo* comes with piano accompaniment, as does the Davidov. Excellent sound.

Rondo in G min. (for cello and orchestra), *Op. 94*.
(M) *** Carlton Dig. 30366 0011-2 [id.]. Tortelier, RPO, Groves – ELGAR: *Cello concerto* **(*); TCHAIKOVSKY: *Rococo variations*. ***

The Dvořák *Rondo* is one of Tortelier's party pieces, and its point and humour are beautifully caught here.

Serenade for strings in E; Serenade for wind in D min., Op. 44.
(M) *(*) Chandos Dig. CHAN 7060 [id.]. Philh. O, Warren-Green.

Christopher Warren-Green's rather languorous approach verges dangerously near sentimentality and, despite glowing sound and fine playing from the Philharmonia strings and wind alike, neither *Serenade* is as effectively characterized as the competition.

Serenade in D min. for wind, Op. 44.
**(*) EMI Dig. CDC5 55512-2 [id.]. Sabine Meyer Wind Ens. – MYSLIVECEK: *Octets Nos. 1–3*. **(*)

In our main volume we list half a dozen versions of the glorious *Serenade for wind* from among the many currently on the market, and this newcomer is a worthy addition. The playing is polished and refined, and the excellent EMI recording makes for pleasurable listening. Perhaps other ensembles bring greater character to this music, István Kertész and the LSO are delightfully fresh, and the Nash have great lightness of touch and zest. The Sabine Meyer Ensemble have elegance but are perhaps a little laid back by comparison with some current rivals (see our main volume) but they give undoubted pleasure.

Slavonic dances Nos. 1–16, Op. 46/1–8; Op. 72/1–8.
500♪ ✿ (M) *** Sony SBK 48161; *SBT 48161* [id.]. Cleveland O, George Szell.

In Szell's exuberant, elegant and marvellously played set of the *Slavonic dances* the balance is close (which means pianissimos fail to register) but the charisma of the playing is unforgettable and, for all the racy exuberance, one senses a predominant feeling of affection and elegance. The warm acoustics of Severance Hall ensure the consistency of the orchestral sound.

Slavonic dances, Op. 72, Nos. 9–16.
(B) *** Decca Eclipse Dig. 448 991-2; *448 991-4* [id.]. RPO, Dorati – GOLDMARK: *Rustic Wedding Symphony*. **(*)

Anyone wanting just the second set of the Dvořák *Slavonic dances* will find that Dorati's performances have characteristic brio; the RPO response is warmly lyrical when necessary, and the woodwind playing gives much pleasure. Sparkle is the keynote, and the Kingsway Hall recording adds suitable atmosphere. The 1983 recording sounds very good in this Eclipse reissue.

Symphonic poems: *The Golden spinning wheel, Op. 109; The Noon witch, Op. 108; The Water goblin, Op. 107; The Wild dove, Op. 110*.
(M) ** Sup. SU 3056-2 011 [id.]. Czech PO, Chalabala.

Originally issued on a pair of LPs, these well-played, idiomatic Supraphon performances of four favourite symphonic poems are eminently recommendable on a single, medium-priced CD for those prepared to accept somewhat emaciated violin timbre when the strings sing out above the stave, and a brass tone with slightly exaggerated brightness. Otherwise the 1961 recording, made in the Dvořák Hall in Prague, has plenty of warmth and atmosphere and is flattering to the delightful contributions of the Czech woodwind and horns. Chalabala's interpretations are thoroughly convincing.

SYMPHONIES

Symphonies Nos. 1–9.
500♪ (M) *** Chandos Dig. CHAN 9008/13 [id.]. SNO, Neeme Järvi.

Järvi has the advantage of outstanding, modern, digital recording, full and naturally balanced. The set is offered at upper mid-price, six CDs for the price of four. Only the *Fourth Symphony* is split centrally between discs; all the others can be heard uninterrupted.

Symphonies Nos. 3 in E flat, Op. 10; 7 in D min., Op. 70.
*** DG Dig. 449 207-2 [id.]. VPO, Myung-Whun Chung.

Myung-Whun Chung and the Vienna Philharmonic couple one of the greatest (and at times most Brahmsian) of the Dvořák symphonies with the 1874 *E flat Symphony*, which brought the young master into Brahms's orbit. The *D minor* contains some of the most profound music of any symphony after Beethoven, and Chung has its measure. His approach is well considered and finely shaped, and yet he manages to make everything sound as fresh and as spontaneous as Dvořák must. The playing in both symphonies is impressive and they deserve – but do not receive – state-of-the-art recorded sound. There needs to be a better-ventilated, more spacious orchestral texture, such as Chandos provide for Bělohlávek. All the same, the stature of the performances is such as to warrant a full three-star recommendation.

Symphony No. 5 in F, Op. 76; Othello overture, Op. 93; Scherzo capriccioso, Op. 66.
500♪ ❁ *** EMI Dig. CDC7 49995-2 [id.]. Oslo PO, Jansons.

Jansons directs a radiant account of this delectable symphony and the EMI engineers put a fine bloom on the Oslo sound. With its splendid encores, equally exuberant in performance, this is one of the finest Dvořák records in the catalogue.

Symphonies Nos. 7 in D min., Op. 70; 8 in G, Op. 88; 9 (New World); Scherzo capriccioso, Op. 66.
(B) *** Decca Double 452 182-2 (2) [id.]. Cleveland O, Christoph von Dohnányi.

Christoph von Dohnányi's Cleveland performances of the last three Dvořák symphonies from the mid-1980s are among his very finest recordings, and they make an admirable Double Decca triptych. Tempi are all aptly judged. The playing of the Cleveland Orchestra is so responsive that the overall impression is one of freshness, and the recording is in the demonstration class, using the acoustics of the Masonic Auditorium to give a convincingly natural balance. Dohnányi's *New World*, superbly played and recorded, like the companion recordings of Nos. 7 and 8, should by rights be a first recommendation, but it fails to observe the first-movement exposition repeat. That said, there is much to praise in this grippingly spontaneous performance, generally direct and unmannered but glowing with warmth. In the first movement Dohnányi, without any stiffness, allows himself relatively little easing of tempo for the second and third subjects, while the great cor anglais melody in the *Largo* and the big clarinet solo in the finale are both richly done, with the ripe and very well-balanced Decca recording adding to their opulence. The sound is spectacularly full and rich. The addition of the *Scherzo capriccioso* is apt when the performance finds an affinity with the *Eighth Symphony* in bringing out the Slavonic dance sparkle and moulding the lyrical secondary theme with comparable affectionate flair.

Symphony No. 8 in G; Legends Nos. 4, 6 & 7, Op. 59; Scherzo capriccioso.
500♪ ❁ (M) *** EMI CDM7 64193-2 [id.]. Hallé O, Sir John Barbirolli.

Symphony No. 8 in G, Op. 88; Slavonic dances Nos. 3, Op. 46/3; 10, Op. 72/2.
(B) **(*) EMI forte CZS5 69509-2 (2). Cleveland O, Szell – BEETHOVEN: *Piano concerto No. 5* etc. ***

Barbirolli's account of this symphony has immense vitality and forward impetus, the kind of spontaneous excitement that is rare in the recording studio, and yet the whole performance is imbued with a delightful, unforced lyricism. The *Scherzo capriccioso* is warm and very exciting too, and the *Legends* make a colourful bonus. It was made in 1957–8 in Manchester's recently rebuilt Free Trade Hall by the Mercury recording team, led by Wilma Cozart Fine. In remastered form it is tremendously real and vivid.

Szell's reading of the *Eighth Symphony* is strong and committed, consistent from first to last, and marvellously played. In sheer adrenalin the interpretation does not quite quite match his earlier, Decca (mono) version in the first two movements but, with full-bodied 1970 sound, it remains both distinctive and very enjoyable. Similarly the pair of *Slavonic dances* are mellower than the earlier complete set on Sony but are still a fine example of Cleveland orchestral bravura. The transfers are first class – this is a richer sound than on many records from this source.

Symphony No. 9 in E min. (From the New World), Op. 95.
(M) *** Decca Phase Four 448 947-2 [id.]. New Philh. O, Dorati – KODALY: *Hary János suite*. ***

Symphony No. 9 (New World); (ii) *Czech suite; Prague waltzes.*
500♪ (B) *** Decca Eclipse Dig. 448 245-2; *448 245-4* [id.]. (i) VPO, Kondrashin; (ii) Detoit SO, Dorati.

Kondrashin's Vienna performance of the *New World Symphony* was recorded in the Sofiensaal. Other performances may exhibit a higher level of tension but there is a natural spontaneity here, with the first-movement exposition repeat fitting naturally into the scheme of things. The cor anglais solo in the *Largo* is easy and songful, and the finale is especially satisfying, with the wide dynamic range adding drama and the refinement and transparency of the texture noticeably effective as the composer recalls ideas from earlier movements. The budget-priced Eclipse CD is enhanced by Dorati's bright, fresh Detroit versions of the *Czech suite* and the even rarer *Prague waltzes* (Viennese music with a Czech accent).

Dorati's performance is immediate and direct, with bold primary colours heightening the drama throughout. Rarely have the Phase Four techniques been used to better artistic effect, and the recording is extremely vivid, without loss of warmth. Not a first choice, perhaps, but eminently recommendable if the excellent Kodály coupling is suitable.

CHAMBER MUSIC

Piano quartets Nos. 1 in D, Op. 23; 2 in E flat, Op. 87.
500♪ ❀ *** Hyperion Dig. CDA 66287 [id.]. Domus.

The Dvořák *Piano quartets* are glorious pieces, and the playing of Domus is little short of inspired. This is real chamber-music-playing: intimate, unforced and distinguished by both vitality and sensitivity. Domus are recorded in an ideal acoustic and in perfect perspective; they sound wonderfully alive and warm.

Piano quintet in A, Op. 81.
** EMI Dig. CDC5 55593-2 [id.]. Rudolf Buchbinder, Alban Berg Qt – SCHUMANN: *Piano quintet.* **

Buchbinder's account of the Dvořák *A major Piano quintet* was recorded at a concert at the Vienna Konzerthaus in 1993 in front of an obviously appreciative audience. Unfortunately, whatever its artistic merits, the recording balance is unsatisfactory, unduly favouring Buchbinder. He is not the last word in imaginative finesse, though his artistry is of a higher order than that of Philippe Entremont in the Schumann coupling, recorded at a much earlier (1985) Carnegie Hall concert. This induces only modified rapture. Fortunately, the catalogue abounds in recordings – Curzon and the VPO Quintet at mid-price on Decca (448 602-2), Pavel Stepán and the Smetana Quartet on Testament (SBT 1074) and Susan Tomes and the Gaudier Ensemble on Hyperion (CDA 66796) – which offer unalloyed pleasure.

Piano quintet in A, Op. 81; Piano trio No. 4 in E min. (Dumky), Op. 90.
(M) **(*) Virgin/EMI Ultraviolet CUV5 61321-2 [id.]. Nash Ens.

It is surprising that the coupling of the *A major Piano quintet* and the *Dumky Trio* has not been chosen more often. The Nash Ensemble offer good, musicianly performances that are eminently well recorded and give satisfaction, without being as memorable as such classic accounts of the quintet as that with Clifford Curzon on Decca.

Piano trios Nos. 1 in B flat, Op. 21; 2 in G min., Op. 26; 3 in F min., Op. 65; 4 in E min. (Dumky), Op. 90.
(M) *** Carlton Dig. 30366 00247-2 (2) [id.]. Solomon Trio.
(B) **(*) Ph. Duo 454 259-2 (2) [id.]. Beaux Arts Trio.

Piano trios Nos. 1–4; 4 Romantic pieces for violin and piano, Op. 75.
** CRD Dig. CRD 3386/7 [id.]. Cohen Trio.

The Solomon Trio (Daniel Adni, Rodney Friend and Raphael Sommer) have the advantage of an outstandingly realistic and well-balanced recording. The resonance seems just right and one can imagine a hall extension behind one's speakers. This is a different group of players from the performers in the earlier, excellent, two-disc set of Beethoven *Piano trios* (Carlton 30366 00107), with only the violinist, Rodney Friend, common to both. But, if anything, these Dvořák performances are even more successful. It is good to welcome the pianist, Daniel Adni, back to the recording studio: it is he who holds the performances together so naturally, so that the players can relax yet bring the music fully to life. While his legato tone is warmly coloured, he can also twinkle delightfully, as in the Scherzo of Op. 21. Indeed the Czech dance movements all lilt most engagingly. The warm tone and musical phrasing of Raphael Sommer, the cellist, is a rewarding feature of the *Adagios* of Opp. 21 and 65; the latter is a performance which brings much subtlety as well as drama and brilliance. The *Dumky* is flexibly quixotic in its spontaneous mood-changes and it combines freshness with communicated affection. This fine Carlton set can be recommended alongside the Trio Fontenay on Teldec, who are also very stimulating but are not recorded quite so beautifully (9031 76458-2 – see our main volume).

The Beaux Arts versions of the *Piano trios* come from the end of the 1960s. The *F minor*, arguably the most magnificent and certainly the most concentrated of the four, is played with great eloquence and vitality, with Bernard Greenhouse's cello solo at the opening of the *Poco adagio* matched by Isidore Cohen's delicacy of feeling. And what sparkling virtuosity there is in the *Scherzo* of the *G minor*, Op. 26. The splendours of the *Dumky* are well realized in an account of great spontaneity and freshness. The pianist Menahem Pressler plays throughout with real effervescence. The recording is naturally balanced and splendidly vivid; only a degree of thinness on the violin timbre, most noticeable on the first disc but also at the first fortissimo of the *Dumky*, gives any grounds for reservation. At Duo price this is excellent value.

The performances by the Cohen Trio are full of life and spirit and are enjoyable also for their warmth. The snag is that, as recorded, Raymond Cohen's violin-tone is excessively thin, and in the end the ear tires of the sound. We have returned to this set several times, but this impression remains unaltered.

Piano trios Nos. 3 in F min., Op. 65; 4 in E min., Op. 90 (Dumky).
*** Hyperion Dig. CDA 66895 [id.]. Florestan Trio.

Eminently satisfying alternative to the Ax/Kim/Ma and Beaux Arts versions. These are musicianly and refined performances that will give much pleasure, and the recording, too, is excellent.

String quartets Nos. 8 in E., Op. 80; 11 in C, Op. 61.
(BB) *** Naxos 8.553372 [id.]. Vlach Qt.

There is nothing 'bargain basement' about these Vlach performances except their price. The playing is cultured and has warmth and vitality, and there can be no grumbles as far as the quality of the recorded sound is concerned. The discrepancy between the numbering of the quartets is accounted for by the fact that the *E major* (No. 8) was written earlier than its companion but published later.

String quartets Nos. 10 in E flat, Op. 51; 12 in F, Op. 96 (American).
(*(**)) Globe mono GLO 6036 [id.]. Netherlands Qt.

The Netherlands String Quartet flourished on the Philips label in the days of mono LP. These recordings come from 1955 and won golden opinions at the time. Listening to them, one wonders whether they have been surpassed – save by the Smetana and Quartetto Italiano in Op. 96. However, the recorded sound calls for some tolerance as the top end of the spectrum tends to be thin almost to the point of shrillness. It is worth taking trouble filtering the top frequencies, as these are very fine performances.

String quartet No. 12 in F (American), Op. 96.
500♪ (M) *** Carlton IMP Dig. 3036 70097-2 [id.]. Delmé Qt – BRAHMS: *Clarinet quintet.* ***

The Delmé Quartet on a superbly recorded Carlton IMP disc at bargain price give a winningly spontaneous-sounding performance, marked by unusually sweet matching of timbre between the players, which brings out the total joyfulness of Dvořák's American inspiration.

Piano duet

Slavonic dances Nos. 1–16, Op. 46/1–8; Op. 72/1–8.
(M) *** DG 449 550-2 [id.]. Alfons and Aloys Kontarsky.
(BB) *** Naxos Dig. 8.553138 [id.]. Silke-Thora Matthies, Christian Köhn.
(B) ** EMI forte CZS5 69311-2 (2). Michel Béroff and Jean-Philippe Collard – BRAHMS: *Hungarian dances* etc. **

This excellently transferred reissue from 1980 takes its place at the top of the list of recommendations for Dvořák's *Slavonic dances* in their original version for piano, four hands, providing some of the most delectable piano duets ever written. Characteristically the excellent Kontarsky brothers offer crisp, clean performances and, more than usually, allow themselves the necessary rubato, conveying affection and joy along with their freshness (sample Nos. 4 and 5 of Op. 46, delightfully contrasted, or for sheer élan the *Furiant* of No. 8). The recording was made in the Berlin Jesus-Christus-Kirche, where the engineers put their microphones in exactly the right place: there is just the right degree of resonance, yet no feeling that they are too near.

Dvořák, like Schubert, had the gift of writing piano-duet music which is at once a joy to performers and to listeners alike. The brilliant piano duo of Matthies and Köhn are most persuasive performers, radiating their own enjoyment, bringing out inner parts, giving transparency to even the thickest textures, subtly shading their tone and, above all, consistently springing rhythms infectiously, with an idiomatic feeling for Czech dance music. The forwardly balanced recording brings out the brightness of the piano while letting warmth of tone come forward in such gentler dances as No. 3 in D. An excellent bargain.

As in the case of the Brahms coupling, enjoyable, sparkling performances from Béroff and Collard are adversely affected by the clangorous nature of the recording, made in the Paris Salle Wagram with the microphones too close.

VOCAL MUSIC

Biblical songs, Op. 99 (B185).

* Berlin Classics Dig. 0091 682 BC [id.]. Theo Adam, Dresden PO, Herbert Kegel – MARTIN: *Sechs Monologe aus Jedermann.* *

The *Biblical Songs* sound a bit Wagnerian here. Theo Adam's recording was made when he was in his early sixties, when his voice had lost some of its freshness. In any event, at full price this is distinctly poor value at only 44 minutes.

(i) *Requiem, Op. 89;* (ii) *6 Biblical songs from Op. 99.*

500♪ ❁ (B) *** DG Double 437 377-2 (2) [id.]. (i) Maria Stader, Sieglinde Wagner, Ernst Haefliger, Kim Borg, Czech PO & Ch., Karel Ančerl; (ii) Dietrich Fischer-Dieskau, Joerg Demus.

This superb DG set from 1959 brings an inspired performance of a work that can sound relatively conventional but which here emerges with fiery intensity, helped by a recording made in an appropriately spacious acoustic that gives an illusion of an electrifying live performance, without flaw. The passionate singing of the chorus is unforgettable, and the soloists not only make fine individual contributions but blend together superbly in ensembles. Ančerl controls his forces with expert precision and the Czech chorus responds to the manner born. As if that were not enough, DG have added Fischer-Dieskau's 1960 recordings of six excerpts from Op. 99. He is at his superb best in these lovely songs. Joerg Demus accompanies sensitively, and the recording balance is most convincing.

(i) *Stabat Mater, Op. 58;* (ii) *Legends Nos. 1–10, Op. 59.*

(B) *** DG Double 453 025-2 (2) [id.]. (i) Mathis, Reynolds, Ochman, Shirley-Quirk, Bav. R. Ch. & SO; (ii) ECO; Kubelik.

Dvořák's devout Catholicism led him to treat this tragic religious theme with an open innocence that avoids sentimentality. Kubelik is consistently responsive and this is a work which benefits from his imaginative approach. The recording, made in the Munich Herkules-Saal, is of very good quality. This set is well worth considering at this reasonable price, especially as the ten *Legends* are played so beautifully by the ECO. This music ought to be better known, with its colourful scoring and folksy inspiration of a high order. One is often reminded of the *Slavonic dances*; although the prevailing mood is more amiable, there is no lack of sparkle. Again very good recording.

Dyson, George (1883–1964)

(i) *Violin concerto. Children's suite* (after Walter de la Mare).

500♪ ❁ *** Chandos Dig. CHAN 9369 [id.]. (i) Mordkovitch; City of L. Sinfonia, Hickox.

Completed in 1941, Dyson's *Violin concerto* is a richly inspired, warmly lyrical work that readily sustains its 43-minute span. The idiom in all four movements is warm and distinctive. Lydia Mordkovitch makes light of the formidable technical difficulties to give a reading both passionate and deeply expressive. The *Children's suite* reflects similar qualities to those in the concerto, not least a tendency to switch into waltz-time and a masterly ability to create rich and transparent orchestral textures, beautifully caught in the opulent Chandos recording. Two rarities to treasure.

(i) *Concerto leggiero* (for piano & strings); *Concerto da camera; Concerto da chiesa* (both for string orchestra).

500♪ ❁ *** Chandos Dig. CHAN 9076 [id.]. (i) Eric Parkin; City of L. Sinfonia, Hickox.

All these pieces belong to the composer's last composing years and date from 1949/51. The writing shows both a strongly burning creative flame as well as new influences from outside. The performances here are wonderfully fresh and committed and the string recording has plenty of bite and full sonority, while the balance with the piano is quite admirable. Highly recommended.

(i; ii) *The Canterbury Pilgrims. Overture at the Tabard Inn;* (i) *In honour of the city.*

*** Chandos Dig. CHAN 9531 (2) [id.]. (i) Yvonne Kenny, Robert Tear, Stephen Roberts; (ii) London Symphony Ch.; LSO, Hickox.

At last Chandos provide us with the long-awaited recording of Dyson's best-known work, preceded by the Overture based on its themes. This orchestral piece is not constructed very succinctly, but it introduces us to the very personable tunes, and the scoring (as in the main work) is vivid. Here the soloists all have major contributions to make, for Dyson's characterization of the individual pilgrims is strong; but the glory of the piece is the choruses, which are splendidly sung here. The recording was made soon after a live performance at the Barbican in September 1996 and carries through the spontaneity of that occasion.

In honour of the city, Dyson's setting of William Dunbar, appeared in 1928, nine years before Walton's version of the same text; Dyson, however, unlike Walton, uses a modern version of the text, as he does in *The Canterbury Tales*, and to fine direct effect. The splendid Chandos recording is fully worthy of the vibrant music-making here.

Elgar, Edward (1857–1934)

'A portrait of Elgar': 3 Bavarian dances, Op. 27; Carissima; Chanson de matin; Chanson de nuit, Op. 15/1–2; Cockaigne overture, Op. 40; Dream children, Op. 43; Enigma variations, Op. 36; Froissart overture, Op. 19; Gavotte (Contrasts), Op. 10/3; Introduction and allegro for strings, Op. 47; May song; Mazurka, Op. 10/1; Nursery suite; Pomp and circumstance marches Nos. 1–5, Op. 39; Rosemary ('That's for remembrance'); Sérénade lyrique; Serenade for strings, Op. 20; Salut d'amour, Op. 12; Spanish Lady (suite); The Wand of youth suite No. 2, Op. 1b.
(B) **(*) Nimbus Dig. NI 1769 (4) [id.]. E. SO or E. String O, William Boughton.

This four-disc set is a counterpart to Nimbus's '*The spirit of England*' (see Concerts, below) and is similarly inexpensive. But there is a small drawback: it is made up of four separate Elgar collections, and Disc 3 (which at 46 minutes is not particularly generous anyway) duplicates the *Chanson de matin* and *Chanson de nuit*, already included on Disc 2 – perverse planning, especially when the first *Wand of Youth suite* is omitted. However, the latter collection (including the *Nursery suite* plus the *Dream children* and most of the miniatures) is particularly attractive, for William Boughton's performances are graceful and sympathetic and have plenty of character. The *Bavarian dances* are winningly relaxed and *The Spanish Lady suite* is well characterized. The *Introduction and allegro* has a ripely overwhelming climax, but the fugal argument is not lost. The *Enigma variations* have many pleasingly delicate touches of colour with the brass and organ making a fine effect in the finale. There is an easy swagger about the *Pomp and circumstance marches*, with the happy lyricism of the trios – not just *Land of hope and glory* – conveying Elgarian joy. The warmly reverberant acoustic of the Great Hall of Birmingham University gives the performances of these larger-scale works a spacious scale that is entirely apt. What is more questionable is the scale conveyed by the recording (in the same acoustic) for the other lighter and more intimate pieces. The manner is sparkling, the playing refined and well detailed, with rhythms nicely sprung, but the large scale implied tends to inflate the music, particularly in the *Wand of youth* excerpts. Nevertheless the relaxed geniality of each performance is likely to quieten most doubts of those attracted to the content of this inexpensive compilation.

'The lighter Elgar': (i) *Beau Brummel: Minuet;* (ii) *Carissima;* (i) *Chanson de matin, Op. 15/2;* (ii) *3 Characteristic pieces, Op. 10: Mazurka; Sérénade mauresque; Contrasts: The Gavottes AD 1700 & 1900;* (i) *Dream children, Op. 43/1–2;* (ii) *May song; Mina; Minuet, Op. 21; Rosemary (That's for remembrance);* (ii; iii) *Romance for bassoon and orchestra, Op. 62;* (i) *Salut d'amour, Op. 12;* (ii) *Sevillana, Op. 7; Sérénade lyrique;* (i; iv) *The Starlight Express, Op. 78:* Organ grinder's songs: *My old tunes; To the children.* (i) *The Wand of Youth suite No. 1:* excerpt: *Sun dance.*
❀ (M) *** EMI CDM5 65593-2 [id.]. (i) RPO, Lawrance Collingwood; (ii) N. Sinfonia, Marriner; with (iii) Michael Chapman; (iv) Frederick Harvey.

The best of Elgar's lighter music has a gentle delicacy of texture and, as often as not, quite a touch of melancholy, which is irresistible to nearly all Elgarians. Its fragile nostalgia has never been better caught than on this beautifully recorded CD which combines almost all the contents of two LPs. The first (originally called '*The miniature Elgar*') was inspired by the famous Ken Russell BBC TV film of Elgar's life, and the orchestral playing under Lawrance Collingwood is especially sympathetic. Frederick Harvey joins the orchestra for two organ grinder's songs from the incidental music for *The Starlight Express*, and they have seldom been sung more winningly on record. They are splendidly alive and with as much interest in the orchestra as in the stirringly melodic vocal line. It is these items one remembers most, but the second collection under Sir Neville Marriner is hardly less successful. Not everything here is on the very highest level of invention, but all the music is pleasing and a good deal of it is delightful in its tender moods and restrained scoring, favouring flute, bassoon and the clarinet in middle or lower register. A boisterous piece like *Sevillana* may be rather conventional but it has Elgar's characteristic exuberance, which represents the other side of the coin. Very much worth having is the rhapsodic *Romance for bassoon and orchestra* with Michael Chapman the elegant soloist, but the whole programme here offers quiet enjoyment and is just the thing for the late evening. The Northern Sinfonia play with style and affection. Throughout, EMI have provided that warm, glowing sound that is their special province in recording Elgar's music, and it is remarkable that Collingwood's recordings, made at Abbey Road in 1964, and the Marriner items, using the Old Banqueting Hall, Jesmond Dene, Newcastle-upon-Tyne, in 1970, match up so well when they are juxtaposed. The CD transfers bring out all the bloom one remembers on the analogue LPs. Not to be missed.

(i) *Cockaigne overture, Op. 40;* (ii) *Cello concerto, Op. 85;* (i) *Enigma variations, Op. 36.*
(M) **(*) Ph. Analogue/Dig. 442 652-2 [id.]. (i) LSO, Sir Colin Davis; (ii) Heinrich Schiff, Dresden State O, Sir Neville Marriner.

Davis's reading of the *Enigma variations* is in the main a traditional one, with each variation carefully shaped, and really first-rate playing from the LSO, contributing both intensity and warmth. In *Cockaigne*, however, Sir Colin is more wilful in his choice of tempi, and this is less evocative than it can be. The mid-1960s recording is full and naturally balanced but lacks something in brilliance. Schiff then gives a warm and thoughtful account of the *Cello concerto*, at his most successful in the lovely slow movement and the epilogue, both played with soft, sweet tone. Other readings convey more of the structural cohesion, but this lyrical, somewhat improvisational view has its place and is easy to enjoy. The digital sound is superb to match the orchestral richness, and the elegiac atmosphere at the opening of the concerto is especially persuasive.

Cockaigne overture, Op. 40; Enigma variations, Op. 36; Introduction and allegro for strings; Serenade for strings, Op. 20.
500♪ ❁ *** Teldec/Warner Dig. 9031 73279-2 [id.]. BBC SO, Andrew Davis.

Andrew Davis's collection of favourite Elgar works is electrifying. The very opening of *Cockaigne* has rarely been so light and sprightly, and it leads on to the most powerful characterization of each contrasted section. The two string works are richly and sensitively done. Similarly the big tonal contrasts in *Enigma* are dramatically brought out, notably in Davis's rapt and spacious reading of *Nimrod*, helped by the spectacular Teldec recording. This is surely a worthy successor to Barbirolli in this repertoire and is an outstanding disc in every way.

(i) *Cockaigne overture, Op. 40;* (ii) *Froissart overture, Op. 19; Pomp and circumstance marches, Op. 39, Nos* (i) *1 in D;* (ii) *2 in A min.; 3 in C min.;* (i) *4 in G;* (ii) *5 in C.*
(M) *** EMI CDM5 66323-2 [id.]. (i) Philh. O; (ii) New Philh. O; Barbirolli.

It is good to have *Cockaigne*, Barbirolli's ripe yet wonderfully vital portrait of Edwardian London, back in the catalogue – one of the finest of all his Elgar records. *Froissart* is very compelling too (though the CD transfer is slightly less flattering here), and Barbirolli makes a fine suite of the five *Pomp and circumstance marches*. The lesser-known Nos. 2 and 5 are particularly gripping, with plenty of contrast in No. 4 to offset the swagger elsewhere. Here the sound is as expansive as you could wish.

Cello concerto in E min., Op. 85.
500♪ ❁ *** EMI CDC7 47329-2 [id.]; *TC-ASD 655*. Du Pré, LSO, Barbirolli – *Sea Pictures*. *** ❁
(M) **(*) Carlton Dig. 30366 0011-2 [id.]. Tortelier, RPO, Groves – DVORAK: *Rondo;* TCHAIKOVSKY: *Rococo variations*. ***
(BB) ** Naxos Dig. 8.550503 [id.]. Maria Kliegel, RPO, Halasz – DVORAK: *Cello concerto*. **

Jacqueline du Pré was essentially a spontaneous artist. Her style is freely rhapsodic, but the result produced a very special kind of meditative feeling; in the very beautiful slow movement, brief and concentrated, her inner intensity conveys a depth of espressivo rarely achieved by any cellist on record.

Tortelier's latest version of the Elgar, now reappearing on Carlton, was originally issued to celebrate the cellist's seventy-fifth birthday in March 1989. It may not be as firm and powerful as his earlier account with Boult: in the finale the septuagenarian shows signs of strain; but the performance has a spontaneity and a new tenderness which make it very compelling.

Maria Kliegel is at her finest, deeply expressive and intense, in Elgar's miraculously compressed slow movement, and again in the comparably meditative epilogue for the finale. There she runs little risk of sounding self-indulgent within a limited span. The lyrical main theme of the first movement by contrast is pulled around in an unconvincing way, and though the virtuoso writing of the scherzo and the finale demonstrate the soloist's agility, her intonation is at times suspect. Flawed as it is – like the Dvořák with which it is coupled – it makes a fair bargain, well recorded in modern, digital sound.

Violin concerto in B min., Op. 61.
500♪ ❁ (M) *** EMI Dig. EMX 2058; *TC-EMX 2058*. Nigel Kennedy, LPO, Handley.
(M) *** Decca 452 696-2 [id.]. Kyung Wha Chung, LPO, Solti – BERG: *Violin concerto*. ***

(i) *Violin concerto in B min., Op. 61; In the South (Alassio): concert overture.*
(B) *** Sony SBK 62745; *SBT 62745* [id.]. (i) Pinchas Zukerman; LPO, Barenboim.

This remains Nigel Kennedy's finest achievement on record, arguably even finer than the long line of versions with star international soloists from either outside or within Britain. With Vernon Handley as guide it is a truly inspired and inspiring performance and the recording is outstandingly faithful and atmospheric. At mid-price it is a supreme Elgarian bargain.

Without loss of body or amplitude, the extra sense of presence in the CD transfer intensifies the impact of Kyung Wha Chung's heartfelt performance, with Solti responding with warmth to the wide-ranging expressiveness of the soloist. Chung's dreamily expansive playing in that middle movement is ravishing in its beauty, not least in the ethereal writing above the stave, and so too are the lyrical pages of the outer movements. The bravura passages draw from her a vein of mercurial fantasy, excitingly volatile, and no other recording brings a wider range of dynamic or tone in the soloist's playing, nor indeed more passionate feeling from soloist and conductor alike.

Zukerman, coming fresh to the Elgar *Violin concerto* in 1976, was inspired to give a reading which gloriously combined the virtuoso swagger of a Heifetz with the tender, heartfelt warmth of the young Menuhin, plus much individual responsiveness. Barenboim is a splendid partner, brilliant but never breathless in the main allegro and culminating in a deeply felt rendering of the long accompanied cadenza, freely expansive yet concentrated. With full but clearly defined recording, naturally balanced, at EMI's Abbey Road studios, this is a version which all Elgarians should seek out, especially at its new bargain price (with cassette equivalent). The coupling is an exciting and virile account of *In the South*, not quite as remarkable as the *Concerto* but a worthwhile bonus, even if the sound is marginally less full.

Enigma variations, Op. 36.
*** Decca Dig. 452 853-2 [id.]. VPO, Solti – BLACHER: *Paganini variations;* KODALY: *Peacock variations.* ***
(M) *** Decca 452 303-2 [id.]. LSO, Monteux – HOLST: *Planets.* ***
(B) *** Carlton Dig. PCD 2051 [id.]. Nat. Youth O of GB, Seaman – R. STRAUSS: *Sinfonia Domestica.* ***

Celebrating his half-century as a Decca artist in 1997, Sir Georg Solti devised this nicely autobiographical collection of three sets of variations: the *Peacock variations* of Kodály representing his Hungarian roots, the lively *Paganini variations* of Blacher a recognition of his years as a German citizen, and finally a tribute to his unique Britishness in Elgar's *Enigma variations*. The disc is also a tribute to the Vienna Philharmonic and Solti's special relationship with that orchestra. In contrast to Solti's brittle Chicago version of 1974, this warmly spontaneous-sounding account of the *Enigma variations* reflects not just the special qualities of this great Viennese orchestra but the way in which Solti has mellowed over the last two decades. This is a heartfelt, incandescent performance, delicate and subtle on detail, and it is the more moving when Solti refuses to over-emote, for example, in the great climax of *Nimrod*, taking it at a flowing speed. The Decca engineers place the orchestra vividly within the unique acoustics of the Musikverein, with close balance avoided and fine sense of spaciousness.

Monteux's *Enigma* remains among the freshest versions ever put on disc and the music is obviously deeply felt. The reading is famous for the real pianissimo which Monteux secures at the beginning of Nimrod, the playing hardly above a whisper, yet the tension electric. Slowly the great tune is built up in elegiac fashion, and the superb climax is more effective in consequence. Differences from traditional tempi elsewhere are marginal and add to one's enjoyment. The vintage Kingsway Hall stereo was outstanding in its day and it has never sounded better than in the present remastering. It is almost impossible to believe that this dates from 1958 and, with its stunning Holst coupling, this is one of the very finest (and most generous – 78 minutes) reissues in Decca's Classic Sound series.

Christopher Seaman and the National Youth Orchestra are inspired to give a wonderfully rich and ardent account of *Enigma*, yet one which opens with persuasively gentle lyricism and produces the most delicate portrayals of *Ysobel* and *Dorabella*, while the great cello variation expands gloriously and *Nimrod* explores the widest gradation of dynamic to reach its climax. The finale is engulfing in its excitement, and Seaman does not forget to add the 'tummy-wobbling' organ reinforcement to the closing pages. The recording is fully worthy of an account which has all the hallmarks of a live performance, even though it was recorded in Watford Town Hall under studio conditions.

(i) *Enigma variations;* (ii) *Falstaff, Op.68.*
(M) *** EMI CDM5 66322-2 [id.]. (i) Philh. O; (ii) Hallé O; Barbirolli.

Ripe and expansive, Barbirolli's view of *Falstaff* is colourful and convincing; it has fine atmospheric feeling too, and the interludes are more magical here than in the Boult version. *Enigma*, too, was a work that Barbirolli, himself a cellist, made especially his own, with wonderfully expansive string-playing and much imaginative detail; the recording was made when he was at the very peak of his interpretative powers. The massed strings have lost some of their amplitude, but detail is clearer and the overall balance is convincing, with the Kingsway Hall ambience ensuring a pleasing bloom.

Falstaff, Op. 68; Imperial march, Op. 32; (i) *Sea pictures, Op. 37.*
(B) *** Sony SBK 63020; *SBT 63020* [id.]. LPO, Barenboim; (i) with Yvonne Minton.

Barenboim's habit of moulding the music of Elgar in flexible tempi, of underlining romantic expressiveness, has never been as convincing on record as here in *Falstaff*, where the big contrasts of texture, dynamic and mood are played for all they are worth. Rarely, even under the composer, has the story-telling element in Elgar's symphonic study been presented so captivatingly. The Gadshill episode with its ambush is so vivid one can see the picture in one's mind's eye. Yvonne Minton uses her rich tone sensitively in Elgar's orchestral song-cycle. There is perhaps less subtlety in her reading than in Janet Baker's, but she responds to this music richly and ardently. Barenboim is a persuasive Elgarian and this makes a most welcome bargain reissue, with his ripe account of the *Imperial march* thrown in for good measure. The CD transfers are excellent, with the warmly atmospheric sound in the *Sea pictures* particularly appealing.

(i; ii) *Introduction and allegro for strings, Op. 47;* (i) *Serenade for strings in E min., Op. 20;* (iii) *Elegy, Op. 58; Sospiri, Op. 70.*
500♪ ❁ *** EMI CDC7 47537-2 [id.]. (i) Sinfonia of L.; (ii) Allegri Qt; (iii) New Philh. O; Barbirolli – VAUGHAN WILLIAMS: *Greensleeves & Tallis fantasias.* *** ❁

Barbirolli brings an Italianate ardour and warmth to this music without in any way robbing it of its Englishness, and the response of the string players, full-throated or subtle as the music demands, was matched by superb analogue recording, notable for its combination of clarity and ambient richness. For CD, the *Elegy* (like the *Serenade*, showing Barbirolli in more gentle and beguiling mood) and the passionate *Sospiri* have been added for good measure. The new CD transfer has retained the fullness, amplitude and analogue ambience and has refocused the upper range most believably. A triumph!

Symphonies Nos.1–2; Cockaigne overture; Pomp and circumstance marches Nos. 1–5.
(B) **(*) Ph. Duo Dig. 454 250-2 (2) [id.]. RPO or LSO, André Previn.

Previn's Philips Duo comes into direct competition with Solti's similar Double Decca coupling (443 856-2), but both conductors provide interpretations which are stimulating as well as individual, Solti the more urgent, Previn the more spacious. Indeed these Previn performances find the conductor as idiomatic and understanding in Elgar as he is in Walton and Vaughan Williams. His view of the opening movement of the *First Symphony* is spacious, with moulding of phrase and lifting of rhythm beautifully judged, to bring natural flexibility within a strongly controlled structure, steadier than usual in basic tempo. Previn's espressivo style tends towards accelerando rather than tenuto, towards fractional anticipation rather than hesitation, which makes for alert allegros and a slow movement that is warm but not self-indulgent. The syncopations of the scherzo/march theme have an almost jazzy swagger, and the reading is crowned by a flowing account of the finale. There Previn confirms his ability to point Elgarian climaxes with the necessary heart-tug, above all in the lovely passage where the main theme is augmented in minims on high violins, here achingly beautiful, neither too reticent nor too heavy-handed.

The opening movement of the *Second* has a similar Elgarian ebb and flow; Previn's warmth is in no doubt, and his expressive flexibility is appealingly free; but one senses an absence of thrust and he does not display as tight a grip on the structure as Solti. Previn's *Larghetto* is deeply felt and is eloquently played by the LSO; however, although the rich *nobilmente* feeling is prevalent, he does not achieve the same degree of intense concentration which makes Solti's view so compelling. Nevertheless, many will warm to Previn's expansive approach, which is again apparent in the bold, purposeful finale. *Cockaigne* is in a similar mould, though attractively affectionate and spirited. The five *Pomp and circumstance marches* are not quite as flamboyant as some versions but are beautifully sprung. The recordings were made at Abbey Road and, if the Philips sound is more refined than the typical Elgar quality from EMI, it certainly does not lack opulence.

Symphony No. 1 in A flat, Op. 55.
500♪ ❁ (B) *** Carlton IMP Dig. PCD 2019 [id.]. Hallé O, James Judd.

James Judd, more than any rival on disc, has learnt directly from Elgar's own recording of this magnificent symphony. Above all, Judd outshines others in the pacing and phrasing of the lovely slow movement which in its natural flowing rubato has melting tenderness behind the passion, a throat-catching poignancy not fully conveyed elsewhere but very much a quality of Elgar's own reading. The refinement of the strings down to the most hushed pianissimo confirms this as the Hallé's most beautiful disc in recent years, recorded with warmth and opulence.

Symphony No. 2 in E flat, Op. 63.
500♪ (B) *** CfP CD-CFP 4544. LPO, Vernon Handley.

Symphony No. 2 in E flat; Cockaigne overture; Dream children No. 1, Op. 43/1.
(M) (**) EMI mono CDM5 66399-2 [id.]. Hallé O, Sir John Barbirolli.

Handley's remains the most satisfying modern version of a work which has latterly been much recorded. What Handley conveys superbly is the sense of Elgarian ebb and flow, building climaxes like a master and drawing excellent, spontaneous-sounding playing from an orchestra which, more than any other, has specialized in performing this symphony. The sound is warmly atmospheric and vividly conveys the added organ part in the bass, just at the climax of the finale, which Elgar himself suggested 'if available': a tummy-wobbling effect. This would be a first choice at full price, but as a bargain CD there are few records to match it.

As in his stereo recording, made a decade later, Barbirolli's 1954 reading is very personal indeed. You might say that Elgar himself, when conducting, ignored many of his own markings, but there is no denying the added beauty and added nobility of performances like Boult's, that maintain a more steady emotional equilibrium. In the first movement Barbirolli's speed is basically slow, then at many points he slows down the tempo still further. Undoubtedly he creates a rapt tension in the passages of pianissimo espressivo and often his own involvement almost carries the day, but inevitably the result is self-conscious and mannered. In the wayward *Larghetto* Barbirolli again varies the pacing excessively, although the climaxes are obviously deeply felt, and the structure of the finale, too, is weakened by the lack of a firm forward pulse. *Cockaigne* is, by contrast, a dramatic and sprightly performance, but the first of the *Dream children* is also invested with added intensity and becomes almost valedictory in feeling. The mono sound is excellent throughout.

Violin sonata in E min., Op. 82.
(BB) *** ASV Quicksilva CDQS 6191 [id.]. Lorraine McAslan, John Blakely – WALTON: *Violin sonata.* ***
(M) **(*) EMI CDM5 66122-2. Yehudi Menuhin, Hephzibah Menuhin – VAUGHAN WILLIAMS: *Sonata* **(*); WALTON: *Sonata.* (**)

This was Lorraine McAslan's début recording from 1985 and, though her performance of Elgar's inspired sonata cannot quite match the virtuoso command and body of tone of Nigel Kennedy's on Chandos (CHAN 8380 – see our main volume), hers is an impressive and warm-hearted version, full of natural imagination and bringing some rapt pianissimo playing in the outer movements. She is helped by the sympathetic partnership of John Blakely, who is attractively incisive. The digital recording is faithful but rather forward, which gives the violin-tone less bloom than it might have. But this coupling with Walton is more than worth its modest cost.

The Menuhins present a large-scale view of this sonata, the least ambitious of Elgar's three late chamber works but one which still brings echoes of the *Violin concerto*. Unfortunately, though slow speeds bring their moments of insight and revelation at the hands of a Menuhin, the result overall is too heavy, and it is marred too by imperfect intonation. The recording is first rate.

(i) *Organ sonata No. 1 in G, Op. 28;* (ii) *Vesper voluntaries, Op. 14: Introduction; Andante.*
(M) *** EMI CDM5 65594-2 [id.]. (i) Herbert Sumsion (organ of Gloucester cathedral); (ii) Christopher Robinson (organ of Worcester Cathedral) – *Choral music.* **(*)

It was a pity that Herbert Sumsion's recording of the *Organ sonata* was not made on the organ at Worcester, for which it was written, but the Gloucester instrument makes a splendidly expansive sound and the gentler pages, glowingly registered, are not as recessed as in some other versions. Sumsion opens grandly and rises to the work's closing climax. His performance is sympathetically idiomatic, though it could perhaps be more flamboyantly extrovert. He is very well recorded, as is Christopher Robinson (who does play at Worcester) in the relatively slight *Voluntaries*, used to make an interlude within the concert of choral music for which the *Sonata* acts as a pendant.

VOCAL MUSIC

Vocal and dramatic music, Volume 1: (1912–1948): (i) *The Apostles: By the wayside.* (ii) *Caractacus: Sword song; O my warriors!* (iii) *Crown of India: Imperial masque. Dream of Gerontius:* (iv) closing scene; (v) *My work is done.* (vi) *Saga of King Olaf: And King Olaf heard the cry!* (vii) *The Starlight Express:* excerpts. (viii) Songs (arranged for orchestra by Haydn Wood): *Like to the damask rose; Rondel; Queen Mary's song; Shepherd's song.* (ix) Motet: *O hearken thou, Op. 64.* Chorus: (x) *The shower, Op. 71/1.*

(***) Elgar Soc./Dutton Lab. mono CDAX 8019 [id.]. (i) Dora Labette, Hubert Eisdell, Dennis Noble, Harold Williams, Robert Easton, Hallé Ch. & O, Harty; (ii) Peter Dawson, O, Barbirolli; (iii) Black Diamonds Band; (iv) Maurice D'Oisly, Clara Butt, Queen's Hall Ch. & O, Sir Henry Wood; (v) Kathleen Ferrier, Gerald Moore; (vi) Tudor Davies, SO, Goossens; (vii) Alice Moxton, Stuart Robinson, O; (viii) Light SO, Haydn Wood; (ix) St George's Chapel Ch., Windsor, Sir Walford Davies; (x) Glasgow Orpheus Ch., Sir Hugh Roberton.

Illustrated with a colourful frontispiece taken from the spectacular painting, 'Elgar's Dream', by Norman Perryman, this is an absolutely fascinating anthology, including some of the earliest recordings of Elgar's music, opening with the Black Diamonds Band (the resident Zonophone 'orchestra' in 1912) making the first and only recording of the *March* from *Crown of India*, called *Imperial masque*. The excerpts from the *Dream of Gerontius* conducted by Sir Henry Wood (1916) are revelatory, with Dame Clara Butt a rich-voiced but not fruity Angel and the tiny chorus making a most convincing impression. Kathleen Ferrier's radiant 1944 performance of the Angel's soliloquy, accompanied by Gerald Moore, is no less treasurable. Peter Dawson projects the *Sword song* from *Caractacus* with typical charisma and makes it sound surprisingly like the *Floral dance*, while no one has ever sung the delightful *Organ grinder's songs* from *The Starlight Express* with such endearing warmth and charm as Stuart Robertson; his colleague, Alice Moxton, has a pretty soubrette delivery that one would not hear today. Finally the famous pre-war Glasgow Orpheus Choir sing *The shower* gently and touchingly, a 1948 recording never before published. Throughout Mike Dutton waves his magic spell over the transfers (the soloist's words are amazingly clear) and, within seconds of starting to listen, one quite forgets any recording inadequacies. Even the 1912 band recording is given fine presence. This disc is available (at a cost of £11 at the time of going to print) directly from The Elgar Society, 2 Marriott's Close, Haddenham, Bucks, HP17 8BT. They have plans for further issues, and we hope they will include the pre-electric abridged recording of *Gerontius* made by Edison Bell Records, which Elgar himself praised in a letter to Edison and which is greatly admired by Jerrold Northrop Moore.

Choral music: *Angelus, Op. 56/1; Ave Maria, Op. 2/2; Ave maris stella, Op. 2/3; Ave verum, Op. 2/1; Give unto the Lord, Op. 74; O hearken thou, Op. 64; Te Deum and Benedictus, Op. 34.*

(M) **(*) EMI CDM5 65594-2 [id.]. Worcester Cathedral Ch., Christopher Robinson; Bramma *Organ sonata No. 1* etc. ***

Elgar was one of a handful of Roman Catholics among our major English composers (Byrd was another). Like Byrd, he wrote much of his early sacred music within a Protestant tradition, so that it was suitable for presentation at the Three Choirs Festivals (the fine *Te Deum*) and even at St Paul's Cathedral (*Give unto the Lord*). *O hearken thou* is a coronation anthem, written in the composer's official capacity for the coronation of George V. The genuinely Catholic works were written during Elgar's apprenticeship at St George's Church, Worcester. Both the *Ave verum* and the *Ave Maria* have a gentle, romantic colouring; but most memorable is the *Angelus*, with its repeated figure like an echoing bell. This was written in Italy in 1909, and it has a touch of Mediterranean sunshine in its mood. There is little in this programme to anticipate the Elgar of *Gerontius*, though much to show an emerging musical individuality. Performances are sympathetic and alive, and the cathedral ambience is highly suitable for the music. The 1969 recording has been transferred admirably to CD. The coupled organ music increases the interest of this generously full reissue (76 minutes).

(i) *The Dream of Gerontius;* (ii) *Cello concerto.*

500♪ (***) Testament mono SBT 2025 (2) [id.]. (i) Heddle Nash, Gladys Ripley, Dennis Noble, Norman Walker, Huddersfield Ch. Soc., Liverpool PO; (ii) Tortelier, BBC SO; Sargent.

It was not until 1945 that the *Dream of Gerontius* was recorded complete for the very first time. Sir Malcolm Sargent was never finer on disc, pacing the score perfectly and drawing incandescent singing from the Huddersfield Choral Society. The soloists too, led superbly by Heddle Nash as Gerontius, have a freshness and clarity rarely matched, with Nash's ringing tenor consistently clean in attack. Though Gladys Ripley's fine contralto is caught with a hint of rapid flutter, she matches the others in forthright clarity, with Dennis Noble as the Priest and Norman Walker as the Angel of the Agony, both strong and direct. The mono recording captures detail excellently, even if inevitably the dynamic range is limited. Having the soloists balanced relatively close allows every word to be heard; in the present transfer, though the chorus lacks something in body, such a climax as *Praise to the Holiest* has thrilling bite. The first and finest of Tortelier's three recordings of the Elgar *Cello concerto* makes an ideal coupling. Like all the Testament transfers of EMI material, it comes with excellent background notes.

(i) *The Kingdom, Op. 51;* (ii) *Coronation Ode, Op. 34.*
(M) *** EMI CMS7 64209-2 [ZDMB 64209]. (i) Margaret Price, Yvonne Minton, Alexander Young, John Shirley-Quirk, LPO Ch., LPO, Boult; (ii) Felicity Lott, Alfreda Hodgson, Richard Morton, Cambridge University Music Soc., King's College, Cambridge, Ch., New Philh. O, Band of Royal Military School of Music, Kneller Hall, Philip Ledger.

Boult was devoted to *The Kingdom*, identifying with its comparative reticence, openly preferring it even to *Gerontius*, and his dedication emerges clearly throughout a glorious performance. It has often been suggested that it is too static, but the Pentecost scene is intensely dramatic, and the richness of musical inspiration in the rest prevents any feeling of stagnation, certainly in a performance as inspired as this. The melody which Elgar wrote to represent the Holy Spirit is one of the noblest that even he created, and the soprano aria *The sun goeth down* (beautifully sung by Margaret Price) leads to a deeply affecting climax. The other soloists also sing splendidly, and the only reservation concerns the chorus, which is not quite as disciplined as it might be and sounds a little too backward for some of the massive effects which cap the power of the work. However, there is no doubt but that the strikingly successful remastering process has brought a gain in presence while retaining the quality of the 1977 original; here the freshening brings better definition without loss of body. The coupling of the *Coronation ode* is handy and certainly welcome, rather than particularly appropriate. It is far more than a jingoistic occasional piece, though it was indeed the work which first featured *Land of hope and glory*. The most tender moment of all is reserved for the first faint flickerings of that second national anthem, introduced gently on the harp to clarinet accompaniment. All told, the work contains much Elgarian treasure, and Ledger is superb in capturing the necessary swagger and panache, flouting all thought of potential bad taste. With recording of outstanding quality – among the finest made in King's College Chapel during the analogue era – and with extra brass bands, it presents a glorious experience. Excellent singing and playing, too, although the male soloists do not quite match their female colleagues. Both works are generously cued.

Sea pictures (song-cycle), *Op. 37.*
500♪ ✿ *** EMI CDC7 47329-2 [id.]; *TC-ASD 655*. Dame Janet Baker, LSO, Barbirolli – *Cello concerto*. *** ✿

(i) *Sea pictures, Op. 37;* (ii; iii) *The Starlight Express: Songs: O children, open your arms to me; There's a fairy that hides; I'm everywhere; Wake up, you little night winds; O stars, shine brightly; We shall meet the morning spiders; My old tunes are rather broken; O think beauty; Dustman, Laughter, Tramp and busy Sweep.* (iii) *Dream children, Op. 43.*
(M) **(*) Decca Dig. 452 324-2 [id.]. (i) Della Jones, RPO; (ii) Alison Hagley, Bryn Terfel; (iii) Welsh Nat. Op. O; all cond. Mackerras – LAMBERT: *The Rio Grande*. **(*)

Like du Pré, Baker is an artist who has the power to convey on record the vividness of a live performance. With the help of Barbirolli she makes the cycle far more convincing than it usually seems, with often trite words clothed in music that seems to transform them. On CD, the voice is caught with extra bloom, and the beauty of Elgar's orchestration is enhanced by the subtle added definition.

These recordings from the early 1990s belong to the short-lived resuscitation of the Argo label, yet they have already reverted to Decca's mid-priced Ovation series. There has never been a more dramatic presentation of the *Sea pictures*. The opening of the *Sea slumber-song* is simple and touching but Mackerras creates a big climax for *Sabbath morning at sea*, and Della Jones brings even more histrionic feeling to the final climax of *The swimmer*. She sings richly throughout and the performance could not be more vivid; however, although *Where corals lie* is obviously deeply felt, one feels that not all the secrets of this music are fully revealed. The vocal numbers from *The Starlight Express* are well sung by Alison Hagley and Bryn Terfel, but why divorce them from the rest of the score? Mackerras is as warmly affectionate in the delicately scored *Dream children* as he is dramatic in the *Sea pictures*, and the recording throughout, made in Brangwyn Hall, Swansea, has plenty of atmosphere and presence.

Enescu, Georges (1881–1955)

7 Chansons de Clément Marot, Op. 15.
(M) *** Unicorn-Kanchana Dig. UKCD 2078 [id.]. Sarah Walker, Roger Vignoles – ROUSSEL: *Mélodies* **(*); DEBUSSY: *Mélodies.* ***

The set of Enescu songs, written in 1908, makes a rare, attractive and apt addition to Sarah Walker's recital of French song. As a Romanian working largely in Paris, Enescu was thinking very much in a French idiom, charming and witty as well as sweetly romantic. Ideal accompaniments and excellent recording.

Eyck, Jakob van (1590–1657)

Der Fluyten Lust-hof (excerpts).
*** Astrée Audivis E 8588 [id.]. Jill Feldman, Sébastien Marq, Rolf Lislevand.

Jakob van Eyck was blind but, as his tombstone stated, 'What God took from his eyes he gave back in his ear'. He began his career as Utrecht's town carilloneur (engineer and tuner, as well as performer); he also played the recorder 'like a bird' in the local park to the delight of the weekend promenaders. *Der Fluyten Lust-hof*, published in two volumes, dates from the middle of the seventeenth century. Van Eyck wrote divisions and improvisations on famous tunes of the time, most of which came from France and England – half a dozen of Dowland's most famous numbers are featured. Jill Feldman sings with engaging purity of line and tone, and she has a nice knack for simple embellishment. She opens the programme with a little French hunting song which is immediately followed by neat recorder divisions on Dowland's *Can shee excuse my wrongs*, transformed into a country dance (Sébastien Marq). Then there is a lute solo (Rolf Lislevand) based on the same Dowland theme, followed by the original song, charmingly sung. The music-making proceeds in a similar manner with *Een Schots Lietjen* ('A little Scots song') presented as a novelty by the recorder over a buzzing (vocal) drone. Van Eyck's recorder variants on Giles Earle's ballad, *When Daphne from faire Phoebus did flie*, bring a surprising, gentle hint of the outline of *Greensleeves*, but this is perhaps less striking when the song itself follows. The programme continues in this vein, with Van Eyck's variations juxtaposed with the originals, always pleasingly sung (Dowland's *Flow my tears* is particularly tender); although this is a lightweight recital, the comparisons are intriguing. The intimacy of the performances is nicely reflected in the recording, which is refined yet with a most natural presence. A pleasing recital for a summer evening.

Falla, Manuel de (1876–1946)

(i) *El amor brujo* (complete); (ii) *Nights in the gardens of Spain.*
500♪ ❁ (M) *** Decca Dig. 430 703-2; *430 703-4* [id.]. (i) Tourangeau, Montreal SO, Dutoit; (ii) De Larrocha, LPO, Frühbeck de Burgos – RODRIGO: *Concierto.* *** ❁

Dutoit's brilliantly played *El amor brujo* has long been praised by us. With recording in the demonstration class, the performance has characteristic flexibility over phrasing and rhythm and is hauntingly atmospheric. The sound in the coupled *Nights in the gardens of Spain* is equally superb, rich and lustrous and with vivid detail. Miss de Larrocha's lambent feeling for the work's poetic evocation is matched by her brilliance in the nocturnal dance-rhythms.

Farrenc, Louise (1804–75)

Nonet for strings and wind in E flat, Op. 38; (i) *Sextet for piano and wind in C min., Op. 40; Trio for flute, cello and piano in E min., Op. 45.*
(M) ** Carlton Dig. 30366 00302 [id.]. (i) Diana Ambache; Ambache Chamber Ens.

Louise Farrenc (born Jeanne-Louise Dumont) studied under Reicha at the Paris Conservatoire. Then, at the age of seventeen, she married a flute player, so it is not surprising that she shows a ready facility in writing for woodwind instruments. Her scoring in the *Sextet* anticipates Poulenc, of nearly a century later, but Farrenc's music here is not witty; indeed it looks back towards Beethoven's *Piano and wind quintet* but without that master's imaginative development of ideas. The Hummelian *Nonet* (scored for five wind instruments and four strings, with double-bass in the place of second violin) is a much more spontaneous piece. It was popular in its day; Joachim presided over its well-attended première in 1850. The *Andante con moto* is a winning set of variations on charmingly *galant* melody, and the bustling Scherzo has a swinging tune for its middle sectiom. Similarly the *Trio* has a songful *Andante* and the Scherzo fizzes with bravura, putting both Diana Ambache and the erstwhile flautist on their mettle. But in the last resort this is well-crafted music without a highly individual voice. The recording, though well balanced, is also too resonant to provide a clear internal focus.

Fasch, Johann (1688–1758)

Chalumeau concerto in B flat, FWV L:B1; Concerto in C min. for bassoon and 2 oboes, FWV L:C2; Concerto in D for 2 horns, 2 oboes & 2 bassoons, FWV L:D14; Trumpet concerto in D, FWV L:D1.
*** DG Dig. 449 210-2 [id.]. Soloists, E. Concert, Pinnock.

Fasch was a contemporary of Telemann; he liked to tell how he passed off an early orchestral suite as being by that master. And he might well have managed the same trick with the present *Suite in G minor*; it is an attractively inventive work, very much in the manner of Telemann, with a perky central *Jardiniers* followed by a touching *Largo*, sustained over gentle harpsichord figurations. The *Gavotte* which follows brings an engaging interplay between oboes and strings. The *Trumpet concerto* is a short, unambitious work and it is not really surprising that it is not often played, though here Mark Bennett makes a fairly good case for it. The *Concerto for chalumeau*, an early clarinet, is altogether more individual, especially the beguiling opening *Largo* which Colin Lawson makes to sound delicately succulent. He is completely in command of his period instrument and is no less winning in the chortling allegro which follows, leading to another nicely decorated slow movement. This work is a real find. The *Concerto* which features a pair of horns makes considerable demands on the players in the jolly allegros which frame a *Largo*, where the sustained upper tessitura brings trills and other ornamentation. The *C minor Concerto for bassoon and two oboes* is more of a concerto grosso and agreeable rather than distinctive. However, the excellence of the performances here and the fine recording make this a collection well worth exploring.

Fauré, Gabriel (1845–1924)

(i) *Ballade for piano and orchestra, Op. 19. Dolly suite;* (ii) *Elégie for cello and orchestra;* (iii) *Fantaisie for flute and orchestra* (orch. I. Aubert). *Masques et bergamasques, Pavane* (orch. H. Rabaud); *Pénélope: Prelude.*
500♪ *** Chandos Dig. CHAN 9416. (i) Kathryn Stott; (ii) Peter Dixon; (iii) Richard Davis; BBC PO, Yan-Pascal Tortelier.

Beautifully played and richly recorded, with Yan-Pascal Tortelier a most understanding interpreter, this neatly brings together the most popular orchestral pieces of Fauré, miniatures which often convey surprising weight of feeling as well as charm, as for example the celebrated *Elégie*, here tenderly played by Peter Dixon. As a Fauré specialist, the soloist, Kathryn Stott, brings out not only the poetry in her freely expressive playing, but the scherzando sparkle of the virtuoso passages. Just as convincing are the *Fantaisie* for flute (soloist Richard Davis) and the ever-popular *Dolly suite*, both arranged by other hands. The four brief movements of *Masques et bergamasques* are charmingly done too.

Elégie, Op. 24.
*** EMI Dig. CDC5 56126-2 [id.]. Han-Na Chang, LSO, Rostropovich – BRUCH: *Kol Nidrei* ***; SAINT-SAENS: *Cello concerto No. 1* ***; TCHAIKOVSKY: *Rococo variations.* *** ❁

Chang is a naturally inspirational artist, and on her sensitive bow the lovely and sometimes elusive *Elégie* is made to sound like a vocal aria, the shaping and use of light and shade unerring, with a dedicated accompaniment from her mentor, Rostropovich. The recorded sound is very beautiful.

(i) *Fantaisie for flute and orchestra, Op. 79* (orch. Aubert); *Masques et bergamasques, Op. 112; Pavane, Op. 50; Pelléas et Mélisande suite, Op. 80.*
*** Decca Dig. 410 552-2 [id.]. (i) Bennett; ASMF, Marriner.

Marriner's Fauré programme was among Decca's earlier CD collections, and it has first-class sound; detail is well defined and there is atmosphere and excellent body. In the past we have undoubtedly underrated the performances; returning to them, we find *Masques et bergamasques* far finer than we had remembered, perhaps the finest version available. William Bennett, too, is most sensitive in the *Fantaisie*, and the *Pelléas* suite is also played with characteristic Academy finesse and warmth.

Masques et bergamasques (suite), *Op. 112; Pavane, Op. 60; Pelléas et Mélisande: Sicilienne.*
** DG Dig. 449 186-2 [id.]. Orpheus CO – RAVEL: *Pavane* etc.; SATIE: *Gymnopédies Nos. 1 & 3.* *(*)

This is the best part of an otherwise disappointing collection. The *Masques Overture* has plenty of spirit and the *Menuet* is engaging; although the recording brings a touch of aggressiveness to the *Gavotte*, the *Pastorale* restores something of the music's serenity, and the *Pavane* and *Sicilienne* are pleasing if not distinctive. However, the total collection plays for only 53 minutes, short measure at premium price.

Piano quartets Nos. 1 in C min., Op. 15; 2 in G min., Op. 45.
500♪ ✿ *** Hyperion CDA 66166 [id.]. Domus.

Domus have the requisite lightness of touch and subtlety, and just the right sense of scale and grasp of tempi. Their nimble and sensitive pianist, Susan Tomes, can hold her own in the most exalted company. The recording is excellent, too, though the balance is a little close, but the sound is not airless.

Piano quintets Nos. 1 in D min., Op. 89; 2 in C min., Op. 115.
500♪ ✿ *** Hyperion Dig. CDA 66766 [id.]. Domus, with Anthony Marwood.

The playing of Domus in these two masterpieces is as light, delicate and full of insight as one would expect. They make one fall for this music all over again, with the pianist, Susan Tomes, at her most sparkling. Excellent sound.

Piano trio in D min., Op. 120.
(B) (*) Sony SBK 62413; *SBT 62413* [id.]. Roth Trio – DEBUSSY; RAVEL: *Quartets.* **(*)

This performance has a certain interest in that it features André Previn playing chamber music in 1961 during his time in Hollywood. He is backwardly balanced, but his colleagues in the Roth Trio do not earn their limelight for, although they often play ardently, their intonation is not always secure.

Violin sonatas Nos. 1 in A, Op. 13; 2 in E min., Op. 108; Andante in B flat, Op. 75; Berceuse, Op. 16; Romance in B flat, Op. 28.
500♪ ✿ *** Decca Dig. 436 866-2 [id.]. Pierre Amoyal, Pascal Rogé.

Readers wanting a modern recording of the two Fauré *Violin sonatas* need look no further. Pierre Amoyal and Pascal Rogé play them as to the manner born. As one would expect, they are totally inside the idiom and convey its subtlety and refinement with freshness and mastery.

PIANO MUSIC

Ballade in F sharp, Op. 19 (original solo piano version); *Barcarolles Nos. 1–13* (complete).
(BB) * Naxos Dig. 8.553634 [id.]. Pierre-Alain Volondat.

In the lowest price-range, the young French pianist Pierre-Alain Volondat couples the *Ballade* in its original solo form and the *Barcarolles*. Unfortunately it is no bargain: the playing is very ordinary and wanting in the subtleties of sonority and nuance so important in this repertoire. With pianists like Collard, Rogé and Crossley in the catalogue, to acquire this would be a false economy. Given the competition, not recommended.

VOCAL MUSIC

La chanson d'Eve, Op. 95; Mélodies: Après un rêve; Aubade; Barcarolle; Les berceaux; Chanson du pêcheur; En prière; En sourdine; Green; Hymne; Des jardins de la nuit; Mandoline; Le papillon et la fleur; Les présents; Rêve d'amour; Les roses d'Isphahan; Le secret; Spleen; Toujours!.
500♪ ✿ *** Hyperion Dig. CDA 66320 [id.]. Dame Janet Baker, Geoffrey Parsons.

Dame Janet Baker gives magical performances of a generous collection of 28 songs, representing the composer throughout his long composing career, including many of his most winning songs. Geoffrey Parsons is at his most compellingly sympathetic, matching every mood. Many will be surprised at Fauré's variety of expression over this extended span of songs.

Requiem, Op. 48.
500♪ *** Teldec/Warner Dig. 4509 90879-2 [id.]. Barbara Bonney, Thomas Hampson, Amb. S., Philh. O, Michel Legrand – DURUFLE: *Requiem.* ***

(i) *Requiem, Op. 48. Masques et bergamasques; Pelléas et Mélisande (suite), Op. 80; Pénélope: Prélude.*
(M) *(*) Decca 452 304-2 [id.]. SRO, Ansermet; (i) with Danco, Souzay, L'Union Chorale de la Tour de Peitz.

Requiem, Op. 48 (1893 version). *Ave Maria, Op. 67/2; Ave verum corpus, Op. 65/1; Cantique de Jean Racine, Op. 11; Maria, Mater gratiae, Op. 47/2; Messe basse; Tantum ergo, Op. 65/2.*
500♪ *** Collegium COLCD 109 [id.]. Ashton, Varcoe, Cambridge Singers, L. Sinfonia (members), Rutter.

(i–iii) *Requiem, Op. 48; Mélodies:* (i; iv) *Aurore; Chanson d'amour; La fée aux chansons; Notre amour; Le secret;* (ii; iv) *Chanson du pêcheur; En sourdine; Fleur jetée; Nell; Poème d'un jour* (3 songs), *Op. 21; Le voyageur.*

** RCA Dig. 09026 68659-2 [id.]. (i) Barbara Bonney; (ii) Håkan Hagegård; (iii) Tanglewood Festival Ch., Boston SO, Ozawa; (iv) Warren Jones.

John Rutter's inspired reconstruction of Fauré's original 1893 score, using only lower strings and no woodwind, opened our ears to the extra freshness of the composer's first thoughts. Rutter's fine, bright recording includes the *Messe basse* and four motets, of which the *Ave Maria* setting and *Ave verum corpus* are particularly memorable. The recording is first rate but places the choir and instruments relatively close.

Michel Legrand uses the full orchestral version of 1900 in the most dramatic way possible. Barbara Bonney's *Pie Jesu* with its simplicity and innocence is very touching. Thomas Hampson makes an eloquent contribution to the *Libera me*, and the flowing choral line shows the subtle range of colour and dynamic commanded by the Ambrosian Singers. With superb, spacious recording this performance is very compelling indeed.

Ozawa also uses the full score. His performance is gentle and recessive, although his performers (including the fine Boston orchestra) rise to the climaxes. When an audience is present, the acoustics of Symphony Hall, Boston, are among the finest in the world, wonderfully warm yet projecting the orchestra with a natural presence and providing the most transparent detail. But empty, the reverberation period is a problem, especially for recording engineers. The chorus here is bathed in a glow of hazy resonance which suits the music but blurs the focus. However, many may like the ecclesiastical, cathedral-like effect, and it ensures that the closing *In Paradisum* is tenderly ethereal. The two sensitive soloists provide the couplings: two separate groups of Fauré songs, also over-resonantly recorded (in Massachusetts and Sweden respectively) – here the piano is most adversely affected. Barbara Bonney responds to Fauré's muse very pleasingly (her lively *La fée aux chansons* and the touching *Le secret* are highlights), Håkan Hagegård less so – his style is very forthright.

It was tempting for Decca to reissue this repertoire in the Classic Sound series. The *Requiem* is very early stereo indeed (1955), but the vividly clear recording only serves to emphasize the rather thin-toned contribution of the chorus. The solo singing is good, but this CD is most notable for the orchestral items, recorded six years later: sympathetic and stylish performances, highly regarded in their day and still sounding well.

Alternative choices for the *Requiem* are legion. Those seeking economy can turn to Jeremy Summerly's direct, unmannered Naxos alternative with the Schola Cantorum of Oxford (8.550765). Gardiner also chooses the original scoring, but using period instruments, and he is also particularly generous and imaginative in his choice of fill-ups (Ph. 438 149-2). The effect with his Monteverdi Choir, augmented by boy choristers from Salisbury, is darkly dramatic, offset by Catherine Bott's radiant *Pie Jesu*. Finally, those who prefer the delightful *Pie Jesu* sung by a boy treble will not be disappointed with Aled Jones, who sings very sweetly in Richard Hickox's easily flowing and spontaneous Conifer version, made at Trinity College, Cambridge, which is also attractively coupled with Duruflé, but not the *Requiem* (74321 15351-2).

Fayrfax, Robert (1464–1521)

Albanus Domini laudans; Ave lumen gratie; Missa Albanus; Antiphons: *Eterne laudis lilium; O Maria Deo grata.*

*** ASV Gaudeamus Dig. CDGAU 160 [id.]. Cardinall's Musick, Andrew Carwood.

This third in Andrew Carwood's outstanding series of church music by the great Tudor composer, Robert Fayrfax, reinforces the impact of the first two with fresh and intense performances, beautifully balanced. The magnificent *Missa Albanus*, written for St Alban's Abbey (where Fayrfax was finally buried) is aptly coupled with two extended antiphons, just as elaborate in their polyphonic complexity. *O Maria Deo grata* is directly associated with this particular Mass, having also been written for St Alban's. Lasting a full 16 minutes, it is an astonishing structure, and has here been realized by Professor Nick Sandon, who has reconstructed the missing parts. *Eterne laudis lilium*, also written for St Alban's, won for Fayrfax the sum of 20 shillings from the much-loved Queen Elizabeth of York, wife of Henry VII, and is a dedicated tribute to St Elizabeth, mother of John the Baptist.

Fernström, John (1897–1961)

Wind quintet, Op. 59.
(BB) ** Naxos Dig. 8.553050 [id.]. Oslo Wind Ens. – KVANDAL; NIELSEN: *Wind quintets.* **

The Swedish composer John Fernström was born in Ichang in China but spent most of his life in southern Sweden. He was active as an orchestral player and manager in Malmö, Lund and Hälsingborg. He composed no fewer than 12 symphonies and a variety of instrumental works in a generally neo-classical style. (Older readers may remember a charming *Concertino for flute, female voices and strings* that was coupled with André Gertler's LP of the Larsson *Violin concerto.*) This *Wind quintet* comes from 1943 and is pleasing and well crafted, though the thematic invention is not particularly individual. Excellent playing from the Oslo Wind Ensemble, but the recording, made in a rather small Norwegian Radio studio, is a bit bright and forward.

Fibich, Zdeněk (1850–1900)

Symphonies Nos. 2 in E flat, Op. 38; 3 in E min, Op. 53.
*** Chandos Dig. CHAN 9328 [id.]. Detroit SO, Järvi.

Neeme Järvi's account of these symphonies comes into direct competition with the Supraphon issue from the Brno orchestra under Jiří Waldhans and Bělohlávek respectively, discussed in our main volume. Generally speaking, the Chandos recording scores in terms of fidelity and space, and the Detroit orchestra respond with enthusiasm to these scores. This disc is more likely to be more persuasive so far as newcomers to this repertoire are concerned. The thematic substance of both works derives from the *Moods, impressions and reminiscences*, the product of the composer's infatuation with Anežka Schulzová.

Piano quintet, Op. 42.
*** ASV Dig. CDDCA 943 [id.]. Endymion Ens. – DOHNANYI: *Sextet.* ***

Fibich's *Piano quintet* is a relatively late piece; it comes from the last decade of his life and has much lively invention and no mean charm. Like the two symphonies listed above, it incorporates some of the thematic ideas which originated from the book of nearly 400 piano miniatures inspired by his infatuation with Anežka Schulzová. She must have been an enchanting young lady. The Endymions give a first-rate account of it and are excellently recorded.

Moods, impressions and reminiscences, Opp. 41, 44, 47 & 57.
*** Chandos Dig. CHAN 9381-2. [id.]. William Howard.

A generally preferable alternative to Rudoslav Kvapil's thoughtful and perceptive recital on Unicorn-Kanchana (DKPCD 9149 – see our main volume). William Howard is equally sensitive to the varying moods of these pieces, and he is much more convincingly recorded. However, it is only fair to point out that the Unicorn CD also includes the *Studies of painting.*

Admirers of this composer will be glad to know that Supraphon are at present recording all the *Moods, impressions and reminiscences* with Marián Lapšanský and have reached No. 125, the third volume, in what will doubtless be nine or ten CDs.

Sárka (opera; complete).
*** Sup. SU 0036-2 612 (2) [id.]. Děpoltová, Zítek, Přibyl, Randová, Brno Janáček Ch., Brno State PO, Jan Stych.

Sárka is Fibich's sixth opera, composed in 1896–7, during the last years of his short life. Some of Fibich's invention is predictable, but there is much that is both endearing and fresh, while the choral writing is distinctly appealing. In addition to the nationalist element, there is also a strong awareness of Wagner. Although it has never caught on outside Czechoslovakia, the opera has been recorded before (by the Prague National Opera under Chalabala) but this new version has the advantage of far superior recording, made in 1978, and an atmospheric and committed performance. Fibich, though a composer of the second order, is nevertheless far from unrewarding and there are many colourful and melodically appealing episodes here, even if the quality of inspiration is not consistent. The cast here is a fine one, and readers who enjoy Czech music will find this set well worth investigation. The transfer to CD is admirably managed – the atmospheric warmth is immediately apparent in the evocative Overture. A full translation is included.

Field, John (1782–1837)

Piano concertos Nos. 3 in E flat; 5 in C (L'incendie par l'orage).
*** Chandos Dig. CHAN 9495 [id.]. Míceál O'Rourke, LMP, Matthias Bamert.

We have already praised Field's *Third E flat Concerto* in its excellent Telarc version by John O'Conor with Mackerras (CD 80370), where it is paired with No. 1. It has one of the composer's most charming *Nocturnes* for its slow movement with a simple string accompaniment, followed by a rhythmically catchy finale. Míceál O'Rourke is well up to form and readily matches the poetry found by O'Conor. The coupling is a concerto which is notable mainly for its histrionic storm effects in the middle of the first movement, which climax with a bold stroke on the tam-tam. After this, the weather breaks and we are ready for the songful *Andante*, featuring a solo clarinet, before the comparatively robust and spirited finale which brings delicacy as well as brilliance of articulation from the soloist, before the clarinet returns to soften the mood. Here O'Rourke's exquisite response is totally beguiling, before the scintillating return to the main theme. Excellent support throughout from Bamert, and first-class recording.

Finzi, Gerald (1901–56)

Dies natalis; Intimations of immortality.
**(*) Hyperion Dig. CDA 66876 [id.]. John Mark Ainsley, Corydon Singers & O, Matthew Best.

Matthew Best, with John Mark Ainsley as soloist in both works, offers the ideal Finzi coupling in the finest and most beautiful of his early works, *Dies natalis*, setting mystical poems of Thomas Traherne, and his most ambitious work, the extended cantata setting Wordsworth's *Intimations of immortality*. Using a relatively small orchestra, this is a more intimate reading of the latter work than on the earlier, EMI recording from Richard Hickox, with speeds less extreme in both directions, yet it conveys an almost comparable concentration. Ainsley has a sweeter if smaller voice than his EMI rival, Philip Langridge, very apt for both works, even if under pressure there is some unevenness. The chorus sings with feeling, though the recording is not ideally clear, with choir and orchestra not as vividly immediate as on the analogue EMI recording which features the Royal Liverpool Philharmonic Choir and Orchestra. That performance is exceptionally committed, with the fervour of the chorus echoing the dedication of the soloist. It is coupled with the Bachian *Grand fantasia and toccata* for piano and orchestra, compellingly played by Philip Fowke, and it remains a marginally stronger recommendation at mid-price (EMI CDM7 64720-2 – see our main volume). Nevertheless, it is very welcome to have new digital recordings of both choral works.

God is gone up; Lo, the full, final sacrifice; Magnificat.
(M) *** EMI Dig. CDM5 65595-2 [id.]. King's College, Cambridge, Ch., Cleobury; Farnes – BAX: *Choral music;* VAUGHAN WILLIAMS: *Mass.* ***

The three Finzi choral pieces with organ accompaniment provide attractive contrasts to the unaccompanied Bax pieces on a beautifully planned disc which shows the King's College choir at its finest and which now includes a beautiful analogue recording of the Vaughan Williams *Mass*, recorded two decades earlier. Both the extended anthem, *Lo, the full, final sacrifice*, setting Richard Crashaw's version of an Aquinas hymn, and the *Magnificat* were commissioned works, the one for St Matthew's, Northampton, the other for Massachusetts; in their rich climaxes they bring out a dramatic side in Finzi along with his gentle beauty, splendidly conveyed by the King's choir. The recording, made in the Chapel, is so nicely balanced that part-writing is clear even against the ample acoustic.

Flotow, Friedrich (1812–83)

Martha (complete).
500♪ (M) *** RCA 74321 32231-2 (2) [id.]. Popp, Soffel, Jerusalem, Nimsgern, Ridderbusch, Bav. R. Ch. and O, Wallberg.

Martha is a charming opera, and the cast of this 1978 recording is as near perfect as could be imagined. Lucia Popp is a splendid Lady Harriet, the voice rich and full yet riding the ensembles with jewelled accuracy. Doris Soffel is no less characterful as Nancy, and Siegfried Jerusalem is in his element as the hero, Lionel, singing ardently throughout. Wallberg's direction is marvellously spirited and the opera gathers pace as it proceeds.

Françaix, Jean (born 1912)

Concertino for piano and orchestra.
*** Decca Dig. 452 448-2 [id.]. Jean-Yves Thibaudet, Montreal SO, Dutoit – HONEGGER: *Concertino* ***; RAVEL: *Concertos.* **

Jean Françaix's delightful *Concertino* comes off well in Thibaudet's hands, as does the no less captivating Honegger. However, the two Ravel *Concertos*, the main works, while very well played and recorded, do not present a strong challenge to existing recommendations. Many collectors will be glad to turn instead to the fine Mercury recording of the Françaix *Concerto* by the composer's daughter, praised in our main volume (434 335-2). This still stands the test of time, and there are no reservations about the Auric, Fetler, Milhaud (*Le boeuf sur le toit*) and Satie (*Parade*) couplings.

Franck, César (1822–90)

Symphonic variations for piano and orchestra.
500♪ ❁ (B) *** Decca 433 628-2 [id.]. Clifford Curzon, LPO, Sir Adrian Boult (with GRIEG: *Concerto* ***; SCHUMANN: *Concerto* **(*)).

Clifford Curzon's 1959 recording of the Franck *Variations* has stood the test of time; even after three decades and more there is no finer version. It is an engagingly fresh reading, as notable for its impulse and rhythmic felicity as for its poetry. The vintage Decca recording is naturally balanced and has been transferred to CD without loss of bloom. The Grieg *Concerto* coupling is hardly less desirable.

Symphony in D min.
(M) *** DG 449 720-2 [id.]. Berlin RSO, Maazel – MENDELSSOHN: *Symphony No. 5.* ***
**(*) Teldec/Warner Dig. 4509 98416-2 [id.]. BPO, Mehta – SAINT-SAENS: *Symphony No. 3.* **(*)
(M) ** Mercury 434 368-2 [id.]. Detroit SO, Paray – RACHMANINOV: *Symphony No. 2.* **
** DG Dig. 437 827-2 [id.]. Boston SO, Ozawa – POULENC: *Organ concerto.* **

(i) *Symphony in D min.;* (ii) *Pièce héroïque* (orch. Charles O'Connell).
500♪ ❁ *** RCA 09026 61967-2 [id.]. (i) Chicago SO, (ii) San Francisco SO, Monteux (with (ii). D'INDY: *Istar* (***)).

Monteux exerts a unique grip on this highly charged Romantic symphony, and his control of the continuous ebb and flow of tempo and tension is masterly, so that any weaknesses of structure in the outer movements are disguised. The splendid playing of the Chicago orchestra is ever responsive to the changes of mood, and the sound is greatly improved.

Maazel's account is beautifully shaped, both in its overall structure and in incidental details. However, though each phrase is sensitively moulded, there is no sense of self-conscious striving for beauty of effect. Maazel adopts a fairly brisk tempo in the slow movement, which, surprisingly enough, greatly enhances its poetry and dignity; his finale is also splendidly vital and succeeds in filtering out the excesses of grandiose sentiment and vulgarity which can disfigure this edifice. The work gains enormously from strong control and deliberate understatement, as well as from the refinement of tone and phrasing which mark this reading, for there is no lack of excitement. The recording, admirably well blended and balanced, is enhanced in this new CD transfer for DG's 'Legendary Recordings' series of 'Originals', and the coupling is aptly chosen, for Mendelssohn's *Reformation Symphony* was another of this conductor's finest DG recordings.

Mehta's live performance brings an individual and powerful reading with highly responsive playing from the BPO, whose playing style has a strong influence over the interpretation. The flexible ebb and flow of pacing, combined with Mehta's firm moulding of phrase, means that when the second subject arrives it rocks to and fro quite slowly and weightily, the bass accented. Resolutely controlled, the outer movements have consistent thrust and generate plenty of adrenalin. The *Allegretto*, taken slowly, is gentle, the cor anglais solo poetically withdrawn. In the finale there is again a pulling back for the brass chorale, but the reprise of the melody from the slow movement slips in naturally. When the forward impetus is restored, Mehta maintains his grip firmly, so that the closing peroration is the more forceful. A compelling version, given full-bodied if not always refined sound, which is worth considering if the coupling is suitable.

Paray's reading is often very exciting; he too understands the emotional ebb and flow of the music, and the tension is well held throughout. Furthermore he gives a genuine Gallic flavour to the phrasing. Mercury's 1959 sound is wide in range and impressive in sonority; if it is a bit grainy on top, that is partly the fault of Franck's unrefined scoring of tuttis.

Considering Ozawa's is a live recording, it is surprising how long it takes for the adrenalin to really start flowing, although the playing of the orchestra is ever persuasive. The first movement isn't without impetus and the conductor's moulding is convincing, but the passion which Munch generated in the same hall 35 years earlier (and which can be sampled inexpensively on RCA Navigator 74321 29256-2) isn't forthcoming. After the elegantly played *Allegretto* things improve considerably in the finale, where at the reprise of the famous chromatic secondary theme of the first movement the Boston string-playing is gloriously warm and full. Of course the DG recording is much smoother than the earlier, RCA balance for Munch, but the hall remains intractable, and the full beauty and natural transparency of the sound which one personally experiences at a Symphony Hall concert is seldom forthcoming on records.

Symphony in D min; (i) *Symphonic variations for piano and orchestra.*
* Sony Dig. SK 58958-2 [id.]. (i) Paul Crossley; VPO, Giulini.

Given the abundance of choice in both works, Giulini is recommendable only to his most fervent admirers, and even they may find their patience strained. This is the slowest account of the *Symphony* now on the market. Paul Crossley is a more than capable soloist – he is often very perceptive and always sensitive in the *Symphonic variations*, but the *Symphony* is not really competitive.

Violin sonata in A.
500♪ ❁ (M) *** Decca 421 154-2. Kyung Wha Chung, Radu Lupu – DEBUSSY: *Sonatas;* RAVEL: *Introduction and allegro* etc. *** ❁

Kyung Wha Chung and Radu Lupu give a glorious account, full of natural and not over-projected eloquence, and most beautifully recorded. The slow movement has marvellous repose and the other movements have a natural exuberance and sense of line that carry the listener with them.

ORGAN MUSIC

Chorales Nos. 1 in E; 2 in B min., 3 in A min.; Pastorale in E, Op. 19; Pièce héroïque in B min.
(B) *(*) EMI forte CZS5 69328-2 (2). Fernando Germani – BACH: *Concertos, BWV 593, 596* etc. **; WIDOR: *Toccata.* **(*)

The huge organ of Selby Abbey dates from 1909, although it was rebuilt in 1948. It is in three sections: on the south side the *Great* and part of the *Pedal* face, across the chancel, the *Choir*, *Swell* and *Solo* and more of the *Pedal*. However, the largest pipes of the *Double Open Diapason* are high up in the nave triforium. Thus is offered in theory a considerably antiphonal interplay, but in effect the long reverberation period of the abbey prevents much point source, and the organ achieves (probably what it was intended to achieve in a period not devoted to clarity of texture) a large-scale – indeed overwhelming – spread of rich sound. The *Pièce héroïque* can never have sounded more massive. As for the remaining works, Germani's rather suave performances are not helped by the generally bland effect of the registration: there is not enough bite in the reeds. Hearing Franck on such a very English organ is not far removed from seeing the composer dressed in a straw hat, blazer and flannels lounging indulgently by the banks of the River Cam. No complaints about the engineering: the CD sounds far more comfortable than the original LP did. However, Peter Hurford's Decca collection of this repertoire still leads the field (444 568-2).

PIANO MUSIC

Choral No. 3; Danse lente; Grand caprice; Les plaintes d'une poupée; Prélude, aria et final; Prélude, choral et fugue.
*** Hyperion Dig. CDA 66918 [id.]. Stephen Hough.

Stephen Hough's impressive recital must now take pride of place among recordings of this repertoire. The *Prélude, choral et fugue* is worthy to rank alongside Murray Perahia's account (coupled with some Liszt, including pieces from the *Années de pèlerinage*), and no praise could be higher. In addition to the piano music, Hough plays his own transcription of the *Third* of the Organ *Chorals*, which in his hands sounds as if it had been written for the piano, so splendidly is it played. A most distinguished record in every way.

Frankel, Benjamin (1906–73)

Symphonies Nos. 1, Op. 33; 5, Op. 46; May Day overture, Op. 22.
*** CPO Dig. 999 240-2 [id.]. Queensland SO, Werner Andreas Albert.

Symphonies Nos. 2, Op. 38; 3, Op. 40.
❁ *** CPO Dig. 999 241-2 [id.]. Queensland SO, Werner Andreas Albert.

Symphonies Nos. 4, Op. 44; 6, Op. 49; Mephistopheles' Serenade and dance, Op. 25.
*** CPO Dig. 999 242-2 [id.]. Queensland SO, Werner Andreas Albert.

It is good that CPO are making available all the Frankel symphonies. The powerfully concentrated *First* leaves no doubt that he was a master symphonist and the *Second* hardly less so. The *Third* with its almost Stravinskian opening is a compelling one-movement work. These have been discussed at greater length in our main volume. The *Fourth Symphony* is arguably one of the very finest of Frankel's works. He conducted a BBC studio performance of it in the 1960s with the Philharmonia Orchestra, as he did of the *Fifth* and *Sixth*, and one would hope that the BBC label may in time release it. During the last decade of his life his symphonies dominated his output, though work on them was disrupted by ill-health. Indeed the *Sixth* (1969) was entirely composed in hospital. Frankel has the breadth of a Mahler and the concentration of a Sibelius without in any sense resembling either master. The *Fourth* (1966) has a more restrained palette yet its invention is both powerful and distinctive. The Scherzo has a memorable delicacy and the elegiac finale has an eloquence that fully justifies William Mann's claims for him as our finest symphonist, albeit after a BBC studio première of the *Fifth* and *Sixth symphonies*. The *Sixth* is dark and powerfully argued and gets very persuasive advocacy from the Queensland orchestra under Werner Andreas Albert, and very fine recording. Readers might well start either with this latest issue or with the coupling of Nos. 2 and 3, which received a Rosette in our main volume.

Bagatelles for 11 instruments (Cinque pezzi notturni), Op. 35; Clarinet quintet, Op. 28; Clarinet trio, Op. 10; Pezzi pianissimi, Op. 41 (for clarinet, cello & piano); *Early morning music.*
*** CPO Dig. 999 384-2 [id.]. Paul Dean, Australian String Qt (members); Queensland Symphony Chamber Players.

The *Clarinet quintet* was composed in 1956 for Thea King in memory of her husband, Frederick Thurston. (She has recorded it for Hyperion, together with works by Lutyens and Maconchy.) It is beautifully crafted and is expertly played by these Australian artists. The *Clarinet trio* is much earlier, being composed in 1940, but Frankel's musical language and fluent invention are already in place. The short but disturbing *Pezzi pianissimi* (1964), written for Thea King and Eleanor Warren, are thoughtful, gentle pieces which resonate in the memory afterwards, as do the *Bagatelles for eleven instruments* of 1959. This work was composed at the time of the *First Symphony* and inhabits the same questing world. Like the symphony, it is serial but not 'atonal' – much in the same way as Frank Martin is. Excellent playing and recording make this a most desirable introduction to a much-neglected and underrated composer whose work is at last gaining ground.

Frescobaldi, Girolamo (1583–1643)

Il Primo Libro de' Madrigale a 5 (1608).
*** Opus 111 Dig. OPS 30-133 [id.]. Concerto Italiano, Rinaldo Alessandrini.

Frescobaldi, born in Ferrara, was 25 when his first book of madrigals was published in 1608. They are songs about lovers, longing, admiring, often not daring to speak directly, about parting and loss, and always about passions unrequited. They produced a glorious stream of lyrical invention and a skill in construction remarkable in a composer at the outset of his career. He left clear instructions for their performance, emphasizing that strict tempo be avoided: 'They can sometimes be slow, sometimes fast and even halting, according to the emotions aroused or the meaning of the words that are sung.' Rinaldo Alessandrini and the Concerto Italiano have been winning golden opinions in this repertoire, and these delightful performances bear out their reputation for fine tuning and blending, and a richly expressive line. They not only give pleasure but should at last put this composer's name firmly in front of the public.

Froberger, Johann (1616–67)

Capriccio in C, FbWV 632; Lamentation sur la mort de Ferdinand III in F, FbWV 633; Partitas: in C, FbWV 612; C min., FbWV 619 ; D, FbWV 611a; E flat, FbWV 631; in G (auff Die Maÿerin), FbWV 606; Toccatas: in A min., FbWV 101; D, FbWV 121; G, FbWV 103; Tombeau sur la mort de M. Blancheroche in C min., FbWV 632.
*** Virgin Veritas/EMI VC5 45259-2. Siegbert Rampe (various harpsichords and virginals).

Lamentation sur la mort de Ferdinand III in F, FbWV 633; Partitas (Suites) Nos. XVIII in G min.; XIX in C min., FbWV 619; XX in D, FbWV 611a; XXX in A min.; Toccatas Nos. II in D min., IX in C; XIV in G, FbWV 103; XVIII in F; Tombeau sur la mort de M. Blancheroche in C min., FbWV 632.
(M) *** HMT Dig. 1901372 [id.]. Christophe Rousset (harpsichord).

Siegbert Rampe brings this rewarding repertoire vividly to life on four different period instruments, each admirably chosen; bearing in mind that slight pitch changes are involved as well as the changing character of the instrument, Rampe proves totally at home with Froberger's often dramatic but also thoughtful, improvisatory style with its closely interwoven arpeggios which have much in common with lute music. He is immediately commanding in the opening *Tombeau sur la mort de M. Blancheroche*, who was a celebrated lutenist and who died after falling down the stairs (the fall is reputedly included in the music), and the similarly meditative *Lamentation for the death of Ferdinand III*. Both these extended valedictions and the intervening *C minor Partita* are played on a double-manual 1628 Ruckers harpsichord, rebuilt a century later in Paris, which produces a satisfying body of tone. The *G major Partita* (*auff Die Maÿerin*), also dedicated to Ferdinand III, is connected with the death of the latter's wife: it is a highly inventive set of variations and, like its companion in E flat major, is played on a Miklis Czech harpsichord, made in Prague in 1671, which gives an appropriately more lightweight effect; its pitch, too, is slightly higher. The three bold *Toccatas* bring plenty of opportunity for invigorating bravura, the *D major* and *G major* presented with a real sense of enjoyment and flair on a tangy Spanish instrument made in 1629, which is in splendid condition. In between comes the reflective and touching *Capriccio in C*, which seems ideally suited to the chosen (1587) virginal, made in Venice by Giovanni Celestini (both these instruments at a slightly lower pitch). The third, very florid *Toccata in A minor* reverts to the Ruckert instrument, as do the two final *Partitas*, which it effectively separates. Both show the composer in characteristic exploratory style. The *Partita in D major* opens with a philosophical *Meditation* by the composer on his own mortality, while the C major work begins with a *Lament for Ferdinand IV*, the young successor to the throne, who died in 1656 and who is finally taken up to heaven by an ascending scale. Each work then follows with extrovert music, a jolly *Gigue*, *Courante* and *Sarabande*. The performances here are outstanding in every way and are documented equally impressively (including pictures of all four instruments used). The recording is very real and believable, but – as always with the harpsichord – it is important not to set the volume control too high.

Needless to say, Christophe Rousset is hardly less impressive in this repertoire. He uses a restored (1652) Couchet double-manual harpsichord which suits all these works admirably in his hands. Its pitch (A392) is the same as Rampe's Prague instrument; in the two *Partitas* which are played by both artists (FbWV 611a and FbWV 619), the effect of Rousset's instrument is brighter than Rampe's Ruckers, which is tuned at A370. This is very effective in the *Gigues*, but some may prefer Rampe's slightly more sonorous effect in the *Allemandes*. If Rousset is often slightly brisker than Rampe, he takes the closing *Sarabande* of the meditative *D major Suite* considerably more slowly. Like Rampe, he is very well recorded and, although he includes slightly less music, his disc is offered at mid-price.

Furtwängler, Wilhelm (1886–1954)

Symphony No. 2 in E min.
(***) Orfeo d'Or mono C 375491B [id.]. VPO, Furtwängler.
* Marco Polo Dig. 8 223436 [id.]. BBC SO, Alfred Walter.

The *Second Symphony* is Furtwängler's masterpiece, and his VPO performance on Orfeo, recorded at the Musikverein in 1953, gives a far better idea of its stature than the earlier (1951) Berlin account which was issued as a commercial recording by DG. It is also vastly superior to a Frankfurt performance Furtwängler conducted with the Hessischen Rundfunks Orchestra in December 1952 which appeared on Fonit Cetra. In intensity of feeling and atmosphere it completely eclipses the modern version on Marco Polo, which has neither. Marco Polo have recorded all the Furtwängler symphonies, but that series does not really do the composer's cause much good. In any event, given the authenticity of the Orfeo account and the decent sound the engineers have produced, why look further? For those who do not know Furtwängler as a composer, the symphony is of Brucknerian proportions and – one is tempted to say – Brucknerian nobility, and lasts almost 80 minutes. Honegger acclaimed it, and so have other great musicians; although his is not a strikingly original voice, it is a profound one.

Gabrieli, Andrea (1520–86)

Aria della battaglia a 8.

(B) ** Decca Eclipse Dig. 448 993-2; *448 993-4* [id.]. Philip Jones Brass Ens., Jones – Giovanni GABRIELI: *Collection.* **(*)

The *Aria della battaglia* is a rambling piece lasting over ten minutes, rather too long to retain the listener's interest – at least in the present performance. It is very well played, without any dramatic dynamic contrasts, and tends to jog along rather than create any great degree of tension. The recording is clear and nicely resonant.

Gabrieli, Giovanni (1557–1612)

(i) *Canzon a 6; Canzon primi toni a 8; Canzon, La Spiritata, a 4; Canzon vigesimasettima a 8; Sonata a 3.* (i; ii) *Canzon per sonar a 4; Canzoni Nos. 4 a 6; 12 a 8; In ecclesiis; Jubilate Deo; O Jesu mi dulcissime; O magnum mysterium; Quem vidistis pastores?; Timor et tremor.*

(B) **(*) Decca Eclipse Dig. 448 993-2; *448 993-4* [id.]. (i) Philip Jones Brass Ens., Jones; (ii) Soloists, King's College, Cambridge, Ch., Cleobury – Andrea GABRIELI: *Aria della battaglia.* **

The first group of *Canzoni* here is played immaculately on modern brass instruments, skilfully balanced and recorded in the Kingsway Hall which gives a nicely resonant bloom, good detail and excellent antiphony. Yet the result is curiously bland. The *Sonata a 3* comes off best; otherwise there seems to be a lack of tension and not the widest range of dynamic.

When one turns to the rest of the programme, recorded four years later in 1986, the results are altogether different. The widely resonant acoustics of King's College Chapel make an admirable alternative to St Mark's for this repertoire. Particularly in the festive motet, *In ecclesiis*, with its three choirs plus organ and instrumental accompaniment, the complex layout is convincing and indeed thrilling (although here the trebles – not quite the strongest contingent this choir has ever fielded – can only just cope); but the Christmas motet, *Quem vidistis pastores?*, with its solo voices from the choir representing the shepherds, is also very well managed. Other highlights include the light and joyful *Jubilate Deo* and the highly atmospheric *O magnum mysterium*; while *Timor et tremor* is richly appealing in texture. The canzoni for brass alone, which act as interludes, are undoubtedly enhanced by the King's ambience, and climaxes have real impact. At Eclipse price this is well worth having for the choral music alone.

Gade, Niels (1817–90)

Andante and allegro (arr. Rachlevsky); *Novelettes, Opp. 53 & 58.*

*** Claves Dig. CD 50-9607 [id.]. Kremlin CO, Misha Rachlevsky.

The *Andante and allegro* is a transcription for full strings of a quartet movement Gade wrote when he was twenty-one. The two sets of *Novelettes* come from 1874 and 1883 and have great allure. This is eminently civilized music, inventive and intelligent, and the performances by the Kremlin Chamber Orchestra under Misha Rachlevsky are beyond praise. It is a joy to hear such natural and beautifully shaped phrasing. The music may not be strong on depth but it is long on charm and delight. The recording is pleasingly natural and warm.

Echoes from Ossian: Overture, Op. 1; Hamlet Overture, Op. 37; Holbergiana, Op. 61; A Summer's day in the country, Op. 55.

** CPO Dig. CPO 999 362-2 [id.]. Rheinland-Pfalz StaatsPhilharmonie, Schmidt.

Both the *Echoes from Ossian Overture* and the much later *Hamlet* are already available on Kitaienko's Chandos recording of the *First Symphony*, so that interest focuses on the two rarities, *A Summer's day in the country*, a five-movement suite written for the Hamburg orchestra in 1879, and the somewhat slighter orchestral suite, *Holbergiana*, written for the bicentenary of the playwright's birth in 1884. (It was for the same celebrations that Grieg composed his suite for piano, *From Holberg's time*, which he subsequently transcribed for strings.) All four movements celebrate a Holberg play, the last being *Maskarade*, on which Nielsen was to base his opera of the same name. *A Summer's day in the country* is the more substantial of the two and its centrepiece, *Solitude of the woods*, is quite captivating. The Rheinland-Pfalz Orchestra play well for Ole Schmidt, and the recording, if not quite of three-star quality, is perfectly natural and well balanced.

(i) *Elverskud (The Elf-King's daughter), Op. 30;* (ii) *Forårs-fantasi (Spring fantasy), Op. 23.*
*** Marco Polo DaCapo Dig. 8.224051 [id.]. (i) Susanne Elmark, Guido Paëvatalu; (i; ii) Kirsten Dolberg; (ii) Anne-Margarethe Dahl, Gert Henning-Jensen, Sten Byriel, Elisabeth Westenholz; (i) Tivoli Concert Ch.; Tivoli SO, Michael Schønwandt.

Gade's *Elverskud*, variously translated as *The Elf-King's daughter*, *The Erl-King's daughter*, *The Fairy spell* or *The Elf-shot* is a work of great charm and the opening of the second half – an evocation of the moonlit world of the fairy hill – is much more than that: it is little short of inspired. This new account under Michael Schønwandt has a good deal to recommend it and it can be seen as a useful alternative to the Chandos version under Dmitri Kitaienko listed in our main volume. In some ways this scores over its rival: the solo singers are generally more satisfying and the conductor keeps a firmer grip on proceedings without any loss of poetic feeling or atmosphere. It also has the advantage of the more adventurous coupling, the *Forårs-fantasi* (*Spring fantasy*), which Gade composed as an engagement present for his fiancée, Sophie. (His wedding present to her was not *The Elf-King's daughter* as erroneously stated in our main volume but the *Fifth Symphony* for piano and orchestra.) It is one of Gade's most delightful inspirations, radiant in its happiness and full of sun. Excellent soloists and very good playing from all concerned. Slightly close recording, but there is still plenty of space round the artists and the texture is reasonably transparent.

Forårs-fantasi (Spring fantasy), Op. 23.
(M) ** EMI CDM5 66000-2 [id.]. Bodil Gøbil, Minna Nyhus, Ole Jensen, Mogens Schmidt Johansen, Eyvind Møller, Danish RSO, Frandsen – NIELSEN: *Hymnus Amoris; Sleep.* **

John Frandsen's performance of Gade's charming *Spring fantasy* first appeared on the Danish Music Anthology label in the 1970s and is new to the EMI catalogue. It is a good performance, fresh, well shaped and decently recorded. Not superior to the new version under Schønwandt listed above, but still eminently worthwhile at mid-price, and attractively coupled.

Galuppi, Baldassare (1706–1785)

Concerto a quattri; (i) *Harpsichord concertos: in C; C min.; F; G.*
(M) *** Erato/Warner 0630 12984-2 (2) [id.]. (i) Edoardo Farina, Sol. Ven., Scimone – *La Caduta di Adamo.* ***

Galuppi was a very considerable figure in his era and undoubtedly had an influence over C. P. E. Bach and Haydn, so it is not before time that we are made more familiar with his music. The present Erato set bears out the favourable impression made by the Virgin CD of two of his motets (see below). The *Concerto a quattri* is as inviting as it is succinct, opening with a graceful *Grave e Adagio*, then moving on to a lively *Spiritoso*. The virtually unknown harpsichord concertos are attractive *galant* works of no mean achievement; the *G major* (which comes first) has a delectably tender Venetian 'serenade' for its central movement, with muted violins and violas singing the melody over a pizzicato bass; the figuration in the spirited finale even suggests mandolins, and the soloist is given a spectacular extended cadenza which calls for (and here receives) the most nimble bravura. The first movement of the *C major Concerto* is totally dominated by the harpsichord, elegantly accompanied by the strings; the slow movement produces a warmly serene melody, taken up thoughtfully by the soloist, and then the keyboard joins the orchestra in a bouncing finale. The jolly and more robust *F major Concerto* is hardly less appealingly melodic, while the *C minor* suggests simmering underlying passions and brings yet another alluring Italianate *Andantino*, full of Mediterranean sunshine. The performances here could hardly be bettered: they have vigour and elegance, they are robust when required and at other times are suitably beguiling. The orchestral sound is pleasingly full and resonant, but the engineers have achieved a nice balance so that the keyboard instrument is in proper scale, yet is never overwhelmed by the tutti. Coupled with the splendid *Adam and Eve* oratorio, this makes a very tempting mid-priced package.

Motets: (i) *Arripe alpestri ad vallem;* (ii) *Confitebor tibi, Domine.*
❀ *** Virgin/EMI Dig. VC5 45030-2 [CDC 45030]. (i) Gérard Lesne, (ii) with Véronique Gens, Peter Harvey; Il Seminario Musicale.

These two very beautiful motets show Galuppi at his most inspired, and they are performed superbly by Gérard Lesne, who is joined by Véronique Gens and Peter Harvey in *Confitebor tibi* (praising God for

His munificence) which brings a skill in its overlapping part-writing worthy of Mozart. The accompaniments from Il Seminario Musicale are refreshingly sensitive, alive and polished, while the recording has a natural presence.

La Caduta di Adamo (The fall of Adam).
(M) *** Erato/Warner 0630 12984-2 (2) [id.]. Mara Zampieri, Susanna Rigacci, Ernesto Palacio, Marilyn Schmiege, Sol. Ven., Scimone – *Concertos.* ***

Galuppi's oratorio, *The fall of Adam*, takes a little while to warm up but then, with the spectacular entry of the Angel of Justice, a Queen of the Night figure producing a similarly histrionic display of coloratura, the drama springs grippingly to life. That role is taken with superb assurance by Susanna Rigacci, but soon Eve (the hardly less impressive Mara Zampieri) is showing her mettle, and Ernesto Palacio (who is at first a shade strenuous) comes into his own in Part II with his touching call for God's forgiveness, *Amare lagrime* ('Bitter tears'). Indeed Part II is a succession of fine numbers, notably Eve's moving cry of despair *Se al Ciel miro* ('When I turn my eyes to heaven I see anger; When I turn, yearning, to my husband, I see betrayal'). The performance is directed with an ideal combination of vigour and expressive feeling by Claudio Scimone, and the 1985 analogue recording is vividly atmospheric. Highly recommended.

Geminiani, Francesco (1687–1762)

Concerti grossi, Op. 2/1–6; Op. 3/1–4.
(BB) *** Naxos Dig. 8.553019 [id.]. Capella Istropolitana, Jaroslav Kreček.

This is part of an ongoing Naxos project to record all Geminiani's concerti grossi using modern instruments but in a style which clearly reflects the freshness and vitality of period-instrument practice. The Capella Istropolitana offer excellent accounts of the whole of Op. 2 and the first four concertos of Op. 3 (with the remainder to follow). Not perhaps quite as characterful as Tafelmusik's version of Op. 2 (Sony SK 48043) but invigoratingly enjoyable and very well recorded.

Concerti grossi, Op. 3/1–6.
(B) (**) Millennium mono MCD 80079. E. Bar. Ens., Herman Scherchen.

Recorded at the same time (September 1954) as Handel's Op. 6, Scherchen's account of Geminiani's Op. 3 is not quite as successful as the Handel (see below), although still very enjoyable for its warmth and breadth of expressive feeling. Tempi are leisured, but the graceful phrasing and the spirited articulation in allegros ensure the listener's pleasure. However, the thinness of the upper strings, as recorded, is more striking here, even if there is underlying body and ambient warmth. The other drawback is the absence of cues for individual movements.

Gerhard, Roberto (1896–1970)

The Duenna (opera; complete).
*** Chandos Dig. CHAN 9520 (2) [id.]. Van Allan, Clark, Glanville, Powell, Archer, Taylor, Roberts, Wade, Opera North Ch., E. N. Philh. O, Antoni Ros Marbá.

Exiled from Spain after the Spanish Civil War, Roberto Gerhard found a permanent home in Cambridge; there, just after the end of the Second World War, he came upon a copy of Sheridan's play, *The Duenna*, originally presented with music by Thomas Linley. He resolved at once to turn it into an opera, being attracted not just by the wit of the dialogue but with its setting in Seville. The opera which resulted was the culmination of a period during the 1940s when the Spanish influence was strongest in his music. Both before and after that time his music reflects far more directly his allegiance to Schoenbergian techniques, but here the hints of atonality simply add extra spice to the Spanish flavours, with sensuously colourful instrumentation and lively dance rhythms.

It makes a highly attractive mixture, and it is sad that such a fine piece – even described as the greatest of all Spanish operas – should have had to wait until 1992 for its first staging. This recording was made in connection with the 1996 revival of the 1992 Opera North production, and though the cast is not as starry as the original one, the teamwork – so important in a lively and fast-moving comedy like this, and here honed to perfection, thanks to stage performances – is what matters, with generally fresh, young voices well contrasted and defined. As the heroine, Donna Luisa, Susannah Glanville sings charmingly, rising to the challenge of her big monologue in Act II, one of the most tenderly lyrical passages in the whole opera, where Gerhard touches deeper emotions than one expects in an eighteenth-century comedy. Richard Van Allan, the one survivor from the original cast, makes an aptly gruff and characterful Don

Jerome, the heavy father, and Neill Archer is an ardent hero. In the title-role of the Duenna, Claire Powell is firm and fruity, delightful in her duet with Don Isaac, the rich Jew who is tricked into marrying her. Their final reconciliation amid the exuberant bustle of the final ensemble scene brings another moving, if brief, moment in a superbly crafted, consistently inspired work, even if there is rather too much reliance on speech over music to fill gaps in the story. The recording, made in the Royal Concert Hall, Nottingham, is vivid and immediate, with fine presence, letting words be heard with commendable clarity even over the richest orchestral background.

Gershwin, George (1898–1937)

(i) *An American in Paris;* (ii) *Piano concerto in F;* (iii) *Rhapsody in blue.*
(M) *** Carlton 3036 007-2 [id.]. (ii–iii) Gwenneth Pryor; LSO, Richard Williams.
(BB) * Naxos Dig. 8.550295 [id.]. (ii–iii) Kathryn Selby; (i) Czech RSO (Bratislava); (ii–iii) Slovak PO; Richard Hayman.

From the opening glissando swirl on the clarinet, the performance of the *Rhapsody in blue* by Gwenneth Pryor and the LSO under Richard Williams tingles with adrenalin, and the other performances are comparable. In the *Concerto*, the combination of vitality and flair and an almost voluptuous response to the lyrical melodies is very involving. *An American in Paris*, briskly paced, moves forward in an exhilarating sweep, with the big blues tune vibrant and the closing section managed to perfection. The performances are helped by superb recording, made in the EMI No. 1 Studio; but it is the life and spontaneity of the music-making that enthral the listener throughout all three works.

The Naxos collection is totally unidiomatic. Everything is well played, even refined (especially the slow movement of the *Concerto*), but the rhythmic feeling of this music eludes these players: the *Rhapsody* is unmemorable and the blues tune in *An American in Paris* is square. Good, modern recording, but the jazzy element is too diluted for this music-making to be fully convincing.

An American in Paris; (i) *Rhapsody in blue.*
(M) *** Sony SMK 47529 [id.]. NYPO, Bernstein; (i) Bernstein (piano) (with BERNSTEIN: *Candide overture; West Side Story: Symphonic dances* ***).

Bernstein's famous 1959 recording of the *Rhapsody in blue* is unsurpassed, and his performance of *An American in Paris* is similarly inspirational. The recording still sounds well. Coupled with his fizzing, early NYPO performance of the *Candide overture* and the *Symphonic dances* from *West Side Story*, this is a record that should be a cornerstone of any collection.

Girl Crazy: suite (orch. Anderson). *Overtures* (orch. Rose): *Oh, Kay!; Funny Face; Let 'em eat cake; Of thee I sing*. Arrangements: *Of thee I sing; Wintergreen for President* (orch. Paul); *3 Preludes* (orch. Stone); (i) *Rhapsody No. 2 for piano and orchestra*.
(M) ** Decca Phase Four 443 900-2 [id.]. (i) Votapek; Boston Pops O, Fiedler.

Arthur Fiedler's performances are played with considerable panache and obvious idiomatic understanding. There are some valuable novelties here. *Wintergreen for President* quotes glibly from a number of other sources (including *The Pirates of Penzance*), and Fiedler readily catches its circus-style roisterous ambience. The *Second Rhapsody*, one of Gershwin's near misses, is given considerable fervour in its advocacy here, with Ralph Votapek's solo contribution sparking off a good orchestral response; but even so it remains obstinately unmemorable. The three piano *Preludes* do not readily transcribe for orchestra but are effective enough. The Phase Four recording is characteristically forwardly balanced but warm and brightly vivid in its colouring.

Rhapsody in blue (original version); *Who cares?* (ballet from Gershwin Songbook, arr. Hershy Kay); arr. of songs for piano: *Clap your hands; Do, do, do it again; Nobody but you; Swanee.*
**(*) Carlton Dig. 30367 0106-2. RPO, Andrew Litton.

Andrew Litton follows in Michael Tilson Thomas's footsteps by adopting the original Whiteman score of the *Rhapsody in blue*. The performance is lively enough and thoughtful too, so it has some elements of the Bernstein approach, particularly in the improvisatory-like passage before the big tune arrives. When it does, its reedy textures emphasize the smaller, less inflated sound which Gershwin originally conceived, while earlier the brass tuttis have a jazzy exuberance, without the players sounding rushed off their feet. In its way, this is very enjoyable and far better recorded than the CBS version, but the rhythmic inflexions are clearly from this side of the Atlantic, and this applies even more strikingly to the (attractively) amiable performance of Hershy Kay's ballet-score adapted from Gershwin's own 'Song Book for Balanchine'.

Litton then usefully plays as solo piano items the four remaining songs which Kay discarded, and very well too.

Oh Kay!

*** Nonesuch/Warner Dig. 7559 79361-2 [id.]. Dawn Upshaw, Kurt Ollman, Adam Arkin, Patrick Cassidy, Robert Westenberg, Liz Larsen, Ch. & O of St Luke's, Eric Stern.

The last in this splendid Nonesuch series of Gershwin musicals is in many ways the finest of all. With the music (including hits like *Someone to watch over me*, *Clap yo' hands*, *Do, do do* and the very catchy *Fidgety feet*) fitting neatly on to one CD, this is a fizzing entertainment. Dawn Upshaw is a highly enticing Kay, and she gets vivid support from Kurt Ollman as Jimmy, Adam Arkin as Shorty McGee and Patrick Cassidy as Larry. The cast could hardly be more naturally at home in Gershwin's sparkling score. Eric Stern directs with great flair and the recording is admirably vivid. Not to be missed.

Porgy and Bess (complete).

500♪ ❁ *** EMI Dig. CDS7 49568-2 (3) [Ang. CDCC 49568]. Willard White, Cynthia Haymon, Harolyn Blackwell, Cynthia Clarey, Damon Evans, Glyndebourne Ch., LPO, Rattle.

Simon Rattle here conducts the same cast and orchestra as in the opera house, and the EMI engineers have done wonders in re-creating what was so powerful at Glyndebourne, establishing more clearly than ever the status of *Porgy* as grand opera, not a mere jumped-up musical or operetta. The impact of the performance is consistently heightened by the subtleties of timing that come from long experience of live performances. Willard White is superbly matched by the magnificent Jake of Bruce Hubbard and by the dark and resonant Crown of Gregg Baker. Cynthia Haymon as Bess is movingly convincing in conveying equivocal emotions. EMI's digital sound is exceptionally full and spacious.

Gibbons, Orlando (1583–1625)

see also in Vocal Recitals, below, under 'Codex'

Almighty and everlasting God; Blessed are all they; Glorious and powerful God; Lord, grant grace; O Lord, how do my woes increase; Sing unto the Lord; This is the record of John; We praise Thee, O Father.

(B) *** Cal. Approche CAL 6621 [id.]. Clerkes of Oxenford, David Wulstan – SHEPPARD: *Mass 'Cantate', Respond: 'Spiritus Sanctus'.* ***

This collection of eight verse-anthems of Orlando Gibbons makes an admirable coupling for some lesser-known music of John Sheppard. They are written for solo groups as well as for the full choir, and often with instrumental accompaniments, and their style obviously recalls similar music by Purcell. By comparison they are not found wanting. They are splendidly sung and recorded, and this is a genuine bargain.

Giordano, Umberto (1867–1948)

Andrea Chénier (complete).

(M) *** RCA 74321 39499-2 (2). Domingo, Scotto, Milnes, Alldis Ch., Nat. PO, Levine.

Andrea Chénier with its defiant poet hero provides a splendid role for Domingo at his most heroic and the former servant, later revolutionary leader, Gérard, is a character well appreciated by Milnes. Scotto gives one of her most eloquent and beautiful performances, and Levine has rarely displayed his powers as an urgent and dramatic opera conductor more potently on record, with the bright recording intensifying the dramatic thrust of playing and singing. Stylishly repackaged in RCA's mid-priced UK Opera Treasury series, this is a clear first choice for this opera on CD. At the time of going to press, it is not listed in the American *Schwann Catalogue*.

Giuliani, Mauro (1781–1828)

(i; ii) *Guitar concertos Nos. 1 in A, Op. 30; 2 in A, Op. 36; 3 in F, Op. 70; Introduction, theme with variations and polonaise (for guitar and orchestra), Op. 65.* (i) *Grande ouverture, Op. 61; Gran Sonata Eroica in A; La Melanchonia; Variations on 'Ich bin a Kohlbauern Bub', Op. 49; Variations on a theme by Handel, Op. 107;* (i; iii) *Variazioni concertanti, Op. 130.*

(B) *** Ph. Duo 454 262-2 (2) [id.]. (i) Pepe Romero, (ii) with ASMF, Marriner; (iii) with Celedonio Romero.

It was a capital idea to combine Giuliani's three engaging guitar concertos on a Duo, and each disc is generously filled out with other concertante and solo music. Romero is a first-rate player, and his relaxed music-making and easy bravura bring an attractive, smiling quality. But what makes the concertos so distinctive are the splendid accompaniments provided by the Academy of St Martin-in-the-Fields under Marriner. The shaping of the naïf contours of Giuliani's orchestral ritornello for the *First Concerto* is deliciously judged, and throughout there are many delightful touches from the orchestra. The finale is irresistibly vivacious, the sparkling orchestral rhythms a constant joy. The *F major Concerto* has comparable charm. Its first movement begins with an engaging little march theme whose dotted contour reminds one of Hummel (the two composers were almost exact contemporaries), and the amiable *Siciliano* which forms the slow movement is matched by an unforceful closing Polonaise. Hummel again comes rhythmically to mind in the first movement of the *Second concerto*, which is for strings alone. The *Andantino* here is pleasingly atmospheric and the final rondo again sparkles rhythmically. The *Introduction, theme with variations and polonaise* (originally conceived for guitar and string quartet) is like a mini-concerto and, if the basic idea of the variations only just rises above the trivial, it is redeemed by a performance of vitality and charm. The Op. 49 *Variations* are agreeable but slight, but the *Sonata Eroica*, although effectively conceived and impressively presented, hardly merits its grand sobriquet as provided by Ricordi when it was published posthumously. The *Variations concertanti* for two guitars, in which Pepe is joined by Celedonio, is a more ambitious late work which exploits the duet variation form with much skill. It is played with affection and ready virtuosity. The mid-1960s recording throughout is warm and refined, very easy on the ear.

Guitar concerto in A, Op. 30.
(B) **(*) Decca Eclipse 448 709-2; *448 709-4* [id.]. Eduardo Fernández, ECO, Malcolm – PAGANINI: *Sonata;* VIVALDI: *Concertos.* **(*)

A rather low-key, essentially chamber performance from the highly musical Fernández, who refuses to show off. He is accompanied elegantly by Malcolm and the ECO and is most naturally recorded. Some might feel the finale should be more extrovert, although it does not lack spirit; on the other hand, the intimacy of this music-making has its own appeal.

Variations on a theme by Handel, Op.107.
(B) *** Sony SBK 62425; *SBT 62425* [id.]. John Williams (guitar) – PAGANINI: *Caprice 24; Grand sonata;* D. SCARLATTI: *Sonatas;* VILLA-LOBOS: *5 Preludes.* ***

The *Variations* are on Handel's famous *Harmonious blacksmith* theme. Their construction is guileless but agreeable, and they are expertly played and well recorded. This is only a small part of a well-planned and exceptionally generous collection devoted mainly to Paganini and Domenico Scarlatti.

Glazunov, Alexander (1865–1936)

(i) *Concerto ballata for cello and orchestra, Op. 108;* (ii) *Piano concerto No. 1, Op. 92.*
*** Chandos Dig. CHAN 9528 [id.]. (i) Dyachkov; (ii) Pirzadeh; I Musici de Montréal, Turovsky – ARENSKY: *Violin concerto.* ***

The highly romantic *First Piano Concerto* which comes from 1910–11, the period in which Glazunov was working on but subsequently abandoned his *Ninth Symphony*, is already well served by Stephen Coombs (see below). The *Concerto ballata* is more of a rarity and, like the *Saxophone concerto*, is the product of the composer's last years in Paris. Apart from Pergamenschikow on Koch, there is no other version of the *Concerto ballata*, and it is a far from negligible piece. Yegor Dyachkov is a fine soloist, and the young Iranian-born Canadian pianist, Maneli Pirzadeh, proves a most poetic and brilliant (yet never ostentatious) exponent of the *Piano concerto*. All in all this makes a highly recommendable coupling.

Piano concertos Nos. 1 in F min., Op. 92; 2 in B flat, Op. 100.
**(*) Hyperion Dig. CDA 66877 [id.]. Stephen Coombs, BBC Scottish SO, Martyn Brabbins – GOEDICKE: *Concertstück.* **(*)

These two piano concertos are ripely lyrical, like a mixture of Brahms and Rachmaninov, but the inspiration is anything but tired or faded. In the *First Concerto*, an extended first movement – with echoes of Rachmaninov's *Second Symphony* – is followed by a long and elaborate set of variations, while the Liszt-like structure of the *Second Concerto* includes the most beautiful slow movement. The two concertos are full of charm and offer civilized discourse with which to beguile the ear. The melodic invention never falls below a certain level of memorability – without ever rising to the heights of distinction. As in his survey of Glazunov's piano music for the same label, Stephen Coombs is a persuasive advocate, though one would occasionally welcome more fire; but he always leaves one with the feeling that this music means more than it does. The BBC Scottish Symphony Orchestra under Martyn Brabbins give sympathetic support, and the only serious reservation one might make concerns the over-resonant recording acoustic.

Violin concerto in A min., Op. 82.
500♪ *** Teldec/Warner Dig. 4509-90881-2 [id.]. Vengerov, BPO, Abbado – TCHAIKOVSKY: *Violin concerto.* ***

Outstanding as Vengerov's Tchaikovsky performance is, his Glazunov is even more exceptional, for he gives a warhorse concerto extra dimensions, turning it from a display piece into a work of far wider-ranging emotions. Above all he makes one appreciate afresh what a wonderful sequence of melodies the composer here offers.

From the Middle Ages, Op. 79; The Kremlin, Op. 30; Poème epique, Op. posth.; Poème lyrique, Op. 12.
(BB) * Naxos Dig. 8.553537 [id.]. Moscow SO, Konstantin Krimets.

None of these is top-drawer Glazunov, and they need the most expert and sympathetic advocacy if they are to win acceptance. This is not in evidence on this disc which, despite its generous playing time and modest price, offers playing that rarely rises above the routine.

From the Middle Ages (suite), *Op. 79; The Sea, Op. 28; Spring, Op. 34; Stenka Razin, Op. 13.*
(M) *** Chandos Dig. CHAN 7049 [id.]. SNO, Järvi.

Although the music is inferior to Tchaikovsky, Glazunov's *From the Middle Ages suite* has charm, and Järvi has the knack of making you think it is better than it is. The tone-poem *Spring* was written two years after *The Sea* and is infinitely more imaginative; in fact it is as fresh and delightful as its companion is cliché-ridden. At one point Glazunov even looks forward to *The Seasons*. *Stenka Razin* has its moments of vulgarity – how otherwise with the *Song of the Volga Boatmen* a recurrent theme? – but it makes a colourful enough opening item for this collection which offers persuasive and very well-recorded performances from the Royal Scottish National Orchestra.

Raymonda (complete ballet).
(BB) **(*) Naxos 8.553503/4 [id.]. Moscow SO, Alexander Anissimov.

In our main edition we gave high praise to the mid-priced Kirov recording of *Raymonda* under Victor Fedotov (Carlton 30366 00067) which includes so much music of charm and grace. That recommendation still stands. This new Naxos version is played elegantly and affectionately, and the Moscow upper strings are fuller and warmer than those of the Kirov players as recorded. It does not lack life. But the Naxos recording, in seeking atmosphere, creates overall a rather less vibrant, less vivid effect than the Kirov version, where the colours are more brightly lit, although this is partly caused by Anissimov's tendency to more luxuriant tempi. The *Entry of the Vassal and Peasants* in Act I is a good deal more lively in Kirov than in Moscow. But that is not to say that the inexpensive Naxos version is not very enjoyable in its more sumptuously spacious manner, for the orchestral playing is very sympathetic.

Scènes de ballet.
(M) ** Revelation RV 10006 [id.]. Moscow RSO, Rozhdestvensky – PROKOFIEV: *Andante for strings* *(*); SIBELIUS: *Symphony No. 7; Rakastava.* (*)

A bizarre coupling. Will collectors of Glazunov's charming ballet music want a late Sibelius symphony, and vice versa? Whatever the thinking behind this coupling (none, we imagine), there are some appealing movements in this score, which was originally (and more appropriately) coupled with Rimsky-Korsakov's *Antar* in the mid-1970s. A decent performance and recording, but coupled with an uncompetitive Sibelius *Seventh*.

The Seasons (ballet; complete), *Op. 67.*
*** Decca Dig. 433 000-2 (2) [id.]. RPO, Ashkenazy – TCHAIKOVSKY: *Nutcracker ballet.* ***
(M) *** EMI CDM5 65911-2. Concert Arts O, Robert Irving – SCARLATTI/TOMMASINI: *Good humoured ladies;* WALTON: *Wise virgins.* ***

The Seasons (ballet), *Op. 67; Concert Waltzes Nos. 1 in D, Op. 47; 2 in F, Op. 51.*
(B) *** EMI forte CZS5 69361-2 (2). Philh. O, Svetlanov – ARENSKY: *Variations on a theme of Tchaikovsky* ***; RIMSKY-KORSAKOV: *Scheherazade.* **

The Seasons is an early work, first performed at St Petersburg in 1900, the choreography being by the famous Petipa. With colourful orchestration, a generous sprinkling of distinctive melody and, at the opening of *Autumn*, one of the most virile and memorable tunes Glazunov ever penned, the ballet surely deserves to return to the repertoire.

Robert Irving's recording with its happily chosen couplings serves to remind us of a first-class ballet conductor of the 1960s, working with both the Sadler's Wells and the New York City companies. His 1960 account has never been surpassed, and the recording, made at New York's Manhattan Center Ballroom, still sounds astonishingly fresh, while the resonant ambience prevents the quality from being too dated. The Concert Arts Orchestra is a pseudonym for a much better-known British combination, and they play with wit, warmth and astonishing precision. The strings are immaculate and there are consistently sensitive and charmingly delicate wind solos. Irving shapes and points the melodies with consummate balletic feeling and his reading is delightfully evocative. The stirring tune of *Autumn* is taken very fast and has strikingly more vitality than with Svetlanov.

Svetlanov's is a classic account of *The Seasons* which stands up very well to rival versions that have appeared in the almost 20 years since it was made, although Ashkenazy's premium-priced version is very beautifully played and has the advantage of digital sound of great allure and warmth. The latter remains first choice, if the coupled *Nutcracker* – which is comparably fine – is also required. Svetlanov's account is played most beautifully. His approach is engagingly affectionate; he caresses the lyrical melodies persuasively so that, if the big tune of the *Bacchanale* has slightly less thrust than usual, it fits readily into the overall conception. The glowing Abbey Road recording is excellent and vividly remastered. It comes in harness with a very Russian *Scheherazade*, which he recorded with the LSO but about which we have some reservations (see below), and Barbirolli's highly persuasive version of the endearing Arensky *Variations* for strings.

PIANO MUSIC

4 Preludes and fugues, Op. 101; Prelude and fugue in D min., Op. 62; in E min. (1926).
*** Hyperion Dig. CDA 66855 [id.]. Stephen Coombs.

The prelude-and-fugue format has attracted relatively few major twentieth-century keyboard composers, apart from Shostakovich. Glazunov's examples are rarely heard but, as Stephen Coombs shows us, their neglect is unjustified. The *D minor Prelude and fugue*, Op. 62, comes from 1899 and is not just a powerful essay in Bachian counterpoint, but a dramatic and compelling piece. As Coombs's notes put it, there is 'nothing dry and dusty about it' at all. Nor for that matter are the set of four, Op. 101, written in 1918. They must have seemed very much out of step in a world where Stravinsky and Prokofiev were the dominant voices of the new music. They are not only intellectually rewarding but they are also artistically most satisfying and inventive pieces. The *E minor* from 1926 opens dramatically and is an impressive piece. When in the past we have written that Glazunov is not at his best in his piano music we obviously did not have the benefit of such persuasive advocacy as this. The recording is eminently satisfactory, without any excessive reverberance.

(i) *Piano sonata No. 2 in E min., Op. 75; Barcarolle sur les touches noires; Idyll, Op. 103. 2 Impromptus, Op. 54; In modo religioso, Op. 38; Prelude and 2 Mazurkas, Op. 25; Song of the Volga boatmen, Op. 97* (arr. Siloti); (ii) *Triumphal march, Op 40.*
*** Hyperion Dig. CDA 66866 [id.]. (i) Stephen Coombs; (ii) Holst Singers, Stephen Layton.

Stephen Coombs really succeeds, where others have not, in making the listener believe that this is music of quality as well as of charm – and indeed much of it is! The *Barcarolle sur les touches noires* and the *Prelude and two mazurkas* are from 1887–8, when Glazunov was in his early twenties; like the *E minor Prelude and fugue*, the *Idyll*, Op. 103, comes from the other end of his career, 1926. The most substantial work on the disc is the *Second Sonata* of 1901, which is better played than by any of its rivals we have heard. The most unusual piece is the transcription of a Wagnerian *Triumphal march*, written for the Chicago Exposition, which eventually introduces *Hail Columbus*, sung in Russian! Not all the music on this generously filled CD is of equal merit but most of it is rewarding, and the recording serves the music well. Admittedly it is slightly over-reverberant so that climaxes in the *Sonata* are opaque, but this should not stand in the way of a strong recommendation.

Tsar Iedesyskiy (King of the Jews).
*** Chandos Dig. CHAN 9467 [id.]. Russian State Symphony Ch. & SO, Rozhdestvensky.
(BB) *(*) Naxos Dig. 8.553575 [id.]. Moscow Cappella & SO, Golovschin.

Glazunov's incidental music to Konstantin Romanov's *Tsar Iedesyskiy* (*King of the Jews*), composed just before the outbreak of the First World War, is new to the catalogue and, although its invention is not always consistent in quality, the score offers considerable artistic rewards. There is an unaffected simplicity that is quite touching, and the naturalness of the musical inspiration outweighs any of its longueurs or miscalculations. Rozhdestvensky shapes each phrase with feeling and imagination, and he gets good results from his chorus and orchestra. Moreover the quality of the recorded sound is first rate in every respect, with well-balanced choral and orchestral forces and a lifelike perspective. There are informative and helpful notes by David Nice. It is in every way superior to the bargain rival on Naxos, which has the merit of economy but offers a performance that is neither as well prepared nor as accomplished as the Chandos.

Glinka, Mikhail (1805–57)

Ruslan and Ludmilla: overture.

❀ (BB) *** Belart 450 017-2. LSO, Solti – MUSSORGSKY: *Khovanshchina Prelude; Night;* BORODIN: *Prince Igor*: excerpts. ***

Solti's electrifying account of the *Ruslan and Ludmilla* overture is probably the most exciting ever recorded (it dates from the mid-1960s) with the lyrical element providing a balancing warmth. The LSO strings are right up on their toes throughout, and it is they to whom we award a Rosette for fizzing ensemble and real sparkle. The recording is brightly lit, but not unacceptably so. The couplings are also very successful.

A Farewell to St Petersburg (song-cycle); *Doubt; Elegy; The fire of longing burns in my heart; How sweet it is to be with you; I recall a wonderful moment; Mary; Say not that it grieves the heart.*

*** Conifer Dig. 75605 51264-2 [id.]. Sergei Leiferkus, Simeon Skigin.

Glinka's songs are grievously (and, after hearing this CD, one could add, unaccountably) neglected on CD. This is the only version of *A Farewell to St Petersburg*, the collection of 12 songs published in 1840, between the two operas, *A Life for the Tsar* (1836) and *Ruslan and Ludmilla*. Christoff included three in his celebrated LP of Glinka songs in the 1960s. Our own authority on Glinka and all things Russian, David Brown, speaks in his sleeve-notes of their 'instant and direct appeal' that transcends any language barrier, and he describes them as having 'a quiet magic of their own, a subtlety and distinctiveness greater than might have been suspected at first hearing'. They may not have the lyrical richness of Tchaikovsky or the psychological depth of Mussorgsky, but they possess great variety of character and develop in a way that only a great melodist could achieve. The aristocrat of Russian baritones, Sergei Leiferkus, is on prime form here and is superbly accompanied by Simeon Skigin. Very natural recorded sound sets the seal on a most distinguished and thoroughly rewarding issue.

Ruslan and Ludmilla (complete).

*** Ph. 446 746-2 (3) [id]. Ognovienko, Netrebko, Diadkova, Bezzubenkov, Gorchakova, Kirov Op. Ch. & O, Gergiev.

(M) **(*) RCA/Melodiya 74321 29348 (3) [id.]. Nesterenko, Rudenko, Yaroslavtsev, Sinyavskaya, Morozov, Fomina, Bolshoi Theatre, Moscow, Ch. & O, Yuri Simonov.

Gergiev in his Kirov recording, done live on stage, launches into this classic Russian opera with a hair-raisingly fast and brilliant account of the overture, and then characteristically brings out the subtlety of much of the writing, as well as the colour. In his concentration he draws the threads of the ramshackle structure together, helped by the staging, even if the sound, transferred at a rather low level, is a little lacking in body. The voices come over well, with Vladimir Ognovienko characterful as Ruslan, bringing out word-meaning, most impressively in his big Act II aria. Anna Netrebko is fresh and bright as Ludmilla, as well as agile, not as shrill as many Russian sopranos; but it is Galina Gorchakova as Gorislava who takes first honours, rich and firm, as is Larissa Diadkova in the travesti role of Ratmir, especially impressive in the delightful duet with Finn (Konstantin Pluzhnikov). A video recording is also available.

The Bolshoi recording on BMG/Melodiya at mid-price brings a warm and convincing account, typical of Bolshoi standards in the late 1970s, with Yevgeni Nesterenko magnificent as Ruslan, rich, firm and heroic. Though Simonov's conducting is not as refined as Gergiev's on Philips, his thrust and purposefulness hold the piece together well and, though the recording is uneven, such a passage as the scene with the head is eerily effective. Another outstanding performance comes from Boris Morozov as the braggart, Farlaf, with his comic patter Rondo in Act II, not just brilliantly agile but resonant too and full of fun, reminding one of Chaliapin's famous recording. Alexei Maslennikov is most affecting in Finn's Ballad, and Nina Fomina is a rich, firm Gorislava. One snag is that Bela Rudenko as Ludmilla is shrill under pressure, and a few cuts are made in Act V; but it is still an enjoyable if uneven set.

Gluck, Christophe (1714–87)

Alessandro (ballet music).

** DG Dig. 445 824-2 [id.]. Col. Mus. Ant., Goebel – REBEL: *Les Elémens* (suite); TELEMANN: *Sonata (Septet) in E min.* **

This is characteristically attractive and spontaneous music, tuneful and nicely scored. But Reinhard Goebel is ill-cast to catch its natural charm. There is no lack of vitality here, and the vigorous writing with trumpets is impressively robust. The second-movement *Allegretto* is neat and sprightly; but if the group's eccentric period-instrument style of phrasing cannot rob the *Andantino* of its essential nobility, their line simply isn't smooth enough to beguile the listener's ear as this music was surely intended to do. The same frequently accented pulse also slightly disturbs the ballet's touching penultimate movement, *Antipoisino*, a graceful slow minuet of much delicacy. Here Roxana, the heroine of the story, saves the day by producing an antidote to restore to life her conqueror husband, Alexander, whom, for both personal and patriotic reasons, she had earlier poisoned! Such were the ways of Asian princesses in ancient times.

Iphigénie en Aulide: highlights.
(M) *** Erato/Warner Dig. 0630 15732-2 [id.] (from complete recording with Van Dam, Von Otter, Dawson, Aler, Monteverdi Ch., Lyon Op. O, Gardiner).

Iphigénie en Aulide was Gluck's first piece in French and it anticipated the *Tauride* opera in its speed and directness of treatment. Gardiner here offers the score as presented in the first revival of 1775. The opera is strongly cast, with Lynne Dawson touching in the title-role and the Monteverdi Choir make a superbly incisive contribution. Those not wanting the complete set (4509 99609-2 – see our main volume) will find these 74 minutes of highlights well selected, and the presentation is admirable, with a full translation and a linking introduction provided for each excerpt. Excellent recording.

Iphigénie en Tauride (complete).
500♪ ✿ *** Ph. Dig. 416 148-2 (2) [id.]. Montague, Aler, Thomas Allen, Argenta, Massis, Monteverdi Ch., Lyon Op. O, Gardiner.

Gardiner's electrifying reading of *Iphigénie en Tauride* is a revelation. Diana Montague in the name-part sings with admirable bite and freshness, Thomas Allen is an outstanding Oreste, characterizing strongly but singing with classical precision. John Aler is a similarly strong and stylish singer, taking the tenor role of Pylade. The recording is bright and full.

Orfeo ed Euridice (complete).
500♪ *** Ph. Dig. 434 093-2 (2) [id.]. Ragin, McNair, Sieden, Monteverdi Ch., E. Bar. Soloists, Gardiner.
*** Teldec/Warner Dig. 4509 98418-2 (2) [id.]. Larmore, Upshaw, Hagley, San Francisco Op. Ch. & O, Runnicles.
(M) ** Van. 08.4040 72 (2) [id.]. Forrester, Stich-Randall, Steffek, V. State Op. Ch. & O, Mackerras.
(M) (**) DG mono 439 711-2 (2) [id.]. Fischer-Dieskau, Stader, Streich, RIAS Chamber Ch., Berlin Motettenchor, Berlin RSO, Ferenc Fricsay.
(M) (**) DG mono 439 101-2 (2) [id.]. Simionato, Jurinac, Sciutti, V. State Op. Ch., VPO, Karajan.

Gardiner's newest set for Philips uses the original Vienna version and could not be more dramatic or deeply expressive. The element of sensuousness, not least in the beautiful singing of the counter-tenor, Derek Lee Ragin, in the title-role, complements the Elysian beauty Gardiner finds in such passages as the introduction to *Che puro ciel*. Sylvia McNair as Euridice and Cyndia Sieden as Amor complete Gardiner's outstanding solo team.

Donald Runnicles, with his San Francisco Opera forces and an excellent cast of principals, conducts a performance based on the 1869 Berlioz edition. The dramatic intensity reflects stage experience, with Runnicles generally adopting speeds a degree broader than those preferred by Gardiner in his EMI set, also based on the Berlioz edition, and with a smoother style. Jennifer Larmore makes a strong and positive Orphée, brilliant in the aria which in this edition ends Act I, rich and warm in rather broad treatment of the big aria, *J'ai perdu mon Eurydice*. Next to von Otter for Gardiner she sounds very feminine, and not quite as flexible. Dawn Upshaw is a charming Eurydice, and Alison Hagley a sweet-toned L'Amour, though she is balanced very backwardly, as is the chorus at times in what is otherwise a good recording. Unlike Gardiner, but like Leppard on Erato, Runnicles includes ballet music at the end.

Mackerras in his mid-1960s Vanguard recording conducts a fresh and intense performance, boldly opting for the Italian version at a time when almost all performances mixed the Vienna and Paris texts. Mackerras makes a concession in including the *Dance of the Furies* and *Dance of the Blessed Spirits* from the Paris version, and his speeds are often very slow by latterday standards. Also his Orfeo, the magnificent Canadian contralto, Maureen Forrester, for all the richness of her singing, follows the oratorio tradition. Good recording for its period.

In his 1957 mono recording, Ferenc Fricsay offers a performance using a baritone hero, and when Dietrich Fischer-Dieskau sings so expressively the result is worth hearing, but this is ruled out as a serious contender. Crisp as the ensemble is, the performing style follows nineteenth-century traditions, although Maria Stader as Eurydice and Rita Streich as Amor both sing very sweetly and movingly.

Using the usual composite text, Karajan in his 1959 Salzburg Festival performance conducts a characteristically dramatic and intense performance with a starry cast, a big-sounding orchestra and few concessions to baroque practice. Sadly, Simionato is a disappointing Orfeo, rich in the lower register but with a pronounced vibrato above.

Godard, Benjamin (1849–95)

Cello sonata in D min., Op. 104; 2 pieces for cello and piano, Op. 61.
*** Hyperion Dig. CDA 66888 [id.]. Lidström, Forsberg – BOELLMANN: *Cello sonata in A min.* etc. ***

An interesting and compellingly played disc of off-beat repertoire. Benjamin Godard was a pupil of Vieuxtemps and a widely respected teacher, best remembered for the occasional salon piece. Godard composed no fewer than eight operas, none of which holds the stage today, although the aria, *Oh! ne t'éveille pas encore*, from *Jocelyn* (1888) is generously represented in the catalogue. The *D minor Sonata* is very much in the Schumann–Brahms tradition and is beautifully crafted and powerfully shaped, as are the *Aubade and Scherzo*, Op. 61. Mats Lidström and Bengt Forsberg play with such passion and conviction that they almost persuade you that this piece is worthy to rank alongside the Brahms sonatas. The recording is just a trifle on the close side, but it produces eminently satisfactory results. Strongly recommended.

Goedicke, Alexander (1877–1957)

Concertstück in D (for piano and orchestra), *Op. 11.*
**(*) Hyperion Dig. CDA 66877 [id.]. Stephen Coombs, BBC Scottish SO, Martyn Brabbins – GLAZUNOV: *Piano concertos Nos. 1 & 2.* **(*)

Alexander Goedicke was three years older than his cousin, Nicolai Medtner, whose shadow served to obscure his talents, and outlived him by six years. This *Concertstück* for piano and orchestra is far from negligible, both in its melodic invention and in its musical structure, and it well deserves to be rescued from the neglect into which it has fallen. Stephen Coombs is a brilliant and sympathetic interpreter of this music and the BBC Scottish Symphony Orchestra under Martyn Brabbins give every support. The recording is too reverberant – and this perhaps inhibits a full three-star recommendation.

Goetz, Hermann (1840–76)

Francesca da Rimini: Overture; Spring overture, Op. 15; (i) *Nenie, Op. 10;* (i–ii) *Psalm 137, Op. 14.*
** CPO Dig. 999 316-2 [id.]. (i) N. German R. Ch.; (ii) Stephane Stiller; N. German R. PO, Hanover, Werner Andreas Albert.

Hermann Goetz enjoys a peripheral hold on the repertory of recorded music, though in recent years CPO have begun to explore his output. He was born in the same year as Tchaikovsky and, had the latter died at the same age as Goetz, we would not have had anything after the *Polish Symphony*. Goetz's admirers included Brahms, who knew his setting of Schiller's *Nenie* and waited a respectful time before embarking on his own version, and George Bernard Shaw, who wrote with enthusiasm about the opera, *Much Ado About Nothing*. The best piece here is *Nenie*, which has a strong sense of purpose and a genuine lyrical flow. The *Francesca da Rimini overture* comes from an opera its composer left unfinished. The musical language is very much in the tradition of Mendelssohn and Spohr, but the invention is of some quality, even if (by comparison with the great masters) a little bland. Good performances from all concerned and decently balanced, well-rounded sound.

Goldmark, Karl (1830–1915)

Violin concerto No. 1 in A min., Op. 28.
500♪ ❁ *** Delos Dig. DE 3156 [id.]. Nai-Yuan Hu, Seattle SO, Schwarz – BRUCH: *Violin concerto No. 2.* *** ❁

Nai-Yuan Hu (pronounced Nigh-Yen Who) makes an outstanding début on CD with a coupling of two underrated concertos which, on his responsively lyrical bow, are made to sound like undiscovered masterpieces. Hu shapes the melodies so that they ravishingly take wing and soar. Moreover Schwarz and the Seattle orchestra share a real partnership with their soloist, helped by a perfectly balanced recording.

Rustic Wedding Symphony, Op. 26.
(B) **(*) Decca Eclipse Dig. 448 991-2; *448 991-4* [id.]. LAPO, López-Cobos – DVORAK: *Slavonic dances Nos. 9–16.* ***

López-Cobos directs a refreshing and attractive reading. In the first movement the generally fast tempi detract from the charm of the piece, but the horns sound as magical as ever and there is sympathetic playing from the Los Angeles orchestra in the central movements. With a lively finale this is easy to enjoy when the digital recording is vivid but naturally balanced. Moreover, this inexpensive reissue offers a considerable Dvořák bonus.

Gottschalk, Louis (1829–69)

(i; iii) *Grande fantaisie triomphale on the Brazilian national anthem* (arr. Adler); (i; iv) *Grande tarantelle for piano and orchestra;* (iii) *Marche solennelle (for orchestra and bands); Marcha triunfal y final de opera;* (iv) *Symphonies Nos. 1 (A Night in the Tropics)* (ed. Buketoff); *2 (A Montevideo);* (i; iv) *The Union: Concert paraphrase on national airs* (arr. Adler); *Variations on the Portuguese national anthem for piano and orchestra* (ed. List). (ii) *5 Pieces* (for piano, 4 hands); (iv; v) *Escenas campestres (Cuban country scenes)*: opera in one Act.
(B) **(*) Carlton/Turnabout 30371 00077 (2) [VoxBox CDX 5009]. (i) Eugene List; (ii) Cary Lewis & Brady Millican; (iii) Berlin SO, Adler; (iv) V. State Op. O, Buketoff; (v) with Paniagua, Estevas, Garcia.

Louis Gottschalk was born in New Orleans of mixed German and French parentage. He studied music in Paris under Charles Hallé and then launched himself on a hugely successful career as composer/conductor/virtuoso pianist. He travelled widely, constantly moving throughout Europe and the USA, appealing to a society whose musical taste was without pretensions. As a touring star (perhaps comparable in many ways to the pop stars and groups of today) he was to some extent an isolated figure, cut off from serious musical influences. His subservience to public taste led to a continual infusion of national and patriotic airs into his scores and his music retained a refreshing naïveté to the last. This pair of Turnabout CDs, packaged in a single jewel-case, offers a distinguished anthology, with obvious dedication from editors and executants alike. Eugene List (as we know from his Gershwin recordings) was just the man to choose as soloist. Whether tongue-in-cheek or not, he manages to sound stylish throughout and in *The Union concert paraphrase*, which is outrageous, he is superb. There is no space here to dwell on the felicities of Gottschalk's elegant vulgarity. If you want Lisztian bravura, try the concertante pieces; if you fancy romanticism mixed with popular national dance rhythms, sample the two symphonies. There is also an imitation of Tchaikovsky's *Marche slave* which does not quite come off. The solo piano pieces (recorded very forwardly) are more variable: *La Gallina* is particularly likeable. The programme ends with some attractive vocal music (the *Escenas campestres*), which is vividly sung. The new CD transfer seems smoother and better focused than the original LPs and the effect is vivid and sparkling, if a little shallow. However, the bright, glittering piano timbre is not out of place here.

Gounod, Charles (1818–93)

Symphonies Nos. 1 in D; 2 in E flat.
*** ASV Dig. CDDCA 981 [id.]. O of St John's, Smith Square, John Lubbock.

Gounod's two symphonies, delightful, lyrical works full of sparkling ideas, were written in quick succession when he was in his mid-thirties, his only extended orchestral works. In No. 1 the effortless flow of first-rate ideas, both of the orchestra and of symphonic form, is very striking and the Bizet *Symphony* immediately springs to mind. In John Lubbock's hands No. 2 brings an unmistakable reminder of early Beethoven. They make an ideal coupling in these beautifully sprung and subtly phrased performances from John Lubbock and the Orchestra of St John's. In their lightness and transparency they bring out the charm of the writing far more than those on the previous version (now withdrawn) from EMI by Plasson and the Toulouse Capitole Orchestra. With this pair of works Lubbock repeats the success he achieved earlier with his splendid coupling of Mendelssohn's *Scottish* and *Italian Symphonies*, and his care for detail and the refreshingly light and polished playing he achieves with the St John's Orchestra is matched by a pervading warmth, helped by the full ambience of the recording.

Faust (complete).
500♪ ❁ *** Teldec/Warner Dig. 4509 90872-2 (3) [id.]. Hadley, Gasdia, Ramey, Mentzer, Agache, Fassbaender, Welsh Nat. Op. Ch. & O, Rizzi.

Rizzi, with an outstanding cast and vividly clear recording, makes the whole score with its astonishing sequence of memorable, tuneful numbers seem totally fresh and new. Jerry Hadley as Faust has lyrical freshness rather than heroic power, brought out in his headily beautiful performance of *Salut! demeure*. The tenderness as well as the bright agility of Cecilia Gasdia's singing as Marguerite brings comparable variety of expression, with the *Roi de Thulé* song deliberately drained of colour to contrast with the brilliance of the *Jewel song* which follows, but it is the commandingly demonic performance of Samuel Ramey as Mephistopheles that sets the seal on the whole set.

Grainger, Percy (1882–1961)

Blithe bells; Colonial song; English dance; Duke of Marlborough's fanfare; Fisher's boarding house; Green bushes; Harvest hymn; In a nutshell (suite); Shepherd's hey; There were three friends; Walking tune (symphonic wind band version); *We were dreamers.*
*** Chandos Dig. CHAN 9493 [id.]. BBC PO, Richard Hickox.

This first disc in Chandos's projected series covering Grainger's complete works could not be more enticing. Hickox is masterly, with rhythms always resilient, both in bringing out the freshness of well-known numbers like *Shepherd's hey* and in presenting the originality and charm of such little-known numbers as *Walking tune*. The BBC Philharmonic is in superb form, warmly and atmospherically recorded. By far the longest item is the suite, *In a nutshell*, which includes pieces like the *Arrival platform humlet*, well known on their own, and which has as its core a powerful and elaborate piece, *Pastoral*, which with its disturbing undertow belies its title.

The Warriors (music for an imaginary ballet).
500♪ *** DG Dig. 445 860-2; *445 860-4* [id.]. Philh. O, Gardiner – HOLST: *The Planets*. ***
Colourful and vigorous, *The Warriors* is described as 'an imaginary ballet for orchestra and three pianos', a characteristically extrovert showpiece, Grainger's largest work. It makes an unexpected and valuable coupling for Gardiner's brilliant account of the favourite Holst work. Dazzling sound.

PIANO MUSIC

Colonial song; Country gardens; Handel in the Strand; Harvest hymn; The hunter in his career; In a nutshell (suite): Gum-suckers' march; In Dahomey (Cakewalk smasher); Irish tune from County Derry; Jutish medley; A march-jig; The merry king; Mock morris; Molly on the shore; Ramble on the last love-duet from Richard's Strauss's *Der Rosenkavalier; A Reel; Scotch strathspey and reel; Shepherd's hey; Spoon river; Walking tune.*
**(*) Hyperion Dig. CDA 66884 [id]. Marc-André Hamelin.

It is good to have as brilliant a pianist as Hamelin turning his attention to Grainger, as unpredictable in his way as Alkan, another speciality of this artist. Hamelin's articulation is phenomenally crisp, and the recording is excellent, but he misses the charm of some of these pieces, when he is often too metrical, pushing ahead a shade too fast in such pieces as *Country gardens* or *Shepherd's hey*, so that rhythms fail to spring infectiously as they should. Yet the choice of items is generous and apt.

Country gardens; In a nutshell (suite); *Gay but wistful; The Gum-sucker's march; Jutish medley; March-jog (Maguire's kick); Molly on the shore; One more day my John; Ramble on the last love-duet in Strauss's 'Der Rosenkavalier'; Sheep and goat walkin' to the pasture; Shepherd's hey; Spoon river; Sussex mummers' Christmas carol; Turkey in the straw; The Warriors.* STANFORD: *Irish dances* arr. GRAINGER: *Leprechaun's dance; A reel.*
*** Nimbus NI 8809 [id]. Percy Grainger (from Duo-Art piano rolls).

We have always been admirers of the Duo-Art player-piano recording system, and here is another remarkably convincing example of modern stereo reproduction from such a source. Grainger's personality leaps out from between the speakers: it is just as if the composer were there in person, yet the original rolls were cut between 1915 and 1929! Rhythms are positive, accents are individual and the playing is always brilliant, if at times splashy. It is good to have such a winningly vigorous *Country gardens* and such a characterful *Shepherd's hey*, while *Sheep and goat walkin' to the pasture* has rhythmical character of the kind that makes one smile. *Turkey in the straw* is thrown off with panache. *Molly on the shore* is infectiously witty, even if it nearly runs away with itself. *Gay but wistful* is neither – nonchalant, rather – but endearing. The lyrical numbers like the touching *Sussex mummers' Christmas carol*, *One more day my John* and the lilting Zanzibar boat song have a winningly relaxed flair, and Grainger makes his arrangement of the Richard Strauss love-duet from *Der Rosenkavalier* sound intimately luscious and deliciously idiomatic. The recording is first class.

VOCAL MUSIC

Anchor song (setting of Rudyard Kipling); *Thou gracious power* (setting of Oliver Wendell Holmes); Arrangements of folk songs: *Afterword; Air from County Derry; Brigg Fair; Early one morning; Handel in the Strand; I'm seventeen come Sunday; The lonely desert-man sees the tents of the Happy Tribes; Marching time; Molly on the shore; 2 Sea chanties; Shallow Brown; Six dukes went a-fishing; There was a pig went out to dig; Ye banks and braes o' bonnie Doon.*

*** Chandos Dig. CHAN 9499 [id.]. Mark Padmore, Stephen Varcoe, Joyful Company of Singers, City of L. Sinf., Hickox; Penelope Thwaites.

In this third infectiously enjoyable disc in Chandos's Grainger series, Richard Hickox – as in his first disc of orchestral pieces – is particularly successful in capturing the exuberance of the composer's inspiration, his joy in sound, his delight in taking you by surprise. It makes a fine counterpart to John Eliot Gardiner's award-winning disc of choral pieces for Philips (446 657-2 – see below), when the duolication of items is minimal. In the darkly intense *Shallow Brown*, Hickox has less prominent janglings in the accompaniment, but he has a clear advantage in opting for an excellent baritone soloist (Stephen Varcoe) instead of a rather uncertain soprano, with an equally fine choral ensemble. Hickox's version of the *County Derry* (the 'Londonderry air') is quite different from Gardiner's, for he has chosen a more extended, much more elaborate setting made in 1920, lasting a full seven minutes in gradual crescendo, the longest item on the disc. *Ye banks and braes* is another item given in a version previously unrecorded, with a whistled descant. Among the items completely new to disc are the *Marching tune* (a Lincolnshire folk-tune made to sound like a lusty Salvation Army chorus with brass accompaniment), and *Early one morning* (with a minor-key cello solo as introduction, before dawn comes up with the tune in the major, when baritone and chorus enter, later with intertwining descants from violin and trumpet). Also most striking is the brief, keenly original choral piece, *The lonely desert-man sees the tents of the Happy Tribes*, here given a dedicated performance, with the tenor intoning a theme from Grainger's orchestral piece, *The Warriors*, and the distant chorus chattering a chant borrowed from his *Tribute to Foster*.

Folksong arrangements: *The Bride's tragedy* (for chorus & orchestra); *Brigg Fair* (for tenor & chorus); *Danny Deever* (for baritone, chorus & orchestra); *Father and daughter* (*A Faeroe Island dancing ballad;* for 5 solo narrators, double chorus, & 3 instrumental groups); *I'm seventeen come Sunday* (for chorus, brass & percussion); *Irish tune from County Derry* (*Londonderry air;* for wordless chorus); *The Lost lady found; Love verses from The Song of Solomon* (for tenor & chamber orchestra); *The merry wedding* (*Bridal dances;* for 9 soloists, chorus, brass, percussion, strings & organ); *My dark-haired maiden* (*Mi nighean dhu;* for mixed voices); *Scotch strathspey and reel – inlaid with several Irish and Scotch tunes and a sea shanty* (orchestral version); *Shallow Brown* (for solo voice or unison chorus, with an orchestra of 13 or more instruments); *The Three ravens* (for baritone solo, mixed chorus & 5 clarinets); *Tribute to Foster* (for vocal quintet, male chorus & instrumental ensemble).

500♪ ❀ *** Ph. Dig. 446 657-2 [id.]. Soloists, Monteverdi Ch., English Country Gardiner O, Gardiner.

It would be hard to imagine a more exhilarating disc of Grainger's music than this collection of 'songs and dancing ballads'. The variety is astonishing even among the folksong settings, which often use melodies transcribed from original sources by Grainger himself. All 14 items, many of them first-ever recordings, bring typically quirky inspirations, superbly interpreted. Even if the choir's attempts at various dialects, from Mummerset onwards, may not be to everyone's taste, the virtuosity of the singing is breathtaking.

Granados, Enrique (1867–1916)

Piano trio, Op. 50.

** Ph. Dig. 446 684-2 [id.]. Beaux Arts Trio – TURINA: *Trios, Opp. 35 & 76.* **

The *Piano trio* is an early work, written when Granados was in his mid-twenties. The composer himself described it as his 'best piece to date' but his finest and most characteristic music was still to come. Refined and sensitive playing from the Beaux Arts, but the recording is not ideal: forwardly balanced and in a reverberant studio, producing some discomfort in climaxes.

Cuentos para la juventud, Op. 1: Dedicatoria. Danzas españolas Nos. 4 & 5, Op. 37/4–5; Tonadillas al estilo antiguo: La maja de Goya. Valses poéticos.

500♪ ❁ (BB) *** RCA Navigator Dig. 74321 17903-2. Julian Bream (guitar) – ALBENIZ: *Collection;* RODRIGO: *3 Piezas españolas.* *** ❁

Like the Albéniz items with which these Granados pieces are coupled, these performances show Julian Bream at his most inspirational. The illusion of the guitar being in the room is especially electrifying in the middle section of the famous *Spanish dance No. 5*, when Bream achieves the most subtle pianissimo. Heard against the background silence, the effect is quite magical.

Graun, Karl Heinrich (1704–1759)

Montezuma: highlights.

(M) *** Decca 448 977-2 (2) [id.]. Elms, Sutherland, M. Sinclair, Ward, Woodland, Harwood, Amb. S., LPO, Bonynge – BONONCINI: *Griselda.* ***

Karl Heinrich Graun was the court composer of Frederick the Great, and it was the Emperor himself who provided the very professional libretto for this work, based on the conquest of Mexico as portrayed in a play by Voltaire. The opera's original success had more to it than royal patronage, and its revival on CD is thoroughly deserved. One serious shortcoming of the full work is the wordiness of the recitatives between numbers (presumably Graun jibbed at cutting any of the royal text) but here the selection, while giving the flavour of recitatives, omits its longueurs. Besides Sutherland who, in the role of Princess Eupaforice, has a stunning aria to sing, Monica Sinclair in the breeches role of the Conquistador, Cortes, is especially impressive. Good singing from the others, too. Richard Bonynge conducts briskly, with a real sense of style, and this tuneful piece is every bit as attractive as the Bononcini opera with which it is coupled. The recording, too, is excellent. A full translation is provided.

Gray, Steve (born 1947)

Guitar concerto (for guitar and small orchestra).

❁ *** Sony Dig. SK 68337 [id.]. John Williams, LSO, Paul Daniel – HARVEY: *Concerto antico.* *** ❁

The lively, bustling first movement of Steve Gray's *Guitar concerto* (1987), written for its performer here, John Williams, is agreeable enough, but the kernel of the work is the long, expressively atmospheric slow movement, which reaches a bold expansive climax. Yet the guitar is often featured in gentle, ruminative, solo cadenza-like writing, very like improvisation, which carries on through the last movement. The effect is haunting, but the jocular finale also brings loudly vociferous, even vulgar, orchestral outbursts – reflecting the composer's jazz-orientated background – and these probably come off better at a concert than on disc. However, the work ends with music of the utmost delicacy. The performance here is surely definitive and the recording first class.

Grieg, Edvard (1843–1907)

At the cradle, Op. 68/5; Country dance; 2 Elegiac melodies, Op. 34; Holberg suite, Op. 40; 2 Melodies, Op. 53.

*** Virgin/EMI Dig. VC5 45224-2. Norwegian CO, Iona Brown – NIELSEN: *At the bier of a young artist* etc. ***

The Norwegian Chamber Orchestra are an excellent group and they collect all of Grieg's music for strings, together with Nielsen's first opus, the *Little Suite* for strings, and his elegiac threnody, *Andante lamentoso* (*At the bier of a young artist*). Very alert and responsive playing, though some may feel that some accents in the opening movement of the *Suite from Holberg's time* are a bit too marked. But this is hardly worth mentioning in a programme that offers such lovely music-making of great feeling and sensitivity. The recording, made in the glorious acoustic of Eidsvoll Church in Norway, is in the demonstration bracket.

(i) *Piano concerto in A min., Op. 16;* (ii) *Peer Gynt: suites Nos. 1 and 2; Prelude; Dance of the Mountain King's Daughter.*

(M) *** Decca 448 599-2 [id.]. (i) Clifford Curzon, LPO; (ii) LSO; Fjeldstad.

(i) *Piano concerto in A min. Lyric pieces: Arietta; Elves' dance; Folk melody, Op. 12/1, 4 & 5; Butterfly; Little bird; To spring, Op. 43/1, 4 & 6; Notturno, Op. 54/4; Gade, Op. 57/2; Sylph; French serenade, Op. 62/1 & 3; Salon, Op. 65/4; Summer evening, Op. 71/2.*
500♪ ❁ (BB) *** Tring Dig. TRPO 24 [id.]. Ronan O'Hora, (i) with RPO, James Judd.

(i) *Piano concerto in A min.;* (ii) *Piano sonata in E min., Op. 7.*
500♪ (M) *** Ph. 446 192-2 [id.]. (i) Kovacevich, BBC SO, Sir Colin Davis; (ii) Zoltán Kocsis – SCHUMANN: *Concerto.* ***

Whether in the clarity of virtuoso fingerwork or the shading of half-tone, Kovacevich is among the most illuminating of the many great pianists who have recorded the Grieg *Concerto*. He plays with bravura and refinement, the spontaneity of the music-making bringing a sparkle throughout, to balance the underlying poetry and, for the mid-priced reissue, Philips have added a performance by Zoltán Kocsis of the *Piano sonata*, recorded digitally at the beginning of the 1980s.

The vintage Decca recoupling is well worthy of the Classic Sound series. The sensitivity of Curzon in the recording studio is never in doubt, and his has been a favourite version of the concerto over a very long period. The performance has always been famous for its freshness, and the sound remains remarkably vivid and immediate. Similarly, in its original format Fjeldstad's *Peer Gynt* was counted to be one of the really outstanding early Decca stereo LPs. The LSO is very sensitive, and the tender string-playing in *Solveig's song* is quite lovely. Fjeldstad's persuasive direction is comparable with that of Beecham, making the listener feel he or she is experiencing this familiar music in a new way. The conductor begins *In the Hall of the Mountain King* rather slowly but builds up a blaze of excitement by the end and quite justifies his conception. The early (1958) Kingsway Hall recording retains its glowing lustre, and only when the violins are under pressure above the stave is there some loss of sweetness. A most rewarding coupling.

The young Manchester pianist, Ronan O'Hora, with a totally sympathetic partner in James Judd, now provides us with a recorded performance which is for the mid-1990s what Solomon and Clifford Curzon were for the later 1950s, Steven Kovacevich for the 1970s, and Perahia for the end of the 1980s. Indeed in imagination and delicacy of feeling, combined with natural, authoritative brilliance, this new performance is unsurpassed.

PIANO MUSIC

Agitato; Album leaves, Op. 28/1 & 4; Lyric pieces, Opp. 43 & 54; Piano sonata in E min., Op. 7; Poetic tone pieces, Op. 3/4–6.
500♪ ❁ *** Virgin/EMI Dig. VC7 59300-2 [id.]. Leif Ove Andsnes.

A notable recital by Grieg's countryman, Leif Ove Andsnes, which has won golden opinions – and rightly so! Andsnes's virtuosity is always at the service of the composer, and he has that ability to make familiar music sound fresh, as if you haven't heard it before.

Lyric pieces, Opp. 12, 38, 43, 47, 54, 57, 62, 65, 68 & 71.
* Finlandia Dig. 0630 14907-2 [id.]. Juhani Lagerspetz.

Grieg's *Lyric pieces* span his whole career, from his halcyon days in Denmark in the mid-1860s through to 1901, six years before his death. They are well represented on CD. Juhani Lagerspetz's survey offers no challenge. He is short on things like charm, grace and poetic feeling and is inclined to be heavy-handed.

Lyric pieces: Op. 12/1; Op. 38/1; Op. 43/1–2; Op. 47/2–4; Op. 54/4–5; Op. 57/6; Op. 62/4 & 6; Op. 65/5; Op. 68/2, 3 & 5; Op. 71/1, 3, 6 & 7.
500♪ (M) *** DG 449 721-2 [id.]. Emil Gilels.

With Gilels we are in the presence of a great keyboard master whose characterization and control of colour and articulation are wholly remarkable. An altogether outstanding record in every way. This recording has been admirably remastered for reissue in DG's 'Originals' series and now sounds better than ever.

VOCAL MUSIC

Haugtussa (song-cycle), *Op. 67; 6 Songs, Op. 48. Songs: Beside the stream; Farmyard song; From Monte Pincio; Hope; I love but thee; Spring; Spring showers; A Swan; Two brown eyes; While I wait; With a waterlily* (sung in Norwegian).
500♪ ❁ *** DG Dig. 437 521-2 [id.]. Anne Sofie von Otter, Bengt Forsberg.

This recital of Grieg's songs by Anne Sofie von Otter and Bengt Forsberg is rather special. Von Otter commands an exceptionally wide range of colour and quality and in Bengt Forsberg has a highly responsive partner. Altogether a captivating recital, and beautifully recorded too.

(i) Peer Gynt: extended excerpts; (ii) *Old Norwegian romance with variations, Op. 51.*
(M) **(*) Ph. Dig. 454 130-2 [id.]. (i) Elly Ameling, San Francisco Ch. & SO, Edo de Waart; (ii) Philh. O, Leppard.

De Waart directs a warmly sympathetic reading of the *Peer Gynt* music, less sharply focused than Järvi or Blomstedt (see our main volume). Ameling, a fine soloist, sings in Norwegian. The *Wedding march* is not included, but the brief unaccompanied choral piece, *Song of the church-goers*, is. Although this selection is not as complete as its two competitors, the disc does find room for the slight but engaging *Old Norwegian romance with variations*. Leppard's phrasing is subtle and he secures beautifully refined playing from the Philharmonia strings. Both recordings are warm and full, if not especially brilliant.

Peer Gynt: suites Nos. 1, Op. 46; 2, Op. 55. Sigurd Jorsalfar: suite.
(B) *** DG Double 447 358-2 (2) [id.]. BPO, Karajan – SIBELIUS: *The Bard* etc. ***

Although Beecham showed a special feeling for this score and his extended selection on EMI (CDM7 64751-2) remains a key recommendation in this repertoire, collectors wanting just the two *Peer Gynt suites* will find Karajan's analogue performances from the early 1970s are still a pretty good bet. They re-emerge here on a DG Double, coupled with a very generous and enticing Sibelius programme. The Grieg performances are highly expressive and superbly played. Anitra dances with allure and there is contrasting simplicity and repose in *Aase's death*. The current transfers are rather brightly lit, but there is no lack of body.

Peer Gynt: suites Nos. 1–2; Lyric pieces: Evening in the mountains; Cradle song, Op. 68/1–2; Wedding day at Troldhaugen, Op. 65/6; Sigurd Jorsalfar suite, Op. 56.
(BB) ** Naxos Dig. 8.550864 [id.]. BBC Scottish SO, Jerzy Maksymiuk.

The *Peer Gynt* music is also presented with admirable simplicity by these excellent Scottish players. But although *Aase's death* brings a rapt closing pianissimo, *In the hall of the Mountain King* could use rather more impetus, and it is the second suite that has the greater character. What makes this disc worth considering is the very beautiful string-playing in the two *Lyric pieces* and the fine performance of the first two numbers from *Sigurd Jorsalfar*, *In the king's hall* engagingly presented and *Borghild's dream* full of atmosphere and drama. The famous *Homage march* is suitably regal but rather too slow and expansive. However, the jolly *Wedding dance* is very spirited.

4 Poems from Bjørnstjerne Bjørnson's Fishermaiden, Op. 21, 6 Songs, Op. 48; Peer Gynt: Solveig's song; Solveig's cradle song. Songs: *At Rodane; A bird song; The first primrose; From Monte Pincio; Hope; I love but thee; I walked one balmy summer evening; Last spring; Margaret's cradle song; On the water; The princess; Spring showers; A Swan; To her II; Two brown eyes; Upon a grassy hillside.*
(BB) **(*) Naxos Dig. 8.553781 [id.]. Bodil Arnesen, Erling Eriksen.

An inexpensive and, at 70 minutes, well-filled CD, beautifully recorded and pleasingly sung. Bodil Arnesen has a voice of great purity and radiance. She sings marvellously in tune, though some may find that in this repertoire she has something of a 'little-girl', innocent quality that does not give the whole picture. This perhaps is troubling when you are listening to all the songs straight off. Taken a group at a time, she will touch most hearts, particularly in the setting of Bjørnson's *Prinsessen* and *Det første møte*. Erling Eriksen is an excellent pianist.

Grofé, Ferde (1892–1972)

Grand Canyon suite.
(M) *(*) Decca Phase Four 448 956-2 [id.]. L. Festival O, Stanley Black – IVES: *Orchestral Set No. 2.* ***

Stanley Black is thoroughly at home in Grofé's picaresque spectacular, but the exaggeratedly forward balance is unrealistic, especially with such a wide panoply of sound; in *On the trail* the bass clarinet is virtually in the listener's lap! Fortissimos are very highly modulated and, although the effect is better contained on CD than it was on LP, the biggest climaxes tend to degenerate into noise. Yet the performance is a colourful one and easy to enjoy, and the Ives coupling shows Stokowski at his most dramatically flamboyant.

Grosz, Wilhelm (1894–1939)

7 Afrika songs, Op. 29; Bänkel und Balladen, Op. 31; Rondels, Op. 11. Hit songs (arr. Robert Ziegler): *Along the Sante Fe Trail; Harbour lights; Isle of Capri; Red sails in the sunset.*
*** Decca Dig. 455 116-2 [id.]. Cynthia Clarey, Kelly Hunter, Jake Gardner, Andrew Shore, Matrix Ens., Ziegler.

It is astonishing to find that the writer of such hit songs of the 1930s as *Isle of Capri* and *Red Sails in the sunset* was a very serious, Vienna-trained composer with a remarkable melodic gift. Exiled first to Britain, later to the United States, he adapted himself readily to new demands but, tragically, he died in his mid-forties and, unlike Kurt Weill or Erich Korngold, has been totally neglected ever since. He is credited with being the first Austrian composer to use a jazz element in his music, and the *Afrika songs* reflect that in settings of poems by black writers, translated into German. The accompaniment has a jazz grouping complementing classical strings and woodwind, with the eight songs linked by imaginative interludes and – last and longest – a haunting, sensuous duet. The three *Rondels* are charming mixtures, similarly sensuous, while the *Ballades* strike a sharper note in their satirical flavour, with echoes of Mahler. Robert Ziegler's arrangements of the hit songs do not precisely imitate the 1930s manner but introduce a Viennese flavour, with hints of Weill. A first-rate team of soloists, as well as fine playing from the Matrix Ensemble.

Haas, Joseph (1879–1960)

Krippenlieder (6 Songs of the Crib), Op. 49.
❁ *** EMI Dig. CDC5 56204-2 [id.]. Bär, Deutsch (with Recital: '*Christmas Lieder*' *** ❁).

Joseph Haas was professor of composition at both Stuttgart and Munich, but his own output has been sadly neglected. These delightful strophic songs are yet another reason why Olaf Bär's collection of German Christmas Lieder is so treasurable. Their romantic melodic style also features a strong folk element, and Haas consistently favours a repeated refrain at the end of each verse. In the lovely opening *Weihnachtslegende* the 'Hosianna! Alleluja!' is very winning indeed, while the somewhat graver closing *Die Heiligen drei König* brings a charming repeated 'Eia Christkindelein, eia'. The simple spontaneity of the melody of *O puer optime!* (Sweet child in poor crib) is hardly less touching, and *Die beweglichste Musika* ('The most nimble music') speaks for itself. Marvellously warm and subtle performances from Bär and Deutsch alike, and splendidly natural recording.

Hahn, Reynaldo (1875–1947)

Piano concerto in E.
*** Hyperion Dig. CDA 66897 [id.]. Stephen Coombs, BBC Scottish SO, Ossonce – MASSENET: *Piano concerto.* ***

Entitled *Improvisation*, the opening movement of this charming work starts with a theme which surprisingly has an English flavour, easily lyrical, leading on to what in effect are a set of variations, full of sharp contrasts and sparkling piano writing. A brief, light-hearted Scherzo leads to a combined slow movement (*Reverie*) and finale (*Toccata*). One might question why a composer best known for miniatures, and above all for his songs, should at the age of 55 launch out so uncharacteristically into a major orchestral work. What Coombs's inspired performance demonstrates, most sympathetically supported by Jean-Yves Ossonce with the BBC Scottish Symphony, is that, though no deep emotions are touched, this is a thoroughly delightful piece, well worth reviving, here perfectly coupled with another concerto that is uncharacteristic of its composer, also written late in his career.

Handel, George Frideric (1685–1759)

see also in Vocal Recitals, below, under 'Codex'

Amaryllis: suite; *The Faithful shepherd:* suite; *The Gods go a-begging:* suite; *The Great elopement:* suite; *The Origin of design:* suite (all arr. Beecham).
(M) (***) Dutton mono CDAX 8018 [id.]. LPO, Sir Thomas Beecham.

Superbly transferred by Dutton, these colourful, ever-charming transcriptions come in vintage performances from the magician himself, made in his LPO days. No one will ever quite match him in bringing out the colour and sparkle of arrangements which boldly fly in the face of all that the purists tell us. As Lyndon Jenkins's admirable note says, the first of the Handel–Beecham suites appeared in 1928: *The Gods go a-begging*, designed as ballet, with movements drawn from various operas, *Alcina*, *Rodrigo*, *Admeto* and *Teseo*, and adding the *Hornpipe* from the *Concerto grosso*, Op. 6/7. After that, Beecham's purloinings are rather harder to identify, and his modifications include a burst of *Rule Britannia* on the final cadence of the *Hornpipe* in *The Great elopement*, hilariously timed. The Dutton transfers let one appreciate the extra frequency-range of the 1945 recording of *The Great elopement*. Otherwise, rather surprisingly, the earliest recordings, dating from January 1933 – *The Origin of design* and two movements from *The Gods go-abegging* – are the most sharply focused, with astonishing body and presence.

Concerto grosso in C (Alexander's Feast); Concerti a due cori Nos. 1 in B flat; 2 in F; 3 in F; Overture in D; Solomon: Arrival of the Queen of Sheba.
(M) *** Ph. 454 131-2 [id.]. ASMF, Marriner.

The *Concerti a due cori* were almost certainly written for performance with the three patriotic oratorios (No. 1 with *Joshua*, No. 2 with *Alexander Babus* and No. 3 with *Judas Maccabaeus*). They are full of good tunes (some very familiar, as they are drawn from the *Messiah*). Handel's scoring is most winning (the horn writing in both the *Second* and *Third Suites* is highly effective) and it is surprising that they are not better known and more popular. The performances here are rich-timbred and stylish, full of warmth, and one reflects how well modern instruments convey the grandeur of Handel's inspiration. This applies equally to the *Overture in D* and the better-known *Concerto grosso* associated with *Alexander's Feast*. Only perhaps in the *Arrival of the Queen of Sheba* does one feel a lighter touch would have been beneficial; Marriner's earlier, Argo recording of this piece was rather more sprightly.

Concerti grossi, Op. 3/1–6; Op. 6/1–12.
500♪ ❁ (M) *** Decca 444 532-2 (3) [id.]. ASMF, Marriner.

This integral recording of the Handel *Concerti grossi* makes a permanent memorial of the partnership formed by the inspired scholarship of Thurston Dart and the interpretative skill and musicianship of (then plain Mr) Neville Marriner and his superb ensemble, at their peak in the late 1960s; the result here very much conjures up the composer's spirit hovering in the background. The three records come at a special lower-mid-price.

Concerti grossi, Op. 3/1–6 & 4b.
(M) *(*) Teldec/Warner 0630 13574-2 [id.]. VCM, Harnoncourt.

Harnoncourt's Op. 3 includes No. 4b, which was in Handel's first edition instead of the present *No. 4 in F major* (HWV 315). With an oboe concerto thrown in, the set originally appeared uneconomically on a pair of CDs. For the reissue the seven concertos are fitted on to a single disc. Tempi on the whole are relaxed and the colouring of the baroque oboes is distinctly attractive. However, although the performances are enjoyable in their leisurely way, the string tuttis are pungently sharp-edged in that so familiar manner from the early days of period performance. Otherwise the sound is good; but this does not compete in a market crowded with excellence. The recordings were made between December 1979 and January 1981.

Concerti grossi, Op. 6/1–12.
(BB) *** Belart 461 329-2 (*Nos. 1–4*); 461 330-2 (*Nos. 5–8*); 461 331-2 (*Nos. 9–12*) (available separately). ECO, Leppard.
(B) (***) Millenium mono MCD 80078 (*Nos. 1–4*); MCD 80123 (*Nos. 5–8*); MCD 80131 (*Nos. 9–12*). E. Bar. O, Hermann Scherchen.
** DG Dig. 447 733-2 (3) [id.]. Orpheus CO.

There are splendid full-priced versions of Handel's Op. 6 – the high-water mark of Baroque orchestral music – notably the highly stimulating I Musici di Montréal under Turovsky who use modern instruments (Chandos CHAN 9004–6) or the excellent period-instrument version by Hogwood and members of the Handel and Haydn Society (O-L 436 845-2), but Leppard's 1967 Philips set is now offered on Polygram's Belart label for little more than the cost of just one of the Chandos or Oiseau-Lyre CDs. Moreover it sounds splendid in its newly remastered format, not in the least dated. The main group is comparatively full-bodied, which means that Leppard's soloists stand out in greater relief. There is grace and elegance here. These performances, too, have plenty of spirit and lively rhythmic feeling, while the richer orchestral texture brings added breadth in slow movements. With the sound newly minted, this is excellent value, though Leslie Pearson's harpsichord continuo is dwarfed by the tuttis. But how beautiful is Handel's famous melody from the very last concerto, marked *Larghetto e piano*, when played so smoothly and lyrically on modern instruments.

Recorded in September 1954, Scherchen's wonderfully warm and affectionate performances are sheer joy. He presents the music on the grandest scale, bringing out the full richness of the lyrical invention (the famous *Largo* from the last of the set is even more graciously beautiful than with Leppard). Indeed the playing of the English Baroque Orchestra (the ECO under a pseudonym perhaps?) is full of grace, while allegros, although leisurely paced, have a balancing rhythmic spring. At cadences Scherchen endearingly produces weighty rallentandos, just as if he was conducting the end of an oratorio aria. The recording is fresh and clear and, although the upper range of the violins is made characteristically thin by the microphones of the time (noticeable at the very opening of the first concerto), there is plenty of body of tone underneath and the ear immediately adjusts because of the attractive ambience. Above all, this highly successful presentation questions the practice of some period-instrument performances. That *Larghetto e piano* from No. 12 sounds so richly Handelian played like this. A set which is well worth considering, not as a first choice, but as a worthwhile back-up.

The Orpheus Chamber Orchestra's performance of Handel's Op. 6 is a disappointment. Immaculate in ensemble, with allegros crisply articulated and lyrically beautiful playing from the members of the concertino, the overall impression is warm but bland. Even the best-known, *No. 5 in D*, which Karajan did so well with larger forces, is only fitfully successful. The elegant finish of the playing in slow movements cannot be gainsaid, although the most famous slow movement of all, the *Larghetto e piano* in No. 12, is curiously lethargic. The recording is very truthful, even if the problem of contrast between solo group and ripieno is not completely resolved.

Organ concertos: Op. 4/1–6; Op. 7/1–6.
500♪ ❁ (M) *** Erato/Warner 4509 91932-2 (2) [id.]. Ton Koopman, Amsterdam Bar. O.
(B) **(*) Decca Double 452 235-2 (2) [id.]. George Malcolm (organ or harpsichord), ASMF, Marriner.

Ton Koopman's paired sets of Opp. 4 and 7 are a remarkable bargain, complete on two CDs in Erato's Duo Bonsai series. They take precedence over all the competition, both as performances and as recordings. The playing has wonderful life and warmth, tempi are always aptly judged and, although original instruments are used, this is authenticity with a kindly presence. Koopman directs the accompanying group from the keyboard, as Handel would have done, and the interplay between soloist and ripieno is a delight.

In the matter of ornamentation and interpolations Malcolm is both imaginative and stylistically impeccable. He plays two of the concertos on the harpsichord (Op. 4/3 and Op. 7/6) and here achieves a near-perfect balance so that the harpsichord is in proper scale with the orchestra without being larger than life. Malcolm's registrations (using the organ of Merton College Chapel for Op. 4, and the instrument at St John the Evangelist, Islington, for Op. 7) are always colourful (notably in Op. 4/4). The lithe, resilient orchestral textures are vigorous in allegros, but in slow movements warmly refined and often subtly shaded, and sometimes the ear craves a more robust effect. Occasionally one feels that this element of sophistication asserts itself too readily. The vintage 1972–3 (originally Argo) recording is warm and full, and this music-making is easy to enjoy.

Royal Fireworks Music; Water music: suites Nos. 1–3 (complete).
❁ *** DG Dig. 435 390-2 [id.]. Orpheus CO.

The conductorless Orpheus Chamber Orchestra are always impressive, but here their playing and ensemble are little short of superlative. It is not always simple to talk of a 'best version' in popular repertoire like this (although for a long time Marriner and his Academy were odds-on favourites), but there is no doubt that these marvellously polished and alive performances sweep the board. Although modern instruments are used, such is the Orpheus sense of baroque style, so crisp and buoyant are the rhythms, that the effect has much in common with a period performance without any of the snags. In short, this is joyously irresistible. And how warmly and elegantly they play the colourful and more intimate dances in the central *G major Suite* of the *Water music*. They begin with a riveting account of the *Royal Fireworks Music*, catching its sense of spectacle, and in the Overture the ear is struck by the solo trumpet's improvised flourish at the lead-in to the main allegro. Strings are used as Handel wished, but the wind and brass dominate, which would have pleased the King. The recording is in the demonstration bracket, and these performances are so fresh that it is like listening to this marvellous music for the very first time.

Water music: suites Nos. 1–3 (complete).
(M) *** Vanguard/Passacaille Dig. 99713 [id.]. Il Fondamento, Paul Dombrecht – TELEMANN: *Water music*. ***

Water music: suites Nos. 1–3 (complete); *Concerto grosso, Op. 3/3, HWV 314.*
(BB) *** BMG Arte Nova Dig. 74321 30498-2. L. Festival O, Ross Pople.

Il Fondamento is an excellent Belgian period-instrument group; under the lively direction of Paul Dombrecht they present Handel's *Water music* with a nice mixture of verve and elegance. The throaty reeds and robust brass ensure a vigorous response, but the more graceful numbers in the centre of the work have pleasing colour and much character. This ranks high among the 'authentic' versions and is made doubly attractive by being coupled at mid-price with Telemann's *Wassermusik*, not perhaps as inspired as Handel's but engagingly inventive and entertaining just the same.

Ross Pople's account of the *Water music* is enjoyably fresh and lively, with crisp and elegant string-playing and impressive contributions from the principal oboe and the horns. The bonus from Op. 3 is well worth having. This is strikingly more characterful than Pople's companion CD of the Boyce *Symphonies*, but the recording, though truthful and well balanced, seems a little studio bound for music originally conceived for open-air performance. Moreover it comes into competition with George Malcolm's superb version of the *Water music* on ASV's Quicksilva super-bargain label, which remains a clear first choice (CDQS 6152).

KEYBOARD MUSIC

Suites Nos. (i) *1 in A;* (ii) *2 in F; 3 in D min.;* (i) *4 in E min.;* (ii) *5 in E;* (i) *6 in F sharp min.; 7 in G min.;* (ii) *8 in F min.*

❁ (B) *** EMI forte CZS5 69337-2 (2). (i) Gavrilov; (ii) Richter.

Suites (i) *Nos. 9 in G min.;* (ii) *10 in D min.; 11 in D min.;* (i) *12 in E min.;* (ii) *13 in B flat;* (i) *14 in G;* (ii) *15 in D min.;* (i) *16 in G min.*

❁ (B) *** EMI forte CZS5 69340-2 (2). (i) Richter; (ii) Gavrilov – BEETHOVEN: *Piano sonata No. 17.* *** ❁

Piano playing doesn't come much better than this! These recordings of the Handel *Keyboard suites* were recorded by Sviatoslav Richter and Andrei Gavrilov at the Château de Marcilly-sur-Maulne during the 1979 Tours Festival, and first appeared in 1983 in a handsome five-LP box, which was treasured by anyone fortunate enough to possess it. They were never reissued as single- or double-pack LPs in the UK and perhaps did not reach as wide a public as they might otherwise have done. They have been slow to reach CD, but EMI have made amends by issuing the set in first-class transfers, and in an economical format – two twin-CDs packaged as one, available separately, and competitively priced – and with Richter's famous 1961 account of Beethoven's *D minor Sonata*, Op. 31, No. 2, thrown in for good measure. There is no need to waste words on the playing, which is balm to the soul. The serenity and tranquillity of the slow movements and the radiance of the faster movements have never before been so fully realized. Not to be missed.

Suite No. 5 in E (includes *The Harmonious blacksmith*).

(B) *** Decca Eclipse Dig. 448 992-2; *448 992-4* [id.]. Alicia de Larrocha, VSO, Uri Segal – MOZART: *Piano concertos Nos. 19 & 22.* ***

Alicia de Larrocha's performance was recorded in the Henry Wood Hall; she gives a robust and vital account of the best-known of Handel's *Suites*, with its famous variations, and again fully justifies the use of the piano for this repertoire. Her performance may not banish memories of Richter (his Touraine performance is now available on an EMI forte reissue) but it is thoroughly enjoyable in its own right. There is plenty of warmth, and the recording is splendidly realistic. This makes a splendid bonus for an outstanding bargain Mozart coupling.

VOCAL MUSIC

Acis and Galatea (complete; arr. Mozart in German).

(M) *** DG Dig. 447 700-2 (2) [id.]. MacDougall, Bonney, Schaefer, Tomlinson, E. Concert Ch. & O, Pinnock.

It may seem perverse for three English-speaking principals to choose to do *Acis and Galatea* in German, but Mozart's arrangement with added woodwind has its own interest, a parallel text to the more radical one he prepared of *Messiah*. Pinnock's performance, well recorded, is as persuasive as one could imagine, with Barbara Bonney an enchanting Galatea and John Tomlinson a characterful Polyphem, clear and precise. Jamie MacDougall as Acis sounds a little gusty at times but makes an attractively ardent hero.

(i) *Apollo e Daphne* (cantata); (ii) *Oboe concerto in G min.*

(B) *** HM Musique d'Abord HMA 1905157 [id.]. (i) Judith Nelson, David Thomas; (ii) Haynes; San Francisco Bar. O; McGegan.

Apollo e Daphne is one of Handel's most delightful cantatas and tells how the determinedly chaste heroine, after an unwelcome and persistent pursuit by her godly suitor, finally escapes a fate worse than death by being transformed into a laurel bush! It has two strikingly memorable numbers, a lovely siciliano for Dafne with oboe obbligato and an aria for Apollo, *Come rosa in su la spina*, with unison violins and a solo cello. Both soloists are first rate, and Nicholas McGegan is a lively Handelian, though the playing of the orchestra could be more polished. The sound is over-resonant but has plenty of atmosphere. For the bargain-priced reissue (retaining the full documentation plus translation) a neat account of Handel's *G minor Oboe concerto* has been added.

Israel in Egypt (oratorio; with *The Lamentations of the Israelites for the Death of Joseph*).
(M) **(*) Virgin/Veritas Dig. VMD5 61350-2 (2) [CDCB 54019]. Argenta, Van Evera, Wilson, Rolfe Johnson, Thomas, White, Taverner Ch. & Players, Parrott.

Parrott directs a clean-cut, well-paced reading which wears its period manners easily. This may lack the distinctive insights of Gardiner's more sharply rhythmic version (Erato 2292 45399-2 – see our main volume) which with modern instruments adopts a similar scale; but with excellent choral and solo singing the performance is unlikely to offend anyone. Good, warm sound. Parrott follows the unique precedent of Handel's very first performance in using as the first part of the oratorio the cantata written on the death of Queen Caroline, *The Lamentations of the Israelites for the Death of Joseph*, with text duly adapted.

Jephtha (oratorio; complete).
(M) ** Teldec/Warner 0630 17426-2 (3) [id.]. Hollweg, Gale, Linos, Esswood, Thomaschke, Mozart Boys' Ch., Arnold Schoenberg Ch., VCM, Harnoncourt.

Harnoncourt's pursuit of extra authenticity, with an orchestra using original instruments, has its snags, and not just in the thin timbre of the strings. Harnoncourt takes a more operatic view of the work than Marriner on the rival version which appeared simultaneously, but he mars the impact of that by too frequently adopting a mannered style of phrasing. The soloists too are on balance far less impressive than those on the Marriner version. The recording acoustic, typically clean, is not helpful in its dryness. With a very full text this makes a long haul, and Gardiner's recording, made live at the 1988 Göttingen Festival, is altogether more exhilarating. His cast, too, is exceptionally fine (Ph. 422 351-2 – see our main volume).

Messiah (complete).
500♪ *** DG Dig. 423 630-2 (2). Augér, Von Otter, Chance, Crook, Tomlinson, E. Concert Ch., E. Concert, Pinnock.
(M) ** Virgin Veritas/EMI VMD5 61330-2 (2) [CDCB 49801]. Kirkby, Emily van Evera, Cable, Bowman, Cornwell, Thomas, Taverner Ch. & Players, Parrott.

Pinnock presents a performance using authentically scaled forces which, without inflation, rise to grandeur and magnificence, qualities Handel himself would have relished. Arleen Augér's range of tone and dynamic is daringly wide, with radiant purity in *I know that my Redeemer liveth*. Anne Sofie von Otter sustains *He was despised* superbly with her firm, steady voice. With full, atmospheric and well-balanced recording, this is a set not to be missed, even by those who already have a favourite version of *Messiah*.

Parrott for EMI has assembled a fine team of performers, as well as his own Taverner Choir and Players. Emma Kirkby is even more responsive here than she was in her earlier recording, for Oiseau-Lyre; but, for all its great merits, the performance lacks the zest and the sense of live communication that mark out a version like Pinnock's, another period performance which also dares to adopt slow, expressive speeds for such arias as *He was despised* and *I know that my Redeemer liveth*. Even at mid-price this is not a strong contender and at full-price Pinnock reigns supreme.

Messiah (slightly abridged).
❁ (B) (***) Dutton Lab. mono 2CDEA 5010 (2) [id.]. Isobel Baillie, Gladys Ripley, James Johnson, Norman Walker, Huddersfield Ch. Soc., Liverpool PO, Malcolm Sargent.

Sargent's first recording of Handel's *Messiah* is not complete. Following his usual performance practice, three numbers are cut from Part II and four from Part III. The recording venue was Huddersfield Town Hall in 1946, when that great Choral Society was still at its peak, and Handel's masterpiece is here brought vividly to life by the most miraculous Dutton Lab. 78-r.p.m. transfer yet. What is so involving is the way this remarkably realistic and present recording (in many ways more vivid than the later stereo set), made in a series of four-minute takes, comes over as an ongoing 'live' performance, from the rich tapestry of the Overture onwards. There must be all sorts of strictures about the style of the performance, not least the slow tempi (especially in Part II) and the orchestration (Sargent uses Prout's edition, plus additions from Mozart's version) and of course its sheer weight and scale – Sargent believed there could never be too many voices. But the chorus sings throughout with enormous conviction and the four fine soloists obviously live their parts; moreover their enunciation is a model and every word is clear. Undoubtedly the star of the performance is Isobel Baillie. Her first entry in *There were shepherds* is a moment of the utmost magic, and what follows is utterly ravishing, while her gloriously beautiful *I know that my Redeemer liveth* has never been surpassed on record. Gladys Ripley sings *He was despised* with moving simplicity and restraint, and she warmly introduces *He shall feed his flock*, sharing it with Baillie, who re-enters exquisitely, like the sun suddenly shining through clouds. Her tonal purity is phenomenal, and it is caught by the current transfer with complete faithfulness. Sargent's tempi for the choruses now sound slow, notably *For unto us a Child is born*, and of course the very grand *Hallelujah*, which is very spacious indeed. But Sargent believes deeply in the music and he carries the listener with him in an ongoing inspired flow. The sound itself is truly astounding! At bargain price this is an essential investment for anyone who loves the English amateur choral tradition.

Messiah (orch. Sir Eugene Goossens): highlights.
(M) *** RCA 09026 68159-2 [id.]. Jennifer Vyvyan, Monica Sinclair, Jon Vickers, Giorgio Tozzi, RPO Ch. & O, Beecham.

Not everyone will want Beecham's complete *Messiah* with its flamboyant orchestration by Sir Eugene Goossens, but many will be intrigued enough to have a sampler; this remastered CD admirably fills the need with 19 key items offered, including the *Overture* and *Pastoral Symphony*. The use of the cymbals to cap the choruses, *For unto us a child is born* and *Glory to God*, is unforgettable. Beecham's tempi are slower (though not for *Hallelujah*!) than we expect today but, given his expansive view of Handel, they are convincingly appropriate. The soloists are excellent and so is the choral singing.

La Resurrezione.
(B) *** HM Musique d'Abord HMA 1907027/8 [id.]. Saffer, George, Nelson, Spence, Thomas, Phil. Bar. O, Nicholas McGegan.

In 1708, halfway through his four-year stay in Italy, the young Handel wrote this refreshingly dramatic oratorio. With opera as such prohibited in Rome, it served as a kind of substitute, not solemn at all, but with dramatic and moving exchanges between the central characters. There is no chorus until the close, but Handel makes up for this with a wonderful palette of orchestra colour in his accompaniments, liberally featuring trumpets, recorders and oboes. McGegan's performance is as lively as one could wish and is excellently cast. Lisa Saffer is an appealing Angel, nimble (in breathtakingly florid coloratura) and touching, especially good in her dialogues with the boldly resonant Lucifer (Michael George). But Judith Nelson is equally affecting as Mary Magdelene, whereas Patricia Spence's dark contralto (as Cleophas) and Jeffrey Thomas's fresh tenor St John bring plenty of dramatic contrast. The sounds from the period instruments of the Philharmonia Baroque Orchestra are ear-tickling, and presumably the soloists join together for the life-assertive closing chorus. Excellent recording, both atmospheric and vivid, makes for a fine bargain alternative to Hogwood (Oiseau-Lyre 421 132-2).

Solomon.
500♪ ❁ *** Ph. Dig. 412 612-2 (2) [id]. C. Watkinson, Argenta, Hendricks, Rolfe Johnson, Monteverdi Ch., E. Bar. Soloists, Gardiner.

This is among the very finest of all Handel oratorio recordings. With panache, Gardiner shows how authentic-sized forces can convey Handelian grandeur even with clean-focused textures and fast speeds. The overriding glory of the set is the radiant singing of Gardiner's Monteverdi Choir. Its clean, crisp articulation matches the brilliant playing of the English Baroque Soloists, and the sound is superb, coping thrillingly with the problems of the double choruses.

Utrecht Te Deum, HWV 278.
(M) *(*) Teldec/Warner Dig. 0630 13573-2 [id.]. Palmer, Lipovšek, Langridge, Equiluz, Moser, Baumann, Arnold Schönberg Ch., VCM, Harnoncourt – BACH: *Magnificat*. *

Handel's magnificent *Utrecht Te Deum* makes a generous coupling for Bach's *Magnificat*, and in a relatively intimate acoustic Harnoncourt sometimes presents allegros briskly and lightly – but, as in the *Magnificat*, that is the exception. The characterful solo singing – the murky-sounding contralto apart – marries oddly with slow, heavy speeds and leaden rhythms, and the chorus, efficient enough, lacks brightness and rhythmic spring. Dryish recording. Simon Preston's Oiseau-Lyre Christchurch version (443 178-2) is the one to go for, or, at mid-price, the reissued Geraint Jones account (DG 453 167-2) – see under 'Codex' in the Vocal Recitals section, below.

OPERA

Agrippina (complete).
*** Ph. Dig. 438 009-2 (3) [id.]. Della Jones, Miles, Lee Ragin, Donna Brown, Chance, Von Otter, Mosley, E. Bar. Soloists, Gardiner.

Agrippina was the second and last of the operas that Handel wrote during his stay in Italy between 1706 and 1710. His libretto was specially written for him by Cardinal Vincenzo Grimani, using historical characters from the time of the Emperor Claudius, in which the immoral goings-on in the court are treated with a lightness and vein of irony that marked operas in the previous century by Monteverdi and Cavalli. Handel responded with a delightful work in which the characters are colourfully drawn, not least Agrippina, the Emperor's scheming wife, here superbly taken by Della Jones, strong and characterful, bringing out the necessary fire and sparkle.

This Gardiner recording, belatedly issued in 1997, some five years after it was completed, comes into direct rivalry with the fine Harmonia Mundi version of 1991 under Nicholas McGegan, fresh and immediate with a generally youthful cast. Not just Della Jones, but most of the other principals are a degree more characterful than their opposite numbers – Derek Lee Ragin as Nero (a counter-tenor clearly preferable to McGegan's soprano), Alastair Miles as the Emperor and Michael Chance as Ottone among them. The Philips sound is warmer and more spacious, with the period instruments sounding sweeter and less abrasive. Gardiner also has an extra ballet movement at the very end after the goddess Juno's epilogue aria, superbly sung here by Anne Sofie von Otter.

Orlando (complete).

*** Erato/Warner Dig. 0630 14636-2 (3) [id.]. Bardon, Mannion, Summers, Joshua, Van der Kamp, Les Arts Florissants, Christie.

William Christie's Erato recording of *Orlando* makes a valuable alternative to the outstanding version, recorded earlier by Christopher Hogwood for Oiseau-Lyre (430 845-2). The most obvious difference is that where Hogwood has a male alto singing the title-role, Christie here opts for a fine mezzo, Patricia Bardon. Her approach is more overtly dramatic than James Bowman's for Hogwood, with moods and passions more positively characterized. The celebrated Mad scene ending Act II illustrates the point perfectly, with Christie and Bardon more violent, using bigger contrasts, ending in a scurrying *accelerando*, whereas the Bowman/Hogwood approach keeps some classical restraint to the end, pointing the drama of the moment in thunder effects. The Erato recording is warm and full, but is not as transparent or well separated as the earlier one, with Christie often opting for marginally broader speeds. The other soloists in the new version are all excellent, readily matching their rivals, not least the contralto, Hilary Summers, as Prince Medoro.

Riccardo Primo (Richard the Lionheart).

*** O-L Dig. 452 601-2 (3) [id.]. Mingardo, Piau, Lallouette, Scaltriti, Brua, Bertin, Les Talens Lyriques, Christophe Rousset.

Recorded in the Abbaye Royale de Fontevrault, where Richard the Lionheart is buried, Christophe Rousset conducts a lively, well-characterized performance of one of the rarest of Handel operas. It was the last but two of the 13 operas which Handel wrote for the Royal Academy of Music in London, and one which aimed to cater for the rival claims of the two leading prima donnas of the day, Francesca Cuzzoni and Faustina Bordoni, as well as for the leading castrato, Senesino. It is one of the most elaborately scored of Handel's operas, even using a sopranino recorder for a delightful bird aria in Act III, for the princess of Navarre, Costanza, Richard's betrothed, Cuzzoni's role. It is a long opera, and you have to wait until Act III for many of the jewels in the score, which then round the piece off with great flair and intensity.

Vocally, the principal glory of this recorded performance is the singing of Sara Mingardo in the title-role, gloriously firm and true. The richness of the sound never gets in the way of flexibility, so that such a showpiece as Richard's Act III aria, *All'orror delle procelle*, has one readily registering what must have been the impact of Senesino in the first performances. In quite a different mood, the duet between Richard and Costanza which ends Act II is enchanting in its poetry, later adapted for Handel's last oratorio, *Jephtha*. Sandrine Piau as Costanza is tenderly expressive, even though (as recorded) the voice, sweet in tone, is yet not perfectly even; and Claire Brua in the Bordoni role of Pulcheria tends to be too gusty to enunciate elaborate divisions clearly. Nevertheless the contrast between the rival ladies is well established. The counter-tenor, Pascal Bertin, is excellent as Oronte, and the two baritone roles are well taken by Roberto Scaltriti (aptly villainous-sounding) and Olivier Lallouette. First-rate, well-balanced sound.

Rinaldo (complete).

(M) *** Sony SM3K 34592 (3) [id.]. Carolyn Watkinson, Cotrubas, Scovotti, Esswood, Brett, Cold, La Grande Ecurie et la Chambre du Roy, Malgoire.

The vigour of Malgoire's direction of an opera which plainly for him is very much alive, no museum piece, makes this a very attractive set, with the one caveat that it has been reissued without a translation (the full libretto is in Italian only). However, this remains an inviting example of period-performance style. The elaborate decorations on *da capo* arias are imaginatively done, but most effectively the famous *Cara sposa* is left without ornamentation, beautifully sung by the contralto Rinaldo, Carolyn Watkinson. The finest singing comes from Ileana Cotrubas, but under Malgoire the whole team is convincing. The bright but spacious recording adds to the projection and liveliness, and the magic sounds associated with the sorceress, Armida, such as the arrival of her airborne chariot, are well conveyed, and throughout Handel's invention is a delight. Well worth having, but it is a pity about the libretto.

Serse (*Xerxes;* complete).
(M) **(*) Sony SM3K 36941 (3) [id.]. Carolyn Watkinson, Esswood, Wenkel, Hendricks, Rodde, Cold, Bridier Vocal Ens., La Grand Ecurie et la Chambre du Roy, Malgoire.

Malgoire's vigorous, often abrasive style in baroque music makes for a lively, convincing performance of one of Handel's richest operas, helped by a fine complement of soloists. Carolyn Watkinson may not be the most characterful of singers in the high castrato role of Xerxes himself, but it is good to have the elaborate roulades so accurately sung. The celebrated *Ombra mai fù* is most beautiful. Paul Esswood is similarly reliable in the role of Arsamene (originally taken by a woman) and the counter-tenor tone is pure and true. Barbara Hendricks and Anne-Marie Rodde are both outstanding in smaller roles, and the comic episodes (most unexpected in Handel) are excellently done, Malgoire's generally heavy rhythmic pulse here paying dividends. There are detailed stylistic points one might criticize in his rendering (for instance the squeeze effects on sustained string notes) but the vitality of the performance is never in doubt, and the somewhat close recording is vivid too. As in the rest of this series of Sony reissues, the snag is the absence of an English translation.

Tamerlano (complete).
(M) **(*) Sony Dig. SM3K 37893-2 (3) [id.]. Ledroit, Elwes, Van der Sluis, Jacobs, Poulenard, Reinhart, La Grande Ecurie et la Chambre du Roy, Malgoire.

Tamerlano is one of Handel's most masterly operas and, though Malgoire's performance is not ideal, this mid-priced reissue from the early 1980s fills an important gap. His style here is less abrasive than it has been on some other opera sets, but one looks in vain for an element of elegance or charm, despite consistently excellent contributions from a good band of soloists, with the two counter-tenors well contrasted – René Jacobs as ever a tower of strength – and with Mieke van der Sluis outstanding among the women. A warning ought to be given that this piece is slow in getting off the ground, although the continuing interchanges in Act I featuring Andronico are splendidly sung, as is his closing aria, *Chi vide mai . . . Benché mi sprezzi*. The music becomes increasingly impressive over Acts II and III, with more ensembles than Handel customarily included. Some arias have been cut, but one has been added in Act I (*Nel mondo e nell abisso*), well sung by the bass, Gregory Reinhardt. Good, clear, but not too dry sound gives a comparatively intimate effect, and the CD transfer is first class. The snag is that, like the other reissues in this series, the full Italian libretto includes no translation.

Arias: (i) *Agrippina: Pur ritorno a rimimiravi. Alexander's Feast: Revenge, Timotheus cries. Belshazzar: Oh, memory still bitter to my soul . . . Oppress'd with never-ceasing grief. Berenice: Si, tra i ceppi.* (ii) *Giulio Cesare: Va tacito e nascosto; Dall'ondoso periglio; Aure, deh per pietà.* (i) *Ottone: Con gelosi sospetti? . . . Dopo l'orrore. Samson: Honour and arms. Saul: To him ten thousands! . . . With rage I shall burst. Serse: Frondi tenere e belle? . . . Ombra mai fù. Solomon: Prais'd be the Lord . . . When the sun o'er yonder hills. Susanna: Down my old cheeks . . . Peace, crown'd with roses.*
(M) **(*) 449 551-2 [id.]. Dietrich Fischer-Dieskau; Munich Bach O; (i) Stadlmair; (ii) Karl Richter.

Opening with an arresting performance of *Revenge, Timotheus cries* from *Alexander's Feast*, this 1977 collection nevertheless emphasizes the lyricism of these excerpts rather than the drama. Fischer-Dieskau is at his finest in the excerpt from *Serse* with its beautifully controlled opening single-note crescendo, which is none other than our old friend, Handel's '*Largo*'. The voice is forwardly balanced and most naturally caught; although the orchestra within the resonant acoustic is quite vividly caught, the modern-instrument textures are full rather than clearly detailed, especially the two *Giulio Cesare* items now added, which were recorded much earlier (in 1969).

Hanson, Howard (1896–1981)

(i) *Piano concerto, Op. 36. For the first time (suite); Merry Mount suite; Mosaics* (with composer's spoken analyses of all three orchestral works, concerning orchestral colour, pitch spectrum, musical form, and 'tone relationships').
(M) *** Mercury 434 370-2 (2) [id.]. Eastman-Rochester O or Philh. O, composer (cond. & narrator); (i) with Alfred Mouledous.

Mercury not only pioneered many of Hanson's major works on record, with the composer conducting the Eastman-Rochester Orchestra, but also invited him to talk about his music. The three orchestral works here seem ideal for the purpose and his 'guide to the instruments of the orchestra' (directly related to the scoring of the *Merry Mount suite*) is particularly instructive, the more so as the microphones have been set up to project solo instruments and groupings of woodwind, brass and strings with extraordinary realism and presence. Elsewhere Hanson discusses orchestral colour (in relation to visual colour) and musical construction in connection with his atmospheric and vividly contrasted set of variations which he calls *Mosaics* (inspired by the mosaics in Palermo Cathedral). More controversially, he expounds on 'tone relationships' as explored in his book, *The Harmonic Materials of Modern Music*. Apparently his work method was to choose a predetermined series of notes for a given composition, rather like a tone row, but which he thinks of as circular, as it is within the normal tonal system. This thesis is related to *For the first time*, in essence a dozen impressionistic vignettes, evoking a day in the life of a (somewhat precocious) child. He wakes to the sound of *Bells*, watches a pair of Irish puppies at play, explores a *Deserted house*, comes across an *Eccentric clock*, meets a group of *Clowns* on their way to the circus, enjoys his mother reading to him the tale of *Kikimora*, watches a *Fireworks* spectacle and so on, then ends his day in the world of *Dreams*. Hanson's invention is fresh and evocative, his scoring felicitous, so all this music is made to serve a double purpose. The four-movement *Piano concerto* is brilliantly played by Alfred Mouledous, especially in the Scherzo, marked *Allegro molto ritmico* (though they are not jazzy rhythms) and the *giocoso* finale, while the slow movement is eloquently expressive. The recordings here were made between 1957 and 1965 (the *Concerto*) and are characteristically vivid, though occasionally very bright on top.

Symphonies Nos. 1 in E min. (Nordic); 2 (Romantic); Elegy in memory of Serge Koussevitzky.
500♪ *** Delos Dig. D/CD 3073 [id.]. Seattle SO, Gerard Schwarz.

Hanson was of Swedish descent and his music has a strong individuality of idiom and colour. The *Second Symphony* is warmly appealing and melodically memorable with an indelible theme which permeates the structure. These Seattle performances have plenty of breadth and ardour, and Schwarz's feeling for the ebb and flow of the musical paragraphs is very satisfying. The recording, made in Seattle Opera House, is gloriously expansive and the balance is convincingly natural.

Symphony No. 3.
(***) Biddulph mono WHL 044 [id.]. Boston SO, Koussevitzky (with MUSSORGSKY: *Khovanshchina: Prelude*. LIADOV: *The enchanted lake*. RIMSKY-KORSAKOV: *Legend of the invisible city of Kitezh: Entr'acte. Dubinushka*. FAURE: *Pelléas et Mélisande: Prélude; la Fileuse; Mort de Mélisande* (**(*)).

(i) *Symphonies Nos. 3; 6;* (ii) *Fantasy-variations on a theme of youth.*
*** Delos Dig. DE 3092 [id.]. (i) Seattle SO; (ii) Carol Rosenberger, NY Chamber Symphony; (i–ii) Schwarz.

The composer himself directed the first public performance of the *Third* in Boston in 1930, and Koussevitzky later performed it a number of times, before making this recording in 1940. Sibelius's influence is obvious, but the construction and Nordic atmosphere are the composer's own, and so too is the rich stream of lyrical melody. Indeed the *Andante tranquillo* brings one of the composer's most memorable themes which returns to provide an apotheosis for the finale. Koussevitzky's reading is powerfully committed, immediately establishing the northern atmosphere of Hanson's sound-world and building the finale steadily to its final climax with gripping concentration. The Boston musicians respond passionately. The Biddulph transfer is very good and any sonic inadequacies are soon overlooked when the music-making is so compulsive. The other pieces, which come before the symphony, are all played superbly, but the sound is more variable. Highlights include the Mussorgsky *Khovanshchina Prelude*, sombrely paced, and the Liadov *Enchanted lake*, both highly evocative and the latter remarkably full and atmospheric. The excerpts from Fauré's *Pelléas et Mélisande* are delicately done, although here climaxes are less refined.

Hanson's spacious symphonic textures call out for stereo, and those seeking a first-class modern recording of the *Third* can turn readily to Schwarz, who has the fullest understanding of this richly lyrical score with its dark undertones. His players are obviously moved by the music's ardour and its Nordic grandeur, especially in the slow movement and finale, which make a profound impact when the Delos sound is so resonantly expansive. The single-movement *Sixth Symphony*, in six continuing sections with a characteristic pervading leitmotiv, was dedicated to Bernstein. It too has a passionate Adagio and Schwarz's performance is hardly less successful. The *Variations* make a suitable bonus, as their mood is often somewhat disconsolate. Carol Rosenberger proves a most sensitive and responsive soloist.

Harris, Roy (1897–1979)

Symphony No. 3.

* Chandos Dig. CHAN 9474 [id.]. Detroit SO, Järvi – COPLAND: *Symphony No. 3.* *(*)

Roy Harris's *Third* is surely the greatest American symphony, its only serious rivals being Piston's *Fourth* and William Schuman's *Third*. Unfortunately, Neeme Järvi's account with the Detroit Symphony Orchestra does not begin to do it justice. There is none of the power or the conviction that Koussevitzky and Bernstein brought to it. The Copland, with which it is coupled, is marginally better but still underpowered. Despite good Chandos recording neither is really recommendable.

Harvey, Richard (born 1953)

Concerto antico (for guitar and small orchestra).

❀ *** Sony Dig. SK 68337 [id.]. John Williams, LSO, Paul Daniel – GRAY: *Concerto.* *** ❀

Richard Harvey's highly atmospheric *Concerto antico* flows over with colour and attractive invention, and it brings a melodic spontaneity which warms the heart and furthers one's hopes for the future of twentieth-century music, written traditionally and seeking a direct, universal appeal. It is easily the best concerto for the guitar since the work by Malcolm Arnold of several decades earlier, admirably written for the soloist and most imaginatively scored in the orchestra. As much a five-movement suite as a concerto, the piece uses old song- and dance-forms, but the composer's ideas are his own – and very tuneful they are, with an element of pastiche in their settings, yet nicely spiced with modern harmonic touches. The first-movement *Alborada* opens at dawn with bells, but it soon bubbles along irresistibly; its minimalist element is expansive rather than simply repetitive. The hauntingly beautiful *Cantilena* slow movement (ten minutes long) gives the piece real substance. Elsewhere the dance-forms often have a rustic, Elizabethan flavour, and the fourth-movement *Forlana* asks the soloist to simulate a lute within a heady melodic cocktail, piquantly exchanging 7/8 and 4/4 rhythms. The brilliant *Lavolta* finale opens with Stravinskian syncopated accents and then introduces a most winning lyricism that alternates lusciously with the rushing *con fuoco* forward momentum. In every way this is a masterly work, and it is played superbly by its commissioner and dedicatee, John Williams, splendidly accompanied by the LSO under Paul Daniel. The recording is in the demonstration bracket and is ideally balanced.

Haydn, Josef (1732–1809)

Cassation in D for 4 horns, violin, viola & bass, Hob Deest; Horn concerto No. 1 in D, Hob VII/d3; Divertimenti: in E flat for 2 horns & string quartet, Hob II/21; in D for 2 horns & string quartet, Hob II/22; in E flat for horn, violin & cello, Hob IV/5.

**(*) Sony Dig. SK 68253 [id.]. Abe Koster, soloists, L'Archibudelli.

After Abe Koster demonstrated his prowess so effectively in the Mozart *Horn concertos*, this collection is something of a disappointment. For one thing, apart from the concerto, the music – in spite of H. C. Robbins Landon's enthusiastic advocacy in the accompanying notes – is far from top-quality Haydn; both the *Divertimenti*, Hob II/21–2, are pre-Esterházy. The performances are very robust, and in at least one instance the horn players are content to play their upper-harmonics with bad tuning rather than lip them (or hand-stop them) into a more exact pitch. Abe Koster manages the high tessitura of the *Concerto* as confidently as those in the basement, and he even manages to play every note of the very difficult solo line of the trio which Haydn called his '*Divertimenti a tre*', Hob IV/5. The horn part immediately travels right up into the stratosphere and the listener is very aware of the continual technical challenge. The result resembles a musical obstacle race for the soloist, with the string players tagging along in the background.

Horn concerto No. 1 in D, Hob. VII/d3.

(M) **(*) Teldec/Warner 0630 12324-2 [id.]. Hermann Baumann, Concerto Amsterdam, Jaap Schröder – DANZI: *Horn concerto in E;* ROSETTI: *Horn concerto in D min.* **(*)

Baumann's 1969 account has crisp, clean, classical lines, emphasized by the rather dry sound of the remastered recording, which gives a bold, open horn-timbre and unexpansive string-timbre. The *Adagio* is rather sombre here (it has some splendidly resonating low notes from the soloist), but the finale is spirited enough.

(i) *Horn concerto No. 2 in D, Hob VII/d4;* (ii) *Oboe concerto in C;* (iii) *Trumpet concerto in E flat.*
(B) ** Carlton Turnabout 30371 00322. Pro Musica O, Reinhardt, with (i) Karl Arnold; (ii) Friedrich Milde; (iii) Walter Gleisle.

The soloists here are uneven but, in a well-planned collection, two of the three performances can be recommended. Friedrich Milde is an excellent oboe player; he has an agreeable tone and assured technique. His phrasing is no less a source of pleasure, especially in the minuet finale, where the solo arabesques around the charming main theme are shaped so stylishly. Gleisle too plays impressively, with bold tone and flexible technique. This is a forthright account of the *Trumpet concerto* but one with plenty of character. The hornist, Karl Arnold, is a much less effective soloist, and he fails to bring the *D major Horn concerto* fully to life. Reinhardt's accompaniments are of a good standard and the recordings are acceptable, although the upper strings have the characteristic Turnabout thinness through being balanced rather too closely.

(i) *Lira concertos Nos. 1 in C, Hob VIIh/1; 3 in G, Hob VIIh/3; 5 in F, Hob VIIh/5.* (ii) *Cassation for lute, violin & cello in C, Hob III/6.*
(B) *** Carlton Turnabout 30371 00312. (i) Hugo Ruf, Chamber Ens. (Susanne Lautenbacher, Ruth Nielen, Franz Beyer, Heinz Berndt, Oswald Uhl, Johannes Koch, Wolfgang Hoffman, Helmuth Irmscher); (ii) Michael Schaffer, Eva Nagora, Thomas Blees.

Haydn's *Lira concertos*, commissioned by King Ferdinand IV of Naples, were written for a curious, obsolete instrument (the 'Lyra Viol') which was a cross between a hurdy-gurdy and a mechanical violoncello. How the problems of intonation were solved – for the pitch of the string notes was achieved mechanically – is difficult to imagine, but the instrument was a favourite of its time. The music Haydn composed for it (or, rather, for two of them, for they were played in duet with a chamber group) is most attractive and is worth reviving. Turnabout employ a modern electronic 'lira' constructed by Johannes Koch. This enables one musician to play both the duet parts (for originally each player had also to turn a handle with one hand in order to work the mechanism). The sound is piquant. It would appear that the drone-like string notes, which were a feature of the original instrument, are played by the orchestra, so that the listener has the best of both worlds. This collection is very entertaining – taken one concerto at a time – not least because the orchestral tuttis are so alive and the recording so expertly balanced. Listeners will be surprised to hear that the second movement of the *Third Concerto* is almost identical with the slow movement of the *Military Symphony*. The *Cassation* is Haydn's own arrangement of his *C major String quartet*, Op. 1/6, which has an appealing central *Adagio*. It makes a neat encore for a very recommendable disc and brings the playing time up to 70 minutes.

Piano concertos in G, Hob XVIII/4; F, Hob XVIII/7; D, Hob XVIII/11.
*** Virgin/EMI Dig. VC5 45196-2 [id.]. Mikhail Pletnev, Deutsche Kammerphilharmonie.

The keyboard concertos are by general consent not the greatest Haydn and, of the three recorded here, one is of doubtful authenticity: the *F major* (XVIII/7 in the Hoboken catalogue) is probably by Wagenseil; and not very much is known about the *G major*, which is very early. In both pieces, as well as in the well-known *D major Concerto*, Mikhail Pletnev offers playing of tremendous character and personality. He is not frightened of being anachronistic, as in the cadenza of the *G major*, yet nor is he out to draw attention to himself. He obviously enjoys a splendid rapport with the Deutsche Kammerphilharmonie, with whom he has recently recorded some Mozart concertos. The sound recording is very alive and present without bringing the players too close, and the colour and feeling Pletnev discovers in these pieces is a source of wonder. This playing is both distinctive and distinguished, and must be a first recommendation in this repertoire.

(i) *Piano concerto in D, Hob XVIII/11;* (ii) *Violin concertos: in C; in G; Hob VIIa/1 & 4;* (ii–iii) *Double concerto for violin and harpsichord in F, Hob XVIII/6.*
*** Sup. Dig. SU 3265-2 [id.]. (i) Bella Davidovich; (ii) Dmitry Sitkovetsky; (iii) Václav Hudeček; Prague CO, Sitkovetsky.

Here is the most winning of Haydn's solo keyboard concertos together with two of the violin concertos, including the *C major* with its engaging, serenade-like, cantabile slow movement. They are impeccably played, with just the right degree of expressive feeling. The piano used by Davidovich has a crisp, clean timbre, rather like a fortepiano, only with more colour, and it suits the dancing outer movements of the *D major* keyboard work quite admirably. But what clinches the appeal of this attractive collection is the delightful account of the *Double concerto*. Here the interplay of piano and violin in Haydn's shared cadenza at the end of the first movement, and in the fine *Largo* with its walking bass followed by solo entries over pizzicatos, is quite perfectly balanced. Indeed this disc makes a splendid case for the use of modern instruments in this repertoire when Sitkovetsky directs the accompanying group so stylishly, and the overall effect is pleasingly intimate, yet also has the most realistic projection.

Trumpet concerto in E flat.

500♪ ❁ *** Ph. Dig. 420 203-2 [id.]. Håkan Hardenberger, ASMF, Marriner – HERTEL ***; HUMMEL *** ❁; STAMITZ: *Concertos.* ***

Hardenberger's playing of the noble line of the *Andante* is no less telling than his fireworks in the finale and, with Marriner providing warm, elegant and polished accompaniments throughout, this is probably the finest single collection of trumpet concertos in the present catalogue.

Violin concertos Nos. 1 in C; 4 in G, Hob VIIa/1 & 4; (i) *Sinfonia concertante in B flat for violin, cello, oboe, bassoon & orchestra, Hob I/105.*

*** Virgin/Veritas EMI Dig. VER5 61301-2. Elizabeth Wallfisch, O of Age of Enlightenment; (i) with Watkin, Robson, Warnock.

Haydn's *Violin concertos* are early works; the *C major* with its winding, serenade-like melody is probably the finer, but the *G major* too has an eloquent *Adagio* and a bustling finale. Wallfisch leads the Orchestra of the Age of Enlightenment from her bow and proves a highly sensitive soloist – these performances are if anything even more impressive than those of the Mozart concertos by the same soloist. Her serenely reflective account of the *Adagio molto* of the *C major* is memorable: the timbre is sweet yet the playing is stylish and perfectly in period. In the *Sinfonia concertante* the smiling interplay of the various wind and string soloists has never been bettered on record and the use of period instruments brings a pleasing intimacy and plenty of spirit. If you want these three works, this is the coupling to go for, and the recording is truthfully balanced and vivid.

Symphonies Nos. 1 – 104; Symphonies A; B. Alternative versions: *Symphony Nos. 22 in E flat (Philosopher),* 2nd version. *Symphony No. 63 in C (La Roxelane),* 1st version. *Symphony No. 53 (L'Impériale):* 3 alternative Finales: (i) *A (Capriccio)*; (ii) *C* (Paris version, attrib. Haydn); *D: Overture in D* (Milanese version). *Symphony No. 103:* Finale (alternative ending). (i) *Sinfonia concertante in B flat for oboe, bassoon, violin and cello.*

500♪ ❁ (B) *** Decca 448 531-2 (33) [id.]. Philh. Hungarica, Antal Dorati; (i) with István Engl, László Baranyai, Igor Ozim, Zóltán Rácz.

An apology is due to our readers concerning this unique recording of the complete Haydn symphonies which was announced by Decca just as we were finalizing the proofs of our 1996 main *Guide*. It was felt that the set was so important that it was vital to include it; we were able to sample the sound of the *Paris Symphonies* (issued separately) and we were assured that the contents were as listed on page 569 of our 1996 edition. In the event, the Editor's overriding dictum, 'Never include a reissue unless you have held it in your hands, studied the new documentation closely and sampled the recorded sound in depth', once again proved itself the only sensible procedure. Everything we said about the records was true – except the list of contents, which proved totally inadequate!

Dorati was certainly ahead of his time as a Haydn interpreter when, in the early 1970s, he made this pioneering integral recording of the symphonies. Superbly transferred to CD in full, bright and immediate sound, the performances are a consistent delight, with brisk allegros and fast-flowing *Andantes*, with textures remarkably clean. The slow, rustic-sounding accounts of Minuets are more controversial, but the rhythmic bounce makes them very attractive too. The set remains the only complete survey and, indeed, is more 'complete' than one could possibly expect. It includes not only the *Symphonies A* and *B* (Hoboken Nos. 106 and 108) but also the *Sinfonia concertante in B flat*, a splendidly imaginative piece with wonderful unexpected touches. Dorati's account – not surprisingly – presents the work as a symphony with unusual scoring, rather than as a concerto. As H. C. Robbins Landon tells us in the accompanying notes, the *Symphonies A* and *B* were omitted from the list of 104 authentic symphonies by error, as the first was considered to be a quartet – wind parts were discovered later – and the second a divertimento. Dorati also includes as an appendix completely different versions of *Symphony No. 22* (*The Philosopher*), where Haydn altered the orchestration (a pair of flutes substituted for the cor anglais), entirely removed the first movement and introduced a new *Andante grazioso*; plus an earlier version of No. 63, to some extent conjectural in its orchestration, for the original score is lost. Of the three alternative finales for *L'Impériale* (No. 53), the first (A) contains a melody which Robbins Landon suggests 'sounds extraordinarily like Schubert'; the second (C) seems unlikely to be authentic; but the third (D) uses an overture which was first published in Vienna. 'In some respects,' Robbins Landon suggests, 'this is the most successful of the three concluding movements'. He feels the same about the more extended finale of the *Drum Roll Symphony*, which originally included 'a modulation to C flat, preceded by two whole bars of rests – a great Falstaffian touch'. But Haydn thought that this made the movement too long and crossed out the whole section. Robbins Landon continues: 'Perhaps, if we may be so bold as to suggest it, Haydn was for once in his life too ruthless here.'

Symphonies Nos. 6 in D (Le Matin); 7 in C (Le Midi); 8 in G (Le Soir).
(M) **(*) Teldec/Warner Dig. 2292 46018-2 [id.]. VCM, Harnoncourt.

Harnoncourt is nothing if not dramatic. He opens No. 6 with an impressively controlled crescendo, beginning from an almost inaudible pianissimo, while the opening of the main allegro is characteristically gruff. But this music-making bursts with vitality, and a soothing flute solo soon appears to calm the listener. How cleverly scored these works are – to seduce the players of the Esterházy orchestra with their consistently rewarding part-writing. The very opening of Harnoncourt's slow movement (of No. 6) is austere but the atmosphere lightens, and it is again a flute which gaily introduces the lively finale, only to be chased off immediately by Harnoncourt's vigorously brusque strings. So it is throughout, with tuttis edgily bold and with plenty of accents, yet with balancing passages of delicacy. It is the solo violin which begins the finale of No. 7 and, when he is peremptorily dispatched by the irate violins, the flute fortunately ventures back. No one could say that these performances lack gravitas and the poised *Andante* of No. 8, where the solo violin re-enters gracefully, is pleasingly elegant, even if the conductor rather over-characterizes the interrupting tuttis. The robust Minuet makes way for an erstwhile double-bass solo in the Trio – which must have surprised the player as much as the listening Prince. The Presto finale opens gently, but Harnoncourt is in his element when the *Tempesta* arrives. The recording is as vivid as the playing; if Harnoncourt's eccentricities prevent an unreserved period-instrument recommendation (which is shared by Goodman (Hyperion CDA 66523) and Pinnock (DG 423 098-2)), this will certainly be welcomed by his admirers. Those preferring modern instruments can turn to Nicholas Ward and the Northern Chamber Orchestra on Naxos, whose performances are both lively and graceful (8.550722).

(i) *Symphonies Nos. 6 in D (Le Matin); 7 in C (Le Midi); 8 in G (Le Soir); 22 in E flat (Philosopher);* (ii) *26 in D min. (Lamentatione);* (i) *31 in D (Horn signal); 43 in E flat (Mercury); 44 in E min. (Trauer-symphonie); 45 in F sharp min. (Farewell);* (ii) *47 in G (Palindrome);* (i) *48 in C (Maria Theresia); 49 in F min. (La Passione); 53 in D (L'Impériale); 55 in E flat (Schoolmaster); 59 in A (Fire); 60 in C (Il distratto); 63 in C (La Roxelane); 69 in C (Laudon); 73 in D (La Chasse); 82 in C (L'ours); 83 in G min. (La poule); 85 in B flat (La Reine); 92 in G (Oxford); 94 in G (Surprise); 96 in D (Miracle); 100 in G (Military); 101 in D (Clock); 103 in E flat (Drum Roll); 104 in D (London).*
(B) **(*) Ph. Analogue/Dig. 454 335-2 (10) [id.]. (i) ASMF, Marriner; (ii) ECO, Leppard (directed from harpsichord).

This fine collection, recorded between 1968 and 1981, is beautifully transferred to CD and offers Philips's most natural sound-quality. Opening with characterful accounts of the three symphonies Haydn composed not long after taking up his appointment at the Esterházy court in 1761, Marriner and Leppard between them offer consistently elegant performances of 29 'named' symphonies, not all of them by any means well known. Marriner has the lion's share; Leppard, conducting from the harpsichord, is in excellent form in the *Lamentatione* and the so-called *Palindrome*, with its set of slow-movement variations on a pair of invertible themes. Under Marriner the Academy playing is more polished and urbane than in the rival accounts under Dorati. Although ultimately there is an earthier quality in the music than Marriner perceives, these are satisfying performances that will give much pleasure, and they often have a compensating charm which Dorati misses (the *Schoolmaster*, for instance). Nos. 44 and 49 are among the highlights, and here Marriner follows Leppard by featuring a discreet harpsichord continuo. Haydn chose No. 44 for performance at his funeral (hence the title) and Marriner shapes the radiantly elegiac slow movement with much tenderness. The richly expressive string phrasing of the opening *Adagio* of the *Farewell Symphony* is superbly contrasted with the genial and buoyant rhythms of the second-movement Allegro. There is some excellent horn playing in both works. On the other hand the *Horn signal* seems curiously undercharacterized. *Il Distratto* and *La Roxelane* both have theatrical connections, and in the former Dorati's account has the greater sense of theatre, while the Academy orchestral playing is more finished. The 'named' *Paris Symphonies* are distinguished by excellent ensemble and keen articulation; they have a winning charm, yet are lively and musical, again offering a distinct alternative to Dorati. No. 94 has a particularly fine performance of the variations which form the slow movement (the 'surprise' itself most effective) and there is most delightful woodwind detail in No. 96 – the oboe solo in the trio of the Minuet is a joy. The playing in the *Clock* is very spruce and clean, and the atmosphere at the opening of the *Drum Roll* is wonderfully caught, while the first movement's second subject shows the fine pointing and lightness of touch which distinguish the music-making throughout. At bargain price the set offers excellent value, and if at times there is just a hint of blandness Marriner has set himself high standards and there is much to admire in each of these performances; if at times they fall short of real distinction, they always rise above the routine.

Symphonies Nos. 82 in C (The Bear); 83 in G min. (The Hen); 84 in E flat; 85 in B flat (La Reine); 86 in D; 87 in A (Paris Symphonies).
(B) ** EMI forte CZS5 69383-2 (2). Menuhin Festival O, Sir Yehudi Menuhin.

Menuhin is well served by the recording engineers, and his readings of all six *Paris Symphonies* remain unfailingly musical. The performances, on a modest scale, are well paced, elegantly phrased and have plenty of vitality. The mid-1970s recording has come up freshly. At the same time, it must be noted that these performances do not captivate or compel the listener in the way one might expect from this great musician. The discs are good value, but Dorati is a much better recommendation at the same price.

Symphonies Nos. 83 in G min. (The Hen); 101 in D (Clock); 104 in D (London).
(M) ** EMI CDM5 66097-2 [id.]. BPO, Karajan.

The very resonant acoustic tells against the success of these performances. Although Karajan points the delightful second subject of the first movement of *The Hen* most delicately, and the *Andante* of the *Clock* is poised and elegant, tuttis are heavy and the very full body of strings is ill-focused. Of course there is plenty of fine playing, but the performance of No. 104 is distinctly ponderous, no match for Karajan's earlier, Vienna recording. His later set of the *London Symphonies* for DG is a much more successful example of big-band Haydn.

Symphonies Nos. 93 in D; 94 in G (Surprise); 97 in C; 99 in E flat; 100 in G (Military); 101 in D (Clock) (London Symphonies).
500♪ ❁ (B) *** Ph. Duo Analogue/Dig. 442 614-2 (2). Concg. O, Sir Colin Davis.

Symphonies Nos. 95 in C min.; 96 in D (Miracle); 98 in B flat; 102 in B flat; 103 in E flat (Drum Roll); 104 in D (London) (London Symphonies).
500♪ ❁ (B) *** Ph. Duo Analogue/Dig. 442 611-2 (2). Concg. O, Sir Colin Davis.

Symphonies Nos. 93 in D; 94 in G (Surprise); 97 in C; 100 in G (Military); 103 in E flat (Drum Roll); 104 in D (London).
(B) *** Decca Double 452 256-2 (2) [id.]. Philharmonia Hungarica, Antal Dorati.

Symphonies Nos. 95 in C min.; 96 in D (Miracle); 98 in B flat; 99 in E flat; 101 in D (Clock); 102 in B flat.
(B) *** Decca Double 452 259-2 (2) [id.]. Philharmonia Hungarica, Antal Dorati.

This Haydn series (recorded between 1975 and 1981) is one of the most distinguished sets Sir Colin Davis has given us over his long recording career, and its blend of brilliance and sensitivity, wit and humanity gives these two-for-the-price-of-one Duo reissues a special claim on the collector who has not already invested in the performances when they cost far more. There is no trace of routine in this music-making and no failure of imagination. A bargain in every sense of the word.

Dorati and the Philharmonia Hungarica, working in comparative isolation in Marl in what was then West Germany (and thus in some ways reflecting Haydn's own experience which caused him to comment, 'I was forced to be original') carried through their monumental project of recording all the Haydn symphonies with consistent zeal and dedication. These final masterpieces are performed with a glowing sense of commitment; and Dorati, doubtless taking his cue from the editor, H. C. Robbins Landon, generally chooses rather relaxed tempi for the first movements – as in No. 93, which is just as deliciously lilting as in Szell's masterly version (SBK 67175 – see our main volume). In slow movements his tempi are on the fast side, but only in No. 94, the *Surprise*, is the result really controversial. Though an extra desk of strings has been added to each section, the results are authentically in scale, with individual solos emerging unforcedly against the glowing acoustic, and with intimacy comes extra dramatic force in sforzandos. A magnificent conclusion to a magnificent project and all the more desirable, now that this series is being economically reissued in Duo format. There is adequate new documentation by Lindsay Kemp.

Symphonies Nos. 94 in G (Surprise); 100 in G (Military); 101 in D (Clock).
(M) *** Ph. 442 649-2 [id.]. Concg. O, Sir Colin Davis.

Sir Colin Davis's recordings from the mid-1970s are eminently recommendable. The Concertgebouw sound is resonant and at times weighty but has good definition and warmth. Those wanting these three favourite named symphonies should be well satisfied, except that all twelve of the *London Symphonies* are available, more economically priced, on a pair of bargain Duos (see above).

CHAMBER MUSIC

Divertimenti Nos. 1–12, Hob III/1–4; Hob II/6; Hob III/6–12.
(BB) *** Arte Nova Dig. 74321 31682-2 (4). Hamburg Soloists, Emil Klein.

These string *Divertimenti* (given that name by Haydn himself) are in fact his earliest string quartets (including Op. 1 and Op. 2). Legend has it that Haydn informed his publisher that he wished the term 'string quartet' to be used only from No. 19 (Op. 9) onwards, in which he finally established a four-movement format. The present works are all symmetrically structured in five movements. Each is framed by two outer *Prestos* within which there is an inner frame of two Minuets and at the centre an *Adagio*, the musical heart of each work, almost always containing the finest music. The other movements are well crafted but relatively conventional, although every so often there is something to catch the ear, for instance the hunting style of the opening movement of the very first work (which recurs in No. 6). The simplicity of the writing probably suits the quartet format (one instrument to a part) better than an expanded instrumentation. But Emil Klein and his excellent Hamburg string group make an elegant case for these chamber orchestral versions, particularly in the cantabile slow movements, which are very beautifully played, although the finales too are often quite infectious. The *Adagios* of Nos. 5 (over a pizzicato accompaniment) and 6 (similar and charmingly delicate) are particularly winning. No. 9 (which has a novel second Minuet, interchanging bowed and pizzicato passages) and No. 11 (with its skipping first movement like a nursery rhyme, fine central *Largo cantabile* and a brief *moto perpetuo* finale) are among the most attractive of the set. They were originally scored to include a pair of horns, but were rearranged into four parts by Haydn's publisher. The extended *Adagio* of No. 10 (9 minutes) is surely worthy of a place in an early Haydn symphony. Inexpensive and with excellent recording, this set is well worth considering.

Piano trios Nos. 1–46, Hob XV:1–41; Hob XIV:C1 in C; Hob XV:C1 in C; Hob XIV6/XVI6 in G; Hob XV:fl in F min.; Hob deest in D (complete).
500♪ ✿ (B) *** Ph. 454 098-2 (9) [id.]. Beaux Arts Trio.

It is not often possible to hail one set of records as a 'classic'. Yet this set can be described in those terms, for the playing of the Beaux Arts Trio is of the very highest musical distinction, and the music is a source of endless delight. The contribution of the pianist, Menahem Pressler, is little short of inspired, and the recorded sound on CD is astonishingly lifelike. The CD transfer has enhanced detail without losing the warmth of ambience or sense of intimacy. Now offered in a bargain box of nine CDs, this is a set no Haydn lover should miss: it is desert island music.

String quartets

String quartets Nos. 31 in E flat; 32 in C; 33 in G min.; 34 in D; 35 in F min.; 36 in A, Op. 20/1–6.
500♪ ✿ *** Astrée Dig. E 8784 (2) [id.]. Mosaïques Qt.

The four players of the Mosaïques Quartet create individual timbres which are pleasing to the ear without any overt opulence, textures which have body and transparency, are perfectly matched and never edgy. The effect is often breathtaking in its rapt concentration. Such is the calibre of this music-making and the strength of insight of these players that the character of these fine, relatively early works is communicated with seemingly total spontaneity.

String quartets Nos. 50–56 (The Seven Last Words of our Saviour on the Cross), Op. 51.
500♪ ✿ *** ASV Dig. CDDCA 853 [id.]. Lindsay Quartet.

No work for string quartet, not even late Beethoven, presents more taxing interpretative problems than Haydn's *Seven Last Words of our Saviour on the Cross*. The recording by the Lindsay Quartet, while offering all the devotional gravity that Haydn demands, brings not just an illuminating variety but also a sense of drama. It is thrilling with so elusive a work to have so complete an answer in a single recording, with sound both well defined and glowingly beautiful, set against an apt church acoustic.

String quartets Nos. 63 in C; 64 in B min.; 65 in B flat, Op. 64/1–3.
*** Hyperion Dig. CDA 67011 [id.]. Salomon Qt.

String quartets Nos. 66 in G; 67 in D (Lark); 68 in E flat, Op. 64/4–6.
*** Hyperion Dig. CDA 67012 [id.]. Salomon Qt.

Like Opp. 54 and 55, Haydn's Op. 64 set was dedicated to the violinist and businessman Johann Tost, who had led the second violins in the Eszterházy orchestra, and they show Haydn at his most inspired. The Salomon performances are well up to the standard of their versions of those earlier works. Their timbre is leaner than that of the estimable Kodály Quartet on Naxos (8.550673/4) but they blend beautifully and have their own insights to offer: their precise ensemble in no way inhibits commitment and feeling.

The second of the two discs is particularly rewarding, with the famous opening movement of the *Lark* readily taking flight and the *Adagio* poised and intense. The Hyperion recording is admirably truthful, but those wanting period performances of these fine works will surely be tempted by the Festetics Harmonia Mundi bargain versions, which are in some ways even more perceptive (HMA 1903040/1).

String quartets Nos. 69–71 (Apponyi), Op. 71/1–3; 72–4, Op. 74/1–3.
(M) *** Arcana Dig. A 918 (2) [id.]. Festetics Qt.

The Festetics Quartet continue their period-instrument Haydn series with – on the whole – beautifully judged performances of Opp. 71 and 74. The playing has the customary animation and finish, with detail perceptively observed, and well-blended yet beautifully transparent textures. As before, there is nothing vinegary here, and phrasing and line are impeccably musical. Minuets are pleasing, without heaviness (sample the Trio of Op. 71/3 for delectable articulation) and finales sparkle. These are three-star performances without a doubt, and the recording could hardly be better judged. One's only reservation concerns slow movements, sometimes a little solemn. The *Largo assai* of Op. 74/3 is just a shade deliberate, and elsewhere one senses that the players are anxious to convey the depth of Haydn's writing. They do, and their thoughtfulness is appreciated – but perhaps this is achieved at the expense of a smidgen of spontaneity. However, one does not want to make too much of this: these CDs give much satisfaction, and certainly the performances have lift-off as well as gravitas.

String quartets Nos. 75 in G; 76 in D min. (Fifths); 77 in C (Emperor); 78 in B flat (Sunrise); 79 in D; 80 in E flat, Op. 76/1–6 (Erdödy Quartets).
500♪ ✿ (BB) *** Naxos Dig. 8.550314; *4550314* (*Nos. 75–77*); 8.550315; *4550315* (*Nos. 78–80*). Kodály Qt.

Haydn's six *Erdödy Quartets*, Op. 76, contain some of his very greatest music, and these performances by the Kodály Quartet are fully worthy of the composer's inexhaustible invention. Their playing brings a joyful pleasure in Haydn's inspiration, every bar of the music springs to life spontaneously, and these musicians' insights bring an ideal combination of authority and warmth, emotional balance and structural awareness.

String quartet No. 76 in D min., Op. 76/2.
**(*) Testament mono SBT 1085 [id.]. Hollywood Qt – HUMMEL: *Quartet in G* *(*); MOZART: *Quartet No. 17.* **(*)

The Hollywood Quartet were recorded at a memorable concert in London's Royal Festival Hall in September 1957, which also included the Mozart coupling and, in the second half of the programme, the Schubert *C major Quintet*. These recordings have never been available before. The playing can only be described as impeccable, not surprisingly so, given the tonal beauty and musical sophistication these artists commanded; and the sound is astonishingly good for the period. There are a couple of minutes of balance test and a brief exchange among the players.

String quartets Nos. 76 in D min. (Fifths); 77 in C (Emperor); 78 in B flat, Op. 76/2-4.
*** EMI Dig. CDC5 56166-2 [id.]. Alban Berg Qt.

The Alban Berg Quartet present the first movement of the *Fifths Quartet* with great energy and vigour. Perhaps they could smile a little more here. Nevertheless this is playing of distinction, bringing impeccable blending and ensemble. They are more relaxed for the opening movement of the *Emperor* and beguilingly pensive at the beginning of the *Sunrise*, although they can be vehemently dramatic too, as in the *Emperor*'s finale, where some listeners might prefer a less aggressive approach. But the three slow movements are played very beautifully, with much delicacy of feeling and sophistication of light and shade, and the rapt pianissimo for the *Adagio* of Op. 70/4 is affectingly intimate. In short this is quartet playing of a high order and, although the recording is brightly lit and the effect a shade too up-front, it is realistic and admirably balanced.

String quartet No. 77 in C (Emperor), Op. 76/3.
(M) * DG Dig. 445 598-2 [id.]. Emerson Qt – MOZART: *String quartets Nos. 17 & 19.* *

The Emerson group produce quartet-playing of remarkable virtuosity and stunning ensemble. One can only wonder in amazement at their brilliance, definition and clarity. However, it is all very thrustful and over-projected, and quite uncongenial as Haydn playing. The Mozart with which it is coupled is even worse. In terms of skill, this deserves more than three stars – but as a musical experience one is at a loss to rate it!

String quartets Nos. 77 in C (Emperor); 78 in B flat (Sunrise), Op. 76/3–4.
(M) *** DG 449 092-2 [id.]. Amadeus Qt – MOZART: *String quartet No. 17.* ***

The Amadeus's 1963 version of the *Emperor*, coupled with Mozart's *Hunt quartet*, was always one of their very best records: it has breadth and warmth, to say nothing of immaculate ensemble. The famous slow movement is particularly successful. The *Sunrise*, which was recorded seven years later, is another finely blended performance, somewhat suaver but still with plenty of vitality in outer movements. Both recordings were truthfully balanced and emerge very successfully on CD.

String quartets Nos. 81 in G; 82 in F, Op. 77/1–2; 83 in D min., Op. 103.
500♪ *** Astrée Dig. E 8799 [id.]. Mosaïques Qt.

Using original instruments to totally convincing effect, the Mosaïques Quartet give outstanding performances of Haydn's last three quartets. They play with much subtlety of colour and dynamic and bring total concentration to every bar of the music.

PIANO MUSIC

Piano sonatas Nos. 20 in B flat, Hob XVI/18; 30 in D, Hob XVI/19; 31 in A flat, Hob XVI/46; 32 in G min., Hob XVI/44.
(B) **(*) Naxos Dig. 8.553364 [id.]. Jenö Jandó.

Jandó continues his Haydn sonata series in his clean, direct style. The first movement of the *G minor Sonata* is particularly appealing, with its neat articulation and tight little runs, and the same might be said of the opening movement of the *A flat major* (No. 31), while its finale is similarly bright and sparkling. But first prize goes to the closing movement of the *D major*, which skips along delightfully and brings quite dazzling dexterity. The thoughtful *Adagio* of the *B flat major*, however, is just a little too studied; but this is not enough of a disadvantage to prevent a recommendation. The piano recording is very realistic.

Piano sonatas Nos. 48 in C, Hob XVI/35; 49 in C sharp min., Hob XVI/36; 50 in D, Hob XVI/37; 51 in E flat, Hob XVI/38; 52 in G, Hob XVI/39.
(M) ** Ph. 442 659-2 [id.]. Ingrid Haebler (fortepiano).

Ingrid Haebler's clean, crisp articulation and bold, somewhat unbending approach seek to project a very classical view of Haydn. Her opening *C major* (Hob XVI/35) has a rhythmic preciseness (with a momentary hint of Dresden china) to remind one a little of Mozart's most famous sonata in the same key, but the opening of the *C sharp minor* is appropriately stronger and darker, and the *Largo e sostenuto* of the *D major* is made to seem quite portentous. She finds a simple lyricism in the *E flat Sonata*, although the closing *Minuet* is again bold and firm. It will be seen that these performances have plenty of character though they are rather unsmiling. The recording is excellent and the fortepiano timbre has body and unexaggerated colour.

VOCAL MUSIC

Canzonettas: Book I: *The mermaid's song; Recollection; Pastoral song; Despair; Pleasing pain; Fidelity, Hob XXVIa/25–30.* Book II: *Sailor's song; The wanderer; Sympathy; She never told her love; Piercing eyes; Content, Hob XXVIa/31–6. The Spirit's song, Hob XXVIa/4; O tuneful voice, Hob XXVIa/42.*
(M) ** Teldec/Warner [id.]. James Griffett, Bradford Tracey (fortepiano).

Haydn's simple, usually strophic settings of English texts were designed for amateur performance. The first six were written for his second visit to London in 1794–5. He sang them himself on one occasion to George III and other members of the Royal Family. They are settings of poems by Anne Hunter, the wife of an eminent London surgeon who had died in between Haydn's two visits. There seems evidence of a romantic attachment between composer and widow. However, of the texts of the second set, written in 1795, only one (*The wanderer*) is by Mrs Hunter; the others draw on Shakespeare and Metastasio. The two remaining songs return to Anne Hunter's words, and the last song, *O tuneful voice*, undoubtedly represents a sad farewell. James Griffet's approach is direct and unaffected and he does not try to put more expression into the words than they will carry. He is admirably accompanied by Bradford Tracey on a Broadwood fortepiano.

The Creation (*Die Schöpfung;* in German).
500♪ (M) *** DG 435 077-2 (2). Janowitz, Ludwig, Wunderlich, Krenn, Fischer-Dieskau, Berry, V. Singverein, BPO, Karajan.
*** DG Dig. 449 217-2 (2) [id.]. McNair, Brown, Schade, Finley, Gilfry, Monteverdi Ch., E. Bar. Soloists, Gardiner.
(B) *** DG Double 453 031-2 [id.]. Blegen, Popp, Moser, Ollman, Moll, Bav. R. Ch. & SO, Bernstein.

(B) **(*) EMI forte CZS5 69343-2 (2). Donath, Tear, Van Dam, Philh. Ch. & O, Frühbeck de Burgos.
(M) ** Teldec/Warner Dig. 2292 42682-2 (2) [id.]. Gruberová, Protschka, Holl, Schönberg Ch., VSO, Harnoncourt.
** Ph. Dig. 446 073-2 (2) [id.]. Orgonasova, Rodgers, Ainsley, Schulte, Vollestad, Gulbenkian Ch., O of 18th Century, Brüggen.
(B) *(*) Carlton Turnabout 30371 00087 [id.]. Mimi Coertse, Julius Patzak, Dezso Ernster, V. Singverein, V. Volksoper O, Horenstein – MOZART: *Coronation Mass*. *(*)

Among versions of *The Creation* sung in German, Karajan's 1969 set remains unsurpassed and, at mid-price, is a clear first choice despite two small cuts (in Nos. 30 and 32). The combination of the Berlin Philharmonic at its most intense and the great Viennese choir makes for a performance that is not only polished but warm and dramatically strong too. The soloists are an extraordinarily fine team, more consistent in quality than those on almost any rival version.

Issued to celebrate the 50th anniversary of the DG Archiv label, Gardiner's version brings the benefit of a period performance on a relatively large scale, involving speeds broader than in direct rival versions, yet with clearer, more detailed recording. Characteristically, Gardiner takes a dramatic view, overtly expressive, vividly pointing the highlights of the Creation story. So the baritone, Gerald Finley, in his narration leading up to the choral cry of *Licht!* ('Light!'), uses an intimate half-tone as if in awe and, with brass clearly defined, the following fortissimo is all the more shattering. Gardiner may not always convey the relaxed joy of Weil's fresh and brisk version on Sony, but the exhilaration and power of Haydn's inspiration, as well as its lyrical beauty, have never been conveyed more tellingly in a period performance on disc, with the Monteverdi Choir singing with virtuoso clarity and phenomenal precision of ensemble. The soloists are outstanding too, though the silvery soprano, Sylvia McNair, does not always sing full out. A first choice among period performances.

Bernstein's DG version, recorded at a live performance in Munich, uses a relatively large chorus, encouraging him to adopt rather slow speeds at times. What matters is the joy conveyed in the story-telling, with the finely disciplined chorus and orchestra producing incandescent tone, blazing away in the big set-numbers, and the performance is compulsive from the very opening bars. Five soloists are used instead of three, with the parts of Adam and Eve sung by nicely contrasted singers, confirming this as an unusually persuasive version, well recorded in atmospheric sound.

Rafael Frühbeck de Burgos directs a genial performance, recorded with richness and immediacy. The soloists are all excellent and, though Helen Donath has a hint of flutter in her voice, she is wonderfully agile in ornamentation, as in the bird-like quality she gives to the aria, *On mighty pens*. The chorus might gain from a more forward balance but their singing is impressive. An enjoyable set, but Karajan at mid-price (DG 435 077-2) remains the primary recommendation, and Dorati's Double Decca set (443 027-2) is a stronger performance than this forte reissue and it also offers the *Salve regina* as a bonus (see our main volume).

Harnoncourt's version with the Vienna Symphony Orchestra was recorded live. It follows the first printed edition of 1800, using the same size of forces as in performances of that date, with a gentle fortepiano replacing harpsichord in recitatives. Compared with the finest versions, the ensemble is on the rough side, and the singing of the male soloists is often rough, too. The tenor Josef Protschka shouts Uriel's first entry but settles down after that; while by far the most distinguished singing of the set comes from Edita Gruberová, dazzling and imaginative, with slightly backward balance helping to eliminate the touch of hardness that the microphone often brings out in her voice. The sound otherwise is full and clear.

Brüggen's Philips version, recorded live in Utrecht in March 1994, brings an alternative period performance, strong and sympathetic with a first-rate team of soloists, fresh and clear, and well focused in the recording. Speeds are unrushed, if generally not quite as broad as Gardiner's, and there is plenty of body in the choral and instrumental sound. Unfortunately, a reverberant acoustic clouds the definition of the chorus, with inner parts obscured in tuttis.

Horenstein's is a fresh and enjoyable performance, given a lively recording. There is not the utmost degree of sophistication; the soloists' runs, for instance, leave something to be desired, especially in the florid music in Part 2. But Mimi Coertse makes an appealing Eve: her *With verdure clad* has real charm. The bass too is good, and both these singers project strong vocal personalities. The choral singing is spirited, and Horenstein directs with spontaneity. It is surprising that such a distinghuised conductor is responsible for the one blot on the performance: his slow and unbuoyant account of *The heavens are telling*, which means that Part 1 ends without the kind of thrill one takes for granted at a live performance.

Masses Nos. (i–iii) *1 in F (Missa brevis), Hob XXII/1;* (i; iii–vi) *1a in G (Rorate coeli desuper), Hob XXII/3; 3 in C: Missa Cellensis in honorem Beatissimae Virginis Mariae (Missa Santae Caecilae), Hob XXII/5;* (i; iii; v–viii) *4 in E flat: Missa in honorem Beatissimae Virginis Mariae (Great organ Mass), Hob XXII/4;* (i; iii; vi; ix; x) *6 in G (Missa Sancti Nicolai), Hob XXII/6;* (xi–xv) *7 in B flat: Missa brevis Sancti Joannis de Deo (Little organ Mass);* (xi; xiii–xviii) *8 in C: Mariazeller Messe, Hob XXII/8;* (xiii–xvii; xix; xx) *9 in B flat: Missa Sancti Bernardi de Offida (Heligmesse), Hob XXII/10;* (ix; xiii–xv; xix; xxi; xxii) *10 in C: Missa in tempore belli (Paukenmesse), Hob XXII/9;* (xvi; xxiii–xxvi) *11 in D min.: Missa in augustiis (Nelson Mass), Hob XXII/11;* (xiii–xv; xxv; xxvii–xxviii) *12 in B flat: Theresienmesse, Hob XXII/12;* (xiii–xvii; xix; xxix) *13 in B flat: Schöpfungmesse (Creation Mass), Hob XXII/13;* (xiii–xvi; xxvii; xxx) *14 in B flat (Harmoniemesse), Hob XXII/14.*

(B) *** Decca 448 518-2 (7) [id.]. (i) Nelson; (ii) Kirkby; (iii) Christ Church Cathedral Ch., AAM, Preston; (iv) Cable; (v) Hill; (vi) Thomas; (vii) Watkinson; (viii); Hogwood (organ); (ix) Minty; (x) Covey-Crump; (xi) Jennifer Smith; (xii) Scott (organ); (xiii) St John's College, Cambridge, Ch.; (xiv) ASMF; (xv) George Guest; (xvi) Watts; (xvii) Tear; (xviii) Luxon; (xix) Cantelo; (xx) McDaniel; (xxi) Partridge; (xxii) Keyte; (xxiii) Stahlman; (xxiv) Wilfred Brown; (xxv) Krause; (xxvi) King's College, Cambridge, Ch., LSO, Willcocks; (xxvii) Spoorenberg; (xxviii) Greevy; Mitchinson; (xxix) Forbes Robinson; (xxx) Young, Rouleau.

Decca's survey of the complete Masses of Haydn, which appeared originally on the Argo and Oiseau-Lyre labels, omits only the newly discovered fragmentary *Missa Sunt bona mixta malis*, Hob XXII/2, of 1768 (available on Sony SK 53368 – see our main volume). Overall this achievement stands alongside Dorati's complete recording of the symphonies (and the Beaux Arts' *Piano trios*) as one of the landmarks of the gramophone during the analogue LP era for, until the original LPs appeared, most of this music was virtually unknown by the ordinary music-lover.

Starting in 1962 with Sir David Willcocks's King's version of the *Nelson Mass*, the production team then moved down the road to St John's for the five remaining magnificent Mass settings which Haydn wrote between 1796 and 1802 for his patron, Prince Esterházy, after his return from London. With changing soloists, of generally consistent quality, George Guest directed a series of performances notable for their fresh directness and vigour, with his St John's Choir showing itself a ready match for the more famous choir at King's College and the sound even more vivid. The recordings were made between 1965 and 1969, with the *Little organ Mass* and *Mariazellermesse* following in 1977. The project was completed over the next two years with the early Masses. But the 'authentic' era had arrived and the orchestra changed from the Academy of St Martin-in-the-Fields to the Academy of Ancient Music. Simon Preston took over, and he directed his Christ Church Cathedral Choir with a comparable freshness and spontaneity to that established at St John's. The engineering team excelled themselves throughout, to produce a well-balanced and spacious yet clearly detailed sound, boldly projected against a nicely resonant acoustic. As with the companion Decca box of the symphonies, H. C. Robbins Landon has provided the notes with his usual spirited scholarship.

(i) *Mass No. 11 in D min. (Nelson): Missa in augustiis, Hob XXII/11;* (ii) *Arianna a Naxos* (orchestral version), *Hob XXVIb/2; Scena di Berenice (Berenice che fai?), Hob XXIVa/10.*

(M) *** Decca Eclipse Dig. 448 983-2; *448 983-4* [id.]. (i) Bonney, Howells, Rolfe Johnson, Roberts, L. Symphony Ch., Hickox; (ii) Arleen Augér, Handel & Haydn Society, Hogwood.

Hickox conducts a lively, well-sung reading of the most celebrated of Haydn's late Masses, most impressive in the vigorous, outward-going music which – with Haydn – makes up the greater part of the service; here the choral singing is little short of glorious. In serene moments the choral sound is slightly recessed, with inner parts less well defined than they might be. The soloists are very good, and Barbara Bonney's purity of line is impressive, although tonally she is a little thin. While in some ways the Willcocks version of 20 years earlier is even finer, in the work's more resplendent moments the London Symphony's choral focus is given greater impact by the more modern digital sound.

What makes the present reissue almost indispensable is the inclusion of Haydn's two major solo cantatas (a full half-hour of wonderful music) which he wrote for his two London visits in the 1790s. The first was written with fortepiano accompaniment (which Haydn himself played in London), and the effective string arrangement had been made by an anonymous hand. Arleen Augér was never more impressive in the recording studio than here. She is superbly dramatic in the cantata which tells of Ariadne abandoned by Theseus on Naxos, and – in melting voice – infinitely touching in the *Scena di Berenice*. Hogwood accompanies most sympathetically and the recording is perfectly balanced. Not to be missed.

The Seasons (Die Jahreszeiten; complete; in German).

500♪ *** DG Dig. 431 818-2 (2). Bonney, Rolfe Johnson, Schmidt, Monteverdi Ch., E. Bar. Soloists, Gardiner.

(B) *** Decca Double 448 101-2 (2) [id.]. Cotrubas, Krenn, Sotin, Brighton Festival Ch., RPO, Dorati.

Even more than usual, Gardiner's studio performance conveys the electricity of a live event. The silver-toned Barbara Bonney and Anthony Rolfe Johnson at his most sensitive are outstanding soloists, and though the baritone, Andreas Schmidt, is less sweet on the ear, he winningly captures the bluff jollity of the role of Simon. The choral singing too is first class.

Dorati brings to the work an innocent dedication, at times pointing to the folk-like inspiration, which is most compelling. This is not as polished an account as Boehm's in the same price-range but, with excellent solo singing and bright chorus work, is enjoyable in its own right. The choruses of peasants in Part 3, for instance, are boisterously robust. Textually there is an important difference in that Dorati has returned to the original version and restored the cuts in the introductions to *Autumn* and *Winter*, the latter with some wonderfully adventurous harmonies. The performance as a whole is highly animated. With Dorati, this is above all a happy work, a point made all the more telling by the immediacy of the new transfer. This is all the more welcome at Double Decca price.

OPERA

L'Anima del filosofo (Orfeo ed Euridice) (complete).
*** O-L Dig. 452 668-2 (2) [id.]. Bartoli, Heilmann, D'Arcangelo, Silvestrelli, AAM, Hogwood.

Haydn wrote his last and grandest opera for London in 1791 but, when the king refused to give the theatre a licence, it was never performed. In 1806 Breitkopf published 11 numbers from the score, but it was not until 1950 that the opera was performed complete, and then with Erich Kleiber conducting and Maria Callas as Euridice. It is a curious piece, quite different in treatment from most operatic versions of the story, with Euridice very much the central figure at the start, leading to her death in Act II. Orfeo consults the Sybil (or Genio in the libretto), goes down to the Underworld, where he loses Euridice a second time, this time irrevocably. He returns almost at once and, forced by the Bacchantes to drink poison, he dies.

Impressed by Handel oratorios and the English choral tradition, Haydn includes many choruses of comment. He also takes the opportunity of writing for a large orchestra, far beyond what he had been used to in Esterháza. The result has many impressive moments, even though Haydn would clearly have modified, and possibly expanded, what he wrote in the light of experience, had it been staged. As it is, a first-rate recording has long been needed, and this one fills the bill very well indeed. Hogwood uses an enlarged Academy, with 12 first violins, and though at times his manner is severe, he paces the piece very effectively, making the most of the drama, even though some key moments are inevitably perfunctory, notably the moment when – in the course of a brief recitative – Orfeo looks back at Euridice, and she is taken from him a second time.

The very opening brings one of the most telling passages, when Euridice in distress flees into the forest, a monologue for which Haydn writes a most adventurous accompanied recitative. Cecilia Bartoli is in her element, passionately expressive, creating a larger-than-life character, as Maria Callas no doubt did too. Orfeo – whom she already loves – rescues her, and the sequence when he pacifies the savage shepherds who have captured her brings another magnetic moment, featuring a harp solo, which then develops into an aria. Euridice's death scene, Orfeo's agony of lament (agitated, and very different from Gluck's *Orfeo* aria, *Che farò*), and a brilliant coloratura aria for the Sybil (dazzlingly done by Bartoli) bring other high points. Though Orfeo's death comes as an anticlimax, the final chorus for the Bacchantes is most memorable, in a minor key, dark and agitated, then fading away to the close, suggesting that Haydn may have had the end of Act II of Mozart's *Idomeneo* in mind. Uwe Heilmann is a most sympathetic Orfeo, musically stylish, even if the microphone catches the hint of a flutter, as it does too with the well-contrasted voices of Ildebrando d'Arcangelo as King Creonte, Euridice's father, and Andrea Silvestrelli as Pluto. The chorus, so important in this work, is fresh and well disciplined.

Heming, Michael (1920–42)

Threnody for a soldier killed in action.
(M) (***) EMI mono CDM5 66053-2 [id.]. Hallé O, Barbirolli – BRITTEN: *Violin concerto* (**); RUBBRA: *Symphony No. 5* etc. (***)

Michael Heming was a kind of Second World War Butterworth, though his gifts did not have time to flower into the fullest blossom. His father, the baritone Percy Heming, and Barbirolli were close friends and, when Michael was killed at El Alamein, Anthony Collins concocted (to use Michael Kennedy's word) the *Threnody for a soldier killed in action* from sketches that the young man had made. Barbirolli and the Hallé Orchestra recorded it in 1945 but it never made inroads into the repertory and, as far as we know, has never been reissued until now. A moving piece in the English pastoral tradition and a welcome fill-up to this interesting disc.

Henze, Hans Werner (born 1926)

The DG Henze Collection
(M) *** DG stereo/mono 449 850-2 (14) [id.]. Various artists.

To mark the occasion of Hans Werner Henze's seventieth birthday, DG have issued a handsomely presented 14-CD set of the repertoire that the composer himself recorded in the heyday of his relationship with the company, plus a handful of others items. DG are wise to make the discs available separately as there are few who would necessarily want or could afford the whole package, even though it is very competitive at mid-price. It is important to note that none of the music Henze has composed in his fifties and sixties is represented in the collection. The most recent work is *Tristan*, a set of preludes for piano, orchestra and electronic tapes, which comes from the mid-1970s. The *Seventh Symphony* is available on EMI (CDC7 54762-2), powerfully presented by Rattle and the CBSO, and presumably the *Eighth* will soon find its way on to disc.

For most collectors the best starting-point, perhaps, would be the symphonies, which come on a two-CD set. Henze recorded the first five with the Berlin Philharmonic in the mid-1960s and followed with the *Sixth*, written in 1968, a few years later. For R.L. the *Third* and *Fourth* remain the most haunting of the set, with the latter casting a particularly powerful spell. It is the product of a refined musical imagination and its expressionist anguish is punctuated by moments of an all-pervasive melancholy which must spring from a deep personal experience. The *First Symphony* is also a delight, springing as it does from an Appolonian neo-classicism reminiscent of Stravinsky and the pale, luminous textures of Frank Martin. The *First Violin concerto* (1947), recorded here with Schneiderhan as soloist, is one of the most rewarding of Henze's early scores, even if his debt to Hindemith is not fully discharged.

The other CDs which would make an excellent introduction to the set include the beautiful *Double Concerto for oboe and harp* (albeit not with Henze himself conducting), played by its dedicatees, Heinz and Ursula Holliger, coupled with one of his most haunting and affecting scores, the *Fantasia for strings*. This was refashioned from a score Henze composed for a film version of Musil's *Der junge Törless* in which, incidentally, they were played on viols. Likewise the beautiful *Five Neapolitan songs* with the young Fischer-Dieskau or the *Cantata della fiaba estrema*, expertly sung by Edda Moser, are wonderful pieces. If you possess the LP originals you will find the transfers, generally speaking, have an admirable clarity, but this is achieved at a certain cost: the LPs have greater openness and depth, with greater space round the aural image and a more subtle placing of instrumental detail.

(i) *2 Ballet variations;* (ii) *Piano concerto No. 2;* (iii) *Tristan* (preludes for piano, tapes and orchestra); (iv) *3 Tientos for guitar.*
(M) **(*) DG mono/stereo 449 866-2 (2) [id.]. (i) RIAS SO, Ferenc Fricsay; (ii) Christoph Eschenbach, LPO; (iii) Homero Francesch, Cologne RSO; (ii; iii) cond. composer; (iv) Siegfried Behrend.

The *Piano concerto* has a deep and brooding lyricism, alternating with considerable violence and tension; but repeated hearing uncovers a vision of great originality and poetry. Eschenbach, for whom the concerto was written in 1967, is the magnificent soloist. The work, almost 50 minutes in length, was inspired by the words of Shakespeare's sonnet: 'The expense of spirit in a waste of shame is lust in action . . . None knows well to shun the heaven that leads men to this hell.' It is an interesting, often moving work, full of a sad eloquence that bursts into occasional bitter outcries of some violence. The beauty of the recording captures all the refinement and delicacy of Henze's textures. The brief *Ballet variations* come from a suite of six written early in the composer's career (1949) as music for a ballet without a narrative, composed while Henze was strongly under the influence of the Stravinsky of the *Danses concertantes*. The three *Tientos* for guitar were originally interludes in *Kammermusik*, a vocal work of a decade later, and, though again brief, are very imaginatively conceived.

Tristan, the other extended work here, is an extraordinary montage which began life as a piano prelude. This the composer sketched in 1972 and he felt the writing had a kinship with Wagner's opera. Later, during a London visit, he had nightmares in which Wagner's hero appeared to inspire further musical associations, and what followed proved itself very much like a musical nightmare. First came an extraordinary mélange of extra-musical sounds, mixed together on tape in a studio in Putney, London, including throwing glass marbles at prepared piano strings and bombarding the strings of a double-bass with tennis balls. A distorted piano performance of Chopin's *Funeral march* was thrown in for good measure, plus a 'computer-analysis' of the first four bars of Wagner's opera. Henze composed the piano preludes and orchestral interludes to go with the taped episodes, and finally he decided to re-make the lunatic tape mélange to fit the composed music more accurately. The resulting work is a six-part structure lasting just over 43 minutes. It opens with a solo piano *Prologue* with woodwind interjections, a *Lament* follows, then the *Preludes* and *Variations*, which feature the orchestra and splice in a quotation from the opening of Brahms's *First Symphony*. Next comes *Tristan's folly*, which draws on the synthesized Chopin excerpts and more distorted Brahms. A bizarre sequence of what the composer calls 'Burlesque dance movements' comes next, ending with a scream of death, with the tape supposedly reproducing the scream of a famous Wagnerian soprano. The closing *Epilogue* leads to rather more distinct distillations of Wagner, a child's heartbeat, bells chiming and so on. It is difficult to take seriously, but it certainly represents a new experience.

(i) *Ode to the west wind* (for cello and orchestra); (ii) *Concerto for double-bass;* (iii) *Violin concerto No. 1.*
(M) *** DG 449 865-2 [id.]. (i) Siegfried Palm; (ii) Gary Karr; (iii) Wolfgang Schneiderhan; (i; iii) Bav. RSO; (ii) ECO; all cond. composer.

The *Violin concerto* dates from the late 1940s and shows the influence of Hindemith still exerted at this time, while the *Ode to the west wind*, inspired by Shelley's poem, was written only a few years later, in 1953. Both works contain pages of some beauty, though the later piece employs a more fragmented and complex style than the predominantly serial *Concerto*. The *Violin concerto* is the more immediately appealing work and has an eloquent slow movement, but both pieces explore a fascinating world of sound; and the performances, apart from having the composer's authority to commend them, are expertly recorded. The *Double-bass concerto* was composed in 1966 for Gary Karr. It is not among the composer's most impressive pieces, though it fascinates by its resourceful treatment of an unpromising solo instrument. The performance is exemplary.

(i) *Double concerto for oboe, harp and strings. Fantasia for strings; Sonata for strings.*
(M) *** DG 449 864-2 [id.]. Zurich Coll. Mus., Paul Sacher, with (i) Heinz and Ursula Holliger.

The language of the *Fantasia*, based on incidental music for a film, is more disciplined and diatonic than is often Henze's wont. It is a moving score with a vein of melancholy that is direct in utterance. The *Double concerto* was inspired by the astonishing artistry and virtuosity of Heinz Holliger on the oboe, who performs it here with his wife, Ursula, on the harp. Highly inventive and resourceful, this performance is authoritative and is given an exemplary recording.

Symphonies Nos. (i) *1–5;* (ii) *6.*
(M) *** DG 449 861-2 (2) [id.]. (i) BPO; (ii) LSO; cond. composer.

These works are the product of a highly sophisticated imagination with a most refined and sensitive awareness of atmosphere and feeling for sonority. There is much nourishment and stimulus to be found here. The *First*, with its cool, Stravinskian slow movement, is a remarkable achievement for a 21-year-old, though we hear it in a revision Henze made early in 1963. There is a dance-like feel to the *Third* (1950), written while Henze was attached to the Wiesbaden Ballet. The *Fourth* was originally intended for the opera *König Hirsch* and was meant to connote 'an evocation of the living, breathing forest and the passing of the seasons'. It is among the most concentrated and atmospheric of his works; there is at times an overwhelming sense of melancholy and a strongly Mediterranean atmosphere to its invention. The *Fifth* embraces the most violent angularity, with passages of exquisite poignancy and tranquillity. It comes from the period of *The Elegy for young lovers* and quotes from one of its arias; the language is strongly post-expressionist. One wonders, however, what its first audience, 'soldiers of the Cuban revolutionary army, sons of workers and students', must have made of the *Sixth Symphony*, composed while Henze was living in Havana! The performances are brilliant and the vivid recordings do not sound their age, those of the first five symphonies being over 35 years old.

VOCAL MUSIC

(i) *Being beauteous;* (ii) *Five Neapolitan songs;* (iii) *Versuch über Schweine (Essay on pigs);* (iv) *Whispers from heavenly death.*
(M) *** DG mono/stereo 449 869-2 [id.]. (i; iv) Edda Moser; (i) RIAS Ch., BPO soloists; (ii) Dietrich Fischer-Dieskau, BPO soloists, Richard Kraus; (iii) Roy Hart, Philip Jones Brass Ens., ECO; (iv) BPO soloists; (i; iii–iv) cond. composer.

The *Versuch über Schweine* ('Essay on pigs') is a work in which Henze gives voice to his political interests. It contains a voice-part that traverses an amazing range and which certainly encompasses an extraordinary variety of timbre. *Being beauteous* is exquisite and quite moving, and *Whispers from heavenly death* is one of the composer's most fascinating works. The singing of Edda Moser is quite phenomenal both in purity of tone and in accuracy of intonation. The performances of all this repertoire could hardly be bettered, and the recording reproduces a wide dynamic range with admirable truthfulness of balance and quality of tone.

(i) *Cantata della fiaba estrema (Cantata of the ultimate fable);* (ii) *Moralitäten (Moralities);* (iii) *Musen Siziliens (Muses of Sicily).*

(M) *** DG 449 870-2 [id.]. (i) Edda Moser, RIAS Ch., Berlin Philh. CO; (ii) Cornelius Schwarz, Dieter Leffler, Andreas Scheibner, Friedemann Jäckel, Titus Paspirgilis, Frieder Lang, Dresden Ch., Leipzig GO; (iii) Dresden Ch., Joseph Rollino, Paul Sheftel, Dresden State O soloists; all cond. composer.

The *Cantata*, a setting of a Roman love-poem, contains moving and often disarmingly simple music with great imaginative resource and subtlety. With Edda Moser the soloist, it cannot fail to communicate vividly. *Moralities* is a setting of 'three scenic plays' which W. H. Auden devised from three of Aesop's fables. Henze scored the work for small orchestra with a narrator, soloists and chorus interchanging the dialogue. Its manner is not in the least intimidating and the result is potently ironic rather than lightly humorous in spirit. The Latin text of the *Muses of Sicily* is taken from the *Eclogues* of Virgil. It opens with a *Pastorale* dialogue between Lycidas and Moeris and ends with the *Song of Silenus*, recounting the creation of the world from the elements of earth, air, sea and liquid. The work is entirely choral (Henze describes it as a concerto) with a vivid accompaniment for two pianos, wind instruments and timpani. The pianos are used very rhythmically, and the combination with timpani inevitably reminds the listener of Bartók, but Henze himself used a term which links the music more readily to Hindemith: he called it *Gebrauchsmusik* ('utility music'). Even if one does not take readily to all this music, Henze could never be less than stimulating. Superb singing and very good recording.

El Cimarrón (autobiography of the runaway slave Esteban Montejo) (recital for four musicians).

(M) *** DG 449 872-2 [id.]. William Pearson, Karlheinz Zoeller, Leo Brouwer, Stomu Yamash'ta, cond. composer.

El Cimarrón, first heard at The Maltings in the Aldeburgh Festival of 1970, represented for Henze a new musical departure, presented at its simplest and most direct. It uses the words of a former slave, born in Cuba over 100 years ago. It is a simple but moving story with a number of left-wing propaganda slants, which fortunately do not get in the way of musical and dramatic expression. The live performance was impressive for the antics of the Japanese percussionist, Stomu Yamash'ta; but on disc the impact of the work is even more intense, because the improvisatory passages have been considerably tightened up, and the story is after all best imagined in the mind's eye – the poetic passage where the runaway lives in the forest, the biting account of the Revolution, the scene of the swaggering Yankees where a four-letter word is inserted (in English) in an otherwise German text. The performance is as near definitive as one could expect, beautifully recorded.

Das Floss der Medusa (The Raft of the Medusa) (oratorio).

(M) *** DG 449 871-2 [id.]. Edda Moser, Dietrich Fischer-Dieskau, Charles Regnier, RIAS Chamber Ch., Members of the St Nikolai Hamburg Youth Ch., N. German R. Ch. & O, cond. composer.

This is a vividly imaginative work, far more approachable than the music Henze was composing before he entered into his latest 'political' period with its extreme left-wing commitment. The scheduled first performance in December 1968 in Hamburg was broken up in a political riot, but a recording had been made earlier and this is now re-released on this disc. Whatever the political bias, the message is both dramatic and moving as told in the tragic story of the crew of a shipwrecked frigate cast adrift and left to die by their officers. Henze has conceived the simple but effective idea of having the members of the crew as represented by the chorus move from one side of the stage to the other, one by one called from the land of the living, over to the side of Death (soprano soloist). A vivid experience, superbly realized.

Der langwierige Weg in die Wohnung der Natascha Ungeheuer (The Tedious way to Natascha Ungueheuer's apartment).

(M) **(*) DG 449 873-2 [id.]. William Pearson, Fires of London, Philip Jones Brass Quintet, Gunter Hampel Free Jazz Ens., Giuseppe Agostini, Stomu Yamash'ta, cond. composer.

Expertly performed though it is, *Der langwierige Weg in die Wohnung der Natascha Ungeheuer* is perhaps the least satisfying or musically substantial of the works in this collection. It was unfortunate that the composer used the word 'tedious' in his title, for the writing has the air of a political tract and comes from the period when the composer was rejecting opera. The work is entitled 'Show for 17 performers', and is an allegory: Natasha Ungeheuer is 'the siren of a false Utopia who constantly lures the leftist intellectual into the cosy situation of so many middle-class socialists, who preach revolution while meanwhile living more or less the same old comfortable life'.

OPERA

Elegie für junge Liebende (Elegy for young lovers) (scenes).
(M) *** DG 449 874-2 [id.]. Fischer-Dieskau, Driscoll, Dubin, Mödl, Berlin RSO & German Op. O, Berlin (members), cond. composer.

Elegie für junge Liebende was completed in 1961, being the composer's fourth extended operatic work. The libretto by W. H. Auden and Chester Kallman is set in a mountain inn, from which the hero and heroine eventually go to their deaths in a storm; but the underlying psychology of the characters, their destinies dominated by the poet, Mittenhoffer, is most complex. So is the construction of the music, both in the variety of forms for the set pieces, and in the way each character is given his or her own musical personality by the individual use of specific instrumentation and note-groupings (intervals, rather than leitmotives). The composer shows his brilliant feeling for orchestral colour and, with Fischer-Dieskau as Mittenhoffer, Martha Mödl as a strong-voiced Carolina (the poet's patron) and Liane Dubin an appealing Elisabeth, the vocal writing is fully characterized. An excellent and enterprising issue.

Der junge Lord.
(M) *** DG 449 875-2 (2) [id.]. Mathis, Grobe, McDaniel, Johnson, Driscoll, German Op., Berlin, Ch. & O, Dohnányi.

As a reaction against his earlier, generally very serious operas, Henze in 1965 completed this piece designed as an *opera buffa*. This is Henze at his most amiable, and it results for much of the time in his Stravinskian side dominating, though he also allows himself a warmer vein of lyricism than usual. The plot in its comedy is consciously cynical, involving a snobbish community duped by a titled Englishman. He introduces an alleged English lord who finally turns out to be an ape. There is an underlying seriousness to the piece, and in this excellent performance, recorded with the composer's approval, the full range of moods and emotions is conveyed. Very good (1967) sound.

Hérold, Ferdinand (1791–1833)

La Fille mal gardée: extended excerpts.
500♪ ❁ (M) *** EMI Dig. CD-EMX 2268 [id.]. RLPO, Wordsworth.

Barry Wordsworth's scintillating account of a generous extended selection from the ballet includes all the important sequences. With playing from the Royal Liverpool Philharmonic Orchestra that combines refinement and delicacy with wit and humour, this is highly recommendable, especially for those enjoying modern, digital sound.

Hildegard of Bingen (1098–1179)

Canticles of ecstasy.
500♪ ❁ *** HM/BMG Dig. 05472 77320-2 [id.]. Sequentia, Barbara Thornton.

Born almost exactly nine centuries ago, Abbess Hildegard of Bingen has over the last decade emerged as one of the great creative figures of medieval times. This is a most moving and beautiful disc. At spacious speeds, with women's voices alone, the elaborate monodic lines soar heavenwards sensuously, matching the imagery of Hildegard's poetry. For a meditative mood this outdoes Gregorian chant. Highly recommended.

Hindemith, Paul (1895–1963)

Kammermusik Nos. 1 (with finale) for twelve solo instruments, Op. 24/1; (i) *4 (Violin concerto);* (ii) *5 (Viola concerto), Op. 36/3–4.*
*** EMI Dig. CDC5 56160-2 [id.]. BPO, Abbado, with (i) Kolja Blacher; (ii) Wolfram Christ.

It is amazing what refinement and point Abbado and the Berlin Philharmonic bring to music which can easily sound just chunky or even stodgy. Hindemith's rhythmic figures never lapse into sewing-machine metricality, with fine shaping of line and phrase. The recording helps, with the chamber textures given transparency, where often – as in Chailly's complete set of all seven *Kammermusik* works on Decca – the sound in its forwardness simulates a full orchestra. The soloists are excellent, with Kolja Blacher finding mercurial lightness in fast movements and warm expressiveness in the lovely *Nachtstuck*. Wolfram Christ, the orchestra's viola principal for many years, is an outstanding artist, flawless in tone and freely expressive.

(i) *Violin concerto;* (ii) *Mathis der Maler (Symphony);* (iii) *Symphonic metamorphosis on themes of Weber.*
500♪ ❁ (M) *** Decca 433 081-2 [id.]. (i) David Oistrakh, LSO, composer; (ii) SRO, Kletzki; (iii) LSO, Abbado.

Oistrakh's performance of the Hindemith *Violin concerto* is a revelation. The composer provides an overwhelmingly passionate accompaniment and the 1962 recording still sounds extraordinarily vivid and spacious. The Rosette is for the concerto but the couplings are well chosen, both also offering vintage late 1960s Decca sound.

Mathis der Maler (symphony).
(M) *** EMI CMS5 66109-2 (2) [id.]. BPO, Karajan – BRAHMS: *Tragic Overture;* BRUCKNER: *Symphony No. 8.* ***
(M) ** DG 439 488-2 [id.]. Boston SO, Steinberg – BUSONI: *Doktor Faust:* excerpt **; PFITZNER: *Palestrina: 3 Preludes* **; WEILL: *Kleine Dreigroschenmusik.* ***

It is good to have Karajan's recording back in the catalogue. It dates from 1957, but it was made in the Berlin Jesus-Christus-Kirche and the sound is impressively spacious, the strings gloriously full. The warm, full-blooded performance is remarkably dramatic and convincing, the central movement very touching. Though Hindemith's markings may occasionally be ignored, Karajan is convincing in everything he does.

The Boston Symphony Orchestra under William Steinberg give a very good account of the *Mathis symphony*, even if it does not quite match in humanity or spontaneity the best of the (now many) current rivals. The 1971 recording sounds eminently acceptable and the interesting couplings undoubtedly enhance the value of this CD.

Sinfonia serena; Symphony (Die Harmonie der Welt).
500♪ ❁ *** Chandos Dig. CHAN 9217 [id.]. BBC PO, Yan Pascal Tortelier.

The *Sinfonia serena* (1946) is a brilliant and inventive score, full of humour and melody. The scoring is inventive and imaginative, the textures varied and full of genial touches. The *Symphony*, *Die Harmonie der Welt* (1951), is another powerful and consistently underrated score. These well-prepared and finely shaped performances are given state-of-the-art recording quality. An outstanding issue.

Symphonic metamorphosis on themes by Weber.
500♪ *** Ph. Dig. 422 347-2 [id.]. Bav. RSO, C. Davis – REGER: *Mozart variations.* *** ❁

Sir Colin Davis's account of the *Symphonic metamorphosis* is first class, though not perhaps as gutsy as Bernstein (DG). However, the reading has plenty of character and enormous finesse and is given state-of-the art Philips recording. Recommended with enthusiasm.

Violin sonatas No 1 in E flat, Op. 11/1; 2 in D, Op. 11/2; 3 in E; 4 in C.
*** BIS Dig. CD 761 [id.]. Ulf Wallin, Roland Pöntinen.

Although Hindemith is more generously represented in the catalogue than he was some years ago, the BIS version of the *Violin sonatas* has the field to itself. True, the short *E major Sonata* of 1935 is available on a Szigeti recital disc (Sony), but none of its companions are. The Op. 11 sonatas date from 1918 when Hindemith was in the army, and while neither is particularly characteristic they are far from negligible. As with all Hindemith, both are well crafted and inventive, even if he has yet to find his voice. The finest of the four is the *C major* of 1939, which is both individual and finely wrought. Ulf Wallin and Roland Pöntinen play this repertoire with real dedication and conviction, and the BIS recording is very lifelike and present. They include a fragment of an alternative finale for the *E flat Sonata*, Op. 11/1, that Hindemith subsequently discarded.

PIANO MUSIC

Ludus tonalis.
*** Decca Dig. 444 803-2 [id.]. Olli Mustonen – PROKOFIEV: *Visions fugitives.* ***

Ludus tonalis; Suite (1922), Op. 26.
**(*) Hyperion Dig. CDA 66824 [id.]. John McCabe.

Hindemith's *Ludus tonalis* – comprising 25 sections – is, in total, not far short of an hour in length. It is a singularly obdurate and unyielding work, far from readily communicative, terse, angular and unseductive in texture. It has been recorded before, but not with more concentration and authority than it is on Hyperion by John McCabe. As if not wishing to compromise himself, instead of coupling it with something a little less formidably intellectual, he offers also the *Suite 1922* which, if anything, is thornier still. So if you are a Hindemith addict, this is surely a disc you will want to explore.

For the general listener, however, Olli Mustonen, using every imaginative device at his disposal, tries to communicate the intricacies and inner detail of Hindemith's argument, as he wends his way through the 25 studies. He uses pianistic colour, even giving hints of wit and irony (neither of which are strong points of this composer), to bring the music to life; as much as it is possible to unravel Hindemith's progression, he manages to do so. He is excellently recorded, and he offers also a fine account of Prokofiev's infinitely more approachable *Visions fugitives* as a palliative.

Hoddinott, Alun (born 1929)

(i; ii) *Concertino for viola and small orchestra, Op. 14;* (iii; iv) *Nocturnes and cadenzas for cello and orchestra, Op. 62;* (v; ii) *Dives and Lazarus* (cantata), *Op. 39;* (vi; iv) *Sinfonia Fidei* (for soprano, tenor, chorus & orchestra), *Op. 95.*
*** Lyrita Analogue/Dig. SRCD 332 [id.]. (i) Erdélyi; (ii) New Philh. O, David Atherton; (iii) Welsh; (iv) Philh. O, Groves; (v) Palmer, Allen, Welsh Nat. Op. Ch.; (vi) Jill Gomez, Burrowes, Philh. Ch.

Two Lyrita CDs now opportunely restore some of the key recordings of Alun Hoddinott's music to the catalogue, and this collection of concertante and vocal works in particular can be recommended both to newcomers and to those who have discovered and enjoyed his distinctly appealing brand of serial lyricism in the past. Csaba Erdélyi, the superb principal viola of the New Philharmonia in the mid-1970s, makes an admirable advocate in the imaginatively conceived *Viola concertino* of 1958, the point of the argument made sharper by the lightness of the string section against a normal woodwind group. By comparison the *Nocturnes and cadenzas* is less easy to come to grips with, presenting a more withdrawn face, not helped by being based on an idea which rather limits the quota of fast music. Nevertheless Moray Welsh excels himself as the cello soloist, making his soliloquy seemingly improvisational, and Sir Charles Groves draws excellent playing from the Philharmonia Orchestra. Not surprisingly, as Hoddinott is a Welshman, he is at his most inspired in his choral music, and particularly so in the succinct and emotionally concentrated cantata, *Dives and Lazarus*. It was originally written for young performers in the Farnham Schools Festival in 1965, but in its vitality it presents no apology and the choral writing is highly individual, especially in the dramatic closing section, *When Lazarus died*, with its exultant '*Allelujas*'.

Sinfonia Fidei (1977) returns to a more conservative idiom than that contained in Hoddinott's purely serial music, but the result is hardly less passionately compelling. This is one of the most impressive of Hoddinott's later works, purposeful and dramatic, and its economy has one immediately following the argument without difficulty. Soloists, chorus and orchestra join to project all this music with the most ardent advocacy and the recordings, spaciously atmospheric, whether analogue or digital, are in every respect first rate. A most rewarding collection, offering music which is worthy of repeated listening.

Symphonies Nos. (i; ii) *2, Op. 29;* (i; iii) *3, Op. 61;* (iv) *5, Op. 81.*
*** Lyrita SRCD 331 [id.]. (i) LSO; (ii) Del Mar; (iii) David Atherton; (iv) RPO, Andrew Davis.

The second of the two Lyrita Hoddinott collections offers three major symphonies, strengthening the composer's claim to be among the most substantial of British figures on the post-war musical scene. The *Second Symphony* dates from 1962 and is clearly the work of a composer who, though a serialist, still retains an allegiance to tonal centres and who uses twelve-note technique as a spur rather than a crutch. Its arguments are not difficult to follow and there is a great outburst of passionate lyricism from the strings at the climax of the *molto adagio*. A high proportion of the music is both slow and solemn and, although the finale is lively, even slightly grotesque, the reservation needs to be stated that Hoddinott might have let his vivid sense of humour have freer rein. Del Mar directs the work confidently, and the LSO respond with eloquence. The *Third Symphony* is even more powerfully wrought, dark in colouring and deeply imaginative. It is well laid out for the orchestra and is perhaps the most completely effective of the three works offered here. Atherton's performance (again using the LSO) is wholly convincing. The *Fifth Symphony* is a more abrasive work than the *Third* and less immediately approachable, although the second of its two movements is laid out in six clearly differentiated sections. It is splendidly powerful, and it reinforces Hoddinott's representation in the catalogue when so impressively played. The vintage recordings of both the *Third* and *Fifth Symphonies* were made by a Decca engineering team in the early 1970s and are spectacularly vivid in their presence, range and definition.

Holbrooke, Joseph (1878–1958)

The Birds of Rhiannon, Op. 87; The Children of Don: Overture, Op. 56; Dylan: Prelude, Op. 53.
** Marco Polo Dig. 8.223721-2 [id.]. Ukraine Nat. SO, Andrew Penny.

Hailed before the First World War in extravagant terms as the composer of 'the Celtic Ring', Holbrooke's music underwent a neglect almost (but not quite) as total as that of his near contemporary, Havergal Brian. Although some of his output was recorded in the days of 78s, both the mono and stereo LP era passed them by. *The Children of Don* (1911) is the first opera of the trilogy, *The Cauldron of Annwyn*, while *Dylan* is the second. Neither overture nor prelude offers particularly memorable or individual ideas and, generally speaking, inspiration is pretty thin. There are touches of Wagner in the former but the musical language is predominantly diatonic, particularly in the tone-poem *The Birds of Rhiannon*. The longest piece is the *Prelude* to *Dylan*, which takes over 20 minutes. It is pretty undistinguished stuff. The whole disc runs to 46 minutes, which is poor value for a premium-price disc. The performances sound a bit under-rehearsed but are adequate (some may find the horn vibrato a bit excessive), and the recording is decent.

(i) *Piano quartet in G min., Op. 21;* (ii) *String sextet in D, Op. 43;* (iii) *Symphonic quintet No. 1 in G min., Op. 44.*
** Marco Polo Dig. 8 223736 [id.]. (i; iii) Endre Hegedüs; (ii) Sándor Papp, János Devich; New Haydn Qt.

All three works come from the early years of the present century, the *Sextet in D major* (1902), the *Symphonic quintet* (1904) and the *Piano quartet in G minor* (1905), though the last began life as a piano trio seven years earlier. Although the music never falls below a certain level of melodic fluency and is expertly crafted, little of it remains in the memory. The musical discourse is civilized and cultured but ultimately is let down by a certain pallor. Probably the most memorable idea comes in the *Lament* that serves as the centrepiece of the *Piano quartet*, though the outer movements rather outstay their welcome. The *String sextet* makes the most immediate and positive impact but, after the CD has come to an end, one realizes why Holbrooke has not stayed the course. Those with a lively musical curiosity should investigate the disc, certainly in preference to the orchestral CD listed above, and the fine Hungarian ensemble play these pieces with appropriate conviction and ardour. Decent recording, much better than for the orchestral disc. An interesting excursion into musical backwaters that are not as stagnant as one might fear, but not sufficiently interesting to warrant any urgency of recommendation.

Holmboe, Vagn (1909–96)

Chamber concertos Nos. (i) *11 for trumpet and orchestra, Op. 44;* (ii) *12 for trombone, Op. 52;* (iii) *Tuba concerto, Op. 152. Intermezzo concertante, Op. 171.*
*** BIS Dig. CD 802 [id.]. (i) Håkan Hardenberger; (ii) Christian Lindberg; (iii) Jens-Bjørn Larsen; Aalborg SO, Owain Arwel Hughes.

During the 1940s, after the success of his *Second Symphony*, Holmboe embarked on a series of 12 *Chamber concertos* for various combinations. The noble neo-baroque *Concerto No. 11 for trumpet* (1948) is not new to the catalogue. There have been two earlier recordings and will doubtless be more, now that Holmboe's music is coming into its own. However, it is unlikely that any will be better than Håkan Hardenberger's account with the Aalborg orchestra, and one is tempted to add that any newcomer will have to be pretty good to match Christian Lindberg's account of the *Twelfth Chamber concerto* (1950), composed in the immediate wake of the *Seventh Symphony*. These are inspiriting and inspiring pieces. The one-movement *Tuba concerto* (1976) is an astonishing piece which explores the virtuoso possibilities of this instrument as do few others. The *Intermezzo concertante* comes from 1987, just before the *Twelfth Symphony*. These are dazzling performances and the orchestral support under Owain Arwel Hughes is first class. The recording is state of the art. Highly recommended.

Symphonies Nos. 11, Op. 141; 12, Op. 175; 13, Op. 192.
*** BIS Dig. CD 728 [id.]. Aarhus SO, Owain Arwel Hughes.

The *Thirteenth Symphony* is an astonishing achievement for a composer in his mid-eighties. There have been octogenarian symphonies (Vaughan Williams's *Ninth*) and even a nonagenarian symphony in Paul Le Flem's *Fourth*, but it is difficult to think of one that sounds more vigorous or powerful than Holmboe's *Thirteenth*, first performed in 1996, some months before his death. It is a veritable powerhouse. The *Twelfth* was commissioned in the composer's eightieth year by BBC Wales, whose orchestra (now the BBC National Orchestra of Wales) had performed no fewer than four of the symphonies in the late 1980s and premièred the *Twelfth* in Cardiff in 1989. It is tautly structured and well argued, though less inspired than the *Eleventh Symphony*, which finds Holmboe at his most visionary. The arabesque that opens the first movement seems as if it is coming from another world. Every credit is due to Owain Arwel Hughes and the Aarhus Symphony Orchestra for their fervent advocacy of this music and to the splendid BIS engineers for the vivid and superbly natural sound. It is good to know that the three *Chamber Symphonies* and the impressive *Nietzsche Requiem* will be issued within the lifetime of this volume.

Holst, Gustav (1874–1934)

Brook Green suite for string orchestra; (i) *Fugal concerto for flute and oboe. The Perfect Fool* (ballet suite), *Op. 39; St Paul's suite for string orchestra, Op. 26/2; A Somerset rhapsody, Op. 21/2.*
500♪ (M) *** EMI CD-EMX 2227; *TC-EMX 2227*. ECO, Sir Yehudi Menuhin.

There are a number of collections of Holst's shorter orchestral works currently available on CD, but none better played or recorded than this and none less expensive. It includes warmly characterized performances of both the works Holst wrote for St Paul's Girls' School, not just the *St Paul's suite* but also the *Brook Green suite*, both sounding fresh, while the rarer *Somerset rhapsody* is also very atmospherically presented.

The Planets (suite).
500♪ *** DG Dig. 445 860 2; *445 860-4* [id.]. Monteverdi Ch. women's voices, Philh. O, Gardiner – GRAINGER: *The Warriors*. ***
(M) *** Decca 452 303-2 [id.]. VPO, Karajan – ELGAR: *Enigma variations*. ***
** Sony SBK 62400; *SBT 62400* [id.]. NYPO & Ch., Bernstein – WALTON: *Façade* (excerpts). ***
(B) * Millennium MCD 80099. V. State Op. O with Ch., Sir Adrian Boult – VAUGHAN WILLIAMS: *Tallis & Greensleeves fantasias*. *(*)

The Planets on DG offers a performance of high voltage, with plenty of panache and an acute feeling for atmospheric colour. Outstandingly enjoyable are the two most extrovert pieces: *Jupiter, the bringer of jollity* has rarely sounded so joyful, with a hint of wildness at the start, and the dancing rhythms of *Uranus* have a scherzando sparkle, with timpani and brass stunningly caught in the full, brilliant recording.

With Karajan at his peak, plus the challenge to an orchestra discovering this music for the first time, this extraordinarily magnetic and powerful 1961 account of *The Planets* is uniquely individual, bringing a rare tension, an extra magnetism, the playing combining polish and freshness. The superb Decca recording – produced by John Culshaw in the Sofiensaal – is fully worthy of reissue in Decca's Classic Sound series. It remains of demonstration quality, with thrilling weight, clarity of focus and sense of presence, and it has never sounded more vivid and more richly atmospheric than in its present transfer. *Mars* is remorselessly paced and, with its whining Wagnerian tubas, is unforgettable, while the ravishingly gentle portrayal of *Venus* brings ardent associations with the goddess of love, rather than seeking a peaceful purity. The gossamer textures of *Mercury* and the bold geniality of *Jupiter* contrast with the solemn, deep melancholy expressed by the VPO strings at the opening of *Saturn*. *Uranus* brings splendid playing from the Vienna brass, given splendid bite.

The Bernstein version of *The Planets* is freer and brasher than Karajan's and not so well recorded, but this bargain reissue is worth considering for the unexpected coupling, 16 movements from Walton's *Façade* entertainment.

Younger readers may not remember that Boult, after making his first mono LP of *The Planets* for Pye (subsequently PRT) with the so-called Philharmonic Promenade Orchestra, in 1959 went to Vienna to make his first stereo version. Boult's trips to Europe have often produced some unexpectedly good records – but not in this instance. The Viennese playing is barely acceptable. The orchestra sounds under-rehearsed: there are fluffs in the strings and a very clumsy principal horn solo at the beginning of *Venus*. In the big, bold tunes the players miss the breadth of the music and sound phlegmatic. Only in *Mars* does the Viennese brass add a characterful hint of Wagner, which was to be amplified in Karajan's inspired later version for Decca with the VPO. The recording is bright and fully acceptable, but this well-transferred CD can be regarded as no more than a curiosity, for the Vaughan Williams couplings are little better.

The Planets (suite); *St Paul's suite* (for strings), *Op. 29*.
(M) *** Carlton Dig. 30366 0432 [id.]. Ladies of New Queen's Hall Ch., New Queen's Hall O, Roy Goodman.

Under Roy Goodman, a conductor more often associated with baroque and classical repertory, the New Queen's Hall Orchestra crowns its achievement so far in a performance favouring instruments of the kind in general use in the first quarter of the twentieth century, the result subtly different from the effect using modern instruments. These players are drawn from among top professional musicians dedicated to the idea of what an orchestra used to sound like, before the latterday emphasis on volume at all costs. They plainly love their art. The result is less aggressive, less brash than usual. Goodman is a persuasive interpreter, generally making a good case for faster speeds than are usual (maybe reflecting Holst's own recording of 1926), even if with less panache in *Jupiter* and *Uranus* than with the finest versions.

Interestingly, although the wooden flutes come from a London manufacturer (Rudall, Carte), all the reed woodwind instruments (and most notably the bassoons) are French. The piston horns (French or British), trumpets (American) and trombones (Boosey & Hawkes) are narrow bore: they do not in any way lack sonority but are without that overwhelming 'fatness' of timbre one associates with wider-bore instruments. The drums will not please environmentalists as they are all covered in animal skins; but the ear registers the difference, and the gut strings bring vividly detailed textures.

The immediate impact with *Mars* is in no doubt. If there is initially less menace than usual, Goodman is tremendously urgent in his pacing, developing great ferocity at the close. One recalls Alan Leo's symbol of the 'destroying angel' in the book on astrology which was the original inspiration for Holst's work. *Venus* with its delicate horn solo and translucent flutes is truly the bringer of peace, and the woodwind colouring and transparency of the strings tickle the ear in *Mercury*.

The opening of *Jupiter* is light and clean, with crisp string articulation characteristic of the lighter sounds of instruments using gut strings. Brass is less forward too, partly a question of recording balance, but also reflecting the use of authentic instruments. Here the bold narrow-bore horns really come into their own, not only in the Holstian rhythmic striding themes but in the support they provide for the great central string tune. The ear continually notices the natural clarity of the sound-picture, not least in *Saturn*, which opens gently and poignantly, with the timpani coming through thrillingly at the climax and the deep bass pedal subtle in its underlining. At the beginning of *Uranus* the chortling bassoons readily recall Dukas's apprentice; the horns are ebullient, the brass – and notably the tuba – making the sharpest, fullest impact. The delicate flutes establish a gentle, lonely mysticism as *Neptune* steals in, the chorus ethereal and perfectly placed in relation to the woodwind. The refreshingly athletic account of the *St Paul's suite* which acts as an encore is a good demonstration of the bright, clean quality of gut strings; only in Holst's combination of *Greensleeves* with the *Dargason* in the finale, does the ear crave a riper sonority. John Boydon's Abbey Road recording does the orchestra full justice, and the back-up notes are well detailed.

The Planets (suite), *Op. 32; Suite de ballet in E flat, Op. 10.*
(BB) ** Naxos Dig. 8.550193 [id.]. Slovak RSO, Bratislava, Adrian Leaper.

On Naxos, the Slovak Radio Orchestra under an English conductor give a direct, straightforward reading, without much subtlety of detail, but strong in effect, helped by excellent, full-bodied, digital recording. The big tune in *Jupiter*, taken spaciously, is sonorously eloquent. The novelty is the inclusion of Holst's early four-movement *Suite de ballet*, written in 1899 and revised in 1912. The invention is attractively robust, apart from the winningly fragile *Valse*, and the work is presented enthusiastically. Good orchestral playing throughout.

(i; ii) *A Choral Fantasia, Op. 51;* (ii) *A Dirge for two veterans;* (iii) *Hymn of Jesus; Ode to Death, Op. 38;* (i; ii) *7 Partsongs, Op. 44.*
500♪ *** Chandos Dig. CHAN 9437 [id.]. (i) Patricia Rozario; (ii) Joyful Company of Singers; (iii) London Symphony Ch.; City of L. Sinf., Hickox.

Richard Hickox proves a passionate advocate of these shorter choral works of Holst, demonstrating that the two Whitman settings, *A Dirge for two veterans* and the *Ode to Death*, are among his finest pieces for voices. That second work is in very much the same vein of inspiration as his masterpiece, the *Hymn of Jesus* and, with the larger forces of the London Symphony Chorus, brings the most powerful performance here.

Honegger, Arthur (1892–1955)

Concertino for piano and orchestra.
*** Decca Dig. 452 448-2 [id.]. Jean-Yves Thibaudet, Montreal SO, Dutoit – RAVEL: *Concertos* **; FRANCAIX: *Concertino*. ***

Honegger's *Concertino* has a gamin-like charm and its jazzy finale has delightful zest and character. Eunice Norton (Honegger's fiancée) recorded it with Ormandy in the days of 78s and Walter Klien made a more than respectable version for Vox in the 1960s (see below). This is probably the best of the few accounts to have appeared since then, and it is much better recorded than the Turnabout reissue. Like the Françaix with which it is coupled, it is an unqualified delight. The main works, the two Ravel *Concertos*, are good but in no way do they challenge existing recommendations, so we hope Decca will one day recouple the two *Concertinos*.

(i) *Concertino for piano and orchestra;* (ii) Piano music: *Album des six: Sarabande. Le cahier Romand: Calme; Un peu animé; Calme et doux; Rythmé; Egal. 2 Esquisses; Hommage à Albert Roussel. 3 Pièces: Prélude; Hommage à Ravel; Danse. 7 Pièces brèves: Souplement; Vif; Très lent; Légèrement; Lent; Rhythmique; Violent. Prélude, Arioso & Fuguette sur le nom de Bach. Toccata et variations.*

(B) *** Carlton Turnabout 30371 00542. (i) Walter Klien, V. Pro Musica, Hollreiser; (ii) Jürg von Vintschger.

This admirable Honegger collection draws on two different Turnabout originals. The *Piano concertino* is a lightweight work that recalls Françaix, but with a dash of added dissonance. It has a haunting central slow section which has bizarre effects in the orchestra, and it flirts with jazz. It is admirably played by Walter Klien, and Hollreiser has the measure of the accompaniment, especially the increase in pace and tension towards the end. Jürg von Vintschger then presents an excellent survey of a neglected aspect of Honegger's output: his solo piano music. It has a mixed cocktail of influences, from Debussy (the *Toccata et variations*) to Poulenc, and even a dash of Satie. Much of it is highly attractive. *Hommage à Ravel* from the *Trois pièces* is beautifully wrought, and the five *morceaux* which make up *Le cahier Romand* are hauntingly atmospheric. Von Vintschger's playing is totally committed – he is right inside the music. The recording, although resonant, is pleasingly full in colour, and readers who want to investigate this side of Honegger's musical personality can do so here at little cost and with remarkably rich rewards.

Pacific 231; Rugby.

(M) ** Sony MHK 62352 [id.]. NYPO, Bernstein – MILHAUD: *Les Choéphores* ***; ROUSSEL: *Symphony No. 3.* **(*)

Leonard Bernstein's 1962 performances sounded pretty strident in their original LP incarnation, though the playing has tremendous character and virtuosity. The engineers have succeeded in taming much of the ferocity, and the present transfer produces more acceptable results.

Symphonies Nos. 2 for strings with trumpet obbligato; 3 (Symphonie liturgique).

500♪ ❁ (M) *** DG 447 435-2 [id.]. BPO, Karajan (with STRAVINSKY: *Concerto in D* ***).

Karajan's accounts of these magnificent symphonies remain in a class of their own. Not even Munch's pioneering recording of the *Symphony No. 2* or its successors comes near to it for sheer poetic intensity, and the *Symphonie liturgique* has likewise never been surpassed. It is luminous, incandescent and moving.

Symphony No. 5 ('Di tre re').

(M) (**) DG Originals mono 449 748-2 [id.]. Lamoureux O, Igor Markevitch – MILHAUD: *Les Choéphores* (**); ROUSSEL: *Bacchus et Ariane: suite No. 2.* **

Markevitch's account of the *Fifth Symphony* with the Orchestre Lamoureux was recorded in the Salle Wagram in 1957 – in mono. The sound has plenty of depth and good perspective; it is a little set back, though there is no lack of impact in tuttis and there is plenty of space round the instruments elsewhere. Markevitch generates plenty of atmosphere, but his approach is more lyrical than, say, Munch's pioneering (1952) record with the Boston orchestra (RCA GD 60085) or the impetuous and dazzling Serge Baudo version with the Czech Philharmonic (Supraphon 11 0667-2); it is probably nearer to the masterly Järvi account on Chandos (CHAN 9176), which has much superior sound. All these alternatives are discussed in our main volume. Markevitch's reading is strongly characterized, but not a first choice.

Christmas cantata (*Cantate de Noël*).

(M) *** EMI Eminence Dig. CD-EMX 2275. Sweeney, Waynflete Singers, Winchester Cathedral Ch., ECO, Neary – POULENC: *Mass; Motets.* ***

A recording of Honegger's charming *Cantate de Noël* to do it full justice. It was the composer's last completed work and deserves to be more popular at the festive season outside France. The recording is impressively wide-ranging and well defined.

Howells, Herbert (1892–1983)

Collegium regale: Te Deum and jubilate; Office of Holy Communion; Magnificat and Nunc dimittis. Preces & Responses I & II; Psalms 121 & 122; Take him, earth for cherishing. Rhapsody for organ, Op. 17/3.

500♪ ❁ *** Decca Dig. 430 205-2 [id.]. Williams, Moore, King's College, Cambridge, Ch., Cleobury.

Here is an unmatchable collection of the settings inspired by the greatest of our collegiate choirs, King's College, Cambridge, presented in performances of heartwarming intensity in that great choir's 1989 incarnation. The boy trebles in particular are among the brightest and fullest ever to have been recorded with this choir. Even those not normally attracted by Anglican church music should hear this.

Hummel, Johann (1778–1837)

(i) *Bassoon concerto in F;* (ii) *Piano concertino in G, Op. 73;* (iii) *Rondo for piano in E (La Galante), Op. 120;* (iv) *Septuor militaire in C, Op. 114.*

(B) *** Carlton Turnabout 30371 00092 [id.]. (i) Zukerman, Württemberg CO, Heilbron, Jörg Faerber; (ii) Galling, Berlin SO, Carl August Bünte; (iii) Galling; (iv) Coll. Con Basso.

It was the Vox Turnabout label in the 1960s which first rediscovered the appeal of the Hummel concertos on LP, and these recordings were much admired when they first appeared. They may not be quite as finished as more modern versions, but they make excellent bargain recommendations. The *Bassoon concerto* is a winner, with all the charm, if perhaps not quite the depth, of the famous work by Mozart. It is played with a real appreciation of its genial humour by George Zukerman, who shows himself also an uncommonly good musician in matters of technique and phrasing. The *Piano concertino* with its immediately catchy dotted melody in the first movement and its amiable chatter is never empty. Again, very good playing from Martin Galling and more than acceptable accompaniments. The recording still sounds very good, pleasingly atmospheric even if the orchestral focus is not absolutely sharp. The *Military septet* is ingeniously scored for the unusual combination of flute, clarinet, trumpet, violin, cello, double-bass and piano. Hummel integrates them with witty skill. The performance is fresh and lively, and this makes a good bonus for the original LP coupling, bringing the playing time up to 77 minutes. Excellent value and most enjoyable.

(i) *Piano concerto in A min., Op. 85;* (i–ii) *Double concerto in G for piano, violin and orchestra;* (iii) *Mandolin concerto in G.*

(B) *(*) Carlton Turnabout 30371 00102 [id.]. (i) Martin Galling; (ii) Susanne Lautenbacher; (i–ii) Stuttgart PO, Paulmüller; (iii) Edith Bauer-Slais, V. Pro Musica O, Hladky.

Hummel's charming *A minor Piano concerto* is much better known now than when it made its LP début in the present version on Turnabout in the 1960s. The work is well played and acceptably recorded. The *Double concerto*, however, is less interesting as a work and, although it is redeemed to some extent by its engaging central *Andante con variazioni*, the performance here is not helped by a highly modulated, resonant recording which places the soloists very near the listener and is unflattering to Susanne Lautenbacher's tone. In the *Mandolin concerto* Hummel exploits the instrument's possibilities skilfully and the invention is agreeable. (Interestingly, the catchy main theme of the first movement is very like the incidental music for the film, *Cinema Paradiso*.) The soloist here makes the most of the work and is well caught by the recording, but the orchestral tuttis are ill-focused and altogether this is much less attractive than the companion Turnabout CD.

Trumpet concerto in E.

500♪ ❁ *** Ph. Dig. 420 203-2 [id.]. Hardenberger, ASMF, Marriner – HAYDN *** ❁; HERTEL ***; STAMITZ: *Concertos.* ***

Hummel's *Trumpet concerto* is usually heard in the familiar brass key of E flat, but the brilliant Swedish trumpeter, Håkan Hardenberger, uses the key of E, which makes it sound brighter and bolder than usual. This is the finest version of the piece in the catalogue, for Marriner's accompaniment is polished and sympathetic.

Piano quintet in E flat, Op.87.

(B) **(*) Hyperion Dyad Dig. CDD 22008 (2) [id.]. Schubert Ens. of L. – SCHUBERT: *Trout quintet;* SCHUMANN: *Piano quintet; Piano quartet.* **(*)

A strong account of an impressive work from the Schubert Ensemble of London, who approach the piece as one in the classical mainstream rather than a *galant* entertainment. There is plenty of energy and commitment, and the brief *Largo* is made a touching interlude; only the finale (admittedly marked *Allegro agitato*) might seem too strongly driven and with not enough balancing elegance. The recording has fine immediacy.

String quartet in G, Op. 30/2.

*(*) Testament mono SBT 1085 [id.]. Hollywood Qt – HAYDN: *Quartet No. 72;* MOZART: *Quartet No. 17.* **(*)

Hummel's charming *G major Quartet* comes with the first half of a 1957 Festival Hall concert. This performance was recorded two years earlier in a Hollywood studio and, though dazzlingly played, is a bit shrill.

Humperdinck, Engelbert (1854–1921)

Christmas Lieder: *Altdeutsches Weihnachtslied; Christkindleins Wiegenlied; Das Licht der Welt; Der Stern von Bethlehem; Weihnachten.*

❀ *** EMI Dig. CDC5 56204-2 [id.]. Bär, Deutsch (with Recital: '*Christmas Lieder*' *** ❀).

These Christmas settings have all the character and charm one would expect from the composer of *Hänsel und Gretel*, and Olaf Bär's warmly flowing line consistently captures their easy lyricism. The *Old German Christmas song* gently recalls *Jesus lieber Jesus mein*, and the bewitching *Christkindleins Wiegenlied* is hardly less memorable; the closing *Weihnachten* has a Schubertian spontaneity of feeling and a lovely tune. Bär's relaxed, affectionate (yet at times dramatic) performances are perfectly judged, and he is beautifully accompanied by Helmut Deutsch. The recording too, is balanced most naturally.

Hänsel und Gretel (complete).

500♪ *** Teldec/Warner Dig.4509 94549-2 (2) [id.]. Larmore, Ziesak, Schwarz, Weikl, Behrens, Tölz Boys' Ch., Bav. RSO, Runnicles.

The success of the Teldec version of *Hänsel und Gretel* is largely due to Donald Runnicles, who adds to the fantasy by giving his soloists an extra degree of freedom, encouraging individual expressiveness. In the casting the emphasis more than ever is on fresh, youthful voices, but here the distinction between boy and girl is sharply drawn. Ruth Ziesak as Gretel and Jennifer Larmore as Hänsel are above all natural-sounding, with little or no feeling of mature opera-singers pretending to be children, yet with no sense of strain and none of the edginess. Fresh clarity marks the other voices too, even that of the Witch as taken by Hanna Schwarz.

Königskinder (complete).

**(*) Calig Dig. CAL 50968/70 (3) [id.]. Moser, Schellenberger, Henschel, Schmiege, Kohn, Munich Boys' Ch., Bav. R. Ch. & O, Fabio Luisi.

It is easy to see why *Königskinder*, for all its many beauties, has never begun to match Humperdinck's masterpiece, *Hänsel und Gretel*, in popularity. Not only is the story of the Prince and the Goosegirl less involving, more disorganized than that of *Hänsel*, the treatment is too long-winded for a fairy-tale opera. The score is as lyrical as you could want, but regularly what in *Hänsel* would have developed into a big tune peters out too soon. Even so, it is good to have a new recording of a rich score, generally well sung and warmly conducted by Fabio Luisi, who captures the buoyancy of much of the writing as well as the lyrical flow. This digital version uses the same choir and orchestra as the earlier, EMI set, recorded in 1976. The venue this time is the Herkules-Saal in Munich instead of the radio studio used by EMI, with sound rather more spacious but not so immediate. An incidental shortcoming in both sets is that the libretto comes in German only, with the Calig libretto omitting even the stage directions. The voices are not specially characterful, but there is no serious weakness. The tenor of Thomas Moser, taking the central role of the Prince, is more heroic than that of his EMI rival, Adolf Dallapozza, with the voice often shaded down beautifully. Though Dagmar Schellenberger as the Goosegirl lacks sweetness, hers is a feeling, well-characterized performance, and she finds a delicate *mezza voce* for the prayer to her parents. Marilyn Schmiege with her warm, firm mezzo makes rather a young Witch, a more equivocal character, not nearly as clearly defined as the Witch in *Hänsel*. All told, this is a performance marked by good teamwork, with the chorus bringing energetic echoes of Smetana's *Bartered Bride* in their brief contributions.

Ibert, Jacques (1890–1962)

Divertissement.

500♪ *** Chandos Dig. CHAN 9023 [id.]. Ulster O, Yan Pascal Tortelier – MILHAUD: *Le Boeuf; Création;* POULENC: *Les Biches.* ***

Yan Pascal Tortelier provides at last a splendid, modern, digital version of Ibert's *Divertissement*. There is much delicacy of detail, and the coupled suite from Poulenc's *Les Biches* is equally delectable.

Complete chamber music

Vol. 1: *Aria for flute, violin & piano; Française* (for solo guitar); *Le jardinier de Samos* (for flute, clarinet, trumpet, violin, cello & percussion); *Jeux* (Sonatine for flute & piano); *2 Movements for wind quartet; Paraboles for 2 guitars; Pastoral for 4 pipes; 3 Pièces brèves for wind quintet; 5 Pièces en trio for oboe, clarinet & bassoon; 6 Pièces for harp.*
*** Olympia Dig. OCD 468 [id.]. Pameijer, Hülsmann, Van Staalen, Grotenhuis, Colbers, Masseurs, Marinissen, Oostenrijk, Gaasterland, Jeurissen, Franssen, De Rijke, Stoop.

Vol. 2: *Ariette* (for solo guitar); *Caprilena for solo violin; Carignane for bassoon & piano; Chevalier errant: L'âge d'or* (for alto sax & piano); *Entr'acte for flute & guitar; Etude-caprice pour un tombeau de Chopin; Ghirlarzana* (both for solo cello); *Impromptu for trumpet & piano; 2 Interludes for flute, violin & harpsichord; String quartet; Trio for violin, cello & harp.*
*** Olympia Dig. OCD 469 [id.]. Franssen, Hülsmann, Gaasterland, Grotenhuis, Bornkamp, Pameijer, Van Staalen, Masseurs, Van Delft, Stoop, New Netherlands Qt.

This pair of Olympia discs offer music which is not only delightful but (for the most part) very little known, with the exception of the *Trois pièces brèves* which are justly familiar. Yet the *Trio for violin, cello and harp* is hardly less distinctive, while the *Cinq Pièces en trio* have a winning pastoral flavour. French composers were especially good at writing Spanish music (Chabrier and Ravel spring immediately to mind), so it is not surprising that Ibert's music featuring the guitar has such southern Mediterranean feeling. But then so do the *Deux Interludes* for flute, violin and harpsichord, another very winning trio and with something of a gypsy flamenco flavour. The two CDs, each lasting around 80 minutes, are arranged in order of composition, so the *Six Pièces* for solo harp come at the beginning to entice the listener with their smooth melodic flow. But there is not a dull or unimaginative item here, and these excellent Dutch players have the full measure of the witty, piquant Poulenc manner. They are very well recorded. This is music to cheer you up on a dull day.

d'India, Sigismondo (*c.* 1582–*c.* 1630)

Il Terzo libro de Madrigali.
(B) **(*) DHM Dig. 05472 77437-2 [id.]. The Consort of Musicke, Anthony Rooley.

Sigismondo d'India's *Third Book of Madrigals* dates from 1615, and their style often echoes the composer's contemporary, Monteverdi. Rooley's Consort blend admirably and sing *a cappella* with remarkable freshness in the early works, if perhaps a little coolly. Rooley feels that the later numbers, from No. 13 onwards, need the support of a discreet continuo, and certainly the singing of these last eight settings seems freer and richer. It was a pity that the bargain reissue did not run to translations, which surely would have been in the proper Baroque Esprit. But this remains an attractive disc.

d'Indy, Vincent (1851–1931)

Symphonie sur un chant montagnard français (Symphonie cévenole).
(M) ** Ph. 454 127-2 [id.]. Bucquet, Monte Carlo Opera O, Capolongo – DUKAS: *L'apprenti sorcier* etc. *** ❁

Marie-Françoise Bucquet is a strong and personable soloist, bringing out the affinities this concertante work has with Franck's *Symphonic variations*. The playing of the Monte Carlo orchestra under Capolongo is supportive, if unrefined, and the performance is at its best in the animated finale. But this is acceptable enough when the Dukas couplings are outstandingly successful.

Symphony No. 2 in B flat, Op. 57; Souvenirs, Op. 52.
**(*) Koch Dig. 37280-2 [id.]. Monte Carlo PO, James DePreist.

The *Second Symphony* remains one of the neglected masterpieces of turn-of-the-century French music. Of the post-Franck school, only the Chausson *Symphony in B flat* has maintained a concert-hall profile, while the symphonies of Dukas and Magnard are hardly ever heard there. Monteux's pioneering performance has been reissued in a 14-CD box – transferred at the wrong pitch – and although it was reissued on LP in the USA, the first stereo version did not appear on the scene until Michel Plasson and the Toulouse orchestra on EMI (see our main volume). Choice between that and this newcomer is a matter of swings-and-roundabouts and should rest perhaps on the coupling. DePreist does not have as fine an orchestra as the Toulouse Capitole, though they play with plenty of commitment, but the recording is slightly more detailed. Plasson's coupling is the ubiquitous *Symphonie sur un chant montagnard français*, an older recording with Aldo Ciccolini and the Orchestre de Paris under Serge Baudo, while DePreist gives us the affecting *Souvenirs* d'Indy composed on the death of his wife, which are not otherwise available. Newcomers to this noble composer may prefer the EMI version, the initiate will opt for the present account. You can't go far wrong with either.

Ireland, John (1879–1962)

Piano concerto in E flat.
500♪ (M) (***) Dutton Lab. mono CDAX 8001 [id.]. Eileen Joyce, Hallé O, Leslie Heward – MOERAN: *Symphony.* *** ❀

Eileen Joyce's 1942 recording of this delightful concerto readily demonstrates the flamboyant romanticism for which she was famous and even a moment or two of fantasy, plus the freshness of discovery. Leslie Heward accompanies with flair, and the orchestral playing is impressive. The superb transfers of the original 78s show the work of Dutton Laboratories at its finest, offering sound that in its body and sense of presence sets new standards in re-creating what it felt like listening to the original 78s.

Five songs to poems by Thomas Hardy; The Advent; Friendship in misfortune; Great things; The Heart's desire; Hymn for a child; I have twelve oxen; Love and friendship; The Merry month of May; My fair; The Sacred flame; The Sally gardens; Santa Chiara; The Scapegoat; The Soldier's return; Spring sorrow.
(M) (**(*)) Saga mono EC 3338-2 [id.]. John Shirley-Quirk, Eric Parkin.

John Shirley-Quirk's performances are as fine as those on his earlier disc of Vaughan Williams and others. Eric Parkin makes a splendidly convincing accompanist, and it is the piano part which constantly impresses with its felicity rather than the vocal line. For all the attractiveness of the idiom, Ireland rarely seems to let himself go with a real tune. The melodic lines are beautiful to look at on paper but, largely through the constant wandering of key, they do not quite add up. One recalls Anna Russell's famous phrase about the modern British 'folksong' that constantly sounds as if it is going to develop into a tune but never quite does. Despite the disappointment, these are finely wrought songs, certain to be interesting to Lieder specialists, and the performances here add to that interest. The recording is more than acceptably clear.

Ives, Charles (1874–1954)

Holidays Symphony.
(B) ** Carlton Turnabout 30371 0011-2 [id.]. Southern Methodist University Ch., Dallas SO, Donald Johanos – COPLAND: *Dance symphony.* **

The so-called *Holidays Symphony* (also known as *New England holidays*) consists of four fine Ives pieces normally heard separately. The first three, *George Washington's birthday*, *Decoration Day* and *The Fourth of July*, with their still-startling clashes of impressionistic imagery, are well enough known. The fourth – full title: *Thanksgiving and/or Forefathers Day* – is a rarity, bringing in a full choir to sing a single verse of a hymn. The performances here are vividly enthusiastic if not absolutely refined. But the recording is impressive with its atmospheric effects, even if not perfectly balanced.

Symphony No. 2; Central Park in the dark; The gong on the hook and ladder; Hallowe'en; Hymn for strings; Tone roads No. 1; The unanswered question.
500♪ *** DG Dig. 429 220-2 [id.]. NYPO, Bernstein.

Bernstein's disc brings one of the richest offerings of Ives yet put on record, offering the *Symphony No. 2* plus six shorter orchestral pieces. They include two of his very finest, *Central Park in the dark* and *The unanswered question*, both characteristically quirky but deeply poetic too. The extra tensions and expressiveness of live performance here heighten the impact of each of the works. The difficult acoustic of Avery Fisher Hall in New York has rarely sounded more sympathetic on record.

Orchestral set No. 2.
(M) *** Decca Phase Four 448 956-2 [id.]. LSO Ch., LSO, Stokowski – GROFE: *Grand Canyon suite.* *(*)

The *Second Orchestral set* consists of three highly evocative pieces crammed with the sort of wild devices that make Ives's music so distinctive. Most memorable is the third of the pieces called (extravagantly) *From Hanover Square North, at the End of a Tragic Day (1915), the Voices of the People Again Rose*. It depicts an incident on the elevated railway on the day when the *Lusitania* was sunk, when the crowd spontaneously started to sing *In the sweet bye and bye*. In such atmospheric music Stokowski's wonderful sense of dramatic development is perfectly exploited. The multi-channel Phase Four recording, made in

1970, is well suited to the music, and the LSO obviously enjoys the experience, not least in the ragtime of the second piece, and the Kingsway Hall ambience ensures plenty of atmosphere, especially in the spectacular choral finale.

Jadin, Hyacinthe (1775–1800)

String quartets, Opp. 1/3; 2/1; 4/1.
*** ASV Gaudeamus Dig. CDGAU 151 [id.]. Rasumovsky Qt – VACHON: *Quartets*. ***

Jadin, of Belgian descent and with the unlikely Christian name of Hyacinthe, was male and was born in Versailles. He died of tuberculosis before he reached his mid-twenties, but he left us piano sonatas, some concertos and three sets of quartets, published annually between 1795 and 1798. He obviously studied the quartets of Haydn and Mozart, for Op. 1/3 is dedicated to the former master. In F minor, it is the most strikingly individual work here, with a well-crafted, Haydnesque first movement with a nice interplay between lead violin and cello, an unusually lyrical second-movement Minuet in the minor key, a pleasing cantabile *Adagio*, and ending with a catchy Polonaise finale (nicely articulated). The chromatic flavour of the opening of Op. 2/1 has just a little in common with Mozart's *Dissonance Quartet*, and the Allegro has a striking cello line; the cello also participates strongly in the *Adagio*. The amiable Op. 4/1 in two movements is attractively lightweight. The Rasumovsky Quartet have obviously lived with this music, and they play it with appealing simplicity and dedication. They are well recorded with plenty of presence and a nice ambient warmth.

Janáček, Leoš (1854–1928)

(i) *Capriccio for piano and wind; Concertino for piano and chamber ensemble;* (ii) *Lachian dances;* (iii) *Sinfonietta;* (iv) *Suite for string orchestra;* (iii) *Taras Bulba;* (v) *Mládí* (suite for wind).
500♪ (B) *** Decca Double Analogue/Dig. 448 255-2 (2) [id.]. (i) Paul Crossley, L. Sinf., David Atherton; (ii) LPO, Huybrechts; (iii) VPO, Mackerras; (iv) LAPO, Marriner; (v) Bell, Craxton, Pay, Harris, Gatt, Eastop.

This Double Decca offers much essential Janáček in absolutely first-class performances and recordings. Paul Crossley is the impressive soloist in the *Capriccio* and the *Concertino*, performances that can be put alongside those of Firkušný – and no praise can be higher. This account of *Mládí* is among the finest available; the work's youthful sparkle comes across to excellent effect here, while the late-1970s analogue sound is very truthful and well balanced. Mackerras's VPO coupling of the *Sinfonietta* and *Taras Bulba* is digital (1980). The massed brass of the *Sinfonietta* has tremendous bite and brilliance as well as characteristic Viennese ripeness. *Taras Bulba* is also given more weight and body than usual, the often savage dance-rhythms presented with great energy.

String quartet No. 1 (Kreutzer sonata).
✿ *** Koch Dig. 3-6436-2 [id.]. Medici Qt – BRITTEN: *Quartet No.3;* JANACEK: *Quartet No. 1;* RAVEL: *Quartet;* SHOSTAKOVICH: *Quartet No. 8;* SMETANA: *Quartet No. 1*. *** ✿

The Medici players grab the listener's attention in the very opening bars, and they give an unsurpassed performance which combines deep feeling with great subtlety of colour. The opening of the third movement is disarming yet gripping in its combination of poignant simplicy and spontaneous, passionate outbursts. The recording could not be more real and tangible.

Glagolitic Mass (original version, ed. Wingfield).
500♪ *** Chandos Dig. CHAN 9310 [id.]. Kiberg, Stene, Svensson, Cold, Danish Nat. R. Ch. & SO, Mackerras – KODALY: *Psalmus hungaricus*. ***

The scholar, Paul Wingfield, has managed to reconstruct Janáček's original score. The added rhythmic complexities of this version, as interpreted idiomatically by Mackerras, often adopting speeds faster than usual, encourage an apt wildness which brings an exuberant, carefree quality to writing which here, more than ever, seems like the inspiration of the moment. The chorus sings incisively with incandescent tone, and the tenor soloist, Peter Svensson, has a trumpet-toned precision that makes light of the high tessitura and the stratospheric leaps that Janáček asks for. The coupling is unexpected but very illuminating, again with the choir and tenor soloist aptly cast. Recorded sound of a weight and warmth that convey the full power of the music.

The Cunning little vixen (complete).

500♪ *** Decca Dig. 417 129-2 (2) [id.]. Popp, Randová, Jedlická, V. State Op. Ch., Bratislava Children's Ch., VPO, Mackerras.

*** Sup. SU 3071/2 612 (2) [id.]. Tattermuschová, Zikmundová, Kroupa, Hlavsa, Prague Nat. Ch. & O, Gregor.

Mackerras's thrusting, red-blooded reading is spectacularly supported by a digital recording of outstanding, demonstration quality. The inspired choice of Lucia Popp as the vixen provides charm in exactly the right measure: sparkling and coquettish, spiteful as well as passionate. The supporting cast is first rate, too. Talich's splendidly arranged orchestral suite is offered as a bonus in a fine new recording.

Janáček's opera is given on Supraphon with plenty of idiomatic Slavonic feeling by the composer's compatriots, with the part of the little vixen here charmingly sung by Helena Tattermuschová. This 1970 recording won a Grand Prix du Disque, plus various other prizes, and deservedly so. As the opening scene immediately demonstrates, the recording is evocatively warm and atmospheric. While the digitally recorded Decca Mackerras set (with Lucia Popp) remains a more obvious first choice, this earlier Czech version can hold its own. While not missing the red-blooded nature of the composer's inspiration, Gregor also captures the woodland ambience with appealing warmth and colour.

Jenůfa (complete).

500♪ ❀ *** Decca Dig. 414 483-2 (2) [id.]. Söderström, Ochman, Dvorský, Randová, Popp, V. State Op. Ch., VPO, Mackerras.

This is the warmest and most lyrical of Janáček's operas, and it inspires a performance from Mackerras and his team which is deeply sympathetic, strongly dramatic and superbly recorded. Elisabeth Söderström creates a touching portrait of the girl caught in a family tragedy. The two rival tenors, Peter Dvorský and Wieslav Ochman as the half-brothers Steva and Laca, are both superb; but dominating the whole drama is the Kostelnitchka of Eva Randová. Some may resist the idea that she should be made so sympathetic but, particularly on record, the drama is made stronger and more involving.

Janiewicz, Feliks (1762–1848)

Divertimento for strings.

(B) *** EMI forte CZS5 69524-2 (2). Polish CO, Maksymiuk – MENDELSSOHN: *String symphonies;* ROSSINI: *String sonatas;* JARZEBSKI: *Tamburetta; Chromatica.* ***

Feliks Janiewicz, born in Poland, travelled widely in Europe before settling in England, where he played in Haydn's London concerts. He then moved to Liverpool (where he married a Miss Eliza Breeze) and ran a music-publishing business, finally ending up in Edinburgh. He was an almost exact contemporary of Rossini, and this delightful work (one of six, written in London around 1805) might well have been another of Rossini's string sonatas, for the writing shares their brilliance and wit. The finale is a *tour de force* of bravura, relished here by this excellent Polish string band. A real find.

Jarzebski, Adam (*c.* 1590–*c.* 1649)

Tamburetta; Chromatica.

(B) *** EMI forte CZS5 69524-2 (2). Polish CO, Maksymiuk – MENDELSSOHN: *String symphonies;* ROSSINI: *String sonatas;* JANIEWICZ: *Divertimento.* ***

Adam Jarzebski spent most of his career in the orchestra of the Warsaw Royal Chapel. These two delightful lollipops show him to be a composer of real personality, the *Tamburetta* bouncing along joyously, with staccato bowing from the Polish strings adding to the rhythmic life, the second changing its mood from dance-like vivacity to stately yet slightly doleful elegance. Marvellous bravura playing from the Polish strings and vividly bright recording add to the music's projection.

Jones, Daniel (1912–93)

Symphonies Nos. (i) *6;* (ii) *9;* (i; iii) *The Country beyond the stars* (cantata).

*** Lyrita SRCD 326 [id.]. (i) RPO, Groves: (ii) BBC Welsh O, Bryden Thomson; (iii) with Welsh Nat. Op. Ch.

Daniel Jones is a much under-rated composer whose symphonies are strikingly coherent and impressively argued. Some might say his voice is not particularly individual, although his chunky scoring creates recognizable textures. The *Sixth Symphony* (1964) is certainly one of his finest, eclectic in style, but the cogency of the argument is matched by his ability to communicate emotional experience. It subdivides into six sections (although unfortunately on the CD there are only three cues) all using the same basic material. The main 'first-movement' *Agitato*, the following *Sostenuto* and the Scherzo, if somewhat conventional in material, are striking in their projection of the composer's personality. The symphony is splendidly played and both Groves and the orchestra show their commitment. The *Ninth Symphony*, written a decade later, is in normal four-movement form, finely crafted and tersely argued, but its material is not quite so strongly personalized. It is very well played by the BBC Welsh Orchestra under Bryden Thomson and truthfully recorded.

The Country beyond the stars is the earliest work here (1958) and is obviously designed to suit the traditional qualities of Welsh choirs: warm, relaxed writing with bursts of eloquent fervour, but always easy on the ear. The Welsh National Opera Chorus do it full justice. The five choral movements are settings of the Breconshire poet, Henry Vaughan, and are divided by a purely orchestral third movement, *Joyful visitors*. It was originally an EMI recording, produced by Brian Culverhouse, and the sound, like Groves's performance, is very fine.

Joplin, Scott (1868–1917)

Rags: *Bethena (concert waltz); Cascades rag; Country club (ragtime two-step); Elite syncopations; The Entertainer; Euphonic sounds (A syncopated novelty); Fig leaf rag; Gladiolus rag; Magnetic rag (syncopations classiques); Maple leaf rag; Paragon rag; Pine apple rag; Ragtime dance; Scott Joplin's new rag; Solace (Mexican serenade); Stoptime rag; Weeping willow (ragtime two-step).*
(M) *** Nonesuch Elektra/Warner 7559 79449-2 [id.]. Joshua Rifkin.

Joshua Rifkin is the pianist whose name has been indelibly associated with the Scott Joplin revival, originally stimulated by the soundtrack music of the very successful film, *The Sting*. His relaxed, cool rhythmic style is at times more subtle than Dick Hyman's more extrovert approach (RCA GD 87993) and, although the piano timbre is full, there is a touch of monochrome in the tone-colour. The current remastering gives the piano a natural presence.

Josquin des Prés (*c.* 1450–1521)

Motets: *Absolom, fili mi; Ave Maria, gratia plena; De profundis clamavi; In te Domine speravi per trovar pietà; Veni, Sanctus Spiritus*. Chansons: *La déploration de la mort de Johannes Ockeghem; El grillo; En l'ombre d'ung buissonet au matinet; Je me complains; Je ne me puis tenir d'aimer; Mille regretz; Petite camusette; Scaramella va alla guerra; Scaramella va la galla.*
*** Virgin Veritas/EMI Dig. VER5 61302-2 [CDC 54659]. Hilliard Ensemble.

Josquin spent much of his life in Italy, first as a singer in the choir of Milan Cathedral and subsequently in the service of the Sforza family. Although Josquin research has become something of a light industry, little of his vast output has reached the wider musical public and still less has been recorded. As Paul Hillier points out in his notes, 'in the carnival songs and frottole we encounter a native Italian style which composers such as Isaac and Josquin may have ennobled but which in turn had its own influence on this music. This fusion of learned polyphony and tuneful rhythmic gaiety laid the foundations of the Italian madrigal.' The chansons recorded here have both variety of colour and lightness of touch, while the motets are sung with dignity and feeling by the Hilliard Ensemble. Indeed, these performances will kindle the enthusiasm of the uninitiated as will few others. The 1983 recording, made in London's Temple Church, is expertly balanced and eminently truthful.

Kabalevsky, Dmitri (1904–87)

The Comedians (suite), *Op. 26: Galop; Gavotte; Epilogue.*
(M) **(*) EMI CDM5 65922-2 [id.]. Hollywood Bowl SO, Alfred Newman – BARTOK: *Miraculous Mandarin;* KHACHATURIAN: *Gayaneh; Masquerade;* SHOSTAKOVICH: *Age of Gold.* **(*)

The brash immediacy of the vibrant playing of the Hollywood orchestra under Newman is emphasized by the close balance and vivid sound. The audacious *Galop* has seldom produced this degree of projection and energy, yet the *Gavotte* has a proper elegance, and the closing movement is as busy as a bee.

Cello concerto No. 2, Op. 77.
**(*) BIS CD 719 [id.]. Lindström, Gothenburg SO, Ashkenazy – KHACHATURIAN: *Cello concerto*. **(*)

Mats Lindström proves an admirably sensitive soloist in Kabalevsky's *Second Concerto*, for the work's unusual structure with its three unbroken sections linked by cadenzas (here individually cued) invites an improvisational approach. Ashkenazy proves an admirable accompanist throughout, providing support and contrast to the solo soliloquies. The recording is of high quality and well balanced but is a shade over-resonant, although the ear adjusts. Not a first choice, but an enjoyable performance, with no lack of spontaneity.

Karamanov, Alemdar (born 1934)

Symphonies Nos. 20 (Blessed are the dead); 23 (I am Jesus).
(M) ** Olympia Dig. OCD 486 [id.]. USSR SO, Vladimir Fedoseyev.

Symphonies Nos. 22 (Let it be); 23.
*** Decca Dig. 452 850-2 [id.]. German SO, Berlin, Vladimir Ashkenazy.

Alemdar Karamanov is another recent discovery among Russian composers. He is not listed in either *Grove* or *Baker's Dictionary*, and he is not mentioned in David Fanning's exhaustive survey in *A Guide to the Symphony*. Born in Simferopol in the Crimea (his father was Turkish), he studied in Moscow with Bogatyrev (the scholar who prepared an edition of Tchaikovksy's *'Seventh' Symphony*) and with Khrennikov and Kabalevsky. He is of a strongly religious temperament and his music found no favour with the Soviet regime, though he did earn the allegiance of Shostakovich, who hailed him as 'one of the most original and unique composers of our time'. In the early 1960s he returned to the Crimea, where he has lived almost as a recluse. He is prolific and has 24 symphonies to his credit, along with three concertos each for the violin and cello, and a variety of other orchestral and choral works.

The present symphonies come from a cycle of six (Nos. 18–23) on the theme of the Apocalypse, written between 1976 and 1980. Nos. 20 and 23 on the Olympia disc were recorded in Moscow in 1982, when their Christian programme was disguised. No. 23 or *I am Jesus* was re-titled *Risen from the ashes*. The music has a certain ecstatic voluptuousness that is reminiscent of Scriabin, but there are also touches of Shostakovich, Rachmaninov and Glière. Karamanov is very imaginative, though a streak of sentimentality comes to the surface – fairly often in the case of No. 20. The Decca performances and recording are vastly superior and make a distinct first choice. The USSR Symphony Orchestra produce rather crude tone at times and there are moments when the wind intonation is flawed. There is a certain pervading sameness about the hot-house atmosphere of this writing and the Szymanowski-like textures, and all three symphonies sound very similar. One wonders how well they will wear on repetition. There is, however, no question as to their interest, and Ashkenazy draws very convincing playing from his fine Berlin orchestra.

Kern, Jerome (1885–1945)

Showboat (complete recording of original score).
500♪ ❁ *** EMI Dig. CDS7 49108-2 (3) [Ang. A23 49108]. Von Stade, Hadley, Hubbard, O'Hara, Garrison, Burns, Stratas, Amb. Ch., L. Sinf., John McGlinn.

In faithfully following the original score, this superb set at last does justice to a musical of the 1920s which is both a landmark in the history of Broadway and musically a work of strength and imagination hardly less significant than Gershwin's *Porgy and Bess* of a decade later. The London Sinfonietta play with tremendous zest and feeling for the idiom; the Ambrosian Chorus sings with joyful brightness and some impeccable American accents. Opposite von Stade, Jerry Hadley makes a winning Ravenal, and Teresa Stratas is charming as Julie, giving a heartfelt performance of the haunting number, *Bill*. Above all, the magnificent black bass, Bruce Hubbard, sings *Ol' man river* and its many reprises with a firm resonance to have you recalling the wonderful example of Paul Robeson, but for once without hankering after the past.

Ketèlbey, Albert (1875–1959)

'Appy 'Ampstead; Bells across the meadows; In a Chinese temple garden; In a monastery garden; In a Persian market; In the mystic land of Egypt; The Phantom melody; Sanctuary of the heart; Wedgwood blue.

(M) *** Decca 444 786-2 [id.]. RPO & chorus, Eric Rogers – *Concert of gypsy violin encores:* Josef Sakonov, L. Festival O. ***

Eric Rogers and his orchestra present the more famous pieces with both warmth and a natural feeling for their flamboyant style, while *Wedgwood blue* is so much the epitome of a salon piece that it becomes a caricature of itself. But in its way it is fetching enough; and the tunes throughout come tumbling out, vulgar but irresistible when played so committedly. The birds twittering in the monastery garden make perfect 'camp' but the playing is straight and committed, and the larger-than-life Phase Four recording suits the music admirably. Moreover it was a happy idea to couple this programme with a collection of Hungarian gypsy fireworks and other favourite lollipops, played with great panache by Josef Sakonov – see Concerts section, below.

Khachaturian, Aram (1903–78)

Cello concerto in E min.

(*) BIS CD 719 [id.]. Mats Lindström, Gothenburg SO, Ashkenazy (with RACHMANINOV: *Vocalise* *) – KABALEVSKY: *Cello concerto.* **(*)

Khachaturian opens his concerto with a flamboyantly rhapsodic sweep, and it is this energetic main theme that dominates. Lindström is carried along by its energy, while sensitive to the sinuous Armenian lyricism of the secondary material and the comparably sinuous Slavic theme for the *Andante*. The vigorous finale has plenty of energy and bravura and, throughout, the combined concentration of Lindström and Ashkenazy prevents the writing from sounding too inflated, even though this is not one of the composer's strongest works. The recording is a bit over-resonant, but otherwise faithful and well balanced. As an encore we are given a fine if restrained account of Rachmaninov's *Vocalise*. An enjoyable if not, in the last resort, memorable coupling.

Piano concerto; Concerto rhapsody for piano and orchestra.

(BB) ** Naxos Dig. 8.550799 [id.]. Oxana Yablonskaya, Moscow SO, Dmitri Yablonsky.

Oxana Yablonskaya is a prodigious player, but she and Yablonsky are prone to over-accentuation and the opening of the work is heavy-going, as is much of the finale. There is no lack of energy and much brilliant pianism, while the music's lyrical side is well understood, with the flexotone not too obtrusive in the slow movement, but the composer's brashness is always very much to the fore. The *Concerto rhapsody for piano and orchestra* is an early work (1955) revised (and no doubt inflated) in 1968 for Nikolai Petrov for whom the prolix bravura of the opening cadenza and the motoric coda of the finale were obviously intended. Its lyrical centrepiece, which again features the flexotone, is endearing in its exotic orientalism, and the glittering – if repetitive and over-extended – finale demands and receives here torrential energy, even if the overall effect of the work is hopelessly garrulous. If only the composer knew when to stop, this could have been a more effective piece. The first modern performance of the *Piano concerto* is provided by the stimulating partnership of Dora Serviarian-Kuhn and Tjeknavorian (on ASV CDDCA 964 – see our main volume).

Gayaneh (ballet): extended suite. *Masquerade* (ballet): suite.

(M) **(*) EMI CDM5 65922-2 [id.]. Hollywood Bowl SO, Alfred Newman – BARTOK: *Miraculous Mandarin;* KABALEVSKY: *The Comedians* (suite); SHOSTAKOVICH: *Age of Gold.* **(*)

Alfred Newman, with brilliant playing from the Hollywood Bowl Orchestra, gives brash, highly energetic accounts of an extended suite of seven numbers from *Gayaneh*, with the *Sabre dance* and *Dance of the Kurds* leaping forward with great zest and the *Russian dance*, which opens with a piquant tic-toc, soon catching up as it noisily gathers pace. The *Galop* from *Masquerade* has similar uninhibited exuberance, but the *Romance*, like the sinuous lyrical numbers in *Gayaneh*, brings a sultry contrasting allure. Both suites generate much excitement and colour, helped by playing which is polished as well as vividly extrovert. The 1959 recording is very brightly lit but gives the strongest projection to this extremely spirited music-making.

Gayaneh (ballet): *suites 1–3.*
(BB) * Naxos Dig. 8. 550800 [id.]. St Petersburg State SO, Anichanov.

These three suites come from Khachaturian's later revisions of his score, and little of what is offered here is of real musical interest. *Gayaneh's solo* from suite No. 1, the *Lullaby* and *Sabre dance* from suite No. 2 and *Gayaneh's Adagio* from suite No. 3 remind us of the quality of the composer's original ideas, and the *Dance of the girls* also has charm. The dozen other items are routine numbers, overscored and containing little music to which one would wish to return. They are played idiomatically and with more conviction than they deserve, and the resonant recording is acceptable.

Klami, Uuno (1900–1960)

Symphony No. 2, Op. 35; Symphonie enfantine, Op. 17.
** Ondine Dig. ODE 858-2 [id.]. Tampere PO, Ollila.

Uuno Klami's musical sympathies were predominantly Gallic and he studied briefly with – or, rather, took advice from – Ravel and Florent Schmitt. Best known for his *Kalevala suite*, which Petri Sakari and the French Radio Orchestra have recorded for Chandos, Klami also composed two symphonies, the second of which he finished at the war's end in 1945. If its tone is predominantly post-romantic in character, its musical coherence is less than impressive. It is stronger on rhetoric than on substance. In its final pages English listeners may well be reminded of Arnold Bax. The *Symphonie enfantine* is a slighter piece from the 1920s, heavily indebted to Ravel, and rather delightful. Though he may be of peripheral importance, Klami's representation on CD is far from negligible, and Tuomas Ollila and the Tampere Philharmonic effectively broaden our picture of him. The Ondine engineers produce sound of exemplary clarity and naturalness.

Kodály, Zoltán (1882–1967)

Dances of Galánta; Dances of Marosszék; Háry János suite; Variations on a Hungarian theme (The Peacock).
500♪ *** Decca Dig. 444 322-2 [id.]. Montreal SO, Dutoit.
(M) *** Decca 425 034-2 [id.]. Philh. Hungarica, Dorati.

Dances of Galánta; Háry János suite; Variations on a Hungarian theme (The Peacock).
*** Telarc Dig. CD 80413. Atlanta SO, Yoel Levi.
** Chandos Dig. CHAN 8877 [id.]. Chicago SO, Neeme Järvi.
** Nimbus Dig. NI 5284 [id.]. Hungarian State SO, Adám Fischer.

Charles Dutoit offers the four most popular of Kodály's orchestral works in richly resonant, purposeful performances, with rhythms crisply sprung and with superb playing from the fine soloists of the Montreal orchestra, helped by recording of demonstration quality, outstanding even by Montreal standards.

Robert Shaw in his Telarc recordings has repeatedly demonstrated what a fine orchestra the Atlanta Symphony is, and here Yoel Levi (who made his recording reputation in Cleveland with a splendid Telarc CD of excerpts from Prokofiev's *Romeo and Juliet* – CD 80089) carries on the good work in a coupling of Kodály's three most popular orchestral works. The digital recording is full and well balanced, and the performances are brilliant and persuasive, with some fine, sensitive playing from the wind principals in particular. The snag is that this issue comes into direct competition with the Decca versions of Charles Dutoit and Antal Dorati, the one with rhythms crisply sprung and with even richer sound and the other with far more idiomatically Hungarian performances, full of flair, and with the 1973 recording still very vivid and sharply focused. Both those Decca discs also offer a bonus in an extra work, the *Marosszék dances*: they are discussed more fully in our main volume.

Järvi conducts the Chicago orchestra in warmly spontaneous readings of the same three works, atmospherically recorded with the orchestra placed at a slight distance. Enjoyable as the performances are, they are not as crisp in ensemble as the best rivals.

Adám Fischer's readings of an identical triptych are more expansive and less tautly dramatic than the rival ones – idiomatic as they are – suffering seriously from distant placing of the orchestra in a washy acoustic.

Háry János suite.
(M) *** Decca Phase Four 448 947-2 [id.]. Netherlands R. O, Dorati – DVORAK: *Symphony No. 9.* ***

The Decca recording is exceptionally vivid and Dorati's direct manner produces the strongest musical characterization. The Phase Four techniques are not exaggerated and they do no harm to Kodály's bright orchestral colours.

Hungarian rondo; Summer evening.
*** DG Dig. 447 109-2 [id.]. Orpheus CO – SUK: *String serenade.* ***

(i) *Hungarian rondo. Summer evening; Symphony.*
**(*) ASV Dig. CDDCA 924 [id.]. (i) Christopher Warren-Green; Philh. O, Yondani Butt.

Nowadays Bartók completely overshadows his distinguished countryman so that we are apt to forget how good so much of Kodály's music is. The *Summer evening* is a beautiful piece and is eminently well served by the Orpheus – as good as (if not better than) the Dorati rival on a Decca Double (443 006-2) – and better recorded. But the pair of Decca discs offer the *Concerto for orchestra*, *Galánta* and *Marosszék dances*, *Háry János suite*, the *Symphony in C*, *Theatre overture* and the *Peacock variations*, with the two discs offered at the same price as this newer issue. At 50 minutes this DG CD offers short measure for a full-price disc.

Yondani Butt's account of *Summer evening* is hardly less impressive, and it comes with a well-characterized account of the *Symphony*, not more impressive than Dorati's version but, of course, a more up-to-date recording. Very good indeed, albeit not quite three-star.

Variations on a Hungarian folksong (The Peacock).
*** Decca Dig. 452 853-2 [id.]. VPO, Solti – ELGAR: *Enigma variations;* BLACHER: *Paganini variations.* ***

It is surprising that Solti waited over 40 years after his 1954 version with the LPO (in mono) before recording Kodály's colourful variations again. Though his interpretation of a fellow-Hungarian composer has altered less between recordings than the Elgar on this same fiftieth-anniversary disc, this performance too has extra warmth and subtlety, with the rhythmic verve just as sharply infectious as before, conveying joy. Vivid sound, capturing the warm acoustic of the Musikverein.

Psalmus hungaricus, Op. 13.
500♪ *** Chandos Dig. CHAN 9310 [id.]. Svensson, Copenhagen Boys' Ch., Danish Nat. R. Ch. & SO, Mackerras – JANACEK: *Glagolitic Mass.* ***

As the unusual but refreshing coupling for the Janáček *Mass*, the *Psalmus hungaricus* is here infected with an element of wildness that sweeps away any idea of Kodály as a bland composer. The glory of the performance lies most of all in the superb choral singing, full, bright and superbly disciplined, with the hushed pianissimos as telling as the great fortissimo outbursts.

Koechlin, Charles (1867–1961)

Horn sonata, Op. 70; 15 Pieces, Op. 180; Morceau de lecture (for horn); *15 Pieces, Op. 180; Sonneries.*
*** ASV Dig. CDDCA 716 [id.]. Barry Tuckwell, Daniel Blumenthal.

Barry Tuckwell has discovered another composer who has a real facility for horn writing, understanding its historical evolution from hand-horn to the modern rotary-valved instrument, yet realizing, as did Britten in his *Serenade*, that with this instrument simplest is best. The *Sonata* is a richly conceived three-movement work, linked by its evocative opening idea, which is echoed in the engaging *Andante* and returns as a haunting postlude at the close of the galumphing finale. The *Morceau de lecture* is freer, more rhapsodic, immediately stretching up ecstatically into the instrument's higher tessitura. The 15 *Pieces* are delightful vignettes, opening with a rapturous evocation, *Dans la forêt romantique*. While some of them are skittish (notably the muted Scherzo (No. 4) or jolly *Allegro vivo* (No. 11), many explore that special solemn melancholy which the horn easily discovers in its middle to lower register, as in Nos. 10 and 12 (both marked *doux*). Two others are for hunting horns, and they robustly use the open harmonics which are naturally out of tune (an effect Britten tried more sparingly), while the 11 brief *Sonneries* are all written for cors de chasse with a similar plangent effect when the tonality is imperfect. Many of the *Sonneries* are in two, three or four parts, which Tuckwell plays by electronic means. This is a collection to be dipped into rather than taken all at once, but Tuckwell's artistry sustains the listener's interest and the fine pianist, Daniel Blumenthal, makes the most of his rewarding part in the *Sonata*. The recording is excellent.

Kokkonen, Joonas (born 1921)

The Last Temptations (opera): complete.
**(*) Finlandia/Warner 1576 51104-2 (2) [id.]. Auvinen, Ruohonen, Lehtinen, Talvela, Savonlinna Op. Festival Ch. & O, Söderblom.

The Last Temptations tells of a revivalist leader, Paavo Ruotsalainen, from the Finnish province of Savo and of his inner struggle to discover Christ. The opera is dominated by the personality of Martti Talvela, and its invention for the most part has a dignity and power that are symphonic in scale. All four roles are well sung, and the performance under Ulf Söderblom is very well recorded indeed.

Kolessa, Mykola (born 1903)

Symphony No. 1.
** ASV Dig. CDDCA 963 [id.]. Odessa PO, Hobart Earle – SKORYK: *Carpathian concerto* etc. **

Mykola Kolessa, now in his nineties, is the grand old man of Ukrainian music. He studied in Prague with Novák and was active as conductor of the Lvov (spelt as Lviv throughout the notes and in the French and German translations). He is not mentioned in *Grove*, but a musicologist and folk-music specialist, Filaret Kolessa (1871–1947), who numbered Bartók among his circle, is listed. Bartók and the French music of the first half of the century were formative influences on Mykola Kolessa. The *First* of his two symphonies was composed in 1950 in the immediate wake of the Zhdanov affair, when any sense of harmonic adventure was discouraged. This piece at times sounds like Glière or Arensky. It is expertly written and is easy to listen to, but it could just as well have been composed in the 1890s or 1910s. Very well played and recorded. The pieces by Kolessa's pupil, Myroslav Skoryk, are more interesting.

Korngold, Erich (1897–1957)

(i) *Cello concerto in C, Op. 37;* (ii) *Piano concerto in C sharp for the left hand, Op. 17. Symphonic serenade for strings, Op. 39; Military march in B flat.*
*** Chandos Dig. CHAN 9508 [id.]. (i) Peter Dixon; (ii) Howard Shelley; BBC PO, Matthias Bamert.

The more one hears of Korngold's lesser-known music the more impressive he seems: more 'gold than corn' rather than the reverse. The least interesting piece is the *Cello concerto*, an adaptation of a short piece he composed in 1946 for the film *Deception* starring Bette Davis and Claude Rains. The work's première, incidentally, was given by Eleanor Aller, later of Hollywood Quartet fame. The *Concerto in C sharp for piano left hand* (1924) is an altogether different matter. Composed, like Ravel's concerto, Prokofiev's *Fourth* and the Strauss *Parergon*, for the one-armed pianist, Paul Wittgenstein, who had lost his right arm during the First World War, it is an extraordinarily imaginative and resourceful work. Although it springs from a post-Straussian world (Gary Graman called it 'a keyboard Salome'), it is full of individual touches. Howard Shelley gives it a radiant performance and is given splendid support. To complaints that the *Military march* (1917) was rather fast, Korngold is said to have replied that it was intended to be played for the retreat! The *Symphonic serenade for strings* was composed after the Second World War and was premièred in 1950 by the Vienna Philharmonic and Furtwängler. It is a very beautiful (as well as beautifully crafted) work with a highly inventive Scherzo and an eloquent, rather Mahlerian slow movement. First-rate playing and opulent, well-balanced recording. Well worth exploring.

Violin concerto in D, Op. 35.
*** Decca 452 481-2 [id.]. Chantal Juillet, Berlin RSO, Mauceri – KRENEK: *Violin concerto* ***; WEILL: *Violin concerto.* **

(i) *Violin concerto;* (ii) *Much Ado About Nothing* (suite), *Op. 11.*
500♪ ✿ *** DG Dig. 439 886-2 [id.]. Gil Shaham; (i) LSO, Previn; (ii) Previn (piano) – BARBER: *Violin concerto.* ***

After settling in America and becoming the most successful of Hollywood film composers, Korngold was never again taken seriously as a composer in his lifetime, much to his chagrin. Ironically, this concerto, increasingly accepted as a masterpiece, draws for its main themes on some of the most succulent ideas from his film music. From Heifetz, the original interpreter, it prompted a big-scaled, full-toned performance, and most interpreters have sought to follow his example. Chantal Juillet by contrast concentrates on the poetry of the work in much gentler treatment, and the natural balance given to the soloist by the Decca engineers in vivid sound enhances that. It may not be as passionate as its rivals, but it is certainly a valid view, no less moving. An imaginative and generous coupling, having violin concertos by two other Central European composers who found refuge in America.

The Israeli violinist, Gil Shaham, gives a performance of effortless virtuosity and strong profile. Shaham is warmer and more committed than Itzhak Perlman in his Pittsburgh recording for EMI, again with Previn conducting (47846-2). There is greater freshness and conviction than in the Perlman. The recording helps, far clearer and more immediate, making this a clear first choice. The suite from Korngold's incidental music to *Much Ado About Nothing* provides a delightful and apt makeweight.

5 Lieder Op. 38; Songs of the Clown, Op. 29.
*** Sony SK 68344 [id.]. Angelika Kirchschlager, Helmut Deutsch – MAHLER: *Lieder und Gesänge.* ***

These two song-groups, written after Korngold went to America – charming miniatures most of them – are tuneful in an innocent way, similar in kind but opposite in scale to Korngold's Hollywood music. Some of them might almost be by British composers of earlier in the century. Even *Come away Death* fails to draw from the composer a deep response (no doubt reflecting his title for the group), gravitating quickly to the major mode. With Op. 29 here receiving its first recording, they add a pointful element to the début recital of this talented, fresh-voiced singer; well worth exploring.

Kreisler, Fritz (1875–1962)

Allegretto in the style of Boccherini; Aucassin and Nicolette; Berceuse romantique; Caprice viennoise; La gitana; Liebesfreud; Liebesleid; Marche miniature viennoise; Menuett in the style of Porpora; Polichinelle; Praeludium and allegro in the style of Pugnani; La Précieuse in the style of Louis Couperin; Rondino on a theme of Beethoven; Schön Rosmarin; Sicilienne and Rigaudon in the style of Francoeur; Syncopation; Tambourin chinois; Tempo di minuetto in the style of Pugnani; Toy-soldiers' march.
*** Decca Dig. 444 409-2 [id.]. Joshua Bell, Paul Coker.

As readily shown by the opening *Praeludium and allegro*, Joshua Bell refuses to treat this music as trivial, and there is a total absence of schmalz. *Tambourin chinois*, impeccably played, lacks something in charm, but not the neatly articulated *La Précieuse*. And what lightness of touch in *Schön Rosmarin*, what elegance of style in the *Caprice viennoise*, what panache in the paired *Liebesfreud* and *Liebesleid*, and how seductive is the simple *Berceuse romantique*, one of the novelties here, like the winning *Toy-soldiers' march* and the unexpected, almost Joplinesque rag, *Syncopation*. The recording is completely realistic.

Krenek, Ernst (1900–1991)

Violin concerto No. 1, Op. 29.
*** Decca 452 481-2 [id.]. Chantal Juillet, Berlin RSO, Mauceri – KORNGOLD: *Violin concerto* ***; WEILL: *Violin concerto.* **

The Krenek *Violin concerto*, buried since its one and only performance in 1924, makes a welcome novelty, generously coupled with better-known concertos by fellow Europeans who also settled in America. Though this is a flawed work, not as tautly structured as it might be, it proves involvingly autobiographical, inspired by the composer's unhappy love-affair with a glamorous violinist, Alma Moodie. The late Berthold Goldschmidt in the liner-notes gives a detailed commentary, having attended the first performance with Alma Moodie (when Krenek ostentatiously kept away). Hearing the 1995 sessions for this recording, his memories came vividly back, so that he can explain how one key passage represents a night journey by train in a sleeping-car. Though the work fades out limply at the end, Chantal Juillet gives a warmly expressive performance, helped by vivid Decca sound, confirming this as a valuable addition to the 'Entartete Musik' series.

Krommer, Franz (1759–1831)

Partitas: in F, Op. 57; E flat, Op. 71; B flat, Op. 78. Marches, Op. 31/3–5.
(BB) *** Naxos Dig. 8.553498 [id.]. Budapest Wind Ens.

The Budapest Wind, led by their exuberant clarinettist, Kálmán Berkes, are a first-rate ensemble, full of spirit and personality. These qualities inform their characterful and lively accounts of these three partitas by Krommer or Krommer-Kramář as he is sometimes known (using both the German and Czech forms of his name). The Budapest team yields nothing in terms of artistic excellence to their full-priced rival, the Sabine Meyer Wind Ensemble, and not a great deal in terms of recording quality. True, the distinguished

German team offer the Op. 76 *Partita* as well, and readers who have acquired that disc (reviewed in our 1992 edition) will not have regretted doing so. But this newcomer has the merit of being every bit as accomplished, arguably more characterful, and certainly less expensive. Recommended.

Kuhlau, Friedrich (1786–1832)

Violin sonatas Nos. 1 in F min., Op. 33; 2 in E flat, Op. 64; 3 in F; 4 in F min.; 5 in C, Op. 79/1–3.
*** CPO Dig. CPO 999 363-2 [id.]. Dora Bratchkova, Andreas Meyer-Hermann.

Kuhlau is best known for his piano sonatinas – with which many novices at the piano are familiar – so this collection of his complete *Violin sonatas* is a delightful surprise. Written between 1820 and 1827, they have much in common with the violin sonatas of Beethoven, and it is surprising how often one is reminded of that master when listening to these attractive and in no way superficial works. The slow movement of the *F minor* and also the finale bring the most striking echoes, but the composer's own personality also emerges strongly, notably in the attractive variations on a Danish folksong which form the slow movement of the *E flat* work and in the *Rondo* finale. The three Opus 79 works are undoubtedly masterpieces, full of life and with invention of a consistently high order. Try the witty finale of Op. 79/1 or the engaging *Andantino* central movement of Op. 79/2, which has a delightful *Polacca* for its closing *Rondo*. The performances by the Bulgarian violinist, Dora Bratchkova, and Andreas Meyer-Hermann (who, like the composer, was born in lower Saxony and later studied in Hamburg) are in every way first rate, and they are most naturally balanced and realistically recorded. If you enjoy the Beethoven violin sonatas, you will certainly enjoy these.

Kvandal, Johan (born 1919)

Wind quintet, Op. 34; 3 Hymn tunes, Op. 23.
(BB) ** Naxos Dig. 8.553050 [id.]. Oslo Wind Ens. – FERNSTROM; NIELSEN: *Wind quintets.* **

The Norwegian composer Johan Kvandal is the son of the composer and Grieg scholar, David Monrad Johansen. He studied in Vienna with Joseph Marx and in Paris with Nadia Boulanger. He has a number of highly imaginative scores to his credit, including *Antagonia*, a memorable, rather Honeggerish concerto for two string orchestras and percussion which was recorded in the 1970s and is well worth tracking down. The *Wind quintet* dates from much the same period as *Antagonia* and was finished in 1971. It was written for the Oslo Wind Quintet for a payment of 25 bottles of red wine. It is well crafted but unmemorable. Excellent playing from the Oslo Wind Ensemble; but the recording, made in a rather small Norwegian Radio studio, is overlit and rather too forward.

Lalo, Eduard (1823–92)

Cello concerto in D min.
*** RCA Dig. 09026 68420-2 [id.]. Ofra Harnoy, Bournemouth SO, Antonio de Almeida – OFFENBACH: *Concerto militaire.* ***

Ofra Harnoy is as thoroughly at home in Lalo as she is in the rare Offenbach coupling. The resonant acoustic adds to the power and expansiveness of Almeida's brass-laden opening tutti and the dialogue which ensues portrays the meek and the powerful, with Harnoy's gentle lyrical insistence finally taming the vehement orchestral gruffness. The delicate melancholy of the *Andante* is engagingly caught, with the central scherzando as light as thistledown, and the finale is vigorously, buoyantly spirited. As usual, the soloist's subtle use of the widest range of dynamic and her ever poetic line give the performance a sense of ongoing spontaneity. Although the degree of reverberation may trouble some listeners, the balance between cello and orchestra is nicely managed.

(i) *Cello concerto in D min.;* (ii) *Symphonie espagnole, Op. 21.*
(B) *(**) Erato/Warner 0630 12740-2 [id.]. (i) Frédéric Lodéon, Philh. O, Dutoit; (ii) Pierre Amoyal, Monte Carlo Op. O, Paray.

Here on Erato is a case where a marvellous solo performance triumphs over indifferent orchestral recording which, in the *Symphonie espagnole*, is boomy in the bass, though the treble is free enough and the solo violin is truthfully caught. Amoyal's account of the solo role is glorious, his playing consistently seductive (and totally free from schmaltz), as well as warm and polished. The infectious finale is like quicksilver and the *Andante* (with rich orchestral brass) has unexpected nobility. Moreover Lodéon's performance of the *Cello concerto* is recommendable in every way – the *Intermezzo* is ravishingly done and the finale spontaneously volatile – with the Philharmonia under Dutoit providing excellent backing. Here the recording, though not brilliant, is much better balanced and it gives the soloist a rich, firmly focused timbre that is most appealing.

Symphonie espagnole, Op. 21.

(M) *** EMI Eminence Dig. CD-EMX 2277 [id.]. Tasmin Little, Royal SNO, Vernon Handley – BRUCH: *Scottish fantasy*. ***

(**(*)) APR Signature mono APR 5506 [id.]. Huberman, VPO, Szell – BEETHOVEN: *Violin concerto*. (***)

(M) *(*) Decca 452 309-2 [id.]. Ruggiero Ricci, SRO, Ansermet – SAINT-SAENS: *Havanaise* etc.; SARASATE: *Carmen (fantasy)* etc. **

Tasmin Little has the gift of sounding totally spontaneous on disc, with no feeling of strict studio manners, here giving a bold and characterful reading of the Lalo, warmly projected and well coupled with Bruch's comparable evocation of Scotland. She is greatly helped by the splendid, keenly polished playing of the Scottish orchestra under Vernon Handley, a most sympathetic partner. Handley is excellent in pointing the rhythms of the fast movements of the Lalo, matching his soloist, and the recording is superb, with brass in particular vividly caught.

When Huberman recorded the *Symphonie espagnole* in 1930, it was common practice to omit the central *Intermezzo*, and so it is here, for that cut allowed the work to fit on to three 78-r.p.m. discs instead of four. Yet as a historic document this makes a welcome coupling for Huberman's classic reading of the Beethoven concerto with the same accompanists. Here more than in the Beethoven, Huberman indulges in surprising swoops of *portamento* – another sign of the times – though always with perfect control to match the sweetly expressive style.

Ricci's is a scintillating performance with as much depth of feeling as the work may reasonably be expected to take, and Ansermet wields his usual expert baton as accompanist. But the recording (as so often with this work) suffers from an unsatisfactory placing of the soloist in relation to the orchestra. The violin is far too close and the orchestral solo voices are pushed into the background. What is more, the violin tone is harder than in the couplings, at times approaching shrillness, and this seems a curious choice for inclusion in Decca's Classic Sound series.

Lambert, Constant (1905–51)

Aubade héroïque; (i) *The Rio Grande; Summer's last will and testament.*

500♪ ❁ *** Hyperion Dig. CDA 66565 [id.]. Sally Burgess, Jack Gibbons, William Shimell, Ch. of Opera North and Leeds Festival, (i) with Jack Gibbons; English N. Philh., Lloyd-Jones.

The Rio Grande, Lambert's jazz-based choral concerto setting a poem by Sacheverell Sitwell, is one of the most colourful and atmospheric works from the 1920s. With Sally Burgess a warmly expressive soloist, sharply dramatic choral singing, and Jack Gibbons the brilliant, keenly responsive pianist, Lloyd-Jones gives a totally idiomatic account of music that requires crisp attack combined with a jazzy freedom of rhythm. The recording in all three works is full, vivid and atmospheric.

Horoscope (ballet): *suite.*

500♪ ❁ *** Hyperion CDA 66436 [id.]. E. N. Philh. O, Lloyd-Jones – BLISS: *Checkmate;* WALTON: *Façade*. ***

The music for *Horoscope* is sheer delight. David Lloyd-Jones is very sympathetic to its specifically English atmosphere. He wittily points the catchy rhythmic figure which comes both in the *Dance for the followers of Leo* and, later, in the *Bacchanale*. Excellent playing and first-class sound.

The Rio Grande.

(M) **(*) Decca Dig. 452 324-2 [id.]. Della Jones, Kathleen Stott, BBC Singers, BBC Concert O, Barry Wordsworth – ELGAR: *Sea pictures* etc. **(*)

With bright, forward recording, this account of *The Rio Grande* is rather more aggressive than the Hyperion one (see above). Wordsworth is also a degree more literal, less idiomatic in the interpretations of jazzy syncopations. The performance is also marginally less warmly expressive, but the power and the colour of the writing come across with fine bite and clarity.

Lambert, Michel (*c.* 1610–96)

Leçons de Ténèbres.
(M) * Virgin Veritas/EMI Dig. VED5 61213-2 (2) [id.]. Noéme Rime, Nathalie Stutzmann, Charles Brett, Howard Crook, with continuo (Philippe Foulon, Mauricio Buraglia, Ivète Piveteau).

Lambert's *Leçons de ténèbres* (three each for Holy Wednesday, Holy Thursday and Good Friday) date from 1689. The settings are austere, with a solo line (here varied among four different artists) plus continuo. While is is very enterprising of Virgin to record this offbeat repertoire, its florid lines and ornamentation mean that any performer has to be very flexible indeed and, above all, the singing has to be perfectly tuned. Here it is not. Indeed the very first *Leçon de Mercredi Saint* (Charles Brett) gets the performance off on to the wrong foot with insecure intonation. Although, later, things improve, this is not a set to recommend with any enthusiasm, for Brett is not the only soloist to be faulted in this way.

Larsson, Lars-Erik (1908–86)

Croquiser, Op. 38; 7 Little fugues with preludes in the old style, Op. 58; Sonatinas Nos. 1, Op. 16; 2, Op. 39; 3, Op. 41.
*** BIS Dig. CD 758 [id.]. Hans Pålsson.

Larsson is better represented in the catalogue than in the concert hall. The eloquent *Violin concerto* of 1953 ought to be a repertory piece, and the *Music for orchestra* (1950) is equally deserving. The piano music is slight but far from insignificant. It is beautifully fashioned, always intelligent and often witty. Hans Pålsson serves it with exemplary taste and expertise. It is well recorded, and those who like Larsson's music need not hesitate.

Lassus, Orlandus (*c.* 1532–94)

(i) *9 Lamentationes Hieremiae*. (ii) *Missa pro defunctis (Requiem)* for 4 voices. (i) *Aurora lucis rutilat* (hymn for Lauds); *Magnificat on Aurora lucis rutilat*. Motets: *Christus resurgens; Regina coeli laetare; Surgens Jesus.*
(B) *** Hyperion Dyad Dig. CDD 22012 (2) [id.]. Pro Cantione Antiqua, (i) Bruno Turner; (ii) Mark Brown.

The competing Harmonia Mundi set of the *Lamentations* is available on a single, premium-priced disc (HMC 901299), whereas for approximately the same cost this Hyperion Dyad offers much more music. Within this set, Bruno Turner's 1981 digital recording of the *Lamentations* is also now accommodated on a single CD, while the second includes a selection of music for Easter Sunday, including the glorious *Aurora lucis rutilat* for two five-part choirs and the *Magnificat* based on the motet, plus Mark Brown's fine performance of the four-part *Requiem*. The performances under Bruno Turner are no less persuasive, expressive and vital. The recording too is spacious and warm. So for that matter is the Harmonia Mundi recording for the Chapelle Royale and Philippe Herreweghe, whose performances of the *Lamentations* are hardly less admirable.

Missa Ad imitationem Vinum bonum; Motet: *Vinum bonum; Missa super Quand'io pens'al martire; Missa super Triste départ.*
*** Decca Dig. 444 335-2 [id.]. King's College, Cambridge, Ch., Stephen Cleobury (with GOMBERT: *Chanson: Triste départ;* ARCADELT: *Madrigal: Quand'io pens'al martire*).

All three Masses here are provided with their source material, and Arcadelt's madrigal, *Quand'io pens'al martire* is particularly beautiful in its own right. Lassus's eight-part motet, *Vinum bonum*, is a lively piece extolling the pleasures of fine wine but also making an association with the miracle at Cana. The Mass itself is similarly strong and extrovert, yet it also has many richly expressive pages and typically imaginative control of sonority: the closing *Agnus Dei* is simple and touching. The King's choristers are on top form throughout and are particularly impressive in the flowing lines of *Missa super Triste départ*. The recording is splendid, with the King's resonance adding colour and atmosphere yet in no way preventing internal clarity.

Missa super Bell' Amfitrit' altera; Psalmus penitentialis VII (Psalm 143); Motets: *Alma redemptoris Mater; Omnes de Saba venient; Salve regina, mater misericordiae; Tui sunt coeli.*
500♪ ❁ (M) *** Decca 433 679-2 [id.]. Christ Church Cathedral, Oxford, Ch., Simon Preston.

The *Mass* is Venetian in style, scored for double choir, each comprising SATB. The seventh *Penitential*

Psalm uses a five-part choir with divided tenors, and at *Sicut erat* expands to a six-part choir with divided trebles. The trebles here are firm in line, strong in tone. Indeed, throughout, the singers produce marvellously blended tone-quality and Simon Preston secures magical results. As if this were not enough, the choir conclude with the four eight-part motets, amazingly rich in texture.

Lawes, William (1602–45)

Consort setts a 5: in A min.; G min. Consort setts a 6: in B flat; in C; in G min.; (i) *2 Ayres for lyra viol; 5 Dances for lyra viol;* (ii) 4 settings of poems by Robert Herrick: *How lillies came white; To Pansies; To Sycamores; To the Virgins, to make much of time.*
** Virgin/EMI Dig. VC5 45147-2 [VC 59021]. Fretwork; Paul Nicholson (organ); (i) Richard Boothby; (ii) with Catherine Bott.

William Lawes was born in Salisbury in 1602. His older brother, Henry, was also a musician, and both eventually found employment with Charles I, who referred to him affectionately as 'the Father of Music'. William was killed by a stray bullet at the siege of Chester and his music was forgotten when Purcell appeared. The current spate of recordings reveals a distinct musical personality, not as strong as Purcell's perhaps, but with an individual lyrical gift and the skill of a musical craftsman. However, apart from the vocal items, this Virgin collection is something of a disappointment. The *Consort setts* in five and six parts are in three movements, usually consisting of a pair of *Fantazies* and an *Aire*. On the evidence here, Lawes seems very concerned to weave his part-writing to achieve the fullest possible sonorities, and the prevailing mood here is sombre. The Fretwork viols are closely balanced, which reduces the dynamic range of the playing, while the organ integrates so well with the vibrato-less string sound that there is a lack of additional colour and possible added brightness. The pieces for lyra viol bring a refreshingly lively 'country dance' contrast, but the highlight of the concert is Catherine Bott's delightful presentation of the four Herrick settings, particularly the third, *To Pansies* ('Ah cruell love'), which is almost operatic. This is a useful disc, but one feels there is more to the *Consort setts* than the present recordings reveal.

Fantasia suites for 2 violins, bass viol and organ Nos. 1–8.
*** Chandos Dig. CHAN 0552 [id.]. Purcell Qt.

Lawes studied with Coperario when the latter was organizing a performing group for Prince Charles which he called 'Coperarios Musique', in which Orlando Gibbons played the organ. Lawes's own *Fantasia suites* are based on those of his mentor and are simpler, usually more extrovert works than the *Consort suites*. They are in three movements, in each case a *Fantazy* followed by two *Aires*, in essence dance movements, alman and galliard, later corant or saraband. The organ does not just play a continuo role but is important in its own right. The music itself is lively in invention and by no means predictable, with surprise moments of passing dissonance, and the composer's individuality comes out in his special brand of lyricism. The performances here have plenty of life, and the recording balance is very successful: the result is enjoyably fresh.

Royal consorts Nos. 1–10.
*** Chandos Dig. CHAN 0584/5 [id.]. Purcell Consort.

Royal consorts Nos. 1 in D min.; 3 in D min.; 6 in D; 7 in A min.; 9 in F.
*** ASV Gaudeamus Dig. CDGAU 146 [id.]. Greate Consort, Monica Huggett.

Royal consorts Nos. 2 in D min.; 4 in D; 5 in D; 8 in C; 10 in B flat.
*** ASV Gaudeamus Dig. CDGAU 147 [id.]. Greate Consort, Monica Huggett.

The ten *Royal Consorts*, even though they are in four rather than five or six parts like the *Setts*, in many ways represent Lawes's most ambitious undertaking. There is evidence that he conceived the works as simple quartets (two violins and two viols) around 1620, but a decade later theorbos (archlutes) were added to provide a basic continuo and increase the range of textural colour, which they certainly do. Each suite is in six or seven movements, the first of which is the most extended, sometimes taking as long as the remaining charming *Aires* and increasingly lively *Almans*, *Corants* and *Sarabands*, all put together. Indeed these opening expressive *Fantazys* or *Pavanes* offer the kernel of the arguments and contain the most adventurous music, combining nobility of feeling with ear-catching contrapuntal lines. Each *Consort* has its own distinct character, but we are offered here two markedly different styles of performance. The playing of the Purcell Consort is notably sprightly, the recording fresh and vividly clear, but within an open acoustic of some depth. The brightness and transparency of the sound, without loss of sonority, means that the individual instruments are cleanly delineated, although blending well together, never better demonstrated than in the splendidly managed *Echo* movement that ends the first work of the series. Monica

Huggett and her Greate Consort are very slightly recessed; their sound is warmer and the expressive music is given a fuller texture by the resonance. Some will feel that, presented in this way, this music is afforded more atmosphere. They also play at a slightly lower pitch, which means that the effect is inevitably mellower when compared directly with the brighter Chandos sound, although on ASV detail is by no means unclear. Both sets of performances are very rewarding, and if we are inclined, marginally, to favour the bright projection and added transparency of Chandos, many collectors will surely respond differently.

Collections

Consort sets a 5: in A min. & C ; Divisions on a Pavan in G min. for 2 bass viols & organ; Royal consorts Nos. 1 in D min.; 6 in D; Set a 4 in G min. (with 2 theorbos); *Lute duets: Alman; 2 Corants.*
(BB) **(*) Naxos Dig. 8. 550601 [id.]. Rose Consort of viols; Jacob Herigan, David Miller (lutes), Timothy Roberts (organ).

Naxos provide an attractive cross-section of Lawes's instrumental music, using an all-viol texture for the string parts in the *Consorts* (with organ where appropriate). The performances make a livelier and more convincing impression than those by Fretwork, although in the *Royal consorts* the well-blended interaction of inner parts is less sharply individual than with the Purcell Consort. Thus the engaging *Echo* movement of the *D minor Consort* is brought off less tellingly here, with a more measured tempo. However, the closing *Aire-Morris* of the *D major Consort* (which ends the programme) is attractively vigorous. The group also include a fascinatingly bravura set of *Divisions for viols and organ* on the same *Pavane* which opens the four-part *Set in G minor*. The pieces for two lutes could have been given more lively projection, although they are well enough played. The excellent balance helps to make this inexpensive sampler recommendable, which readers might well try.

Leclair, Jean-Marie (1697–1764)

Trio sonatas: in D (première récréation de musique d'une exécution facile), Op. 6; in A, Op. 14; Double violin sonata in D, Op. 3/6.
**(*) Chandos Dig. CHAN 0582 [id.]. Coll. Mus. 90 (Simon Standage, Micaela Comberti, Jane Coe, Nicholas Parle).

The pair of *Trio sonatas* prove to be elegant and tuneful French suites and, although the composer advertised the *D major* as making few technical demands on the players, it is by no means simplistic and the extensive decorated *Chaconne* with which it ends (splendidly played here) is hardly music for beginners! The *Double violin sonata* opens with a tenderly melancholy *Andante* but proves a lively and engaging work with a dancing finale, even though the central *Largo* is again rather doleful. In short this is all highly attractive music with a consistently high standard of invention, and it is played on period instruments with fine style and much vitality. The recording cannot be faulted. The sole reservation, and it is not unimportant, is that Simon Standage's timbre has a characteristic cutting edge which some ears may find wearing after a time.

Lecuona, Ernesto (1895–1963)

Danzas Afro-Cubanas; Gardenia; Noche de Estrellas; Porcelana China (Danza de Muñecos); Polka de los Enanos; (i) *Rapsodia Cubana; Valses Fantásticos; Vals del Nilo; Yo te Quiero Siempre.*
** BIS Dig. CD 794 [id.]. Thomas Tirino, (i) with Polish Nat. RSO, Michael Bartas.

Ernesto Lecuona hails from Cuba and made a career for himself outside Latin and Central America. His reputation extended to Spain and France as well as North America, and he numbered Ravel and Gershwin among his admirers. A pupil of Joaquín Nin, he founded the Havana Symphony Orchestra and the Lecuona Cuban Boys Band and also served as an honorary cultural attaché in Washington (as at one time had the pianist, Jorge Bolet). He was active in both the Columbia and RCA recording studios until the 1930s when he concentrated on composing. He obviously enjoyed a strong technique, particularly for the left hand, for which he writes with both virtuosity and ingenuity. With the exception of the *Rapsodia Cubana*, which is conspicuously slight in invention, this is light music in the Latin-American style but distinguished by an inventive and resourceful use of rhythm. Thomas Tirino is equal to its demands, although this recording – which emanates from New York and Katowice, not BIS's usual venues – is not three-star. Nor is the music; however, although it is all very limited, there are rewarding moments of sophistication.

Lehár, Franz (1870–1948)

The Czarevitch (sung in English).
*** Telarc Dig. CD 80395 [id.]. Nancy Gustafson, Jerry Hadley, Naomi Itami, Lynton Atkinson, Jeffrey Carl, ECO, Bonynge.

Telarc here follows up its brilliant Gilbert and Sullivan series under Sir Charles Mackerras with parallel recordings, not just of the *Land of Smiles* but also of *The Czarevitch*, each offering the score virtually complete on a single disc. Though it lacks the really memorable melodies which make the finest Lehár operettas so winning, *The Czarevitch* is a delightful piece which, with Richard Bonynge as a most understanding conductor, is full of charm and sparkle, with Russian colour from balalaikas nicely touched in. Anyone wanting this in English translation will not be disappointed, with the second couple of principals readily matching up to Jerry Hadley and Nancy Gustafson.

The Land of smiles (sung in English).
*** Telarc Dig. CD 80419 [id.]. Nancy Gustafson, Jerry Hadley, Naomi Itami, Lynton Atkinson, ECO, Bonynge.

Richard Bonynge proves as warmly understanding of the Lehár idiom as he is in Bellini, while Jerry Hadley winningly takes the Tauber role of Prince Sou-Chong. He also provides a new translation, with the hit-number, 'You are my heart's delight', becoming *My heart belongs to you*, with diction commendably clear. Nancy Gustafson makes a bright heroine and Lynton Atkinson sings with winning lightness in the second tenor-role. Recommended.

The Merry Widow (Die lustige Witwe; complete, in German).
500♪ ❁ *** EMI CDS7 47178-8 (2) [Ang. CDCB 47177]. Schwarzkopf, Gedda, Waechter, Steffek, Knapp, Equiluz, Philh. Ch. and O, Matačić.

Matačić provides a magical set, guaranteed to send shivers of delight through any listener with its vivid sense of atmosphere and superb musicianship. It is one of Walter Legge's masterpieces as a recording manager, creating a sense of theatre that is almost without rival in gramophone literature. The CD opens up the sound yet retains the full bloom, and the theatrical presence and atmosphere are something to marvel at.

Leoncavallo, Ruggiero (1858–1919)

I Pagliacci (complete).
(M) *** DG 449 727-2 [id.]. Carlyle, Bergonzi, Taddei, Panerai, La Scala, Milan, Ch. & O, Karajan.
(***) EMI mono CDS5 56287-2 (2). Callas, Di Stefano, Gobbi, La Scala, Milan, Ch. & O, Serafin – MASCAGNI: *Cavalleria rusticana*. (***)
(B) *(*) Ph. Duo 454 265-2 (2) [id.]. Stratas, Domingo, Pons, Rinaldi, La Scala, Milan, Ch. & O, Prêtre – MASCAGNI: *Cavalleria rusticana*. *(*)

Karajan's *Pagliacci* has dominated the catalogue for three decades alongside its natural operatic partner, *Cavalleria rusticana*, so it is apt that DG have chosen it for separate reissue in their series of 'Originals', freshly remastered. Karajan does nothing less than refine Leoncavallo's melodrama, with long-breathed, expansive tempi and the minimum of exaggeration. Karajan's choice of soloists was clearly aimed to help that – but the passions are still there; and rarely if ever on record has the La Scala Orchestra played with such beautiful feeling for tone-colour. Bergonzi is among the most sensitive of Italian tenors of heroic quality, and it is good to have Joan Carlyle as Nedda, touching if often rather cool. Taddei is magnificently strong, and Benelli and Panerai could hardly be bettered in the roles of Beppe and Silvio. The combined set remains available (and unsurpassed) but on three records at premium price – although, as well as *Cav.*, DG provide a splendid set of performances of operatic intermezzi as a filler. However, the separate *Pagliacci* is something of a bargain.

It is thrilling to hear *Pagliacci* starting with the Prologue sung so vividly by Tito Gobbi. Di Stefano, too, is at his finest, but the performance inevitably centres on Callas and there are many points at which she finds extra intensity, extra meaning. Serafin's direction is strong and direct. The mono recording is dry, with voices placed well forward but with choral detail blurred, and this set is still overpriced.

The Prêtre version is taken from the soundtrack of Zeffirelli's film of the opera, and is principally remarkable for the large-scale heroic performance, superbly sung, of Plácido Domingo as Canio. Much of the rest is less recommendable. Juan Pons sings the *Prologue* impressively and exploits his fine baritone as Tonio; but Teresa Stratas and Alberto Rinaldi (Silvio) both suffer from uneven vocal production, with Stratas's earthy timbres going raw under pressure. Even at Duo price this is not very recommendable, and the extra clarity and presence of CD serve only to underline the vocal flaws. A synopsis is offered in lieu of a libretto.

I Pagliacci: highlights.
(M) **(*) EMI CDM5 66048-2 [id.]. Scotto, Carreras, Nurmela, Allen, Amb. Op. Ch., Philh. O, Muti – MASCAGNI: *Cavalleria rusticana:* highlights. **(*)

Muti uses the original text, which is often surprisingly different, with Tonio instead of Canio delivering (singing not speaking) the final *La commedia è finita*. It is an urgent performance and very involving, but the rendering of the Prologue by Kari Nurmela brings a coarse start to the proceedings.

Leoni, Franco (1884–1949)

L'Oracolo (opera): complete.
*** Decca 444 396-2 [id.]. Sutherland, Gobbi, Van Allan, Tourangeau, Davies, John Alldis Ch., Finchley Children's Music Group, Nat. PO, Bonynge.

L'Oracolo, heard first at Covent Garden in 1905, the work of a contemporary of Puccini who settled in London, tells the lurid story of the wicked Cim-Fen, who finally gets strangled, to the delight of everyone, with his own pigtail. In the meantime the heroine goes mad after the murder of her beloved, and the whole drama is set against sound-effects which are superbly caught in this brilliant first recording, made in the Kingsway Hall in 1975. The very opening – three bangs on the bass drum, two crowings of a cockerel and a great jabber in Chinese from the chorus – might almost be a hi-fi demonstration, and the Decca engineers have certainly seized their chance.

The piece gives marvellous opportunities not only to the veteran Tito Gobbi (relishing the character's wickedness) but also to Joan Sutherland, specialist in mad scenes, and to Richard Van Allan as the doctor who finally dispatches Cim-Fen. If Leoni's actual idiom is rather too bland for so dark a story, and his melodies, although often lusciously attractive, never quite come up to Puccini standard, the piece makes a fine compact entertainment in such a performance as this, directed with passionate conviction by Richard Bonynge, with superb playing from the National Philharmonic. Even though it is reissued at full price, this enterprising set is well worth having: it grows more compelling on repeated hearings. A full libretto is provided.

Le Roux, Gaspard (d. *c.* 1705)

Pièces de clavecin: Suites Nos. 1–7.
*** O-L Dig. 443 329-2 [id.]. Christophe Rousset (harpsichord).

Christophe Rousset, playing a Hemsch harpsichord reputed to have been used by Le Roux himself, here adds to his laurels and our knowledge of French keyboard literature with this vivid and surprisingly individual music of an almost unknown composer. If you enjoy Rameau and have already investigated Rousset's companion collection of the music of Pancrace Royer (436 127-2 – see out main volume), this is the composer to try next. The music for the most part is undemanding, but never trivial.

Liadov, Anatol (1855–1914)

Baba-Yaga, Op. 56; The enchanted lake, Op. 62; Kikimora, Op. 63; A musical snuff-box, Op. 32; 8 Russian folksongs, Op. 58.
(M) *(*) Virgin/EMI Ultraviolet Dig. CUV5 61322-2. Bergen PO, Kitaienko – STRAVINSKY: *Firebird suite* etc. *(*)

Although the *Musical snuff-box* has charm, and Kitaienko's performances are not without atmosphere, they lack sparkle, and the Naxos Slovak collection of these same miniatures listed in our main volume (8.550328) is not only preferable, it is also cheaper.

Ligeti, György (born 1923)

(i) *Cello concerto;* (ii) *Piano concerto;* (iii) *Violin concerto.*
*** DG Dig. 439 808-2 [id.]. (i) Queras; (ii) Aimard; (iii) Gawriloff; Ens. InterContemporain, Boulez.

Sony are at present gathering together a comprehensive Ligeti Edition, which we hope to survey next time. Meanwhile those interested in sampling the music of this famous exponent of the avant garde could not do better than try this concertante triptych which won the *Gramophone* magazine's Contemporary Music Award in 1996. The composer's imaginative inventiveness is never in doubt, but his musical purpose is not always easy to fathom. All the performers believe that this music has an underlying profundity; all three performances are musically and technically impressive and communicate strongly.

Liszt, Franz (1811–86)

Piano concertos Nos. 1 in E flat; 2 in A.
** Telarc Dig. CD 80429 [id.]. André Watts, Dallas SO, Litton – MACDOWELL: *Piano concerto No. 2 in D min.* *(*)

Piano concertos Nos. 1–2; Totentanz.
500♪ ✿ *** DG Dig. 423 571-2 [id.]. Zimerman, Boston SO, Ozawa.

Krystian Zimerman's record of the two *Concertos* and the *Totentanz* is altogether thrilling, and he has the advantage of excellent support from the Boston orchestra under Ozawa. It has poise and classicism and, as one listens, one feels this music could not be played in any other way – surely the mark of a great performance! This record is outstanding in every way, and it now makes a first choice for this repertoire.

These are barnstorming performances by André Watts, made to seem even more overwhelming by the powerful projection of the Telarc sound and the resonant acoustic. This is not to say that the music's gentler poetic episodes, and the two slow movements in particular, do not bring a sensitive response from both pianist and conductor, but the lyrical music is quite dwarfed by the thunderous rhetoric. There is plenty of excitement, but it all becomes a bit wearing, and a similar approach to the MacDowell coupling is unacceptable.

Piano concerto No. 1 in E flat.
(M) *** DG 449 719-2 [id.]. Argerich, LSO, Abbado – CHOPIN: *Piano concerto No. 1.* ***

(i) *Piano concerto No. 1 in E flat; Fantasia in E min. on Hungarian folksongs; Hungarian rhapsodies Nos. 8–11, 13.*
(M) (***) Sony mono MHK 62338 Claudio Arrau, (i) with Phd. O, Ormandy.

For some reason Martha Argerich (in 1968) recorded only Liszt's *First Concerto* and not the *Second.* However, in the *E flat Concerto* there is an excellent partnership between the pianist and Abbado, and this is a performance of flair and high voltage which does not ever become vulgar. It is very well recorded and, in this reissue coupled with Chopin for DG's 'Legendary Recordings' series of 'Originals', it sounds better than ever.

These Arrau recordings come from 1952 and have not been in circulation here for many years. The *E flat Concerto* was done in one take and prompted Ormandy to say after the playback, 'Well, what is there to say? We're done. It can't be better than this!' The rest of the programme has just as much electricity. Arrau had an aristocratic poise and a refined musicianship which were unique in this repertoire. The sound is amazingly good.

Symphonic poems: *Ce qu'on entend sur la montagne (Bergsinfonie); Festklänge; Hunnenschlacht; Die Ideale; Von der Wiege bis zum Grabe;* (i) *Dante symphony.*
(B) *** EMI forte CZS5 68598-2 (2). Leipzig GO, Masur; with (i) Arndt, Leipzig Thomaskirche Ch.

On the whole Masur's survey of Liszt's symphonic poems is the finest we have had so far. The performances have a dramatic vitality that eludes Haitink, and the Leipzig orchestra's playing is even finer than that of the LPO on Philips. Some of the earlier pieces, such as *Ce qu'on entend sur la montagne* and *Festklänge*, suffer not only from formal weakness but also from a lack of interesting melodic invention. However, these performances – and, whatever one may think of it, this music – cast a strong spell, and with rare exceptions Masur proves a most persuasive advocate. It is the rich sonority of the lower strings, the dark, perfectly blended woodwind-tone and the fine internal balance of the Leipzig Gewandhaus Orchestra that hold the listener throughout. In the *Dante Symphony* Barenboim's BPO account takes pride of place, but that is on a single full-priced disc. Masur is by no means completely upstaged. He does not shirk the robust diabolism, and the closing section brings a radiantly ecstatic contribution from the Leipzig choir, led by the excellent treble, Volker Arndt. The recordings are well balanced and refined, and the CD transfers are vivid: strings and brass alike have fine presence and sonority. Liszt's influence was enormous in his lifetime – on Wagner, the Russians, the French – and listening to these performances one realizes that his personality has lost none of its magnetism, even in a field that he was slow to conquer.

PIANO MUSIC

Complete piano music, Vol. 39: *Années de pèlerinage, 1st year (Switzerland); 3 Morceaux suisses.*
** Hyperion Dig. CDA 67026 [id.]. Leslie Howard.

With Volume 39 of his continuing Liszt survey Leslie Howard moves on to the first year of the *Années de pèlerinage*, for the most part playing the second versions. But this is music we know well in the hands of artists like Wilhelm Kempff. Howard provides thoroughly musical performances, but without finding the degree of poetry and magic that these evocative pieces deserve. The three *Morceaux suisses* come off brightly and quite spontaneously. Liszt's descriptive powers are more literally used here, with a storm graphically depicted in the second, *Un soir dans la montagne*.

Complete piano music, Vol. 40: *Ballade No. 2* (first version); *Festmarsch zur Säkularfeier von Goethes Geburtstag; Seconde Marche hongroise; Nocturne (Impromptu);* Concert paraphrases and transcriptions: *Galop russe* (Bulhakov); *Gaudeamus igitur* (2 versions: *Paraphrase; Humoreske*); *Lyubila ya* (Wielhorsky); *La Marche pour le Sultan Abdul Médjid-Khan* (Donizetti); *Seconda Mazurka di Tirindelli; Le Rossignol-Air russe* (Alyabiev); *Una stella amica-Valzer* (Pezzini).
** Hyperion Dig. CDA 67034 [id.]. Leslie Howard.

This collection is described as *Pièces d'occasion*, and much of the music here is desperately trivial. Liszt's paraphrase on *Gaudeamus igitur* at nine minutes outlasts its welcome, while the second version, called *Humoreske*, is even less entertaining. Howard takes everything fairly seriously and, though his playing is secure technically, he seldom dazzles the ear, which is surely what the composer would have done.

Complete piano music, Vol. 41: Recitations with piano: (i) *A holt költo szerelme (The Dead poet's love);* (ii) *Helge's Treue (Helge's loyalty); Lenore; Der traurige Mönch (The Sad monk);* (iii) *Slyepoi (The Blind man).*
*(**) Hyperion Dig. CDA 67045 [id.]. Leslie Howard, with (i) Sandor Eles; (ii) Wolf Kahler; (iii) Yuri Stepanov.

A real curiosity, but essentially a specialist compilation. While one is willing to follow an opera libretto alongside a recording, to have to listen to a spoken poetic narrative in German, Hungarian or Russian alongside its musical illustration while following the translation is a different matter. Certainly the ballades here are not lacking in melodrama. *Lenore*, whose lover fails to come back from the wars, cries out blasphemously against God. Night falls, and she hears the sound of hooves clip-clopping: there he is on his horse to take her to the bridal bed. They travel 'a hundred miles' through the night, later followed by demons, and at the end of the journey her lover is no more than a brittle skeleton. All the lurid tales here obviously excited Liszt's imagination, and Howard rises to the occasion. But one wonders how often one would want to return to a CD of this kind.

Complete piano music, Vol. 42: Concert paraphrases: AUBER: *Tyrolean melody* from *La Fiancée; Tarantelle di bravura* from *Masaniello*. BELLINI: *Réminiscences des Puritains; Introduction et Polonaise* from *I Puritani; Grosse Concert-fantaisie* on *La Sonnambula*. DONIZETTI: *Réminiscences de Lucrezia Borgia: Grandes fantaisies I & II*. MEYERBEER: *Réminiscences des Huguenots*. (i) MOZART: *Song of the two armed men* from *Die Zauberflöte* (piano duet). RAFF: *Andante finale* and *Marsch* from *König Alfred*. VERDI: *Coro di festa e marcia funebre* from *Don Carlos; Salve Maria de l'opéra de Jérusalem* from *I lombardi* (two versions). WAGNER: *Pilgrims' chorus* from *Tannhäuser; Am stillen Herd – Lied* from *Die Meistersinger*.
** Hyperion Dig. CDA 67101/2 [id.]. Leslie Howard, with (i) Philip Moore.

Liszt wrote his concert paraphrases in order to present his audiences with music they would hear but rarely in the opera house. To come off, they need to be played with dazzling virtuosity and – above all – real charisma. Leslie Howard is reliably equal to most of their technical demands but he does not titillate the ear, and much of this music tends to lose the listener's attention. These records have been praised elsewhere, but for us they did not prove very stimulating listening. For instance, Howard takes the *Pilgrims' chorus* from *Tannhäuser* unbelievably slowly; he is at his best in the Bellini items. As a sound document to demonstrate the range of Liszt's operatic interest this is valuable, but the playing is seldom very exciting in itself.

Complete piano music, Vol. 43: *Années de pèlerinage, 1st Year, Switzerland: Au bord d'une source* (with coda for Sgambati). *Années de pèlerinage, 2nd Year, Italy; Supplement: Venezia e Napoli.*
**(*) Hyperion Dig. CDA 67107 [id.]. Leslie Howard.

This is one of Howard's more spontaneous recitals. *Au bord d'une source* comes off delightfully, and the brief nine-bar additional coda which Liszt wrote for his friend, the young composer/pianist Giovanni Sgambati, makes a charming (if superfluous) postlude. Howard is also at his best in the *Venezia e Napoli Supplement*, in which the closing *Tarantella* sparkles iridescently. The earlier pieces of the *Second Year* come off well enough, but the *Dante Sonata* needs more grip and fire than Howard finds for it. Excellent recording.

Complete piano music, Vol. 44: Concert paraphrases: BEETHOVEN: *Symphonies Nos. 3 (Marche funèbre); 5–7* (complete) (first versions); *No. 6 (fifth movement)* (second version); *No. 7* (fragment); *Adelaïde* (two versions); *Fantasy* from *Ruins of Athens* (first version). BERLIOZ: *Marche au supplice* from *Symphonie fantastique* (second version). LISZT: *Cadenza for 1st movement of Beethoven's Piano concerto No. 3*.
** Hyperion Dig. CDA 67111/3 [id.]. Leslie Howard.

Once again these recordings are valuable as documentation in showing how brilliantly Liszt transcribed Beethoven's orchestral works, preserving all the important detail. But Leslie Howard seems concerned to lay the music out before us with care for every bit of that detail, without seeking to create enough thrust to take the music onwards. The account of the *Fifth Symphony*, which opens the first disc, has almost no adrenalin whatsoever and proceeds onward as a very routine affair, while the *Marche funèbre* from the *Eroica* is similarly very literal in feeling. The *Pastoral Symphony* might be thought to work well with a simple, straightforward approach, especially when Howard's playing of the Scherzo and the storm sequence generates proper bravura. But then the *Shepherd's hymn of thanksgiving* is presented with little warmth of feeling. The opening of the *Seventh* has a false start, for we are first given only a fragment. When Howard begins again, the *Introduction* seems to go on for a long time but the allegro has momentum, and the other movements have more life than the other symphonies – especially the Scherzo, which really sparkles – although the articulation in the finale could be cleaner. The programme ends with excerpts from Berlioz's *Symphonie fantastique*, with first the *idée fixe* languorously turned into a 'nocturne' (which does not work especially well), followed by a bold, lively *Marche au supplice* which at least ends the programme vigorously. As with the rest of this series, the recording is excellent.

Other piano music

Années de pèlerinage, 2nd year (Italy); Supplement: Venezia e Napoli.
500♪ ✽ (BB) *** Naxos Dig. 8.550549 [id.]. Jenö Jandó.

Jandó offers Lisztian playing of the highest order, confirming the *Années de pèlerinage* as being among the supreme masterpieces of the piano. Clearly Jandó sees the *Dante sonata* as the climactic point of the whole series. His performance has tremendous dynamism and power. One has the sense of Liszt himself hovering over the keyboard.

(i) Concert paraphrases of opera: BELLINI: *Réminiscences de 'Norma'*; BERLIOZ: *Bénédiction et Serment, 2 motifs de 'Benvenuto Cellini'*; DONIZETTI: *Réminiscences de 'Lucia di Lammermoor'*; VERDI: *Miserere du 'Trovatore'*; WAGNER: *Liebestod from 'Tristan und Isolde'*; WEBER: *'Oberon' overture*. (ii) *Etudes d'exécution transcendante d'après Paganini: Nos. 1, Preludio; 2 in E flat; 3, La Campanella; 4, Vivo; 5, La Chasse; 6, Theme with variations.*
(B) ** Carlton/Turnabout 30371 00342. (i) Alfred Brendel; (ii) Louis Kentner.

On the evidence of this Turnabout reissue, operatic style (especially Donizetti, Bellini, and early Verdi) is not Brendel's special métier. He plays strongly and emotionally but does not easily catch the spirit of the music. The most enjoyable performance here is the transcription of Weber's *Oberon overture*, which is played with appealing delicacy and charm. There are no such disappointments in Louis Kentner's accounts of the *Transcendental studies*, however. While the playing avoids display for its own sake, there is no lack of brilliance, and *La Chasse* sparkles delightfully. The closing variations on Paganini's most famous *Study* are played with bold panache. The recording is a bit clattery on top but has plenty of supporting sonority.

Concert paraphrases: (i) BELLINI: *Réminiscences de Norma*. GOUNOD: *Faust: Waltz*. MEYERBEER: *Le Prophète: The Skaters (Illustration No. 2)*. (ii) SCHUMANN: *Widmung*. (i) TCHAIKOVSKY: *Eugene Onegin: Polonaise*. (iii) VERDI: *Aida: Danza sacra e duetto final. Don Carlo: Coro di festa e marcia funèbre. Ernani. I Lombardi: Salve Maria de Jérusalem. Rigoletto. Miserere du Trovatore*. WAGNER: (iv) *Der fliegende Holländer: Spinning chorus;* (v) *Lohengrin: Elsa's bridal procession. Parsifal: Feierlicher marsch*.
(B) **(*) Ph. Duo 456 052-2 (2) [id.]. (i) Michele Campanella; (ii) Misha Dichter; (iii) Claudio Arrau; (iv) Alexander Uninsky; (v) Zoltán Kocsis.

Michele Campanella offers dextrous accounts of the Bellini, Gounod, Meyerbeer and Tchaikovsky items; even if he is rhythmically a touch heavy-handed, his glittering upper tessitura is compensation. When Kocsis takes over, his eloquence is remarkable, and the solemn march from *Parsifal* (which Liszt totally rewrote in his transcription) is the highlight of the collection. In his Verdi selection Arrau characteristically refuses to indulge in display for its own sake, even in these deliberate showpieces. His technique (in 1972) is effortlessly superb and, if there is inevitably a lack of sheer excitement, he shows what inner intensity some of this music contains in deeply expressive playing. The recording throughout is very good, outstanding for Arrau and Kocsis.

Etudes d'exécution transcendante (complete).
*** Teldec/Warner 4509 98415-2 [id.]. Boris Berezovsky.

This must surely be how Liszt himself sounded. Boris Berezovsky's performances show astonishing flair and technical assurance. His charisma in the bravura writing is very commanding indeed, yet in *Feux follets* he plays with the utmost delicacy, and the ruminative poetry of *Ricordanza* is melting. The piano is recorded boldly and brilliantly, not as full and sonorous as with Arrau, but there is no lack of pianistic colour in the gentler lyrical writing. The colour portrait of Liszt on the back of the accompanying booklet demonstrates why so many women succumbed to his physical charms!

Etudes d'exécution transcendante No. 10; Hungarian rhapsody No. 12; La leggierezza; Liebestraüme No. 3; Waldesrauschen.
(M) * Revelation Dig. RV 10031 [id.] Evgeni Kissin – SCHUMANN: *Etudes symphoniques* etc. *

These performances come from recitals this charismatic young Russian gave in 1984 and 1989, when he was thirteen and eighteen respectively. The playing is dazzling, but the recorded sound is close and crude and does not begin to do justice to the sound we know he produces.

Etudes d'exécution transcendante d'après Paganini: Nos. 3 (La Campanella); 5 (La Chasse). Etudes d'exécution transcendante: Feux follets; Polonaise No. 2 in E.
(M) *** Nimbus Dig. NI 8810 [id.]. Ferruccio Busoni (piano) – BACH: *Chaconne;* CHOPIN: *Preludes.* **

Very convincingly reproduced from a 1915 Duo-Art piano-roll, in first-class digital sound, this gives a stunning impression of Busoni's transcendental technique in music which calls for the kind of scintillating virtuosity this remarkable artist could so readily provide. Occasionally in *Feux follets* he seems somewhat wilful, but the bravura is prodigious, and the two *Paganini studies* are superb, while there is some glittering upper tessitura in the central section of the characterful *Polonaise*. Fascinating.

Hungarian rhapsodies Nos. 1–19; Rhapsodie espagnole.
(B) *** DG Double 453 034-2 (2) [id.]. Roberto Szidon.

Roberto Szidon offers Liszt playing of the highest order. He has flair and panache, genuine keyboard command and, when required, great delicacy of tone. He is well recorded too, and this DG Double is not only inexpensive but also provides (as does Cziffra on EMI) an excellent version of the *Rhapsodie espagnole*. Cziffra's performances (on CZS5 69003-2 – discussed in our main volume) are from an artist of an even more volatile personality, but Szidon is by no means upstaged: his style is equally valid and his approach is always imaginatively illuminating. There is a further alternative set from Michele Campanella on a Philips Duo (438 371-2) which has no want of technical command or finesse, but in the last resort his playing has less panache even though he is given the best recorded sound of all.

Vanguard 'Alfred Brendel collection': *Hungarian rhapsodies Nos. 2–3, 8, 13, 15 (Rákóczy march); Csárdás obstinée.*
(M) *** Van. 08 4024 71 [OVC 4024]. Brendel (also on 08 9163 72, with CHOPIN: *Andante spianato; Polonaises* **).

This is one of Brendel's finest records from the 1960s. It remains available singly, but now also comes (as part of Vanguard's 'Alfred Brendel collection') in a slip-case with a Chopin recital recorded at around the same time. However, this is rather less enticing and the separate Liszt issue is the one to go for.

Piano sonata in B min.
(B) *** EMI forte CZS5 69527-2 (2). Anievas – CHOPIN: *Sonata No. 3* **; RACHMANINOV: *Preludes Nos. 1–24* etc. **(*)

Anievas gives a fine and memorable performance, notable for its thoughtfulness and its subtlety in the control of tension. The lyrical impulse is finely balanced to bring out the music's poetry as well as its fire and strength. There may be more flamboyant interpretations available which more readily project the music's bravura, but few other recorded performances are as satisfying or are more successful in revealing the work's stature. The recording too is generally very good and, although the reverberation prevents absolute clarity in the bass in florid passages, the effect is firmer in the excellent CD transfer.

Piano sonata in B min.; Berceuse; Concert study: Gnomenreigen. Liebestraum No. 3 in A flat; Valse oubliée No. 1.
(M) *** Decca 452 306-2 [id.]. Clifford Curzon (with SCHUBERT: *Impromptu in A flat, D.935/2*).

Curzon shows an innate understanding of the *Sonata*'s cyclic form, so that the significance of the principal theme is brought out subtly in relation to the music's structural development. There are only a few performances to compare with this and none superior, and Decca's recording matches the playing in its excellence. The shorter pieces too are imaginatively played. The excellent recording was made in the Sofiensaal in 1963, but the fairly close microphones create something of a studio effect. For the reissue in Decca's Classic Sound series, Curzon's warm and beautiful account of Schubert's *A flat Impromptu* has been added. This was recorded at The Maltings, and here the sound is noticeably richer and has a fuller sonority.

Miscellaneous recitals

Piano sonata; Années de pèlerinage, 1st Year: Au bord d'une source; 2nd Year: Sonetto 104 del Petrarca; 3rd Year: Les jeux d'eau à la Ville d'Este; Concert paraphrases: Die Forelle; Erlkönig (Schubert); *Réminiscences de Don Juan* (Mozart); *Rigoletto* (Verdi). *Consolation No. 3; Etudes d'exécution transcendante d'après Paganini: La campanella. Etudes de concert: Gnomenreigen; Un sospiro. Harmonies poétiques et religieuses: Funérailles. Hungarian rhapsody No. 12 in C sharp min.; Liebesträume No. 3 in A flat; Mephisto waltz No. 1.*
500♪ (B) *** Decca Double Dig. 444 851-2 (2). Jorge Bolet.

The full range of the late Jorge Bolet's achievement for Decca in the music of Liszt is admirably surveyed here, ending with his commanding account of the *Sonata*. He can be romantic without sentimentality, as in the *Consolation*, *Un sospiro* or the most famous *Liebesträume*, yet can dazzle the ear with bravura or beguile the listener with his delicacy of colouring, as in the *Années de pèlerinage*. All the recordings here save the Mozart *Concert paraphrase* are digital and are as clear and present as one could wish.

Litolff, Henri (1818–91)

Concerti symphoniques Nos. 2 in B min., Op. 22; 4 in D min., Op. 102.
*** Hyperion Dig. CDA 66889 [id.]. Peter Donohoe, Bournemouth SO, Litton.

The *Fourth Concerto symphonique* is the source of the famous Litolff *Scherzo*, so often heard in the days of 78s. The complete work has been recorded before, by Gerald Robbins with the Monte Carlo Opera Orchestra under Eduard van Remoortel; it was issued on a Genesis LP, when we dismissed the first movement as rhetorical, the slow movement as uninspired, and the finale empty. But what a difference a really fine performance makes! Indeed we have to revise our view of the music. The first movement is certainly rhetorical but opens with endearing flamboyance under the baton of Andrew Litton, while the passage-work scintillates in the hands of Peter Donohoe. The secondary material has both delicacy and charm. The famous *Scherzo* which follows is taken a fraction too fast and loses some of its poise, the articulation not always absolutely clean; but one adjusts to the breathless virtuosity, and it remains the work's finest inspiration. The *Adagio religioso* opens with some lovely horn-playing, its solemn mood nicely offset later by the pianistic decoration. The finale, marked *Allegro impetuoso*, is certainly all of that, with more twinkling bravura from Donohoe.

The *Second Concerto* (which comes first on the disc) is also well worth having. Its opening *Maestoso* (16 minutes) is hopelessly inflated, but the Bournemouth orchestra present it with confident flamboyance, and Donohoe shows us that the Chopinesque secondary material is engaging. He finds all its charm alongside its brilliance. The second movement is another scintillating Scherzo, introduced humorously by the bassoon, and, if not quite as memorable as its more famous companion, it has a tripping centrepiece worthy of Saint-Saëns, especially as presented here. The quietly reflective *Andante* is again melodically appealing and winningly decorated by the piano; the Rondo finale bounces along gaily, and again the ear is drawn to the affectionately polished orchestral response alongside the sparkling solo contribution. With a warm, naturally balanced recording, this entertaining Hyperion CD is one of the year's surprises and very much worth having.

Lloyd, George (born 1913)

Symphony No. 8.
*** Troy Dig. TROY 230 [id.]. Philh. O, composer.

After his severe depression and nervous breakdown, Lloyd gave up composing entirely for many years, earning his living instead as a mushroom farmer, only gradually turning back to composition. The *Eighth Symphony*, written in 1961 – the first to be heard in public – is a product of that long recuperative period, and in the openness of inspiration (passionately English) it both belies earlier depression and testifies to the success of composition as therapy. Linked by a six-note leitmotif, the work holds well together. Even if the scherzando finale is arguably a little too long for its material, the elliptical first movement (opening and closing atmospherically and with a richly memorable secondary theme) and the eloquently sustained *Largo* both show the composer at his finest. Sir Edward Downes, who gave the first broadcast performance in 1977, subsequently made a fine LP of the work for Lyrita, but that has long been out of the catalogue and is now inevitably superseded by the composer's own highly spontaneous and very well-played Philharmonia account. The recording, made in the spacious acoustics of Watford Town Hall, is first class.

VOCAL MUSIC

A Litany.
**(*) Troy Dig. 200 [id.]. Janice Watson, Jeremy White, Guildford Choral Soc., Philh. O, composer.

A Litany, a setting of 12 verses from the John Donne poem, is currently Lloyd's most recent work. Completed in 1995, it was first performed in London in 1996 and was recorded soon afterwards. If anything, the recording is more successful than that first performance, with the choir enthusiastically at home in music which communicates readily, even if the soloists are less than ideal, both having rather wide vibratos. *A Litany* is not as inspired as the *Symphonic Mass*. It is unfortunate that the very opening brings a curious reminder of *The Phantom of the Opera* and *Belshazzar's Feast* with a whiff of Ketèlbey for good measure. But the music soon settles down and there is much fine choral writing in the first two sections, even if it is the third, unaccompanied, section, 'a song of thanks to the Virgin', that is the heart of the piece. The finale is quixotic in its mood changes but ends very positively. The spacious recording is well up to Albany's usual high standard.

A Symphonic Mass.
500♪ ❀ *** Albany Dig. TROY 100 [id.]. Brighton Festival Ch., Bournemouth SO, composer.

George Lloyd's *Symphonic Mass* is the composer's masterpiece. Written for chorus and orchestra (but no soloists) on the largest scale, the work is linked by a recurring main theme, a real tune which soon lodges insistently in the listener's memory, even though it is modified at each reappearance. The performance is magnificent and the recording is fully worthy, spaciously balanced within the generous acoustic of the Guildhall, Southampton, and overwhelmingly realistic, even in the huge climax of the *Sanctus* with its shattering percussion.

Locatelli, Pietro (1695–1764)

L'Arte del violino Op. 3: Concertos Nos. 8 in E min.; 11 in A; 12 in D.
(B) *** Carlton Turnabout 30371 00352. Susanne Lautenbacher, Mainz CO, Günter Kehr.

There is a fine complete set of Op. 3, played on period instruments by Elizabeth Wallfisch (Hyperion CDA 66721/3) and praised in our main volume. However, many collectors will surely welcome just a sampler taken from Susanne Lautenbacher's earlier Vox set from the 1960s. The three concertos here are well chosen. No. 11 has a fine central *Largo* and No. 12 a lively, Handelian opening theme; and all have impressive solo *Capriccios* in which Susanne Lautenbacher can demonstrate what were considered violin 'fireworks' in the early eighteenth century. Her lyrical playing brings a pleasingly full timbre, and Kehr and the Mainz Chamber Orchestra provide well-upholstered accompaniments. The recording is first class.

Concerti grossi, Op. 1/1–12.
(BB) *** Naxos Dig. 8.553445/6 [id.]. Capella Istropolitana, Jaroslav Kreček.

Locatelli's Op. 1 first appeared in 1721 but was revised in 1729 when their composer settled in Amsterdam. Though indebted to Corelli (with the eighth of the set ending with a Christmas *Pastorale* which is beautiful in its own right), they have a style and personality of their own. Their invention is vigorous, their expressive range appealing. If you enjoy *concerti grossi* you won't be disappointed here. The Capella Istropolitana play with crisp attack, plenty of sparkle and resilient rhythms; the style of the slow movements reveals a keen identity with the lessons of period performances, even though modern instruments are used and phrasing is unexaggerated by bulges. The recording is admirable, with textures clear and with attractive, light sonorities. Most enjoyable and highly recommended.

6 Introduttioni teatrali, Op. 4/1–6; 6 Concerti grossi, Op. 4/7–12.
*** Hyperion Dig. CDA 67041/2 [id.]. Raglan Bar. Players, Elizabeth Wallfisch.

There is simply no better introduction to the music of Locatelli than his superbly invigorating collection of six *Theatrical introductions*. They are essentially (highly inventive) small-scale *concerti grossi*, with a concertino of four players, written in the fast–slow–fast manner of an Italian overture. Indeed the finale of No. 5 reminds one of the fifth *concerto grosso* of Handel's Op. 6.

We have already highly praised an earlier recording of these stimulating works by the Freiburg Baroque Ensemble (DHM 0542 77207-2) to which we have given a Rosette. We have no reason to withdraw that, but whereas the Freiburg players provide interludes in their survey by playing three *Trio sonatas*, the Raglan Baroque Players instead offer the other six *Concerti grossi* which make up the rest of Locatelli's Op. 4. They too show him on his finest form, particularly the *Concerto No. 8 in F à immitazione de Corni da caccia*, where the opening *Grave* is quite profound, and then in later movements the solo violin of the concertino uses double-stopping ingeniously to depict a pair of horns. The remaining works are not as novel as this, but No. 10 (*Da Camera*) is a reworking of the *Sixth Sonata* of Locatelli's Op. 8 (see below) and includes the remarkable *Minuetto* with extended bravura variations, which are superbly played here by Elizabeth Wallfisch. No. 11 opens with another remarkably sombre *Grave* and then produces a jewelled sequence of brief movements (five in all). The final concerto of the set features four solo violins and was surely influenced by Vivaldi's famous work in this format which he included in *L'Estro armonico*. It deserves to be better known. The playing of the Raglan Baroque Ensemble, directed from the violin by the estimable Elizabeth Wallfisch, is supremely vital and expressively alive. The aural brightness is rather more sharply etched than in the DHM set, which competes in the first half of the work, but by no means unacceptably when the basic sonorities are so full and the ambience so appealing.

Violin sonatas (for 1 or 2 violins) *and continuo, Op. 8/1–10.*
*** Hyperion Dig. CDA 67021/2 [id.]. Locatelli Trio.

Locatelli's Op. 8 consists of six works for solo violin, of which the last is the most impressive with its closing *Aria di minuetto* with eight variations, demanding considerable bravura from the soloist. All the sonatas start with a slow, expressive introduction, with faster movements following. The remaining works are *Trio sonatas*; with their format of (usually) four (or sometimes five) movements, they offer the composer even greater opportunities for variety and he is obviously intending to please his cultivated listeners. The very agreeable (penultimate) *Cantabile* of No. 7, for instance, is followed by an unusual *Allegro* alternating more sustained passages with bursts of activity. But the invention in these later works is deft in imaginative touches, and the contrapuntal writing is genially spirited. Provided you don't respond adversely to Elizabeth Wallfisch's tendency in playing to bulge very slightly on expressive phrasing, the performances are admirable, crisply detailed and refreshingly alive. The Hyperion recording is well up to standard.

Locke, Matthew (*c*. 1621–77)

Psyche.
*** O-L Dig. 444 336-2 [id.]. Catherine Bott, Christopher Robson, Andrew King, Paul Agnew, Michael George, Simon Grant, Julia Gooding, Helen Parker, Julian Podger, Ch. & New L. Cons., Pickett.

Psyche dates from 1675, a year after Locke's success with his similar drama with music, *The Tempest*. But he worked on *Psyche* (broadly based on the Lully equivalent) in partnership with Giovanni Draghi, who provided the instrumental parts of the score, which are now lost. So they have been inspirationally reconstituted by Philip Pickett and Peter Holman by making arrangements from Draghi's keyboard music, and the result is very vivid and colourful. The vocal music is very engaging too, from the *Chorus of Nymphs* to the Forge scene, complete with anvil noises. The soloists all rise to the occasion, especially Catherine Bott who is perfectly cast as Venus. Michael George is also splendid, and there is no weak link here, while the New London Chorus obviously enjoy themselves and make a lively contribution. This is not on the level of Purcell, but it still makes a most enjoyable entertainment.

Loewe, Carl (1796–1869)

Ballads and Lieder: *Archibald Douglas; Canzonette; Die drei Lieder; Edward; Elvershöh; Erlkönig; Freibeuter; Frühzeitiger Frühling; Der getreue Eckart; Gottes ist der Orient!; Die Gruft der Liebenden; Gutmann und Gutweib; Der heilige Franziskus; Heinrich der Vogler; Herr Oluf; Hinkende Jamben; Hochzeitlied; Ich denke dein; Im Vorübergehen; Kleiner Haushalt; Lynkeus, der Türmer, auf Fausts Sternwarte singend; Meeresleuchten; Der Mohrenfürst auf der Messe; Der Nöck; Odins Meeresritt; Prinz Eugen; Der Schatzgräber; Süsses Begräbnis; Tom der Reimer; Der Totentanz; Trommelständchen; Turmwächter Lynkeus zu den Füssen der Helena; Die Uhr; Die wandelnde Glocke; Wandrers Nachtlied; Wenn der Blüten Frühlingsregen; Der Zauberlehrling.*
(M) *** DG 449 516-2 (2) [id.]. Fischer-Dieskau, Demus.

For the most part this set was recorded in 1968–9, with a second group of songs added a decade later. With the great German baritone consistently in fine voice, it makes an ideal selection of some of Loewe's most memorable songs and ballads. Fischer-Dieskau, admirably accompanied by Jörg Demus, gives performances which have the commitment and intensity of spontaneous expression while remaining flawlessly controlled and strongly thought through. This alternative setting of the *Erlkönig*, preferred by many in the nineteenth century, is in its way as dramatic as Schubert's, if musically less subtle. The following *Edward* is also extraordinarily dramatic, while the magnificent *Die Uhr* ('The timepiece') opens lightly but develops an unexpected depth of feeling. The story-telling in other songs is also so graphic that it might be thought that even a non-German speaker would have little need to refer to the translations. However, it is an excellent feature of the set that these are provided in full. Splendidly vivid recording: if you enjoy Schubert, you can hardly fail to relish the best of Loewe.

Ludford, Nicholas (1485–1557)

Masses; Magnificat benedicta & Motets (complete).
500♪ ❁ (M) *** ASV/Gaudeamus CDGAX 426 (4) [id.]. The Cardinall's Musick, Andrew Carwood.

This four-CD box gathers together the four splendid discs of Ludford's music performed by Carwood and his excellent group of singers, who are individually as impressive as in the blended whole. This is music of remarkably passionate feeling, and it brings to life a composer who spent much of his working life in St Stephen's Chapel at St Margaret's, Westminster. His music is little short of extraordinary, and we hope our Rosette will tempt collectors to explore it, either through this comprehensive box or by trying one of the individual issues (CDGAU 131, CDGAU 132, CDGAU 133 and CDGAU 140).

Lully, Jean-Baptiste (1632–87)

Atys: highlights.
(B) *** HM Dig. HMT 7901249 [HMC 901249] (from complete recording, with Guy de Mey, Agnès Mellon, Les Arts Florissants, cond. Christie).
(B) *** HM Dig. HMX 290844/46 (3) [id.] (from complete recording, cond. Christie) – CAMPRA: *Idomenée:* highlights; RAMEAU: *Castor et Pollux:* highlights. ***

Atys remains one of Christie's greatest successes on record; it is full of good things, and many of them are also included on the single-disc highlights selection (notably the delightful Sleep scene of Act III). With consistently fine singing and superb recording, this disc contains about a third of the opera (68 minutes).

This CD is also offered as part of one of Harmonia Mundi's enterprising 'Trios', in this case offering three discs of operatic highlights together in a slip-case at bargain price. But unlike its companions, *Idomenée* and *Castor et Pollux*, no translation is included for *Atys*. Christie's performance is highly recommended by us (on HMC 901257/9), with Guy de Mey memorable in the principal role, and this 68-minute selection includes the remarkable 'Sleep fantasy' in Act III. Taken as a package with its two companions, this collection of highlights costs only a fraction of the price of the three-disc complete set.

Lumbye, Hans Christian (1810–74)

Amager polka; Amelie waltz; Champagne galop; Columbine polka mazurka; Copenhagen Steam Railway galop; Dream pictures fantasia; The Guard of Amager (ballet): *Final galop. Helga polka mazurka; Hesperus waltz; Lily polka (dedicated to the ladies); Queen Louise's waltz; Napoli* (ballet): *Final galop. Salute to August Bournonville; Salute to our friends; Sandman galop fantastique.*
500♪ ❁ *** Unicorn Dig. DKPCD 9089 [id.]. Odense SO, Peter Guth.

This superb Unicorn collection offers 75 minutes of the composer's best music, with wonderfully spontaneous performances demonstrating above all its elegance and gentle grace. It opens with a vigorous *Salute to August Bournonville* and closes with a *Champagne galop* to rival Johann junior's polka. But Lumbye's masterpiece is the unforgettable *Copenhagen Steam Railway galop*, a whimsical yet vivid portrait of a local Puffing Billy. The little engine wheezingly starts up and proceeds on its journey, finally drawing to a dignified halt against interpolated cries from the station staff. Because of the style and refinement of its imagery, it is much the most endearing of musical railway evocations, and the high-spirited lyricism of the little train racing through the countryside, its whistle peeping, is enchanting.

Lutoslawski, Witold (1913–94)

(i) *Chain II; Interlude; Partita. Musique funèbre; Symphony No. 4.*
(BB) *** Naxos Dig. 8.553202 [id.]. (i) Bakowski; Polish Nat. RSO, Wit.

This is the most approachable of the first issues in Naxos's adventurous Lutoslawski series. The *Symphony No. 4* is his culminating masterpiece which, in its concentration over two linked movements, seems to echo Sibelius's *Seventh.* The darkly intense *Funeral music* in memory of Bartók is another beautiful and concentrated work, while the two violin concertante works, *Chain II* and *Partita*, here come with the separating *Interlude*, similarly thoughtful, which Lutoslawski wrote as a link. In almost every way, not least in the playing of the violinist, Krzysztow Bakowski, these Polish performances match and even outshine earlier recordings conducted by the composer, helped by full, brilliant sound.

Piano concerto.
*** Koch Dig. 3-6414-2 [id.]. Ewa Kupiec, Bamberg SO, Judd – SZYMANOWSKI: *Symphony No. 4.* **

Ewa Kupiec gives a magnetic performance of this difficult concerto, with its fragmentary writing in slow movements and chattering passage-work in the second-movement Scherzo. Even more than the dedicatee, Krystian Zimerman, or Piotr Paleczny in the previous recordings, she finds fun in the Scherzo and, warmly supported by Judd and the Bamberg orchestra, gives point and purpose to the seemingly improvisatory writing of the other movements. Excellent sound. The Szymanowski symphony with its important piano part makes an interesting but ungenerous coupling.

(i) *Piano concerto. Little suite; Symphonic variations; Symphony No. 2.*
(BB) *** Naxos 8.553169 [id.]. (i) Paleczny; Polish Nat. RSO, Wit.

The *Symphonic variations*, more tonal than most of Lutoslawski's works, make an attractive introduction to the second of Naxos's discs in what aims to cover his complete orchestral music. The *Little suite* is an approachable work too, before the much tougher and more substantial symphony and concerto, which make up the great part of the disc. In two massive movements, *Hesitant* and *Direct*, the *Symphony No. 2* is an uncompromising piece, and here is helped by a purposeful, very well-rehearsed performance. The *Piano concerto*, originally written for Krystian Zimerman, is even more elusive, often fragmentary, but again the performance is magnetic, with the pianist, Piotr Paleczny, playing with a clarity and brilliance that sound totally idiomatic. Excellent sound, with good presence.

MacDowell, Edward (1861–1908)

Piano concertos Nos. 1 in A min., Op. 15; 2 in D min., Op. 23.
500♪ ❁ *** Olympia Dig. OCD 353 [id.]. Donna Amato, LPO, Paul Freeman.

Of MacDowell's two *Piano concertos* the *First* is marginally the lesser of the two: the melodic content, though very pleasing, is slightly less memorable than in the *Second*. Donna Amato's scintillating performance is entirely winning, and she is equally persuasive in the *A minor*. A highly rewarding coupling in all respects.

Piano concerto No. 2 in D min., Op. 23.
*(*) Telarc Dig. CD 80429 [id.]. André Watts, Dallas SO, Andrew Litton – LISZT: *Piano concertos Nos. 1–2.* **

No one could say that Watts and Litton are not committed in their approach to this concerto, or that there is a lack of adrenalin. But they treat this endearingly light-hearted piece as if it were Busoni and give it the full barnstorming treatment, like the two Liszt *Concertos* with which it is coupled. The result fails to dazzle; instead it overwhelms the music with rhetoric, and the resonant recording amplifies the effect. At the moment, Earl Wild's definitive version of the *Concerto* on Chesky (CD 76) is very difficult to obtain. Fortunately Donna Amato's coupling of both the *First* and *Second Concertos* on Olympia can be recommended without reservation.

Machaut, Guillaume de (*c.* 1300–1377)

Ballades, motets, rondeaux & virelais: *Amours me fait desirer; Dame se vous m'estés lointeinne; De Bon Espoir – Puis que la douce rousee; De toutes flours; Douce dame jolie; Hareu! hareu! le feu; Ma fin est mon commencement; Mes esperis se combat; Phyton le mervilleus serpent; Quant j'ay l'espart; Quant je suis mis au retour; Quant Theseus – Ne quier veoir; Se ma dame m'a guerpy; Se je souspir; Trop plus est belle – Biauté paree – Je ne sui mie certeins.*
(M) *** Virgin Veritas/EMI VED5 61284-2 (2). Early Music Cons. of L., David Munrow (within Recital: '*The art of courtly love*' ***).

This collection is within 'Guillaume Machaut and his age', which is itself part of David Munrow's wide-ranging collection, 'The art of courtly love' – see below under Vocal Recitals. Treasures here include cantatas with James Bowman and Charles Brett beautifully matched as soloists. Everything reveals both the remarkable individuality of Guillaume de Machaut as a highly influential composer who spanned the first three-quarters of the fourteenth century, and the life and energy which Munrow consistently brought to early music, even if in some items he arguably goes too far in pepping it up, as in presenting *Dame se vous m'estés* as a bagpipe solo! Excellent CD transfers.

Messe de Nostre Dame (with Plainsong for the Proper of the *Mass of Purification for the Purification of the Virgin (Candlemas)*.
**(*) HM Dig. HMC 901590 [id.]. Soloists, Ens. Organum, Marcel Péres.

Messe de Nostre Dame; Le Lai de la Fonteinne (The Lay of the Fountain); Rondeau: *Ma fin est mon commencement (My end is my beginning).*
**(*) Hyperion Dig. CDA 66358 [id.]. James, Stafford, Covey-Crump, Potter, Padmore, Nixon, Hillier, George, Hilliard Ens., Paul Hillier.

Messe de Nostre Dame. Le Livre dou Voir dit (excerpts): *Plourez dames; Nes qu'on porroit* (ballades); *Sans cuer dolens* (rondeau); *Le lay de bonne esperance; Puis qu'en oubli* (rondeau); *Dix et sept cinq* (rondeau).
(BB) **(*) Naxos Dig. 8.553833 [id.]. Oxford Camerata, Jeremy Summerly.

With his *Messe de Nostre Dame* (dedicated to the Virgin Mary), Guillaume de Machaut wrote the first known complete setting of the Ordinary of the Mass: *Kyrie*, *Gloria*, *Credo*, *Sanctus* and *Agnus Dei*. He chose to finish with his own simple interpolation: *Ite missa est*, which very briefly tells us, 'The mass is ended; thanks be to God.' Machaut's writing is full of extraordinary, dissonant clashes and sudden harmonic twists which are immediately resolved, so the music is both serene and plangently stimulating: here is an epoch-making work of great originality. Both the Hilliard Ensemble and the Oxford Camerata present the Mass as it stands (and therefore they have room for extra items), whereas Marcel Péres has inserted the plainsong for the Proper of the Mass, taken from the Candlemas liturgy for the Purification of the Virgin, which is presented in the same florid style as is Machaut's setting of the Ordinary.

Of the three performances here, Jeremy Summerly's account is undoubtedly the most eloquently serene; it is beautifully controlled and modulated, rather after the fashion of the famous Willcocks/King's College accounts of the Byrd Masses. The harmonic pungencies are cleanly presented but unexaggerated and – compared with Hillier and (especially) Péres – the music's lines, although by no means bland, flow in relative tranquillity. Obviously much care went into the preparation of the recording, made in conjunction with BBC Radio 3 and France Musique. Reims Cathedral was chosen for the recording location because that was where the work was first performed, and even the choice of the actual recording site – in front of the organ, immediately east of the choir step – sought to produce a similar acoustic effect to what Summerly feels the composer would have experienced; and the effect is affectingly beautiful. The singers apparently experimented freely with plicas – notational signs indicating some kind of ornament – the meaning of which is uncertain but which appear frequently; but there is none of the audacious decoration which is so striking on the Harmonia Mundi version.

Hillier's approach certainly does not lack repose or linear beauty, but he presses the music onwards with a much greater sense of drama than obtains in Oxford. His *Kyrie* is three minutes shorter than Summerly's, and the *Gloria* brings freely passionate accelerandos, which are highly involving but may or may not be authentic. The Hilliard group is superbly recorded with a strong presence, and there is no doubt that the music's unexpected dissonances are more dramatically brought out here than on Naxos.

However, the boldness of effect produced by the Ensemble Organum under Marcel Péres in every way dramatically upstages its two competitors. In his (confident and very interesting) notes, Péres laments that 'The art of ornamentation is little practised by performers today, which is much to be regretted. Ornamentation is essential, for it creates the active force of the work.' And in this performance it certainly does – to an extraordinary degree. The Ensemble Organum tangibly includes a Corsican element, and the dark pungency of male timbre and twirling embellishments, with suggestions of micro-intervals, bring a distinctly Arabian flavour, an almost Muslim character to the ornamentation. The singing itself is powerfully resonant and the dissonances ring out boldly. After this the other performances sound a bit like milk and water, and there is no doubt that the Harmonia Mundi performance is unforgettably stimulating. But is it what Machaut intended? We simply do not know. Certainly this is a record to hear and be thrilled by, if hardly a 'library' addition for a collection. The recording is splendid. Although there are no extra items, at the time of review the Harmonia Mundi issue (in a box) includes a 78-minute sampler 'Portrait' of excerpts from other recordings of early music by this same group. However, this bonus item may not continue for the lifetime of this book.

On Naxos the coupled chansons were recorded, equally effectively, at the BBC's Maida Vale studio; they celebrate Machaut as poet/lover as well as composer and, at its modest price, the disc is worth having for these alone. Indeed *Le Livre dou voir dit* is one of the most remarkable cycles of poems of the Middle Ages. Its 9,094 lines of verse, arranged in octosyllabic rhyming couplets, were inspired by the passionate love between the elderly composer (Machaut was in his sixties when he wrote all the music here) and his adolescent student admirer, Péronne d'Armetières. It draws on their correspondence, which frequently shared poems, some set to music by Machaut and intended for his beloved to sing. The music itself is lighter in lyrical feeling than the Mass and its melodic and harmonic style, while recognizably similar, is far less plangent.

In the first two ballades here (*Plourez dames*, written in 1362, and *Nes qu'on porroit* of a year later) the lyrics are pervaded with melancholy and longing, and the settings share the same flowing melodic idea. *Sans cuer doleur* is still dolorous, but the lovers have now spent some time together and Machaut is lamenting their separation. (Its rondeau setting, with a haunting refrain, was apparently written earlier but was chosen by the composer to send back to Péronne because of its appropriate lyrics.) *Puis qu'en oubli sui de vous dous amis* ('Since I am forgotten by you, sweet friend') is particularly touching, given a darkness by its low-pitched line, but its languishing is not to be taken too seriously, for in the final rondeau included here, *Dix et sept*, Machaut encodes the name of his beloved in the figures.

Their relationship lasted about four years and fired the composer to what was his richest and most fruitful period of composition. His feelings are admirably detailed in the ambitious 20-minute *Lay de bonne esperance* ('Lay of good hope') with 12 stanzas telling how his new-found love aroused him from despairing lethargy when 'shot through the heart by a pair of eyes, grey-green, piercing, charming, striking, smiling and gay . . . my lady, through her sweet smiling look, made a dart of burning desire and of hope'. Machaut continues in praise of her beauty and his joy in loving and, finally, his refreshment and reward 'that I was a true lover'. It is a poem of extraordinary passion and eloquence, and it is a pity that the solo performance here, though well enough sung by Matthew Brook, does not have sufficient vocal charisma or charm to carry such an extended monologue. Never mind, the rest of the programme is very well managed, and this is certainly one of Naxos's real bargains.

The solo singing in the extra items on the Hyperion disc is very impressive indeed, as might be expected from the cast-list. *Le Lai de la Fonteinne* is another elaborate poem of 12 stanzas in praise of the Virgin, six polyphonic, six monodic, beautifully sung by Mark Padmore, Rogers Covey-Crump and John Potter, while the shorter rondeau, an expressive piece if restlessly so, is ingeniously constructed, and is a 'crab' canon by inversion, in that the imitating part, instead of being presented straightforwardly, is written backwards and upside down – appropriately so, to fit the text: 'My end is my beginning.'

MacMillan, James (born 1959)

(i) *The Berserking* (a concerto for piano and orchestra); (ii) *Britannia; Sinfonietta; Sowetan spring.*
*** RCA Dig. 09026 68328-2 [id.]. Royal SNO; (i) with Peter Donohoe, Stenz; (ii) composer.

James MacMillan is a composer with a demon when it comes to vivid communication. In their widely contrasted ways, all four of the works here have an agenda, political and social, yet the high-voltage electricity which results is very different from propaganda music, whether of the right or left, when so colourfully each work reflects the composer's intensely personal responses. So *The Berserking* – a term drawn from frenzied Viking warriors – was written in response to MacMillan's frustration as an ardent Scot to his compatriots' 'seeming facility for shooting themselves in the foot'. The manically energetic first movement of this 33-minute piano concerto – brilliantly played by Peter Donohoe – may represent 'swaggering futility', but it is exciting music in its own right, and it resolves on two slower, more contemplative movements which finally bring peace in a modal mood not all that distant from Vaughan Williams. Similarly *Britannia*, with its ironic references to English music from *Knees up Mother Brown* to *God save the Queen* and *Cockaigne*, proves to be a thoroughly enjoyable Ivesian fantasy. Implanted in the meditations of the one-movement *Sinfonietta* is a violent, ironic reference to an Ulster marching song, which serves to intensifiy the beauty of the rest. Only the very serious agenda of *Sowetan spring* results in an obsessive piece with too much reliance on minimalism, though that too is memorable. With superb performances, brilliantly recorded, this is a disc to attract more than the devotee of new music.

Mahler, Gustav (1860–1911)

Symphony No. 1 in D (Titan); (i) *Lieder eines fahrenden Gesellen.*
(M) **(*) DG 449 735-2 [id.]. Bav. RSO, Kubelik, (i) with Dietrich Fischer-Dieskau.

Kubelik gives an intensely poetic reading. He is here at his finest in Mahler and though, as in later symphonies, he is sometimes tempted to choose a tempo on the fast side, the result could hardly be more glowing. The rubato in the slow funeral march is most subtly handled. In its CD reissue the quality is a little dry in the bass and the violins have lost some of their warmth, but there is no lack of body. In the *Lieder eines fahrenden Gesellen* the sound is fuller, with more atmospheric bloom. No one quite rivals Fischer-Dieskau in these songs, and this is a very considerable bonus, especially at 'Originals' price.

Symphonies Nos. 1 in D; (i) *2 in C min. (Resurrection).*
(B) **(*) Decca Double 448 921-2 (2) [id.]. (i) Harper, Watts, London Symphony Ch.; LSO, Solti.

Solti's 1966 account of No. 2 remains a demonstration of the outstanding results Decca were securing with analogue techniques at that time, although the brilliance of the fortissimos may not suit all ears. Helen Watts is wonderfully expressive, while the chorus has a rapt intensity that is the more telling when the recording perspectives are so clearly delineated. The London Symphony Orchestra play Mahler's *First* like no other orchestra. They catch the magical opening with a singular, evocative quality, at least partly related to the peculiarly characteristic blend of wind timbres, and throughout there is wonderfully warm string-tone. Solti's tendency to drive hard is felt only in the second movement, which is pressed a little too much, although he relaxes beautifully in the central section. Especially memorable are the poignancy of the introduction of the *Frère Jacques* theme in the slow movement and the exultant brilliance of the closing pages. Excellent value, although Solti's individual mid-priced record of the *First Symphony* (417 701-2) is still more tempting.

Symphonies Nos. (i) *2 (Resurrection);* (ii) *4 in G.*
(B) ** DG Double 453 037-2 (2) [id.]. (i) Neblett, Horne, Chicago Ch. & SO; (ii) Von Stade, VPO, Abbado.

Abbado's version of the *Resurrection Symphony* proves a performance of extremes, with variations of tempo more confidently marked than is common but with concentration so intense that there is no hint of self-indulgence. The delicacy of the Chicago orchestra in the second and third movements is as remarkable as its precision, while the great contrasts of the later movements prove a challenge not only to the performers but also to the DG engineers, who produce sound of the finest analogue quality. Generally the singing is as splendid as the playing but, if there is even a minor disappointment, it lies in the closing pages which are just a little contained. However, the later recording of the *Fourth* is disappointing, above all in the self-consciously expressive reading of the slow movement. There is much beauty of detail, but the Vienna Philharmonic has played and been recorded better than this.

Symphony No. 2 in C min. (Resurrection); Symphony No. 5 in C sharp min. (*Adagietto* only).
*** Conifer Dig. 75605 51277-2 (2) [id.]. Benita Valente, Maureen Forrester, LSO, Gilbert Kaplan.

A Mahler *Second* with a difference. This two-CD set includes an important visual component: a set of some 150 photographs and paintings of Mahler which can be reproduced on either the Apple Macintosh or MS-DOS personal computers with a CD-ROM drive, as well as an excellent transfer of the Welte-Mignon piano-rolls that Mahler made, a collage of reminiscences by musicians who played under Mahler, and a pocket-sized reproduction of the 1897 first edition of the score. The ample notes also reproduce some of the photographs found on the CD. The latter reproduce quite superbly and are copiously annotated in French, German and English. They are accompanied by the *Adagietto* from the *Fifth Symphony* but this can presumably be switched off if you find it distracting. The performance of the *Adagietto* opens the first disc and then, after the reminiscences and the piano-rolls, comes the first movement of the *Second Symphony*. The remainder follows on the second CD, together with the photographs, many of great interest. Gilbert Kaplan is not a professional conductor but has immersed himself in Mahler and Mahleriana. His performances of both the *Second Symphony* and the *Adagietto* from the *Fifth* are not only thoroughly idiomatic and full of enthusiasm but totally compelling. He gets keenly dramatic and highly responsive playing from the LSO, and the recording quality (when played on high-grade equipment rather than through computer loudspeakers as one might be tempted to do after sampling the photos) is of demonstration quality. We commented favourably on the performance in our main edition when it appeared on the Carlton label but, given the interest of the additional material, we would be inclined to upgrade it to three stars, for the performance and recording are certainly second to none.

Symphony No. 3 in D min.
500♪ *** Ph. Dig. 432 162-2 (2) [id.]. Jard van Nes, Tölz Boys' Ch., Ernst-Senff Ch., BPO, Haitink.

With the Berlin Philharmonic producing glorious sounds, recorded with richness and immediacy, Haitink conducts a powerful, spacious reading. It culminates in a glowing, concentrated account of the slow finale, which gives the whole work a visionary strength often lacking. The mystery of *Urlicht* is then beautifully caught by the mezzo soloist, Jard van Nes.

(i) *Symphony No. 4 in G;* (ii) *Lieder eines fahrenden Gesellen.*
500♪ ❁ (M) *** Sony SBK 46535 [id.]. (i) Judith Raskin, Cleveland O, Szell; (ii) Frederica von Stade, LPO, Andrew Davis.

George Szell's 1966 record of Mahler's *Fourth* represented his partnership with the Cleveland Orchestra at its highest peak and the digital remastering for CD brings out the very best of the original recording. The performance remains uniquely satisfying: the music blossoms, partly because of the marvellous attention to detail (and the immaculate ensemble), but more positively because of the committed and radiantly luminous orchestral response to the music itself. In the finale Szell found the ideal soprano to match his conception.

Symphony No. 5 in C sharp min.
500♪ ❁ (M) *** EMI CDM7 64749-2 [id.]. New Philh. O, Barbirolli.
* DG Dig. 453 416-2 [id.]. VPO, Boulez.

Barbirolli's famous (1969) version is on any count one of the greatest, most warmly affecting performances ever committed to disc, expansive, yet concentrated in feeling: the *Adagietto* is very moving. The recording was made in Watford Town Hall and has been remastered most successfully. A classic version, and still a fine bargain.

'Emotionally sterile' was one verdict on Boulez's Mahler, and it must be conceded that, as in much of his music-making, Boulez's approach is (to say the least) dispassionate, like an aerial survey that indicates the nature of the terrain but does not allow one to experience it. As always, Boulez has impressive control and produces some glorious sounds from the Vienna Philharmonic, but there is little soul here, and few Mahlerians are likely to warm to this performance.

Symphony No. 6 in A min.
500♪ *** DG 415 099-2 (2) [id.]. BPO, Karajan (with *5 Rückert Lieder* **(*)).

With superlative playing from the Berlin Philharmonic, Karajan's reading of the *Sixth* is a revelation, above all in the slow movement, which emerges as one of the greatest of Mahler's slow movements, and the whole balance of the symphony is altered. Though the outer movements firmly stamp this as the darkest of the Mahler symphonies, in Karajan's reading their sharp focus makes them both compelling and refreshing. The superb DG recording, with its wide dynamics, adds enormously to the impact. Christa Ludwig's set of the *Five Rückert Songs* has been added as a bonus.

Symphony No. 7 in E min.
*** DG Dig. 419 211-2 (2) [id.]. NYPO, Bernstein.

Bernstein's *Seventh* on DG, recorded from live performances, remains a clear first choice for this symphony. It is quite riveting from first to last, ending with a searingly exciting account of the finale. None of the more recent versions quite measures up to this, although Sinopoli's highly individual, emotionally fraught, and certainly controversial version (also on DG, 437 851-2) is disturbingly powerful, and it includes Bryn Terfel's magnificent interpretation of the *Kindertotenlieder*. This leaves the reissue of Abbado's very commanding reading with the Chicago Symphony, which makes a clear first choice in the mid-price-range (DG 445 513-2). Against this, Chailly's Decca set, although it has keenly idiomatic playing from the Concertgebouw Orchestra, seems comparatively lightweight, although its unusual coupling of Diepenbrock's *Im grossen Schweigen* may be a bonus for some collectors (444 446-2). Haitink's third version of the work on Philips is paired with the *Adagio* from the *Tenth Symphony* but this *Seventh* is curiously uninvolving and is not even absolutely immaculate in ensemble. Moreover it lacks the spontaneity of his earlier versions (Ph. 434 997-2).

Symphony No. 8 (Symphony of 1000).
500♪ ✿ *** DG Dig. 435 433-2 (2) [id.]. Studer, Blasi, Jo, Lewis, Meier, Nagai, Allen, Sotin, Southend Boys' Ch., Philh. Ch. & O, Sinopoli.

Giuseppe Sinopoli crowns his Mahler cycle with the Philharmonia in a ripely passionate account of this most extravagant of the series, recorded with a richness and body that outshine any digital rival. The chorus sings with fine control and incandescent tone, from the hypnotic first entry through to a thrilling final crescendo on '*Alles vergangliche*'.

(i) *Symphony No. 9;* (ii) *Kindertotenlieder.*
(B) (**) Carlton VoxBox mono/stereo CDX2 5509 (2) [id.]. (i) VSO; (ii) Norman Foster, Bamberg SO; Jascha Horenstein.

Symphony No. 9; (i) *Kindertotenlieder; 5 Rückert Lieder.*
(B) *** DG Double 453 040-2 (2) [id.]. BPO, Karajan; (i) with Christa Ludwig.

Fine as Karajan's other Mahler recordings have been, his two accounts of the *Ninth* transcend them. In the earlier, analogue version it is the combination of richness and concentration in the outer movements that makes for a reading of the deepest intensity, while in the middle two movements there is point and humour as well as refinement and polish. Helped by full, spacious recording, the sudden pianissimos which mark both movements have an ear-pricking realism such as one rarely experiences on record, and the unusually broad tempi are superbly controlled. In the finale Karajan is not just noble and stoic; he finds the bite of passion as well, sharply set against stillness and repose. The earlier (1980) analogue performance makes a remarkable bargain, reissued as a DG Double and costing half as much as the later, digital recording. Moreover the performances of the *Kindertotenlieder* and *Rückert Lieder* have a distinction and refinement of playing which stand out above all. Ludwig's singing is characterful too, with the poise and stillness of the songs beautifully caught. Even if the microphone conveys some unevenness in the voice, the recording is rich and mellow to match the performances.

Horenstein's was the first LP version of this most visionary of Mahler's symphonies, and the interpretation still stands comparison with the many fine versions that have appeared since. Where, rather surprisingly, it falls down in comparison with the dedicated interpretations of Walter and Karajan is in the slow finale, where Horenstein tends to overload the emotion and to use too overtly expressive a style. Later in his career his manner grew more restrained, and no doubt a re-recording would have been very different. The interpretation is not helped by the Vox mono sound which, though clean enough, is forwardly balanced and allows no true pianissimo; nor indeed can it expand to a real fortissimo. But so committed an interpretation from one of the great Mahlerian conductors is well worth considering, though it is a pity that it would not fit on a single CD. Norman Foster's resonantly dark bass baritone suits the coupled song-cycle and his melancholy response is sensitive enough, but there is too little variety of colour and mood.

Lieder eines fahrenden Gesellen.
* Sup. Dig. SU 3026-2 [id.]. Iván Kusnjer, Czech PO, Bělohlávek – MARTINU: *Symphony No. 6.* **

Iván Kusnjer brings little variety of colour or dynamics to the *Lieder eines fahrenden Gesellen*; he sings pretty well *fortissimo* throughout. Not recommendable in spite of Bělohlávek's supportive accompaniment. Obviously a non-starter at full price, but it might possibly have been worth considering at mid- or bargain-price for the sake of the coupling.

Lieder eines fahrenden Gesellen; Lieder und Gesänge (aus der Jugendzeit); Im Lenz; Winterlied.
500♪ ❀ *** Hyperion CDA 66100 [id.]. Dame Janet Baker, Geoffrey Parsons.

Dame Janet presents a superb collection of Mahler's early songs with piano. The performances are radiant and deeply understanding from both singer and pianist, well caught in atmospheric recording. A heart-warming record.

Lieder und Gesänge.
*** Sony Dig. SK 68344 [id.]. Angelika Kirchschlager, Helmut Deutsch (with Alma MAHLER: *5 Lieder*) – KORNGOLD: *5 Lieder, Op. 38; Songs of the Clown.* ***

Angelika Kirchschlager from Salzburg is one of the most talented Lieder singers of her generation, fresh, bright and girlish of tone and with keen insight into word-meaning. In Mahler's youth songs she may not have the subtlety of Dame Janet Baker in the same repertory, with tonal contrasts far more limited, but the girlishness and direct approach are arguably more apt for these early songs with their folk flavours, often settings of *Des Knaben Wunderhorn*. The five additional songs by Alma Mahler were written in the early years of her marriage to Gustav: charming inspirations, tuneful and direct but full of subtle modulations, and quite unlike her husband's work. They make an attractive extra item in this impressive début recording.

Das Lied von der Erde.
500♪ (B) *** BBC Radio Classics BBCRD 9120 [id.]. J. Baker, Mitchinson, BBC N. SO, Leppard.
(M) ** Decca 452 301-2 [id.]. Fischer-Dieskau, King, VPO, Bernstein.

Taken from a performance for radio in the Free Trade Hall, Manchester, the Leppard version offers Dame Janet Baker at her very peak in 1977, giving one of the most moving and richly varied readings of the contralto songs ever. The final *Abschied* has a depth and intensity, a poignancy and, at the end, a feeling of slipping into the unconscious, that set it above even Dame Janet's earlier recording with Haitink.

Bernstein's 1966 recording brings tempi which, although personal, are only occasionally wilful, nearly always suiting the music naturally, so that the tenor songs sparkle as they should and, though the final *Abschied*, taken at a very slow tempo indeed, puts extra strain on everybody, Bernstein's intensity carries the performance through. Doubts do arise over the soloists. James King is a strong-voiced tenor, but his phrasing and word-pointing at times sound comparatively stiff. Fischer-Dieskau is as sensitive as ever, but it is doubtful whether even he can match the finest contralto in the role, for one needs a lightening of tone in the even-numbered songs rather than – as here – a darkening. Nor can a baritone voice give quite such precision to the notes which Mahler's rounded melodies clearly need. John Culshaw produced and the Decca engineers gave Bernstein a ravishing recording aura in the Sofiensaal in which the sound of the Vienna Philharmonic was ravishingly beautiful. However, for once the remastering for Decca's Classic Sound series is not entirely flattering: there is no lack of body and warmth, but the resonant focus is not always absolutely refined.

Marek, Czeslaw (1891–1985)

Meditations, Op. 14; Sinfonia, Op. 28; Suite for orchestra, Op. 25.
*** Koch Dig. 36429-2. Philh. O, Gary Brain.

Czeslaw Marek was a Polish-born Swiss composer who, when he died in 1985 at the age of 94, left a handful of finely crafted, warmly post-Romantic works which virtually no one had heard. Modest to a fault, and happily rich enough not to care, he gave up composing in 1940 and refused even to promote any performances of his music, let alone recordings. This first of seven discs covering his complete works offers ripely convincing performances in spectacular sound of three richly orchestrated works. Earliest is the four-movement suite, *Meditations*, written in 1913, with very skilful orchestral writing for a 22-year-old. The *Suite*, Op. 25, dates from 1926, consisting of five colourful and atmospheric movements, with a hint of neo-classicism in the romantic mixture. Most rewarding of all is the inspired one-movement *Sinfonia* of 1929, over half an hour long, echoing Sibelius's *Seventh* in its formal control and concentration. This was one of the works which in 1928 vied with Atterburg's *Symphony No. 6* and Havergal Brian's *Gothic Symphony* for the first prize in the Schubert centenary competition.

Martin, Frank (1890–1974)

Concerto for 7 wind instruments, percussion and strings; Etudes; (i) *Polyptique for violin and two string orchestras.*

❀ *** DG Dig. 435 383-2 [id.]. (i) Marieke Blankestijn; COE, Thierry Fischer.

This is a remarkable record and quite in a class of its own. The *Polyptique* is a work of serene profundity, inspired by a polyptych, a set of very small panels depicting scenes from the Passion which Martin saw in Siena. It is a work of great power and is played with rapt concentration and dedication by Marieke Blankestijn and the European Chamber Orchestra under Thierry Fischer. In the *Concerto for seven wind instruments, percussion and strings* there is a lightness of accent and refinement of tone and dynamics that are quite exceptional, and the *Etudes pour cordes* similarly outclasses its predecessors. The tone is pure and there is the widest possible range of timbre, colour and dynamics without ever the slightest hint of self-consciousness. Music of great quality, playing of great artistry, and recording to match.

Concerto for 7 wind instruments, percussion and strings; Passacaglia; Petite symphonie concertante for harp, harpsichord, piano & double string orchestra.

(M) **(*) Dinemic Dig. DCCD 012 [id.]. Geneva CO, Thierry Fischer.

This Geneva account of the *Petite symphonie concertante* is more atmospheric and spacious than the performance directed by the composer himself. In fact this is the best reading (as opposed to performance) now before the public. The balance is not ideal (the piano looms far too large in the aural picture *vis-à-vis* the other soloists) and the strings sound under-strength. Thierry Fischer has recorded the *Concerto for seven wind instruments* before with the Chamber Orchestra of Europe on DG (see above) and, although this is not quite as distinguished, it is very good indeed – and a good deal cheaper. The soloists and orchestra are better balanced than in the *Petite symphonie concertante*. In the gravely eloquent *Passacaglia* one also feels the need for a greater body of string-tone. Make no mistake, however: these are all perceptive performances and are well recorded. Excellent value.

(i) *Violin concerto;* (ii) *Etudes for strings*; (iii) *Maria-Triptychon.*

*(*) New Albion NA 086CD [id.]. Stuart Canin; (i) Berkeley SO; (ii) New Century CO; (iii) Sara Ganz.

Stuart Canin studied with Galamian in his native New York and now teaches on the west coast of America. His version of Frank Martin's beautiful concerto is easily the best recorded and is far from negligible artistically. Even so, the 1955 Schneiderhan/Ansermet record on Decca (448 264-2 – see our main volume) is ultimately more satisfying despite its less flattering sound. Though they are accomplished, neither the Berkeley orchestra nor the New Century Chamber Orchestra is in the first flight, and in the *Etudes for strings* their playing does not begin to match that of their finest rivals. Similarly Sara Ganz and Canin do not pose a serious challenge in the *Maria-Triptychon* to the Chandos alternative (CHAN 9411). Not without merit, but far from ideal.

The Four elements; (i) *In terra Pax.*

*** Chandos Dig. CHAN 9465 [id.]. LPO, Bamert; (i) with Howarth, Jones, Mill, Williams, Roberts, Brighton Festival Ch.

The Four elements is a work of immediate appeal and brings continuing rewards. It is certainly the best point to begin a further exploration of Frank Martin's world, once you have discovered the *Petite symphonie concertante*. *In terra Pax*, too, is a noble work, and if the singers are not quite as impressive as the cast of Ansermet's pioneering recording, this still makes a key coupling in the growing Martin discography. Bamert and his team are thoroughly sympathetic in every respect, and the Chandos recording is superior to the Ansermet original, good though that was.

Symphonie concertante (arr. of *Petite symphonie concertante* for full orchestra); *Symphony; Passacaglia.*

❀ *** Chandos Dig. CHAN 9312 [id.]. LPO, Matthias Bamert.

The *Symphony* is one of the composer's most haunting works. The slow movement has an otherworldly quality, suggesting some verdant, moonlit landscape, strongly related in its muted colouring to the world of Debussy's *Pelléas et Mélisande*. The composer's arrangement of the *Petite symphonie concertante* into a purely orchestral piece quite transforms the work's sound and texture and makes a fascinating comparison with the original. The *Passacaglia* is another very successful orchestral transciption of an organ piece. All this music is very sensitively played by the LPO under Bamert, and the Chandos recording is exemplary.

Cantate pour le 1er août; Chansons: *Sonnet; Le coucou; Ode; Le petit village; Janeton; Petite église; Ste Charlotte avait voulu. Mass for double choir;* (i) *Ode à la Musique. Songs of Ariel.*
*** Collins Dig. 1467-2 [id.]. (i) Simon Birchall; The Sixteen, Harry Christophers.

The most substantial work here is the *Mass for double choir*, which Martin composed in the 1920s but kept in a drawer until the 1960s. It is a beautiful work and well represented in the catalogue. Harry Christophers and The Sixteen give us a performance that can rank alongside any of them, and which has the additional attraction of couplings that are not otherwise available. The *Fünf Gesänge des Ariel*, written in 1950 for Felix de Nobel's celebrated Nederlands Kamerkoor, served as a kind of sketch for episodes in *The Tempest*, but it is marvellous in its own right. All of the vocal writing is resourceful and much of it inspired. Both the *Trois Chansons* of 1931 to texts by Ronsard and the 1944 *Chansons* are pleasing, though not perhaps as inventive as the *Ode à la musique*, a setting of some verses by the composer Machaut. Splendid singing from all concerned, including the baritone Simon Birchall in the *Ode à la musique*. This, incidentally, is a later piece, written just before *Les quatres éléments*. The *Cantate pour le 1er août* was written during the war years and comes between *Le vin herbé* and *Der Cornet*, though it does not match their level of inspiration. In every respect, however, this is a rewarding and beautiful record that will give all who value this great composer much satisfaction.

6 Monologues from Everyman.
* Berlin Classics Dig. 0091 682 BC [id.]. Theo Adam, Dresden PO, Herbert Kegel – DVORAK: *Biblical songs.* *

The *Six Monologues from Everyman*, one of the great song-cycles of the twentieth century, is well served on disc (see our main volume). The recent Chandos issue is probably best value. Theo Adam's recording was made when he was in his early sixties, when his voice had lost some of the bloom of youth. Apart from its artistic considerations, this is poor value at 44 minutes considering it retails at premium price.

Martinů, Bohuslav (1890–1959)

Piano concertos Nos. 2; 3; 4 ('Incantation').
500♪ ❁*** RCA Dig. 09026 61934-2 [id.]. Rudolf Firkušný, Czech PO, Libor Pešek.

The present set by Rudolf Firkušný, who premièred all three concertos and was the dedicatee of No. 3, was well worth waiting for. Firkušný is its ideal advocate. He makes a stronger case for the *Second Piano concerto* than any previous pianist, and the brightly optimistic *Third* is hardly less persuasive. Part of the success of these performances is the quality of the orchestral support. The recording is very good indeed.

Symphonies Nos. 1–4.
500♪ *** BIS Dig. CD 362/3 [id.]. Bamberg SO, Järvi.

Martinů always draws a highly individual sound from his orchestra and secures great clarity, even when the score abounds in octave doublings. He often thickens his textures in this way, yet, when played with the delicacy these artists produce, they sound beautifully transparent. The BIS recording is in the demonstration class.

Symphony No. 6 (Fantaisies symphoniques).
** Sup. Dig. SU3026-2 [id.]. Czech PO, Bělohlávek – MAHLER: *Lieder eines fahrenden Gesellen.* *

Jiří Bělohlávek's Supraphon account is every bit as good as his earlier, Chandos performance, and the recording is both more detailed and present. But while the Chandos alternative (CHAN 8897 – see our main volume) is coupled more generously and logically with the Janáček *Sinfonietta* and Suk's captivating *Fantastic Scherzo*, this comes with an inadequate account of the Mahler Wayfarer songs. At full price this is, alas, a non-starter.

Musique de chambre No. 1; Nonet; La revue de cuisine; Les rondes.
** Kontrapunkt Dig. 32227 [id.]. Danish Chamber Players.

The *Musique de chambre No. 1* is a late work from the last year of Martinů's life and it is full of inventive resource. It is scored for clarinet, violin, viola, cello, harp and piano, and the delicate exchanges between harp and piano are handled very imaginatively. *Les rondes* is a suite of dances for oboe, clarinet, bassoon, trumpet, two violins and piano which comes from much the same period as *La revue de cuisine*. Neither has been recorded before and they are well worth exploring. Both the *Nonet* and *La revue de cuisine* are coupled on a Hyperion disc (CDA 66084) by the Dartington Ensemble, where they are much better recorded. Expert and vital though the Danish performances are, the recording is not open enough, and the overall effect, particularly in the *Nonet*, is distinctly claustrophobic.

Oboe quartet (for oboe, violin, cello & piano); *Piano quartet; String quintet; Viola sonata.*
(BB) *** Naxos 8.553916 [id.]. Artists of 1994 Australian Festival of Chamber Music.

The best thing here is the captivating *Oboe quartet*, which is quite a discovery. Like the fine *Viola sonata* and the early *String quintet* whose slow movement is crossed by the shadow of Martinů's master, Roussel, it is not otherwise represented. Its appearance at budget price is doubly welcome in that the performances are lively and spirited and the recording eminently natural. The wartime *Piano quartet No. 1* is in the catalogue, coupled with the Suk *Piano quartet*, but that CD is currently at full price. The *Oboe quartet* is a must, not only for special admirers of the composer but for the wider musical public too.

Martucci, Giuseppe (1856–1909)

(i) *Piano concerto No. 2 in B flat, Op. 66;* (ii) *Le canzone dei ricordi.*
*** Sony Dig. SK 64582 [id.]. (i) Carlo Bruno; (ii) Mirella Freni; La Scala, Milan, PO, Riccardo Muti.

Riccardo Muti has already recorded the *Giga* from Op. 61, the *Notturno*, Op. 70, No. 1, and the *Novelletta*, Op. 82, with the same La Scala forces on a valuable disc containing also Busoni's *Turandot* suite and Casella's delightful *Paganiniana*. The *Second Piano concerto in B flat* is a massively powerful work whose first movement alone runs to 23 minutes. It is Brahmsian in both its scope and scale; however, although it is indebted to him, there is far more to it than that: this is Brahms distilled through very individual filters, and there is no question of the extraordinary mastery with which the composer unfolds his argument. No doubts either about the virtuosity and sensibility which the impressive soloist brings to bear. Carlo Bruno's name is at present unfamiliar to us but he is a commanding artist whom we would like to hear on more familiar terrain. The performance exhibits infinitely greater authority and finesse than Francesco Caramiello and d'Avalos on ASV, and it is recorded with far greater subtlety and naturalness. It emerges as a far more interesting piece. (The ASV is inclined to be a bit close and leaves nothing in reserve.) From the solo writing in the *Concerto* it is obvious that Martucci possessed a formidable pianistic technique – and he was, of course, a celebrated conductor. (He gave the Italian première of *Tristan*.) Mirella Freni brings to *Le canzone dei ricordi* all the warmth and delicacy of feeling this lovely score calls for. Muti conducts with evident conviction and gets very fine results from the Milan orchestra. Strongly recommended.

Mascagni, Pietro (1863–1945)

Cavalleria rusticana (complete).
(M) *** RCA 74321 39500-2. Scotto, Domingo, Elvira, Amb. Op. Ch., Nat. PO, Levine.
(***) EMI mono CDS5 56287-2 (2). Callas, Di Stefano, Panerai, Ch. & O of La Scala, Milan, Serafin – LEONCAVALLO: *I Pagliacci.* (***)
**(*) Decca 444 391-2 [id.]. Varady, Pavarotti, Bormida, Cappuccilli, Gonzales, Nat. PO, Gavazzeni.
(B) *(*) Ph. Duo 454 265-2 (2) [id.]. Obraztsova, Domingo, Barbieri, Bruson, Gall, La Scala, Milan, Ch. & O, Prêtre – LEONCAVALLO: *I Pagliacci.* *(*)

Now reissued at mid-price (pleasingly presented in a slip-case with libretto) in RCA's Opera Treasury series, this now stands as a clear first recommendation for Mascagni's red-blooded opera, with Domingo giving a heroic account of the role of Turiddù, full of defiance. Scotto is strongly characterful too, and James Levine directs with a splendid sense of pacing, by no means faster than his rivals (except the leisurely Karajan) and drawing red-blooded playing from the National Philharmonic. The recording is vivid and strikingly present in its CD transfer. At the time of going to press, this recording is not listed in the American *Schwann Catalogue*.

Dating from the mid-1950s, Callas's performance as Santuzza reveals the diva in her finest form, with edginess and unevenness of production at a minimum and with vocal colouring at its most characterful. The singing of the other principals is hardly less dramatic and Panerai is in firm, well-projected voice.

With Pavarotti loud and unsubtle as Turiddù – though the tone is often most beautiful – it is left to Julia Varady as Santuzza to give the 1976 Decca recording under Gavazzeni its distinction. Though her tone is not heavyweight, the impression of youth is most affecting; the sharpness of pain in *Voi lo sapete* is beautifully conveyed, and the whole performance is warm and authentic. Cappuccilli's Alfio is too noble to be convincing, and the main claim to attention lies in the brilliant forward recording. This set is now issued separately, but remains at full price.

Taken from the soundtrack of a Unitel television film (like the companion version of *Pag.*), the Prêtre set can be recommended to those who want a reminder of the film, and maybe also to those who want to hear Domingo in ringing voice; but otherwise the flaws rule it out as a serious contender. Obraztsova's massive and distinctive mezzo is certainly characterful but sounds edgy and uneven, hardly apt for the role. One or two moments are memorable – for example, the agonized utterance of the curse *A te la mala Pasqua*, not fire-eating at all – but she, like some of the others, equally unsteady, looked better than they sound. Fedora Barbieri, a veteran of veterans among mezzos, makes a token appearance as Mamma Lucia. The recording is full and atmospheric with the sound effects needed for television. Even at Duo price this is not very tempting, for the coupled *Pagliacci* is hardly more impressive. A brief synopsis is offered in lieu of a libretto.

Cavalleria rusticana: highlights.
(M) **(*) EMI CDM5 66048-2 [id.]. Caballé, Carreras, Varnay, Manuguerra, Hamari, Amb. Op. Ch., Philh. O, Muti – LEONCAVALLO: *I Pagliacci:* highlights. **(*)

Caballé is in good form here and receives good support from the rest of the cast. With Muti conducting strongly, this a recommendable sampler of a highly dramatic performance, vividly recorded.

Mason, Daniel Gregory (1873–1953)

(i) *Prelude and fugue for piano and orchestra, Op. 20;* (ii) *String quartet in G min. (based on Negro themes), Op. 19.*
(B) ** Carlton/Turnabout 30371 00282. (i) Mary Louise Boehm, Westphalian SO, Landau; (ii) Kohon Qt – BEACH: *Piano concerto.* **

Daniel Gregory Mason was an academic (head of the Music Department at Columbia University). His music is agreeable and well crafted but eclectic: the *Fugue* recalls César Franck and the *Quartet* is Dvořákian and is also well supplied with American spirituals. It is very well played by the Kohon Quartet and the recording is good, if a shade too forward. This is enjoyable music, even if it is not very individual.

Massenet, Jules (1842–1912)

Piano concerto in E flat.
*** Hyperion Dig. CDA 66897 [id.]. Stephen Coombs, BBC Scottish SO, Ossonce – HAHN: *Piano concerto in E.* ***

Massenet, much the most successful French opera composer of his day, unexpectedly completed this substantial concerto at the age of sixty, and received little appreciation. Based on sketches written many years earlier, before his operatic career took off, it regularly reveals Massenet's love of the keyboard, and in a performance like Stephen Coombs's the result is a delight. One might argue that the light manner and lack of weight in the argument do not match the impressive scale of the work – which may have disconcerted early critics – but the writing is full of attractive ideas. That is so, even when in the Slovak dance of the finale the main theme barely skirts banality, providing an extra challenge for Coombs to magick it with sparkling articulation. As in the Hahn concerto – an apt coupling, when it occupies a similar place in that composer's career – Jean-Yves Ossonce is a most sympathetic accompanist, drawing idiomatic playing from the BBC Scottish Symphony, helped by warm, well-balanced sound.

Hérodiade: highlights.
*** EMI Dig. CDC5 55613-2 [id.] (from complete set with Studer, Denize, Heppner, Hampson, Van Dam, Capitole Toulouse Ch. & O, Plasson).

The EMI set of *Hérodiade* is our first choice for this opera and the highlights are well enough chosen, though at full-price the disc is not particularly generous measure (67 minutes) and provides only a synopsis without translation.

Thérèse (complete).
*** Decca 448 173-2 [id.]. Huguette Tourangeau, Ryland Davies, Louis Quilico, Linden Singers, New Philh. O, Bonynge.

This story of the French Revolution, depicting a conflict of love and loyalty, has so many parallels with Puccini's *Tosca* and Giordano's *Andrea Chénier* of the previous decade that it is surprising Massenet chose it. He was then (1905) at the end of his career and was freshly inspired by the charms of a young mezzo-soprano, Lucy Arbell, who by all accounts was (vocally at least) unworthy of his attentions. The result was this passionate score, compressed and intense, lacking only the last degree of memorability in the melodies that make Massenet's finest operas so gripping. Bonynge is a splendid advocate, amply proving how taut and atmospheric the writing is. There is some first-rate singing from the three principals.

The vivid vintage recording, produced by James Walker in the Kingsway Hall in 1973, is excellent, and the reissue now includes a libretto with a new translation.

Mathias, William (1934–92)

(i; ii) *Dance overture, Op. 16;* (iii; ii) *Divertimento for string orchestra, Op. 7;* (i; ii) *Invocation and dance, Op. 17;* (iv; ii) *'Landscapes of the mind': Laudi, Op. 62; Vistas, Op. 69.* (iii; ii) *Prelude, Aria and Finale for string orchestra, Op. 25;* (v) *Sinfonietta, Op. 34.*
*** Lyrita SRCD 328 [id.]. (i) LSO; (ii) David Atherton; (iii) ECO; (iv) New Philh. O; (v) Nat. Youth O of Wales, Arthur Davison.

As this collection readily bears out, William Mathias is a composer of genuine talent, versatile as well as inventive. The joyful *Dance overture* is vividly scored, rather after the manner of Malcolm Arnold, and the *Invocation and dance* has genuine spontaneity. The *Divertimento* and *Prelude, Aria and Finale* have a family likeness in presenting workmanlike Hindemithian arguments in fast movements and warm lyricism in slow ones, although the *Aria* is restrained and ethereal. The colourful, extrovert *Sinfonietta* was written for the Leicestershire Schools Symphony Orchestra in 1967. Its *Lento* has a delectable blues flavour, and the finale too is popularly based rhythmically, with its lively and sometimes pungent syncopations. Undoubtedly the two most remarkable works here are the two pieces described by their composer as 'Landscapes of the mind'. *Laudi*, written in 1973, a 'landscape of the spirit', opens with temple bells and then contrasts bold cross-rhythms with gently voluptuous string sonorities, closing with a serene yet sensuous benediction, somewhat after the manner of Messiaen. The even more mystically evocative *Vistas* was inspired by the composer's visit to the USA in 1975. Here an Ivesian influence is unmistakable and, though there are ambiguous bursts of energy, the sections of restrained scoring, with evocatively distant trumpet-calls, are luminously atmospheric. Performances throughout are of the highest calibre with Atherton at his most perceptive, and the recordings (engineered by Decca for the most part) are outstanding.

Matthews, Colin (born 1946)

Hidden variables; Memorial; Quatrain; Machines and dreams.
*** Collins Dig. 1470-2 [id.]. LSO, Michael Tilson Thomas.

Like Knussen's excellent disc for DG, this grouping of orchestral pieces by Matthews, each lasting between 10 and 16 minutes, demonstrates his impressive range of expression. Regularly his writing reveals his joy in sound, his love of mixing unexpected colours, whether inventively dallying with minimalism in *Hidden variables* or searching more deeply in *Memorial* (written in memory of Britten, to whom he was musical amanuensis over the last years) and *Quatrain*. In many ways most striking of all is *Machines and dreams*, a toy symphony written for the Festival of Children at the Barbican in London in 1991. The disc contains the live recording made then, with a virtuoso children's ensemble playing the toy instruments alongside the full London Symphony Orchestra. If the humour may initially seem naïve, it grows on you with repetition, such is the wit and sense of fun behind Matthews's use of bird noises (with affectionate nods in the direction of Messiaen), toy pianos, sirens, football rattles, metronomes, and so on. The wonder is that poetry emerges too. An intriguing disc, very well performed and brilliantly recorded.

Broken symmetry; 4th Sonata for orchestra; Sun dances.
*** DG Dig. 447 067-2 [id.]. London Sinf., Oliver Knussen.

These three fine works, given superb performances by Oliver Knussen and the London Sinfonietta, present a strong portrait of an outstanding and imaginative composer, each taken from a different period of his career. The *Fourth Sonata*, from the mid-1970s, presents Matthews's response to minimalism in its repetitive rhythms but with ideas kept continually alert in a well-planned structure. *Sun dance*, from the mid-1980s, is a ballet for ten instruments which brilliantly transcends that limitation of forces. *Broken symmetry*, from the early 1990s, is a scherzo movement for large orchestra, leading to a dramatic conclusion. The excellent recording brings both bloom and sharp focus.

Mayerl, Billy (1902–59)

All-of-a-twist; Autumn crocus; Bats in the belfry; The harp of the winds; Insect oddities: Praying mantis; Wedding of an ant. Jazzaristrix; The Jazz master; Jill all alone; Look lively; Loose elbows; Marigold; Railroad rhythm; Shallow waters; Sweet William. Arrangements: *Body and soul; Limehouse blues; Peg o' my heart; Phil the Fluter's ball; Smoke gets in your eyes.*
(M) *** Virgin/EMI Ultraviolet Dig. CUV5 61323-2 [id.]. Susan Tomes.

Billy Mayerl believed he had achieved a specially English style of jazz. During the 1920s and 1930s his name was a household word, and 20,000 students enrolled in his mail-order School of Music to learn syncopated piano. He left an indelible legacy of light pieces of high quality, with writing that is often much more complex and sophisticated than the rags of Joplin and his contemporaries. His most famous lyrical numbers, such as *Marigold* and *Autumn crocus* (to quote Susan Tomes) combine 'a blend of elegance, wistfulness, nonchalance and high spirits – qualities which stamped his whole output'. The best of his pieces sound surprisingly undated, and in the hands of this stunning pianist they emerge with a refreshing spontaneity. The flashing cross-syncopations of *Bats in the belfry* and *All-of-a-twist* emerge with dazzling rhythmic freedom, for indeed this brilliant and talented artist has those 'Loose elbows' (readily demonstrable in the infectious piece of that name), which are an essential part of the Mayerl style. The gentle numbers, like *Jill all alone* and *Shallow waters*, are as winning as the picaresque *Insect oddities*. The transcriptions all emerge magnetically, and the easy, flowing flexibility of the playing is as remarkable as the dash and verve of the bravura, so well displayed in the closing *tour de force* of *Railroad rhythm*. The recording is splendidly real.

Medtner, Nikolai (1880–1951)

Violin sonata No. 3 (Sonata epica), Op. 57.
*** Erato/Warner Dig. 0630 15110-2 [id.]. Repin, Berezovsky – RAVEL: *Violin sonata.* ***

Vadim Repin and Boris Berezovsky make a formidable partnership, and they give what is arguably the most sensitive and certainly the most persuasive account of the *Sonata epica* since David Oistrakh and Alexander Goldweiser's celebrated Melodiya LP. Composed in the years preceding the Second World War, Medtner's third and last *Violin sonata* runs for three-quarters of an hour, but in the hands of these artists it does not outstay its welcome. They bring to it a wide range of colour and dynamics and infuse every phrase with life. Repin uses the Guarneri which belonged to Isaac Stern for almost half a century, and it sounds magnificently responsive in his hands. Very natural recording-balance adds to the pleasure this CD gives.

Mendelssohn, Felix (1809–47)

(i; ii) *Capriccio brillant in B min. for piano and orchestra, Op. 22;* (iii) *Piano concerto in A min.* (for piano and strings); (i; iv) *Piano concertos Nos. 1 in G min., Op. 25; 2 in D min., Op. 40;* (iii; v) *Double piano concerto in E* (for two pianos and strings); (i; ii) *Rondo brillant in E flat for piano and orchestra, Op. 29;* (vi) *Rondo capriccioso in E, Op. 14.*
(B) *** Decca Double 452 410-2 (2) [id.]. (i) Peter Katin; (ii) LPO, Martinon; (iii) John Ogdon, ASMF, Marriner; (iv) LSO, Anthony Collins; (v) with Brenda Lucas; (vi) Jorge Bolet.

This well-filled Double Decca conveniently gathers together all Mendelssohn's major concertante works for the piano except the *Double concerto in A flat* (which is available on a Hyperion disc: CDA 66567 – see our main volume). However, the present compilation is tempting in its own right, as Katin's early (1956) performances of the two best-known solo concertos have come up very freshly on CD; the ambient warmth of the recording disguises its age and the piano recording is excellent. Katin has the full measure of these remarkably similar works. His crisp passage-work prevents the outer movements from becoming either lifeless or brittle, and he offers a pleasingly light touch in the finales (indeed the last movement of Op. 25 scintillates). In both slow movements his style is sensitive without sentimentality, a feature mirrored in the excellent accompaniments. The two concertante occasional pieces were recorded earlier (1954) and Katin is in sparkling form. Here a mono master is used; but this is an amazing example of the way Arthur Haddy's Decca recording team could use the Kingsway Hall ambience to give an impression of stereo. So warmly convincing is the ambient effect that the ear is readily fooled unless one listens carefully, for the piano-sound and the balance are both excellent. The ambitious and successful *A minor Concerto* was written when the composer was thirteen and the *Double concerto* comes from approximately two years later. These delightful concertante rarities both have engaging ideas and are played with great verve and spirit by John Ogdon and his wife. The orchestral playing is equally lively and fresh throughout, and the vivid (originally Argo) 1969 Kingsway Hall recording has hardly dated. Jorge Bolet (recorded digitally in 1985) offers the solo *Rondo capriccioso* as a closing encore and immediately establishes his credentials of easy bravura applied with the lightest of touch.

Capriccio brillant in B min., Op. 22; Piano concertos Nos. 1 in G min., Op. 25; 2 in D min., Op. 40; Rondo brillant in E flat min., Op. 29; Serenade and allegro giocoso in B min., Op. 43.
(M) ** Ph. Dig. 454 685-2. Jean-Louis Steuerman, Moscow CO, Orbelian.

Jean-Louis Steuerman is a first-rate pianist and he is given brilliant support by the Moscow Chamber Orchestra under Constantine Orbelian. The recording, too, is most vivid. The snag is the barnstorming, Lisztian style of the performances, which are involving but emotionally too inflated for the lyrical flow of Mendelssohn's two simple concertos. Even so, Steuerman's bravura is very impressive, though the forceful accompaniments lack charm, and at times become almost aggressive. Most successful is the ambitiously romantic slow movement of the *D minor Concerto* and the three shorter encores, especially the *Capriccio brillant*.

Piano concertos Nos. 1 in G min., Op. 25; 2 in D min., Op. 40; Capriccio brillant in B min., Op. 22.
500♪ ❀ *** Chandos Dig. CHAN 9215 [id.]. Howard Shelley, LMP.

Piano concertos Nos. 1–2; Capriccio brillant, Op. 22; Rondo brillant in E flat, Op. 29.
500♪ (BB) *** Naxos Dig. 8.550681-2 [id.]. Benjamin Frith, Slovak State PO (Košice), Robert Stanovsky.

Howard Shelley offers marvellous playing in every respect: fresh, sparkling and dashing in the fast movements, poetic and touching in the slower ones. The London Mozart Players are a group of exactly the right size for these works and they point rhythms nicely and provide the necessary lift.

But Benjamin Frith on Naxos is a hardly less personable and nimble soloist: he is sensitively touching in the slow movements and makes much of the fine *Adagio* of No. 2. The Slovak orchestra accompany with vigour and enthusiasm, and if the effect is at times less sharply rhythmic this is partly the effect of a somewhat more reverberant acoustic.

Double piano concertos: in A flat; in E.
(BB) *** Naxos Dig. 8.553416 [id.]. Benjamin Frith, Hugh Tinney, Dublin R. & TE Sinfonietta, O Duinn.

This Naxos disc challenges comparison with the outstanding Hyperion issue coupling these same two charming double concertos (CDA 66567). Mendelssohn wrote them in his early teens for his sister Fanny and himself to play, and the wonder is that the earlier of the two, written when he was fourteen, a very expansive structure of over 40 minutes, is the more identifiably Mendelssohnian, with a slow movement and finale based on material that might have been written many years later. If the Irish players are not quite as persuasive as their Scottish counterparts on Hyperion, their playing is just as refined, and Frith and Tinney are a fair match for Coombs and Munro, less powerful but just as magnetic and even more poetic. The transparent recording helps, very appropriate for such youthful music.

2 Concert pieces for clarinet and basset horn: in F min., Op. 113; in D min., Op. 114.
(B) *** Hyperion Dyad Dig. CDD 22017 (2) [id.]. Thea King, Georgina Dobrée, LSO, Francis (with Concert – see below ***).

These Mendelssohn duets for clarinet and basset horn are most diverting, with their jocular finales; and they are played with a nice blend of expressive spontaneity and high spirits. Georgina Dobrée proves a nimble partner for the ever-sensitive Thea King. This is part of an excellent two-disc set, including other attractive concertante works by Max Bruch, Crusell, Spohr and other less familar names.

Violin concerto in E min., Op. 64.
500♪ (M) *** Sony Dig. SMK 64250 [id.]. Cho-Liang Lin, Philh. O, Tilson Thomas – BRUCH: *Concerto;* VIEUXTEMPS: *Concerto No. 5.* ***
(BB) *** Belart 461 355-2. Campoli, LPO, Boult – BEETHOVEN: *Violin concerto.* ***
** Hänssler Dig. 98.934 [id.]. Sitkovetsky, ASMF, Marriner – BRAHMS: *Violin concerto.* **

Cho-Liang Lin's vibrantly lyrical account now reappears with the Bruch *G minor* plus the Vieuxtemps No. 5, to make an unbeatable mid-priced triptych. They are all three immensely rewarding and poetic performances, given excellent, modern, digital sound, and Michael Tilson Thomas proves a highly sympathetic partner in the Mendelssohn *Concerto*.

It is good to have Campoli's delightful performance back in the catalogue. His perfectly formed tone and polished, secure playing are just right for the Mendelssohn *Concerto*, and this is a delightful performance, notable for its charm and disarming simplicity. The 1958 (originally Decca) recording is brightly lit in the CD transfer, and the vividness is marred by a degree of roughness in the orchestral focus;

but no matter, this very inexpensive record gives much pleasure and is a fine reminder of a superb violinist.

Sitkovetsky's is a sweetly lyrical reading of the Mendelssohn. He broadens romantically for the second subject, and he takes the central *Andante* at an easily flowing tempo that avoids sentimentality, before adopting a challengingly fast tempo for the finale, readily measuring up to all the virtuoso demands. There are more individual and more compelling readings than this but, with a good coupling, very vividly recorded and with superb playing from the Academy, it makes a fair recommendation.

(i) *Violin concerto in E min., Op. 64;* (ii) *A Midsummer Night's Dream: Overture, Op. 21; Scherzo; Intermezzo; Nocturne; Wedding march, Op. 61.*
(B) *** Erato/Warner Bonsai 4509 94578-2 [id.]. (i) Pierre Amoyal, Bamberg SO, Guschlbauer; (ii) LPO, Leppard.

Leppard's *Overture* and suite from *A Midsummer Night's Dream* is drawn from a highly praised complete recording made in 1978 and very well recorded. Two soloists are here credited on the insert leaflet, although no vocal items have been included, which was a pity for they were well sung and there would have been plenty of room for them, as the playing time of this disc is only fractionally over an hour. Leppard gives the music sparkle and resilience, taking the *Nocturne* with its horn solo persuasively at a flowing tempo, though the *Wedding march* is here relatively heavy. Not surprisingly, Pierre Amoyal gives a fresh, sympathetic account of the *Violin concerto*, with a tenderly simple account of the slow movement and a scintillating finale. Guschlbauer provides good support, and the 1973 recording is good, so even as it stands this makes quite a good bargain recommendation.

Symphonies for strings Nos. 1 in C; 6 in E flat; 7 in D min.; 12 in G min.
*** BIS Dig. CD 683 [id.]. Amsterdam New Sinf., Lev Markis.

Symphonies for strings Nos. 2 in D; 3 in E min.; 9 in C; 10 in B min.
*** BIS Dig. CD 643 [id.]. Amsterdam New Sinf., Lev Markis.

Symphonies for strings Nos. 4 in C min.; 5 in B flat; 8 in D; 11 in F.
*** BIS Dig. CD 748 [id.]. Amsterdam New Sinf., Lev Markis.

String symphonies Nos. 1–12 (complete); *No. 13 (Sinfoniesatz) in C min.*
*** RCA Dig. 09026 68069-2 (3) [id.]. Hanover Band, Roy Goodman.

Mendelssohn's early symphonies for strings, lost for 150 years, were rediscovered in 1950. The first ten were student works and the last two, together with the virtually unknown *Symphony movement in C minor* (No. 13), had all been completed before their young composer reached the age of fourteen. The special novelty on the RCA set is the fully scored version (for woodwind, brass and timpani) of No. 8, one of the more ambitious of the series, with a performance time of 30 minutes. Mendelssohn rewrote the Trio of the very jolly Minuet and uses the woodwind and horns most effectively throughout: this is a splendid movement which could readily fit into one of the later, mature symphonies. Otherwise the composer left the music very much as it had been in its original string version. The curiously dolorous *Adagio* still emphasizes the string section, with the movement dominated by three violas, underpinned by the two bassoons which are used to darken the sonority still further. The finale makes good use of both the brass and the woodwind and, in its confident contrapuntal writing and full-bodied scoring, undoubtedly recalls Mozart's *Jupiter Symphony*. It was completed in 1822. The last 49 bars of the orchestration have been lost but, as the string parts survive, the orchestration was completed by Fritz Behrend for performance on modern instruments. However, he did not allow for the natural limitations of the brass instruments available in Mendelssohn's time, and there has been some further editing for the present recording. What is surprising in the performance here is the way that Goodman has been content to have the wind detail comparatively recessed within the hall resonance instead of being projected more vividly. The first six symphonies are in three-movement, Italian overture form; then, from No. 7 onwards, Mendelssohn moves into the four-movement format of the Haydn and Mozart symphonies, often with a slow introduction. No. 11, the most ambitious (40 minutes 32 seconds), has five, with a second-movement Scherzo and fourth-movement Minuet which frame the beautiful, serene central *Adagio* (in layout recalling Haydn's early Divertimenti/ Quartets). Its Scherzo (*Commodo Schweizerland*), like the Scherzo in No. 9 (whose charming, Laendler-like Trio is called *La Suisse*), was influenced by a summer holiday in Switzerland, and it draws on a Swiss wedding dance-song, *Bin alben e warti Tachter gsi*, which is given extra brilliance by the use of triangle, cymbals and timpani. *No. 12 in G minor* brings an extraordinary intensity of expression in its solemn *Andante*, while its splendidly crafted finale confidently and fascinatingly looks back to Mozart's penultimate *G minor Symphony*. The arresting *Symphoniesatz*, too, is remarkably imaginative in its construction and towards the close even anticipates a style of writing which its young composer would use later in his teenage years.

Bustling energy and drive are the keynote of Goodman's period-instrument performances. Allegros sparkle and the comparatively brief *Andantes* of the earliest works are sensitively presented, even if one feels here that the music could occasionally smile more. But the later symphonies, which have brought maturity from experience, are superbly characterized. The playing is as alert and vigorous as ever, yet Goodman's readings balance energy with gravitas and weight, and their persuasive, expressive feeling shows the players as totally involved in this remarkable, precocious writing. All in all, this admirably documented RCA set upstages all the current competition in these works, although those wanting modern-instrument performances will find William Boughton's series with the English String Orchestra also very enjoyable, if more modest in its scholarship (Nimbus NI 5141/2/3, available separately).

We welcomed the first of the BIS Mendelssohn *String symphonies* to appear (comprising Nos. 2, 3, 9, 10) in our main volume; the remaining instalments by this fine Amsterdam ensemble fully live up to the expectations it aroused. The playing of the Amsterdam New Sinfonietta is vibrant and alive, and the recording has a warmth and clarity that give the set the edge over its current rivals. This music is full of charm, and the quality of Mendelssohn's youthful invention is little short of astonishing.

Symphonies for string orchestra Nos. 2 in D; 3 in E min.; 5 in B flat; 6 in E flat.
(B) *** EMI forte Dig. CZS5 69524-2 (2). Polish CO, Maksymiuk – JANIEWICZ: *Divertimento;* JARZEBSKI: *Chromatica; Tamburetta;* ROSSINI: *String sonatas.* ***

This collection of the boy Mendelssohn's early *String symphonies* (written when he was only twelve) is most invigorating. These earlier symphonies from the series of 12 may look to various models from Bach to Beethoven, but the young composer keeps showing his individuality and, however imitative the style, the vitality of the invention still bursts through. The slow movement of *Symphony No. 2*, for example, is a Bachian meditation that in its simple beauty matches later Mendelssohn. The Polish strings are set in a lively acoustic, giving exceptionally rich sound, but the playing also has plenty of dash.

Symphonies Nos. 1–5; Overtures: *Athalia* (also *War march of the priests*); *Calm sea and a prosperous voyage, Op. 27; The Hebrides (Fingal's Cave), Op. 26.*
(B) *** Decca Analogue/Dig. 448 514-2 (3) [id.]. Ghazarian, Gruberová, Krenn, V. State Op. Ch. (in *No. 2* (*Hymn of Praise*)); VPO, Dohnányi.

Dohnányi's Decca set (which includes also two key overtures, plus the lesser-known *Athalia* and the *War march of the priests*) brings performances which are fresh and direct, often relying on faster and more flowing speeds than in Abbado's full-price set, more clearly rebutting any idea that this music might be sentimental. The most striking contrast comes in the *Hymn of praise*, where Dohnányi's speeds are often so much faster than Abbado's that the whole character of the music is changed, as in the second-movement Scherzo, sharp in one, gently persuasive in the other. Many will prefer Dohnányi in that, particularly when the choral sound is brighter and more immediate too. The vintage recordings were made in the Sofiensaal between 1976 and 1978, and the two overtures and the *Italian Symphony* are digital, the Decca engineers producing sound which was among the finest of its period and which sounds excellent on CD. The snag of the set is that Dohnányi, unlike Abbado, omits exposition repeats, which in the *Italian Symphony* means the loss of the substantial lead-back passage in the first movement. However, attractively packaged in a bargain box, this is still rather enticing. The *Reformation Symphony* comes off particularly well.

(i) *Symphonies Nos. 1 in C min., Op. 11;* (ii) *2 in B flat (Hymn of Praise), Op. 52;* (i) *3 in A min. (Scottish), Op. 56; Overture The Hebrides (Fingal's Cave), Op. 26.*
(B) *** Ph. Duo 456 071-2 (2) [id.]. LPO; (i) Haitink; (ii) M. Price, Burgess, Jerusalem, LPO Ch., Chailly.

(i) *Symphonies Nos. 4 in A (Italian), Op. 90; 5 in D min. (Reformation), Op. 107; Calm sea and prosperous voyage overture, Op. 27;* (ii–iii) *Violin concerto in E min.;* (iii–iv) *A Midsummer Night's Dream: Overture, Op. 21; Incidental music, Op. 61.*
(B) *** Ph. Duo 456 074-2 (2) [id.]. (i) LPO; (ii) Grumiaux; (iii) Concg. O; (iv) with Woodland, Watts, Women of Netherlands R. Ch.; all cond. Haitink.

When Bernard Haitink in 1980 was prevented from rounding off his planned Mendelssohn symphony cycle with the Symphony No. 2 (*Lobgesang – Hymn of Praise*), Riccardo Chailly stepped in to record it in his place. This compilation brings together what, despite the change of conductor, is an outstanding cycle, fresh and energetic, with a geniality that regularly puts a smile on Mendelssohn's face. If one compares this with rival cycles at mid-price, this one is more warmly expressive, more lightly pointed than either Sawallisch's (the previous Philips cycle) or Dohnányi's on Decca, both of which seem plainer, even at times fierce, next to this. Only in the first movement of the *Italian Symphony* does Haitink press too hard, and even then he has time to spring rhythms. Broadly, Chailly follows a similar pattern in *Lobgesang*, another excellent performance with an outstanding trio of soloists, helped by full and vivid sound, though the fine chorus is backwardly balanced. The fourth disc contains Haitink's brilliant

Concertgebouw version of the *Midsummer Night's Dream* incidental music – ten movements, including a dazzling account of the Overture – as well as the excellent Grumiaux version of the *Violin concerto*, also with Haitink and the Concertgebouw, with 1960s sound still fresh and clear.

Symphonies Nos. 1 in C min., Op. 11; 5 in D (Reformation), Op. 107; Octet, Op. 20: Scherzo.
(M) *** DG Dig. 445 596-2 [id.]. LSO, Abbado.

The *First* and *Fifth* are Mendelssohn's least-played and least-recorded symphonies, so Abbado's coupling is very welcome. The youthful *First* has plenty of C minor bite. The toughness of the piece makes one wonder that Mendelssohn ever substituted the *Scherzo* from the *Octet* for the third movement (as he did in London), but Abbado helpfully includes a sparkling version of that extra Scherzo so that on CD, with a programming device, you can readily make the substitution yourself. His direct manner suits the *Reformation Symphony* equally well. Brightly lit, early-digital recording (1984), but with the warm ambience of St John's, Smith Square, adding overall bloom.

Symphonies Nos. 3 (Scottish); 4 (Italian), Op. 90.
500♪ *** Decca Dig. 433 811-2 [id.]. San Francisco SO, Herbert Blomstedt.
(BB) *** Belart 450 099-2. LSO, Abbado.
(BB) ** Naxos Dig. 8.553200 [id.]. Nat. SO of Ireland, Reinhard Seifried.

(i) *Symphonies Nos. 3 in A min. (Scottish), Op. 56;* (ii) *4 in A (Italian), Op. 90;* (i) *Hebrides overture (Fingal's cave), Op. 26.*
(M) *** DG Originals 449 743-2 [id.]. BPO, Karajan.
(M) ** Mercury 434 363-2 [id.]. (i) LSO, Dorati; (ii) Minneapolis SO, Skrowaczewski.

Of all the many discs coupling Mendelssohn's two most popular symphonies, the *Scottish* and the *Italian*, there is none finer than Blomstedt's. Not only does he choose ideal speeds – not too brisk in the exhilarating first movement of the *Italian* or sentimentally drawn out in slow movements – he conveys a feeling of spontaneity throughout, springing rhythms infectiously. The sound is outstandingly fine, outshining any direct rival.

Karajan's 1971 account of the *Scottish* is justly included among DG's 'Originals', as it is one of his finest recordings. The performance contains some slight eccentricities of tempo: the opening is rather measured, but affectionately so, while the closing pages of the finale are taken with exuberant brilliance. The orchestral playing is superb – the pianissimo articulation of the strings is a pleasure in itself – and the conductor's warmth and direct eloquence, with no fussiness, are irresistible. The Scherzo is marvellously done and becomes a highlight, while there is no doubt that Karajan's coda has splendid buoyancy. The coupling was originally just this very characterful and evocative account of *Fingal's Cave*, but now the *Italian Symphony* has been added, recorded two years later. This is also played very beautifully and brilliantly but, good though the performance is, it does not quite match that of the *Scottish* and it is just a shade wanting in spontaneity and sparkle.

Abbado's outstanding Decca recording of the *Scottish Symphony* (now reissued on Belart) is beautifully played and the LSO responds to his direction with the greatest delicacy of feeling, while the *Italian Symphony* has a comparable lightness of touch, matched with lyrical warmth. The vintage (1968) Kingsway Hall recording is first class; however, the absence of the first-movement exposition repeat in the *Scottish Symphony* (though not in the *Italian*) is a drawback.

The first movement of Dorati's (1956) *Scottish*, though exciting, is hard driven, and the reading never quite recovers, although – more surprisingly – the swinging tune at the end of the finale is presented quite steadily and the coda does not take off. Skrowaczewski's *Italian* is briskly paced but extremely well played, with the Minneapolis strings on their toes in lightly articulating the outer movements. Neither conductor observes the first-movement exposition repeat. Easily the finest performance here is Dorati's *Fingal's Cave*, warmly romantic (the LSO lower strings playing beautifully in the expansive opening), exciting without being forced. The recordings are acceptable but not among the finest on this label.

Though Seifried draws refined playing from the Irish orchestra in readings with few idiosyncrasies, built on unexceptionable speeds, the impact of the performances is seriously diminished by the recording, with the orchestra set distantly in a reverberant acoustic and transferred at a very low level so that details often disappear, with tuttis growing opaque. Even in the super-bargain category there is a much more recommendable version in Lubbock's account with the Orchestra of St John's, warm and clear on Quicksilva (CDQS 6004), and at mid-price there is David Chernak's vital and strikingly fresh coupling on Meridian (CDE 84261).

Symphony No. 4 in A (Italian), Op. 90.
500♪ (M) *** DG Dig. 445 514-2 [id.]. Philh. O, Sinopoli – SCHUBERT: *Symphony No. 8.* *** ❁

Sinopoli's great gift is to illuminate almost every phrase afresh. His speeds tend to be extreme – fast in the first movement but with diamond-bright detail, and on the slow side in the remaining three. Only in the heavily inflected account of the third movement is the result at all mannered but, with superb playing from the Philharmonia and excellent Kingsway Hall recording, this rapt performance is most compelling.

Symphony No. 5 in D (Reformation), Op. 107.
(M) *** DG 449 720-2 [id.]. BPO, Maazel – FRANCK: *Symphony in D min.* ***

The *Reformation Symphony* springs grippingly to life in Maazel's hands. The Berlin Philharmonic brass make an immediate impact in the commanding introduction and the orchestral playing throughout continues on this level of high tension. The finale is splendidly vigorous, the chorale, *Ein' feste Burg is unser Gott*, ringing out resplendently. If ever one were choosing a 'best buy' for this individual symphony, Maazel's interpretation would rank very high on the list. It was aptly chosen for reissue in DG's series of 'Legendary Recordings', and the Franck coupling is hardly less impressive. The recording is spacious and has been vividly enhanced by the DG CD transfer.

CHAMBER MUSIC

Cello sonata No. 2 in D, Op. 58.
(M) *** Mercury 434 377-2 [id.]. Starker, Sebók – BRAHMS: *Cello sonatas.* ***

Starker and Sebók give an outstanding account of Mendelssohn's finest *Cello sonata*, spontaneously full of ardour, yet with plenty of light and shade in the central movements, and topped by a sparkling finale, which yet retains the lyrical feeling. The 1962 recording is truthful and admirably balanced within a warm acoustic with a clear focus.

Octet in E flat, Op. 20; String quintet No. 1 in A, Op. 18.
500♪ (M) *** Virgin Veritas/EMI Dig. VC5 45168-2. Hausmusik.

Using period instruments, the British-based group, Hausmusik, gives a most refreshing performance of the *Octet* and couples it with another miraculous masterpiece of Mendelssohn's boyhood. The period performance gives extra weight to the lower lines compared with the violins, with the extra clarity intensifying the joyfulness of the inspiration. At mid-price, a clear first choice for the *Octet*.

Piano trios Nos. 1 in D min. Op. 49; 2 in C min., Op. 66.
(M) **(*) Virgin/EMI Ultraviolet Dig. CUV5 61312-2. Grieg Trio.
** Globe Dig. GLO 5156 [id.]. Julian Reynolds, Johannes Leertouwer, Viola de Hoog.

Very good performances from the Grieg Trio, recorded five years ago but not issued before – or, if it was, not submitted for review. They give thoroughly musical accounts of both trios, yet they are obviously fired more greatly by the *C minor*, in which they play the *Andante* with a simple expressive warmth and the Scherzo generates great bravura. Although not quite as distinctive as the Beaux Arts (which periodically goes in and out of the catalogue), this remains a strongly recommendable alternative. The pianist does not quite match Menahem Pressler in sparkle or charm (but then who does?) but in any event he is an elegant player. But the Grieg Trio are let down by the recording, which is much too resonant for detail to emerge as clearly as it should and which thickens the overall textures.

Julian Reynolds plays an Erard piano made in Paris in 1837, which in every respect matches the piano the composer himself played and admired. Nevertheless, by today's standards it has a rather dead timbre and does not help these period performances to really sparkle, particularly as overall the Utrecht recording is opaque. The playing has enormous energy; indeed the fast pacing often seems to press the music on too hard, although the brilliance of execution is in no doubt. Opus 66 is the stronger of the two performances. But, apart from the use of the Mendelssohnian piano, this is in no way a distinctive coupling.

Piano trio No. 2 in C min., Op. 66.
*** Ph. Dig. 432 125-2 [id.]. Beaux Arts Trio – SMETANA: *Piano trio in G min.* ***

Although most collectors will probably want the Mendelssohn *Piano trios* together (and there is a fair choice of such a coupling, if nothing that really stands out), those happy to take the *C minor Trio* alone, coupled with Smetana, will find the Beaux Arts distinguished in all respects and very well recorded.

String quartets Nos. 1 in E flat, Op. 12; 2 in A min, Op. 13; 6 in F min., Op. 80.
*** Decca Dig. 436 325-2 [id.]. Ysaÿe Qt.

String quartets Nos. 3 in D; 4 in E min., Op. 44/1–2.
*** Decca Dig. 440 369-2 [id.]. Ysaÿe Qt.

String quartet No. 5 in E flat, Op. 44/3; 4 Pieces, Op. 81.
*** Decca Dig. 452 049-2 [id.]. Ysaÿe Qt.

We welcomed the first issue in the Ysaÿe Quartet's Mendelssohn cycle, comprising *Nos. 3 in D* and *4 in E minor*, Op. 44/1–2, in our 1994 edition, and the remaining two live up to the expectations these aroused. There is plenty of life, without the slightly overdriven quality that worried us to some extent in the mid-price DG set by the Melos Quartet. As we said of their predecessors, these are urbane and cultured performances, as befits this civilized and endearing music. The Decca recording is eminently satisfactory. This makes a good alternative to the Coull versions on Hyperion, although the latter also include the early (1823) *Quartet*, which gives the Hyperion set an added advantage (CDS 44051/3).

Songs without words, Books 1–8 (complete); *No. 49 in G min., Op. posth.*
(B) **(*) Hyperion Dyad Dig. CDD 22020 (2) [id.]. Lívia Rév.

Lívia Rév is a thoughtful, sensitive and aristocratic artist. Her survey of the *Songs without words* has charm and warmth, and she includes a hitherto unpublished piece. The set is handsomely presented and the recording is warm and pleasing; it is, however, somewhat bottom-heavy. Yet the slightly diffuse effect suits the style of the playing. This might well now be seriously considered at its new price, especially by those who enjoy intimate music-making and want digital sound with its silent background.

Songs without words, Books 1–8 (complete); *Albumblatt, Op. 117; Gondellied; Kinderstücke, Op. 72; 2 Klavierstücke.*
(B) *** DG Double 453 061-2 (2) [id.]. Daniel Barenboim.

This 1974 set of Mendelssohn's complete *Songs without words*, which Barenboim plays with such affectionate finesse, has dominated the catalogue for nearly two decades. For this reissue the six *Kinderstücke* (sometimes known as 'Christmas pieces') have been added, plus other music, so that the second of the two CDs plays for 73 minutes. The sound is first class. At DG Double price (two CDs for the price of one) this sweeps the board in this repertoire, and it is good to see that the back-up documentation has now been restored.

A Midsummer Night's Dream: Overture, Op. 21; Incidental music, Op. 61 (complete; with melodramas and text).
*** DG Dig. 439 897-2 [id.]. Kathleen Battle, Frederica von Stade, Tanglewood Festival Ch., Boston SO, Ozawa (with excerpts from play spoken by Dame Judi Dench).

(i) *A Midsummer Night's Dream: Overture, Op. 21; Incidental music, Op. 61* (including spoken passages with the melodramas); *Symphony No. 4 (Italian).*
*** Sony SK 62826. (i) Sylvia McNair, Angelika Kirchschlager, Kenneth Branagh (speaker), Ch.; BPO Abbado.

Like the Sony version below, Ozawa's virtually complete performance presents Mendelssohn's enchanting incidental music – which is most beautifully played throughout by the Boston Symphony Orchestra – complete with the Shakespearean text, which is spoken over the melodramas by Judi Dench. With two excellent soloists and a fine choral contribution, the only omission here is the brief excerpt which is No. 6 in the score; but the fragmentary reprise of the *Wedding march*, and the two little comic snippets, the Bergomask (*Dance of the clowns*) and ironic little *Funeral march*, intended for the Rude Mechanicals' 'Pyramus and Thisbe' playlet, are included, whereas they are missing in the competing Sony version with Kenneth Branagh. Judi Dench speaks the Shakespeare text in the simplest way, without any of Branagh's occasional exuberance of style, and in her performance Shakespeare's words seem to glow as magically as Mendelssohn's music. This means that Mendelssohn's little melodramas become so much more than orchestral snippets. At the very end of the play, when Dench speaks Puck's closing words to the audience, and Ozawa plays Mendelssohn's ravishingly gentle orchestral coda – repeating music which has already entranced the ear at the close of the Overture – it is quite extraordinarily touching. The recording is first class, one of the finest made in Symphony Hall in recent years, and the balance, with Dench's narration quite intimate but with every word clear, is very well judged indeed. Of course if you choose Branagh on Sony, you get a symphony thrown in for good measure. This DG alternative has no coupling and plays for only 56 minutes, but every one of them is delightful.

It certainly makes an attractive package having Mendelssohn's *Midsummer Night's Dream* music dramatically presented (with Kenneth Branagh taking every role from Titania to Puck), and then very generously coupled with Mendelssohn's most popular symphony. Sony have managed to squeeze in 50 minutes of the incidental music, which means that the only omissions are the fragmentary reprise of the *Wedding march* and the two little comic pieces, *Bergomask* and *Funeral march*, intended for the Rude Mechanicals' Pyramus and Thisbe episode. Some may resist Branagh's style – burring his 'r's for a Mummerset Puck, coming near to an Olivier imitation in Oberon's final speech – but in his versatility he is very persuasive. Having speech over music in melodrama certainly makes sense of the more fragmentary passages of the score which most other discs omit. Abbado's performances are a delight, fresh and transparent in the fairy music, with generally fast speeds made exhilarating, never breathless. The chorus is balanced atmospherically, with the two excellent soloists, Sylvia McNair and Angelika Kirchschlager, set more forwardly. The recording, made live in the Philharmonie in Berlin, is rather more vivid, a degree less recessed than in the symphony, where the orchestra is placed at a slight distance. Abbado's reading has changed little since his LSO recording of 1985, a fresh, beautifully sprung reading. By any reckoning he remains one of the most persuasive interpreters of this delectable work.

A Midsummer Night's Dream: Overture Op. 21; (i) *Incidental music, Op. 61. Octet in E flat, Op. 20* (string orchestra version).

**(*) Decca Dig. 440 296-2 [id.]. (i) Lynne Dawson, Dalia Schaechter, Berlin R. Women's Ch.; Berlin Deutsches RSO, Berlin, Ashkenazy.

Ashkenazy is given an attractive, warm, spacious recording, not sharply detailed but not blurred either. The orchestral playing is polished and sympathetic, if not always with the very lightest touch, and the same comment applies to the solo singing, especially that of the mezzo, Dalia Schaechter. But this is enjoyably spontaneous, as is the full-blown, Romantic account of the *Octet*. In both cases the charm of the Scherzo is not missed, but that for the *Octet* loses some of its sparkle when so well nourished.

(i) *A Midsummer Night's Dream: Overture, Op. 21; Incidental music, Op. 61;* (ii) *Die erste Walpurgisnacht, Op. 60.*

*** Teldec/Warner Dig. 9031 74882-2 [id.]. (i) Coburn, Van Magnus, Bantzer (speaker); (ii) Remmert, Heilmann, Hampson, Pape; Arnold Schoenberg Ch., COE, Harnoncourt.

Harnoncourt gets the best of both worlds, simultaneously visiting both Mendelssohn's fairy kingdom and his not-too-serious evocation of satanic revelry and the traditional religious response. Soloists, chorus and a narrator for the Shakespearean text (translated into German) all participate in this vivid, condensed version of the *Midsummer Night's Dream* incidental music which manages to include the *Overture*, *Scherzo*, *Nocturne*, *Intermezzo* and *Wedding march*, plus the vocal numbers, including the finale. Harnoncourt is nothing if not dramatic in the *Overture*, with the feather-light violins opening *pianopianissimo* and the tuttis strong and rhythmic. The playing of the COE is of a virtuoso order and the *Scherzo* is wonderfully light and crisp in articulation. With excellent contributions from soloists and chorus, the vocal music goes very well, too – though, like the spoken Shakespearean text, it is disconcerting not to have it in English. After the serene close, the atmosphere changes abruptly for Mendelssohn's Ballade, *Die erste Walpurgisnacht*, which has never before been performed so dramatically on record.

As a boy, Mendelssohn became a favourite visitor of the poet, Goethe, and later he repaid the affection in his setting of an early and rather curious Goethe poem about Druids and their conflict with early Christians seen – perhaps unexpectedly – from the point of view of the Druids. But then maybe the young composer found the situation had an affinity with Jewish persecution through the ages. Written in 1831–2, it is not great music, but in Harnoncourt's hands its drama is vividly evoked, especially in the two remarkable choruses, the first for the oppressed Druid women, *Schlachten sie schon unsre Kinder!* ('They are slaughtering our children') and the bizarre, even ferocious, tarantella-like *Kommt mit Zacken und mit Gabeln* ('Come with prongs and forks'), when the Druid guards decide to simulate devils and witches from hell to make fools of their Christian conquerors. In this they succeed only too well, and they are left offering a closing supplication to their own deity, which recalls *Die Zauberflöte*. Harnoncourt directs the work with great gusto. He has an excellent team of soloists, with Thomas Hampson standing out, while the singing of the Arnold Schoenberg Choir is unforgettably vivid, helped by an exceptionally lively and spacious recording. This is one of Harnoncourt's very finest records.

Merbecke, John (*c.* 1505–*c.* 1585)

Missa per Arma Iustitie; Antiphona per arma iustitie (plainsong); Ave Dei patris filia; Domine Ihesu Christe; A virgin and mother.
*** ASV/Gaudeamus Dig. CDGAU 148 [id.]. Cardinall's Musick, Andrew Carwood.

The Tudor composer John Merbecke was a polyphonic master to bracket with his exact contemporary, Thomas Tallis, but his Latin church music has largely disappeared, perhaps destroyed by him after he became a devout Calvinist. This disc brings together all the major items that survive, a magnificent extended setting of the Mass and two splendid anthems, one early and direct in its polyphony, the other dauntingly complex. In the hands of Andrew Carwood and his fine choral group, Cardinall's Musick, the disc proves as revelatory and as beautiful as their previous, highly acclaimed issues of earlier Tudor masters, Nicholas Ludford and John Fayrfax.

Messiaen, Olivier (1908–92)

Turangalîla Symphony.
500♪ *** Decca Dig. 436 626-2 [id.]. Jean-Yves Thibaudet, Takashi Harada, Concg. O, Chailly.

Chailly's powerful, dramatic reading with the Concertgebouw makes an outstanding first choice. The richness of the sound goes with beautiful balance, fine clarity and a keen sense of presence, heightening the impact of Chailly's clean-cut, brilliant interpretation.

(i) *Quatuor pour la fin du temps (Quartet for the end of time);* (ii) *Le merle noir.*
500♪ (M) *** EMI CDM7 63947-2 [id.]. (i) Gruenberg, De Peyer, Pleeth, Béroff; (ii) Zöller, Kontarsky.

Messiaen's visionary and often inspired piece was composed during his days in a Silesian prison camp. The 1968 EMI account, led by Erich Gruenberg and with Gervase de Peyer the inspirational clarinettist, is in the very highest class, the players meeting every demand the composer makes upon them, and the fine, clear Abbey Road recording gives the group striking presence while affording proper background ambience. The bonus, *Le merle noir*, exploits the composer's love of birdsong even more overtly and is splendidly played and recorded here.

PIANO MUSIC

4 Etudes de rythme; Petites esquisses d'oiseaux; 8 Préludes; Vingt regards sur l'Enfant Jésus.
(M) *** Erato/Warner 4509 96222-2 (3) [id.]. Yvonne Loriod.

The 1973 recording by Yvonne Loriod – the composer's second wife – of *Vingt regards* has long been considered very special in its understanding and feeling for the composer's musical sound-world. The piano recording is full but is otherwise acceptable rather than outstanding – yet the magnetism of the playing overcomes the lack of the sharpest focus. This now returns to the catalogue at mid-price, coupled with other key repertoire played with equal distinction.

ORGAN MUSIC

Apparition de l'Eglise éternelle; L'Ascension; Diptyque; Messe de la Pentecôte.
*** Decca Dig. 436 400-2 [id.]. Thomas Trotter (organ of Eglise-Collegiate Saint-Pierre de Douai, France).

Thomas Trotter here proves himself a hypnotic interpreter of Messiaen, creating muted but hauntingly iridescent colouring, and he controls the elliptical crescendo and decrescendo of the ecstatic *Apparition de l'Eglise éternelle*, moving it steadily onwards to its remorselessly achieved climax and sombre closing section. *L'Ascension* was first an orchestral work, but the opening, depicting the *Majesty of Christ*, is made totally commanding in its organ sonorities. The spectacular third section, *Transports de joie*, newly composed for the organ, brings the most thrilling sounds, before the ethereal restraint of the closing *Prière*. The *Diptyque* has a more down-to-earth appeal and is almost amiable in its first part, then reverting to a more typical, quietly sustained penitential close. In short, this superbly recorded collection holds the listener in its thrall, and Trotter surely makes a perfect choice of organ for this programme.

Apparition de l'Eglise éternelle; La Nativité du Seigneur.
**(*) EMI mono CDC5 55222-2 [id.]. Composer (organ of L'Eglise de la Sainte-Trinité, Paris).

Issued separately in EMI's 'Composers in Person' series, these performances are totally authoritative and convincing, for the composer was an admirable exponent of his own music. It is part of Messiaen's four-disc mid-priced survey of his complete organ music (EMI CZS7 67400-2), and the 1956 mono recording is first class. However, we see no reason why this separate CD should have been issued at premium price.

Le banquet céleste; Les corps glorieux (7 Visions brèves de la Vie des Ressuscités); Verset pour la fête de la dédicace.
**(*) Decca Dig. 448 064-2 [id.]. Thomas Trotter (organ of St Fridolins-Münster, Bad Säckingen, Germany).

The *Verset pour la fête de la dédicace* was composed as an examination test-piece in 1960 and it is not, perhaps, essential listening, but both *Le banquet céleste* and, more importantly, *Les corps glorieux* are. Thomas Trotter's recital, recorded at the Klais organ of St Fridolins-Münster, Bad Säckingen, is impeccably played, but the acoustic environment is not ideal for this repertoire. The sound has the clarity of a cold digital recording and has little atmosphere or resonance. Every detail clearly registers but does not add up to a satisfactory picture. One observes Messiaen's world but is not drawn into it in the way one experiences the more atmospheric recordings listed in our main volume.

La Nativité du Seigneur (9 meditations); Le banquet céleste.
500♪ ❀ *** Unicorn Dig. DKPCD 9005 [id.]. Jennifer Bate (organ of Beauvais Cathedral).

'*C'est vraiment parfait!*' said Messiaen after hearing Jennifer Bate's Unicorn recording of *La Nativité du Seigneur*, one of his most extended, most moving and most variedly beautiful works. For the CD issue, *Le banquet céleste* also provides an intense comment on the religious experience which has inspired all of the composer's organ music. The recording of the Beauvais Cathedral organ is of demonstration quality.

Miaskovsky, Nicolai (1881–1950)

Cello concerto in C min., Op. 66.
*** DG Dig. 449 821-2 [id.]. Mischa Maisky, Russian National O, Mikhail Pletnev – PROKOFIEV: *Sinfonia concertante.* ***

Mischa Maisky shows admirable finesse and restraint in Miaskovsky's elegiac concerto. Those who find him sometimes too gushing, too ready to lay bare his breast, will be pleasantly surprised. Like the Prokofiev coupling, this is a strongly characterized performance that gets to the heart of this beautiful piece. Pletnev keeps a firm grip on proceedings, and the Russian National Orchestra play with impeccable taste and aristocratic feeling. This concerto has a sense of nostalgia, a longing for a past that is lost beyond recall, and an overwhelming melancholy that at times calls the Elgar concerto to mind. Rostropovich's 1956 recording still sounds good, and it is coupled with an attractive Taneyev novelty; indeed we gave it a Rosette in our main volume, and it comes at mid-price (EMI CDM5 65419-2). Julian Lloyd Webber's Philips version is also competitive, coupled with Tchaikovsky's *Rococo variations* and a brief *Adagio* of Shostakovich (Ph. 434 106-2); but the present issue will now probably be a first choice for many collectors. It is well recorded and, though the soloist is forwardly balanced, it is not at the expense of orchestral detail.

Cello sonata No 1 in D, Op. 12.
*** Virgin/EMI Dig. VC5 45119-2. Truls Mørk, Jean-Yves Thibaudet – RACHMANINOV: *Cello sonata* etc. ***

The Norwegian cellist, Truls Mørk, plays this lovely piece with both feeling and restraint. No doubt the most logical choice in this work is Marina Tarasova on Olympia, for she also offers its later companion in *A minor*, Op. 81, and the beautiful and elegiac *Cello concerto* (ODD 530 – see our main volume). For those wanting the present coupling, however, these artists give a very fine account both of the *Sonata* and of the Rachmaninov coupling. They are well balanced too.

Milhaud, Darius (1892–1974)

(i) *Le boeuf sur le toit, Op. 58;* (ii; iv) *Le carnaval d'Aix* (for piano and orchestra), *Op. 83b.* (ii; v) *Concerto for percussion and small orchestra, Op. 109.* (iii; vi) *Piano concerto No. 2, Op. 228.* (ii; vii) *Concerto No. 1 for viola and orchestra of soloists, Op. 109.* (iii; viii) *Suite cisalpine sur les airs populaires Piémontais* (for cello and orchestra), *Op. 332;* (ii) *Symphonies pour petite orchestra Nos. 1–5, Opp. 43, 49, 74–5;* (ii; ix) *No 6* (with vocal soloists), *Op. 79; L'Homme et son désir (ballet)* for soprano, contralto, tenor, bass and orchestra, *Op. 48.* (vi) (Piano) *La Muse ménagère.*

(B) **(*) Carlton VoxBox CDX 5109 (2) [id.]. R. Luxembourg O, cond. (i) Froment; (ii) composer; (iii) Bernard Kontarsky; with (iv) Carl Seeman; (v) Fauré Daniel; (vi) Grant Johannesen; (vii) Ulrich Koch; (viii) Thomas Blees; (ix) Doemer, Klein, Arend, Koster.

This valuable box combines the contents of three LPs, with the greater part of the contents conducted by the composer, and with Froment's spirited *Le boeuf sur le toit* thrown in for good measure, all deriving from the archives of Radio Luxembourg. The authenticity of the performances can be in no doubt and the sound is good – with the proviso that, because of the source, the recordings (from either 1969 or 1972) are closely balanced and never allow a real pianissimo to register. This means that, with little or no dynamic range, the music-making can become wearing to listen to after a time. *Le carnaval d'Aix*, an attractive, spontaneous piece, written in Paris in 1926 for the composer's forthcoming visit to the USA, is particularly vivid. The *Second Piano concerto* (1941) is a jazzy work with obvious associations with the Ravel concerto. Grant Johannesen plays it brilliantly, but the accompaniment under Bernard Kontarsky is undistinguished and the recording shallow (although not enough to preclude enjoyment when the pianist is so sympathetic). The finale sounds very much of a scramble here. As we know from his other Turnabout recordings, Thomas Blees is a first-class cellist, and he is persuasive in the rather jolly *Suite cisalpine* in spite of a much too forward balance. Five of the *Six symphonies for small orchestra* were written between 1917 and 1922, and No. 6, which includes four (wordless) voices, was added in 1923. The frugal instrumentation varies with each work and matches the economy of the writing. Each symphony has three movements, but they are very brief, sometimes no more than a minute in length. Yet the character of each work is strong, from the charming opening *Le Printemps* to the *Fifth*, for ten wind instruments, which is very Stravinskian. The *Sixth*, the longest, uses the vocal timbres effectively, but in the recording the singing is not ideally flexible, and in the finale of No. 4 (for strings alone) the fugal writing shows that the orchestra is not of the front rank. The best is the *Third*, subtitled *Serenade*; but all are highly agreeable. *L'Homme et son désir* comes from 1918 and is an evocative score inspired by Milhaud's contact with the sounds of the Brazilian jungle. Its performance has a strong projection and the sound is undoubtedly vivid. Perhaps the most effective part is the very opening. The solo piano work, *La Muse ménagère*, paints a series of simple domestic scenes from *Getting up* to *Reading at night*, and it produces surprisingly sensitive and poetic miniatures. They are played with great affection by Johannesen and the recording of his piano is excellent. With all the reservations about the narrowed range of dynamic (and this *is* a problem), the interest of the repertoire is such as to make this inexpensive box an essential purchase for any admirer of Milhaud, very like EMI's 'Meet the Composer' series, only much less expensive.

Le boeuf sur le toit, Op. 58; La création du monde, Op. 81.

500♪ *** Chandos Dig. CHAN 9023 [id.]. Ulster O, Yan Pascal Tortelier – IBERT: *Divertissement*; POULENC: *Les Biches*. ***

A most engaging account of *Le boeuf sur le toit* from Tortelier and his Ulster players, full of colourful detail, admirably flexible, and infectiously rhythmic. Perhaps *La création du monde* is without the degree of plangent jazzy emphasis of a French performance, but its gentle, desperate melancholy is well caught, and the playing has plenty of colour rhythmic subtlety.

(i) *Concerto for 2 pianos and orchestra, Op. 226. Protée – symphonic suite No. 2, Op. 57;* (ii) *Suite provençale, Op. 187:* excerpts.

(B) ** BBC Radio Classics 15656 91862 [id.]. (i) Geneviève Joy, Jacqueline Robin; BBC SO, composer; (ii) BBC Concert O, Ashley Lawrence (with AURIC; POULENC; TAILLEFAIRE; HONEGGER: *Les Mariés de la Tour Eiffel* **).

These performances were recorded at the BBC's Maida Vale Studios during Milhaud's guest appearances with the BBC Symphony Orchestra in 1969 when he was in his late seventies. He recorded the high-spirited and lightweight *Double concerto* commercially with Geneviève Joy, but this BBC account has great spontaneity, as does his considerably earlier and imaginative *Protée*. The remainder of the disc is taken up with movements from the *Suite provençale* and odd numbers from *Les Mariés de la Tour Eiffel* with Ashley Lawrence and the BBC Concert Orchestra, recorded in 1974, not long after Milhaud's death. Decent rather than distinguished recording, with a rather tubby percussion sound.

Symphonies Nos. 1 (1939); *2* (1944); *Suite provençale.*
500♪ ❀ *** DG Dig. 435 437-2 [id.]. Toulouse Capitole O, Michel Plasson.

The Orchestre du Capitole de Toulouse and Michel Plasson play these melodious scores with total commitment and convey their pleasure in rediscovering this music. The recording is very natural with a refined tone and well-balanced perspective. The delightful *Suite provençale* is as good as a holiday in the south of France – and cheaper!

VOCAL MUSIC

Les Choéphores, Op. 24.
(M) *** Sony MHK 62352 [id.]. Vera Zorina (narr.), McHenry Boatwright, Irene Jordan, Virginia Babikian, NY Schola Cantorum, NYPO, Bernstein – HONEGGER: *Rugby, Pacific 231* **; ROUSSEL: *Symphony No. 3.* **(*)
(M) (**) DG Originals mono 449 748-2 [id.]. Geneviève Moizan, Hélène Bouvier, Heinz Rehfuss, Claude Nollier, Chorale de L'Université, Lamoureux O, Igor Markevitch – HONEGGER: *Symphony No. 5* (**); ROUSSEL: *Bacchus et Ariane: Suite No. 2.* **

Les Choéphores is the second part of Milhaud's setting of Paul Claudel's translation of the *Oresteia* of Aeschylus. It was composed in 1915 at the height of the First World War and comprises seven scenes which cover the same events as are depicted in Strauss's *Elektra*. Milhaud scores the work for large forces, including a spoken role – effectively declaimed on Sony by Vera Zorina – plus soloists, chorus and orchestra. It marked a bold and radical departure in Milhaud's style, making use of polytonality, choral speech and arresting dramatic effects. It is a work of stark intensity, and the sleeve quotes the critic Alfred Frankenstein as hailing it as 'absolutely sensational'. Bernstein's 1961 performance never appeared on this side of the Atlantic on LP, though the Honegger and Roussel items (from much the same period) did. The performance is thrilling and the recording sounds excellent for the period. This is an important issue, much enhanced by the interest of the Roussel coupling and the excellence of the presentation.

Markevitch's 1957 recording has a lot going for it. The performance is strongly characterized, though less virtuosic than Leonard Bernstein's vivid stereo account, made in New York four years later. The mono recording is well balanced with plenty of front-to-back depth and good perspective, though it has the inevitable tonal frailty one might expect after 40 years. The soloists are generally good, but Bernstein scores with the superiority of the orchestral playing and the choral singing.

Moeran, Ernest J. (1894–1950)

2 Pieces for small orchestra: (i) *Lonely waters; Whythorne's shadow.*
(M) **(*) EMI Dig. CDM7 64200-2 [id.]. (i) Ann Murray; ECO, Tate – BAX: *3 Pieces;* BRIDGE: *There is a willow;* BUTTERWORTH: *Banks of green willow* etc. **(*)

The two Moeran pieces in Tate's English recital present a complete contrast with each other, the first atmospheric and impressionistic, the second reflecting the composer's interest in the Elizabethan madrigal. They are given finely judged, refined performances, warmly recorded.

Symphony in G min.
500♪ ❀ *** Dutton Lab. mono CDAX 8001 [id.]. Hallé O, Leslie Heward – IRELAND: *Piano concerto.* (***)

There is always something special about first recordings, but this is remarkable in more than one respect. First, it is a wonderful performance of a great British symphony. Secondly, it celebrates a great British conductor, working at white-hot intensity, who died (so prematurely) just over a year after the original 78s appeared. No praise can be too great for Michael Dutton's CD transfer, made direct from the 78-r.p.m. shellac pressings, using the Cedar system to suppress the surface noise, yet providing sound for which no apologies whatsoever need to be made.

Monteverdi, Claudio (1567–1643)

Madrigals and motets (collection)

Disc 1: Madrigals: *Addio Florida bella; Ahi com'a un vago sol; E così a poco a poco torno farfalla; Era l'anima mia; Luci serene e chiare; Mentre vaga Angioletta ogn'anima; Ninfa che scalza il piede; O mio bene, a mia vita; O Mirtillo, Mirtill'anima mia; Se pur destina; Taci, Armelin deh taci; T'amo mia vita; Troppo ben può questo tiranno amore.*

Disc 2: Madrigals: *Bel pastor dal cui bel guardo; Lamento d'Arianna; Non è gentil cor; O come sei gentile; Ohimé, dov'é il mio ben; Zefiro torna* (with Benedetto FERRARI: *Queste pungenti spine* (cantata); (attributed FERRARI): Final duet for MONTEVERDI: *L'Incoronazione di Poppea: Pur ti miro, pur ti godo*).

Disc 3: Motets for 1, 2 & 3 voices: *Confitebor tibi Domine* (solo); *Duo seraphim* (a 3); *Ego flos campi* (solo); *Fugge, anima mea* (a 2); *Jubilet; Laudate Dominum; Nigra sum* (all three solos); *O beata viae* (a 2); *O quam pulchra es* (solo); *Pulchra es, amica mea* (a 2); *Salve, O Regina* (solo).
(B) **(*) HM Analogue Dig. HMX 290841/3 [id.]. Concerto Vocale, René Jacobs.

One of Harmonia Mundi's bargain 'trios', this Monteverdi programme is presented by the Concerto Vocale directed by the distinguished counter-tenor, René Jacobs, whose vocal artistry and virtuosity dominate many of the performances. It offers an admirable, inexpensive survey of Monteverdi's music, both his madrigals and his church music. The disc called *'Un concert spirituel'* is the highlight of the set and might have received a Rosette as an independent issue. It opens with the remarkable and beautiful *Duo seraphim* which juxtaposes overlapping long notes and rapid virtuoso diminutions, suggesting angels' wings as well as a celestial chorale. The music becomes quite sublime when on the words '*tres sunt*' a third voice enters to symbolize the Trinity. The two-part *O beata viae* begins lightly, with the vocal parts in imitation before its character becomes more reflective; the moods then alternate; and these contrasts of serenity with bravura outbursts are even more striking in the *Salve, O Regina*. Both the solo *Confitebor tibi Domine* and the duet *Fugge, anima mea* are in essence miniature cantatas, with complex duets followed by solos which additionally bring a violin obbligato. This was originally played by the soloist, who was expected to be an instrumentalist as well as a singer. *Pulchra es* is the first of Monteverdi's chamber duets, with the second voice entering unexpectedly to fill out the texture richly. The dramatically expressive *Nigra sum* soon becomes lyrically quite sensuous, especially at the decorated closing section, and *O quam pulchra es* is very like one of the composer's operatic laments, and very touching. Both are set to words from the Song of Songs. Their dolorous feeling is well caught by Jacobs, whose decoration is very assured. *Laudate Dominum* and *Jubilet* both have joyful dancing rhythms, but are again interrupted by passages of virtuoso recitative; the latter ends with jubilant '*Allelujas*'. Both are sung delightfully by Judith Nelson, and altogether this makes an outstanding concert, with imaginatively varied continuo accompaniments (including organ as well as harpsichord). They are recorded in an atmospheric acoustic, adding bloom to voices and instruments alike, without clouding detail.

The first madrigal collection is also available separately on a bargain Musique d'Abord CD (HMA 190184). It is a highly attractive collection of generally neglected items, briskly and stylishly performed, and, with continuo accompaniment, the contrasting of vocal timbres is achieved superbly. Again excellent recording.

The third programme offers repertoire that is more familiar, including the famous *Lamento d'Arianna*. However, here Jacobs allots the lead vocal role to Helga Müller-Molinari, whose general approach is too redolent of grand opera always to carry conviction, while her opulent voice does not blend readily with the instrumental support. The interest of this disc is greatly increased by the inclusion of music by Benedetto Ferrari, a Venetian composer of the generation following Monteverdi, and also a playwright and theorbo player. He is best remembered for a handful of operas and his three books of *Musiche varie*. His *Queste pungenti spine* is a spiritual cantata which comes from the 1637 book and is accompanied on the CD by the final duet from *L'Incoronazione di Poppea*, which has been attributed to him by some scholars. Listening to the one, it is very difficult to believe he really did compose the other, for the Monteverdi madrigals are on a much higher level of inspiration.

Ab aeterno ordinata sum; Confitebor tibi, Domine (3 settings); *Deus tuorum militum sors et corona; Iste confessor Domini sacratus; Laudate Dominum, O omnes gentes; La Maddalena: Prologue: Su le penne de venti. Nisi Dominus aedificaverit domum.*
500♪ ❁ *** Hyperion Dig. CDA 66021 [id.]. Kirkby, Partridge, Thomas, Parley of Instruments.

There are few records of Monteverdi's solo vocal music as persuasive as this. The performances are outstanding, with the edge on Emma Kirkby's voice attractively presented in an aptly reverberant acoustic.

Madrigals, Book 2 (complete).
*** Opus 111 Dig. OPS 30-111 [id.]. Concerto Italiano, Rinaldo Alessandro.

Rinaldo Alessandro and his superb Concerto Italiano are singing their sunny Italianate way through Monteverdi's complete madrigal sequence. Apart from being of Italian birth, all the performers here have studied early Italian and therefore bring a special idiomatic feeling to the words. The Second Book, about half of whose five-part settings are from Tasso, demands and receives a simpler style of presentation than the later works, and there is radiant freshness about the singing here which is particularly appealing. The recording has the most pleasing acoustic.

Madrigals, Book 4 (complete).
*** Opus 111 Dig. OPS 30-81 [id.]. Concerto Italiano, Rinaldo Alessandro.

The Fourth Book, published in 1603 and again for five voices, marks an added richness of expressive feeling over Monteverdi's earlier settings, well recognized by Rinaldo Alessandro and his superbly blended vocal group. This series goes from strength to strength and can be strongly recommended. The recording continues to match the singing in excellence.

Madrigals, Book 5 (complete).
❁ *** Opus 111 Dig. OPS 30-166 [id.]. Concerto Italiano, Rinaldo Alessandro.

Book 5 marks a turning point in Monteverdi's madrigal output, for the last six works bring an obligatory continuo and are very much freer in style, even semi-operatic in their use of freely individual vocal solos, usually contrasted with more sustained concerted passages, as in the very beautiful *Ahi com'a un vago sol cortese giro* ('Alas, how from just one lovely, courteous glance from those two lovely eyes'). The remarkable closing setting, *Questi vaghi concenti* ('These sweet harmonies'), splendidly sung here, is in essence a seven-minute cantata for nine voices, with instrumental ritornellos; this alternates lively solos against sustained writing for the ensemble, often treated as a pair of imitating choral groups. The collection overall is unified by being based on a series of texts from Guarini's *Pastor fido* ('Faithful shepherd'), a dramatic poem telling of the continuing emotional difficulies of two pairs of lovers, Amarilli and Mirtillo, Dorinda and Silvio. The famous opening dialogue diptych, *Cruda Amarilli*, followed by *O Mirtillo, Mirtillo anima mei* brings first a richly dolorous expressive serenity, then an introduction of plangent dissonances as Amarilli asks plaintively, 'And why do you, treacherous Love, unite us when Destiny divides us?' But the following pair of madrigals, the languishing *Era l'anima mia* and Dorinda's heartfelt opening plea, *Ecco, Silvio, colei ch'in odio hai tanto*, are remarkable for balancing sweetness with a new degree of voluptuous espressivo, admirably suggested by the Italian painting which adorns the front of the disc, an elegant naked lady, her Italianate female charms perfectly proportioned, conveying both innocence and promise. The performances by this superb Italian vocal group, at one moment blending richly together, at another asserting solo individuality, cannot be too highly praised, and again they are beautifully recorded.

Madrigals (Duets and solos): *Chiome d'oro, bel thesoro; Il son pur vezzosetta pastorella; Non è di gentil core; O come sei gentile, caro augellino; Ohimè dov'è il mio ben?; Se pur destina e vole il cielo, partenza amorosa*. Sacred music: *Cantate Domino; Exulta, filia Sion; Iste confessoe II; Laudate Dominum in sanctis eius; O bone Jesu, o piissime Jesu; Sancta Maria, succurre miseris; Venite, siccientes ad aquas Domini*. (Opera) *Il Ritorno d'Ulisse in patria: Di misera regina (Penelope's lament)*.
(M) *** Carlton Dig. 30366 00442 [id.]. Emma Kirkby, Evelyn Tubb, Consort of Musicke, Rooley.

Those who have enjoyed the delightful artistry of Emma Kirkby will surely revel in this collection, mostly of duets in which she is joined by Evelyn Tubb. The two voices are admirably matched and both artists ornament their lines attractively and without overdoing it. Evelyn Tubb is given a solo opportunity in Penelope's lament from *Il ritorno d'Ulisse*, which she sings dramatically and touchingly. Anthony Rooley's simple accompaniments with members of the Consort of Musicke are also imaginatively stylish. We are pleased to report that the current reissue has been properly documented with notes and full translations.

Selva morale e spirituale: *Beatus vir a 6; Confitebor tibi; Deus tuorum militum a 3; Dixit Dominus a 8; Domine a 3; Jubilet tota civitas; Laudate dominum a 5; Laudate pueri a 5; Magnificat a 8; Salve Regina a 3*.
** EMI CDC 7 47016-2 [id.]. Kirkby, Rogers, Covey-Crump, Thomas, Taverner Cons. Ch. and Players, Parrott.

Parrott's 1982 collection returns to the catalogue, still at full price and with its catalogue number unchanged. There is some fine singing from Emma Kirkby and Nigel Rogers, and the recorded sound is very good. The performances really need more breadth and grandeur, and there is at times a somewhat bloodless quality about the singing of some of the pieces; but there is enough to admire, such as the attractive account of *Salve Regina* and the opening *Dixit Dominus*. The CD adds to the clarity and presence but tends to emphasize minor faults of balance between instruments and voices, and it suggests to the ear that a little more spaciousness in the acoustic would have given the music-making (even with these comparatively small numbers) more amplitude. Even so, this collection is worth considering.

Vespro della Beata Vergine (Vespers).
500♪ ❁ *** DG Dig. 429 565-2 (2) [id.]. Monoyios, Pennicchi, Chance, Tucker, Robson, Naglia, Terfel, Miles, H. M. Sackbutts & Cornetts, Monteverdi Ch., London Oratory Ch., E. Bar. Soloists, Gardiner.
(M) *** Virgin Veritas/EMI Dig. VMD5 61347-2 (2). Kirkby, Nigel Rogers, Davis Thomas, Taverner Ch., Cons. & Players, Parrott.

Vespro della Beata Vergine (with *Magnificat*).

(B) ** Sony SB2K 62656 (2) [id.]. Prosper, Albert, Levitt, Melvin Brown, Drake, Gregg Smith Singers, Gregg Smith, Texas Boys' Ch., George Bragg, Columbia Bar. Ens., Craft – J. S. BACH: *Cantatas Nos. 131 and 198.* **

Gardiner's second recording of the *Vespers* vividly captures the spatial effects that a performance in the Basilica of St Mark's, Venice, made possible. It would be hard to better such young soloists as the counter-tenor Michael Chance, the tenor Mark Tucker and the bass Bryn Terfel. Without inflating the instrumental accompaniment – using six string-players only, plus elaborate continuo and six brass from His Majesties Sackbutts and Cornetts – he combines clarity and urgency with grandeur. Gardiner (as before) does not include plainchant antiphons, and so has room on the two discs for the superb alternative setting of the *Magnificat*, in six voices instead of seven, in another dedicated performance.

Though Andrew Parrott uses minimal forces, with generally one instrument and one voice per part, so putting the work on a chamber scale in a small church setting, its grandeur comes out superbly through its very intensity. Brilliant singing here by the virtuoso soloists, above all by Nigel Rogers, whose distinctive timbre may not suit every ear but who has an airy precision and flexibility to give expressive meaning to even the most taxing passages. Fine contributions too from Parrott's chosen groups of players and singers, and warm, atmospheric recording. At mid-price this is very competitive.

Craft's version of the *Vespers* dates from 1967. It is very well recorded for its period, and there are some impressive sonorities here. Modern instruments are used and Craft's sense of style is not lacking; his tempi are usually well judged. Although the end effect is of a chamber performance, the refined choral singing gives pleasure, the playing of the trumpets is not lacking in splendour, and the close of the *Magnificat* is impressively spacious. The fresh-voiced Gloria Prosper stands out among the soloists, who are all good. At bargain price this might well be considered if the coupled Bach cantatas are acceptable.

OPERA AND OPERA BALLET

Il ballo delle ingrate; Il combattimento di Tancredi e Clorinda; Tirsi e Clori (opera-ballets).

500♪ ❁ *** O-L Dig. 440 637-2 [id.]. Bott, King, Ainsley, Bonner, George, New London Consort, Pickett.

The star of this outstanding Monteverdi disc is Catherine Bott, as she is of so many discs from Pickett and the New London Consort. It is both apt and attractive that for once one has all three of these inspired opera-ballets, a generous triptych. Pickett characteristically presents them with a sharp clarity and concern for dramatic bite, to match and outshine any of the various rivals in each work. First-rate, well-balanced sound.

Il ballo delle ingrate; Sestina: Lagrime d'amante al sepolcro dell'amata.

(M) *** HM Dig. HMT 1901108 [id.]. Mellon, Laurens, Reinhardt, Feldman, Les Arts Florissants, Christie.

William Christie directs refreshingly dramatic accounts of both *Il ballo delle ingrate* and the complex but very beautiful *Sestina*. His performers have been chosen for character and bite, but all sing impressively. Some may find the lovely final lament of *Il ballo* too plaintive, but it is certainly touching and in keeping with the rest of the performance. In the glorious *Sestina* the richness of Christie's interpretation makes for compelling listening, and both performances are beautifully and vividly recorded. With full translations included, this is a fine bargain.

L'Incoronazione di Poppea.

500♪ *** DG Dig. 447 088-2 (3) [id.]. McNair, Von Otter, Hanchard, Chance, D'Artegna, E. Bar. Soloists, Gardiner.

With an exceptionally strong and consistent cast in which even minor roles are taken by star singers like Catherine Bott and Nigel Robson, Gardiner presents a purposeful, strongly characterized performance. He is helped by the full and immediate sound of the live recording, made in concert at the Queen Elizabeth Hall, and there are clear advantages in having a counter-tenor as Nero instead of a mezzo-soprano, particularly one with a slightly sinister timbre like Dana Hanchard. So in the sensuous duet which closes the opera, the clashing intervals of the voices are given a degree of abrasiveness, suggesting that, though this is a happy and beautiful ending, the characters still have their sinister side.

Orfeo (complete).

500♪ *** O-L Dig. 433 545-2 (2) [id.]. Ainsley, Gooding, Bott, Bonner, George, Grant, New L. Cons., Pickett.

Pickett has not tried to treat *Orfeo* with kid gloves but has aimed above all to bring out its freshness, not caring quite so much about pinpoint ensemble, preferring less extreme speeds and characteristically relying more on dramatic contrasts in instrumentation. He has the cornetts, sackbutts and a rasping regal organ playing at a lower pitch than usual, deducing that transposition from Monteverdi's use of high clefs. The result is all the more darkly menacing. As Orfeo, John Mark Ainsley is crisply flexible in the elaborate decorations of *Possente spirto*, Orfeo's plea to Charon. Catherine Bott is outstanding among the others, establishing the characterful style of the solo singing from the start.

Il ritorno d'Ulisse in patria: highlights.
(M) **(*) Teldec/Warner 0630 15799-9 [id.] (from complete set with Eliasson, Lerer, Hansen, Hansmann, Van Egmond, Junge Kantorei, VCM, Harnoncourt).

A comprehensive (76-minute) selection from Harnoncourt's sympathetic 1971 performance (2292 42496-2 – see our main volume), dominated by Norma Lerer's touching Penelope, although Sven Olof Eliasson's Ulisse is not ideally pure of tone. The documentation includes a full translation.

Mozart, Wolfgang Amadeus (1756–91)

Cassations Nos. 1 in G, K.63; 2 in B flat, K.100; 3 (Serenade) in D, K.100.
(BB) *** Naxos Dig. 8.550609 [id.]. Salzburg CO, Harald Nerat.

The super-budget Naxos label issues a great many recorded performances that are inexpensive but are otherwise of only moderate appeal; every now and then, however, a winner appears – and this is one of them. For all their charms, these early *Cassations* (otherwise miniature serenades or divertimenti) are not likely to be a top priority for many collectors but, played with style and excellently recorded, they are very attractive at Naxos price, and they would still be so if they cost more. They were probably written in Salzburg in 1769, when Mozart was in his early teens, but in many ways they are forward-looking. Nos. 1 and 2 each have seven movements, No. 3 extends to eight. The *First* has two delightful slow movements: a delicate *Andante* and the second introduces a cantilena for solo violin (well played here by Georg Hölscher). K.99 is just as engaging and follows the pattern with a further pair of *Andantes*, and so does the *Third* (which Mozart described as a Serenade), but it is scored more ambitiously, using trumpets as well as horns. All three make enjoyable listening, and all three are here given lively, nicely turned performances, very well – if resonantly – recorded. This admirable disc is certainly worth its modest cost and nicely fills a gap in the catalogue.

Bassoon concerto in B flat, K. 191.
(B) **(*) Carlton Turnabout 30371 00662. George Zukerman, Württemberg CO, Jörg Faerber – WEBER: *Bassoon concerto in F* etc. **

George Zukerman was for some time the principal bassoonist of the CBC Radio Orchestra and he is a soloist of the very front rank. His flexible phrasing and sweetness of tone are a constant source of pleasure and, if he emphasizes the lyrical side of the bassoon's character rather at the expense of the secondary, humorous role, there is no lack of high spirits in the finale. The only reservation about this otherwise admirable performance is Zukerman's decision to add fairly long cadenzas to each movement, which would be more sensible in a concert performance than for repeated listening on a record. The recording is of Turnabout's best quality.

(i) *Bassoon concerto;* (ii) *Clarinet concerto;* (iii) *Oboe concerto, K.314.*
500♪ *** Decca Dig. 443 176-2 [id.]. (i) David McGill; (ii) Franklin Cohen; (iii) John Mack; Cleveland Orchestra, Dohnányi.

In this favourite trio of Mozart concertos for reed instruments, Christoph von Dohnányi and the Cleveland Orchestra successfully follow up their record of the *Flute and harp concerto* and *Sinfonia concertante for violin, viola and orchestra* (see below) with an impressive showcase disc using three more soloists from the orchestra. It is beautifully recorded and attractively balanced. Even if the overall impression here is very much of orchestral principals stepping forward under the conductor, this remains very enjoyable music-making by musicians who are clearly at one with Mozart.

(i) *Clarinet concerto in A, K.622;* (ii) *Flute and harp concerto in C, K.299;* (iii) *Serenade No. 13 in G (Eine kleine Nachtmusik), K.525.*
(M) **(*) Belart 450 035-2. (i) Harold Wright, Boston SO, Ozawa; (ii) Karl-Heinz Zöller, Nicanor Zabaleta, BPO, Märzendorfer; (iii) VPO, Karl Boehm.

Harold Wright's Boston performance of the *Clarinet concerto* is thoroughly musical and well recorded. The warm tone of the clarinet is especially appealing and the soloist enterprisingly plays his own cadenza in the slow movement. However, Ozawa's accompaniments, though well fashioned and neatly laid out, are rather matter-of-fact, and the overall orchestral effect is accomplished rather than inspired. There are no strictures about the Zöller/Zabaleta account of the *Flute and harp concerto*. The flautist is a most sensitive player and his phrasing is a constant source of pleasure, while Zabaleta's sense of line knits the overall texture of this solo-duet most convincingly. Märzendorfer conducts with both warmth and lightness; the outer movements have an attractive rhythmic buoyancy. The early-1960s recording is clear and clean, if not as rich as we would expect today. Of the many excellent versions of Mozart's famous *Night music* in the catalogue, Karl Boehm's 1976 performance is among the finest: polished and spacious, with a graceful *Andante* and a neat, lightly pointed finale. The sound is warm and pleasing, though at the very opening the ear picks up a slight lack of cleanness in the bass focus. But it is of little moment and soon dissipates. Excellent value.

(i) *Clarinet concerto in A, K.622* ; (ii) *Serenade No. 10 for 13 wind instruments, K.361: Adagio* (only).
*** EMI Dig. CDC5 55155-2 [id.]. Sabine Meyer; (i) Dresden State O, Hans Vonk; (ii) with Wind Ens. – STAMITZ: *Clarinet concerto No. 10*; WEBER: *Clarinet concerto No. 1.* ***

Using the original basset clarinet, Sabine Meyer gives a highly seductive performance of Mozart's beautiful concerto and at the same time accompanies herself by directing a rich-textured modern-instrument orchestral backing from the excellent Dresden orchestra, resonantly recorded. The solo playing has much warmth and great finesse, bringing the most sophisticated use of colour and light and shade. Indeed some listeners may feel that this music-making has an element of self-consciousness, especially at the gentle muted reprise of the *Adagio*. But the finale trips along gracefully and her beauty of tone and line is enticing, and it is good to have a performance of such individuality. She participates also in a sonorously solemn account of the *Adagio* from the so-called *Gran Partita*, in which she joins the principal oboe (Diethelm Jonas) to lead the plaintive melodic flow. The couplings, too, are very impressive. Those wanting a somewhat more classically orientated account can turn to Thea King on Hyperion, whose coupling is the *Clarinet quintet* (see below).

(i) *Clarinet concerto;* (ii) *Clarinet quintet in A, K.581.*
500♪ *** Hyperion Dig. CDA 66199 [id.]. Thea King, (i) ECO, Tate; (ii) Gabrieli Qt.

Thea King's coupling brings together winning performances of Mozart's two great clarinet masterpieces. She steers an ideal course between classical stylishness and expressive warmth, with the slow movement becoming the emotional heart of the piece. The Gabrieli Quartet is equally responsive in its finely tuned playing. For the *Clarinet concerto* Thea King uses an authentically reconstructed basset clarinet such as Mozart wanted. With Jeffrey Tate an inspired Mozartian, the performance – like that of the *Quintet* – is both stylish and expressive, with the finale given a captivating bucolic lilt. Excellent recording.

(i) *Flute and harp concerto in C, K.299;* (ii) *Oboe concerto in C, K.271.*
*** Chandos Dig. CHAN 9051 [id.]. (i) Susan Milan, Skaila Kanga; (ii) David Theodore; City of L. Sinf., Hickox – SALIERI: *Double concerto.* ***

A warmly elegant modern-instrument account of this beguiling concerto, with the delicate interweaving of flute and harp given a delightful bloom by the resonant recording, although this means that the orchestral image is also expansive, and some ears might prefer lighter textures and more transparency. Susan Milan is a very appealing flautist and takes an exquisite lead in the graceful *Andante*, so elegantly paced by Hickox. The finale is agreeably lighthearted. The *Oboe concerto* is equally sensitive, again with the line of the *Adagio* delectably sustained by David Theodore, whose creamy tone is so enticing. His pert articulation in the finale is a sheer joy. Both soloists play their own cadenzas. Again the ear notices the very resonant orchestral sound, but in all other respects this is highly recommendable and it has a charming surprise for its coupling.

(i) *Flute and harp concerto in C, K.299;* (ii) *Violin concerto No. 5 in A, K.219.*
*(*) Carlton Turnabout 30371 00182. Württemberg CO, Jörg Faerber, with (i) Jean Patéro, Helga Storck; (ii) György Pauk.

This was a recommendable account of the *Flute and harp concerto* in its day. Although the recording sounds dated in the matter of thin violins, the flute and harp are well balanced and delicately played; but the coupling with a single violin concerto seems a bit perverse. However, Pauk is a good player and this is a neat, stylish performance, accurate in intonation and with unindulgent sensitivity in the slow movement. He is well supported by Faerber, but once again the orchestra sounds thin on top.

Horn concertos Nos. 1–4.
(M) **(*) Teldec 0630 17429-2 [id.]. Herman Baumann, VCM, Harnoncourt.

Horn concertos Nos. 1 in D, K.412 (with *Rondo*, reconstr. J. Humphries); *2–4 in E flat, K. 417, K.447 & K.495; Concert rondo in E flat, K.371* (reconstr. J. Humphries); *Rondo in D, K.514* (completed Süssmayer).
❀ *** O-L Dig. 443 216-2 [id.]. Anthony Halstead, AAM, Hogwood.

We owe something of an apology to Anthony Halstead. His splendid complete set of Mozart's *Horn concertos* was recorded in the summer of 1993 and issued in 1994 but has not been noticed by us until now. It takes its place fairly easily at the top of the list. Not only are the performances special, but textually this set comes closest to Mozart's intentions. Also, by using two different hand-horns, Halstead shows us the full range of tonal possibilities of the eighteenth-century instrument. For the earlier works, K.371, K.417 and K.447, he favours a modern copy of a Bohemian hand-horn of Mozart's own time; for K.495 and the *D major Concerto*, another copy of a more sophisticated and slightly smaller-bore Raoux instrument of 1795, to which most virtuosi of the time, including the famous Giovanni Punto, turned in the latter part of the century. It is easier to hand-stop, its tone is slightly more golden and its execution smoother. Listening to the glorious slow movement of K.495, with its chromatic touches and flowing line, the ear can readily perceive the difference, although Halstead presents the earlier works with effortless virtuosity and much sophistication of light and shade. The stopped notes are not disguised but seem so readily part of the music's progress that one feels that Mozart instinctively realized exactly what was available to him as part of the horn's natural harmonic series when writing the horn parts. The *D major Concerto*, always described as No. 1, is a later work which Mozart did not finish until 1791. He began the closing *Rondo* but left the scoring unfinished; it was completed, after the composer's death, by Süssmayer, who added material of his own. The result is undoubtedly charming and more substantial than Mozart's reconstructed original, which John Humphries has completed for this recording by returning to the composer's draft. It seems likely that Mozart's choice of the lower, D major key (rather than E flat) for this work was to accommodate Leutgeb (the virtuoso and friend for whom the concertos were written) who was now in his mid-fifties and whose embouchure was probably becoming less secure on high notes. The *Concert Rondo*, K.371, is part of a much earlier concerto which Mozart began to write in 1781.

For all this information we are indebted to the fascinating notes accompanying the CD, written jointly by Humphries and Halstead. As for the playing itself, it cannot be praised too highly for its imaginative musical phrasing, technical fluency and spontaneity. Hogwood moreover provides splendidly alert and sympathetic accompaniments. They are beautifully recorded, with the horn aptly balanced, and so pleasing is the orchestral sound that, apart from the transparent detail, one would hardly believe one was listening to period instruments.

Like Halstead, Hermann Baumann successfully uses the original hand-horn, without valves, for which the concertos were written, and the result is not achieved at the expense of musical literacy or expressive content. Baumann lets the listener hear the stopped effect only when he decides that the tonal change can be put to good artistic effect. In his cadenzas he also uses horn chords (where several notes are produced simultaneously by resonating the instrument's harmonics), but as a complement to the music rather than as a gimmick. Unfortunately the remastering has not been entirely successful: the original recording was mellow and reverberant; now it is noticeably drier. The solo horn is given a bold – indeed, rather too tangible – presence, yet its outline is not absolutely sharp, while there is also some roughness of focus in the strings.

Tuckwell (on Collins 1153-2) still reigns supreme for a first-class modern-instrument version of these works, and he also includes all the additional movements. Dennis Brain's famous set with Karajan remains very special, and EMI now offer a good, new transfer of that 1954 mono set, which adds a distinguished earlier recording of the *Piano and wind quintet*, K.452, in which Dennis also participated (CDC5 55087-2).

Piano concertos Nos. 1–6; 8–9; 11–27; Rondos Nos. 1–2, K.382 & 386.
500♪ ❀ (M) *** Sony Analogue/Dig. SX12K 46441 (12). Murray Perahia, ECO.

The Perahia set on twelve mid-priced CDs is a remarkable achievement; in terms of poetic insight and musical spontaneity, the performances are in a class of their own. There is a wonderful singing line and at the same time a sensuousness that is always tempered by spirituality. This is an indispensable set in every respect.

Piano concertos Nos. (i) *1–4;* (ii) *5;* (iii) *6;* (ii) *8–9;* (iv) *11;* (iii) *12;* (iv) *13–16;* (iii) *17;* (iv) *18;* (iii) *19;* (ii) *20;* (iii) *21;* (iv) *22;* (iii) *23;* (iv) *24;* (ii) *25;* (iii) *26;* (ii) *27; Concert rondos for piano and orchestra: in D, K.382; in A, K.386;* (ii; v) *Double piano concerto in E flat, K.365;* (ii; v; vi) *Triple concerto in F (Lodron), K.242.*
(B) **(*) Ph. 454 352-2 (10) [id.]. Ingrid Haebler ((i) fortepiano or (ii–iv) piano), with (i) V. Capella Academica, Edward Melkus; (ii–vi) LSO; (ii) Galliera; (iii) Rowicki; (iv) Sir Colin Davis; (v) Ludwig Hofmann; (vi) Sas Bunge.

Piano concertos No. 20 in D min., K.466; 21 in C, K.467.
(BB) **(*) Belart 450 055-2 (from above). Ingrid Haebler, LSO; (i) Galliera; (ii) Rowicki.

Ingrid Haebler recorded the Mozart concertos with the LSO for Philips between 1965 and 1968, alternating among three different conductors, then completing the set in 1973 with eminently stylish accounts of the first four concertos played appropriately on the fortepiano, accompanied by Melkus and his excellent Vienna Capella Academica. Her readings of the remainder are distinguished by a singular poise, meticulous finger-control and great delicacy of touch. She is less concerned with dramatic intensity; but with her carefully delineated boundaries she undoubtedly gives considerable pleasure by her restrained sensibility and musicianship. She is helped throughout by finely judged recordings, warm and spacious yet crystal clear, and the orchestral response is most sympathetic, particularly in the concertos conducted by Rowicki and Davis. She is at her most characteristic in the early masterpiece, No. *9 in E flat*, K.371, with a clean, classical approach; her account of K.413 (No. 11) is also beautifully alert and the slow movement immediately impresses with its poetry; but eventually the lack of forward movement becomes more obvious. It would be difficult to imagine a more poised account of No. *17 in G major*; the playing may lack the ultimate in forward drive, but Haebler plays lovingly and with great poetry, even if one regrets a certain want of temperament. Both the *B flat Concerto* (No. 18) and the great *E flat Concerto* (No. 22) show her at her finest: she is unfailingly musical and, though she is meticulous in her attention to detail, this does not detract from the scale of the music; the fine accompaniments from Davis contribute to the success of these performances. Haebler's tempi in the *D minor concerto* (No. 20) are warmly relaxed and on the leisurely side. She displays much delicate colouring, but more forward movement throughout, and greater tautness in the finale would have been welcome. She is just a bit *too* relaxed, and matters are not helped by Galliera, who keeps his players on too slack a rein. The first movement of K.467 (No. 21) is a little straitlaced, without the breadth and dignity that some artists have brought to it or the urgency that one has from others. Haebler plays her own cadenzas – and very good they are – but in the heavenly slow movement she is not as imaginative as either Kovacevich or Casadesus, to name but two fine alternative versions, although Rowicki's direction is again excellent. Rowicki also directs the *A major Concerto* (No. 23), and this is undoubtedly a most enjoyable performance, although there are preferred versions available. In the *C minor Concerto* (No. 24) she plays with the clarity of articulation and sense of poise that one has come to take for granted from her, but she tends to scale down the dark sense of passion in this work, though Davis's strong and virile accompaniment prevents any real loss of gravitas. Galliera is at the helm in No. 25, but Haebler's rather self-conscious contribution does not encompass sufficient depth to excite enthusiasm. The first movement of the *Coronation Concerto* (No. 26) is straightforward and dignified, but in the main theme of the slow movement she exaggerates staccato markings and even plays the top A of the theme staccato. The *Double* and *Triple concertos* are given fresh, unaffected readings, and Haebler and Hofmann and, in the latter, Sas Bunge play splendidly; but other versions have more personality and inner life. To sum up: as a complete survey this cannot measure up to Perahia, who remains first choice on 12 mid-priced discs (SX12K 46441), even if Sony's recordings do not consistently match the Philips sound-quality. But Haebler has her own insights to offer, she is a highly individual Mozartian and there is much here to give pleasure when the recorded sound is so good.

For those wanting a characteristic sample of the series, Belart have made available a super-bargain coupling of the two top favourite concertos, *Nos. 20 in D minor* and *21 in C major*, the latter with its 'Elvira Madigan' associations – although Haebler's exquisitely dispassionate view of the famous *Andante* would hardly have been suitable for the sound-track. The recordings are beautifully transferred.

Piano concerto No. 6 in B flat, K.238.
(M) **(*) Decca 448 598-2 [id.]. Vladimir Ashkenazy, LSO, Schmidt-Isserstedt – BACH: *Clavier concerto No. 1* **(*); CHOPIN: *Piano concerto No. 2.* ***

This is an eloquent performance of a charming work, beautifully accompanied. The 1968 recording is excellent for its period, though perhaps an unexpected choice for reissue in Decca's Classic Sound series. The coupled Chopin concerto is the highlight of this reissue.

Piano concertos Nos. 8 in C (Lützow), K.246; 9 in E flat (Jeunehomme), K.271; Concert rondo No. 2 in A, K.386.
500♪ ❁ (M) *** Decca 443 576-2 [id.]. Ashkenazy, LSO, Kertész.

Ashkenazy's earlier, 1966 coupling with Kertész, which includes also the *A major Concert rondo*, originally earned the LP a Rosette, and we see no reason not to carry it forward. Ashkenazy has the requisite sparkle, humanity and command of keyboard tone, and his readings can only be called inspired. He is very well supported by the LSO under Kertész.

Vanguard 'Alfred Brendel Collection': *Piano concertos Nos. 9 in E flat, K.271; 14 in E flat, K.449.*
(M) *** Van. 08.4015.71 [OVC 4015]. Brendel, I Solisti di Zagreb, Janigro.

Brendel's 1968 performance of No. 9 is quite outstanding, elegant and beautifully precise. The classical-sized orchestra is just right and the neat, stylish string-playing matches the soloist. Both pianist and conductor are sensitive to the gentle melancholy of the slow movement, and in the contrasting middle section of the finale Brendel's tonal nuance is beautifully shaded. The performance of K.449 is also first rate, with a memorably vivacious finale. Altogether this is an outstanding reissue with natural sound which hardly shows its age in the clean remastering.

Piano sonata No. 8 in A min., K.310; Fantasia in C min., K.396; Rondo in A min., K.511; 9 Variations on a Minuet by Duport, K.573.
(M) *** Van. 08.4025.71 [OVC 4025]. Alfred Brendel.

Vanguard '*Alfred Brendel Collection*', Vol. 1: Mozart.
(M) *** Van. 08.9161.72 (2) [OVC 9172]. as above.

Brendel's strikingly fresh 1968 Mozart performances, which are among his finest on record, are now gathered together in a slip-case as part of Vanguard's '*Alfred Brendel collection*'. There is no financial advantage in buying the discs together, but admirers of this artist will undoubtedly want both. On the solo disc the *Fantasia* is predictably imaginative, but so is the set of *Variations*, in which the care with shaping and detail raises the interest of the listener and the stature of the music. The analogue recording is firm and full, drier than in the concertos.

Piano concertos Nos. 9 in E flat (Jeunehomme), K.271; 21 in C, K.467.
(B) **(*) Erato/Warner 0630 12812-2 [id.]. Maria-João Pires, Gulbenkian Foundation, Lisbon, CO, Guschlbauer.

These were among Pires' earlier series of Mozart recordings, made in the 1970s, and they are both stylish and sensitive. There is an element of reserve in the performance of the *Jeunehomme* – that is until the buoyant finale, which has plenty of youthful high spirits. Her seriousness of approach suits K.467 much better, and in both concertos she is well served both by Guschlbauer's warm yet alertly supportive accompaniments and by the Erato engineers. However, even at bargain price, this is not distinctive.

Piano concertos Nos. 16 in D, K.451; 20 in D min., K.466.
(M) *(*) DG Dig. 445 597-2 [id.]. Rudolf Serkin, LSO, Abbado.

Serkin's digital recordings of the Mozart piano concertos for DG in the early 1980s showed a sad decline in his pianism. Those who are prepared to bear with the prosaic playing for the sake of the musical insights that do emerge will have no quarrels with this issue technically, recorded when the pianist was about eighty years of age.

Piano concertos Nos. 17 in G, K.453; 19 in F, K.459.
(M) *** Carlton/Turnabout 30371 00162. Alfred Brendel, V. Volksoper O, Paul Angerer or Wilfried Boettcher.

Brendel was an inspired Mozartian when he made his earlier Mozart recordings for the Vox Turnabout label at the end of the 1950s and the beginning of the 1960s; these performances have a radiant freshness and spontaneity which he did not quite match in his later, Philips versions. The recording is on the thin side in the matter of violin timbre, although it has a good ambience; and at Brendel's entry one forgets this fault, for the piano is realistically recorded and very convincingly balanced in relation to the orchestra. Brendel is helped by a vivacious orchestral contribution in both works, with the strings neat, graceful and polished. Brendel's phrasing of the second subject of the first movement of the *G major* is a delight, and the *Andante*, too, is a constant source of pleasure, while both soloist and orchestra share in the high spirits of the finale. The opening movement of No. 19 sounds particularly fresh, and the genial lightness of touch which soloist and orchestra show in the shaping of the melodic line is immediately felt from the opening. There is some very pleasing wind-playing throughout this performance, and the finale is particularly felicitous.

Piano concertos Nos. 17 in G, K.453; 27 in B flat, K.595.
(B) *** Carlton Turnabout 30371 0059-2. Walter Klien, Minnesota O, Skrowaczewski.

Walter Klien's performances were upstaged by those of Brendel, recorded for Vox at around the same time, and (as far as we can trace) this excellent coupling has never been issued in the UK before. Klien receives superior accompaniments from the excellent Minnesota Orchestra under Skrowaczewski, and he is given a very much-better-than-average Turnabout recording. The performance of K.595 is particularly fine, the first movement full of imaginative touches, the slow movement exquisite; and the finale, played with an engagingly light touch, has a delightfully spontaneous-sounding cadenza. No. 17 is also most enjoyable, if not quite as fine, the *Andante* thoughtful and the finale sparkling. Admirers of Klien should not miss this disc.

Piano concertos Nos. 19, K.459; 20, K.466; 21, K.467; 23, K.488; 24, K.491; Concert rondos Nos. 1–2, K.382 & 386.
500♪ ❁ (B) *** Ph. Duo 442 269-2 [id.]. Alfred Brendel, ASMF, Marriner.

This must be the Mozartian bargain of all time, five piano concertos and two concert rondos – all for the cost of one premium-price CD. A Rosette then for generosity, to say nothing of the distinction of the performances. Indeed the playing exhibits a sensibility that is at one with the composer's world and throughout the set the Philips sound-balance is impeccable.

Piano concertos Nos. 19 in F, K.459; 22 in E flat, K.482.
(B) *** Decca Eclipse Dig. 448 992-2; *448 992-4* [id.]. Alicia de Larrocha, VSO, Uri Segal – HANDEL: *Keyboard suite No. 5.* ***

Alicia de Larrocha can hold her own against most of her rivals in terms of both scale and sensitivity, though her K.482 is perhaps not as completely integrated or as touching as the Perahia, which has particularly eloquent playing from the ECO wind. She is also on good form in the *F major*; the Decca recording is beautifully transparent and clear, as well as being warmly resonant, which increases the tinge of romantic feeling in these performances. The sound is particularly natural, with the upper range smooth yet well defined. Although the ear is drawn slightly to the forward balance of the woodwind, the piano-image is most believable, the treble pellucid with no edge. At Eclipse price this is very competitive indeed, especially with the attractive Handelian bonus.

Piano concertos Nos. (i) *19 in F, K.459;* (ii) *27 in B flat, K.595. Piano sonata No. 2 in F, K.280.*
(M) **(*) DG mono/stereo 449 722-2 [id.]. Clara Haskil; (i) BPO, (ii) Bav. State O; (i–ii) Ferenc Fricsay.

Clara Haskil was at her finest in the music of Mozart, as this CD readily demonstrates, and K.595 is an outstanding performance, with an exquisitely played *Larghetto* and wonderfully fluent passage-work from the pianist in the first movement, with every bar alive. On the whole Fricsay accompanies impressively here, but at the opening of K.459 the orchestral articulation is rhythmically flabby, especially compared with the clean solo entry, and this cannot match De Larrocha and Segal on Decca. However, the central *Allegretto* redeems the performance, and both finales sparkle. So too does Haskil's buoyant finale for the *F major Sonata*, full of joy, following a predictably thoughtful *Adagio*. The piano recording is good throughout, but the orchestra could do with a stronger profile in both works, although the 1957 mono sound is perfectly acceptable. The sonata (1961) is stereo.

Piano concertos Nos. 20 in D min., K.466; 21 in C, K.467.
500♪ ❁ *** DG Dig. 419 609-2 [id.]. Malcolm Bilson (fortepiano), E. Bar. Soloists, Gardiner.

(i) *Piano concertos Nos. 20–21;* (ii) *Fantasia in D min., K.397.*
(B) **(*) DG 439 491-2 [id.]. (i) Géza Anda, Salzburg Camerata Academica; (ii) Kempff.

These are vital, electric performances by Bilson and the English Baroque Soloists, expressive within their own lights, neither rigid nor too taut in the way of some period Mozart, nor inappropriately romantic. This is a disc to recommend even to those who would not normally consider period performances of Mozart concertos.

The *D minor* is one of Géza Anda's stronger performances, with solo playing that is both stylish and spontaneous. No. 21 is notable for its poised introduction to the famous slow movement. One notices a certain rhythmic rigidity, and a lighter touch in the finale would have been acceptable, but on the whole this is satisfying, and the remastered DG recording (from the 1960s) sounds particularly fresh. The *Fantasia* is a real bonus: Wilhelm Kempff's disarming simplicity of style hides great art. This playing is in a class of its own.

Anda re-recorded these two concertos later for RCA with comparable success. Some might argue with justice that the DG versions have slightly more character, but the RCA disc is both stylish and enjoyable, and it is now in the very lowest price-range and includes Jochum's account of *Eine kleine Nachtmusik* (Navigator 74321 17888-2 – see our main volume).

(i) *Piano concertos Nos. 20 in D min., K.466; 21 in C, K.467; 23 in A, K.488; 24 in C min., K. 491; 25 in C, K. 503.*
500♪ ❁ (B) *** Double Decca Analogue/Dig. 452 958-2 (2). Vladimir Ashkenazy, Philh. O.

This set – with two CDs offered for the price of one – deserves to be successful and is highly recommendable on all counts. With five of the greatest Mozart piano concertos included, this is real bounty. Ashkenazy's

A major is beautifully judged, alive and fresh, yet warm – one of the most satisfying accounts yet recorded, even finer than Brendel's. The recording focuses closely on the piano, yet no orchestral detail is masked and the overall impression is very bright and lifelike.

Piano concertos Nos. 20 in D min., K.466; 21 in C, K.467; 25 in C, K.503; 27 in B flat, K.595.
(B) **(*) DG Double 453 079-2 (2) [id.]. Friedrich Gulda, VPO, Abbado.

Abbado had much greater luck in his Mozartian partnership with Gulda than he was to experience with Serkin a decade or so later, but even so it was a pity that these two discs (from the mid-1970s) had to be reissued in tandem, for the first is much more successful than the second. Gulda uses a Bösendorfer and in Nos. 20 and 21 his tone is crisp and clear with just a hint of a fortepiano about it, admirably suited to these readings, which have an element of classical restraint; yet at the same time they are committed and do not lack warmth. Abbado's accompaniment is first class, and the orchestral wind-playing is delightful. In Nos. 25 and 27, however, Gulda is strangely cool, though he disciplines his responses impressively and there is no basic want of feeling or finesse, as for instance in the second group of the first movement of K.503, although overall there is a lack of charm. There are felicitous moments elsewhere, but the account of K.595 does not compare with the finest available, despite very good playing from the Vienna Philharmonic. The digital transfer is bright and clear, but there is also a certain shallowness of sonority.

Piano concertos Nos. 20 in D min., 23 in A, K.488 (with vocalized *Preludes* and *'Song for Amadeus'*: vocal and piano improvisations on the *Adagio* from *Piano sonata No. 2 in F, K.280*).
*(**) Sony SK 62601 [id.]. Chick Corea, St Paul CO, Bobby McFerrin (cond. and vocalist).

This is no ordinary coupling of two favourite Mozart concertos, for Bobby McFerrin is no ordinary musician, but a gifted musical evangelist who seeks to draw the attention of those who would not venture inside a concert hall. A totally inexperienced (and unprejudiced) listener attending one of his concerts would almost certainly respond to his charismatic music-making and surely come away wanting to hear more. Chick Corea, too, is a sensitive Mozartian, even if his style defies convention, and these are enjoyably individual concerto performances, spontaneously sympathetic, with the *A major Concerto* the more successful of the two. Each is introduced by a 'Prelude' – a brief *a cappella* vocal and piano improvisation, which is magnetic but should have been cued separately instead of leading straight into the first movement of the concerto. Moreover Corea's improvised cadenzas are wholly his own and are unashamedly out of period, even with a jazz inflexion, and the embellishments elsewhere also have 'blue' notes, although these are applied more to the *D minor Concerto* than to the *A major*, where the touching simplicity of the slow movement is pretty much left to speak for itself. The closing improvisatory duo on the *Adagio* from the *F major Piano sonata*, called '*A song for Amadeus*', readily demonstrates McFerrin's unique vocal skills in a wordless melisma, with a timbre not too unlike that of a counter-tenor. Purists should stay away from this unique twentieth-century Mozartian excursion; others may find it fascinating, although the orchestral accompaniment for the first movement of the *D minor Concerto* is rhythmically rather eccentric. The recording is fair, not ideally clear in projecting the orchestra.

Piano concertos Nos. 20 in D min., K.466; 27 in B flat, K.595.
❀ (M) *** Decca 417 288-2 [id.]. Clifford Curzon, ECO, Britten.

In September 1970 Clifford Curzon went to The Maltings at Snape, and there with Benjamin Britten and the ECO he recorded these two concertos. K.595, the last concerto of all, was always the Mozart work with which he was specially associated and, not surprisingly – when he was the most painfully self-critical and mistrusting of recording artists – he wanted to do it again. Just before he died, in September 1982, sessions had been organized to make such a recording (as they had on several previous occasions). But it was not to be, and anyone hearing this magical record, full of the glow and natural expressiveness which always went with Britten's conducting of Mozart, will recognize both performances as uniquely individual and illuminating, with Curzon at his very finest. The record was kept from issue on LP until after Sir Clifford's death, when it received its Rosette from us. It now arrives on CD still sounding full and beautiful.

(i) *Piano concertos Nos. 21 in C, K.467; 23 in A, K.488; 27 in B flat, K.595; Symphony No. 40 in G min., K.550; Masonic funeral music, K.477.*
* ECM Dig. 449 670-2 (2) [id.]. Keith Jarrett, Stuttgart CO, Dennis Russell Davis.

Keith Jarrett has given us some excellent Bach but, on the evidence of these performances, he is much less naturally attuned to Mozart. The effect is precise but deadpan; pacing is leisured and, in spite of judicious decoration, there is an almost total absence of sparkle. The result refuses to spring to life and even becomes boring. The weighty orchestral image within a resonant recording does not help. They play the other works well enough, but without any kind of distinction.

Piano concertos Nos. 21 in C, K.467; 25 in C, K.503.
500♪ ❀ (B) *** Ph. 426 077-2. Kovacevich, LSO, C. Davis.

The partnership of Kovacevich and Davis almost invariably produces inspired music-making. Their balancing of strength and charm, drama and tenderness, make for performances which retain their sense of spontaneity but which plainly result from deep thought, and the weight of both these great C major works is formidably conveyed. The 1972 recording is well balanced and refined.

(i) *Piano concertos Nos. 21 in C, K.467; 26 in D (Coronation), K.537;* (ii) *12 Variations on 'Ah, vous dirai-je, Maman', K.265.*
500♪ ❀ (B) *** Sony SBK 67178 [id.]. (i) Robert Casadesus, Columbia SO or Cleveland O, Szell; (ii) André Previn (piano).

The ravishing slow movement of K.467 has never sounded more magical than here, and Casadesus then takes the finale at a tremendous speed; but, for the most part, this is exquisite Mozart playing, beautifully paced and articulated. For the *Coronation concerto* Casadesus and Szell are again inspired to a totally memorable performance, and again the slow movement is captivating: Casadesus's Mozart may at first seem understated, but the imagination behind his readings is apparent in every phrase. And as if this were not enough for a bargain reissue, Sony have added a superb account of the *'Ah, vous dirai-je' variations* ('Twinkle, twinkle, little star') from the young André Previn, recorded in Hollywood in 1962.

Piano concertos Nos. 22 in E flat, K.482; 25 in C, K.503.
(M) *** Carlton/Turnabout 30371 00372. Alfred Brendel, VCO or V. Pro Musica O, Paul Angerer.

Another unforgettable early Brendel coupling, recorded in 1958 but with the sound very respectable in its CD transfer. The string-tone remains thin, but the *E flat Concerto* is better focused than on LP and the excellent wind-playing is well caught. Brendel plays the first movement of K.482 with authority, the *Andante* variations very beautifully and the finale enchantingly. Paul Angerer brings plenty of character and imagination to the accompaniments and is especially good in shaping the more serious *Andantino cantabile* episode which is Mozart's surprise in the otherwise sprightly finale. No. 25 shows Brendel at his most commanding, and Angerer sets the scene admirably with an imposing opening, even if the recording focus is less clean in this work. Again the solo phrasing is eminently stylish, with the secondary lyrical theme of the first movement giving much pleasure, the *Andante* classically serene and the finale given the lightest touch.

Piano concertos Nos. (i–ii) *23 in A, K.488;* (iii; ii) *24 in C min., K.491;* (iv) *Double piano concerto in E flat, K.365.*
(B) **(*) Sony SBK 63037; *SBT 63037* [id.]. Robert Casadesus; with (i) Columbia SO; (ii) Szell; (iii) Cleveland O; (iv) Gaby Casadesus, Phd. O, Ormandy.

Casadesus's pre-war account of K.491 with Eugene Bigot was one of the glories of the Columbia catalogue, and his post-war LP was no less fine. Perhaps memory deceives, for the present account does not seem to scale quite those heights, but it is still pretty marvellous, especially the *Larghetto*, and the slightly overdriven precision of Szell hardly detracts from its merits. K.488 is certainly impressive too, and here the Columbia Symphony Orchestra is a more modest-sized group. The finale is taken very fast indeed, but the orchestra manage to stay with their brilliant soloist; however, a little more poise would have been advantageous. The remastering is very successful: the sound has more refinement than on LP and is certainly vivid. Alas, the *Double concerto* is a non-starter. In the outer movements the closely balanced pianos are made to sound aggressively hard and Ormandy's string section is fierce and inflated. The performance is lively enough, but unbeguiling. But the disc is well worth having for the two solo works.

(i) *Piano concertos Nos. 23 in A, K.488; 24 in C min., K.491. Piano sonata No. 14 in C min., K.457.*
(M) *** Carlton/Turnabout 30371 00172. Walter Klien; (i) V. Volksoper O, Peter Maag.

Walter Klien's characteristically sympathetic performance of the *A major Concerto* is worthy to rank alongside Kempff. The approach is essentially simple, but the lyrical flow is beautifully sustained throughout and the glowing beauty of the slow movement gives great pleasure. The recording too is remarkably good. The orchestra sounds somewhat less full-bodied in K.457 but Maag's opening tutti has plenty of character. At his first entry Klien's piano image seeks to contrast the meek with the powerful; although the possibilities of contrast are fully exploited, during the movement the soloist's contribution expands to match that of the orchestra. The slow movement again shows the felicity of the partnership and the wind-playing is nicely pointed. Indeed Maag's direction is distinguished throughout and, if the strings are not immaculate in refinement, this is still a treasurable Turnabout, made the more attractive by Klien's outstandingly fine performance of the *C minor Sonata*, which is given first-class recording.

Piano concertos Nos. 23 in A, K.488; 26 in D (Coronation), K.537.
(M) ** Teldec/Warner Dig. 4509 97483-2 [id.]. Friedrich Gulda, Concg. O, Harnoncourt.

Friedrich Gulda discreetly participates in the orchestral ritornelli. The playing of the Concertgebouw Orchestra is careful in handling both balance and nuances, and Nikolaus Harnoncourt is particularly successful in conducting the *Coronation concerto*. Gulda gives an admirably unaffected and intelligent account of the *A major*, which is enjoyable – as, for that matter, is his reading of the *Coronation* – but it does not constitute a challenge to such rivals as Perahia or Brendel.

Piano concerto No. 27 in B flat, K.595; (i) *Double piano concerto in E flat, K.365.*
500♪ ❀ (M) *** DG 419 059-2 [id.]. Emil Gilels, VPO, Boehm, (i) with Elena Gilels.

Gilels's is supremely lyrical playing that evinces all the classical virtues. No detail is allowed to detract from the picture as a whole; the pace is totally unhurried and superbly controlled. All the points are made by means of articulation and tone, and each phrase is marvellously alive, while Boehm and the Vienna Philharmonic provide excellent support. The performance of the marvellous *Double concerto* is no less enjoyable.

Violin concertos

Violin concertos Nos. 1 in B flat, K.207; 2 in D, K.211; 3 in G, K.216; 4 in D, K.218; 5 in A (Turkish), K.219; Adagio in E, K.261; Rondos: in B flat, K.269; in C, K.373.
(M) *** Virgin/EMI VCD5 45214-2 (2) [id.]. Christian Tetzlaff, Deutsche Kammerphilharmonie.
(B) **(*) EMI forte Dig. CZS5 69355-2 (2). Zimmermann, Württemberg CO, Faerber.

Christian Tetzlaff is a first-class player and an equally first-class Mozartian. He plays all five concertos with great freshness and he simulateously directs the Deutsche Kammerphilharmonie in polished and sympathetic accompaniments. His pacing of allegros is brisk, but exhilaratingly so, and his expressive phrasing in slow movements matches the clean, positive style of his contribution to faster movements. The performances seem to get better as he works his way through the set, and the recording balance is excellent. However, he enters a very competitive field. For a somewhat lower cost on a Philips Duo one can get Grumiaux, who is unsurpassed; and that set includes also the *Sinfonia concertante in E flat*, K.364 (see below). We also have a very soft spot for the Decca Double, similarly priced, in which the excellent Mayumi Fujikawa offers all the repertoire above and she is given a vintage Decca analogue sound of striking warmth and naturalness (440 621-2).

Frank Peter Zimmermann is a highly talented German whose account of these concertos is also most impressive. His interpretations do not quite match those of Grumiaux (with whom, at the price, he comes into direct competition), Stern, Perlman, or even the sparkling Fujikawa on a Double Decca; but they are distinguished by fine musicianship and an effortless technical command. Zimmermann uses cadenzas by Zukerman and Oistrakh in No. 2 and Joachim in No. 4. The digital recordings have agreeable warmth and freshness and are very well balanced. Jörg Faerber is an excellent partner and gets extremely alive playing from the Württemberg orchestra. Not a first recommendation then, but certainly worth considering,

(i) *Violin concertos Nos. 1–5;* (ii) *Adagio in E, K.261; Rondo in C, K.373;* (i; iii) *Sinfonia concertante in E flat, K.364.*
500♪ (B) *** Ph. Duo 438 323-2 (2) [id.]. Arthur Grumiaux, (i) LSO, C. Davis; (ii) New Philh. O, Leppard; (iii) with Arrigo Pellicia.

Violin concertos Nos. 1-5; (i) *Sinfonia concertante for violin, viola and orchestra in E flat, K.364.*
(B) ** DG Dig. 453 043-2 (2) [id.]. Gidon Kremer, (i) Kim Kashkashian; VPO, Harnoncourt.

Grumiaux's accounts of the Mozart *Violin concertos* come from the early 1960s and are among the most beautifully played in the catalogue at any price. The orchestral accompaniments have sparkle and vitality, and Grumiaux's contribution has splendid poise and purity of tone.

However expert the playing, the Gidon Kremer performances are not especially individual. The *B flat Concerto* (No. 1) is curiously uninvolving. Harnoncourt is nothing if not eccentric in his approach to Mozart. His opening movement of No. 2 is brisk and clean, then the slow movement is purposefully moulded. In No. 3 the first movement flows at just the right pace, and then in the *Andante* a comma is placed to romanticize the climbing opening phrase of the main theme slightly. But with Kremer playing sweetly throughout, such individual touches may be found very acceptable (including a long cadenza in the first movement) when there is plenty of vitality and Harnoncourt's tuttis are always strong. Finales are attractively spirited, with some fine wind solos from the Viennese players. However, there are much more rewarding accounts of the *Sinfonia concertante* available. The recordings are pleasingly warm.

Violin concerto No. 3 in G, K.216.

500♪ (B) *** EMI forte CZS5 69331-2 (2) [id.]. David Oistrakh, Philh. O – BEETHOVEN: *Triple concerto;* BRAHMS: *Double concerto;* PROKOFIEV: *Violin concerto No. 2.* ***

David Oistrakh was at his finest in this beautiful 1958 performance of Mozart's *G major Concerto.* His supple, richly toned yet essentially classical style suits the melodic line of this youthful work and gives it the stature of maturity. The orchestral contribution is directed by the soloist himself and is surprisingly polished.

Violin concerto No. 5 in A (Turkish), K.219.

500♪ (M) *** DG 447 403-2 [id.]. Wolfgang Schneiderhan, BPO, Jochum – BEETHOVEN: *Violin concerto.* *** ❁

Schneiderhan plays with effortless mastery and a strong sense of classical proportion, and the Berlin orchestra support him well. The recording is realistically balanced, and this makes a generous coupling for his famous record of the Beethoven, made six years earlier.

(i) *Concertone in C, K.190;* (ii) *Sinfonia concertante in E flat, for violin, viola and orchestra, K.364.*

500♪ ❁ *** DG 415 486-2 [id.]. Perlman, Zukerman, Israel PO, Mehta.

The DG version of the *Sinfonia concertante* was recorded in Tel Aviv at the Huberman Festival in December 1982. It is balanced with the soloists a fraction too near the microphones. The performance is in a special class and is an example of 'live' recording at its most magnetic, with the inspiration of the occasion caught on the wing. The *Concertone* is also splendidly done; the ear notices the improvement in the sound-balance of the studio recording of this work. But the *Sinfonia concertante*, with the audience incredibly quiet, conveys an electricity rarely caught on record.

Divertimenti

Divertimenti for strings Nos. 1–3, K.136–8; Serenade No. 13 (Eine kleine Nachtmusik), K.525.

*** Collins Dig. 1378-2 [id.]. Consort of L., Robert Haydon Clark.

Robert Haydon Clarks's alert and sparkling accounts of the three string *Divertimenti* (or so-called 'Salzburg symphonies') remind us of Marriner's early analogue set with the ASMF. They are hardly less polished and are warmly stylish and very crisply played indeed. There is no need for original instruments when a modern string group can sound as fresh as this. *Eine kleine Nachtmusik* is equally persuasive. Moreover the conductor has here interpolated the 'missing' Minuet and Trio. In fact, as the accompanying notes readily admit, it is most unlikely to be the correct replacement, but it works rather well in context. Excellent, vividly real recording.

Serenades

(i) *Serenades Nos. 4 in D, K.237 (with March in D, K.237); 5 in D, K.204 (with March in D, K.215); in D (Serenata Notturna), K.239;* (ii; iii) *7 in D (Haffner), K.250;* (ii–iv) *9 in D (Posthorn), K.320;* (v) *10 in B flat for 13 wind instruments (Gran Partita), K.361; 11 in E flat, K.375; 12 in C min., K.388;* (i) *13 in G (Eine kleine Nachtmusik), K.525.*

(M) ** Teldec/Warner Dig.4509 95986-2 (5). (i) VCM; (ii) Dresden State O; (iii) with Thomas Zehetmair; (iv) Peter Damm; (v) V. Mozart Wind Ens.; all cond. Harnoncourt.

The two early *Serenades* are introduced boldly with their associated *Marches.* They are superbly played but are presented in Harnoncourt's strongly accented, dramatic style; the kind of affectionate elegance and warmth that Boskovsky brought to this repertoire in his vintage years with Decca is seldom very apparent. The effect here does not lack brilliance, but there is little coaxing, and a human dimension is rarely forthcoming. The *Serenata notturna* is no more beguiling.

In both the *Haffner* and *Posthorn Serenades* Harnoncourt's soloist is Thomas Zehetmair, who gives a splendid account of himself. Harnoncourt offers an eminently spacious and expressive view of the former, at times somewhat idiosyncratic. (He puts the brakes on the trio sections of the Minuets of movements 3, 5 and 7, and the phrasing is mannered.) The *Posthorn Serenade* is little different. The ample acoustic of Dresden helps to inflate these performances, which are quite unlike those we are used to from this conductor.

The account of the *Serenade for 13 wind instruments* is even more controversial. The actual playing of the Vienna Mozart Wind Ensemble is exemplary and the wind blends beautifully. The opening is double-dotted, as authorized in the New Mozart Ausgabe, but tempi will doubtless worry many collectors. The allegro of the first movement is far from *molto* – but that in itself would not disturb those familiar with, say, Furtwängler's classic account. What renders this version unacceptable is the grotesque tempo of the third movement (*Adagio*) and (even more so) of the second Minuet. The treatment of the C minor section in the *Romance* is also very heavy-handed, The playing itself is first class. The two other *Wind serenades* are hardly less individual. Harnoncourt begins K.375 with an eccentrically slow tempo for the first movement. Though he regularly adopts a moulded style, he brings out the tonal contrasts between instruments, never blending. Otherwise allegros are generally on the fast side, well pointed and with fine rhythmic flair; and the whole of K.388 is lively and colourful. *Eine kleine Nachtmusik*, however, brings more eccentricity. It is indulgently mannered in the trio of the Minuet, which is taken at a much slower tempo; the reprise sounds faster than it is. On the other hand, the finale is quite leisured and very neatly articulated. But this is not a set to be recommended generally with any confidence.

Serenade No. 7 in D (Haffner), K.250; March in D, K.249.
*** Sony Dig. SK 66270 [id.]. Isaac Stern, Franz Liszt CO, Rampal.

Serenade No. 7 in D (Haffner), K.250; Serenata notturna in D, K.239.
(M) **(*) Erato/Warner Dig. 0630 13737-2 [id.]. Pavlo Beznosiuk, Amsterdam Bar. O, Koopman.

Easily the finest of recent accounts of the delightful *Haffner Serenade* is the new Sony version from the Franz Liszt Chamber Orchestra. Here Isaac Stern teams up with his old friend, Jean-Pierre Rampal, who puts down his flute to direct a performance which combines vigour and energy with elegance and grace. Clearly he knows all about period manners, and his tempo in the opening movement's *Allegro molto* marginally upstages Koopman; yet that engaging little '*moto perpetuo*' theme in the violins could not be played more neatly. Stern's solo contribution is a bit thin in timbre but his phrasing is sure, and what makes this performance so enjoyable is the warmth and elegance of the playing of the Liszt Chamber Orchestra in the three movements which follow the miniature violin concerto: indeed the first Minuet is truly *galant*, as Mozart indicated. The finale fizzes with energy and geniality, with nice trills from bassoons and flutes adding to the sense of high spirits.

Koopman's account is bolder and his accents are much more robust than Rampal's, especially in Minuets; indeed the energetic timpani are little short of explosive. But he has an excellent violin soloist in Pavlo Beznosiuk, and he too ensures that the delectable *moto perpetuo* sparkles daintily. The extra transparency means that detail registers throughout. The timpani come through strongly and cleanly in the *Serenata notturna* and tend to dominate aurally, but the string playing remains elegantly turned.

Serenade No. 9 in D (Posthorn), K.320; (i) *Bassoon concerto in B flat, K.191.*
**(*) RCA Dig. 09026 61927-2 [id.]. (i) Eberhard Marschall; Bav. R. O, Sir Colin Davis.

Sir Colin Davis's account of the *Posthorn Serenade* cannot be faulted save in one respect. The recording was made 'live' and it is admirably paced and elegantly played, and the *Concertante* section which features a group of wind players (instead of the solo violin which Mozart had interpolated in previous serenades) is pleasingly colourful. The *Andantino* is warmly played and has both poise and gravitas, very like the slow movement of a symphony. In the Trio of the second Minuet the posthorn poops away nicely. The finale sounds weighty when trumpets and drums enter, but the strings play with vigour and grace. The snag is the ample resonance of the Dresden acoustic (the more remarkable as there is an audience present) which, while flattering the whole orchestra, inflates the textures in a way we do not expect today in a work of this kind. The *Bassoon concerto* is similarly affected and the first tutti sounds overblown. But the bassoonist, Eberhard Marschall, is such a personable and characterful player that one cannot help but revel in his solo contribution, while Davis shapes the central *Andante* with appealing breadth. The Minuet finale rounds the work off with much flair from all concerned.

Serenade No. 9 in D (Posthorn); Idomeneo (ballet music), K.367; 2 Marches in D, K.335/1–2.
**(*) O-L Dig. 452 604-2 [id.]. AAM, Hogwood.

If you are a follower of Hogwood's Mozart, this will not disappoint. The playing has style and finesse; it is also strong in character. Indeed the *Serenade* (with its pair of bold Marches which act as introduction and postlude) is unusually symphonic in feeling; although the graceful secondary material is well appreciated, some listeners might feel that the music could smile more. However, when it finally appears, the posthorn makes a vibrant impression. The recording is excellent.

Serenades Nos. 10 in B flat for 13 wind instruments, K.361; Serenade No. 12 in C min., K.388.
** RCA Dig. 09026 60873-2 [id.]. Wind Ensemble of Bav. RSO, Sir Colin Davis.

Although both were recorded live, the *C minor Serenade* comes off slightly more spontaneously than the so-called *Gran Partita*, although neither account really sparkles. The resonant acoustic does not help, although it certainly provides a ripe sonority. In both works there is plenty of light and shade. The closing sequence of movements of the *B flat Serenade*, from the *Romance* through the *Theme and variations* to the robust closing *Rondo*, brings much fine solo playing; but overall this is not a distinctive coupling.

Serenades Nos. 11 in E flat, K.375; 12 in C min., K.388; Overtures: Le nozze di Figaro (arr. Vent); *Don Giovanni* (arr. Triebensee); *Die Zauberflöte* (arr. Heidenreich).
*** Hyperion Dig. CDA 66887 [id.]. E. Concert Winds.

One of the most enjoyable records of Mozart's wind music to appear for a long time. Fresh, spirited playing; firmly focused and well blended sound both from the players and from the engineers. A delight!

(i) *Sinfonia concertante for violin, viola and orchestra in E flat, K.364;* (ii) *Sinfonia concertante for oboe, clarinet, horn, bassoon and orchestra in E flat, K.297b.*
*** DG Dig. 429 784-2 [id.]. (i) Todd Phillips, Maureen Gallagher; (ii) Stephen Taylor, David Singer, William Purvis, Orpheus CO.

(i) *Sinfonia concertante for violin, viola and orchestra in E flat, K.364;* (ii) *Sinfonia concertante for oboe, clarinet, horn, bassoon and orchestra in E flat, K.297b;* (iii) *Rondo in B flat for violin and orchestra, K.269.*
(B) ** Sony SBK 67177; *SBT 67177* [id.]. (i) Druian, Skernick, Cleveland O (members), Szell; (ii) De Lancie, Gigliotti, Jones, Garfield, Phd. O, Ormandy; (iii) Zukerman, ECO, Barenboim.

(i) *Sinfonia concertante for violin, viola and orchestra in E flat, K. 364;* (ii) *Duos for violin and viola Nos. 1–2, K.423–4.*
(M) ** Cal. Approche Dig. CAL 6230 [id.]. Jan Talich Jr & Sr, Talich CO, Kurt Redel.

The performances from members of the Orpheus Chamber Orchestra have an appealing warmth and intimacy. The dialogue between the violin and viola soloists in K.364 is both lively and very sensitive, with a warm expansiveness for the lovely secondary group, while the slow movement brings a comparably felt espressivo, and the finale is buoyant. This is most satisfying, and the comparable work with wind soloists gives a similar feeling of a chamber performance, with the soloists not lacking individuality but blending exceptionally well as a team. Here the first movement is briskly paced, the *Adagio* is warm and leisurely, and the finale light and graceful. The recording is very truthful and the warm acoustic gives pleasing inner definition. The competing performances led by Christopher Warren-Green, with the London Chamber Orchestra, have an even stronger profile, the effect bolder, less intimate. Either record will provide comparable satisfaction and the character of each has its own individuality. The Virgin Ultraviolet reissue, however, has a considerable price advantage (CUV5 61205-2).

Szell's 1963 account of K.364 was a serious contender in its day, with fine playing from Rafael Druian and Abraham Skernick, tender in the slow movement, and with a vivacious finale to round off the performance. The recording is too closely balanced but otherwise good. Ormandy's wind soloists in K.297b blend well together but display less individuality than usual in the *Adagio*; their playing has more diversity of character in the finale. Zukerman and Barenboim then provide a sprightly encore.

The Calliope Approche version for the Talich duo, *père et fils*, with their eponymous Chamber Orchestra is also very fresh, and it too has a nice feeling of intimacy, although orchestral tuttis have an even stronger profile than with the Orpheus group. The snag is that the violin timbre of Jan Talich Junior is very thin and seems to catch the microphone. Also many collectors will want something more substantial than the *Duos* for a coupling, delightful though they are. As it happens, in some ways they come off more successfully than the major work.

(i) *Sinfonia concertante for violin, viola and orchestra in E flat, K.364. Symphonies Nos. 23 in D, K.181; 36 (Linz).*
**(*) Sony Dig. SK 66859 [id.]. (i) Rainer Kussmaul, Wolfram Christ; BPO, Abbado.

Following the pattern of his three earlier discs of Mozart made in Berlin for Sony, this offers an attractive mixture, rather weightier than before, this time recorded under studio conditions, not live. The *Sinfonia concertante* features two of the orchestra's distinguished principals. Both Kussmaul and Christ are outstanding artists, each with individual expressive imagination but who co-ordinate with Abbado as they would simply as members of the orchestra. Those used to performances with regular virtuoso soloists may think this lacking a little in character, but the cohesion and intensity are most impressive, making this a symphony with soloists. The *Linz Symphony* brings a purposeful reading at rather fast speeds, culminating in a buoyant account of the finale. The most surprising performance is of the little *Symphony No. 23*, well under ten minutes long, which – with no sense of incongruity – Abbado relates to the two later masterpieces, with plenty of light and shade and an exuberant account of the military-sounding *Presto* finale. Excellent Berlin recording.

Sinfonia concertante in E flat for oboe, clarinet, horn, bassoon and orchestra, K.297b.
(M) ** EMI CDM5 66101-2 [id.]. Steins, Stähr, Hauptmann, Braun, BPO, Karajan – BRAHMS: *Violin concerto.* *(*)

Karajan's EMI recording of the *Sinfonia concertante* comes from the same period as his late Mozart symphonies and has much the same character. The Berlin wind soloists play beautifully and the accompaniment is warm; Karajan's spacious tempo and the weightiness of the presentation prevent any real lightness of touch, even though the solo contribution to the finale is eminently elegant.

(i) *Sinfonia concertante in E flat, K.297b;* (ii) *Piano and wind quintet in E flat, K.452.*
❀ (***) Testament mono STB 1091 [id.]. (i) Dennis Brain, Cecil James, Sidney Sutcliffe, Bernard Walton, Philh. O, Karajan; (ii) Gieseking, Philh. Wind Ens. – BEETHOVEN: *Piano and wind quintet.* (***) ❀

The Mozart *Quintet* is one of the classic chamber-music recordings of all time. Gieseking and members of the Philharmonia Wind (Dennis Brain, Sidney Sutcliffe, Bernard Walton and Cecil James) recorded it over 40 years ago, and in terms of tonal blend and perfection of balance and ensemble it has few rivals, although among modern versions Perahia's account with members of the ECO remains very highly recommendable at mid-price, also coupled with Beethoven (see below).

To the original quintet coupling Testament have added the *Sinfonia concertante* for wind, which these distinguished players recorded with Karajan in 1953, a performance of comparable stature. Not to be missed. The mono sound comes up wonderfully fresh in this Testament transfer. This is a full-price reissue and is worth every penny of the asking price.

SYMPHONIES

Symphonies Nos. 1–47 (including alternative versions); in C, K.35; in D, K.38; in F, K.42a; in B flat, K.45b; in D, K.46a (K.51); in D, K.62a (K.100); in B flat, K.74g (K.216); in F, K.75; in G, K.75b (K.110); in D, K.111a; in D, K.203, 204 & 196 (121); in G, K.425a (K.444); in A min. (Odense); in G (New Lambacher).
(B) *** O-L Analogue/Dig. 452 496-2 (19) [id.]. AAM, Schröder, Hogwood.

The monumental complete recording of the Mozart symphonies, using authentic manners and original instruments, made between 1978 and 1985, now returns as a complete set on 19 bargain-priced CDs. With Jaap Schröder leading the admirably proportioned string group (9,8,4,3,2) and Christopher Hogwood at the keyboard, this was a remarkably successful joint enterprise. The playing has great style, warmth and polish and, if intonation is not always absolutely refined, that is only to be expected with old instruments. The survey is complete enough to include No. 37 – in fact the work of Michael Haydn but with a slow introduction by Mozart. The *Lambacher* and *Odense Symphonies* are also here, plus alternative versions, with different scoring, of No. 40; while the *Paris Symphony* is given two complete performances with alternative slow movements. Although Pinnock's more recent recording remains first choice (see below), it is much less comprehensive, and Hogwood's overall achievement is remarkable. The recording is well balanced and has plenty of ambience, the CD transfers are very successful, and the accompanying documentation is very good.

Symphonies Nos. (i) *1 in E flat, K.16; 4 in D, K.19; in F, K.19a; 5 in B flat, K.22; 6 in F, K.43; 7 in D, K.45; in G (Neue Lambacher); in G (Alte Lambacher), K.45a; in B flat, K.45b; 8 in D, K.48; 9 in C, K.73; 10 in G, K.74; in F, K.75; in F, K.76; in D, K.81; 11 in D, K.84; in D, K.95; in C, K.96; in D, K.97; 12 in G, K.110; 13 in F, K.112; 14 in A, K.114; 15 in G, K.124; 16 in C, K.128; 17 in G, K.129; 18 in F, K.130; 19 in E flat, K.132* (with alternative slow movement); *20 in D, K.133; in D, K.161 & 163; in D, K.111 & 120; in D, K.196 & 121; in C, K.208 & 102. Minuet in A, K.61g/1.* (ii) *21 in A, K.134; 22 in C, K.162; 23 in D, K.181; 24 in B flat, K.182; 25 in G min., K.183; 26 in E flat, K.184; 27 in G, K.199; 28 in C, K.200; 29 in A, K.201; 30 in D, K.202; 31 in D (Paris), K.297* (with alternative slow movement); *32 in G, K.318; 33 in B flat, K.319; 34 in C, K.338; 35 in D (Haffner), K.385; 36 in C (Linz), K.425; 38 in D (Prague), K.504; 39 in E flat, K.543; 40 in G min., K.550; 41 in C (Jupiter), K.551.*
(B) **(*) Ph. 454 085-2 (12) [id.]. (i) ASMF, Marriner; (ii) Concg. O, Krips.

The first half of this box is a reissue of Volume 1 of the Philips Complete Mozart Edition. Marriner's recordings confirm the Mozartian vitality of the performances and their sense of style and spontaneity. The Philips engineers respond with alive and vivid recording. Except perhaps for those who insist on original instruments, the finesse and warmth of the playing here is a constant joy. The Dutch players for Krips also bring warmth, as well as proving characteristically stylish in phrasing and execution. Quick movements can be bracingly vigorous. Both the previously underrated *No. 28 in C* and the first great masterpiece in A major, both aptly paced, are very persuasively done, with an almost ethereal delicacy from the strings in the beautiful *Andante* of No. 29 and the horns thrusting exuberantly in the coda of the finale. Although Krips's Mozartian sensibility never deserts him, the readings of some of the later symphonies are somewhat wanting in character, however, and do not do full honour to the fine Mozartian that Krips was. No. 39 goes well enough and the first movement of the *G minor* is not pressed too hard, but in the *Jupiter* Krips holds the tension much more slackly. The ample Concertgebouw sound, with its resonant bass, emphasizes the breadth of scale of the music-making, yet the digital remastering gives an attractive freshness to the violins, although the Minuets sound well upholstered. Throughout, the orchestral playing is a pleasure in itself, especially nimble in finales, which are never raced.

Symphonies Nos. 1–41.
(B) **(*) DG 453 231-2 (10) [id.]. BPO, Karl Boehm.

Boehm's Mozart symphony recordings with the Berlin Philharmonic, made between 1959 and 1968, were in fact just as much a pioneering project, setting the pattern for Antal Dorati's Haydn series for Decca, completed five years later. All the earlier symphonies were recorded in intensive sessions in March and November 1968, a real voyage of discovery, with performances warm and genial, with bold contrasts of dynamic and well-sprung rhythms. On matters of scholarship these performances may have been supplanted by a whole series of recordings since, but as a welcoming way to investigate Mozart early and late they certainly hold their place, with hardly a hint of routine in the playing. As with Dorati in Haydn, Minuets are slow by today's standards, but it is interesting to find some of the Minuets in the early symphonies taken more briskly, almost as fast Laendlers. This latest CD reissue, on ten discs instead of twelve, also brings the advantage of fuller and more forward transfers, with good body and presence. The new bargain box, unlike the previous one, has essays on Boehm as Mozartian by Peter Cosse and Mozart as symphonist by Heinz Becker. An excellent bargain, and not just for the historical specialist, but for all Mozartians.

Symphonies Nos. 16 in C, K.128; 17 in G, K.129; 18 in F, K.130; 19 in E flat, K.132; 20 in D, K.133; 21 in A, K.134; 22 in C, K.162; 23 in D, K.181; 24 in B flat, K.182; 25 in G min., K.183; 26 in E flat, K.184; 27 in G, K.199; 28 in C, K.200; 29 in A, K.201.
500♪ *** DG Dig. 439 915-2 (4). E. Concert, Trevor Pinnock.

This invigorating DG box of the Salzburg Symphonies is a splendid follow-up to Pinnock's collection of the earlier juvenile works (DG 437 792-2). The playing has polish and sophistication, fine intonation and spontaneity and great vitality, balanced by warm, lyrical feeling in slow movements. Indeed the account of *No. 29 in A major* is among the finest available (on either modern or original instruments) and the earlier A major work (No. 21) is very impressive too, as is the G minor, K.183, and the very 'operatic' *No. 23 in D major*. Another clear first choice, and not only for authenticists.

Symphonies Nos. 25 in G min., K.183; 29 in A, K.201; 31 in D (Paris), K.297.
(M) **(*) DG 449 552-2 [id.]. BPO, Karl Boehm.

These three symphonies come from the complete box (see above) that Boehm recorded in the 1960s. The playing of the Berlin Philharmonic is quite superlative, but here enjoyment is occasionally marred by the want of spontaneity that sometimes distinguished Boehm's direction. Marriner, for instance, is far more spirited in No. 25, though the orchestral playing is less cultured. The easy-going tempi are acceptable until the finale, which is very slow. The finales of Nos. 29 and 31 are more lively, but the weighty opening of the *Paris* will not appeal to everyone, although the violins articulate gracefully, and the Berlin wind phrase exquisitely throughout the disc. The mid-1960s recording is full-bodied (perhaps too much so for today's ears) and does not sound too dated.

Symphonies Nos. 29 in A, K.201; 31 in D (Paris), K.297; 34 in C, K.338.
(M) (***) Dutton Lab. mono CDEA 5008 [id.]. LPO, Sir Thomas Beecham.

In Dutton's budget-priced Essential Classics series it is good to welcome these incomparable performances, which date from between 1937 and 1940. Although Beecham re-recorded many Mozart symphonies with the RPO after the war, he never returned to Nos. 29 or 34. Beecham's are elegant and cultivated accounts which in many ways are unique, though No. 29 brings one of his most controversial readings. One can readily accept the absence of exposition repeats and can adjust to Beecham's expansiveness and affectionate manner in all the slow movements, but in No. 29 the pace of the opening movement is eccentrically slow, even if Beecham is very persuasive in his pointing. In his note Lyndon Jenkins points out that Beecham had conducted No. 29 four times in the month before he recorded it, which must mean that the speeds were well calculated. In the finales by contrast Beecham prefers really fast speeds, exhilarating in all three here. The superb new transfers are fuller and have much finer presence, transparency and, above all, body than the earlier, EMI versions that appeared some years ago.

Symphonies Nos. 29 in A, K.201; 35 (Haffner), K.385; 36 (Linz); 38 (Prague); 39 in E flat, K.543; 40 in G min., K.550; 41 in C (Jupiter) (with rehearsal sequences for Nos. 39–41).
(M) ** EMI CMS5 66113-2 (3) [CDMD 66113]. BPO, Karajan.

Symphonies Nos. 29 in A, K.201; 35 in D (Haffner), K.385; 36 in C (Linz), K.425.
(M) ** EMI CDM5 66098-2 [id.]. BPO, Karajan.

Symphonies Nos. 38 in D (Prague), K.504; 39 in E flat, K.543 (with rehearsal extracts).
(M) ** EMI CDM5 66099-2 [id.]. BPO, Karajan.

Symphonies Nos. 40 in G min., K.550; 41 in C (Jupiter), K.551 (with rehearsal extracts).
(M) ** EMI CDM5 66100-2 [id.]. BPO, Karajan.

Reissued as part of EMI's Karajan Edition, Karajan's set has the rehearsal sequences for the last three symphonies thrown in for good measure – and they are certainly of interest (they are included on the individual issues as well as in the collection). Moreover, the different microphone placing means that the sound-balance is brighter, leaner-textured than in the actual recording sessions. However, as the conductor's comments are spoken in German, the non-linguist will be able to follow his intentions only with some difficulty, fascinating as is his attention to detail. This is large-orchestra Mozart, the reverberant acoustic of the Jesus-Christus-Kirche (which the EMI recording team never handled as well in eighteenth-century scores as their DG counterparts did later) giving considerable breadth and impact, but also a cushioned thickness of texture to the orchestral sound. The interpretations too have plenty of weight, although Karajan also shows poise and grace: the opening of No. 36 is especially fine. Undoubtedly the best of the set is *No. 39 in E flat*, in which the playing has superb polish and refinement of tone, and few readers will find much to quarrel with in Karajan's interpretation. The same might be said, if perhaps to a somewhat lesser extent, of *No. 40 in G minor* and certainly of the *Jupiter*. Again the playing of the orchestra is a joy in itself and the interpretations are purposeful and considered, even if they do not have the sparkle and naturalness of the very finest recorded performances of these works. No. 29, however, was not part of the original LP set: it was made in the Grünewaldkirche in 1960, and here the sound is fresher. It is a warm, polished performance, realized with much finesse, and it has plenty of life. Yet in the last analysis this music-making is wanting in the final touch of spontaneity and fire; for all the magnificent orchestral playing, the listener is sometimes left vaguely dissatisfied, and not only by the lack of transparency in the orchestral textures.

Symphonies Nos. 29 in A, K.201; 41 in C (Jupiter); Serenade No. 13 in G (Eine kleine Nachtmusik), K.525.
(***) Testament mono/stereo SBT 1093 [id.]. Philh. O, Klemperer.

Klemperer's 1954 Mozart symphony recordings of Nos. 29 and 41, unavailable for many decades, marked the turning-point in his accident-prone career. They were the very first recordings which he made with the Philharmonia Orchestra – from then on providing the focus of his work, belatedly establishing him as a central interpreter of the great German classics. Only the first movement of No. 29 bears out the later image of Klemperer as slow and rugged. After that, all is exhilaration, with superlative playing from the Philharmonia, with rhythms beautifully sprung and phrases elegantly turned. The *Jupiter* in particular is electrifying, one of the very finest versions on disc, both powerful and polished, while *Eine kleine Nachtmusik* (in stereo) for once is made to sound like late Mozart, both strong and elegant. Outstanding transfers.

Symphonies Nos. 31 in D (Paris), K.297; 32 in G, K.318; 33 in B flat, K.319; 34 in C, K.338; 35 in D (Haffner), K.385; 36 in C (Linz), K.425; 38 in D (Prague), K.504; 39 in E flat, K.543; 40 in G min., K.550; 41 in C (Jupiter), K.551.
500♪ *** DG Dig. 447 043-2 (4). English Concert, Pinnock.

Among period performances of Mozart symphonies Pinnock's stand out above all others, and this four-disc collection covering the masterpieces from the *Paris* to the *Jupiter* can be warmly recommended not just to period enthusiasts but also to non-specialist collectors. It is the joy and exhilaration in Mozart's inspiration that consistently bubble out from these performances, even from the dark *G minor* or the weighty *Jupiter*. The rhythmic lift which Pinnock consistently finds is infectious throughout, magnetizing the ear from the start of every movement, and few period performances are as naturally and easily expressive as these. Allegros are regularly on the fast side but never hectically so, and it is a measure of Pinnock's mastery that when in a slow movement such as that of the *Prague* he chooses an unusually slow speed, there is no feeling of dragging. Where Gardiner in these same works exaggerates the dynamic contrasts, Pinnock keeps them firmly in the eighteenth-century tradition, with textural contrasts more clearly integrated. The performances are all billed as being 'directed from the harpsichord', but that continuo instrument is never obtrusive, and one can only register surprise that such subtlety and exuberance have been achieved without a regular conductor. Clear, well-balanced sound, with the orchestra in some symphonies set more distantly than in others.

Symphonies Nos. 35 in D (Haffner), K.385; 36 in C (Linz), K.425; 38 in D (Prague), K.504; 39 in E flat, K.543; 40 in G min., K.550; 41 in C (Jupiter), K.551.
(B) *** DG Double 453 046-2 (2) [id.]. BPO, Karajan.

Here is Karajan's big-band Mozart at its finest. Although there may be slight reservations about the Minuet and Trio of the *Linz*, which is rather slow (and the other minuets are also somewhat stately), overall there is plenty of life here, and slow movements show the BPO at their most graciously expressive. The opening of the *G minor* may not be quite dark enough for some tastes. The *Jupiter*, although short on repeats, has weight and power as well as surface elegance. The remastered sound is clear and lively, full but not over-weighted.

Symphonies Nos. 36 in C (Linz), K.425; 38 in D (Prague), K.504.
(M) ** DG Dig. 445 566-2 [id.]. VPO, James Levine.

One tends to produce a double-take when reading Levine's timing for this pairing of two favourite symphonies: 77 minutes, all but ten seconds. The reason is that he plays every repeat in sight, in *Minuets*, slow movements and finales alike, so that the slow movement of the *Linz* runs to 13½ minutes! The performances are characteristically lively and are marked by superb VPO playing. But listeners will surely feel, however much they may love Mozart, that this is surely too much of a good thing.

Symphonies Nos. (i) *38 in D (Prague), K.504; 39 in E flat, K.543;* (ii) *40 in G min., K.550; 41 in C (Jupiter), K.551.*
(B) ** Decca Double Dig. 448 924-2 (2). (i) Chicago SO; (ii) COE; Sir Georg Solti.

It would be easy to underestimate Solti's Chicago performances of Mozart, for the Decca sound brings a very bright sheen to the upper strings. Solti's approach is in no way glossy; indeed, there is a sense of serious purpose here, notably in the first movement of No. 39, while both slow movements are beautifully played, the phrasing supple and sensitive. The vigour of the opening of the *Prague* is undoubtedly exhilarating, and the finales of both works are alert and sparkling. On the whole, No. 39 is the more memorable: even if the Minuet sounds a bit heavy, the *Andante* shows Solti and his orchestra at their finest. For the two final symphonies Solti turned to the talented young players of the Chamber Orchestra of Europe, recorded at the Alte Oper in Frankfurt, and they respond acutely to his direction with finely disciplined ensemble, paradoxically producing an interpretation which in many places is uncharacteristic of the conductor, unforced and intimate rather than fiery. The middle movements of No. 40 are disappointing for opposite reasons, the *Andante* too self-consciously pointed, and the Minuet too heavy. The *Jupiter* is plainer and much more successful, brightly detailed and crisply articulated. The recording has plenty of bloom on the sound as well as good detail.

Symphonies Nos. 38 in D (Prague), K.504; 39 in E flat, K.543.
500♪ *** Virgin/EMI Dig. VC7 59561-2 [id.]. Sinfonia Varsovia, Sir Yehudi Menuhin.

Menuhin's Mozart with this hand-picked orchestra – of which he is the Principal Conductor – has a clear place for those who, resisting period instruments, yet want many of the benefits of an authentic approach without sacrificing sweetness of string sound. It may be surprising to some that Menuhin is such a complete classicist here, with speeds on the fast side. Yet he does not sound at all rushed.

Symphonies Nos. 40 in G min., K.550; 41 in C (Jupiter), K.551.
500♪ ❀ (M) *** DG Dig. 445 548-2 [id.]. VPO, Bernstein.

Symphonies Nos. 40 in G min., K.550; 41 in C (Jupiter), K.551; Overture: La clemenza di Tito.
**(*) Decca Dig. 448 062-2 [id.]. Mozarteum Camerata Academica, Salzburg, Sándor Végh.

Bernstein's electrifying account of No. 40 is keenly dramatic, individual and stylish, with the finale delightfully airy and fresh. If anything, the *Jupiter* is even finer: it is exhilarating in its tensions and observes the repeats in both halves of the finale, making it almost as long as the massive first movement.

Sándor Végh is a musician of stature, and both symphonies are played impressively. They are strongly characterized and every phrase is carefully thought out. Some may find them a little studied and regret that the music does not flow with that instinctive naturalness that you find in a Bruno Walter, a Beecham or a Colin Davis. Yet on balance there is much that is revealing here, and the quality of the playing is exemplary. Not what is known as 'a library choice', perhaps, but a version that will provoke thought and repay study. There is great sparkle in the overture to *La clemenza di Tito*, and the Decca recording is firm and vivid.

CHAMBER MUSIC

Complete quintets

(i) *Adagio and fugue in C min., K.546;* (ii) *Adagio and rondo in C for glass harmonica, flute, oboe, viola & cello;* (iii) *Clarinet quintet in A, K.581;* (iv) *String quintets Nos. 4 in G min., K.516; 5 in D, K.593; 6 in E flat, K.614.*
(B) **(*) Ph. Duo 456 058-2 [id.]. (i) Italian Qt; (ii) Hoffman, Nicolet, Holliger, Schouten, Decroos; (iii) Jack Brymer, Allegri Qt; (iv) Grumiaux Trio, Gérecz, Lesueur.

(i) *Horn quintet in E flat, K.407;* (ii) *Piano and wind quintet in E flat, K. 452;* (iii) *String quintets Nos. 1 in B flat, K.174; 2 in C min., K.406; 3 in C, K.515; Adagio in B flat for 2 clarinets & 3 bassett horns.*
(B) **(*) Ph. Duo 456 055-2 (2) [id.]. (i) Timothy Brown, ASMF Chamber Ens.; (ii) Ingrid Haebler, Bamberg Wind Qt (members); (iii) Grumiaux Trio, Gérecz, Lesueur; (iv) Netherlands Wind Ens.

The six Mozart *String quintets* are available in a mid-priced box, together with a radiant account of the *Clarinet quintet* (with Bohuslav Zahradnik the sensitive soloist), on three Calliope discs which cost approximately the same as the pair of Duos above (see below). The Calliope set was awarded a Rosette in our main edition and in the long run will prove a far better investment. Moreover, bargain hunters preferring the Grumiaux ensemble's immensely civilized (1973) survey of just the *String quintets* will find them also available on three mid-priced discs, as Volume 11 of the Philips Mozart Edition (422 511-2).

Of the additional music above, the *Adagio and fugue* is not strictly a quintet at all, or the Quartetto Italiano would not have been able to present it so effectively without assistance. The *Adagio and rondo* for glass harmonica, however, proves a welcome bonus, with Bruno Hoffman playing that rare instrument, so titillating to the ear if heard in fairly brief spans. The *Adagio in B flat* for clarinets and basset horns is also a charmer for similar reasons when performed so delectably by the Netherlands group. Of the other major works, Brymer's reading of the *Clarinet quintet* is warm and relaxed and very agreeable, if not distinctive. Timothy Brown is a personable soloist and the *Horn quintet* is given a well-projected and lively account. However, in spite of Ingrid Haebler's characteristically stylish contribution to the *Piano and wind quintet*, the Bamberg performance does not take flight, a straightforward rather than an imaginative account. Throughout all four CDs the recordings are admirably balanced and given high quality analogue sound.

Clarinet quintet in A, K.581.
(BB) **(*) Belart 450 056-2. Jack Brymer, Allegri Qt – SCHUBERT: *Trout quintet.* ***

Brymer's interpretation of the *Clarinet quintet* is warm and leisurely, and he chooses slow tempi throughout. With his tone so succulent, and with velvety support from the Allegri Quartet, he is almost entirely successful in sustaining them although, as the finale proceeds, the forward flow of the music is reduced to a near crawl before the quickening at the coda. The recorded sound is warm and flattering, and this is still very beguiling.

(i) *Clarinet quintet in A, K.581;* (ii) *Flute quartet No. 1 in D, K.285;* (iii) *Oboe quartet in F, K.370.*
(B) **(*) EMI Dig. CDZ5 69702-2 [id.]. (i) Nicholas Carpenter; (ii) Jaime Martin; (iii) Jonathan Kelly; Brindisi Qt (members).

The three soloists introduced here in EMI's Debut series are all principals with various British orchestras. Each is a first-rate artist and all three performances here are fresh and enjoyable, with the *Flute quartet* the most successful of the three, perhaps because its charming, serenade-like *Adagio*, with the soloist poised over a pizzicato accompaniment, cannot fail to beguile the listener. In both the other works the slow movements, although played persuasively, are just a little plain; to make up for it, all three finales are sprightly, with that of the *Clarinet quintet* being particularly successful. The members of the Brindisi Quartet provide admirable support, and the recording is excellent, vivid and transparent.

(i) *Clarinet quintet in A, K.581;* (ii) *Horn quintet in E flat, K.407;* (iii) *Oboe quartet in F, K.370.*
500♪ (M) *** Ph. 422 833-2. (i) Antony Pay; (ii) Timothy Brown; (iii) Neil Black; ASMF Chamber Ens.

It is a delightful idea to have the *Clarinet quintet*, *Oboe quartet* and *Horn quintet* on a single CD. Here, Antony Pay's earlier account of the *Clarinet quintet*, played on a modern instrument, with the Academy of St Martin-in-the-Fields players must be numbered among the strongest now on the market for those not insisting on an authentic basset clarinet. Neil Black's playing in the *Oboe quartet* is distinguished, and again the whole performance radiates pleasure, while the *Horn quintet* comes in a well-projected and lively account with Timothy Brown. The recording, originally issued in 1981, is of Philips's best.

(i) *Clarinet quintet in A, K.581;* (ii) *Violin sonatas in F, K.376; E flat, K.481.*
(M) *** Cal. Approche CAL 6628 [id.]. (i) Bohuslav Zahradnik, Talich Qt; (ii) Peter Messiereur, Stanislav Bogunia.

The *Clarinet quintet* is exquisitely done. Bohuslav Zahradnik's contribution has much delicacy of feeling and colour; he is highly seductive in the slow movement, and even in the finale the effect is gentle in the most appealing way without any loss of vitality. The recording balance is exemplary. The two *Violin sonatas* are also beautifully played in a simple, direct style that is wholly persuasive. The recording is clearly detailed and well balanced, if slightly more shallow.

Clarinet trio in E flat (Kegelstatt), K.498.
** Sony Dig SK 57499 [id.]. Stoltzman, Ax, Ma – BEETHOVEN; BRAHMS: *Clarinet trios.* ***

The Brahms and Beethoven trios come off better than the Mozart *Kegelstatt Trio*. Yo-Yo Ma plays the viola part on the cello, which presents no problems. However, the performance is not without tiny little mannerisms (particularly from this great cellist), which diminish pleasure.

(i) *Flute quartets Nos. 1 in D, K.285; 2 in G, K.285a; 3 in C, K.285b; 4 in A, K.298*; (ii) *Andante for flute and orchestra in C, K.315.*
(B) *** DHM 05472 77442-2 [id.]. Barthold Kuijken; (i) Members of Coll. Aur.; (ii) La Petite Band.

The Collegium Aureum set is the only bargain version using period instruments. Kuijken plays a beguilingly soft instrument from Dresden, made by August Grenser in 1789, and the effect has great charm, even to ears not much enamoured of period instruments. The playing of the three string instruments is also very smooth and accomplished, and the ensemble is beautifully recorded in a warm acoustic. The pitch is lower by a semitone, but few listeners will mind this. The *Andante for flute and orchestra* makes an engaging encore.

(i) *Flute quartets Nos. 1–4;* (ii) *Oboe quartet in F, K.370.*
(M) *** DG 453 287-2 [id.]. (i) Andreas Blau; (ii) Lothar Koch; Amadeus Qt (members).

The flute was not Mozart's favourite wind instrument, yet he wrote some delightful music for it, none more so than these delectably elegant quartets. On DG, although the flute dominates, the other instruments are not over-weighted. The phrasing throughout breathes naturally. The enchanting slow movement of K.285, in which the flute cantilena is floated over a pizzicato accompaniment, is beautifully done, and the ear is caught by the gracious shaping of the *galant* themes used as the basis for variations in the second movement of K.285c or the no less charming opening movement of K.298. Blau is a fine artist and the Amadeus accompany him with subtlety and distinction. These performances are matched by the refinement of Koch in the *Oboe quartet*. With creamy tone, nice embellishments (especially in the finale) and very stylish phrasing, he is splendid. The Amadeus accompany with sensibility and here the string part-writing has rather more interest and the balance is flawless. The excellent analogue recordings date from the late 1970s. Other recommended versions of the flute works have no extra work, so this superior, mid-priced DG disc is very competitive indeed.

(i) *Horn quintet in E flat, K.407;* (ii) *Oboe quartet in F, K.370; String quartet No. 17 in B flat (Hunt), K.458.*
** ASV Dig. CDDCA 968 [id.]. (i) Stephen Bell; (ii) Nicholas Daniel; Lindsay Qt.

This is not one of the more successful of the Lindsay offerings. Why, for instance, choose the much-recorded *Hunt String quartet* instead of another work that includes a solo wind instrument? The performance of K.458 is immaculate and spirited but not especially penetrating. In both the *Oboe quartet* and the *Horn quintet* it is the slow movements and finales that are most successful. In the first movement of K.407 Stephen Bell's spreading timbre lacks something in refinement: this is a case where the wide bore of the German horn is obviously less attractive than that of a more authentic narrow-bore instrument for which Mozart's quartet was written.

(i) *Oboe quartet in F, K.370. String quartets Nos. 20 in D, K.499; 22 in B flat, K.589.*
(**(*)) Globe mono GLO 6037 [id.]. (i) Jaap Stotijn; Netherlands Qt.

The dated sound should not deter any readers who care about style from investigating this disc. This fine Dutch quartet were wonderfully classic Mozartians, and their accounts of both quartets offer many musical rewards. The two *String quartets* were recorded in 1954, only two years after the ensemble was formed, and the *Oboe quartet* dates from 1956, so that the sound is constricted in frequency-range. The Netherlands Quartet was led by Nap de Klijn, and their second violin was Jaap Schröder, who went on in the following decade to concentrate on early music.

(i) *Piano quartets Nos. 1–2;* (i) *Horn quintet in E flat, K.407.*
500♪ ✿ (M) *** Decca mono 425 960-2 [id.]. (i) Clifford Curzon, Amadeus Qt; (ii) Dennis Brain, Griller Qt.

All versions of the Mozart *Piano quartets* rest in the shadow of the recordings by Clifford Curzon and members of the Amadeus Quartet. No apologies need be made for the 1952 mono recorded sound. The performances have a unique sparkle, slow movements are elysian. One's only criticism is that the *Andante* of K.478 opens at a much lower dynamic level than the first movement, and some adjustment of the controls needs to be made. The *Horn quintet* coupling was recorded in 1944 and the transfer to CD is even more miraculous. The slight surface rustle of the 78-r.p.m. source is in no way distracting and Dennis Brain's performance combines warmth and elegance with a spirited spontaneity, and the subtleties of the horn contribution are a continuous delight. A wonderful disc that should be in every Mozartian's library.

Piano trios Nos. 1 in B flat, K.254; 2 in G, K.496; 3 in B flat, K.502; 4 in E, K.542; 5 in C, K.548; 6 in G, K.564.
(M) *** Teldec/Warner Dig. 0630 12336-2 (2). Trio Fontenay.

The Trio Fontenay have already given us excellent accounts of the Brahms and Dvořák *Piano trios* and they are equally happy in the music of Mozart. As before, the splendid pianist, Wolf Harden, dominates the music-making by strength of personality, although the others are well in the picture, and the playing of the cellist, Niklas Schmidt, is notable. The playing of this group is consistently fresh and spontaneous: the *Allegretto* finale of the *G major*, K.496, has a seemingly improvisational freedom and the *E major*, K.542, which opens the second disc, is particularly memorable, the opening *Allegro* light and sparkling, with a delightful *Andante grazioso* to follow and a very spirited finale. Indeed these musicians are completely at one with Mozart and the recording is truthful and well balanced. Although the Beaux Arts set remains very tempting on a Philips Duo (and it throws in the *Clarinet trio* for good measure – see our main volume), this Teldec set has the advantage of modern digital recording and carries the strongest recommendation at mid-price. The only snag is the absence of accompanying musical notes.

Piano and wind quintet in E flat, K.452.
500♪ (M) *** Sony Dig. SMK 42099 [id.]. Perahia, members of ECO – BEETHOVEN: *Quintet.* ***

An outstanding account of Mozart's delectable *Piano and wind quintet*, with Perahia's playing wonderfully refreshing in the *Andante* and a superb response from the four wind soloists. They are well balanced, with the piano against the warm but never blurring acoustics of The Maltings at Snape.

String quartets Nos. 14 in G, K.387; 15 in D min., K.421; 16 in E flat, K.428; 17 in B flat (Hunt), K.458; 18 in A, K.464; 19 in C (Dissonance), K.465 (Haydn Quartets).
✿ (M) *** Astrée Audivis Dig. E 8596 (3) [id.] (*K.387 & K.421:* E 8746; *K.428 & K.458:* E 8747; *K.464 & K.465:* E 8748). Mosaïques Qt.

(i) *String quartets Nos. 14–19 (Haydn Quartets)*; also *String quartet No. 3 in G, K.156;* (ii) *Violin sonata No. 18 in G, K.301.*
(M) *** Cal. CAL 3241/3 [id.]. (i) Talich Qt; (ii) Peter Messiereur, Stanislav Bogunia (with HAYDN: *String quartet No. 74 in G min., Op. 74/3* **(*)).

The set of six quartets dedicated to Haydn contains a high proportion of Mozart's finest works in the genre and, although we have long had a special liking for the Chilingirian performances on CRD, this new set by the Mosaïques Quartet must take pride of place, the more particularly as it is offered at mid-price. As with their previous award-winning performances of Haydn, this is playing of great distinction which offers new insights in every one of the six quartets. Phrasing is wonderfully musical, textures are elegantly blended, there is great transparency yet a full sonority, and this music-making unfolds freshly and naturally with absolutely none of the disadvantages one usually associates with period performances. Slow movements have great concentration and often rapt intensity, yet allegros are alert and vital and finales are a joy. None more so than the closing movement of K.387, which opens delicately but develops a striking impetus, and then the secondary theme dances liltingly. The *Hunt* brings a comparable rhythmic lightness in outer movements and a gently sustained *Adagio*. The first movement of K.428 is thoughtful, yet strong and penetrating, the *Andante* has a powerful atmosphere, while the genial touch in the finale wittily reminds us of Haydn. The underlying tautness at the opening of the *Dissonance Quartet* and the plangent textures possible with original instruments are the more telling when the mood suddenly lightens at the allegro, and this performance again makes the strongest contrast between the profound slow movement and the vigorously extrovert yet engagingly neat closing *Allegro molto*. The recording is first class, real and present, while allowing the widest range of dynamic. The three CDs are separately packaged but come in a slip-case so we assume that later they will be available separately.

The performances by the Talich Quartet are immaculate in ensemble and the performances have a special kind of shared intimacy which is yet immediately communicative. There is complete understanding of what Mozart is trying to say and a warmth and elegance of phrasing which is totally appealing. The analogue recordings are beautiful, very smooth on top, the balance slightly middle- and bass-orientated. The set has now been issued complete on three mid-priced discs with a pair of bonuses. The *Violin sonata* follows after the *Dissonance Quartet*; after the finale of the *Hunt*, K.458, and a pause of about 12 seconds, the Haydn quartet, Op. 74/3, begins, with a level disconcertingly higher and the transfer more immediate. This too is a fine performance – but be prepared! Perhaps the *Dissonance* could have a stronger profile but it, too, is beautifully played and recorded.

This set tends to upstage most of the competition on modern instruments, although the Chilingirians (at full price) on CRD play with unforced freshness and vitality and offer even finer recording. They are worth the extra cost and rightly received a Rosette in our main edition (CRD 3362/4).

String quartets Nos. 15 in D min., K.421; 21 in D, K.575.
*** DG Dig. 449 136-2 [id.]. Hagen Qt.

The Hagen Quartet here reinforce their Mozartian credentials. Their set of the first 13 *Quartets* from K.80 through to K.173 (plus the three Salzburg *String divertimenti*, K.136/8) struck an excellent balance between naturalness of utterance and sophistication of tone (DG 431 645-2 – see our main volume). In both the quartets recorded here, they are highly sensitive to dynamic markings without ever exaggerating them. They are pensive and inward-looking (at times as if they are viewing Mozart through Schubertian eyes) and they make the listener think anew about this great music. A rewarding and interesting coupling, and much to be preferred to other recent versions such as the Ysaÿe and Emerson Quartets. Exemplary recorded sound.

String quartet No. 16 in E flat, K.428; String quintet No. 3 in C, K.515.
** ASV Dig. CDDCA 992 [id.]. Lindsay Qt.

This latest offering from the Lindsays is a disappointment. They play with fine ensemble and genuine affinity for the music, but they seem to be following period-instrument manners and the phrasing is distorted by curious lunges which accord ill with a smooth Mozartian line. The *C major Quintet* opens enticingly, but in both works it is the relatively straightforward minuets and finales which give the most pleasure, although the *Andante* of the *Quintet* has rapt concentration. Good, present recording.

String quartet No. 17 (Hunt), K.458.
(M) *** DG 449 092-2 [id.]. Amadeus Qt – HAYDN: *String quartets Nos. 77–78.* ***
**(*) Testament mono SBT 1085 [id.]. Hollywood Qt – HUMMEL: *Quartet in G* *(*); HAYDN: *Quartet No. 76.* **(*)

The Amadeus, recorded in 1963, give a strikingly fine account of the *Hunt*, famous in its day. The reading is well characterized and, though there are some touches that will not have universal appeal (in the slow movement, for example, these artists do not always allow the music to speak for itself), this is, generally speaking, a most satisfying version, notable for a finely blended and naturally balanced recording, which has been transferred beautifully to CD.

The Hollywood Quartet's performance was recorded at a memorable concert in London's Royal Festival Hall in September 1957, and also included the Haydn coupling. The performance is as impeccable as one would expect from these artists and the sound astonishingly good for the period.

String quartets Nos. 17 in B flat (Hunt), K.458; 19 in C (Dissonance), K.465.
(M) * DG Dig. 445 598-2 [id.]. Emerson Qt – HAYDN: *String quartet No. 77.* *

The Emersons are stunningly articulate performers; they are meticulous too: every 't' is crossed and every 'i' dotted. In terms of sonority and ensemble the listener is bowled over by their virtuosity. But this is eminently self-aware, over-projected playing that might possibly be appropriate in William Schuman or Elliott Carter but is totally out of place in Mozart. They are not helped by a rather unspacious (though not unacceptable) recorded sound.

(i) *String quintets Nos. 1–6;* (ii) *Clarinet quintet in A, K.581.*
500♪ ✽ (M) *** Cal. CAL 9231/3 [id.]. Talich Qt, with (i) Bohuslav Zahradnik; (ii) Karel Rehak.

Glorious performances from the augmented Talich Quartet, with both the *C major* and *G minor* (together on the first disc), unforgettable in their expressive warmth, matching of timbre and easy, unforced spontaneity. The *Adagio* of the *G minor* is raptly beautiful. The second disc, which includes the *Clarinet quintet* in a gently radiant account featuring Bohuslav Zahradnik as the soloist, has been praised above in its separate issue; suffice it to say that the third disc, containing K.593 and K.614, is equally rewarding.

String quintets (Nos. 2) in C, K.515; (3) in G min., K.516; (5) in D, K.593; (6) in E flat, K.614.
(B) **(*) Hyperion Dyad Dig. CDD 22005 [id.]. Salomon Qt, Simon Whistler.

The Salomon Quartet use period instruments, and this Dyad reissue comes into direct competition with the mid-priced Virgin Veritas collection of the same four quintets by Hausmusik. The Salomon group, understandably, are at their very best in the *G minor Quintet*, with the beauty of the *Adagio* sensitively caught. The final work is also splendidly played, but the *C major* and *D major Quintets* are cooler. The Hyperion recording is excellent, and this Dyad costs the same as a single premium-priced CD; but on almost all counts Hausmusik, who are also most realistically recorded, find greater depth in this music and in particular bring out a hauntingly dark yet gentle melancholy in slow movements, while finales bounce along joyfully (VCD 45169-2 – see our main volume).

Violin sonatas Nos. 17 in C, K.296; 18 in G, K.301; 19 in E flat, K.302; 20 in C, K.303; 21 in E min., K.304; 22 in A, K.305; 23 in D, K.306; 24 in F, K.376; 25 in F, K.377; 26 in B flat, K.378; 27 in G, K.379; 28 in E flat, K.380; 32 in B flat, K.454; 33 in E flat, K.481; 34 in A, K.526; Violin sonatina in F, K.547.
(B) *** Decca 448 526-2 (4) [id.]. Szymon Goldberg, Radu Lupu.

This was one of Radu Lupu's first recordings for Decca and he plays with uncommon freshness and insight, while Szymon Goldberg brings a wisdom, born of long experience, to these sonatas which is almost unfailingly revealing. Lupu gives instinctive musical support to his partner and both artists bring humanity and imagination to their performances. In short this is very distinguished and admirably fills an important gap in the catalogue. There is no better sampler than the third of the four discs, in which the delightful closing *Theme and variations* of the *A major Sonata*, K.305, shows the complete rapport shared by these artists, to be followed memorably by the ambitious opening *Adagio* of the *G major*, K.379, which sounds so like Beethoven. Another set of variations which completes this work is presented with disarming simplicity. The poised beauty of the *Andante* of the *E flat Sonata*, K.380, then leads to a winningly sparkling closing Rondo. The recordings were made in the Kingsway Hall in 1974 and were expertly balanced by Christopher Raeburn. They have been most naturally transferred to CD, and this Decca bargain box can be given the strongest recommendation.

Violin sonatas Nos. 18 in G, K.301; 21 in E min., K.304; 23 in A, K.306; 26 in B flat, K.378; 27 in G, K.379.
(**(*)) Globe mono GLO 6039 [id.]. Nap de Klijn, Alice Heksch.

Elegant playing from this fine duo, recorded in 1951–3, one of the earliest versions of the Mozart *Sonatas* to make use of the fortepiano. Nap de Klijn was a wonderful player, and both he and Alice Heksch were so impressed by the sound of the Stein fortepiano they heard in Salzburg in 1950 that they commissioned a copy, which is used here. The playing is tremendously alive and sensitive, and only the slightly acidulated top tempers an enthusiastic recommendation.

PIANO MUSIC

Piano duet

Sonatas for piano duet: in C, K.19d; in B flat, K.358; in G, K.357; in D, K.381; in D, K.448 (for 2 pianos); in F, K.497; in C, K.521.
(M) *** Teldec/Warner Dig. 0630 12335 [id.]. Güher & Süher Pekinel.

This excellent duo are in their element in Mozart. Their playing is full of life and spirit, yet their vigour never rides roughshod over Mozart. The *Andante* of K.381 is beautifully poised, while the *molto allegro* finale of its *D major* companion (for two pianos) is memorably bold, rhythmic and infectious. Excellent, modern, digital recording makes this a first recommendation for this repertoire, even if the documentation is totally inadequate.

Solo piano music

Piano sonatas Nos. 1–10.
❁ (B) *** Carlton VoxBox CDX 5026 (2) [id.]. Walter Klien.

Piano sonatas Nos. 11–18; Fantasia in C min., K.475.
❁ (B) *** Carlton VoxBox CDX 5046 (2) [id.]. Walter Klien.

Walter Klien's set was first issued on Turnabout LPs at the beginning of the 1970s as part of his integral recording of all Mozart's piano music; it now reappears, beautifully transferred to CD, with greater naturalness than before. Moreover all 18 *Sonatas* (including the *F major*, which is an amalgam of the

Allegro and Andante, K.533, with the *Rondo*, K.494), plus the *Fantasia in C minor*, K.475, have been successfully accommodated on four bargain-priced discs. Klien is an outstanding Mozartian; his playing has consistent freshness and is in exemplary taste. It gives enormous pleasure and is at times slightly more robust in its vitality than the playing of Mitsuko Uchida, whose complete Philips set on five mid-priced CDs, digitally recorded, remains our first recommendation in this repertoire. There is nothing remotely self-conscious about Klien's style; the phrasing is unfailingly musical and every detail is beautifully placed without there being the slightest suggestion of preciosity. One has only to sample the opening allegro of the initial sonata included in the first box (*No. 5 in G*, K.283) or the delightful *Andante* which follows, to discover the disarming simplicity of Klien's style and the magic which invests his phrasing, or the spirited articulation of the outer movements of the *C major*, K.309, to find out how special is this music-making. The second box begins with the glorious *A major*, K.311, with its lovely opening *Andante with variations*. Klien captures the grazioso mood of the theme to perfection and later, in the famous closing *Rondo alla Turca*, his buoyant accenting is hardly less captivating. The balance is rather forward (the piano seems just behind the speakers and the sound-image is widely spread), but the tone is rounded and full, and the brightness in the treble never becomes brittle. There is a minimum of background, which never becomes obtrusive.

Piano sonatas Nos. 1–18; Fantasia in C min., K.475.
(M) ** Nimbus NI 1775 (6) [id.]. Marta Deyanova.

Marta Deyanova is an excellent Mozartian and she has her own distinct insights to offer in these sonatas: her style is crisp and clean, without artifice. There is an attractive sense of poise, as at the opening of the *F major*, K.289, while the *Adagio* of the same work is a fine demonstration of her thoughtful lyricism in slow movements, full of imaginative touches of light and shade, yet never precocious or out of style. But while we enjoyed these performances a great deal, the characteristically resonant recording which Nimbus seem to favour for their piano records slightly blurs the outlines of the playing, and the empty hall effect will not be to all tastes.

Piano sonatas Nos. 8 in A min., K.310; 11 in A, K.331; 13 in B flat, K.333; 14 in C min., K.457; Adagio in B min., K.540; Fantasia in C min., K.475; Rondo in A min., K.511; 9 Variations in D on a minuet by Dupont, K.573.
(B) **(*) Ph. Duo Analogue/Dig. 454 244-2 (2) [id.]. Alfred Brendel.

The recordings of the *A major Sonata*, K.331, and the *B flat*, K.333, come from 1971 and 1975 respectively and they show Brendel at his very finest, while (not to be forgotten) the *B minor Adagio* is also memorable. So thoughtful and illuminating are Brendel's insights in these works that, even if you possess other versions of them, this will uncover new areas of feeling. K.331, with its engaging opening theme and variations and justly famous *Alla turca* finale, is a joy. The analogue recording, too, is most realistic. However, the *A minor*, K.310, and the *C minor*, recorded digitally in the following decade, are more controversial. The pianism is masterly, as one would expect from this great artist, but both performances strike one as the product of excessive ratiocination. There is no want of inner life, the texture is wonderfully clean and finely balanced, but the listener is too aware of the mental preparation that has gone into it. The first movement of the *A minor* has immaculate control but is more than a little schoolmasterly, particularly in the development. The staccato markings in the slow movement are exaggerated and the movement as a whole is unsmiling and strangely wanting in repose. Brendel seems unwilling to seduce us by beauty of sound, and the result is self-conscious playing, immaculately recorded. Fortunately he is back on form in the *Fantasia in C minor*, the *Rondo* and the *Variations*.

Piano sonatas No. 8 in A min., K.310; 11 in A, K.331; 15 in F, K.533.
500♪ ❀ *** Sony Dig. SK 48233 [id.]. Murray Perahia.

Murray Perahia celebrates his return to the recording studios with this recital, which is easily the finest Mozart sonata record for some years. Such is his artistry that one is never consciously aware of it. Again we have the old story of the search for truth producing beauty almost as a by-product.

Piano sonata No. 17 in B flat, K.570.
(***) Testament mono STB 1089 [id.]. Emil Gilels – CHOPIN: *Sonata No. 2;* SHOSTAKOVICH: *Preludes and fugues Nos 1, 5 & 24.* (***)

The *B flat Sonata* was recorded in Paris at the Théâtre des Champs-Elysées in March 1954. The sound is a little dry and close, but the playing has a simplicity and poetry that completely transcend sonic limitations.

ORGAN MUSIC

Andante in F, K.616; Fantasia in F min. (Adagio and allegro), K.594; Fantasia in F min. (Allegro and Andante), K.608 (all for musical clock; ed. Trotter). *Adagio in C, K.356* (originally for glass harmonica). Organ pieces: *Adagio in B min., K.40; Andantino in E flat, K.236; Fugue in C min., K.401; Gigue in G, K.574; Prelude (Fantasia) and fugue in C, K.394; Suite, K.399: Overture. Molto allegro in G, K.72a; 4 Pieces from London Notebook, K.15.*
*** Decca Dig. 443 451-2 [id.]. Thomas Trotter (organ of Nederlands Hervormde Kerk, Farsum).

Mozart is never really thought of as a composer for the organ, but he loved its challenge and, whenever he travelled, always made the point of seeking out a local instrument. The problem for us was that he liked best of all to improvise and seldom wrote anything down. Until now, the only 'organ works' we have had on record have been the three pieces he wrote for Count Deym's mechanical organ attached to a clock. Mozart had no opinion of the mechanism for which his music was commissioned and is known to have wished the pieces were intended for a large instrument. These two major *Fantasias* sound quite splendid on the Dutch organ here and Thomas Trotter plays them with great flair, while he finds an entirely suitable registration for the ocarina-like *Andante*, K.616, with its charming decorative effects. The *Adagio for glass harmonica* is also sweetly evoked. Of the other pieces, four are engagingly simple miniatures from the Notebook of Mozart's first juvenile visit to London in 1764. The other, much later, works include a splendid *Fugue in G minor*, K.401, which he finished, all but the eight-bar coda, later added by Stadler; and there is also a lollipop *Gigue in G major*, K.574, written for the Court organist in Dresden, probably in 1789. But the most remarkable remaining piece here is the masterly *Prelude and fugue in C*, K.394, whose dazzling passage-work reminds one just a little of Bach's most famous *D minor Toccata*, although the joyous bravura style is all Mozart's own. It is an extraordinary piece, and Thomas Trotter's account of it is a *tour de force*. The recording is wonderfully vivid, sonorous and clear.

VOCAL MUSIC

Concert arias: *Ah! lo previdi . . . Ah, t'invola, K.272; Alma grande e nobil core, K.578; A questo seno . . . Or che il cielo, K.374; Bella mia fiamma . . . Resta, o cara, K.528; Betracht dies Herz und frage mich, K.42; Misera, dove son! . . . Ah! non son io che parlo, K.369; Vado, ma dove? o Dei!, K.583*
(M) *** DG 449 723-2 [id.]. Gundula Janowitz, VSO, Wilfried Boettcher.

In 1966 when this recording was made (in the Grosser Saal of the Vienna Musikverein) Gundula Janowitz's voice combined a glorious tonal beauty with a surprising degree of flexibility so that Mozart's cruelly difficult divisions – usually written deliberately to tax the original ladies involved – present no apparent difficulty. Janowitz is helped by a flattering, reverberant acoustic, but there is no mistaking the singer's ability to shade and refine the tone at will. An excellent collection of delightful concert arias that are too often neglected nowadays, thanks to the vagaries of modern concert-planning.

Masonic music

Music for Masonic occasions: *Adagio in B flat* (for 2 clarinets & 3 basset horns); *Adagio and fugue in C min.* (for string quartet), *K.546; Adagio and rondo in C* (for flute, oboe, viola, cello & celesta), *K.617; Canonic adagio in F* (for 2 basset horns and bassoon), *K.410; Masonic funeral music (Maurerische Trauermusik), K.477;* (Vocal): *Ave verum corpus, K.618; De profundis clamavi (Psalm 129), K.92; Dir, Seele des Weltalls, K.429; Die ihr des unermesslichen Weltalls Schöpfer ehrt, K.619; Die ihr einen neuen Grade, K.468; Ihr unsre neuen Leiter, K.484; Lasst uns mit geschlungnen Händen, K.623a; Laut verkünde unsere Freude, K.623; Die Maurerfreude, K.471; O heiliges Band, K.148; Santa Maria, Mater Dei, K.272; Zerfliesset Heut', geliebte Brüder, K.483.*
(B) **(*) Carlton/Turnabout 30371 00157 (2) [VoxBox CDX 5055]. Equiluz, Resch, Hoppe, V. Volksoper Ch. & O, Maag; K. Rapf; Wind Ens. (with *Musical joke, K.522* – Ens., Günter Kehr).

This may be thought an ingenious way of collecting some of Mozart's shorter works together; but in fact, whether or not all this music was intended for Masonic purposes by its composer (*De profundis*, for instance, was written when Mozart was only fifteen), it is now used by the Viennese Lodge of which the conductor (an excellent Mozartian) is himself a member. If perhaps the best-known music comes off least well, much of the rest is attractive, especially the miniature cantatas. The instrumental music creates pleasing interludes, although Mozart would have been surprised to hear the *Adagio and rondo in C* in this format (charming as it is), since the celesta was a discovery of Tchaikovsky's for the *Nutcracker* ballet! Nevertheless the recording is excellent – the acoustic has the right degree of spaciousness – and the performers catch the moods of the music, sombre or joyful, and make up in vitality and commitment what they lack in polish. For this reissue a small ensemble led by Günter Kehr (one instrument to a part) provides a respectable and lively account of *A Musical joke*, with the humorous 'wrong notes' coming over bold and strong. The sound is acceptable, if a bit thin on top.

Mass No. 16 in C (Coronation), K.317.

(B) **(*) DG Double 453 016-2 (2) Tomowa-Sintow, Baltsa, Krenn, Van Dam, V. Singverein, BPO, Karajan – BEETHOVEN: *Missa solemnis*. ***

(B) *(*) Carlton/Turnabout 30371 00087. Wilma Lipp, Christa Ludwig, Murray Dickie, V. Oratorio Ch., Pro Musica SO, Vienna, Horenstein – HAYDN: *The Creation*. *(*)

Karajan's 1976 recording of the *Coronation Mass* is a dramatic reading, lacking something in rhythmic resilience perhaps; but, with excellent solo singing as well as an incisive contribution from the chorus, there is no lack of strength and the score's lyrical elements are sensitively managed. The current remastering has further improved the sound.

The striking thing about the Turnabout performance of the *Coronation Mass* is the good teamwork of the soloists. Each is rather less effective on his or her own, but the composite singing is most enjoyable. The recording is well focused, open and clear, but in the last resort this is not distinctive.

Masses Nos. 16 in C (Coronation), K.317; 17 in C (Missa solemnis), K.337; (i) *Epistle sonatas Nos. 16, K.329; 17, K.336.*

**(*) Virgin Veritas/EMI Dig. VER5 61244-2 [id.]. Patrizia Kwella, Ulla Groenwold, Christoph Prégardien, Franz-Josef Selig, Cologne Chamber Ch., Coll. Cartusianum, Peter Neumann.

Peter Neumann directs a most enjoyably spirited account of the *Coronation Mass* and couples it with the much rarer *Missa solemnis*, K.336, which is on a similar scale and which is also very well sung. The singers, a well-blended team, are balanced somewhat backwardly within an ecclesiastical acoustic, which takes off a little of the bite from the chorus too, but the effect remains vivid. Hogwood's version of the *Coronation Mass* (paired with the *Vespers*) is even finer, and he has Emma Kirkby as a radiant soprano soloist (O-L 436 585-2). But that is at full price, and Patrizia Kwella makes fine solo contributions to both the Virgin performances.

Mass No. 18 in C min. (Great), K.427.

500♪ *** DG Gold Dig. 439 012-2 [id.]. Hendricks, Perry, Schreier, Luxon, V. Singverein, BPO, Karajan.

In his (1982) digital recording of the *C minor Mass* Karajan gives Handelian splendour to this greatest of Mozart's choral works and, though the scale is large, the beauty and intensity are hard to resist. Solo singing is first rate, particularly that of Barbara Hendricks, the dreamy beauty of her voice ravishingly caught.

Requiem Mass (No. 19) in D min., K.626.

(M) *** Virgin/EMI Dig. CUV5 61260-2 [id.]. Yvonne Kenny, Alfreda Hodgson, Arthur Davies, Gwynne Howell, N. Sinfonia Ch., London Symphony Ch., N. Sinfonia, Richard Hickox.

(BB) *(*) Naxos Dig. 8.550235 [id.]. Hajóssyova, Horská, Kundlák, Mikuláš, Slovak PO & Ch., Košler.

Requiem Mass (No. 19) in D min., K.626; Kyrie, K.341.

*** HM Dig. HMC 901620 [id.]. Sibylla Rubens, Annette Markert, Ian Bostridge, Hanno Müller-Brachmann, La Chapelle Royale Coll. Vocale, O des Champs Elysées, Herreweghe.

Gardiner (on Ph. 420 197-2) with characteristic panache gives one of the most powerful performances ever of Mozart's *Requiem*, and this will be first choice for those preferring a period performance. However, for those seeking a modern-instrument account, Richard Hickox's excellent version on Virgin's mid-priced Ultraviolet label matches any in the catalogue. With generally brisk speeds and light, resilient rhythms, it combines gravity with authentically clean, transparent textures in which the dark colourings of the orchestration, as with the basset horns, come out vividly. All four soloists are outstandingly fine, and the choral singing is fresh and incisive, with crisp attack. The voices, solo and choral, are placed rather backwardly; otherwise the recording is excellent.

Herreweghe is arresting from the very dramatic opening bars, and in the work's central Sequenz (*Dies irae*; *Tuba mirum*; *Rex Tremendae*; *Recordare*; *Confutatis* and the moving *Lacrimosa*) he achieves a remarkable emotional thrust. The orchestra gives weighty support, and one is hardly aware that this is a period-instrument performance, with the horns and trumpets capping climaxes forcefully. The soloists make an excellent team, singing with individuality (especially Ian Bostridge) but also blending together. The sound is spacious, but there is no feeling that the choral impact is blunted. After Süssmayer's completion, it seems entirely appropriate to end the record with the simple and very touching *Kyrie*, K.341, which is from Mozart's own hand.

Though the chorus and soloists are first rate on the Naxos issue, recorded in Bratislava, the style of the performance is on the heavy side, with generally slow speeds and rhythms that are often square and plodding. The four soloists are all firm and fresh-toned, though their tuning together is not always impeccable.

(i) *Thamos, King of Egypt* (incidental music), *K.345;* (ii) *Der Schauspieldirektor*.
(M) **(*) Teldec/Warner Dig. 4509 95979-2 [id.]. (i) Perry, Mühler, Van Alterna, Thomaschke, Van der Kamp, Netherlands Chamber Ch.; (ii) Nador, Láki, Hampson, Van der Kamp; Concg. O, Harnoncourt.

Originally issued at premium price without a coupling, this mid-priced reissue is now rather more competitive when it also includes a perfectly adequate complete performance of the vocal numbers from *Der Schauspieldirektor*. It is brightly sung, with a well-chosen pair of female adversaries, even though it is no match for the Decca version with Te Kanawa and Gruberová, both in sparkling form (see below). Comedy is perhaps not Harnoncourt's strong point; his accompaniments, as usual, are well laced with accents. However, he directs a spirited account of the *Thamos* incidental music, now thought to date from rather later than originally estimated and here made to seem strong and mature in incisive, sharply articulated performances. Playing is excellent and, though chorus and soloists are rather backwardly placed in a reverberant acoustic, the singing is enjoyable too.

OPERA

Così fan tutte (complete).
500♪ *** Decca Dig. 444 174-2 (3). Renée Fleming, Anne Sofie von Otter, Frank Lopardo, Olaf Bär, Adelina Scarabelli, Michele Pertusi, COE, Solti.
500♪ ❁ (M) *** EMI CMS7 69330-2 (3) [Ang. CDMC 69330]. Schwarzkopf, Ludwig, Steffek, Kraus, Taddei, Berry, Philh. Ch. & O, Boehm.
**(*) EMI Dig. CDS5 56170-2 (3) [id.]. Hillevi Martinpelto, Hagley, Murray, Streit, Finley, Allen, OAE, Rattle.

In contrast to his prickly and straight-faced recording of the early 1970s, Solti's digital *Così*, recorded live at the Royal Festival Hall in 1994, is as sparkling and full of humour as you could want. With the youthful and starry cast acting the story out on stage so as to sharpen the dramatic point, Solti takes a fast and light approach which yet has none of his old fierceness. The speeds may challenge the singers, notably in the many ensembles, but Solti gives his performers every consideration in moulding the arch of phrases or in allowing time for elaborate decorations.

Boehm's classic set has been handsomely repackaged and remains a clear alternative choice, despite the attractions of the new Gardiner version. Its glorious solo singing is headed by the incomparable Fiordiligi of Schwarzkopf and the equally moving Dorabella of Christa Ludwig; it remains a superb memento of Walter Legge's recording genius and still bears comparison with any other recordings made before or since.

Following the impressive versions of John Eliot Gardiner and Sir Georg Solti, Sir Simon Rattle offers this sizzling account of *Così*, also recorded live, with the period instruments of the Orchestra of the Age of Enlightenment. In its often hectic speeds from the overture onwards, it may miss some of the sparkle of the piece, but Rattle knows how to bring out the emotional high points, so that the superb Fiordiligi, Hillevi Martinpelto, at a measured speed sings with aching beauty in *Per pietà*. With less pointed playing, the set may not replace Gardiner, Boehm or Solti, but the cast is the most consistent of the three, including Thomas Allen as a masterly Alfonso, Kurt Streit a clear-toned Ferrando and Gerald Finley a youthfully ardent Guglielmo. It is refreshing too to have a soprano Dorabella, particularly when the lovely timbre of Alison Hagley's voice is clearly contrasted with the brighter tones of Martinpelto. As ever, Ann Murray is a characterful Despina. The acoustic of Symphony Hall, Birmingham, adds brightness to the sound, though this is not focused quite as well as Birmingham recordings made without an audience.

Così fan tutte: highlights.
(BB) **(*) Belart 450 114-2 (from complete recording, with Janowitz, Fassbaender, Prey, Schreier, Grist, VPO, cond. Boehm).
(M) **(*) Teldec/Warner Dig. 0630 15809-9 [id.] (from complete recording, with Margiono, Delores Ziegler, Anna Steiger, Van der Walt, Cachemaille, Hampson, Netherlands Op. Ch., Concg. O, Harnoncourt).

These Belart highlights come from Karl Boehm's third (DG) recording of the opera and, with 72 minutes of music included, it makes an attractive memento. It was recorded live during the Salzburg Festival performance on the conductor's eightieth birthday. It has a splendid cast, and the zest and sparkle of the occasion come over delightfully. Even if at times ensemble leaves a good deal to be desired, at super-budget price it makes a genuine bargain.

Harnoncourt, the period-instrument specialist, as in his other Mozart opera recordings here favours an orchestra of modern instruments while adopting speeds of period style. He gives a quirkily magnetic reading and many will be glad of a fairly comprehensive sampler (74 minutes), especially when – as usual with the Warner Classics Opera Collection series – it is documented with a full translation and linking narrative. Though *O soave sia il vento* is raced along, Fiordiligi's great Act II aria, *Per pietà*, is taken very slowly indeed. Even so, Charlotte Margiono sustains the line immaculately, and she is similarly accommodating over another of Harnoncourt's eccentricities, making the emphatic opening of Fiordiligi's other big aria, *Come scoglio*, into a hushed meditation. There is no real weak link in the cast, but Harnoncourt's perverse tempi prevent a full recommendation for the complete set.

Don Giovanni (complete).

500♪ *** EMI CDS7 47260-8 (3) [Ang. CDCC 47260]. Waechter, Schwarzkopf, Sutherland, Alva, Frick, Sciutti, Taddei, Philh. Ch. & O, Giulini.

(M) **(*) Decca 448 973-2 (3) [id.]. Bacquier, Sutherland, Lorengar, Horne, Krenn, Gramm, Monreale, Grant, Amb. S., ECO, Bonynge.

** Telarc Dig. CD 80420 (3) [id.]. Skovhus, Corbelli, Brewer, Lott, Focile, Chiummo, Scottish Chamber Ch. and O, Mackerras.

** Accent Dig. ACC 99116/8 (3) [id.]. Van Mechelen, Claessens, Vink, Hogman, Argenta, Schäfer, Van der Kamp, La Petite Bande, Kuijken.

The classic Giulini/EMI recording sets the standard by which all other recordings have come to be judged. Elisabeth Schwarzkopf, as Elvira, emerges as a dominant figure to give a distinctive but totally apt slant to this endlessly invigorating drama. The young Sutherland may be relatively reticent as Anna but, with such technical ease and consistent beauty of tone, she makes a superb foil. Taddei is a delightful Leporello, and each member of the cast – including the young Cappuccilli as Masetto – combines fine singing with keen dramatic sense.

Richard Bonynge's reading of *Don Giovanni*, recorded in 1968 and originally dismissed as too lightweight, was in many ways ahead of its time, using a chamber orchestra, with plentiful appoggiaturas in the vocal lines, even if some *Andantes* are on the slow side. The Kingsway Hall recording vividly captures an ideal scale. Though the overture is rather underpowered, tension never lapses after that, and the cast is exceptionally strong, finer than in most modern versions. Sutherland is commanding as Donna Anna, even finer than for Giulini on EMI. Gabriel Bacquier, at his peak as the Don, makes a vigorous hero, with Donald Gramm a firm if sober-sided Leporello and Werner Krenn an outstanding, heady-toned Ottavio, while Clifford Grant sings with thrillingly black tone as the Commendatore. Pilar Lorengar, with a hint of flutter in the voice, is a vulnerable rather than a biting Elvira, while the choice of Marilyn Horne as a full mezzo Zerlina, strange by latterday standards, follows historic precedent, with the singer scaling her powerful voice down. A mid-priced set for more than Sutherland devotees.

Sir Charles Mackerras follows up his earlier recordings of Mozart operas with the Scottish Chamber Orchestra for Telarc with a vividly dramatic account of *Don Giovanni*, perfectly paced, with modern instruments echoing period practice. The teamwork is excellent but, individually, the casting is flawed. Bo Skovhus as Giovanni may be seductive in expression, but the sound too often grows woolly under pressure. Felicity Lott, as recorded, is in disappointing voice as Elvira, not nearly as sweet as usual; there is also too much acid in the soprano tones of Christine Brewer as Donna Anna, though Nuccia Focile makes a characterful Zerlina. Ambient recording, better controlled than in some previous issues in this series.

Sigiswald Kuijken's live recording with a well-matched Belgian team is marked by speeds more measured and closer to tradition than are usual in period performance. Textures are light and transparent, but the dramatic impact remains powerful – as at the very start of the overture – thanks to a wide-ranging recording. The snag for many will be that Kuijken uses the original Prague score, involving the omission of Ottavio's *Dalla sua pace* and – even more seriously – Elvira's *Mi tradi*, with no appendix included for those who want those favourite numbers. One misses *Mi tradi* the more when the Elvira of Christina Hogman brings the most satisfying singing in the set, with tone firm and full. As recorded, Nancy Argenta as Zerlina, charming as ever, sounds more grainy than usual, while Elena Vink's dramatic performance as Anna is marred by edginess under pressure. Werner van Mechelen's singing as Giovanni is not always well focused, fluttery at times, and the most striking of the men is Harry van der Kamp as the Commendatore.

Don Giovanni: highlights.

(B) ** Sony SBK 62663; *SBT 62663* [id.] (from complete set, with Raimondi, Moser, Te Kanawa, Berganza, Riegel, Van Dam, King, Paris Op. Ch. & O, Maazel).

This bargain Sony set of highlights generously (79 minutes) represents the performance which Lorin Maazel directed so strongly and urgently for the Losey film of the opera. An obvious strength is the line-up of three unusually firm basses: José van Dam a saturnine Leporello, Malcolm King a darkly intense

Masetto, and Ruggero Raimondi a heroic Giovanni. With Kiri Te Kanawa a radiant Elvira, the dramatic scale is certainly impressive, although neither Teresa Berganza as a mezzo Zerlina nor Edda Moser as Donna Anna matches her. Unfortunately the recording, made in a Paris church, has the voices close against background reverberation. However, the presentation is very good for a bargain CD with an excellent cued synopsis, and this is well worth its modest cost.

Die Entführung aus dem Serail (complete).

500♪ *** DG Dig. 435 857-2 (2) [id.]. Orgonasova, Sieden, Olsen, Peper, Hauptmann, Mineti, Monteverdi Ch., E. Bar. Soloists, Gardiner.

(M) *** Teldec/Warner Dig. 2292 42643-2 (2) [id.]. Kenny, Watson, Schreier, Gamlich, Salminen, Zurich Op. Ch. & Mozart O, Harnoncourt.

Gardiner's overture immediately establishes the extra zest of the performance, with wider dynamic contrasts, more body in the sound, and with more spring in the rhythm and a keener sense of fun. So Konstanze's great heroic aria, *Martern aller Arten*, has tremendous swagger; thanks also to glorious singing from Luba Orgonasova, at once rich, pure and agile, the close is triumphant; and in the other great aria, *Traurigkeit*, she is warmer too, less withdrawn. As Belmonte, Stanford Olsen for Gardiner is firm and agile, and though Cornelius Hauptmann, Gardiner's Osmin, lacks a really dark bass, he too is firm and characterful. Add to that a recording which gives a clearer idea of staging, and you have a version of *Entführung* to be recommended as first choice even for those who would not normally go for a period performance.

Harnoncourt's version establishes its uniqueness at the very start of the overture, tougher and more abrasive than any previous recording, with more primitive percussion effects than we are used to in his Turkish music. It is not a comfortable sound, compounded by Harnoncourt's often fast allegros, racing singers and players off their feet. Slow passages are often warmly expressive, but the stylishness of the soloists prevents them from seeming excessively romantic. The men are excellent: Peter Schreier singing charmingly, Wilfried Gamlich both bright and sweet of tone, Matti Salminen outstandingly characterful as an Osmin who, as well as singing with firm dark tone, points the words with fine menace. Yvonne Kenny as Constanze and Lillian Watson as Blonde sound on the shrill side, partly a question of microphones. Readers will note that this has now been reissued on two (instead of three) CDs, and at mid-price. There is also a highlights disc (75 minutes) on Teldec 0630 13811-9.

Idomeneo (complete).

500♪ ❁ *** DG Dig. 431 674-2 (3) [id.]. Rolfe Johnson, Von Otter, McNair, Martinpelto, Robson, Hauptmann, Monteverdi Choir, E. Bar. Soloists, Gardiner.

*** DG Dig. 447 737-2 (3) [id.]. Bartoli, Domingo, Vaness, Grant Murphy, Hampson, Lopardo, Terfel, Met. Op. Ch. & O, Levine.

(B) (**) DG mono 447 662-2 (3) [id.]. Kmentt, Haefliger, Grümmer, Lorengar, Capecchi, V. State Op. Ch., VPO, Fricsay.

With its exhilarating vigour and fine singing, Gardiner's aim has been to include all the material Mozart wrote for the original 1781 production, and he recommends the use of the CD programming device for listeners to select the version they prefer. Gardiner's Mozartian style is well sprung and subtly moulded rather than severe. The principals sing beautifully, notably Anne Sofie von Otter as Idamante and Sylvia McNair as Ilia, while Anthony Rolfe Johnson as Idomeneo is well suited here, with words finely projected. The electrifying singing of the Monteverdi Choir adds to the dramatic bite.

From the very opening of the overture it is clear what tense dramatic control James Levine has over this masterpiece of an *opera seria*, reflecting in the recording his experience in the opera house. It stands as his finest Mozart opera performance on disc. The superb sound helps, fuller and more vivid than in any previous recording, with the Met. Orchestra both stylish and incisive, and with woodwind principals outstanding. The text is roughly that of the Munich first performance, with Elettra given her culminating aria and Arbace both of his, and with recitatives given nearly complete – as satisfying and practical a solution to the textual problem as could be devised.

The cast is not just starry but stylish, with Plácido Domingo a commanding Idomeneo, giving a noble, finely controlled performance, which makes it a pity that the shorter version of his big aria, *Fuor del mar*, is preferred. Carol Vaness is a powerful, dramatic Elettra, well focused, and Cecilia Bartoli characterizes well as Idamante, wonderfully pure-toned in the Trio, while Heidi Grant Murphy is a charmingly girlish Ilia with a light, bright soprano. Completing this unrivalled team, you have Thomas Hampson as a superb Arbace and Bryn Terfel commanding in the brief solo given to the Oracle. The Met. chorus, like the orchestra, is incisively dramatic. John Eliot Gardiner's splendid DG Archiv set includes almost every textual alternative, but for those who prefer modern rather than period instruments and who fancy an exceptionally powerful line-up of soloists this is a clear choice.

Fricsay's live recording from the 1961 Salzburg Festival is intensely dramatic and offers some fine singing from such soloists as Elisabeth Grümmer as Elettra and Pilar Lorengar as Ilia. Sadly, Waldemar Kmentt is a strained Idomeneo and, worst of all, the Paumgartner text used by Fricsay is impossibly corrupt, with numbers cut, rearranged and altered. Having Idamante as a tenor remains a drawback too, even with Ernst Haefliger, and live recording involves varying balances and intrusive audience noises.

Idomeneo: highlights.

(M) **(*) Teldec/Warner 0630 15802-9 [id.] (from complete recording, with Hollweg, Trudeliese Schmidt, Yakar, Palmer, Equiluz, Tear, Estes, Zurich Opera Ch. & Mozart O, Harnoncourt).

Using a text very close to that of the Munich première of Mozart's great *opera seria*, and with the role of Idamante given to a soprano instead of being transposed down to tenor register, Harnoncourt presents a distinct view, one which in principle is preferable to general modern practice, and it is well worth sampling. This is hardly a performance to warm to, but it is refreshing and alive. The vocal cast is good, with Werner Hollweg a clear-toned, strong Idomeneo and Felicity Palmer finding the necessary contrasts of expression as Elettra. However, it is surprising that in an account which aims at authenticity, appoggiature are so rarely used. The selection runs to 72 minutes and the excellent documentation includes a translation.

Le nozze di Figaro (complete).

500♪ *** Decca Dig. 410 150-2 (3). Te Kanawa, Popp, Von Stade, Ramey, Allen, Moll, LPO & Ch., Solti.

500♪ ❁ (B) *** CfP CD-CFPD 4724; *TC-CFPD 4724* (2). Sciutti, Jurinac, Stevens, Bruscantini, Calabrese, Cuénod, Wallace, Sinclair, Glyndebourne Ch. & Festival O, Gui.

(M) (**(*)) EMI mono CHS5 66080-2 (3) [CDHC 66080]. Kunz, Seefried, Schwarzkopf, Schöffler, Gueden, V. State Op. Ch., VPO, Furtwängler.

Solti opts for a fair proportion of extreme speeds, but they underline the quintessential happiness of the entertainment. Samuel Ramey makes a virile Figaro, superbly matched to the most enchanting of Susannas on record, Lucia Popp, who gives a sparkling and radiant performance. Thomas Allen's Count is magnificent too. Frederica von Stade is a most attractive Cherubino, even if *Voi che sapete* is too slow; but crowning all is the Countess of Kiri Te Kanawa, challenged by Solti's spacious tempi in the two big arias, but producing ravishing tone, flawless phrasing and elegant ornamentation throughout. With superb, vivid recording this now makes a clear first choice for a much-recorded opera.

The effervescent 1955 stereo Glyndebourne recording makes a bargain without equal on only two CDs from CfP. Just as Sesto Bruscantini is the archetypal Glyndebourne Figaro, Sena Jurinac is the perfect Countess, with Graziella Sciutti a delectable Susanna and Risë Stevens a well-contrasted Cherubino, vivacious in their scenes together. Franco Calabrese as the Count is firm and virile. The only regret is that Hugues Cuénod's brilliant performance of Basilio's aria in Act IV has had to be omitted (as it so often is on stage) to keep the two discs each within the 80-minute limit. There is no libretto; instead a detailed synopsis is provided. But this set costs little more than a third of the price of the Decca/Solti version.

Furtwängler's vintage recording of *Figaro* from the Salzburg Festival was made by Austrian Radio in 1953, the only year when he conducted it there. Fascinatingly, at the conductor's insistence the performance is in German, reverting to the pre-war custom in Salzburg. It is a revelation to compare his reading of *Figaro* with Karajan's in the EMI studio recording made only a year earlier with the same orchestra, the Vienna Philharmonic, and with three of the same principals: Elisabeth Schwarzkopf as the Countess, Irmgard Seefried as Susanna and Erich Kunz as Figaro. Next to Furtwängler, Karajan – who recorded the opera without the secco recitatives – sounds stiff and plain, surprisingly lacking in humour. By contrast, many of Furtwängler's speeds are very broad though, even at their most extreme, there is always a lift to the rhythm to give Mozartian sparkle. The result is an exceptionally warm and relaxed reading, in which all the principals joyfully bring out the comedy, Kunz and Seefried above all. Schwarzkopf is in superb voice, rich and full, more creamy-toned than with Karajan, though her later performance on Giulini's 1959 recording is finest of all. Hilde Gueden as Cherubino and Paul Schoeffler as the Count are also most characterful, even if Schoeffler no longer sounds young. The snag is that, even with Basilio's and Marcellina's arias cut in the last act – as habitually they were in those days – the performance stretches to three CDs. Also, as with other EMI historic issues, no libretto is provided, just a detailed synopsis.

Le nozze di Figaro: highlights.

(M) *** EMI CDM5 66049-2 [id.] (from complete recording, with Schwarzkopf, Moffo, Cossotto, Taddei, Waechter, Philh. Ch. & O, cond. Giulini).

*** Teldec/Warner Dig. 0630 13808-9 [id.] (from complete recording, with Scharinger, Bonney, Margiono, Hampson, Lang, Moll, Langridge, Netherlands Op. Ch., Concg. O, Harnoncourt).

** DG Dig. 449 838-2 [id.] (from complete recording, with McNair, Gallo, Studer, Skovhus, Bartoli, V. State Op. Ch., VPO, Abbado).

The Giulini CD makes a clear first choice for a highlights CD from *Nozze di Figaro*. The selection may play for only 62½ minutes but every item is treasurable, not least *Non più andrai*, the Countess's two arias, and the long excerpt from the Act II finale. The new transfer is extremely vivid, and the synopsis relates the excerpts to the narrative.

Harnoncourt's *Nozze di Figaro* is relaxed and sparkling – one of his very best Mozart opera sets, with Barbara Bonney a charmingly provocative Susanna and Anton Scharinger a winning Figaro. Thomas Hampson proves a dominant Count and Charlotte Margiono a tenderly sweet Countess. The 76-minute selection of highlights (like the others in the Teldec series) comes with a full translation and can be recommended in its own right.

The DG alternative offers only 70 minutes and does not have a full translation, only a synopsis. It will primarily be of interest to admirers of Abbado, although his approach is unsparkling and curiously literal. The cast is young and uneven, with the women principals standing out.

Il rè pastore (complete).
** Teldec/Warner Dig. 4509 98419-2 (2) [id.]. Saccà, Murray, Mei, Nielsen, Schäfer, VCM, Harnoncourt.

Harnoncourt's set, in contrast with Sir Neville Marriner's outstanding version in the Philips Mozart series (422 535-2), offers a performance, recorded live in the Vienna Musikverein, using period instruments. Characteristically in Mozart opera, Harnoncourt takes a tough, vigorous view even of this unpretentious serenata, the last of Mozart's boyhood stage-works, pressing home allegros vigorously, with the horn and trumpet parts brightly brought out and with timpani added. This means that he misses the tenderness of such numbers as Agenore's first aria (where Marriner at a far slower tempo uses muted strings), though he relaxes for the most celebrated aria, Aminta's *L'amero*, beautifully sung by Ann Murray, the most characterful singer in the cast. Otherwise, the Marriner cast is preferable in every detail, with neither tenor – Roberto Saccà as Alessandro and Markus Schäfer as Agenore – stylish or agile enough. With its reverberation, the recording enhances the big-scale impression, with occasional audience noises intruding.

(i–v; viii) *Der Schauspieldirektor*. Concert arias: (ii; vii; ix) *Misera, dove son!, K.369; Un moto di gioia, K.579; Schon lacht der holde Frühling, K.580*. (i; vii; ix) *Vado, ma dove? oh Dei!, K.583; Bella mia fiamma, addio, K.529; Nehmt meinen Dank, ihr holden Gonner!* (iv; vi; x) *Die Entführung: Ha! Wie will ich triumpheren*. (v; viii) *Le nozze di Figaro: Overture*.
(M) *** Decca Dig. 452 624-2 [id.]. (i) Te Kanawa, (ii) Gruberová, (iii) Heilmann, (iv) Jungwirth; (v) VPO; (vi) V. Haydn O; (vii) V. CO; (viii) Pritchard; (ix) Fischer; (x) Kertész.

This Decca recording of the four musical numbers from *Der Schauspieldirektor* (presented 'dry' with no German dialogue) was made only six months before Sir John Pritchard died, an apt last offering from him, a great Mozartian. Having two such well-contrasted star sopranos adds point to the contest, and the performances are a delight, though the recorded sound is not as well focused as usual from this source. The *Figaro overture*, also conducted by Pritchard, is another completely new item. The rest is reissue material, with three concert arias each from Gruberová and Dame Kiri, taken from Decca's 1981 boxed set of the collected arias. Manfred Jungwirth's bitingly dark account of Osmin's aria from *Entführung* dates from ten years before that, a welcome extra. The single mid-priced disc comes with full translations and note and the reissue is something of a bargain.

Die Zauberflöte (complete).
500♪ *** Ph. Dig. 426 276-2 (2) [id.]. Te Kanawa, Studer, Lind, Araiza, Bär, Ramey, Van Dam, Amb. Op. Ch., ASMF, Marriner.
*** DG Dig. 449 166-2 (2); Video VHS 072 447-3 [id.]. Oelze, Schade, Sieden, Peeters, Finley, Backes, Monteverdi Ch., E. Bar. Soloists, Gardiner.
(M) **(*) DG Originals 449 749-2 (2) [id.]. Lear, Peters, Wunderlich, Fischer-Dieskau, Crass, Hotter, BPO, Boehm.
(B) (***) Dutton mono 2CDEA 5011 (2) [id.]. Lemnitz, Roswaenge, Hüsch, Berger, Strienz, BPO, Beecham.
(B) ** Decca Double 448 734-2 (2) [id.]. Gueden, Lipp, Simoneau, Berry, Böhme, V. State Op. Ch., VPO, Karl Boehm.

Marriner directs a pointed and elegant reading of *Zauberflöte*, bringing out the fun of the piece, and the cast is the finest in any modern recording. Dame Kiri lightens her voice delightfully, while Olaf Bär, vividly characterful, brings the Lieder-singer's art to the role of Papageno. Araiza's performance is subtle and conveys much feeling. Cheryl Studer as Queen of the Night is easily the finest among modern recordings; and Samuel Ramey gives a generous and wise portrait of Sarastro. This is now the finest digital version, superbly recorded.

John Eliot Gardiner rounds off his outstanding series for DG Archiv of Mozart's seven great mature operas with an electrifying account of *Zauberflöte*. In almost every way it surpasses even the finest period-performance rivals, even though the generally inspired casting is marred by the underpowered and uneven Sarastro of Harry Peeters. The recording was made in studio conditions over the same period as staged performances at the Ludwigsburg Festival, getting the best of both worlds. William Christie in his Erato version, based similarly on live festival performances, is more relaxed in his approach, bringing out more fun in the piece, but Gardiner, at once more daring in his choice of speeds, both fast and slow, finds more depth, drawing more polished and incisive playing from his English Baroque Soloists. One can appreciate far more clearly in this bigger-scale view the other essential elements in Mozart and Schikaneder's complex entertainment, not just an allegory involving masonic ritual, but above all an intensely human quest, with the plight of the heroine, Pamina, involving us if anything even more than that of the hero, Tamino.

In this Gardiner is helped enormously by his choice of singer as Pamina, a young German soprano with a ravishingly pure and sweet voice, flawlessly controlled, Christiane Oelze. [In the agonized Act II aria, *Ach, ich fühl's*, she conveys a depth of emotion rarely matched. Also superb is the American soprano who takes the role of Queen of the Night. With a voice as full and silvery as it is flexible, Cyndia Sieden has none of the tinkly shallowness of many coloraturas, while the Tamino of Michael Schade has youthful freshness combined with keen imagination; though there are more characterful Papagenos than Gerald Finley, few sing as freshly and cleanly as he. With recording clear and well balanced, the set offers an incidental practical advantage in putting the spoken dialogue on separate tracks, so that it can readily be programmed out. Recommended strongly alongside Marriner's modern-instrument version.

One of the glories of Boehm's DG set is the singing of Fritz Wunderlich as Tamino, a wonderful memorial to a singer much missed. Fischer-Dieskau, with characteristic word-pointing, makes a sparkling Papageno on record and Franz Crass is a satisfyingly straightforward Sarastro. The team of women is well below this standard – Lear taxed cruelly in *Ach, ich fühl's*, Peters shrill in the upper register (although the effect is exciting), and the Three Ladies do not blend well – but Boehm's direction is superb, light and lyrical, but weighty where necessary to make a glowing, compelling experience. Fine recording, enhanced in this new transfer for reissue as one of DG's 'Originals'. It is now divested of its previous coupling of *Der Schauspieldiretor* and fitted on to two instead of three CDs.

Beecham's magical pre-war set of *Zauberflöte* has had three earlier CD transfers, all of them seriously flawed, which makes it specially welcome that Mike Dutton comes up with a transfer which at last does justice to the original sound, full and vivid; and the two discs are offered at bargain price. There is glorious singing from Tiana Lemnitz as Pamina, brilliant coloratura from Erna Berger as Queen of the Night, and sharp characterization from Gerhard Hüsch as Papageno. Helge Roswaenge is a Germanic Tamino and Wilhelm Strienz a firm but lugubrious Sarastro. No spoken dialogue, but much warmth and sparkle.

The principal attraction of this Decca reissue from the earliest days of stereo, apart from its modest cost, is the conducting of Karl Boehm. With surprisingly good recording quality (vintage 1955), vivid, warm and full in the bass, that might well be counted recommendation enough, in spite of the absence of dialogue, particularly when the Tamino of Léopold Simoneau and the Papageno of Walter Berry are strongly and sensitively sung. But the rest of the singing is variable, with Hilde Gueden a pert, characterful Pamina, unhappy in the florid divisions, and Wilma Lipp an impressive Queen of the Night, but Kurt Böhme a gritty and ungracious Sarastro. For its age the sound is remarkably atmospheric. No libretto/ translation is provided, but there is a good synopsis, and it is a pity that it is not cued.

Arias: *Artaserse: Per pietà, bell'idol mio. Il barbiere di Siviglia: Schon lacht der holde Frühling* (arr. BEYER). *Demofoonte: Se tutti i mali miei. Didone abbandonata: Basta, vincesti . . . Ah, non lasciarmi. I due baroni di Rocca Azzura: Alma grande e nobil core. A questo seno deh vieni . . . Or che il cielo a me ti rende. Ezio: Misera, dove son? . . . Ah! non son io che parlo. Le nozze di Dorina: Voi avete un cor fedele. Le nozze di Figaro: Un moto di gioia*. Arias from: *Der Schauspieldirektor; Die Entführung aus dem Serail.*

(M) *** Decca Analogue/Dig. 448 249-2 [id.]. Edita Gruberová, VCO, Fischer.

This collection comes from a box, covering all the Mozart arias and concert arias for soprano, which first appeared at the beginning of the 1980s. It brings brilliant and charming performances from Gruberová, full of sparkle and character, and superbly articulated. Among the other rare items it includes an alternative aria for Susanna in *Figaro*, *Un moto di gioia*. The excerpts from *Der Schauspieldirektor* and *Die Entführung* come from much later but are also impressively sung.

Arias from: *Don Giovanni; Die Entführung aus dem Serail; La finta giardiniera; Il rè pastore; Le nozze di Figaro; Il sogno di Scipione; Die Zauberflöte. Concert aria: Nehmt meinen Dank.*
*** Decca Dig. 452 602-2 [id.]. Renée Fleming, O of St Luke's, Mackerras.

Renée Fleming has rarely sounded quite so beautiful on disc as in this wide-ranging collection of Mozart arias, one of the finest available. If it is disappointing not to have her singing the role of the Countess in *Figaro*, the two Susanna items are both welcome – *Deh vieni* bringing out her most golden tone and the big alternative aria, *Al desio*, challenging her to her most brilliant singing. Her account of La Fortuna's aria from *Il sogno di Scipione* is commanding too, and her ornamentation is phenomenally crisp and brilliant throughout, not least in *Ach ich liebte* from *Entführung*. The only reservations come with the brisk treatment, period-style, of Pamina's *Ach, ich fühl's* and the lovely aria from *Zaïde*, both of which could be much more tenderly expressive. Excellent, stylish accompaniment and first-rate recording.

Muldowney, Dominic (born 1952)

(i) *Piano concerto;* (ii) *Saxophone concerto*.
(M) *** EMI CDM5 66528-2 [id.]. (i) Peter Donohoe, BBC SO, Mark Elder; (ii) John Harle, L. Sinf., Diego Masson.

Dominic Muldowney, born in 1952 and music director at the National Theatre since 1976, has latterly become a composer laudably concerned with direct communication to a wide range of listeners. These two colourful and dramatic concertos are excellent examples of his more recent style, far more approachable than his earlier work. His *Piano concerto* is a formidable work in a continuous half-hour span of many different sections. It uses Bachian forms, along with tough Bachian piano figuration, to move kaleidoscopically in a kind of musical collage of references to different genres, including jazz and the popular waltz. With Peter Donohoe giving one of his finest performances on record, and with colourful playing from the BBC Symphony Orchestra under Mark Elder, the piece emerges powerfully, with occasional gruff echoes of Hindemith. The *Saxophone concerto* (written for the outstanding virtuoso of the instrument, John Harle, who plays it on the record) is a more compact, strongly characterized work in three movements, each throwing up a grateful number of warm, easy tunes without any sense of compromise or incongruity. Warm, well-balanced recording.

Mussorgsky, Modest (1839–81)

The Capture of Kars (Triumphal march); St John's night on the bare mountain (original score); *Scherzo in B flat. Khovanshchina: Prelude to Act I;* (i) *Introduction to Act IV. The Destruction of Sennacherib.* (i; ii) *Joshua.* (i) *Oedipus in Athens: Temple chorus. Salammbô: Priestesses' chorus* (operatic excerpts all orch. Rimsky-Korsakov).
500♪ ❁ (M) *** RCA 09026 61354-2 [id.]. (i) London Symphony Ch.; (ii) Zehava Gal; LSO, Abbado.

The *Khovanshchina Prelude*, very beautifully played indeed, is well enough known, but it is good to have so vital and pungent an account of the original version of *Night on the bare mountain*. Best of all are the four choral pieces; they are immediately attractive and very Russian in feeling. The recording is first rate. This is one of the most attractive Mussorgsky records in the catalogue.

Night on the bare mountain; Khovanshchina: Prelude (both arr. Rimsky-Korsakov).
(BB) *** Belart 450 017-2. LSO, Solti – GLINKA: *Ruslan and Ludmilla: overture* *** ❁; BORODIN: *Prince Igor:* excerpts. ***

Solti's *Night on the bare mountain* can stand up to all the competition in its vintage (1967) recording with its fine amplitude and great brilliance. This remains one of Solti's finest analogue recordings, offering also the highly atmospheric *Khovanshchina Prelude*, which is beautifully played.

Night on the bare mountain (trans. Tchernov).
500♪ ❁ *** Teldec/Warner Dig. 4509 96516-2 [id.]. Boris Berezovsky – BALAKIREV: *Islamey*. *** ❁

This remarkable transcription by Konstantin Tchernov sounds hardly less dazzling in Berezovsky's hands than the outstanding *Islamey* with which it is coupled. The engineers capture very good piano-sound.

(i) *Night on the bare mountain* (arr. Rimsky-Korsakov); (ii) *Pictures at an exhibition* (orch. Ravel).
500♪ *** DG Dig. 429 785-2 [id.]. NYPO, Sinopoli – RAVEL: *Valses nobles et sentimentales*. **(*)

Sinopoli's electrifying New York recording of Mussorgsky's *Pictures at an exhibition* not only heads the list of modern digital versions but also it again displays the New York Philharmonic as one of the world's great orchestras, performing with an epic virtuosity and panache that recall the Bernstein era of the 1960s. *A Night on the bare mountain* is comparably vibrant, with the Rimskian fanfares particularly vivid and the closing pages full of Russian nostalgia.

A night on the bare mountain; Pictures at an exhibition; Khovanshchina, Act IV: Entr'acte. Boris Godunov: symphonic synthesis (all arr. and orch. Stokowski).
*** Chandos Dig. CHAN 9445 [id.]. BBC PO, Matthias Bamert.

These highly characteristic transcriptions all come from the peak period of Stokowski's association with the great orchestra he helped to create in Philadelphia. The skilfully tailored 24-minute *Boris Godunov* synthesis dates from November 1936, the *Pictures from an exhibition* from 1939, and *Night on bald mountain* (the correct title, and nearer the original Russian meaning) was scored for Disney in 1940. Anyone who has seen *Fantasia* will find the music indelibly associated with the imagery of the film, and the spectacularly plangent orchestration (especially the highly individual use of the percussion) is in many respects nearer to Mussorgsky's *St John's night on the bare mountain* than the Rimsky version, with Rimsky's interpolated brass fanfares omitted. Thus Mussorgsky's satanic conception makes a spectacularly sinister impact, with the coda by contrast sumptuously romantic. (One wonders why Matthias Bamert chose not to tack on Schubert's *Ave Maria*, as Stokowski did for the film.) The sombre power of the operatic synthesis from *Boris Godunov*, with its Kremlin bells and chanting monks, and the haunted portrait of Boris himself, are also gripping, while the *Entr'acte* from *Khovanshchina* is even finer, one of Stokowski's most telling transcriptions, rich in its sonorities and played very tellingly under Bamert. We like the vividness of Stokowski's *Pictures* too, particularly the way in which the the unison horns swell out vocally near the climax of *Bydlo*, while to choose a cor anglais for the main theme in *The old castle* is every bit as telling as Ravel's saxophone, perhaps more so. Not surprisingly, Stokowski scores for the violins rather more readily than Ravel, as instanced by the opening *Promenade*. The one moment when Ravel's orchestration is truly inspired is the interchange between *Goldenberg and Schmuyle*; Stokowski has the solo trumpet echoed by the woodwind and the effect is mockingly bizarre, but less bleatingly obsequious than Ravel's version. However, the *Catacombs* sequence makes a sumptuously weighty impact, and *Baba-Yaga* is grotesquely pointed with imaginative orchestral comments. Two numbers are omitted: *Tuileries* and *Limoges*; according to Edward Johnson's authoritative notes, Stokowski considered them 'too French' and 'not Mussorgskian'. *The Great Gate of Kiev*, massively scored, including tolling bells and organ, makes a huge final apotheosis. In all, this record is a great success, for the Chandos sound is fully worthy and would surely have delighted the old orchestral magician with its richness of amplitude – the effect far preferable to the somewhat bloated Phase 4 quality of Stokowski's own earlier recordings for Decca.

Pictures at an exhibition (orch. Ravel).
500♪ ✿ (M) *** RCA 09026 61401-2 [id.]. Chicago SO, Fritz Reiner – RESPIGHI: *The Fountains of Rome; The Pines of Rome*. *** ✿
(M) (***) Mercury mono 434 378-2 [id.]. Chicago SO, Rafael Kubelik – BARTOK: *Music for strings, percussion and celesta*. (***)

Reiner's 1957 Chicago performance brings the advantage of the rich acoustics of Symphony Hall. The finale climax of *The Great Gate of Kiev* shows the concentration of the playing. The remastering is fully worthy, and there is excellent documentation.

Kubelik's famous (1951) mono version of Ravel's masterly scoring was the Mercury recording which coined the term (and subsequent trademark) 'Living presence', taken from Howard Taubman's review in *The New York Times*. The realism of the recording (in spite of some thinness in the top range of the strings) still has the power to astonish. It is most naturally balanced and, although without the additional illumination of stereo, still conveys much of the splendid acoustic of Chicago's Orchestral Hall. The success of the record is not just technical, but musical too. The performance has great freshness with not a hint of routine anywhere; there are many subtleties, particularly as one picture or promenade is dovetailed into another. The melancholy of *The old castle* is touchingly caught and the tuba solo of *Bydlo* is similarly dolorous, even if the playing here is slightly below par technically, while the musical portrayal of Samuel Goldenberg is made to seem peculiarly Hebraic. The orchestral virtuosity in *Tuileries*, *Limoges* and the *Chicks' ballet* is not overt but has a Ravelian delicacy; similarly, the central section of *Baba Yaga* has a gently sinister quality that is very telling. The brass at the climax of *The Great Gate of Kiev* is splendid; if the tam tam does not come through in the way it does on the equally famous Telarc stereo record, the majesty of the dénoucment is very tangible.

Pictures at an exhibition (original piano version).
500♪ ❁ *** Virgin/EMI Dig. VC7 59611-2 [id.]. Mikhail Pletnev – TCHAIKOVSKY: *Sleeping Beauty*: excerpts. *** ❁
* DG Dig. 437 667-2 [id.]. Ivo Pogorelich – RAVEL: *Valses nobles et sentimentales*. *

Pletnev's account is easily the most commanding to have appeared since Richter, a re-creation rather than a performance. Pletnev does not hesitate to modify the odd letter of the score in order to come closer to its spirit. *The Great Gate of Kiev* is extraordinarily rich in colour. An altogether outstanding issue.

Pogorelich's version is for the most dedicated admirers of the pianist only. There is abundant pianistic skill and some considerable imagination in the handling of keyboard colour, but this artist's posturing is insupportable. No challenge to existing recommendations.

The Complete Songs.
500♪ ❁ (M) (***) EMI mono CHS7 63025-2 (3) [Ang. CHS 63025]. Boris Christoff, Alexandre Labinsky, Gerald Moore, French R. & TV O, Georges Tzipine.

The Mussorgsky songs constitute a complete world in themselves, and they cast a strong spell: their range is enormous and their insight into the human condition deep. Christoff was at the height of his vocal powers when he made the set with Alexandre Labinsky, his accompanist in most of the songs; and its return to circulation cannot be too warmly welcomed. This was the first complete survey, and it still remains the only really recommendable set.

Song-cycles: *The Nursery; Songs and dances of death*. Songs: *Darling Savishna; Forgotten; The He-Goat; The Puppet-show; Mephistopheles' Song of the flea*.
500♪ ❁ *** Conifer Dig. 7605 51229-2 [id.]. Sergei Leiferkus, Semion Skigin.

These are impressive performances; not only does Sergei Leiferkus make a beautiful sound, but his singing has immense character and power. He seems to command an unlimited range of colour and to be able to draw forth all the drama and variety of vocal timbre these songs demand. In Semion Skigin he has a pianist of commanding dramatic talent and, at the same time, exemplary restraint.

Song-cycles: *The Nursery; Sunless; Songs and dances of Death*. Songs: *Gopak; Hebrew song; Song of the flea*.
*** Sony Dig. SK 66858 [id.] Marjana Lipovšek, Graham Johnson.

Marjana Lipovšek always imparts intensity and meaning to the music she sings. (Her account of Frank Martin's *Die Weise von Liebe und Tod des Cornet Christoph Rilke* remains one of the most haunting and moving of all recordings of twentieth-century song-cycles.) Her mezzo has a sumptuous yet subtle quality, and the rapport between her and partner, Graham Johnson, is close. His playing is of the highest imaginative order. Although *The Nursery* has been recorded by a number of female singers (Galina Vishnevskaya, Margaret Price and others), the bulk of the songs on this disc fall within the preserve of the male singer. Yet even if you are collecting Sergei Leiferkus's magisterial survey of the complete songs on Conifer, this recital is still well worth your attention. Lipovšek brings special musical and poetic insights to all this repertoire; her range of colour and sonority is impressively wide, and she and Johnson remain admirably free of the constraints of the bar line. In a word, their interpretations aspire to the quality of a pitched poetic speech. The recording has plenty of bloom, and the balance between singer and pianist is very natural. A lovely recital.

Boris Godunov (original version; complete).
500♪ *** Sony Dig. S3K 58977 (3) [id.]. Kotcherga, Leiferkus, Lipovšek, Ramey, Nikolsky, Langridge, Slovak Philharmonic Ch., Bratislava, Tölz Boys' Ch., Berlin RSO, Abbado.

In Claudio Abbado's performance the urgency of the composer's inspiration is conveyed as never before on disc, without reducing the epic scale of the work or its ominously dark colouring. Vocally, the performance centres on the glorious singing of Anatoly Kotcherga as Boris. Rarely has this music been sung with such firmness and beauty as here and, so far from losing out dramatically compared with rivals who resort to *parlando* effects for emphasis, the performance gains in intensity. The other principal basses, Samuel Ramey as the monk, Pimen, and Gleb Nikolsky as Varlaam, are well contrasted. The tenor, Sergei Larin, sings with beauty and clarity up to the highest register as the Pretender, while Marjana Lipovšek is a formidably characterful Marina, if not quite as well focused as usual. Having Philip Langridge as Shuisky and Sergei Leiferkus as Rangoni reinforces the starry strength of the team. The sound is spacious, full and glowing.

Boris Godunov: highlights.
(M) ** Erato/Warner Dig. 0630 13812-9 [id.] (from complete recording, with Raimondi, Polozov, Vishnevskaya, Plishka, Tesarowicz, Riegel, Gedda, Washington Ch. Arts Soc. & Ontario Soc. Nat. SO, Rostropovich).

Recorded live in Washington, Rostropovich's recording, using Mussorgsky's original score unadulterated by Rimsky-Korsakov, sounds very much like what it is: a well-drilled concert performance with some fine choral singing. This perhaps matters less on a highlights CD, and Raimondi's warmly Italianate voice in the name-part brings out the lyricism of the lines more often barked or grunted. But although Boris's death scene is wonderfully controlled in hushed intensity, the Tsar's inner agony is missing. The Coronation scene, too, lacks something in weight. The documentation includes a translation without the original Russian, a sensible enough decision.

Mysliveček, Josef (1737–81)

Octets Nos. 1 in E flat; 2 in E flat; 3 in B flat.
**(*) EMI Dig. CDC5 55512-2 [id.]. Sabine Meyer Wind Ens. – DVORAK: *Serenade in D min.* **(*)

The Sabine Meyer Wind Ensemble offer three charming *Octets* by Mysliveček as their fill-up to an eminently satisfying if laid-back account of the Dvořák *Wind serenade*. Too many claims should not be made for this music, which is of no great substance but is nevertheless genuinely charming, particularly in the slow movements. The excellent, well-balanced EMI recording makes for pleasurable listening.

Nielsen, Carl (1865–1931)

Aladdin (suite); *A fantasy-journey to the Færoes* (rhapsodic overture); *Helios Overture; Maskarade: Overture; Prelude to Act II, Dance of the cockerels. Pan and Syrinx; Saga-drøm.*
*** DG Dig. 447 757-2 [id.]. Gothenburg SO, Järvi.

Of the anthologies of Nielsen's orchestral music other than the symphonies, this is now the best on offer. The performances are vital and affectionate, with the orchestra playing with their usual finesse and enthusiasm. Both *Pan and Syrinx* and *Saga-drøm* are atmospheric. Two minor reservations: the *Helios Overture* is too swiftly paced (the sun rises over the Aegean in fast-forward mode). The recording is very fine indeed, though comparison of the *Aladdin suite* which the same orchestra and recording team made in the early 1980s reveals an even greater warmth and expansiveness alongside the rest of the programme.

At the bier of a young artist; Little suite for strings, Op. 1.
*** Virgin/EMI Dig. VC5 45224-2. Norwegian CO, Iona Brown – GRIEG: *At the cradle* etc. ***

The Norwegian Chamber Orchestra are an excellent group and their account of Nielsen's first opus, the *Little suite for strings*, is about the best in the catalogue. His moving elegy, the *Andante lamentoso* (*At the bier of a young artist*) is equally eloquent in their hands. The recording, made in the glorious acoustic of Eidsvoll Church in Norway, is very real and tangible. Very strongly recommended.

Violin concerto, Op.33.
500♪ ❀ *** Sony Dig. SK 44548 [id.]. Cho-Liang Lin, Swedish RSO, Salonen – SIBELIUS: *Violin concerto.* *** ❀
* Teldec/Warner Dig. 0630 13161-2 [id.]. Maxim Vengerov, Chicago SO, Barenboim – SIBELIUS: *Violin concerto.* *

Cho-Liang Lin brings as much authority to Nielsen's *Concerto* as he does to the Sibelius. His perfect intonation and tonal purity excite admiration, but so should his command of the architecture of this piece. Salonen is supportive here and gets good playing from the Swedish Radio Symphony Orchestra.

If dazzling technique were all that counted, Vengerov's performance would score top rating. This artist can certainly play the violin! But musically this is all far too self-aware and narcissistic. It does not come anywhere near the touching freshness and innocence of Nielsen's inspiration and in no way challenges Cho-Liang Lin on Sony.

Symphonies Nos. (i) *1 in G min., Op. 7;* (ii) *2 (Four Temperaments), Op. 16;* (iii) *3 (Sinfonia espansiva), Op. 27;4 (Inextinguishable), Op. 29;* (i) *5, Op. 50;* (iii) *6 (Sinfonia semplice).*
500♪ *** Decca Dig. 443 117-2 (3) [id.]. San Francisco SO, Blomstedt (with Kromm, McMillan in No. 3).

Blomstedt's complete Decca set appears at a modest discount and is pretty well self-recommending. All six are among the finest available, and the reservation concerning No. 6, where a broader tempo would have helped generate greater evocation in the opening movement, is relatively insignificant against the overall success of this series.

Symphony No. 1 in G min., Op. 7.
*(*) Classico Dig. CLASSCD 115 [id.]. Copenhagen PO, Okko Kamu – SIBELIUS: *Symphony No. 7*. *(*)

Taken on its merits, this is a very well-played account, and very decently recorded into the bargain. Kamu's reading stands up well to its rivals – and, to go no further than his countrymen Berglund and Salonen, his conception of the symphony to be preferred. But at full price and 52 minutes' duration, however, this is an uneconomic buy. Those who want one Nielsen symphony are more likely to want another rather than the Sibelius, which is less impressive. Decent recording.

(i) *Symphonies Nos. 1 in G min., Op. 7; 5, Op. 50;* (ii) *Helios overture, Op. 17.*
500♪ ❁ (M) (***) Dutton Lab. mono CDLXT 2502 [id.]. Danish State RSO; (i) Thomas Jensen; (ii) Erik Tuxen.

These are exemplary transfers of the première recording of the *First Symphony* and the first LP recordings of the *Fifth* and the *Helios Overture*. Jensen and Tuxen both played under Nielsen, and their performances have a special authenticity. The quality of these Decca recordings is captured with absolute fidelity in these stunning transfers. An indispensable issue that belongs in every Nielsen collection.

Symphonies Nos. (i) *2 (The Four Temperaments);* (ii) *4 (Inextinguishable).*
❁ (***) Dutton Lab. mono CDCLP4001 [id.]. Danish State RSO; (i) Thomas Jensen; (ii) Launy Grøndahl.

Both Launy Grøndahl and Thomas Jensen played under Nielsen, and the latter had an exceptionally good feeling for Nielsen's tempi. The *Second Symphony* (*The Four Temperaments*) was the first Nielsen symphony to be recorded and dates from 1947. (An earlier version by the same forces was made in 1944 but for some reason it was never released.) The *Fourth*, recorded in 1951, under Launy Grøndahl has the ring of authenticity that communicates immediately. Its fire and temperament remain undimmed and unsurpassed to this day. The Dutton transfers do full justice to these masters: the Grøndahl comes from tape and the Jensen from shellac discs. Neither has ever sounded better. An essential element in any Nielsen collection.

Symphony No. 4 (Inextinguishable), Op. 29.
(B) **(*) BBC Radio Classics 15656 91882 [id.]. Hallé O, Sir John Barbirolli – SIBELIUS: *Symphony No. 5*. **(*)

Sir John Barbirolli's account with the Hallé Orchestra comes from a (1965) Promenade Concert during Nielsen's centenary year. Sir John recorded the *Fourth* for Pye in 1959, but this is far more satisfactory in every way, certainly as far as the sound is concerned. It has warmth and body, though it is naturally not as wide-ranging or transparent as a modern recording; but most readers should find it very serviceable. The notes quote a review of a 1959 Barbirolli concert performance: 'the whole frame of the symphony quivers with the vigour which propels it'. Newspapers' music critics wrote well in those days, and this verdict is certainly on target.

Symphony No. 4 (Inextinguishable), Op. 29; Little suite for strings, Op. 1; (i) *Hymnus amoris.*
*** Decca Dig. 452 486-2 [id.]. Danish Nat. RSO, Ulf Schirmer; (i) with Barbara Bonney, John Mark Ainsley, Lars Pedersen, Michael Hansen, Danish Nat. R. Ch., Copenhagen Boys' Ch.

Ulf Schirmer shows a natural affinity for Nielsen and turns in an intensely felt and freshly thought-out account of Nielsen's *Fourth Symphony*. He occasionally emphasizes *ritardandi* markings, but these are rarely intrusive and readers can be assured that his performance has the ring of conviction. The Danish National Radio Orchestra play very well for him, and they are excellently recorded too. Some may find the dynamics rather extreme, though this will not worry those with high-grade, wide-ranging equipment. The very top is a bit overlit and hard but is easily tamed. The recording quality is not as refined as the Neeme Järvi/Gothenburg (DG) or Stockholm/Rozhdestvensky (Chandos), but the performance is more characterful. Indeed it is the most enjoyable version of the work since Blomstedt's San Francisco version on the same label. Instead of another symphony, Schirmer gives us Nielsen's early cantata, *Hymnus amoris*, composed between the *First* and *Second Symphonies*, one of his warmest and most open-hearted scores. It gets a good performance and recording, with excellent and responsive singing from the distinguished soloists, and there is a persuasive account of Nielsen's first published opus, the endearing *Little suite for strings*. Eminently recommendable for those who feel attracted by this particular coupling.

CHAMBER MUSIC

(i) *Duet in A for two violins;* (ii) *Fantasistykke for clarinet and piano;* (iii; iv) *Piano trio in G;* (v) *String quartet in D min.;* (iii) *Violin sonata in G min. (1881–2);* (vi) *Polka.*

** Kontrapunkt Dig. 32231 [id.]. (i) Bjarne Hansen, Peder Elbæk; (ii) Asger Bondo, Rosalind Bevan; (iii) Hansen, Bevan; (iv) Svend Winsløw; (v) Carl Nielsen Qt; (vi) Fünen Trio.

The manuscripts of Nielsen's juvenilia were all deposited in the Royal Library, Copenhagen, and while there is abundant evidence of musical talent there is nothing that is remotely individual. The *Quartet in D minor* was the student piece he took with him to show Gade and which gained him entrance to the Copenhagen Conservatoire. The *Piano trio*, his only attempt at the medium, and the *Violin sonata* are also completely derivative. The disc also includes a few bars of the very earliest fragment, a piece of dance music written when he was nine. The performances are very good and so, too, is the recording; but this is only for those with a specialized interest in Nielsen. The composer would probably be horrified at the thought that these sketches were in the public domain.

Wind quintet, Op. 43.

(BB) ** Naxos Dig. 8.553050 [id.]. Oslo Wind Ens. – FERNSTROM; KVANDAL: *Wind quintets.* **

A very good account of the *Wind quintet* from these Oslo players, recorded in a rather small Norwegian Radio studio. The sound is bright and forward. It does not displace either the Sony digital version by the Vienna/Berlin Ensemble (SK 45996) or the mid-priced Melos performance (coupled with the Janáček *Concertino* and *Mládi* on EMI CDM5 65304-2) but is worth the asking price. Neither of the couplings is of comparable stature, but those with a taste for music off the beaten track will doubtless welcome them.

Piano and organ music. (i) *Chaconne, Op. 32;* (ii) *Commotio;* (iii) *Festival prelude;* (iv) *Humoresque-Bagatelles, Op. 11;* (iii) *Little preludes for organ;* (v) *Piano music for young and old;* (iv) *5 Piano pieces, Op. 3;* (vi) *Suite, Op. 45;* (viii) *Symphonic suite, Op. 11;* (vi) *Theme and variations, Op. 40; Three pieces, Op. 59.*

(**) Danacord mono DACOCD 363/64 (2) [id.]. (i) France Ellegaard; (ii) Finn Viderø; (iii) Niels Otto Raasted, Grethe Krogh; (iv) Galina Werschenska; (v) Eyvind Møller; (vi) Arne Skjold Rasmussen; (vii) Hermann D. Koppel.

This pair of discs restores to circulation many performances that are of more than merely documentary or historical interest. The earliest performances are by the Russian-born pianist, Galina Werschenska, a pupil of Glazunov who settled in Denmark in 1930 and whose sensitive accounts of the Opp. 3 and 11 pieces were made in 1937 and 1945 respectively. The latter, oddly enough, sounds less fresh than the former. France Ellegaard's early Decca LP of the *Chaconne* is finely played, dynamic nuances are scrupulously observed and there is a pleasing spontaneity. Perhaps the greatest interest attaches to Arne Skjold Rasmussen's recordings of the *Suite*, Op. 45, originally called *Suite luciferique* after the bearer of light and not the prince of darkness, the noble *Theme and variations*, Op. 40, and the radical *Three pieces*, Op. 59, of his last years. All these come from 1952–3 and so are not to be confused with the three-LP set that Skjold Rasmussen made by Fona in Scandinavia and Vox Turnabout in the 1960s. Skjold Rasmussen has almost unique authority in this area. Less impressive, perhaps, is Finn Viderø's 1960 live performance of *Commotio*, recorded at Batell Chapel, Yale, which does not make as strong an impact as the première recording by Georg Fjelrad or Grethe Krogh's 1965 account. All the same this is a set that will interest Nielsen lovers with a sense of historical perspective and it forms a useful appendix to Leif Ove Andsnes's splendid Virgin CD (see below).

Chaconne, Op. 32; Humoresque-bagatelles, Op. 11; 5 Pieces, Op. 3; 3 Pieces, Op. 59; Suite luciferique, Op. 45.

500♪ ❁ *** Virgin/EMI Dig. VC5 45129-2 [id.]. Leif Ove Andsnes.

This music is quite wonderful; the early pieces have great charm and the later *Suite* and the *Three Pieces*, Op. 59, great substance. Now at last they have found a princely interpreter in the Norwegian, Leif Ove Andsnes. Indeed these are performances of eloquence and nobility that are unlikely to be surpassed for some years to come.

VOCAL MUSIC

Hymnus Amoris, Op. 12 (1896–7); Sleep, Op. 18 (1903–4).

(M) ** EMI CDM5 66000-2 [id.]. Kirsten Schulz, Bodil Gøbil, Tonny Landy, Bent Norup, Mogens Schmidt Johansen, Hans Christian Andersen, Copenhagen Boys' Ch., Danish RSO, Mogens Wöldike – GADE: *Forårs-fantasi.* **

Neither of these lovely cantatas is otherwise available at mid-price and both are eminently worth acquiring.

These finely shaped performances were recorded by these artists and Mogens Wöldike in 1977 when he was in his eighties, but they still have an appealing freshness. Neither is superior to the Chandos accounts listed in our main edition, which also offer *Springtime on Fünen* and the late *Motets*, Op. 55; but for readers who have neither of those, this would make a perfectly acceptable buy.

Saul and David (complete).
500♪ ❀ *** Chandos Dig. CHAN 8911/12 [id.]. Haugland, Lindroos, Kiberg, Westi, Ch. & Danish Nat. RSO, Järvi.

Nielsen's first opera has the merit of an outstanding Saul in Aage Haugland. The remainder of the cast is very strong and the powerful choral writing is well served by the Danish Radio Chorus. It convinces here in a way that it rarely has before, and the action is borne along on an almost symphonic current that disarms criticism. A marvellous set.

Novák, Vitězslav (1870–1949)

Eternal longing, Op. 33; In the Tatra mountains, Op. 26; Slovak suite, Op. 32.
*** Virgin/EMI Dig. VC5 45251 [id.]. RLPO, Libor Pešek.

After the First World War, Novák's star began to wane as Janáček's began to make its ascent. Although Novák is not quite as visionary or as revolutionary as the latter, he is a composer of real stature. *The Storm* (now back in the Supraphon catalogue – see below) is a masterpiece! Novák's two best-known tone-poems date from the first years of the century – as, for that matter, does the enchanting *Slovak suite*. *In the Tatra mountains* (1902) might be thought of as a kind of Bohemian *Alpine Symphony* and is no less striking, while *Eternal longing* (1903–4) blends expressionism and impressionism in a wholly individual fashion. The *Slovak suite* has a refreshing spontaneity and fertility of invention, second only to his master, Dvořák. Libor Pešek and the Liverpool orchestra put us firmly in their debt with this issue. Both performance and recording are first rate.

The Storm, Op. 42.
(M) *** Sup. SU 3088-2 211 [id.]. Soloists, Czech PO Ch. & O, Košler.

The Storm is arguably Novák's finest composition, and this was its first stereo recording, made in 1978. It is a work of great beauty and imagination, scored with consummate mastery and showing a lyrical gift of a high order. It has warmth and genuine individuality; the idiom owes something to Richard Strauss as well as to the Czech tradition, and there is an impressive command of both melody and structure. This is noble, moving and powerful music – very different from, say, Janáček but recognizably from the same part of the world, and equally fresh. The performance is fully worthy and has splendid dramatic feeling, helped by good soloists and a fine chorus. The recording, too, is admirably balanced, and there is considerably more depth on this vivid CD transfer than on LP, and plenty of weight, even if the soloists are rather too forward. This is one of the best Supraphon reissues for some time.

Nyman, Michael (born 1948)

(i) *Piano concerto;* (ii) *On the Fiddle; Prospero's Books.*
(B) *** Tring Dig. TRP 097 [id.]. (i) Peter Lawson; (ii) Jonathan Carney; RPO, Carney.

Michael Nyman's brand of minimalism has been most effective in illustrating a whole sequence of films, including the Oscar-winning *The Piano*, in which this concerto was evocatively used. This Tring version of that work, with Peter Lawson a fine, muscular soloist, costs only a third as much as the Argo issue with the composer conducting (443 382-2) and is just as powerful as that original, helped by fuller and more immediate sound. (However, for R.L. the sound-picture is too forward and over-resonant: minimalist music needs the widest range of dynamic to make its fullest effect.) The most attractive of the three pieces (and the shortest) is the trilogy, *On the fiddle*, drawn from Nyman's music for three films directed by Peter Greenaway (*Full fathom five* comes from *The Tempest*, *Angelfish decay* uses a sequence from *A Zed and Two Noughts* and *Miserere paraphrase* derives from *The Cook, The Thief, His Wife and Her Lover*). Here, with the solo violin taking a central role, Nyman reverts to warmly melodic writing, and the RPO leader, Jonathan Carney, is a most persuasive advocate, both as soloist and as conductor. The music for the Shakespeare-based film with John Gielgud, *Prospero's Books*, is more conventionally minimalist, with nagging repetitions at generally fast speeds. This too is magnetic in its way, using a smaller ensemble. An excellent bargain for anyone who has responded to Nyman's film music.

Ockeghem, Johannes (*c.* 1410–97)

Ave Maria; Intemerata Dei mater; Missa Ecce ancilla Domini.
*** Proudsound Dig. PROUCD 133 [id.]. The Clerks' Group, Edward Wickham (with JOSQUIN DES PREZ: *Déploration sur la mort de Johannes Ockeghem;* OBRECHT: *Salve Regina*).

While his anniversary year may not attract as much attention as those of Brahms and Schubert, the great Renaissance master is receiving greater exposure. This CD is as good an entry point into Ockeghem's world as any. The *Missa Ecce ancilla Domini* is generally thought of as one of his most characteristic Masses. The Clerks' Group and Edward Wickham are totally inside the idiom and their phrasing seems to come almost by second nature. Wickham presents a more convincing picture of Ockeghem's sound-world than almost any of his rivals.

Requiem; Motet and *Missa Fors seulement.*
*** ASV Gaudeamus CDGAU 168 [id.]. Clerks' Group, Edward Wickham.

Ockeghem's *Requiem* (the first known setting which survives in manuscript form) is one of the great riddles of medieval liturgical music. Its various surviving movements are very different in style, notation and part writing and (rather like the Du Fay *St Anthony Mass* – see above) it was long thought that the manuscript might be a collection of fragments from a number of different works. But whether or not this is so and despite those striking musical differences – the bare consecutive fifths in the *Introitus* contrasting with the vastly richer style of the closing *Offertorium* – the *Requiem* seems to hold together with a curiously convincing unity. Certainly every bar of the music is memorable, especially in such a dedicated performance as we have here. The Clerks' Group under Edward Wickham offer fine blending and tuning, clearly detailed inner parts and a richly flowing line which is seemingly ideally paced. In addition we are offered the *Kyrie, Gloria* and *Credo* of the *Missa Fors seulement*, plus the rondeau on which it is based, and further arrangements of the latter by Pierre de la Rue and Antoine Brumel, which offer more splendid music to intrigue the inquisitive ear.

Offenbach, Jacques (1819–80)

Andante for cello and orchestra; Concerto militaire in G for cello and orchestra (completed Jean-Max Clément).
*** RCA Dig. 09026 68420-2 [id.]. Ofra Harnoy, Bournemouth SO, Antonio de Almeida – LALO: *Concerto.* ***

The *Concerto militaire* dates from 1847. No complete autograph score exists; although there is a set of the original orchestral parts in existence, their current whereabouts is uncertain. The published score, as recorded here, is revised by the French cellist, Jean-Max Clément, who orchestrated the last two movements, using the piano score and keeping to the style and scale of the opening movement. He also reconstructed the solo part (notably in the finale, where he provides the cadenza), which appears never to have been written out in full by its composer: it bristles with bravura, sometimes in registers more in keeping with a violin than a cello! The composer himself richly revised the scoring of the second-movement *Andante* as an independent piece, and it is presented here separately, after the complete performance of the concerto. It has a glorious main theme, and in Harnoy's ravishing performance it is the highlight of this CD. The first movement of the concerto opens with an extended and characteristically Offenbachian tutti – robbed a little of its sparkle here by a somewhat over-resonant recording. This first introduces the dotted march theme which affords the work its title (the composer's own idea), but then comes the soaring secondary theme which is even more memorable. Harnoy has the full measure of the work: she essays the technical hurdles of the solo part with aplomb, yet her lyrical lines, the true stuff of operetta, soar ardently; her playing imaginatively uses the widest range of dynamic to add to the sense of spontaneity. The jaunty finale is full of high spirits. Almeida accompanies sympathetically and persuasively, and cello and orchestra are naturally balanced, but it is a pity that the otherwise agreeable acoustic of the Wessex Hall in the Poole Arts Centre has also afforded such a high degree of resonance.

Gaîté parisienne (ballet, arr. Rosenthal): complete.
500♪ ✿ (M) *** RCA 09026 61847-2 [id.]. Boston Pops O, Arthur Fiedler – ROSSINI/RESPIGHI: *Boutique fantasque.* ***
(M) * Mercury 434 365-2 (2) [id.]. Minneapolis SO, Dorati – ADAM: *Giselle* **(*); Johann STRAUSS: *Graduation ball.* *

Fiedler's *Gaîté parisienne* is irresistible – one of his very finest records. The orchestra are kept exhilaratingly on their toes throughout and are obviously enjoying themselves, not least in the elegantly tuneful waltzes and in the closing *Barcarolle*. John Pfeiffer's superb new transfer makes the recording sound remarkably fresh and full. Unbelievably it dates from 1954, one of the very first of RCA's 'Living Stereo' records and still one of the finest.

Dorati conducts with plenty of spirit but is let down by a close, impossibly dry recording with lustreless violins. The orchestra sounds as if it is in a studio cushioned in cotton wool.

Les Contes d'Hoffmann (complete).

500♪ ❀ *** Decca 417 363-2 (2) [id.]. Sutherland, Domingo, Tourangeau, Bacquier, R. Suisse Romande and Lausanne Pro Arte Ch., SRO, Bonynge.

** Erato/Warner Dig. 0630 14330-2 (3) [id.]. Alagna, Van Dam, Dessay, Jo, Vaduva, Dubose, Sénéchal, Bacquier, Lyon Opéra Ch. & O, Kent Nagano.

On Decca Joan Sutherland gives a virtuoso performance in four heroine roles, not only as Olympia, Giulietta and Antonia but also as Stella in the *Epilogue*. Bonynge opts for spoken dialogue, and puts the Antonia scene last, as being the more substantial. His direction is unfailingly sympathetic, while Sutherland is impressive in each role, notably as the doll Olympia and in the pathos of the Antonia scene. As Giulietta she hardly sounds like a *femme fatale*, but still produces beautiful singing. Domingo gives one of his finest performances on record, and so does Gabriel Bacquier. It is a memorable set, in every way, much more than the sum of its parts.

Nagano, like Jeffrey Tate on his 1992 Philips set (already deleted), uses the authoritative edition prepared by Michael Kaye, but with the Guiraud recitatives rather than spoken dialogue. With 1,600 extra autograph pages available, it makes a very long entertainment and, in one respect, the characterization of Giulietta in the Venice Act, the extra material distorts the result, particularly when as here the role is taken by a light, bright-toned coloratura like Sumi Jo. Another problem is that Offenbach at his death left multiple versions of particular numbers; though Kaye's judgement is good, it is a pity on a recording that the spurious but delightful *Scintille, diamant* is not included even in an appendix, though inconsistently he does include the similarly spurious sextet in the Giulietta scene, taken at high speed. Brisk speeds are the rule throughout the performance, with a dry acoustic and no sound effects, preventing a theatrical atmosphere being conveyed. Though this is claimed as a first recording of the complete grand opera version, there is little grandeur. Sadly, the brightness of sound gives an edge to the voices, so that Roberto Alagna's tenor loses its velvet tones and too often sounds taut and dry. It means that one hardly ever sees this Hoffmann as a lover and seducer, rather as just a braggart. Equally, the three singers taking the roles of the heroines all have their moments of shrillness – even Sumi Jo who, with her light, bright coloratura, turns Giulietta from a *femme fatale* into a coquette. Natalie Dessay, the Olympia, and Leontina Vaduva, the Antonia, are both young singers who have begun to make their mark on disc, but their characterizations are muted, hardly distinctive. Nevertheless, José van Dam is as incisive and strong as ever in the three villainous roles, only occasionally betraying that he is not as young as when he appeared in the Cambreling set. It is also good to welcome such veterans as Michel Sénéchal and Gabriel Bacquier in character roles, adding necessary spice. But the Bonynge set on Decca still reigns supreme.

La Périchole: highlights.

(M) *** Erato/Warner 0630 15735-9 [id.] (from complete recording, with Crespin, Vanzo, Bastin, Friedmann, Trigeau, Rhine Op. Ch., Strasbourg PO, Lombard).

Though both Régine Crespin in the title-role and Alain Vanzo as her partner, Piquillo, were past their peak at the time this Erato recording was made (1977), Crespin remains fresh and Vanzo produces heady tone in his various arias, some of them brilliant. Lombard secures plenty of life from his Strasbourg team and they are well projected by a vivid recording. While the complete set is very much worth having (2292 45686-2 – see our main volume), this 67-minute selection can be strongly recommended too, as the documentation includes the essential translation.

Orff, Carl (1895–1982)

Carmina Burana.

*** EMI Dig. CDC5 55392-2 [id.]. Natalie Dessay, Thomas Hampson, Gérard Lesne, Choeur d'enfants de Midi-Pyrénées, Orféon Donostiarra, Toulouse Capitole O, Plasson.

(BB) ** Naxos Dig. 8.550196 [id.]. Jenisová, Dolezal, Kusnjer, Slovak Philharmonic Ch., Czech RSO (Bratislava), Gunzenhauser.

Carmina Burana is very well served on CD. Blomstedt's Decca version (430 509-2) is consistently exhilarating, and the male, female and boy choristers all enjoy themselves hugely – as they should with such stimulating words to sing. Ormandy and his Philadelphians too have just the right panache to bring off this wildly exuberant picture of the Middle Ages, and there is no more enjoyable bargain version (Sony SBK 47688).

But Michel Plasson's new EMI performance, recorded in Toulouse, is rather special. It is sumptuously packaged, as CDs seldom are, and the design is suitably hedonistic, with a golden, slimly statuesque female form to represent the *Cours d'amours*. Moreover, not only is the choral singing extraordinarily vivid, it is as seductively warm in pianissimos as it is incisively vibrant in fortissimos, with a wonderful shout at the close of *Were diu werly alle min* ('Were the world all mine'). The three soloists are the finest on record. Plasson opens deliberately, with strongly marked accents, but the performance immediately takes off, and his control of tempo and pacing is as subtle as it is seemingly spontaneous. Thomas Hampson's tender first entry, *Omnia sol temperat* ('The sun rules over all'), is matched by his great vigour in the *Tavern scene*, *Estuan interius* ('Burning inside . . .'). The orchestral introduction for the *Song of the roast swan* is bizarrely piquant and Gérard Lesne's alto timbre is uniquely suited to its wailing upper tessitura, while the orchestra adds sinister little snarls. Hampson's unctuous, larger-than-life Abbot is given enthusiastic support from the chorus, and they expand boisterously for *In taberna quando sumus*. The trebles open *Amor volat undique* with knowing Gallic delicacy, helped by the daintiness of the flutes, and Lesne and Hampson combine to make the sequence *Si puer cum puella* ('If a boy with a girl . . .') quite delectable, topped by Natalie Dessay's tenderly ravishing *Stetit puella*, which is to be followed later by her moment of tender submission (*Dulcissime*) with its thrilling upward leap. The choral *Tempus est iocundum* brings the fullest expression of sexual rapture ('Oh, oh, oh, I am bursting out all over'), into which the trebles from the Midi-Pyrénées enter with enthusiasm, if without quite the knowing exuberance which English boy-trebles bring to it. (One thinks of the splendid Previn version which is now due for mid-priced reissue.) But Plasson's closing *Ave formosissima – O Fortuna* has splendid grandeur, and this outstandingly recorded new version must go straight to the top of the list.

The Slovak Chorus sing Orff's hedonistic cantata with lusty, Slavonic enthusiasm, and it is a pity that some of the score's quieter passages are somewhat lacking in bite because of the resonance. But the Tavern scene comes across especially vividly and the culminating *Ave formosissima* and *O Fortuna* are splendidly expansive. The soprano, Eva Jenisová, is the most impressive of the three soloists, who generally do not match their Western rivals. This is an enjoyable performance, with exciting moments, but the Ormandy version is worth the extra outlay.

Catulli Carmina.

(M) *** DG 449 097-2 [id.]. Arleen Augér, Wieslaw Ochman, Berlin Op. Ch., 4 pianos & percussion, Jochum – EGK: *The Temptation of St Anthony.* ***

Catulli Carmina; Trionfo di Afrodite.

❀ *** EMI Dig. CDC5 55517-2 [id.]. Dagmar Schellenberger, Lothar Odinius, Linz Mozart Ch., Munich R. O, Franz Welser-Möst.

Orff's sequel to *Carmina Burana* (using much the same formula, but with the accompaniment scored for four pianos and percussion) cannot match its predecessor in memorability, but for anyone hypnotized by the composer's vital rhythmic ostinatos this is the work to recommend next, and certainly so in Franz Welser-Möst's vibrant performance, complete with enthusiastic crowd noises and superlative choral singing that in its sharpness and precision lifts the music clear of banality. The soloists, too, are excellent, the soprano, Dagmar Schellenberger, revelling in the sensuous upper tessitura which is so like the music for the Girl in the Red Tunic in *Carmina Burana*.

Trionfo di Afrodite, the third work in Orff's sequence, is a wedding cantata, and here the composer is in fresh imaginative form, exploring the marriage rites of Ancient Greece by combining two dramatic choral odes by Catullus in Greek style with poems by Sappho and a chorus from Euripides's *Hippolytus*. It is scored for large orchestra, including three pianos and plentiful percussion; with more nagging rhythmic repetitions it pays its hedonistic tribute to the pleasures of love in a similarly exhilarating manner. Although it opens in the familiar Orff style with alternating choruses of eager young men and willing virgins, there is an added dimension in the tender writing, when young men and maidens alike consider the implications of the forthcoming nuptials, ending with an extraordinary closing choral glissando. The meeting of bride and groom is remarkably evocative, the soprano soaring up into the highest tessitura and the tenor, Lothar Odinius, attractively light-voiced and confident in writing which often lies high up in his register; the choral commentary here is very gentle. The vibrant *Invocation to Hymenaeus* brings a curious reminder of *Petrushka* but stirringly returns us to Orff's world of ostinatos until the arrival of the bride at the wedding chamber brings a series of spoken exhortations by the leader of the guests with vehement choral interruptions, preparing for the wedding ritual and considering the change of status and behaviour that the wedding will bring to the young couple. There follows a chorus, first touching then ardent, celebrating marital bliss. The bridegroom then joins his bride admiringly in the wedding chamber, to which she responds with wordless coloratura. The work ends dramatically with a vision of Aphrodite, which brings an immensely bold closing chorus and a final explosion of enthusiasm from the assembled guests. It is an extraordinary dramatization, and it is brought thrillingly to life by Welser-Möst and his combined soloists, singers and orchestra, working splendidly as a team and superbly recorded. An unforgettable sonic experience.

Until the arrival of the Welser-Möst version, Jochum's performance of *Catulli Carmina* was never surpassed. His chorus sings with sharp, rhythmic point and, if imagination is called for in such music, Jochum matches flexibility with a spark of humour in his control of mechanistic rhythms. His soloists are individual and sweet-toned. The recording is very fine, although even on CD evocative pianissimos sound a little recessed.

Paganini, Niccolò (1782–1840)

Violin concerto No. 4 in D min.; Sonata Varsavia (orch. & arr. Pietro Spada).
* Ph. 446 718-2 [id.]. Gidon Kremer, VPO, Muti.

Paganini's *Fourth Concerto* only reappeared in 1954; it was premièred by Grumiaux and later recorded by Szeryng. Muti genially makes the very most of its rather pompous opening tutti and Kremer has no problems with its many technical challenges, showing real affection for the innocent melody of the *Adagio flexibile con sentimento*, which he reprises exquisitely, and despatches the brilliant finale with aplomb. But for his first-movement cadenza he makes a collage from Paganini's theme plus motives from Schnittke's *A Paganini* for violin solo, opening with a passage of aggressive atonality. This might work as an outrageous surprise at a live performance, but on record it is not something to which one warms or willingly returns, and thus Kremer quite ruins the first movement. Only the solo part survives of the four-movement *Sonata Varsavia*, plus an inauthentic manuscript of a version for violin and piano. In the arrangement offered here, Pietro Spada has resourcefully embellished and wittily recomposed the textures of the orchestral ritornelli which separate the passages of solo fireworks, and the result is a complete success. Of the four movements the third, *Tema polacca*, is particularly winning. What a pity about that cadenza!

24 Caprices, Op. 1.
*** Telarc Dig. CD 80398 [id.]. James Ehnes.

James Ehnes is Juilliard-trained and has technique to burn. He tosses off these pieces with great bravura and aplomb. His playing has real personality, even if others have managed to find greater subtlety and delicacy. Accardo plays them as if they are more than bravura pieces and, as we say in our main volume, invests them with an eloquence far beyond the sheer display they offer. All the same, there is much to relish in his youthful ardour and the splendid sound the Telarc engineers give us.

Caprice No. 24, Op. 1/24; Grand sonata in A.
(B) *** Sony SBK 62425; *SBT 62425* [id.]. John Williams (guitar) – GIULIANI: *Variations on a theme by Handel;* D. SCARLATTI: *Sonatas;* VILLA-LOBOS: *5 Preludes.* ***

Grand sonata in A.
(B) **(*) Decca Eclipse 448 709-2; *448 709-4* [id.]. Eduardo Fernández – GIULIANI; VIVALDI: *Concertos.* **(*)

John Williams is in excellent form in the *Grande sonata*, with its charming central *Romanza* and ingenuous closing *Andantino variato* (originally a duo for guitar and violin), and the famous *Caprice*, for violin solo, both arranged by Williams. The recording is only marginally balanced too forwardly and is otherwise truthful. Most enjoyable.

Fernández's playing is rightly much admired by fellow guitarists. His technique is immaculate and his somewhat self-effacing approach always puts the composer first. He is beautifully recorded and the effect is engagingly intimate to suit the gentle, improvisatory nature of his playing, especially the pensive central *Romanza*. Some might feel that the finale needs more extrovert feeling, but there is certainly no lack of dash or bravura.

Palestrina, Giovanni Pierluigi di (1525–94)

Masses: *Ecce ego Joannes; Sine nomine.*
(BB) *** Belart 461 018-2. Mary Thomas, Jean Allister, Edgar Fleet, Christopher Keyte, Carmelite Priory Ch., London, John McCartney – VICTORIA: Mass & Motet: *O quam gloriosum.* ***

The reissue of these distinguished (originally Oiseau-Lyre) recordings by the London Carmelite Priory

Choir under John McCartney, made in the early 1960s, is very welcome indeed on Polygram's super-budget label, Belart. The two works offered here make a good foil for each other, for they are contrasted in style and texture. The Mass 'without name' is a small-scale work, whereas *Ecce ego Johannes* is more ambitious and dramatic. Both are beautifully sung and very well recorded. With the availablity of this record so inexpensively and with extra works by Victoria (not on the original LP) included for good measure, one hopes that more music-lovers will be tempted to sample this wonderfully expressive and rewarding music.

Mass & Motet: *Assumpta est Maria.* Motets: *Ave Maria; Beata es, Virgo Maria; Hodie gloriosa semper Virgo Maria; Regina coeli; Magnificat septimi toni.*
(B) **(*) EMI Dig. CDZ5 69703-2 [id.]. Clare College, Cambridge, Ch., Timothy Brown.

This is an exceptionally well-chosen collection, mainly of shorter works, but also including the splendid *Missa Assumpta est Maria* which was not published in the composer's lifetime but survives in the music library of the Sistine Chapel. The programme ends with an equally fine *Magnificat* setting. We are familiar with the excellent Clare College Choir and their rich sound, partly achieved by using women's voices, from earlier recordings under their previous director, John Rutter. This EMI Debut CD introduces their new conductor, Timothy Brown, and the choir responds expressively to his melismatic direction, immediately arresting in the beautiful opening motet with which the Mass is associated. The choir is beautifully recorded, and the only minor criticism is the relatively resticted dynamic range, which may partly be caused by the microphone placing, but which certainly reduces the dramatic contrast of the singing. But this remains a thoroughly worthwhile bargain disc, although it is a pity that the documentation has so little to say about the music.

Missa Papae Marcelli; Alma redemptoris Mater; Magnificat 1 toni; Nunc dimittis. Stabat mater; Surge illuminare.
500♪ *** Ph. Dig. 454 994-2 [id.]. Tallis Scholars (with ALLEGRI: *Miserere* ***).

The Tallis Scholars are here recorded in the Basilica of Maria Maggiore in Rome, where Palestrina was a choirboy and, later, master of the choristers. The most celebrated of Palestrina's masses, *Missa Papae Marcelli*, receives as eloquent a performance as any in the catalogue. The Tallis Scholars have wonderful fluidity and the sense of movement never flags in this finely tuned, well-paced reading. Much the same goes for the remaining motets here and, of course, for the Allegri *Miserere*, which had a unique association with the Sistine Chapel until Mozart heard it and wrote it down from memory for performance elsewhere. As the recording was made before an audience, there is applause, which is quite inappropriate and very tiresome. In every other respect this is a first-class issue and can be warmly recommended. It should be noted that it is also available on videotape (GIMVP 994) and laserdisc (GIMLD 994).

Panufnik, Andrzej (1914–91)

Violin concerto.
(M) *** EMI CDM5 66121-2. Menuhin, Menuhin Festival O, composer – L. BERKELEY: *Concerto;* WILLIAMSON: *Concerto.* ***

The *Violin concerto* presents an interesting structure in three movements, the meatiest in argument being the finale, the only quick movement. It requires the imagination and commitment of a Menuhin to sustain the first two movements, starting with a quasi-cadenza *senza misura*. After that the central *Adagio* is sweeter, more obviously lyrical before the toughness of the finale. A valuable work, outstandingly performed and very well recorded (at Abbey Road in 1975).

Parry, Hubert (1848–1918)

Symphony No. 2 in F min. (Cambridge); Overture to an unwritten tragedy; Symphonic variations in E.
(BB) **(*) Naxos Dig. 8.553469 [id.]. Royal SNO, Andrew Penny.

Challenging the outstanding Parry series from Chandos conducted by Matthias Bamert, Naxos here offers a very acceptable alternative to the *Symphony No. 2*, similarly coupled with the *Symphonic variations* and with an extra item in the *Overture*. The playing of the Royal Scottish National Orchestra is just as polished as that of the LPO on Chandos, but Penny's manner is less warmly expressive at speeds generally a little faster, and the recorded sound is rather less opulent.

PIANO MUSIC

Hands across the centuries (suite); *10 Shulbrede tunes; Theme and 19 variations in D min.*
*** Priory Dig. PRCD 451 [id.]. Peter Jacobs.

It has to be said, on the evidence of this very enjoyable recital, that Parry is a much more rewarding piano composer than his contemporary, Stanford (see below). Shulbrede Priory was the remains of a substantial twelfth-century Augustinian settlement, turned into a country house, where the composer's married daughter lived with her family. Parry was captivated by its charm and atmosphere when he first paid a visit there in 1902 and he returned frequently. In 1914 he published a set of ten delightful miniatures which showed his affection and the strong spell the house wielded over him. The style of the ten Shulbrede tunes may be eclectic, but how colourful and warmly melodic they are, some associated with his grandchildren, two with their obviously very feminine mother, 'Dolly', plus a sparkling evocation of *Bogies and Sprites that gambol by night* (obviously not malignant) and a touchingly romantic portrayal of the high-vaulted *Prior's chamber*. The mock-baroque *Hands across the centuries suite* is hardly less diverting, its invention equally varied, and it does not attempt to remain in the harmonic era of bygone days. The more ambitious *Theme and variations* is rather prolix but is very well organized. Peter Jacobs, obviously enjoying himself, plays all this music with flair and the nimblest fingers (very necessary at times) and there is never a dull bar here. Excellent natural recording, too. A real find – you should try it, if you admire Parry.

Pärt, Arvo (born 1935)

And one of the Pharisees; (i) *The Beatitudes; Cantate Domino (Psalm 95);* (ii) *De Profundis (Psalm 129); Magnificat; 7 Magnificat Antiphons;* (i) *Missa Sillabica. Solfeggio; Summa (Credo).*
*** HM Dig. HMU 907182 [id.]. Theatre of Voices, Paul Hillier; (i) with Christopher Bowers-Broadbent (organ); Dan Kennedy (percussion).

The cover of this CD indicates that it includes just *De Profundis*, whereas this 76-minute collection covers a very wide range of Pärt's choral output, from the short *Solfeggio* of 1964, which seems to float in space, to *The Beatitudes* (1990) of which this is the recording première. This work opens in stillness and calm but, as so often with this composer, leads on to a great climax, here over an organ pedal; then, after an exultant 'Amen', the organ has a brief but prolix postlude. *De Profundis* (1980), which opens the concert so eloquently, brings a similarly elliptical structure, based on a simple climbing phrase in the bass answered by a falling sequence in the upper parts; it again uses an organ pedal to underpin the climax; then the organ disappears before the descent. The organ reappears in the *Missa Sillabica* (1977), heard here in a slightly revised version, which is a fine example of Pärt's use of the simplest means to communicate his expression of the liturgical text, the repetitions within the 'Credo' a characteristic example. *And one of the Pharisees* is a setting for three voices of a text from chapter 7 of St Luke's Gospel and its powerful medieval atmosphere, including solo chants, reminds us of the link which Pärt's litugical music has with the distant past. The *Seven Magnificat Antiphons* are brief choral vignettes of considerable diversity, with a great surge of sound in *O Schlüssel Davids* and plangent passing dissonances in the final *O Emmanuel*. The concert closes with the essentially serene *Magnificat*, evocatively distanced at the opening, but again with an exulting climax. The performances here could hardly be more powerful or atmospheric, yet they are firmly controlled. They are magnificently recorded.

(i) *Cantus in memory of Benjamin Britten; Festina lente; Summa;* (i; ii) *Tabula rasa;* (ii) *Fratres; Spiegel im Spiegel.*
500♪ (M) *** EMI Dig. CD-EMX 2221; *TC-EMX 2221*. (i) Bournemouth Sinf., Richard Studt; (ii) Tasmin Little, Martin Roscoe.

An admirable and enterprising compilation from EMI Eminence to tempt those who have not yet sampled this composer's highly individual sound-world with its tintinnabulation (ringing bells). In the two chamber works Tasmin Little holds the listener's attention by the intensity of her commitment and the powerful projection of her playing. But most striking of all is the ambitious *Tabula rasa* with strong contrasts between the erupting energy of the opening *Ludus* and the aptly named second-movement *Silentium* which, of course, isn't silent but spins a compulsive atmospheric web.

Patterson, Paul (born 1947)

Concerto for orchestra, Op. 45; Europhony, Op. 55; (i) *Missa brevis, Op. 54.*
(M) *** EMI Dig. CDM5 66529-2 [id.]. LPO, Owain Arwel Hughes; (i) with LPO Ch.

This disc offers representative examples of Patterson's recent work, much more approachable in idiom than his earlier music. The gem of the collection is the *Missa brevis*, using a seemingly simple style boldly and freshly. It must be as grateful for the singers as it is for the listener, with moments of pure poetry as in the *Benedictus*. The two orchestral pieces, though less individual, are colourful and immediately attractive. Their openness of idiom conceals the ingenuity of their construction, with *Europhony* clearly developing on variation form. Vigorous performances and wide-ranging recording.

Pergolesi, Giovanni (1710–36)

(i–ii) *Stabat Mater;* (i) *Salve Regina in C min.*
*** O-L Dig. 425 692-2 [id.]. (i) Emma Kirkby; (ii) James Bowman; AAM, Hogwood.

In our main volume we gave a strong recommendation to Abbado's modern-instrument performance of Pergolesi's *Stabat mater*, with Margaret Marshall and Terrani, memorable for its great intensity and ardour (DG 415 103-2). However, those preferring a period-instrument version will find James Bowman and Emma Kirkby make a splendid partnership. There is both grace and expressive intensity in their singing, and their embellishments are stylistically impeccable. Hogwood accompanies committedly and his Academy of Ancient Music does not lack fullness of sonority. Emma Kirkby then sings the shorter *Salve Regina* very touchingly. On the whole this is preferable to the competing authentic Hyperion version (CDA 66294), although there the couplings are more generous.

Pettersson, Allan (1911–80)

Symphonies Nos. 7; 11.
*** BIS Dig. CD 580 [id.]. Norrköping SO, Leif Segerstam.

The music of Allan Pettersson inspires partisan feeling. When Antal Dorati's LP of the *Seventh Symphony* first appeared, it was greeted with acclaim by Swedish audiences, for long force-fed on a diet of serialist and post-serialist fodder, who fell ravenously on its direct, post-Mahlerian language. The *Seventh* is probably the finest of his symphonies and it was not long before its success had fostered a Pettersson fever which prompted the composer, never very prone to self-criticism, to embark on no fewer than nine others. Many music-lovers respond to his music with great warmth, while others find his soul-searching, navel-gazing agonizing insufferably self-pitying. There seems to be no middle course, and if you are among his admirers the present CD, which shows him at his best, can be recommended. Segerstam and his fine Norrköping players bring great feeling to the *Seventh* and give the somewhat shorter *Eleventh Symphony* the most sympathetic advocacy. If you want to explore further, you could try the *Fifth Symphony* and the amorphous *Viola concerto* – very well played by Nobuko Imai (BIS CD 480), but the present disc seems the best possible place to start.

Symphony No. 9.
*** CPO Dig. CPO 999 231-2. Berlin RSO, Alun Francis.

Pettersson's *Ninth Symphony* (1970) was composed in the valley of the shadow of death and has had a powerful effect on many of his admirers. Paul Rapaport reported in *Fanfare* magazine that 'listening to this symphony has *understandably* [my italics, not his] caused some people not to eat or speak for hours or even longer'. True, it *is* difficult to know what to say after hearing it except to call for a very stiff drink. Life being short and sweet, one can only say that the 70 minutes which it takes to unfold seem like eternity. Not surprisingly, given the sudden beatification he received with the *Seventh Symphony* and the enthusiasm with which his supporters hailed him, fame went to Pettersson's head and he began to assume that any utterance from his pen, irrespective of quality, had to be committed to paper, and that his every quaver was significant. The three stars are for the performance and recording, so that admirers of the composer can proceed accordingly.

Pfitzner, Hans (1869–1949)

Violin concerto in B min., Op. 34.

*(*) Carlton Turnabout 30372 00402. Susanne Lautenbacher, Philh. Hungarica, Günther Wich – VOLKMANN: *Konsertstück* etc. **

Pfitzner's *Violin concerto* comes from 1923 and belongs to the same period as his magnificent *Von Deutsche Seele*, once available on DG coupled with Schoeck's *Lebendig begraben*. (Let's hope that that will reappear on one of DG's 'Originals'.) The *Violin concerto* is something of a rarity, understandably so since its solo part is demanding without offering the opportunities for empty, virtuosic display. It is a long work (of some 35 minutes) whose three movements are played without a break. There is some remarkable writing here, in particular in the searching slow movement. Susanne Lautenbacher gives a brave account of the solo part, even if she is not always in total agreement with the orchestra on matters of intonation. Generally speaking the playing is rough-and-ready and is recommendable only *faute de mieux*. The recordings come from the 1960s and are sub-fusc, and it is worth mentioning that nowhere on either the sleeve or the disc is their provenance mentioned. The uninitiated may well be deceived into thinking it is 1996 (the only date to appear), though their ears will quickly undeceive them, and the presentation is poor. Were it not for the interest of the music itself, this would rate only one star.

Das Herz: Liebesmelodie (Love theme); *Das Kaethchen von Heilbronn: Overture. Palestrina: Preludes to Acts I, II & III.*

(*) DG Dig. 449 571-2 [id.]. German Opera, Berlin, O, Thielemann – R. STRAUSS: *Capriccio* etc. *

Strauss, when told that his contemporary, Pfitzner, found composing very hard, is alleged to have replied, 'Then why does he bother?' Yet if Pfitzner's opera *Palestrina* is flawed dramatically and is overlong, it includes some fine music, and anyone fortunate enough to have seen the recent productions at Covent Garden and Rome with Christian Thielemann at the helm will know of his dedication to this score. Thielemann believes passionately not only in Strauss but in Pfitzner too, and here he confirms the impression he created in those live performances in spacious and concentrated readings of the three *Palestrina Preludes*. The playing is passionate yet at the same time restrained. The *Love theme* from Pfitzner's last opera, and the extended prelude to his early opera, *Das Kaethchen von Heilbronn*, if overlong, are more sparkling than the rest. Both add to a fairly persuasive portrait, though the Strauss items prove much more memorable, and one has the feeling that this is not music to which one would return very often. The Orchestra of the Berlin Deutsches Oper does not possess the opulent string-tone found at the *Philharmonie* but they play with conviction. The DG recording is very good without being state of the art.

Palestrina: 3 Preludes.

(M) ** DG 439 488-2 [id.]. Bav. RSO, Leitner – BUSONI: *Dr Faust* **; HINDEMITH: *Mathis Symphony* **; WEILL: *Kleine Dreigroschenmusik*. ***

Ferdinand Leitner's version of the three *Preludes* was recorded in 1958 and originally appeared in harness with the *Symphony in C*, Op. 46. It is well enough played, though Kubelik in the complete recording and Christian Thielemann with the Orchestra of the Deutsches Oper, Berlin, make a stronger impression.

String quartets: in D, Op. 13; in C min., Op. 50.

*** CPO Dig. CPO 999 072-2 [id.]. Franz Schubert Qt.

We think of Pfitzner primarily as a composer of opera and Lieder, but this first-class CPO string quartet coupling serves to show him as a composer of fine chamber music in the mainstream of the German romantic tradition. The two works are aptly paired to span his career; the *D major*, from 1903, was dedicated to Alma Mahler. The opening is gentle and elegiac, the mood nostalgic to contrast with the lighthearted scherzando second movement (*mit Humour*), with its forceful descending 'Three blind mice' introduction. The third movement is pensively contrapuntal, but simple cheerfulness returns in the finale. The *C minor Quartet*, written 40 years later, carries a mood of resignation which hauntingly dominates the first and third movements, but the *Andantino*, which comes second, jauntily restores the composer's good humour, and the finale is also optimistic, even quoting from Schubert. Altogether these are two thoroughly rewarding works, finely crafted, with a ready flow of appealing variations and subtly individual harmonic progressions. They are splendidly played by the richly blended Schubert Quartet, whose chording is immaculate and who respond to the bittersweet, *fin de siècle* flavour of the writing. Excellent, realistic recording. A find.

Piston, Walter (1894–1976)

(i; ii) *Capriccio for harp and strings;* (ii) *3 New England sketches;* (iii) *Serenata;* (ii) *Symphony No. 4.*
500♪ ❀ *** Delos Dig. DE 3106 [id.]. (i) Wunrow; (ii) Seattle SO; (iii) NY CO; Gerard Schwarz.

Piston's *Fourth* is arguably the finest American symphony, as powerful in its forward sweep as the Harris *Third* and better held together than either Barber's *First* or Copland's *Third*. The remaining pieces, not only the *New England sketches* but also the inventive *Capriccio for harp and strings*, are well worth seeking out. The fine recording and Gerard Schwarz's natural and unforced direction make this a most desirable CD. The slow movement of the *Serenata*, equally well played by New York forces, is quite inspired.

The Incredible flutist (ballet; complete); *New England sketches; Symphony No. 6* (1955).
500♪ *** RCA Dig. RD 60798 [60798-2-RC]. St Louis SO, Leonard Slatkin.

Walter Piston's ballet, *The Incredible flutist*, is one of the most refreshing and imaginative of all American scores. The most powerful work on Slatkin's disc is the *Sixth Symphony*, about which there is an inexorable sense of logic and inevitability. Piston is a cultivated, refined symphonist who does not wear his heart on his sleeve. The playing of the St Louis orchestra under Leonard Slatkin both here and in the *New England sketches* is sensitive and brilliant.

Ponchielli, Amilcare (1834–86)

La Gioconda (complete).
500♪ *** Decca Dig. 414 349-2 (3) [id.]. Caballé, Baltsa, Pavarotti, Milnes, Hodgson, L. Op. Ch., Nat. PO, Bartoletti.
*** EMI CDS5 56291-2 (3). Callas, Cossotto, Ferraro, Vinco, Cappuccilli, La Scala, Milan, Ch. & O, Votto.

The colourfully atmospheric melodrama of this opera gives the Decca engineers the chance to produce one of their most vivid opera recordings. Caballé is just a little overstressed in the title-role but produces glorious sounds. Pavarotti has impressive control and heroic tone. Commanding performances too from Milnes as Barnaba, Ghiaurov as Alvise and Baltsa as Laura, firm and intense all three. Bartoletti proves a vigorous and understanding conductor, presenting the blood and thunder with total commitment but finding the right charm in the most famous passage, the *Dance of the hours*.

Maria Callas gave one of her most vibrant, most compelling, most totally inspired performances on record in the title-role of *La Gioconda*, with flaws very much subdued. The challenge she presented to those around her is reflected in the soloists – Cossotto and Cappuccilli both at the very beginning of distinguished careers – as well as the distinctive tenor Ferraro and the conductor Votto, who has never done anything finer on record. The recording still sounds well, though it dates from 1959.

Poulenc, Francis (1899–1963)

(i) *Aubade;* (ii) *Double piano concerto in D min.; Sinfonietta.*
*** Virgin/EMI VCS5 45028-2. (i–ii) Jean-Bernard Pommier, with (ii) Anne Queffélec; City of London Sinf., Richard Hickox.

Jean-Bernard Pommier gives a thoroughly idiomatic and incisive account of the *Aubade*, and both he and Anne Queffélec play the *Concerto for two pianos* to the manner born. They have the measure of the pastiche Mozart slow movement and the quasi-Gamelan first. Good though the Duchable–Collard performance was – we gave it a Rosette in its bargain double-pack format – this has the better recording. Hickox gives an affectionate and charming account of the *Sinfonietta* that matches – almost – the splendid account from the Orchestre National under Dutoit. Very recommendable.

Les biches (ballet suite).
500♪ *** Chandos Dig. CHAN 9023 [id.]. Ulster O, Yan Pascal Tortelier – IBERT: *Divertissement*; MILHAUD: *Le boeuf; La création.* ***

Yan Pascal Tortelier and the Ulster Orchestra give an entirely winning account of Poulenc's ballet suite, and the playing is equally polished and crisply articulated. The lovely *Adagietto* is introduced with tender delicacy, yet reaches a suitably plangent climax. Top-drawer Chandos sound.

Bucolique (from *Variations sur le nom de Marguerite Long*); (i) *Concert champêtre. 2 Marches et un intermède; Fanfare; Pièce brève sur le nom d'Albert Roussel; Sinfonietta; Suite française.*
✪ *** Decca Dig. 452 665-2 [id.]. (i) Pascal Rogé; Fr. Nat. O, Charles Dutoit.

The major works here are the *Sinfonietta* and the *Concert champêtre*. The *Sinfonietta*, commissioned to mark the first anniversary of the BBC's Third Programme and dedicated to his fellow-composer, Auric, comes off marvellously. For those who entertain doubts as to its quality, this version by Charles Dutoit and the Orchestre National de France should be mandatory listening; it is certainly among the most persuasive accounts in the catalogue. In the *Concert champêtre* Pascal Rogé proves as fine a clavecinist as pianist and his account, equally strong on charm and elegance, ranks high among present recommendations. The smaller pieces greatly enhance the already strong attractions of this disc. All of them are imaginative, none more so than *Bucolique* from the *Variations sur le nom de Marguerite Long*. The excellence of the performances is matched by first-rate and meticulously balanced Decca sound.

(i) *Concert champêtre;* (ii) *Organ concerto in G min.;* (iii) *Piano concerto.*
** Virgin/EMI Dig. VCS 45067-2. (i) Maggie Cole; (ii) Gillian Weir; (iii) Jean-Bernard Pommier; City of London Sinf., Hickox.

This Virgin coupling of the *Concert champêtre* and the concertos for piano and organ originally appeared in 1990. For all their merits, none of the performances is a first recommendation, though Gillian Weir's account, recorded at the Royal Festival Hall in London, comes near. Maggie Cole is unequally balanced, and neither she nor Hickox's orchestra is well served by the recording (made at Henry Wood Hall) which is over-reverberant and opaque. Jean-Bernard Pommier is a more than capable player, but the performance as a whole is short of an essential ingredient in Poulenc's music, namely charm. The *Organ concerto* is worth three stars but its companions rate only one.

Organ concerto in G min.
** DG Dig. 437 827-2 [id.]. Simon Preston, Boston SO, Ozawa – FRANCK: *Symphony in D min.* **

Unlike its Franck coupling, the Preston/Ozawa account of the *Organ concerto* is not recorded live, but the hall acoustic still proves somewhat intractable, and the sound is not entirely convincing in fortissimos. However, the slightly harsh tinge given to the organ in the complicated tuttis of the finale (even though it is a little uncomfortable) has a distinctly Gallic character. The performance here is certainly spirited, while there is some engaging registration from Preston in the *Andante* section and a warmly elegant string response.

(i) *Double piano concerto in D min. Capriccio d'après le bal masqué; L'embarquement pour Cythère; Sonata for piano* (4 hands).
** Ph. Dig. 426 284-2 [id.]. Katia & Marielle Labèque, (i) with Boston SO, Ozawa.

The Labèque sisters turn in a flashy, rather brilliant account of the concerto and, strangely enough, they are long on energy and short on charm. Despite the bright, well-lit recording, there is something unappealing here, but fans of this partnership may well think differently.

CHAMBER MUSIC

Sonata for piano (4 hands); *Sonata for 2 pianos. Badinage; Capriccio; Elégie; L'Embarquement pour Cythère; 3 Feuillets d'album; 5 Impromptus; Promenades.*
(M) ** EMI CDM7 63946-2 [id.]. Jacques Février, Gabriel Tacchino.

Jacques Février was a close collaborator of the composer and recorded the *Concerto for two pianos* with him only a year before Poulenc's death. His authority notwithstanding, there are more accomplished versions of this repertoire now on the market from Rogé, Crossley and others.

(i) *3 Mouvements perpétuels;* (ii) *Le Bal masqué;* (iii) *Le Bestiare; Cocarde;* (iv) *Le Gendarme incompris;* (iii) *4 Poèmes de Max Jacob;* (ii) *Rapsodie nègre (1919).*
*** Decca Dig. 452 666-2 [id.]. (ii–iv) François Le Roux; (iv) Dominique Visse, Lambert Wilson; (i–ii) Pascal Rogé; Fr. Nat. O (members), Charles Dutoit.

An engaging and charming addition to the growing representation of Poulenc in the Decca catalogue. Most of these pieces are early (1917–21) settings of Apollinaire, Cocteau and Max Jacob and are offered together with the later, better-known and always captivating *Le Bal masqué*. Such was the popularity of the *Trois Mouvements perpétuels* that Poulenc orchestrated them in 1925 and made a second arrangement for nine instruments, as offered here. *Le Bestiare* is recorded in its original form for baritone and a small instrumental ensemble without piano. This is one of the few pieces on this CD in which Pascal Rogé does not participate. *Le Gendarme incompris* ('The misunderstood policeman') is a spoken entertainment, a *comédie-bouffe*, lasting about 20 minutes, a curtain-raiser interspersed with some songs for boarding schools to words by Cocteau and Raymond Radiguet (1903–23). As always with Poulenc there is a lot of charm, but an undercurrent of deeper feeling too. Elegant and polished performances, expertly balanced by the Decca engineers.

Violin sonata.
*** Sony Dig. SK 66839 [id.]. Cho-Liang Lin, Paul Crossley – DEBUSSY: *Violin sonata;* RAVEL: *Violin sonatas & Tzigane.* ***

Cho-Liang Lin and Paul Crossley give a vibrant, well-argued account of Poulenc's characterful and pungent *Sonata*, to which Sony accord excellent recording. They are much better balanced than are Frank Peter Zimmermann and Alexander Lonquich, to which we rather generously accorded three stars. Though that performance has charm and personality, the rather prominently balanced piano spoils it. The main rivals are Chantal Juillet and Pascal Rogé on Decca (443 968-2), and there is a spirited bargain challenge from Dong-Suk Kang and Pascal Devoyon on Naxos (8.550276 – see Instrumental Recitals, below). However, this present issue has much going for it: apart from the quality of the playing and the exemplary recorded sound, there is the generous programme on offer.

Improvisations Nos. 1–3; 6–8; 12–13; 15; Mouvements perpétuels; 3 Novelettes; Pastourelle; 3 Pièces; Les soirées de Nazelles; Valse.
500♪ ❁ *** Decca Dig. 417 438-2 [id.]. Pascal Rogé.

This music is absolutely enchanting, full of delight and wisdom; it has many unexpected touches and is teeming with character. Rogé is a far more persuasive exponent of it than any previous pianist on record; his playing is imaginative and inspiriting, and the recording is superb.

Mass in G; 4 Motets pour le temps de Noël.
(M) *** EMI Eminence Dig. CD-EMX 2275. Mark Harris, Winchester Cathedral Ch., Neary – HONEGGER: *Christmas cantata.* ***

The shadow of Stravinsky hovers over the *G major Mass*, and it is rather more self-conscious than his later choral pieces, certainly more so than the delightful *Quatre Motets pour le temps de Noël*. Martin Neary gets excellent results from the Winchester Cathedral Choir and his fine treble, Mark Harris. The EMI recording is also first rate, with well-defined detail and firm definition. The reissue offers only 58 minutes but is recommendable in every other respect.

Power, Leonel (d. 1445)

Missa, Alma redemptoris mater. Motets: *Agnus Dei; Ave Regina; Beata viscera; Credo; Gloria; Ibo michi ad montem; Quam pulchra es; Salve Regina; Sanctus.*
*** Virgin Veritas/EMI Dig. VER5 61345-2. Hilliard Ens., Hillier.

Power was a contemporary of Dunstable and was born probably in the mid-1370s. One of the leading composers represented in the Old Hall MS. (some 20 pieces are attributed to him), Power spent the last years of his life at Canterbury, but the music on this disc is earlier, coming from the period before 1413. The *Missa, Alma redemptoris mater* is probably the earliest, in which all the Mass sections are linked by a common cantus firmus and there is also a complex mathematical design. The music is of an austere beauty that is quite striking, as indeed is the remarkable singing of the Hilliard Ensemble. The digitally remastered recording comes from the early 1980s and is vivid and present. Strongly recommended.

Praetorius, Michael (1571–1621)

Christmas motets and chorale concertos: *In dulci jubilo; Joseph, lieber Joseph mein; Der Morgenstern ist aufgedrungen; Nun komm der Heiden Heiland; Omnis mundus jocundetur; Psalitte; Puer natus: Ein Kind geborn zu Bethlehem; Singet und klinget; Vom Himmel hoch; Wachet auf, ruft uns die Stimme; Wie schön leuchtet der Morgenstern. Missa gantz Teudsch: Kyrie eleison.*
**(*) MDG Dig. 614 0660-2 [id.]. Hassler Consort, Franz Rami.

The skill of Praetorius as a polyphonist is readily demonstrated in the more ambitious works here, with the settings varying within the chorale concertos between three and fifteen parts. Indeed the busy contrapuntal textures of the opening *Wachet auf* stretch up to nineteen different lines. They are full of interest, and *Nun komm der Heiden Heiland* is similarly lively and inventive. *Puer natus est* (à 3, 7 and 11) alternates slow and jolly, energetic sections very appealingly, while the two movements from the *Mass* show the composer at his most unconventionally individual: both are unexpectedly vigorous, with echoes in the solo vocal parts of the *Kyrie* and the *Gloria* more rhythmically forceful with alternating declamatory passages. But it is the simpler and more lyrical settings that one remembers most affectionately. *In dulci jubilo* for double choir with solo lines simply embellished is quite delightful, and the solo interweaving at the opening of *Joseph, lieber Joseph mein* is equally lovely. The brief *Psallitte*, lightly sprung in its rhythms, is also memorable. *Der Morgenstern* is first heard in a simple evocative presentation then, in the chorale variations which follow, it is expanded, but not too flamboyantly. Of the two closing items *Omnis mundus jocundetur* is appealingly carol-like, pastoral in feeling, in spite of its complexity of texture. *Singet und klinget* reintroduces the melody, so associated with this composer, which we have heard before as the basis for *Joseph, lieber Joseph mein*. The performances here are on a chamber scale, with solo voices well matched and blended, if lacking something in individuality. But the freshness of the music-making is never in doubt and, although the balance is immediate, the recording is very good, integrating the various textural strands within a pleasing acoustic, even if the sound tends to congeal a little rather than separating out naturally.

Dances from Terpsichore (Suite de ballets; Suite de voltes). (i) Motets: *Eulogodia Sionia: Resonet in laudibus; Musae Sionae: Allein Gott in der Höh sei Ehr; Aus tiefer Not schrei ich zu dir; Christus der uns selig macht; Gott der Vater wohn uns bei; Polyhymnia Caduceatrix: Erhalt uns, Herr, bei deinem Wort*.

**(*) Virgin Veritas/EMI VER5 61289-2 [CDM 61289]. Early Music Cons. of L., Munrow; (i) with boys of the Cathedral and Abbey Church of St Alban.

Terpsichore is a huge collection of some 300 dance tunes used by the French Court dance bands of Henri IV. They were enthusiastically assembled by the German composer, Michael Praetorius, who also harmonized them and arranged them in four to six parts; however, any selection is conjectural in the matter of orchestration. One of the great pioneers of the 'authentic' re-creation of early music, David Munrow's main purpose was to bring the music fully to life and, at the same time, imaginatively to stimulate the ear of the listener. This record, made in 1973, is one of his most successful achievements. Munrow's instrumentation is imaginatively done: the third item, a *Bourrée* played by four racketts (a cross between a shawm and comb-and-paper in sound), is fascinating. The collection is a delightful one. After this stimulating aural feast, Munrow offers six of the composer's eloquent motets, the finest of which is *Erhalt uns, Herr, bei deinem Wort* for four choirs, each with its own accompanying instrumental group, although the shorter *Gott der Vater wohn uns bei* for double choir is hardly less resplendent, and the joyful *Allein Gott in der Höh sei Ehr* (for counter-tenor and triple choir) is also most stimulating, with crumhorns added to the third accompanying group. The only snag is the lack of a really clean focus in the CD transfer, especially in the exultant closing *Christus der uns selig macht*. The Abbey Road acoustic is reverberant, creating a wide amplitude, and the remastering has not altogether been a success in trying to sharpen up the focus. But the result remains rich in amplitude, and this inspired music, which often reminds the listener of Giovanni Gabrieli, is sung superbly by the choir.

Christmas music: *Polyhymnia caduceatrix et panegyrica Nos. 10, Wie schön leuchtet der Morgenstern; 12, Puer natus in Bethlehem; 21, Wachet auf, ruft uns die Stimme; 34, In dulci jubilo*.

(M) *** Virgin Veritas/EMI VM5 61353-2. Taverner Cons. Ch. & Players, Parrott – SCHUTZ: *Christmas oratorio*. ***

This is the finest collection of Praetorius's vocal music in the current catalogue. The closing setting of *In dulci jubilo*, richly scored for five choirs and with the brass providing thrilling contrast and support for the voices, has great splendour. Before that comes the lovely, if less ambitious *Wie schön leuchtet der Morgenstern*. Both *Wachet auf* and *Puer natus in Bethlehem* are on a comparatively large scale, their combination of block sonorities and florid decorative effects the very essence of Renaissance style. The recording is splendidly balanced, with voices and brass blending and intertwining within an ample acoustic, and all the more welcome in this mid-priced Veritas reissue.

Prokofiev, Serge (1891–1953)

Andante for strings, Op. 50 bis.

(M) *(*) Revelation RV 10006 [id.]. Moscow RSO, Rozhdestvensky – GLAZUNOV: *Scènes de ballet* **; SIBELIUS: *Symphony No. 7; Rakastava*. (*)

The *Andante for strings* is a transcription Prokofiev made of the slow movement of his *First String quartet*, Op. 50, which was written in 1930. It is a beautiful piece and Rozhdestvensky shapes it with real eloquence. (It was previously coupled with his 1970s' account of the *Third Symphony*.) The sound is perfectly acceptable but not distinguished – and it is difficult to detect any improvement on the original LP. What a weird coupling though!

Chout, Op. 21; The Prodigal son, Op. 46 (both complete).
(M) ** Koch/Consonance 81-5004 [id.]. Moscow R. & TV SO, Rozhdestvensky.

The reissuing at mid-price of the old HMV/Melodiya LPs of the complete scores of Prokofiev's ballets, *Chout* and *The Prodigal son*, makes better sense than his symphonies. Neither are as well represented in the catalogue as are the symphonies, and neither is otherwise coupled together. Of course there are better (and three-star) versions (Järvi on Chandos, for one) but, despite some raw-sounding brass and less-than-opulent sound, this is a useful reissue.

Cinderella (ballet; complete), *Op. 87; Summer night: suite, Op. 123.*
500♪ ❁ *** DG Dig. 445 830-2 (2) [id.]. Russian Nat. O, Mikhail Pletnev.

Pletnev produces playing of terrific life, lightness of touch, poetic feeling and character. Quite simply the best-played, most atmospheric and affecting *Cinderella* we have ever had on disc.

Piano concertos Nos. 1–5.
(B) *** Double Decca 452 588-2 (2) [id.]. Ashkenazy, LSO, Previn.
(B) ** BMG/Melodiya Twofer 74321 30645 (2) [id.]. Victoria Postnikova, USSR MoC SO, Gennady Rozhdestvensky.

Piano concertos Nos. 1 in D flat, Op. 10; 3 in C, Op. 26; 4 in B flat, Op. 53.
500♪ (BB) *** Naxos Dig. 8.550566 [id.]. Kun Woo Paik, Polish Nat. RSO (Katowice), Antoni Witt.

Piano concertos Nos. 2 in G min., Op. 16; 5 in G, Op. 55.
500♪ (BB) *** Naxos Dig. 8.550565 [id.]. Kun Woo Paik, Polish Nat. RSO (Katowice), Antoni Witt.

(i) *Piano concertos Nos. 1–5;* (ii) *Autumnal, Op. 8;* (iii) *Overture on Hebrew themes, Op. 34.*
(M) *** Decca 448 126-2 (*Nos. 1, 2 & 4*); 448 127-2 (*Nos. 3 & 5; Autumnal; Overture*) [id.]. (i) Ashkenazy, LSO, Previn; (ii) LSO, Ashkenazy; (iii) Puddy, Ashkenazy & Gabrieli Qt.

Ashkenazy is a commanding soloist in both the *First* and *Second Concertos*, and his virtuosity in the *First* is quite dazzling. If he is curiously wayward in the opening of the *Second*, there is no question that this too is a masterly performance. The best-known, the *Third Concerto*, is keen-edged and crisply articulated, and the only reservation here concerns the slow movement, in which the piano entry immediately after the theme is uncharacteristically mannered. However, Ashkenazy is undoubtedly authoritative in No. 4 and he gives an admirable account of No. 5: every detail of phrasing and articulation is well thought out, and yet there is no want of spontaneity or any hint of calculation. Throughout, Previn and the LSO accompany sympathetically, and the recently remastered recording makes the most of the vintage mid-1970s Kingsway Hall sound. The criticisms are minor and should not inhibit readers from acquiring these most distinguished performances, for Ashkenazy has great panache. The early *In Autumn* is eminently worth having, as is the chamber performance of the *Overture on Hebrew Themes*. The concertos alone are also available on a Double Decca.

Kun Woo Paik's playing throughout these five concertos has exhilarating bravura. Tempi are dangerously fast at times and occasionally he has the orchestra almost scampering to keep up with him, but they do, and the result is often electrifying. In short, with vivid recording in the Concert Hall of Polish Radio, which has plenty of ambience, this set is enormously stimulating and a remarkable bargain.

The Melodiya recordings come from 1983–7. Given the poetic fantasy and formidable technical address Postnikova commands, one might have had high expectations of this cycle, yet it is curiously disappointing and at times even pedestrian. Of course there are good things but, without beating about the bush, the fact remains that there are better versions of all five individual concertos available, and the same applies should you want them as a complete set. The recordings are serviceable.

Piano concertos Nos. 2 in G min., Op. 16; 3 in C, Op. 26.
** Hyperion Dig. CDA 66858 [id.]. Nikolai Demidenko, LPO, Alexander Lazarev.

Nikolai Demidenko is a commanding artist whose dazzling technique and virtuosity are never in doubt and whose artistry compels admiration. Yet neither of these performances really challenges existing recommendations. In the *Second Concerto in G minor* Demidenko suffers by comparison with, say, Kun Woo Paik (Naxos), Yefim Bronfman (Sony) and Ashkenazy (Decca) – to choose three from all price ranges. Demidenko begins impressively but there is something curiously self-conscious that does not convince. Although he can produce beautifully coloured playing at the pianissimo level, he produces distinctly unpleasing, not to say ugly, tone above forte. In the popular *C major Concerto* there is even stronger competition, and again there is some forced tone in the exuberant lead-in to the second group of the first movement. The London Philharmonic and Lazarev give generally good support, and the recording is well balanced.

(i) *Piano concerto No. 5 in G, Op. 55. Piano sonata No. 8 in B flat, Op. 84; Visions fugitives, Op. 22/3, 6 & 9.*
(M) *** DG Originals 449 744-2 [id.]. Richter, (i) with Warsaw PO, Rowicki.

Richter's account of the *Fifth Piano concerto* is a classic. It was recorded in 1959, yet the sound of this excellent CD transfer belies the age of the original in its clarity, detail and vividness of colour. In any event it cannot be recommended too strongly to all admirers of Richter, Prokofiev and great piano-playing. Richter then plays the *Eighth Sonata* and the excerpts from the *Visions fugitives* with comparable mastery, the latter deriving from a live recital. In both cases the recording is surprisingly good.

Violin concertos Nos. 1 in D, Op. 19; 2 in G min., Op. 63.
500♪ ✿ *** Sony SK 53969 [id.]. Cho-Liang Lin, LAPO, Esa-Pekka Salonen – STRAVINSKY: *Violin concerto.* ***

The two Prokofiev concertos are among the composer's most richly lyrical works, and Lin brings out their romantic warmth as well as their dramatic bite. Salonen's understanding support culminates in ravishing accounts of both works.

Violin concerto No. 1 in D, Op. 19.
*** Teldec/Warner Dig. 4509 92256-2 [id.]. Maxim Vengerov, LSO, Rostropovich – SHOSTAKOVICH: *Violin concerto No. 1.* ***

Maxim Vengerov's coupling missed inclusion in our main volume, but it hardly needed additional advocacy from us as it not only won the *Gramophone*'s Concerto Award in 1995, but was also voted 'Record of the Year'. Vengerov's magnetism in both concertos is in no doubt; his playing is full of life and spontaneous feeling, helped by Rostropovich's highly supportive accompaniments. In the Prokofiev, Julian Rachlin displays rather more poetic subtlety (Sony SK 66567) but his pairing is with Tchaikovsky, and many will feel that Vengerov's Shostakovich coupling is even more appropriate, while his performance has its own special character and insights. The recording is excellent too.

Peter and the wolf, Op. 67.
500♪ ✿ (M) *** Virgin/EMI Dig. CU5 61137-2 [id.]. Gielgud, Ac. of L., Richard Stamp – SAINT-SAENS: *Carnival.* ***
** Cala Dig. CACD 1022 [id.]. Ben Kingsley (nar.), LSO, Mackerras – BRITTEN: *Young person's guide;* DUKAS: *L'apprenti sorcier.* **

(i) *Peter and the wolf;* (ii) *Lieutenant Kijé* (suite).
(M) **(*) Decca Phase Four 444 104-2 [id.]. (i) Sean Connery (nar.), RPO; (ii) Netherlands R. PO; Dorati – BRITTEN: *Young person's guide.* **(*)

Sean Connery uses a modern script by Gabrielle Hilton which brings a certain colloquial friendliness to the narrative and invites a relaxed style, to which the actor readily responds. If you can accept such extensions as 'dumb duck' and a pussy cat who is 'smooth, but greedy and vain', you will not be disappointed with Connery's participation in the climax of the tale, where Dorati supports him admirably. Both *Peter and the wolf* and *The Young person's guide to the orchestra* start with the orchestra tuning up, to create an anticipatory atmosphere, and the introductory matter is entirely fresh and informal. In *Lieutenant Kijé* Dorati is characteristically direct, with everything boldly characterized, and he secures excellent playing from the Netherlands orchestra. As with *Peter and the wolf*, the extremely vivid Decca Phase Four recording (not unnaturally balanced but ensuring every detail is clear) gives the performance a strong projection.

Although Ben Kingsley's narration has a gentle charm, it lacks pace and vividness. He is at his best in the moments of high drama (when the wolf makes its sinister walk round the tree) and pathos, as in his gentle assurance that the duck inside the wolf is still alive. But with the masterly storytelling of Sir John Gielgud available at mid-price, this Cala disc has comparatively little to recommend it.

Romeo and Juliet (ballet), *Op. 64* (complete).
500♪ (B) *** EMI forte CZS5 68607-2 (2). LSO, Previn.

Previn and the LSO made their recording in conjunction with live performances at the Royal Festival Hall, and the result reflects the humour and warmth which went with those live occasions. Previn's pointing of rhythm is consciously seductive, whether in fast, jaunty numbers or in the soaring lyricism of the love music. The Kingsway Hall recording quality is full and immediate, yet atmospheric too. A very real bargain.

Romeo and Juliet (ballet), *Op. 64:* highlights.
500♪ *** Sony Dig. MK 42662 [id.]. BPO, Salonen.

With magnificent playing from the Berlin Philharmonic Orchestra, Esa-Pekka Salonen's set seems marginally a first choice for those wanting merely a full-priced single disc of excerpts from Prokofiev's masterly score.

Sinfonia concertante for cello and orchestra, Op. 125.
*** DG Dig. 449 821-2 [id.]. Mischa Maisky, Russian Nat. O, Pletnev – MIASKOVSKY: *Cello concerto.* ***

Mischa Maisky is often over-emotional, but in Prokofiev's masterpiece his intensity is not misplaced. This is a highly characterful account that can withstand the most exalted comparisons. Pletnev and the Russian National Orchestra give a superb account of themselves and produce a real Prokofievian sonority, full of the mordant flavour the composer commands and with a splendid rhythmic spring. Judging from this, Pletnev would do a superlative Prokofiev symphony cycle, and one can only hope that DG will let him start with the *Sixth* and *Seventh*, written at roughly the same period. The Miaskovsky coupling enhances the attractiveness of this CD which, for the *Sinfonia concertante*, will now be a first choice for many collectors.

Symphonies Nos. 1–7; (i) *Lieutenant Kijé (suite), Op. 60.*
*** Chandos Dig. CHAN 8931/4 [id.] (without *Lieutenant Kijé*). SNO, Järvi.
(B) ** DG 431 614-2 (4) [id.]. BPO, Ozawa; (i) with Andreas Schmidt.

Obviously there can be no comparison here with the Ukraine orchestra (see below) and one would expect the Berlin Philharmonic under Seiji Ozawa to be a sure-fire recommendation in this repertoire. However, the synthetic DG balance manages to rob the Berlin strings of their opulence and sheen, and the recorded sound, though well enough detailed, lacks transparency and air. Nor does Ozawa bring an idiomatic approach or any special insights to the cycle. In the *Second Symphony*, in addition to the undistinguished recording there is a curious lack of conviction and personality about the performance. One has only to hear conductors like Karajan in Nos. 1 and 5 (DG 437 253-2), Abbado in No. 3 (Decca 448 579-2), Ashkenazy in 6 and 7 (Decca 443 325-2) to realize that there is more to this music than Ozawa finds; and those wanting a complete cycle can rest content with Järvi on Chandos. As performances they are the equal of the best, and the recordings are of the highest quality.

Symphonies Nos. 1 in D, Op. 25 (Classical); 2 in D min., Op. 40; Autumn, Op. 8; Dreams, Op. 6.
(BB) * Naxos Dig. 8.553053 [id.]. Ukraine Nat. SO, Theodore Kuchar.

Symphonies Nos. 3 in C min., Op. 44; 7 in C sharp min., Op. 131.
(BB) (*) Naxos Dig. 8.553054 [id.]. Ukraine Nat. SO, Theodore Kuchar.

Symphony No. 5 in B flat, Op. 100; The Year 1941, Op. 90.
(BB) (*) Naxos Dig. 8.553056 [id.]. Ukraine Nat. SO, Theodore Kuchar.

Symphony No. 6 in E flat min., Op. 111; Waltz suite, Op. 110.
(BB) * Naxos Dig. 8.553069 [id.]. Ukraine Nat. SO, Theodore Kuchar.

The Naxos cycle has had an indifferent press but, at its competitive price, it perhaps deserves better than to be dismissed out of hand. Even so, it is not so much of a bargain as all that! The *Fourth Symphony* has not yet appeared, and when it does the set will run to five CDs – or even six if Naxos decide to issue the original (1930) version and the post-war revision separately. The first disc brings two early rarities, *Autumn* and *Dreams*, as well as the *First* and *Second Symphonies*. It soon becomes evident that the Ukraine National Orchestra is not in the first rank. Interpretatively things are less impressive: the *Classical Symphony* is heavy-handed and ponderous in Kuchar's hands. Each movement (with the exception of the finale) is too slow. The latter has some sparkle, but the rest is hard work. In the first movement of the *Second Symphony* the strings, which are not the weightiest, are rather swamped by the brass, and the imaginative set of variations which comprise the second movement are distinctly lacklustre in this performance.

The *Third*, related as it is to the opera, *The Fiery Angel*, is undoubtedly one of Prokofiev's most extraordinary creations, and the *Seventh* with its touch of bitter-sweetness is consistently underrated. To anyone traversing the complete cycle, the weaknesses of the orchestra will now become all too apparent, and the playing has far too little punch and the conducting too little imagination. Neither score deserves such routine phrasing. The *Fifth* is so generously represented on CD, even at mid-price, that any newcomer has to be very good indeed to pose an effective challenge. This cannot even be classified as *vin ordinaire*; it is very ordinary indeed, and not even the presence of a rarity, *The Year 1941*, lifts this to a really recommendable category. The *Sixth Symphony* fares better, not so much in matters of orchestral finesse as in interpretative intention. However, intentions and deeds are two different things and, even though the playing has more character and conviction than the *Fifth*, it never rises to anything like distinction. Nor does the recording.

Symphonies Nos. 1 in D (Classical), Op. 25; 5 in B flat, Op. 100.
500♪ (M) *** DG 437 253-2 [id.]. BPO, Karajan.
(M) ** BMG/Melodiya Dig. 74321 32042-2 [id.]. Moscow Philh. O, Dmitri Kitaienko.

Symphonies Nos. 1 in D (Classical), Op. 25; 5 in B flat, Op. 100; Russian overture, Op. 72.
(BB) ** Belart 461 320-2. LSO or LPO, Walter Weller.

Karajan's 1979 recording of the *Fifth* is in a class of its own. The playing has wonderful tonal sophistication, and this remains among the most distinguished *Fifths* ever recorded; it is coupled with Karajan's 1982 digital recording of the *Classical Symphony*, in which his performance is predictably brilliant.

Weller's performance of the *Classical Symphony* is excellent, perhaps lacking the last degree of imagination, but with first-class playing from the LSO. The *Fifth Symphony* also has undoubted merits, and again the LSO are in top form; but Weller's reading is let down by a slow movement which lacks real bite and forward impetus (it is much slower than the metronome marking). Weller also makes too much of the *l'istesso tempo* in the Scherzo. The *Russian overture* (played by the LPO) has plenty of vitality. What makes this disc worth considering for super-bargain hunters is the Decca recording, which is strikingly vivid and well balanced too.

Given the current competition, Dmitri Kitaienko's accounts of the *First* and *Fifth Symphonies* with the Moscow Philharmonic are little more than also-rans. With Karajan, Previn, Ormandy and Koussevitzky in the catalogue, all at modest prices, these performances are unlikely to prompt the pulse to beat faster.

Symphonies Nos. 1 in D (Classical), Op. 25; 7 in C sharp min., Op. 131.
(M) *(*) Koch/Consonance 81-5006 [id.]. Moscow RSO, Rozhdestvensky.

These performances appeared on the HMV/Melodiya label in the early 1970s and they did admirable service at the time, even if the Moscow Radio Orchestra was not the last word in finesse. Their reappearance, while welcome, finds them in a far more competitive climate and, although they are good, they would no longer be the first recommendation they once were. It is possible to imagine better transfers; an A/B sample of the *Seventh Symphony* against the HMV LP is not to the advantage of the newcomer.

Symphonies Nos. 2 in D min., Op. 40; 3 in C min., Op. 44.
(M) * Koch/Consonance 81-5007 [id.]. Moscow RSO, Rozhdestvensky.

The sound here does not wear its years well, though the performance – particularly in the second movement of No. 2 – is very immediate and convincing. No. 3 sounds earlier than the 1971 LP and is much rougher and more constricted. Sonically, it is only marginally better than the Revelation disc listed below. The *Second Symphony* is probably worth considering at mid-price, but the *Third* rates only half a star!

Symphony No. 3 in C min., Op. 44.
(M) * Revelation RV 10025 [id.]. USSR State SO, Gennady Rozhdestvensky – SHOSTAKOVICH: *Symphony No. 5.* *

Rozhdestvensky's account of the *Third Symphony* comes from 1961 and is in its way quite electrifying. It is full of character and has a hell-for-leather quality which is communicative. The *Third Symphony* was a great rarity at this time and was probably new to the players too. The grim sound-quality is such as to rule it out as more than a one-star recommendation. But readers should try to hear it for themselves as it has tremendous fire, and this may for some collectors outweigh the abysmal sound.

Symphonies Nos. 3 in C min., Op. 44; 4 in C, Op. 47.
*(*) DG Dig. 437 838-2. BPO, Ozawa.

It is no good pretending that the Ozawa–Berlin set is more successful in its parts than it is in the whole. The *Third* does not begin to match the Riccardo Muti version with the Philadelphia Orchestra, coupled with No. 1 (Ph. 432 992-2), which is our first recommendtion for this coupling, and in the *Fourth* Neeme Järvi is much to be preferred. The sound does not flatter the Berlin Philharmonic, whose strings do not have the freshness and bloom one looks for.

Symphony No. 5 in B flat, Op. 100; Lieutenant Kijé (suite), Op. 60.
(M) **(*) EMI Eminence Dig. CD-EMX 2273. RPO, Vernon Handley.

Symphony No. 5 in B flat, Op. 100; Scythian suite, Op. 20.
*** EMI Dig. CDC7 54577-2 [id.]. CBSO, Simon Rattle.

Rattle's brilliantly recorded account of the *Fifth Symphony* with the CBSO is very fine indeed, full of fire and vitality; given the quality of the sound, it must rank along with the best now available. The slow movement comes off particularly well – though perhaps it is invidious to single out one particular movement, for these are really stimulating performances with many imaginative touches. Thoroughly recommendable. Having the full five-movement *Lieutenant Kijé suite* as well as the *Fifth Symphony* makes a stimulating coupling on Vernon Handley's EMI disc with the RPO. The amiability of the *Kijé* performance, colourful in its illustration of the different situations, spreads over into the *Symphony*. This is a more easy-going reading than most, beautifully played but putting an emphasis on expressiveness rather than on dramatic bite. The Scherzo is jolly in an easily jazzy way rather than sharp; and, for all its seductive beauty, the slow movement is rather too soft-grained for Prokofiev, partly a question of the recording acoustic in St Augustine's Church, Kilburn. In the relaxed account of the finale, the marking *giocoso* is characteristically what Handley emphasizes. An agreeable version for those who fancy the coupling, even if this account of the *Symphony* misses some of its darker side.

(i) *Symphony No. 5 in B flat, Op. 100;* (ii) *Scythian suite, Op. 20;* (iii) *Dreams, Op. 6;* (iv) *The white swan, Op. 7* (for female chorus).
(B) ** BBC Radio Classics 15656 91462 [id.]. (i) Leningrad PO; (ii) LSO; (iii) BBC SO, with Alan Civil; (iv) BBC SO Ch.; all cond. Rozhdestvensky.

Gennady Rozhdestvensky's account of the *Fifth Symphony* with the Leningrad Philharmonic comes from a 1971 Promenade Concert. The performance is eminently satisfactory and the analogue BBC recording is more than acceptable. One of the main attractions of the disc lies in the interest of the couplings. The *Scythian suite*, recorded with the LSO at London's Royal Festival Hall in 1976, has appropriate energy and savagery, but the sound is less spacious and open and the dynamic range less wide-ranging. The other two pieces are rarities and, though there are alternative versions of *Dreams*, there is none of *The white swan*, a setting of Konstantin Balmont which Rozhdestvensky himself has reconstructed from the autograph. Even readers who already have the *Fifth Symphony* may well want to consider this for the sake of the additional music.

PIANO MUSIC

10 Pieces from Romeo and Juliet, Op. 75; War and peace: Waltz, Op. 96/1. The Love of three oranges, Op. 33b: Scherzo; March. 6 Pieces from Cinderella, Op. 102.
*** Decca Dig. 452 062-2 [id.]. Vladimir Ashkenazy.

Ashkenazy's recital concentrates on Prokofiev's music for the stage in the composer's own adroit transcriptions for the keyboard. Excerpts from two operas, including the beguiling *Waltz* from *War and peace*, the ten pieces from *Romeo and Juliet* and six from *Cinderella*, make an attractive and appealing hour's listening, particularly when they are as well characterized and vividly recorded as they are here. If this programme appeals, there is no need to hesitate.

Piano sonatas Nos. 2 in D min., Op. 14; 3 in A min., Op. 28; 5 in C, Op. 38; 9 in C, Op. 103.
*** Sony Dig. SK53273 [id.]. Yefim Bronfman.

We are almost spoilt for choice in the Prokofiev *Sonatas*. There are fine complete sets by Boris Berman and Frederic Chiu, not to mention Gavrilov's splendid accounts of Nos. 3, 7 and 8 on DG, and outstanding individual sonatas: Pogorelich's *Sixth* and both Pollini's and Richter's *Seventh*. We complained of short measure in the *Seventh* and *Eighth Sonatas* in our main volume, but there need be no such caveat here. Bronfman is highly articulate and meticulously attentive to details of dynamics and phrasing. The brittle rhythms and the energy of the writing are always effectively conveyed. He plays the earlier (and in many respects finer) version of the inventive *Fifth Sonata*. The recorded sound is excellent, and readers wanting this particular coupling need not hesitate. A good three-star recommendation, and the equal of any of the modern versions now on the market.

Piano sonata No. 6 in A, Op. 82.
500♪ ✿ *** DG Dig. 413 363-2 [id.]. Pogorelich – RAVEL: *Gaspard de la nuit.* ***

Pogorelich's performance of the *Sixth Sonata* is quite simply dazzling; indeed, it is by far the best version of it ever put on record. It is certainly Pogorelich's most brilliant record so far and can be recommended with the utmost enthusiasm in its CD format.

Visions fugitives, Op 22.
*** Decca Dig. 444 803-2 [id.]. Olli Mustonen – HINDEMITH: *Ludus tonalis.* ***

You are not likely to buy Mustonen's CD for this Prokofiev coupling, but rather to enjoy this attractive suite as an antidote to Hindemith's much more intractable *Ludus tonalis*. If you venture so bravely into Hindemith's world you will find Mustonen's account of the *Visions fugitives* perceptive, strongly characterized and vividly coloured. It is also very well recorded.

VOCAL MUSIC

(i) *Alexander Nevsky, Op. 78;* (ii) *Lieutenant Kijé, Op. 60; Scythian suite, Op. 20.*
500♪ (M) *** DG 447 419-2 [id.]. (i) Elena Obraztsova; London Symphony Ch., LSO; (ii) Chicago SO; Claudio Abbado.

Abbado's performance of *Alexander Nevsky* culminates in a deeply moving account of the tragic lament after the battle (here very beautifully sung by Obraztsova), made the more telling when the battle itself is so fine an example of orchestral virtuosity. The chorus is as incisive as the orchestra. A fine account of *Lieutenant Kijé* and what is probably the best version of the *Scythian suite* to appear in many years make this a desirable reissue in DG's Legendary Recordings series.

The Fiery Angel (complete).
500♪ ✿ *** Ph. Dig. 446 078-2 (2) [id.] (Video 070 198-3; LD 070 198-1). Gorchakova, Leiferkus, Pluzhnikov, Ognovanko, soloists; Kirov Op. Ch. & O, Gergiev.

Impressive as Neeme Järvi's 1990 recording for DG of this elusive but powerful opera is, Gergiev's with Kirov forces is even finer. From the very outset the style is declamatory in a way that recalls Mussorgsky. Indeed, in terms of fantasy and sheer imaginative vision, *The Fiery Angel* reaches heights which Prokofiev never surpassed, and its atmosphere resonates for a long time.

War and peace (complete).
500♪ ✿ (M) *** Erato/Warner 2292 45331-2 (4) [id.]. Vishnevskaya, Miller, Ciesinski, Tumagian, Ochman, Ghiuselev, Smith, Paunova, Petkov, Toczyska, Zakai, Gedda, Fr. R. Ch. & Nat. O, Rostropovich.

War and Peace is not just epic in scale but warmly approachable, with a fund of melody rarely matched this century. Rostropovich's complete account on record, flawed in some of the casting, nevertheless confirms equally that this is one of the great operatic masterpieces of the century. It was natural that Rostropovich's wife, Galina Vishnevskaya, should sing the central role of Natasha. It is extraordinary how convincingly this mature soprano in her early sixties characterizes a young girl; there may be raw moments, but she is completely inside the role. The Hungarian baritone, Lajos Miller, is a clear-voiced Andrei and Wiesław Ochman is a first-rate Pierre, while Nicola Ghiuselev is a noble Kutuzov, in some ways the most impressive of all.

Puccini, Giacomo (1858–1924)

(i) *Messa di gloria;* (ii) *Capriccio sinfonico; Preludio sinfonico.*
(B) **(*) Erato/Warner 0630 12818-2 [id.]. (i) Johns, Huttenlocher, Ch. & O of Gulbenkian Foundation, Lisbon, Corboz; (ii) Monte-Carlo Op. O, Scimone.

The Lisbon performance from Corboz is more affectionate than Scimone's mid-priced digital version, also on Erato (4509 96367-2 – see our main volume), but that has a stronger profile and remains a preferable choice. Nevertheless there is splendid choral singing in Lisbon, and the reverberant recording has been made to sound firmer and cleaner on CD, while the sound is impressively full. The present reissue has a price advantage, and the coupling includes two fascinating early orchestral works, with the *Capriccio sinfonico* suddenly producing out of a hat the famous theme that was to become the Bohemian motif of *La Bohème*. The playing of the Monte Carlo orchestra is committed, if not very polished.

La Bohème (complete).
*** EMI Dig. CDC5 56120-2 [Ang. CDCB 56120]. Vaduva, Alagna, Swenson, Hampson, Keenlyside, Ramey, L. Voices, boys from L. Oratory School, Philh. O, Pappano.
(B) *** Decca Double 448 725-2 (2) [id.]. Tebaldi, Bergonzi, Bastianini, Siepi, Corena, D'Angelo, St Cecilia Ac. Ch. & O, Serafin.
(***) EMI mono CDS5 56295-2 (2). Callas, Di Stefano, Moffo, Panerai, La Scala, Milan, Ch. & O, Votto.
(M) **(*) RCA 74321 39496-2 (2) [09026 61725-2]. Caballé, Domingo, Milnes, Raimondi, Alldis Ch., Wandsworth School Boys' Ch., LPO, Solti.

** Erato/Warner Dig. 0630 10699-2 (2) [id.]. Te Kanawa, Leech, Titus, Quilico, Gustafson, Amb. S., St Clement Danes School Ch., LSO, Kent Nagano.

(M) ** Nimbus mono NI 7862/3 [id.]. Albanese, Gigli, Oili, Menotti, Baracchi, Baronti, La Scala, Milan, Ch. & O, Berrettoni.

Pappano's recording of *Bohème* is the finest in over 20 years or even longer – sumptuously played and recorded, and characterfully sung by a starry cast. Above all, it is conducted with ever-fresh imagination by Antonio Pappano, who brings out not just subtle emotions alongside high passion, but also the fun of the piece in lightly sprung rhythms. This is a performance in which nothing is routine and where, over and over again, you hear Puccini afresh. It is Pappano's gift – and one registers it from the start – that extremes are made to sound totally natural, not forced or self-conscious, whether of extreme speeds, both fast and slow, of extreme dynamics, superbly caught by the engineers, or of extreme flexibility in rubato. So the exchanges when Mimì arrives have the most moving intimacy at the gentlest pianissimo, with the singers given full expressive freedom within a purposeful frame. The great set-piece numbers at the end of Act I, *Che gelida manina*, *Mi chiamano Mimì* and *O soave fanciulla*, then have the freshness of genuine emotion – of Rodolfo tenderly concerned, of Mimì vulnerable, of their realization of love swelling in a radiant, towering crescendo. Alagna's tenor may not be velvety, but it has a fine tonal range with a heroic ring, and Vaduva is similarly characterful rather than just sweet. The others make a superb team, virtually incomparable today – Ruth Swenson using her dramatic timbres most delicately even in the outburst of the waltz song, Thomas Hampson a swaggering Marcello, with Samuel Ramey and Simon Keenlyside characterfully contrasted as the other two Bohemians, all relishing the fun. With the Philharmonia inspired to playing of consistent flair, notably the woodwind soloists, this is a version to stand alongside the classics of the past.

Tebaldi's Decca set with Bergonzi dominated the catalogue in the early days of stereo; technically it was an outstanding recording in its day, and it still sounds astonishingly vivid, with a very convincing theatrical atmosphere. At Double Decca price, it is one of the great operatic bargains in the current catalogue. Vocally the performance achieves a consistently high standard, with Tebaldi as Mimì the most affecting. Carlo Bergonzi is a fine Rodolfo; Bastianini and Siepi are both superb as Marcello and Colline, and even the small parts of Benoit and Alcindoro (as usual taken by a single artist) have the benefit of Corena's magnificent voice. The veteran Serafin was more vital here than on some of his records. The recording, not far off 40 years old, has its vividness and sense of stage perspective enhanced on CD. The set comes with a perfectly adequate cued synopsis, for *La Bohème* is an exceptionally easy opera to follow.

Callas, flashing-eyed and formidable, may seem even less suited to the role of Mimì than to that of Butterfly, but characteristically her insights make for a vibrantly involving performance. Though Giuseppe di Stefano is not the subtlest of Rodolfos, he is in excellent voice here, and Moffo and Panerai make a strong partnership as the second pair of lovers. Votto occasionally coarsens Puccini's score but he directs with energy. The comparatively restricted dynamic range means that the singers appear to be 'front stage', but there is no lack of light and shade in Act II.

The glory of Solti's set of *Bohème* is the singing of Montserrat Caballé as Mimì, an intensely characterful and imaginative reading which makes you listen with new intensity to every phrase, the voice at its most radiant. Domingo is unfortunately not at his most inspired. *Che gelida manina* is relatively coarse, though here as elsewhere he produces glorious heroic tone, and he never falls into vulgarity. The rest of the team is strong, but Solti's tense interpretation of a work he had never conducted in the opera house does not quite let either the full flexibility of the music or the full warmth of romanticism have their place. The recording, however, is both vivid and atmospheric, and this recording is welcome back to the catalogue, pleasingly packaged in RCA's mid-priced Opera Treasury series. At the moment it remains at full price in the USA.

Kent Nagano conducts a strong, lusty performance, very well played, and recorded in full and brilliant upfront sound in the same venue as Pappano's EMI version, Abbey Road studios. With a strong cast it would normally be a fair contender, but next to Pappano it sounds heavy-handed, even coarse, lacking the tenderness which marks so much of the EMI set. Partly because of the close balance of voices, there are few pianissimos, with Richard Leech singing out well, but sounding lusty and charmless in *Che gelida manina* and with Dame Kiri Te Kanawa underlining *Mi chiamano Mimì* heavily at a slow speed. As recorded, she sounds too mature for an ingénue Mimì, not at all vulnerable; though the rest make up a strong cast, there is little feeling of a dramatic presentation, rather a concert account.

It is good to have the classic recording with Gigli restored to the catalogue in Nimbus's Prima Voce series, when EMI's own CD transfer, drier and less atmospheric, has been deleted. The Nimbus transfer process (recording an acoustic-horn gramophone in a large room) works well here, with plenty of body in the sound, without too much masking of reverberation, and with a bloom on the voices. The glory of the set is Gigli's Rodolfo, with a chuckle in the voice bringing out the fun, while Gigli uses his pouting manner charmingly, with the occasional sob adding to the charm. He adds little touches, as when he murmurs '*Prego*' when ushering Mimì out, before she discovers she has lost her key. He dwarfs the others, with even Albanese a little shrill as Mimì.

La Bohème: highlights.
(M) **(*) EMI CDM5 66050-2 [id.] (from complete set, with Freni, Gedda, Adani, Sereni, Mazzoli; cond. Schippers).

The selection from the Schippers set is not generous (59 minutes), and Freni is balanced rather closely, but she and Gedda make an impressive pair of lovers and there is much that is memorable here, not least the closing scene. As usual with this series, a synopsis places each excerpt in context.

La Fanciulla del West (The Girl of the Golden West) complete.
500♪ ❁ (M) *** Decca 421 595-2 (2) [id.]. Tebaldi, Del Monaco, MacNeil, Tozzi, St Cecilia Ac., Rome, Ch. & O, Capuana.

The Decca set of *La Fanciulla del West* has been remastered for CD with spectacular success. Tebaldi gives one of her most warm-hearted and understanding performances on record, and Mario del Monaco displays the wonderfully heroic quality of his voice to great – if sometimes tiring – effect. Cornell MacNeil as the villain, Sheriff Rance, sings with great precision and attack, with Tozzi singing beautifully. Capuana's expansive reading is matched by the imagination of the production, with the closing scene wonderfully effective.

Gianni Schicchi (complete).
500♪ (M) *** RCA Dig. 74321 25285-2 [id.]. Panerai, Donath, Seiffert, Bav. R. Ch., Munich R. O, Patanè.
*(*) Decca Dig. 444 395-2 [id.]. Nucci, Freni, Alagna, Maggio Musicale Fiorentino O, Bartoletti.

The RCA (formerly Eurodisc) recording of *Gianni Schicchi* brings a co-production with Bavarian Radio, and the recording is vivid and well balanced. Central to the performance's success is the vintage Schicchi of Rolando Panerai, still rich and firm. He confidently characterizes the Florentine trickster in every phrase, building a superb portrait, finely timed. Peter Seiffert as Rinuccio gives a dashing performance, consistently clean and firm of tone, making light of the high tessitura and rising splendidly to the challenge of the big central aria. Helen Donath would have sounded even sweeter a few years earlier, but she gives a tender, appealing portrait of Lauretta. Though Italian voices are in the minority, it is a confident team. In its reissued form, access to the disc has been greatly improved and there are now seven cues.

Madama Butterfly (complete).
500♪ *** DG Dig. 423 567-2 (3) [id.]. Freni, Carreras, Berganza, Pons, Amb. Op. Ch., Philh. O, Sinopoli.
(B) *** Decca Double 452 594-2 (2) [id.]. Tebaldi, Bergonzi, Cossotto, Sordello, St Cecilia, Rome, Ac. Ch. & O, Serafin.
(***) EMI mono CDS5 56298-2 (2). Callas, Gedda, Borriello, Danieli, La Scala, Milan, Ch. & O, Karajan.
(M) ** RCA 74321 39497-2 (2) [6160-2-RC]. Leontyne Price, Richard Tucker, Philip Maero, Rosalind Elias, RCA Italiana Ch. and O, Leinsdorf.

However expansive his speeds, Sinopoli is never sentimental or self-indulgent. Puccini's honeyed moments are given, not sloppily, but with rapt intensity. They are then set the more movingly against the biting moments, from the opening fugato of Act I, sharply incisive, through to the final aria, tough and intense. As she was for Karajan in his classic Decca set, Freni is a model Butterfly; though the voice is no longer so girlish, she projects the tragedy even more weightily than before. José Carreras is similarly presented as a large-scale Pinkerton. Juan Pons is a virile Sharpless and Teresa Berganza an equally positive, unfruity Suzuki. This is a set which in its spacious but intensely concentrated way brings a unique and unforgettable experience. But it is on three CDs.

Serafin's sensitive and beautifully paced reading finds Tebaldi at her most radiant. Though she was never the most deft of Butterflies dramatically (she never actually sang the role on stage before recording it), her singing is consistently rich and beautiful, breathtakingly so in passages such as the one in Act I when she tells Pinkerton she has changed her religion. The excellence of the Decca engineering in 1958 is amply proved in the CD transfer, the current remastering now providing full, atmospheric sound from the very beginning, opening out further as the orchestration grows fuller, with voices very precisely and realistically placed. At Double Decca price this is a pretty formidable bargain. First choice for this opera rests with the DG Sinopoli set with Freni, Carreras and Berganza. However, like the radiant Karajan alternative in which Freni is paired with Pavarotti (417 577-2), this involves three premium-priced discs, thus costing about three times as much as the Tebaldi version, which is now very highly recommendable.

Callas's view, aided by superbly imaginative and spacious conducting from Karajan, gives extra dimension to the Puccinian little woman, and with some keenly intelligent singing too from Gedda as

Pinkerton this is a set which has a special compulsion. The performance projects the more vividly on CD, even though the lack of stereo in so atmospheric an opera is a serious disadvantage.

Leontyne Price was in glorious voice when, in July 1962, she recorded this opera under Erich Leinsdorf. This is a weighty portrait of Butterfly, with Price's gloriously rich, creamy tone seamlessly controlled, even if occasionally she indulges in unwanted portamenti. The obvious snag is that some of the vocal acting sounds too crude for Puccini's little woman, and Tucker is at times similarly coarse as Pinkerton. Added to that, what puts the set finally out of court is Leinsdorf's metrical and unresilient conducting, and with that rigidity comes a straitjacketing of emotion. However, the current mid-priced UK reissue in RCA's Opera Treasury series means that the set can certainly be recommended to admirers of Leontyne Price, for the remastering is vividly atmospheric.

Manon Lescaut (complete).

500♪ *** Decca Dig. 440 200-2 (2) [id.]. Freni, Pavarotti, Croft, Taddei, Vargas, Bartoli, NY Met. Op. Ch. & O, Levine.

(***) EMI mono CDS5 56301-2 (2). Callas, Di Stefano, Fioravanti, La Scala, Milan, Ch. and O, Serafin.

With Luciano Pavarotti as a powerful Des Grieux, James Levine conducts a comparably big-boned performance of *Manon Lescaut*, bringing out the red-blooded drama of Puccini's first big success, while not ignoring its warmth and tender poetry. The impact is enhanced by exceptionally full, vivid sound, with the voices balanced close, well in front of the orchestra.

It is typical of Callas that she turns the final scene into the most compelling part of the opera. Serafin, who could be a lethargic recording conductor, is here electrifying, and Di Stefano too is inspired to one of his finest complete opera recordings. The cast-list even includes the young Fiorenza Cossotto, impressive as the singer in the Act II *Madrigal*. The recording – still in mono, not a stereo transcription – minimizes the original boxiness and gives good detail.

(i) *La Rondine* (complete). (ii) *Le Villi: Prelude, L'Abbandono; La Tregenda; Ecco la casa . . . Torna al felice*. (iii) Song: *Morire!*.

*** EMI Dig. CDS5 56338-2 (2) [id.]. (i–iii) Roberto Alagna; (i) Gheorghiu, Mula-Tchako, Matteuzzi, Rinaldi; (i–ii) London Voices, LSO, Pappano; (iii) Pappano (piano).

Puccini's ill-timed attempt to outshine Lehár in an operetta-like subject has long been counted a failure. The two previous recordings have each modified that idea, but Pappano on this EMI issue transforms the work, revealing it to be another masterpiece. He is aided by the partnership of Angela Gheorghiu, most moving in the Violetta-like role of the heroine, Magda, and of Alagna as the ardent young student she falls in love with. Puccini cunningly interweaves elements not just of *La Traviata* but of *The Merry Widow* and *Fledermaus*, not to mention earlier Puccini operas, with a melodic style for the most part simpler than before, with one striking theme following another in profusion, each subtly interwoven.

Pappano consistently brings out the poetry, drawing on emotions far deeper than are suggested by this operetta-like subject, thanks also to Gheorghiu's superb performance, translating her mastery as Violetta to this comparable character, tenderly expressive, as in Magda's first big solo, *Che il bel sogno di Doretta*. Consistently she makes you share the courtesan's wild dream of finding her young student. Most striking of all is the way she convinces you of her heartbreak, when in Act III she finally gives up Ruggero, not through any opposition from his family, but out of love for him, knowing the liaison would ruin him.

As Ruggero, the hero, Alagna winningly characterizes the ardent young student, singing in his freshest voice. What will specially delight Puccinians in this set is that he is given an extra aria about Paris, *Parigi e un citta*, which transforms his otherwise minimal contribution to Act I. Adapting it from a song, Puccini included it in the 1920 Viennese version of the score but never incorporated it in the original, Italian version, as it certainly deserves. The role of the poet, Prunier, is also transformed thanks to the casting of the clear-toned William Matteuzzi in what is normally a comprimario role. Not only is his relationship with Magda beautifully drawn, his improbable affair with the skittish maid, Lisette (clone of Adèle in *Fledermaus*), is made totally convincing too, mirroring Magda's affair. Inva Mula-Tchako is equally well cast in that soubrette role, bright, clear and vivacious, with Alberto Rinaldi making the sugar-daddy, Rambaldo, the dull dog intended.

The fill-ups are welcome too, particularly as neither of the rival sets has any. The exccrpts from *Le Villi*, warm and dramatic, include two orchestral showpieces. Alagna also gives a ringing account of Roberto's aria, as he does of the song, *Morire!* – with Pappano at the piano – the source of the extra aria for Ruggero included in the main opera.

Suor Angelica (complete).

(M) **(*) RCA 74321 40575-2. Popp, Lipovšek, Schiml, Jennings, Bav. R. Ch., Munich R. O, Patanè.

Patanè's performance is idiomatic and consistently well placed. Neither Lucia Popp as Angelica nor

Marjana Lipovšek as the vindictive Zia Principessa is ideally cast – the one overstressed, the other sounding too young – but these are both fine artists who sing with consistent imagination, and the recording is pleasingly atmospheric. There is a libretto/translation provided, and the only snag is the lack of cueing: only two tracks are indicated, one 28 minutes into the opera and the second 12 minutes later.

Il Tabarro (complete).

(M) *** RCA 74321 45081-2. Nimsgern, Tokody, Lamberti, Pane, Bav. R. Ch., Munich R. O, Patanè.

Patanè in his larger-than-life direction may at times run the risk of exaggerating the melodrama, but the result is richly enjoyable. Ilona Tokody, already well known from Hungaroton opera sets, makes a powerful, strongly projected Giorgetta, somewhat showing up the relative weakness of the tenor, Giorgio Lamberti, as her lover, Luigi. His over-emphatic underlining mars his legato, but the main love-duet comes over with gutsy strength. Siegmund Nimsgern makes a powerful Michele, a shade too explosive in the climactic final aria, but generally firm and clean in his projection, making the character more sinister. The full and brilliant recording has voices set convincingly on a believable stage, well balanced against the orchestra, the effect appealingly atmospheric. There is a libretto/translation and the reissue is much more generously cued than before, providing ten tracks in all.

Tosca (complete).

500♪ ❁ *** EMI mono CDS5 56304-2 (2). Callas, Di Stefano, Gobbi, Calabrese, La Scala, Milan, Ch. and O, De Sabata.

(B) *** Decca Double 452 620-2 (2) [id.]. Leontyne Price, Di Stefano, Taddei, V. State Op. Ch., VPO, Karajan.

(M) *** RCA 74321 39503-2 (2) [RCD-2-0105]. Leontyne Price, Domingo, Milnes, Plishka, Alldis Ch., Wandsworth School Boys' Ch., New Philh. O, Mehta.

** Teldec/Warner Dig. 0630 12372-2 (2) [id.]. Malfitano, Domingo, Raimondi, Rome RAI Ch. & SO, Mehta.

There has never been a finer recorded performance of *Tosca* than Callas's first, with Victor de Sabata conducting and Tito Gobbi as Scarpia. Gobbi makes the unbelievably villainous police chief into a genuinely three-dimensional character, and Di Stefano as the hero, Cavaradossi, was at his finest. The conducting of De Sabata is spaciously lyrical as well as sharply dramatic, and the mono recording is superbly balanced in Walter Legge's fine production. Though there is inevitably less spaciousness than in a stereo recording, the voices are caught gloriously.

Now reissued on a Double Decca, Karajan's Vienna set is unbeatable value. Karajan deserves equal credit with the principal singers for the vital, imaginative performance, recorded in Vienna. Taddei himself has a marvellously wide range of tone-colour, and though he cannot quite match the Gobbi snarl he has almost every other weapon in his armoury. Leontyne Price is at the peak of her form and Di Stefano sings most sensitively. The sound of the Vienna orchestra is enthralling – both more refined and richer than usual in a Puccini opera – and it sounds quite marvellous in its digitally remastered format, combining presence with atmosphere and making a superb bargain.

Price made her second complete recording of *Tosca* (for RCA) ten years after the first under Karajan, and the interpretation remained remarkably consistent, a shade tougher in the chest register – the great entry in Act III a magnificent moment – and a little more clipped of phrase. That last modification may reflect the relative manners of the two conductors – Karajan more individual in his refined expansiveness, Mehta more thrustful. On balance, taking Price alone, the preference is for the earlier set, but Mehta's version also boasts a fine cast, with the team of Domingo and Milnes at its most impressive. The recording, too, is admirable, even if it yields to the Decca in atmosphere and richness. The current reissue in RCA's Opera Treasury series (at the moment for the UK only) is very agreeably packaged. The set remains at premium price in the USA.

The Teldec set offers a remastered version of the television soundtrack for the recording made on site in Rome at the very venues and times of day specified in the libretto. If that was a gimmick, it led to a powerful and compelling account of the opera, well conducted by Mehta. This audio recording cannot really compete with the finest studio versions when – no doubt for reasons of matching sight to sound – the voices are unnaturally close, with the orchestra set well behind. The sense of presence and the warmth of tone are impressive, but Plácido Domingo's performance is made to sound less subtle than it is. The vibrant Catherine Malfitano is better treated, with the voice very well caught – upfront sound for a tough, upfront character – but Raimondi's Scarpia sounds less sinister when heard at such close range.

Tosca (complete; sung in English).

*** Chandos Dig. CHAN 3000 (2) [id.]. Eaglen, O'Neill, Yurisich, Geoffrey Mitchell Ch., Peter Kay Children's Ch., Philh. O, Parry.

With opera in English, a neglected cause, the Peter Moores Foundation here sponsors the most persuasive example yet on CD of opera in translation. Above all, it offers the first recording to demonstrate the powers of Jane Eaglen at full stretch in one of the most formidable, vocally satisfying portrayals of the role of Tosca in years. The thrilling security with which she attacks one top note after another is a delight, vehement in presenting Tosca's jealousy. She is well matched by Dennis O'Neill as Cavaradossi, aptly Italianate in every register, with only occasional unevenness. Gregory Yurisich makes a powerful Scarpia, younger-sounding than most, and a plausible lover, with David Parry proving an outstanding Puccinian, pacing the score masterfully to heighten tensions, helped by opulent recording.

Turandot (complete).

500♪ *** Decca 414 274-2 (2) [id.]. Sutherland, Pavarotti, Caballé, Pears, Ghiaurov, Alldis Ch., Wandsworth School Boys' Ch., LPO, Mehta.

(***) EMI mono CDS5 56307-2 (2) [id.]. Callas, Fernandi, Schwarzkopf, Zaccaria, La Scala, Milan, Ch. & O, Serafin.

(M) ** RCA 09026 62687-2 [5932-2-RC]. Nilsson, Bjoerling, Tebaldi, Tozzi, Rome Op. Ch. & O, Leinsdorf.

Joan Sutherland gives an intensely revealing and appealing interpretation, making the icy princess far more human and sympathetic than ever before, while Pavarotti offers a characterization equally imaginative, beautiful in sound, strong on detail. Mehta directs a gloriously rich and dramatic performance, superlatively recorded, still the best-sounding *Turandot* on CD.

With Callas, the character seems so much more believably complex than with others, and this 1957 recording is one of her most thrillingly magnetic performances on disc. Schwarzkopf provides a comparably characterful and distinctive portrait as Liù, far more than a Puccinian 'little woman', sweet and wilting. Eugenio Fernandi sounds relatively uncharacterful as Calaf, but his timbre is pleasing enough. By contrast, Serafin's masterly conducting exactly matches the characterfulness of Callas and Schwarzkopf, with colour, atmosphere and dramatic point all commandingly presented. With such a vivid performance, the 1957 mono sound hardly seems to matter, although the choral passages tend to overload at climaxes.

On RCA, Birgit Nilsson is certainly an icy princess. She has power and attack, even if some of her top notes are too hard to be acceptable even from the Princess Turandot. Tebaldi, in fine voice as Liù, is warm and sympathetic, and Bjoerling is a splendid Calaf. This was one of his last recordings (in 1959), but he was as clear-voiced and youthful-sounding as ever. The rest of the cast matches this standard, but Leinsdorf's conducting is chilly, and the recording, not too cleanly focused in its CD format, like the performance lacks ripeness and warmth.

Turandot: highlights.

(M) ** EMI CDM5 66051-2 [id.] (from complete set, with Caballé, Carreras, Freni; cond. Lombard).

It is difficult to enthuse about a highlights CD that plays for only 53 minutes, even if key items are included and put in narrative perspective by the synopsis. So this will mainly be of interest to Caballé admirers (although the recording does not particularly flatter her).

Purcell, Henry (1659–95)

3 Fantasias for 5 viols; 9 Fantasias for 4 viols; Fantasia on one note for 5 viols; In nomine for 6 viols; In nomine for 7 viols.

500♪ *** Virgin Veritas/EMI Dig. VC5 45062-2 [CDC 45062]. Fretwork.

(i) *3 Fantasias for 5 viols; 9 Fantasias for 4 viols; Fantasia on one note for 5 viols; In nomine for 6 viols; In nomine for 7 viols;* (ii) Duet: *How pleasant is this flowery plain;* Verse anthem: *In thee, O Lord, do I put my trust;* Song: *Oh! what a scene does entertain my sight;* Drinking song: *'Tis wine was made to rule the day;* Trio: *When the cock begins to crow.*

500♪ (M) (***) DG mono 447 156-2 [id.]. (i) Schola Cantorum Basiliensis, August Wenzinger; (ii) Saltire Singers, Instrumental Ens., Hans Oppenheim.

The Purcell *Fantasias* and *In nomines* are among the most searching and profound works in all music, and the inspired performances by Wenzinger's group have never been surpassed: ethereal, infinitely touching in their refined delicacy of texture. Although this disc is mono, in no way is it technically inferior, and its natural balance and ambience almost bring an illusion of stereo.

The players of Fretwork use viols with a concern for matching, tuning and balance which is quite exceptional, and their natural expressiveness matches the deeper implications of these masterpieces in microcosm. This makes a superb modern successor to the earlier recordings by Wenzinger and his Schola Cantorum Basiliensis and by Harnoncourt, both included in DG's Archiv Purcell Collection.

Anthems: *Man that is born of woman; O God, thou has cast us out; Lord, how long wilt thou be angry?; O God, thou art my God; O Lord God of hosts; Remember not, Lord, our offences; Thou knowest, Lord, the secrets of our hearts*. Verse anthems: *My beloved spake; My heart is inditing; O sing unto the Lord; Praise the Lord, O Jerusalem; They that go down to the sea in ships. Morning Service in B flat: Benedicte omnia opera; Cantate Domino; Deus miscreatur; Magnificat; Nunc dimittis. Evening service in G min.: Magnificat; Nunc dimittis. Latin Psalm: Jehovah, quam multi sunt hostes mei. Te Deum and Jubilate in D.*

500♪ (M) *** DG 447 150-2 (2) [id.]. David Thomas, Christ Church Cathedral, Oxford, Ch., E. Concert, Simon Preston.

The admirable Christ Church two-disc collection of anthems, verse-anthems and excerpts from service settings was recorded in the London Henry Wood Hall in 1980. With some of the music not otherwise available, it is self-recommending. Apart from David Thomas's fine contribution (in the verse-anthems) the soloists come from the choir – and very good they are too, especially the trebles. The performances are full of character, vigorous yet with the widest range of colour and feeling, well projected in a recording which simulates a cathedral ambience yet is naturally focused and well detailed – analogue sound at its best.

Come, ye sons of art away; Ode on St Cecilia's Day: Welcome to all the pleasures. Of old when heroes thought it base (Yorkshire Feast song).

*** DG Dig. 427 663-2 [id.]. J. Smith, Priday, Amps, Chance, Wilson, Ainsley, George, Richardson, E. Concert Ch., E. Concert, Pinnock.

Pinnock directs exuberant performances. The weight and brightness of the choral sound go with infectiously lifted rhythms, making the music dance. The soloists are all outstanding, with the counter-tenor duetting of Michael Chance and Timothy Wilson in *Sound the trumpet* delectably pointed. The coupling, the neglected *Yorkshire Feast song*, is full of wonderful inspirations, like the tenor and counter-tenor duet, *And now when the renown'd Nassau* – a reference to the new king, William III.

STAGE WORKS AND THEATRE MUSIC

'Sweeter than roses': *Bonduca: O lead me to some peaceful gloom. The Fairy Queen: Thrice happy lovers; O let me weep. Henry II, King of England: In vain 'gainst love I strove. The History of King Richard III: Retir'd from any mortal's sight. King Arthur: Fairest isle. The Married Beau: See where repenting Celia lies. Oedipus: Music for a while. Pausanias: Sweeter than roses. Rule a Wife and have a Wife: There's not a swain. Sir Anthony Love: Pursuing beauty. The Tempest: Dear pretty youth. Timon of Athens: The cares of lovers. Tyrannic love: Ah! how sweet it is to love.* LOCKE: *My lodging it is on the cold ground.*

*** O-L Dig. 443 699-2 [id.]. Catherine Bott, instrumental ens. (with BLOW: *Lovely Selina.* DRAGHI: *Where are thou, God of dreams?* COURTEVILLE: *Creep, creep, softly creep.* ECCLES: *The Villain: Find me a lonely cave.* WELDON: *The Tempest: Dry those eyes; Halcyon days*).

Catherine Bott is in splendid form in this delightful collection of English Restoration theatre music which is dealt with more fully in our Vocal Recitals listing below.

Dido and Aeneas (complete).

500♪ ❁ (M) *** Decca 425 720-2. Dame Janet Baker, Herincx, Clark, Sinclair, St Anthony Singers, ECO, Anthony Lewis.

Janet Baker's 1962 recording of *Dido* is a truly great performance. The radiant beauty of the voice is obvious enough, but the emotion is implied, as it should be in this music, not injected in great uncontrolled gusts. Like most vintage Oiseau-Lyre recordings, this was beautifully engineered.

The Fairy Queen (complete).

500♪ *** DG Dig. 419 221-2 (2) [id.]. Harrhy, Jennifer Smith, Nelson, Priday, Penrose, Stafford, Evans, Hill, Varcoe, Thomas, Monteverdi Ch., E. Bar. Soloists, Gardiner.

Gardiner's performance is a delight from beginning to end, for, though authenticity and completeness reign, scholarship is worn lightly and the result is consistently exhilarating, with no longueurs whatever. The fresh-toned soloists are first rate, while Gardiner's regular choir and orchestra excel themselves, with Purcell's sense of fantasy brought out in each succeeding number. Beautifully clear and well-balanced recording.

(i) *The Indian Queen* (incidental music); (ii) *King Arthur* (complete).

500♪ ❁ (M) *** Decca 433 166-2 (2) [id.]. (i) Cantelo, Wilfred Brown, Tear, Partridge, Keyte, St Anthony Singers, ECO, Mackerras; (ii) Morison, Harper, Mary Thomas, Whitworth, Wilfred Brown, Galliver, Cameron, Anthony, Alan, St Anthony Singers, Philomusica of L., Lewis.

With stylish singing and superb direction and accompaniment, this is an invaluable reissue. Charles Mackerras shows himself a strong and vivid as well as scholarly Purcellian. The Rosette, however, is for the pioneering 1959 set (also Oiseau-Lyre) of *King Arthur*, fully worthy to stand alongside the companion recording of *Dido and Aeneas*, made three years later – see above. Here the success of the interpretation does not centre on the contribution of one inspired artist, but rather on teamwork among a number of excellent singers and on the stylish and sensitive overall direction of Anthony Lewis.

King Arthur (complete).
500♪ ❁ *** Erato/Warner Dig. 4509 98535-2 (2) [id.]. Gens, McFadden, Padmore, Best, Salomaa, Les Arts Florissants, William Christie.

Christie brings out the jollity behind much of the piece. Few will resist *Your hay it is mow'd* when the chorus even includes 'gentlemen of the orchestra' in the last verse. Unlike the earlier, Gardiner version (also Erato), this one does not in that character number have the bass soloist (Petteri Salomaa) singing in a broad Mummerset dialect, but it is still earthy enough. Christie's soloists are generally warmer and weightier than Gardiner's, notably Véronique Gens as Venus, sustaining Christie's exceptionally slow speed for *Fairest isle*. The vigour of Purcell's inspiration in this semi-opera has never been more winningly conveyed in a period performance on disc, with full-bodied instrumental sound set against a helpful but relatively dry acoustic, giving immediacy to the drama.

King Arthur: highlights.
(M) *** Erato/Warner Dig. 0630 15736-9 [id.] (from complete recording, with Jennifer Smith, Fischer, Priday, Ross, Stafford, Elliott, Varcoe, Monteverdi Ch., E. Bar. Soloists, Gardiner).

A 64-minute highlights disc from *King Arthur* is a novelty, but as the selection includes all the key items (including Philadel's chorus with the spirits and the Frost scene) some collectors could be attracted to it. Gardiner's soloists are all good, although the men are more strongly characterful than the ladies and it is the choral singing which one remembers. The recording is spacious and the documentation is very full indeed.

Rabaud, Henri (1873–1949)

Divertissement sur des chansons russes, Op. 2; Eglogue, Op. 7; Mârouf, savetier du Caire: dances; Symphonic poem after Lenau's Faust (Procession nocturne), Op. 6; Suites anglaises Nos. 2–3.
** Marco Polo Dig. 8.223503 [id.]. Rheinland-Pfalz PO, Segerstam.

Henri Rabaud is best known for his opera, *Mârouf, savetier du Caire*, though it has not been available since the days of LP. He himself recorded the *Procession nocturne* in the days of shellac, and this has been transferred to CD; but otherwise his music has enjoyed little exposure on records. Now that Pierre Dervaux's EMI record with the Orchestre Philharmonique du Pays de Loire is difficult to get hold of, Leif Segerstam's recording with the Baden-Baden or Rheinland-Pfalz Philharmonic has the field more or less to itself. Rabaud was not prolific, for the bulk of his time was consumed by conducting and by his administrative duties at the Paris Conservatoire, of which he was director during the inter-war years. (He had a short spell with the Boston Symphony just before Monteux took it over in the early 1920s.) The *Eglogue* was Rabaud's first orchestral piece, written in Italy during his period as a Prix de Rome scholar, and derives its inspiration from the first *Eclogue* of Virgil. The dances from *Mârouf, savetier du Caire* have an appropriately oriental flavour since the opera itself is based on an episode from the *Arabian Nights*. The *Procession nocturne* is a tone-poem based on the same Lenau poem which inspired Liszt's *Nächtlige Zug* and is the most atmospheric of the pieces on this disc. The *Suites anglaises* are arrangements of Byrd, Farnaby and other Elizabethan composers that Rabaud made for a 1917 production of *The Merchant of Venice*. Like Roger-Ducasse, Rabaud's music is not strongly personal, but it is distinctly Gallic and well worth investigating. As with their Koechlin (*Le livre de la jungle* and *Les heures persanes*) and Florent Schmitt's *La tragédie de Salomé*, Segerstam and his orchestra show a real sympathy with this turn-of-the-century French repertoire, and they are decently recorded too.

Rachmaninov, Sergei (1873–1943)

(i) *Piano concertos Nos 1–4;* (ii) *Rhapsody on a theme of Paganini.*
(B) *** BMG/Melodiya Twofer Dig. 74321 40068-2 (2). Victor Eresko; (i) USSR SO, Gennady Provotorov; (ii) Leningrad PO, Vladimir Ponkin.

Issued as a 'Twofer', two discs for the price of one, the Melodiya digital versions of the four Rachmaninov

Piano concertos (1984) plus the *Paganini rhapsody* (1983) make an excellent bargain in performances full of flair. The notes give no information about the pianist, Victor Eresko, but he proves a formidable virtuoso who in No. 3 opts for the weightier and more difficult of Rachmaninov's two cadenzas: even in that he betrays no strain whatever, not just technically brilliant but spontaneously expressive through thickets of notes. In his articulation Eresko plays with the crispest definition, not just in bravura passage-work, but magically in the light, quicksilver skeins of notes so characteristic of Rachmaninov, and in such movements as the finales of Nos. 3 and 4 he points rhythms with a sparkle of wit, making most others seem a little plain. He also brings off the virtuoso codas to each of these works with splendid panache, to set this up as a most attractive set, well recorded and a first-rate bargain. Ashkenazy and Previn on their Double Decca (444 839-2) omit the *Rhapsody*, but another obvious competitor who does not is the vintage version by Earl Wild, now on two mid-priced Chandos discs (CHAN 6605 and 6607); but that involves cuts in No. 3. So in most respects this Melodiya set has the bargain field to itself.

Piano concertos Nos. (i) *1 in F sharp min., Op. 1;* (ii) *3 in D min., Op. 30.*
(BB) ** Belart 461 348-2. (i) Peter Katin, LPO, Boult; (ii) Alicia de Larrocha, LSO, Previn.

Boult brings a sympathetic freshness to the *First Concerto* and his conducting is matched by Katin's spirited and mercurial playing. The pianist does not attempt a conventional bravura style, and some may be disappointed on this account, but in this, the shortest of Rachmaninov's concertos, the added clarity and point given to so many passages more than make amends (if indeed amends need be made). The orchestra responds well but does not always play with perfect precision. However, the early-1970s Decca stereo is excellent: bright, with good definition and balance. The 1975 recording of the *Third Concerto* is even finer, warm and glowing. Alicia de Larrocha is a cultured player whom we do not associate with barn-storming bravura; she gives an individual performance, full of imaginative detail, but not one which holds together very cohesively, despite Previn's understanding accompaniment.

Piano concerto No. 2 in C min., Op. 18.
*** Hänssler Dig. CD 98.932 [id.]. Garrick Ohlsson, ASMF, Marriner – TCHAIKOVSKY: *Piano concerto No. 1.* ***

Ohlsson and Marriner combine to give a satisfyingly romantic account of this favourite concerto, and they are able to relax in the outer movements without loss of grip or tension. The climax of the first movement is broad and very powerful, and the finale, while not lacking brilliance, makes the very most of Rachmaninov's great secondary melody with a gorgeously expansive final presentation; the coda is then satisfyingly positive, rather than being rushed off its feet. The *Adagio* is equally persuasive, creating a simple lyrical flow, with the reprise tenderly beautiful, rapt in its gentle concentration. The recording is full-bodied and natural and is admirably balanced. If you want a modern, digital recording of this coupling, this Hänssler CD is hard to beat.

(i) *Piano concerto No. 2 in C min., Op. 18;* (ii) *Rhapsody on a theme of Paganini, Op. 43.*
(M) *** Decca 448 604-2 [id.]. Julius Katchen; (i) LSO, Solti; (ii) LPO, Boult – DOHNANYI: *Variations on a nursery tune.* ***

Katchen re-recorded the *C minor Concerto* with Solti in stereo in 1958, seven years after his mono recording with Fistoulari, and the *Paganini variations* with Boult the following year. Even today the Kingsway Hall stereo is impressively rich and full, especially in the famous *Eighteenth Variation*. If there remains something very special about Katchen's earlier mono versions (Dutton CDLXT 2504 – see our main volume), most listeners will revel in the vintage sound of this remake, fully worthy of reissue in Decca's Classic Sound series. Katchen's performances of both works offer drama and excitement in plenty – the outer movements of the *Concerto* reach the highest peak of excitement, with bravura very much to the fore. Solti makes a splendid partner here; Boult sees that the *Rhapsody* is superbly shaped and has diversity and wit as well as romantic flair. With three works offered, this reissue can be recommended very highly.

(i) *Piano concerto No. 2 in C min., Op. 18; Rhapsody on a theme of Paganini, Op. 43;* (ii) *Preludes: Op. 3/2; Op. 23/4; Op. 32/10.*
(B) ** DG 449 843-2 [id.]. (i) Vásáry, LSO, Ahronovitch; (ii) Lazar Berman.

The partnership of the impetuous Ahronovitch and the more introvert pianist works well enough in the *Concerto*. The first movement has a fine climax, but after that the tension is lower and the languorous *Adagio* does not distil the degree of poetry achieved elsewhere. The conductor's chimerical style is better suited to the *Rhapsody*, with its opening faster than usual and with strong contrasts of tempo and mood between brilliant and lyrical variations. The sound of the recordings is very good. The *Preludes* provide a useful bonus, but this reissue is hardly a front runner.

Piano concertos Nos. 2 in C min., Op. 18; (ii) *3 in D min., Op. 30.*
(B) ** Sony SBK 63032; *SBT 63032* [id.]. (i) Gary Grafman; (ii) André Watts; (i–ii) NYPO; (i) Bernstein; (ii) Ozawa.

Another disc, cashing in on the success of the film *Shine* and tackily entitled 'Rachmaninov goes to the cinema', couples the *D minor* in André Watts's very good account with the New York Philharmonic under Ozawa, made in 1969, with the 1964 Gary Grafman/Bernstein version. They also throw in the 18th Variation from the *Paganini variations*, which has frequently been plundered for soundtracks. It is perfectly good value for money, accepting that it is at bargain price, but there are much better things around.

Piano concerto No. 3 in D min., Op. 30.
500♪ *** Ph. 446 673-2 [id.]. Martha Argerich, Berlin RSO, Chailly – TCHAIKOVSKY: *Piano concerto No. 1.* ***

(i) *Piano concerto No. 3 in D min., Op. 30. Barcarolle in G min., Op. 23/5; Mélodie in E, Op. 3/3; Preludes: in C sharp min., Op. 3/2; in G min., Op. 23/5; in G sharp min., Op. 32/12.*
*** Decca Dig. 448 401-2 [id.]. Shura Cherkassky, (i) with RPO, Temirkanov.

(i) *Piano concerto No. 3 in D min. 5 Études-tableaux, Op. 33/1–3 & 6; Op. 39/6.*
**(*) EMI Dig. CDC5 56350-2 [id.]. Leif Ove Andsnes, (i) Oslo PO, Paavo Berglund.

(i) *Piano concerto No. 3 in D min. Preludes: in C sharp min., Op. 3/2; in G min., Op. 23/5; in G; in G sharp min., Op. 32/5 & 12; Piano sonata No. 2 in B flat min., Op. 36.*
(**) RCA Dig. 74321 40378-2 [id.]. David Helfgott; (i) with Copenhagen PO, Horvat.

There are few finer examples of live recording than Martha Argerich's electrifying performance of Rachmaninov's *Third Piano concerto*, recorded in Berlin in 1982. Her volatility and dash are entirely at one with the romantic spirit of this music, and her interpretation is so commanding that individual eccentricities seem a natural part of the chimerical musical flow. The recording is very good; the strings might have been better flattered in the studio but the overall sound-picture satisfyingly demonstrates the skill of the Philips engineering team.

Shura Cherkassky's playing could always be relied on for both individuality and finesse. His account of the Rachmaninov *Third Piano concerto* appeared at about the same time as his version of the Rubinstein *Fourth*. The latter caught our last deadline, but this newcomer missed it. It is something of a *tour de force* for an octogenarian and, although there are others with greater fire and zest, this has a poetic grace which in its way is rather special. Nothing Cherkassky did was without its special musical insights, and readers who respond to Cherkassky's pianism should snap up this last opportunity of hearing him, for he made no more records after this.

EMI have transferred Leif Ove Andsnes's aristocratic account of the *Third Piano concerto* with Berglund and the Oslo orchestra from Virgin to their red label. His playing is cultivated and he brings finesse and refined musicianship to all he does. Berglund is conscientious and supportive, but workmanlike rather than inspired. Unencumbered in the *Etudes-tableaux*, Andsnes's imagination is able to take free wing.

David Helfgott's record needs no advocacy from us – it is already a world bestseller. We would like to be able to recommend it. The biographical film, *Shine*, about the early life of the pianist and his struggles to regain a place on the concert platform after his disastrous childhood experiences, excites one's admiration. But the live performance here of the 'key' work in his career leaves a great deal to be desired. One remembers that Rachmaninov himself (who had a prodigious technique) was intimidated by Horowitz's dazzling account of the concerto. Alas, Helfgott for all his commitment plays with a lack of inhibition which is too often technically wide of the mark. He is heard at his best in the *Preludes*, for the *Sonata* is not really very cohesive either.

Piano concertos Nos. 3 in D min, Op. 30; 4 in G min., Op. 40.
(M) **(*) Van. Classics Dig. 99091 [id.]. Nikolai Lugansky, Russian State Ac. SO, Ivan Shpiller.

It is odd to look back at the 5th edition of *Grove's Dictionary of Music and Musicians* to see in what low esteem Rachmaninov was held in the 1950s. Eric Blom, no less, wrote of his 'artificial and gushing tunes' and more or less wrote off the *Fourth Concerto* altogether, 'as a failure from the start'. Nikolai Lugansky is a young Russian pianist of quality, born in 1972 (which makes him a year or so younger than Evgeni Kissin and Leif Ove Andsnes). These performances do not have the slightest trace of ostentation. He produces a wonderful sound, allows phrases to breathe naturally and the music to unfold freely. In short he is content to serve Rachmaninov rather than his own ego. He plays the cadenza that Rachmaninov himself recorded rather than the overblown alternative favoured by the majority of pianists these days, and in the *Fourth Concerto* his playing is wonderfully fluid. There is ample virtuosity, but it takes second place to poetic fantasy. To put it in a nutshell, Lugansky is a real artist whose thoughts about the music carry more weight for this listener than many barnstorming virtuosi. There are drawbacks, however, for the orchestral playing is not of comparable distinction. The strings of the Russian Academic Symphony Orchestra do not produce as sumptuous or opulent a tone as they did in the days of Svetlanov, and the horn vibrato may worry some collectors; moreover the recording is not in the very first flight, though it is far from inadequate. Both these shortcomings should produce a two-star rating, but the artistic merits of Lugansky's unfailingly musical and aristocratic playing just carry it across into a three-star bracket.

Piano concerto No. 4 in G min., Op. 40.
500♪ ❁ *** EMI CDC7 49326-2 [id.]. Michelangeli, Philh. O, Gracis – RAVEL: *Piano concerto in G.* *** ❁

This is one of the most brilliant piano records ever made. It puts the composer's own recorded performance quite in the shade, and the Ravel coupling is equally illuminating. The recording does not quite match the superlative quality of the playing but still sounds pretty good.

Symphonic dances, Op. 45; (i) *The Bells, Op. 35.*
(M) **(*) BMG/Melodiya 74321 32046-2 [id.]. (i) Shumskaya, Dovenman, Bolshakov, Russian State Chamber Ch. Moscow PO, Kyrill Kondrashin.

Kondrashin's classic 1969 performance with the Moscow Philharmonic returns in a less than distinguished transfer. One wonders whether the impression, that our LPs sounded better, is deceptive – until you hear them side by side. All the same, this is an electrifying performance and, like *The Bells*, which comes from 1966, shines through all sonic limitations.

Symphonies Nos. 1 in D min., Op. 13; 2 in E min., Op. 27; 3 in A min., Op. 44.
(B) **(*) Carlton VoxBox CDX 5034 (2) [id.]. St Louis SO, Leonard Slatkin.

Symphonies Nos 1–3; Vocalise, Op. 34/14.
(B) ** BMG/Melodiya Twofer 74321 40065-2 (2) [id.]. USSR SO (No. 1); Bolshoi Theatre O (No. 2); USSR R. & TV Large SO (No. 3); Svetlanov.

Having all three of Rachmaninov's *Symphonies* in ripely idiomatic performances on two budget-priced VoxBox discs makes an excellent bargain, even if the recording lacks something in immediacy. Recorded between 1976 and 1979, they reveal that already, early in his career as the St Louis music director, Slatkin had welded this second-oldest American orchestra into a most responsive ensemble, able in Rachmaninov's ripest melodies to play with both polish and a warmly flexible expressiveness. The sound in No. 1, presumably recorded last, is rather fuller and more forward than in the other two symphonies, but there is plenty of detail in each. This does not match the digital Double Decca reissue (448 116-2) of Ashkenazy's performances in the same price range, which remains a primary recommendation; but it is of comparably excellent value, especially for admirers of Slatkin.

Though recorded in the 1960s, Svetlanov's readings of the Rachmaninov symphonies, at one time available from EMI on LP, come in full-bodied, atmospheric sound. This version of No. 1 stands among the very finest ever, warm and concentrated and full of panache, not least in the celebrated theme at the start of the finale. No. 3 is first rate too, persuasively done with resonant strings. In No. 2 Svetlanov is rather heavier-handed, and he is not helped by an acid clarinet in the slow movement. Though the finale is exhilarating, it brings the fatal snag that the recapitulation is drastically cut. Otherwise this economically priced reissue would be very competitive.

Symphony No. 2 in E min., Op. 27.
500♪ (M) *** Carlton Dig. PCD 904 [id.]. LSO, Rozhdestvensky.
(M) Mercury ** 434 368-2 [id.]. Detroit SO, Paray – FRANCK: *Symphony.* **

Symphony No. 2 in E min.; The Rock, Op. 7.
(M) ** Sony SMK 57650 [id.]. St Petersburg Philharmonic Ac. SO, Dmitriev.

Symphony No. 2 in E min.; Vocalise, Op. 34/14.
* Erato/Warner Dig. 4509 96360-2 [id.]. Bolshoi SO, Lazarev.

Rozhdestvensky gives a very Tchaikovskian reading of Rachmaninov's *E minor Symphony*. There is plenty of vitality but, with the big string melodies blossoming voluptuously, the slow movement, after a beguiling opening clarinet solo, has a climax of spacious intensity, its power almost overwhelming. The finale is flamboyantly broadened at the end, and the feeling of apotheosis is very much in the Tchaikovsky mould.

Alexander Dmitriev offers exactly the same coupling as Mikhail Pletnev and the Russian National Orchestra on DG (439 888-2) and, although the latter is to be preferred, Dmitriev makes a far from negligible alternative. His players have the cumbersome name of the St Petersburg Philharmonic Academic Symphony Orchestra (though it used to be known as the Leningrad Radio or the Leningrad Symphony) and they produce excellent results. Like Pletnev, Dmitriev does not wear his heart on his sleeve; he is concerned about the overall shape of a paragraph rather than dwelling on individual beauty of incident. The rather recessed sound diminishes the appeal of the disc, but it still has much to recommend it.

Paul Paray's Rachmaninov *Second* was one of the first in stereo (1957). The performance is a vivid one, the Detroit orchestra play very well for him, and there is no lack of passion; yet something is missing. The conductor does not always display a natural feeling for Rachmaninov's yearning, winding string cantilena. Sometimes he seems to break the long melodic line into little phrases in order to increase the intensity, but with the opposite effect. This is enjoyable, but it is not among the finest early versions.

Alexander Lazarev and the Bolshoi Orchestra are at full price and are somewhat uncompetitive. This is an also-ran, the performance wanting in drive and personality. It is no match for Pletnev (in the same price-bracket), while Rozhdestvensky still makes an obvious first choice at mid-price (Carlton PCD 904).

Symphony No. 3 in A min., Op. 44; Isle of the dead, Op. 29; Vocalise, Op. 34/14.
❀ (M) (***) RCA mono 09026 62532-2 [id.]. Phd. O, Sergei Rachmaninov.

RCA deserve congratulations for making these wonderful recordings available on a separate CD, an immense boon for those who cannot afford the ten-CD Complete Rachmaninov Edition. Rachmaninov's own recording of the *Third Symphony*, *Isle of the dead* and *Vocalise*, made in 1939 and 1929 respectively, are an indispensable part of any serious collector's library. They also sound magnificent – and not simply for their age. Only one conductor has ever matched these: Koussevitzky, whose Boston performances from the 1940s (never issued commercially and not currently available) are electrifying. The rest (even by such idiomatic interpreters as Ormandy and Previn) pale by comparison.

Cello sonata in G min., Op. 19; 2 Pieces, Op. 2; Vocalise, Op. 34/14.
*** Virgin/EMI Dig. VC5 45119-2 [CDC 45119]. Truls Mørk, Jean-Yves Thibaudet – MIASKOVSKY: *Cello sonata No. 1.* ***

The gifted Norwegian cellist Truls Mørk plays with a restrained eloquence that is totally compelling. The demanding (and commanding) piano part is given with authority and conviction by Thibaudet, and they handle the companion pieces excellently. The value of this well-recorded and well-balanced issue is enhanced by the attractive Miaskovsky coupling.

PIANO MUSIC

Music for 2 pianos: (i) *Suites Nos. 1–2, Opp. 5 & 17; Symphonic dances, Op. 45; Russian rhapsody;* (Solo piano) *Etudes-tableaux, Op. 33; Variations on a theme by Corelli, Op. 42.*
500♪ (B) *** Decca Double 444 845-2 (2) [id.]. Vladimir Ashkenazy, (i) with André Previn.

The colour and flair of Rachmaninov's writing in the two *Suites* (as inspired and tuneful as his concertos) are captured with wonderful imagination. The two-piano version of the *Symphonic dances* produced a work which in pianistic detail as well as sharpness of argument is masterly. Ashkenazy and Previn are challenged to a dazzling performance, and they are hardly less persuasive in the coupled *Russian rhapsody*, an early piece, well worth hearing in a performance as fine as this. Ashkenazy's superb solo performances of the *Etudes-tableaux* and the *Corelli variations* (a rarity and a very fine work) cap the appeal of this bargain Double. The recording throughout is superb.

Etudes-Tableaux, Opp. 33/2 & 8; 39/3–5; Morceaux de Fantaisie, Op. 3; Preludes, Opp. 23/1, 3, 5, 7 & 10; 32/6, 8, 10 & 12.
** Hyperion Dig. CDA 66713 [id.]. Nikolai Demidenko.

In this recital Nikolai Demidenko enters hotly contested terrain. There are perceptive and intelligent touches, but also a good deal that is detached or mannered. He can produce some ugly tone above *forte* (as in the third *Prelude* of Op. 23), though there are moments of great tenderness. He is well enough recorded, but he does not begin to challenge Howard Shelley on the same label or Gavrilov, Ashkenazy or Richter in this repertoire.

24 Preludes (complete); *3 Nocturnes; Polka de WR.*
(B) **(*) EMI forte CZS5 69527-2 (2). Agustin Anievas – CHOPIN: *Sonata No. 3* **; LISZT: *Sonata.* ***

24 Preludes (complete); *Piano sonata No. 2 in B flat min., Op. 36.*
500♪ (BB) *** Decca Double 443 841-2 (2) [id.]. Vladimir Ashkenazy.

There is superb flair and panache about Ashkenazy's playing. At Double Decca price, this sweeps the board. Ashkenazy's poetic feeling is second to none.

Anievas recorded the Rachmaninov *Preludes* in the early 1970s, but they were soon withdrawn and, later, Ashkenazy's set dominated the catalogue. Anievas certainly has the measure of all this music, although in the lyrical *Preludes* he returns to the coaxing style of the *Nocturnes* and, though he is gently persuasive and undoubtedly poetic, the effect is Chopinesque. His bravura is never barnstorming (Richter creates an altogether more hair-raising effect in the *B flat Prelude*, Op. 23/2) but Anievas finds plenty of colour and much variety of character in these so varied pieces, and he is well recorded.

Piano sonata No. 2 in B flat min., Op. 36 (original version); *Etudes-tableaux, Op. 33/1, 39/4 & 7; Morceaux de fantaisie, Op. 3/3 & 5; Preludes, Op. 23/1 & 7; 32/2, 6, 9 & 10.*
500♪ ❀ *** Ph. Dig. 446 220-2 [id.]. Zoltán Kocsis.

Be it in the smaller, reflective pieces or in the bigger-boned *B flat minor Sonata*, Zoltán Kocsis's piano speaks with totally idiomatic accents, effortless virtuosity and a keen poetic feeling. This is a most distinguished offering and is recommended with enthusiasm. Excellent recording.

VOCAL MUSIC

The Bells, Op. 35.
*** Telarc Dig. CD 80363 [id.]. Renée Fleming, Karl Dent, Victor Ledbetter, Atlanta Ch. & SO, Robert Shaw – ADAMS: *Harmonium.* ***

The Bells, Op. 35; 3 Russian songs, Op. 41.
500♪ (M) *** Decca Dig. 436 482-2 [id.]. Natalia Troitskaya, Ryszard Karczykowski, Concg. Ch. & O, Ashkenazy.

Ashkenazy's volatile Russian style is eminently suitable for Rachmaninov's masterly cantata. His tenor soloist has just the right touch of temperament, and in the slow movement Natalia Troitskaya's contribution combines Slavonic feeling with freshness. The chorus respond readily to the black mood of the Scherzo and bring a melancholy intensity to the finale. The Decca recording is superb.

Robert Shaw conducts a colourfully expansive performance of Rachmaninov's cantata – which is not to say that the Scherzo is not vividly exciting. The special melancholy of the finale is touchingly conveyed, with a fine orchestral response as well as an ardent contribution from the choir, bringing a powerful climax. All three soloists are impressive and if Renée Fleming, who sings beautifully, is not especially Slavonic, in the closing *Lento lugubre* the baritone, Victor Ledbetter, catches the darkly expressive mood admirably. While this is not superior to Ashkenazy, who leads the field at mid-price, he has a quite different coupling, and anyone wanting the spectacular Adams work should be well satisfied with Shaw's Rachmaninov.

Liturgy of St John Chrysostom, Op. 31.
500♪ ❀ (B) *** EMI forte CZS5 68664-2 (2). Maximova, Zorova, Vidov, Stoytsov, Petrov, Bulgarian R. Ch., Milkov.

It would be difficult to imagine this superbly recorded performance being bettered and, although the spacious tempi (which are sustained with continuing concentration) mean that the performance, which takes 97 minutes, stretches to a pair of CDs, the set is offered in EMI's forte series so that the two discs are offered for the price of one. It is a pity that a full text with translation is not included, but the presentation is otherwise fully acceptable.

Vespers, Op. 37.
500♪ ❀ *** HM Chant du Monde Russian Season Dig. LDC 288050 [id.]. St Petersburg Capella, Chernuchenko.

Rachmaninov's *Vespers* – more correctly the 'All-night vigil' – rank not only among his most soulful and intensely powerful music but are also the finest of all Russian choral works. The St Petersburg Capella offer singing of an extraordinarily rapt intensity. The dynamic range is enormous, the perfection of ensemble and blend and the sheer beauty of tone such as to exhaust superlatives, and it is hard to imagine that their singing can be surpassed. The recording does them justice and is made in a suitably atmospheric acoustic.

Rameau, Jean Philippe (1683–1764)

Pièces de clavecin en concert Nos. 1–5.
(B) *** HM Dig. HMX 2901418 [HMC 901418]. Christophe Rousset, Ryo Terakado, Kaori Uemura.

The instrumental *Pièces de clavecin* usually include a flute, but they are equally valid in this format with baroque violin and viola da gamba. The Harmonia Mundi team are attractively spirited and rhythmically buoyant; the effect with period instruments brings a slightly abrasive edge at times, but not disagreeably so. The star here is Christophe Rousset, whose very imaginative contribution lights up this music-making. The recording is realistic, the balance excellent. At bargain price this is well worth considering.

Grand motets: *In convertendo; Quam dilecta. Laboravi.*
(B) *** HM HMT 7901078 [HMC 901078]. Gari, Monnaliu, Ledroit, De Mey, Varcoe, Chapelle Royale Ch., Ghent Coll. Voc., Herreweghe.

These two motets are among Rameau's finest works. The Ghent Collegium Vocale is stiffened by forces from La Chapelle Royale in Paris. They produce excellent results, and the soloists are also very fine indeed. The instrumental ensemble includes several members of La Petite Bande, so its excellence can almost be taken for granted. The brief *Laboravi* makes an appealing little encore. This CD is even more attractive at bargain price.

OPERA-BALLET

(i) *Anacréon* (opéra-ballet; complete); (ii) *Le berger fidèle* (cantata).
*** DG Dig. 449 211-2 [id.]. (i–ii) Véronique Gens; (ii) Thierry Félix, Annick Massis, Rodrigo del Pozo, Ch.; Les Musiciens du Louvre, Marc Minkowski.

Rameau composed two works on the theme of the ancient Greek poet, Anacreon, famed for his devotion to Cupid and Bacchus. This is the second, originally designed as an *acte de ballet* to a libretto by P.-J. Bernard and composed in 1757. The music has both vivacity and charm, and they are fully revealed in this splendidly alive, DG Archiv performance from Minkowski and his excellent Choeur and Musiciens du Louvre, who are given first-class recording. The plot asks the question: can love and wine coexist? There is real drama at the opening of Scene 2 when Anacreon's unremitting wining and dining is interrupted by the angry arrival of Bacchus's Priestess (the excellent Véronique Gens) to destroy a statue of Cupid and abduct Anacreon's neglected lover, Lycoris. Scene 3 opens with an atmospheric evocation reminiscent of Vivaldi: *Sommeil-Pluie* (delicate pizzicati) -*Orage*; here as elsewhere the ear is caught by the contributions from the petites flûtes (transverse baroque piccolos), which so enhance the orchestral colour, chattering away in their obbligatos for the arias and returning piquantly to add brightness to the closing *Contredanse* after the problem has been resolved with the very happy compromise: wine should be one of the joys of lovers, not an alternative diversion! As an encore, Véronique Gens sings very affectingly an equally inspired 15-minute solo cantata which juxtaposes happiness and sacrifice with all the drama of the operatic stage. Once again the power of love wins out and tragedy is averted. This fine coupling now replaces Christie's earlier, Harmonia Mundi version of *Anacréon* with Les Arts Florissants (HMC 90190).

Castor et Pollux (complete).
*** HM Dig. HMC 901435/7 [id.]. Crook, Corréas, Mellon, Gens, Schirrer, Brua, Piau, Les Arts Florissants Ch. & O, William Christie.

Recorded in 1992, following staged performances at the Aix-en-Provence Festival a year earlier, Christie's performance of Rameau's second *tragédie en musique* uses the original 1733 text, quite different from the 1754 text recorded for Erato by Charles Farncombe (4509 95311-2). Christie's performance consistently benefits from the dramatic timing, not least in the fluently alert and idiomatic exchanges in recitative, as well as in the broad, expressive treatment of set numbers like Telaire's lament, *Tristes apprets*, beautifully sung by Agnès Mellon. With such fine sopranos as Véronique Gens and Sandrine Piau in relatively small roles, the cast has no weakness. Howard Crook has the clear tenor needed for the role of Castor (who appears very late in the drama), with Jérôme Corréas a stylish Pollux. The sound is a little drier and less warm than is usual with Christie, but it is fresh and immediate and has plenty of body, with military percussion beautifully caught. This is now a clear first choice.

Castor et Pollux: highlights.
(B) *** HM Dig. HMX 290844/46 (3) [id.] (from above set; cond. Christie) – CAMPRA: *Idomenée:* highlights; LULLY: *Atys:* highlights. ***

This is one of Harmonia Mundi's enterprising 'Trios', compiling three discs of operatic highlights at bargain price, in this case with full documentation, including translation. *Castor et Pollux* is a masterpiece, vividly recorded, and this 70-minute selection, if taken with its two companions, costs but a fraction of the price of the three-disc complete set.

Hippolyte et Aricie (complete).
*** Erato/Warner Dig. 0630 15517-2 (3) [id.]. Padmore, Panzarella, Hunt, Naouri, James, Les Arts Florissants, William Christie.

It was through *Hippolyte et Aricie* that, in Anthony Lewis's 1965 Oiseau-Lyre recording (still available on Decca 444 526-2), Christie first discovered Rameau while still a student at Harvard. His love for the piece brims out from his superb recording, which has the benefit of using the text specially prepared for the complete Rameau Edition by Sylvie Bouissou. In this, as she explains in a note, she aims to restore fully the original (1733) edition, long buried, which was later altered and modified, not for artistic reasons, but under pressure from a conservative public. Marc Minkowski in his fine, crisply alert DG Archiv recording (445 853-2) uses a text substantially similar, and both of them – unlike Lewis – include the Prologue. The contrasts with Minkowski are striking, for Christie, using rather larger forces to produce warmer textures and timbres, consistently brings out the sensuous beauty of much of the writing as well as its dramatic point. At speeds fractionally broader, he bounces rhythms more infectiously and allows himself more flexible phrasing, regularly more relaxed in his manner, without undermining the classical purity of style. Though Anne-Maria Panzarella as Aricie is not as golden in tone as Véronique Gens for Minkowski, she is fresh and bright, responding immediately to Christie's timing which more consistently seems geared to stage presentation, with a conversational quality given to passages of recitative. Mark Padmore is a more ardent Hippolyte than his opposite number and Lorraine Hunt a weightier, more deeply tragic Phèdre, with Eirian James a warm Diana and Laurent Naouri as Thésée weightier than Russell Smythe. The Erato sound too is warmer and more immediate than the DG Archiv.

Rangström, Ture (1871–1947)

Symphonies Nos. 3 in D flat (Song under the Stars); (i) *4 in E flat (Invocatio)*.
** CPO Dig. CPO 999 369-2 [id.]. (i) Mark Fahlsjö; Norrköping SO, Michail Jurowski.

The Swedish composer Ture Rangström is best remembered for his 200 or so songs. This disc leaves no doubt that his gifts were lyrical rather than symphonic. The *Third Symphony* (1929) takes one of his songs, *Bön till natten* ('Prayer to the night') as its starting point, but the result is terribly inflated. The *Fourth Symphony* (1933–6) is best described as a suite for orchestra and organ. Its invention is very uneven, though there is a charming *Intermezzo*, which forms the central movement. Good performances and recordings, but neither work is remotely convincing symphonically.

Rautavaara, Einojuhani (born 1928)

Angels and visitations; (i) *Violin concerto. Isle of bliss.*
✿ *** Ode Dig. ODE 881-2 [id.]. (i) Elmar Oliveira; Helsinki PO, Leif Segerstam.

Rautavaara's wholly original *Violin concerto* is truly memorable and must surely be ranked alongside other outstanding modern works in this form by Samuel Barber and Christopher Headington. Like their music, it is hauntingly accessible and wholly grips the listener. It moves from an ethereal opening cantilena, through a series of colourful events and experiences until, after a final burst of incandescent energy, it makes a sudden but positive homecoming. The soloist must be able to float in space, move forward in a seemingly spontaneous melisma, create a sense of rhapsodical freedom in the capricious solo cadenza in the Scherzo (where he is joined by other instrumentalists) and add his own extemporisation to the later, very free cadenza, following after what the composer calls the 'moonlit scene', then encompass the fierce bravura of the closing section, with its chimerical *moto perpetuo* rhythms. The lively opening of the *Isle of bliss* is deceptive, for the music centres on a dreamy, sensual romanticism and creates a rich orchestral tapestry with a sense of yearning ecstasy, yet overall it has a surprisingly coherent orchestral structure. *Angels and visitations* is close to the visions of William Blake and (as the composer tells us) brings a sense of 'holy dread'. The extraordinary opening evokes a rustling of angels' wings, which is then malignantly transformed, becoming a ferocious multitude of bumblebees. It is a passage of real imaginative power, in some ways comparable to the storm sequence in Sibelius's *Tapiola*. The work is in a kind of variation form and moves from the ethereal nature of angels to demons quite readily, while later taking on board forceful rhythmic influences from Stravinsky's *Rite of spring* and *Petrushka*. Its orchestration and impact are spectacular, hardly music for a small flat! Elmar Oliveira is the inspired soloist in the *Violin concerto*, floating his line magically and serenely in the opening *Tranquillo* and readily encompassing the work's adventurous shifts of colour and substance. Segerstam provides a shimmering backing and directs a committed and persuasively spontaneous orchestral response throughout all three works. The recording is superbly balanced, spacious and vivid in detail.

Symphony No. 7 (Angel of Light); (i) *Annunciations*.
*** Ondine Dig. ODE 869-2 [id.]. (i) Kari Jussila; Helsinki PO, Leif Segerstam.

The *Seventh Symphony* is the more substantial piece and is both powerful and atmospheric. There is a good deal of Sibelius in its first movement and there is a pervasive sense of nature. Rautavaara betrays some affinities with the minimalists but offers greater musical substance. *Annunciations* for organ, brass quintet, winds and percussion, written in 1976–7, strikes a more dissonant note but it is brilliant and well thought out. Kari Jussila is the virtuoso soloist, and the Helsinki orchestra under Segerstam are eminently well served by the Ondine engineers.

Ravel, Maurice (1875–1937)

Alborada del gracioso; Une barque sur l'océan; Boléro; (i) *Piano concerto in G; Piano concerto for the left hand. Daphnis et Chloé* (complete ballet); *L'Eventail de Jeanne: Fanfare. Menuet antique; Ma Mère l'Oye* (complete); *Pavane pour une infante défunte; Rapsodie espagnole; Le tombeau de Couperin; La valse; Valses nobles et sentimentales.*

500♪ ❁ (M) *** Decca 421 458-2 (4). Montreal SO with Ch. and (i) Pascal Rogé; Dutoit.

Anyone coming new to this repertoire will find Dutoit's four-disc mid-price box unbeatable value: the orchestral playing is wonderfully sympathetic and the recording ideally combines atmospheric evocation with vividness of detail. In the concertos, Pascal Rogé finds gracefulness and vitality for the *G major* work and, if there is less dynamism in the *Left-hand concerto*, there is no lack of finesse. The balance is very realistic and the recording throughout is in the demonstration class.

Alborada del gracioso; Une barque sur l'océan; Ma Mère l'Oye (complete ballet); *Pavane pour une infante défunte; Le tombeau de Couperin.*

**(*) Erato/Warner Dig. 0630 14331-2 [id.]. Lyon Opéra O, Kent Nagano.

Nagano displays a lightness of touch in *Le tombeau de Couperin* which eludes the Orpheus Chamber Orchestra, and the Lyon orchestra play sensitively for him. They are naturally recorded, too: *Une barque sur l'océan* is most evocative. But the full magic of *Ma Mère l'Oye* is not distilled here, and the *Alborada* lacks glitter.

Alborada del gracioso; Pavane pour une infante défunte; Rapsodie espagnole; Valses nobles et sentimentales.

500♪ ❁ (M) *** RCA GD 60179 [60179-2-RG]. Chicago SO, Reiner – DEBUSSY: *Ibéria.* *** ❁

These performances are in an altogether special class. In the *Rapsodie espagnole*, the *Prélude à la nuit* is heavy with fragrance and atmosphere; never have the colours in the *Feria* glowed more luminously, while the *Malagueña* glitters with iridescence. No one captures its sensuous atmosphere as completely as did Reiner, and the recorded sound with its natural concert-hall balance is greatly improved in terms of clarity and definition.

Boléro; Jeux d'eau (orch. Viacava); *Ma Mère l'Oye: suite;* (i) *Tzigane. La vallée des cloches* (orch. Grainger); *La valse;* (ii) *5 Mélodies populaires grecques.*

**(*) Cala Dig. CACD 1004 [id.]. (i) Stephanie Chase; (ii) Sally Burgess; Philh. O, Geoffrey Simon.

A record of unusual interest in that it offers orchestral transcriptions of two Ravel piano pieces that are new to the catalogue: Viacava's orchestration of *Jeux d'eau*, made in 1951, and Percy Grainger's exotic and imaginative scoring of *La vallée des cloches* from 1944. The test of good orchestration is to convey the illusion that the music could have existed in no other form, as do Ravel's own transcriptions of *Alborada del gracioso* and *Ma Mère l'Oye*, and it is a tribute to Viacava's cunning and expertise that he succeeds as well as he does (albeit not completely) to disguise the keyboard origins of *Jeux d'eau*. Percy Grainger's *La vallée des cloches* is quite remarkable, calling as it does on an exotic array of glockenspiel, vibraphone, marimba, celeste, dulcitone and other 'tuneful percussion' (to quote Grainger's own heading on the score), including the strings of a piano struck by a mallet. It is not perhaps wholly Ravel in sensibility, but it is highly effective in its own right. Geoffrey Simon directs good performances from the Philharmonia, though his *Ma Mère l'Oye* doesn't banish memories of Giulini, Cluytens or Dutoit. Simon's two soloists in the *Cinq mélodies populaires grecques* and *Tzigane* are excellent, and the recording is very good indeed. The liner-notes by Grant Cathro are full of insights into Ravel's music and are very perceptive.

Boléro; Ma mère l'Oye (complete); *La valse.*

(M) **(*) Ph. 442 548-2 [id.]. LSO, Pierre Monteux.

Monteux's 1964 version of the complete *Ma Mère l'Oye* is a poetic, unforced reading, given naturally balanced sound. *La valse* is impressive too, and *Boléro* has well-sustained concentration, even though some will raise an eyebrow at the slight quickening of pace in the closing pages. These three recordings are taken from a Philips original which has responded well to its digital remastering, retaining its warmth while obtaining a clearer profile. However, this now seems rather short measure.

Piano concerto in G.
500♪ ❀ *** EMI CDC7 49326-2 [id.]. Michelangeli, Philh. O, Gracis – RACHMANINOV: *Concerto No. 4.* *** ❀

Michelangeli plays with superlative brilliance which yet has great sympathy for the tender moments. The exquisite playing in the slow movement makes up for any deficiencies of dimensional balance. The recording has been remastered very successfully and is of high quality: clear, with bold piano timbre and excellent orchestral detail.

Piano concerto in G; Piano concerto for the left hand in D.
** Decca Dig. 452 448-2 [id.]. Thibaudet, Montreal SO, Dutoit – HONEGGER; FRANCAIX: *Concertinos.* ***

** Ph. Dig. 446 713-2 [id.]. Zoltán Kocsis, Budapest Festival O, Iván Fischer – DEBUSSY: *Fantasy for piano & orchestra.* ***

Jean-Yves Thibaudet is an elegant player and, as readers who know his survey of the keyboard music will know, is thoroughly inside Ravel's idiom. These are eminently accomplished and often beautiful performances, but they strike few resonances in the memory once they are over. It would be unfair to call them bland, and they are certainly not characterless, but they are not in any way special. Suffice it to say that others dig deeper into these scores (particularly the *Concerto for the left hand*), and Pascal Rogé remains much more satisfying (Decca 410 230-2 – see our main volume).

Zoltán Kocsis, too, offers some superb pianism in his accounts of the two concertos but he is, surprisingly enough, not always responsive to the wide range of colour and dynamics in both scores, and the glorious slow movement of the *G major Concerto* is curiously wanting in that dreamy, sensuous quality which Argerich or Rogé bring to it. The orchestral playing is polished and spirited, but the performances as a whole disappoint.

Daphnis et Chloé (ballet; complete).
500♪ ❀ (M) *** RCA 09026 61846-2 [id.]. New England Conservatory & Alumni Ch., Boston SO, Munch.
(M) * Ph. Dig. 454 684-2 [id.]. Tanglewood Ch., Boston SO, Haitink.

Charles Munch's Boston account is one of the great glories of the 1950s, superior in every way to his later version from the 1960s. The playing in all departments of the Boston orchestra is simply electrifying. The sound here may not be as sumptuous as the Monteux on Decca, but the richness of colour lies in the playing, and there is a heady sense of intoxication that at times sweeps you off your feet, and the integration of the chorus is impressively managed, with the ballet ending in tumultous orchestral virtuosity.

Haitink's version brings a powerful performance, marked by extremes of tempo and dynamic. Its directness is matched by the superb playing of the Boston orchestra, but sadly this is one of the relative failures by the Philips engineers working in Boston. The sound, at rather a low level, lacks body and is curiously misty, giving the Boston strings an acid edge which scarcely reflects their beauty. First choice for Ravel's lustrous score rests with Dutoit and his Montreal forces, giving a wonderfully luminous recording (Decca 400 055-2), or with Munch in Boston.

Ma Mère l'Oye (complete); *Le tombeau de Couperin; Valses nobles et sentimentales.*
500♪ ❀ *** Decca Dig. 410 254-2 [id.]. Montreal SO, Dutoit.

A few bars of this Decca record leave no doubt as to its excellence. This offers demonstration quality, transparent and refined, with the textures beautifully balanced and expertly placed. The performances too are wonderfully refined and sympathetic. *Ma Mère l'Oye* is ravishingly beautiful, its special combination of sensuousness and innocence perfectly caught.

Pavane pour une infante défunte; Le tombeau de Couperin.
*(*) DG Dig. 449 186-2 [id.]. Orpheus CO – FAURE: *Masques et bergamasques* etc. **; SATIE: *Gymnopédies Nos. 1 & 3.* *(*)

Impeccable ensemble, but the Orpheus performances are curiously unsympathetic. The opening *Prélude* of *Le tombeau de Couperin* sounds just that bit breathless; the *Forlane* and *Menuet* lack poise; and the buoyant *Rigaudon* brings a touch of aggression in the recorded sound. The *Pavane pour une infante défunte*, too, lacks subtlety of feeling.

Tzigane (for violin and orchestra).
(M) *** EMI CDM5 66058-2 [id.]. Itzhak Perlman, O de Paris, Barenboim – SAINT-SAENS: *Havanaise;* VIEUXTEMPS: *Violin concertos Nos. 4 & 5.* ***

Perlman's classic (1974) account of Ravel's *Tzigane* for EMI is marvellously played; the added projection of the CD puts the soloist believably at the end of the living-room. The opulence of his tone is undiminished by the remastering process and the orchestral sound retains its atmosphere, while gaining in clarity.

CHAMBER MUSIC

Introduction and allegro for harp, flute, clarinet and string quartet.
500♪ ❁ (M) *** Decca 421 154-2. Osian Ellis, Melos Ens. – DEBUSSY; FRANCK: *Sonatas*. *** ❁

The beauty and subtlety of Ravel's sublime septet are marvellously realized by this 1962 Melos account. The interpretation has great delicacy of feeling, and the recording hardly shows its age at all.

(i) *Piano trio in A min.;* (ii) *String quartet in F;* (iii) *Violin sonata in G.*
(M) **(*) Ph. 454 1342-2 [id.]. (i) Beaux Arts Trio; (ii) Italian Qt; (iii) Grumiaux, Hajdu.

Ravel's *String quartet* usually comes in harness with the Debussy *Quartet*; here it is offered as part of a triptych of Ravel's key chamber-works. The performance by the Quartetto Italiano has long been praised by us. The Beaux Arts give a predictably fine account of the *Trio*, and the only slight criticism would be an occasional want of charm by the violinist, Daniel Guilet, but that is a small reservation. In the *Violin sonata* Grumiaux's playing has great finesse and beauty of sound. The recordings date from 1966 and are very naturally balanced, but the CD transfer demonstrates their age by a degree of shrillness of the fortissimo string-timbre.

String quartet in F.
❁ *** Koch Dig. 3-6436-2 [id.]. Medici Qt – BRITTEN: *Quartet No. 3;* JANACEK: *Quartet No. 1;* SHOSTAKOVICH: *Quartet No. 8;* SMETANA: *Quartet No. 1*. *** ❁
(B) **(*) Sony SBK 62413; *SBT 62413* [id.]. Tokyo Qt – DEBUSSY: *Quartet* **(*); FAURE: *Piano trio*. (*)

In the hands of the Medici players the opening of the Ravel *Quartet* is utterly magical, its subtlety of atmosphere and gentle radiance caught with a perfection rare in the concert hall, let alone on record. This is a great performance of a masterly work, for the *Assez vif – très rhythmé* brings comparable finesse and concentration, while the stillness at the opening of the *Très lent* make one hold one's breath at the music's *tendresse*. The recording is completely tangible: it is as if these players were at the end of one's room.

The Tokyo Quartet play with great finesse and tonal beauty, especially in the warm yet refined account of the *très lent*. They certainly observe the marking of the finale, *vif et agité* and perhaps elsewhere there could be a touch more poise. But their music-making is thoroughly alive. The sound is very good.

(i; ii) *Violin sonata (1897); Violin sonata in G;* (i; iii) *Sonata for violin and cello;* (i; ii) *Berceuse sur le nom de Gabriel Fauré; Kaddish; Pièce en forme de habanera; Tzigane.*
*** Decca Dig. 448 612-2 [id.]. (i) Chantal Juillet; (ii) Pascal Rogé; (iii) Truls Mørk.

Violin sonata (1897); Violin sonata in G; Tzigane; Berceuse sur le nom de Gabriel Fauré.
*** Sony Dig. SK 66839 [id.]. Cho-Liang Lin, Paul Crossley – DEBUSSY; POULENC: *Violin sonatas*. ***

Violin sonata in G.
*** Erato/Warner Dig. 0630 15110-2 [id.]. Vadim Repin, Boris Berezovsky – MEDTNER: *Sonata No. 3 (Sonata epica)*. ***

There are some admirable recent accounts of the Ravel *G major Sonata* to be had, including Christian Tetzlaff and Leif Ove Andsnes (Virgin) and Schlomo Mintz and Yefim Bronfman, now at mid-price and attractively coupled with the two Prokofiev *Sonatas* (DG), both three-star recommendations. But the Sony issue is if anything even more competitively coupled, for it offers very good value in terms of playing time and, more importantly, artistic satisfaction. Cho-Liang Lin plays with his usual effortless virtuosity and impeccable taste, and he is well supported by Paul Crossley. The early (1897) *Sonata* has rarely sounded more captivating. Sony provide these artists with exemplary recorded sound.

The Decca is an all-Ravel record and, in addition to the two *Sonatas*, gives us the *Tzigane*, a handful of other shorter pieces and the *Sonata for violin and cello*. Chantal Juillet and Pascal Rogé present a *Tzigane* with a difference in that Rogé uses a piano luthenal (an instrument modified to sound like a cimbalom, which was used in the first performance in 1922) and Juillet sounds more zigeuner-like than most of her rivals. Their accounts of the two *Sonatas* are predictably cultured and (equally unsurprisingly) beautifully recorded. Pascal Rogé scores over Cho-Liang Lin's partner in terms of sheer responsiveness, and Chantal Juillet and Truls Mørk are first rate in the *Duo sonata*. Strongly recommended, if this programme is suitable.

Vadim Repin and Boris Berezovsky on Erato offer an unusual coupling. It is difficult to see what the Medtner *Sonata* has in common with the Ravel. This reservation apart, these two artists give a vitally alert and highly sensitive account of the piece, which can hold its own alongside the current competition. They command a wide range of colour and dynamics, infuse every phrase with life, and have the full measure of the 'Blues' movement. Repin plays the Guarneri with which Isaac Stern delighted us for almost half a century and it sounds magnificently responsive in his hands. Very good and completely natural recording.

PIANO MUSIC

A la manière de Borodine; A la manière de Chabrier; Gaspard de la nuit; Jeux d'eau; Menuet antique; Menuet sur le nom de Haydn; Miroirs; Pavane pour une infante défunte; Prélude; Sérénade grotesque; Sonatine; Le tombeau de Couperin; Valses nobles et sentimentales.
500♪ *** Decca Dig. 433 515-2 (2) [id.]. Jean-Yves Thibaudet.

A la manière de Borodine; A la manière de Chabrier; Gaspard de la nuit; Jeux d'eau; Menuet antique; Menuet sur le nom de Haydn; Miroirs; Pavane pour une infante défunte; Prélude; Sonatine; Valses nobles et sentimentales.
(M) *(*) EMI Classics CMS5 68565-2 (2). Samson François.

Thibaudet exhibits flawless technique, perfect control, refinement of touch and exemplary taste. He distils just the right atmosphere in *Oiseaux tristes* and *Une barque sur l'océan* – but then, one might as well choose any other piece from *Miroirs*, and his *Gaspard* can hold its own with any in the catalogue. The recording is of real distinction too.

Samson François enjoyed cult status in the France of the 1960s. This was, of course, before the arrival on the scene of such artists as Michel Béroff, Jean-Philippe Collard and Pascal Rogé. It is difficult to understand why François was singled out for such admiration as his Ravel is often downright insensitive. He was at his best in the *Concerto for the left hand*, not represented in this collection; but elsewhere he is distinctly cavalier about dynamic markings and tends to confuse *pianissimo* with *mezzo-forte*. The transfers are decent and can be recommended to his admirers.

Gaspard de la nuit.
500♪ *** DG Dig. 413 363-2 [id.]. Pogorelich – PROKOFIEV: *Sonata No. 6.* *** ✿

Pogorelich's *Gaspard* is out of the ordinary; this is piano playing of astonishing quality. The control of colour and nuance in *Scarbo* is dazzling and its eruptive cascades of energy and dramatic fire have one sitting on the edge of one's seat.

Valses nobles et sentimentales.
* DG Dig 437 667-2 [id.]. Ivo Pogorelich – MUSSORGSKY: *Pictures.* *

Pogorelich pulls the *Valses nobles* around in the most insufferable and affected fashion. The second of the *Valses* virtually grinds to a halt, and there is little that is noble here but much that stretches the listener's kindliest sentiments towards the artist. The pianism is sophisticated, but this issue is strictly for fans of Pogorelich rather than admirers of Ravel. Very good recording.

VOCAL MUSIC

Mélodies: *Ballade de la Reine; Morte d'Aimer; Canzone italiana; Chanson du rouet; Chanson espagnole; Chanson française; Chanson hébraïque; Chansons madécasses; 5 mélodies populaires grecques; 2 Epigrammes de Clément Marot; 2 Mélodies hébraïques; Don Quichotte à Dulcinée; Un grand sommeil nuit; Les grands vents venus d'outremer; Histoires naturelles; Manteau de fleurs; Noël des jouets; Rêves; Ronsard à son âme; Sainte; Scottish song; Shéhérazade* (complete); *Si morne!; Sur l'herbe; Tripatos; 3 Poèmes de Stéphane Mallarmé; Vocalise en forme de Habanera.*
(B) *** EMI Dig. CZS5 69299-2 (2). Norman, Mesplé, Lott, Berganza, Van Dam, Bacquier, Capitole Toulouse O or Paris CO, Plasson; Dalton Baldwin (piano).

With a composer whose expressive range in song-form (or mélodie) might have seemed limited, it is an excellent idea in the EMI set to have six strongly contrasted singers, each given an apt area to cover. So Teresa Berganza as well as singing *Shéhérazade* has two songs inspired by Spain, the *Vocalise in the form of an Habanera* and the *Chanson espagnole* from the set of five *Chants populaires*, each of which is allotted to a different singer. Felicity Lott's *Chanson écossaise* is a rarity, *Ye banks and braes* sung in a convincing Scots accent. For all the shallowness of Mady Mesplé's voice, it works well in the *Mélodies populaires grecques*, while Jessye Norman, rich-toned if not quite as characterful as usual, has the *Chansons madécasses* as well as lesser-known songs. It is the contribution of the two men that provides the sharpest illumination: José van Dam magnificently dark-toned in the *Don Quichotte* songs and the *Mélodies hébraïques* (making *Kaddish* thrillingly powerful in its agony of mourning), while Gabriel Bacquier twinkles in Figaro tones in the point songs. Excellent sound, and the pair of CDs particularly generous

(136 minutes) in offering the contents of three LPs and now being offered as an inexpensive Rouge et Noir reissue.

'Chant d'amour': 4 Chansons populaires; 2 Mélodies hébraïques; Tripatos; Vocalise-étude en forme de Habanera.
*** Decca Dig. 452 667-2; *452 667-4* [id.]. Cecilia Bartoli, Myung-Whun Chung – BIZET; BERLIOZ; DELIBES: *Mélodies.* ***

Cecilia Bartoli is just as much at home in the music of Ravel as she is with the songs of the other composers represented in this outstanding recital of French songs. Myung Whun-Chung, too, proves himself a natural accompanist.

OPERA

L'enfant et les sortilèges (complete).
500♪ ❁ (***) Testament mono SBT 1044 [id.]. Nadine Sautereau, André Vessières, Solange Michel, Denise Scharley, Yvon Le Marc'Hadour, Joseph Peyron, Martha Angelici, French Nat. R. Ch. and O, Ernest Bour.

Testament here offer a superlative transfer of the unsurpassed first recording of Ravel's charming one-acter under Ernest Bour. There is a magic about this performance that completely captivates the listener. Each part could not be improved upon in character, subtlety and style. The singing and playing of the French Radio forces are vital and imaginative. With no stars but with no weak link, the singers make an outstanding team, helped by sound which, with background hiss eliminated, has astonishing presence. No other version casts quite such a strong spell.

Rawsthorne, Alan (1905–71)

(i) *Piano concerto No. 2;* (ii) *Concerto for 2 pianos.*
(B) ** BBC Radio Classics 15656 91762 [id.]. John Ogdon, (i) BBC SO; (ii) with Brenda Lucas, LPO; both cond. Pritchard – SIMPSON: *Piano concerto.* **

Rawsthorne's *Second Piano concerto* of 1951 is neither as individual nor as haunting as the *First*, but it is highly pianistic and accomplished. Ogdon's performance comes from a 1983 Promenade concert and found this great pianist taking plenty of risks. The later *Concerto for two pianos* comes from a 1968 Prom and is less successful both as a work and as a recording, for the two players are less sharply in focus. Geoffrey Tozer on Chandos (CHAN 9125) remains the prime recommendation for all three concertos (on a single CD) which, apart from the more vivid recording quality, has the added virtue of demonstrating that the *First Concerto* is an underrated masterpiece.

Rebel, Jean-Féry (1661–1747)

Les caractères de la Danse; Les Elémens; Le tombeau de M. de Lully.
*** Erato/Warner Dig. 2292 45974-2 [id.]. Les Musiciens du Louvre, Marc Minkowski.

Les Elémens (suite).
** DG Dig. 445 824-2 [id.]. Col. Mus. Ant., Goebel – GLUCK: *Alessandro* (ballet); TELEMANN: *Sonata (Septet) in E min.* **

The earliest piece on this Erato CD is the eloquent trio sonata, *Le tombeau de M. de Lully*, which was written on the death of the great French composer whose pupil Rebel had become as a boy of eight. The last and most substantial is *Les Elémens* which, the excellent notes tell us, is one of the most original works of the period. It was first performed in 1737 as a divertissement following a performance of Lully's *Cadmus et Hermione*. The opening movement, *Le cahos*, was added the following year and 'in the estimation of the greatest connoisseurs, is one of the most beautiful symphonic works that exist in this genre', to quote a contemporary review. With its representation of chaos in which all the notes of the harmonic scale are heard simultaneously, it is certainly quite astonishing in effect. The performance and recording are of the highest quality, and this is to be preferred to the rival accounts from Christopher Hogwood and the Academy of Ancient Music, and Reinhard Goebel and the Musica Antiqua Köln.

The Cologne Musica Antiqua are surely the most aggressive among all period-instrument groups, and they could well win a prize for their explosive representation of *Le cahos*. But later, although they manage to paint Rebel's whimsical picture of the birds in the trees (*Ramade*) and follow on with an equally accurate portrait of *Rossignols*, when they come to the *Loure* the heavy accents make it seem as if the dancing is taking place in boots, and the solid, trumpeting hand horns add to the feeling of clumsy peasantry. They do, however, manage a charming accelerando for the *Caprice*.

Reger, Max (1873–1916)

Variations and fugue on a theme by Mozart, Op. 132.
500♪ ✪ *** Ph. Dig. 422 347-2 [id.]. Bav. RSO, C. Davis – HINDEMITH: *Symphonic metamorphosis*. ***
(M) (**) DG Originals 449 737-2 (2) [id.]. BPO, Boehm – BEETHOVEN: *Missa solemnis*. (**)

Sir Colin Davis's whole performance has a radiance and glow that does full justice to this masterpiece, which is not only scored with great delicacy but has wit and tenderness in equal measure. The Philips recording is state of the art. Recommended with enthusiasm.

Recorded in 1956, this Boehm version must have just missed being in stereo. The sound is good and the orchestral playing is first class, but the performance is curiously uninvolving. Boehm gets off on the wrong foot by taking Mozart's theme (from the *A major Piano sonata*, K.331) remarkably slowly.

(i) *Variations and fugue on a theme of Mozart, Op. 132;* (ii) *4 Tone-poems after Böcklin, Op. 128.*
*(*) Berlin Classics 0021772BC [id.]. (i) Dresden State O; (ii) Dresden PO; Heinz Bongartz.

Cultured and musical performances of these beautiful scores from the Dresden orchestras under Heinz Bongartz, who has an obvious feeling for Reger. He gets eloquent playing from the Staatskapelle, Dresden, in the *Mozart variations*, though the fugue is less successful. The *Böcklin pictures* are imaginatively done, though the actual quality of the playing does not match that of the Concertgebouw Orchestra for Neeme Järvi on Chandos (CHAN 8794 – see our main volume). The recordings date from the 1960s and lack the bloom of their more modern rivals. However, there is plenty of detail, and the overall sound is well balanced. Two stars for the performance and one for the eminently serviceable recorded sound.

Christmas Lieder: *Christkindleins Wiegenlied; Ehre sei Gott in der Höhe! Maria am Rosenstrauch; Morgengesang; Uns ist geboren ein Kindelein.*
✪ *** EMI Dig. CDC5 56204-2 [id.]. Bär, Deutsch (with Recital: '*Christmas Lieder*' *** ✪).

One does not think of Max Reger as a composer of light-hearted Christmas Lieder, and indeed his contribution sustains the most serious mood of any of the songs in Olaf Bär's superb recital, especially the closing *Ehre sei Gott in der Höhe!* But even here the imagination of Bär's word-colouring and his wide range of dynamic prevents any feeling of heaviness, while the strong postlude on the piano is satisfyingly positive. The opening *Morgengesang*, describing the 'morning star', brings a delightfully fresh spontaneity, and *Mary in the Rosebower* has a gentle, rocking lyricism, beautifully realized in Helmut Deutsch's flowing accompaniment.

Reicha, Antonín (1770–1836)

(i) *Sinfonia concertante in G for flute, violin and orchestra. Symphony in E flat, Op. 41; Overture in D.*
*** MDG Dig. MDG 335 0661-2 [id.]. (i) Ida Bieler, Jean-Claude Gérard; Wuppertal SO, Peter Gülke.

Reicha is one of the most interesting and influential of Beethoven's lesser contemporaries and, anyone listening to the present disc might venture to add, a strong personality in his own right. The first movement of the *Sinfonia concertante* brings engaging textures but is otherwise relatively conventional. The other two movements are a different matter. The *galant Andante* brings a charming little violin melody over a tick-tock flute accompaniment; later the two instruments change roles. The *Overture in D minor* is, remarkably, in 5/8 time and its nagging ostinato main theme is at first quite catching. The snag is that, despite its variety of colour, it is a shade over-long. The *Symphony* is a different matter. Its main allegro is very confidently constructed in a style very like the later symphonies of Haydn and Mozart. The *Andante un poco adagio* doesn't disappoint, while the progress of the lively finale (again following a Haydn model, but by no means unoriginal) isn't predictable either. The composer keeps a card or two up his sleeve until the very end. A real discovery, which invites repeated hearings. The orchestra proves to be a surprisingly fine ensemble and, with two first-class soloists here, offers a rewarding collection, well recorded.

Flute quartets Nos. 1 in E min., Op. 98; 2 in A; 3 in D, Op. 98/1–3.
*** MDG Dig. MDG 311 0630-2 [id.]. Konrad Hünteler, Rainer and Jürgen Küssmaul, Roel Dietiens.

The music of the Bohemian composer, Antonín Reicha, has a familiar ring to it, yet its craftsmanship and elegance of form are a constant pleasure, and the composer's ideas are by no means lacking in individuality. In the opening *Quartet*, a particularly fine piece, one thinks often of Mozart, who also wrote some delightful works for the same combination of instruments, and Reicha's invention is seldom inferior. The piquant opening of the *Second Quartet* has a Bohemian insouciance, but Mozart is again recalled very distinctly in the Minuet. In the *Third Quartet* the quaint little tune, marching along slowly and elegantly, which forms the basis for virtuoso roulades for the flute soloist in the opening *Adagio un poco Andante* is Bohemian in spirit, and its charm is almost matched by the following Allegro. The finale, marked *Folie harmonique*, begins with little shudders, perhaps at the thought of the witty fugal writing that is subsequently to appear in the string parts. Throughout all three works the solo flute part demands, and receives, the utmost virtuosity from its performer, here Konrad Hünteler, who usually dominates – but sometimes effectively blends with – his colleagues, all excellent players. The vivid recording completes the listener's pleasure.

Wind quintets: in F (1811); in E flat; in B flat, Op. 88/2 & 5; in D; in A, Op. 91/3 & 5.
(B) *** Hyperion Dyad Dig. CDD 22006 (2) [id.]. Academia Wind Quintet of Prague.

This Dyad combines two separate collections, recorded in 1987 and 1989 respectively. The second disc, which includes the rather more ambitious *A major* and *B flat major Quintets* (the latter has a highly unusual opening movement, continually alternating allegros and adagios), is, if anything, even more rewarding than the first. Czech wind-playing in Czech wind music has a deservedly high entertainment rating, and the present performances are no exception. The music itself has great charm and geniality; it is ingenuous yet cultivated, with some delightful, smiling writing for the bassoon. The players are clearly enjoying themselves, yet they play and blend expertly. The sound too is admirable.

Respighi, Ottorino (1879–1936)

Ancient airs and dances: suites Nos. 1–3.
(BB) ** Naxos Dig. 8.553564 [id.]. Nat SO of Ireland, Rico Saccani.

On Naxos a clear, direct, well-played account, somewhat lacking in atmosphere. This is partly caused by the effect of the closely balanced, bright, clean recording. The Orpheus Chamber Orchestra account on DG is far more satisfying and, although it costs much more, it also includes *The Birds suite* and the *Three Botticelli pictures*, which are equally impressive (see below).

(i) *Ancient airs and dances: suites Nos. 1–3;* (ii) *Belfagor:* overture; (iii) *The Birds* (suite); (ii) *The Fountains of Rome; The Pines of Rome;* (iii) *3 Botticelli pictures (Trittico Botticelliano).*
(B) **(*) EMI forte Dig. CZS5 69358-2 (2). (i) LACO, or (iii) ASMF; Marriner; (ii) LSO, Gardelli.

Sir Neville Marriner's account of the suites of dances is attractively light and gracious, offering an almost French elegance, with pleasingly transparent textures. *The Birds* and *Trittico Botticelliano* are no less delightful, and they are beautifully recorded. So far so good; but Lamberto Gardelli's performances of *The Pines* and *Fountains of Rome*, though warmly sympathetic and finely played, bring less of a feeling of drama. There are some lustrous sounds here, but these accounts generate neither the atmospheric magic nor electricity experienced in the competing versions from Reiner or Karajan. The *Belfagor overture* is an acceptable bonus, a dramatic and lively piece, strongly characterized and vivid.

Ancient airs and dances: suites Nos. 1 & 3; The Birds (Gli uccelli); 3 Botticelli pictures (Trittico Botticelliano).
500♪ ❁ *** DG Dig. 437 533-2 [id.]. Orpheus CO.

These pieces are stunningly played by this remarkable, conductorless ensemble. Their ensemble is terrific, rhythms wonderfully articulate and the music has a sense of joy and vitality. Sensitive accounts of the *Trittico Botticelliano* and an exhilarating, songful one of *The Birds*. Very fine recording, too.

Ancient airs and dances: suite No. 3 for strings; The Fountains of Rome; The Pines of Rome.
(M) *** DG 449 724-2 [id.]. BPO, Karajan (with BOCCHERINI: *Quintettino;* ALBINONI: *Adagio in G min.* (arr. Giazotto) ***).

Karajan's highly polished, totally committed performances of the two most popular Roman pieces are well supplemented by the *Third suite* of *Ancient airs and dances*, brilliantly played and just as beautifully transferred, more impressive in sound than many more recent Karajan recordings. In the symphonic poems Karajan is in his element, and the playing of the Berlin Philharmonic is wonderfully refined. The opening of the *Ancient airs* brings ravishing tone from the Berlin Philharmonic strings, and they sound even more lavish in Giazotto's famous arrangement of Albinoni's *Adagio*. That has been added as a bonus for this remastered reissue in DG's 'Legendary Recordings' series of 'Originals', while Boccherini's *Quintettino* makes an engaging additional lollipop.

3 Botticelli pictures; (i) *Aretusa;* (ii) *Lauda per la Nativita del Signore;* (i) *Il tramonto.*
500♪ ❁ *** Collins Dig. 1349-2 [id.]. (i) Dame Janet Baker; (ii) Patricia Rosario, Louise Winter, Lynton Atkinson, Hickox Singers; City of L. Sinfonia, Hickox.

This collection is crowned by the contributions of Dame Janet Baker, who gives ravishing performances of two of Respighi's warm and sensitive settings of Shelley poems. *Aretusa* was the first work in which Respighi established his mature style. *Il tramonto* ('The sunset') is just as beautiful. *Lauda* is a nativity cantata which touchingly presents the story as a simple pastoral sequence, with the tenderly expressive woodwind accompaniment suggesting rustic pipe music. The *Trittico Botticelliano* establishes its seductiveness in the shimmering sounds at the very opening of the first movement, *Primavera*.

Feste romane; The Fountains of Rome; The Pines of Rome (symphonic poems).
*** EMI Dig. CDC5 55600-2 [id.]. Oslo PO, Mariss Jansons.
*** Conifer Dig. 75605 51292 [id.]. Santa Cecilia Ac. O, Gatti.

Respighi's Roman trilogy is hardly neglected on CD. Our main volume lists no fewer than eight highly recommendable issues, and there are some two dozen alternatives currently available. 1996–7 has brought several spectacular versions from such masterly maestros as Maazel and Sinopoli, but none that we have heard is quite in the same category as the two listed above. These both challenge the very best of the competition. Jansons's splendidly vivid account of the *Feste romane* first appeared in 1990 together with the second suite from *Daphnis et Chloé* and Dukas's *L'Apprenti sorcier*. Both the newcomers, *The Pines* and *The Fountains*, are equally magnificent, and Jansons has their measure. There is more to this music than just colour, Mediterranean atmosphere and virtuoso orchestration. One expects the latter from a pupil of Rimsky-Korsakov, but there is a rather special quality of bitter-sweetness and a sense of longing and nostalgia that are beautifully realized here. The orchestral playing is of the first order, marvellous wind and brass throughout; and the Oslo recording scores over its immediate rival in having the deeper and more sumptuous acoustic ambience.

Daniele Gatti also brings something special to all three works: a rapt intensity, an extraordinary feeling for atmosphere and a total dedication to these glowing, richly coloured scores that is completely involving. The Santa Cecilia Orchestra plays wonderfully for him, and the Conifer recording, while not quite as spacious and open as the Oslo, is very well detailed. The wide dynamic range needs some help in some of the *pianopianissimo* sections, at the end of the *Fountains*, for example, where you will need to adjust the volume control. However, except for this, these Gatti performances have the edge on the Jansons and would ultimately be a first choice.

The Fountains of Rome; The Pines of Rome.
500♪ ❁ (M) *** RCA 09026 61401-2 [id.]. Chicago SO, Fritz Reiner – MUSSORGSKY: *Pictures at an exhibition.* *** ❁

Reiner's legendary recordings of *The Pines* and *Fountains of Rome* were made in Symphony Hall, Chicago, on 24 October 1959, and the extraordinarily atmospheric performances have never been surpassed since. The turning on of the Triton fountain brings an unforced cascade of orchestral brilliance, while the triumphal procession of Neptune's chariot across the heavens which forms the powerful centrepiece of the Trevi portrait has an overwhelmingly spacious grandeur. The marvellous orchestral playing is matched by the skill of RCA's new generation of transfer engineers, who have put it all on CD with complete fidelity.

Riisager, Knudåge (1897–1974)

Erasmus Montanus overture, Op. 1; Etudes (ballet; complete); *Qarrtsiluni, Op. 36.*
*** Chandos Dig. CHAN 9432 [id.]. Danish Nat. RSO, Rozhdestvensky.

Both the *Etudes* and *Qarrtsiluni* are classics of the Danish ballet and have been recorded before but never as successfully as here. Knudåge Riisager was born in Estonia of Danish parents and spent the bulk of his working life in the Danish Ministry of Finance. He pursued his musical studies in Paris with Roussel and Paul Le Flem, and his admiration for *Les six* is evident in the elegance and wit that distinguish the *Etudes* (1948), a pastiche based on Czerny, and *Qarrtsiluni* (1938). There is a zest and sparkle about his music, though it neither aims for nor has any great depth. The *Erasmus Montanus overture* is a highly accomplished first opus, written when its composer was 23. Attractive but slight music, neatly performed and superbly recorded. Let us hope that someone will revive his delightful *Schlaraffenland* (*A Fool's Paradise*).

Rimsky-Korsakov, Nikolay (1844–1908)

Le Coq d'or; The Maid from Pskov; Pan Voyevoda: suites.
❀ *** Impetus Kontrapunct Dig. 32247 [id.]. Odense SO, Edward Serov.

Serov is a complete master of the repertoire, and the playing of the Odense orchestra is glorious, the glowing woodwind palette matched by the most seductive and transparent string textures (especially in portraying Queen Shemakha in *Le Coq d'or*). Serov's performance is every bit as fine as Pletnev's on DG, and the recording here is even more luxuriant. Indeed it is very much in the demonstration bracket, and Serov's exciting account of *The marriage feast and lamentable end of Tsar Dodon* makes an unforgettable impact. *The Maid of Pskov* brings another memorably sinuous melody in its *Overture*, and the final movement of the suite, *The Tsar hunting in the wood and Tempest*, has much of the imaginative pictorial evocation and imagery of Berlioz's *Royal hunt and storm*. Again it is superbly presented, as is the hardly less attractive *Pan Voyevoda* which opens with a pastoral evocation rather like Wagner's *Forest murmurs*, and has a passionate central *Clair de lune* framed by three brilliantly scored *Russian dances*, an engaging *Krakowiak*, and a more robust *Mazurka* and *Polonaise*. Very highly recommended: marvellous music, its magic fully realized, and sound which could hardly be bettered.

Scheherazade (symphonic suite), *Op. 35*.
(M) *** RCA 09026 68168-2 [id.]. Chicago SO, Fritz Reiner – STRAVINSKY: *Chant du rossignol.* ***
(B) ** EMI forte CZS5 69361-2 (2). LSO, Svetlanov – ARENSKY: *Variations on a theme by Tchaikovsky;* GLAZUNOV: *The Seasons; Concert waltzes.* ***

Scheherazade; Capriccio espagnol, Op. 34.
500♪ ❀ *** Telarc Dig. CD 80208 [id.]. LSO, Sir Charles Mackerras.

Mackerras's reading combines gripping drama with romantic ardour, subtlety of colour with voluptuousness; he is helped by a wonderfully beguiling portrait of Scheherazade herself, provided by his orchestral leader, in this case Kees Hulsmann. The charming closing reverie, with the Sultan lying peacefully satiated in the arms of his young wife, their themes blissfully intermingled, is unforgettable. After an appropriate pause, Mackerras then delivers a thrilling bravura account of *Capriccio espagnol*, lushly opulent in the variations, and carrying all before it in the impetus of the closing *Fandango asturiano*. Telarc's digital recording is very much in the demonstration class.

Reiner's first movement opens richly and dramatically and has a strong forward impulse. Sidney Harth, the orchestral leader, naturally balanced, plays most seductively. Reiner's affectionate individual touches have much in common with Beecham's (full-price) version and sound almost as spontaneous; the finale, brilliant and very exciting, has a climax of resounding power and amplitude. The Chicago Hall acoustics provide the orchestra with plenty of body (the brass-laden introduction is weightily arresting), yet in John Pfeiffer's newest transfer detail is more clearly focused and immediate, while the strings retain all their bloom in the third movement. Above all, Reiner's is a virtuoso reading with phenomenally crisp ensemble, to have one relishing not just the brilliance but the individual finesse of the Chicago orchestra and its principals. The new coupling also shows Reiner and his orchestra at their finest, and it is particularly appropriate, for Stravinsky's glittering orchestral palette in *Le chant du rossignol* owes much to Rimsky.

Svetlanov's version of this perennial favourite with the LSO was made in 1978. But it is disappointing, despite John Georgiadis's subtly seductive image of Scheherazade herself. The broad, powerful opening movement, taken very spaciously indeed, is balanced by a finale which is almost aggressively brilliant. The inner movements are extremely volatile, with much ebb and flow of tempo, not always convincing, so that they are less contrasted than usual. The LSO wind solo playing is impressive, but the strings sometimes have an almost febrile timbre which is less than glamorous. Svetlanov's conception undoubtedly brings out the Russianness of the score, and it is certainly vivid; but in such a competitive field this could hardly be a strong contender, which is a pity when the Arensky and Glazunov couplings are so seductive.

Sinfonietta on Russian themes, Op. 31.
*(*) Finlandia/Warner Dig. 0630 14910-2 [id.]. Norwegian R. O, Ari Rasilainen – BALAKIREV: *Overture on three Russian tunes;* BORODIN: *Symphony No. 1 in E flat.* *(*)

Rimsky's *Sinfonietta* (1884) was based on an earlier string quartet. It is agreeably fashioned and, among other folk themes, features (in the *Andante*) a familiar melody that Stravinsky used (even more effectively) in his *Firebird* ballet. The pastoral opening movement (which includes a striking horn tune) is too like the central movement to offer sufficient variety, and the Scherzo-finale is repetitive. The work is warmly and elegantly presented, but a bit more robust vitality would not have come amiss; the warmly comfortable recording, too, lacks the kind of bite and projection that would have helped the music to spring more vividly to life.

Symphonies Nos. 1 in E min., Op. 1; 2 (Antar), Op. 9; 3 in C, Op. 32; Capriccio espagnol, Op. 36; (i) *Piano concerto in C sharp min., Op. 30. Russian Easter festival overture, Op. 36; Sadko, Op. 5.*
(M) **(*) Chandos Dig. CHAN 7029 (3) [id.]. (i) Geoffrey Tozer; Bergen PO, Kitaienko.

Kitaienko makes the most of Rimsky's *First Symphony*, as he does of *Antar*, its exoticism well conveyed. Indeed he draws very good playing from the Bergen Philharmonic throughout. In the *Third Symphony* he is comparably successful in the opening movement, and the lustrous colours of the secondary material glow appealingly, but the Scherzo lacks sparkle. Similarly, while he gets very lively results in the *Capriccio espagnol*, *Sadko* takes a while to warm up, although it has a spectacular close. With Tozer at the keyboard he shares a warmly lyrical view of the *Piano concerto* but, partly because of the resonant sound, the finale lacks something in sparkle. Malcolm Binns on Hyperion is much more successful in this comparatively elusive work. His version is coupled with the two essays in this form of Balakirev (CDA 66640 – see our main volume).

Symphonies Nos 1–3; Scheherazade, Op. 35.
(B) ** BMG/Melodiya Twofer 74321 40065-2 (2) [id.]. USSR SO, Svetlanov.

In the Rimsky-Korsakov symphonies, Svetlanov is a most persuasive interpreter, pointing rhythms and phrasing more subtly than such a rival as Kitaienko on Chandos. Unfortunately the recorded sound is less full and immediate than many from this source, though not seriously enough to mar enjoyment. Ironically, it is the earliest recording, that of *Scheherazade*, made in 1969, that has the most body, with impressive weight and dynamic range. The performance is superb, warmly expressive and spontaneous-sounding, with an excellent, warm reading of the love scene of the third movement. The one reservation is that the ensemble is less crisp than in the finest latterday versions.

Symphonies Nos. 1 in E min., Op. 1; 2 in F sharp min., Op. 9 (Antar).
*** RCA Dig. 09026 62558-2 [id.]. State SO of Russia, Yevgeni Svetlanov.

Yevgeni Svetlanov's later digital accounts of the first two symphonies have much the same merits as his *Third* (RCA 09026 61684-2 – see our main volume) and, like that CD, may well be a first choice for some collectors. Begun when he was only seventeen and completed four years later, in 1865, when it was re-scored and premièred by Balakirev, it was subjected to a thoroughgoing revision in 1884 and transposed up a semitone from E flat to E minor. The *Second (Antar)*, written in 1868, was revised no fewer than three times, in 1876, 1897 and 1903. For his Philharmonia version on Hyperion, Svetlanov opted for the 1897 edition, but here he goes back to 1876. (Even in 1876 Rimsky-Korsakov knew how to write for the orchestra!) The Philharmonia have the greater polish and finesse, but the Russians respond well to Svetlanov's impulsive and full-blooded approach. The recording, made while the orchestra was on tour in France, is very good indeed, and despite one or two interpretative exaggerations this rates a three-star recommendation.

OPERA

Sadko (complete).
500♪ *** Ph. Dig. 442 138-2 (3) [id.]. Galusin, Tsidipova, Tarassova, Minjelkiev, Gergalov, Grigorian, Alexashin, Diadkova, Boitsov, Bezzubenkov, Ognovenko, Gassiev, Putilin, Kirov Op. Ch. & O, Gergiev.

Sadko is full of melodic inspiration and atmosphere. Whatever its dramatic weaknesses, the score is full of glorious musical invention, sumptuously orchestrated, which puts the listener completely under its spell. The Sadko of Vladimir Galusin is very good, indeed most of the roles are well sung. The conducting of Valery Gergiev is one of the highlights of the performance: he brings great warmth and feeling for colour to the opera. The recording is very good. There is an excellent video (070 439-1 for the laserdisc; 070 439-3 for the VHS cassette), well directed for the cameras by Brian Large; both sound and vision are particularly impressive on Laserdisc.

Rodgers, Richard (1902–79)

'Rodgers and Hammerstein songs' from: *Allegro; Carousel; The King and I; Me and Juliet; Oklahoma!; The Sound of Music; South Pacific; State Fair.*
*** DG Dig. 449 163-2; *449 163-4* [id.]. Bryn Terfel, Opera North Ch., E. N. Philh., Paul Daniel.

Even among many enticing crossover discs this stands out. Bryn Terfel masterfully embraces the Broadway idiom, projecting his magnetic personality in the widest range of songs, using a remarkable range of tone, from a whispered head voice (as he does magically at the end of *Some enchanted evening*) to a tough, almost gravelly fortissimo at climaxes, from the biting toughness of *Nothing like a dame* or Billy Bigelow's big soliloquy in *Carousel* (using a very convincing American accent) to the warmth of *If I loved you* and *You'll never walk alone* (with chorus). It is a comment on the quality of performance that in that final item you get the authentic gulp in the throat without any hint of sentimentality. Specially welcome are the rarities, including one number from *Me and Juliet* and four from the stylized and underprized *Allegro*, including the powerfully emotional *Come home*. With excellent sound and fine playing from Opera North forces under Paul Daniel, this is a wide-ranging survey of Rodgers and Hammerstein (supplemented by first-rate notes) to have one valuing their achievement more than ever. It deserves the widest circulation.

Rodrigo, Joaquín (born 1902)

Concierto de Aranjuez (for guitar and orchestra).

500♪ ❀ (M) *** Decca Dig. 430 703-2; *430 703-4* [id.]. Carlos Bonell, Montreal SO, Dutoit – FALLA: *El amor brujo* etc. *** ❀

Decca have reissued the much-praised Bonell/Dutoit recording of the *Concierto*, now re-coupled with Alicia de Larrocha's splendid digital recording of Falla's *Nights in the gardens of Spain* plus Dutoit's outstanding complete *El amor brujo*. This is a very attractive pairing and the reasons for the success of the Rodrigo performance remain unaltered: an exceptionally clear, atmospheric and well-balanced digital recording plus Bonell's imaginative account of the solo part, and the strong characterization of the orchestral accompaniments by Charles Dutoit and his excellent Montreal orchestra.

(i) *Concierto pastoral* (for flute and orchestra); *Fantasia para un gentilhombre* (arr. Galway for flute and orchestra); (ii) *Concierto de Aranjuez* (for guitar and orchestra).

(M) *** RCA Analogue/Dig. 09026 68248-2 [id.]. (i) James Galway, Philh. O, Mata; (ii) Kazuhito Yamashita, Paillard CO, Paillard.

The *Concierto pastoral* was composed for James Galway in 1978. Its spikily brilliant introduction is far from pastoral in feeling, but the mood of the work soon settles down. At first hearing, the material seems thinner than usual, but Rodrigo's fragmented melodies and rhythmic ostinatos soon insinuate themselves into the listener's memory. The slow movement is especially effective, with a witty scherzando centrepiece framed by the *Adagio* outer sections. Galway's performance is truly superlative, showing the utmost bravura and matching refinement. He is beautifully recorded, and the small accompanying chamber orchestra is well balanced. The arrangement of the *Fantasia* is a very free one, necessitating re-orchestration, exchanging clarinet and horn instrumentation for the original scoring for trumpet and piccolo. The solo part too has been rewritten and even extended, apparently with the composer's blessing. The result is, to be honest, not an improvement on the original. But Galway is very persuasive, even if there is a persistent feeling of inflation. The brilliant Japanese guitar player, Kazuhito Yamashita, is not mentioned at all on the front of the CD, yet he contributes a memorable solo contribution to the famous *Concierto de Aranjuez*, especially in the slow movement, where he adds a cadenza. The finale too has plenty of adrenalin. Paillard and his orchestra support him well enough, although the orchestral playing at times lacks refinement. But this digitally recorded performance is full of life and may be regarded as a bonus.

Solo guitar music

Tres Piezas españolas.

500♪ ❀ (BB) *** RCA Navigator Dig. 74321 17903-2. Julian Bream (guitar) – ALBENIZ: *Collection;* GRANADOS: *Collection*. *** ❀

Rodrigo's *Three Spanish pieces* are characteristically inventive, the central *Passacaglia* quite masterly and the closing *Zapateado* attractively chimerical in Julian Bream's nimble figers. This 1983 recording has been added to what was already one of the finest of all recorded guitar recitals of Spanish music. An outstanding bargain in every way.

Rosetti, Antonio (*c*. 1750–92)

Horn concerto in D min., Kaul III:43.

(M) **(*) Teldec/Warner 0630 12324-2 [id.]. Hermann Baumann, Concerto Amsterdam, Jaap Schröder – DANZI: *Horn concerto in E;* HAYDN: *Horn concerto in D*. **(*)

The Bohemian composer, born Franz Anton Rössler, who adopted an Italian name, wrote prolifically and attractively for the horn: the present concerto is characteristic of the taxing melodic line he provides for the soloist, with high-ranging, lyrical tessitura contrasting with florid arpeggios. He was especially good at rondo finales, and the present example shows him at his melodically most exuberant. Baumann's recording could do with more warmth in the orchestra: the string-tone is close-miked and rather dry, while the horn-timbre by contrast resonates openly; but this makes an attractive collection, despite the less than ideal orchestral sound.

Rossini, Gioacchino (1792–1868)

La Boutique fantasque (ballet, arr. Respighi) complete.

(B) **(*) Decca Eclipse Dig. 448 984-2; *448 984-4* [id.]. Nat. PO, Bonynge – CHOPIN: *Les Sylphides*. **(*)

Bonynge goes for sparkle and momentum above all in Respighi's brilliant and sumptuous rescoring of Rossini, a magical ballet if ever there was one. The Decca compact disc has great brilliance and the orchestral colours glitter and glow within the attractive resonance of Kingsway Hall, although there is a degree of digital edge on the treble. Bonynge's exuberance is certainly exhilarating when the sound is so spectacular.

La Boutique fantasque: extended suite.

500♪ (M) *** RCA 09026 61847-2 [id.]. Boston Pops O, Arthur Fiedler – OFFENBACH: *Gaîté parisienne*. *** ❁

Fiedler offers nearly half an hour of the ballet, not missing out much of importance. The performance sparkles, the playing has warmth and finesse and the Boston acoustics add the necessary atmosphere at the magically evocative opening. John Pfeiffer's remastering of this 1956 recording leaves little to be desired and the coupling is indispensable.

String sonatas Nos. 1–6 (complete).

500♪ (B) *** Decca Double 443 838-2 (2) [id.]. ASMF, Marriner (with CHERUBINI: *Etude No. 2 for French horn and strings* (with Barry Tuckwell); BELLINI: *Oboe concerto in E flat* (with Roger Lord); DONIZETTI: *String quartet* ***).

(D) *** EMI forte Analogue/Dig. CZS5 69524-2 (2). Polish CO, Maksymiuk – MENDELSSOHN: *String symphonies;* JANIEWICZ: *Divertimento;* JARZEBSKI: *Chromatica; Tamburetta*. ***

We have a very soft spot for the sparkle, elegance and wit of these ASMF performances of the Rossini *String sonatas*. Marriner offers them on full orchestral strings but with such finesse and precision of ensemble that the result is all gain. The 1966 recording still sounds remarkably full and natural, with other music added. Apart from the Donizetti *Quartet*, which has an appropriately Rossinian flavour, the two minor concertante works are well worth having, with both Barry Tuckwell (in what is in essence a three-movement horn concertino) and Roger Lord in excellent form.

Jerzy Maksymiuk with the Polish Chamber Orchestra consistently chooses challengingly fast speeds, and the playing is bracingly brilliant. Though some of the fun is lost, the wit remains, and these virtuoso performances are still most enjoyable for their exhilarating dash. Nos. 2, 3, 4 and 5 were recorded in analogue sound, earlier than the rest, but the difference is minimal and no one will complain at the quality, which is excellent. A fine alternative to the Marriner versions, and made the more attractive by the couplings, notably the Janiewicz *Divertimento*, so like Rossini in style, and also the two Jarzebski lollipops which stand out for their strength of personality.

Stabat Mater.

500♪ ❁ *** Chandos Dig. CHAN 8780 [id.]. Field, Della Jones, A. Davies, Earle, London Symphony Ch., City of L. Sinfonia, Hickox.

This is a most winning account; all four soloists are first rate, not Italianate of tone but full and warm, and the London Symphony Chorus sings with fine attack as well as producing the most refined pianissimos in the unaccompanied quartet, here as usual given to the full chorus rather than to the soloists. Full-bodied and atmospheric sound.

OPERA

Overtures: *Il barbiere di Siviglia; La cambiale di matrimonio; L'inganno felice; L'Italiana in Algeri; La scala di seta; Il Signor Bruschino; Tancredi; Il Turco in Italia*. (i) *Introduction, theme and variations for clarinet and orchestra in E flat*.

❁ (M) *** DG Dig. 445 569-2 [id.]. Orpheus CO; (i) with Charles Neidlich.

This crackingly good CD by the conductorless Orpheus Chamber Orchestra has always been one of the most enjoyable collections of Rossini overtures ever put on disc; at mid-price and with Charles Neidlich's scintillating account of the concertante clarinet work also included, it is irresistible. The wit of the latter is caught with such sparkle and humour that one cannot help but smile with pleasure. In the overtures the orchestra displays astonishing unanimity of style and ensemble. Not only is the crispness of string phrasing a joy, but the many stylish wind solos have an attractive degree of freedom. These are performances that in their refinement and apt chamber scale give increasing pleasure with familiarity. The DG recording is marvellously real, with the perspective perfectly judged.

Overtures: *Il barbiere di Siviglia; La Cenerentola; La gazza ladra; La scala di seta; Il Signor Bruschino; William Tell.*
500♪ ✿ (M) *** RCA GD 60387 [60387-2-RG]. Chicago SO, Fritz Reiner.

As with the others in RCA's remastered Reiner/Chicago series, the 1958 sound-quality has been improved phenomenally; the *galop* in the *William Tell overture* is all-engulfing, a thrilling moment indeed. But it is the sparkle and vivacity of these performances that one remembers above all – and, in *La Cenerentola*, the wit, as well as fizzing orchestral bravura. One would have liked the opening flourish of *La scala di seta* to be neater – it is presented too lavishly here – but this is the solitary reservation over a magnificent achievement.

Overtures: *La gazza ladra; L'Italiana in Algeri; Semiramide; Il Signor Bruschino; William Tell.*
500♪ (B) **(*) EMI forte CZS5 69364-2 (2) [id.]. RPO, Sir Colin Davis – BEETHOVEN: *Symphony No. 7* *** ✿; SCHUBERT: *Symphony No. 9.* ***

Sir Colin Davis's 1962 collection, recorded at Abbey Road, brings playing that is admirably stylish with an excellent sense of nuance. *Semiramide* is superb, reminding one of Beecham, as does the spunky opening of *The Thieving Magpie*. *William Tell* is pretty good too, the opening beautifully played. In *Il Signor Bruschino* it seems as if the bow-tapping device is done by the leader alone, which is rather effective.

Il barbiere di Siviglia (complete).
500♪ *** Decca Dig. 425 520-2 (3) [id.]. Bartoli, Nucci, Matteuzzi, Fissore, Burchuladze, Ch. & O of Teatro Comunale di Bologna, Patanè.
*** EMI CDS5 56310-2 (2). Callas, Gobbi, Alva, Ollendorff, Philh. Ch. & O, Galliera.
(M) *** RCA 09026 68552-2 (3) [id.]. Merrill, Peters, Valletti, Tozzi, Corena, Met. Op. Ch. & O, Leinsdorf.
(M) *(*) EMI CMS5 66040-2 (2) [Ang. CDMB 66040]. Sills, Gedda, Milnes, Capecchi, Raimondi, John Alldis Ch., LSO, Levine.

Cecilia Bartoli gives a winningly provocative characterization. Like the conductor, Bartoli is wonderful at bringing out the fun. So is Leo Nucci, and he gives a beautifully rounded portrait of the wily barber. Burchuladze, unidiomatic next to the others, still gives a monumentally lugubrious portrait of Basilio, and the Bartolo of Enrico Fissore is outstanding, with the patter song wonderfully articulated at Patanè's sensible speed.

Gobbi and Callas were here at their most inspired and, with the recording quality nicely refurbished, the EMI is an outstanding set, not absolutely complete in its text, but so crisp and sparkling it can be confidently recommended. Callas remains supreme as a minx-like Rosina, summing up the character superbly in *Una voce poco fa*. The early stereo sound comes up very acceptably on a pair of CDs, clarified to a degree, presenting a uniquely characterful performance with new freshness and immediacy.

When this 1958 Leinsdorf set first appeared, it was greeted with approbation for its completeness. With a playing time of 160 minutes, it was first issued on four LPs; now it comes on three mid-priced CDs. However, much material which is almost always omitted in the opera house here finds its way back. Moreover the cast is consistently impressive. Roberta Peters sparkles as Rosina, her voice always sweet and her coloratura (not always avoiding intrusive aitches) exquisitely agile and pointed. Robert Merrill could be a more genuinely comic Figaro, but his vocal acting is certainly impressive and his voice is beautifully focused. Valletti, Corena and Tozzi are all splendid. Leinsdorf manages to provide genuine lightness and so convey the proper sparkling style. Within the fairly wide reverberation the sound remains clear, and the CD transfer has not lost its original bloom. While our first choice for this opera remains with Bartoli and Nucci on Decca, this RCA reissue is well worth having in its own right.

Levine conducts vigorously in this EMI (originally Angel) version from the mid-1970s, but neither the singing of Beverly Sills nor that of Nicolai Gedda can be commended with any enthusiasm, the one unpleasing in tone for all its brilliance, the other seriously strained – a reminder, no more, of what Gedda's voice once was. Sherrill Milnes makes a strong, forthright Figaro, in every way the centre of attention here, and Ruggero Raimondi is a sonorous Basilio. Good recording and a full translation.

Il barbiere di Siviglia: highlights.
*** Teldec/Warner Dig. 0630 13815-9 [id.] (from complete recording, with Hagegård, Larmore, cond. López-Cobos).

Teldec offers a generous and comprehensive 76-minute selection from a performance which is outstanding in every way. Jennifer Larmore is an enchanting Rosina; the dry-toned Figaro, Håkan Hagegård, brings out the opera's humour, and Raúl Giménez makes a stylishly attractive hero. López-Cobos directs zestfully and the ensembles are as infectious as they are spirited. A full translation is included.

La Cenerentola (complete).
500♪ *** Decca Dig. 436 902-2 (2) [id.]. Bartoli, Matteuzzi, Corbelli, Dara, Costa, Banditelli, Pertusi, Teatro Comunale (Bologna) Ch. & O, Chailly.

Chailly's version has the effervescence of a live performance, with none of the disadvantages of a live recording. Cecilia Bartoli, one of the most vibrantly exciting singers of the younger generation, makes an inspired Cenerentola. Her tone-colours are not just more sensuous than those of her rivals: her imagination and feeling for detail add enormously to her vivid characterization, culminating in a stunning account of the final rondo, *Non più mesta*. The rest of the cast has been just as carefully chosen, with William Matteuzzi as an engaging prince, sweeter of tone and more stylish than his direct rivals. Few Rossini opera-sets have such fizz as this, and the recording is one of Decca's most vivid. The video was recorded more recently at the Houston Grand Opera with Bartolli, Corbelli, Dara and Pertusi continuing in the principal roles and Bruno Campanella conducting with fine spirit. Visually the production is a delight. Subtitled in English, this is very highly recommended (Decca 071 444-3).

La Cenerentola: highlights.
(M) *** Teldec/Warner Dig. 0630 15804-9 [id.] (from complete recording, with Larmore, Giménez, Quilico, Corbelli, Scarabelli, ROHCG Ch. & O, Rizzi).

On Carlo Rizzi's Teldec version with Covent Garden forces, Jennifer Larmore makes an enchanting heroine, both tenderly expressive in cantilena and flawlessly controlled through the most elaborate coloratura passages. The rest of the cast was chosen just as effectively and there is no weak link; throughout, Rizzi brings out the sparkle. With vivid recording and nearly 75 minutes of music included, this makes a splendid choice for a disc of highlights, especially for collectors who have the competing Decca set with Cecilia Bartoli. As usual with the Warner Opera Collection series, a full translation is included.

L'Italiana in Algeri (complete).
500♪ ✿ *** DG 427 331-2 (2) [id.]. Baltsa, Raimondi, Dara, Lopardo, V. State Op. Konzertvereinigung, VPO, Abbado.

Abbado's brilliant version was recorded in conjunction with a new staging by the Vienna State Opera. Agnes Baltsa is a real fire-eater in the title-role, and Ruggero Raimondi with his massively sepulchral bass gives weight to his part without undermining the comedy. The American tenor, Frank Lopardo, proves the most stylish Rossinian, singing with heady clarity, while both buffo baritones are excellent too.

L'Italiana in Algeri: highlights.
(M) *** Erato/Warner 0630 15738-9 [id.] (from complete recording, with Horne, Palacio, Ramey, Trimarchi, Battle, Zaccaria, Prague Ch., Sol. Ven., Scimone).

Scimone's highly enjoyable version is beautifully played and Marilyn Horne makes a dazzling, positive Isabella, while Samuel Ramey is splendidly firm as Mustafa. Domenico Trimarchi (Taddeo) and Ernesto Palacio (Lindoro) do not let the side down, and at mid-price this selection (73 minutes) is excellent value with its full translation. However, the comparable Sony highlights disc (SMK 53504) remains a marginal first choice – see our main volume – although the documentation is less complete.

Tancredi (complete).
500♪ (B) *** Naxos Dig. 8.660037/8 [id.]. Podles, Jo, Olsen, Spagnoli, Di Micco, Lendi, Zaccaria, Capella Brugensis, Brugense Coll. Instrumentale, Alberto Zedda.
** RCA Dig. 09026 68349-2 (3) [id.]. Kasarova, Mei, Vargas, Peeters, Cangemi, Bav. R. Ch., Munich R. O, Roberto Abbado.

The enterprise of Naxos in recording one of the rarer operas of Rossini is triumphantly rewarded, for this set completely displaces the rival version from Sony, and the eminent Rossini scholar and conductor, Alberto Zedda, proves a far more resilient, generally brisker and lighter Rossini interpreter than his counterpart. Sumi Jo completely outshines Lella Cuberli as the heroine, Amenaide, in dazzlingly clear coloratura, as well as imaginative pointing of phrase, rhythm and words; but it is the tenor, Stanford Olsen, who offers some of the freshest, most stylish and sweetly tuned singing from a Rossini tenor in recent years. An Italian libretto is provided but no translation. Instead, a helpful synopsis is geared to the different tracks on the discs.

Extravagantly presented on three full-priced discs, the RCA set of *Tancredi* is yet valuable for including the two alternative endings which Rossini wrote, the one happy, the other tragic in reflection of the original Voltaire, respectively for Venice and Ferrara. Alternative arias are also given on the third disc. Sadly, there is little else to recommend this in preference to the splendid two-disc Naxos version at bargain price, except the contribution of the characterful and vibrant Vesselina Kasarova in the title-role. Her control of florid writing is formidable, with crisply executed trills, though otherwise her Naxos rival, Ewa Podles, weightier and richer of tone, is far from outshone. None of the others quite matches the Naxos cast, with Ramón Vargas effortful and heavy-handed next to Stanford Olsen, Eva Mei gusty next to Sumi Jo, and Harry Peeters wobbly and uncertain next to Niccola Zaccaria. Nor is Roberto Abbado as light-handed as Alberto Zedda, though the Munich Radio Orchestra has some fine wind soloists.

Il Turco in Italia.
(***) EMI mono CDS5 56313-2 (2). Rossi-Lemeni, Callas, Gedda, Stabile, Ch. & O of La Scala, Milan, Gavazzeni.

Callas was at her peak when she recorded this rare Rossini opera in the mid-1950s. As ever, there are lumpy moments vocally, but she gives a sharply characterful performance as the capricious Fiorilla, married to an elderly, jealous husband and bored with it. Nicola Rossi-Lemeni as the Turk of the title is characterful too, but the voice is ill-focused, and it is left to Nicolai Gedda as the young lover and Franco Calabrese as the jealous husband to match Callas in stylishness. It is good too to have the veteran Mariano Stabile singing the role of the Poet in search of a plot. Walter Legge's production has plainly added to the sparkle. On CD the original mono recording has been freshened and given a degree of bloom, despite the closeness of the voices. It is a vintage Callas issue, her first uniquely cherishable essay in operatic comedy.

Il viaggio a Reims (complete).
500♪ ❀ *** DG Dig. 415 498-2 (2) [id.]. Ricciarelli, Valentini Terrani, Cuberli, Gasdia, Araiza, Giménez, Nucci, Raimondi, Ramey, Dara, Prague Philharmonic Ch., COE, Abbado.

This DG set is one of the most sparkling and totally successful live opera recordings available, with Claudio Abbado relishing the sparkle of the comedy; the line-up of soloists here could hardly be more impressive, with no weak link. Abbado's brilliance and sympathy draw the musical threads compellingly together with the help of superb, totally committed playing from the young members of the Chamber Orchestra of Europe.

Collections

L'assedio de Corinto: Avanziam' . . . Non temer d'un basso affetto! . . . I destini tradir ogni speme . . . Signormche tutto puio . . . Sei tu, che stendi; L'ora fatal s'appressa . . . Giusto ciel. La Donna del lago: Mura Felici; Tanti affetti. Otello: Assisa a pie d'un salice. Tancredi: Di tanti palpiti.
500♪ ❀ (M) *** Decca 421 306-2 [id.]. Marilyn Horne, Amb. Op. Ch., RPO, Henry Lewis.

Marilyn Horne's generously filled recital disc brings one of the most cherishable among all Rossini aria records ever issued. The voice is in glorious condition, rich and firm throughout its spectacular range, and is consistently used with artistry and imagination, as well as brilliant virtuosity in coloratura. By any reckoning this is thrilling singing, and the sound is full and brilliant, showing its age hardly at all.

Roussel, Albert (1869–1937)

Bacchus et Ariane (complete ballet), *Op. 43*; *Le festin de l'araignée (The spider's feast), Op. 17.*
❀ *** Chandos Dig. CHAN 9494 [id.]. BBC PO, Yan Pascal Tortelier.

Tortelier offers the best *Bacchus et Ariane* yet – and what a marvellously inventive and resourceful score it is. The BBC Philharmonic play with tremendous zest and give a sensitive and atmospheric account of *Le festin de l'araignée*. They offer us the complete banquet, not just the chosen dishes on the set menu! Splendid recording and performances of rewarding and colourful music that deserves to be more widely heard.

Bacchus et Ariane: Suite No. 2.
(M) ** DG Originals 449 748-2 [id.]. Lamoureux O, Igor Markevitch – HONEGGER: *Symphony No. 5;* MILHAUD: *Les Choéphores.* (**)

Markevitch's spirited and atmospheric account of the second suite from *Bacchus et Ariane* comes from

1960 and, unlike its companions (Honegger's *Fifth Symphony* and Milhaud's *Les Choéphores)*, is in stereo. It is very well played and recorded with plenty of space round the aural image, but the sound naturally lacks the body and focus of a modern recording, although it is fully acceptable.

Symphonies Nos. 1 (La poème de la forêt), Op. 7; 2 in B flat, Op. 23; 3 in G min., Op. 42; 4 in A, Op. 53.
500♪ *** RCA Dig. 09026 61511-2 (2) [id.]. R. France PO, Janowski.

The Roussel symphonies have not been ideally served on disc, and the present set is a source of celebration and is well worth having. On this showing Marek Janowski has a natural feel for the Roussel idiom. The set is neatly packaged (two discs in the space of one) and the recording, made in the Salle Olivier Messiaen of Radio France, has plenty of body, presence and detail. This is now the standard recommendation for these rewarding and resourceful scores.

Symphony No. 3 in G min., Op. 42.
(M) **(*) Sony MHK 62352 [id.]. NYPO, Leonard Bernstein – HONEGGER: *Rugby; Pacific 231* **; MILHAUD: *Les Choéphores.* ***

A vividly characterized and enormously vital account of Roussel's magnificent *Third Symphony*. It was Bernstein's mentor, Koussevitzky, who commissioned the work for the fiftieth anniversary of the Boston Symphony Orchestra, and Bernstein's reading is as highly charged as one could wish for. The performance comes from 1961 and in the original LP format was shrill and reverberant. The present transfer has tamed some though not all of its ferocity and cleaned up some of the detail. Though the recording is not perfect, this is still the best performance of the symphony in the current catalogue, and it comes with a Milhaud rarity new to these shores.

Songs: *Jazz dans la nuit, Op. 38; Light, Op. 19/12; 2 Mélodies, Op. 20; 2 Poèmes chinois, Op. 35.*
(M) **(*) Unicorn-Kanchana Dig. UKCD 2078 [id.]. Sarah Walker, Roger Vignoles – DEBUSSY: *Mélodies;* ENESCU: *Chansons.* ***

Sarah Walker may not plumb the full emotions of some of the deceptively deep songs in her Roussel group – *Light*, for example – but the point and charm of *Jazz dans la nuit* are superbly caught, and the group makes an attractive and generous coupling for the Debussy and Enescu songs, all superbly recorded, with Vignoles a most sensitive accompanist.

Rubbra, Edmund (1901–86)

Symphonies Nos. 2 in D, Op. 45; 6, Op. 80.
*** Chandos Dig. CHAN 9481 [id.]. BBC Nat. O of Wales, Richard Hickox.

Neither symphony is new to the catalogue, but neither has been better served either by the performers or by the engineers. The *Second Symphony* dates from 1937 and, even though Rubbra thinned out the scoring when he revised it in 1950, the textures remain opaque in climaxes. Richard Hickox and his fine players do however make the score more lucid than Handley's Lyrita recording from the 1970s. The performance is meticulously prepared and yet flows effortlessly, and the slow movement speaks with great eloquence. The heart of the *Sixth Symphony* is the serene *Canto* movement which is not dissimilar in character to the *Missa in honorem Sancti Dominici* (which Hickox, incidentally, recorded in the 1970s). It is arguably the finest of the cycle after No. 9, and Hickox and his fine players do it proud. So, too, do the Chandos engineers.

Symphonies Nos. 4, Op. 53; 10 (Sinfonia da camera), Op. 145; 11, Op. 153.
500♪ *** Chandos Dig. CHAN 9401 [id.]. BBC Nat. O of Wales, Hickox.

Richard Hickox is a thoroughly dedicated and sympathetic advocate of Edmund Rubbra's music, and he offers a particularly imaginative account of the *Eleventh Symphony* in one movement. The *Fourth Symphony*, a wartime work, has great serenity and tranquillity. Its opening is among the most beautiful in all English music of our time. Hickox's account of the *Fourth* is totally convincing, and the Chandos recording is excellent in every respect, with plenty of warmth and transparency of detail.

Symphony No. 5 in B flat, Op. 63; Loth to depart (Improvisations on virginal pieces by Giles Farnaby), Op. 50/4.
(M) (***) EMI mono CDM5 66053-2 [id.]. Hallé O, Barbirolli – BRITTEN: *Violin concerto* (**); HEMING: *Threnody for a soldier killed in action.* (***)

This is the very first recording of any Rubbra symphony. Made in 1950, it originally appeared on seven 78-r.p.m. discs with the haunting *Loth to depart* as a fill-up. Although it has reappeared on LP both in the early 1950s and in HMV's British Music series in the late 1960s, it has never sounded as fresh and 'present' as it does in Andrew Walter's exemplary transfer. Sir Adrian Boult gave its première in 1949 but Barbirolli was quick to take it up, and his spacious and affectionate reading stands up well nearly half a century after its composition.

(i) *Symphony No. 9 (Sinfonia sacra), Op. 140. The Morning Watch for chorus and orchestra, Op. 55.*
500♪ ❁ *** Chandos Dig. CHAN 9441 [id.]. (i) Lynne Dawson, Della Jones, Stephen Roberts; BBC Nat. Ch. of Wales, BBC Nat. O of Wales, Hickox.

The *Ninth Symphony*, arguably Rubbra's greatest work, has long gone unrecognized, but there is no doubt that this is Rubbra's most visionary utterance. This is an unqualified masterpiece; indeed it is a work which can withstand the most exalted comparisons and emerge unscathed. Subtitled *The Resurrection*, it was inspired by a painting of Donato Bramante and has something of the character of the Passion, which the three soloists relate in moving fashion. *The Morning Watch*, a setting of Henry Vaughan for chorus and orchestra, which was originally to have formed part of a choral fifth symphony, is another score of great nobility. Both works are superbly served here by all these fine musicians, and the Chandos recording is no less magnificent.

Rubinstein, Anton (1829–94)

Piano sonatas Nos. 1 in E min., Op. 12; 2 in C min., Op. 20; 3 in F, Op. 41; 4 in A min., Op. 100.
(B) *** Hyperion Dyad Dig. CCD 22007 (2) [id.]. Leslie Howard.

Leslie Howard copes with the formidable technical demands of these *Sonatas* manfully. He proves highly persuasive in all four works, though the actual invention is scarcely distinguished enough to sustain interest over such ambitious time-spans. Rubinstein wrote these pieces for his own use, and doubtless his artistic powers and strong personality helped to persuade contemporary audiences. The 1981 recordings sound excellent, and this set is more enticing as a Dyad, with two discs offered for the price of one. Returning to these works, one is surprised to find how enjoyable the music is, with some good lyrical ideas, phrased romantically, to balance the arrestingly flamboyant rhetoric which Leslie Howard obviously relishes.

Rutter, John (born 1943)

(i) *Gloria;* (ii) Anthems: *All things bright and beautiful; For the beauty of the earth; A Gaelic blessing; God be in my head; The Lord bless you and keep you; The Lord is my Shepherd; O clap your hands; Open thou my eyes; Praise ye the Lord; A prayer of St Patrick.*
500♪ *** Coll. Dig. COLCD 100; *COLC 100* [id.]. Cambridge Singers, (i) Philip Jones Brass Ens.; (ii) City of L. Sinfonia, composer.

The resplendent *Gloria* is a three-part piece, and Rutter uses his brass to splendid and often spectacular effect. The anthems are diverse in style and feeling and, like the *Gloria*, have strong melodic appeal – the setting of *All things bright and beautiful* is delightfully spontaneous. It is difficult to imagine the music receiving more persuasive advocacy than under the composer, and the recording is first class in every respect.

(i) *Requiem; I will lift up mine eyes.*
500♪ *** Coll. Dig. COLCD 103; *COLC 103* [id.]. (i) Ashton, Dean; Cambridge Singers, City of L. Sinfonia, composer.

John Rutter's melodic gift, so well illustrated in his carols, is here used in the simplest and most direct way to create a small-scale *Requiem* that is as beautiful and satisfying in its English way as the works of Fauré and Duruflé. Caroline Ashton's performance of the delightful *Pie Jesu* is wonderfully warm and spontaneous, most beautifully recorded on CD, and *I will lift up mine eyes* makes a highly effective encore piece.

Sæverud, Harald (1897–1992)

Symphony No. 6 (Sinfonia dolorosa), Op. 19; Galdreslåtten, Op. 20; Kjæmpevise-slåtten, Op. 22; Peer Gynt Suites Nos. 1 & 2, Op. 28.
*** BIS Dig. CD 762 [id.]. Stavanger SO, Alexander Dmitriev.

Norway is currently celebrating the centenary of their strongly characterful and independent-minded composer, Harald Sæverud, and this BIS record brings some of his best-known works to the catalogue. The *Peer Gynt* music, written for a post-war production of Ibsen's play, could not be further removed from Grieg's celebrated score. It is earthy and rambunctious and it makes Grieg sound positively genteel. It calls to mind Robert Simpson's felicitous phrase about Sæverud's 'rich and salty sense of humour that often warms his asperities', and so does the delightful, inventive and wholly original *Galdreslåtten*. The *Sixth Symphony* (*Sinfonia dolorosa*) is a short but intense piece from the war years, dedicated to a close friend who perished in the resistance, and the *Kjæmpevise-slåtten* ('Ballad of Revolt') comes from the same years. It is an inspiriting work, an outraged, combative reaction to the sight of the Nazi occupation barracks near his Bergen home. Eminently satisfactory performances from the Stavanger orchestra under Alexander Dmitriev, brought vividly to life by the BIS recording team.

Saint-Saëns, Camille (1835–1921)

(i) *Caprice andalou, Op. 122; Morceau de concert, Op. 62: Romance, Op. 36* (all for violin and orchestra); *Morceaux de concert:* (ii) *for harp and orchestra, Op. 64;* (iii) *for horn and orchestra, Op. 94; Romance for horn and orchestra, Op. 48. Spartacus: overture.*
*** EMI Dig. CDC5 55587-2 [id.]. (i) Olivier Charlier; (ii) M. Nordmann; (iii) R. Vlatkovič; O de Paris Ens., Kantorow.

Saint-Saëns seldom disappoints, and this proves to be an appealing collection of concertante miniatures. His ready melodic flow and natural craftsmanship are always endearing, and the *Morceau de concert* for violin and orchestra, if lacking the memorability of the *Introduction and rondo capriccioso*, and the *Caprice andalou*, if not matching the *Havanaise*, both bring much to delight the ear from the charm of the one and the gentle, voluptuous languor of the other. The *Romance*, too, brings another striking melody in its central section. The two works for horn and orchestra (another *Romance* and *Morceau*) are both more romantically robust and, with the concertante works for violin alternating, this makes a most agreeable entertainment when both Olivier Charlier and Radovan Vlatkovič are such persuasive soloists. The other *Morceau*, for harp and orchestra, brings a delicate secondary tune which is perhaps the most appealing of all the melodies offered here. With its slow central interlude and jaunty finale this is more like a fully-fledged concerto and the composer's invention does not flag; moreover his lightweight scoring always allows the harp to shine through. The overture *Spartacus* brings no anticipations of Khachaturian. Indeed its style veers nearer to that of Lalo (especially in brass sonorities towards the end), though it is scored more lightly and felicitously than one would expect from that composer. It also brings a melodic whiff of Verdi in its secondary string tune. If perhaps a shade overlong, it is presented persuasively by Kantorow and his players. The recording, made in the Salle Wagram, is very satisfactory.

Carnival of the animals.
500♪ (M) *** Virgin/EMI Dig. CUV7 61137-2 [id.]. Anton Nel, Keith Snell, Ac. of L., Richard Stamp – PROKOFIEV: *Peter.* *** ❁

Richard Stamp directs an outstanding version of Saint-Saëns's witty zoology, full of affectionate humour. Throughout, one responds to the polished overall presentation and sense of fun; although some may feel that the recording is rather resonant, it adds a genial warmth to the vitality of the proceedings.

Cello concerto No. 1 in A min., Op. 33.
*** EMI Dig. CDC5 56126-2 [id.]. Han-Na Chang, LSO, Rostropovich – BRUCH: *Kol Nidrei* ***; FAURE: *Elégie* ***; TCHAIKOVSKY *Rococo variations.* *** ❁

Han-Na Chang's account of the Saint-Saëns *Concerto* is second to none, full of ardour, yet light-hearted in its bravura: the swirling energy of the opening is echoed brilliantly by the orchestra. The *Allegretto* then steals in daintily, with the cello response exquisitely fragile. The return of the opening theme is joyously exhilarating, the lyrical interludes sensitively contrasted, and the piece ends in joyful high spirits. Chang's delicacy of feeling, natural sense of line and wide range of dynamic show an instinctive musicianship and a mastery of her instrument that recalls the young Menuhin, while the sophistication of the performance is extraordinarily mature, helped in no small part by Rostropovich's always supportive accompaniment and the superb playing of the LSO. The EMI Abbey Road recording is first class in every way and beautifully balanced.

(i) *Cello concerto No. 1 in A min., Op. 33;* (ii) *Piano concerto No. 2 in G min., Op. 22;* (iii) *Violin concerto No. 3, Op. 61.*
500♪ ❁ (M) *** Sony Dig. SMK 66935 [id.]. (i) Yo-Yo Ma, O Nat. de France, Maazel; (ii) Cécile Licad, LPO, Previn; (iii) Cho-Liang Lin, Philh. O, Tilson Thomas.

Three outstanding performances from the early 1980s are admirably linked together in this highly desirable CBS mid-price reissue. Yo-Yo Ma's performance of the *Cello concerto* is distinguished by fine sensitivity and beautiful tone, while Cécile Licad and the LPO under Previn turn in an eminently satisfactory reading of the *G minor Piano concerto* that has the requisite delicacy in the Scherzo and seriousness elsewhere. Cho-Liang Lin's account of the *B minor Violin concerto* with the Philharmonia Orchestra and Michael Tilson Thomas is exhilarating and thrilling; indeed, this is the kind of performance that prompts one to burst into applause; his version is certainly second to none and is arguably the finest yet to have appeared.

Piano concertos Nos. 1–5.
500♪ (B) *** Decca Double 443 865-2 (2); *443 865-4* [id.]. Pascal Rogé, Philh. O, RPO or LPO, Dutoit.

Played as they are here, these concertos can exert a strong appeal: Pascal Rogé brings delicacy, virtuosity and sparkle to the piano part and he receives expert support from the various London orchestras under Dutoit. Altogether delicious playing and excellent piano-sound from Decca, who secure a most realistic balance. On CD the five *Concertos* are successfully accommodated on two discs and the digital remastering is wholly successful, retaining the bloom of the analogue originals, yet producing firmer detail and splendid piano-sound. Now reissued as a Double Decca set (two CDs or cassettes for the price of one) the value is obvious.

Violin concertos Nos. (i) *1 in A, Op. 20;* (ii) *3 in B min., Op. 61.*
(M) *** Decca Dig./Analogue 448 128-2 [id.]. Kyung Wha Chung; (i) Montreal SO, Dutoit; (ii) LSO, Foster – CHAUSSON: *Poème;* VIEUXTEMPS: *Violin concerto No. 5.* ***

Saint-Saëns's *First Violin concerto* is a miniature – in three sections, but playing altogether for only just over 11 minutes. Kyung Wha Chung presents it delightfully, equally at home in its persuasively simple lyricism and in the energetic bravura of the outer sections. Charles Dutoit provides an admirable accompaniment. She then gives a characteristically passionate account of the *B minor Concerto*, the finest of Saint-Saëns's violin concertos, so intense that even a sceptical listener will find it hard not to be convinced that this is a great work. Such music needs this kind of advocacy and Miss Chung is splendidly backed up by the LSO under Lawrence Foster. The 1975 analogue recording is slightly less flattering to her than the 1980 digital sound in Montreal, but remains full and clear.

Danse macabre, Op. 40; (i) *Havanaise, Op. 83; Introduction and Rondo capriccioso, Op. 28. La jeunesse d'Hercule, Op. 50; Marche héroïque, Op. 34; Phaéton, Op. 39; Le rouet d'Omphale, Op. 31.*
500♪ (M) *** Decca 425 021-2 [id.]. (i) Kyung Wha Chung, RPO; Philh. O; Charles Dutoit.

A splendidly conceived anthology. The symphonic poems are beautifully played, and the 1979 Kingsway Hall recording lends the appropriate atmosphere. Charles Dutoit shows himself an admirably sensitive exponent, revelling in the composer's craftsmanship and revealing much delightful orchestral detail in the manner of a Beecham. Decca have now added Kyung Wha Chung's equally charismatic and individual 1977 accounts of what are perhaps the two most inspired short display-pieces for violin and orchestra in the repertoire.

Havanaise, Op. 83.
(M) *** EMI CDM5 66058-2 [id.]. Itzhak Perlman, O de Paris, Barenboim – RAVEL: *Tzigane;* VIEUXTEMPS: *Violin concertos Nos. 4 & 5.* ***

Perlman plays this Saint-Saëns warhorse with splendid panache and virtuosity on EMI; his tone and control of colour in the *Havanaise* are ravishing. The digital remastering brings Perlman's gorgeous fiddling right into the room, at the expense of a touch of aggressiveness when the orchestra lets rip; but the concert-hall ambience prevents this from being a problem.

Havanaise, Op. 83; Introduction and Rondo capriccioso, Op. 28.
(M) ** Decca 452 309-2 [id.]. Ruggiero Ricci, LSO, Gamba – LALO: *Symphonie espagnole* *(*); SARASATE: *Carmen (fantasy)* etc. **

Ricci is on excellent form here, and he is well supported by the LSO under Gamba. His *Introduction and Rondo* is well shaped and brilliantly interpreted, but the *Havanaise* is surely too fast for comfort. The languid feeling, suggestive of a warm relaxing atmosphere, certainly lies within the playing, but the overall effect is rather too streamlined. Better sound and balance here than in the Lalo coupling, but this is hardly a candidate for Decca's Classic Sound series.

Symphony No. 2 in A min., Op. 55; Phaéton, Op. 39; Suite algérienne, Op. 60.
*** ASV Dig. CDDCA 599 [id.]. LSO, Butt.

Symphonies Nos. 2 in A min.; (i) *3 in C min., Op. 78.*
*** Chandos Dig. CHAN 8822 [id.]. Ulster O, Yan Pascal Tortelier; (i) with Gillian Weir.

If you want the *Second Symphony*, it is particularly well played by the LSO under Butt, with the freshness of a major orchestra discovering something unfamiliar and enjoying themselves. The companion pieces are also thoroughly enjoyable and are just as attractively presented. The recording is warmly atmospheric.

Yan Pascal Tortelier's performance of the *Second* is also very attractive and very well recorded; but Yondani Butt's account of this work has greater freshness, and the slightly less reverberant ASV recording contributes to this.

If, however, your main interest lies with the *Third Symphony*, this extra resonance proves no disadvantage, and the Chandos CD must be strongly recommended. Not long before we went to print, E.G. conducted a side-by-side comparison of all the available recordings of the *Organ Symphony* except the more recent issues discussed below. He came out in favour of the Tortelier version as a 'best buy', both for the appeal of the performance overall and for the state-of-the-art Chandos recording, with its extremely spectacular and impressively balanced finale. Which is not to say that I.M.'s favourite, with the Berlin Philharmonic in cracking form under Levine, is not also in the running – if you prefer a sparkling version of Dukas's *Sorcerer's apprentice* as coupling (DG 419 617-2).

Symphony No. 3 in C min., Op. 78.
**(*) Teldec/Warner Dig. 4509 98416-2 [id.]. BPO, Mehta – FRANCK: *Symphony in D min.* **(*)

Symphony No. 3 in C min.; Carnival of the animals; Cyprès et Lauriers, Op. 156.
** Carlton Dig. 30366 00012 [id.]. Kynaston, Youngho & Jingho Kim, Philh. O, Djong Victorin Yu.

(i) *Symphony No. 3 in C min.; Cyprès et Lauriers, Op. 156. La Foi, 3 tableaux symphoniques, Op. 130.*
(M) *** EMI Dig. CDC5 55584-2 (2) [id.]. Toulouse Capitole O, Plasson; (i) with Matthias Eisenberg.

(i) *Symphony No. 3 in C min. Danse macabre, Op. 40; Phaéton, Op. 39; Samson et Dalila: Danse bacchanale.*
*** Sony SK 53979 [id.]. (i) Newman; Pittsburgh SO, Maazel.

Maazel's new Sony recording must go the the top of the list for audacious spectacle in the finale. The recording, rich and spacious, was made in the Heinz Hall in Pittsburgh, employing similar microphone techniques to those used by the RCA engineers in the late 1960s for Reiner's Symphony Hall recordings in Chicago. The organ part, admirably played by Anthony Newman, was recorded in the Church of St Ignatus Loyola in New York City, and laminated on afterwards. It makes a superb impact. The first entry is impressive indeed, and the following organ statement of the finale's main theme, with the two pianos rippling in the backgound and topped by the cymbals, has never been presented more tellingly on record. The performance overall is direct and exciting, with the *Poco adagio* initially solemn, then touchingly tranquil, and the wide dynamic range enables Maazel to achieve subtle pianissimo effects, notably in the gentle closing section of the hitherto vigorous Scherzo. The finale is a *tour de force*. Maazel presses the music onwards thrillingly to its close, the trombones very much to the fore, as in the climax of the first movement, and the tuba also very tangible. The close is overwhelming, cymbals ringing out, and the downward descent of the organ pedals underlining the whole edifice, while Maazel's accelerando in the coda tautens the excitement even further. *Phaéton*, too, has never come off more effectively on record, and its portrayal of its hero's attempts to drive his father, Helios's, chariot across the heavens is touchingly followed by a lamenting postlude from strings and horns after the epic thunderbolt climax. *Danse macabre* is similarly spirited (with a fine violin solo), and there is real abandon at the close of the *Bacchanale* from *Samson and Dalila*.

Michel Plasson and the Orchestre du Capitole de Toulouse offer a particularly interesting package. Their account of the *Symphony No. 3*, made in the Basilique Notre-Dame La Daurade, Toulouse, with Matthias Eisenberg, is first rate and the recording first class, although brightly lit. The only snag is the plangent, reedy sound of the Puget organ, very French and somewhat harsh. It is truthfully reproduced, but will not appeal to all ears and will probably reproduce differently on different equipment. But its spectacular impact cannot be denied. The symphony comes in a two-for-the-price-of-one format with two rarities, *Cyprès et Lauriers*, whose high opus number indicates its lateness in Saint-Saëns's output, and *La Foi*, three symphonic tableaux drawn from incidental music for Eugène Brieux's play, *False Gods*. With *Cyprès et Lauriers*, Saint-Saëns returned to the medium of organ and orchestra for the first time since the *Third Symphony*. It was completed to celebrate the ending of the 1914–18 war and is extravagantly scored: its first movement (*Cyprès*) is for organ solo, and here the organ sounds just right. The second (*Lauriers*) brings trumpet fanfares and a general sense of spectacle: clearly Saint-Saëns is greatly enjoying his bursts of rhetoric, and so do we. Indeed the work's rumbustious close is thoroughly endearing. *La Foi*, which runs for just over 30 minutes, comes on the second CD and has some of the fey, oriental charm that characterizes the *Egyptian piano concerto* (No. 5). Thoroughly convincing performances, and *La Foi* is well worth hearing. This is certainly excellent value.

Under Mehta, the first-movement allegro of the symphony immediately takes wing and very soon expands to become weighty too – the horns sing out vociferously at the climax, with the trumpets following. The *Poco adagio* makes a serene, cantabile contrast, its climactic ardour affecting. The bustling energy of the Scherzo is well caught, with the detail of the piano figurations sparkling, and Daniel Chorzempa's powerful organ entry certainly makes one sit up. The tension is well held, and the BPO produces a characteristically full body of sound, while Mehta ensures a spontaneous quickening for the coda. Sonically this is spectacular too, though not quite as overwhelming as Maazel's recent Pittsburgh recording for Sony, which also has the edge as a performance. But then that does not offer the Franck symphony as well.

Djong Victorin Yu's recording was made in the Royal Festival Hall and is notable for its refined detail although, surprisingly, at the massive organ entry the two pianos are no clearer than in Maazel's Pittsburgh version, and the end result of the (by no means unexciting performance) is much less overwhelming. The *Carnival of the animals* is fresh but not distinctive either, and the main interest of this full-priced Carlton CD is the inclusion of Saint-Saëns's *Cyprès et Lauriers*, written to celebrate the signing of the Treaty of Versailles at the end of the First World War. After a solemn *Poco adagio* its roisterous Allegro skirts vulgarity by a small margin – an infectiously rumbustious dialogue between organ and orchestra complete with trumpet fanfares which could surely become a popular 'hit' if given sufficient exposure. It is most invigorating in the splendidly committed account given here, and the recording is first class.

CHAMBER MUSIC

Violin sonatas Nos. 1 in D min., Op. 75; 2 in E flat, Op. 102; Berceuse, Op. 38; Introduction and Rondo capriccioso, Op. 28 (arr. Bizet).
** ASV Dig. CDDCA 892 [id.]. Xue-Wei, John Lenehan.

Of Saint-Saëns's two *Violin sonatas* the second is the more appealing with its simple *Andante* and closing *Allegro grazioso*, in which Xue-Wei seems thoroughly at home. He is also delightfully nimble in the Scherzo (as is his fine partner, John Lenehan) and he manages the *moto perpetuo* finale of the *First sonata* with equal facility. Before that comes the lovely *Berceuse* which shows Xue-Wei's tone at its most appealing, but in the opening *Introduction and Rondo capriccioso*, played with real sparkle, the close microphones are unflattering to the violin's upper range.

Salieri, Antonio (1750–1825)

(i) *Fortepiano concerto in B flat;* (ii) *Double concerto for flute and oboe in C. Sinfonia in B flat (La Tempesta di mare).*
(M) ** Erato/Warner Dig. 0630 12987-2 [id.]. (i) Badura-Skoda; (ii) Hoogendoorn & Borgonovo; Sol. Ven., Scimone.

Salieri certainly did not poison Mozart but, listening to this well-crafted but somewhat empty music, one could well imagine that he might have wanted to, out of sheer envy. For his writing skilfully goes through all the motions of the eighteenth-century concerto and sinfonia without much hint of real inspiration. The *Double concerto* is his best-known work and has been recorded before. Its chatter is pleasant enough, but here the effect is rather like a couple of old gossips meeting at a vicarage fête. The *Fortepiano concerto* is conventional: its first-movement secondary theme has a touch of charm, but the closing Minuet with variations is a routine affair. The *Sinfonia* is the freshest piece in the programme, but it is of doubtful attribution: it might as easily have been written by Salieri's elder brother, who lived in Italy. Indeed its character is different from the two companion works. The sparkling if repetitive first movement (presumably this is the supposed tempest) has a sunny Italian quality, the central *Andante* a courtly, old-fashioned elegance and the finale is really rather neat. It is played here with much vigour, and Scimone is just as persuasive in the two concertos; moreover his soloists are excellent. So is the recording.

Double concerto in C for flute and oboe.
*** Chandos Dig. CHAN 9051 [id.]. Susan Milan, David Theodore, City of L. Sinf., Hickox – MOZART: *Flute and harp concerto; Oboe concerto.* ***

Salieri's innocently insubstantial *Double concerto* is quite transformed by the charisma and sheer style of the solo playing from Susan Milan and David Theodore. The catchy little triplet figure which dominates the first movement is articulated with engaging crispness, and a dialogue which can too easily sound garrulous here is full of charm. The exquisite playing of Theodore in the simple melody of the *Largo* and the perfect blending of the two soloists turns it into a really memorable slow movement, and the flute and oboe chase each other round engagingly in their winning decorations of the nicely poised Minuet finale.

Hickox's accompaniment is both polished and genial, and the recording casts a pleasing glow over the whole proceedings.

Sarasate, Pablo (1844–1908)

Carmen (fantasy), Op. 25 (arr. Zimbalist); *Zigeunerweisen, Op. 10/1.*
(M) ** Decca 452 309-2 [id.]. Ruggiero Ricci, LSO, Gamba – LALO: *Symphonie espagnole* *(*); SAINT-SAENS: *Havanaise* etc. **

Ricci plays with dazzling virtuosity an arrangement by Zimbalist that adds further embellishments to Sarasate's brilliant fantasia. *Zigeunerweisen* has plenty of gypsy fire and an opulent lyrical line. The solo violin is placed rather near to the microphones but can stand the scrutiny, even if the 1959 sound is not as flattering as the quality EMI provide for Perlman (CDC7 47101-2 – see our main volume).

Satie, Erik (1866–1925)

Gymnopédies Nos. 1 & 3 (orch. Debussy).
*(*) DG Dig. 449 186-2 [id.]. Orpheus CO – FAURE: *Masques et bergamasques* etc. **; RAVEL: *Pavane* etc. *(*)

The oboe playing in the first of the *Gymnopédies* is curiously lethargic; the third brings ethereal sounds from the violins and is more appealing. But this is not overall a very recommendable (53-minute) collection.

PIANO MUSIC

Piano, 4 hands: (i) *La Belle excentrique; 3 Morceaux en forme de poire.* Solo piano: *Caresse; Croquis et agaceries d'un gros bonhomme en bois; Danse de travers; Descriptions automatiques; Fantaisie valse; Passacaille; Les pantins dansent; 1ère Pensée Rose + Croix; Petite ouverture à danser; Pièces froides I: Airs à faire fuir. II: Danse de travers. Poudre d'or; Prélude de la porte héroïque du ciel; Prélude en tapisserie; Valse ballet; 3 Valses distinguées du précieux dégoûté.*
*** Virgin/EMI VC7 59296-2. Anne Queffélec; (i) with Catherine Collard.

Although we continue to think very highly of Pascal Rogé's pair of Decca records of this repertoire (410 220-2 and 421 713-2), anyone seeking a single representative Satie collection will find this 72-minute recital by Anne Queffélec hard to beat. She can be quirky, as in the opening *Croquis et agaceries d'un gros bonhomme en bois* or, more particularly, the satirical *Valse ballet*; she is engagingly cool in the *Pièces froides*; her accounts of the *Caresse* and *Les pantins dansent* are quite haunting, while the *Petite ouverture à danser* has much charm. She does not miss that bitter-sweet melancholy which is special to the composer, so well expressed in *Son binocle*, the delicate second number of *Les trois valses distinguées*. The *Première pensée Rose + Croix* is wonderfully poised, when it can sound static, and her simple serenity extends also to the *Prélude de la porte héroïque du ciel*. The little French valse, *Poudre d'or*, is played with a nice mixture of insouciance and glitter. In the *Trois morceaux en forme de poire* and the lively *La Belle excentrique* she is partnered by the excellent Catherine Collard, and how brilliantly they end the concert with that final quartet of sparkling vignettes, opening with the dazzling *Grande ritournelle* and ending with the irrepressible *Can-can 'grand-mondain'*. The recording is excellent and, although this collection omits the famous *Gymnopédies* and *Gnossiennes*, they are readily available on Rogé's fine Decca recital (410 220-2) which duplicates only one item here (the *Prélude en tapisserie*).

Avant-dernières pensées; Chapitres tournés en tous sens; Croquis et agaceries d'un gros bonhomme en bois; Danses gothiques; Descriptions automatiques; Embryons desséchés; Enfantillages pittoresques; 3 Gnossiennes; 3 Gymnopédies; Heures séculaires et instantanées; Menus propos enfantins; 5 Nocturnes; 4 Ogives; Les pantins dansent; Passacaille; Peccadilles importunes; Pièces froides; Prélude en tapisserie; 4 Preludes; Préludes de la porte héroïque du ciel; Premier menuet; Rêverie de l'enfance de Pantagruel; 3 Sarabandes; Sonatine bureaucratique; Sports et divertissements; Trois valses du précieux; Véritables préludes flasques; Vieux séquins et vieilles cuirasses.
(B) **(*) Carlton VoxBox CDX 5011 (2) [id.]. Frank Glazer.

Vox offers a great deal of Satie's solo piano music on two CDs in excellent performances by Frank Glazer, and this VoxBox scores over the competition by offering much more music (though, curiously, not the last three *Gnossiennes*). Glazer seems to penetrate the character of each of these aphoristic and haunting miniatures with genuine flair and insight. His are searching and sympathetic performances; the recording, although rather reverberant and a little veiled in the treble, is full-bodied and faithful. The Vox CD transfer slightly enhances the original piano-sound and there is no drying-out of timbre or ambience. Some of these pieces are insubstantial, but those attracted to the idiom of the music will find this a safe investment.

Chapitres tournées en tous sens; Croquis et agaceries d'un gros bonhomme en bois; Descriptions automatiques; Embryons desséchés; Enfantillages pittoresques; 6 Gnossiennes; 3 Gymnopédies; Menus propos enfantins; Passacaille; Pas trop vif; 6 Pièces de la période; Ragtime Parade; Véritables préludes flasques.
(BB) (*) Naxos Dig. 8.550305 [id.]. Klára Körmendi.

Klára Körmendi's recital on Naxos is not really recommendable. The playing is less at fault than the recording. The sound itself is very hard and unappealing, and it is very difficult to derive much pleasure from it.

Sauer, Emil von (1862–1942)

Piano concerto No. 1 in E min.
*** Hyperion Dig. CDA 66790 [id.]. Stephen Hough, CBSO, Lawrence Foster – SCHARWENKA: *Piano concerto No. 4.* ***

Winner not only of the *Gramophone*'s Concerto Award, but also voted Record of the Year in 1996, this potent coupling of Sauer and Scharwenka surely combines every feature of the 'Romantic concerto', from flamboyant display to beguiling lyricism. As a greatly admired virtuoso, Emil von Sauer was an able exponent of the Scharwenka concerto; and his own work, although lighter in feeling, makes comparable demands on the dexterity of the soloist. Its delightful melodic vein and style have much in common with Saint-Saëns, especially in the Scherzo, although the touching *Larghetto amoroso* also evokes the poetic atmosphere of Chopin. The good-natured finale is relished here by soloist and orchestra alike, and Stephen Hough sparkles his way through its glittering upper tessitura. Altogether this makes a perfect foil for the more ambitious concerto with which it is paired. Splendid recording, with a nice sense of scale.

Saxton, Robert (born 1953)

(i) *Chamber symphony (Circles of light);* (ii) *Concerto for orchestra; The Ring of eternity;* (i) *The Sentinel of the rainbow.*
(M) *** EMI Dig. CDM5 66530-2 [id.]. (i) L. Sinf.; (ii) BBC SO; Knussen.

Robert Saxton is one of the most immediately communicative of the younger generation of British composers, using the orchestra with a panache that plainly reflects his own pleasure in rich and colourful sound. These four works, all written between 1983 and 1986, bring fine examples, notably the *Concerto for orchestra*, first given at the Proms in 1984. Its four linked sections broadly follow a symphonic shape, as do those of the *Chamber symphony* of 1986, which uses smaller forces, with solo strings. That later work has the title *Circles of light* and was inspired by a quotation from Dante, when in the *Divine Comedy* he looks into the eyes of his beloved, Beatrice, and links what he sees to the movement of the heavens. The other two works, both lasting around 15 minutes, also have evocative titles and are linked in the composer's mind to the *Concerto for orchestra* to form a sort of trilogy. Oliver Knussen draws intense, committed playing both from the BBC Symphony Orchestra in the *Concerto for orchestra* and *The Ring of eternity*, and from the London Sinfonietta in the chamber-scale works. Full, warm recording.

Scarlatti, Alessandro (1660–1725)

Cantatas: *Clori e Mirtillo; E pur vuole il cielo e amore; Ero e Leandro; Filli che esprime la sua fede a Fileno; Marc'Antonio e Cleopatra; Questo silenzio ombroso.*
*** Virgin/Veritas/EMI Dig. VC5 45126-2. Gérard Lesne, Sandrine Piau, Il Seminario Musicale.

These six cantatas again bring together Gérard Lesne and his well-matched partner, Sandrine Piau. Each has a solo item, but the most striking works are those in which they join together. As so often with this repertoire, the texts dramatize the problems of lovers who are unable to be together or who destiny insists must part. The most dramatic of these is the dialogue between Antony and Cleopatra at the moment when he has to leave for Rome. They argue their different viewpoints in closely intertwined duets, and finally Cleopatra yields; Sandrine Piau creates a tender frisson with her last solo line: *Ti saro fida sempre in vita e in morte* ('I shall be true to you in life and death'). The opening, much shorter, pastoral cantata here, *Questa silenzio ombroso* ('This shady quietude'), is a deeply expressive duet which lightens as the soprano line describes the sweetly lamenting nightingale. *Filli che esprime la sua fede a Fileno*, an expression of steadfast love, has a long instrumental introduction for violin and flute which comes off well, as does the skipping closing section; but in the melancholy central aria there is a watery obbligato flute and, although the timbre is perfectly matched to Lesne's vocal line, some listeners may regret that the flautist (by the nature of his instrument) is unable to offer reliable intonation. Both vocal artists are on top form, and the simple continuo accompaniments are admirably played by Il Seminario Musicale. This is specialized repertoire, perhaps not to all tastes; but Lesne and Piau are exceptional artists.

Scarlatti, Domenico (1685–1757)

The Good-humoured ladies (ballet suite; arr. Tommasini).
(M) *** EMI CDM5 65911-2. Concert Arts O, Robert Irving – GLAZUNOV: *The Seasons;* WALTON: *Wise virgins*. ***

Scarlatti's music in Tommasini's witty arrangement chatters along very like a group of dear old ladies gossiping over their cups of tea. Irving points this up most beautifully and (especially in the finale) offers some very brilliant orchestral playing, while the *Andante* (from the *Sonata in B minor*, Kk 87) is touchingly tender. The recording is first class and completely belies its age (1961).

Keyboard sonatas, Kk. 1, 3, 8–9, 11, 17, 24–5, 27, 29, 87, 96, 113, 141, 146, 173, 213–14, 247, 259, 268, 283–4, 380, 386–7, 404, 443, 519–20, 523.
500♪ *** Virgin/EMI Dig. VCD5 45123-2 (2) [ZDCB 45123]. Mikhail Pletnev (piano).

What a happy idea to record a carefully chosen selection of some of Scarlatti's finest and most adventurous sonatas, stretching over two CDs, giving the fullest opportunity to demonstrate the extraordinary range of this music in a recital-length programme playing for 140 minutes. The performances throughout are in the very front rank, played very freely and with consistent imagination, not least the dazzling closing work in *D major*, Kk. 29, with its contrasts of mood and semi-improvisatory feeling. Pletnev is beautifully recorded.

Keyboard sonatas, Kk. 32, 64, 69, 87, 133, 146, 160, 198, 208, 213, 380, 429, 466, 481, 511, 517; Toccata in D min.
(B) **(*) Cal Approche CAL 6670 [id.]. Inger Södergren.

The ever sensitive Inger Södergren gives an appealing recital of 16 well-contrasted *Sonatas* plus a brilliant account of the highly individual *Toccata in D minor*. Some might feel that her gentle, almost wistful treatment of the lyrical sonatas errs towards being too romantic but her crisp articulation in the lively pieces is unimpeachable, and she is very well recorded.

Keyboard sonatas, Kk. 159, 175, 208, 213, 322 & 380 (arr. for guitar).
(B) *** Sony SBK 62425; *SBT 62425* [id.]. John Williams (guitar) – GIULIANI: *Variations on a theme by Handel;* PAGANINI: *Caprice; Grand sonata;* VILLA-LOBOS: *5 Preludes*. ***

Guitar arrangements of Scarlatti sonatas have their charms when played by an artist as imaginative as John Williams. He manages by percussive plucking to sound at times almost like a harpsichord, while his gentle playing is always beguiling especially in the delightful *D major Sonata*, Kk 159. The recording is faithful, somewhat close and larger than life, but never unacceptably so. This diverse and well-planned recital (76 minutes) is very enjoyable indeed.

Stabat Mater in C min.
(B) **(*) Sony SBK 48282; *SBT 48282* [id.]. BBC Singers, John Poole – VIVALDI: *Stabat Mater; Dixit Dominus*. **(*)

A thoroughly musical, if not distinctive, performance from the BBC Singers, who blend well together and are realistically recorded. An attractive coupling for two enjoyable period performances of Vivaldi.

Scharwenka, Franz Xaver (1850–1924)

Piano concerto No. 4 in F min., Op. 82.
*** Hyperion Dig. CDA 66790 [id.]. Stephen Hough, CBSO, Lawrence Foster – SAUER: *Piano concerto No. 1*. ***

Scharwenka, famous virtuoso pianist as well as composer and teacher (admired by Busoni and Liszt), wrote four piano concertos; this, his finest, dates from 1908. It was very famous in its time and its composer was later to play it triumphantly in New York (in 1910) with Gustav Mahler conducting. It is ambitiously flamboyant and on the largest scale: in four movements, with the first lasting nearly 19 minutes. Its invention, which manages a potent mix of bravura and lyricism, readily holds the attention, with plenty of interest in the bold orchestral tuttis. The second-movement *Allegretto* has much charm and is very deftly scored; a full flood of romanticism blossoms in the *Lento* slow movement. The stormy *con fuoco* finale combines a touch of wit and more robust geniality with glittering brilliance and power; and all four movements make prodigious technical and artistic demands on the soloist, to which Stephen Hough rises with great technical aplomb and consistent panache; he also plays with fine poetic sensibility. He is given vigorously committed support by Lawrence Foster and the CBSO and a first-class Hyperion recording. Winner not only of the *Gramophone* Concerto Award, this was also that magazine's Record of the Year in 1996, and deservedly so.

Scheidt, Samuel (1587–1654)

Ludi musici (Hamburg, 1621): excerpts.
*** Audivis Astrée Dig. ES 8559 [id.]. Hespèrion XX, Jordi Savall.

The music of Samuel Scheidt exists on the periphery of the catalogue, but he deserves to be better known; this excellent and rewarding anthology will serve any collector very well as an introduction. Although he studied briefly under Sweelinck in Amsterdam in 1608–9, Scheidt spent his life in Halle, both as organist and for five years as Kapellmeister, interrupted in 1625 when the Court left Halle, not to return until 1638. He published four collections of instrumental music between 1621 and 1624 under the title *Ludi musici* but only the First Book survives, and all these pieces are drawn from it. In 1636 Scheidt's four children died in the plague, but that lay in the future. For all its good nature, his music has a melancholy streak. It is immediately striking in the touchingly expressive extended opening of the *Paduan à 4* (from Cantus IV) with its gentle, lyrical flow and passing dissonances. The music becomes more positive and lively in its second half, then reverts to its doleful opening mood. The later *Paduan* (from Cantus V) is also very touching, and this writing has much in common with Dowland's *Lachrimae*. Scheidt actually draws on Dowland in his spirited *Battle galliard*, so characteristic of its time. Other English tunes are featured in his canzons, notably in the delightful five-part *Canzon* (from Cantus XXVI). The courants, too, are generally light-hearted; that from Cantus XI is played delicately on a double harp, but there is also a touching *Courant dolorosa* for viols in Cantus IX. All this music is played with characteristic finesse, nicely judged espressivo and plenty of vitality by the superb Jordi Savall and Hespèrion XX, and the viol sound is smooth and pleasingly natural, with none of that scratchiness which comes from too close microphones.

Schickele, Peter (born 1935)

Oboe concerto.
(M) *** Carlton Fanfare Dig. 30366 0065-2 [id.]. Pamela Pecha, Moscow PO, Paul Freeman – VAUGHAN WILLIAMS: *Oboe concerto;* R. STRAUSS: *Oboe concerto.* ***

Peter Schickele (also known as P. D. Q. Bach) is a professional American musical joker, but his humour does not cross the Atlantic very comfortably, so he is not well known in the UK. He studied composition under Milhaud, so it is not surprising that his well-crafted and highly spontaneous concerto has its exotic side, especially in its central *Chant*. But Schickele's invention throughout the piece is ear-tickling and this work is in every way winning, ending with a touching *Epiloque*. It is a pity that the very sparse notes provided with this CD do not provide more information about its gestation, but they do tell us that the present performer is its dedicatee, and she gives it a performance of great character and immediate appeal. She is both well accompanied and vividly recorded.

Schmidt, Franz (1874–1939)

Das Buch mit sieben Siegeln (The Book with 7 seals).
*** Calig Dig. CAL 50 978/9 [id.]. Fontana, Hintermeier, Azesberger, Büchner, Holl, Hollzer, V. Singverein, VSO, Stein; Martin Haselböck (organ).
(M) (***) Sony mono SM2K 68442 (2) [id.]. Gueden, Malaniuk, Dermota, Wunderlich, Berry, V. Singverein, VPO, Mitropoulos; Alois Forrer (organ).

Given the recent interest in Schmidt's symphonies, it is no surprise that attention should now shift to his oratorio, *Das Buch mit sieben Siegeln* (*The Book with 7 seals*). After he finished the *Fourth Symphony* in

1933, he devoted his remaining creative years to this setting of the *Revelation of St John the Divine*, completing it in 1937. The Calig recording comes from a concert performance, given in the Grosser Musikvereinsaal in Vienna in May 1996, and so has the advantage of modern recorded sound. The mid-price Sony version comes from Austrian Radio tapes of a live performance, given as part of the Salzburg Festival in August 1959, with an illustrious line-up under the legendary Dmitri Mitropoulos. The Sony is a mono recording but, given the eloquence and dedication of Mitropoulos's conducting, any sonic limitations are soon forgotten. Under his inspired direction every phrase means something. There is nothing routine and much that is inspired – certainly the singing of Anton Dermota, who took part in the first performance in 1938 and thus brings special authority to the role. It is difficult to grade these recordings. Given its fervour and intensity, the Mitropoulos cannot have fewer than three stars despite the mono sound. Horst Stein's 1996 performance is also impressive and certainly carries a full three-star recommendation. With neither version can one go very far wrong.

Schmitt, Florent (1870–1958)

Deux mirages.

(M) *** EMI CDM5 65996-2 [id.]. John Ogdon – DUKAS; DUTILLEUX: *Sonatas*. ***

Florent Schmitt's piano music is not well served on CD, so that John Ogdon's splendid account of the *Deux mirages* is all the more welcome. The first was written in 1920 and is an elegy for Debussy. Like so much of Florent Schmitt's music, it is strong on atmosphere and makes for compelling listening. The second is a dazzling virtuoso piece, written for Cortot and inspired by the legend of Mazeppa. Ogdon takes its formidable technical hurdles in his stride. The disc also brings impressive accounts of the Dukas and Dutilleux *Sonatas* and deserves the strongest recommendation.

Schnittke, Alfred (born 1934)

Symphony No. 1.

*** Chandos Dig. CHAN 9417 [id.]. Russian State SO, Gennady Rozhdestvensky.

Schnittke's *First Symphony* dates from 1969–72 and is a huge radical canvas lasting some 68 minutes. In his essay on 'The Symphony in the Soviet Union' in *A Guide to the Symphony*, David Fanning writes that it 'contains a whole lexicon of advanced devices – the theatricality of American happenings with the players entering one by one and leaving at the end only to enter again as if to restart the whole process, the aleatory (chance) elements of the Polish school, and the multiple quotations of Berio's *Sinfonia* plus a cadenza for jazz violin'. As for the aleatory elements, one is reminded of Hans Keller's remark: 'If there are no wrong notes, then how can there be right ones?' It is essentially a musical gesture, a tirade rather than a symphony of protest and anger, that must have set off powerful resonances in the 1970s Soviet scene, in much the same way as did Solzhenitzyn's writings, but which sounds pretty thin a quarter of a century on. Rozhdestvensky's performance is committed, and the recording, made at a public performance in the Moscow Conservatoire in 1988, is well detailed. There is more rhetoric than substance here. The three stars are allotted for the performance and recording; for the composition the stars can be aleatoric!

(i) *Symphony No. 4;* (ii) *3 Sacred Hymns.*

*** Chandos Dig. CHAN 9463 [id.]. (i) Jaroslav Zdorov, Dmitri Pianov; (i–ii) Russian State Symphonic Cappella; (i) Russian State SO; Valery Polyansky.

The *Fourth Symphony* draws on Christian (Catholic, Lutheran and Russian Orthodox) and Jewish chant and is avowedly religious in programme, reflecting episodes in the life of the Virgin Mary. It lasts 40 minutes and is scored for two singers, one a counter-tenor, chorus and orchestra; it also makes inventive and colourful use of keyboard sonorities. Readers with a keen interest in Schnittke will find both the performance and the recording to be of high quality. Others may share our less enthusiastic response to the piece: it seems too concerned with gesture and essentially empty of musical substance. The *Three Sacred Hymns* for *a cappella* choir from 1983 are both eloquent and beautiful.

Schoeck, Othmar (1886–1957)

(i) *Horn concerto, Op. 65. Prelude for orchestra, Op. 48;* (ii) *Serenade for oboe, cor anglais and strings, Op. 27. Suite in A flat for strings.*

** CPO Dig. CPO 999 337-2 [id.]. (i) Bruno Schneider; (ii) Silvia Zabarella, Martin Zuchner; Coll. Musik, Winterthur, Werner Andreas Albert.

The major work here is the five-movement *Suite in A flat for strings*, which Schoeck composed in 1945. Although it is not quite as poignant as *Sommernacht*, also for strings, composed a few months earlier, there is some imaginative and expressive writing. The second movement, *Pastorale tranquillo*, has that sense of melancholy and nostalgia so characteristic of Schoeck. In it he imagined 'the peace and deep stillness of the forests', and the movement was apparently much admired by Schoeck's countryman, Honegger. The middle movement, a *March*, has something of the sardonic humour of Prokofiev. The slightly later *Concerto for horn and strings* (1951) is well played by Bruno Schneider and is an appealing piece that will strike a responsive chord among all who care for late Strauss. The *Serenade for oboe, cor anglais and strings* is a five-minute interlude which Schoeck composed for a much-truncated production of his opera, *Don Ranudo*, at Leipzig in 1930. The *Prelude for orchestra* (1930) is new to records and serves as a reminder that Schoeck was at one time a pupil of Reger. Its textures lack transparency, but this is in part due to the rather opaque recording, made in a radio studio. It is perfectly acceptable, but the strings could do with more bloom and tuttis need to open out a little more. A useful issue, now that Howard Griffiths's recording of the *Suite* with the ECO on Novalis, coupled with the glorious *Violin concerto*, is no longer in circulation.

Schoenberg, Arnold (1874–1951)

Chamber Symphonies Nos. 1–2; (i) *Piano concerto, Op. 42.*
*** Ph. Dig. 446 683-2 [id.]. (i) Alfred Brendel; SW German RSO, Baden-Baden, Michael Gielen.

Alfred Brendel has been a lifelong champion of the *Piano concerto*: this is his third recording and it is undoubtedly the most telling, partly because the knotty orchestral textures are brightly revealed in a recording which is admirably clear yet does not lack fullness, while the balance with the piano is admirable. The performance is strong, impassioned in the *Adagio*, with the mixtures of *grotesquerie* and *giocoso* nicely juxtaposed in the finale, where Brendel's contribution is quite brilliant. Michael Gielen is a committed partner, subtle in his rhythmic inflexions and bringing plenty of vitality to the accompaniment, matching Brendel's dash in the last movement. The choice of coupling seems apt when the two *Chamber Symphonies* have never been more enjoyable on record, their diverse moods and amazing range of colouring caught with lyrical warmth and detail finely and affectionately observed. The orchestral playing is of the very highest calibre. Indeed Gielen finds both charm and gaiety (rare commodities with Schoenberg) in the *con fuoco* finale of No. 2, although of course the movement ends in dark melancholy. Again first-rate recording. A major addition to the Schoenberg discography.

(i) *Pelleas und Melisande* (symphonic poem), *Op. 5;* (ii) *Verklaerte Nacht, Op. 4.*
(B) ** Sony SBK 63035; *SBT 63035* [id.]. (i) O de Paris, Barenboim; (ii) NYPO, Boulez.

Barenboim's 1977 recording of Schoenberg's extended symphonic poem is not without atmosphere or ardour, but it is distantly balanced within the blurring acoustics of Notre Dame, Paris, and lacks tangibility, besides being opaque. When one turns to *Verklaerte Nacht*, the effect is infinitely more vivid. Boulez secures highly responsive playing from the strings of the New York Philharmonic, and he has the passionate measure of the composer's sensuously poetic evocation to the full. This must yield place to Sinopoli, who offers the same coupling at premium price (DG 439 942-2 – see our main volume). However, it is still Karajan who reigns supreme in this repertoire; his superb Berlin Philharmonic performances are linked with the *Orchestral variations*, Op. 31, Berg's *Lyric suite* and three *Orchestral pieces*, plus music by Webern, on three mid-priced discs which form a cornerstone for any collection of music by the composers of the so-called Second Viennese School (DG 427 424-2).

Variations for orchestra, Op. 31; Verklaerte Nacht, Op. 4.
500♪ ❁ *** DG 415 326-2 [id.]. BPO, Karajan.

Karajan's version of *Verklaerte Nacht* is altogether magical and very much in a class of its own. There is a tremendous intensity and variety of tone and colour: the palette that the strings of the Berlin Philharmonic have at their command is altogether extraordinarily wide-ranging.

Verklaerte Nacht, Op. 4 (string sextet version).
500♪ ❁ (***) Testament mono SABT 1031. Hollywood Qt, with Alvin Dinkin, Kurt Reher – SCHUBERT: *String quintet*. (***) ❁

This almost flawless performance enjoyed the imprimatur of Schoenberg himself, who supplied the sleeve-note for it (reproduced in the excellent booklet), the only time he ever did so. The sound is remarkably good and very musical. Recommended with enthusiasm.

Schubert, Franz (1797–1828)

BICENTENARY COLLECTIONS

DG '*Schubert Masterworks*'

(B) ** DG 453 660-2 (20) [id.]. Various artists, as below.

Although, as can be seen below, there are many fine recordings included in DG's celebratory box of Schubert 'Masterworks', there are also a few which are less recommendable and, although the purchase of the complete set represents a considerable saving, collectors would do far better to pick and choose. There is no additional booklet with the slipcase, and the great drawback to the individual CDs in this set is the documentation, which, for a company of the calibre of DG, is unbelievably sparse. Each CD has an attractively illustrated booklet using various pictures of the composer and of contemporary life, from 'A Schubert evening in a Viennese town-house' to (less appropriately) 'Ball game in Atzenbrugg'. But the documentation is restricted to a single, brief, autobiographical note about the composer, which is repeated with each CD, with nothing further added about the music.

(i) *Konzertstück in D, D.345; Rondo in A for violin and strings, D.438;* (ii) *Duo in A, D.574; Fantasy in C, D.934.*

(M) *** DG analogue/Dig. 453 665-2 [id.]. Gidon Kremer, with (i) LSO, Emil Tchakarov; (ii) Valery Afanassiev.

This is not only one of Kremer's most impressive records, it happily fills a gap in the catalogue in combining two of Schubert's most engaging concertante works with a pair of his finest works for violin and piano, the *Duo* from 1817 and the *Fantasy* from a decade earlier. All four have that freshness and (at times) innocence of invention which make Schubert's instrumental music so engaging, yet Kremer and Afanassiev (a splendid partnership) treat the *Duo* as a major sonata by observing the first-movement exposition repeat. They also show imaginative flair in the *Fantasy*, especially in its chimerical *Allegretto*. The concertante pieces are equally successful, the recording is excellent, and this was an excellent choice for including within DG's special bicentenary collection.

Symphonies Nos. 1 in D, D.82; 2 in B flat, D.125; Rosamunde: Overture (Die Zauberharfe), D.644.

(M) **(*) DG 453 661-2 [id.]. BPO, Boehm.

Symphonies Nos. 3 in D, D.200; 4 in C min. (Tragic), D.417; Rosamunde: Ballet music Nos. 1–2, D.797.

(M) ** DG 453 662-2 [id.]. BPO, Boehm.

Symphonies Nos. 5 in B flat, D.485; 6 in C, D.589.

(M) *** DG 453 663-2 [id.]. BPO, Boehm.

Symphonies Nos. 8 in B min. (Unfinished), D.759; 9 in C (Great), D.944.

(M) *** DG 453 664-2 [id.]. BPO, Boehm.

Boehm's cycle of the Schubert symphonies was recorded over a decade between 1963 and 1973, and the Berlin Philharmonic plays with striking warmth and finesse throughout. Boehm does not smile as often as Schubert's music demands – especially by the side of Beecham in Nos. 3 and 5, but he is always sympathetic. Certainly the Berlin wind are a joy to listen to, and it is only in the early symphonies that he does not quite capture the youthful sparkle of these delightful scores, although in its way No. 1 is brightly and elegantly done and No. 2 also is characteristically strong; both are classical in spirit. No. 4 offers splendidly disciplined playing, but this is not one of the more characterful interpretations of the set. It is good that Boehm's warmly graceful account of No. 5 and the glowing performance of No. 6, one of Schubert's most genial works, are coupled together, for both symphonies show Boehm at his best, taking an easy-going view, with relaxed tempi that never grow heavy. The remastered sound is remarkably fine, fresher and clearer and without loss of bloom, although the focus in No. 6 is not absolutely sharp.

Boehm capped his series with an outstanding account of the *Unfinished Symphony* and one of the finest of all recorded performances of the *Great C major*. The *Unfinished* combines deep sensitivity and great refinement, and the points of detail as well as the overall warmth keep this version among the very finest on record. The opening of the development – always a key point – is magically done, and, throughout, the superb recording quality gives unusual clarity while allowing the Berlin Philharmonic ensemble its natural opulence. Boehm's performance of the *Ninth*, recorded three years earlier, stands in the lyrical Furtwängler tradition rather than in the forceful Toscanini stream, but it is the balance between the conflicting interests in this symphony which distinguishes Boehm's reading. His modification of tempo in the various sections of the first movement is masterly in its finesse, often so subtle that it requires close attention to spot it. In the slow movement the rhythmic spring to the repeated quavers is delectable, with the Berlin players really on their toes. Nor is there any lack of drama in the performance, for the playing is marvellous throughout. Only in the finale, taken rather fast, is the playing slightly less gripping, and even there one has excitement in plenty. The recording is very good indeed and in its CD transfer sounds fresh, warm and full. One notes, however, that on its last appearance this coupling appeared on DG's bargain Classikon label, so now it costs more – but it's well worth it.

(i) *Arpeggione sonata, D.821;* (ii) *Piano quintet in A (Trout), D.667. Adagio in E flat ('Notturno')* (for piano trio), *D.897.*
(M) **(*) DG 453 667-2 [id.]. (i) Pierre Fournier, Jean Fonda; (ii) Christoph Eschenbach, Koeckert Qt.

Pierre Fournier made one of the key modern arrangements of the *Arpeggione sonata* for cello (also used by Tortelier) and he gives this a wholly persuasive account. He is beautifully balanced and recorded. Alongside it comes an enjoyably alert performance from Christoph Eschenbach and members of the Koeckert Quartet of the *Trout*. There is a good deal of sparkle and character – the variations are given plenty of individual interest, the outer movements striking momentum – and Eschenbach himself plays with genuine elegance. The recording acoustic is clear and rather dry; some may find it a trifle unexpansive. The *Notturno* has the advantage of a warmer acoustic and is played most sympathetically.

(i) *Octet in F, D.803;* (ii) *Introduction and variations for flute and piano on 'Trock'ne Blumen'* from *Die schöne Müllerin, D.802.*
(M) *** DG 453 666-2 [id.]. (i) V. Chamber Ens.; (ii) Aurèle Nicolet, Karl Engel.

The Vienna Chamber Ensemble do not overlap in personnel with the New Vienna Octet, who have recorded this work for Decca, though their performance has a similar polish and urbane Viennese warmth. This is mellifluous Schubert, and very engaging it is: fresh and elegant. This dates from 1980, and the CD transfer maintains the smoothness and realism of the LP. Very enjoyable. The innocent set of variations on a melancholy little tune makes a slight but pleasing encore.

Piano trios Nos. 1 in B flat, D.898; 2 in E flat, D.929.
(M) ** DG 453 671-2 [id.]. Trio di Trieste.

The Trio di Trieste give eminently lively and sensitive accounts of these *Trios*, and they are well recorded, although the ear notices that the microphones are close at the very opening of the *B flat trio*. These performances are not distinctive, but they are thoroughly serviceable.

String quartets Nos. 12 in C min. (Quartettsatz), D.703; 15 in G, D.887.
(M) ** DG 453 670-2 [id.]. Melos Qt.

There are many points of interest here, even if there are some mannered touches. The recording, however, is a little hard and close, and it inhibits a whole-hearted recommendation.

String quartets Nos. 13 in A min. (Rosamunde), D.804; 14 in D min. (Death and the Maiden), D.810.
(M) ** DG 453 669-2 [id.]. Melos Qt.

It is a pity that the quality of the recorded sound is not more appealing in this coupling, though remastering has brought added presence. Generally speaking, the Melos Quartet's playing is impressive enough, but they wear their hearts a little too much on their sleeves; the slow movements are just a shade too sentimental.

String quintet in C, D.956.
(M) **(*) DG 453 668-2 [id.]. Melos Qt, Mstislav Rostropovich.

Rostropovich plays as second cello in the Melos performance, and no doubt his influence from the centre of the string texture contributes to the eloquence of the famous *Adagio* which, like the performance as a whole, is strongly, even dramatically, characterized. The emphasis on the rhythmic articulation of the outer movements leaves no doubt as to the power of Schubert's writing, and there is no lack of atmosphere in the opening and closing sections of the slow movement. The recording is live and immediate. A fine version, but not a first choice.

(i) *Allegro in A min., Lebenstürme, D.947;* (ii) *Divertissement à l'hongroise in G min., D.818; Fantasia in F min., D.940;* (i) *Marche militaire in D, D.733/1; Rondo in A, D.951.*
(M) ** DG 453 675-2 [id.]. (i) Paul Badura-Skoda, Jörg Demus; (ii) Alfons and Aloys Kontarsky.

The *Fantasia* is one of Schubert's greatest works for piano duet; from the Kontarskys we have a bright, aggressive performance, but one almost totally lacking in charm and poetry. The technique is formidable, as is the unanimity between two players who in twentieth-century music have few rivals; but here they make Schubert sound relatively heartless, whatever the incisive strength of the performance. The recording is bright to match. The playing of Badura-Skoda and Demus, on the other hand, has the right lightness of touch and a feeling for the delicacy and individual nuance of the phrases. The players communicate their enjoyment too as the music passes from one to the other.

Fantasy in C (Wanderer), D.760; 4 Impromptus Nos. 1–4, D.899; 5–8, D.935.
(M) **(*) DG 453 762-2 [id.]. Wilhelm Kempff.

Predictably fine playing from Kempff, and many individual moments of special pleasure: the gentle opening theme of D.899/1, the curving arches of triplets in the second of the set, the lovely way Kempff floats the flowing tune of the *G flat major* over its accompaniment, and the exquisite playing at the reprise of the first section of the *A flat* (all these from D.899). But elsewhere Kempff's approach is sometimes more classical than romantic and the phrases are presented concisely, rather than allowed to unfold lovingly. Often the second presentation of a theme is marginally more relaxed. But all the pieces are characterized very individually. The recordings of the *Impromptus* are admirably faithful and beautifully transferred, if a little dry in acoustic. In the *Wanderer fantasy* high drama is missing, but the result is compelling, with a moulding of the structure which gives a complete illusion of spontaneity.

Piano sonatas Nos. 19 in C min., D.958; 20 in A, D.959.
(M) *** DG 453 673-2 [id.]. Wilhelm Kempff.

Kempff is never less than illuminating in Schubert, and these highly spontaneous performances are nicely turned and well shaped, as one would expect from so authoritative a Schubertian, and there are numerous imaginative insights. The recording gives pleasingly realistic sound, even if is not of DG's very finest.

Piano sonata No. 21 in B flat, D.960; 6 Moments musicaux, D.780.
(M) **(*) DG 453 674-2 [id.]. Daniel Barenboim.

To say that Barenboim gives a Kempff-like reading of Schubert's greatest sonata, D.960, is not to deny his characteristic individuality but to point out that his is a reflective, lyrical view of the work, marked by clean semi-quaver work and sharp dynamic contrasts. Yet the slightest sense of artifice is destructive in this composer, and Barenboim's delivery of the first movement's opening statement is just a shade self-conscious. The artless grace and Blake-like innocence of this idea do not quite come across here. The second movement is slow and concentrated, the Scherzo light and sparkling with a real sense of joy. The finale is sharpened with clear-cut contrasts, yet there is curious inelegance in the second subject, an obtrusive left-hand staccato at the end of the first half of the theme. In the *Moments musicaux* Barenboim's mood is often thoughtful and intimate; at other times we are made a shade too aware of the interpreter's art, and there is an element of calculation that robs the impact of freshness. The recording is excellent.

Choruses: *Chor der Engel, D.440; Das Dörfchen, D.598; Gesang der Geister über den Wassern, D.714; Glaub, Hoffnung und Liebe, D.954; Gondelfahrer, D.809; Jägerlied, D.201; Kantate für Irene Kiesewetter, D.936; Klage um Ali Bey, D.140; Lützows wilde Jagd, D.205; Die Nacht, D.983C; Die Nachtigall, D.724; 23rd Psalm, D.706;* (i) *92nd Psalm, D.953.*
(M) **(*) DG 453 679-2 [id.]. Austrian R. Ch., ORF SO (members), Gottfried Preinfalk, with (i) Rudolph Katzböck.

An enjoyable and well-planned programme of Schubert's shorter choral works, including the engaging *Song of the Spirits over the waters*, the *Jägerlied* and *Lützows wilde Jagd* (complete with horns) and a pair of fine Psalm settings. Sympathetic if not distinctive performances, flattered by the warm recording acoustic.

Mass No. 6 in E flat, D.950.
(M) **(*) DG Dig. 453 680-2 [id.]. Mattila, Lipovšek, Hadley, Pita, Holl, V. State Op. Ch., VPO, Abbado.

Abbado takes a spacious rather than a dramatic view of Schubert's most popular setting of the Mass, making the music look forward to Bruckner. This is quite unlike the performance from Bruno Weil on Sony (see below) but is intriguing in its way. With first-rate singing from soloists and chorus it is certainly stimulating, with well-balanced digital sound, but it would not be a prime choice.

Die schöne Müllerin, D.795; An die Musik; Du bist die Ruh; Erlkönig; Heidenröslein; Der Musensohn.
✿ (M) *** DG 453 676-2 [id.]. Dietrich Fischer-Dieskau, Gerald Moore.

With the transfer barely giving an indication of its analogue source back in 1972, Fischer-Dieskau's classic version of *Die schöne Müllerin* remains among the very finest ever recorded. Though he had made several earlier recordings, this is no mere repeat of previous triumphs, now combining his developed sense of drama and story-telling, his mature feeling for detail and yet spontaneity too, helped by the searching accompaniment of Gerald Moore. It is a performance with premonitions of *Winterreise*. With extra Lieder added to fill out the recital, this is now one of the most cherishable of Fischer-Dieskau's many superb Schubert CDs.

(i) *Schwanengesang, D.957;* (ii) *Ave Maria (Ellens Gesang III); Die Forelle; Gretchen am Spinnrade; Die Junge Nonne; Wiegenlied.*
(M) ** DG Analogue/Dig. 453 678-2 [id.]. (i) Hermann Prey, Leonard Hokanson; (ii) Gundula Janowitz, Irwin Gage.

Prey's recording of *Schwanengesang* was made live at a recital at the 1978 Hohenems Festival. It gains little in intensity from that and suffers from inevitable vocal shortcomings (the early songs a little cautious) and rather humdrum accompaniment. The other favourite songs, very well sung by Janowitz, make an attractive supplement.

Winterreise (complete).
(M) *** DG 453 677-2 [id.]. Dietrich Fischer-Dieskau, Daniel Barenboim.

Fischer-Dieskau's fifth recording of Schubert's greatest cycle, made in 1979, has the voice still in superb condition. Prompted by Barenboim's spontaneous-sounding, almost improvisatory accompaniments, it is highly inspirational. In expression this is freer than the earlier versions and, though some idiosyncratic details will not please everyone, the sense of concentrated development is irresistible. The recording is very natural and beautifully balanced. However, the last appearance of this version was on DG's bargain Classikon label, so the present reissue brings a price increase. In any case, first choice remains with either Fischer-Dieskau's early-1970s set with Gerald Moore (DG 415 187-2) or his later collaboration with Brendel, which produced an exceptionally moving performance, full of new insights (Ph. 411 463-2).

Decca '*Masterworks*'
(B) **(*) Decca Analogue/Dig. 452 389-2 (12) [id.].

As with their comparable Brahms compilation, Decca have delved into their back-catalogue to celebrate the bicentenary of Schubert's birth. For collectors understandably not willing to take the plunge into the contents of all 12 well-filled CDs, the music is all available separately in a series of Double Deccas.

Volume I: *Symphonies Nos.* (i; iii) *4 in C min. (Tragic), D.417; 5 in B flat, D.485;* (i; iv) *8 in B min. (Unfinished), D.759;* (ii; iv) *9 in C (Great), D.944;* (i; v) *Rosamunde: Overture (Die Zauberharfe); Entr'acte to Act III; Ballet music No. 2, D.797.*
(B) *** Decca Double 452 390-2 (2) [id.]. (i) VPO; (ii) LSO; (iii) Kertész; (iv) Krips; (v) Monteux.

Apart from a few extreme tempi – a fast minuet in No. 4, a fast first movement and a slow start to the second in No. 5 – the Kertész performances of the symphonies offer attractive, stylish Schubert playing. He does not always find the smile in Schubert's writing, but the playing of the Vienna Philharmonic is beyond reproach and the recordings are exemplary for their day (1970). Krips then directs an unforced, very satisfying account of the *Unfinished*, helped by excellent playing and good (1969) recording. However, this lacks some of the bite which even this symphony should have. The same conductor's reading of the *Great C major* is a different matter, one of the very finest performances of this much-recorded symphony ever put on record. It has a direct, unforced spontaneity which shows Krips's natural feeling for Schubertian lyricism at its most engaging. The playing is polished yet flexible, strong without ever sounding aggressive. The pointing of the trio in the Scherzo is delectable, and the feathery lightness of the triplets in the finale makes one positively welcome every single one of its many repetitions. As a whole, this reading represents the Viennese tradition at its very best. The early (1958) stereo sounds amazingly good, and the set is worth acquiring for this performance alone.

Volume II: (i) *Arpeggione sonata, D.821* (arr. for cello); (ii) *Fantasy in C, D.934;* (iii) *Octet, D.803;* (iii; iv) *Piano quintet in A (Trout), D.667.*
(B) **(*) Decca Double 452 393-2 (2) [id.]. (i) Rostropovich, Britten; (ii) Goldberg, Lupu; (iii) V. Octet; (iv) Curzon.

Even if Clifford Curzon's 1957 recording of the *Trout* sounds its age because of thin violin-timbre, it remains a classic performance in every respect. A similar comment might be made about the Vienna recording of the *Octet*, made in the Sofiensaal in the same year, which also has somewhat meagre violin-timbre. But the performance has the glow of the Vienna Octet at its peak under the leadership of Willi Boskovsky. The horn has a Viennese fruitiness, but that only makes the performance more authentic. The account of the *Fantasy in C* by Goldberg and Lupu has a comparable Schubertian freshness, and here the 1979 recording is first class, as it is in Rostropovich's account of the *Arpeggione sonata*, which is undoubtedly charismatic but very much more idiosyncratic.

Volume III: (i) *String quartets Nos. 12 (Quartettsatz);* (ii) *14 (Death and the Maiden);* (iii) *15 in G;* (i; iv) *String quintet in C, D.956.*
(B) **(*) Decca Double 452 396-2 (2) [id.]. (i) Weller Qt; (ii) VPO Qt; (iii) Gabrieli Qt; (iv) Gürtler.

In the *Death and the Maiden* the Vienna players' homogeneity is such that one hears one instrument rather than four, and one senses one mind rather than the four usually sympathetic minds of a great quartet. Admittedly Boskovsky, the first violinist, plays wonderfully in the variations, but he is *primus inter pares* for the greater part of the time. The tempi are generally excellent, and the slight but effective holding back of the Scherzo lends it a much more telling character. The *G major Quartet* is another of Schubert's most profound and searching utterances, and the Gabrieli players have its measure. Their performance is compelling from beginning to end, and it has genuine sensitivity and depth of feeling. The inspired *String quintet* and the remarkable *Quartettsatz* also brings fine playing by the Weller Quartet, though they are a trifle sweet and suave; other performances of the former are much more searching. The Decca engineers have achieved a natural balance and the most realistic quality of sound throughout.

Volume IV: (i) *Piano sonata No. 21, D.960;* (ii) *Fantasia in C (Wanderer), D.760;* (iii) *Impromptus Nos 1–4, D.899; 5–8, D.935; Moments musicaux 1–6, D.780.*
(B) **(*) Decca Double Analogue/Dig. 452 399-2 (2) [id.]. (i) Curzon; (ii) Ashkenazy; (iii) Schiff.

Not surprisingly, Curzon's is a memorable account of the *B flat Sonata*. Tempi are aptly judged, detail is finely drawn but never emphasized at the expense of the architecture as a whole, and the piano sounds very truthful in timbre. Ashkenazy gives a predictably fine account of the *Wanderer fantasy* but is let down somewhat by the clangorous recording. The *Impromptus* and *Moments musicaux*, however, as played most sympathetically by András Schiff, are most satisfactorily recorded and they laid the foundations for his Schubertian odyssey. The performances are idiomatic, intelligent and humane, and no one who has found satisfaction in Schiff's current survey of the sonatas will be disappointed by them.

Volume V: *Die schöne Müllerin, D.795; Winterreise, D.911; An die Laute, D.905; Der Einsame, D.800; Die Taubenpost, D.957/14.*
(B) **(*) Decca Double 452 402-2 (2) [id.]. Pears, Britten.

Schubert's darkest song-cycle, *Winterreise*, was in fact originally written for high, not low, voice; quite apart from the intensity and subtlety of the Pears/Britten version, it gains enormously from being at the right pitch throughout. When the message of these poems is so gloomy, a dark voice tends to underline the sombre aspect too oppressively, where the lightness of a tenor is even more affecting. That is particularly so in those songs in which the wandering poet in his despair observes triviality – as in the picture of the hurdy-gurdy man in the last song of all. What is so striking about the Pears performance is its intensity. One continually has the sense of a live occasion. As for Britten, he re-creates the music, sometimes with a fair freedom from Schubert's markings but always with scrupulous concern for the overall musical shaping and sense of atmosphere. The sprung rhythm of *Gefror'ne Tränen* is magical in creating the impression of frozen drops falling, and almost every song brings similar magic. Pears is imaginative too in *Die schöne Müllerin*, if for once in rather gritty voice; and Britten again brings a composer's insight to the accompaniments. Other versions provide more charm in this most sunny of song-cycles, but the Pears/Britten partnership remains uniquely valuable. The transfers of both cycles have fine presence and realism. However, *Winterreise* is still available separately at mid-price (Decca 417 423-2) and is even more recommendable in this form.

Volume VI: (i) *Masses Nos. 4 in C, D.452;* (ii) *5 in A flat, D.678;* (iii) *6 in E flat, D.950;* (iv) Part songs: *Christ ist erstanden, D.440; Gott meine Zuversicht (Psalm 23), D.706; Nachthelle, D.892; Ständchen, D.921.*
(B) ** Decca Double 452 405-2 (2) [id.]. (i) Bryn-Julson, Jan de Gaetani, Rolfe Johnson, King, L. Sinf. Ch. & O, Atherton; (ii) Eathorne, Greevy; (ii–iii) Evans, Keyte; (iii) Palmer, Watts, Bowen; (ii–iii) St John's College Ch., ASMF, Guest; (iv) Elizabethan Singers, Louis Halsey; Viola Tunnard (piano).

David Atherton's lively account of the last of Schubert's four early Masses, the *C major*, D.452, has refreshment to offer but is not noticeably inspired by any of the detailed sentiments of the liturgy. George Guest's performances of the two later Masses are faithful but lack the distinction which marked his recordings of the Haydn Masses on the same label; neither the singing nor the playing in the *A flat Mass* is in the least routine, but the music-making lacks a really individual profile. The *E flat Mass* is more successful: the freshness of the singing here (the chorus far more important than the soloists) and the resilient playing of the Academy make their mark when the mid-1970s (originally Argo) recording is also very fine. Nevertheless the current period performances under Bruno Weil find an added dimension in these richly rewarding masterpieces, and the singing and playing on Sony are little short of inspired (see below). The part songs, recorded much earlier in 1967, are splendidly sung, even if Helen Watts, the soloist in *Ständchen*, sounds just a little matronly; and it is difficult to imagine the musical listener not responding to them with the warmth of feeling that this open-hearted music inspires.

ORCHESTRAL MUSIC

(i–ii) *Konzertstück in D, D.345; Polonaise in B flat, D.580; Rondo in A, D.438;* (i; iii) *Rondo brillant in B min., D.895;* (iv) *Notturno in E flat, D.897.*
(M) *** Teldec/Warner Dig. 0630 14538-2 [id.]. (i) Zehetmair; (ii) Deutsche Kammerphilharmonie; (iii) David Levine; (iv) Haydn Trio.

This was the nearest Schubert came to writing a violin concerto. None of this music is ambitious but it all has a characteristic charm, especially when played with such a light touch. Indeed Zehetmair is the ideal soloist, sweet-toned and stylish. The engaging *Polonaise* is placed between the *Konzertstück* and *Rondo*, both with slow introductions. Zehetmair ably directs his own orchestral accompaniments; then comes the sparkling *Rondo brillant* for violin and piano in which David Levine is a fine partner. As the measure is short, Teldec have added on the *Notturno* for piano trio, most persuasively presented by the Haydn Trio of Vienna.

Symphonies Nos 1–6; 8 (Unfinished); 9 (Great).
*** RCA Dig. 09026 62673-2 (4) [id.]. Dresden State O, Sir Colin Davis.

Symphonies Nos. 1–6; 8–9; Grand Duo in C, D.812 (orch. Joachim); *Rosamunde overture (Die Zauberharfe), D.644.*
500♪ *** DG Dig. 423 651-2 (5) [id.]. COE, Abbado.

Symphonies Nos. 1–6; 8 (Unfinished); 9; Rosamunde: Overture (Die Zauberharfe) & ballet music.
(M) **(*) EMI CMS5 66114-2 (4) [CDMD 66114]. BPO, Karajan (with WEBER: *Der Freischütz: Overture* **(*)).

Symphonies Nos. 1 in D, D.82; 2 in B flat, D.125.
(M) **(*) EMI CDM5 66102-2 [id.]. BPO, Karajan (with WEBER: *Der Freischütz: Overture* **(*)).

Symphonies Nos. 3 in D, D.200; 4 in C min. (Tragic), D.417; Rosamunde: Ballet music 1–2.
(M) ** EMI CDM5 66103-2 [id.]. BPO, Karajan.

Symphonies Nos. 5 in B flat, D.485; 6 in C, D.589; Rosamunde: Overture (Die Zauberharfe), D.644.
(M) **(*) EMI CDM5 66104-2 [id.]. BPO, Karajan.

Symphonies Nos. 8 in B min. (Unfinished), D.759; 9 in C (Great), D.944.
(M) **(*) EMI CDM5 66105-2 [id.]. BPO, Karajan.

Abbado's is an outstanding set. Rarely has he made recordings of the central Viennese classics which find him so naturally sunny and warm in his expression. Speeds are often on the fast side but never feel breathless, and the recording is refined, with fine bloom on the string-sound. Textually too, the Abbado set takes precedence over its rivals and there are certain fascinating differences from what we are used to. The five CDs are now also available separately – see below.

Sir Colin Davis's Dresden cycle of the Schubert symphonies, neatly fitted on four discs (offered for the price of three) despite observing all repeats, is issued to celebrate the Schubert bicentenary in 1997. It makes a glowing tribute that regularly reveals Davis drawing magnetic and intense playing from the Dresden orchestra, with the polish of the ensemble adding to the impact, never making the results sound self-conscious. In the youthful symphonies, Nos. 1–3, Davis does not forget that these were written soon after Beethoven's *Seventh* and *Eighth*. For their time, both offer ambitiously extended arguments, and in some details Schubert seems to have learnt from both Beethoven works. So Schubert's marking of *Allegretto* for the slow movement of No. 3 clearly reflects Beethoven's similar marking for his second movements in both those symphonies. It follows that Davis refuses to regard these as merely elegantly Mozartian, but genuinely Schubertian, with romantic melodies naturally and affectionately drawn out.

In the middle symphonies Davis seems happier bringing out the elegance and charm, but then crowns the cycle with a radiant reading of the *Unfinished*, always warm but with an element of toughness, marked by high dynamic contrasts. In the *Great C major* Davis observes every repeat and, though the playing is as refined as in the rest of the cycle, the tensions are not quite so keen. All the same, this is a most distinguished cycle, helped by glowing sound, with the warm acoustic of the St Lukas Church adding to the weight and scale. Abbado's superb, keenly concentrated cycle with the COE still is not surpassed, using a smaller ensemble in a drier acoustic, but sunny and naturally warm in expression. But his set, which includes the *Grand Duo*, runs to five premium-priced discs and so costs considerably more. When the four Davis discs are made available separately, the first one (coupling Nos. 1, 3 and 8) will make an excellent and generous sampler. The Abbado series is already available on separate discs: Nos. 1–2 (DG 423 652-2); 3–4 (DG 423 653-2); 5–6 (423 654-2); the *Unfinished* and the *Grand Duo* (423 655-2) all highly recommendable, and the *Ninth* particularly so (423 656-2).

Karajan presents a most polished and beautiful set of Schubert symphonies. Now reissued as part of EMI's Karajan Edition, they were recorded in the latter part of the 1970s in the Philharmonie. The point and elegance of the Berliners' playing in the early symphonies is most persuasive, yet the results are never mannered. Undoubtedly many ears will react adversely to the reverberant acoustic for giving the impression of too large a band, one which rather lacks the brightness and transparency one associates with Schubert's songful writing; and the *Fourth Symphony*, the *Tragic*, finds Karajan less compelling. The *Unfinished*, dating from 1975, with Berlin refinement at its most ethereal, has an other-worldly quality, rapt and concentrated. The first movement is the original first take restored. There were technical problems with it and so Karajan re-recorded the movement a month later. Those problems have now been solved by the current re-mix, with excellent results. The *Great C major* (1977) is also compelling, but here some may find that the reverberant acoustic gives the impression of too much weightiness. But this is not a superficial reading: it has plenty of impetus and power, while the *Andante* has freshness too. The finale has undoubted thrust, although tuttis bring a degree of heaviness, caused as much by the sound itself as by the playing. The disc which includes the first two symphonies opens with a weightily dramatic performance of Weber's *Der Freischütz overture*, recorded digitally in 1981.

Symphonies Nos. 1 in D, D.82; 5 in B flat; Overture in the Italian style in D, D.590; Overture Des Teufels Lustschloss, D.84.
(M) *** Carlton Dig. 30367 01272 [id.]. E. Sinfonia, Sir Charles Groves.

This coupling of the *First* and *Fifth Symphonies* gets Groves's cycle off to an excellent start. First-movement allegros (exposition repeats included) have weight, yet rhythms are nicely sprung. Both *Andantes* are gracious and well paced, and the finale of No. 1 dances airily. The Minuet/Scherzo of No. 5 is particularly attractive; the Trio with its glowing horns flows agreeably. The two *Overtures* are a distinct asset: the piece in Italian style is relaxed and sunny, while the drama and pathos of *Des Teufels Lustschloss* ('The Devil's Pleasure Castle') are well caught with some fine, sonorous brass. It is the elegance and warmth of the orchestral playing which contribute so much to these performances, as does the first-rate Abbey Road recording, which has both body and glowing detail.

Symphonies Nos. 2 in B flat, D.125; 6 in C, D.589; Overture Die Zwillingsbrüder.
(M) ** Carlton Dig. 30367 01282 [id.]. E. Sinfonia, Sir Charles Groves.

Groves's account of the *Second Symphony* is alert and well played but a little plain. The finale (marked *Presto vivace*) is neatly articulated by the strings but is a bit too slow. The conductor readily shows his affection in No. 6, and he finds much of its charm. The Scherzo is pleasingly vigorous to offset the graceful finale but, heard alongside Boehm or Beecham, the playing here is less spontaneous in feeling. The overture brings some fine wind-playing but could be more spirited. Very good recording.

Symphonies Nos. 3 in D, D.200; 4 in C min. (Tragic), D.417; Overtures: Der häusliche Krieg, D.787; In the Italian style in C, D.591; Der Teufel als Hydraulicus, D.4.
(M) **(*) Carlton Dig. 30367 01292 [id.]. E. Sinfonia, Sir Charles Groves.

Groves is in good form in this extremely generous anthology. First movements are a little lacking in rhythmic point, but the *Allegretto* of No. 3 has plenty of charm and the *Andante* of the *Tragic* is gentle and gracious; both finales are vivaciously done. The two unknown overtures are a real bonus. *Der häusliche Krieg* (only rediscovered in the early 1960s) opens with an attractive horn chorale and later becomes quite jolly; *Der Teufel als Hydraulicus* is only half its length but is agreeable enough. It is the earliest of Schubert's orchestral works, written when the composer was fourteen. The *Italian overture* is also affectionately done.

Symphonies Nos. 3 in D, D.200; 5 in B flat, D.485; 6 in C, D.589.
500♪ ✽ (M) *** EMI CDM7 69750-2. RPO, Beecham.

Beecham's are magical performances in which every phrase breathes. There is no substitute for imaginative phrasing and each line is shaped with affection and spirit. The sound is now just a shade drier in Nos. 3 and 6 than in their last LP incarnation but is generally faithful and spacious. This is an indispensable record for all collections and a supreme bargain in the Schubert discography.

Symphonies Nos. 3 in D, D.200; 8 in B min. (Unfinished), D.759.
(M) **(*) DG Originals 449 745-2 [id.]. VPO, Carlos Kleiber.

Carlos Kleiber's 1979 Schubert coupling has been greatly admired in some quarters, so it is not surprising that DG have chosen it for reissue in their series of 'Originals'. Kleiber is certainly a refreshingly unpredictable conductor; sometimes, however, his imagination goes too far towards quirkiness, and that is certainly so in the slow movement of No. 3, which is rattled through jauntily at breakneck speed. The effect is bizarre even for an *Allegretto*, if quite charming. The Minuet too becomes a full-blooded Scherzo, and there is little rest in the outer movements. The *Unfinished* brings a more compelling performance, but there is unease in the first movement, where first and second subjects are not fully co-ordinated, the contrasts sounding a little forced. The recording brings out the brass sharply, and is of wide range.

Symphonies Nos. 5 in B flat, D.485; 8 in B min. (completed by Brian Newbold).
**(*) Virgin Veritas/EMI Dig. VER5 61305-2 [CDM 61305]. OAE, Mackerras.

Though not as magnetic as his account of No. 9, Mackerras's performance of No. 5 has comparable qualities of freshness and resilience. Tempi are only marginally brisker than traditional performances, and the slow movement has grace if not quite the degree of warmth that Boehm and Walter find. The special claims of the Veritas reissue is that the *'Unfinished' Symphony* is here heard as finished by Brian Newbold. However, although he uses the composer's music, the result cannot match the first two movements in dramatic intensity, a point emphasized by Mackerras's vibrantly powerful reading. He opens in the mysterious depths with the darkest *pianopianissimo*, and the plangent period timbres bring a real sense of *Sturm und Drang*, with powerful contrasts and strong, forceful accents in the second movement. Excellent recording. A stimulating coupling but not, perhaps, a first choice.

Symphonies Nos. 5 in B flat, D. 485; 8 in B min. (Unfinished), D. 759; 9 in C (Great), D. 944.
(B) *** Decca Double Dig. 448 927-2 (2) [id.]. VPO, Solti.

This Double Decca combining three favourite Schubert symphonies is one of the most attractive of all Solti's many reissues on the Decca label. There have been more charming versions of No. 5 but few that so beautifully combine freshness with refined polish. The *Unfinished* has Solti adopting measured speeds but with his refined manner keeping total concentration. The *Great C major Symphony* is an outstanding version, among the very finest, beautifully paced and sprung in all four movements, and superbly played. It has drama as well as lyrical feeling, but above all it has a natural sense of spontaneity and freshness. The recordings all confirm the Vienna Sofiensaal as an ideal recording location, and the glowing detail, especially in No. 9, is a source of consistent pleasure.

Symphony No. 8 in B min. (Unfinished), D.759.
500♪ ✿ (M) *** DG Dig. 445 514-2 [id.]. Philh. O, Sinopoli – MENDELSSOHN: *Symphony No. 4 (Italian).* ***

Sinopoli secures the most ravishingly refined and beautiful playing; the orchestral blend, particularly of the woodwind and horns, is magical. It is a deeply concentrated reading of the *Unfinished*, bringing out much unexpected detail, with every phrase freshly turned in seamless spontaneity.

Symphonies Nos. 8 in B min. (Unfinished); 9 in C (Great).
(B) *** RCA Twofer Dig. 09026 68314-2 (2) [id.]. BPO, Günter Wand.

In a two-disc format, two for the price of one, Günter Wand offers visionary performances of both works, superbly played in live Berlin performances and glowingly recorded. Wand's magnetism, the dedication he conveys, depends not on any self-consciously expressive gestures but on direct response to the music and to Schubert's detailed markings. Consistently he makes the playing sound spontaneous, even in the tricky problems of speed-changes in the *Great C major*. In the manner of his generation he does not observe exposition repeats in the outer movements or second-half repeats in the Scherzo, but this is a beautifully co-ordinated, strong and warm reading. The *Unfinished* is just as magnetic, again with no exaggeration, but with every interpretative problem solved as though it did not exist. An outstanding issue if you want this coupling.

Symphony No. 9 in C (Great).
500♪ (M) *** Virgin Veritas/EMI Dig. VER5 61245-2 [CDM 61245]. O of Age of Enlightenment, Mackerras.
500♪ (B) *** EMI forte CZS5 69364-2 (2) [id.]. Cleveland O, George Szell – BEETHOVEN: *Symphony No. 7* *** ✿; ROSSINI: *Overtures.* **(*)
(M) **(*) Ph. Dig. 442 646-2 [id.]. ASMF, Marriner.
(M) ** Carlton Dig. 30367 001162 [id.]. E. Sinfonia, Sir Charles Groves.

In the first recording to use period instruments, Sir Charles Mackerras and the Orchestra of the Age of Enlightenment on the Virgin Classics label give a winning performance, one that will delight both those who prefer conventional performance and devotees of the new authenticity. The characterful rasp and bite of period brass instruments and the crisp attack of timpani are much more striking than any thinness of string-tone. It is a performance of outstanding freshness and resilience.

Szell's Cleveland account was his second in stereo with that orchestra. It was made in Severance Hall by an EMI team led by Peter Andry and it has the hallmarks of an HMV recording from the beginning of the 1970s, with a wider dynamic range than Szell usually enjoyed and with better overall balancing. Szell's powerful reading provides a reminder that the parallels between him and another great disciplinarian conductor, Toscanini, were sometimes significant. Szell's approach is similarly direct, but lyrical feeling underlies the surface brightness and the crisply sprung rhythms are exhilarating. But it is in the hectic triplets of the finale that the orchestra is unmatched in precision, with a sparkling lightness of articulation that is a joy to the ear.

Taken from his collected edition of Schubert symphonies, Sir Neville Marriner's account of the *Great C major* makes up for any lack of weight with the fresh resilience of the playing, consistently well sprung. All repeats are observed, bringing the timing of the *Symphony* to over an hour; however, the fill-up offered with the full-priced issue (a two-movement fragment, D.615, written just after the *Sixth Symphony* and orchestrated by Brian Newbold) has now been omitted and, although the recording is first rate, this makes the present reissue distinctly less tempting in a competitive market-place.

Groves gives a straightforward, direct account of Schubert's *Ninth*, negotiating the tempo changes confidently and maintaining a strong lyrical flow. The English Sinfonia play well for him but, although the finale goes well, the reading as a whole has no special insights to offer; there are more gripping versions available. Excellent recording.

CHAMBER MUSIC

Arpeggione sonata in A min., D.821; Cello sonatinas Nos. 1–3, D.384–5 & D.408.
*** Channel Classics Dig. CCS 9696 [id.]. Pieter Wispelwey, Paolo Giacometti.

The simple charms of Schubert's *Arpeggione sonata* are often elusive, but not here. The highly musical Pieter Wispelwey has the full measure of Schubert's innocent lyricism, and the pianist's light touch in the finale is especially persuasive. Indeed Paolo Giacometti makes one of the most convincing cases for the use of the fortepiano in Schubert that we have yet encountered, and the restored instrument itself, originally built by Salvatore Lagrassa around 1815, has a remarkable range of colour. So often a fortepiano is desperately lacking in sonority – and, indeed, any kind of timbre at all – but Signor Lagrassa obviously knew a thing or two about creating a sunny palette. Pieter Wispelwey's tone, using gut strings, always sings and, even using a minimum of vibrato, he constantly cajoles the ear, while his phrasing has an appealing simplicity. Thus the three violin *Sonatinas* are made to sound convincing in these cello transcriptions, especially the *G minor*, D.408, in which the *Andante* and finale are endearing. The recording is forwardly but truthfully balanced. Recommended.

Arpeggione sonata in A min., D.821. Songs arr. Maisky: *Die schöne Müllerin, D.795: Der Neugierige; Der Müller und der Bach. Winterreise, D.911: Tauschung; Der Leiermann. Schwanengesang, D.957: Ständchen; Am Meer. Allerseelen; An die Musik; Du bist die Ruh; Der Einsame; Die Forelle; Heidenröslein; Litanei auf das Fest; Nacht und Träume; Nur wer die Sehnsucht kennt.*
** DG Dig. 449 817-2 [id.]. Mischa Maisky, Daria Hovora.

Mischa Maisky complements his recording of the *Arpeggione sonata* with the musical – if reticent – Daria Hovora as partner, with a dozen or more transcriptions for cello of Schubert songs. Maisky has already recorded the *Arpeggione* with Martha Argerich on Philips, coupling it with the Schumann *Fantaisiestücken* (see our main volume) and it is difficult to understand why he should want to re-record it so soon, particularly as that version is so good. Readers wanting this work should acquire Pieter Wispelwey (see above) or the Maisky–Argerich disc (412 230-2) or consider the Rostropovich–Britten version on Decca (443 575-2). In the song transcriptions he is mellifluous and highly professional. His beauty of tone is not in question, but his all-purpose expressiveness which at times becomes gushing is less pleasing. In his bicentenary year Schubert deserves something better than this.

Duo sonata (for violin and piano) *in A, D.574; Fantasy in C, D.934; Rondo in B min., D.895.*
** Nimbus Dig. NI 5044 [id.]. Thomas Brandis, Bruno Canino.

None of these works is generously represented in the current catalogue at present, and all have moments of charm and indeed sublimity. The performances here are persuasive and intelligent, but they are recorded in a reverberant acoustic and the microphones appear to be too close to the violin so that, although this is not a period performance, Brandis's tone sounds edgy. In the end this effect tires the ear, although authenticists might not be too disturbed.

Octet in F, D.803.
(M) *** Teldec/Warner Dig. 0630 14543-2 [id.]. Berlin Soloists.
(B) * Sony Dig. SBK 62655; *SBT 62655* [id.]. Cleveland Octet.

(i) *Octet in F;* (ii) *Minuet and Finale in F for wind octet, D.72.*
500♪ ❁ (B) *** Decca Eclipse Dig. 448 715-2; *448 715-4* [id.]. (i) Vienna Octet; (ii) Vienna Wind Soloists.

As a companion disc to their equally delectable version of the Beethoven *Septet*, the Vienna Octet give a gloriously warm-hearted and sparkling account of Schubert's *Octet*. This is quite irresistible, and the two charming miniatures from Schubert's youth make a delightful encore. Demonstration sound-quality and the lowest possible price take this straight to the top of the list.

The Berlin Soloists give a strong and stylish performance which, on a bigger scale than most, designedly brings out the symphonic power of a piece lasting over an hour. Every single repeat is observed and, with such distinguished playing, that length is readily sustained. This is very well characterized, not just in the big, symphonic movements but in the charming *Andante variations* too. Though the sound is not always ideally sweet on string-tone, the recording is full and clear, and at mid-price this remains competitive, despite the bare minimum of documentation included.

The Sony Cleveland digital version, although polished, is a non-starter. The balance is close, which does not flatter the violins in the opening movement. The following *Adagio* is sluggish and the performance is entirely lacking in the feeling of joy and high spirits which characterize this delightful work. Even the finale fails to take off.

Piano quintet in A (Trout) D.667.
500♪ *** Decca Dig. 411 975-2 [id.]. András Schiff, Hagen Qt.
(BB) *** Belart 450 056-2. Ingrid Haebler, Arthur Grumiaux, Georges Janzer, Eva Czako, Bernard Cazauran – MOZART: *Clarinet quintet.* **(*)
(B) **(*) Hyperion Dyad Dig. CDD 22008 (2) [id.]. Schubert Ens. of L. – HUMMEL: *Piano quintet;* SCHUMANN: *Piano quintet; Piano quartet.* **(*)

András Schiff and the Hagen Quartet give a delectably fresh and youthful reading of the *Trout quintet*, full of the joys of spring, but one which is also remarkable for hushed concentration, as in the exceptionally dark and intense account of the opening of the first movement. The Scherzo brings a light, quick and bouncing performance, and there is extra lightness too in the other middle movements. Alongside Brendel (but no other current rivals), this version observes the exposition repeat in the finale, and with such a joyful, brightly pointed performance one welcomes that.

There is some admirably unassertive and deeply musical playing from Miss Haebler and from the incomparable Grumiaux. These artists do not try to make 'interpretative points' but are content to let the music speak for itself. The quality of the recorded sound is good. Recoupled with Jack Brymer's beguilingly leisurely account of the *Clarinet quintet*, this makes a genuine bargain on Polygram's Belart label.

A lively, immediate account from the Schubert Ensemble of London, strongly led by the pianist, William Howard. The first movement is brisk but committed, and the famous variations are well characterized. There are more touching accounts on record but few more vivaciously spontaneous, with a vivid recording to match.

(i) *Piano quintet in A (Trout), D.667. String quartet No. 14 in D min. (Death and the Maiden), D.810.*
(M) **(*) DG Originals 449 746-2 [id.]. Amadeus Qt, with (i) Gilels, Zepperitz.

In the 1975 recording of the *Trout* there is a masterly contribution from Gilels, and the Amadeus play with considerable freshness. The approach is very positive, not as sunny and spring-like as in some versions, but rewarding in its seriousness of purpose. The recording balance is convincing and the remastering creates a firm and vivid sound-image. The Amadeus's account of the *Death and the Maiden quartet* was their first analogue recording of this work in 1959. The unanimity of ensemble is remarkable. The quartet play as one in dealing with the finer points of phrasing, for example at the very beginning of the variations. The early DG stereo, too, is commendable. But, although one cannot fault these players' sensitivity to Schubertian line and nuance, in the last resort this performance has not the depth of the very finest versions.

(i) *Piano quintet in A (Trout), D. 667. String quartets Nos. 13 in A min., D.804; 14 in D min. (Death and the Maiden), D.810; 15 in G, D.887;* (ii) *String quintet in C, D.956.*
(M) ** EMI CMS5 66144-2 (4) [CDMD 66144]. Alban Berg Qt, with (i) Leonskaja, Hörtnagel; (ii) Heinrich Schiff.

Compilations of this kind always bring the inherent danger that a single performance may be much less successful than the rest and so reduce the appeal of the set as a whole. If EMI had included just the string works here, this box would have been very attractive. But the *Trout* (in which the quartet are joined by Elisabeth Leonskaja and Georg Hörtnagel) brings the keenest disappointment. Despite the excellence of the recording and some incidental beauties, it remains a curiously uninvolving performance with routine gestures. There is little real freshness here and Leonskaja's playing is not rich in sensitivity or in variety of colour.

The *A minor Quartet*, however, is beautifully managed, though the slow movement (with the theme of the *Rosamunde Entr'acte*) is very fast indeed. The exposition repeat is omitted in the first movement of *Death and the Maiden* but otherwise this, too, is a very impressive performance. The playing is breathtaking in terms of tonal blend, ensemble and intonation throughout both these works; if at times one is not always totally involved (except perhaps in the Minuet and Trio of the *A minor*) there is much to relish and admire. In the *G major* the Alban Berg players are most dramatic. Indeed they tend to over-dramatize: pianissimos are the barest whisper and ensemble has razor-edged precision. Yet again they do not observe the exposition repeat in the first movement. They are strikingly well recorded, however, and beautifully balanced; but the sense of over-projection somehow disturbs the innocence of some passages.

In the great *C major Quintet*, where they are joined by Heinrich Schiff, they produce a timbre which is richly burnished and full-bodied. Once more there is no first-movement exposition repeat, but theirs is still a most satisfying account, strongly projected throughout. Given the sheer polish and gorgeous sound that distinguishes such playing, this account ranks high among current recommendations and the recording is admirable. But as a collection this must be approached with some caution.

(i) *Piano quintet in A (Trout);* (ii) *String quartet No. 14 in D min. (Death and the Maiden), D.810.*
(M) *** Ph. 442 656-2 [id.]. (i) Beaux Arts Trio with Samuel Rhodes & Georg Hörtnagel; (ii) Italian Qt.

From the augmented Beaux Arts Trio comes one of the most delightful and fresh *Trouts* now available. Every phrase is splendidly alive, there is no want of vitality and sensitivity, and a finely judged balance and truthful (1976) recording make it a most desirable version. The Italian Quartet's version of the *Death and the Maiden* dates from a decade earlier, but the recording was first class in its day, and this sounds every bit as good as the *Trout*. The performance remains one of the finest available. The slow movement is particularly eloquent, showing a notable grip in the closing pages.

Piano trios Nos. 1 in B flat, D.898; 2 in E flat, D.929.
**(*) Sony Dig. SK 62695 [id.]. Jos van Immersel, Vera Beths, Anner Bylsma.

Piano trios Nos. 1–2; Adagio in E flat ('Notturno') (for piano trio), *D.897; Sonata in B flat* (for piano trio), *D.28.*
(M) *** Teldec/Warner Dig. 0630 12337-2 (2) [id.]. Haydn Trio of Vienna.
**(*) Teldec/Warner 4509 94558-2 (2) [id.]. Trio Fontenay.

(i) *Piano trios Nos. 1–2; Adagio in E flat ('Notturno')* (for piano trio), *D.897; Sonata in B flat* (for piano trio), *D.28;* (ii) *String trios: in B flat* (in one movement), *D.471; in B flat, D.581.*
500♪ (B) *** Ph. Duo 438 700-2 (2) [id.]. (i) Beaux Arts Trio; (ii) Grumiaux Trio.

The Beaux Arts set of the Schubert *Piano trios* from the late 1960s is another of the extraordinary bargains now offered on the Philips Duo label. The performances provide impeccable ensemble with the pianist, Menahem Pressler, always sharply imaginative and the cellist, Bernard Greenhouse, bringing simple dedication to such key passages as the great slow-movement melody of the *Trio No. 2 in E flat*. The *Notturno*, played here with great eloquence, recalls the rapt, hushed intensity of the glorious slow movement of the *String quintet*. What makes the set doubly attractive is the inclusion of the two much rarer *String trios*, also early works from 1816/17. Given such persuasive advocacy, both pieces cannot fail to make a strong impression.

The Haydn Trio of Vienna are a highly musical and well-integrated group who undoubtedly are at one with the Schubertian spirit. Their playing is full of vigour and their characterization is strong and often robust, yet with a balancing intimacy. Both slow movements are beautifully yet simply played and the cellist, Walter Schulz, is not wanting in the *Andante* of D.929, while the Scherzo which follows sparkles lightly as it should: here the excellent pianist, Heinz Medjimorec, is delectably nimble. In the *Notturno* the contrast is very marked between the hushed opening and the assertive middle section. With excellent, well-balanced, modern digital recording this stands high among current lower-priced recommendations, although one regrets that the accompanying documentation is inadequate.

There are many felicities of detail in the performances from the Trio Fontenay and their affectionate lyricism certainly does not lack warmth. But at times they over-dramatize and at others there is a feeling that phrasing is somewhat indulgent, as for instance with Niklas Schmidt's beautifully timbred yet almost sensuous cello solo in the *Andante* of the *B flat Trio*. The rapt opening of the *Notturno* needs a greater feeling of Schubertian innocence: a serenity without too much *espressivo*. The first movement of the *B flat Trio* certainly has a strong impulse (some may think it almost goes over the top) and the Scherzo is treated as an opportunity for extrovert virtuosity. Excellent recording, but these performances lack the springlike freshness of the competing Viennese group, or indeed the famous Beaux Arts set on Philips.

Those wanting period performances of the Schubert *Piano trios* will not find Immersel, Beths and Bylsma lacking in character, although textures are lean and the approach is less strong on charm than it is on vigour and drama. There could be more lyrical give-and-take in the slow movement of the *B flat Trio*; however, there is nicely judged delicacy of feeling and plenty of concentration for the delightful *Andante con moto* slow movement of the *E flat Trio*, and the Scherzo which follows has an attractively light touch (as indeed does the Scherzo of D.898). The recording is well balanced and realistic.

Piano trio No. 1 in B flat, D.898.
(B) *** EMI forte CZS5 69367-2 (2). David Oistrakh, Sviatoslav Knushevitzky, Lev Oborin – BEETHOVEN: *Archduke trio* ***; BRAHMS: *Violin sonatas Nos. 1–2.* **(*)

Schubert's music needs warmth and humanity, and this well-integrated Russian team on the bargain forte reissue give both these qualities in abundance. They strive for beauty of tone and accuracy of ensemble (both of which they achieve with apparent ease) and imbue the music with just that essence of clarity and warmth that it demands by right. The tempi are extremely sensible, and in more than one way sensitive, and the Scherzo is handled in masterly fashion by all three players. Excellent piano-tone and a good round sound from the strings. The encores are beautifully played and, if the couplings are suitable, this makes a fine bargain.

String quartets

String quartets Nos. 1 in G min., D.18; 13 in A min., D.804; Overture in B flat (fragment), *D.470.*
*** MDG Dig. MDG 307 0602-2 [id.]. New Leipzig Qt.

String quartets Nos. 5 in B flat, D.68; 10 in E flat, D.87; in C min. (fragment), *D.103.*
*** MDG Dig. MDG 307 0605-5 [id.]. New Leipzig Qt.

String quartets Nos. 6 in C, D.74; 8 in B flat, D.112; in B flat (fragment), *D.470.*
*** MDG Dig. MDG 307 0606-5 [id.]. New Leipzig Qt.

String quartet No. 14 in D min. (Death and the Maiden), D.810; Minuet, D.86; Minuets and German dances, D.89.
*** MDG Dig. MDG 307 0604-2 [id.]. New Leipzig Qt.

String quartet No. 15 in G, D.887; Fragment, D.2c; String trio, D.472.
*** MDG Dig. MDG 307 0601-2 [id.]. New Leipzig Qt.

(i) *String quintet in C, D.956. Fragment, D.3; Overture, D.8a.*
*** MDG Dig. MDG 307 0603-2 [id.]. (i) Michael Sanderling; New Leipzig Qt.

The New Leipzig Quartet offer an ideal approach. They have great sweetness of tone, like the post-war Barylli Quartet, yet they are not sugary; they give us a wide dynamic range without drawing attention to themselves, and they seem totally inside the Schubert tradition. They have much greater warmth than the Melos of Stuttgart on DG and are far removed from the overpowering jet-setting quartet-machines which are so admired these days. Theirs is humane music-making which conveys some sense of period and naturalness of expression. The *Quintet* may not be as intense as some versions but it is still very rewarding. The recordings are very good and the set has the merit of including various less familiar fragments. A thoroughly musical and well-recorded series.

String quartets Nos. 9 in G min., D.173; 13 in A min., D.804.
(M) **(*) Teldec/Warner 0630 13575-2 [id.]. Alban Berg Qt.

The Alban Berg Quartet add to their laurels in this 1975 Schubert coupling, with more superb playing, finely integrated ensemble matched to genuine depth of feeling. The *A minor Quartet* has its slow movement based on Schubert's famous '*Rosamunde*' melody, and the eloquence of the playing here is gloriously natural and unforced. The *Andantino* of the *G minor* is also memorably done, and the crisp articulation in the finale is a joy. The recording was admirably balanced, but the slight snag is that the CD transfer has added an edge to the quartet's strong attack, which is immediately noticeable in the opening movement of the *A minor*, which comes first on the record. Some ears will adjust to this, but it brings a degree of aggressiveness to the playing.

String quartets Nos. 10 (7) in E flat, D.87; 13 in A min., D.804.
❀ *** Audivis Astrée Dig. E 8580 [id.]. Mosaïques Qt.

The splendid period-instrument Mosaïques Quartet, having been hugely successful in Haydn and highly rewarding in Mozart, now move on to Schubert with equally impressive results. Above all these performances, so notable for their points of closely observed detail, are highly spontaneous. The very opening of the *E flat Quartet* (published posthumously as No. 10, but actually the seventh in order of composition, and written in 1816) is warmly inviting, and the players have the full measure of the songful serenity of its lovely *Adagio*. The profundities of the *A minor* are fully understood by this highly sensitive group: the first-movement exposition repeat is observed and the recapitulation is particularly memorable. There is dramatic intensity as well as charm in the famous ('*Rosamunde*') *Andante*, and the subtleties of the highly original Minuet are nicely caught, with the finale following gracefully: the delicacy of the shading of the playing here is a marvel. A superb disc, beautifully recorded.

String quartets Nos. 12 in C min. (Quartettsatz), D.703; 13 in A min., D.804; 14 in D min. (Death and the Maiden); 15 in G, D.887.
500♪ ❁ (B) *** Ph. Duo 446 163-2 (2) [id.]. Italian Qt.

The Italian Quartet's 1965 coupling of the *Quartettsatz* and the *Death and the Maiden quartet* was counted the finest available in its day, with the famous variations played with great imagination and showing a notable grip in the closing pages. These players' understanding of Schubert is equally reflected in their performance of the *A minor Quartet*, recorded a decade later. The familiar '*Rosamunde*' slow movement is beautifully paced. The 1976 sound, too, is first class. The *G major Quartet* is, if anything, even finer. The 1977 recording still sounds remarkably real and present.

String quartets Nos. 12–15; (i) *String quintet in C, D. 956.*
(M) *** Nimbus Dig. NI 1770 [id.]. Brandis Qt, (i) with W.-S. Yang.

This is a first-class set in every way and an excellent recommendation for those wanting digital recordings of the late *Quartets* plus the *Quintet* in a mid-priced box. The Brandis Quartet, a fine Central European group, have warmth and they bring a natural eloquence to all these quartets which are all the more potent for being free of interpretative point-making. In the great *C major Quintet*, with beautiful matching, they again convey spontaneous expressiveness, and they are not afraid to linger a little over the first movement's lovely second-subject melody. Their slow movement, played freely, has rapt tension but, again, also conveys warmth, rather an ethereal, withdrawn atmosphere which communicates in a quite individual way. They are very naturally recorded.

String quartet No. 15 in G, D.887; (i) *Notturno for piano trio, D. 897.*
*** Decca Dig. 452 854-2 [id.]. Takács Qt, (i) with Andreas Haefliger.

As in their performance of the *String quintet* (Decca 436 324-2), the Takács Quartet play very freely, using the widest range of dynamic, with the leader often dropping to a withdrawn pianissimo with seeming spontaneity, so that the result does not seem mannered or self-conscious. The opening of the *Andante* brings the most delicate entry from the cello, gentle and restrained, and the Scherzo, too, opens with a gossamer touch, although the finale dances with joyful vigour. In the *Notturno* Andreas Haefliger weaves his piano figurations with comparable finesse. The top-quality recording has fine presence, yet the quartet image is set slightly back.

String quintet in C, D.956.
(B) (***) Millennium mono MCD 80124 [id.]. V. Konzerthaus Qt.
** HM Dig. HMC 901494 [id.]. Melos Qt, Wolfgang Boettcher.
** DG Dig. 439 774-2 [id.]. Hagen Qt, Heinrich Schiff (with BEETHOVEN: *Grosse Fuge* ***).
** Sony Dig. SK 53983 [id.]. Stern, Lin, Laredo, Ma, Robinson – BOCCHERINI: *String quintet in E.* **(*)

The Vienna Konzerthaus Quartet are right inside this music and they give a simple, direct and refreshingly unexaggerated reading of great appeal. There is real tension here, and it is a pity that the early recording-balance prevents a real pianissimo registering in the slow movement where there is no lack of intensity; otherwise the sound is excellent and, even as it stands, this is a most rewarding version.

Finely blended timbre, strikingly sweet and smooth on top, from the Melos group. In the first movement they are a shade too dulcet for music which has great underlying tensions, but they certainly achieve a rapt pianissimo in the *Adagio*, although later the playing seems a shade too bitingly vehement, if not as aggressive-seeming as the Hagen version.

The Hagen Quartet play with great concentration and immaculate ensemble. They are obviously highly involved, yet they seriously overdramatize the music, especially in the matter of exaggerated dynamic contrast, which spoils the effect of the hushed pianissimo they achieve in the *Adagio*. The coupled *Grosse Fuge* of Beethoven is superbly done, but this Schubert performance is not comfortable to live with.

Isaac Stern and his colleagues certainly find plenty of energy for their performance of the great *C major String quintet*, particularly in the Scherzo, but the rapt concentration of pianissimo playing which is so necessary to capture the work's special magic, particularly in the slow movement, eludes them; this is simply a strong, well-played performance, rather too closely balanced. First choice among modern recordings of this extraordinary work still rests with the Lindsay Quartet (ASV CDDCA 537), although the Cleveland Quartet's version (to which Ma also contributes) offers a strong challenge at mid-price (Sony SMK 39134). Both these are digital with the obvious advantage of a silent background, but we also have a special affection for the much older, analogue Saga version by the augmented Aeolian Quartet, where the playing brings hushed pianissimos of the most intense beauty (EC 3368-2).

Violin sonatinas Nos. 1–3; Rondo in B min. (Rondeau brillant), D.895; Duo in A (Grand duo), D.574; Fantasie in C, D.934.
(M) *** Sony Stern Edition IV Dig./Analogue SM2K 64528 (2) [id.]. Isaac Stern, Daniel Barenboim (with: HAYDN: *Violin concerto in C, Hob VIIa/1* with Chamber O **).

It is good to have these 1988 Stern recordings reissued at mid-price in time for the bicentenary. The performances have a natural warmth and plenty of character, yet there is an unaffected simplicity and directness of style which suits the three early *Sonatinas*, written in 1816 but not published until two decades later. One has only to sample the *Andante* of the *G minor*, D.408, or the sturdy opening of the *Allegro* of the *Rondo brillant* to appreciate the affinity these artists have with Schubert's muse. The *Grand duo* (the title was invented by Diabelli for the work's posthumous publication) dates from little more than a year later, but both artists provide the necessary added flair (especially in the Scherzo) for this rather more ambitious piece. The gentle, mysterious opening of the *Fantasie* is superbly caught and the lilting *Allegretto* makes a perfect foil for the songful *Andantino* (which readily takes wing on Stern's bow). The finale is a joy. The Haydn *Concerto*, excellently recorded in mono in 1947, is a very acceptable bonus. Stern directs the work himself and the highlight of the performance is his touching account of the *Adagio*, although the accompanying guitar-like orchestral pizzicatos could ideally have had a lighter touch. A superb set just the same.

PIANO MUSIC

Piano music for four hands

Andantino varié in B min., D.823; Duo in A min., D.947; Fantasia in F min., D.940; Grand duo sonata in C, D.812; 3 Marches militaires, D.733; 6 Polonaises, D.824; Rondo in A, D.951; Variations on an original theme in A flat, D.813.
500♪ (M) *** Erato/Warner 0630 11231-2 (2). Anne Queffélec & Imogen Cooper.

It is good to have a thoroughly recommendable mid-priced set of Schubert's music for piano/four hands, including the greatest work ever written for the genre, the *F minor Fantasia*. The slighter pieces also come off well: the *Variations* are beautifully played and have an engaging innocence, while the most famous *Marche militaire* sparkles. The 1978 analogue recording is well balanced, clear and natural, the acoustic neither over-reverberant nor too confined.

Solo piano music

(i) *Allegretto in C min., D.915; 12 German dances, D.790;* (ii) *Impromptus Nos. 1–4, D.899; 5–8, D.935;* (i) *3 Klavierstücke, D.946;* (iii) *6 Moments musicaux, D.780; 12 Valses nobles, D.969.*
(B) ** EMI CZS5 69561 (2) [CDZB 69561]. (i) Cyprien Katsaris; (ii) Agustin Anievas; (iii) Andor Foldès.

It is very tempting for record companies to use more than one artist when compiling a back-catalogue, two-disc recital, but the results too often are of varying calibre; so it is here in this otherwise generous and well-planned programme.

Agustin Anievas opens the collection with the first *C minor Impromptu* of D.899, playing dramatically and with poise, and his digital dexterity in the following *E flat major* is impressive; but there is no Schubertian coaxing until the glorious *G flat* work, and he makes less than he might of the striding theme which underlies the following piece in A flat. The tendency for the otherwise truthful Abbey Road 1976 recording to harden in *fortes* is not helpful. In short, this playing is fresh but not touched with real distinction, although the simplicity of presentation of the second set, D.935, is quite appealing. When one turns to Cyprien Katsaris for the *Allegretto* and three late *Klavierstücke*, the playing is much more penetrating, while the charming *German dances* bring an agreeably lighter touch. Not surprisingly, Andor Foldès's set of the six *Moments musicaux* has much Schubertian lyrical feeling, besides offering the most realistic recording (made in Berlin earlier in the decade).

Fantasia in C (Wanderer), D.760; Andante in A, D.604; Allegretto in C min., D.915; 3 Klavierstücke (Impromptus), D.946; Scherzo in B flat, D.593/1; 13 Variations on a theme by Anselm Hüttenbrenner in A min., D.576.
(M) *** DG 453 289-2 [id.]. Wilhelm Kempff.

Although there is no lack of strength in the *Wanderer fantasia*, the high drama which such a pianist as Sviatoslav Richter finds is missing; but the result with Kempff is equally compelling, with a moulding of the structure which gives the illusion of spontaneity. Kempff then injects all his habitual magic into the other often deceptively simple pieces. His playing is utterly disarming in the second of the three *Klavierstücke*, which were written in the last year of Schubert's life, easy, happy inspirations that wear greatness easily. The *Andante* and *Allegretto* are engaging too, and the *Scherzo* hops along winningly, more like a Laendler, while the *Hüttenbrenner variations* (echoes here of the *Allegretto* of Beethoven's *Seventh Symphony*) are more decoratively insubstantial; but whatever the tone of Schubert's voice, Kempff's crystal touch and natural intensity make for pure delight. Excellent analogue recording (from 1967–71) naturally transferred.

Fantasia in C (Wanderer), D.760; Impromptus, D.899; Impromptus, D.935; 3 Klavierstücke, D.946; Moments musicaux, D.780.
(*) Hyperion Dig. CDA 67091/2 (2) [id.]. Nikolai Demidenko.

There is little of the sublime or of the grace with which Schubert is so abundantly endowed in Nikolai Demidenko's recital. It goes without saying that there are some felicitous touches, as one would expect from so intelligent a player, but they are relatively few. There is much more that is prosaic and penny-plain. Given the abundant alternatives from such eminent Schubertians as Perahia, Lupu and Brendel, listed below and in our main volume, among whom it is difficult to choose, there is little here that need detain us. The Hyperion recording is first rate.

Fantasia in C (Wanderer), D.760; Impromptus, D.899/3 & 4; Piano sonata No. 21 in B flat, D.960.
500♪ ❁ *** RCA RD 86257 [RCA 6257-2-RC]. Artur Rubinstein.

Rubinstein plays the *Wanderer fantasia* with sure magnificence and, particularly in the variations section, he is electrifying. The two *Impromptus* are played with the most subtle shading of colour and delectable control of rubato, and the superb account of the *Sonata* shows Rubinstein as a magically persuasive Schubertian. The 1965 sound is remarkably real, with fine presence and little shallowness.

Impromptus Nos. 1–4, D.899; 5–8, D.935.
500♪ *** Sony Dig. SK 37291 [id.]. Murray Perahia.

Perahia's account of the *Impromptus* is very special indeed and falls barely short of greatness. Directness of utterance and purity of spirit are of the essence here. The CBS recording is very good, truthful in timbre.

Impromptus Nos. 1–4, D.899; 5–8, D.935; 3 Klavierstücke (Impromptus), D. 946; 6 Moments musicaux, D.780; 12 German dances, D.790; 16 German dances, D.783.
❁ (B) *** Ph. Duo 456 061-2 (2) [id.]. Alfred Brendel.

Brendel's analogue set of the *Impromptus* is magical, and the *Moments musicaux* are among the most poetic in the catalogue.It is difficult to imagine finer Schubert playing than this; to find more eloquence, more profound musical insights, one has to go back to Edwin Fischer – and even here comparison is not always to Brendel's disadvantage. The *Klavierstücke* are searching, with Brendel going even deeper than in his earlier recording on Turnabout, and in his hands the *German dances*, although retaining their underlying charm, sound anything but trivial. The recordings date from the early 1970s and offer Philips's very finest analogue quality; the remastering is expert and the focus is very slightly cleaner, without any loss of bloom.

Piano sonatas

Piano sonatas Nos. 1 in E, D.157; 2 in C, D.279; 3 in E, D.459; 4 in A min., D.537; 5 in A flat, D.557; 6 in E min., D.566; 7 in E flat, D.568; 9 in B, D.575; 11 in F min., D.625; 13 in A, D.664; 14 in A min., D.784; 15 in C, D.840 (Relique); 16 in A min., D.845; 17 in D, D.850; 18 in G, D.894; 19 in C min., D.958; 20 in A, D.959; 21 in B flat, D.960.
500♪ (M) *** DG 423 496-2 (7) [id.]. Wilhelm Kempff.
(M) *** Decca Dig. 448 390-2 (7) [id.]. András Schiff.

Wilhelm Kempff's cycle was recorded over a four-year period (1965–9). DG has now collected the sonatas into a seven-CD box and those wanting a comprehensive survey of this repertoire need look no further. There is no individual overview of the whole cycle that has been musically as consistently satisfying as Kempff's. The recordings are not state of the art (there is an occasional hint of shallowness) but they are very acceptable indeed and there is a wisdom about his playing which puts it in a special category.

With the collection (like Kempff's survey) including the *First Sonata*, D.157 (written when the composer was eighteen), and also the fragment of the *Eighth* (which Kempff omits), Schiff sets the seal on his seven-CD survey for Decca which has excited golden opinions. In his note he calls them 'among the most sublime contributions written for the piano' – and he plays them as if they are, too. Schiff has some distinguished rivals and the complete set from Kempff remains very special indeed – Kempff has never been surpassed in the great *B flat Sonata*. Yet Schiff's is a survey that blends pianistic finesse with keen human insights. He has a good feeling for the architecture of these pieces and he invests detail with just the right amount of feeling. The modern, digital recordings, made in the Brahms-Saal of the Musikverein in Vienna, are eminently satisfactory. Readers considering adding a new cycle to their collections need have no serious qualms about starting here, especially with the CDs conveniently packaged in a mid-priced box. They are still available separately at full price.

Piano sonatas, Vol. 1: *Nos. 3 in E, D.459; 5 in A flat, D.557; 18 in G, D.894.*
(M) *** EMI Eminence Dig. CD-EMX 2279 [id.]. Martino Tirimo.

Martino Tirimo may have made his name on disc with his Debussy and prize-winning Rachmaninov, but there are few more thoughtful pianists than he. Following the publication of his ur-text edition of all 21 of Schubert's *Piano sonatas* (which includes completions of movements left as fragments), this is the first disc in what is planned as a uniquely complete recorded cycle. Though the sound is less immediate and more reverberant than on rival discs, Tirimo not only reveals new textual points but consistently matches great Schubertians like Kempff, Brendel and Schiff, in readings marked by delicate phrasing and bold choice of speeds. So in the late *G major Sonata* Tirimo is initially gentler than his rivals, both in the expansive first movement and in the lyrical *Andante*, playing with a velvet legato; but then in fast speeds for the *Allegro* Minuet and the *Allegretto* finale, he heightens the drama. Most impressive too is the natural weight and gravity he brings to the central *Adagio* in the five-movement *Sonata No. 3 in E*, a problematic work which Tirimo discusses most illuminatingly in his notes.

Piano sonatas, Vol. 2: *Nos. 2 in C, D.279; 17 in D, D.850.*
(M) *** EMI Eminence Dig. CD-EMX 2278 [id.]. Martino Tirimo.

This second disc in Tirimo's cycle closely follows the first, both in the authority of the playing and – rather less happily – in the reverberant recording. Here too there is a late sonata, the great *D major*, with Tirimo bringing out the dramatic contrasts, springing rhythms persuasively and illuminating new textual points, notably in the second-movement *Andante*. *No. 2 in C*, a striking teenage inspiration, is the more impressive when it comes in a version with the witty *Allegretto* finale completed by Tirimo. He also includes an alternative version of the Minuet, with a different Trio.

Piano sonatas, Vol. 3: *Nos. 1 in E, D.157; 9 in F sharp min., D.571* (completed Tirimo); *19 in C min., D.958.*
(M) *** EMI Eminence Dig. CD-EMX 2280 [id.]. Martino Tirimo.

The *Sonata in F sharp minor* (No. 9) opens hauntingly. It was written in 1817, and the unfinished first movement became separated from the *Allegro* (finale) and Scherzo, which existed independently; more musical detective work isolated the slow movement, and the work has now been put together and completed most successfully by Tirimo: it is one of the illuminating performances here. The trickling theme of its Scherzo is charmingly Schubertian. The *First (E major) Sonata* was written soon after the composer's eighteenth birthday. The opening is boldly classical, but Schubertian fingerprints appear in the lilting secondary material, and the disconsolate *Andante in E minor* is very touching in Tirimo's hands. The recording remains truthful and one soon adjusts to the resonance.

Piano sonatas, Vol. 4: *Nos. 4 in A min., D.537; 11 in C, D.613* (complete Tirimo); *20 in A, D.959.*
(M) *** EMI Eminence Dig. CD-EMX 2281 [id.]. Martino Tirimo.

The *Sonata in C*, D.613, dates from the year after the *F sharp minor* (on the previous disc). The *Adagio* was the only completed movement of the three and was published independently in 1869. It is one of Schubert's finest and is played very winningly here. The other two movements had to wait 28 years before being printed in the complete edition of Schubert's works. Tirimo successfully completed the first movement (which the composer left at the end of the development section) and the engaging *Allegretto* finale. There is much else to delight the listener in his playing here, especially the subtle lilt at the opening of the central movement, marked *Allegretto quasi Andantino*, while his veiled tone in the touching *Andantino* of the *A major Sonata* is matched by the sparkling, light-hearted Scherzo. Excellent if noticeably resonant sound.

Piano sonata No. 5 in A flat, D.557; 2 Scherzi, D.593.
(M) *** Decca 448 129-2 [id.]. Radu Lupu – BRAHMS: *Piano sonata No. 3.* ***

In the little three-movement *A flat Sonata* Lupu strikes the perfect balance between Schubert's classicism and the spontaneity of his musical thought, and at the same time he leaves one with the impression that this achievement is perfectly effortless. The *Andante* unfolds with appealing delicacy and the finale combines delicacy with strength. The two *Scherzi* are hardly less successful, the first particularly light and charming, the second rather more quixotic in mood. The analogue recording from the mid-1970s is as natural and fresh as the performances themselves.

Piano sonatas Nos. 13 in A, D.664; 14 in A min., D.784; Hungarian melody, D.817; 12 Waltzes, D.145.
500♪ ❁ (M) *** Decca 443 579-2 [id.]. Ashkenazy.

A magnificent record in every respect. Ashkenazy is a great Schubertian who can realize the touching humanity of this giant's vision as well as his strength. There is an astonishing directness about these performances and a virility tempered by tenderness.

Vanguard 'Alfred Brendel collection': *Piano sonatas Nos. 15 in C (Unfinished), D.840; 19 in C min., D.958; 16 German dances, D. 783.*
(M) *** Van. 08 4026 71 [id.]. Alfred Brendel (also on 08 9165 72 with SCHUMANN: *Etudes symphoniques; Fantasia in C* ***).

Brendel's fine performances from the 1960s (discussed in our main volume) are now additionally available in a slip-case coupled with Schumann as part of Vanguard's 'Alfred Brendel collection'.

Piano sonata No. 20 in A, D.959; Impromptus Nos. 1–4, D.935.
(B) *(*) Sony SBK 63042; *SBT 63042* [id.]. Rudolf Serkin.

In its day (the mid-1960s), Serkin's account of the *A major Sonata* was a much-praised performance by a much-admired pianist. But we must confess to holding a minority view, for the playing seems far less sensitive than one expects from an artist of this stature. Of course there are moments of poetry, and his command of the structure is impressive enough, but his fortissimos are brutally ugly (and that isn't only the fault of the hard, close recording). A great disappointment, and the *Impromptus*, too, are no match for those from Brendel.

Piano sonata No. 21 in B flat, D.960.
500♪ (M) *** Decca 448 578-2 [id.]. Clifford Curzon – BRAHMS: *Piano sonata No. 3* etc. ***

Piano sonata No. 21; Allegretto in C min., D.915; 12 Ländler, D.790.
500♪ ❁ *** EMI Dig. CDC5 55359-2 [id.]. Kovacevich.

Stephen Kovacevich's account of the great *B flat major Sonata* is one of the most eloquent accounts on record of this sublime sonata and one which is completely free of expressive point-making. Indeed it is the most searching and penetrating account of the work to have appeared in recent years and, given the excellence and truthfulness of the recording, must carry the strongest and most enthusiastic recommendation.

Curzon's is also among the finest accounts of the *B flat Sonata* in the catalogue. Tempi are aptly judged and everything is in fastidious taste. Detail is finely drawn but never emphasized at the expense of the architecture as a whole. It is beautifully recorded, and the piano sounds very truthful in timbre.

VOCAL MUSIC

Lieder on record (1898–1952): Volume 1, 1898–1929 (all with piano unless otherwise indicated): *Ave Maria* (1898) Edith Clegg; sung in English. *Ungeduld* (1901) Paul Knüpfer. *Heidenröslein* (1902) Minnie Nast. *Litanei* (1901); *Ständchen: Zögernd leise* – with Hofoper Ch. & O, Bruno Seidler (1908) both Marie Götze. *Ständchen* (sung in English): *Hark, hark! the lark* (1902) David Bispham. *Die schöne Müllerin: Der Neugierige* (1902) Franz Naval. *Rastlose Liebe* (1902); *Die Allmacht* (1910) both Edyth Walker. *Erlkönig* (1906); *Du bist die Ruh; Die Liebe* (1907) all three Lilli Lehmann. *Der Wanderer* (1902) Ernst Wachter. *Schwanengesang: Abschied* (1904); *Winterreise: Der Leiermann* (1934) both Harry Plunket-Greene; sung in English. *An die Leier* (1909) Pauline Cramer. *Die Forelle* (1902) Leopold Demuth. *Schwanengesang: Am Meer* (1904) Gustav Walter. *Die junge Nonne* (1907) Susan Strong (with orchestra). *Der Wanderer* (1906); *Schwanengesang: Aufenthalt* (1912); *Winterreise: Der Leiermann* (1910) all three Lev Sibiriakov; sung in Russian. *Frühlingsglaube* (1910) Heinrich Hensel. *Der Kreuzzug* (1905) Wilhelm Hesch. *Schwanengesang: Ständchen* (1907 with orchestra) & *Liebesbotschaft* (1909) both Leo Slezak. *An die Musik; Du bist die Ruh* (1911 – both with Arthur Nikisch, piano); *Suleika II* (1929 – with Coenraad V. Bos, piano); *Ellens Gesang* (1939 – with Gerald Moore, piano) all four Elena Gerhardt. *Die schöne Müllerin: Das Wandern* (1914); *Winterreise: Der Leiermann* (1928) both Sir George Henschel

(accompanying himself on the piano). *Die schöne Müllerin: Der Müller und der Bach* (1911) Elise Elizza. *An die Musik; Gruppe aus dem Tartarus* (1910) both Ottilie Metzger. *Sei mir gegrüsset* (1921) Friedrich Brodersen. *Die schöne Müllerin: Undgeduld & Wohin?* (1922–3) both Frieda Hempel. *Gruppe aus dem Tartarus* (1924); *Erlkönig* (1936, with Gerald Moore) both Alexander Kipnis. *Du bist die Ruh* (1924); *Die Liebe hat gelogen* (1927, with Edwin Schneider) both John McCormack. *Im Abendrot; Verklärung* (1929) both Aaltje Noordewier-Reddingius. *Winterreise: Rückblick; Frühlingstraume & Mut!* (1927) all three Richard Tauber, with Mischa Spoliansky. *Gretchen am Spinnrade; Mignon II* (1928) both Meta Seinemeyer, with O, Frieder Weissmann. *Die Forelle; Lachen und Weinen* (1928); *Winterreise: Der Lindenbaum* (1931) all three Vanni Marcoux, with Piero Coppola; sung in French. *An die Musik* (1926) Ursula van Diemen, with Arpád Sándor. *Memnon* (1932) Harold Williams, with Herbert Dawson. *Das Lied im Grünen* (1930) Sigrid Onegin, with Clemens Schmalstich. *Schwanengesang: Der Doppelgänger. Der Tod und das Mädchen* (1930 with O, Eugene Goossens) both Feodor Chaliapin (sung in Russian). *Schwanengesang: Aufenthalt; Ihr Bild. Die schöne Müllerin: Pause* (1928) all three Hans Duham, with Ferdinand Foll. *Sei mir gegrüsset; Auf dem Wasser zu singen; Geheimes* (1927) all three Lotte Lehmann with O, Manfred Gurlitt. *Winterreise: Der Lindenbaum. Der Tod und das Mädchen* (1926) both Julia Culp, with Fritz Lindemann.
(M) (***) EMI mono CHS5 66150-2 (3) [CDHC 66154].

The first item in this fascinating historical survey really offers a frisson to the listener, even though it is a very swoopy account of *Ave Maria* sung in English. It is what is thought to be the very first recording of a Schubert song, delivered in 1898 by Edith Clegg, a contralto known only for having sung at Covent Garden in 1909. From then on the focus grows ever clearer, both in sound and in vocal technique, with even the second item, *Ungeduld* from *Die schöne Müllerin*, recorded by the German bass, Paul Knüpfer, in 1901 with a forwardness and clarity that defy the years.

Each item brings its revelations, with the American, David Bispham, singing *Hark, hark! the lark* in 1902 in a prim D'Oyly Carte English accent; the soprano, Lilli Lehmann, in 1906 giving an intensely dramatic account of *Erlkönig*; Harry Plunket-Greene (born 1865), vivid in 1934 electrical recording, characterfully giving *Der Leiermann* from *Winterreise* in English, every word clear, but with an Irish accent, the narrative effect like a folksong; Lev Sibiriakov transforming the same song to become intensely Russian (again extraordinarily vivid recording, made in St Petersburg by Fred Gaisberg); and Sir George Henschel (born 1850) at 78 recording that same song in the original German with a firmness and point for any modern singer to envy. It is amazing to think that the tenor, Gustav Walter, who was recorded in a ringing account of *Am Meer* at the age of 70, was born in 1834, within six years of Schubert's death.

It is a set which telescopes history and tells, among much else, what store all these vintage singers set by firm, clear delivery with not a hint of a wobble among them. Quite apart from such starry names as Chaliapin, Tauber and McCormack, Alexander Kipnis (who gives another memorable account of *Erlkönig*), the brilliant Frieda Hempel and the golden-toned Meta Seinemeyer demand special mention. Anyone listening to these 65 items, lasting 3½ hours, will be amazed at the riches, with freshness the keynote, stylistically flawed only occasionally in sentimental *rallentandos*. Texts are given in the booklet but, alas, none of the potted biographies from the original LP set nor (worse still) an index of songs. Unmissable just the same.

Lieder on record, 1898–1952: Volume 2, 1929–52: *Schwanengesang: Der Atlas* (1930); *Erlkönig* (orch. Berlioz); *Schwanengesang: Der Doppelgänger* (1934) all three Charles Panzéra, with O, Piero Coppola (sung in French). *Die Forelle* (1927); *Der Hirt auf dem Felsen* (1929) both Lotte Schöne, the second with Berlin State Op. O, Leo Blech); *Schwanengesang: Am Meer* (1929) Friedrich Schorr, with Robert Jäger. *Gretchen am Spinnrade* (1929) Dusolinna Giannini, with Michael Raucheisen. *Erlkönig* (1930) Georges Thill, with Henri Etcheverry (baritone), C. Pascal (treble) & O. *Der Tod und das Mädchen* (1929) Maria Oiszewska, with George Reeves. *Nachtviolen; An die Geliebte; Das Heimweh* (1938) all three Elisabeth Schumann, with Leo Rosenek. *Der Jüngling an der Quelle* (1936) Elisabeth Schumann, with Elizabeth Coleman. *An die Nachtigall* (1933); *Der Schmetterling* (1937) both Elisabeth Schumann, with George Reeves. *Der Musensohn* (1932) Therese Behr-Schnabel, with Artur Schnabel. *An die Laute; Am See* (1932); *Der Wanderer an den Mond* (1937) all three Karl Erb, with Bruno Seidler-Winkler. *Schwanengesang: Frühlingssehnsucht* (1937) Karl Erb, with Gerald Moore. *Auflösung; Schwanengesang: Liebesbotschaft* (1935); *Wiegenlied: Schlafe, schlafe; Wiegenlied: Wie sich der Auglein* (1933) all five Ria Ginster, with Gerald Moore. *Ganymed; Rosamunde: Der Vollmond strahlt. Winterreise: Das Wirthaus* (1938); *Schwanengesang: Kriegers Ahnung* (1937) all four Herbert Janssen, with Gerald Moore. *Mignon I; Nachtstücke; Die junge Nonne* (1937) all three Susan Metcalfe-Casals, with Gerald Moore. *Erlkönig* (1937) Marta Fuchs, with Michael Raucheisen. *Schwanengesang: Die Taubenpost* (1937) both Gerhard Hüsch, with Gerald Moore. *Lied eines Schiffers; Widerschein* (1939) both Gerhard Hüsch, with Hanns Udo Müller. *Auf dem Wasser zu singen* (1943) Frida Leider, with Michael Raucheisen. *Die schöne*

Müllerin: Halt!; Eifersucht und Stolz (1945); *Schäfers Klagelied* (1949) all three Aksel Schiotz, with Gerald Moore. *Die Vögel; Liebhaber in allen Gestalten* (1948) both Elisabeth Schwarzkopf, with Gerald Moore; *Seligkeit* (1946) Elisabeth Schwarzkopf, with Karl Hudez. *Im Frühling; Auf der Bruck* (1950) both Peter Pears, with Benjamin Britten. *Der Hirt auf dem Felsen* (1947) Margaret Ritchie, with Reginald Kell (clarinet) & Gerald Moore. *Schwanengesang: Ihr Bild* (1947) Julius Patzak, with Hermann von Nordberg. *Auf dem Wasser zu singen* (1948) Irmgard Seefried, with Gerald Moore. *Heidenröslein* (1947) Irmgard Seefried, with Hermann von Nordberg. *Am Bach im Frühling; Gruppe aus dem Tartarus; Meerstille; Wandrers Nachtlied I–II* (1949) all five Hans Hotter, with Gerald Moore. *An die Leier* (1949) Flora Nielsen, with Gerald Moore. *Prometheus* (1949) Bernhard Sönnerstedt, with Gerald Moore. *Aus Heliopolis I* (1949) Endré Koréh, with Hermann von Nordberg. *Die schöne Müllerin: Am Feierabend; Trock'ne Blumen. Nacht und Träume. Schwanengesang: Das Fischermädchen* (1951) all four Dietrich Fischer-Dieskau, with Gerald Moore. *Die Allmacht; Frühlingsglaube; Wandrers Nachtlied II* (1952) Kirsten Flagstad, with Gerald Moore.
(M) (**(*)) EMI mono CHS5 66154-2 (3) [CDHC 66154].

This second volume in EMI's historic survey of Schubert song on record brings almost comparable delight, even if there are fewer surprises when many, if not most, of the singers are already familiar from their recordings. The 64 items lead up to the two great exponents of Lieder in our time, Schwarzkopf and Fischer-Dieskau, here both vividly characterful at the start of their recording careers. In timbre the charming Lotte Schöne might almost be mistaken for the even more sparkling Elisabeth Schumann, here represented in five brief songs. Naturally German singers predominate, but some of the most cherishable items are from non-German singers: Charles Panzéra and Georges Thill from France (heard in a version of *Erlkönig*, sung very dramatically in French as a trio with Henri Etcheverry and a boy treble), Peter Pears and Margaret Ritchie from Britain, as well as transatlantic singers like Dusolina Giannini (fresh and powerful in *Gretchen am Spinnrade*), Flora Nielsen and Susan Metcalfe-Casals, whose very rare recordings, privately made for her by EMI, are a revelation. The only disappointments are the recordings of Therese Behr-Schnabel (accompanied by her husband), recorded when she was 58, and Herbert Janssen, whose rapid flutter in the voice is distracting among performances of immaculate firmness. The programme ends with three songs from Kirsten Flagstad, in 1953 past her prime but still commanding. Excellent transfers, as in the first volume, with the same reservations over documentation.

The Graham Johnson Schubert Lieder Edition

(Volumes Nos. 1–23 are covered in our main volume)

Lieder, Vol. 24: *Goethe Schubertiad: An Mignon; An Schwager Kronos; Bundeslied; Erlkönig; Ganymed; Geistes-Gruss; Gesang der Geister über den Wassern* (2 versions); *Der Goldschmiedsgesell; Der Gott und die Bajadere; Hoffnung; Jägers Abendlied* (2 versions); *Mahomets Gesang; Mignon (So lasst mich scheinen); Rastlose Liebe; Der Rattenfänger; Schäfers Klagelied; Der Schatzgräber; Sehnsucht* (2 versions); *Sehnsucht (Nur wer die Sehnsucht kennt); Tischlied; Wer nie sein Brot mit Tränen ass.*
*** Hyperion Dig. CDJ 33024 [id.]. Christine Schäfer, John Mark Ainsley, Simon Keenlyside, Michael George, L. Schubert Chorale, Stephen Layton; Graham Johnson.

This collection, drawn from Schubert's many settings of Goethe, aims to celebrate the important role the poet's works played in the composer's life. Graham Johnson in his notes makes high claims: 'It was the collaboration between Schubert and Goethe which allowed song with piano to become an enduring and valid means of musical expression on a large emotional scale.' Sadly, Goethe himself was indifferent to the inspired efforts of this then-obscure composer, but it did not affect the intensity of Schubert's response to the words. This selection, like that of Volume 28, devoted to Schiller, is related to the life of the poet and includes many fascinating items, not least those in which Schubert set a text more than once. There are half a dozen of them here, including two quite different settings of *The Song of the Spirits over the Waters*, each completed by other hands. The second, for male chorus, is particularly powerful. Also fascinating is the version of *Erlkönig* here, with three singers taking part, characterizing the different voices in the story, a practice which Schubert himself sanctioned. (This is also included in Volume 2 of EMI's historical Lieder collection, with Georges Thill leading a performance in French.) All the singers here are ideally responsive, with Michael George reining in a voice weightier than the rest.

Lieder, Vol. 25: (i) *Die schöne Müllerin* (song-cycle); (ii) with additional poems by Wilhelm Müller.
❀ *** Hyperion Dig. CDJ 33025 [id.]. (i) Ian Bostridge, Graham Johnson; (ii) read by Dietrich Fischer-Dieskau.

For this first of the big song-cycles in his comprehensive Schubert edition for Hyperion, Graham Johnson could not have chosen his singer more shrewdly. It is a delight to have in Ian Bostridge a tenor who not only produces youthfully golden tone for this young man's sequence but who also gives an eagerly detailed account of the 20 songs, mesmeric at the close, to match even the finest rivals. With the help of Johnson's keenly imaginative accompaniment, Bostridge's gift for changing face and conveying mood makes the story-telling exceptionally fresh and vivid. The bonus is also to have Dietrich Fischer-Dieskau (now retired from singing) reciting the Müller poems which Schubert failed to set. Johnson is at his most inspired too in his detailed notes, which will be a revelation even to experienced Schubertians.

Lieder, Vol. 26: *'An 1826 Schubertiad': 2 Scenes from Lacrimas* (*Schauspiel*); *4 Mignon Lieder* of Wilhelm Meister. Lieder: *Abschied von der Erde; An Sylvia; Das Echo; Der Einsame; Grab und Mond; Mondenschein; Nachthelle; Des Sängers Habe; Ständchen; Totengräberweise; Trinklied; Der Wanderer an den Mond; Widerspruch; Wiegenlied.*
*** Hyperion Dig. CDJ 33026 [id.]. Christine Schäfer, John Mark Ainsley, Richard Jackson. L. Schubert Chorale, Layton; Graham Johnson.

Starting with *Der Einsame*, sung by Richard Jackson, one of the most haunting of Schubert songs, here is a Schubertiad that brings its measure of darkness, relying entirely on Lieder which Schubert wrote in 1825 and 1826. By then he was writing fewer songs than before, but was hitting the mark every time. It ends in sombre tones with *Abschied von der Erde* ('Farewell to the Earth'), not a song at all but a melodrama for reciter and piano, which Richard Jackson narrates as effectively as one could imagine. Christine Schäfer and Richard Jackson between them perform most of the programme, with John Mark Ainsley contributing just one or two, including *To Sylvia*. That is one of the three Shakespeare settings which come as a lightweight interlude. Schäfer's contributions shine the most brightly, not least the hypnotic *Wiegenlied*, to words by Seidl. Graham Johnson's notes include a survey of Schubert's career in 1825–6, a list of the songs written then, and his brilliant analysis of each item.

Lieder, Vol. 27: *Abendröte cycle of Friedrich von Schlegel* (complete). Other settings of Friedrich von Schlegel: *Blanka; Fülle der Liebe; Im Walde; Der Schiffer*. Settings of August von Schlegel: *Lebensmelodien; Lob der Tränen; Sonnets I–III; Sprache der Liebe; Wiedersehn.*
*** Hyperion Dig. CDJ 33027 [id.]. Matthias Görne, Christine Schäfer, Graham Johnson.

When the young German baritone, Matthias Görne, made his début at Wigmore Hall, deputizing on a gala occasion, it was instantly obvious that here was a major new Lieder singer. He makes an inspired choice for this fine disc in Graham Johnson's collected edition of the Schubert songs, now firmly established as one of the most important projects being undertaken by any record company. With a masterly feeling for words and vocal line Görne brings out the full charm of these settings of poems by the von Schlegel brothers, Friedrich as well as August, the translator of Shakespeare. The seven songs to words by August are rounded off with three settings of his translations of Petrarch sonnets, while Johnson, prompted by circumstantial evidence, has ingeniously assembled a cycle of 11 Friedrich von Schlegel settings, *Abendröte* ('Sunset'), with Christine Schäfer as soloist in three of them, though not in the best-known of them, *Die Vogel* ('The Bird'), a favourite with both Elisabeth Schumann and Elisabeth Schwarzkopf. Görne and Johnson regularly demonstrate what masterpieces even some of the least known and briefest songs are. Johnson's notes are, as ever, a model, explaining why belated publication of particular songs has unfairly brought about neglect.

'A Voyage of discovery' (a selection from the first 27 volumes of the Hyperion Schubert Edition).
(B) *** Hyperion Dig. HYP 200 [id.]. Various artists; Graham Johnson.

This is a delightful sampler, featuring the widest range of the fine Lieder singers whom Graham Johnson has assembled for his magnificent project. Dame Janet Baker, Dame Margaret Price and Dame Felicity Lott are on the list, with Peter Schreier, Christoph Prégardien, Brigitte Fassbaender, Elly Ameling and the late Arleen Augér among the distinguished singers from outside Britain. Inspired newcomers include Christine Schäfer, Matthias Görne and, in some ways most striking of all, Ian Bostridge, who contributes three songs. Sarah Walker has the longest item, a serenade, *Ständchen*, quite different from the famous one, with male chorus as backing. What – understandably – are missing are the texts and detailed notes which Johnson provides for the individual discs, but the booklet includes full details of each of the first 27 discs.

'The Songmakers' Almanac Schubertiade': I, *'Lebensmut': Die junge Nonne; Der zürnende Diana; Vom Mitleiden Mariä; Lachen und Weinen; Selige Welt; Mignon und der Harfner; Auflösung; Lebensmut; Weilkommen und Abscheid*. II, *'Nacht und Träume': An die Laute; Wiegenlied; Ellens Gesang II; Nacht und Träume; Licht und Liebe; Ständchen (Horch! horch! die Lerch); Der Tod und das Mädchen; Der Winterabend; Abschied von der Erde*. III, *'Das Lied im Grünen': Fischerweise; Das Lied im Grünen; Der Schiffer; Nähe des Geliebten; Frühlingsglaube; Wandrers Nachtlied; Im Frühling; Wehmut; Auf der Bruck*. IV, *'An mein Klavier': An mein Klavier; Zum Punsche; Geheimnis; Viola; Der Hochzeitsbraten*.
(B) **(*) Hyperion Dyad CDD 22020 (2) [id.]. Felicity Lott, Ann Murray, Anthony Rolfe Johnson, Richard Jackson; Graham Johnson.

Recorded in 1983, this two-disc collection in Hyperion's two-for-the-price-of-one Dyad series presents over two hours of songs arranged by related groups – 'The romantic struggle', 'Serenades and lullabies', 'Nature and love', 'At home with the Schubertians'. That was the way Graham Johnson devised his immensely popular Songmakers' Almanac concerts, making this a forerunner of his brilliantly conceived recorded edition of the complete songs. Johnson's notes, including comments on individual items and full texts, observe a similar pattern to that adopted in the main edition, though a song like the Seidl *Wiegenlied* is allowed only three of its stanzas, not all five. The analogue recording, given an AAD transfer to CD, is not quite as clean as in the main edition, with a halo of sound round the voices, not quite sharply focused enough. But with such inspired performances one's ear quickly adjusts, to give a delightful impression of just such live events as the original Schubertiads. Left to the end are the two items which are by far the longest: the poignant *Viola*, a ballad telling of an abandoned flower, with Ann Murray a charming soloist, and the convivial *Hochzeitsbraten* ('Wedding dish'), featuring the other three soloists. All four singers are at their freshest, with Ann Murray in particularly fine voice, taking on many of the most challenging songs.

Secular vocal music and Part-songs: *Die Advocaten; An den Frühling; Andenken; Bardengesang; Bergknappenlied; Bootsgesang; Coronach; Die Entfernten; Dessen Fahne; Donnerstürme wallte; Das Dörfchen; Dreifach ist der Schritt der Zeit* (2 versions); *Ein jugendlicher Maienschwung; Eisiedelei; Erinnerungen; Ewige Liebe; Fischerlied; Flucht; Frisch atmet des Morgens lebendiger Hauch; Frühlingsgesang; Frühlingslied* (2 versions); *Geist der Liebe; Der Geistertanz; Gesang der Geister über den Wassern; Goldner Schein; Der Gondelfahrer; Gott in der Natur; Grab und Mond, Hier strecket, Hier unarmen sich getreue Gatten; Im Gegenwärtigen Vergangenes; Jünglingswonne; Klage um Ali Bey; Lacrimosa son io* (2 versions); *Leise, leise, lasst uns singen; Liebe; Liebe säusein die Blätter; Lied im Freien; Lutzows wilde Jagd; Mailied* (3 versions); *Majestät'sche Sonnenrose, Mirjums Siegesgesang; Mondenschein; Der Morgernstern; Die Nacht; Nachtgesang im Walde, Nachthelle; Die Nachtigall; Nachtmusik; Naturgenuss; Nur wer die Sehnsucht kennt; La Pastorella al prato; Punschlied; Räuberlied; Ruhe, schönstes Glück der Erde; Schlachtegesang; Der Schnee zerrinnt; Selig durch die Liebe; Ständchen (Zögernd leise); Das stille Lied; Thronend auf erhab'nem Sitz; Totengräberlied; Trinklied* (4 versions); *Trinklied aus dem 16 (Jahrhundert); Trinklied im Mai; Trinklied im Winter; Unendliche Freude* (2 versions); *Vorüber die stöhnende Klage; Wehmut; Wein und Liebe; Wer die steile Sternenbalm; Widerhall; Widerspruch; Wilkommen, lieber schöner Mai; Zum Rundetanz; Zur guten Nacht; Die zwei Tugendwege*.
(M) *** EMI CMS5 66139-2 (4) [CDMD 66139]. Hildegard Behrens, Brigitte Fassbaender, Peter Schreier, Dietrich Fischer-Dieskau, Capella Bavariae, Bav. R. Ch. & SO, Sawallisch.

Schubert's part-songs make up a sizeable proportion of his total output, and this outstanding four-disc collection, superbly performed and recorded with Sawallisch the most understanding guide, both as pianist and conductor, brings out many rare treasures. Many are jolly ballads to celebrate life's simple pleasures, like the opening 'Song in the open air'; others are more expressively eloquent, such as *Ruhe, schönstes Glück der Erde* ('Rest, greatest earthly blessing'), the joyous *Gott in der Natur*, and the evocative male-voice chorale, *Nachtmusik*. On the other hand, *Die Advocaten* is a light-hearted trio in which a pair of lawyers wonder whether their fees are going to be paid; their client, Mr Sempronius, then arrives to do so, if reluctantly, and they are all bewitched by the clink of coins. The longest item, *Miriam's Song of triumph, on a Biblical subject*, is almost a miniature oratorio. Two striking Psalm-settings and the *Hymn to the Holy Ghost* (with brass accompaniment) have been omitted from the original LP collection but are now included on Sawallisch's EMI set of Schubert's religious music. Another substantial piece to cherish here is the version of *The Song of the Spirits over the Waters* with eight-part chorus and strings, as well as the atmospheric *Nachtgesang im Walde*, with horns accompanying a male-voice ensemble. Not surprisingly, horns also provide a lively opening for the gleeful and much briefer *Lützows wilde Jagd*, which begins the fourth disc. The highly imaginative setting of *Wehmut*, which comes near the end of the collection, has a haunting tolling bell effect, achieved in the voices alone. The tiny songs designed for Schubert and his friends to sing together, many of them drinking songs, add to the delight of the collection.

Highly recommended to any Schubertian eager for new discovery. The transfers to CD could hardly have been managed more naturally, and the singers are given a fine presence.

Miscellaneous vocal recitals

'A Schubert evening': (i) *Abendstern; Am Grabe Anselmos; An die Nachtigall; An die untergehende Sonne; Berthas Lied in der Nacht; Delphine; Ellens Gesang* from *The Lady of the Lake (Raste Krieger; Jäger von der Jagd; Ave Maria); Epistel an Herrn Josef von Spaun; Gondelfahrer; Gretchen am Spinnrade; Hin und wieder; Iphigenia; Die junge Nonne; Kennst du das Land; Liebe schwärmt; Das Mädchen; Das Mädchens Klage; Die Männer sind méchant; Mignon Lieder I–III (Heiss mich nicht reden; So lasst mich scheinen; Nur wer die Sehnsucht kennt); Schlummerlied; Schwestergruss; Strophe von Schiller (Die Götter Griechenlands); Suleika songs I–II (Was bedeutet die Bewegung; Ach, um deine feuchten Schwingen); Wiegenlied; Wiegenlied (Schlafe, schlafe).* 'Favourite Lieder': (ii) *An die Musik; An Sylvia; Auf dem Wasser zu singen; Du bist die Ruh; Die Forelle; Frühlingsglaube; Heidenröslein; Litanei; Der Musensohn; Nacht und Träume; Rastlose Lied; Der Tod und das Mädchen.*

500♪ ❁ (B) *** EMI forte CZS5 69389-2 (2) [CDFB 69389]. Dame Janet Baker, with (i) Gerald Moore; (ii) Geoffrey Parsons.

This astonishingly generous collection, offered on EMI's two-for-the-price-of-one forte label, combines a pair of recitals recorded by Dame Janet at two different stages in her career, in 1970 and a decade later. The first collection ranges wide in an imaginative *Liederabend* of Schubert songs that includes a number of comparative rarities. With Gerald Moore (who returned to the studio out of retirement especially for the occasion) still at his finest, this is a profoundly satisfying collection. The later (1980) recital with Geoffrey Parsons is treasurable. Take a poll of favourite Schubert songs and a high proportion of these would be in the dozen offered in the 1980 group. With a great singer treating each with loving, detailed care, the result is a charmer of a recital. The later recording is of fine EMI vintage and catches the more mature voice naturally and with rather more presence than a decade earlier. It is a pity that, because the set is so economically priced, there are no translations, but this remains an unmissable reissue.

Lieder: *An die Laute; An die Leier; An die Musik; An Silvia; Auf der Bruck; Du bist die Ruh; Erlkönig; Das Fischermädchen; Die Forelle; Ganymed; Gruppe aus dem Tartarus; Heidenröslein; Lachen und Weinen; Litanei auf das Fest; Meeres Stille; Der Musensohn; Rastlose Liebe; Schäfers Klagelied; Ständchen; Die Taubenpost; Der Tod und das Mädchen; Der Wanderer; Wandrers Nachtlied.*

500♪ *** DG Dig. 445 294-2 [id.]. Bryn Terfel, Malcolm Martineau.

Bryn Terfel's DG disc of Schubert confirms how this young Welsh bass-baritone has an exceptional gift to project his magnetic personality with comparable intensity, whether in opera or in Lieder, whether live or on disc. Terfel emerges as a positive artist, giving strikingly individual and imaginative readings of these 23 favourite songs, and it is a measure of his magnetism that the result is so dramatically compelling. Full, firm sound.

An die Laute; An die Musik; An Silvia; Der Einsame; Im Abendrot; Liebhaber in allen Gestalten; Lied eines Schiffers an die Dioskurern; Der Musensohn; Ständchen (Leise flehen meine Lieder).

(M) *** DG Originals 449 747-2 [id.]. Fritz Wunderlich, Hubert Giesen – BEETHOVEN: *Lieder;* SCHUMANN: *Dichterliebe.* ***

Few tenors have matched the young Wunderlich in the freshness and golden bloom of the voice. The open manner could not be more appealing here in glowing performances, well coupled with other fine examples of this sadly short-lived artist's work. Truly this disc is a candidate for inclusion in DG's series of 'Legendary performances'.

Church music

6 Antiphons for the Blessings of the Branches on Palm Sunday; Auguste jam coelestium in G, D.488; Deutsche Messe, D.872 (with Epilogue, The Lord's Prayer); Graduale in C, D.184; Hymn to the Holy Ghost, D.964; Kyries: in D min., D.31; F, D.66; Lazarus, D.689; Magnificat in C, D.486; Offertorium (Totus in corde) in C, D.136; Offertorium (Tres sunt) in A min., D.181; 2 Offertoriums (Salve Regina) in F, D.223 & A, D.676; Psalm 23, D.706; Psalm 92, D.953; Salve Reginas: in B flat, D.106; in C, D.811; Stabat Mater in G min., D.175; Tantum ergo (3 settings) *in C, D.460/1 & D.739; Tantum ergo in D, D.750.*

(M) *** EMI Dig./Analogue CMS7 64783-2 (3) [CDMD 64783]. Popp, Donath, Rüggerberg, Venuti, Hautermann, Falk, Fassbaender, Greindl-Rosner, Dallapozza, Araiza, Protschka, Tear, Lika, Fischer-Dieskau, Capella Bavariae, Bav. R. Ch. & SO, Sawallisch.

Volume two of Sawallisch's great and rewarding Schubertian survey has much glorious music, sung with eloquence and richly recorded in the Munich Hercules Hall. Even some of the shortest items – such as the six tiny *Antiphons*, allegedly written in half an hour – have magic and originality in them. Plainer, but still glowing with Schubertian joy, is the so-called *Deutsche Messe*. The *Magnificat*, too, is a strongly characterized setting, and even the three settings of St Thomas Aquinas's *Tantum ergo* (all in C) have their charm. There are other surprises. The lovely setting of the *Offertorium in C (Totus in corde)* is for soprano, clarinet and orchestra, with the vocal and instrumental lines intertwining delectably, while the no less appealing *Auguste jam coelestium* is a soprano–tenor duet. The *Salve Regina in C*, D.811, is written for four male voices, *a cappella*, and they again contribute to the performance of *Psalm 23*, where Sawallisch provides a piano accompaniment. The religious drama, *Lazarus*, has the third CD to itself. Schubert left it unfinished and, though no more dramatic than his operas, it contains much delightful music. With Robert Tear in the name-role, Helen Donath as Maria, Lucia Popp as Jemima, Maria Venuti as Martha, Josef Protschka as Nathanael and Fischer-Dieskau as Simon, it is very strongly cast and the performance is splendid; indeed the singing is outstanding from chorus and soloists alike throughout this set, and the warm, well-balanced recording adds to one's pleasure.

Masses Nos. 1–6 (complete); *Kyries in B flat, D.45; D min., D.49; Offertorium in B flat, D.963; Salve Reginas: in F, D.379; in B flat, D.386; Stabat Mater in F min., D.383; Tantum ergo in E flat, D.962.*
(M) *** EMI Dig./Analogue CMS7 64778-2 (4) [CDMD 64778]. Popp, Donath, Fassbaender, Dallapozza, Schreier, Araiza, Protschka, Fischer-Dieskau, Bav. R. Ch. & SO, Sawallisch.

Sawallisch's highly distinguished survey of Schubert's church music was recorded in the early 1980s. This first volume is centred on his major Mass settings, especially his masterpiece in this form, the *E flat Mass*. Though the chorus is not flawless here, the performances are warm and understanding. The earlier Mass settings bring superb, lively inspirations, not to mention the separate *Kyries* and *Salve Reginas*. Excellent, cleanly focused sound, for the most part digital, with the benefit of the ambience of the Munich Herkules-Saal.

Masses Nos. 1–6 (complete).
*** Sony S4K 62778 (4) [id.]. Alexander Nader, Thomas Puchegger, Georg Leskovich, Jörg Hering, Kurt Azesberger, Harry van der Kamp, Belà Fischer, Albin Lenzer, Benjamin Schmidinger, treble soloists from V. Boys' Ch., Ch. Viennensis, OAE, Weil.

Masses Nos. 1 in F, D.105; 2 in G, D.167.
*** Sony Dig. SK 68247 [id.]. Nader, Puchegger, Leskovich, Hering, Azesberger, Van der Kamp, V. Boys' Ch., Ch. Viennensis, OAE, Bruno Weil.

Masses Nos. 3 in B flat, D.324; 4 in C, D.452.
*** Sony Dig. SK 68248 [id.]. Nader, Puchegger, Leskovich, Fischer, Hering, Van der Kamp, V. Boys' Ch., Ch. Viennensis, OAE, Bruno Weil.

(i) *Mass No. 5 in A flat, D.678* (2nd version); *Deutsche Messe, D.872.*
*** Sony Dig. SK 53984 [id.]. (i) Treble soloists from V. Boys' Ch. (Stefan Preyer, Thomas Weinnhappel), Hering, Van der Kamp; V. Boys' Ch., Ch. Viennensis, OAE, Bruno Weil.

Mass No. 6 in E flat, D.950.
*** Sony Dig. SK 66255 [id.]. Schmidinger, Lenzer, Hering, Azesberger, Van der Kamp, V. Boys' Ch., Ch. Viennensis, OAE, Bruno Weil.

Bruno Weil draws incandescent performances of all six of Schubert's *Masses* from his fine team, helped by sound that is clearer and more detailed than on direct rival recordings. The combination of Viennese choirs – with the trebles of the Vienna Boys' Choir outstandingly full and fresh – and of a British period orchestra works superbly, making one appreciate, even more than with the Sawallisch versions, how seriously this area of Schubert's oeuvre has been underappreciated, both in the early works and in the two mature masterpieces in A flat and E flat. In the earlier *Masses* and in the simple chordal writing of the *Deutsche Messe* the presence of boys adds to the impression of liturgical performances, fresh and dedicated. In the *Sixth Mass in E flat*, with his direct manner and brisk speeds, Weil reinforces the originality of Schubert's inspiration in this last and greatest of his Mass settings, written in the last year of his life. In particular the complex contrapuntal writing comes over with new bite and attack, making one register this as a Mass worthy of being bracketed with the greatest. With Sawallisch in his superb series for EMI, now reissued at mid-price, the approach is smoother, more expansive and in some ways more refined, more moulded in its expressiveness, but Weil's forthright manner could not be more winning. A set to recommend enthusiastically, not least to those who have dismissed Schubert's religious writing as uninspired. The recordings were made (unexpectedly) in Vienna's Casino Zögernitz (SK 68247/8), the Haydn-Saal of the

Schloss Esterházy, Eisenstadt (SK 66255) and the Schloss Grafenegg, Reitschule, Austria (SK 53984); and they are consistently balanced very realistically. The sound has plenty of weight and sonority and a very convincing ambience. The one possible snag is the relatively short measure compared with the Sawallisch set: SK 66255 (the *Mass in E flat*) has a playing time of barely 48 minutes. However, such is the quality of the music-making that, for once, this seems unimportant.

The CDs are available separately, and those looking for a place to start might choose SK 53984, which couples the delightful *Deutsche Messe*, with its simple chordal settings of German words, with the A flat masterpiece which is Schubert's *Missa Solemnis*. It helps that Weil uses the second version of the work, with the *Credo* more compact. As ever, he draws inspired playing and singing from his Austro-British team, with the bright, full treble sound of the Vienna Boys cleanly set against the period instruments of the Orchestra of the Age of Enlightenment, both beautifully balanced in a recording with plenty of bloom on the sound, yet with good detail.

Mass No. 5 in A flat, D.678.
** Teldec/Warner Dig. 4509 98422-2 [id.]. Soloists, Schoenberg Ch., COE, Harnoncourt.

Harnoncourt's live recording brings a characteristically intense and dedicated reading but, as with the parallel recording of the *E flat Mass*, the recording fails to convey enough inner detail, with tuttis unclear, if satisfyingly weighty. Particularly with no fill-up, this cannot quite compare either with Weil's period performance or with Sawallisch's more spacious, traditional performance.

Mass No. 6 in E flat, D.950.
** Teldec/Warner Dig. 0630 13163-2 [id.]. Orgonasova, Remmert, Van der Walt, Holzmair, Scharinger, Schoenberg Ch., COE, Harnoncourt.

Harnoncourt has a special affection for Schubert's Masses, and in his live recording from Graz he draws a dedicated performance from his fine team of singers and players. The line-up of soloists is first rate, and the Arnold Schoenberg Choir is among the finest in the world, but the recording is much less clear than it should be, with plenty of weight in tuttis but little inner detail, and with some haze round the solo voices. The fine playing of the COE is what impresses most, but again this hardly matches either Weil's period performance or Sawallisch's more spacious, traditional version on EMI.

Song-cycles: (i) *Die schöne Müllerin, D.795* (with spoken *Prologue* and *Epilogue*); *Schwanengesang, D.957; Winterreise, D.911.* (ii) *Einsamkeit, D.620.*
(M) **(*) EMI CMS5 66146-2 (3) [CDMC 66146]. Dietrich Fischer-Dieskau, (i) Gerald Moore; (ii) Karl Engel.

Fischer-Dieskau's EMI recordings of the three song-cycles were made around the time of the great baritone's fortieth birthday in 1961–2 and represent the second wave of his Schubert interpretations. He was to re-record them, again with Gerald Moore, for DG with even greater thought and refinement, but the direct power of expression here is superb, too. For *Die schöne Müllerin*, he also included spoken versions of the *Prologue* and *Epilogue* (taken from the songs in Wilhelm Müller's cycle) which Schubert did not set. The snag is that in the case of *Die schöne Müllerin* the 1985 digital remastering has caused the voice to sound edgy and peaky at climaxes, although the other cycles, transferred later, are altogether smoother.

As an added bonus, following after *Schwanengesang*, we are offered a rarity: Schubert's 1818 setting of Johann Mayrhofer's poem in twelve stanzas, *Einsamkeit* ('Solitude'). At nearly 19 minutes, this is almost a mini-cycle in itself, moving on from its thoughtful opening to consider zestful youth, full of activity, the happiness of comradeship (celebrated with a charming waltz rhythm), longing and requited ecstasy, gloom, freedom and ambition, finally returning to the solitude of old age. The setting does not, perhaps, represent Schubert at his greatest, but Fischer-Dieskau follows the poet's mood-changes dramatically and with characteristic sensitivity, and the listener is thoroughly involved. The sound is excellent, and it is a pity that for this reissue EMI did not cue the individual verses. However, full translations are included. Nevertheless our prime recommendation remains with Fischer-Dieskau's later, DG recordings, again with Gerald Moore: *Die schöne Müllerin* (DG 415 186-2); *Schwanengesang*, plus seven other favourite songs (DG 415 188-2); *Winterreise* (DG 415 187-2).

Song-cycles: *Die schöne Müllerin; Schwanengesang* (with also: *Im Freien; Der Wanderer an den Mond; Das Zügenglöcklein*); *Winterreise*. Lieder: *Alinde; An den Monde; An die Leier; An die Laute; An die Musik; An Silvia; Dass sie hier gewesen; Der Einsame; Die Forelle; Frühlingsglaube; Im Frühling; Der Schiffer; Schwanengesang; Sei mir gegrüsset*. Goethe Lieder: *Ganymed; Geheimes; Heidenröslein; Liebhaber in allen Gestalten; Der Musensohn; Rastlose Liebe; Wandrers Nachtlied*.
(M) *** EMI CMS5 66145-2 (4) [CDMD 66145]. Olaf Bär, Geoffrey Parsons.

Die schöne Müllerin was the first of the cycles which Olaf Bär recorded, in 1986 in Dresden, with the voice fresher and more velvety than later. The tone is all the better-suited to this young man's cycle, even more when contrasted with Fischer-Dieskau's in the companion box of EMI's Schubert Edition, especially when the digital recording is so flattering to Bär's warmly beautiful lyrical flow. In *Winterreise*, recorded two years later, again with Geoffrey Parsons a masterful accompanist, Bär again finds a beauty of line and tone to outshine almost everyone, and his singing is both deeply reflective and strongly dramatic, if without quite the power of Fischer-Dieskau's poetic projection or the sheer intensity of Britten and Pears (see above). Yet the darkness of the close is given the electricity of live communication and the sound is again outstanding, with the voice again seeming wonderfully natural and the balance with the piano bringing intimacy in a helpful atmosphere. The third disc, recorded in 1989, amplifies the collection of late songs, posthumously published as *Schwanengesang*, with three well-chosen extra items from the same period, notably *Der Wanderer an den Mond*, where Bär brings out the agony and weariness of the traveller addressing the moon. The singing throughout is characteristically sensitive and dramatic, with *Ständchen* strong and passionate rather than light and charming. The fourth disc offers 21 miscellaneous songs, most of them favourites, including 7 Goethe settings. Recorded in 1991–2, they show the voice grittier than earlier, but still searchingly expressive, with Geoffrey Parsons again the most understanding accompanist. Admirers of Bär, among whom we may be counted, will find this set a splendid survey of his Schubertian achievement, made the more attractive by the high quality of the recording.

Schwanengesang; 5 Lieder: *Am Fenster; Herbst; Sehnsucht; Der Wanderer an den Mond; Wiegenlied, D.867*.
500♪ ✿ *** DG Dig. 429 766-2 [id.]. Brigitte Fassbaender, Aribert Reimann.

Brigitte Fassbaender gives a totally distinctive and compelling account of *Schwanengesang*, proving stronger and more forceful than almost any rival. She turns what was originally a relatively random group of late songs into a genuine cycle, by presenting them in a carefully rearranged order and adding five other late songs. Her magnetic power of compelling attention is intensified by the equally positive accompaniment of Aribert Reimann. The celebrated Schubert *Serenade* to words by Rellstab is far more than just a pretty tune, rather a passionate declaration of love; and Fassbaender builds her climax to the cycle round the final Heine settings, heightening their dramatic impact by the new ordering.

Winterreise (song-cycle), *D. 911*.
*** Ph. Dig. 446 407-2 [id.]. Wolfgang Holzmair, Imogen Cooper.

Wolfgang Holzmair with his high, almost tenor-like baritone gives a young man's view of this darkest of song-cycles, full of musical poetry. With not a hint of grit in the firm, clear voice, he may lack the darker tones of a Fischer-Dieskau, but with his direct manner and keen concentration and with fine feeling for detailed word-meaning, he conveys a chill, a sense of numbness that builds up superbly to the final song, *Der Leiermann*, taken (like many others) rather more flowingly than usual. Imogen Cooper is a splendid partner, bringing a soloist's imagination to bear on the often plain accompaniments. An excellent recommendation for anyone who welcomes a relatively restrained reading, beautifully sung, which is yet magnetic from first to last.

OPERA

Alfonso und Estrella (complete).
*** Berlin Classics BC2156-2 (3) [id.]. Schreier, Mathis, Prey, Adam, Fischer-Dieskau, Berlin R. Ch. & State Op. O, Suitner.

It is strange that Schubert, whose feeling for words in lyric poetry drew out emotions which have natural drama in them, had little or no feeling for the stage. Had his operas been produced, no doubt he would have learnt how to use music more positively; as it is, this tale of royal intrigue in medieval times goes its own sweet way without ever buttonholing the listener as opera should. Once that is said, it contains a stream of delightful music, Schubert at his most open and refreshing; under Suitner's direction it here receives a sparkling performance, excellently cast. Edith Mathis makes a sweet heroine, and Peter Schreier sings radiantly, as if in an orchestrated *Schöne Müllerin*. The reconciliation of the two principal male characters, Froila and Mauregato, is most touching as sung by Fischer-Dieskau and Prey. The recording is richly atmospheric and is splendidly transferred to CD, and a full translation is included.

Schumann, Robert (1810–56)

Piano concerto in A min., Op. 54.

500♪ (M) *** Ph. 446 192-2 [id.]. Kovacevich, BBC SO, Sir Colin Davis – GRIEG: *Concerto; Sonata.* ***

Our primary recommendation for this favourite Romantic concerto remains with the successful symbiosis of Stephen Kovacevich and Sir Colin Davis, who give an interpretation which is both fresh and poetic, unexaggerated but powerful in its directness and clarity, and the spring-like element of the outer movements is finely presented by orchestra and soloist alike. The sound has been admirably freshened, and this is even more attractive at mid-price.

Violin concerto in D min., Op. posth.

500♪ *** Decca Dig. 444 811-2 [id.]. Joshua Bell, Cleveland O, Christoph von Dohnányi – BRAHMS: *Violin concerto.* ***

(B) **(*) EMI forte CZS5 69334-2 (2). Gidon Kremer, Philh. O, Muti – BRAHMS: *Violin concerto* *(*); SIBELIUS: *Concerto.* **

With Dohnányi and the Cleveland Orchestra adding to the weight and drama, Joshua Bell in a commanding performance defies the old idea of this as an impossibly flawed piece, bringing out charm as well as power. With full-bodied, well-balanced recording, this is a disc which offers an apt and generous coupling, with both concertos in versions not easily surpassed.

The vein of introspection in the Schumann *Violin concerto* seems to suit Gidon Kremer, who gives a generally sympathetic account of it and has very good support from the Philharmonia Orchestra under Riccardo Muti. It is not Schumann at his most consistently inspired, but there are good things in it, including a memorable second subject and a characteristic slow movement. The recording is full-bodied, vivid and convincingly balanced. However, the coupled pair of concertos are much less recommendable and, although the sonata recital with Gavrilov (for details, see under the Brahms coupling) brings much to praise, overall this forte set joins the 'curate's eggs' of which the bargain catalogue has no shortage.

Symphonies Nos. 1–4.

500♪ (B) *** RCA 74321 20294-2 (2). Phd. O, James Levine.

(B) **(*) DG Double Dig. 453 049-2 (2) [id.]. VPO, Bernstein.

Symphonies Nos. 1–4: Manfred overture, Op. 115.

(M) **(*) Sony MH2K 62349 (2) [id.]. Cleveland O, George Szell.

Symphonies Nos. 1 in B flat (Spring); 2 in C; 3 (Rhenish); 4 in D min. (original Leipzig version); *Overture, scherzo and finale, Op. 52.*

500♪ ✿ *** RCA Dig. 09026 61931–2 (2) [id.]. Hanover Band, Goodman.

Roy Goodman's versions on period instruments are a revelation, not just an academic exercise. Few period performances of nineteenth-century works can match these refreshing accounts, either for the vigour and electricity of the playing or for the new perceptions given. Convincingly Goodman shows how these works are far more cohesive in their often volatile inspiration than many used to think. Textures are clarified, but never to reduce the impact of the music, rather to give them exceptionally clean-cut terracing of sound, thanks also to the satisfyingly beefy recording. The first disc contains the three works dating from 1841, not just the *Spring Symphony* (No. 1) and the *Overture, scherzo and finale* but the original Leipzig version of the *Symphony No. 4*, usually heard in the revision of ten years later, with each sequence made very convincing by Goodman, particularly the big crescendo into the finale. Brahms preferred this earlier version, and here one registers why.

The Dresden CDs of the Schumann symphonies under Sawallisch are as deeply musical as they are carefully considered; the orchestral playing combines superb discipline with refreshing naturalness and spontaneity (EMI CMS7 64815-2). These recordings have dominated the catalogue, alongside Karajan's interpretations (DG 429 672-2) above all other recordings on modern instruments, though Roy Goodman's RCA version on period instruments is even more revelatory.

Yet the RCA bargain 'Symphony Edition' brings a splendid set of Schumann to cap them both. Recorded in a glowingly warm acoustic, the Philadelphia Orchestra has seldom sounded so rich-textured over recent years. The strings expand gloriously in the *Adagio* of No. 2; the brass produce the most expansive sonorities in the *Rhenish*. The performances are as vital as they are warm, and Levine usually produces accelerandos at the ends of outer movements to increase the excitement. The series is capped with a superb version of No. 4, where the powerful link into the finale brings brass playing to remind one not only of Wagner but of the *Ring*, and the very flexible account of the finale itself is not only thrilling but in its control of tempo shows that Levine has listened to the famous Furtwängler interpretation, absorbed its detail and made it his own. The two discs are available separately at mid-price: *Symphonies Nos. 1* and *3* (74321 20295-2) and *Symphonies Nos. 2* and *4* (74321 20296-2).

Szell's set of Schumann symphonies was recorded in pairs, in 1958 (Nos. 1–2) and 1960 (Nos. 3–4). Over the years the individual works have been available only very sporadically in the UK and we cannot trace making a previous assessment of No. 2, with which Szell began his cycle in October 1958. It proves to be a thrilling performance of great power and strong forward thrust, yet the eloquent *Adagio* expands gloriously and brings the most ardent response from the Cleveland strings, matched by few other versions.

Szell is at his most incisive and the orchestra are at their warmest in No. 1, truly a *Spring Symphony* in this exhilarating yet romantic reading. The account of the *Rhenish* is even finer, marvellously full of life. The playing is breathtaking, with the horns gloriously full-blooded. No. 4 is strong and dramatic, not as weighty as some, but equally convincing. The Cleveland players dig deep into the emotions of this music and Szell's flexibility of tempo in the finale, rather after the Furtwängler tradition, is made to seem spontaneous, such is the urgency of the overall performance. The *Manfred overture* is a great success, too. The remastering has quite transformed the recording, which throughout all four symphonies produces a richly opulent sound. The usual Cleveland problem of the close balance with the absence of any real pianissimos remains, but so does the ample hall ambience, and these vigorously passionate readings triumph over such a drawback. Szell proves himself an outstanding exponent of Schumann, able to stand alongside the finest interpreters of his day, and, were it not for the reduced range of dynamic, this set would have earned a Rosette. The two discs are packaged in an attractive stiff cardboard container, opening up like a book, with fine documentation.

Bernstein's VPO recordings from 1984–5 have the extra voltage which comes with live music-making at its most compulsive, and it is a pity that Bernstein, who displays a natural response to Schumann, seeks to impose personal idiosyncrasies on the performances that are not as convincing as Furtwängler's. Bernstein seems reluctant to let the music speak for itself, with heavily underlined expressiveness. The first movement of the *Spring Symphony* is pushed very hard, and the *Second Symphony* also brings the same larger-than-life projection. Slow movements are obviously deeply felt and have both warmth and humanity. In the *Rhenish Symphony* Bernstein's expressive indulgences are by no means as disruptive as some reviews have indicated, and the slight exaggeration at the climax of the fourth movement (said to be inspired by the sight of Cologne Cathedral) is forgivable when the brass playing is so overwhelmingly powerful. The outer movements of the *Fourth* are not allowed to move forward at a steady pace, but the *Romanze* has warmth and charm, even if the phrasing at the opening has an element of self-consciousness. The big transitional climax before the finale is massively conceived, yet lacks the spine-tingling sense of anticipation that Furtwängler generates at this point. Even so, with splendid orchestral playing and much engaging detail, there is a great deal to admire throughout these performances, and the resonant acoustic of the Grossersaal of the Musikverein gives the music-making a robust immediacy.

Symphony No. 1 in B flat (Spring), Op. 38.

500♪ (M) *** DG 447 408-2 [id.]. BPO, Karajan – BRAHMS: *Symphony No. 1.* ***

Karajan is totally attuned to Schumann's sensibility and he provides a strong yet beautifully shaped performance of the *Spring Symphony*. The very opening is electrifying with the Berlin Philharmonic giving of their finest, and the sound is an obvious improvement on the previous CD incarnation of this well-balanced analogue recording from the early 1970s, adding body and weight to the clear, fresh detail.

CHAMBER MUSIC

Piano quartet in E flat, Op. 47; Piano quintet in E flat, Op. 44.

(B) **(*) Hyperion Dyad Dig. CDD 22008 (2) [id.]. Schubert Ens. of L. – HUMMEL: *Piano quintet;* SCHUBERT: *Trout quintet.* **(*)

Lively, committed performances from the Schubert Ensemble of London. Although led by the excellent pianist, William Howard, this is playing from a balanced team which communicates directly and with both slow movements bringing a warmly expressive response and nicely observed detail. There are more individual versions of both works; however, if this inexpensive Dyad compilation seems tempting, the overall standard of musicianship is commendable and the amiable momentum of the music-making is enjoyable. Good if not outstanding recording. The Beaux Arts Philips CD remains first choice for this coupling (420 791-2 – see our main volume).

Piano quintet in E flat, Op. 44.
** EMI Dig. CDC5 55593-2 [id.]. Philippe Entremont, Alban Berg Qt – DVORAK: *Piano quintet in A.* **

The Schumann *Piano quintet* was recorded at a concert these artists gave in Carnegie Hall in 1985, where, to judge from the enthusiastic applause, it was a great success. Philippe Entremont is a fine pianist but not as sensitive to nuances of colour and dynamics as many of his colleagues. His insights are certainly not of the same order as Menahem Pressler's (Beaux Arts) or other rivals listed in earlier editions. The EMI recording is very good and the Alban Berg play with a little more spontaneity than they do in the studio, but this is not a first choice.

Piano trios Nos. 1 in D min., Op. 63; 2 in F, Op. 80.
(M) **(*) Virgin/EMI Dig. CUV5 61313-2. Grieg Trio.

These mid-price accounts of the first two Schumann *Trios* are new recordings and not reissues, as is the case of the 1992 Brahms *Trios* on the same label, also played by the Grieg Trio. Their approach to Schumann is admirably forthright and well characterized. The pianist Vebjørn Anvik is a commanding player (sometimes open to the criticism of being too assertive) but always intelligent. The playing of his two partners, Søvr Sigerland and Ellen-Margarete Flesjø, has splendid spirit and sensitivity. The recording is a shade lacking in transparency in the middle and lower register, thanks to a rather resonant acoustic, but this is not a serious hindrance to one's pleasure. The Beaux Arts offering on two CDs of all three *Piano trios* plus the *Fantasiestücke*, Op. 88, remains a first recommendation at premium price (Ph. 432 165-2), but this Ultraviolet version is to be preferred to the overbright Fontenay on Teldec; and no one investing in this coupling is likely to be disappointed in the least.

PIANO MUSIC

Arabeske, Op. 18; Faschingsschwank aus Wien, Op. 26; Kinderszenen, Op. 15; Papillons, Op. 2; Piano sonata No. 2 in G min., Op. 22.
(B) ** Carlton Turnabout 30371 0019-2 [id.]. Walter Klien.

Klien, always a thoughtful artist, is at his best in the *Arabeske*, and especially in the *Kinderszenen* which he plays very beautifully. He is also impressive in the *G minor Sonata*, and especially so in the beautiful *Andantino*. But the impulsive manner in the *Faschingsswank aus Wien* is not helped by a hard recorded quality, and the same is true for *Papillons*, where the sound is only marginally more congenial.

Carnaval, Op. 9; Etudes symphoniques, Op. 13; Kinderszenen, Op. 15.
(B) ** Cal. Approache CAL 6650 [id.]. Inger Södergren.

Inger Södergren is surprisingly impetuous in the *Kinderszenen* and, while the gentle pieces (including *Träumerei*) are touching, in what the French on this CD call '*sur le cheval de bois*', she gallops very boisterously indeed. *Carnaval* has a similarly impulsive character and certainly does not lack vitality, but it is in the *Etudes symphoniques* that one finds her at her most penetrating. The piano sound is good but a trifle hard at higher dynamic levels.

Davidsbündlertänze, Op. 6; Kreisleriana, Op. 16.
(B) *(*) Carlton Turnabout 30371 0041-2 [id.]. Walter Klien.

The strong impulse of Walter Klien's playing, coupled with a rather hard, bold piano-image, misses some of the lyrical flow of the *Davidsbündlertänze*. Klien is at his best in the work's more thoughtful moments, and here the piano-tone is fully acceptable. *Kreisleriana* is full of Schumannesque poetic feeling, even if at times Klien's impulsiveness nearly carries him away. The sound is fuller in this work.

Etudes symphoniques.
(B) *** EMI forte Dig. CZS5 69521-2 (2). Alexeev – BRAHMS: *Fantasias* etc. ***

Dimitri Alexeev combines the virtuoso technique which the work demands with supreme musicality and poetic feeling, the performance providing a structural cohesion not always in evidence. The digital recording, made several years later than that of the coupling, is excellent in bringing out the warmth of the piano-tone. This is a first-rate bargain.

Etudes symphoniques, Op. 13; Abegg variations, Op. 1; Widmung (trans. Liszt).
(M) * Revelation Dig. RV10031 [id.]. Evgeni Kissin – LISZT: *Etudes d'exécution transcendante No. 10* etc. *

If you are tempted, as we would be, to buy this version of the Schumann *Symphonic studies*, be warned: the sound is close and crude. Kissin was seventeen when he made this recording, the other items having been made when he was thirteen! The playing is amazing, worth three stars and more, but the sound does not begin to do him justice.

Vanguard 'Alfred Brendel edition': *Etudes symphoniques; Fantasy in C, Op. 17.*
(M) *** Van. 08 9165 72 (2). Brendel – SCHUBERT: *Piano sonatas Nos. 15 & 19* etc.

Brendel's opening phrase of the *Symphonic studies* is immediately individual, and yet in essence these readings from the 1960s are not wayward, even though they are strongly personalized. There are other ways of approaching Schumann (Kempff's, for instance), but in Brendel's hands the music's structure emerges anew and has the emotional grip one associates with Beethoven. Excellent recording to match the playing.

Fantasia in C, Op. 17; Faschingsschwank aus Wien (Carnival jest from Vienna), Op. 26; Papillons, Op. 2.
500♪ (M) *** EMI CDM7 64625-2 [id.]. Sviatoslav Richter.

Richter's phrasing, his magnificent control of dynamics, his gift for seeing a large-scale work as a whole – all these contribute towards the impression of unmatchable strength and vision. The recording is faithful, with genuine presence. The account of *Papillons* is beguilingly subtle in control of colour.

Kinderszenen, Op. 15; Sonata No. 1 in F sharp min., Op. 11; Waldszenen, Op. 82.
500♪ *** Decca Dig. 421 290-2 [id.]. Vladimir Ashkenazy.

Ashkenazy has his finger(s) on the pulse of Schumann's inspiration. The playing is very natural and all the more impressive for that. He proves a sound guide in the *Waldszenen*, and his *Kinderszenen* is one of the most appealing in the catalogue, again with a naturalness and directness that are attractive. The Decca recording is excellent.

Kinderszenen, Op. 15; Kreisleriana, Op. 16; Novelette in F, Op. 21/1.
(M) *** DG Dig. 445 599-2 [id.]. Vladimir Horowitz.

The subtle range of colour and articulation in *Kreisleriana* is remarkable, but then Horowitz plays in the studio just as if he were in front of a live audience, and the freshness and accuracy would be astonishing if we had not heard him repeating the trick. He was over eighty when he recorded the *Novelette* but the playing betrays remarkably little sign of frailty, and the recording given him by the DG engineers was among the finest he ever received. *Kinderszenen*, however, comes from a live recital, recorded in the Vienna Musikverein in 1987, a delightfully innocent performance never making pianistic points but letting the music speak for itself. The recording is good, but the audience's bronchial afflictions are inevitably a nuisance, even during the early spring of the year! An unmissable collection, just the same.

VOCAL MUSIC

Dichterliebe, Op. 48.
(M) *** DG Originals 449 747-2 [id.]. Fritz Wunderlich, Hubert Giesen – BEETHOVEN; SCHUBERT: *Lieder.* ***

Wunderlich, had he lived, would no doubt have surpassed this early recording of a favourite Schumann song-cycle but, even with an often unimaginative accompanist here, his freshness is most endearing, irresistible with so golden a voice.

Dichterliebe, Op. 48; Liederkreis, Op. 39.
500♪ *** Ph. Dig. 416 352-2 [id.]. Dietrich Fischer-Dieskau, Alfred Brendel.

Fischer-Dieskau, in inspired collaboration with Alfred Brendel, brings an angry, inconsolable reading, reflecting the absence of fulfilment in the poet's love. The Op. 39 *Liederkreis* also brings inspired, spontaneous-sounding performances, with the voice here notably fresher.

Frauenliebe und Leben (song-cycle), *Op. 42.*
500♪ ❁ (M) *** Saga EC 3361-2 [id.]. Dame Janet Baker, Martin Isepp (with Lieder recital ***).

Janet Baker's range of expression in her earlier, Saga recording of the Schumann cycle runs the whole gamut from a joyful golden tone-colour in the exhilaration of *Ich kann's nicht fassen* through an ecstatic half-tone in *Süsser Freund* (the fulfilment of the line *Du geliebter Mann* wonderfully conveyed) to the dead, vibrato-less tone of agony at the bereavement in the final song. Martin Isepp proves a highly sensitive and supportive partner, and the recording balance has been improved immeasurably by the CD transfer.

Scenes from Goethe's Faust.
500♪ ❁ (M) *** Decca 425 705-2 (2). Harwood, Pears, Shirley-Quirk, Fischer-Dieskau, Vyvyan, Palmer, Aldeburgh Festival Singers, ECO, Britten.

In 1972, soon after a live performance at the Aldeburgh Festival, Britten inspired his orchestra and his fine cast of singers to vivid performances, which are outstandingly recorded against the warm Maltings acoustic. This is magnificent music, and readers are urged to explore it – the rewards are considerable.

Schurmann, Gerald (born 1928)

6 Studies of Francis Bacon for large orchestra; Variants for small orchestra.
**(*) Chandos Dig. CHAN 9167 [id.]. BBC SO, composer.

Inspired by the fantastic, often violent or painful paintings of Francis Bacon, Schurmann here writes a virtuoso orchestral showpiece, full of colourful effects. The vigour of the writing is admirably caught in this performance under the composer, as it is too in the often spiky writing of *Variants* for a rather smaller orchestra, set against passages of hushed beauty. First-rate recording from 1979, made at All Saints', Tooting; but this CD is offered at premium price and has a total playing time of barely 50 minutes.

Schütz, Heinrich (1585–1672)

Christmas story (Weihnachthistorie).
(M) *** Virgin Veritas/EMI VM5 61353-2 [CDM 61289]. Kirkby, Rogers, Thomas, Taverner Cons., Taverner Ch., Taverner Players, Parrott – PRAETORIUS: *Christmas motets.* ***

Christmas story (Weihnachthistorie); 3 Cantiones sacrae (1625); Psalm 100.
(BB) *** Naxos Dig. 8.553514 [id.]. Agnew, Crookes, MacCarthy, Oxford Camerata, Summerly.

The reissued EMI version of Schütz's *Christmas story*, now on Virgin Veritas, has the advantage of three first-class soloists, all of whom are in excellent voice. One is soon gripped by the narrative and the beauty and simplicity of the line. There is no sense of austerity here, merely a sense of purity, with the atmosphere of the music beautifully captured by these forces under Andrew Parrott. Apart from a rather nasal edge on the violin tone, it is difficult to fault either this moving performance or the well-balanced and refined recording.

Summerly with his talented group of 10 singers – two of them doubling as soloists – give a compelling reading of Schütz's vivid and compact telling of the *Christmas story*. Aptly austere in its overall manner, with clear instrumental accompaniment, it yet brings out the beauty and vigour of the numbers depicting the different groups, in turn the angels, the shepherds and the wise men. The scholarly credentials are impeccable, with excellent notes provided, and the recording, made in Hertford College, Oxford, is full and vivid. The motets and the psalm-setting make a welcome fill-up.

(i) *Christmas story (Weihnachthistorie);* (ii) *Easter oratorio (Historia der Auferstehung Jesu Christ). Cantiones sacrae: Quid commisisti* (cycle of five 4-part motets). (iii) *Deutsches Magnificat.* Motets for double choir: *Ach, Herr, straf mich nicht* (Psalm 6); *Cantate Domino* (Psalm 96); *Herr unser Herrscher* (Psalm 8); *Ich freu mich des* (Psalm 122); *Unser Herr Jesus Christus.*
(B) **(*) Decca Double 452 188-2 (2) [id.]. Heinrich Schütz Ch., with (i) Partridge, Palmer, soloists, Instrumental Ens., Philip Jones Brass Ens.; (ii) Pears, Tear, Langridge, Elizabethan Consort of Viols, London Cornett & Sackbutt Ens.; (iii) Symphoniae Sacrae Chamber Ens., all cond. Norrington.

Norrington's Argo recordings of the *Christmas story* and the *Easter oratorio* were made before he espoused the cause of original instruments. The former offers some extremely fine singing from Ian Partridge as the Evangelist, while Peter Pears shows impressive authority and insight as well as singing beautifully in the same role for the companion work. The Heinrich Schütz Choir phrases with great feeling and subtlety; indeed, some may feel that their singing is a little too self-consciously beautiful for music that is so pure in style. A similar comment might be made about the double motets, although the sense of joy expressed in the *Quid commisisti* cycle (from the 1625 *Cantiones sacrae*) communicates strongly. The *Deutsches Magnificat* is given with admirable authority and is one of the best things in this very generous (146-minute) collection. Indeed this set offers much to enjoy and admire, and the vintage recordings, made between 1969 and 1975, have fine sonority, with the ambitious double motets given a proper sense of spectacle.

Easter oratorio (Historia der Auferstehung Jesu Christ).
(M) ** Erato/Warner 0630 11230-2 [id.]. Kurt Widmer, Jan Caals, Bernadette Degelin, Musica Polyphonica, Louis Devos.

The period performance from Devos has authority and a convincingly austere atmosphere. There is some fine singing here, especially from the choir; but not all will take to Kurt Widmer's slightly precious vocal style as Evangelist. The recording is very good, but the 49-minute playing time is less praiseworthy.

The Resurrection; Meine Seele erhebt den Herren.
(M) *** HM Dig. HMT 7901311 [id.]. Concerto Vocale, René Jacobs.

René Jacobs's account of Schütz's *Historia der Auferstehung Jesu Christi* with the Concerto Vocale is a performance of great accomplishment and taste, and quite beautifully recorded. This performance still gives great pleasure, as does the lively account of *Meine Seele erhebt den Herren* from the second Book of the *Symphoniae sacrae* (1647). This makes a fine mid-priced alternative to Bernius's excellent Sony version, which includes also the *Christmas story* (SK 45943).

Der Schwanengesang (Opus ultimum; reconstructed by Wolfgang Steude).
(M) *** Virgin Veritas/EMI VED5 61306-2 (2). Hannover Knabenchor, Hilliard Ens., L. Bar., Heinz Hennig.

Schütz's *Opus ultimum* is a setting of Psalm 119, the longest psalm in the psalter, which he divides into 11 sections. He finishes off this 13-part motet cycle with his final setting of Psalm 100, which he had originally composed in 1662, and the *Deutsches Magnificat.* Wolfram Steude's note recounts the history of the work, parts of which disappeared after Schütz's death; and his reconstruction of two of the vocal parts is obviously a labour of love. The project was undertaken in celebration of the European Music Year in 1985, and the recording a co-production with North German Radio. The performance is a completely dedicated one, with excellent singing from all concerned and good instrumental playing, and the conductor, Heinz Hennig, secures warm and responsive singing from his Hannover Knabenchor. The acoustic is spacious and warm and the recording balance well focused. The sound is firm, clear and sonorous. This rare set is welcome back to the catalogue on Virgin Veritas at mid-price.

Scriabin, Alexander (1872–1915)

Piano concerto in F sharp min., Op. 20.
*(*) Hyperion Dig. CDA 66680 [id.]. Nikolai Demidenko, BBC SO, Alexander Lazarev – TCHAIKOVSKY: *Piano concerto No. 1.* *(*)

One would expect Nikolai Demidenko to have something special to say about the Scriabin *Concerto*, but his performance is curiously unimpressive. True, there are some lovely touches in the slow movement, but these are often spoilt by mannered phrasing. His brilliance can also border on brutality in the more virtuosic episodes. Even though there is relatively little competition, this does not rate a two-star grading. Ashkenazy is superior – not to mention the Solomon account, which that great pianist refused to pass. Decent, but not outstanding, recording.

(i) *Piano concerto in F sharp min., Op. 20;* (ii) *Poème de l'extase, Op. 54;* (i) *Prometheus – The poem of fire, Op. 60.*
500♪ *** Decca 417 252-2 [id.]. (i) Ashkenazy, LPO; (ii) Cleveland O; Maazel.

Ashkenazy plays the *Piano concerto* with great feeling and authority. *Prometheus* too, powerfully atmospheric and curiously hypnotic, is given a thoroughly poetic and committed reading and Ashkenazy copes with the virtuoso obbligato part with predictable distinction. Maazel's 1979 Cleveland recording of *Le Poème de l'extase* is a shade too efficient to be really convincing. The playing is often brilliant and the recording is very clear but the trumpets are rather forced and strident. However, it can be regarded as a bonus for the other two works.

Symphonies Nos. 1 in E, Op. 26; 2 in C min., Op. 29; 3 in C min. (Le divin poème), Op. 43; 4 (Poème de l'extase), Op. 54.
(B) **(*) Ph. Duo 454 271-2 (2) [id.]. Frankfurt RSO, Eliahu Inbal.

Symphonies Nos. 1–3; Poème de l'extase; (i) *Prometheus.*
500♪ *** EMI CDS7 54251-2 (3) [CDC 54251]. Toczyska, Myers, Westminster Ch. (in *No. 1*), Phd. O, Muti, (i) with Alexeev.

Muti's complete set of the Scriabin symphonies can be recommended almost without reservation; overall the sound is as vivid and richly coloured as the performances. With the two additional symphonic poems (*Le Poème de l'extase* white-hot with passionate intensity, yet masterfully controlled) now added, this is an impressive achievement.

For those wanting a modest-priced set of the three Scriabin symphonies plus the *Poème de l'extase*, the Inbal/Frankfurt set, recorded in 1978–9, has the field to itself. This same orchestra went on later to re-record the symphonies under Kitaienko, but that set stretches to three (bargain) discs, to include also *Prometheus* and the early, Chopinesque *F sharp Piano concerto* (RCA 74321 20297-2). Moreover, Kitaienko does not shrink from adding to the percussion at will. Not content with that, he goes even further and adds a chorus at the closing section of the *Poème de l'extase*! The Philips Frankfurt recordings are full, smooth and clear and the orchestral playing is refined and committed, albeit less intoxicatingly vivid than in Muti's full-priced EMI set, which is distinctly superior. The *Poème de l'extase* is beautifully played and has plenty of atmosphere and, if it is not as passionately voluptuous as in Muti's hands, it makes a considerable impression and is pleasingly lacking in vulgarity. Overall, this Philips Duo remains a valuable and recommendable alternative investment for those with limited budgets.

Piano sonatas Nos. 1–10; Sonate-fantaisie in G sharp min.
500♪ *** Hyperion Dig. CDA 67131/2 [id.]. Marc-André Hamelin.

Marc-André Hamelin commands the feverish intensity, the manic vision, wide dynamic range and fastidious pedalling that Scriabin must have. There are other fine Scriabin cycles and, of course, celebrated accounts of single sonatas from Horowitz, Richter and Sofronitzky, but of newer cycles Hamelin's must now be a first recommendation.

Piano sonatas Nos. 2 in G sharp min., Op. 19; 5 in F sharp, Op. 53; 6 in G, Op. 63; 7 in F sharp ('White Mass'), Op. 68; 9 in F ('Black Mass'); Fantaisie in B min., Op. 28.
(BB) ** Naxos Dig. 8.553537 [id.]. Bernd Glemser.

This is announced as being the first volume of the complete Scriabin *Sonatas* and for those who want merely to get to know the notes, as it were, this would make an eminently serviceable choice at its modest asking price. Bernd Glemser is a young German pianist of obvious talent who shows a natural sympathy for this repertoire. He commands a keen imagination, a wide range of keyboard colour and he possesses an impressive technical address. No one buying these sonatas will feel short-changed – but of course they will not feel as satisfied as they would by such rivals as Marc-André Hamelin (Hyperion), Roberto Szidon (DG) or Ashkenazy (Decca), all three-star recommendations. It goes without saying that Horowitz and Richter in No. 9 are in a class of their own in terms of their almost demonic vision and electrifying pianism. There are times (as in the recent Vlach's Dvořák *Quartets*) when Naxos produce at bargain price something which is as good as a full-price recommendation. Bernd Glemser's accounts are very recommendable at the price but cannot be a three-star recommendation.

Sheppard, John (*c.* 1515–*c.* 1559)

Aeterne rex altissime; Audivi vocem de coelo; Beata nobis gaudia; Dum transisset Sabbatum (1st & 2nd settings); *In manus Tuas* (2nd & 3rd settings); *Gaude, gaude, gaude Maria; Hostis Herodes impie; Impetum fecerunt unanimes; In manus Tuas* (3rd setting); *Libera nos, salva nos* (2nd setting); *Sacris solemniis; Sancte Dei pretiose; Spiritus sanctus procedens* (2nd setting).
Second Service: *Magnificat; Nunc dimittis. Te Deum laudamus.*
Western Wynde mass.
(B) *** Hyperion Dyad Dig. CDD 22022 (2) [id.]. The Sixteen, Harry Christophers.

Ave maris stella. Cantate mass. Motets: *Deus tuorum militum* (1st setting); *Filiae Hierusalem venite; Haec dies; In manus Tuas Domine* (1st setting); *In pacem in idipsum; Jesu salvator saeculi, redemptis; Jesu salvator saeculi verbum; Justi in perpetuum vivent; Laudem dicite Deo; Libera nos, salva nos* (1st setting); *Paschal Kyrie; Regis Tharsis et insulae; Salvator mundi, Domine; Spiritus sanctus procedens* (1st setting); *Verbo caro factus est.*
✿ (B) *** Hyperion Dyad Dig. CDD 22021 (2) [id.]. The Sixteen, Harry Christophers.

All the music here is of such high quality and it is so superbly sung and recorded that it seems only sensible to consider these two Dyad reissues together. The first collection listed (CD 22022) will be especially attractive for some collectors, as the second of the two discs includes Sheppard's *Western Wynde mass*. However, this is a less elaborate setting of this famous theme than some others, notably that of John Taverner, for until the closing *Agnus Dei* Sheppard consistently places the melodic line on top, whereas Taverner moves the tune about within the lower parts. Nevertheless Sheppard's setting has an appealingly simple beauty, while the extended *Te Deum laudamus* which closes the programme is even richer in its harmonic progressions. The soaring second version of *Dum transisset Sabbatum* and the third version of the sombre *In manus Tuas* (with their characteristic momentary dissonances) which precede the Mass are also memorable. The companion disc offers ten more responsories, all of high quality and offering considerable variety, from the flowing antiphon, *Libera nos, salva nos*, and the gently serene second setting (for Palm Sunday) of *In manus Tuas Domine* and the more adventurous *Gaude, gaude, gaude Maria* on to the particularly rich upper lines of the first, Easter Day, setting of *Dum transisset Sabbatum* and the imaginatively contrasted *Sacris solemniis* with its fluent imitation in the upper voices.

However, we have given our Rosette to the companion set (CD 22021), for it includes Sheppard's glorious six-voiced *Cantate mass*, much more complex than *Western Wynde* and, with its glowingly textured polyphony, surely among his most inspired works. Before that on the first CD come eleven responsories, all showing the composer at his most concentrated in inspiration. The Sixteen consistently convey the rapturous beauty of Sheppard's writing, above all in the ethereal passages in the highest register, very characteristic of him. Even there, the Sixteen's sopranos seem quite unstressed by the tessitura. There are not many more beautiful examples of Tudor polyphony than this.

Mass 'Cantate'; Respond: 'Spiritus Sanctus'.
(B) *** Cal. Approche CAL 6621 [id.]. The Clerkes of Oxenford, Wulstan – GIBBONS: *Hymns*. ***

John Sheppard's *Cantate Mass* appears in the Hyperion Dyad collection, above; but for those looking for a less expensive way of examining his claims to musical mastery, the present Calliope Approche bargain reissue is ideal. The *Mass*, sung here a third higher than the manuscript indicates, and involving the sopranos in formidable problems of tessitura, is among the most distinctive of Sheppard's works, presenting surprises in a way uncommon in civilized polyphonic writing. The textures here are refreshingly clear, helped by the superb performances of the Clerkes of Oxenford. The five-part *Spiritus Sanctus* is less striking but makes an excellent bonus, equally well recorded.

Shostakovich, Dmitri (1906–75)

The Age of gold (suite), *Op. 22.*
(M) **(*) EMI CDM5 65922-2 [id.]. Philh. O, Irving – BARTOK: *Miraculous Mandarin:* suite. KABALEVSKY: *The Comedians* (suite); KHACHATURIAN: *Gayaneh; Masquerade:* suites. **(*)

The *Age of gold* is early Shostakovich, 1929 vintage, and the idiom is very much a cynical Russian pastiche of smart 1920s music from the West. Here the Philharmonia players are in their element, boisterously turning the barbs of satire into fun. The audacious *Polka* is given an English wit, matching Shostakovich with Lord Berners and Walton's *Façade*, while the closing dance with its boisterous accordions and piercing piccolos generates irrepressible energy. In between comes the *Adagio* where, with the most delicate solo playing from the oboe and principal violin, Irving creates an enchantingly fragile balletic atmosphere. The 1960 Kingsway Hall recording is remarkably full and clear.

Ballet suites Nos. 1–5, Festive overture, Op. 96, Katerina Ismailova: suite.
500♪ *** Chandos Dig. CHAN 7000/1 [id.]. RSNO, Järvi.

This highly entertaining set generally represents Shostakovich in light-hearted, often ironic mood, throwing out *bonnes-bouches* like fireworks and with a sparkling vividness of orchestral colour. The *Ballet suites* were the composer's way of satirically but anonymously re-using material from earlier works which lay unperformed for political reasons. The playing is perceptive and full of flair. The recording is spectacular and resonantly wide-ranging in the Chandos manner.

Cello concertos Nos. 1 in E flat, Op. 107; 2, Op. 126.
500♪ *** Ph. Dig. 412 526-2 [id.]. Heinrich Schiff, Bav. RSO, Maxim Shostakovich.

Schiff's superbly recorded account does not displace Rostropovich in the *First*, but it can hold its own. The *Second Concerto* is a haunting piece, essentially lyrical; it is gently discursive, sadly whimsical at times and tinged with a smiling melancholy that hides deeper troubles. The recording is enormously impressive.

Piano concertos Nos. 1–2; The Unforgettable year 1919, Op. 89; The Assault on beautiful Gorky (for piano and orchestra).
500♪ (B) *** CfP Dig. CD-CFP 4547; *TC-CFP 4547*. Alexeev, Philip Jones, ECO, Maksymiuk.

Alexeev is a clear first choice in both *Concertos*, and his record would sweep the board even at full price. The digital recording is excellent in every way and scores over its rivals in clarity and presence. There is a fill-up in the form of a miniature one-movement *Concerto* from a film-score called *The Unforgettable year 1919*.

Violin concertos Nos. 1 in A min., Op. 99; 2 in C sharp min., Op. 129.
500♪ *** Virgin/EMI Dig. VC7 59601-2 [CDC 59601]. Sitkovetsky, BBC SO, Andrew Davis.

Virgin's coupling by Sitkovetsky and the BBC Symphony Orchestra under Andrew Davis is impressive and intense; there is no doubt as to its excellence, it has tremendous bite. It is also splendidly recorded, and takes its place at the top of the list.

Violin concerto No. 1 in A min., Op. 99.
*** Teldec/Warner Dig. 4509 92256-2 [id.]. Maxim Vengerov, LSO, Rostropovich – PROKOFIEV: *Violin concerto No. 1.* ***

Maxim Vengerov's pairing of Shostakovich with Prokofiev was the *Gramophone*'s 1995 Record of the Year. Vengerov comes into direct competition with Perlman in Shostakovitch's *A minor Concerto*, yet his playing can dazzle the ear equally tellingly; he also really gets under the skin of the concerto and finds an added depth of poetic feeling, while fully retaining all the music's thrust and spontaneity. Rostropovich and the LSO give splendid support, and this Teldec disc becomes a first recommendation, except for those wanting both Shostakovich concertos together on a single CD.

'The Dance album': The Bolt: ballet suite, Op. 27a (1934 version); *The Gadfly* (extended excerpts from the film score), *Op. 97* (original orchestration); *Moscow-Cheryomushki* (suite from the operetta), *Op. 105.*
*** Decca Dig. 452 597-2 [id.]. Phd. O, Riccardo Chailly.

André Kostelanetz has already offered us a vivacious sampler of Shostakovich's entertainment music (see below), but surprisingly little of it is duplicated here. Chailly in fact offers 13 items from *The Gadfly* and reveals it to be far finer music than hitherto suspected, partly by using the original scoring. Erez Ofer, the Concertmaster of the Philadelphia Orchestra, plays the violin solo, the famous *Romance*, with delectable delicacy of feeling. For all his sophistication of detail and expressive expansiveness, Chailly doesn't miss out on the witty audacity. The opening number of *Moscow-Cheryomushki*, *A spin through Moscow* (when the chauffeur borrows the boss's car), has great energy and élan, the *Polka* from *The Bolt* combines wit with narrowly avoided vulgarity, and the boisterous opening of the following *Variations* will disappoint nobody. But, apart from the tunefulness, what one remembers most here is the superb playing of the Philadelphia Orchestra: the sonorous brass and vivid woodwind, while the strings haven't sounded like this in decades. The Decca team have found a new recording venue in New Jersey, and it is a joy to hear the luscious violins in *The Tango* from *The Bolt*, or *Montanelli* from *The Gadfly*; while the full body of tone in melancholy response to *The slap in the face* and the soft-voiced cellos and violas in *Gemma's room* recall the Stokowskian era.

Symphonies Nos. 1–15; (i; ii) *From Jewish folk poetry;* (ii) *6 Poems of Marina Tsvetaeva.*
500♪ (B) *** Decca Dig./Analogue 444 430-2 (11) [id.]. Varady, Fischer-Dieskau, Rintzler; (i) Söderström, Karczykowski; (ii) Wenkel; Ch. of LPO or Concg. O; LPO or Concg. O, Haitink.

No one artist or set of performances holds all the insights into this remarkable symphonic canon, but what can be said of Haitink's set is that the playing of both the London Philharmonic and the Concertgebouw orchestras is of the highest calibre and is very responsive; moreover the Decca recordings, whether analogue or digital, are consistently of this company's highest standard, outstandingly brilliant and full. All in all, a considerable achievement. The eleven discs are now offered together at bargain price, but they also remain available separately at mid-price.

(i) *Symphony No. 1 in F min., Op. 10;* (ii) *Festive overture, Op. 96.* Collection: *The Age of gold, Op. 22: Polka. Ballet suite No. 1: Galop; Music-box waltz; Dance. Ballet suite No. 2: Polka; Galop. The Gadfly, Op. 97a: Introduction; Barrel organ waltz; Nocturne; Folk festival; Galop. Moscow-Cheryomushki: Overture waltz; Galop.*
❁ (B) *** Sony SBK 62642; *SBT 62642* [id.]. (i) Phd. O, Ormandy; (ii) Columbia SO, André Kostelanetz.

Ormandy and the Philadelphia Orchestra recorded this version of the *First Symphony* in the presence of the composer in 1959, and their endeavours have never been surpassed. It is a beautifully proportioned, tense and vivid account, with everyone doing their utmost to get things right. The sound, too, is excellent. Still, after 37 years, a front-runner in spite of some excellent successors. The coupling could not have been better chosen: a suite of Shostakovichian orchestral lollipops selected by Kostelanetz, a dab hand at this kind of audacious light music. Readers who know the *Polka* from *The Age of gold* will know what to expect. Kostelanetz opens with a fizzing account of the *Festive overture*, Op. 96. Then comes the series of miniatures – mixed up to provide maximum contrast. Many of the pieces were virtually unknown when these performances first appeared in 1965, and even today few of them are familiar to the wider public. The fast numbers (like the Offenbachian *Galop* from *The Gadfly*) are redeemed from vulgarity by momentum and brilliant scoring, many of them suggesting the composer thumbing his nose at the Soviet authorities, and there is no better example than the *Moscow-Cheryomushki Overture waltz* with its trombone glissandi accompanying a very Russian dance-accelerando, followed by the equally infectious potpourri called *Folk festival*. But the gentler pieces are more memorable still: the hauntingly tender *Nocturne* from *The Gadfly* and the delicious *Barrel organ waltz* from the same source, matched by the *Music-box waltz* from the *Ballet suite No. 1.* Kostelanetz plays this music for all it's worth, and if again the recording is brash, this time it fits the music like a glove.

Symphonies Nos. 4 in C min., Op. 43; 10 in E min., Op. 93.
(B) *** Sony SB2K 62409 (2) [id.]. Phd. O, Ormandy.

The *Fourth* was the symphony which Shostakovich withdrew on the eve of its première, to be replaced later by the *Fifth* as 'a Soviet artist's reply to just criticism'. Ormandy pioneered the work in the West. His reading of this strange and powerful symphony is less subtle than Kondrashin's Russian account, less refined than Haitink, but it is thoroughly convincing and has the Philadelphia Orchestra playing both brilliantly (witness the frenzied string passage at the climax of the first movement) and with real depth of feeling. The combination of irony, anguish and plangent lyricism, as in the central *Moderato*, is strongly characterized, while the curiously subdued atmosphere of the march which opens the finale is remarkably well caught. The 1963 recording, made in Philadelphia Town Hall, is spaciously full and vivid; it sounds excellent in the current CD transfer.

Ormandy went on to record No. 10 with equal success in the same venue in 1968, and again he makes a case for treating the work with a passion that is apt for Tchaikovsky. The result is not as refined in its effect as Karajan's DG version, but it still makes a compelling, indeed massive, impact, notably in the long first and third movements. Ormandy's control of string phrasing is again immaculate and his great orchestra is never less than convincing and is often superbly brilliant in the precision of its virtuosity. This makes a thoroughly worthwhile bargain coupling.

Symphony No. 5 in D min., Op. 47.
(M) * Revelation RV 10025 [id.]. USSR State SO, Yuri Temirkanov – PROKOFIEV: *Symphony No. 3.* *

(i) *Symphony No. 5;* (ii) *Hamlet* (film incidental music), *suite, Op. 116.*
500♪ (BB) *** RCA Navigator 74321 24212-2 [id.]. (i) LSO, Previn; (ii) Belgian RSO, José Serebrier.

Previn's RCA version, dating from early in his recording career (1965), remains at the top of the list of bargain recommendations. This is one of the most concentrated and intense readings ever, superbly played by the LSO at its peak. Only in the hint of analogue tape-hiss and a slight lack of opulence in the violins does the sound fall short of the finest modern digital recordings – and it is more vividly immediate than most. The new coupling is appropriate. *Hamlet* obviously generated powerful resonances in Shostakovich's psyche and he produced vivid incidental music; with atmospheric recording, this 28-minute suite makes a considerable bonus.

Temirkanov's account of the *Fifth Symphony* derives from a concert performance in 1981 and, though less prone to expressive exaggeration than some of his more recent recordings, it is still uncompetitive, even at mid-price. He wears his heart on his sleeve in the *Largo* and, though there are some good things, readers are better advised to turn elsewhere. Decent recording quality.

Symphonies Nos. 5 in D min.; 6 in B min., Op. 54.
500♪ ❁ (B) (***) Dutton Lab. mono CDAX 8017 [id.]. Phd. O, Stokowski.

Stokowski's electrifying première of the *Fifth* has never been surpassed on record, notably for the intensity and beauty of the string playing in the first and third movements. The new Dutton transfer is little short of miraculous in its vividness and presence, and the quality of the recording is astonishing. Stokowski's *Sixth* was made in 1940, only a few months after the work was premièred, and it is powerfully atmospheric, the lines wonderfully sustained and the playing at times frighteningly intense. This performance has a special ring of authenticity.

Symphony No. 8 in C min., Op. 65.
500♪ *** Ph. Dig. 422 442-2 [id.]. Leningrad PO, Mravinsky.
(M) * Ph. Dig. 454 683-2 [id.]. BPO, Bychkov.

Mravinsky's live recording in full, clear, digital sound gives a superb idea of the magnetism of his reading, demonstrating the firm structural strength while plumbing the deep personal emotions in this stressed wartime inspiration. It is a great performance.

Bychkov's version is a non-starter. It is full of agogic point-making, especially in the outer movements; although very well played, it does not even begin to compare with Mravinsky's superb digital Decca recording, which remains a clear first choice. At mid-price Haitink's strongly architectural Concertgebouw reading is also unusually satisfying (Decca 425 071-2).

Symphony No. 10 in E min., Op. 93.
500♪ *** DG Gold Dig. 439 036-2 [id.]. BPO, Karajan.

Symphony No. 10 in E min., Op. 93; The Age of gold: suite, Op. 22.
(**(*)) Testament mono STB 1078 [id.]. Philh. O, Efrem Kurtz.

At the opening Karajan distils an atmosphere as concentrated as it is bleak and unremitting, while in the

Allegro the Berlin Philharmonic leave no doubts as to their peerless virtuosity. Everything is marvellously shaped and proportioned, and the early (1981) digital sound is made firmer by this 'original-image' bit re-processing.

Efrem Kurtz's recording of the *Tenth Symphony* appeared early in 1956 in the immediate wake of Mitropoulos's pioneering version with the New York Philharmonic. It is not as searingly powerful as the latter, but it is a distinctive reading and there is outstanding playing from the Philharmonia. (Some of its principals are listed: Sidney Sutcliffe (oboe), Bernard Walton (clarinet) and Dennis Brain leading the horn section.) The span of the opening slow movement is not easy to sustain, but Kurtz was scrupulous in carrying out the composer's markings, and his concern extends to the spirit as well as the letter of the score. If not the equal of Mitropoulos or Karajan, this is a *Tenth* worth hearing. The four movements from *The Age of gold* are characterfully shaped and expertly played by the Philharmonia. Reissued at full price with a brilliantly clear transfer which nevertheless produces an uncomfortably shrill treble, notably affecting the high violins.

Symphony No. 11 in G min., Op. 103 (The Year 1905).
*** Testament STB 1099 [id.]. Fr. R. O, André Cluytens.

Cluytens's recording of the *Eleventh Symphony* was made only a few months after its première and was recorded in Paris in the presence of the composer, a day or so after he had recorded the two *Piano concertos* with the same artists. It was issued in mono on three sides, the fourth being left blank and, thanks to its uncompetitive format, did not survive long in the catalogue. It appears now in stereo for the very first time and sounds astonishingly fine. Indeed it stands up to modern competition very well. Shostakovich called the *Eleventh* his 'most Mussorgskian work' and, as emerges in Elisabeth Wilson's *Shostakovich: A Life Remembered*, it was clear to Soviet audiences that its 'sub-text' was not so much the abortive February rebellion of the title as the events in Budapest, where the Soviet Union had just suppressed the Hungarian uprising.

(i) *Symphony No. 15 in A, Op. 141;* (ii) *From Jewish folk poetry* (song-cycle), *Op. 79.*
500♪ ❁ (M) *** Decca Analogue/Dig. 425 069-2 [id.]. (i) LPO; (ii) Söderström, Wenkel, Karczykowski, Concg. O; Haitink.

Haitink makes the first movement sound genuinely symphonic, bitingly urgent; after the Wagner quotations which open the finale, his slow tempo for the main lyrical theme gives it heartaching tenderness, not the usual easy triviality. The playing of the LPO is excellent, with refined tone and superb attack, and the recording is both analytical and atmospheric. The CD includes a splendidly sung version of *From Jewish folk poetry*.

CHAMBER MUSIC

Piano trio No. 2 in E min., Op. 67; Viola sonata, Op. 147 (arr. Shafran); (i) *7 Romances on Verses by Alexander Blok, Op. 127.*
** Chandos Dig. CHAN 9526 (2) [id.] (i) Joan Rodgers; Bekova sisters.

There are some 18 rival accounts of the poignant and concentrated wartime *Piano trio in E minor* and roughly a dozen of Shostakovich's last work, the *Viola sonata*, Op. 147, in its original form. Daniel Shafran's arrangement does not seem to be in the repertory of the great cellists of the day, and it will hardly be a high priority for Shostakovich collectors. Neither of these performances is of negligible accomplishment – but nor, on the other hand, are they exceptional. The disc is worth considering for the sake of the *Seven Romances on Verses by Alexander Blok*, Op. 127, for soprano and piano trio, which is less well represented on disc. Good singing from Joan Rodgers and fine Chandos recording: the main question will be whether you can justify duplicating the *E minor Trio* for their sake.

String quartets Nos. 1–15; (i) *Piano quintet in G min.* (ii) *2 Pieces for string octet, Op. 11.*
(M) *** BMG/Melodiya 74321 40711-2 (6) [id.]. Borodin Qt; with (i) Sviatoslav Richter; (ii) Prokofiev Qt.

Originally issued on EMI and now reappearing on BMG/Melodiya, the Borodin Quartet's second recording of Shostakovich's complete *String quartets* is an economical investment when purchased complete. The present recordings are made in a generally drier acoustic than their predecessors, and Nos. 3 and 5 suffer noticeably in this respect. However, the ears quickly adjust and the performances can only be described as masterly. The Borodins possess enormous refinement, an altogether sumptuous tone and a perfection of technical address that is almost in a class of its own – and what wonderful intonation! These and the Bartók six are the greatest quartet cycles produced in the present century and are mandatory listening. The *Piano quintet* was recorded at a public concert at the Moscow Conservatoire, and it goes without saying that with Richter at the helm the account is a powerful one, although the quality of the sound here is noticeably dry and forward. The *Two Pieces for string octet* are now added to the second CD.

String quartet No. 8 in C min., Op. 110.
❁ *** Koch Dig. 3-6436-2 [id.]. Medici Qt – BRITTEN: *Quartet No. 3;* JANACEK: *Quartet No. 1;* RAVEL: *Quartet;* SMETANA: *Quartet No. 1.* *** ❁

Immediately creating a powerful atmospheric spell at the opening, attacking the second movement with great ferocity and finding a bleak emptiness of constituents for the other-worldly closing obituary, this is a performance of rapt dedication and concentration, given a recording which achieves a remarkably natural presence.

PIANO MUSIC

24 Preludes and fugues, Op. 87.
500♪ ❁ (M) *** BMG/Melodiya 74321 19849-2 (3) [id.]. Tatiana Nikolayeva.

In this repertoire, the first choice must inevitably be Tatiana Nikolayeva, 'the onlie begetter', as it were, of the *Preludes and fugues*. Her reading has enormous concentration and a natural authority that is majestic. There is wisdom and humanity here, and she finds depths in this music that have eluded most other pianists who have offered samples.

Preludes and fugues, Op. 87, Nos. 1 in C; 5 in D; 24 in D min.
(***) Testament mono STB 1089 [id.]. Emil Gilels – CHOPIN: *Sonata No. 2;* MOZART: *Piano sonata No. 17.* (***)

These three *Preludes and fugues* were recorded in New York in 1955. The sound is a little dry and close, but the playing is magisterial.

OPERA

Lady Macbeth of Mtsensk (complete).
500♪ ❁ *** EMI CDS7 49955-2 (2) [Ang. CDCB 49955]. Vishnevskaya, Gedda, Petkov, Krenn, Tear, Amb. Op. Ch., LPO, Rostropovich.

Rostropovich, in his finest recording ever, proves with thrilling conviction that this first version of Shostakovich's greatest work for the stage is among the most original operas of the century. Vishnevskaya is inspired to give an outstanding performance and provides moments of great beauty alongside aptly coarser singing; and Gedda matches her well, totally idiomatic.

Sibelius, Jean (1865–1957)

(i) *The Bard, Op. 64; En Saga, Op. 9;* (ii) *Finlandia, Op. 26; Kuolema: Valse triste, Op. 44;* (i) *4 Legends, Op. 22;* (ii) *Tapiola, Op. 112.*
(B) *** DG Double 447 358-2 (2) [id.]. (i) Helsinki R. O, Kamu; (ii) BPO, Karajan – GRIEG: *Peer Gynt suites* etc. ***

Okku Kamu offers an exceptionally fine account of *The Bard*, and *En Saga* is hardly less admirable. His set of the four *Legends* is very good indeed. He handles pictorial detail most imaginatively, and the Helsinki Radio Orchestra responds with enthusiasm and good ensemble to his lively direction. Although his account of *Lemminkäinen and the Maidens of Saari* is a trifle brisk it is certainly exciting, and the famous *Swan* glides in sombrely. The engineers produce a well-balanced and truthful sound-picture and the CD transfer is firm and clear. Karajan's performances come from the mid-1960s. *Finlandia* and *Tapiola* are still among the finest accounts available, and the rather slow *Valse triste* is certainly seductive. Good transfers.

Violin concerto in D min., Op. 47.
500♪ ❁ *** Sony Dig. SK 44548 [id.]. Cho-Liang Lin, Philh. O, Salonen – NIELSEN: *Violin concerto.* *** ❁
*** EMI CDC5 56150-2 [id.]. Perlman, Pittsburgh SO, Previn – TCHAIKOVSKY: *Violin concerto.* ***
(B) ** EMI forte CZS5 69334-2 (2). Gidon Kremer, Philh. O, Muti – BRAHMS: *Violin concerto* *(*); SCHUMANN: *Concerto.* **(*)
* Teldec/Warner Dig. 0630 13161-2 [id.]. Maxim Vengerov, Chicago SO, Barenboim – NIELSEN: *Violin concerto.* *

Cho-Liang Lin's playing is distinguished not only by flawless intonation and an apparently effortless virtuosity but also by great artistry. The slow movement has tenderness, warmth and yet restraint with not a hint of over-heated emotions. Lin encompasses the extrovert brilliance of the finale and the bravura of the cadenza with real mastery. The Philharmonia Orchestra rise to the occasion under Esa-Pekka Salonen, and the recording is first class.

Itzhak Perlman plays the work as a full-blooded virtuoso showpiece and the Pittsburgh orchestra under André Previn support him to the last man and woman. He makes light of all the fiendish difficulties in which the solo part abounds and takes a conventional view of the slow movement, underlining its passion, and he gives us an exhilarating finale. The sound is marvellously alive and thrilling, though the forward balance is very apparent. This has now been recoupled with the Tchaikovsky concerto, but still at full price.

Kremer presents the *Concerto* essentially as a bravura concerto, and his is a vibrantly extrovert reading. While the recording balance places the soloist well forward, the orchestral texture has plenty of impact and good detail, and the fortissimo brass blaze out excitingly. There is undoubted poetry in the slow movement and throughout Muti gives his soloist splendid support. Other versions, however, are more searching and have more character, albeit in very different ways. The sonata recital with Gavrilov (see under the Brahms coupling) does increase the appeal of this forte collection, but none of the main concertante works is a top recommendation.

Among the profusion of Sibelius concertos Maxim Vengerov's Chicago account is dazzling and brilliant. He is much and (for the most part) rightly admired, but the Sibelius is all too glib and flashy to challenge the innumerable accounts that are currently available. Barenboim gets good playing from the Chicago orchestra and the recording, too, is very full-bodied and present. The Nielsen coupling has little to recommend it.

(i) *Violin concerto. Symphony No. 2 in D, Op. 43.*
** RCA Dig. 09026 61701-2 [id.]. (i) Spivakov; St Petersburg PO, Temirkanov.

Although Temirkanov's reading of the symphony is free from the expressive exaggeration that disfigured his Tchaikovsky, it is not a performance of any great stature; nor is Spivakov's (albeit accomplished) account of the concerto in any way memorable. Good playing from the St Petersburg orchestra and good recording do not make the claims of this CD very strong.

(i) *Violin concerto in D min., Op. 47; 6 Humoresques, Op. 87/1–2; Op. 89/3–6;* (ii) *Finlandia, Op. 26.*
(B) **(*) Erato/Warner 0630 12746-2 [id.]. (i) Amoyal, Philh. O, Dutoit; (ii) Helsinki PO, Kamu.

Amoyal's interpretation of the concerto can hold its own with most now available. He brings a splendid ardour, refined taste and great purity of tone to it, and it goes without saying that he surmounts its many technical hurdles with aplomb. He is free from that slight suggestion of the *zigeuner* which disfigures some accounts and he has greater spirituality than Kremer. The finale perhaps lacks the sheer excitement of Heifetz, whose pupil he was in the late 1960s; nevertheless it is good, and in the slow movement Amoyal has nobility and warmth. The recording is very natural, with a decent perspective and balance. For the bargain-priced reissue the surprisingly rarely recorded *Six Humoresques* have been added, improvisationally free and chimerical performances that catch the music's atmospheric delicacy, while the winningly extrovert No. 5 has plenty of verve and bravura. Okko Kamu's account of *Finlandia*, if not distinctive, generates undoubted excitement, and the recording effectively combines brilliance with sonority.

En Saga, Op. 9; Finlandia, Op. 26; Karelia suite, Op. 11; (i) *Luonnotar, Op. 70; Tapiola, Op. 112.*
500♪ (M) *** Decca Dig. 430 757-2 [id.]. Philh. O, Ashkenazy, (i) with Elisabeth Söderström.

These are all digital recordings of the first order: Decca sound at its very best. The performances are among the finest available, especially *En Saga*, which is thrillingly atmospheric, while the *Karelia suite* is freshly appealing in its directness. The climax of *Tapiola* is almost frenzied in its impetus – some may feel that Ashkenazy goes over the top here; but this is the only real criticism of a distinguished collection and a very real bargain. These recordings are all also available on a Double Decca, paired with Horst Stein's accounts of *Night ride and sunrise*, *Pohjola's daughter* and the four *Legends* (452 576-2). However, the playing of the Suisse Romande Orchestra in the last-named does not match that of the Philharmonia for Ashkenazy, and the single disc is the one to go for.

Finlandia, Op. 26; Karelia suite, Op. 11; Kuolema: Valse triste, Op. 44; Legends: The Swan of Tuonela; Lemminkäinen's return, Op. 22/2 & 4; Pohjola's daughter, Op. 49.
(BB) * Naxos Dig. 8.550103 [id.]. Czech RSO, Kenneth Schermerhorn.

It seems a remarkable achievement to produce a dull performance of *Finlandia*, but this one gets bogged down at the very beginning, and it is not helped by the rather opaque, bass-heavy recording. Moreover the opening of the *Intermezzo* of *Karelia* does not manage to generate much tension, and the *Alla marcia* also fails to lift off, again not helped by the sound. *Lemminkäinen* returns with a fair degree of enthusiasm and *Pohjola's daughter* builds to a quite impressive climax, although the performance is in no way distinguished. *The Swan of Tuonela* is more involving in its atmospheric evocation. But there are far finer versions of all this music on record, and this Naxos disc is a non-starter, even at budget price.

Finlandia, Op. 26; Karelia suite, Op. 11; Scènes historiques: Festivo, Op. 25/3; The Chase; Love song; At the drawbridge, Op. 66/1–3; The Tempest (incidental music): *suites Nos. 1–2, Op. 109.*
500♪ ❁ (M) (***) EMI mono CDM7 63397-2 [id.]. RPO, Beecham.

Beecham's mono performance of the incidental music for *The Tempest* is magical – no one has captured its spirit with such insight. The four *Scènes historiques* are beautifully done, with the most vivid orchestral colouring. No apologies whatsoever need be made about the sound here, though in the *Intermezzo* from *Karelia* (which has a 78-r.p.m. source) the quality is curiously crumbly at the opening and close: surely a better original could have been found.

4 Legends, Op. 22; Night ride and sunrise, Op. 55; (i) *Luonnotar, Op. 70.*
**(*) Virgin/EMI Dig. VC5 45213-2 [CDC 45213]. (i) Solveig Kringelborn; Royal Stockholm PO, Paavo Järvi.

4 Legends, Op. 22; Tapiola, Op. 112.
500♪ *** Ondine ODE 852-2 [id.]. Helsinki PO, Leif Segerstam.

Segerstam's performances of both the *Legends* and *Tapiola* are first class. This is now a first recommendation for the *Legends*, while *Tapiola* is the best since Karajan.

Paavo Järvi, son of the Estonian-born Neeme Järvi, draws fine and responsive playing from the Royal Stockholm Philharmonic and his account of the *Four Legends* can hold its own alongside current rivals. *The Swan of Tuonela* is atmospheric with the cor anglais solo beautifully played and, although *Lemminkäinen in Tuonela* does not have the dark, brooding concentration of Jensen's pioneering disc, it comes off very well indeed. *Luonnotar* is even more spacious than Järvi *père*, though Solveig Kringelborn does not make as strong an impression as her Finnish colleague on the Gothenburg DG recording. A good *Night ride and sunrise*, though again not quite a first choice. The recording has not the bloom and sense of space that Chandos gave the orchestra in their Nielsen cycle with Rozhdestvensky. This is well detailed and present but has less depth.

Pelléas et Mélisande: suite; *Scènes historiques:* suites Nos. 1 & 2, *Opp. 25 & 66.*
* Chandos Dig. CHAN 9483 [id.]. Danish Nat. RSO, Leif Segerstam.

Leif Segerstam and the Danish Radio Orchestra are beautifully recorded and their playing radiates genuine enthusiasm. Segerstam indulges in some pretty weird things in the *Pelléas et Mélisande* music. *At the castle gate* is too slow and the *Mélisande* movement is dreadfully slow. So, too, is the middle section of *Festivo* from the first set of *Scènes historiques*. When there are so many selfless performances of the *Pelléas* music to be found (Petri Sakari, also on Chandos (CHAN 9158)), let alone such a magical one of the *Scènes historiques* as the Beecham, why bother with this?

SYMPHONIES

Symphonies Nos. 1–7.
500♪ (M) *** Decca Dig. 421 069-2 (4). Philh. O, Ashkenazy.

Symphonies Nos. 1 in E min., Op. 39; 4 in A min., Op. 63.
(BB) *** Belart 461 325-2. VPO, Maazel.

Symphonies Nos. 2 in D, Op. 43; 3 in C, Op. 32.
(BB) **(*) Belart 461 321-2. VPO, Maazel.

Symphonies Nos. 5 in E flat, Op. 82; 6 in D min., Op. 104; 7 in C, Op. 105.
(BB) *(**) Belart 461 323-2. VPO, Maazel.

Symphonies Nos. 1–7; In Memoriam, Op. 59; The Tempest: suite No.1, Op. 109/2.
(M) *(*) Chandos Dig. CHAN 7054 (4) [id.]. Danish Nat. RSO, Leif Segerstam.

Ashkenazy's Sibelius series makes a rich and strong, consistently enjoyable cycle. Ashkenazy by temperament brings out the expressive warmth, colour and drama of the composer rather than his Scandinavian chill, reflecting perhaps his Slavonic background. The recordings are full and rich as well as brilliant, most of them of demonstration quality, even though they date from the early digital period.

The finest of Lorin Maazel's performances, which originated on the Decca label in the 1960s, are the *First* and *Fourth Symphonies*. The *First* has freshness and power to commend it, along with careful attention to both the letter and the spirit of the score; the *Fourth* brings comparable concentration: the first movement is as cold and unremitting as one could wish, and throughout the work Maazel identifies with the atmosphere and mystery of this music. In both symphonies the Vienna Philharmonic responds with enthusiasm and brilliance and the Decca engineers produce splendid detail, while the overall sound has fine body. The *Second* is excellent too and is beautifully played. Maazel's reading, however, leans more to the romantic view of the work: the Tchaikovskian inheritance is stressed rather than the classical forebears, which is why it is a great favourite with I. M. The finale with ripe, vintage Decca recording is sumptuously gripping. The *Third* has a very good first movement, but the second is faster than ideal; it is not quite poetic or reflective enough. Even so, Maazel keeps a firm grip on the outer movements, and his build-up in the finale is most impressive. The *Fifth* and, more particularly, the *Sixth* do not come off so well. Maazel sounds relatively uninvolved in both works. His *Seventh Symphony*, however, proved another landmark in the Sibelius discography: it has great majesty and breadth. These three records together now cost little more than the price of a single premium-priced disc and represent the least expensive way to survey this repertoire. Certainly the first two discs are genuine bargains.

Even though it has the advantage of very good Chandos digital recording from the beginning of the 1990s, this Segerstam box, even at mid-price, is a non-starter. Segerstam pulls the *First Symphony* mercilessly out of shape. He is more intrusive than almost any rival maestro, and his posturing in the finale is simply insupportable. The account of the *Second Symphony* is more successful, broadly expansive and warm-hearted, but not a little self-indulgent, particularly in the slow movement with its exaggerated climax. In the *Third*, Segerstam sets out at exactly the right pace, but it is not long before the brakes are applied. The natural flow of the movement is impeded by similarly disruptive changes of tempo. Despite some imaginative touches in the slow movement and good orchestral playing, this is not a reading with which it would be easy to live. The first movement of the *Fifth* never really flows, nor is the slow movement allowed to speak for itself. The finale virtually grinds to a halt at letter N; *un pochettino largamente* becomes very *molto* indeed. The *Seventh* gets pulled about too, though the majestic ending comes off well, and the conductor also inflates *In Memoriam* to almost twice its normal length.

The *Fourth* and the *Sixth* are Segerstam's two more successful performances; the former has many insights and in the latter he conveys a strong sense of atmosphere and is attentive to detail, although towards the end of the first movement he abruptly pulls back. However, the passage leading up to that (letter M in the score) is imaginatively done. As in the *Fourth*, the insights outweigh the moments of wilfulness, and it is good to hear the slow movement played at a really leisurely pace (even though he perhaps overdoes it). Throughout the cycle the playing of the Danish Radio Symphony Orchestra is sensitive and responsive, but first choice for a mid-priced box of these symphonies still rests with Ashkenazy on Decca (421 069-2), although Gibson, also on Chandos, might be considered, for his set takes up only three discs (CHAN 6559 – see our main volume).

Symphonies Nos. 1 in E min., Op. 39; 4 in A min., Op. 63.
❀ *** RCA Dig. 09026 68183-2 [id.]. LSO, Sir Colin Davis.

Sir Colin Davis's account of the *Fourth Symphony* is the most powerful to have appeared since the mid-1960s when the Karajan and Maazel versions made so strong an impression. It has a depth and eloquence that mark it out from any of its current rivals. There is a total identification with the spirit of this score, and an imaginative insight that goes deeper than his earlier account with the Boston Symphony from the 1970s. This is now the one to have. The *First Symphony* is hardly less impressive; the LSO play with feeling and virtuosity. To top it all, RCA give them splendid recorded sound.

Symphonies Nos. 1 in E min.; 7 in C, Op. 105.
500♪ ❀ (***) Beulah mono 1PD 8 [id.]. LSO, Anthony Collins.

Symphonies Nos. 1–7; Nightride and sunrise, Op. 55; Pelléas et Mélisande: suite, Op. 46; Pohjola's daughter, Op. 49.
(M) (***) Beulah mono 1–4PD 8 (4) [id.]. LSO, Collins.

There are those who (justly) count Anthony Collins's magnificent account of the *First Symphony* of 1952, with its haunting, other-worldly opening clarinet solo, as the finest ever put on disc, for the tension throughout the performance is held at the highest level. The closely integrated *Seventh* is also well understood by Collins, and once again the closing moments of the symphony are drawn together very impressively. The Decca recording remains remarkably vivid. Sibelians should also note that Collins's accounts of the other symphonies (with the fill-ups) have been added to this CD to make a four-disc set in a slip-case at a saving on the price of the individual records.

Symphonies Nos. 2 in D; 6 in D min., Op. 104.
500♪ *** RCA Dig. 09026 68218-2 [id.]. LSO, Sir Colin Davis.

The *Sixth* is a work for which Colin Davis has always shown a special affinity and understanding. Its purity of utterance and harmony of spirit give it a special place in the canon. There is no playing to the gallery and there is a grandeur and a natural distinction about the playing.

Symphony No. 3 in C, Op. 52; Finlandia, Op. 26; Karelia suite, Op. 11; Kuolema: Valse triste, Op. 44/1; Legend: The Swan of Tuonela, Op. 22/2.
** Sony Dig. SK 61963 [id.]. Pittsburgh SO, Lorin Maazel.

Given the quality of Maazel's first Sibelius cycle with the Vienna Philharmonic, made by Decca during the 1960s (see above), this new survey from Pittsburgh continues to disappoint. There are good things, of course, and the sense of momentum in the first movement is generally well sustained, though he pulls back rather more than he did at the end of the exposition and at the very end of the movement. The slow movement is on the brisk side – as indeed it was last time around. Whatever its merits, we are so spoilt for choice that any newcomer would have to be outstanding to be an effective challenge to Colin Davis, Blomstedt or Ashkenazy. *The Swan* comes off well, and so do the outer movements of the *Karelia* suite (the *Ballade* tends to sag).

Symphonies Nos. 3 in C, Op. 52; 5 in E flat, Op. 82.
500♪ *** RCA Dig. 09026 61963-2 [id.]. LSO, Sir Colin Davis.

Sir Colin Davis's account of the *Third Symphony* has a majesty and power that have few rivals. His *Fifth*, too, has tremendous grandeur as well as a feeling for the natural symphonic current that flows in these wonderful works. The recording has a splendour worthy of the music and the players.

Symphonies Nos. 3 in C, Op. 52; 6 in D min., Op. 104.
**(*) Decca Dig. 448 817-2 [id.]. San Francisco SO, Herbert Blomstedt.

Blomstedt is very impressive in this coupling, and so is the Decca recording. They are both performances of integrity and musicianship. All the same, Sir Colin Davis on RCA is ultimately finer and is to be preferred, although his couplings are different (see our main volume). He has deeper and more poetic insights than Blomstedt.

Symphonies Nos. 4 in A min., Op. 63; 6 in D min., Op. 104.
** Finlandia Dig. 0630 14951-2 [id.]. COE, Paavo Berglund.

Symphonies Nos. (i) *4 in A min.;* (ii) *6 in D min., Op. 104;* (i) *The Bard, Op. 64; Lemminkäinen's return, Op. 22/4; The Tempest: Prelude.*
500♪ ❁ (M) (***) EMI mono CDM7 64027-2 [id.]. (i) LPO, (ii) RPO, Sir Thomas Beecham.

In its colour Beecham's account of the *Fourth Symphony* reflects his feeling that, far from being an austere work, as is often claimed, it is ripely romantic. No performance brings one closer to the music, while the recording, made over fifty years ago, sounds astonishingly fresh. Beecham's 1947 account of the *Sixth Symphony* was said to be Sibelius's favourite recording of all his symphonies. Its eloquence is no less impressive. In the three shorter works on the disc Beecham's rhythmic sharpness and feeling for colour vividly convey the high voltage of Sibelius's strikingly original writing.

Surely not the start of another Sibelius cycle from Paavo Berglund! The ways of record companies are mysterious indeed: this is his fourth account of the *Fourth Symphony* and his third of the *Sixth*! The Chamber Orchestra of Europe play attentively, and as usual Berglund is dedicated and selfless in his interpretative approach. This is Sibelius straight and without frills, eminently well prepared and, as far as it goes – which is not far enough – satisfactory. But there are depths in both scores that remain unplumbed and heights that remain unscaled. Excellent and naturally balanced recording, but ultimately this is not a patch on the first recommendations listed in our main volume, let alone Sir Colin Davis's recent accounts of both symphonies.

Symphonies Nos. 4 in A min.; 7 in C; Kuolema: Valse triste.
500♪ ❁ (M) *** DG 439 527-2 [id.]. BPO, Karajan.

For many Karajan's celebrated 1965 account of the *Fourth Symphony* remains the finest version on record, and it certainly ranks along with the Beecham as among the most insightful. The performance is undoubtedly a great one. The *Seventh Symphony* is perhaps less successful though it comes off better than in Karajan's Philharmonia version, and the *Valse triste* is seductive. An indispensable record.

Symphony No. 5 in E flat, Op. 82.
(B) **(*) BBC Radio 15656 91882 [id.]. Hallé O, Sir John Barbirolli – NIELSEN: *Symphony No. 4.* **(*)

This broadcast performance of the *Fifth Symphony* comes from the 1968 Prom season, a year after his last EMI recording of the work. The sound may not be as wide-ranging or the textures as detailed or transparent as one might find in a studio recording, but there is warmth and body here. Sir John's view of the symphony is well known, and it is good to have him so commanding in the heat of the concert hall.

Symphonies Nos. 5 in E flat, Op. 82; 6 in D min., Op. 104; 7 in C, Op. 105; Finlandia, Op. 26; The Oceanides, Op. 73; Tapiola, Op. 112.
(B) **(*) EMI forte Dig. CZS5 68646-2 (2). Helsinki PO, Berglund.

This forte double completes Berglund's Sibelius cycle, which is now among the least expensive recommendable sets of the symphonies in the catalogue. Nos. 1–4 are on a companion forte reissue (CZS5 68643-2 – see our main volume). Sober, straightforward, powerful readings which maintain the high standards of performance and recording that have consistently distinguished Berglund's EMI Sibelius records. There is a good feeling for the architecture of this music and no want of atmosphere. In the *Fifth Symphony*, the development section of the first movement has a mystery that eluded Berglund first time around, and there is splendid power in the closing pages of the finale. The *Sixth* is particularly fine, though the Scherzo may strike some listeners as too measured. The *Seventh* is arguably one of the finest now before the public: it has real nobility and breadth, and Berglund has the full measure of all the shifting changes of mood and colour. Moreover the Helsinki orchestra play magnificently and seem to have a total rapport with him. Berglund's account of *The Oceanides* is splendidly atmospheric and can be put alongside Rattle's, which is praise indeed! The recording is well detailed and truthful, and the perspective natural. *Tapiola* is given its impact by a spacious ruggedness, and the very close of the work has a moving intensity. All the same, despite the very good recorded sound and the economical price and packaging, these cannot be recommended in preference to or even alongside the earlier Colin Davis set with the Boston Symphony, which is similarly priced and packaged on a pair of Philips Duos (446 157-2 and 446 160-2). That is the one to go for.

Symphony No. 7 in C, Op. 105.
*(*) Classico Dig. CLASSCD 115 [id.]. Copenhagen PO, Okko Kamu – NIELSEN: *Symphony No. 1.* *(*)

A decent, well-shaped but ultimately run-of-the-mill performance – and hardly competitive, given the quality of its rivals. At full price and 52 minutes' playing time, it is unlikely to challenge existing recommendations.

Symphony No. 7 in C, Op. 105; Rakastava, Op. 16.
(M) (*) Revelation RV 10006 [id.]. Moscow RSO, Rozhdestvensky – GLAZUNOV: *Scènes de ballet* **; PROKOFIEV: *Andante for strings.* *(*)

Rozhdestvensky shapes the *Seventh Symphony* in noble fashion but the trombone has a ruinous and crude vibrato. *Rakastava* is beautifully played, but the sound on both recordings leaves a lot to be desired. The symphony was made 1962 and *Rakastava* a year later. But what a weird coupling!

(i) *Piano quintet in G min.; Piano trio in C (Lovisa). String quartet in E flat.*
*** Finlandia/Warner Dig. 4509 95858-2 [id.]. Sibelius Ac. Qt, (i) with Tawaststjerna.

The early *Quartet* is Haydnesque and insignificant, and the *Lovisa Trio*, so called because it was written in that small town in the summer of 1888, offers only sporadic glimpses of things to come. The *Piano quintet* is given a fine performance on Finlandia, and there is little to choose between it and the more expansive Goldstone/Gabrieli account on Chandos (CHAN 8742). Readers will note the new catalogue number.

VOCAL MUSIC

Kullervo Symphony, Op. 7.
*** Finlandia/Warner Dig. 0630 14906-2 [id.]. Groop, Hynninen, Polytech Ch., Finnish RSO, Jukka-Pekka Saraste.

Sibelius's early symphony has been well served on CD, but Jukka-Pekka Saraste's performance with Finnish Radio forces is arguably the best of the current performances. It has a more urgent sense of movement and a greater dramatic intensity than those by his countrymen, Paavo Berglund (EMI) and Leif Segerstam (Chandos), and it has a rougher, tougher centre and seems more in tune with the essential character of the work than Salonen's (Sony). Jorma Hynninen is common to all these performances save Segerstam and, though his voice has lost some of the bloom of his first recording of the piece, he remains pretty commanding. Monica Groop is also in excellent voice. Saraste, whose recent set of the symphonies, recorded in St Petersburg with the same orchestra, was nothing special, produces altogether excellent results here. He shares the same venue (the Cultural House in Helsinki) with Berglund's 1985 recording but, although the sound is not as transparent or well ventilated as the EMI nor the choral singing as well focused, everything is so much more musically alive. This must be the preferred version now, though rumour has it that Sir Colin Davis and the LSO are recording it – and if it is anything like their 1992 London performance, it will be difficult to beat.

Simpson, Robert (born 1921)

Piano concerto.
(B) ** BBC Radio Classics 15656 91762 [id.]. John Ogdon; Bournemouth SO, Silvestri – RAWSTHORNE: *Piano concertos.* **

Here is Robert Simpson's only piano concerto, played by its dedicatee, John Ogdon, who gave its première at the 1967 Cheltenham Festival. This performance with the Bournemouth orchestra under Constantin Silvestri was given in Bristol later that year. It is a one-movement work which seems designed to explore the instrument's percussive potential rather than its lyrical possibilities. Ogdon plays it marvellously, but listening to it again after the passage of nearly 30 years makes one realize why it has never entered the repertory. It finds Simpson in unremittingly aggressive mode and offers all too few moments of respite. Eminently acceptable sound for the period.

Symphonies Nos. 1; 8.
*** Hyperion Dig. CDA 66890 [id.]. RPO, Vernon Handley.

Robert Simpson's *First Symphony* was a dissertation he submitted for his doctorate of music at Durham University, and his first work to reach the gramophone. Sir Adrian Boult recorded it with the LPO in 1956. It is a one-movement work, albeit in three sections, powerfully constructed and forcefully argued. It holds up to the test of time remarkably well and better than much other music of the 1950s. Vernon Handley gives a spacious and magisterial account of it, and the Hyperion recording illuminates so much of the detail which Boult's old mono recording left uncharted. Like the *First Symphony*, the *Eighth* received its première from a Danish orchestra (the former under Launy Grøndahl, the latter under Jerzy Semkow). One critic has pointed to the *Eighth* as seeming to embody some 'colossal inner rage' and, like the *Fifth*, it undoubtedly has a combative tumult that rarely passes into tranquillity. Handley makes out a strong case for both scores, and the sound is absolutely first class. An indispensable issue for anyone who cares about the post-war symphony in Britain.

Symphony No. 9.
500♪ ✿ *** Hyperion Dig. CDA 66299 [id.]. Bournemouth SO, Vernon Handley (with talk by the composer).

What can one say about the *Ninth* of Robert Simpson, except that its gestures are confident, its control of pace and its material are masterly? It is a one-movement work, but at no time in its 45 minutes does it falter – nor does the attention of the listener. The CD also includes a spoken introduction to the piece that many listeners will probably find helpful. It is played superbly by the Bournemouth Symphony Orchestra under Vernon Handley, and is no less superbly recorded.

Symphony No. 10.
*** Hyperion Dig. CDA 66510 [id.]. RLPO, Handley.

The *Tenth Symphony* (1988) will be a tough nut to crack for many collectors. Simpson is a real symphonist and his musical argument is unfailingly concentrated. The *Tenth*, like its predecessor, has a Beethovenian strength and momentum. It lasts almost an hour and is not the ideal starting place from which to explore this composer's world. But make no mistake: it is a work of stature, and it is very well played and recorded here.

String quartets Nos. 2; 5.
*** Hyperion Dig. CDA 66386 [id.]. Delmé Qt.

The *Second Quartet* is a spirited one-movement work which comes from 1953, between the *First* and *Second Symphonies*. It is, like most of Simpson's music in this medium, thought-provoking and full of character. The *Fifth*, composed over 20 years later in 1974, is one of the three modelled on Beethoven's *Rasumovsky Quartets* – in this case, Op. 59, No. 2 – and even emulates the phrase structure of the Beethoven. It is a long and powerfully sustained piece, which receives expert advocacy from the Delmé Quartet and excellent Hyperion sound.

Sinding, Christian (1856–1941)

Suite (for violin and orchestra), *Op. 10*.
(M) *** EMI CDM5 66060-2 [id.]. Perlman, Pittsburgh SO, Previn – BARTOK: *Violin concerto No. 2;* CONUS: *Violin concerto*. ***

Heifetz recorded this dazzling piece in the 1950s, and it need only be said that Perlman's version is not inferior. Such is the velocity of Perlman's first movement that one wonders whether the disc is playing at the right speed.

Skoryk, Myroslav (born 1938)

Carpathian concerto; Hutsul triptych.
** ASV Dig. CDDCA 963 [id.]. Odessa PO, Hobart Earle – KOLESSA: *Symphony No. 1*. **

Myroslav Skoryk is now in his late fifties, a pupil of the veteran Ukrainian composer Mykola Kolessa, with whose *First Symphony* (1950) his pieces are coupled. Skoryk teaches composition at Lvov and has a considerable output to his credit, including two piano concertos, two violin concertos and a good deal of music for the theatre. The *Hutsul triptych* (1965) derives from a score Skoryk composed for the film, *Shadows of forgotten ancestors*, by Sergei Paradhzhanov. It is colourful, often atmospheric and inventive, not unlike some Shchedrin. The *Carpathian concerto* (1972) is an expertly scored orchestral piece with strong folkloric accents – and some cheap orientalism. Not a good piece nor strongly individual, but the centrepiece of the *Hutsul triptych* is worth hearing.

Smetana, Bedrich (1824–84)

Má Vlast (complete).
500♪ *** Sup. Dig. 11 1208-2 [id.]. Czech PO, Kubelik.
500♪ (BB) *** Naxos Dig. 8.550931 [id.]. Polish Nat. RSO (Katowice), Antoni Wit.

Rafael Kubelik's Czech version is special, imbued with passionate national feeling, yet never letting the emotions boil over. The recording is vivid and full but not sumptuous, yet this suits the powerful impulse of Kubelik's overall view, with the build-up to the exultant close of *Blaník* producing a dénouement of great majesty.

Antoni Wit and his excellent Polish National Radio Orchestra also give us a superbly played and consistently imaginative account of Smetana's *Má Vlast*, a work whose patriotic aspirations can so readily turn into rhetoric. Not here, however. The warm resonance of the Concert Hall of Polish Radio in Katowice seems right for this very individual reading, full of fantasy, which goes automatically to the top of the list alongside Kubelik's distinguished, and justly renowned, 1990 Czech Philharmonic version on Supraphon, which is rather special.

Piano trio in G min., Op. 15.
*** Ph. Dig. 432 125-2 [id.]. Beaux Arts Trio – MENDELSSOHN: *Piano trio No. 2*. ***
**(*) MDG MDGL 3247 [id.]. Trio Parnassus – ARENSKY: *Piano trio in D min*. **(*)

The Beaux Arts account is not to be confused with the 1972 recording which they coupled with the Chopin *Trio* in the same key. It is the top recommendation for those wanting this coupling. They are very well recorded and are more restrained than their rivals on MDG.

The Trio Parnassus play very much in the nineteenth-century manner and tend to underline and italicize, but they give a likeable and convincing performance, very alive and vivid. Their coupling, the Arensky *D minor Trio*, may well sway some readers in their favour.

String quartet No. 1 (From my life).
✿ *** Koch Dig. 3-6436-2 [id.]. Medici Qt – BRITTEN: *Quartet No. 3;* JANACEK: *Quartet No. 1;* RAVEL: *Quartet;* SHOSTAKOVICH: *Quartet No. 8*. *** ✿

Smetana's masterly autobiographical *Quartet* brings a performance of dramatic intensity and spontaneous warmth from the Medici, who are in inspired form throughout all five works in this outstanding set. They capture the touch of irony as well as the high spirits in the Scherzo and move us greatly in their deeply felt response to the beautiful, valedictory *Largo sostenuto*, while the sudden, violent change of mood in the finale is profoundly affecting. The recording has remarkable presence and realism.

Polkas and dances: *Bear; Furiant; Grain dance; Hop dance; Lancer; Little hen; Little onion; Neighbour's dance; Polkas Nos. 1–4; Stamping dance; Stepping dance.*
(***) (M) EMI mono CDM5 66069-2 [id.]. Rudolf Firkušný – DEBUSSY: *Recital.* (***)

Artistically this is in a class of its own. Firkušný certainly captures the spirit of his great countryman and brings zest and joy into his playing. The music, too, has great sparkle and wit. These performances originally appeared on a mono Capitol LP in the 1950s but they sound very well in the present transfer. This is really distinguished playing in the three-star category, and the inevitable sonic limitations should not inhibit collectors from investigating it.

The Bartered Bride (complete, in Czech).
500♪ *** Sup. Dig. 10 3511-2 (3) [id.]. Beňačková, Dvorský, Novák, Kopp, Jonášová, Czech Philharmonic Ch. and O, Košler.

The digital Supraphon set under Košler admirably supplies the need for a first-rate Czech version of this delightful comic opera. The performance sparkles from beginning to end, with folk rhythms crisply enunciated in an infectiously idiomatic way. The cast is strong, headed by the characterful Gabriela Beňačková as Mařenka and one of the finest of today's Czech tenors, Peter Dvorský, as Jeník. Miroslav Kopp in the role of the ineffective Vašek sings powerfully too. The libretto has been improved and is clear and easy to use.

Smyth, Ethel (1858–1944)

String quartet in E min.; String quintet in E, Op. 4.
*** CPO Dig. 999352-2 [id.]. Augmented Mannheimer Qt.

These two works, given warmly expressive performances by a fine German quartet, represent Dame Ethel Smyth at opposite ends of her composing career. The *Quintet* of 1884 may suggest Dvořák's *American Quartet* and *New World Symphony* in its first movement, but the Smyth *Quintet* was written before either of those works, a strongly built piece with substantial outer movements framing three interludes, including a brief, magical *Adagio* which breathes the air of late Beethoven. Even more delightful and refreshing is the *Quartet*, begun in 1902 but not completed until ten years later. You could never imagine this often jaunty, amiable music coming from such a firebrand campaigner for women's rights. Instead of an allegro first movement, Smyth opts for an easy-going *Allegretto*, while the beautiful, peacefully lyrical slow movement equally belies the composer's political image.

Soler, Antonio (1729–83)

see Vocal Recitals, below, under 'Codex'

Spohr, Ludwig (1784–1859)

Double quartet in D min., Op. 65.
(M) ** EMI CDM5 65995-2 [id.]. Gervase de Peyer, Melos Ens. – BERWALD: *Septet* ***; WEBER: *Clarinet quintet.* **(*)

The main interest of Spohr's *Double quartet* lies in its inherent antiphony, which is skilfully managed. This is what might be described as a well-wrought piece but, apart from theScherzo which is quite catchy, the rest of the music is pleasant but unmemorable. The performance has plenty of character, but the recording, though clear and quite full, sounds a little edgy in the present transfer.

Stamitz, Carl (1745–1801)

Bassoon concerto in F.
(B) ** Carlton/Turnabout 30371 0006-2. George Zukerman, Württemberg CO, Heilbronn, Jörg Faerber – DITTERSDORF: *Double-bass concerto* etc. **

Stamitz's *Bassoon concerto* is a very much slighter work than its companion for cello, agreeable without being in any way individual, until the final rondo, which George Zukerman enjoys so much that he makes us smile too.

Cello concerto in A.

(B) **(*) Carlton Turnabout 30371 0023-2. Thomas Blees, Württemberg CO, Jörg Faerber – DANZI: *Cello concerto in E min.;* WEBER: *Grand potpourri for cello and orchestra.* **(*)

Thomas Blees is an uncommonly good cellist, and he gives a highly eloquent account of the fine slow movement of Stamitz's *Cello concerto* and a beautifully turned performance of the delightfully gay finale. The recording balances him rather too near the microphones, but his timbre is well focused (the buzziness of the cello-tone present on the old LP pressing has been cured in the CD transfer). This is a three-star performance and, although the orchestral sound could do with more body, this work is very much worth investigating.

(i) *Clarinet concerto No. 3 in B flat.*

(M) **(*) Carlton/Turnabout 30371 00222. David Glazer, Innsbruck SO, Robert Wagner – WEBER: *Clarinet concerto* etc. **

Stamitz's *B flat Clarinet concerto* is one of his more individual works, despite its obvious debt to Mozart, and it shows a touch of humour in its passage-work for the soloist. David Glazer's performance is a very good one, and the Turnabout recording is warm and quite vivid, if not refined. The Weber couplings too are well chosen and generous.

Clarinet concerto No. 10 in B flat.

*** EMI Dig. CDC5 55155-2 [id.]. Sabine Meyer, ASMF, Iona Brown – MOZART: *Clarinet concerto* etc.; WEBER: *Clarinet concerto No. 1.* ***

Stamitz wrote a fair number of clarinet concertos, of which this is a typical example. The slow movement is plain beside that of its Mozart coupling, but Sabine Meyer presents it persuasively and makes much of the genial passage-work of the outer movements, and especially the roulades of the dancing finale. She is stylishly accompanied and excellently recorded.

Stanford, Charles (1852–1924)

3 Motets, Op. 38: Beati quorum via; Coelos ascendit; Justorum animae. Anthems: *For lo, I raise up; Glorious and powerful God; How beautiful are their feet; If ye then be risen with Christ; The Lord is my Shepherd; Ye choirs of new Jerusalem; Ye holy angels bright.* (Organ) *Preludes and fugues in B and C, Op. 193/2–3.*

*** CRD Dig. CRD 3497 [id.]. New College, Oxford, Ch., Higginbottom; Paul Plummer or Andrew Smith (organ).

Edward Higginbottom and his splendid choir never made a finer record than this. The opening exultant *If ye then be risen with Christ* with its richly expansive closing picture of 'Christ sitting at the right hand of God' and resplendent repeated 'Amens' is matched by the soaring upper lines of the even more ambitious *Ye holy angels bright*, with its wide range of dynamic and mood. No less impressive are the splendours of *Glorious and powerful God* and *Ye choirs of new Jerusalem*, although the more succinct *How beautiful are their feet* is hardly less powerful. The beautiful setting of the 23rd Psalm is as affecting as the floating expressive lines of *Beati quorum via* ('Blessed are they whose way is undefiled') with its simple imitation and gentle echoes on the word 'via'. However, the joyful '*Alleluias*' which close *Coelos ascendit hodie Jesus Christus Rex gloria* do not make as strong an antiphonal effect as they might. The two organ *Preludes and fugues* are well placed to provide stimulating interludes. They are admirably played by Andrew Smith, who does not get a mention on the front or back of the booklet (only in small print inside). His equally unnoticed colleague, Paul Plummer, also makes an impressive contribution to the closing *For lo, I raise up*, where the choral response is thrillingly ecstatic, surging forward to its climax, then falling back to peaceful serenity for its benediction: 'But the Lord is in his holy temple: let all the earth keep silence for him.' All this music shows Stanford at his most confidently inspired, readily carrying the listener with him, when the performances are so secure and committed and superbly recorded in the Chapel of New College, Oxford.

3 Motets, Op. 38: Beati quorum via; Coelos ascendit; Justorum animae. Anthems: *For lo, I raise up, Op. 145; The Lord is my Shepherd. Bible songs: A song of peace; A song of wisdom, Op. 113/4 & 6.* Hymns: *O for a closer walk with God; Pray that Jerusalem. Magnificat for double chorus, Op. 164; Morning, Communion and Evening services in G, Op. 81: Magnificat and Nunc dimittis. Morning, Communion and Evening services in C, Op. 115: Magnificat and Nunc dimittis.* (Organ) *Postlude in D min.*

(M) *** EMI Dig. CDC5 55535-2 [id.]. John Mark Ainsley, King's College, Cambridge, Ch., Stephen Cleobury (organ); James Vivian (organ accompaniments).

Framed by eloquently beautiful settings of the *Magnificat* and *Nunc dimittis* from 1902 and 1909 respectively (Alastair Hussain the radiantly secure treble soloist in the former), this 75-minute collection – the hundredth issue in EMI's distinguished British Music series – celebrates Stanford's remarkable achievement within the Anglican tradition over a quarter of a century, from his lovely (1886) anthem, based on the 23rd Psalm, and the three Latin Motets of 1892 to the thrilling *For lo, I raise up* of 1914 (with the King's group sounding even more incisive, though not more impassioned, than their colleagues at New College, partly a question of a more forward balance). The concert is climaxed by the large-scale *a cappella* Latin *Magnificat for double choir* of 1918, dedicated to Parry, which is sung magnificently. The style of the Latin motets varies from homophony to simple polyphony and *Coelos ascendit hodie* uses an antiphonal double choir of eight parts for the '*Alleluias!*'. Included also are rarer repertoire: the two Hymns (1910), *Pray that Jerusalem* and *O for a closer walk with God*, the former more ardent than one might expect, the latter simple and touching. The two *Bible songs*, written a year earlier, are for tenor soloist with organ, here the sensitive John Mark Ainsley, with the *Song of wisdom* gaining in momentum and confidence as it proceeds. Needless to say, the King's performances under Stephen Cleobury are splendid in every way and the recording, while fully retaining the rich ambience of the famous chapel, controls the resonance so that there is no blurring of focus. The stirring *Postlude in D minor* (1908), which Cleobury himself plays, is used as a central interlude. James Vivian, the current organ scholar, impressively provides some of the accompaniments which are usually important in their own right and make bravura demands on the player. Highly recommended alongside the CRD collection above. Both CDs are well worth having, even though some duplication is involved.

(i) *Requiem, Op. 63;* (ii) *The Veiled Prophet of Khorassan* (excerpts).
*** Marco Polo 8.223580/1 [id.]. (i) Frances Lucy, Colette McGahon, Peter Kerr, Nigel Leeson-Williams, RTE Philharmonic Ch.; (ii) Virginia Kerr; Nat. SO of Ireland, cond. (i) Adrian Leaper; (ii) Colman Pearce.

Stanford's magnificent *Requiem* (1897) was composed in honour of the painter, Lord Leighton, who died in 1896. It is a powerfully conceived and moving work, integrating the soloists as a team with the choir in a particularly satisfying way. The contrasts of the writing, from the ethereal opening of the *Kyrie* to the blazing fortissimo of the *Tuba mirum*, are superbly caught here, the best recording we have had from Marco Polo and surely in the demonstration bracket. With fine solo singing to match the fervour of the chorus, Adrian Leaper can be congratulated on the great success of the first recording of a work that should surely be in the general choral repertoire. The exotic suite from Stanford's first opera, *The Veiled Prophet of Khorassan*, makes an agreeable if not distinctive encore. It is a pity that the *Requiem* is just a minute or so too long to fit on a single CD.

Stenhammar, Wilhelm (1871–1927)

(i) *Symphonies Nos. 1 in F; 2 in G min., Op. 34; Serenade for orchestra, Op. 31* (with *Reverenza* movement); *Excelsior Overture, Op. 13; The Song (Sången): Interlude, Op. 44; Lodolezzi sings (Lodolezzi sjunger): suite;* (ii) *Piano concertos Nos. 1 in B flat min., Op. 1;* (iii) *2 in D min., Op. 23;* (iv) *Ballad: Florez och Blanzeflor;* (v) *2 Sentimental Romances;* (vi) *Midwinter, Op. 24; Snöfrid, Op. 5.*
(M) *** BIS Dig. BIS CD 714/716 [id.]. (i) Gothenburg SO, Neeme Järvi; (ii) Love Derwinger; (iii) Cristina Ortiz; (iv) Peter Matthei; (v) Ulf Wallin; (vi) Gothenburg Ch.; (ii–v) Malmö SO, Paavo Järvi.

Järvi's performances are now repackaged at a distinctly advantageous price; this is the most comprehensive compilation of Stenhammar's orchestral music now on the market. All the performances and recordings are of high quality. All the recordings are digital save for that of the *First Symphony*, which comes from a 1982 concert performance and has great warmth and transparency. Recommended with enthusiasm.

Symphony No. 2 in G min., Op. 36; Excelsior! Overture.
(BB) **(*) Naxos Dig. 8.553888 [id.]. Royal SNO, Petter Sundkvist.

Petter Sundkvist's account of Stenhammar's glorious *Second Symphony* is absolutely first class interpretatively, though it is rather let down by the quality of sound, which does not match that of his Gothenburg rivals. It is the first recording of a Stenhammar symphony by a non-Swedish orchestra and the first to embody all the corrections the composer made in the autograph score. It is a meticulous, dedicated account which radiates an understanding of and love for this music. Everything is beautifully proportioned and well held together. Sundkvist also gives us an exhilarating account of the early, post-Wagnerian *Excelsior! Overture*. The Royal Scottish National Orchestra respond with enthusiasm. It is a safe recommendation at the price, but the sound is not three-star.

CHAMBER MUSIC

(i) *Allegro brillante in E flat; Allegro ma non tanto;* (ii; iii) *Violin sonata in A min., Op. 19*; (iii) *Piano sonata in A flat, Op. 12.*
** BIS Dig. CD 764 [id.]. (i) Tale Qt (members); (ii) Tale Olsson; (iii) Lucia Negro.

All this music comes from the 1890s, before Stenhammar's personality was fully formed. The *A flat Sonata*, written in the same year (1895) as the better-known and somewhat Brahmsian *Three Fantasies*, Op. 11, was criticized by Nielsen as being too indebted to Beethoven and Mendelssohn; though derivative, it has some pleasing invention and a good feeling for form. Lucia Negro recorded it way back in the early 1980s but she plays it with even greater authority and sensitivity now. The *Violin sonata* comes from 1899 and was written for Stenhammar's chamber-music partner, the composer Tor Aulin. The *Allegro ma non tanto* is the first movement of a projected piano trio (1895); and little is known about the even earlier *Allegro brillante* fragment. The pianist, who is unfailingly responsive, rather swamps her partners here and in the *Violin sonata*, thanks to a less than satisfactory balance.

String quartets Nos. (i) *1 in C, Op. 2;* (ii) *2 in C min., Op. 14;* (iii) *3 in F, Op. 18; 4 in A min., Op. 25;* (i) *5 in C (Serenade), Op. 29;* (ii) *6 in D min., Op. 35.*
(M) *** Cap. CAP 21536 (3) [id.]. (i) Fresk Qt; (ii) Copenhagen Qt; (iii) Gotland Qt.

The *First Quartet* shows Stenhammar steeped in the chamber music of Beethoven and Brahms, though there is a brief reminder of the shadow of Grieg; the *Second* is far more individual. By the *Third* and *Fourth*, arguably the greatest of the six, the influence of Brahms and Dvořák is fully assimilated, and the *Fourth* reflects that gentle melancholy which lies at the heart of Stenhammar's sensibility. The *Fifth* is the shortest; the *Sixth* comes from the war years when the composer was feeling worn out and depressed, though there is little evidence of this in the music. The Copenhagen Quartet play this marvellously. Performances are generally excellent, as indeed is the recording, and it is good to have this thoroughly worthwhile set at mid-price.

Sterndale Bennett, William (1816–75)

Piano concertos Nos. 1 in D min., Op. 1; 3 in C min., Op. 9.
500♪ ❁ *** Lyrita Dig. SRCD 204 [id.]. Malcolm Binns, LPO, Nicholas Braithwaite.

David Byers, who has edited the concertos, speaks of Bennett's 'gentle lyricism, the strength and energy of the orchestral tuttis'; and they are in ample evidence here. No praise can be too high for the playing of Malcolm Binns whose fleetness of finger and poetic sensibility are a constant source of delight, and for the admirable support he receives from Nicholas Braithwaite and the LPO. The engineers produce sound of the highest quality. A most enjoyable disc.

Stradella, Alessandro (1644–82)

Motets: *Benedictus Dominus Deo; Chare Jesu suavissime; Crocifissione e morte di N. S. Giesù Christo; Lamentatione il Mercoledì Santo; O vos omnes qui transitis.*
*** Virgin/Veritas/EMI VC5 45175-2. Gérard Lesne, Sandrine Piau, Il Seminario Musicale.

Throughout his life, Alessandro Stradella was associated with scandals, both financial and sexual, and he was finally murdered, although the reasons for his assassination are obscure. He was a highly successful composer and professional arranger (of opera) and wrote church music which combined drama with remarkable serenity and expressive beauty. *Benedictus Dominus Deo* is a particularly beautiful duet cantata in which God is thanked for sending his son to earth to redeem mankind. *O vos omnes*, a solo cantata, is shorter but no less potent. The text first expresses a languishing adoration of Jesus, with sensuous use of descending chromatics, and the work ends with lively *Alleluias*. Lesne is a master of this repertoire, and in the former cantata he is radiantly joined by Sandrine Piau, who then goes on to dominate the joyously lyrical *Chare Jesu suavissime*, sweetly praising Saint Philip Neri. These works are framed by the more austere *Crocifissione e morte di N. S. Giesù Christo* (which has a memorably eloquent instrumental introduction, after which the solo line is both grave and plaintive) and the closing *Lamentatione for Ash Wednesday*, which is also restrained but touching beautiful. The accompaniments, by a small, authentic-instrument group, are very sensitive indeed. This is perhaps specialist repertoire, but Gérard Lesne has made it his own and his artistry is unsurpassed.

Straus, Oscar (1870–1954)

Marches: *Einzugs; Bulgaren; Die Schlossparade. Menuett à la cour*. Polka: *G'stellte Mäd'ln. Rund um die Liebe* (Overture); Waltzes: (i) *L'Amour m'emporte. Alt-Wiener Reigen; Eine Ballnacht; Der Reigen; Didi;* (i) *Komm, komm, Held meiner Träume; Tragante; Valse lente; Walzerträume*.
*** Marco Polo Dig. 8.223596 [id.]. (i) Veronika Kincses; Budapest Strauss SO, Alfred Walter.

It is good to have Oscar Straus (with one 's') represented in the Marco Polo series of Viennese dance music; even though he is no relation to the famous Strauss family, his style of writing echoed theirs, also absorbing influences from Lehár. His great hit was the operetta, *A Waltz Dream* (1907), which had a first run in Vienna of 500 performances. His *Walzerträume* is deftly based on the main theme from the operetta, and the *Einzugs-Marsch* comes from the same source. But he could also manage a neat polka and score it very prettily, as is instanced by *G'stellte Mäd'ln*, while the *Alt-Wiener Reigen waltz* is also full of charm and is played here very seductively. *Komm, komm, Held meiner Träume* is of course the famous 'Come, come, my hero', which comes from a parody operetta based on George Bernard Shaw's *Arms and the Man*. In 1908 it was a flop in Vienna, under its title *Der tapfere Soldat* ('The brave soldier') but was a resounding success in England and the USA later, when its title was changed to *The Chocolate Soldier* and its hit song took the world by storm. It is nicely sung here in soubrette style by Veronika Kincses. The light-hearted *Didi waltz* is all that survives from a much less successful attempt to adapt Sardou's *Die Marquise* for the operetta stage. The *Valse lente*, with its bewitchingly gentle charm (presented most daintily by Walter), sounds rather like Delibes; this and the elegant *Menuett à la cour* both come from a fairy-tale ballet (*The Princess of Tragant*) in which all the characters are puppet-like and behave like stiff automata until Prince Kreisler, the hero, breaks the spell. The whole company then dance the joyfully vigorous *Tragant waltz*. *Eine Ballnacht*, similarly gay, celebrates the 'operetta of dreams' which Straus confected in the darkest days of the First World War, to cheer up the Viennese after four years of increasing deprivation. When the Second World War broke out, the now-world-renowned composer fled, first briefly to Paris, then to America. But he returned home when peace was resumed and wrote an engaging hit, sung first by Danielle Darrieux in a 1952 French film, *Madame de . . .*, and here by Veronika Kincses, and he capped his movie career with a Parisian-style waltz, *Der Reigen*, for the famous Max Ophüls film, *La Ronde*, the song eventually becoming better-known than the movie. The programme opens with a pot-pourri overture irresistibly full of sumptuous and light-hearted melody. It is infectiously played here, like the rest of the programme, by the first-class Budapest Strauss Symphony Orchestra, conducted with affection and great élan by Alfred Walter – easily the best CD he has made so far. The recording, too, is gorgeously sumptuous, and this is a marvellous disc to cheer you up on a dull day. Highly recommended.

Strauss, Johann Jr (1825–99)

Volume 46: March: *Vaterländischer*. Polkas: *Pawlowsk; Pizzicato* (with Josef); *Probirmamsell*. Quadrilles: *Marien; Annika*. Romance: *Sehnsucht*. Waltzes: *Cagliostro; Engagement; Greeting to America*. (i) Gradual: *Tu qui regis totum orbem*. SCHUMANN, arr. Johann Strauss: *Widmung*.
*** Marco Polo Dig. 8.223246 [id.]. Slovak RSO (Bratislava), Michael Dittrich; (i) with Slovak Philh. Ch. (members).

Michael Dittrich is on top form in Volume 46 of this ongoing series, opening vivaciously with a musical switch in march form, beginning with the *Radetzky* 'fanfare' and proceeding to quote intriguing snippets from all kinds of sources, including the Austrian national anthem. The *Greeting to America waltz* has a very appropriate and recognizable introduction and is as attractive as the delightfully scored *Engagement waltz*, also written for America. The *Marien-Quadrille* is another charmer, and we learn from the excellent notes that the famous *Pizzicato polka*, a joint effort between Johann and Josef, was composed in Pavlosk on a Russian tour in 1869. The transcription of Schumann's love song, *Widmung*, was made by Johann in 1862 as a tribute to his new bride, Jetty, who was a singer, but the *Romance* (*Sehnsucht*) was written as a more robust cornet solo. The Gradual, *Tu qui regis totum orbem* ('Thou who rulest the whole world'), is a surprise inclusion from the eighteen-year-old composer – an offertory sung in conjunction with the performance of a Mass by his teacher, Professor Dreschler – and very pleasing it is. The concert ends with one of the deservedly better-known waltzes, taken from the operetta *Cagliostro in Wien* and played in an elegantly vivacious but nicely flexible style, like the rest of this very appealing programme, one of the very best of the Marco Polo series. The recording is excellent.

Volume 47: Ballet music from *Die Fledermaus;* from *Indigo und die vierzig Räuber* (arr. Schönherr). *Eine Nacht in Venedig: Processional march.* GOUNOD, arr. Johann STRAUSS: *Faust (Romance). Quadrille on themes from Faust.* Marches: *Kaiser Alexander Huldinungs; Kaiser Frans Joseph Jubiläums; Der Zigeunerbaron.* Waltzes: *Coliseum waltzes; Farewell to America; Sounds from Boston.*
*** Marco Polo Dig. 8.223247 [id.]. Bratislava City Ch., Slovak RSO (Bratislava), Johannes Wildner.

This is another very attractive compilation with many beguiling novelties. After the brief but lively march from *Der Zigeunerbaron* comes *Farewell to America*, an agreeable pastiche waltz which waits until its coda to quote *The Star-spangled Banner*. The following *Faust Romance* is a robust flugelhorn solo, based on an aria which was later to disappear from Gounod's revision of his score. The lively *Quadrille*, however, includes many favourite tunes from the opera and genially climaxes with the *Soldiers' chorus*. Strauss's own ballet-music, written to be played during Orlofsky's supper party in *Die Fledermaus*, is today almost always replaced by something briefer. It includes a number of short national dances (not forgetting a *Schottische*), and the *Bohemian dance* is in the form of a choral polka, actually sung here ('Marianka, come here and dance with me'), while the Hungarian finale reprises the music from Rosalinde's *Csárdás*. On the other hand, Schönherr's audaciously scored (some might say over-scored) 11-minute *mélange* of tunes from *Indigo and the Forty Thieves* is at times more like Offenbach than Strauss: it coalesces the good tunes and presents them in a glittering kaleidoscope of orchestral colour. The engaging *Coliseum waltzes* which follow uncannily anticipate the *Blue Danube*, complete with an opening horn theme. *Sounds from Boston*, written for the composer's Boston visit in 1872, is another pastiche waltz of considerable charm, resulting as much from its delicacy of scoring as from its ready melodic flow: the orchestral parts were discovered, hidden away in the music library of the Boston Conservatory. The ideas come from earlier waltzes and almost none of them are familiar. All this music is liltingly and sparklingly presented by the Slovak Radio Orchestra, and no one could accuse the conductor, Johannes Wildner, of dullness.

Volume 48: Complete Overtures, Volume 1: *Concert overture: Opéra comique* (arr. Pollack). *Intermezzo* from *Tausend und eine Nacht.* Overtures: *Blindekuh; Cagliostro in Wien; Der Carneval in Rom; Die Fledermaus; Indigo und die vierzig Räuber. Prince Methusalem; Das Spitzentuch der Königen.*
**(*) Marco Polo Dig. 8.223248 [id.]. Slovak State PO (Košice), Alfred Walter.

Collections of operetta overtures are almost always entertainingly tuneful, and this one is no exception. It begins with a curiosity that may or may not be authentic, an *Overture comique* written by the young Johann Jr for large harmonium (a kind of orchestrion) and piano, and afterwards arranged by the Strauss scholar, Fritz Lange, for violin and piano. None of the ideas it contains can be traced to the composer's notebooks, but the piece is attractive and is well put together in the form of a concert overture. It is heard here in a new arrangement (following the Lange manuscript) by Christopher Pollack. *Indigo und die vierzig Räuber* ('Indigo and the forty thieves') is also interesting in that Strauss omits the waltz rhythm altogether, which makes its lightly rhythmic progress seem rather Offenbachian. The *Intermezzo* from *1001 Nights* is a just favourite, although Walter's languorous performance could use a little more lift, and *Die Fledermaus* is a fairly routine performance. However, Walter conducts the other overtures very agreeably and makes the most of their pretty scoring. The waltzes are always coaxed nicely, particularly that in *Cagliostro in Wien*, and the playing has charm; yet one feels that some of the livelier ideas might have been given a bit more zip.

Volume 49: Complete overtures, Volume 2: *Aschenbrödel (Cinderella): Quadrille.* Overtures: *Die Göttin der Vernunft (The Goddess of reason); Der lustige Krieg. Jabuka: Prelude to Act III. Eine Nacht in Venedig: Overture* and *Prelude to Act III.* Overtures: *Simplicius; Waldmeister; Der Zigeunerbaron.*
**(*) Marco Polo Dig. 8.223275 [id.]. Slovak State PO (Košice), Alfred Walter.

Alfred Walter's second collection of overtures has distinctly more sparkle than the first. He is always good with waltzes and there are quite a few here, if only in snippet form. The pair included in *A Night in Venice* are presented with appealing delicacy, while *The Goddess of reason* brings a waltzing violin solo complete with cadenza and, at the close, another waltz which swings splendidly. *Zigeunerbaron* is the best-known piece here, and it is laid out elegantly and is beautifully played. But Walter is inclined to dally by the wayside: in the theatre a performance like this would not hold the attention of the audience. *Simplicius* is much more lively, with a march near the beginning, and *Waldmeister* has real verve, with the horns skipping along nicely towards the end. What one rediscovers on listening through this pair of discs is not only the fecundity of Johann's invention and the charm of his orchestration, but also the felicitous way he turns a pot-pourri into a naturally spontaneous sequence of ideas. The recording throughout both collections is first class, spacious and with a ballroom warmth.

Volume 50: (i) *Am Donaustrand;* (i) *Erste Liebe (Romanze); Erster Gedanke;* (i) *Ein gstanzi von Tanzl; Die Fledermaus: Csárdás and New Csárdás. Frisch gewagt* (Galop); *Da nicken die Giebel* (Polka-Mazurka); *Die Göttin der Vernunft* (Quadrille); (i) *Dolci pianti;* Waltzes: (i) *Frühlingstimmen;* (i) *King Gretelein; Nachgelassener; Odeon-Waltz;* (i) *Wo die Citronen blüh'n;* (i) *Wenn du ein herzig Liebchen hast.*
*** Marco Polo Dig. 8.223276 [id.]. (i) Marilyn Hill Smith; Slovak RSO (Bratislava), Christian Pollack.

Marilyn Hill Smith was on hand for this collection, so one wonders why the opening *Csárdás* from *Die Fledermaus* is the orchestral version (arranged by Hans Swarowsky); but the excellent Christian Pollack makes a good case for it, his ebb and flow of mood and tempo very engaging. Hill Smith sings a number of items, and her light soubrette is just right for this repertoire. She presents *Wo die Citronen blüh'n* with much vivacity and is hardly less sparkling in the famous *Voices of spring*. Moreover she offers as a charming vignette *Dolci pianti* (a song which Strauss composed for his singer-wife, Jetty), for which she has also provided the accompanying translation. The rest of the programme is agreeable, but there are no lost masterpieces here. Pollack makes the most of the waltzes and is especially characterful in the polka-mazurka, *Da nicken die Giebel*, which sounds a bit like a slow waltz with extra accents. Again, first-rate recording.

Volume 51: *Auf der Alm* (Idyll); *Fürstin Ninetta* (Entr'acte); Galop: *Liebesbotschaft;* (i) Choral polka: *Champêtre (Wo klingen die Lieder)*. Polka-mazurka: *Promenade-Abenteuer*. (ii) *Romance No. 2 for cello and orchestra*. Choral waltz: (i) *An der schönen, blauen Donau.* Waltzes: *Centennial; Enchantment; Engagement; Farewell to America; Manhattan; Tauben*. Songs: (iii) *Bauersleut' im Künstlerhaus; D'Hauptsach* (both arr. Rott).
❀ *** Marco Polo Dig. 8.223279 [id.]. Slovak RSO (Bratislava), Jerome Cohen; with (i) Slovak Philharmonic Ch.; (ii) Ivan Tvrdik; (iii) Adrian Eröd.

It is rather appropriate that Volume 51 should be special, and so it is. It opens with the enchanting choral *Polka mazurka champêtre*, introduced by the horns and gloriously sung by a male chorus with a nicely managed diminuendo at the coda. And it ends with Strauss's masterpiece, the *Blue Danube*, also for male-voice choir and sung with an infectious lilt, to leave the listener in high spirits. All the other half-dozen waltzes here are virtually unknown, and every one is delightful. The opening strain of *Manhattan* is ear-catching and Cohen later (rarely in this series) indulges himself in some affectionate rubato which is most seductive. The *Centennial* and the (well-named) *Enchantment waltzes* are again most affectionately presented, and their beguiling introductions are in each case followed by a string of good tunes. The *Engagement waltz* opens more grandly, but then the atmosphere lightens, and there is plenty of sparkle. *Farewell to America* (a pot-pourri) brings the American National Anthem delicately and nostalgically into the coda. The *Romance No. 2 for cello and orchestra*, tastefully played by Ivan Tvrdik, is surprisingly dolorous at its opening, then produces a romantic flowering, before ending nostalgically. The *Liebesbotschaft Galop* then arrives to cheer us all up, and it is followed by yet another unknown waltz, *Tauben*, in which Cohen coaxes the opening quite ravishingly. Of the two brief baritone solos the second, *D'Hauptsach*, has a most pleasing melody. No other record in the series so far offers such a fine package of unexpected delights or more hidden treasure, and there could be no better advocate than the present conductor, Jerome Cohen. He has the advantage of spacious, naturally balanced recording. A Rosette then for the sheer enterprise of the first half-century of this series and also for the special excellence of this collection with its discovery of six remarkably fine waltzes.

Graduation ball (ballet; arr. Dorati)
(M) * Mercury 434 365-2 (2) [id.]. Minneapolis SO, Dorati – ADAM: *Giselle* **(*); OFFENBACH: *Gaîté parisienne*. *

Dorati conducts his own ballet arrangement with plenty of spirit, although at times his approach seems ungracious and lacking in geniality. But this is at least partly the fault of the dry recording, with the Minneapolis violins robbed of almost all their lustre.

'1987 New Year Concert in Vienna': Overture: *Die Fledermaus*. Polkas: *Annen; Pizzicato* (with Josef); *Unter Donner und Blitz; Vergnügungszug*. Waltzes: *An der schönen, blauen Donau;* (i) *Frühlingsstimmen*. J. STRAUSS Sr: *Beliebte Annen* (polka); *Radetzky march*. Josef STRAUSS: *Ohne Sorgen polka;* Waltzes: *Delirien; Sphärenklänge*.
500♪ ❀ *** DG Dig. 419 616-2 [id.]. VPO, Karajan; (i) with Kathleen Battle.

In preparation for this outstanding concert, which was both recorded and televised, Karajan re-studied the scores of his favourite Strauss pieces. The concert itself produced music-making of the utmost magic; familiar pieces sounded almost as if they were being played for the first time. Kathleen Battle's contribution to *Voices of spring* brought wonderfully easy, smiling coloratura and much charm. *The Blue Danube* was, of course, an encore, and what an encore! Never before has it been played so seductively on record. This indispensable collection makes an easy first choice among any Strauss compilations ever issued.

'New Year's concert '97': March: *Russischer*. Polkas: *Die Bajadere; Bluette; Fata Morgana; Neue Pizzicato; Patronessen; 's gibt nur a Kaiserstadt, 's gibt a Wien!*. Waltzes: *An der schönen, blauen Donau; Freuet euch des Lebens; Hofballtänze; Motoren*. Josef STRAUSS: Polkas: *Carrière; Eingesendet; Frauenherz; Vorwärts!*. Waltz: *Dynamiden*. STRAUSS, Johann Sr: *Radetzky march* (with SUPPE: *Light cavalry overture*. HELLMESBERGER: Polka: *Leichtfüssig*).
*** EMI Dig. CDC5 56336-2 [id.]. VPO, Riccardo Muti.

Riccardo Muti here breaks away from his more usual severity into music-making wreathed in smiles. In the subtlety of his rhythmic pointing he transcends even what we expect of the Vienna Philharmonic in waltz-time. Muti in his approach to this repertory regularly concentrates on the refinement of the writing, bringing out inner strands, graduating pianissimos, encouraging the Vienna Philharmonic's reputation as the most refined orchestra in the world. In recent years the programmes have been including more and more rarities from the countless scores in the Strauss archives, yet this programme goes further than ever before. In its 100 or so minutes the rarities vastly outnumber the well-known favourites, making this an issue to attract far more than the usual devotees of the Viennese New Year. There are no fewer than eight Strauss items entirely new to these concerts, and it is only at the end, as the traditional second encore, when Muti (with a spoken greeting) introduces the *Blue Danube*, that we are on familiar ground. Add to that Suppé's *Light cavalry overture*, transformed from its military band associations, and you have a mixture guaranteed to delight, helped by vivid recording with plenty of air round the sound.

Overtures: *Die Fledermaus; Waldmeister. Perpetuum mobile*. Polkas: *Eljen a Magyar!; Pizzicato* (with Josef); *Tritsch-Tratsch; Unter Donner und Blitz; Vergnügungszug*. Waltzes: *Accelerationen; An der schönen, blauen Donau; G'schichten aus dem Wienerwald; Kaiser; Morgenblätter; Rosen aus dem Süden*. Josef STRAUSS: Polkas: *Frauenherz; Die Libelle; Ohne Sorgen; Die tanzende Muse*. Waltzes: *Aquarellen; Delirien; Sphärenklänge; Transaktionen*. Johann STRAUSS, Sr: *Radetzky march*.
(B) **(*) DG Double Dig. 453 052-2 (2) [id.]. VPO, Maazel.

The presence of a New Year's Day audience is most tangible in the *Pizzicato polka*, where one can sense the intercommunication as Maazel manipulates the rubato with obvious flair. He also gives a splendid account of *Transaktionen*, which has striking freshness and charm. The *Waldmeister* overture is a delightful piece and readily shows the conductor's affectionate response in its detail, while the opening of the *Aquarellen waltz* brings an even greater delicacy of approach and the orchestra responds with telling pianissimo playing. For the rest, these are well-played performances of no great memorability. The digital sound is brilliant and clear, somewhat lacking in resonant warmth.

Polkas: *Fledermaus* (from *Die Fledermaus*); *Kriegsabenteuer* (from *Der Zigeunerbaron*); *Pizzicato* (with Josef); *Unter Donner und Blitz*. Waltzes: *Accelerationen; Rosen aus dem Süden; 1001 Nacht; Wo die Zitronen blüh'n*. Eduard STRAUSS: Polka: *Bahn frei*. Waltz: *Doktrinen*. Josef STRAUSS: Waltzes: *Dynamiden; Sphärenklänge*.
500♪ ✿ (M) *** RCA 09026 61688-2 [id.]. Boston Pops O, Arthur Fiedler.

Arthur Fiedler, the doyen of the Boston Pops, never made a better record than this. He shapes the introductions to these famous walzes with captivating charm; his dancing rubato brings an authentic Viennese feel and gives the impression of total spontaneity. Obviously the waltzes by Josef and Eduard especially command his affection, and all polkas go with a swing. Eduard's *Bahn frei* sizzles with energy – an exhilarating showstopper. Strauss records don't come any better than this, and the warm Boston acoustics, superbly caught in the early days of stereo (1956–9), add a special allure to all this music-making.

Die Fledermaus (complete).
500♪ *** Ph. Dig. 432 157-2 (2) [id.]. Kiri Te Kanawa, Gruberová, Leech, Wolfgang Brendel, Bär, Fassbaender, Göttling, Krause, Wendler, Schenk, V. State Op. Ch., VPO, Previn.
** Teldec/Warner Dig. 2292 42427-2 (2) [id.]. Gruberová, Bonney, Hollweg, Protschka, Kmentt, Lipovšek, Netherlands Op. Ch., Concg. O, Harnoncourt.

André Previn here produces an enjoyably idiomatic account of Strauss's masterpiece, one which consistently conveys the work's exuberant high spirits. Dame Kiri Te Kanawa's portrait of Rosalinde brings not only gloriously firm, golden sound but also vocal acting with star quality. Brigitte Fassbaender is the most dominant Prince Orlofsky on disc. Edita Gruberová is a sparkling, characterful and full-voiced Adèle; Wolfgang Brendel as Eisenstein and Olaf Bär as Dr Falke both sing very well indeed. Richard Leech as Alfred provides heady tone and a hint of parody. Tom Krause makes a splendid Frank, the more characterful for no longer sounding young. This now goes to the top of the list of latterday *Fledermaus* recordings.

Harnoncourt, with characteristic concern for scholarship in his version with the Concertgebouw

Orchestra, presents the first recording to use a really full, authentic text, as published in the new editions, including the complete ballet in Act II. The singing cast is very strong, with consistently fresh, clean voices, very well recorded in crisply focused sound. Harnoncourt's direction is unfailingly pointed too, with textures exceptionally clear, and the bright, incisive manner allows the necessary lightness. What nevertheless tends to be missing is Viennese fizz and vivacity. Some of the aura of a scholarly approach seems to reduce the high spirits, though individual singers give deliciously characterized performances, notably Barbara Bonney as Adèle and Marjana Lipovšek as Orlofsky. Edita Gruberová, similarly characterful, reveals a different side, both to her voice and to her personality, from what we have come to expect: weightier, more dramatic, but unfortunately with a beat beginning to develop in the lower and middle registers. Curiously, instead of spoken dialogue, separate bands are provided containing comment and narration, but non-German speakers can easily programme them out. There is a mid-priced highlights disc (72 minutes) which might be considered (Teldec 0630 13816-9).

Der Zigeunerbaron: highlights.
**(*) Teldec/Warner Dig. 4509 98821-2 [id.] (from complete set, with Coburn, Lippert, Schasching, Hamari, Holzmair, Oelze, Von Magnus, Lazar, Arnold Schönberg Ch., VSO, Harnoncourt).

Though the Harnoncourt *Zigeunerbaron* brings uneven casting, his conducting is sparklingly fresh and there is much to enjoy in this generous (71 minutes) set of highlights which has a great advantage, not shared by the complete set from which it derives, of not being overladen with German dialogue. However, unusually for this Telarc series, no translations are provided.

Strauss, Josef (1827–70)

Volume 4: March: *Osterreichscher Kronprinzen;* Polkas: *La Chevaleresque; Jockey; Schlarffen; Titi; Wiener Leben;* Quadrilles: *Genovefa; Turner. Ständchen;* Waltzes: *Freudengrüsse; Frohes Leben; Vereins-Lieder.*
**(*) Marco Polo Dig. 8.223564 [id.]. Slovak RSO (Bratislava), Michael Dittrich.

Josef usually proves most reliable in his polkas, and *Schlarffen* is one of his finest, while the *Titi polka* is delicious, with the portrait of that pretty bird implied in the scoring rather than with any imitations. Both are very infectious as presented here by the excellent Michael Dittrich, and the better-known *Jockey* bursts with vivacity. The *Turner Quadrille* is also captivating in its swinging rhythm, with some whistling piccolo embroidery near the close. The waltzes *Vereins-Lieder* and *Freudengrüsse*, however, are light-hearted without being truly memorable. *Frohes Leben* has more striking ideas. The programme ends with a simple *Serenade* that might or might not have been intended as a tribute to Wagner.

Volume 5: *Defilier* (March); Polkas: *Die Gazelle; Maiblümchen; Die Marketenderin; Mignon; Vorwärts;* Quadrilles: *Csikos; Die Grossherzogin von Gerolstein;* Waltzes: *Dynamiden (Geheime Anziehungskräfte); Flammen; Huldigungslieder.*
**(*) Marco Polo Dig. 8.223565 [id.]. Slovak State PO (Košice), Christian Pollack.

The very fetching *Die Grossherzogin quadrille* gets this programme off to a good start. In English, of course this comes out as *The Grand Duchess of Gerolstein* and the piece is an agreeable pot-pourri of the many excellent tunes from Offenbach's operetta, presented one after another with little or no attempt at tailoring and with brief pauses in between. Pollack (as elsewhere) chooses a dancing tempo and one wants to get up and join in. The polka, *Marketenderin* ('Camp follower' – in this case a vivacious lady, generous with her favours) is charming too, though it reminds the listener a little of a more famous piece by Johann. *Vorwärts* ('Forward') then goes with a swing and is delightfully scored – one of Josef 's very best. *Mignon* is very catchy too, and *Die Gazelle* has something of the grace of its title. Of the three waltzes included here, there is one masterpiece: *Dynamiden*, with its ravishing cantabile is fully worthy of Johann, and it is beautifully played. *Huldigungslieder* also begins impressively and has rather a good opening waltz-tune, but it is slightly less memorable overall. *Flammen* surprises the listener by opening with a fast, polka-like introduction. The main strain is very agreeable and there are some engagingly fresh ideas later on. Pollack takes the polka-mazurkas at dance tempi with a strong accent on the first beat, which is obviously authentic; but for concert perfomance a slightly faster tempo might have been more effective, and this especially applies to *Maiblümchen*, which closes the concert. Nevertheless this is one of the most rewarding Josef Strauss collections so far in the series.

Volume 6: March: *Victor*. Polkas: *Carrière; Causerie; Figaro; Joujou; Tanz-Regulator; Waldröslein. Musen quadrille*. Waltzes: *Die Industriellen; Krönungslieder; Nilfluthen*.
**(*) Marco Polo Dig. 8.223566 [id.]. Slovak State PO (Košice), John Georgiadis.

Of the three waltzes here, the first, *Die Industriellen*, is marginally the most beguiling, and Georgiadis has its measure, both at the lilting opening tune and in its engaging secondary scalic figure that rises and falls in a busy little group of notes. *Nilfluthen* ('Nile waters') was written for the Concordia Ball, held during the celebrations for the opening of the Suez Canal (Emperor Franz Josef was there). It, too, has a nifty main theme and there is nothing in the least Egyptian about its style. *Krönungslieder* opens with a regal fanfare (it celebrated a royal political settlement in 1867 between the Austrian Empire and Hungary, when the Emperor and Empress were crowned in Budapest); but after that it is a routine sequence. Of the polkas, the *Causerie* ('Chatting') is the most ingenuously charming, while *Carrière* is one of Josef's most infectious galops. John Georgiadis is thoroughly at home here, and this music is all stylishly presented and again very well recorded.

Strauss, Richard (1864–1949)

An Alpine Symphony; Don Juan, Op. 20.
500♪ *** Decca Dig. 421 815-2. San Francisco SO, Blomstedt.

Blomstedt's *Alpine Symphony* is superbly shaped and has that rare quality of relating part to whole in a way that totally convinces. He gets scrupulously attentive playing from the San Francisco orchestra and a rich, well-detailed Decca recording.

Also sprach Zarathustra; (i) *Burleske for piano and orchestra; Don Juan, Op. 20.*
*** EMI Dig. CDC5 56364-2 [id.]. (i) Emanuel Ax; Phd. O, Sawallisch.

Also sprach Zarathustra, Op. 30; Till Eulenspiegel; Salome: Dance of the seven veils.
**(*) Decca Dig. 452 603-2 [id.]. BPO, Solti.

Solti's eightieth-birthday Strauss collection is a disappointment. For one thing, the recording, although brilliant, is not very sumptuous; *Also sprach Zarathustra*, despite the superb playing of the Berlin Philharmonic, is interpretatively no advance on his earlier, more ripely expansive, Chicago version. For about the same cost Solti admirers can get a Double Decca which includes this, *Don Juan* and *Till Eulenspiegel*, recorded in Chicago, an opulent version of the *Alpine Symphony* (not taking too long over the climb) with the excellent Bavarian Radio Symphony Orchestra, plus a characteristically urgent *Ein Heldenleben* with the VPO, which would seem a much stronger recommendation altogether (440 618-2).

The new Philadephia Orchestra recording of *Also sprach Zarathustra* is a different matter. One of Sawallisch's finest recordings with this orchestra, it is passionate yet nobly contoured, and the famous opening is extremely spectacular and expansive. The recording was made in the New Jersey Studios at Collingswood (where Decca followed on with their splendid Shostakovich sessions). It is good, too, to have a fine, modern version of the witty *Burleske*, with Emanuel Ax giving a sparkling account of the solo piano part. This was originally premièred only seven months after *Don Juan* was first heard under the composer's baton, so the coupling is apt. Sawallisch's view of the latter is spacious rather than hard-driven, but the climax is thrilling, with the orchestra again giving of their best.

(i) *Also sprach Zarathustra; Death and transfiguration; Don Juan; Ein Heldenleben; Till Eulenspiegel;* (ii) *Der Rosenkavalier: Waltz sequence.*
500♪ (B) *** Ph. Duo Dig./Analogue 442 281-2 (2) [id.]. Concg. O, (i) Haitink; (ii) Jochum.

Haitink's performances are undoubtedly distinguished, superbly played, persuasively and subtly characterized. He finds added nobility in *Death and transfiguration*, while there is no lack of swagger in the accounts of both the *Don* and *Till*. The easy brilliance of the orchestral playing is complemented by the natural spontaneity of Haitink's readings, seamless in the transition between narrative events, without loss of the music's picaresque or robust qualities. An indispensable set, and one of the finest of all the Duo bargains.

Also sprach Zarathustra, Op. 30; Ein Heldenleben, Op. 40.
500♪ ❁ (M) *** RCA 09026 61494-2 [id.]. Chicago SO, Fritz Reiner.
(M) *** Ph. Dig. 442 645-2 [id.]. Boston SO, Ozawa.

These were the first stereo sessions the RCA engineers arranged with Fritz Reiner, after the company had taken over the Chicago orchestra's recording contract from Mercury. A wonderful performance that ranks alongside the very best ever committed to disc. *Ein Heldenleben* shows Reiner in equally splendid form. There have been more incisive, more spectacular and more romantic performances, but Reiner achieves an admirable balance and whatever he does is convincing. If anything, the recording sounds even better than *Also sprach* and the warm acoustics of Orchestra Hall help convey Reiner's humanity in the closing pages of the work.

Ozawa's 1981 recording of *Also sprach Zarathustra* became one of the first demonstration records for compact disc, and even for today's ears the depth and unforced firmness of the organ pedal sound leading on to an extraordinary crescendo cannot fail to bring a shiver to the nape of the listener's neck. The solo strings are balanced rather close, but otherwise this is a wonderfully warm and natural sound, with both a beguiling bloom and fine inner clarity. Ozawa as a Strauss interpreter goes for seductive phrasing and warmth rather than high drama or nobility, but this remains one of his finest achievements at Boston. Ozawa's view of *Heldenleben* is similarly free-flowing, lyrical and remarkably unpompous. He consistently brings out the joy of the virtuoso writing, and though the playing of the Boston orchestra is not quite as immaculate as in the companion version of *Zarathustra* the richness and transparency are just as seductive, superbly caught by the Philips engineers. There is a remarkable sense of presence and reality. This will admirably suit those needing a recommendable mid-priced disc of these two works, although Reiner's RCA analogue interpretations are even more distinctive, and the early Chicago Hall stereo is also remarkably fine (9026 61494-2 – see our main volume).

(i) *Horn concertos Nos. 1 in E flat, Op. 11; 2 in E flat;* (ii) *Duet concertino for clarinet and bassoon. Wind serenade in E flat, Op. 11.*

500♪ (M) *** EMI Dig. CD-EMX 2238 [id.]. (i) David Pyatt; (ii) Joy Farrall, Julie Andrews; Britten Sinfonia, Nicholas Cleobury.

David Pyatt gives ripely exuberant performances of Strauss's two *Horn concertos*. The outer movements of the gently rapturous *Duet concertino* are presented with enticing delicacy of texture, and the slow movement again brings a most touchingly doleful opening solo, this time from the bassoonist, Julie Andrews. Cleobury and the Britten Sinfonia give sensitive support throughout, and the early *Serenade* is also made the more attractive by the lightness of touch of the wind blending, its sonorities always fresh.

Oboe concerto.

(M) *** Carlton Fanfare Dig. 30366 0065-2 [id.]. Pamela Pecha, Moscow PO, Paul Freeman – VAUGHAN WILLIAMS: *Oboe concerto*; SCHICKELE: *Oboe concerto*. ***

(i) *Oboe concerto. Ein Heldenleben, Op. 40.*

**(*) EMI CDC5 56149-2 [id.]. (i) Richard Woodhams; Phd. O, Wolfgang Sawallisch.

(i) *Oboe concerto. Metamorphosen for 23 solo strings.*

**(*) Ph. Dig. 446 105-2 [id.]. Heinz Holliger, COE.

The received wisdom might be to expect that Holliger would be an easy first choice here. He is never less than masterly and the assurance of his playing is remarkable. But, as with his earlier, analogue recording, there is a hint of efficiency at the expense of ripeness, and in the slow movement he fails to convey a sheer love for the music in its most absolute sense, which prevents this from being quite the ideal version one had hoped for. He is not helped by being balanced rather too closely and the effect is not flattering to his timbre. As an apt coupling he takes up the baton and directs a very well-controlled and thoughtfully shaped performance of the *Metamorphosen*, but once again there is an absence of ripeness, and the recording, while it reveals every strand of detail, brings a degree of excess digital definition to the climax.

Pamela Pecha was co-principal of the Cleveland Orchestra for 12 years, the first woman in the orchestra's wind section, and she gives a completely persuasive account of the Strauss *Concerto*, the opening easily flexible and the slow movement warmly songful. Paul Freeman and the Moscow Philharmonic Orchestra provide an accompaniment which does not miss the work's essential mellow dimension, and the recording has a glowing ambience which suits the music far better than the rather cool effect of the Philips sound-balance for Holliger. Moreover the Carlton couplings are particularly attractive.

As one would expect from a great Strauss conductor, there is much to relish in Sawallisch's account of *Ein Heldenleben*, and he secures playing of great refinement and culture from the Philadelphia Orchestra. At the same time one misses some of the bold rhetoric and heroic gestures that are to be found in many of the classic *Heldenlebens* of the past, such as Beecham, Krauss, Kempe and, above all, Karajan's 1959 version, which still has the power to thrill in a way which ultimately eludes this performance. The less than state-of-the-art recorded sound and a synthetic balance do not help. Ormandy's account with this great orchestra (Sony SBK 48272; *SBT 48272*), made in the 1960s, is more compelling – see our main volume – and that offers also Szell's equally outstanding versions of *Don Juan* and *Till*). Incidentally, one feature of the present *Heldenleben* should be mentioned: Sawallisch restores the original ending, which is far lower-keyed than the familiar, more imposing apotheosis. Richard Woodhams, the orchestra's principal oboe, is an eloquent soloist in the concerto.

Violin concerto in D min., Op. 8.
(B) **(*) Decca Eclipse Dig. 448 988-2; *448 988-4* [id.]. Boris Belkin, Berlin RSO, Ashkenazy – BRAHMS: *Violin concerto*. ***

It is good to have a thoroughly recommendable bargain version of Strauss's engaging early concerto. Though not quite a match for Xue Wei on ASV (CDDCA 780 – see our main volume), partly because just occasionally his intonation is not absolutely immaculate, Belkin finds much charm in the Mendelssohnian second group of the opening movement, and he plays the *Lento* with an appealing fragile tenderness, then following with fairy-light articulation in the dancing finale. Ashkenazy provides a gracefully supportive accompaniment and the Decca sound is excellent, although perhaps the soloist is a trifle too closely miked – perhaps because the recording was made in the Berlin Jesus-Christus Kirche.

(i) *Death and transfiguration; Sinfonia domestica, Op. 53;* (ii) *Salome's dance of the seven veils.*
500♪ ✿ (B) *** Sony SBK 53511; *SBT 53511* [id.]. (i) Cleveland O, Szell; (ii) Phd. O, Ormandy.

Szell's *Death and transfiguration* dates from 1957 and it is still unsurpassed. The opening has the most compelling atmosphere and the triumphant closing pages are the more effective for Szell's complete lack of indulgence. The *Sinfonia domestica*, recorded in 1964, is less naturally balanced: the engineers seem more concerned with making every detail tell, but the performance brings such powerful orchestral playing, with glorious strings especially in the passionate *Adagio*, that criticism is disarmed: there is certainly no lack of body here. The programme ends with an extraordinarily voluptuous Philadelphia performance of *Salome's dance*, which conjures up a whole frieze of naked female torsos. Ormandy directs with licentious abandon, and the orchestra responds with tremendous virtuosity and ardour, unashamedly going over the top at the climax.

Don Quixote, Op. 35.
(M) *** EMI CDM5 66106-2 [id.]. Rostropovich, BPO, Karajan – WAGNER: *Die Meistersinger: Overture; Tannhäuser: Overture and Venusberg music*. ***

The Karajan/Rostropovich account of *Don Quixote* is predictably fine. The recorded sound (1975) is impressively remastered, spectacular in its realism, with well-defined detail, superb warmth and body, and fine perspective, its only failing a tendency for Rostropovich to dominate the aural picture. He dominates artistically, too. His Don is superbly characterized, and the expressiveness and richness of tone he commands are a joy in themselves. There are moments when one wonders whether the intensity of his response does not lead to over-emphatic tone, but in general both the cello and viola soloists and the Berlin orchestra under Karajan silence criticism. Even if you already have Karajan's earlier (1969) version with Fournier for DG, which is in some ways subtler (429 184-2, paired with *Death and transfiguration*), this EMI version is not to be missed, and the Wagner couplings are also of the highest calibre.

(i) *Don Quixote, Op. 35;* (ii) *Burleske.*
(M) *** RCA 09026 61796-2 [id.]. (i) Janigro; (ii) Byron Janis; Chicago SO, Fritz Reiner.

(i) *Don Quixote, Op. 35. Don Juan, Op. 20.*
(M) *** RCA 09026 68170-2 [id.]. Chicago SO, Fritz Reiner, (i) with Antonio Janigro.

Even at full price, Reiner's *Don Quixote* was a top recommendation. Reiner was a masterly Straussian and this 1959 version was one of the very finest of RCA's Chicago Hall recordings. Antonio Janigro plays stylishly and with assurance; if he brings less intensity than Fournier to the ecstatic solo cadenza in Variation V, his contribution to the close of the work is distinguished. The recording has been freshly remastered for its new coupling with *Don Juan* and detail seems even more refined, though there is no loss of amplitude in climaxes: the ride through the air (track 10) is remarkly expansive. *Don Juan* dates from the earliest days of stereo (1959) and is most famous for its superbly thrilling climax in which the great horn-theme leaps out unforgettably, thrustfully echoed by the strings. But the lustre of the strings is hardly less remarkable, and again John Pfeiffer's new transfer is enormously improved over its first presentation on CD (RD 85408), with greater transparency not achieved at the expense of body of tone. Byron Janis's account of the *Burleske* is undoubtedly distinguished, but this is also available on RCA's super-bargain Navigator label, coupled with Mahler (74321 21286-2), and most collectors are likely to choose the newer pairing of *Don Quixote* with *Don Juan*.

Ein Heldenleben, Op. 40.
(M) *** EMI CDM5 66108 [id.]. BPO, Karajan – WAGNER: *Der fliegende Holländer: Overture; Parsifal: Preludes*. ***
(M) *** DG 449 725-2 [id.]. BPO, Karajan – WAGNER: *Siegfried idyll*. ***

The 1974 EMI Karajan *Heldenleben* is superlatively recorded and lavishly transferred to CD. The performance shows a remarkable consistency of approach on Karajan's part and an equal virtuosity of technique and even greater sumptuousness of tone on the part of the Berlin Philharmonic than the earlier, DG performance; indeed the sound is remarkably vivid. Some have found the playing marginally less spontaneous, but it is gloriously ardent and, listening to it objectively, there seems little difference between the two readings. Couplings might dictate a choice; both discs offer the music of Wagner; the EMI is the more generous: an electrifying *Flying Dutchman overture*, and glorious playing (and recording) in the two *Parsifal Preludes*.

Although Karajan's 1959 *Heldenleben* cannot quite match his later EMI version in sumptuousness it still sounds remarkably impressive. Its selection for reissue in DG's series of 'Originals' seems particularly apt, since this was not only the first post-war recording Karajan made for DG but also his very first in stereo. It is a superb performance. Playing of great power and distinction emanates from the Berlin Philharmonic and, in the closing section, an altogether becoming sensuousness and warmth. The remastering makes the most of the ambient atmosphere and, while not losing body, firms up the orchestral detail. The new coupling of Wagner's *Siegfried idyll*, in which Karajan was unsurpassed, could not be more appropriate.

Metamorphosen for 23 solo strings.
*** DG Dig 447 744-2 [id.]. Dresden State O, Sinopoli – BRUCKNER: *Symphony No. 8.* ***

Sinopoli has the measure of Strauss's lament for the destruction of Germany's artistic heritage in the closing days of the Second World War. In his hands *Metamorphosen* has a simplicity of utterance and a natural, unforced quality that is most impressive. The strings of the Staatskapelle Dresden produce a magnificent sonority, and the DG engineers do them proud. The sound has detail and presence, as well as warmth.

Sinfonia domestica, Op. 53; Death and transfiguration, Op. 24.
(M) *** EMI CDM5 66107-2 [id.]. BPO, Karajan – WAGNER: *Lohengrin: Preludes; Tristan und Isolde: Prelude & Liebestod.* ***
(D) *** Carlton Dig. PCD 2051 [id.]. Nat. Youth O of GB, Seaman – ELGAR: *Enigma variations.* ***
*** RCA Dig. 09026 68221-2 [id.]. Bav. RSO, Lorin Maazel.

Sinfonia domestica, Op. 53; (i) *Parergon zur Sinfonia domestica, Op. 73.*
*** DG Dig. 449 188-2 [id.]. (i) Gary Graffman; VPO, Previn.

Strauss's *Sinfonia domestica* is quite admirably served by Karajan's mid-priced 1973 recording, which now re-emerges as part of EMI's Karajan Edition, coupled with some superb Wagner performances. The playing is stunningly good and the sumptuous Berlin strings produce tone of great magnificence. EMI provide a recording (made in the Salle Wagram, Paris, in 1973) not quite as sumptuous as the Berlin recordings mentioned above but of wide range, superbly focused detail and warm ambience.

Absolutely no apologies need be made for the playing of the National Youth Orchestra in 1993. The strings may not be quite as opulent as those of the Berlin Philharmonic, but they still sound pretty good, and the whole performance glows with life. Not surprisingly, these young players respond readily to the orgasmic passion of the 'Love scene', but the wind soloists also revel in the charming detail of the opening movement. The joyous apotheosis is splendidly managed and overall Christopher Seaman holds the structure together with admirable cohesion. The recording, made in Watford Town Hall, approaches the demonstration bracket.

Maazel's account on RCA with yet another *Death and transfiguration* from his baton is better recorded than on his 1983 DG version, and the playing of the Bavarian orchestra is both subtle and refined and is in every way equal to the virtuosic demands of this score. Thoroughly recommendable and free of any overblown exaggeration.

André Previn has the more logical and useful coupling in the 1924 *Parergon* on themes from the symphony that Strauss composed for the one-armed Paul Wittgenstein, for whom Ravel, Pfitzner and Prokofiev also wrote concert pieces. Previn gives the Vienna Philharmonic its head in repertoire that they know inside out. A thoroughly musical and enjoyable account, enhanced by the *Parergon*, in which Gary Graffman proves an eloquent soloist. It is a strong work given with great character here, and more convincing than Malcolm Frager's for Kempe. Neither version is to be preferred to the Karajan, but both are thoroughly enjoyable.

Violin sonata in E flat, Op. 18.
(M) (***) RCA mono 09026 61763-2 [id.]. Heifetz, Brooks Smith – BRAHMS: *Piano trio No. 1;* DOHNANYI: *Serenade.* (***)

Heifetz's legendary recording of the Strauss *Sonata* with Brooks Smith, which has never been surpassed, was made in 1954 and comes with his 1941 recordings of the Brahms *B major Trio* with Rubinstein and Feuermann and a masterly account with Primrose and Feuermann of the Dohnányi *Serenade for string trio*. Self-recommending.

VOCAL MUSIC

Lieder: *Alerseelen; All' mein' Gedanken; Befreit; Cäcilie; Efeu; Heimliche Aufforderung; Herr Lenz; Hochzeitlich; Junggesellenschwur; Liebeshymnus; Mein Auge; Meinem Kinde; Nachtgang; Nichts; Das Rosenband; Sehnsucht; Ständchen; Traum durch die Dämmerung; Waldseligkeit; Wasserrose; Weihnachtsgefühl; Winternacht.*
(M) *** EMI Eminence Dig. CD-EMX 2250 [id.]. Simon Keenlyside, Malcolm Martineau.

Keenlyside follows up the success of his fine Schubert recital, also for EMI Eminence (CD-EMX 2224), with this excellent collection of Strauss Lieder, beautifully sung, again with Malcolm Martineau a most sensitive accompanist. Try the highly distinctive, intimate reading of *Ständchen* ('Serenade'), with Keenlyside singing almost in a half-tone and with Martineau playing magically. The fine-spun legato of *Waldseligkeit* and the poise of *Meinem Kinde* are equally impressive. Keenlyside uses a head voice for the gentle top notes of *Allerseelen* ('All Saints' Day'), but then finds plenty of power, sharply focused, in songs like *Befreit*. The sequence is rounded off with two exhilarating songs, *Cäcilie* and *Herr Lenz* (with its pun on the name Strauss – nosegay). Though this comes at mid-price, text and translations are provided. Excellent EMI sound.

Enoch Arden, Op. 38.
*(*) Litmus LIT 101-2 [id.]. Nicholas Garrett, Peter Hewitt.

Tennyson wrote *Enoch Arden* in the year of Strauss's birth and, though it is virtually unread now, it was a bestseller in the year of its publication, and was much admired during the poet's lifetime. It tells of a fisherman who was shipwrecked and believed drowned. On his return, after many years, he discovers that his wife has happily remarried and, so as not to disturb her new-found happiness, he resolves to keep his survival secret. In our own age, melodrama (spoken words over a musical accompaniment) has fallen out of fashion, but a few years before the poet's death Strauss set the poem in a German translation. Nicholas Garrett and Peter Hewitt have revived it in English. It takes 75 minutes and rather outstays its welcome. Nicholas Garrett is an excellent narrator and Peter Hewitt gives capable support. However, the condition of the Steinway on which he is recorded is not ideal, and nor is the acoustic environment. Spoken voice and piano are well balanced. An interesting curiosity, but no more.

Four Last songs; Die heiligen drei Könige. Capriccio (opera): *Moonlight music and monologue* (closing scene); *Metamorphosen for 23 solo strings.*
(M) *** DG Dig. 445 599-2 [id.]. Anna Tomowa-Sintow, BPO, Karajan.

Before he made this recording of the closing scene from *Capriccio* with Anna Tomowa-Sintow, Karajan, supreme Straussian, had never previously conducted Strauss's last opera. It is a ravishing performance with one of his favourite sopranos responding warmly and sympathetically; if lacking the final touch of individual imagination that such inspired music cries out for, one senses the close rapport between conductor and singer. Similarly in the other late, great masterpiece, the *Four Last songs*, Tomowa-Sintow's lovely, creamy-toned singing tends to take second place in the attention, almost as if the voice was a solo instrument in the orchestra, and the result is undoubtedly very touching. The orchestral version of Strauss's nativity-story song makes an attractive extra item. The recording is warm, lacking a little in a sense of presence, but compensating in atmosphere. For this reissue Karajan's 1980 digital account of *Metamorphosen* has been added; it has even greater emotional urgency than his earlier, analogue version, recorded in 1971, and there is a marginally quicker pulse. Here the digital recording is rather more sumptuous.

Four Last songs; Orchestral Lieder: *Das Bächlein; Freundliche Vision; Die heiligen drei Könige; Meinem Kinde; Morgen; Muttertändelei; Das Rosenband; Ruhe, meine Seele; Waldseligkeit; Wiegenlied; Winterweihe; Zueignung.*
✿ *** EMI CDC7 47276-2 [id.]. Elisabeth Schwarzkopf, Berlin RSO or LSO, Szell.

For the reissued CD version of Schwarzkopf's raptly beautiful recording of the *Four Last songs*, EMI have added not just the old coupling of Strauss orchestral songs but also the extra seven which she recorded three years later in 1969, also with George Szell conducting, but with the LSO instead of the Berlin Radio Symphony Orchestra. There are few records in the catalogue which so magnetically capture the magic of a great performance, with the intensity of Schwarzkopf's singing in all its variety of tone and meaning perfectly matched by inspired playing.

(i) *Four Last songs;* Orchestral Lieder: *Befreit; Cäcilie; Muttertändelei; Waldseligkeit; Wiegenlied. Der Rosenkavalier: suite.*
**(*) RCA Dig. 09026 68539-2 [id.]. (i) Renée Fleming; Houston SO, Eschenbach.

Renée Fleming with her rich, mature soprano gives warmly sympathetic readings of the *Four Last songs*, thrilling in climaxes as the voice is allowed to expand, and full of fine detail, even if these readings lack the variety of a Schwarzkopf. The five separate orchestral Lieder also bring a wide expressive range, with *Waldseligkeit* beautifully poised, and ending boldly on *Cäcilie*. The singer is not helped by the way that Eschenbach makes the accompaniments seem a little sluggish, polished though the playing is. Something of the same lack of thrust marks his account of Strauss's own arrangement of the *Rosenkavalier* excerpts, despite beautiful playing from the Houston orchestra. How much more welcome would it have been to have had extra items from the singer.

Four Last songs; Lieder: *Cäcilie; Meinem Kinde; Morgen; Ruhe, meine Seele; Wiegenlied; Zueignung.*
500♪ ❁ *** Ph. Dig. 411 052-2 [id.]. Jessye Norman, Leipzig GO, Masur.

Strauss's publisher Ernest Roth says in the score of the *Four Last songs* that this was a farewell of 'serene confidence', which is exactly the mood Jessye Norman conveys. The start of the second stanza of the third song, *Beim Schlafengehen*, brings one of the most thrilling vocal crescendos on record, expanding from a half-tone to a gloriously rich and rounded forte. In concern for word-detail Norman is outshone only by Schwarzkopf, but both in the *Four Last songs* and in the orchestral songs the stylistic as well as the vocal command is irresistible.

OPERA

Ariadne auf Naxos (complete).
500♪ ❁ (***) EMI mono CDS5 55176-2 (2) [CDCB 55176]. Schwarzkopf, Schock, Rita Streich, Dönch, Seefried, Cuénod, Philh. O, Karajan.

Elisabeth Schwarzkopf makes a radiant, deeply moving Ariadne. Rita Streich was at her most dazzling in the coloratura of Zerbinetta's aria and, in partnership with the harlequinade characters, sparkles engagingly. But it is Irmgard Seefried who gives perhaps the supreme performance of all as the Composer, exceptionally beautiful of tone, conveying a depth and intensity rarely if ever matched. The fine pacing and delectably pointed ensemble add to the impact of a uniquely perceptive Karajan interpretation. Though in mono and with the orchestral sound a little dry, the voices come out superbly. However, this has now reverted to full price.

Capriccio: Prelude. Feuersnot: Love scene. Guntram: Prelude.
*** DG Dig. 449 571-2 [id.]. German Opera, Berlin, O, Thielemann – PFITZNER: *Das Herz* etc. **(*)

These Strauss items, two of them rare, make an excellent coupling for the Pfitzner which Thielemann chose for his début recording with DG. Though in the *Feuersnot* Love scene the orchestra of the Deutsches Opera in Berlin is not quite as poised or refined as the Staatskapelle in Dresden for Sinopoli, the thrust and passion are even greater, with a freer expressiveness. Excellent sound.

Elektra (complete).
❁ *** DG Dig. 453 429-2 (2) [id.]. Marc, Schwarz, Voigt, Jerusalem, Ramey, V. State Op. Konzertvereinigung, VPO, Sinopoli.
** Teldec/Warner Dig. 4509 99175-2 (2) [id.]. Polaski, Meier, Marc, Botha, Struckmann, German Op. Ch. & Berlin State O, Barenboim.

Sinopoli directs an incandescent performance of *Elektra*, at once powerful and sensuous, vividly recorded in full-bodied sound, and with a team of principals unmatched since Solti's classic recording with Birgit Nilsson. Alessandra Marc, a fine Chrysothemis in the Barenboim version, is here much more aptly cast in the title-role, instantly establishing her command in the opening monologue, magnetically done. Where she scores even over Nilsson is in the warmth and beauty of tone. Not only are the dramatic outbursts thrillingly projected with firmly focused tone, she is just as compelling in gentler moments, whether reflecting the creepily sinister side of Elektra's character or in her radiant ecstasy following her recognition of her brother, Orest. The glorious solo ending with the rapturous cry of '*Seliger*' ('happier') has never been caught so seductively on disc as here, with Sinopoli drawing glowing playing from the Vienna Philharmonic, if anything even more persuasive than he was in his recording of *Salome*. Deborah Voigt as Chrysothemis is clear and firm too, well contrasted, and Hanna Schwarz is a powerful Klytemnestra, with bitingly well-focused tone. Having such a fine, heroic tenor as Siegfried Jerusalem in the small role of Aegist is another tribute to the casting, crowned by the choice of Samuel Ramey as a warm and strong Orest, a perfect foil for Alessandra Marc. The performance is rounded off with a thrilling account of the final scene, capturing Elektra's hysterical joy with rare intensity.

Barenboim says he aims to achieve maximum transparency in this complex score; but in the context of this recording, which has the orchestra distantly balanced, that sounds like an excuse. Whatever the explanation, the lack of weight in the slightly cloudy orchestral sound seriously reduces the impact of

Barenboim's direction, so that such great moments as the recognition scene between Elektra and Orest lack the emotional thrust needed. It does not help either that in moments of mounting tension Barenboim tends to keep the pulse very steady, instead of pressing forward. Deborah Polaski, in her finest recording yet, makes an impressive Elektra, cleanly focused, pure-toned where necessary (as in her ecstatic solo after the recognition) but able to expand in dramatic weight. Next to her, the Chrysothemis of Alessandra Marc sounds too mature and mezzo-ish, an older, not a younger sister; but Waltraud Meier is in splendid voice as Klytëmnestra, sinister and evil-sounding in every phrase, making her confrontations with Elektra the most memorable passages. The Orest of Falk Struckmann is a dull dog, with a gritty voice that cuts through textures, but who conveys little feeling. Not by any means a first choice.

Feuersnot: Love scene. Die Frau ohne Schatten: Symphonic fantasy. Salome: Dance of the seven veils.
*** DG Dig. 449 216-2 [id.]. Dresden State O, Sinopoli – WEBER: *Overtures: Der Freischütz; Oberon.* ***

Sinopoli has already shown us in his complete recording of *Salome* for DG (431 810-2), made in Berlin, how warmly sympathetic he is to Strauss's operatic music. With his Dresden orchestra the results are, if anything, even more sensuous, not least in *Salome's dance*, when ravishing string-tone is perfectly married to Sinopoli's moulded and flexible style. The Love scene from Strauss's very first opera, *Feuersnot*, is drawn from the closing pages of the opera, a delectable lollipop that ought to be much better known. Much the longest piece on the disc is the *Symphonic fantasy* from *Die Frau ohne Schatten*, which Strauss put together in 1946 at a time when complete performances of this favourite of his among his operas looked unlikely. Again Sinopoli's concentration and the gorgeous playing of the orchestra, sumptuously recorded, give cohesion to an obviously sectional piece. Odd as the coupling with Weber overtures is, the results are equally superb.

Die Frau ohne Schatten.
500♪ ❁ *** Decca Dig. 436 243-2 (3) [id.]. Behrens, Varady, Domingo, Van Dam, Runkel, Jo, VPO, Solti.
(M) ** DG 449 584-2 (3) [id.]. Fischer-Dieskau, Borkh, Bjoner, Mödl, Jess Thomas, Hotter, Bav. State Op. Ch. & O, Keilberth.

In the Heldentenor role of the Emperor, Plácido Domingo gives a performance that is not only beautiful to the ear beyond previous recordings but which has an extra feeling for expressive detail, deeper than that which was previously recorded. Hildegard Behrens as the Dyer's wife is also a huge success; her voice has rarely sounded so beautiful on record. Julia Varady as the Empress is equally imaginative, with a beautiful voice, and José van Dam with his clean, dark voice brings a warmth and depth of expression to the role of Barak, the Dyer, which goes with a satisfyingly firm focus. With the Vienna Philharmonic surpassing themselves, and the big choral ensembles both well disciplined and warmly expressive, this superb recording is unlikely to be matched, let alone surpassed, for many years. Solti himself is inspired throughout.

There are many cuts in this 1964 DG set, and that alone will deter most Straussians. Moreover Keilberth is no more vital and inspired than he was in the companion set of *Arabella*, also made during the celebration period after the opening of the new post-war Munich Opera House. It is a pity that these two factors tend to rule the set out, for the singing is mostly very good, and it is marvellous to hear the central part of Barak sung with such freshness and beauty by Fischer-Dieskau, while Jess Thomas is also in fine voice as the Emperor. Considering the circumstances of the performance, the recording too is most creditable and it has been given a first-class CD transfer.

Der Rosenkavalier (complete).
500♪ ❁ *** EMI CDS7 49354-8 (3) [Ang. CDCC 49354]. Schwarzkopf, Ludwig, Stich-Randall, Edelmann, Waechter, Philh. Ch. & O, Karajan.

Karajan's 1956 version, one of the greatest of all opera recordings, is in a class of its own, with the patrician refinement of Karajan's spacious reading combining with an emotional intensity that he has rarely equalled. Matching that achievement is the incomparable portrait of the Marschallin from Schwarzkopf, bringing out detail as no one else can, yet equally presenting the breadth and richness of the character, a woman still young and attractive. Christa Ludwig with her firm, clear mezzo tone makes an ideal, ardent Octavian and Teresa Stich-Randall a radiant Sophie, with Otto Edelmann a winningly characterful Ochs, who yet sings every note clearly.

Salome (complete).
500♪ *** DG. Dig. 431 810-2 (2) [id.]. Studer, Rysanek, Terfel, Hiestermann, German Opera, Berlin, Ch. & O, Sinopoli.

The glory of Sinopoli's DG version is the singing of Cheryl Studer as Salome, producing glorious sounds throughout. Her voice is both rich and finely controlled, with delicately spun pianissimos that chill you the more for their beauty, not least in Salome's attempted seduction of John the Baptist. Sinopoli's reading is often unconventional in its speeds, but it is always positive, thrusting and full of passion, the most opulent account on disc, matched by full, forward recording. As Jokanaan, Bryn Terfel makes a compelling recording début, strong and noble. Among modern sets this makes a clear first choice.

Die schweigsame Frau (complete).
(M) **(*) EMI CMS5 66033-2 (3) [Angel CDMC 66033]. Adam, Scovotti, Burmeister, Trudeliese Schmidt, Dresden State Op. Ch. & State O, Janowski.

Strauss was already seventy when he tackled this exuberant comic opera, with its libretto by Stefan Zweig based on Ben Jonson's *Epicoene*. It is evidence of Strauss's energy that he revelled in the heavy task of composing and scoring so much fast, brilliant and complex music, the ensembles pointed by touches of neo-classicism. You might count it all a lot of fuss over not very much, and this version is not quite as persuasive as it might be, with a church acoustic giving bloom but blurring some detail. Janowski conducts an efficient rather than a magical performance, and Theo Adam's strongly characterized rendering of the central role of Dr Morosus is marred by his unsteadiness. Jeanette Scovotti is agile but shrill as the Silent Woman, Aminta. A valuable set of mixed success. The CD transfer brings the usual advantages but underlines the oddities of the recording. The reissue (unlike the previous full-priced set) includes a libretto/booklet with full English translation.

Stravinsky, Igor (1882–1971)

(i) *Apollo;* (ii) *The Firebird; Petrushka* (1911 score); *The Rite of spring* (complete ballets).
500♪ ❁ (B) *** Ph. Duo 438 350-2 [id.]. (i) LSO, Markevitch; (ii) LPO, Haitink.

Markevitch gives a gravely beautiful reading of *Apollon musagète*, and the slightly distanced balance is surely ideal, for the focus is excellent. No more refined account of *The Firebird* has ever been put on record than Haitink's analogue version. The sheer savagery of *Kashchei's dance* may be a little muted, but the sharpness of attack and clarity of detail make for a thrilling result, while the magic and poetry of the whole score are given a hypnotic beauty, with the LPO at its very finest. In *Petrushka* the rhythmic feeling is strong, especially in the Second Tableau and the finale, where the fairground bustle is vivid. The natural, unforced quality of Haitink's *Rite* also brings real compulsion. Other versions may hammer the listener more powerfully, thrust him or her along more forcefully; but the bite and precision of the playing here are most impressive. Outstanding value.

Le baiser de la fée (Divertimento); The Soldier's tale: suite; Suites for orchestra Nos. 1–2; Octet.
500♪ (M) *** Decca Dig. 433 079-2 [id.]. L. Sinf., Chailly.

Chailly's version of the *Le baiser de la fée* divertimento, admirably fresh, is superbly played and Decca's recording is in the finest traditions of the house. The two *Orchestral suites* provide a kaleidoscopic series of colourful vignettes. The 1922 *Octet* is given a performance of infectious virtuosity, with individual bravura matched by polished ensemble and fine tonal blending. The surprisingly little-recorded concert suite from *The Soldier's tale*, added for this reissue, makes an impressive finale. Throughout the programme, the CD is very much in the demonstration class.

Capriccio for piano and orchestra; Concerto for piano and wind instruments; Movements for piano and orchestra; Symphonies of wind instruments.
500♪ *** Sony Dig. SK 45797 [id.]. Paul Crossley, L. Sinf., Salonen.

This is the sort of repertoire in which Esa-Pekka Salonen excels and in which Paul Crossley is also expert. All three performances can hold their own with the best, as indeed can the *Symphonies of wind instruments*. It is good to make the acquaintance of this CD, which can be confidently recommended to all lovers of the composer. Excellent digital recording too.

Le chant du rossignol (Song of the nightingale): symphonic poem.
(M) *** RCA 09026 68168-2 [id.]. Chicago SO, Fritz Reiner – RIMSKY-KORSAKOV: *Scheherazade* ***

Le Rossignol is an underrated Stravinsky work and its derivative opening (with its overtones of Debussy's *Nuages* and the Rimskian flavour of the opening Act) have led to its virtues being undervalued. Among them is the extraordinarily rich fantasy and vividness of colouring; this symphonic poem, which Stravinsky made from the material of his opera, deserves a much more established place in the concert repertoire. Lorin Maazel made a justly famous DG recording of it with the Berlin Radio Symphony Orchestra, and Ansermet's Decca version was equally renowned for its iridescent Decca sound. Both at the time eclipsed

Reiner's version of 1956, yet in its currently remastered form it is surely second to none, bringing astonishingly full and vivid sound, full of presence, an excellent coupling for his strong and dramatic reading of *Scheherazade*. Where this transitional work – composed over two separate periods – often seems to lack something in thrust, Reiner's virile, sharply focused reading relates it more clearly than usual to the *Rite of spring*. Not just in Solti's reign but in Reiner's too this was a supreme orchestra. The virtuosity of the playing and the clarity of its direction are arresting, while the refined yet glittering detail of the orchestral palette in the work's five (titled) closing sections is most evocative.

Violin concerto in D.

500♪ (M) (***) Sony mono SMK 64505 [id.]. Stern, Columbia SO, composer (with ROCHBERG: *Violin concerto* *(**)).

500♪ *** Sony Dig. SK 53969 [id.]. Cho-Liang Lin, LAPO, Esa-Pekka Salonen – PROKOFIEV: *Violin concertos Nos. 1 & 2.* *** ❁

Stern's 1951 mono recording with the composer has never been surpased and seldom approached. The outer movements have an exhilarating combination of rhythmic bite and wit, and the two central arias bring a very special subtlety of colour and feeling. The sound is of the highest quality: no apologies whatsoever need be made for it. Listening to the record lifts the spirits, and we would have given it a Rosette were it not for the Rochberg coupling, which (as music) is very much of the second grade, even if Stern's performance is not.

As in the two Prokofiev concertos, so in the Stravinsky Lin plays with power and warmth, while Salonen terraces the accompaniment dramatically, with woodwind and brass bold and full.

The Firebird (complete); *Le chant du rossignol; Fireworks; Scherzo à la russe.*

500♪ ❁ (M) *** Mercury 432 012-2 [id.]. LSO, Dorati.

The Firebird (ballet; complete); *Scherzo à la Russe.*

(M) ** Ph. Dig. 454 682-2 [id.]. BPO, Haitink.

We missed Haitink's 1991 digital recording of *The Firebird* the first time around. But it proves disappointing, curiously lacking in magnetism and glitter, and although climaxes bring more adrenalin and greater sonic brilliance one is conscious of the microphones, and neither performance nor recording can compare with Dorati's electrifying Mercury version with the LSO of three decades earlier. That offered not only the *Scherzo* as coupling, but also a comparably compelling version of *Le chant du rossignol*, with *Fireworks* thrown in as a final encore.

Ballets: *The Firebird* (suite; 1919 version); *Jeu de cartes; Petrushka* (1911 version); (i) *Pulcinella* (1947 version); *The Rite of spring.*

(B) *** DG Double 453 085-2 (2) [id.]. LSO, Abbado; (i) with Teresa Berganza, Ryland Davies, John Shirley-Quirk.

An attractive compilation of essential Stravinsky at a very reasonable price. The highlight here is *Petrushka*, while both the *Firebird suite* and *Jeux de cartes* are given stunning performances. The LSO plays with superb virtuosity and spirit. The neo-classical score of *Pulcinella* is given a surprisingly high-powered reading. But if Abbado is in danger of over-colouring, the bite and flair are entirely convincingly Stravinskian, with rhythms sharply incisive. Not just the playing but the singers too are outstandingly fine. Abbado's feeling for atmosphere and colour is everywhere in evidence, heard against an excellently judged perspective. There is a degree of detachment in Abbado's reading of *The Rite of spring*, although his observance of markings is meticulous and the orchestra obviously revels in the security given by the conductor's direction. The recording here is multi-miked, and the effect is less exciting than one would have expected. Nevertheless this is a worthwhile investment if taken as a whole.

Firebird (ballet): *suite; 4 Norwegian moods.*

(M) *(*) Virgin/EMI Ultraviolet Dig. CUV5 61322-2. Bergen PO, Kitaienko – LIADOV: *Baba-Yaga* etc. *(*)

Kitaienko's performances of the *Norwegian moods* bring a pleasingly folksy evocation; but the *Firebird suite*, although similarly colourful, seriously lacks dramatic profile. Both works are pleasingly recorded, but this is not in any way a distinctive record.

Petrushka (1911 version; complete). *The Firebird: suite* (1919). *Fireworks; Pastoral* (arr. Stokowski).

500♪ ❁ (***) Dutton Lab. mono CDAX 8002 [id.]. Phd. O, Stokowski (with: SHOSTAKOVICH: *Prelude in E flat min., Op. 34/14,* arr. Stokowski (***)).

Stokowski's 1937 version of *Petrushka* is very special indeed, the sound tremendously present and amazingly detailed for its period – high fidelity even by today's standards – and the performance is marvellously characterized and full of atmosphere: indeed it is difficult to think of a portrayal of Petrushka himself that is more poignant, keenly felt or brilliantly coloured. (Perhaps Bernstein's CBS account from the 1960s comes closest.) The playing of the Philadelphia Orchestra is quite stunning, and the Dutton transfer gets far more detail on to CD than the RCA rival (see below); it is also smoother on top. The 1935 *Firebird suite* (its ending cut, to fit on a 78-r.p.m. side) takes wing too – equally strongly characterized and full of atmosphere. A marvellous collection – indeed, a desert island disc.

Petrushka (ballet; 1911 version); *Symphony in three movements*.
** Everest EVC 9042 [id.]. LSO, Eugene Goossens.

Goossens made one of the first recordings of *Petrushka* in the days of pre-electric 78s, and his long affection for the score comes out in this vivid 1959 version, very well recorded for its time. This was highly regarded in the early days of stereo, and it is still enjoyably alive and dramatic. The *Symphony* is not as strong a performance, for the playing of the LSO here is less than brilliant.

Petrushka (1947 version); (i) *Pulcinella* (complete ballets).
*** Decca Dig. 443 774-2 [id.]. Concg. O, Chailly; (i) with Anna Caterina Antonacci, Pietro Ballo; William Shimell.

A splendid new *Petrushka* from Chailly, vividly characterized and with genuine pathos in Petrushka's cell scene. The orchestral playing is superb and the Decca engineers, always famous for this score, not content to rest on their laurels have pulled out all the stops, providing glittering detail, yet making full use of the warm Concertgebouw ambience. *Pulcinella* is equally winning, perhaps not as high-powered as the Abbado version, but with some splendidly incisive string-playing and plenty of rhythmic lift. There is charm and wit here, as well as drama. No complaints about the strong vocal contributions, and again the recording is in the demonstration bracket.

The Soldier's tale (*L'histoire du soldat*; complete).
*** Nimbus Dig. NI 5063 [id.]. Christopher Lee, SCO, Lionel Friend
*** Chandos Dig. CHAN 9189 [id.]. Aage Haugland, SNO, Järvi.
** Astrée Valois/Audivis Dig. V 4805 [id.]. Carole Bouquet, Gérard Depardieu, Guillaume Depardieu, Instrumental Ens., Mintz.

With the actor Christopher Lee both narrating and taking the individual parts, the Nimbus issue brings an attractively strong and robust reading, lacking the last degree of refinement but with some superb solo playing – from the violinist, for example. The recording is vivid and full of presence, with the speaking voice related to instruments far better than is usual. For a version in English, it makes an excellent investment.

The Chandos version provides an excellent alternative to the highly recommendable Nimbus version in English, in which Christopher Lee characterizes vividly, bringing out the sinister side of the story. Unlike the Chandos, that uses a version of the text helpfully amended from the original. Aage Haugland takes a more forthright view than Lee, with the Soldier less of a cockney and with the Devil given a crypto-French accent as a very oily character. Where the Chandos scores is in the sharper focus of the performance, generally brisker and tauter at faster speeds, helped by a close recording which yet has plenty of air round the sound.

Recorded live at the Théâtre des Champs-Elysées in 1996, the Astrée version can be recommended to those who want the original French text, with Carole Bouquet as a quicksilver narrator. Her delivery is often so fast and slurred, at least in the passages without music, that it may disconcert those who are not very fluent in French. Gérard Depardieu characterizes the Devil well, if not with all the sinister overtones one expects, and his son gives an engaging portrait of the Soldier. Shlomo Mintz directs an idiomatic performance of the score, not helped by very close and dry recording.

(i) *Symphony in C; Symphony in 3 movements;* (ii) *Symphonies of wind instruments; Scherzo fantastique, Op. 3.*
500♪ (M) *** Decca Dig. 436 474-2 [id.]. (i) SRO; (ii) Montreal SO; Dutoit.

The *Symphony in C* and *Symphony in three movements* are both exhilarating pieces and Dutoit punches home their virile high spirits and clean-limbed athleticism. The *Symphonies of wind instruments*, the work Stravinsky composed in 1920 in memory of Debussy, is given a very effective and crisp performance, and the sparkling *Scherzo fantastique* also demonstrates the greater polish of the Montreal players.

CHAMBER AND INSTRUMENTAL MUSIC

Concerto for two pianos; Sonata for two pianos; The Rite of spring.
(BB) * Naxos Dig. 8.553386 [id.]. Benjamin Frith, Peter Hill.

Benjamin Frith and Peter Hill are both brilliant players, though their *Rite of spring* needs higher voltage and more colour. Much the same might be said of the *Concerto for two pianos*. Ultimately, though, it is not on artistic grounds that this remains a one-star recommendation, but because of the recording quality. The acoustic is badly cramped and wanting in space and ambience. Ashkenazy and Gavrilov (Decca 433 829-2) are well worth the extra outlay – see our main volume.

(i) *Divertimento* (from *Le baiser de la fée*); *Duo concertante; Suite italienne;* (ii) *Mavra: Chanson russe.*
(M) *** EMI Analogue/Dig. CDM5 66061-2 [id.]. Itzhak Perlman, with (i) Bruno Canino; (ii) Samuel Sanders (with RACHMANINOV: *Vocalise, Op. 34/14;* Songs: *It's peaceful here* (arr. Heifetz); *Daisies* (arr. Kreisler) ***; TCHAIKOVSKY: *Andante cantabile* from *Op. 11; Chanson sans paroles* (arr. Kreisler); *Souvenir d'un lieu cher: Mélodie, Op. 42/2* (arr. Flesch) **).

The *Italian suite* was arranged from the Pergolesi-based ballet, *Pulcinella*, while the *Duo concertante* was written after the *Violin concerto* and for the same artist, Samuel Dushkin. The *Divertimento* is arranged from movements of the Tchaikovsky-derived ballet, *The fairy's kiss*. Stravinsky toured with Dushkin in the early 1930s, including the *Suite italienne* and the *Divertimento* in his concert programmes. (He recorded not only the *Violin concerto* but also the *Duo concertante* for Columbia with him.) Perlman plays all this music with warmth and understanding, and his achievement in the *Duo concertante*, which has often seemed a dry work, is particularly remarkable. Bruno Canino makes a sympathetic partner and the 1974 recording, originally excellent, has been clearly and cleanly transferred to CD, the sound more strongly etched than on LP. Perlman's seductively slinky account of the *Chanson russe* from *Mavra* was recorded four years later, and the two Rachmaninov songs, which are played with a delightful flowing lyricism, are digital; but in all these cases the sound is warmer and smoother. In Tchaikovsky's *Andante cantabile* Perlman seems determined to avoid any possible suggestion of sentimentality and the result is perhaps a shade cool; however, the *Chanson sans paroles* has real panache and the phrasing of the *Mélodie* from the *Souvenir d'un lieu cher* is equally appealing. Samuel Sanders gives admirable support, although he is made to sound a little self-effacing by the recording balance. But the Stravinsky collection remains one of Perlman's most rewarding achievements among his many recordings of instrumental duos.

VOCAL MUSIC

(i) *Mass;* (ii) *Les Noces.*
500♪ (M) *** DG 423 251-2 [id.]. (i) Trinity Boys' Ch., E. Bach Festival O; (i, ii) E. Bach Festival Ch.; (ii) Mory, Parker, Mitchinson, Hudson; Argerich, Zimerman, Katsaris, Francesch (pianos), percussion; cond. Bernstein.

In the *Mass* the style is overtly expressive, with the boys of Trinity Choir responding freshly, but it is in *Les Noces* that Bernstein conveys an electricity and a dramatic urgency which give the work its rightful stature as one of Stravinsky's supreme masterpieces, totally original and – even today – unexpected, not least in its black-and-white instrumentation for four pianos and percussion. The star pianists here make a superb, imaginative team.

OPERA

Oedipus Rex (opera-oratorio).
500♪ *** Sony Dig. SK 48057 [id.]. Cole, Von Otter, Estes, Sotin, Gedda, Chéreau, Eric Ericson Chamber Ch., Swedish RSO & Ch., Salonen.

Salonen with his Swedish forces and an outstanding cast, more consistent than any previous one, conducts the strongest performance yet on disc of this landmark of modern opera. He offers an ideal combination of rugged power and warmth, delivered expressively but without sentimentality. The singing of the two principals, Vinson Cole as Oedipus and Anne Sofie von Otter as Jocasta, conveys the full depth of emotion behind the piece. With recorded sound both dramatically immediate and warm, and with splendid narration in French from Patrice Chéreau, this displaces all rivals, even the composer's own American version.

Stravinsky Edition, Volume 9: *The Rake's progress* (complete).
500♪ (M) *** Sony SM2K 46299 (2) [id.]. Young, Raskin, Reardon, Sarfaty, Miller, Manning, Sadler's Wells Op. Ch., RPO, composer.

The Rake's progress (complete).
*** Erato/Warner Dig. 0630 12715-2 (2) [id.]. Hadley, Upshaw, Lloyd, Ramey, Collins, Bumbry, Lyon Opera Ch. & O, Kent Nagano.
** Ph. Dig. 454 431-2 (2) [id.]. Rolfe Johnson, McNair, Adams, Bostridge, Henschel, Plishka, Tokyo Op. Singers, Saito Kinen O, Ozawa.

It was a splendid idea to get Stravinsky to come to London to record *The Rake's progress*. The casting is uniformly excellent with the Rake of Alexander Young dominating but Judith Raskin an attractive heroine. Regina Sarfaty's Baba is superbly characterized and her anger at being spurned just before the 'squelching' makes a riveting moment. The composer conducts with warmth as well as precision, both chorus and orchestra respond persuasively, and the CD transfer is excellent. A clear first choice.

Kent Nagano, with his Lyon Opera forces and an outstanding cast of soloists, directs a fresh and crisp account of Stravinsky's neo-Mozartian score, springing rhythms lightly to make the music sparkle, while timing the dramatic moments to bring out deeper emotions. In the title-role Jerry Hadley, with his fresh, clear tone, is aptly youthful-sounding and brings out the pathos of the final scenes when struck insane by Nick Shadow. Samuel Ramey is powerful and sinister in that devilish role, as he was in the earlier, Chailly version, and Dawn Upshaw makes a tenderly affecting Anne Trulove, bringing out the heroine's vulnerability. Robert Lloyd as Trulove and Anne Collins as Mother Goose are both very well cast, and the veteran, Grace Bumbry, makes a fruity Baba the Turk. Excellent ensemble from the Lyon Opera chorus, though the balance is a little backward. Otherwise first-rate sound, making this a good, modern, digital alternative to the composer's own version.

Seiji Ozawa follows up his successful recording of *Oedipus Rex* with *The Rake's progress*, similarly timing the sessions to fit in with live performances. With forward sound – except for the far too distant chorus – the result has power but lacks something of the point and refinement of the Nagano version, with ensemble less sharply focused. The warmth and sweetness of Sylvia McNair's soprano suit the role of Anne but she lacks the tenderness of her finest rivals; and the close balance brings out a gritty quality in Anthony Rolfe Johnson's voice when under pressure, sounding no longer young. Nevertheless his characterization is splendid, but Paul Plishka as Nick Shadow is most disappointing, not dark or sinister enough and far too wobbly. Others are good, notably Jane Henschel as Baba the Turk and Ian Bostridge as Sellem the auctioneer.

Strozzi, Barbara (*c.* 1619–64)

Sacri musicali affetti, Libro I, *Op. 5* (extracts): *Erat Petrus; Hodie oritur; Mater Anna; Nascente Maria; O, Maria; Parasti cor meum; Salve Regina; Salve sancta caro.*
500♪ ❁ *** HM Dig. ED 13048 [id.]. Maria Cristina Kiehr, Concerto Soave (with: GIANONCELLI: *Tastegiatas 1–2;* BIAGIO MARINI: *Sonate da chiesa e da camera; Sinfonia secondo tuono;* TARQUINIO MERULA: *Capriccio cromatico; Canzon* ***).

Barbara Strozzi's many Marian celebrations, with their ripely expressive chromaticism, portray the Madonna as a warm, feeling creature with whom any normal woman could identify, rather than a chaste icon. The opening *Salve Regina* with its sighing phrases and melancholy descending scale is wonderfully tender, yet the music has a life-celebrating vitality too. The motet *Erat Petrus* (the Gospel story of Peter set free from prison) is virtually an operatic scena; it matches both Cavalli and Monteverdi in its dramatic confidence, set with great rhythmic variety and using a dialogue device between 'two' voices with aplomb. Perhaps most remarkable of all is the ravishing F minor *Parasti cor meum*, bringing sliding chromatic glissandi – surely a perfect illustration of the Italian word, *affetti*. Maria Kiehr's singing here is unforgettable, as is her bravura decorative flair; indeed her ornamentation is a model of expressive understanding throughout. She is beautifully accompanied by the appropriately named Concerto Soave. To make the programme even more enjoyable, the vocal items are interspersed with admirably chosen intrumental pieces by Strozzi's contemporaries, featuring – as do the accompaniments – chamber organ as well as harpsichord and the usual continuo instrumentation of the time. The recording is admirably balanced and very natural. This is a treasurable collection and a musical revelation.

'To the unknown goddess': Cantate, ariette e duetti, Op. 2: L'amante segreto . . . Voglio, voglio morire; Amor dormiglione . . . Amor, non dormir più; La fanciuletta semplice . . . Spesso per entro al petto; Gite o giorni dolenti; Giusta negativa . . . Non mi dite ch'io canti; La sol, fa, mi, re do . . . La mia donna perchè canta. Cantate ariete a una, due e tre voci, Op. 3: Ardo in tacito foco. Diporti di Euterpe, Op. 7: Appresso ai molli argenti; Lagrime mie . . . Lagrime mie, a che vi trattenete; Pensaci ben mio core; Tradimento.

(M) *** Carlton Dig. 30366 00412 [id.]. Catherine Bott, Paula Chateauneuf; Timothy Roberts; Frances Kelly.

Having discovered the extraordinarily individual seventeenth-century female Venetian composer Barbara Strozzi (adopted daughter of Monteverdi's librettist) through her religious music, here is an opportunity to sample her secular love songs. The very first in this recital, *Ardo in tacito foco* ('The heart forbids the tongue to pronounce the beloved's name') immediately displays her characteristic languishing musical device of a chromatically inclined downward scale, while the opening of the Lamento, *Lagrime mie, a che vi trattenete* ('My tears, why do you hold back'), with its equally luscious chromatic sighs, is just as affecting. Catherine Bott revels in its yearning line, with her embellishments adding to the languor. But there is considerable variety of mood here. *La fanciuletta semplice* ('The simple girl') and *Amor dormiglione* are both charmingly fresh and uncomplicated; the latter has a dancing, upward, vocal arpeggio, while *La, sol, fa, mi, re, do* is like a sparkling folksong. *L'amante segreto*, however, is a lovely, lyrical song, soaring up high, with a sad coda. Most eloquent of all is the closing *Appresso ai molli argenti* ('Close to the soft banks of a murmuring stream') with its remarkable word-imagery set with real imaginative flair. Catherine Bott is as much a master of this repertoire as her predecessor, Maria Cristina Kiehr, was with the *Sacri musicali affetti*. She encompasses its florid upper tessitura with freshness and ease, she responds readily to moments of sensuality, and her bravura decorated runs are remarkably secure. The small accompanying group (archlute or guitar, harpsichord and double harp) is just right, and so is the recording balance. Strongly recommended, especially if you have already tried the Harmonia Mundi disc.

Suk, Josef (1874–1935)

Asrael Symphony, Op. 27.

500♪ ✿ *** Chandos Dig. CHAN 9042 [id.]. Czech PO, Bělohlávek.

Jiří Bělohlávek, the principal conductor of the Czech Philharmonic, draws powerfully expressive playing from the orchestra in a work which in its five large-scale movements is predominantly slow. Next to Pešek's fine Liverpool performance, the speeds flow a degree faster and more persuasively, and the ensemble, notably of the woodwind, is even crisper, phenomenally so. It helps too that the sound is warmer, closer and more involving than the refined but more distant Virgin recording.

Serenade for strings, Op. 6.

*** DG Dig. 447 109-2 [id.]. Orpheus CO – KODALY: *Hungarian rondo* etc. ***

We are currently spoiled for choice for recordings of this lovely *Serenade*, and this is as good as (if not better than) any of our current recommendations. Probably the best is Bělohlávek, coupled with *A Fairy-tale* and discussed in our main volume (Chandos CHAN 9063). The Orpheus Chamber Orchestra play with scrupulous care for detail, and the textures are clean and fresh. Splendid recording, but this is relatively short measure.

String quartets Nos. 1 in B flat, Op. 11; 2, Op. 31; Ballade; Barcarolle; Meditation on the Czech choral, St Wenceslas, Op 35a; Minuet.

✿ *** CRD Dig. CRD 3472 [id.]. Suk Qt.

The early *B flat Quartet* was written (in 1896) before the tragedy that overtook the composer in his thirties. It is essentially a sunny work, yet its *Adagio* has a remarkable potency of elegiac feeling, which is very affecting in a performance as ardently responsive as that by the eponymous Suk Quartet on CRD. They also catch the lighted-hearted delicacy of the opening movement and the blithe gaiety of the closing *Allegro giacoso* to perfection.

The *Second Quartet*, composed 15 years later, is far more concentrated than its predecessor, and it reflects something of the melancholy spirit of the *Asrael Symphony* of only a few years earlier. Its expressive opening (a series of descending chords), which runs through the whole work, was originally intended for a piece called *Mysterium*. The *Quartet* is a single-movement work lasting about half an hour; its thematic material is curiously haunting and in some ways its boldness and forward-looking writing suggest that Janáček's quartets are just around the corner. The performance here is not only deeply moving and seemingly spontaneous, it is wonderfully full of observed detail, while the *Adagio* section, which recurs, brings a profound intensity of feeling. What haunting music this is! Of the other works here the simple *Meditation* on a hymn to the patron saint of Bohemia is the most affecting, and again it is played very touchingly. Suk also wrote three more pieces for the medium. One was a reworking of the final movement of the Op. 11 *Quartet* but it was never used (or published). The agreeable *Minuet in G* is an arrangement for string quartet of the second movement of the piano *Suite*, Op. 21. The *Barcarolle* is a charming piece of juvenilia, a real lollipop, to show the composer's ready melodic facility. It is derived from the second movement of Suk's first serious attempt at quartet writing, and the only part of the work that he allowed to be published (in 1928), in a piano arrangement. The original version is played here. CRD have something of a reputation for recording chamber music, but they have never made a better record than this superb collection, produced by Jeremy Hayes and engineered by Bob Auger. The beauty and internal transparency of string texture is matched by the natural presence of the group itself.

Sullivan, Arthur (1842–1900)

Ballet music

L'Ile enchantée (complete ballet); *Thespis*: suite.
**(*) Marco Polo 8.2234560 [id.]. RTE Concert O, Dublin, Andrew Penny.

Sullivan wrote a great deal of ballet and incidental music, and much of it is totally unknown; so we are indebted to Marco Polo for moving across the Channel from the Strausses in Vienna to provide us with a survey nearer home. *L'Ile enchantée* was written to be fitted into a Covent Garden production of Bellini's *La Sonnambula* in 1864. Its somewhat Verdian style, using lyrical brass solos as well as engaging woodwind (as in the *Mazurka* variation, which is Delibesian), would have fitted well into its Bellinian slot, and the score is quite lively, with a splendid final *Galop*. *Thespis* was an early Gilbert and Sullivan creation which did not survive, and the very introduction of the ballet suite unmistakably establishes the jolly rhythmic pattern we associate with the Savoy Operas, while its closing *Galop* has a character which draws on both influences. Andrew Penny changes from Malcolm Arnold to Sullivan with equally sympathetic results. He secures bold, lively playing from the Dublin orchestra, and the resonant recording is very suitable, if without the lustrous glow we associate with Decca's ballet records.

King Arthur (incidental music): suite; *Macbeth* (incidental music): suite; *The Merry Wives of Windsor* (incidental music): suite.
*** Marco Polo Dig. 8.223635 [id.]. Margaret MacDonald, RTE Chamber Ch. & Concert O Dublin, Andrew Penny.

This is perhaps the finest of the four Marco Polo records of Sullivan's music, showing the composer at his most pleasingly inventive and appealing. The opening *Chorus of Lake Spirits* in *King Arthur* might well have come out of *Patience* (they sound very much like lovesick maidens). But the following, more confident *Unseen spirits* would have fitted more readily into *Iolanthe*. The *Chaunt of the Grail* begins as an engaging little march, nicely scored, which is joined by the full chorus and expands impressively. The *May song* is charming, and the more doleful (but not tragic) *Funeral march* and final chorus round the selection off splendidly. The music for *Macbeth* brings a fine Overture (which was published) with some striking brass writing, and the *Introduction to Act IV* has a rather good tune (though hardly with the flavour of Shakespearean tragedy). But easily the finest number is the deliciously fairy-like, Mendelssohnian *Chorus of the Spirits in the Air*, while the following *Chorus of Witches and Spirits* sounds more like the opening of the Act I finale to another Savoy Opera. All the music for *The Merry Wives of Windsor* sounds as if it were part of an operetta. The scena '*As I am a true spirit, welcome!*', sung very nicely by Margaret MacDonald with chorus, is a highlight; but Sullivan also included a Swinburne setting as an additional song for Mistress Anne Page which is more ambitious, and the closing *Dance* with chorus rounds the whole programme off in exhilarating fashion. Sullivan's flow of attractive ideas makes for a most enjoyable 50 minutes, and all the performers rise to the occasion. The recording is excellent.

The Merchant of Venice (Masquerade); *Henry VIII* (incidental music): suite. *Overture: The Sapphire necklace: Overture in C (In Memoriam).*
** Marco Polo Dig. 8.223461 [id.]. Emmanuel Lawler, RTE Concert O, Dublin, Andrew Penny.

We have had both the rather inflated but at times quite engaging *In Memoriam Overture* and excerpts from Sullivan's incidental music for *The Merchant of Venice* before. But here is a more extended suite which includes a solo tenor *Barcarolle* with a strong flavour of *The Gondoliers*. It comes after some evocative writing for woodwind and horns has set the late-evening Venetian scene. There are plenty of good ideas here, and nice orchestral touches, with quirky bassoons in the *Grotesque dance*, some delicately pointed string-writing in the *Waltz*, and a grand G&S style finale to round things off spiritedly. The *Henry VIII* incidental music was commissioned for a production of Shakespeare's play in Manchester, on which the curtain went up in 1877. The music was confined to Act V. The suite opens with regal trumpet fanfares and the scoring is well laced with brass (which made it popular on the bandstand) but it is also notable for a pleasing tenor contribution, *King Henry's song* (well sung here by Emmanuel Lawler), which shows how readily Sullivan could spin a ballad. *The Sapphire necklace* had a very chequered career. The opera for which it was written was never produced and the score disappeared. The overture was published for military band use in an arrangement by Charles Godfrey. No orchestral parts survive, so the present orchestral version is a re-arrangement of the military band score! It opens with sonorous trombone chords, then string pizzicatos over which a rather engaging minuet theme emerges on the clarinet. There is another neat little tune later, using woodwind and strings very charmingly. The piece is well constructed and has a rumbustious ending, but it would have been more effective had it been shorter. It is much more redolent of the Savoy Theatre than of Covent Garden. Andrew Penny secures lively, well-played performances throughout; but in the last resort this is a disc for curious Sullivan fans rather than for the general collector.

Victoria and Merrie England (complete ballet).
*** Marco Polo 8.223677 [id.]. RTE Sinf., Dublin, Andrew Penny.

Victoria and Merrie England was not a ballet as we understand it today, but a uniquely British combination of mime to music, speciality dances, grand tableaux and, most important, military costumes designed for the girls of the *corps de ballet* to reveal as much of their nether limbs as was deemed respectable. It was written to celebrate Queen Victoria's Diamond Jubilee and so was also well laden with patriotism. Essentially a historical cavalcade, its six principal scenes dealt in turn with Ancient Britain, May Day in Queen Elizabeth's time, The Legend of Herne the Hunter, Christmas revels in the time of Charles II, the Coronation of Queen Victoria and, finally, a celebration of Britain's Glory, with a military parade and the entrance of Britannia. All in all it was more of a pantomime than a ballet. It opened in May 1897 at London's Alhambra Theatre, the traditional site for such Victorian musical extravaganzas, and played for six months, during which time the Prince of Wales and other members of the Royal Family visited the show 19 times.

Then, unbelievably, the score and orchestral parts were lost. Fortunately the whole ballet had been published as a piano solo, and Sullivan himself selected three orchestral suites for concert use. However, assiduous research sponsored by the Sullivan Society finally enabled the assembling of a complete score, edited by Roderick Spencer. Scenes 1, 2 and 4 largely use Sullivan's own orchestration; Scenes 3, 5 and 7 are more conjectural; the scoring of Scene 8 has been determined from the piano reduction; only Scene 6 had to be completely re-orchestrated from the piano transcription. Was it worth all the effort? Well, yes, it's engaging stuff, with plenty of allusions to the Savoy Operas, notably the opening of the May Day festivities on the village green in Scene 2, and the *Maypole dance* which closes that scene, while the *Galop and Dance of Nymphs and Hunters* which ends Scene 5 is very like a G&S patter song. Sullivan's invention, if not always of his highest quality, maintains a pretty good standard, with plenty of jolly tunes and jaunty ideas. Whoever was responsible for the scoring, it works well, particularly the atmospheric opening scene in Ancient Britain, which immediately produces a striking, melancholy tune with harp for the Druids, while in the *Rites of the Mistletoe*, *Rule Britannia* creeps in for the first time on the trumpet. The Windsor Forest setting for the *Herne the Hunter* sequence obviously stimulated Roderick Spencer's imagination for, after the introductory storm, the pastoral instrumentation here is delightful, with the clarinet piping over shimmering strings. This leads to one of the best tunes of the whole piece, the delicate *Waltz of the Wood Nymphs*, which has much in common with Geoffrey Toye's *Haunted ballroom*. Sullivan used his *Imperial march* for the Coronation scene. But it is the final section, 'Britain's Glory', which is the most robustly enjoyable, with the entrance of English, Irish, Scottish and Colonial troops celebrated with a series of folk tunes, wittily climaxed with 'For he is an Englishman' borrowed from *HMS Pinafore* and sentimentally followed with *There's no place like home*, and finally a brassy version of the National Anthem. It's all very endearing, and Andrew Penny presents it with warm affection and much gusto. It isn't great music but it is good fun.

OPERA

HMS Pinafore (complete; with dialogue).
500♪ ❁ (M) *** Decca 414 283-2. Reed, Skitch, Round, Adams, Hindmarsh, Wright, Knight, D'Oyly Carte Op. Ch., New SO of L., Godfrey.

HMS Pinafore.
500♪ ❁ *** Telarc Dig. CD 80374 [id.]. Suart, Allen, Evans, Schade, Palmer, Adams, Ch. & O of Welsh Opera, Mackerras.

Sir Charles Mackerras here gives an exuberant reading of the first operetta of the cycle. The lyricism and transparency of Sullivan's inspiration shine out with winning freshness. The casting is not just starry but inspired. So in such a number as Captain Corcoran's *Fair moon to thee I sing* one relishes the pure beauty of the melody as sung by Thomas Allen, sharpened by innocent send-up in Gilbert's verses. Rebecca Evans is an appealing Josephine and Richard Suart a dry Sir Joseph Porter. Michael Schade is heady-toned as the hero, Ralph Rackstraw, while among character roles Felicity Palmer is a marvellously fruity Little Buttercup, with Richard van Allan as Bill Bobstay and the veteran, Donald Adams, a lugubrious Dick Deadeye. As with the previous CDs of *Mikado* and *Pirates of Penzance*, Telarc squeezes the whole score on to a single CD, vividly recorded.

HMS Pinafore is in our view the finest of all the D'Oyly Carte stereo recordings. While Owen Brannigan, on EMI, without the benefit of dialogue conveys the force of Dick Deadeye's personality remarkably strongly, Donald Adams's assumption of the role on Decca (which does have the dialogue) is little short of inspired, and his larger-than-life characterization underpins the whole piece. The rest of the cast make a splendid team: Jean Hindmarsh is a totally convincing Josephine – she sings with great charm – and John Reed's Sir Joseph Porter is a delight.

The Mikado (complete, but without Overture).

500♪ ❁ *** Telarc Dig. CD 80284 [id.]. Donald Adams, Rolfe Johnson, Suart, McLaughlin, Palmer, Van Allan, Folwell, Welsh Nat. Op. Ch. and O, Mackerras.

With the overture omitted (not Sullivan's work) and one of the stanzas in Ko-Ko's 'little list' song (with words unpalatable today), the whole fizzing Mackerras performance is fitted on to a single, very well-filled disc. The cast, with no weak link, is as starry as those in EMI's 'Glyndebourne' series of G&S recordings of thirty years ago, yet, far more than Sir Malcolm Sargent on those earlier recordings, Mackerras is electrically sharp at brisk speeds, sounding totally idiomatic and giving this most popular of the G&S operettas an irresistible freshness at high voltage. Donald Adams is as firm and resonant as he was in his D'Oyly Carte recording, made no less than 33 years earlier.

Suppé, Franz von (1819–95)

Overtures: *Beautiful Galathea; Boccaccio, Light cavalry; Morning, noon and night in Vienna; Pique dame, Poet and peasant.*

500♪ (M) *** Mercury 434 309-2 [id.]. Detroit SO, Paul Paray – AUBER: *Overtures*. *** ❁

Listening to Paray, one discovers a verve and exhilaration that are wholly Gallic in spirit. His chimerical approach to *Beautiful Galathea* (with a wonderfully luminous passage from the Detroit strings near the very opening) is captivating, and the bravura violin playing in *Light cavalry* is remarkably deft. With its splendid Auber coupling this is one of Mercury's most desirable reissues.

Overtures: *Die Frau Meisterin; Die Irrfahrt um's Glück; Light cavalry; Morning, noon and night in Vienna; Pique dame; Poet and peasant; Tantalusqualen; Wiener-Jubel (Viennese Jubilee).*

500♪ ❁ *** EMI Dig. CDC7 54056-2 [id.]. ASMF, Marriner.

Marriner's collection of Suppé *Overtures* goes straight to the top of the list. It is expansively recorded in EMI's No. 1 Studio and, played up to concert volume on big speakers, it produces the most spectacular demonstration quality. The performances have tremendous exuberance and style: this is one of Marriner's very best records.

Szymanowski, Karol (1882–1937)

(i) *Violin concertos Nos. 1, Op. 35; 2, Op. 61. Concert overture, Op. 12.*
*** Chandos Dig. CHAN 9496 [id.]. (i) Lydia Mordkovitch; BBC PO, Sinaisky.

(i) *Violin concertos Nos. 1, Op. 35; 2, Op. 61;* (ii) *Romance, Op. 23; 3 Paganini caprices, Op. 40.*
*** EMI Dig. CDC5 55607-2 [id.]. Zehetmair, (i) CBSO, Rattle; (ii) Silke Avenhaus.

At long last these concertos are coming into their own and one can expect other musicians to take up their challenge. They will have to be good to dislodge Thomas Zehetmair's deeply felt versions with Rattle and the CBSO. Rattle conjures up the Szymanowskian sound-world with real flair, and the soloist characterizes each phrase with impeccable instinct. The engineers deliver first-rate sound in both works and in the four violin and piano makeweights, in which Zehetmair is well supported by the young German pianist, Silke Avenhaus.

Lydia Mordkovitch is also admirably suited, full-toned and red-blooded, for these exotic concertos, helped by playing, richly recorded, from the BBC Philharmonic under Vassily Sinaisky, the orchestra's Principal Guest Conductor. Together they bring out to the full the sensuousness of the *First Concerto* as well as its elusive charm, a highly original one-movement span leading to an extraordinary, gentle ending. That work is strongly contrasted, not just with the early and extrovert *Concert overture*, an illuminating coupling, but with the *Second Concerto*. By then (1932), Szymanowski's style had acquired nationalistic flavours, Bartók-style, while remaining rich and distinctive.

Symphonies Nos. 2 in B flat, Op. 19; (i) *4 (Sinfonia concertante).*
*** Chandos Dig. CHAN 9478 [id.]. (i) Howard Shelley; BBC PO, Vassily Sinaisky.

The *Second* and *Fourth Symphonies* are two decades apart. There is a lot of Scriabin, Strauss and Reger in the *Second* (1910–11) but the scoring is congested. Szymanowski overhauled the orchestration in 1930 with the aid of Grzegorz Fitelberg, who made the pioneer recording in 1955, but the climaxes are still opaque. The soft-focus recording is less clearly defined than, say, Dorati's brightly lit, well-detailed account on Decca, but it presents a more atmospheric aural picture. Vassily Sinaisky is a highly sympathetic interpreter of the piece, and this BBC version must be a prime recommendation. So, too, is the coupling, the *Sinfonia concertante* (1932). Howard Shelley produces a quality of sound that is as luminous and every bit as refined and velvet-toned as the two rivals from Piotr Paleczny (on EMI and BBC). The balance between piano and orchestra is particularly well managed, and the lush orchestral textures are more lucid than we have heard them elsewhere.

Symphony No. 4 (Sinfonia concertante).
** Koch 3-6414-2 [id.]. Ewa Kupiec, Bamberg SO, Judd – LUTOSLAWSKI: *Piano concerto.* ***

As she shows in her inspired account of the Lutoslawski concerto, with which this symphony is coupled, Ewa Kupiec is a pianist with a formidable technique, who conveys a feeling of spontaneous expressiveness even when taxed by bravura writing. Though this is not as purposeful a performance as that of the Lutoslawski – largely a question of the orchestra not sounding so well attuned – this makes an unusual if rather ungenerous coupling of two concertante works for piano by Polish composers of successive generations. First-rate sound.

INSTRUMENTAL MUSIC

Mythes, Op. 30; Kurpian folk song; King Roger: Roxana's aria (both arr. Kochanski).
500♪ ❁ (M) *** DG 431 469-2. Kaja Danczowska, Krystian Zimerman – FRANCK: *Violin sonata.* ***

Kaja Danczowska brings vision and poetry to the ecstatic, soaring lines of the opening movement of *Mythes*, *The Fountains of Arethusa*. Her intonation is impeccable, and she has the measure of these other-worldly, intoxicating scores. There is a sense of rapture here that is totally persuasive, and Krystian Zimerman plays with a virtuosity and imagination that silence criticism. An indispensable issue.

PIANO MUSIC

12 Etudes, Op. 33; Masques, Op. 34; Mazurkas, Op. 50/7, 13 & 15; Op. 62/1–2; Métopes, Op. 29.
*** EMI Dig. CDC5 55390-2 [id.]. Mikhail Rudy.

Mikhail Rudy has a natural feel for Szymanowski's sound-world and his sensibility. He plays with great flair and is well recorded. This can be recommended alongside (though not necessarily in preference to) Dennis Lee's Hyperion recital (CDA 66409).

Mazurkas, Opp. 50 & 62.
** Mer. Dig. CD84323 [id.]. Kaoru Bingham.

The late *Mazurkas*, Op. 50, were inspired by Szymanowski's contact with the folk music of the Goral mountains in southern Poland and are elliptical and strangely elusive in character. Kaoru Bingham exhibits genuine feeling for this repertoire, and she is recorded more than decently. No one wanting this repertoire is likely to be disappointed, though her playing does not quite have the depth and intensity of Dennis Lee's highly recommendable Szymanowski recital on Hyperion, which includes the four *Etudes*, Op. 4, the *Fantasy*, Op. 14, *Masques*, Op. 34, and *Métopes*, Op. 29 (CDA 66409 – see our main volume).

Tallis, Thomas (*c.* 1505–85)

Gaude gloriosa; Loquebantur variis linguis; Miserere nostri; Salvator mundi, salva nos, I and II; Sancte Deus; Spem in alium (40-part motet).
500♪ ❁ *** Ph. 454 906-2 [id.]. Tallis Scholars, Phillips.

Within the admirably suitable acoustics of Merton College Chapel, Oxford, the Tallis Scholars give a thrilling account of the famous 40-part motet, *Spem in alium*, in which the astonishingly complex polyphony is spaciously separated over a number of point sources, yet blending as a satisfying whole to reach a massive climax. The *Gaude gloriosa* is another much recorded piece, while the soaring *Sancte Deus* and the two very contrasted settings of the *Salvator mundi* are hardly less beautiful.

Tartini, Giuseppe (1692–1770)

Violin concertos, Volume 1: *Concertos in D, D.15; in G, D.78 & D.80; in A min., D.115; in B flat, D.123.*
** Olympia Dig. OCD 475 [id.]. Gordan Nikolitch, Orchestre d'Auvergne, Arie van Beek.

Violin concertos, Volume 2: *Concertos: in C, D.12; in D min., D.45; in E, D.51; in B flat, D.117.*
** Olympia Dig. OCD 476 [id.]. Gordan Nikolitch, Orchestre d'Auvergne, Arie van Beek.

Tartini wrote over 135 violin concertos, of which 100 still remain unpublished. The present series from Olympia suggests that a complete survey is under way, and it will be interesting to see if Tartini's fecundity matches that of Vivaldi. As it so happens, the opening of the first concerto in Volume 1 (D.15, *in D major*) and the sparkling finale of the (*G major*, D.78), with its echo effects in the solo line, are both surprisingly like Vivaldi, but the companion *G major* work, D.80, has a rather beautiful *Andante*, which has Tartini's firm personal imprint. Nikolitch plays it ethereally. But it may not belong to the work, for there is a second, less striking *Grave*, which is here added as an appendix. The *A minor Concerto* opens with a rather fine *Cantabile* before the *Allegro assai* gets under way, and this work brings another slow movement of some distinction. The finale dances pleasingly, with an interesting solo part, and this is one of the best concertos of the series so far.

The opening *B flat major Concerto* on the second disc (D.117) has a particularly attractive contrapuntal first movement and a touching *Largo*. Tartini wrote alternative slow movements for the *C major* work, D.12, each given a sobriquet, taken from the libretto of a long-forgotten opera of the period. Both are in siciliano form, while the *Adagio* of the *E major*, D 51, is subtitled *Tortorella bacie*, and this reference to an unidentified turtle-dove (a human one perhaps?) brings another affectingly simple melody. Although Nikolitch with his pure, vibrato-less line finds an austere beauty for all three, it is a pity his playing is so withdrawn. This is music which calls for more warmth, dazzle and charm and, although the Orchestre d'Auvergne accompanies spiritedly and the recording is very good, there is a missing dimension here.

Tavener, John (born 1944)

(i) *Eternal memory for cello and strings;* (ii) *The Hidden treasure* (for string quartet); (iii) *Svyati (O Holy one)* for cello and chorus; (iv) *Akhmatova songs* for soprano and cello. *Chant* for solo cello.
*** RCA Dig. 09026 68761-2 [id.]. Steven Isserlis; with (i) Moscow Virtuosi, Spivakov; (ii) Daniel Phillips, Krista Feeney, Todd Phillips; (iii) Kiev Chamber Ch., Mykola Gobdych; (iv) Patricia Rosario.

All this music is constructed simply (simplistically, some might say) and is based for the most part on a simple rising and falling scalic sequence, in the case of the *Svyati* and *Eternal memory* seemingly linked thematically (both of them faintly recalling the opening of the slow movement of Bruckner's *Seventh Symphony*). Their atmosphere is extraordinarily magnetic. *Eternal memory* moves on from *The Protecting veil* and the composer describes its evocation as 'the remembrance of death; the remembrance of Paradise lost': its serene outer sections frame a more troubled centrepiece, 'grotesque, dance-like and rough'. *The Hidden treasure* for string quartet still has a dominating cello role and might be described as a religious pilgrimage, closing with a mystical transformation. In the *Akhmatova songs* the rising and falling sequence is floridly ornamented, with sinuous chromatic glissandi and half-notes in the Eastern manner; and the singer is required to soar up ecstatically to the top of her range, which Patricia Rosario manages confidently. *Svyati* returns to a simple but radiant dialogue, alternating cello soliloquy with a mystical choral response. Steven Isserlis has never made a finer record than this and he gives the feeling of quiet improvisation (especially in his solo *Chant*); throughout, the singing and playing capture the music's atmosphere superbly. The beautiful recording has a natural presence.

(i) *The Protecting veil* (for cello and orchestra); *Thrinos*.
500♪ *** Virgin/EMI Dig. VC7 59052-2 [id.]. Steven Isserlis, (i) LSO, Rozhdestvensky – BRITTEN: *Cello suite No. 3*. ***

In the inspired performance of Steven Isserlis, dedicatedly accompanied by Rozhdestvensky and the LSO, *The Protecting veil* has an instant magnetism, at once gentle and compelling. Tavener's simplicity of idiom has you escaping at once into a spiritual world, sharing his visions. Much is owed to the performance, with Isserlis a commanding soloist. He is just as compelling in the other two works on the disc, not just the Britten but also the simple lyrical lament, *Thrinos*, which Tavener wrote especially for him. Excellent recording.

VOCAL MUSIC

The Akathist of Thanksgiving.
500♪ ❁ *** Sony Dig. SK 64446 [id.]. Bowman, Wilson, Westminster Abbey Ch., BBC SO & Singers, Martin Neary.

Even among Tavener's many works inspired by his Russian Orthodox faith, *The Akathist of Thanksgiving* stands out for its concentrated intensity. The recording was taken live from the performance given in January 1994 at Westminster Abbey. The result on disc is both warmly atmospheric and well defined, with high dynamic contrasts involving not just choral forces but strings, heavy brass and percussion. Martin Neary proves an inspiring conductor, drawing incandescent tone from the choirs, thrillingly reinforced by the underlying weight of instrumental sound.

Taverner, John (*c*. 1495–1545)

Mass: The Western Wynde; Christe Jesu pastor bone; Dum transisset Sabbatum; Kyrie Le Roy; Mater Christie.
(B) *** Decca Double 452 170-2 (2) [id.]. King's College, Cambridge, Ch., Willcocks – BYRD: *Masses for 3, 4 and 5 voices* etc. ***

John Taverner's remarkable individuality is admirably shown by this excellent King's concert. The *Western Wynde Mass* (so called because of its use of this secular tune as a constantly recurring ground) is a masterpiece of the highest order. Its lines soar to express rich expressive feeling, particularly in the *Sanctus*, and overall it is hauntingly memorable. The other music here also shows the composer's wide range of expressive power: the motets are by no means dwarfed by the Mass and are works of great beauty in their own right. With first-class King's performances, appropriately more extrovert in feeling than the coupled music of Byrd, this makes an outstanding collection, with the highly evocative 1961 (originally Argo) recording giving the trebles an abundant body of tone.

Tchaikovsky, Peter (1840–93)

Andante cantabile, Op. 11; Nocturne in C sharp min., Op. 19/4; Souvenir de Florence, Op. 70; Variations on a rococo theme, Op. 33; Eugene Onegin: Lensky's aria.
*** DG Dig. 453 460-2 [id.]. Mischa Maisky, Orpheus CO.

If in the central cello repertory Mischa Maisky can seem dangerously wilful, Tchaikovsky here suits him perfectly. Understandably, with him as star, the *Rococo variations*, not the longest work, get top billing here, and they receive a warmly persuasive reading, at once impulsive and freely expressive. Long versed in conductorless playing, the brilliant Orpheus Chamber Orchestra follow him loyally, as they do in the other concertante items, as arranged by the composer. In the celebrated *Andante cantabile* Maisky uses full tone for the opening melody and then most beautifully begins the middle section in a hushed pianissimo. Paradoxically, much the longest work, the *Souvenir de Florence*, is the one which gives Maisky the least to do as soloist. The original string sextet version is here adapted for full strings, with Maisky coming to the fore only in the second movement. There, when the violin and cello lines soar in duet over guitar-like pizzicatos as a sort of serenade, the full violins take the upper line, with Maisky in solo below, easily holding his own. With such forces the movement works up to an overwhelming climax. The playing is just as rich and persuasive, with finely polished ensemble. Excellent recording, warm and well balanced.

Capriccio italien, Op. 45; Manfred Symphony, Op. 58; Romeo and Juliet (fantasy overture); Serenade for strings in C, Op. 48; The Tempest, Op. 18.
(B) *** BMG/Melodiya Twofer 74321 34164-2 (2). USSR SO, Svetlanov.

Svetlanov's recordings of the major Tchaikovsky orchestral works, made in the late 1960s, still stand up well to current competition; the remastering for CD is highly successful, retaining the vividness and colour and minimizing any coarseness. Their reissue on three 'Twofers' (as BMG/Melodiya have designated their two-for-the-price-of-one double-CD packs) makes a genuine bargain.

The vibrant brass-playing opening of *Capriccio italien* immediately establishes the very Russian credentials of these performances, yet the strings bring both panache and warmth too, while the final tarantella generates a sudden burst of adrenalin at the close. But the key work here is *Manfred*, and Svetlanov provides a superb account, strong and uninhibited, among the finest available: the orchestral playing has splendid colour and urgency, with plenty of passion from the strings. The full-blooded Russian recording is entirely appropriate and, while the work's weaker moments are not totally disguised, this is altogether very satisfying. *Romeo and Juliet* has similar red-blooded romanticism, and *The Tempest*, too, with its memorably ecstatic love theme, is passionate in a characteristically Russian way. This emphasizes the melodrama of the piece – better this, however, than undercharacterization – and the opening and closing sections depicting Prospero's magic island are evocatively done, with thrustful horn playing. The *Serenade for strings* is a spacious account; Svetlanov seeks Mozartian elegance in the first movement by not pressing too hard. The *Waltz* is beautifully turned, and in the *Elegy* the Slavonic ardour preserves a deep melancholy rather than seeking extrovert passion. The finale has plenty of vigour but the breadth of the reading is preserved, and with fine string playing this is a most attractive performance.

Piano concerto No. 1 in B flat min., Op. 23.
*** Hänssler Dig. CD 98.932 [id.]. Garrick Ohlsson, ASMF, Marriner – RACHMANINOV: *Piano concerto No. 2.* ***
500♪ *** Ph. 446 673-2 [id.]. Martha Argerich, Bavarian RSO, Kondrashin – RACHMANINOV: *Piano concerto No. 3.* ***
*(*) Hyperion Dig. CDA 66680 [id.]. Nikolai Demidenko, BBC SO, Alexander Lazarev – SCRIABIN: *Piano concerto.* *(*)

It is good to have a really splendid, modern coupling of these two most popular romantic concertos from Ohlsson and Marriner that can measure up to the finest versions from the past, presented in naturally balanced, modern, digital recording of the very highest quality. The Tchaikovsky opens with a commanding melodic sweep, and the first movement allegro is as full of poetic detail as it is exciting, leading on to the cadenza in the most spontaneous way. The *Andante semplice* is charmingly light-hearted and, after the scintillating centrepiece, is very tender at its reprise. The dancing finale brings all the bravura you could ask for, and in the coda Ohlsson broadens the pace of those furious octaves and ends the concerto with a sense of weight and power as well as excitement. The battle is over, the pianist clearly winning on the home straight.

Argerich's Philips issue comes from a live performance given in October 1980, full of animal excitement, with astonishingly fast speeds in the outer movements. The impetuous virtuosity is breathtaking, even if passage-work is not always as cleanly articulated as in her superb studio performance for DG; but you will find few more satisfying performances on record than either of these.

One would expect Nikolai Demidenko to bring something special to this great concerto, but his performance is curiously uninvolving though undoubtedly virtuosic. His brilliance can also border on brutality when it comes to fortissimo passages. Decent but not outstanding recording.

Piano concertos Nos. 2 in G, Op. 44; 3 in E flat, Op. 75.
500♪ ❁ *** EMI Dig. CDC7 49940-2 [id.]. Donohoe, Bournemouth SO, Barshai.

Donohoe's much-praised recording of Tchaikovsky's *Second Piano concerto* is coupled with his excellent account of the *Third*. This superb recording of the full, original score of the *Second* in every way justifies the work's length and the unusual format of the slow movement, with its extended solos for violin and cello; these are played with beguiling warmth by Nigel Kennedy and Steven Isserlis. Peter Donohoe plays marvellously and in the finale he is inspired to bravura which recalls Horowitz in the *B flat minor Concerto*. The recording has a fine, spacious ambience and is admirably realistic and very well balanced.

Violin concerto in D, Op. 35.
500♪ *** Teldec/Warner Dig. 4509 90881-2 [id.]. Vengerov, BPO, Abbado – GLAZUNOV: *Violin concerto.* ***
*** EMI CDC5 56150-2 [id.]. Perlman, Phd. O, Ormandy – SIBELIUS: *Violin concerto.* ***

Vengerov's inspired Tchaikovsky reading immediately establishes itself as a big performance, both in the daring manner and in the range of dynamic of the playing. For all his power and his youthfully eager love of brilliance, Vengerov is never reluctant to play really softly. The finale is sparklingly light. The close brings an eruption of excitement, as in a live performance.

Taken from an analogue original of the late 1970s, Perlman's Philadelphia version sounds all the fuller and more natural in its CD format, with the soloist balanced less aggressively forward than usual; in clarity and openness, however, it cannot match the finest digital recordings on compact disc. Perlman's expressive warmth goes with a very bold orchestral texture from Ormandy and the Philadelphia Orchestra, and anyone who follows Perlman – in so many ways the supreme violin virtuoso of our time – is not likely to be disappointed. The old coupling of just the *Sérénade mélancolique* has now been more generously replaced with the Sibelius concerto, but this disc remains at full price.

(i) *1812 Overture; Capriccio italien.*
500♪ ❀ (M) *** Mercury 434 360-2 [id.]. (i) Bronze French cannon, bells of Laura Spelman Rockefeller Memorial Carillon, Riverside Church, New York City; Minneapolis SO, Dorati (with separate descriptive commentary by Deems Taylor) (with BEETHOVEN: *Wellington's victory* *** ❀).

Just as in our listing of this famous Mercury record we have placed *1812* first, so in the credits the cannon and the glorious sounds of the Laura Spelman Carillon take precedence, for in the riveting climax of Tchaikovsky's most famous work the effects completely upstage the orchestra. This is not to suggest that Dorati's performance is in any way lacking. Indeed he makes a great deal of the character and colour of the Russian folk material on which the composer draws so tellingly. But at the end, when the carillon floods into the listener's room and the cannon open fire, the effect is quite overwhelming.

(i) *1812 Overture* (arr. Buketoff). *Sleeping Beauty* (ballet), *Op. 66:* excerpts; *The Voyevoda* (symphonic ballad), *Op. 78;* (i; ii) *Moscow* (coronation cantata).
**(*) Delos Dig. DE 3196 [id.]. Dallas SO, (i) and Ch.; (ii) with Svetlana Furdui and Vassily Gerello; Andrew Litton.

Tchaikovsky's *Voyevoda* was under-rated – even by the composer who, soon after he had written it, destroyed the score. Fortunately the orchestral parts survived. Taken from Pushkin, it has a rather similar plotline to *Francesca da Rimini*. This time, however, it is a provincial governor (*voyevoda*), who returns from a journey to discover his wife in the arms of her lover, but the retribution he seeks is ironically unsuccessful and the bullet intended for the lover kills the voyevoda instead. The score's central section depicts the love scene in the garden before the dénouement; its atmosphere (with scoring delicately including the celesta) is much more restrained than with *Francesca* and there is a sinuously sinister passage featuring the bass clarinet while the voyevoda plots his revenge before the fatal shot is fired and the music swiftly terminates. The work is maturely imbued with potent Tchaikovskian melancholic atmosphere and its invention is often memorable. It is most persuasively played by the excellent Dallas Symphony under Andrew Litton. He is equally impressive in a rather arbitrary set of excerpts from the *Sleeping Beauty* ballet, presented with elegance, character and – where necessary – passion, although one has to comment that collectors interested in the two principal novelties will surely already have the *Sleeping Beauty* in some form or other. The programme opens with a choral *1812* in Ivor Buketoff's arrangement which returns to the words of the original folksongs on which the music is based. So the very opening becomes a chorus (instead of lower strings), as does the more lilting of the two lyrical tunes in the middle and the work closes with '*God save our gracious Tsar*'. At the close the Dallas chorus sings with an expansiveness that tends almost to overwhelm cannon and carillon. Tchaikovsky's cantata, *Moscow*, was an 1883 commission for the coronation of Alexander III. It is an essentially lyrical work and, when sung with such feeling (especially from two ardently Slavonic soloists, who are perfectly cast), it becomes an attractive novelty, yet here has real depth of feeling. The recording throughout, as one expects from Delos in Seattle, is rich and spacious: the chorus could perhaps have more bite, but they are very well balanced.

Manfred Symphony; The Tempest, Op. 18.
500♪ *** DG Dig. 439 891-2 [id.]. Russian Nat. O, Pletnev.

Since the coming of stereo there has never been a shortage of good recordings of *Manfred*, but Pletnev's tends to trump what has gone before. The actual sounds of the Russian orchestra, the wind as well as the ardent strings, add a touch of plangent colouring to Tchaikovsky's inspired scoring, but Pletnev identifies with the ongoing sweep of the work, yet he can relax glowingly in the pastoral evocation of the slow movement. In *The Tempest* Pletnev again carries the piece through on a wave of passionate romantic feeling. The recording is first class.

The Nutcracker (ballet), *Op. 71* (complete).
*** Decca Dig. 433 000-2 (2) [id.]. Finchley Children's Music Group, RPO, Ashkenazy – GLAZUNOV: *The Seasons* (complete). ***

(B) *** BMG/Melodiya Twofer 74321 40067-2 (2). Bolshoi Theatre Children's Ch., Bolshoi Theatre O, Rozhdestvensky.

Among premium-priced versions Ashkenazy's digital *Nutcracker* holds its place at the top of the list, ideally coupled with Glazunov's *Seasons*, an equally enticing performance. Both have the advantage of state-of-the-art Decca sound.

We enthused about Rozhdestvensky's recording when it originally appeared on HMV in the mid-1970s, and it remains among the most vital accounts of the ballet in the catalogue. It has a very strong Russian colouring, nowhere more strikingly different from a Western approach than in the *Waltz of the snowflakes*, with the children's voices singing lustily. The timbres of woodwind and brass are robustly textured, the colouring bold. The *March* has a more military brassiness than usual – and very arresting it is, quite unlike the more piquant stylization one normally expects. In fortissimos the trombones make a strong impression. The strings have added bite yet are expansive too, but there is never the slightest hint of sentimentalizing the music, while the opening party scene conveys the rumbustious character of adults and children enjoying themselves. The big climaxes have plenty of excitement, and in the characteristic dances of the *Divertissement* the orchestral palette has never glowed more vividly. The result is refreshingly spontaneous and full of character. Every point of Tchaikovsky's music tells, and the sheer life of the playing disarms any criticism. The excellent recording actually dates from 1960 and the present transfer brings a consistently lively projection without detracting from the theatrical atmosphere.

Nutcracker suite; Sleeping Beauty: suite; Swan Lake: suite.
500♪ ❁ (M) *** DG 449 726-2 [id.]. BPO, Rostropovich.
(M) **(*) Decca 448 592-2 [id.]. VPO, Karajan.

Rostropovich's account of the *Nutcracker suite* is enchanting. The *Sleeping Beauty* and *Swan Lake* selections are hardly less distinguished, and in the former the *Panorama* is gloriously played. The CD remastering, which was always outstanding, now approaches demonstration standard.

This triptych was made during Karajan's Decca period in the 1960s. As reissued in Decca's Classic Sound series, the recording is very satisfactory indeed; tuttis are well focused by the digital transfer, and the glowing ambience of the Sofiensaal flatters the strings and adds to the woodwind colourings, particularly in the *Nutcracker suite*, which is altogether less bland here than in Karajan's later re-recording with the BPO. Overall this disc offers very fine playing from the VPO and, although the atmosphere is generally relaxed (especially in *Sleeping Beauty*), there is a persuasive balancing warmth.

(i) *Romeo and Juliet* (fantasy overture, ed. Stokowski). (ii) *Sleeping Beauty* (ballet), *Op. 66* (excerpts); *Swan Lake* (ballet), *Op. 20* (excerpts).
(M) *(**) Decca Phase Four 448 950-2 [id.]. (i) SRO; (ii) New Philh. O; Stokowski.

Stokowski plays both ballet suites with great panache, generating a consistently high level of adrenalin. The orchestral playing under his direction is characteristically fine, and no one knew better than he how to shape a Tchaikovsky melody or indeed (and here he uses the possibilities of artificial balancing unashamedly) how to reveal a felicitous detail of scoring. It is a pity that the Phase Four techniques have contributed a gloss of artificial brilliance to reduce the naturalness of the strings, but this music-making remains utterly magnetic and often thrilling (witness the finale of *Swan Lake* or the introduction to the *Sleeping Beauty*). The selections are not predictable; indeed the *Panorama* from *Sleeping Beauty* is a surprising omission. However, for Stokowski aficionados the collector's item here is *Romeo and Juliet*. Stokowski held the view that Tchaikovsky wanted to finish his fantasy overture in a gently elegiac mood and that the final loud orchestral chords were a sop to public taste. So, being a law unto himself, he recorded the overture without the ending indicated in the score, adding an emphasized percussive crash before the funeral procession. The performance itself has a languorously passionate climax, but the brightly lit Phase Four sound is not refined enough to please the ear consistently.

The Sleeping Beauty (ballet), *Op. 66* (complete).
500♪ (BB) *** Naxos Dig. 8.550490/2 [id.]. Slovak State PO (Košice), Andrew Mogrelia.

Andrew Mogrelia conducts Tchaikovsky's score with an ideal combination of warmth, grace and vitality. Moreover the Slovak State Philharmonic prove to be an excellent orchestra for this repertoire, with fine wind-players and equally impressive string principals for the important violin and cello solos. The Naxos digital recording is full and brilliant without being overlit, and the acoustics of the House of Arts in Košice bring a spacious ambience. A clear first choice among all available recordings, irrespective of cost.

Suites Nos. 1 in D min., Op. 43; 2 in C (Caractéristique); 3 in G, Op. 55; 4 in G (Mozartiana), Op. 61.
(B) *** Ph. Duo 454 253-2 (2) [id.]. New Philh. O, Antal Dorati.

Dorati's highly distinguished set of the four underrated *Orchestral suites* of Tchaikovsky come from the late 1960s. They have never sounded better than in the present CD transfer: the sound has some lack of transparency and ultimate vividness, but it is pleasingly naturally balanced. Dorati was a masterly ballet conductor and he brings out the balletic feeling, in the first two suites especially, and revels in the infinitely inventive orchestral detail which shows the composer consistently seeking subtle new orchestral colourings, not least in the *Scherzo burlesque* of the *Second Suite* with its folksy accordions, while in the final wild *Danse baroque* there is even an anticipation of Stravinsky's *Petrushka*. *Mozartiana* is also neatly and stylishly done. In the *Third Suite* Svetlanov's Russian recording demonstrates more Slavic temperament, but Dorati is thoroughly at home in the justly famous *Theme and variations*, capped by a splendid closing *Polacca*: the Philips recording expands impressively here and rises to the occasion. At Philips Duo price this is very recommendable indeed and is a source of much enjoyment.

Suite No. 4 (Mozartiana), Op. 61; The Seasons, Op. 37b (orch. A. Gauk).
*** Chandos Dig. CHAN 9514 [id.]. Detroit SO, Neeme Järvi.

The special delight here is the orchestration of Tchaikovsky's piano suite, *The Seasons*. It was made at the height of the Second World War by the Soviet conductor, Alexander Gauk, presumably for a ballet. Gauk devises characteristically Tchaikovskian sounds in all 12 numbers, adding colour and atmosphere, enhancing the contrasting character of each movement, reinforcing each evocative title. So, taking an obvious enough cue, the flute intensifies the melodic line in the *Song of the lark* (March) and in the fanfares of *The hunt* (September). The brass writing has distant echoes of the *Fourth Symphony*. Most magical of all is the *Barcarolle* for June, with sensuous string-writing and a brief part for the celesta, bringing *Nutcracker* associations. *The Seasons* suite is almost twice as long as the coupling, the orchestral *Suite No. 4*, *Mozartiana*, which Järvi has already recorded for Chandos with the Philharmonia as a coupling for the Tchaikovsky *Piano concerto No. 1*. If the Detroit recording is a degree less transparent, the performance, like the acoustic, is even warmer, aptly Tchaikovskian even more than it is elegantly Mozartian, with the soaring melody of the *Preghiera* third movement (as arranged from Mozart's *Ave verum*) made lovingly expressive rather than classically restrained. The long set of variations which makes up the finale is then given a strong and beefy performance, bringing out the jollity in these often trivial variants.

Swan Lake (ballet), *Op. 20* (complete).
500♪ *** Decca Dig. 436 212-2 (2) Montreal SO, Dutoit.
(B) **(*) DG Double 453 055-2 (2) [id.]. Boston SO, Ozawa.

Dutoit offers the original score virtually complete, as Tchaikovsky conceived it. Dutoit's performance, without lack of drama, emphasizes the warmth and grace of the music, its infinite variety. With wind solos of much character, and warm, nicely turned string phrasing and pacing which alternates bursts of liveliness within a romantically mellow basic conception, Dutoit's reading is easy to enjoy.

Ozawa's version omits the Act III *Pas de deux* but otherwise plays the complete original score. His performance is certainly alive and often vigorous (as at the opening *Allegro giusto*). But it has not quite the verve of Lanchbery's CfP version; Ozawa's approach is more serious, less flexible. Yet the playing of the Boston orchestra is strikingly polished and sympathetic, and there are many impressive and enjoyable things here, with wind (and violin) solos always giving pleasure. The end result is a little faceless, in spite of a spectacular, wide-ranging analogue recording, as vivid as it is powerful, and admirably transferred to CD.

Swan Lake (ballet): highlights.
(M) **(*) Ph. 442 546-2 [id.]. LSO, Monteux.

The expansive acoustic suits Monteux's approach, which is warmly affectionate rather than seeking the highest adrenalin levels, though it does not lack vitality. The LSO playing is beautifully turned, and only perhaps in the finale, which Monteux paces slowly and grandly, does the slight lack of concentration and bite in the music-making affect the directness of Tchaikovsky's inspiration. And even here the spacious (1962) sound, with its sonorous brass, still makes a good effect. The disc offers just short of an hour of music.

SYMPHONIES

Symphonies Nos. 1–6.
*** DG Dig. 449 967-2 (5) [id.]. Russian Nat. O, Mikhail Pletnev.

Symphonies Nos. 1–6; Capriccio italien; Manfred Symphony.
500♪ ❁ (M) *** Chandos Dig. CHAN 8672/8 [id.]. Oslo PO, Jansons.

Symphonies Nos. 1–3; Francesca da Rimini, Op. 32.
(B) **(*) BMG/Melodiya Twofer 74321 34163-2 (2) [id.]. USSR SO, Svetlanov.

Symphonies Nos. 4–6 (Pathétique); Andante cantabile in B flat, Op. 11; The Voyevoda, Op. 78.
(B) **(*) BMG/Melodiya Twofer 74321 40066-2 [id.]. USSR SO, Svetlanov.

Jansons's Tchaikovsky series, which includes *Manfred*, is self-recommending. The full romantic power of the music is consistently conveyed and, above all, the music-making is urgently spontaneous throughout, with the Oslo Philharmonic Orchestra always committed and fresh, helped by the richly atmospheric Chandos sound. The seven separate CDs offered here are packaged in a box priced as for five premium discs.

Native Russian artists always bring something special to the Tchaikovsky symphonies. Think of the impact that Yevgeni Mravinsky and the Leningrad Philharmonic made on their first visits to the West in the late 1950s and their subsequent recordings. We know from his transcriptions of *The Sleeping Beauty* and *Nutcracker* that Pletnev has an intuitive grasp of the kind of sonority Tchaikovsky had in mind and that he can summon forth from the piano all the subtlety of colour and dynamic range of the whole orchestral palette. The same goes for his baton. His survey of the six numbered symphonies – he has already given us *Manfred* and wisely excludes the Bogatyriev reconstruction of the so-called *Seventh in E flat* – is spread over five CDs. Nos. 2 and 4 are accommodated on one CD and the remainder are allotted one CD each.

Pletnev's readings have all the innate aristocratic feeling Tchaikovsky could ask for, but at no time does Pletnev wear his heart on his sleeve. The wide dynamic spectrum and clarity of articulation that distinguish his pianism are clearly in evidence, but virtuosity, brilliance and colour are never there at the expense of artistic truth. Some may feel (and indeed have felt) that the emphasis in the *First Symphony* is too much on the *rêveries* of the title, and Tchaikovsky's rhetoric might be handled more convincingly; but, for the most part, Pletnev's approach throughout the cycle is the reverse of the overblown. Indeed the highly charged, high-voltage sound which we associate with Mravinsky surfaces in the *Pathétique*, but otherwise he sets greater store by classicism, carefully balanced proportions and a masterly sense of line. DG have accorded the cycle very fine and well-detailed sound. The set comes with copious scholarly annotation by Richard Taruskin. Not a first recommendation perhaps, but there are many new insights here in which the experienced Tchaikovskian will take much pleasure.

Svetlanov's are performances of much temperament and fire, though the orchestral playing is a little variable. With fast tempi in the outer movements the *First Symphony* comes fully alive, with the atmosphere of the Russian winter felt in the *Adagio*. The Scherzo is beautifully managed and the finale – after the noble and restrained opening – has the quality of genuine Russian dance so that one can imagine the Cossack boots kicking. The *Little Russian* has plenty of character too. Svetlanov takes the *Andantino* very slowly but retains the charm, and he does not let the finale get out of hand. The *Polish Symphony* is a performance of strong contrasts between the inner and outer movements. The orchestral playing is somewhat variable and ensemble is less than perfect. The *Alla tedesca* is a little slow and slightly ponderous, but everywhere else the music's characterization is apt and the rhetoric of the finale is again well handled.

The *Fourth*, bold and direct, stands out among the last three symphonies, very well held together. In the finale Svetlanov makes no pause each time the second subject appears. The *Fifth*, however, while it has a fine lyrical impulse, is surprisingly undramatic. When the motto theme should storm into the middle of the slow movement it makes its entrance and there is comparatively little impact. The Waltz is elegantly done, but the opening of the finale languishes a bit and the movement really comes to life only when the allegro proper begins.

The *Pathétique* is much more convincing, with a beautifully moulded second subject. The Scherzo-march is somewhat relaxed but the finale is powerfully controlled and eloquent. The extra items are well worth having, especially the rare *Voyevoda*, while the middle section of *Francesca da Rimini* has a unique lyrical fervour. The sound throughout is bright and full-blooded to match the performances and, even taking our reservations into account, this set is worth its modest asking price.

Symphonies Nos. 1 in G min. (Winter daydreams), Op. 13; 2 in C min. (Little Russian), Op. 17.
(BB) **(*) Belart 461 322-2. VPO, Lorin Maazel.

It is good news that, having restored Maazel's Sibelius symphonies to the catalogue, Polygram's super-bargain Belart label is now beginning on his hardly less successful Tchaikovsky cycle, also made with the VPO in the 1960s. In the first two symphonies Maazel's performances clearly look forward to the emotional tautness of the mature symphonies from the *Fourth* onwards, rather than seeking to bring out the charm of the young composer's earliest essays in symphonic form. But if the first movement of the *Winter daydreams Symphony* is driven hard and the Mendelssohnian quality of the opening is not as warmly evocative as with Pletnev, Maazel is altogether happier with the rhetoric than the Russian conductor, and the finale is particularly successful: even Tchaikovsky's somewhat academic fugato section is made to come off, with short stabbing emphases of each entry of the theme. There is also evidence of the care with which Maazel has studied the score. Much felicitous detail emerges afresh and the delightful Scherzo comes to life splendidly, with a real feeling displayed for the line of the waltz which forms its centrepiece, and the movement's coda is delectably neat. The slow movement is not as dreamy as one might ask, but it is not without atmosphere, and the style of the playing, with strong, thrusting horns for the final statement of the main theme, is convincing enough in the context of the other movements. The *Little Russian Symphony* is presented with similar hard-driving brio. The charming *Andantino marziale* is nicely done, but the Scherzo is vivid rather than gay, and the finale is exciting without being genial. The performance is not helped by the spectacularly resonant (and brilliantly engineered) analogue recording, which has a degree of harshness and tends to prevent the music from smiling. Excellent value just the same: a disc that is well worth trying when it costs so little.

Symphonies Nos. (i) *2 (Little Russian), Op. 17;* (ii) *4 in F min.*
500♪ ✿ (B) *** DG 429 527-2. (i) New Philh. O; (ii) VPO, Claudio Abbado.

Abbado's coupling of Tchaikovsky's *Second* and *Fourth Symphonies* is one of the supreme bargains of the current catalogue. His account of the *Little Russian Symphony* is very enjoyable. But this is merely a bonus for an unforgettable account of the *Fourth Symphony*, unsurpassed on record. It was recorded in 1975 in the Musikverein and still sounds very good indeed.

Symphonies Nos. 4–6.
(B) *** DG Double 453 088-2 [id.]. BPO, Karajan.
(B) *** Decca Double 443 844-2 (2) [id.]. Philh. O, Ashkenazy.

Who would have thought in the early days of CD that one day we would be offered Karajan's outstanding Berlin Philharmonic performances of the three last symphonies for the cost of one premium-priced CD! Karajan's 1977 analogue version of No. 4 (the most atmospherically recorded of the three) is undoubtedly more compelling than his previous recordings and also is in most respects preferable to the newer, digital, Vienna version. It is the vitality and drive of the performance as a whole that one remembers, although the beauty of the wind-playing at the opening and close of the slow movement can give nothing but pleasure. Similarly the 1976 reading of the *Fifth* stands out from his other recordings. The first movement is unerringly paced and has great romantic flair; in Karajan's hands the climax of the slow movement is grippingly intense, though with a touchingly elegiac preparation for the horn solo at the opening. The Waltz has character and charm too – the Berlin Philharmonic string-playing is peerless – and in the finale Karajan drives hard, creating a riveting forward thrust.

Karajan had a special affinity with Tchaikovsky's *Pathétique symphony* (and – remembering Furtwängler's famous 78-r.p.m. set – so has the Berlin Philharmonic Orchestra). He has recorded it five times in stereo. For many the 1977 version is the finest. With a brilliant – even too brilliant – recording of the widest dynamic range (though not an especially sumptuous lower resonance) the impact of Tchaikovsky's climaxes – notably those of the first and third movements – is tremendously powerful, the articulation of the Berlin players precise and strong. The climactic peaks are created with fierce bursts of tension, and the effect on the listener is almost overwhelming. In the 5/4 movement Karajan allows the middle section to increase the elegiac feeling, against a background of remorseless but distanced drum-beats, like a tolling bell. The finale has great passion and eloquence, with two gentle sforzandos at the very end to emphasize the finality of the closing phrase. The digital remastering of the analogue recordings is eminently satisfactory.

Ashkenazy's set makes a genuine alternative bargain on Double Decca, although the layout splits No. 5 across the two discs between the second and third movements. Apart from the emotional power and strong Russian feeling of the readings, the special quality which Ashkenazy conveys is spontaneity. The freshness of his approach, his natural feeling for lyricism on the one hand and drama on the other, is consistently compelling, even if at times the orchestral ensemble is not always immaculate. The late-1970s Kingsway Hall recording quality is full and atmospheric, with the strings full, the brass sonorous and a satisfyingly resonant, Tchaikovskian ambience. This could be a best buy for those wanting all three symphonies in modern stereo (but not digital) versions, as the sound is more sumptuous than that provided by DG for Karajan.

(i) *Symphony No. 4 in F min., Op. 36;* (ii) *Francesca da Rimini, Op. 32.*
(M) ** Mercury 434 373-2 [id.]. (i) LSO; (ii) Minneapolis SO; Antal Dorati – BORODIN: *Prince Igor: Overture.* **

Dorati's performance of the *Fourth Symphony* is assured and often exciting but sounds a little cut and dried. The climaxes are tense but, like the accelerandos, well controlled. The finale comes off very well indeed. If you like your Tchaikovsky not too frenetic, you may enjoy this very much, and it is certainly a performance to live with, especially when the 1960 Mercury recording, made in Wembley Town Hall, is so full-blooded and with the right kind of ambience. However, *Francesca da Rimini* was recorded (two years earlier) in Minneapolis, and the evocative, sustained writing of the middle section is not helped by the dry, lustreless acoustic. The climax is exciting but without the coloration of resonance. Tchaikovsky's method of building up a climax by throwing short repeated figures at great speed into an orchestral maelstrom loses all its effect and tends to become just a pointless succession of notes. The coupled *Prince Igor* overture is much more successful.

Symphony No. 5 in E min., Op. 64; The Tempest, Op. 18.
(M) **(*) Virgin/EMI Ultraviolet Dig. CUV5 61325 [CDC 59598]. Bournemouth SO, Andrew Litton.

Symphony No. 5; (i) *Eugene Onegin: Tatiana's letter scene.*
500♪ ❁ (M) *** EMI Dig. CD-EMX 2187. LPO, Sian Edwards; (i) with Eilene Hannan.

Sian Edwards conducts an electrifying and warm-hearted reading of Tchaikovsky's *Fifth*, which matches any version in the catalogue, particularly when it comes with an unusual and exceptionally attractive fill-up, Tchaikovsky's greatest inspiration for soprano, *Tatiana's letter scene*. That is freshly and dramatically sung, in a convincingly girlish impersonation, by the Australian, Eilene Hannan.

Litton is surprisingly slow and steady in the first movement of the *Fifth*. There is a case – as Klemperer and Boehm both showed in their different ways – for taking a squarely symphonic view, but Litton's reading lacks the high voltage of his finest Tchaikovsky performances. The other three movements are first rate. The slow movement brings a beautiful horn solo, with the sound exquisitely distanced and with Litton sustaining his slow *Andante* well. At a well judged speed, the Waltz third movement is then delightfully fresh and delicate in a simple way, and the finale, again on the broad side, is warm rather than ominous, with very clean articulation in the playing and fine detail. Atmospherically recorded with slightly distanced sound in the Virgin manner, and transferred at a lower level than the rival issues, this version certainly has its attractions, despite that first movement, particularly when it has so rare and generous a fill-up. The Shakespearean symphonic fantasy, *The Tempest* – not to be confused with the much less ambitious overture of the same name, written for Ostrovsky's play – is given a glowing performance, passionately committed yet refined, to suggest a forgotten masterpiece.

Symphony No. 6 (Pathétique); Francesca da Rimini.
(B) ** Decca Eclipse Dig. 448 994-2; *448 994-4* [id.]. Montreal SO, Dutoit.

The Montreal sound for Dutoit is gloriously rich and resonant but, rather as in his earlier version of the Tchaikovsky *Fifth*, Dutoit's reading, warmly expressive, yet lacks the final bite of tension which in Tchaikovsky is such an essential ingredient. He leaves you feeling that the performance is too well controlled, not daring enough. *Francesca da Rimini* has both weight and strength, backed up by a recording of spectacular range, but with less variation of tension than in the finest versions.

Symphony No. 6 in B min. (Pathétique), Op. 74; Romeo and Juliet (fantasy overture).
(M) *** DG Masters Dig. 445 601-2 [id.]. Philh. O, Sinopoli.

If one divides interpreters of this *Symphony* into those who tend to press ahead in stringendo and those who hold back in ritenuto, Sinopoli – perhaps surprisingly after his Elgar *Second* – is firmly in the former group. What is striking here is the passion of the playing of the Philharmonia, recorded with the most satisfying opulence. Sinopoli's reading of the opening movement is beautifully shaped, with the second subject introduced very tenderly. He adopts slow speeds for the middle two movements but sustains them well, with the 5/8 rhythm of the second brought even closer than is common to the feeling of a waltz. In the march of the third movement, many will prefer Sinopoli's broader view, with a slight easing on the big, swaggering, fortissimo entries leading to a satisfying culmination. The finale brings a highly eloquent response from the Philharmonia strings and the result is very moving. The big advantage that Sinopoli has in this mid-priced reissue is that it is generously coupled with *Romeo and Juliet*, which is also very exciting. Even if there is a hint of self-consciousness at the first entry of the love theme, there is plenty of uninhibited passion in the later repeats. In short this is one of the finest of recent versions of the

Pathétique, and it is highly recommendable (a favourite of I.M.'s). Excellent recording, but this is not a first choice for all of us; that rests with Pletnev (Virgin VC7 59661-2), to which R.L. gave a Rosette, or Jansons (Chandos CHAN 8446), which remains E.G.'s choice.

Variations on a rococo theme for cello and orchestra, Op. 33.
✪ *** EMI Dig. CDC5 56126-2 [id.]. Han-Na Chang, LSO, Rostropovich – BRUCH: *Kol Nidrei;* FAURE: *Elégie;* SAINT-SAENS: *Cello concerto No. 1.* ***
500♪ ✪ (M) *** DG 447 413-2 [id.]. Rostropovich, BPO, Karajan – DVORAK: *Cello concerto.* *** ✪
(M) *** Carlton Dig. 30366 0011-2 [id.]. Tortelier, RPO, Groves – DVORAK: *Rondo in G min.* ***; ELGAR: *Cello concerto in E min.* **(*)

Han-Na Chang gives a memorably beautiful performance of the Tchaikovsky *Rococo variations*. This phenomenally gifted 13-year-old Korean-born cellist has the most ravishing tone and a wonderfully musical sense of line. Rostropovich sets the scene with an affectionate elegance (or, rather, the first horn of the LSO does, and how gracefully he does it); and then Chang introduces Tchaikovsky's theme with disarming simplicity, with the first variation following with a natural, spontaneous flow and the third generating just the right degree of energy. The fourth, *Andante grazioso*, introduced very gently, is quite ethereal and No. 6, where Tchaikovsky turns the melody into a nostalgic Russian folksong, even more touchingly seductive. Of course the finale has the expected dash, and the crispest articulation. It is a pity she didn't choose to record the original version – but then nor did Rostropovich himself – and her performance is hardly less sophisticated in detail than his famous DG version and quite as endearing. The LSO are inspired by Chang to give a wonderfully sensitive accompaniment, and the recording is in the demonstration class.

Like Chang, Rostropovich uses the published score rather than the original version which more accurately reflects the composer's intentions. But this account, with Karajan's glowing support, is so superbly structured in its control of emotional light and shade that one is readily convinced that this is the work Tchaikovsky conceived. The recording (made in the Jesus-Christus Kirche) is beautifully balanced and is surely one of the most perfect examples of DG's analogue techniques.

Tortelier's version on the Carlton label is warm and red-blooded, if technically not as flawless as his earlier reading, but the recording is pleasantly atmospheric, slightly distanced so that the tenderness of the performance is brought out the more.

CHAMBER MUSIC

(i) *String quartets Nos. 1–3*; (ii) *Souvenir de Florence, Op. 70.*
(B) ** Decca Double 452 614-2 (2) [id.]. (i) Gabrieli Qt; (ii) ASMF, Marriner.

The Gabrielis give finely conceived performances of the three *String quartets*, producing well-blended tone-quality. Their ensemble is excellent, and they are completely inside the music. The recordings are clean and alive, but ideally the upper range could be projected less forcefully, and the CD transfer emphasizes the fierceness. While first choice inevitably rests with the Borodin Quartet (BMG/Melodiya 74321 18290-2 – a mid-priced set which includes the *Souvenir de Florence*), this is recommendable as an inexpensive Double Decca alternative. Certainly the *Souvenir de Florence* is an attractive proposition, played by a full body of strings, especially when they are an ensemble of the calibre of the Academy of St Martin-in-the-Fields; the one snag is that their version has been subjected to some tactful cutting.

PIANO MUSIC

The Seasons, Op. 37b.
*(*) Chandos Dig. CHAN 9309 [id.]. Luba Edlina – BORODIN: *Petite suite.* **

Luba Edlina's account of *The Seasons* comes up against some pretty stiff competition, not least from the Pletnev all-Tchaikovsky disc on Virgin, which is in a class of its own (VC5 45042-2). She does not match him in terms of colour or imagination and, although the Chandos recording is very natural, this disc does not have strong claims on the collector.

Sleeping Beauty (excerpts) arr. Pletnev.
500♪ ✪ *** Virgin/EMI Dig. VC7 59611-2 [id.]. Mikhail Pletnev – MUSSORGSKY: *Pictures at an exhibition.* *** ✪

In the present transcription Pletnev gives us about 30 minutes of *The Sleeping Beauty* in a dazzling performance. In sheer clarity of articulation and virtuosity this is pretty remarkable – also in poetry and depth of feeling. An altogether outstanding issue and in every way a *tour de force*.

Piano sonatas: in C sharp min., Op. 80; in G, Op. 37; Allegro (1863–4) (completed Leslie Howard).
** Hyperion Dig. CDA 66939 [id.]. Leslie Howard.

On the face of it a highly appealing prospect. Leslie Howard is an intelligent guide in this repertoire, and his completion of the fragment, an *Allegro in F minor* of some 172 bars, comprising an exposition with a fair amount of the development, puts us in his debt. The *C sharp minor Sonata* comes from 1865 but it is the *G major*, Op. 37, of 1878 which is the more important and the better recorded of the two. Leslie Howard brings an excellent technical address to these pieces but less poetic insight and imagination. This is recommendable but, one must add, not to those who have heard Richter, Pletnev or Berezovsky play these pieces.

OPERA

Eugene Onegin (complete).
500♪ *** Decca 417 413-2 (2) [id.]. Kubiak, Weikl, Burrows, Reynolds, Ghiaurov, Hamari, Sénéchal, Alldis Ch., ROHCG O, Solti.

Solti, characteristically crisp in attack, has plainly warmed to the score of Tchaikovsky's colourful opera, allowing his singers full rein in rallentando and rubato to a degree one might not have expected of him. The Tatiana of Teresa Kubiak is most moving, with her golden, vibrant voice rising impressively to the final confrontation of Act III. The Onegin of Bernd Weikl offers firm singing that yet has authentic Slavonic tinges. Onegin becomes something like a first-person story-teller. The rest of the cast is excellent, with Stuart Burrows as Lensky giving one of his finest performances on record yet. Here, for the first time, the full range of musical expression in this most atmospheric of operas is superbly caught.

Iolanta (complete).
*** Ph. Dig. 442 796-2 (2) [id.]. Gorchakova, Alexashkin, Hvorostovsky, Grigorian, Kirov Op. Ch. & O, Gergiev.
(B) ** CPO Dig. CPO 999 456-2 (2) [id.]. Gurevich, Katchinian, Ben, Denolfo, ECOV Ch., Warsaw PO, Hans Rotman.

Gergiev and his outstanding Kirov team give a warm, idiomatic reading of Tchaikovsky's charming fairy tale opera of the blind princess. Bringing out the atmospheric beauty of the score, it completely outshines the existing Rostropovich version on Erato, where, quite apart from incidental flaws, Galina Vishnevskaya sounds far too mature for a young princess. Here, by contrast, Galina Gorchakova gives the most moving portrait of the heroine, tender and vulnerable, with words delicately touched in. As Vaudémont, the knight who falls in love with her, Gegam Grigorian sings with rather tight, very Russian tenor-tone, not always pleasing but with a fine feeling for the idiom and a natural ease in high tessitura. Dmitri Hvorostovsky sings nobly and heroically as Robert, his more vigorous friend and rival, while Sergei Alexashkin sings with dark, grainy – again very Russian – tone as King René, Iolanta's father. Above all, the exchanges between characters consistently convey the feeling of stage-experience. The recording, not ideally clear but well balanced, was made in the theatre but under studio conditions. The first disc, containing three-quarters of the music, takes the story to the end of the long Iolanta/Vaudémont duet.

The CPO version, with two discs offered for the price of one, makes a fair alternative to the Kirov set, brightly recorded in upfront sound, with a cast that rivals the Russian one. Under Hans Rotman the performance, well played, brings out the passion of the score, but less subtly, less idiomatically. As Iolanta, Michaela Gurevich sings tenderly in tones rather similar to Gorchakova's but with more edge. Ian Denolfo as Vaudémont is warmer and firmer than his Russian rival but is strained on top; Alexander Ben as Robert is just as strong and urgent as Hvorostovsky, while Arutiun Katchinian is on the light side as the King.

The Queen of Spades (Pique Dame) (complete).
500♪ *** Ph. Dig. 438 141-2 (3) [id.]. Grigorian, Putilin, Chernov, Solodovnikov, Arkhipova, Gulegina, Borodina, Kirov Op. Ch. & O, Gergiev.

When each new recording of this opera for many years has been flawed, it is good that Gergiev and his talented team from the Kirov Opera in St Petersburg have produced a winner. It is good to have the veteran Irina Arkhipova singing powerfully and bitingly in that key role, while the other international star, Olga Borodina, is unforgettable as Pauline, singing gloriously with keen temperament. Otherwise Gergiev's chosen team offers characterful Slavonic voices that are yet well focused and unstrained, specially important with the tenor hero, Herman, here dashingly sung by Gegam Grigorian. As the heroine, Lisa, Maria Gulegina sings with warm tone and well-controlled vibrato, slightly edgy under pressure.

Telemann, Georg Philipp (1681–1767)

Alster (Overture) suite; La Bouffonne suite; Triple horn concerto in D; Grillen-Symphonie.
*** Chandos Dig. CHAN 0547 [id.]. Coll. Mus. 90, Standage.

This collection offers some of Telemann's most colourful and descriptive music, often quite bizarrely scored. The *Triple horn concerto* opens the programme with the hand-horns rasping boisterously. Then comes *La Bouffonne suite* with its elegant *Loure* and the extremely fetching *Rigaudon*, while the work ends with a touchingly delicate *Pastourelle*, beautifully played here. The *Grillen-Symphonie* ('Cricket symphony') is quite exotically painted, with a piquant dialogue between upper wind and double-basses in the first movement, while the second has unexpected accents and lives up to its name *Tändelnd* (Flirtatious). The work ends with a rustic peasant dance. The horns (four of them) re-enter ambitiously at the colourful *Overture* of the *Alster suite*, add to the fun in the *Echo* movement, and help to simulate the Hamburg glockenspiel which follows. The entry of the Alster Shepherds brings a piquant drone effect, but best of all is the wailing *Concerto of frogs and crows*, with drooping bleats from the oboe and then the principal horn. Apart from the special effects, the suite also has one of the composer's most tenderly fragile slow movements for muted strings (*Der ruhende Pan*) and it again ends with a general dance. Standage and his group make the very most of Telemann's remarkable orchestral palette and play with great vitality as well as finesse. This is one of the most entertaining Telemann collections in the catalogue, and it is splendidly recorded.

(i) *Concert sonata for trumpet & strings in D;* (ii) *Trumpet concertos: in E min.; in G;* (iii) *Triple concerto for trumpet & 2 oboes in D;* (iv) *Concerto for 3 trumpets, 2 oboes, timpani & strings in D.*
(M) *** Erato/Warner Dig./Analogue 0630 13743-2 [id.]. Maurice André, (i) Vienna Soloists; (ii) Franz Liszt CO, Budapest, Frigyes Sándor; (iii) Pierlot, Chambon, Hogne, Jean-François Paillard CO, Paillard; (iv) Touvron, Lionel André, Arrignon, Chavana, Ens. O, Jean-Pierre Wallez.

The concerto for three trumpets, two oboes and strings (recorded digitally in 1982) has some very attractive textures and the invention is fresh; the companion work for trumpet and a pair of oboes (which have the *Siciliano* third movement to themselves) is scored in a similarly imaginative way, with the accompaniment reduced to a single bassoon (which at times is almost an additional soloist) and continuo. André scales down his tone where necessary to balance with the woodwind. Both this and the rest of the programme is analogue, from the 1970s. The *Concert sonata* (here reconstructed by Fernand Oubradous) has a highly expressive, very Italianate *Largo* (the harpsichord just about peeps in here) and a joyous finale, which André relishes, but with plenty of necessary light and shade. The remaining works are true solo concertos of high calibre: the cantabile line of the melancholy *Andante* of the *G major* is played very touchingly; the rondo finale is simulataneously *galant* and regal. The mood then changes again for the warmly expressive *Andante* which opens the *E minor Concerto*; its second movement is a catchy *moto perpetuo*. André negotiates it skilfully – and particularly so the recitativo by which it is interrupted in the middle. After the noble following *Largo*, the work is capped by a crisply buoyant finale, by no means predictable in its progress. These are all memorable works, showing their composer to be a leading figure in baroque trumpet repertoire. In the multiple concerto, Wallez's accompaniment is not strong in personality, but all the other concertos are given excellent support. Highly recommended.

Concerto for 3 oboes & 3 violins in B flat, TWV 44:43; (i) *Concerto for recorder, bassoon & strings in F; Concerto for 4 violins in G, TWV 40:201; Overture (Suite) in F for 2 horns, violins & continuo, TWV 44:7.*
(M) *** Teldec/Warner 0630 12320-2 [id.]. VCM, Harnoncourt, (i) with Frans Brüggen, Otto Fleischmann.

One of the best Telemann discs currently available. The five-movement Overture or Suite featuring a pair of horns shows the composer at his most characteristic (natural horns are used), and the performances are most persuasive. The oboes also sound splendidly in tune, which is not always the case with the baroque instrument, and phrasing is alive and sensitive. Indeed these performances are extremely fine, and only the *Concerto for recorder and bassoon* lets the disc down a little; it is also not as well played as the others. The quality is good and the digital remastering has not tried to clarify artificially what is basically a resonant recording with inner detail mellowed by the ambience. Outlines, however, are cleaner and one would not guess that this dates from 1966.

(i–iii) *Double concerto in E min. for recorder and transverse flute;* (iv) *Viola concerto in G;* (i; v) *Suite in A min. for flute and strings;* (iii) *Overture des Nations anciens et modernes in G.*
500♪ ❁ (M) *** Teldec/Warner 9031 77620-2 [id.]. (i) Frans Brüggen, (ii) Franz Vester, (iii) Amsterdam CO, André Rieu; (iv) Paul Doctor, Concerto Amsterdam, Brüggen; (v) SW German CO, Friedrich.

All these works show Telemann as an original and often inspired craftsman. His use of contrasting timbres in the *Double concerto* has considerable charm; the *Overture des Nations anciens et modernes* is slighter but is consistently and agreeably inventive, and the *Suite in A minor*, one of his best-known works, is worthy of Handel or Bach. Frans Brüggen and Franz Vester are expert soloists and Brüggen shows himself equally impressive on the conductor's podium accompanying Paul Doctor, the rich-timbred soloist in the engaging *Viola concerto*. The sound, splendidly remastered, is unbelievably good, with fine body and presence: it is difficult to believe that these recordings are now three decades old.

(i) *Viola concerto in G;* (ii) *Triple violin concerto in F;* (iii) *Suite in F for 4 horns, 2 oboes & strings;* (i) *Suite for viola da gamba & strings in D.*
(B) ** Carlton/Turnabout 30371 00422. (i) Ernst Wallfisch, Württemberg CO, Faerber; (ii) Lautenbacher, Schaefer, Egger, Stuttgart Soloists; (iii) Spach, Roth, Schollmeyer, Balser, Sous, Bogacchi, Mainz CO, Kehr.

The *Viola concerto in G* is well known as one of Telemann's most striking works, and the *Concerto in F for three violins* has a similar attractive affinity with Bach. The expressive slow movement is notable. The *Suite in D major*, with the viola da gamba not always used in a concertante role, is another inventive collection of dance movements, and the *Suite in F* using four horns and a pair of oboes is one of Telemann's most striking and original works. Its programme conjures up Greek mythology, but transferred to the Alster riverside in Hamburg. There are echoes, shepherds, swans and nymphs, but the most striking and original item is a concert given by frogs and crows. The music is not, strictly speaking, imitative and the writing for the horns is surprisingly modern. The playing here is always alive and musicianly; the recording has a pleasing ambience but is not always absolutely refined in the upper range. The CD transfer, however, greatly improves the focus of the original LP, and this enterprising collection remains very viable.

(i) *Viola concerto in G;* (ii) *Suite in A min. for recorder and strings; Tafelmusik,* Part 2: (iii) *Triple violin concerto in F;* Part 3: (iv) *Double horn concerto in E flat.*
500♪ ❁ (BB) *** Naxos Dig. 8.550156; *4550156* [id.]. (i) Kyselak; (ii) Stivín; (iii) Hoelblingova, Hoelbling, Jablokov; (iv) Z. & B. Tylšar, Capella Istropolitana, Richard Edlinger.

Our Rosette is awarded for enterprise and good planning – to say nothing of good music-making. It is difficult to conceive of a better Telemann programme. Ladislav Kyselak is a fine violist and is thoroughly at home in Telemann's splendid four-movement concerto; Jiři Stivín is an equally personable recorder soloist in the masterly *Suite in A minor*; his decoration is a special joy. The *Triple violin concerto* with its memorable *Vivace* finale and the *Double horn concerto* also show the finesse which these musicians readily display. Richard Edlinger provides polished and alert accompaniments throughout. The digital sound is first class.

Overture (Suite) in B flat (La Bourse); Suites in C and G.
(M) *** Vanguard/Passacaille Dig. 99710 [id.]. Il Fondamento, Paul Dombrecht.

Paul Dombrecht and Il Fondamento follow up the success of their *Water music* coupling with characterful period-instrument performances of three more of Telemann's suites. Each is in its usual form: French overture followed by various dances, sometimes given epithets. The *C major Suite* (which comes last on this CD) is one of the most sprightly and its third number (*Les étudiants galliards*) is something of a hit. There is also a fine *Sarabande*, while the penultimate *Canaries* and closing *Air Italien* also have much charm. The *Overture in B flat* is also a suite of dances, and every number is given a sobriquet, such as the charming *Le repos interrompu, La guerre en la paix* and, more remarkably, *L'Espérance de Mississippi*. Its overall title, *La Bourse*, is associated with the ground floor of the composer's mansion, where he lived between 1712 and 1721, which at that time housed the Hamburg Stock Exchange. Excellent recording, but a collection to be played just one suite at a time!

Water music (Hamburger Ebb' und Fluth).
(M) *** Van./Passacaille Dig. 99713 [id.]. Il Fondamento, Paul Dombrecht – HANDEL: *Water music.* ***

Telemann's *Water music* is rightly one of his most popular works, and it is good to have a thoroughly recommendable period-instrument performance available at mid-price and aptly coupled with Handel. The playing is of a high standard and the reed instruments of Il Fondamento are characterful. Telemann's invention is of a very high standard, not only for the vivacious numbers but also for the expressive writing: the Loure (*Der Verliebte Neptunes*) is quite memorable. But most striking of all is the Gigue entitled *Ebbe und Fluth*, which ingeniously suggests the shifting currents of the Alster. The recording is excellent.

CHAMBER MUSIC

Essercizii musici (Solos 1–12; Trio sonatas 1–12; complete).
**(*) DHM Dig. 054472 77361-2 (4) [id.]. Camerata Köln.

The *Essercizii musici* almost certainly date from 1739–40. The collection includes twelve pieces for solo instruments (violin, flute, viola da gamba, oboe, harpsichord) with bass continuo, alternating with a similar number of trio sonatas, using combinations of the same instruments. As usual with Telemann, the stylistic and melodic variety is remarkable and his invention seems inexhaustible: he was justly proud of the part-writing in the trio sonatas exhibited here. The Cologne group uses period instruments in winningly polished fashion. The oboist, Hans-Peter Westermann, is a particularly fine baroque player, and the solos and sonatas featuring the oboe are among the highlights of the set, as are the *Trios No. 11*, which also includes a flute alongside the oboe, and the delightful *No. 12*, with its busy obbligato harpsichord. Here the *Mesto* third movement is quite haunting. The *Trio No. 8* for flauto dolce (Michael Schneider) also has a neatly contrived harpsichord part and the performance sparkles. More rarely, there are two *Solo Harpsichord suites* (Nos. 6 and 12), and they show Telemann to be a dab hand at keyboard writing. They are persuasively and flexibly played by Sabine Bauer. Indeed all these performances are refreshingly alive, with no lack of light and shade. The balance is perhaps a trifle close (which reduces the dynamic range a bit) although detail is admirably clear. The set, offering nearly four hours of music, is not to be taken all at once but, dipped into, gives much to tickle the ear.

Der getreue Music-Meister (complete).
500♪ ❁ (B) *** DG 447 722-2 (4) [id.]. Mathis, Töpper, Haefliger, Unger, McDaniel, Würzburg Bach Ch., Instrumental soloists, including Linde, Tarr, Melkus, Schäffer, Elza van der Ven, Ulsamer.

We award a Rosette for sheer enterprise to DG's Archiv division in recording (in 1966–7) a 'complete' version of Telemann's *Der getreue Music-Meister* ('The constant Music Master') which has been called the first musical periodical. Other composers were invited to contribute, thus the present box includes a lute piece by Weiss, a *Gigue sans basse* by Pisandel and an ingenious choral canon by Zelenka. There is also a great deal of refreshing instrumental music of Telemann with the widest variety of instrumentation, with various combinations of recorder, flute, oboe, chalumeau, bassoon, trumpet and various stringed instruments, including a *Burlesque suite* for 2 violins ingeniously depicting scenes from *Gulliver's Travels*. The operatic arias from *Eginhard*, *Belsazar* and *Sacio* are of considerable interest, while the comic fable from *Aesopus* concerns 'The she-goat's wooing of the lion'. Sixty-two pieces are recorded here. Performances are almost invariably of excellent quality, and Edith Mathis and Ernst Haefliger stand out among the vocal soloists. Excellent documentation includes full vocal texts. The recording sounds delightfully fresh and natural.

(i) *6 Paris quartets (Nouveaux quatuors en six suites)* (1738): *Nos. 1 in D min.; 2 in A min.; 3 in G; 4 in B min.; 5 in A; 6 in E min.;* (ii) (Orchestral) *Suites: in E flat (La Lyra) for strings;* (iii) *in F for solo violin, 2 flutes, 2 oboes, 2 horns, strings & timpani.*
500♪ ❁ (M) *** Teldec/Warner 4509 92177-2 (2) [id.]. (i) Quadro Amsterdam (Frans Brüggen, Jaap Schröder, Anner Bylsma, Gustav Leonhardt); (ii) Concerto Amsterdam, Frans Brüggen; (iii) with Schröder.

When these records first appeared, we commented: 'The performances are of such a high order of virtuosity that they silence criticism, and Frans Brüggen in particular dazzles the listener.' Moreover the recording is of the very first class, beautifully balanced and tremendously alive. To fill out the space on the second CD, we are offered a pair of orchestral suites. The *Suite in F* is the more ambitious. The *La Lyra Suite in E flat major* is hardly less resourceful and in the third movement, *La Vielle*, Telemann gives a more than passable imitation of a hurdy-gurdy.

Quartets: in A min., for recorder, oboe, violin, and continuo; D min., for 2 flutes, bassoon and continuo; Bassoon sonata in F min.; Trio sonatas: in A min. & C min., for recorder, oboe and continuo.
** Ph. Dig. 454 154-2 [id.]. Philidor Ensemble.

An intimate, elegantly played (period instruments seldom seem to offer technical problems these days) collection for the late evening. The style is laid back and rather doleful. A more spirited, extrovert feeling at times might have been helpful, to provide more variety of mood. The recording cannot be faulted.

Sonata (Septet) in E min.
** DG Dig. 445 824-2 [id.]. Col. Mus. Ant., Goebel – GLUCK: *Alessandro* (ballet); REBEL: *Les Elémens*. **

As always, Telemann's scoring is unpredictable: his *Septet Sonata* is in a sense a quintet, for the upper parts are played by pairs of oboes and violins in unison, with obbligato parts for the two violas over the continuo bass. The Cologne group ensure that the blend is fairly abrasive and, although they open eloquently with the *Gravement*, when they come to the fourth movement marked *Tendrement*, their period line quite misses the point, even though the accompanying notes emphasize Telemann's attraction to this elegant feature of French eighteenth-century taste.

Tippett, Michael (born 1905)

Concerto for double string orchestra; Fantasia concertante on a theme of Corelli; (i) *Songs for Dov.*
(M) *** Virgin/EMI Ultraviolet Dig. CUV5 61326-2. SCO, composer, (i) with Nigel Robson.

It is particularly valuable to have the *Concerto for double string orchestra*, which Tippett had never previously recorded himself. Interpreting his own youthful inspiration, the nonogenarian gives delightfully pointed readings of the outer movements, bringing out the jazzy implications of the cross-rhythms, not taking them too literally, while the lovely melody of the slow movement has never sounded more warmly expressive. The Scottish Chamber Orchestra plays with comparable passion in the *Fantasia concertante*, a related work from Tippett's middle period, while Nigel Robson is a wonderfully idiomatic and convincing tenor soloist in the difficult vocal lines of the three *Songs for Dov*. Warm, full recording.

Piano sonatas Nos. 1 (Fantasy-Sonata); 2–3.
*** Chandos Dig. CHAN 9468 [id.]. Nicholas Unwin.

Apart from John Ogdon's account of Nos. 1 and 2, which are available as part of a competitive package comprising the *Piano concerto*, the *Concerto for double string orchestra*, the *Fantasia concertante on a theme of Corelli* and the *First Quartet*, the main competition here is from Paul Crossley's fine set of all four *Sonatas* on CRD. (Nos. 3 and 4 were composed with him in mind.) Nicholas Unwin is an impressive player and has all the technical resources for these pieces at his command. He has an exceptionally wide range of colour, though at times Crossley has more subtlety and delicacy when Tippett's fantasy takes wing. The Chandos recording is quite superb. Crossley's set takes two CDs, but if you happen not to need or want the *Fourth* this is a viable alternative.

A Child of our time (oratorio).
(M) **(*) Carlton Dig. 30367 0205-2 [id.]. Armstrong, Palmer, Langridge, Shirley-Quirk, Brighton Festival Ch., RPO, Previn.

(i) *A Child of our time* (oratorio); (ii) *The Weeping Babe.*
(BB) **(*) Belart 461 123-2. (i) Morison, Bowden, Lewis, Standen, RLPO Ch. & O, Pritchard; (ii) Cantelo, John Alldis Ch., Sir Colin Davis.

Previn's is a colourful and winning performance, warmer and more expressive than Davis's, predictably helped by the conductor's natural understanding of jazz rhythms. This is a reading which leaves you in no doubt as to the depth of emotion felt by the composer; but ensemble is not always ideally crisp, the chorus is set rather backwardly and the soloists, a less polished if just as characterful team as Davis's, have uneven moments. The digital recording is unobtrusively natural, if slightly recessed.

It is good to have a super-bargain version of Tippett's oratorio, and if the (originally Argo) recording is not modern – it dates from the late 1950s – it sounds remarkably clear in its CD format and is not without atmosphere. There is even a case for preferring this Pritchard performance, despite the less crisp ensemble, to Sir Colin Davis's Philips version, coupled at premium price with *The Knot Garden* (446 331-2). Pritchard's approach is more feeling and sympathetic, and after all this is music which speaks of deep emotion. Elsie Morison and Richard Lewis both sing most beautifully. The brief fill-up, *The Weeping Babe*, was recorded a decade later. It is a setting of some Edith Sitwell poems, a wartime piece of lyrical simplicity, and is excellently sung by the Alldis Choir. This is highly recommendable; however, first choice for *A Child of our time* must rest with the composer's own version, which has full, modern sound (Collins 1339-2).

The Midsummer marriage (complete).
500♪ ❁ *** Lyrita SRCD 2217 (2) [id.]. Remedios, Carlyle, Burrows, Herinx, Harwood, Watts, Ch. & O of ROHCG, Sir Colin Davis.

That Tippett's visionary conception, created over a long period of self-searching, succeeds so triumphantly on record – if anything with greater intensity than in the opera house – is a tribute above all to the exuberance of the composer's glowing inspiration, his determination to translate the beauty of his vision into musical and dramatic terms. There are few operas of any period which use the chorus to such glorious effect, often in haunting offstage passages, and, with Sir Colin Davis a burningly committed advocate and with a cast that was inspired by live performances in the opera house, this is a set hard to resist, even for those not normally fond of modern opera. The singing is glorious, the playing magnificent and the recording outstandingly atmospheric, and the new Lyrita transfer brings an extraordinary sense of realism, the feeling of sitting in the stalls inside an opera house with quite perfect acoustics – even though the recording was made in Wembley Town Hall.

Tomkins, Thomas (1572–1656)

Music for viols: *Almain in F* (for 4 viols); *Fantasias 1, 12 & 14* (for 3 viols); *Fantasia* (for 6 viols); *Galliard: Thomas Simpson* (5 viols & organ); *In Nomine II* (for 3 viols); *Pavane in A min.* (for 5 viols & organ); *Pavane in F; Ut re mi (Hexachord fantasia)* (both for 4 viols); (Keyboard) (i) *Fancy for two to play. Pavan and galliard: Earl Strafford.* (Organ) *In nomine; Miserere; Voluntary;* Verse anthems: *Above the stars; O Lord, let me know mine end; Thou art my King.*

❀ (BB) *** Naxos Dig. 8.550602 [id.]. Rose Consort of Viols, Red Byrd; Thomas Roberts; (i) with John Bryan.

This well-planned Naxos programme is carefully laid out in two parts, each of viol music interspersed with harpsichord and organ pieces and ending with an anthem. It gives collectors an admirable opportunity to sample, very inexpensively, the wider output of Thomas Tomkins, an outstandingly fine Elizabethan musician whose music is still too little known. Born in Gloucester, he spent his career both as 'instructor choristarum' at Worcester Cathedral and as a member of the Chapel Royal, helping to supervise the music at the coronation of Charles I. But with the arrival of Cromwell he withdrew from public life. (The organ he installed at Worcester was removed.) Best known for his magnificent church music, it is refreshing to discover what he could do with viols, experimenting with different combinations of sizes of instrument, usually writing with the polyphony subservient to expressive harmonic feeling, as in the splendid and touching *Fantasia for 6 voices*. Perhaps the most remarkable piece here is the *Hexachord fantasia*, where the scurrying part-writing ornaments a rising and falling six-note scale (hexachord). Tomkins's keyboard and organ music is similarly full of character (the *Fancy for two to play* especially so). His *Pavans* are solemn, even stately, yet his *In nomine* setting for viols is quite lively. The performances here are expert and warmly musical, and they make very enjoyable listening. The two five-part verse anthems and *Above the stars*, which is in six parts, are accompanied by five viols; they are performed colloquially, with counter-tenor lead for *Above the stars* and a bass soloist in *Thou art my King*; both parts are demanding and are attractively sung here. This well-recorded collection, like Naxos's early Telemann collection (8.550156), earns its Rosette not just for the stimulation it brings, but for the enterprise shown.

Trunk, Richard (1879–1968)

7 Christmas Lieder, Op. 71: Advent; Weihnachten; Maria; In der Krippe; Die heiligen drei Könige; Idyll; Christbaum.

❀ *** EMI Dig. CDC5 56204-2 [id.]. Olaf Bär, Helmut Deutsch (with Recital: '*Christmas Lieder*' *** ❀).

These delightful Christmas settings by Richard Trunk are the surprise at the centre of Olaf Bär's superb collection of German Christmas songs. Trunk, a pupil of Rheinberger, lived in America for a period, returning to Germany after the outbreak of the First World War, and he established himself as conductor and academic in Cologne. His remarkable feeling for words and easy melodic lyricism are very much in the mainstream of German Lieder and, even if the style of the music is more eclectic, its invention is engagingly individual and never flags. Olaf Bär gives inspired performances, relishing the countless subtleties in the marriage of text and vocal line, especially in the dramatic tale of the meeting between the *Drei Könige* and Herod. But the highlight is the masterly *Idyll*, picturing Mary beneath a lime tree rocking her son to sleep with four angels on guard overhead. The setting is magically evocative and should be far better known.

Turina, Joaquín (1882–1949)

Piano trios Nos. 1, Op. 35; 2, Op. 76; Circulo, Op. 91.

** Ph. Dig. 446 684-2 [id.]. Beaux Arts Trio – GRANADOS: *Trio.* **

The *First Piano trio* comes from 1927 and was premièred in London with the composer himself at the piano. (Turina was a formidable pianist and at his first Paris concert in 1907 played the Brahms, Franck and Schumann *Quintets*!) This Trio is demanding and original, opening with a fugue and prelude and having as its central movement a set of variations. The *Piano Trio No. 2 in B minor* shows something of Turina's debt to Ravel, as indeed does the *Circulo*, a fantasy written just before the outbreak of the Spanish Civil War, its three movements depicting sunrise, midday and sunset. The performances have plenty of subtlety and refinement but the recording is not really three-star, the piano being a bit forward in relation to its companions and the piano-sound in climaxes being accommodated uncomfortably.

Turnage, Mark-Anthony (born 1960)

(i) *Dispelling the fears;* (ii) *Night dances;* (iii) *Your Rockaby.*
*** Argo Dig. 452 598-2 [id.]. (i) Hardenberger, Wallace, Philh. O, Harding; (ii) Hulse, Tunstall, Constable, Wallace, L. Sinf., Knussen; (iii) Robertson, BBC SO, Andrew Davis.

Turnage is a natural communicator who can happily draw on the widest range of influences and produce music that, for all its modernity, is immediately enjoyable to more than the specialist. These three works offer an impressive survey of his orchestral progress from 1981, when he wrote *Night dances*, to the mid-1990s, when he completed *Your Rockaby*. It helps that jazz and popular music provide an important strand in Turnage's writing. *Night dances* has a movement directly drawing on Miles Davis, and *Your Rockaby* is in effect a saxophone concerto, while the bluesy lyrical passage at the end of *Dispelling the fears* provides a welcome resolution to what is otherwise a tough piece. It is a mark of Turnage's genuine originality that the different sources of inspiration coalesce into a satisfying stylistic whole. With starry soloists, these are performances which consistently bring home the power and concentration of the music, helped by cleanly focused recording.

Vachon, Pierre (1731–1803)

String quartets, Op. 5/2; Op. 7/2.
*** ASV Gaudeamus Dig. CDGAU 151 [id.]. Rasumovsky Qt – JADIN: *Quartets.*

Although none of the works on this disc are masterpieces, the music provides us with an interesting and enjoyable sampler of the French school of quartet writing at the end of the eighteenth century. Vachon, born in Arles, was a frequent visitor to London, playing in his own concertos at the Haymarket Theatre. He wrote his quartets in a *galant* style which the French called the *quatuor concertant ou dialogué*. Op. 5 and Op. 7 were both published in London during the composer's first visit, at the beginning of the 1770s. The second of his Op. 5 quartets is in G minor and its first movement (of three) is a good example of his simplistic dialogue style, while its *Andante grazioso* is quite appealing, the finale a slow, gracious Minuet. The layout of the charming *Andantino* of Op. 7/2 anticipates the Rondo style of the finale. The performances here are polished and well recorded. Distinctly enjoyable in its innocuous way.

Vaňhal, Johann Baptist (1739–1813)

Symphonies: in A min.; C (Sinfonia comista);·D min.; E min.; G min.
**(*) Teldec/Warner Dig. 0630 13141-2 [id.]. Concerto Köln.

Vaňhal (or Wanhal, as he himself signed his name) was born in Bohemia but spent the bulk of his life in Vienna, where these works were composed during the 1760s and 1770s. This was the period of the so-called 'Sturm und Drang' symphonies, works in a minor key with a keen, driving intensity, of which Haydn's *La Passione* is a good example. Vaňhal's symphonies were widely heard at this time and the great French Mozart scholar, Georges de Saint-Foix, cited his *D minor symphony* (albeit not the one on this disc) as an influence on Mozart's little *G minor Symphony*, K.183. These are works of vivid and lively invention which also embrace a wide diversity of approach. The *C major* (*Sinfonia comista*), one of his later symphonies, differs from its companions in its richness of scoring and programmatic inspiration. The Concerto Köln play with tremendous spirit, enthusiasm and style. The recording is too forwardly balanced so that the tuttis are at times a little rough. Not that this greatly inhibits a three-star recommendation for what is a very interesting recording of repertoire which is not otherwise available at present.

Vaughan Williams, Ralph (1872–1958)

Oboe concerto.
(M) *** Carlton Fanfare Dig. 30366 0065-2 [id.]. Pamela Pecha, Moscow PO, Paul Freeman – R. STRAUSS: *Oboe concerto;* SCHICKELE: *Oboe concerto.* ***

Pamela Pecha gives a particularly attractive account of this sometimes elusive concerto, managing its opening cantilena with pleasing spontaneity and revelling in its folksong element. The effect is both fresh and warm-hearted. She is accompanied excellently, and the recording has a glowing ambience which flatters all concerned.

Fantasia on Greensleeves; (i) *Fantasia on a theme of Thomas Tallis.*

500♪ ❁ *** EMI CDC7 47537-2 [id.]. Sinfonia of L., (i) with Allegri Qt; Barbirolli – ELGAR: *Introduction and allegro* etc. *** ❁

(B) *(*) Millennium MCD 80099. V. State Op. O, Sir Adrian Boult – HOLST: *The Planets.* *

Barbirolli's is a quite outstanding performance of the *Tallis fantasia*, one of the great masterpieces of all music. The wonderfully ethereal and magically quiet playing of the second orchestra is another very moving feature of this remarkable performance. The remastered CD retains all the warmth, amplitude and ambient bloom of the superb (1963) recording. The delightful *Greensleeves fantasia* makes an irresistible bonus, presented with pleasing freshness.

Recorded in 1959, the players of the Vienna State Opera Orchestra find hardly more affinity with the music of Vaughan Williams than they do with Holst, although the ensemble is better. Despite Boult's special efforts, the solo string quartet in the *Tallis fantasia* fail to respond to the hushed, ethereal quality of the writing (especially the cellist, whose phrasing is awkwardly angular). *Greensleeves*, too, is comparatively graceless.

(i) *Fantasia on Greensleeves; Fantasia on a theme by Thomas Tallis;* (ii) *The Lark ascending.*

(B) *** Sony SBK 62645; *SBT 62645* [id.]. (i) Phd. O, Ormandy; (ii) Rafael Druian; Cleveland Sinf., Louis Lane – DELIUS: *Brigg Fair; Dance Rhapsody No. 2* etc. ***

These thoroughly recommendable performances from 1963 demonstrate the special feeling American musicians can find for English music. In the *Tallis fantasia* Ormandy (like Barbirolli) characteristically underlines the drama of a work that is often regarded as delicate and atmospheric. Some listeners might object to the lustiness of the first climax, but it is utterly convincing in its passionate richness. Moreover the smaller contrasting string group is better balanced here and makes a more ethereal contrast than in Ormandy's later, RCA version. The recording of *The Lark ascending* was made during the period when Louis Lane was a colleague of George Szell at Cleveland and the orchestra was at the peak of its form. Rafael Druian is the highly poetic violin soloist, a performance that has never been surpassed for its delicate sustained pianissimos, even though the balance is fairly close. The orchestral playing, besides being polished, has both character and atmosphere. The CD transfers have expanded the original sound most strikingly. With highly romantic Delius performances as coupling, this is one of the most desirable of Sony's 'Esssential Classics'.

Film music: *Coastal Command* (suite); *Elizabeth of England: Three Portraits. 49th Parallel: Prelude. The Story of a Flemish Farm* (suite).

**(*) Marco Polo 8.223665 [id.]. RTE Concert O, Dublin, Andrew Penny.

Vaughan Williams's wartime film music was of the highest quality, and it is every bit as memorable as the finest scores of Walton. Older readers will remember what an impression the Powell/Pressburger movie *49th Parallel* (1941) made in the early years of the war, and the inspirational feeling of the *Prelude* with its nostalgic patriotic feeling. *Coastal Command* (1942) was a dramatized documentary which, Betjeman-like, poetically centred on the romantic profiles of the Catalina flying-boats. The music is remarkably evocative, even away from the visual images, and there are echoes from the composer's symphonic writing and also from *Job*. But the even more imaginative (1943) score for *The Story of a Flemish Farm* (a true story about personal sacrifice which enabled a wartime escape to England) brings many such resonances. The masterly evocation of *Dawn in the barn* clearly anticipates the *Sixth Symphony*, while the haunting sequence, *The Dead Man's Kit*, evokes the *Sinfonia antartica*. *Elizabeth in England* (1955–7), another documentary, narrated by Alec Clunes, reminisces about the past as well as celebrating the present. The music has its Elizabethan hey-nonny flavour, but there is a haunting *Poet* sequence which introduces a magically gentle tune, later to be used in the *Sea Symphony*. Finally comes a celebration of *The Queen* which has not only regality but also at its centre a quietly thoughtful reverie of restrained nobility. Andrew Penny is a splendid advocate, and these performances teem with life and are equally eloquent in their mood-painting. The recording is bright and quite full, but a bit two-dimensional; the more exuberant scoring needs rather more amplitude.

Job (A masque for dancing); (i) *The Lark ascending.*

(BB) *** Naxos Dig. 8.553955 [id.]. E. N. Philh., Lloyd-Jones, (i) with David Greed.

In this splendid account of Vaughan Williams's masterly ballet score, David Lloyd-Jones – at super-budget price on Naxos – virtually upstages the competition. He gives a performance tingling with drama, yet with much delicacy of feeling. The opening scene is particularly atmospheric and the *Saraband of the Sons of God* brings a noble dignity, especially when it returns expansively on the full brass. There is much fine orchestral playing: the principal oboe's contributions throughout and the solo violin in scene vii are touchingly fragile, while Job's comforters are portrayed with delectably oily saxophone-playing. The big climaxes bring a superb brass contribution; indeed the brass almost submerge the organ at the vision of Satan. The dance rhythms are caught superbly – bitingly so in *Satan's dance of triumph*, genially Holstian in the *Galliard of the Sons of the Morning*. The Epilogue is touchingly ethereal. The recording, made in Leeds Town Hall, has an ideal spaciousness, yet combines vivid detail with glowing textures. For an encore the orchestral leader, David Greed, provides an exquisitely delicate portrayal of the *Ascending lark*, not as charismatic perhaps as Iona Brown's version (see Concerts section), but with a remarkably sustained closing *piano-pianissimo*.

Symphonies Nos. 1–8; Partita for double string orchestra.
(BB) (***) Belart mono 461 422-2 (5). Baillie, Cameron, Ritchie, Gielgud, LPO Ch., LPO, Boult.

In some ways Boult's mono set of the Vaughan Williams *Symphonies* (No. 8 is in stereo) is unsurpassed, and the recording still sounds amazingly realistic, especially in the *Sea Symphony*, a demonstration LP in its day. The composer was present at the recording sessions and the orchestral playing was notable for its inspirational intensity. The five discs are handsomely packaged in a strong cardboard box with an engaging portrait of the young composer on the front. A set which is as indispensable as it is inexpensive. The discs are all available separately as follows: the *Sea Symphony* (450 144-2); the *London Symphony* (461 008-2); the *Pastoral Symphony* and No. 5 (461 118-2); Nos. 4 and 6 (461 117-2); and Nos. 7 and 8 (see below) on 461 116-2. Boult's first recording of No. 9 is on Everest (EVC 9001).

Symphonies Nos. 1–9; (i) *Flos campi; Serenade to music.*
500♪ (M) *** EMI Dig./Analogue CD-BOXVW 1 (6) [id.]. Soloists, Liverpool Philharmonic Ch., RLPO, Vernon Handley; (i) with Christopher Balmer.

Handley's set consists of the six individual CDs in a blue slipcase, and it will especially suit those needing both economy and modern, digital sound; only the *Sinfonia Antartica* is analogue – and that is still a fine modern recording, offering also the orchestral version of the *Serenade to music* as a fill-up. In all his Vaughan Williams recordings Handley shows a natural feeling for expressive rubato and is totally sympathetic. Many of his performances are first or near-first choices and No. 5 is outstanding in every way. This disc also includes a very successful account of *Flos campi*.

A London Symphony (No. 2); Symphony No. 8 in G min.
500♪ ✿ (M) *** EMI CDM7 64197 2 [id.]. Hallé O, Sir John Barbirolli.

Barbirolli's 1957 recording of the *London Symphony* was an inspirational performance, entirely throwing off the fetters of the studio. The reading gathers power as it proceeds and the slow movement has great intensity and eloquence, with the Hallé strings surpassing themselves. The recording, besides having a wide dynamic range, has plenty of atmosphere and warmth. The digital remastering is wholly successful, with the background subdued. The new coupling of the *Eighth Symphony* makes the CD doubly attractive, and this record was made by Mercury engineers. It is a robust performance rather than a subtle one, but full of character and feeling, matched by most vivid sound.

Symphony No. 5 in D; (i) *Flos campi* (suite).
500♪ ✿ (M) *** EMI Dig. CD-EMX 9512; TC-EMX 2112 [Ang. CDM 62029]. RLPO, Handley; (i) with Christopher Balmer & Liverpool Philharmonic Ch.

Vernon Handley's disc is outstanding in every way, a spacious yet concentrated reading, superbly played and recorded, which masterfully holds the broad structure of this symphony together, building to massive climaxes. The warmth and poetry of the work are also beautifully caught. The rare and evocative *Flos campi*, inspired by the Song of Solomon, makes a generous and attractive coupling, equally well played, though the viola solo is rather closely balanced. The sound is outstandingly full, giving fine clarity of texture.

(i) *Sinfonia antartica (No. 7); Symphony No. 8 in D min.*
(BB) *** Belart mono/stereo 461 116-2. LPO, Boult; (i) with Margaret Ritchie, LPO Ch.; superscriptions spoken by Sir John Gielgud.

Boult's 1953 performance of the *Sinfonia antartica* has never been surpassed; the superbly atmospheric mono recording, with its translucent icy vistas and Margaret Ritchie's floating, wordless soprano voice sounding quite ethereal, remains a model of balancing. Boult and the LPO achieve the highest level of concentration throughout, and the evocation of the frozen landscapes and the shifting ice-floes is as compelling as his control of the structure of a work that is never easy to hold together, while the organ entry at the climax of *Landscape* is a truly engulfing moment. Sir John Gielgud's superscriptions (from the score) act as moving preludes. The *Eighth Symphony*, summoned as it were by bells, is early stereo (1956). Only the first and last movements make use of the full orchestra (which includes a remarkable array of tonal percussion) while the middle two movements are scored for wind instruments alone (Scherzo) and strings alone (*Cavatina*). The LPO plays beautifully, and the Decca engineers seem to have relished the challenge of balancing these unusual sounds of glissando tubular bells, tuned gongs, vibraphone, xylophone, and all the other exotic ingredients. The string-tone sounds far fuller and more expansive than it did when this recording last appeared, on a Decca Ace of Diamonds CD; and altogether this caps this remarkably successful series of Belart super-bargain reissues.

Symphony No. 9 in E min.; Job (A masque for dancing).
**(*) Teldec/Warner Dig. 4509 98463-2 [id.]. BBC SO, Andrew Davis.

It was a promising idea to couple Vaughan Williams's early (1930) ballet score (intended for Diaghilev but rejected as being 'too English') with the last of his symphonies, written 27 years later. The 'Masque for dancing' (as the composer described it) vividly depicts the biblical narrative, while originally the symphony's atmosphere was inspired by the cathedral city of Salisbury, with direct reference in the second movement to the heroine's fate in the Thomas Hardy novel, *Tess of the D'Urbervilles*. The BBC Symphony Orchestra play both scores splendidly, and the recording is spacious. However, as in Davis's other Vaughan Williams records, the orchestra is set back and some of the impact is lost, especially in the nightmarish Scherzo; the performance too, although finely shaped, lacks the ultimate degree of concentration. *Job* is very successful, and no one could say that the spectacular organ entry (recorded earlier by Andrew Davis in Cambridge's King's College Chapel and effectively dubbed in) does not make a huge impact, while Job's comforters are strongly characterized and the serene closing music, including the lovely *Pavane of the Sons of the Morning*, is radiantly presented.

Violin sonata in A min.
(M) **(*) EMI CDM5 66122-2. Yehudi Menuhin, Hephzibah Menuhin – ELGAR: *Sonata* **(*); WALTON: *Sonata*. (**)

The late Vaughan Williams *Sonata* is an unexpected piece for the Menuhins to record and, though in the first movement (as in the Elgar) their tempo is controversially slow, giving the music unexpected weight, the whole performance makes a fine illumination of an elusive piece, not least from the pianist, who copes splendidly with the often awkward piano-writing. The recording is first rate.

Mass in G min.
(M) *** EMI CDM5 65595-2 [id.]. King's College, Cambridge, Ch., Willcocks – BAX; FINZI: *Choral music*. ***

Here with the finest band of trebles in the country Sir David Willcocks captures the beauty of the Vaughan Williams *Mass* more completely than any rival, helped by the fine, atmospheric, analogue recording. This is a work which, on the one hand, can easily seem too tense and lose its magic or, on the other, fall apart in a meandering style; Willcocks admirably finds the middle course. Although recorded two decades before the Bax and Finzi couplings, the remastered analogue sound is by no means second best.

On Wenlock Edge (song-cycle from A. E. Housman's *A Shropshire Lad*); (i) *10 Blake songs for voice and oboe. 4 Hymns: (Lord, come away!; Who is this fair one?; Come love, come Lord; Evening hymn);* Songs: *Merciless beauty;* (ii) *The new ghost; The water mill.*
500♪ (M) *** EMI CDM5 65589-2 [id.]. Ian Partridge, (i) Janet Craxton, Music Group of London; (ii) Jennifer Partridge.

The EMI mid-priced CD is an outstandingly beautiful record, with Ian Partridge's intense artistry and lovely individual tone-colour used with compelling success in Vaughan Williams songs both early and late. With playing from the Music Group of London which matches the soloist's sensitivity, the result is atmospheric and moving. The *Ten Blake songs* come from just before the composer's death: bald, direct settings that with the artistry of Partridge and Craxton are darkly moving.

Velasquez, Glauco (1884–1914)

Album-leaves Nos. 1–2; Brutto Sogno; Canzone Strana; Danse de silphes; Devaneio; Divertimento No. 2; Impromptu; Melancolia; Minuetto e Gavotte Moderni; Petite Suite; Prelúdios Nos. 1–2; Prelúdio e Scherzo; Rêverie; Valsa lenta; Valsa romântica.
** Marco Polo Dig. 8.223556 [id.]. Clara Sverner.

Glauco Velasquez was an illegitimate child, born in Naples to a Brazilian mother and fathered by a Portuguese singer. When their relationship collapsed, his mother took the boy to Brazil, where he was brought up in ignorance of his father's identity. He soon showed musical aptitude, and by his mid-twenties he had attracted some attention in musical circles with his piano miniatures, recorded here. Their heady melancholy is beguiling and their chromaticism remarkable, considering their provenance. At times he comes close to early and middle-period Scriabin, though there is some flavour of his part-native, part-adoptive country. The best of these pieces have a personality and charm that are conveyed effectively by Clara Sverner, and they are very well recorded. Not a three-star record perhaps, but an unusually interesting one.

Verdi, Giuseppe (1813–1901)

Overtures and Preludes: *Aida* (Prelude); *Alzira; Aroldo* (Overtures); *Attila; Un ballo in maschera* (Preludes); *La battaglia di Legnano; Il Corsaro* (Sinfonias); *Ernani* (Prelude); *La forza del destino* (Overture); *Un giorno di regno; Giovanna d'Arco* (Sinfonias); *Luisa Miller* (Overture); *Macbeth; I Masnadieri* (Preludes); *Nabucco* (Overture); *Oberto, Conte di San Bonifacio* (Sinfonia); *Rigoletto; La Traviata* (Preludes); *I vespri siciliani* (Overture).
(B) *** DG Double 453 058-2 (2) [id.]. BPO, Karajan.

It is good to have Karajan's complete set of Overtures and Preludes back in the catalogue. The 1975 recording was one of the very best made in the Philharmonie: the sound combines vividness with a natural balance and an attractive ambience. As we have commented before, the performances have an electricity, refinement and authority that sweep all before them. The little-known overtures, *Alzira*, *Aroldo* and *La battaglia de Legnano*, are all given with tremendous panache and virtuosity. Every bar of this music is alive and, with all the exuberance, Karajan skirts any suggestion of vulgarity. Try the splendid *Nabucco* or the surprisingly extended (8-minute) *Giovanna d'Arco* to discover the colour and spirit of this music-making, with every bar spontaneously alive, while there is not the faintest suggestion of routine in the more familiar items. As a DG Double this is even more strongly recommendable.

Overtures and Preludes: *Aida* (Prelude); *Alzira; Aroldo* (Sinfonias); *Atilla* (Prelude); *Un ballo in maschera* (Sinfonia); *Il corsaro* (Prelude); *Luisa Miller* (Sinfonia); *Oberto, conte di San Bonifacio* (Sinfonia); *La Traviata* (Preludes); *I vespri siciliani* (Sinfonia).
(BB) **(*) Naxos Dig. 8.553018 [id.]. Hungarian State Op. O, Pier Giorgio Morandi.

Overtures and Preludes: *La battaglia di Legnano* (Sinfonia); *Don Carlos* (Prelude); *I due Foscari; Ernani* (Preludes); *La forza del destino; Un giorno di regno (Il finto Stanislao); Giovanna d'Arco; Macbeth* (Sinfonias); *I masnadieri* (Prelude); *Nabucco* (Overture); *Rigoletto* (Prelude).
(BB) **(*) Naxos Dig. 8.553089 [id.]. Hungarian State Op. O, Pier Giorgio Morandi.

Morandi has served his time conducting at La Scala and he gives ripely robust accounts of these colourful overtures and sinfonias, with excellent playing from his Hungarian musicians, notably from the strings in the *Traviata* and *Aida Preludes* and from the brass in *Nabucco*. *La forza del destino* ends the second disc strongly. Full-bloodedly resonant sound (with the second collection at times marginally sharper in definition) means that this pair of bargain discs is worth anyone's money, even if the readings are not as dramatically individual as those of Karajan.

Overtures and Preludes: *Alzira;* (Overture); *Attila* (Prelude); *La battaglia di Legnano* (Overture); *Il corsaro; I due Foscari; Ernani* (Preludes); *Un giorno di regno (Il finto Stanislao); Giovanna d'Arco* (Overtures); *Macbeth* (Prelude with ballet music); *I Masnadieri* (Prelude); *Nabucco; Oberto* (Overtures).
*** Chandos Dig. CHAN 9510 [id.]. BBC Philh. O, Edward Downes.

Edward Downes's programme opens with the little-known *Oberto* and follows with the spirited *Un giorno di regno*; but its highlight is *Nabucco* with its diginified brass sonority. Throughout, these extremely lively performances combine panache and virtuosity with string playing which uses a very wide dynamic range. The crescendo at the opening of *Giovanna d'Arco* is most dramatic. Some of the shorter Preludes are very evocative, notably the brief *Macbeth Prelude*, while the ballet music is both dramatic and colourful, if hardly subtle. *I Masnadieri* closes with a languorous cello solo (very nicely played here). *La battaglia di Legnano* which ends the 76-minute programme has plenty of full-blooded brass at the opening and close. The recording shows Chandos engineering at its most spectacular, but where are *La forza del destino*, *I vespri siciliani* and *Luisa Miller*? All these are included in Karajan's comprehensive, mid-priced, two-disc DG set which, if not recorded as opulently as this Chandos CD, are marvellously authoritative (453 058-2). The other extremely viable alternative is the pair of Naxos bargain discs re-listed above.

Overtures and Preludes: *Aida* (Prelude); *Attila* (Overture); *Un ballo in maschera* (Prelude); *La battaglia di Legnano; La forza del destino; Giovanna d'Arco; Luisa Miller* (Overture); *I Masnadieri* (Prelude); *Nabucco* (Overture); *La Traviata* (Preludes to Acts I & III); *I vespri siciliani* (Overture).
**(*) Sony Dig. SK 68468 [id.]. La Scala PO, Riccardo Muti.

As he demonstrates in the opening *Forza del destino overture*, where the arching string-melody is elegantly and sensuously shaped, Muti offers warmly romantic performances, full of colourful detail, rather than grippingly dramatic music-making after the fashion of Toscanini. The result is very attractive, with more languorous string-playing in the *Traviata Preludes* and much delicacy in the *Introduction* to Act I of *Aida*. The woodwind make a glowing contribution to *Giovanna d'Arco*, and the brass come into their own in *Nabucco* and *La battaglia di Legnano*. With spaciously natural sound this is easy to enjoy, but Karajan remains first choice for this repertoire.

Overtures and Preludes: *Alzira* (Overture); *Un ballo in maschera; Il corsaro; I due Foscari; Ernani* (Preludes); *Il finto Stanislao; La forza del destino* (Sinfonias); *I lombardi alla prima crociata* (Act III, scene iii); *Macbeth* (Prelude); *Oberto, Conte di San Bonifacio* (Sinfonia); *Rigoletto* (Prelude); *Stiffelio* (Overture).
** Sony Dig. SK 62373 [id.]. La Scala PO, Riccardo Muti.

The La Scala Orchestra are obviously completely at home in this music and there is no lack of polish, vigour or melodrama. But with so many brief Preludes included, all of which, while effective in the theatre, are heard less often independently, this is not a very substantial programme. After a series of short-winded pieces, Muti ends with *Stiffelio* but, lively and tuneful as it is, this can hardly be regarded as one of the composer's most sophisticated overtures. The La Scala recording is resonantly full but not nearly as brilliant or colourful as the Chandos sound for Downes.

Requiem Mass.
*** Chandos Dig. CHAN 9490 [id.]. Michele Crider, Markella Hatziano, Gabriel Sade, Robert Lloyd, L. Symphony Ch., LS0, Hickox.
(B) **(*) DG Double 453 091-2 (2) [id.]. Freni, Ludwig, Cossutta, Ghiaurov, V. Singverein, VPO, Karajan – BRUCKNER: *Te Deum.* **(*)

(i) *Requiem Mass;* (ii) *4 Sacred pieces.*
500♪ *** Ph. Dig. 442 142-2 (2) [id.]. (i) Orgonasova, Von Otter, Canonici, Miles; (ii) Donna Brown; Monteverdi Ch., ORR, Gardiner.

It says much for Richard Hickox's recording for Chandos with the LSO and London Symphony Chorus that in important ways – not just practically as the only modern single-disc version – it marks the first of what could be a new generation of readings of Verdi's choral masterpiece. His pacing flows more freely than has become the rule in latterday performances, yet there is never a feeling of haste, simply of heightened intensity when his control of rubato and phrase is so warmly idiomatic. These are very much the speeds which made the vintage Serafin recording of 1939 so compelling (still available on a fine Dutton transfer – CDLX 7010), but with singing from the London Symphony Chorus infinitely finer than that of Serafin's Italian chorus. In their fire they rival Giulini's classic Philharmonia set (EMI CDS7 47257-8), even outshining that in luminosity, thanks in part to the spacious and full recording which, in a reverberant church acoustic, yet reveals ample detail. The other key comparison is with John Eliot Gardiner's Philips recording using a chorus of 70 and period forces, more radically presenting a new approach. Gardiner may be even more transparent in texture but too often his highly detailed reading seems self-conscious next to Hickox's, which in its urgency is as spontaneous-sounding as Giulini's.

Gardiner, using period forces, is searingly dramatic and superbly recorded, with fine detail, necessary weight and atmospheric bloom. It can still be recommended as a fine alternative among modern digital recordings even to collectors not drawn to period performance. The soloists make a characterful quartet, with the vibrant Orgonasova set against the rock-steady von Otter, and with Canonici bringing welcome Italianate colourings to the tenor role. The *Four Sacred pieces* are equally revealing. The longest and most complex, the final *Te Deum*, is the most successful of all, marked by thrillingly dramatic contrasts, as in the fortissimo cries of '*Sanctus*'.

With only Robert Lloyd an established name on disc, Hickox may seem to lose out on his quartet of soloists next to Giulini or even Gardiner. In fact they provide his crowning glory, as consistent and well matched a team as any, naturally balanced and more idiomatically Italianate than Giulini's or Gardiner's. The warm-toned soprano, Michele Crider, has a glorious chest register, and the mezzo, Markella Hatziano, amply confirms the unforgettable impression she made as Dido in concert performances of Berlioz's *Trojans* for Colin Davis, while the tenor, Gabriel Sade, sings with clear, heady beauty, not least in a radiant *Ingemisco*. As for Robert Lloyd, he gives one of his noblest, most commanding performances. This issue is a winner in every way, not just for economic reasons.

Karajan's earlier recording of the *Requiem* has been greatly enhanced in its CD transfer, with the whole effect given greater presence and immediacy. He has a fine team of soloists, too. However, Karajan's reading still smooths over the lines of Verdi's masterpiece. The result is often beautiful, but, apart from the obvious climaxes, such as the *Dies irae*, there is a lack of dramatic bite. However, with two discs offered for the price of one and with Bruckner's *Te Deum* thrown in for good measure, many collectors may be tempted to try this.

OPERA

Aida (complete).

500♪ (M) *** EMI CMS7 69300-2 (3) [Ang. CDMC 69300]. Freni, Carreras, Baltsa, Cappuccilli, Raimondi, Van Dam, V. State Op. Ch., VPO, Karajan.

(M) ** RCA 74321 39498-2 (3) [6198-2-RC]. Leontyne Price, Bumbry, Domingo, Milnes, Raimondi, Sotin, Alldis Ch., LSO, Leinsdorf.

(**) EMI mono CDS5 56316-2 (3). Callas, Tucker, Barbieri, Gobbi, La Scala, Milan, Ch. & O, Serafin.

On EMI, Karajan's is a performance of *Aida* that carries splendour and pageantry to the point of exaltation. On record at least, there can be little question of Freni lacking power in a role normally given to a larger voice, and there is ample gain in the tender beauty of her singing. Carreras makes a fresh, sensitive Radames, Raimondi a darkly intense Ramphis and Van Dam a cleanly focused King, his relative lightness no drawback, while Baltsa as Amneris crowns the whole performance with her fine, incisive singing. Despite some over-brightness on cymbals and trumpet, the Berlin sound for Karajan, as transferred to CD, is richly and involvingly atmospheric, most strikingly in the scenes of pageant which have rarely been presented on record in greater splendour.

There is much to commend in Leontyne Price's 1971 recording of *Aida*, reissued at mid-price in RCA's Opera Treasury series, though currently remaining at full price in the USA; with a fine cast, it is a set that might be worth considering. But inevitably it comes into direct comparison with Price's earlier set (Decca 417 416-2 – see our main volume), and by that standard it is a little disappointing. Price's voice is not as glowing as it was and, though there are moments when she shows added insight, it is the earlier performance which generates more electricity and has more dramatic urgency. Domingo makes a warm and stylish Radames, Milnes a strong if hardly electrifying Amonasro and Bumbry a superb, imaginative Amneris. It is a pity that the recording, by the most recent standards, does not capture the glamour of the score. Most of the earlier sets are more impressive in sound.

The Nile Scene has never been performed more powerfully and characterfully on record than in this vintage La Scala set. Though Callas is hardly as sweet-toned as some will think essential for an Aida, her detailed imagination is irresistible, and she is matched by Tito Gobbi at the very height of his powers. Tucker gives one of his very finest performances on record, and Barbieri is a commanding Amneris. The mono sound is more than acceptable, but this remains at full price.

Un ballo in maschera (complete).

(M) *** DG Dig. 449 588-2 (2) [id.]. Domingo, Barstow, Nucci, Quivar, Sumi Jo, V. State Op. Konzertvereinigung, VPO, Karajan.

(***) EMI mono CDS5 56320-2 (2). Callas, Di Stefano, Gobbi, Ratti, Barbieri, La Scala, Milan, Ch. & O, Votto.

Recorded in Vienna early in 1989, *Un ballo in maschera* was Karajan's last opera recording and it makes a fitting memorial, characteristically rich and spacious, with a cast – if not ideal – which still makes a fine team, responding to the conductor's single-minded vision. Standing out vocally is the Gustavo of Plácido Domingo, strong and imaginative, dominating the whole cast. He may not have the sparkle of Pavarotti in this role, but the singing is richer, more refined and more thoughtful. Amelia is Josephine Barstow's finest achievement on record, and dramatically she is most compelling. Leo Nucci, though not as rough in tone as in some of his other recent recordings, is over-emphatic, with poor legato in his great solo, *Eri tu*. Sumi Jo, a Karajan discovery, gives a delicious performance as Oscar the page, coping splendidly with Karajan's slow speed for her Act I solo. Florence Quivar produces satisfyingly rich tone as Ulrica. Though the sound is not as cleanly focused as in the Decca recording for Solti, it is warm and full.

Votto's 1956 recording, with voices as ever set rather close but with a fair amount of space round them, is among the best of the sets with Callas from La Scala, and CD focuses its qualities the more sharply. Cast from strength with all the principals – notably Gobbi and Giuseppe di Stefano – on top form, this is indispensable for Callas's admirers.

Don Carlo (complete; in French).
*** EMI Dig. CDS5 56152-2 (3) [CDCC 56152]. Alagna, Van Dam, Hampson, Mattila, Meier, Ch. de Théâtre du Châtelet, O de Paris, Antonio Pappano.

Recorded live at the Châtelet Théâtre in Paris, the EMI set of the full five-Act version makes a clear first choice for anyone wanting this epic opera in the original French. Pappano may not include as much of the extra and optional material as Abbado has on his four-disc DG Scala set (the only rival in French), but his judgement on the text is good, with one or two variants included. The whole performance sounds more idiomatic, helped by a cast more fluent in French than Abbado's. Regularly Pappano conveys the dramatic thrust more intensely. Often he is lighter in rhythmic touch, naturally impetuous as well as expressive, inspiring his players as well as his singers, an exceptionally strong team.

Roberto Alagna is both youthfully lyrical and heroic, defying the idea that his tenor would lack the power for this role. Thomas Hampson as Posa and José van Dam as King Philip are both centrally strong and expressive, projecting firmly, even if there have been more individual readings of both roles. Waltraud Meier is not caught at her best as Eboli, sounding gusty in the Veil song, even if she relishes the drama of *O don fatale*. As the Grand Inquisitor, Eric Halfvarson is not quite steady enough, even if (thanks to Pappano) the confrontation with the King is thrilling. Crowning the whole performance is the Elisabeth of Karita Mattila, giving her most commanding performance to date. The tender intensity and detailed expressiveness of her singing goes with the most beautiful tonal range, culminating in a magnificent account of her big Act V aria, sure and true as well as deeply moving. The live recording brings some odd balances, with the sound transferred at a lowish level. The choruses of the *Auto da fé* scene (with bells chiming before the music starts) lack the bite you have in the finest studio performances – if not the Abbado. Even so, the opera-house atmosphere, vividly caught, amply compensates for any shortcoming.

Don Carlos (complete).
(M) (**) DG mono 447 655-2 (2) [id.]. Fernandi, Siepi, Bastianini, Jurinac, Simionato, Steffanoni, V. State Op. Ch., VPO, Karajan.

Karajan's DG set of the four-Act version was recorded live at the Salzburg Festival in 1958 and, despite the lovely singing of Sena Jurinac as the Queen, it cannot compare with his Berlin performance of 20 years later on EMI, recorded in the studio but with the Salzburg Festival cast of that year. Simionato, Bastianini and Siepi were all among the finest Italian singers of their day, but in this opera their performances are generalized rather than illuminating. For a live recording of its period the sound is good.

Falstaff (complete).
(M) **(*) Decca 417 168-2 (2) [id.]. Sir Geraint Evans, Ligabue, Freni, Kraus, Elias, Simionato, RCA Italiana Op. Ch. & O, Solti.

We owe an apology to the late Sir Geraint Evans in missing Decca's reissue of his irresistible assumption of the role of Verdi's Falstaff, in partnership with Sir Georg Solti. Their set, originally issued by RCA, comes up as sparkling as ever on a pair of mid-priced CDs. There is an energy, a sense of fun, a sparkle that outshine rival versions, outstanding as they may be. Evans never sounded better on record, and the rest of the cast live up to his example admirably. Solti drives hard, and almost any comparison with the ancient Toscanini set will show his shortcomings, but it is still an exciting and well-pointed performance, the rest of the cast well contrasted. Although Giulini still leads the premium-priced versions (DG 410 503-2) the Decca set is still very much worth considering.

La forza del destino (complete).
500♪ (M) *** RCA 74321 39502-2 (3). Leontyne Price, Domingo, Milnes, Cossotto, Giaiotti, Bacquier, Alldis Ch., LSO, Levine.

James Levine directs a superb performance. The results are electrifying. Leontyne Price recorded the role of Leonora in an earlier RCA version made in Rome in 1956, but the years have hardly touched her voice, and details of the reading have been refined. The roles of Don Alvaro and Don Carlo are ideally suited to the regular team of Plácido Domingo and Sherrill Milnes so that their confrontations are the cornerstones of the dramatic structure. Fiorenza Cossotto makes a formidable rather than a jolly Preziosilla, while on the male side the line-up of Bonaldo Giaiotti, Gabriel Bacquier, Kurt Moll and Michel Sénéchal is far stronger than on rival sets. In a good, vivid transfer of the mid-1970s sound, this is a strong, well-paced version with an exceptionally good and consistent cast. Now reissued at mid-price in RCA's UK Opera

Treasury series, and quite stylishly re-packaged, it makes an unmissable bargain, although for the moment it remains at full price in the USA.

La forza del destino (slightly abridged).
(***) EMI mono CDS5 56323-2 (3). Callas, Tucker, Tagliabue, Nicolai, Rossi-Lemeni, Capecchi, La Scala, Milan, Ch. & O, Serafin.

Though there are classic examples of Callas's raw tone on top notes, they are insignificant next to the wealth of phrasing which sets a totally new and individual stamp on even the most familiar passages. Apart from his tendency to disturb his phrasing with sobs, Richard Tucker sings superbly; but not even he – and certainly none of the others (including the baritone Carlo Tagliabue, well past his prime) – begin to rival the dominance of Callas. Serafin's direction is crisp, dramatic and well paced, again drawing the threads together. The 1955 mono sound is less aggressive than many La Scala recordings of this vintage and has been freshened on CD.

Macbeth (complete).
500♪ *** Ph. Dig. 412 133-2 (3) [id.]. Bruson, Zampieri, Shicoff, Lloyd, German Op. Ch. & O, Berlin, Sinopoli.
(M) *** DG 449 732-2 (2) [id.]. Cappuccilli, Verrett, Ghiaurov, Domingo, La Scala, Milan, Ch. and O, Abbado.

Even more than his finest rivals, Sinopoli presents this opera as a searing Shakespearean inspiration, and Renato Bruson and Mara Zampieri respond vividly. Zampieri's voice may be biting rather than beautiful but, with musical precision an asset, she matches exactly Verdi's request for the voice of a she-devil. Neil Shicoff as Macduff and Robert Lloyd as Banquo make up the excellent quartet of principals, while the high voltage of the whole performance clearly reflects Sinopoli's experience with the same chorus and orchestra at the Deutsche Oper in Berlin.

At times Abbado's tempi are unconventional, but with slow speeds he springs the rhythm so infectiously that the results are the more compelling. The whole performance gains from superb teamwork, for each of the principals – far more than is common – is meticulous about observing Verdi's detailed markings, above all those for *pianissimo* and *sotto voce*. Verrett, hardly powerful above the stave, yet makes a virtue out of necessity in floating glorious half-tones, and with so firm and characterful a voice she makes a highly individual, not at all conventional Lady Macbeth. As for Cappuccilli, he has never sung with such fine range of tone and imagination on record as here, and Plácido Domingo makes a real, sensitive character out of the small role of Macduff. Excellent recording, splendidly remastered as one of the first operas to be included in DG's 'Legendary Recordings' series, and now at mid-price and on two discs.

Nabucco (complete).
500♪ *** DG Dig. 410 512-2 (2) [id.]. Cappuccilli, Dimitrova, Nesterenko, Domingo, Ch. & O of German Op., Berlin, Sinopoli.

Even the thrill of the great chorus *Va, pensiero* is the greater when the melody first emerges at a hushed pianissimo, as marked, sound almost offstage. Dimitrova is superb in Abigaille's big Act II aria, noble in her evil, as is Cappuccilli as Nabucco, less intense than Gobbi was on Gardelli's classic set for Decca, but stylistically pure. The rest of the cast is strong too, including Domingo in a relatively small role and Nesterenko superb as the High Priest, Zaccaria. Bright and forward digital sound, less atmospheric than the 1965 Decca set with Gobbi and Suliotis, conducted by Gardelli.

Otello (complete).
500♪ *** DG Dig. 439 805-2 (2) [id.]. Domingo, Studer, Leiferkus, Ch. & O of Bastille Opera, Myung-Whun Chung.
(M) *** RCA 74321 39501-2 (2) [RCD2-2951]. Domingo, Scotto, Milnes, Amb. Op. Ch., Nat. PO, Levine.

Plácido Domingo's third recording of *Otello* proves to be his finest yet, more freely expressive, even more involved than his previous ones; the baritonal quality of his tenor now brings new darkness, with the final solo, *Niun mi tema*, poignantly tender. Cheryl Studer gives one of her finest performances as Desdemona, the tone both full and pure, while Sergei Leiferkus makes a chillingly evil Iago, the more so when his voice is the opposite of Italianate, verging on the gritty, which not everyone will like. With plenty of light and shade, Myung-Whun Chung is an urgent Verdian, adopting free-flowing speeds yet allowing Domingo full expansiveness in the death scene. This now makes a pretty clear first choice for this much-recorded opera.

On RCA, Domingo as Otello combines glorious heroic tone with lyrical tenderness. Scotto is not always sweet-toned in the upper register, and the big ensemble at the end of Act III brings obvious strain; nevertheless, it is a deeply felt performance which culminates in a most beautiful account of the all-important

Act IV solos, the *Willow song* and *Ave Maria*, most affecting. Milnes too is challenged by his role: this Iago is a handsome, virile creature beset by the biggest of chips on the shoulder. In the transfer of the 1977 analogue original the voices are caught vividly and immediately, and the orchestral sound too is fuller and cleaner than in many more recent versions. Now reissued in RCA's Opera Treasury series, this becomes really competitive and is a clear first choice among mid-priced versions. In the USA it remains at full price for the moment.

Rigoletto (complete).

500♪ *** Ph. Dig. 412 592-2; *412 592-4* (2) [id.]. Bruson, Gruberová, Shicoff, Fassbaender, Lloyd, St Cecilia Ac., Rome, Ch. & O, Sinopoli.

(***) EMI mono CDS5 56327-2 (2). Gobbi, Callas, Di Stefano, La Scala, Milan, Ch. & O, Serafin.

(M) *(*) EMI CMS5 66037-2 (2) [Ang. CDMB 66037]. Milnes, Sills, Kraus, Ramey, Amb. Op. Ch., Philh. O, Rudel.

Edita Gruberová makes the heroine a tender, feeling creature, emotionally vulnerable yet vocally immaculate. Similarly, Renato Bruson as Rigoletto responds to the conductor, combining beauty with dramatic bite. Even more remarkable is the brilliant success of Neil Shicoff as the Duke, more than a match for his most distinguished rivals. Sinopoli's speeds, too, are unconventional at times, but the fresh look he provides makes this one of the most exciting Verdi operas on disc, helped by full and vivid recording, consistently well balanced.

There has never been a more compelling performance of the title-role in *Rigoletto* than that of Gobbi on his classic La Scala set of the 1950s. At every point, in almost every single phrase, Gobbi finds extra meaning in Verdi's vocal lines, with the widest range of tone-colour employed for expressive effect. Callas, though not naturally suited to the role of the wilting Gilda, is compellingly imaginative throughout, and Di Stefano gives one of his finer performances. The transfer of the original mono recording is astonishingly vivid in capturing the voices, but this remains at full price.

Rudel's late-1970s version on EMI, well recorded, can be recommended to devotees of Beverly Sills but not really to anyone else. This was her last major opera recording before her retirement, and the voice as recorded was no longer beautiful, the tone shallow and often tremulous. Milnes as Rigoletto is just as strong as in the earlier Sutherland/Bonynge set on Decca, and Kraus also effectively repeats the success of his singing on two earlier sets. But with Rudel's refreshing direction at times marred by excessive tensions, this is a reissue of limited value.

Rigoletto: highlights.

(M) *(*) Teldec/Warner Dig. 0630 15807-9 [id.] (from complete recording, with Leech, Agache, Vaduva, Ramey, Larmore, Welsh Nat. Op. Ch. & O, Rizzi).

This is not one of Carlo Rizzi's more impressive opera recordings. In the title-role Alexander Agache has the benefit of a glorious voice, but his characterization of the hunchback is sketchy, lacking bite and conviction. Richard Leech sings strongly as the Duke, but without charm. As Gilda, Leontina Vaduva uses her light, sweet, pretty voice very capably, poised as well as agile, but she is not helped by the general slackness.

Simon Boccanegra (complete).

500♪ ❁ (M) *** DG Originals 449 752-2 (2) [id.]. Freni, Cappuccilli, Ghiaurov, Van Dam, Carreras, La Scala, Milan, Ch. and O, Abbado.

Abbado's 1977 recording of *Simon Boccanegra* is one of the most beautiful Verdi sets ever made. Under Abbado the playing of the orchestra is brilliantly incisive as well as refined, so that the drama is underlined by extra sharpness of focus. The cursing of Paolo after the great Council Chamber scene makes the scalp prickle, with the chorus muttering in horror and the bass clarinet adding a sinister comment, here beautifully moulded. Cappuccilli, always intelligent, gives a far more intense and illuminating performance than the one he recorded for RCA earlier in his career. He may not match Gobbi in range of colour and detail, but he too gives focus to the performance; and Ghiaurov as Fiesco sings beautifully too. Freni as Maria Boccanegra sings with freshness and clarity, while Van Dam is an impressive Paolo. With electrically intense choral singing as well, this is a set to outshine even Abbado's superb *Macbeth* with the same company, superbly transferred to CD (see above). It had already been awarded a Rosette at full price, and the set is now all the more desirable at mid-price.

La Traviata (complete).

500♪ ❁ *** Decca Dig. 448 119-2 (2) [id.]. Gheorghiu, Lopardo, Nucci, ROHCG Ch. & O, Solti.

(**) EMI mono CDS5 56330-2 (2). Callas, Kraus, Sereni, Ch. & O of San Carlos Op., Lisbon, Ghione.

In a magnetic reading Solti treats the piece, not with his old fierceness, but with refinement and tenderness as well as emotional weight. As on stage, Gheorghiu brings heartfelt revelations, using her rich and vibrant, finely shaded soprano with consistent subtlety. Frank Lopardo emerges as a fresh, lyrical Alfredo with a distinctive timbre, passionate and youthful-sounding too. Leo Nucci, a favourite baritone with Solti, provides a sharp contrast as a stolid but convincing Germont. This is now a leading contender among all the many rival sets and for many it will be a first choice. A video version – taken from a single performance, not (like the CDs) an edited compendium of a series – is also offered (VHS 071 431-3; Laserdisc 071 428-1), letting one appreciate how Gheorghiu's physical beauty matches her voice, and how elegant and atmospheric Richard Eyre's Covent Garden production is.

Recorded at a live performance in March 1958, Callas's Lisbon-made version is uniquely valuable in spite of very rough sound. Here, far more than in her earlier, Cetra recording of this opera, one can appreciate the intensity which made this one of her supreme roles, with exquisite detail conveying fleeting emotions even in such an obvious passage as the *Brindisi*. Kraus is a fresh, stylish Alfredo, Sereni a positive Germont, more characterful than in the EMI set with De los Angeles. For Callas admirers – who will not object to the occasional ugliness – it is an essential set. However, the extraneous noises in this live recording – like the prompter's constant groaning – as well as the tape background and the crumbling at climaxes, are made all the clearer on CD; what matters is the vivid sense of presence, with Callas at her most vibrant. A unique historical document.

La Traviata: highlights.

*** Teldec/Warner Dig. 0630 13817-9 [id.] (from complete set, with Gruberová, Shicoff, Zancanaro, Amb. S., LSO, Rizzi).

This makes a fine recommendation for a selection of highlights (72 minutes) when Rizzi's Teldec set brings fine singing from a well-matched cast, and Gruberová is memorably touching in the opera's closing scene. A full translation is included.

Il Trovatore (complete).

500♪ ❁ (M) *** RCA 74321 39504-2 (2) [6194-2-RC]. Leontyne Price, Domingo, Milnes, Cossotto, Amb. Op. Ch., New Philh. O, Mehta.

(***) EMI mono CDS5 56333-2 (2). Callas, Barbieri, Di Stefano, Panerai, La Scala, Milan, Ch. & O, Karajan.

(B) * Decca Double 448 743-2 (2) [id.]. Tebaldi, Del Monaco, Savarese, Simionato, Maggio Musicale Fiorentino Ch. & O, Erede.

The soaring curve of Leontyne Price's rich vocal line is immediately thrilling in her famous Act I aria, and it sets the style of the RCA performance, full-bodied and with the tension consistently held at the highest levels. The choral contribution is superb; the famous *Soldiers*' and *Anvil choruses* are marvellously fresh and dramatic. When *Di quella pira* comes, the orchestra opens with tremendous gusto and Domingo sings with a ringing, heroic quality worthy of Caruso himself. There are many dramatic felicities, and Sherrill Milnes is in fine voice throughout; but perhaps the highlight of the set is the opening section of Act III, when Azucena finds her way to Conte di Luna's camp. The ensuing scene with Fiorenza Cossotto is vocally and dramatically quite electrifying.

The combination of Karajan and Callas is formidably impressive. There is toughness and dramatic determination in Callas's singing, whether in the coloratura or in the dramatic passages, and this gives the heroine an unsuspected depth of character which culminates in Callas's fine singing of an aria which used often to be cut entirely – *Tu vedrai che amore in terra*, here with its first stanza alone included. Barbieri is a magnificent Azucena, Panerai a strong, incisive Count, and Di Stefano at his finest as Manrico. On CD the 1956 mono sound, though dry and unatmospheric, is one of the more vivid from La Scala at that period.

Even at Double Decca price this Tebaldi/Del Monaco *Trovatore* is a non-starter. Del Monaco has exactly the right heroic tone-colour for Manrico, and it was a great pity that he failed so lamentably to do much more than bawl away. It is all very exciting for a few minutes but so wearing after a time. Tebaldi, as always, has some lovely moments, but in the last resort there is some lack of imagination in her interpretation. Her singing generally is technically flawless, but one rarely feels that new insight into the meaning of a phrase which many less reliable singers sometimes give. About the best singing in the set comes from Simionato. The conducting too does not have quite the lift and dramatic tension this opera above all calls for, although the early stereo (1956) is effective enough in conveying atmosphere. There is no libretto, merely an uncued synopsis.

Il Trovatore: highlights.

** Decca Dig. 452 200-2 [id.] (from complete recording, with Pavarotti, Banaudi, Verrett, Nucci, Maggio Musicale Fiorentino Ch. & O, Mehta).

Pavarotti's is a bravura performance as Manrico, even if he indulges in vocal mannerisms that on disc more than in live performance grow irritating. Antonia Banaudi sings accurately but, next to Pavarotti, is unmemorable. Shirley Verrett and Leo Nucci are as reliable as ever, and Mehta is vital as well as brisk in an opera that brings out the best in him; but this performance cannot match his classic reading for RCA with Leontyne Price and the young Domingo. Moreover, although the Decca disc is at premium price, there is no translation, only a synopsis.

Victoria, Tomás Luis de (*c.* 1548–1611)

see also in Vocal Recitals, below, under 'Codex'

Missa Ave maris stella; O quam gloriosum est regnum (motet); *Missa O quam gloriosum.*
500♪ ❁ *** Hyperion CDA 66114 [id.]. Westminster Cathedral Ch., David Hill.

The Latin fervour of the singing is very involving; some listeners may initially be surprised at the volatile way David Hill moves the music on, with the trebles eloquently soaring aloft on the line of the music. The spontaneous ebb and flow of the pacing is at the heart of David Hill's understanding of this superb music.

Mass and Motet: *O magnum mysterium.* Mass and Motet: *O quam gloriosum. Ardens est cor meum; Ave Maria.*
(BB) *** Naxos Dig. 8.550575 [id.]. Oxford Camerata, Jeremy Summerly (with Alonso LOBO: *Versa est in luctum* ***).

These Masses are already familiar from recordings by David Hill's Westminster Cathedral Choir. But this Naxos coupling is by no means second best. Like David Hill, Jeremy Summerly moves the music of each Mass on fairly briskly until the *Sanctus* and *Agnus Dei*, when the spacious *espressivo* of the singing makes a poignant contrast. The two motets on which the Masses are based are sung as postludes and very beautiful they are, especially the idyllic *O magnum mysterium.* Finally the short *Versa est in luctum* (a setting of a section of the Requiem Mass) by Alonso Lobo, a Spanish contemporary, ends the concert serenely. The recording is excellent and this is a fine bargain.

Mass and Motet: *O quam gloriosum.*
(BB) *** Belart 461 018-2. Mary Thomas, Jean Allister, Edgar Fleet, Christopher Keyte, Carmelite Priory Ch., London, John McCartney – PALESTRINA: Masses: *Ecce ego Joannes; Sine nomine.* ***

Like the Palestrina couplings, this paired Mass and motet are exceptionally distinguished performances, and they are made the more attractive (in all three cases) by this ideal recorded presentation which couples the motet which is musically connected with each Mass, something which we expect these days as a matter of course but which happened less frequently in the early 1960s, when these recordings first appeared. The sound is remarkably fine, for the microphone placing has been well calculated to the acoustic so that, while the part-writing can be heard clearly, the overall blend is tonally beautiful.

Vieuxtemps, Henri (1820–81)

Violin concertos Nos. 4 in D min., Op. 41; 5 in A min. (Grétry), Op. 37.
(M) *** EMI CDM5 66058-2 [id.]. Itzhak Perlman, O de Paris, Barenboim – RAVEL: *Tzigane;* SAINT-SAENS: *Havanaise.* ***

Vieuxtemps wrote six violin concertos, and it is surprising that so few violinists have attempted to resurrect more than the odd one. This coupling of the two best-known is not only apt; it presents superbly stylish readings, with Perlman both aristocratically pure of tone and intonation and passionate of expression. In his accompaniments Barenboim draws warmly romantic playing from the Paris orchestra. The 1976–7 recording, as usual with Perlman, balancing the soloist well forward, now sounds a little dated, with a touch of shrillness on the upper range of the violin. However, this remains a three-star record, the more so for its inclusion of two of Perlman's very finest recordings as couplings.

Violin concerto No. 5 in A min., Op. 37.
(M) *** Decca 448 128-2 [id.]. Kyung Wha Chung, LSO, Foster – CHAUSSON: *Poème;* SAINT-SAENS: *Violin concertos Nos. 1 & 3.* ***

Even more than the Saint-Saëns *Third concerto*, which forms the major coupling, the Vieuxtemps No. 5 needs persuasive advocacy, and that is certainly what Kyung Wha Chung provides, not just in her passionate commitment in the bravura sections but also in the tender expressiveness of the slow movement, so much more compelling than the usual, more extrovert manner. The 1974 Kingsway Hall recording has lost perhaps a little of its original allure in the matter of the solo violin timbre but is otherwise very satisfactory.

Villa-Lobos, Heitor (1887–1959)

Piano concertos Nos. 1-5.
(B) *** Decca Double Dig. 452 617-2 (2) [id.]. Cristina Ortiz, RPO, Miguel Gómez-Martínez.

What emerges from the series of concertos, as played by Cristina Ortiz here, is that the first two are the most immediately identifiable as Brazilian in their warm colouring and sense of atmosphere, even though the eclectic borrowings are often more unashamed than later, with many passages suggesting Rachmaninov with a Brazilian accent. No. 3, the work Villa-Lobos found it hard to complete, tends to sound bitty in its changes of direction. No. 4, more crisply conceived, has one or two splendid tunes, but it is in No. 5 that Villa-Lobos becomes most warmly convincing again, returning unashamedly to more echoes of Rachmaninov. With Ortiz articulating crisply, there is much to enjoy from such colourful, undemanding music, brilliantly recorded and sympathetically performed. Now at Double Decca price, this entertaining set is worthy of a place in all but the smallest collections.

5 Preludes for guitar.
(B) *** Sony SBK 62425; *SBT 62425* [id.]. John Williams (guitar) – GIULIANI: *Variations on a theme by Handel;* PAGANINI: *Caprice No. 24; Grand sonata;* D. SCARLATTI: *Sonatas.* ***

Although John Williams is balanced a shade too closely, he is very well recorded; his playing, improvisationally spontaneous and full of magical evocation, is of the highest level of mastery. A lower-level setting compensates for the balance and enables this artist's playing to register effectively. These are as perfect and as finely turned as any performances in the catalogue.

String quartets Nos. 2 (1915); 7 (1941).
** Marco Polo Dig. 8.223394 [id.]. Danubius Qt.

The *Seventh Quartet* comes from 1941 – a good vintage for Villa-Lobos – and is conceived on an ambitious scale. Like the *Second Quartet* of Bloch, it is not far short of 40 minutes. Unlike Villa-Lobos's music from the 1930s, this is less exotic in feel, and his discovery of Bach in the *Bachianas Brasileiras* also makes itself felt here. There is an abundance of melodic invention and contrapuntal vitality, even if his musical thinking remains essentially rhapsodic. The Danubius Quartet give a straightforward but somewhat languid account of the piece, and their performance could do with stronger projection. The wartime *Second Quartet* is much shorter and is of less interest. Reservations aside, admirers of this extraordinary composer will not want to be without this more than serviceable CD.

Cirandas; Rudepoêma.
*** ASV Dig. CDDCA 957 [id.]. Alma Petchersky.

We liked the first instalment of ASV's collection of the piano music (on CDA 607) and find no reason for disappointment in this splendid successor, which can be recommended with real enthusiasm. Not only is the playing first class, but the music itself is of much interest. *Rudepoêma* (1921–6) is a musical portrait of Artur Rubinstein and is full of temperament and virtuosity. Alma Petchersky rises to its innumerable challenges with great spirit and panache. The *Cirandas* (1926), which make formidable technical demands on the pianist, are despatched with great brilliance and no mean poetic feeling. Alma Petchersky is very well recorded and, if the standards of this series are maintained, future issues will be self-recommending.

Vivaldi, Antonio (1675–1741)

L'Estro armonico (12 Concertos), Op. 3.
(B) ** EMI forte CZS5 69376-2 (2). Virtuosi di Roma, Fasano.

Fasano's performances are certainly musically fresh and enjoyable, but the contrasts between orchestra and solo groups, and between first and second violins in the orchestra, lose some of their effect through being minimized by the recording balance. These contrasts are the very stuff of which concerti grossi are made, and it is a pity when the chance is missed to make the most of this. One can, of course, identify when the concertino and the ripieno are playing, but here the dynamic result is not as stimulating as it should be. The recording, from the beginning of the 1960s, now sounds a little dated in the matter of the smoothness of the string-timbre, and this cannot compare with Marriner's ASMF set, offered at the same price on a Double Decca. Moreover, this also includes a bouquet of extra wind concertos (443 476-2).

La Stravaganza (12 concertos), *Op. 4* (complete).
❀ (B) *** Decca Double 444 821-2 (2). Soloists, ASMF, Marriner.

Marriner's performances make the music irresistible. The solo playing of Carmel Kaine and Alan Loveday is superb and, when the Academy's rhythms have such splendid buoyancy and lift, it is easy enough to accept Marriner's preference for a relatively sweet style in the often heavenly slow movements. The recording, made in St John's, Smith Square, in 1973/4, is of the very highest quality and the CD transfers are in the demonstration class.

The Trial between harmony and invention (Il Cimento dell'armonia e dell'invenzione) 12 concertos, Op. 8.
(M) **(*) Teldec/Warner 0630 13572-2 (2) [id.]. Alice Harnoncourt, Jürg Schaeftlein, VCM, Harnoncourt.

The Teldec complete set is undoubtedly original in approach and full of character; there is, however, an element of eccentricity in Harnoncourt's control of dynamics and tempi, with allegros often aggressively fast and chimerical changes of mood that are not always convincing. Alice Harnoncourt's timbre is leonine and her tone production somewhat astringent, bringing out the pithiness of timbre inherent in her baroque instrument. The dramatic style of the solo playing is certainly at one with the vivid pictorialism of Vivaldi's imagery. The shepherd's dog in *Spring* barks vociferously, and the dance rhythms at the finale of the same concerto are extremely invigorating. The interpretative approach throughout emphasizes this element of contrast. The languorous opening of *Summer* makes a splendid foil for the storm and the buzzing insects, yet the zephyr breezes are wistfully gentle. The continuo uses a chamber organ to great effect, and picaresque touches of colour are added to the string textures. Concertos Nos. 9 and 12 are played on the oboe by Jürg Schaeftlein, who makes a first-class contribution; and this choice of instrumentation further varies the colouring of Vivaldi's score. The sound is bright, vivid and clean, if dry-textured and sometimes fierce in the Telefunken manner. The two discs, originally issued separately, are now in a box together.

The Four Seasons, Op. 8/1–4; Violin concertos in E flat (La tempesta di mare), RV 253; in C, (Il Piacare), RV 180.
*** Ph. Dig. 446 699-2 [id.]. Mariana Sirbu, I Musici.

The Four Seasons; Concerto for strings (Alla rustica) in G, RV 151.
(BB) ** Naxos Dig. 8.550056 [id.]. Takako Nishizaki, Capella Istropolitana, Gunzenhauser.

Mariana Sirbu has a beautiful tone and an admirable line, and she can be expressive and vigorous by turn, without putting the timbre under strain. I Musici are thoroughly at home and sound fresh in a work which they must have played countless times. All the points of programmatic detail are nicely observed, from the bold shepherd's dog onwards (and they are also fully detailed in the accompanying notes). The sensuous somnambulance of the slow movement of *Summer* is as nicely delineated as the icicles of *Winter* and the gusting winds, which bring plenty of drama. In short this is a first-olass modern-instrument performance, with the lute and harpsichord continuo adding modestly to the effect of slow movements. The two bonus concertos are similarly well played, and the recording is natural, with fine projection. This would grace any collection, yet there are even more characterful versions available. On Sony, Tafelmusik, with Jeanne Lamon the ever-imaginative soloist, provide a superb period-instrument performance (SK 48251), while for those preferring the fuller texture of modern instruments the chimerical solo playing of Marieke Blankestijn (with the COE), who provides the same bonuses as Sirbu, is the perfect alternative (Teldec 4509 91683-2). There are also plenty of superb, less expensive versions, but for those you must consult our main volume.

The super-bargain Naxos version is given first-class digital sound, warm, fresh and well balanced (though the continuo does not come through very impressively). Takako Nishizaki plays beautifully, displaying an appropriate degree of bravura, and the accompaniment under Stephen Gunzenhauser is modest in scale and pleasingly finished. These are amiably musical performances, but Vivaldi's pictorial imagery is understated: the shepherd's dog has obviously just returned from an exhausting spring walk and *Winter* has seemingly been mellowed by the depletion of the ozone layer.

La Cetra, Op. 9; (ii) *Double oboe concerto in D min., RV 535;* (iii) *Piccolo concerto in C, RV 443.*
500♪ ❀ (B) *** Decca Double 448 110-2 (2) [id.]. (i) Iona Brown, ASMF; (ii) Neil Black; (iii) Celia Nicklin; both with ASMF, Marriner.

Iona Brown, for some years the leader of St Martin's Academy, here acts as director in the place of Sir Neville Marriner. So resilient and imaginative are the results that one hardly detects any difference from the immaculate and stylish Vivaldi playing in earlier Academy Vivaldi sets. There is some wonderful music here; the later concertos are every bit the equal of anything in *The Trial between harmony and invention*, and they are played gloriously. The recording too is outstandingly rich and vivid, even by earlier Argo standards with this group.

6 Flute concertos, Op. 10.
(M) *** Carlton Dig. 30367 0021-2 [id.]. Judith Hall, Divertimenti of L., Paul Barritt.

Judith Hall's record of the Op. 10 *Flute concertos* is fresh and brightly recorded. She plays with considerable virtuosity and a great deal of taste. The Divertimenti of London is a modern-instrument group and the players are both sensitive and alert. It is almost impossible to suggest a clear first choice in this repertoire, but the DG set from Patrick Gallois and the splendid Orpheus Chamber Orchestra is arguably the lightest and most spirited of any. But that comes at premium price (437 839-2), and at mid-price Judith Hall is very competitive.

6 Flute concertos, Op. 10; Flute concertos: in A min., RV 108; in D, RV 429; in G, RV 438; in A min., RV 440; in C min., RV 441; (i) *Double flute concerto in C, RV 533. Piccolo concerto in A min., RV 445.*
(B) *** Ph. Duo 454 256-2 (2) [id.]. Severino Gazzelloni, I Musici; (i) with Marja Steinberg.

This Duo set purports to contain Vivaldi's 'complete flute concertos', but it is an unlikely claim: the works for sopranino recorder, RV 443 and 444, are not here, nor is the arrangement of *La Notte* (RV 104) which includes also a bassoon. However, the solo flute version is (Op. 10/2) and, with its movements representing ghosts (*Fantasmi*) and sleep (*Il sonno*), is a masterpiece by any standards. A Duo collection entirely made up of concertante works for flute might be thought a rather daunting prospect, but Gazzelloni is an artist of such quality and poetry that such doubts are banished. And it must be added that these concertos all show Vivaldi in the best light, not only in the best-known, *La tempesta di mare* and *Il gardellino*, from Op. 10, but in many of the miscellaneous concertos, too: witness the delicate slow movement of the *A minor*, RV 440, the touching *Largo* of the *C minor*, RV 441, or the lively opening movements of the *D major*, RV 429, and *A minor*, RV 108, which also brings another pensive central *Largo* and a gaily dancing finale. These modern-instrument performances have elegance, and Gazzelloni's playing is masterly: his tone is admirably fresh and clean, while I Musici give him splendid support. Indeed the accompaniments have splendid life and detail, and the balance and analogue recordings (from the 1960s and 1970s) are of a high order.

Complete bassoon concertos

Bassoon concertos: in C, RV 466; in C, RV 467; in C, RV 474; in F, RV 486; in F, RV 487; in F, RV 491; in A min., RV 499; in A min., RV 500.
**(*) ASV Dig. CDDCA 971 [id.]. Daniel Smith, ECO, Ledger.

Bassoon concertos: in C, RV 469; in C, RV 470; in C, RV 472; in C, RV 476; in C, RV 479; in D min., RV 481; in F, RV 488; in G, RV 494.
**(*) ASV Dig. CDDCA 972 [id.]. Daniel Smith, ECO, Ledger.

Bassoon concertos: (i) *in C, RV 471; in C, RV 475;* (ii) *in C, RV 477;* (i) *in F, RV 490; in G min., RV 495; in G min., RV 496;* (ii) *in B flat (La Notte), RV 501.*
*** ASV Dig. CDDCA 973 [id.]. Daniel Smith; (i) Zagreb soloists, Tonko Ninič́; (ii) ECO, Ledger.

Bassoon concertos: in C, RV 478; in C, RV 480; in E flat, RV 483; in F, RV 485; in A min., RV 497; in A min., RV 498; in B flat, RV 502.
*** ASV Dig. CDDCA 975 [id.]. Daniel Smith, Zagreb soloists, Tonko Ninič́.

Bassoon concertos: in C min., RV 480; in E min., RV 484; in F, RV 489; in G, RV 492; in G, RV 493; in B flat, RV 503; in B flat, RV 504.
*** ASV Dig. CDDCA 974 [id.]. Daniel Smith, Zagreb soloists, Tonko Ninič́.

The bassoon seems to have uncovered a particularly generous fund of inspiration in Vivaldi, for few of his 37 concertos for that instrument are in any way routine. Daniel Smith's achievement in recording them all is considerable, for he plays with constant freshness and enthusiasm. His woody tone is very attractive and he is very well caught by the engineers. This set can be welcomed almost without reservation and, dipped into, the various recordings will always give pleasure. We have listened to every one of these concertos and have come up smiling. Daniel Smith is a genial and personable player and he has considerable facility; even if some of the more complicated roulades are not executed with exact precision, his playing has undoubted flair. He is balanced well forward, but the orchestral accompaniment has plenty of personality and registers well enough. As can be seen, ASV have remastered the set to fit on five instead of six CDs, each with more than 70 minutes' playing time. About halfway through the sessions the Zagreb soloists take over the accompaniments and offer alert, vivacious playing that adds to the pleasure of the performances.

It infects Daniel Smith too, and he responds with even greater vigour and rather more polish, while overall there is plenty of affectionate warmth. CDDCA 974, the last of the series, is the record to begin with if you intend sampling this enterprising ASV series. Almost all the works here show Vivaldi at his most pleasingly spontaneous. Smith and the Zagreb group rise to the occasion, and the recording is characteristically vivid.

Bassoon concertos: in C, RV 472; in D min., RV 482; in E min., RV 484; in F, RV 491; in G, RV 494; in G min., RV 495; in A min., RV 499.
*** Ph. Dig. 446 066-2 [id.]. Klaus Thunemann, I Musici.

In the late 1980s Klaus Thunemann gave us a first instalment of Vivaldi's *Bassoon concertos* and it was very highly praised in these pages (Ph. 416 355-2). This second bunch is no less outstanding. He makes every work seem a masterpiece. His virtuosity is remarkable, and it is always at the composer's service. Moreover the polish of the playing is matched by its character and warmth. I Musici are on their finest form, and all the slow movements here are touchingly expressive: his timbre has more colour than that of Danny Bond (with Hogwood – see below) and his ease of execution adds to our enjoyment. The Philips recording is in the demonstration bracket and is ideally balanced.

Guitar concertos: in D, RV 93; in A min., RV 108; (i) *with bassoon: in E, RV 265; in G, RV 435;* (ii) *Double guitar concerto in G, RV 532;* (iii) *Double concerto in D min. for viola d'amore and guitar, RV 540;* (iv) *Trio for violin, guitar and continuo in C, RV 82.*
*** RCA Dig. 09026 68291-2 [id.]. Angel Romero, ASMF; with (i) Graham Sheen; (ii) Lito Romero; (iii) Norbert Blume; (iv) Kenneth Sillito, John Constable.

Guitar concertos: in D, RV 93; in C, RV 425; in G min. (La notte), RV 439; (i) *Double concerto in D min. for viola d'amore and guitar, RV 540; Trios: in C, RV 82; in G min., RV 85.*
** Ph. Dig. 434 082-2 [id.]. Pepe Romero, I Musici; (i) with Massimo Paris.

Most of the Vivaldi concertos which are played on the guitar are arrangements. RV 93 and RV 532 were originally written for mandolins, and RV 540 was conceived for viola d'amore and lute. The others works were written for various instruments, usually flute or violin. However, they all work well on the guitar – and especially as presented here by Angel Romero and members of the ASMF, who obviously seek to convey a transparency of effect normally associated with period instruments. Romero produces a light, mandolin-like sound on his guitar, and the Academy players scale down their timbres to match. The result is delightful. Both *Double concertos* come off particularly well and Norbert Blume plays so gently and sweetly on the viola d'amore that it balances adroitly with the plucked instrument. One understands from his timbre how the viola d'amore was so admired in Vivaldi's time. The recording is first class, and this is by far the finest CD of this repertoire we have yet heard, especially as all the music is so attractive.

Comparison with the Pepe Romero partnership with I Musici is instructive. Pepe also seeks an intimate guitar-image, but his instrument is heard within a warmer, more resonant ambience, and the sound is much less clear and clean, almost romantic in effect. In the *Double concerto for viola d'amore and guitar*, the rich-toned stringed instrument dominates and in the slow movement the guitar is confined to a secondary role. I Musici produce full textures and, although they play as beautifully as always, the ear craves more clearly focused internal detail. This is certainly enjoyable, but alongside the RCA disc it is very much second best.

Guitar concertos: in D, RV 93 (arr. Malipiero); *in A* (arr. Pujol from *Trio sonata in C, RV 82*); (i) *Double concerto for guitar and viola d'amore in D min., RV 540* (arr. Malipiero).
(B) **(*) Decca Eclipse 448 709-2; *448 709-4* [id.]. Eduardo Fernández, ECO, Malcolm, (i) with Norbert Blume – GIULIANI: *Concerto;* PAGANINI: *Sonata.* **(*)

Eduardo Fernández is a musician's guitarist whose playing is consistently refined and sensitive, always responsive to the composer's needs, if at times perhaps a little too self-effacing. Yet the performance of the *Double concerto for guitar and viola d'amore* is winningly intimate, particularly in the very gentle central *Largo*, in which Fernández is perfectly balanced with Norbert Blume. The solo concertos are enjoyable in a similarly refined manner, with bravura unexaggerated and Malcolm always providing the most understanding and polished accompaniments, the recording is first class and beautifully balanced.

Concertos for lute and mandolin: *Lute concerto in D, RV 93; Mandolin concerto in C, RV 425; Double mandolin concerto in G, RV 532; Double concerto in D min. for viola d'amore, lute and strings, RV 540; Concerto in C for 2 recorders, 2 violins 'in tromba marina', 2 mandolins, 2 theorbos, 2 salmoé, cello and strings, RV 558. Trios: in C, RV 82; in G min., RV 85, for violin, lute and continuo.*
**(*) Teldec/Warner Dig. 4509 91182-2 [id.]. Il Giardino Armonico, Giovanni Antonini.

For those who prefer original instruments, here is the repertoire offered above, and more besides, in period performances from the pioneering Italian group in this field. The opening of the multiple-instrument concerto, including two long, single-string violins '*in tromba marina*', is strikingly gutsy, although the accompanying notes do not explain what was used to replace the salmoé which are obsolete and cannot even be identified with certainty. The playing throughout has lots of energy, and textures are fresh and transparent, with slow movements appealingly fragile. The *Largo* duet between lute and viola d'amore in RV 540 is delightful, as are the pair of *Trios* which bring similar delicacy of texture. The one snag is the curious flowing dynamic surge in the allegros which some listeners will find disconcerting. Otherwise, with the excellent recording we take for granted with Das Alte Werk, this can be recommended.

Concertos for strings: in C, RV 113 & RV 114; in D min., RV 127; in F, RV 138; in G (Alla Rustica), RV 151; in G min., RV 153, RV 156 & RV 157; in A min., RV 161; in B flat, RV 167.
(BB) **(*) Naxos Dig. 8.553742 [id.]. Accademia I Filarmonici, Alberto Martini.

The Accademia I Filarmonica is Italy's equivalent of the North American Orpheus group, a conductorless chamber orchestra, to some extent led from the bow by Alberto Martini. They do not use period instruments, but their style, brisk and athletic, with comparatively lean textures, is well removed from that of I Musici. They make the most of this group of Vivaldi's string concertos – which might equally well have been called sinfonias. The only famous one is *Alla Rustica*, which is vigorously done. Slow movements are delicate in texture with the harpsichord continuo coming through naturally. Not all this music is equally appealing, but the best movements are quite indelible, for instance the jogging opening allegro of RV 113 and its minor-key *Grave* slow movement, and the gay, *moto perpetuo* finale of the *D minor* work, RV 127, which ends the programme. Excellent recording, but a disc to be dipped into rather than played through.

Viola d'amore concertos: in D, RV 392; in D min., RV 393, RV 394 & RV 395; in A, RV 396; in D min., RV 397.
**(*) Hyperion Dig. CDA 66795 [id.]. Catherine Mackintosh, OAE.

The viola d'amore was greatly admired in Vivaldi's time for its 'sweetness' of tone, apparently sweeter than that of the contemporary violin. Yet to today's ears its character is more plangent, and that especially applies to performance style on a baroque instrument. As can be seen, Vivaldi favoured the key of D minor above others for his concertos for that instrument, and it must be said that they are generally more limited in appeal than most of his violin concertos. Catherine Mackintosh gives expert performances with the Orchestra of the Age of Enlightenment, but her astringent timbre means that one needs to approach these concertos singly, in contrast with those for other instruments.

Violin concertos: in C, RV 187; in C, RV 195; in C min., RV 197; in D, RV 209; in D min., RV 242; in B flat, RV 364.
** RCA Dig. 09026 68433-2 [id.]. Pinchas Zukerman, ECO.

These concertos are played with bright, easy virtuosity and no lack of expressive warmth. But the end result is bland.

Miscellaneous concertos

(i) *Bassoon concertos: in C, RV 474; in F, RV 489; in A min., RV 498; Concerto for violin, 2 horns, cello, bassoon & strings in F, RV 571; Concerto for violin, 2 oboes, 2 recorders, bassoon & strings, RV 577; Concerto for violin, 3 oboes, 2 recorders, bassoon & strings, RV 576.*
*** O-L Dig. 436 867-2 [id.]. (i) Danny Bond; soloists, AAM, Hogwood.

Vivaldi's music was never more attractive than in his composite concertos for multiple instruments, when his ear obviously revelled in the contrasting timbres of recorder, bassoon, sometimes horns, and stringed instruments. The opening movement of the *G minor Concerto*, RV 576 (which is presented first on the disc), is particularly ear-catching. Here the wind also play in the slow movement, and the organ continuo adds further colour, whereas in RV 571 Simon Standage takes a solo violin role. In the outer movements of this concerto the horns make an attractively robust contribution. To provide extra variety here, three fine *Bassoon concertos* are interspersed among the multiple works, with Danny Bond providing a woodily authentic timbre. The doleful *Andantes* are appealing in RV 474 and RV 489, whereas in RV 498 the chugging solo part in the opening movement is most winning. The playing here is all expert, as is the balance; this is a collection which in its piquant variety of colouring will appeal to all Vivaldians who enjoy period instruments.

Double concertos: for 2 cellos in G min., RV 531; for violin, cello and strings in F (Il Proteo ò sia il mondo rovescio), RV 544; in A for 2 violins (per eco in lontano), RV 552; Triple concertos: for 3 violins in F, RV 551; for violin and 2 cellos in C, RV 561. Quadruple concerto for 2 violins & 2 cellos in D, RV 564.
*** Teldec/Warner Dig. 4509 94552-2 [id.]. Christophe Coin and soloists, Il Giardina Armonico, Antonini.

An exceptionally rewarding collection of concertos for multiple, stringed instruments, made the more striking by the inclusion of RV 544 with its curious sub-title evoking Proteus, who changed shape, and an upside-down world. But all the concertos here show Vivaldi's invention at its most diverse, with textures ever intriguing the ear (not least the work which features a favourite baroque device by designating one violin '*per eco in lontano*'). Christophe Coin leads an excellent team of soloists and the imaginative continuo (organ, harpsichord and arch-lute) adds to the colour of performances which are full of life, yet which also reveal the music's more subtle touches and are remarkably free from the exaggerated stylistic devices too often associated with period instruments. The recording is excellent.

Double cello concerto in G min., RV 531; Lute concerto in G, RV 93; Double mandolin concerto in G, RV 532; Recorder concertos: in C min., RV 441; in C, RV 443. Trio for violin, lute & continuo in G min., RV 85.
(M) *** DG Dig. 445 602-2 [id.]. Demenga, Häusler, Söllscher, Copley, Camerata Bern, Füri.

An excellent mid-priced digital collection, assembled from various records made by the Camerata Bern, which will especially suit those who like their Vivaldi on original instruments. Söllscher's account of the *Duet concerto* for mandolins (in which he takes both solo roles) is quite outstanding, and there is some breathtaking virtuosity from Michael Copley in the *Recorder concertos*. Further variety is provided by the *Trio*, which is also an attractive work. The well-balanced recording has splendid presence and realism.

Flute concerto in G min. (La Notte), Op. 10/2, RV 439; Oboe concerto in A min., RV 463; Concertos for strings: in G min., RV 156; in D min. (Madrigalesco), RV 329; Double trumpet concerto in C, RV 537; Violin concerto in G, Op. 11/4, RV 308; Quadruple violin concerto in B min., Op. 3/10, RV 580.
(M) ** EMI Eminence Dig. CD-EMX 2210. Soloists, Hanover Band, Anthony Halstead.

An attractive clutch of concertos, including several of Vivaldi's best, although it is a pity that the version of *La Notte* was not chosen which includes also a bassoon. The period performances are lively, spick and span but are a little lacking in individuality of personality. The recording is excellent.

Concerto for 2 flutes, 2 oboes, 2 clarinets, bassoon, 2 violins & strings in C (Per la Solennità di San Lorenzo), RV 556; Violin concertos: in D (Fatto per la Solennità della S. Lingua di S. Antonio), RV 212; in F (per la Solennità di San Lorenzo), RV 286; in C (in due cori, Per la S.S. ma Assontione di Maria Vergine), RV 581; Double concerto for violin, oboe & strings in B flat (Funèbre), RV 579.
(M) *** Erato/Warner 0630 13744-2 [id.]. Sol. Ven., Claudio Scimone.

Although the presentation of this CD describes it as a collection of 'solemn concertos' and there is much of the composer's finest expressive writing here, there is also a great deal that is vivid and lively too. Indeed this is an exceptionally stimulating collection of music written for performance on various religious feast-days, and all these works have the composer's imagination working at full stretch. The *Violin concerto in C*, RV 581, is for two string orchestras with echo effects. The *Concerto funèbre* is atmospheric in a darkly expressive way. Using muted strings in the acompaniments plus additional instruments, it is one of the composer's most strikingly original works. The *Violin concerto in D*, RV 212, brings remarkable violin cadenzas in the outer movements, with the soloist soaring up like a bird in the finale. The multiple concerto, RV 556, which is listed first, ends the concert in a blaze of florid colour, with the clarinets standing out – they were novel instruments at the time of composition – in the *Allegro molto*, and they are featured again in the finale; but, more strikingly, in the slow movement the principal clarinet has an important cantilena solo over pizzicato strings. The modern-instrument performances under the ever-reliable Claudio Scimone are excellent, with first-rate solo playing, and the balance is always well managed. The sound too is pleasingly warm yet not clouded.

Double concertos: for 2 cellos in G min., RV 531; for 2 oboes in D min., RV 523; for 2 violins in C, RV 505; in D, RV 511; Triple concerto for oboe & 2 violins, RV 554.
*** Chandos Dig. CHAN 0528 [id.]. Coe, Warkin, Robson, Latham, Standage, Comberti, Coll. Mus. 90, Standage.

Period-instrument performances are increasingly identified with the style of their performing groups, and that of Simon Standage's Collegium Musicum 90 is particularly invigorating, undoubtedly stylish and with no lack of expressive feeling. The rhythmic crispness and buoyancy and the somewhat plangent string-sound have lots of character so that, with excellent soloists, this group of concertos – all showing

Vivaldi at his most athletic – has an obvious appeal. The ripe sound of the baroque oboes and the crunchy cello timbre are particularly characterful, although the tingling astringency characteristic of the accompanying group is even more strongly focused in the solo playing for the concertos for two violins, and especially in the busy finale of RV 511. The recording is of Chandos's top baroque quality.

Concerto per l'Orchestra di Dresda in G min. (for 2 recorders, 2 oboes & bassoon), RV 577; Concerto per la Solennità di S. Lorenzo in C, RV 556; Chamber concerto for recorder, oboe, violin, bassoon & continuo in D (La pastorella), RV 95; Flute concerto in G min. (La Notte), Op. 10/2, RV 439; Concerto for strings (Sinfonia) in C, RV 114; Quadruple concerto for 2 violins and 2 cellos in G, RV 575.
(M) *** Virgin Veritas/EMI Dig. VER5 61275-2. Soloists, Taverner Players, Andrew Parrott.

This is a particularly winning collection – an hour of Vivaldi at his most creative. The opening Dresden concerto with its interplay between the wind groups, but including also solo violin obbligati, is particularly original; then comes the delightful pastoral chamber concerto, with its rustic woodwind charm. This has a particularly engaging siciliano for the solo recorder as its central *Largo*, so nicely played (and decorated) here by Marion Verbruggen, while the imitative finale is hardly less endearing. The two-movement 'Sinfonia', RV 114, is also notable for its inventive finale – in the form of a ciaconna. *La Notte* is (by common consent) among Vivaldi's most imaginative works for flute; its descriptive evocations are atmospherically caught by the Taverner Players, notably '*Ghosts*' and '*Sleep*' which is so reminiscent of the *Four Seasons*, The following concerto for a pair each of violins and echoing cellos at times sounds more like a concerto grosso. The grand opening of the *Concerto for S. Lorenzo* is Handelian, but Vivaldi's own personality reasserts itself firmly in the following allegro. The work is richly scored and, apart from the main protagonists – a pair of solo violins – features recorders, oboes and (a great novelty at that time) clarinets, with ear-catching results. This is its first recording in its original form; Vivaldi, for practical reasons, later dispensed with the clarinets. It makes a splendid conclusion to an outstanding concert, very well laid out, beautifully and authentically played, and excellently recorded.

Concertos and cantatas: (i) *Lute concerto in D, RV 93; Double mandolin concerto in G, RV 532;* (ii) *Recorder concertos: in A min., RV 108; in G min. (La Notte), RV 439*. (i) Cantatas: *All'ombra di sospetto, RV 678; Lungi dal vago volto, RV 680; Vengo a voi, luci adorate, RV 682.*
*** O-L Dig. 433 198-2 [id.]. (i) Tom Finucaine; (ii) Philip Pickett; (iii) Catherine Bott; New L. Consort, Pickett.

Philip Pickett here attempts an alternative to the usual practice of offering a straightforward collection of mixed Vivaldi concertos on disc by interspersing instrumental with vocal music. The cantatas here are light and very florid and make a good foil for the piquant concerto works on recorder and mandolin; and how good it is to hear RV 93 actually played on the intimate lute. Catherine Bott sings with charm and nicely judged expressive feeling. Her virtuosity is amazing, especially in the sparklingly florid upper tessitura of the second part of *All'ombra di sospetto – O quanti amanti . . . Menti contenti* ('Oh, how many lovers are caught by cunning wiles . . . Joys based on falsehood are veritable torments'). The second cantata, *Lungi dal vago volo*, about a lover's longing and rejoicing, is an engaging duet between solo voice and solo violin, and they intertwine most felicitously. With excellent playing and very good recording, this makes a diverting mixture and it will be interesting to see if such an experiment is a success.

CHAMBER MUSIC

Cello sonatas Nos. 1 in B flat, RV 47; 3 in A min., RV 43; 4 in B flat, RV 45; 5 in E min., RV 40; 6 in B flat, RV 46.
*** RCA Dig. 09026 60430-2 [id.]. Ofra Harnoy, Colin Tilney, Miham Tetel.

Vivaldi's nine *Cello sonatas* are among his most inspired chamber works. Ofra Harnoy plays six of them with a deftly paced vigour and brings to the slow movements beautiful tone and a restrained simplicity of line which catches their expressive feeling to perfection. Here Colin Tilney's discreet continuo support is played on the organ, very effectively balanced to give the right degree of support; it also blends admirably with the cello. In allegros the harpsichord comes through less tellingly. However, Harnoy's response is so sympathetic to the composer's muse that one feels any grumbling about this is splitting hairs. In all other respects the recording is excellent.

Those wedded to original instruments will find a highly recommendable complete set is available on CRD by the excellent L'Ecole d'Orphée (CRD 3440/1).

'Manchester' violin sonatas (for violin and continuo) *Nos. 1–12* (complete).
**(*) Arcana Dig. A 4/5 [id.]. Fabio Biondi, Alessandri, Naddeo, Pandolfo, Lislevand.
** HM Dig. HMU 907089/90 [id.]. Romanesca.

The so-called 'Manchester' *Sonatas* were discovered as recently as 1973 in Manchester's Henry Watson Music Library. All the works are in four movements, with an opening Prelude, a following Corrente or Allemanda, then a slow movement, and a closing dance movement, often a Corrente or a Giga; but in three instances the Allemanda forms the finale. Within these simple structures Vivaldi wrote music of high quality and offering much refreshment. We have no doubt which we prefer of these two period-instrument performances, although neither is ideal; and it would be illuminating to hear these works played on modern instruments. Romanesca are recorded fairly dryly, though they are very well balanced. Although Nigel North's archlute, theorbo or guitar makes a very pleasing contribution and John Toll's harpsichord is nicely in the picture, the sound of Andrew Manze's baroque violin is somewhat raw, even though he plays expertly. On the other hand, the Romanesca phrasing has marginally less of that curious accented lunging currently in favour with period groups, which is at times more noticeable on the Arcana set. However, one adjusts to this when Fabio Biondi's tone is so much sweeter and her colleagues are afforded an altogether warmer sound by the more expansive ambience of the Arcana recording. Tempi are generally faster with Romanesca, appreciably so in the Correntes, and often to stimulating effect. But overall the Arcana version is the more persuasive.

VOCAL MUSIC

Sacred music, Volume 1: *Credo in unum Deum, RV 591; Dixit Dominus, RV 594; Kyrie eleison, RV 587; Lauda Jerusalem, RV 608; Magnificat, RV 610.*

*** Hyperion Dig. CDA 66769 [id.]. Susan Gritton, Lisa Milne, Caroline Denley, Lynton Atkinson, David Wilson-Johnson, Choristers and Ch., King's Consort, Robert King.

Hyperion are beginning a new series to cover all the key sacred choral works of Vivaldi, and the performances on this first volume could not be more auspicious. We already know from Negri's fine analogue series for Philips how inspired so much of this repertoire is, and the present disc readily bears this out. All the music here is for double choir except the simple *Credo*, which is without soloists but has great intensity of feeling expressed in the *Et incarnatus est* and *Crucifixus*. Apart from the splendidly grand and masterly *Dixit Dominus,* RV 594 (gloriously sung here), there are two fine, shorter works which also include double string orchestra: the *Kyrie eleison* and the *Lauda Jerusalem*. But most striking of all is Vivaldi's first setting of the *Magnificat* – in G minor, dating from around 1715 although revised in the 1720s – made memorable by its highly individual chromatic writing, immediately obvious at the opening, but also adding to the poignancy of the *Et misericordia*. This is followed by a burst of energy at the *Fecit potentiam* and the unison *Deposit potentes*. Robert King has gathered an excellent team of soloists for this collection (witness the following soprano duet, *Esurientes*, which is delightful), but it is the stirringly eloquent choral singing one remembers most, vividly directed by King and splendidly balanced and recorded.

Sacred music, Volume 2: Motets: (i) *Canta in prato, ride in monte, RV 623;* (ii) *Clarae stellae, scintillate, RV 625;* (ii) *Filiae maestae Jerusalem, RV 638;* (i) *In furore iustissimae irae, RV 626;* (iii) *Longe mala, unbrae, terrores, RV 629;* (i) *Nulla in mundo pax sincera, RV 630.*

*** Hyperion Dig. CDA 66779 [id.]. (i) Deborah York; (ii) James Bowman; (iii) Catherine Denley; King's Consort, Robert King.

We have already discovered the quality of Vivaldi's motets from an excellent Erato recital which offers a quartet of them, sung with agile charm by Cecilia Gasdia (4509 96966-2). That is exactly what they require, for they are in essence concertos for voice, but generally with a recitative between the first movement and slow movement. All the works here have considerable appeal and are very well sung indeed, but those for the soprano, the very agile Deborah York, are the most memorable. The opening of *In furore iustissimae irae* ('In wrath and most just anger') is delivered with dramatic venom, but then the Largo, *Tune meus fletus* ('Then shall my weeping'), follows exquisitely. The closing staccato *Alleluia* is remarkably like a violin part, and Vivaldi uses the same device for the opening of *Canto in prato*, which has no slow movement; here the *Alleluia* is engagingly melismatic. The other highlight of the collection is James Bowman's *Filiae maestae Jerusalem* which brings a touching Larghetto, *Silenti Zephyri* ('Let the winds be hushed'). The closing soprano cantata opens with a gentle siciliana with a typically evocative string accompaniment: *Nulla in mundo pax sincera* ('There is no unblemished peace in the world'). The nimble following aria depicts a hidden snake waiting for the unwary, and the closing, fast-flowing *Alleluia* requires real virtuosity from the singer, and it certainly sparkles here. Altogether this is a first-class collection, and it is excellently recorded.

Sacred music, Volume 3: *Beatus vir* (two versions), *RV 597 & RV 598; Crediti propter quod, RV 605; Dixit Dominus, RV 595; Domine ad adjuvandum, RV 593.*
*** Hyperion Dig. CDA 66789 [id.]. Susan Gritton, Catrin Wyn-Davies, Catherine Denley, Charles Daniels, Neal Davies, Michael George, King's Consort and Ch., Robert King.

Vivaldi's two settings of the *Beatus vir* are quite different. RV 597 is for double choir and is on an ambitious scale; it even has a kind of leitmotif, a refrain that reappears in various sections of the work. RV 598 is in a single movement and is written for soloists and a single choir, rather in the manner of a concerto grosso. The present setting of *Dixit Dominus* for single chorus (but with sopranos sometimes divided) was rediscovered only in the late 1960s – in Prague's National Library. *Domine ad adjuvandum* is a superbly concentrated short work for double choir, based on Psalm 69. It is in three brief sections and, after the soprano's *Gloria patri*, there is a spectacular contrapuntal closing section which makes one smile at its sheer bustle. The performances here are well up to the standard of this excellent series, and the soloists manage to rise to the vocal bravura, especially in duets. The Hyperion recording is of high quality, although ideally one would have welcomed more choral bite.

Beatus vir, RV 597; Gloria in D, RV 589.
(BB) **(*) Naxos 8.550687 [id.]. Anna Crookes, Jayne Quitaker, Carys-Anne Lane, Caroline Trevor, Oxford Schola Cantorum, N. CO, Ward.

This Naxos coupling of what are probably the two favourite Vivaldi choral works is beautifully recorded and well worth its modest cost. Although some listeners will want greater attack in the famous opening and closing sections of the *Gloria* and in the *Potens in terra* in the companion work, these spacious performances, directed by Nicholas Ward, are still warmly enjoyable, partly because of the freshness of the solo contributions, but also because the choral singing has considerable intensity, especially in the continual return of the haunting *Beatus vir* chorale ('Blessed is the man that feareth the Lord; He hath great delight in his commandments') in RV 589. The *Paratum cor eius*, too, brings a surge of choral feeling, and the chorus rises to the occasion for the splendid closing *Gloria Patri*. Full translations are included; full marks, Naxos!

(i) *Dixit Dominus in D, RV 594;* (ii) *Stabat Mater, RV 621.*
(B) **(*) Sony SBK 48282; *SBT 48282* [id.]. (i) Hill Smith, Bernardin, Partridge, Caddy; (i–ii) Watts; E. Bach Festival ((i) Ch., O, Malgoire – D. SCARLATTI: *Stabat Mater*. **(*))

Malgoire's overemphatic style of baroque playing, with first beats of bars heavily underlined, is inclined to be wearing, but these fine works make an excellent coupling, and the singing is first rate, from both the chorus and the soloists in the better-known setting of *Dixit Dominus*, and particularly from Helen Watts in the moving sequence of solo items that makes up the *Stabat Mater*. Reverberant, church-like acoustic.

(i) *Gloria in D, RV 588; Gloria in D, RV 589;* (ii; iii) *Beatus vir in C, RV 597; Dixit dominus in D, RV 594;* (iv; iii) *Magnificat in G min., RV 610.*
500♪ (B) *** Decca Double Dig./Analogue 443 455-2 (2) [id.]. (i) Russell, Kwella, Wilkens, Bowen, St John's College, Cambridge, Ch., Wren O, Guest; (ii) Jennifer Smith, Buchanan, Watts, Partridge, Shirley-Quirk, ECO, Cleobury; (iii) King's College, Cambridge, Ch.; (iv) Castle, Cockerham, King, ASMF, Ledger.

The two settings of the *Gloria* make an apt and illuminating pairing. Both in D major, they have many points in common, presenting fascinating comparisons, when RV 588 is as inspired as its better-known companion. Guest directs strong and well-paced readings, with RV 588 the more lively. Good, warm recording to match the performances. *Dixit dominus* cannot fail to attract those who have enjoyed the better-known *Gloria*. Both works are powerfully inspired and are here given vigorous and sparkling performances with King's College Choir in excellent form under its latest choirmaster. But what caps this outstanding Vivaldi compilation is the earlier King's account of the inspired *Magnificat in G minor*. Ledger uses the small-scale setting and opts for boys' voices in the solos such as the beautiful duet (*Esurientes*) which is most winning.

(i) *Stabat Mater in F min., RV 621; Cessate omai cessate, RV 684; Filiae mestae in C min., RV 638. Concerto for strings in C, RV 114; Sonata al Santo Sepolcro in E flat, RV 130.*
*** HM Dig. HMC 901571 [id.]. (i) Andreas Scholl; Ens. 415, Banchini.

Chiara Banchini and Ensemble 415 have recently given us some fine period-instrument performances, but none is finer than this; yet it is the superb contribution of counter-tenor Andreas Scholl which earned this disc the *Gramophone*'s 1996 Baroque Vocal Award. His tenderly expressive account of the *Stabat Mater* is infinitely touching, while the pastoral cantata, *Cessate omai cessate*, is, dramatically and lyrically, hardly less involving. Here Vivaldi's imaginative accompaniments are relished by the accompanying group, and they are equally on their toes in the similarly contrasted string works. The recording is first class and, although the programme lasts less than an hour, the music-making throughout is outstandingly communicative.

OPERA

L'Incoronazione di Dario (complete).

(B) **(*) HM Dig. HMC 1901235/7 [id.]. Elwes, Visse, Lesne, Ledroit, Verschaeve, Poulenard, Mellon, Nice Bar. Ens., Bezzina.

Set in the fifth century B.C. at the Persian court, this Vivaldi opera involves the conflict which followed the death of King Cyrus and the succession of Darius. Written in 1717, it is one of Vivaldi's earlier operas, in places reflecting the great oratorio he had written the year before, *Juditha triumphans*, reworking three numbers. The opera here receives a lively performance, generally well sung. John Elwes as Darius himself, though stylish, does not sound as involved as some of the others, notably the male alto, Dominique Visse, who is superb both vocally and dramatically as the female confidante, Flora. Reliable singing from the whole cast, and first-rate recording. The full libretto is provided only in Italian, with translated summaries of the plot in English, French and German. However, this reissue on Harmonia Mundi's bargain Musique d'abord label is very tempting.

Volkmann, Robert (1815–83)

(i) *Konsertstück for piano and orchestra, Op. 42;* (ii) *Cello concerto, Op. 33.*

(M) ** Carlton/Vox Turnabout 30372 00402. (i) Jerome Rose, Radio Luxembourg SO, Pierre Cao; (ii) Thomas Blees, Hamburg SO, Alois Springer – PFITZNER: *Violin concerto.* *(*)

Robert Volkmann was a contemporary of Schumann and a friend of Brahms and was much admired in his day. Born in Saxony, he studied in Leipzig and held various teaching appointments in Prague and Budapest. The *Konsertstück in C minor* for piano and orchestra comes from 1860 and makes formidable demands on the virtuosity of the soloist; these are admirably met by Jerome Rose. Like the somewhat earlier *Cello concerto*, it is heavily indebted to Schumann. The recordings come from the 1960s and are rough-and-ready. Presentation is poor: while it lists all the artists, the front cover mentions only the *Konsertstück*. The late lamented Harold Truscott was a great champion of Volkmann; but if these pieces were his only representation in the catalogue, one would be tempted to agree with Sir George Grove's verdict, 'Fluent, graceful, clever and not without originality, it misses the qualities that make music immortal.'

Voříšek, Jan Václav (1791–1825)

Fantasia in C, Op. 12; 6 Impromptus, Op. 7; Piano sonata in B flat, Op. 20; Variations in B flat, Op. 19.

*** Collins Dig. 1458-2 [id.]. Artur Pizarro.

Jan Václav Voříšek is among the most interesting of Beethoven's Bohemian contemporaries and, had he lived longer, might have developed into a major creative figure. Artur Pizarro offers exactly the same programme here as Raduslav Kvapil on Unicorn (DKPCD 9145), and the two make interesting and in some ways complementary alternatives. To put it roughly, Pizarro seems to lay greater stress on the poetic and inward-looking side of Voříšek's personality, while Kvapil gives greater weight to classical symmetry and restraint. The recording is exemplary.

12 Rhapsodies, Op. 1; Le Désir, Op. 3; Le Plaisir, Op. 4.

*** Collins Dig. 1477-2 [id.]. Artur Pizarro.

In 1813 Voříšek left Prague to study law in Vienna, but he lost no time in furthering his musical studies with Hummel. In 1814 he met Beethoven, who found his twelve *Rhapsodies*, Op. 1, 'well worked out' (*brav gearbeitet*) for so young a man. Some of the pieces are Beethovenian and others, like Nos. 8 and 9, even look forward to Schumann. *Le Désir* and *Le Plaisir* were published in 1820 and their poetic fantasy is well conveyed by Pizarro in this excellently recorded and highly recommendable disc.

Wagner, Richard (1813–83)

(i) *A Faust overture; Overtures: Der fliegende Holländer; Rienzi; Lohengrin: Prelude to Act I;* (ii) *Prelude to Act III. Tannhäuser: Overture and Grand march.*
(B) *** Sony SBK 62403; *SBT 62403* [id.]. (i) Cleveland O, Szell; (ii) Phd. O, Ormandy.

Szell's Wagner collection, recorded in Severance Hall in 1965, remains one of his most impressive records and is worthy to rank alongside his electrifying programme of excerpts from the *Ring* (SBK/*SBT* 48175 – see below). The inclusion of the still rarely heard *Faust overture* is most welcome. Hearing this searingly dramatic and intense work, one again wonders why it has not become a repertory piece. It was conceived in 1840 at the time of the *Dutchman* – which is also included here – and rewritten in 1855 during the composition of the *Ring*. To describe the playing of the Cleveland Orchestra as brilliant is inadequate, for the precision and beauty of tone clothe deeper understanding. Though, characteristically, the pianissimos are not always as hushed as they might be, the body of orchestral tone is gloriously expansive. However, there is one fascinating anomaly in the *Faust overture* for which there seems no feasible explanation. As a reader (Douglas Bertram) has pointed out, in the chord on the first beat after figure 'F' in the score, the violins clearly play E natural, when it should surely be E flat. Toscanini plays E flat and that sounds correct and logical when related to what follows. But then why did Szell, so meticulous in matters of detail, get it wrong? Of course it hardly affects the overall validity of the performance, yet it remains a fascinating musical conundrum. The concert opens with Ormandy's physically thrilling account of the *Tannhäuser overture*, followed by the *Grand march* (sumptuous Philadelphia strings), and he also contributes an ebullient *Lohengrin* Act III *Prelude*. The Philadelphia recordings are less refined but the concert overall makes for a rich experience.

Siegfried idyll.
(M) *** DG 449 725-2 [id.]. BPO, Karajan – R. STRAUSS: *Ein Heldenleben.* ***

Karajan's account of Wagner's wonderful birthday present to Cosima is unsurpassed; it has never sounded better than in this new transfer for DG's series of 'Legendary Recordings', aptly coupled with Strauss's *Ein Heldenleben*, Karajan's very first stereo recording for DG.

Der fliegende Holländer: Overture. Götterdämmerung: Siegfried's funeral music; Finale. Die Meistersinger: Overture. Tristan und Isolde: Preludes, Acts I & III; Liebestod. Die Walküre: Ride of the Valkyries.
(M) ** DG Dig. 445 571-2 [id.]. O de Paris, Barenboim.

Barenboim's 1982 Wagner collection was rather successful. He achieved fairly idiomatic playing from the French orchestra and there is no lack of warmth or tension, particularly in the excerpts from *Tristan*. The three excerpts from the *Ring*, recorded the following year, are less telling. Here the orchestra particularly the brass section – does not sound authentic, and the recording acoustic is not helpful, failing to give the necessary resonance to the brass sounds.

Der fliegende Holländer: Overture. Parsifal: Preludes to Acts I & III.
(M) *** EMI CDM5 66108-2 [id.]. BPO, Karajan – R. STRAUSS: *Ein Heldenleben.* ***

These recordings come from 1974 and are magnificently played and sumptuously recorded. There is urgency and edge in *The Flying Dutchman*, which is very exciting, and the string playing in the *Parsifal Preludes* is nobly shaped; if here perhaps the very last degree of tension is missing, the Berlin strings create a glorious sound.

Götterdämmerung: Dawn and Siegfried's Rhine journey. Lohengrin: Preludes to Acts I & III. Die Meistersinger: Prelude to Act I. Das Rheingold: Entry of the Gods into Valhalla. Rienzi: Overture. Siegfried: Forest murmurs. Tannhäuser: Overture. Die Walküre: Ride of the Valkyries; Wotan's farewell and Magic fire music.
500♪ (B) *** EMI forte Dig. CZS5 68616-2 (2). BPO, Tennstedt.

This EMI forte double combines two highly successful collections from the early days of the digital era. The recordings were made in the Philharmonie between 1981 and 1983; they could ideally be more opulent in the middle and bass, but the brilliance is demonstrable, and there is weight, too, and fine detail, especially in the atmospheric *Forest murmurs*. Moreover the orchestral playing is superb and the sense of spectacle is in no doubt. Tennstedt amalgamates something from the combined Furtwängler and Klemperer traditions with his broad, spacious readings, yet the voltage is consistently high.

Götterdämmerung: Dawn and Siegfried's Rhine journey; Siegfried's death and funeral music. Die Meistersinger: Prelude. Das Rheingold: Entry of the Gods into Valhalla. Siegfried: Forest murmurs. Tristan und Isolde: Prelude & Liebestod. Die Walküre: Wotan's farewell and Magic fire music.
500♪ ❁ (M) *** Sony SBK 48175; *SBT 48175* [id.]. Cleveland O, Szell.

The orchestral playing here is in a very special class. Its virtuosity is breathtaking. Szell generates the greatest tension, particularly in the two scenes from *Götterdämmerung*, while the *Liebestod* from *Tristan* has never been played on record with more passion and fire. The *Tristan* and *Meistersinger* excerpts have been added to the contents of the original LP, and the improvement in quality with the latest remastering for CD is little short of miraculous.

Götterdämmerung: Dawn and Siegfried's Rhine journey; Siegfried's death and funeral music. Die Meistersinger: Prelude. Das Rheingold: Entrance of the gods into Valhalla. Siegfried: Forest murmurs. Die Walküre: The Ride of the Valkyries.
(M) *(**) Decca Phase Four 443 901-2 [id.]. LSO, Stokowski.

This collection of *Ring* excerpts was first issued in 1966 and was not one of Decca's most successful Phase Four recordings. There is a shrill, superficial brilliance and patches of roughness in the highly modulated recording – but no matter, this is vintage Stokowski. He is at his most electrifying in *Siegfried's Rhine journey*, while the gods enter Valhalla like a procession of Roman juggernauts. The opening *Ride of the Valkyries* is especially affected by the top-heavy balance (though the flute and piccolo detail is aurally fascinating), but *Forest murmurs* with its chirruping birds has never sounded more atmospherically potent. The *Mastersingers prelude* was recorded 'live' at the London Festival Hall in 1972 and, if the orchestra is made to seem much too close, the overall balance is better and the sound somewhat more refined. The performance is full of adrenalin but has warmth and grandeur too, with some glorious playing from the LSO strings. The applause is justified.

Lohengrin: Preludes to Acts I & III. Tristan und Isolde: Prelude & Liebestod.
(M) *** EMI CDM5 66107-2 [id.]. BPO, Karajan – R. STRAUSS: *Sinfonia domestica*. ***

These Karajan performances (again from 1974) are in a class of their own. The body of tone produced by the Berlin Philharmonic gives a breathtaking richness to the climaxes. That of the first *Lohengrin Prelude* is superbly graded, and in the *Tristan Liebestod* the orgasmic culmination is quite overwhelming, as is the thrilling brass playing in the famous *Lohengrin* Act III *Prelude*.

Die Meistersinger: Overture. (i) *Tannhäuser: Overture and Venusberg music.*
(M) *** EMI CDM5 66106-2 [id.]. BPO, Karajan, (i) with German Op. Ch. – R. STRAUSS: *Don Quixote*. ***

Further excerpts from Karajan's outstanding (1974) sessions: a superb sense of timing and spaciousness is applied to the *Tannhäuser* excerpts, and the *Die Meistersinger Prelude* has a similar imposing breadth. The sound is excellent.

OPERA

Der fliegende Holländer (complete).
500♪ (M) *** Ph. Dig. 434 599-2 (2) [id.]. Estes, Balslev, Salminen, Schunk, Bayreuth Festival (1985) Ch. & O, Nelsson.
*** Sony Dig. S2K 66342 (2) [id.]. Morris, Voigt, Heppner, Rootering, Svendén, Groves, Met. Op. Ch. & O, James Levine.

Woldemar Nelsson conducts a performance even more glowing and responsively paced than those of his starrier rivals. The cast is more consistent than any, with Lisbeth Balslev as Senta firmer, sweeter and more secure than any current rival, raw only occasionally, and Simon Estes a strong, ringing Dutchman, clear and noble of tone. Matti Salminen is a dark and equally secure Daland and Robert Schunk an ardent, idiomatic Erik. The chorus is superb, wonderfully drilled and passionate with it.

James Levine directs his Metropolitan Opera forces in a weighty, exceptionally spacious reading, warmly and atmospherically recorded, with a first-rate cast of soloists. Levine's speeds are even slower than Karajan's in his EMI recording, and markedly slower than those of Woldemar Nelsson in his live Bayreuth recording, which is otherwise a first choice. Levine sustains concentration strongly, even when – as in the Spinning Chorus – the speed is eccentrically slow. His springing of rhythms too helps to disguise slow speeds. His view is clearly that this early opera should be treated as being in the same bracket as the mature Wagner, and his principals respond to the challenge in performances that bring out the brooding intensity of both the Dutchman and Senta. So James Morris in the title-role makes the Dutchman into a Wotan-like figure, weighty if slightly gritty of tone. Deborah Voigt finds a stillness and repose in Senta's meditations in her Ballad, producing radiant sounds. Ben Heppner is a superb Erik, with heroic tone clear and fresh, while Jan-Hendrik Rootering is a warm, benevolent Daland. Excellent choral singing and fine playing. The Nelsson version remains a safer recommendation, more bitingly dramatic (unless you find stage noises too distracting), but this Levine set makes a powerful alternative.

Der fliegende Holländer: highlights.
(M) **(*) EMI Dig. CDM5 66052-2 [id.] (from complete set with Van Dam, Vejzovic, Moll, Hofmann; cond. Karajan).
**(*) Sony Dig. SK 61969 [id.] (from above complete recording with James Morris, Debora Voigt, Ben Heppner; cond. Levine).

This EMI highlights disc is only slightly more generous than most of the rest of the series (67 minutes) but will be useful for those wanting to sample Karajan's 1983 recording, particularly as José Van Dam as the Dutchman and Kurt Moll as Daland are both so impressive, and Senta's ballad (Dunja Vejzovic) is very movingly sung. The synopsis relates each excerpt to the narrative.

The highlights Sony CD is generously selected (76 minutes) and includes the Overture. But there is no translation and the synopsis is not cued.

Götterdämmerung (complete).
*** Decca 455 569-2 (4) [id.]. Nilsson, Windgassen, Fischer-Dieskau, Frick, Neidlinger, Watson, Ludwig, V. State Op. Ch., VPO, Solti.

Solti's *Götterdämmerung* represented the peak of his achievement in recording the *Ring* cycle. His reading had matured before the recording was made. He presses on still, but no longer is there any feeling of over-driving, and even the *Funeral march* is made into a natural, not a forced, climax. There is not a single weak link in the cast. Nilsson surpasses herself in the magnificence of her singing: even Flagstad in her prime would not have been more masterful as Brünnhilde. As in *Siegfried*, Windgassen is in superb voice; Frick is a vivid Hagen, and Fischer-Dieskau achieves the near impossible in making Gunther an interesting and even sympathetic character. As for the recording quality, it surpasses even Decca's earlier achievement, and the CDs have again been remastered to improve the sound and clean up background noise even further; the new presentation nostalgically reflects the original LP issues.

Lohengrin (complete).
500♪ *** DG Dig. 437 808-2 (3) [id.]. Jerusalem, Studer, Meier, Welker, Moll, Schmidt, V. State Op. Ch., VPO, Claudio Abbado.
(M) ** DG 449 591-2 (3) [id.]. James King, Janowitz, Thomas Stewart, Gwyneth Jones, Bav. R. Ch. & SO, Kubelik.

Abbado keeps Wagner's square rhythms flowing more freely, allowing himself a greater measure of rubato. That Abbado's speeds are generally faster than Solti's (with the Act III *Prelude* a notable exception, where Abbado's compound time is more springy) means that the complete opera is squeezed on to three instead of four discs, giving it the clearest advantage. For the general collector this will now be first choice. As Elsa, matching her earlier, Bayreuth performance on Philips, Cheryl Studer is at her sweetest and purest, bringing out the heroine's naïvety touchingly. Though there are signs that Siegfried Jerusalem's voice is not as fresh as it once was, he sings commandingly, conveying both beauty and a true Heldentenor quality. Among the others, Waltraud Meier as Ortrud and Kurt Moll as King Heinrich are both superb.

In Kubelik's DG set, the performance of Gundula Janowitz as Elsa is ravishing, with a constant stream of glorious tone over the widest range, and deeply expressive phrasing. For her alone this set is one for Wagnerians to hear. James King is an imaginative Lohengrin, but Thomas Stewart's Telramund has nothing like the dramatic intensity one ideally requires. Gwyneth Jones as the wicked Ortrud provides a sad showing. The pain of her performance, with many passages completely out of control, would be enough to turn most collectors away, and, though Kubelik's interpretation begins dramatically and is often dedicated and thoughtful, it cannot compare with Kempe's, which glows with expressive conviction. A vivid CD transfer makes the most of the lively 1971 recording.

Die Meistersinger von Nürnberg (complete).
*** Decca Dig. (numbered presentation edition) 452 606-2 (4) [id.]. Van Dam, Heppner, Mattila, Opie, Lippert, Vermillion, Pape, Chicago SO Ch. & O, Solti.
500♪ *** DG 415 278-2 (4) [id.]. Fischer-Dieskau, Ligendza, Lagger, Hermann, Domingo, Laubenthal, Ludwig, German Op. Ch. & O, Berlin, Jochum.
*** Calig CAL 50971-74 (4) [id.]. Stewart, Crass, Hemsley, Konya, Unger, Janowitz, Fassbaender, Bav. R. Ch. & O, Kubelik.

This is the only Wagner opera that Sir Georg Solti has recorded a second time, a work which 'I think I love more than anything else which Wagner wrote'. That love comes over from first to last in this glowing performance. By comparison, his earlier, Vienna recording is stiff and metrical, often fierce, with bright, upfront recording, where this new live recording, made in Orchestra Hall, Chicago, is mellower, with plenty of air round the sound, enhancing the extra warmth, relaxation and subtlety of the performance. Though speeds are often a shade faster than before, the degree of urgency also reflects the new warmth and flexibility. Central to the success of the new performance is the singing of Ben Heppner as Walther, not just heroic but clear and unstrained, ardently following Solti's urgency in the *Prize song*, a performance more beautiful than any of recent years except his own for Sawallisch. Karita Mattila sings with comparable beauty as Eva. Though she is still young, her firm, clear voice is more mature, almost mezzo-ish at times, than one expects of an Eva, and she too naturally surges forward in the great solo of the *Quintet*. For some the controversial element will be the Sachs of José van Dam, clean and sharply focused rather than weighty, not quite the wise, old, genial Sachs in his duet with Eva in Act II. This is again unconventional casting which yet brings new beauty and new revelation, as in the hushed pianissimo at the end of the *Fliedermonolog* when he tells of the bird singing. With René Pape a powerful Pogner, Alan Opie a clean-cut, unexaggerated Beckmesser with plenty of projection, and Herbert Lippert and Iris Vermillion excellent as David and Magdalene, it is a cast to rival any on disc, making this a clear recommendation if you want a digital recording.

Jochum's is a performance which, more than any, captures the light and shade of Wagner's most warmly approachable score, its humour and tenderness as well as its strength. The cast is the most consistent yet assembled on record. Caterina Ligendza's Eva is an appealing performance, and the choice of Domingo for Walther is inspired. The key to the set is of course the searching and highly individual Sachs of Fischer-Dieskau, and Horst Laubenthal's finely tuned David matches this Sachs in applying Lieder style. The recording balance favours the voices, but on CD they are made to sound slightly ahead of the orchestra. There is a lovely bloom on the whole sound.

The Calig issue, belatedly issued on commercial disc, offers one of the very finest performances of *Meistersinger* ever recorded, with a cast unmatched on record for its characterful consistency. It is a radio recording, made in Munich in October 1967, and the vividness of the sound is astonishing, with more realism and presence than in almost any recent digital recording. There is plenty of body in the orchestral and choral sound; but what above all makes the results so involving is the immediacy of the voices, placed in front of the orchestra but with plenty of bloom, so that one registers their expressions, as though face to face. Even the mêlée at the end of Act II emerges vividly. This is also one of Kubelik's most inspired recordings, incandescent in the way it builds up to the big emotional climaxes, just as in a live performance. When it comes to the casting, every single voice has been chosen not only for its firmness and clarity, with no wobbling or straining, but also for the central aptness of voice to character. It would be hard to think of a more radiant and girlish Eva than Gundula Janowitz, and the Hungarian tenor, Sandor Konya, too little heard on record, is a glowing Walther, beautiful in every register if not quite as subtle as the leading Walther today, Ben Heppner. Thomas Stewart as Hans Sachs is similarly unstrained, using his firm, dark baritone with warm expressiveness, while Thomas Hemsley has rarely been so impressive on disc, a sharp-focused Beckmesser who conveys the ironic humour but who never guys the role. Franz Crass is a fine, dark Pogner, and it would be hard to find a match for Gerhard Unger as David or Brigitte Fassbaender as Magdalene, with the upfront sound heightening their subplot. A Wagner production as consistent as this is an extreme rarity, the more surprising to find in what began as a radio recording.

Parsifal (complete).

500♪ ✽ *** DG Dig. 413 347-2 (4) [id.]. Hofmann, Vejzovic, Moll, Van Dam, Nimsgern, Von Halem, German Op. Ch., BPO, Karajan.

Communion, musical and spiritual, is what this intensely beautiful Karajan set provides. The playing of the Berlin orchestra is consistently beautiful. Kurt Moll as Gurnemanz anchors the work vocally. José van Dam as Amfortas is also splendid. The Klingsor of Siegmund Nimsgern could be more sinister, but the singing is admirable. Dunja Vejzovic makes a vibrant, sensuous Kundry. Only Peter Hofmann as Parsifal leaves any disappointment, but his natural tone is admirably suited to the part and he is never less than dramatically effective. The four CDs are still among DG's finest so far.

Das Rheingold (complete).

*** Decca 455 556-2 (2) [id.]. London, Flagstad, Svanholm, Neidlinger, VPO, Solti.

The first of Solti's cycle, recorded in 1958, *Rheingold* remains in terms of engineering the most spectacular on CD. The immediacy and precise placing are thrilling, while the sound-effects of the final scenes, including Donner's hammer-blow and the Rainbow bridge, have never been matched since. Solti gives a magnificent reading of the score, crisp, dramatic and direct. Vocally, the set is held together by the unforgettable singing of Neidlinger as Alberich. He vocalizes with wonderful precision and makes the character of the dwarf develop from the comic creature of the opening scene to the demented monster of the last. Flagstad learned the part of Fricka specially for this recording, and her singing makes one regret that she never took the role on the stage. George London is sometimes a little rough, but this is a dramatic portrayal of the young Wotan. Svanholm could be more characterful as Loge, but again it is a relief to hear the part really sung. An outstanding achievement. Newly remastered and with the original artwork restored, the set has now been fitted on to a pair of CDs (instead of three).

Der Ring des Nibelungen (complete).
500♪ ❁ (M) *** Decca 455 552-2 (14) [id.]. Nilsson, Windgassen, Flagstad, Fischer-Dieskau, Hotter, London, Ludwig, Neidlinger, Frick, Svanholm, Stolze, Böhme, Hoffgen, Sutherland, Crespin, King, Watson, Ch. & VPO, Solti.

Solti's was the first recorded *Ring* cycle to be issued. Whether in performance or in vividness of sound, Solti's remains the most electrifying account of the tetralogy on disc, sharply focused if not always as warmly expressive as some. Solti himself developed in the process of making the recording, and *Götterdämmerung* represents a peak of achievement for him, commanding and magnificent. The recordings have again been carefully remastered to make the very most of the original analogue sound and clean up as many of the background noises as possible. Each Act of the cycle is now heard without interruption. This remains a historic set that is as central today as when it first appeared.

Siegfried (complete).
*** Decca 455 564-2 (4) [id.]. Windgassen, Nilsson, Hotter, Stolze, Neidlinger, Böhme, Hoffgen, Sutherland, VPO, Solti.

Siegfried has too long been thought of as the grimmest of the *Ring* cycle, but a performance as buoyant as Solti's reveals that, more than in most Wagner, the message is one of optimism. Each of the three Acts ends with a scene of triumphant optimism. Solti's array of singers could hardly be bettered. Windgassen is at the very peak of his form, lyrical as well as heroic. Hotter has never been more impressive on record, his Wotan at last captured adequately. Stolze, Neidlinger and Böhme are all exemplary, and predictably Joan Sutherland makes the most seductive of woodbirds. With singing finer than any opera house could normally provide, with masterly playing from the Vienna Philharmonic and with Decca's most vivid recording, this is a set likely to stand comparison with anything the rest of the century may provide. As with the rest of the series, the present newly remastered CDs have cleaned up background noises and enhanced the transfer of the sound itself.

Tannhäuser (Paris version; complete).
500♪ *** DG. Dig. 427 625-2 (3) [id.]. Domingo, Studer, Baltsa, Salminen, Schmidt, Ch. & Philh. O, Sinopoli.

Plácido Domingo here produces sounds of much power as well as beauty. Giuseppe Sinopoli makes his most passionately committed opera recording yet, warm and flexible, always individual, with fine detail brought out, always persuasively, and never wilful. Agnes Baltsa is not ideally opulent of tone as Venus, but she is the complete seductress. Cheryl Studer gives a most sensitive performance, creating a movingly intense portrait of the heroine, vulnerable and very feminine. Matti Salminen in one of his last recordings makes a superb Landgrave and Andreas Schmidt a noble Wolfram.

Tristan und Isolde (complete).
500♪ (M) *** EMI CMS7 69319-2 (4) [Ang. CDMD 69319]. Vickers, Dernesch, Ludwig, Berry, Ridderbusch, German Op. Ch., Berlin, BPO, Karajan.

Karajan's is a sensual performance of Wagner's masterpiece, caressingly beautiful and with superbly refined playing from the Berlin Philharmonic. Dernesch as Isolde is seductively feminine, not as noble as Flagstad, not as tough and unflinching as Nilsson; but the human quality makes this account if anything more moving still, helped by glorious tone-colour through every range. Jon Vickers matches her in what is arguably his finest performance on record, allowing himself true pianissimo shading. The rest of the cast is excellent too. The recording has been remastered again for the present reissue, making this an excellent first choice, with inspired conducting and the most satisfactory cast of all.

Tristan und Isolde: highlights.
(M) *** Teldec/Warner Dig. 0630 15808-9 [id.] (from complete set, with Meier, Jerusalem, Lipovšek, Salminen, Struckmann, Berlin State Op. Ch., BPO, Barenboim).

Barenboim's 76-minute selection (which originally appeared at full price) is generous enough and has the advantage of excellent documentation, with a full translation. If you need a selection from this opera, the present performance and recording are very fine, and this is a clear first choice for a highlights disc.

Die Walküre (complete).
*** Decca 455 559-2 (4) [id.]. Nilsson, Crespin, Ludwig, King, Hotter, Frick, VPO, Solti.

Solti sees Act II as the kernel of *Die Walküre*, perhaps even of the whole *Ring* cycle, with the conflict of wills between Wotan and Fricka making for one of Wagner's most deeply searching scenes. That is the more apparent when the greatest of latterday Wotans, Hans Hotter, takes the role, and Christa Ludwig sings with searing dramatic sense as his wife. Before that, Act I seems a little underplayed. This is partly because of Solti's deliberate lyricism – apt enough when love and spring greetings are in the air – but also (on the debit side) because James King fails both to project the character of Siegmund and to delve into the word-meanings as all the other members of the cast consistently do. Crespin has never sung more beautifully on record, but even that cannot cancel out the shortcoming. As for Nilsson's Brünnhilde, it has grown mellower, the emotions are clearer, and under-the-note attack is almost eliminated. The newly remastered set sounds better than ever.

Operatic scenes: *Götterdämmerung: Immolation scene. Tristan und Isolde: Prelude and Liebestod. Die Walküre: Hojotoho!*
**(*) Sony Dig. SK 62032 [id.]. Jane Eaglen, ROHCG O, Elder – BELLINI: Scenes from *Bianca e Fernando* etc. **(*)

Jane Eaglen with her rich, powerful voice copes splendidly with three of the most formidable passages which Wagner ever wrote for soprano: *Isolde's Liebestod* (preceded by the *Tristan Prelude*), *Brünnhilde's Immolation scene* and her cries of *Hojotoho!* in *Walküre*. The bright clarity of her top notes, fearlessly attacked with pinging precision, is thrilling, and she rounds off both the *Tristan* and *Götterdämmerung* solos with tenderness and great beauty, but with speeds so relentlessly steady there is a static feeling, so that the music rather fails to carry you on, lacking the necessary thrust – partly the fault of Elder's conducting. Yet, in coupling with Bellini scenes, this is an impressive demonstration of a young singer's potential.

Wallace, William (1860–1940)

Symphonic poems Nos. 1, The Passing of Beatrice; 3, Sister Helen; 5, Sir William Wallace; 6, Villon.
*** Hyperion Dig. CDA 66848 [id.]. BBC Scottish SO, Martyn Brabbins.

This highly enjoyable Hyperion collection is something of a surprise. Like Hamish McCunn, William Wallace was born in Greenock, near Glasgow. Moreover he was a remarkable master of all trades, a captain in the RAMC, a doctor and an eye surgeon, a classical scholar, poet and dramatist and, last but by no means least, a composer. At the end of his dedicated service during the First World War he turned to music and became Professor of Harmony and Composition at the Royal Academy of Music. The fifth of his symphonic poems was premièred at Sir Henry Wood's Queen's Hall Promenade Concerts in 1905, only a month after the 600th anniversary of the death of his eponymous Scottish hero, whose name has recently been made famous again by the film, *Braveheart*. The composition's full title is *Sir William Wallace, Scottish hero, freedom-fighter, beheaded and dismembered by the English*. The music is not as melodramatic as it sounds. Its Scottish character is immediately obvious at the brooding opening; the main theme, 'Scots wha' hae', emerges only slowly but is celebrated more openly towards the end of a piece which does not close with triumphant celebration, as there was nothing triumphant about the hero's fate. *Villon*, an irreverent medieval poet, was a hero of a different kind, and Wallace's programme draws on the thoughts of his philosophical ballads (which are named in the synopsis) in music which is both reflective and vividly colourful. The very romantic *Passing of Beatrice* is a sensuous vision of Paradise, lusciously Wagnerian with an unashamedly Tristanesque close, reflecting the heroine's final transformation. The scoring is sensuously rich yet it retains also the spiritually ethereal quality of the narrative, rather as Wagner does in *Parsifal*. The final piece here is based on Rossetti and its full title is *Sister Helen, Villainess, murdering by sorcery; insane with jealous and frustrated love*. What is so remarkable is not only the quality of the musical material throughout these works, but also the composer's skill and confidence in handling it: they are musically every bit as well crafted as the symphonic poems of Liszt. Clearly the BBC Scottish Symphony Orchestra enjoy playing them, and Martyn Brabbins shapes the musical episodes skilfully to balance the warm lyricism and drama without becoming too histrionically melodramatic. The result is remarkably satisfying. There are no masterpieces here but all this music is well worth a hearing, and it is splendidly played and recorded.

Wallace, William Vincent (1812–65)

Maritana (opera; complete).

**(*) Marco Polo Dig. 8.223406-7 [id.]. Cullagh, Lee, Clarke, Caddy, RTE Philharmonic Choir and Concert O, O Duinn.

Along with Balfe's *Bohemian Girl* and Benedict's *Lily of Killarney*, Wallace's *Maritana* marked a breakthrough in opera in Britain, and it held the stage for over 50 years. This lively recording, with Irish artists celebrating this nineteenth-century Irish composer, helps to explain the work's attractions, regularly reminding the modern listener of Gilbert and Sullivan. The big difference is that where G & S present a parody of grand opera, with tongue firmly in cheek, Wallace is intensely serious, with the big melodramatic moments quickly becoming unintentionally comic. To compound the similarity with G & S, the story, like that of the *Yeomen of the Guard*, depends on the heroine, by contract, marrying a man condemned to death who then escapes his punishment. What matters is that there are many more good tunes than that of the still-remembered aria for the heroine, *Scenes that are brightest*, and the ensembles in this winning performance are always fresh and lively. The soloists too all have voices which focus cleanly, even if they are not specially distinctive. The recording is bright and forwardly balanced, with words crystal clear. Worth investigating as a period piece.

Walton, William (1902–83)

'Walton edition': (i; ii) *Viola concerto;* (i; iii) *Violin concerto;* (iv) *Coronation marches: Crown imperial; Orb and sceptre; Façade (suites Nos. 1–2); Hamlet: Funeral march. Henry V* (scenes from the film with Sir Laurence Olivier & chorus; suite, arr. Mathieson); *Johannesburg festival overture; Partita for orchestra; Portsmouth Point overture; Richard III: Prelude & suite. Spitfire prelude and fugue; Symphony No. 1 in B flat min.;* (v) *The Wise Virgins (ballet suite)* & (iv) *Sheep may safely graze;* (iv; vi) *Belshazzar's Feast.*

500♪ (M) *** EMI stereo/mono CHS5 65003-2 (4) [CDHD 65003]. (i) Sir Yehudi Menuhin; (ii) New Philh. O; (iii) LSO; (iv) Philh. O; (v) Sadler's Wells O; (vi) with Donald Bell, Philh. Ch.; all cond. composer.

EMI follows up its revelatory Elgar Edition with this handsome Walton Edition, bringing together the composer's own EMI recordings not previously available on CD, with some of the most important dating from the mono interregnum before stereo arrived. The big revelation is Walton's own recording of the *First Symphony*, made in mono in October 1951. *Belshazzar* and the *Symphony* make up the first disc, very generous measure, and all four discs are very well filled indeed. The second disc, entirely stereo, couples Menuhin's recordings of the *Violin* and *Viola concertos* with his version of the *Partita*, made in 1959. The third disc, mono except for Walton's scintillating account of the *Johannesburg Festival overture* and the *Hamlet Funeral march*, brings together the shorter pieces. The final disc contains the film music. Most important is the belated restoration of the complete Henry V sequence with Laurence Olivier, recorded in 1946. The transfer is again first rate, with the atmospheric quality of the writing vividly caught, even if the mono sound lacks a little in body. The sound of arrows at the climax of the Agincourt charge has never been matched on subsequent recordings. What consistently comes out throughout the set is that in his seemingly reticent way Walton was just as inspired a conductor of his own music as Elgar was of his.

(i) *Cello concerto. Symphony No. 1 in B flat min.*

500♪ *** Decca Dig. 443 450-2 [id.]. (i) Robert Cohen; Bournemouth SO, Litton.

Andrew Litton's coupling of the *Symphony No. 1* and the *Cello concerto* crowns his formidable achievement as principal conductor of the Bournemouth Symphony Orchestra. In the *First Symphony*, Litton's success lies not just in his ability to screw up tension to breaking point but also in his treatment of the jazzy syncopations which are a vital element in this music. Like Previn – and, for that matter, Walton himself – Litton treats the jazz rhythms with a degree of idiomatic freedom, consistently making the music crackle with electric energy. The exceptionally full and vivid recording brings out the opulence as well as the sensuousness of Walton's orchestration. In the *Cello concerto* Robert Cohen for Litton is mercurial as well as tender, following a deep, hushed, meditative approach. The way that Cohen makes the opening note of the slow finale seem to emerge from afar is magical.

Viola concerto.

* Revelation RV 10010 [id.]. Yuri Bashmet, USSR State SO, Gennadi Rozhdestvensky – BRITTEN: *Spring Symphony.* **(*)

Yuri Bashmet and Gennadi Rozhdestvensky obviously have great affection for the *Viola concerto*, but the first movement is marred by self-indulgent rubato at the start, though Bashmet is commanding throughout, always imaginative. More seriously, in the 1988 Moscow Radio recording the soloist is balanced far too close, with the rather rough orchestra dimly heard from behind. Nevertheless, an interesting coupling for an electrifying account of Britten's *Spring Symphony*.

(i) *Viola concerto;* (ii) *Violin concerto.*
500♪ *** EMI Dig. CDC7 49628-2 [id.]. Nigel Kennedy, RPO, Previn.
(B) ** BBC Radio Classics 15656 91732 [id.]. (i) Peter Schidlof, BBC SO, C. Davis; (ii) Iona Brown, LSO, Downes.

Kennedy's achievement in giving equally rich and expressive performances of both works makes for an ideal coupling, helped by the unique insight of André Previn as Waltonian, and there are few Walton records as richly rewarding as this, helped by warm, atmospheric sound.

It is specially good to have Iona Brown's warm and purposeful reading of the *Violin concerto* on disc, full of temperament, a live broadcast from Cheltenham, recorded in 1967. The late Peter Schidlof of the Amadeus Quartet is also a warm and sympathetic interpreter of Walton in the *Viola concerto*, though some of the impact is lost through the often cloudy recording, made at an Albert Hall Prom in 1972. The meditative epilogue is especially beautiful, but the Scherzo, taken at a dangerously fast tempo, sounds scrappy, with the viola articulation unclear and the orchestral ensemble ragged. Nevertheless the warmth and thrust of the performance make it well worth hearing.

(i) *Viola concerto;* (ii) *Symphony No. 1;* (iii) *3 Songs from Façade.*
500♪ ✿ (M) (***) Dutton Lab. mono CDAX 8003 [id.]. (i) Riddle, LSO, composer; (ii) LSO, Harty; (iii) Dora Stevens, Foss.

This first ever recording of the *Viola concerto*, made for Decca in December 1937 with Walton conducting the LSO and with Frederick Riddle as soloist, puts a totally different complexion on the piece from usual. Riddle's performance has never been surpassed. It is coupled ideally with the very first recording of Walton's *First Symphony*, made in 1935 by the LSO under Sir Hamilton Harty. Though the playing is not always as polished as in modern versions, the emotional thrust under Harty is uniquely powerful. Again the sound is beefy and full.

(i) *Violin concerto;* (ii; iii) *Capriccio burlesco;* (iv; iii) *Façade suite No. 1; Johannesburg festival overture.*
(B) *** Sony SBK 62749; *SBT 62749* [id.]. (i) Francescatti, Phd. O, Ormandy; (ii) Orchestra; (iii) André Kostelanetz; (iv) NYPO.

Zino Francescatti's 1959 recording of the Walton *Violin concerto* with Eugene Ormandy and the Philadelphia Orchestra comes close to matching the power and thrust of both the Heifetz versions which preceded it. In a first-rate transfer to CD on a bargain-price reissue in Sony's Essential Classics series, it is very well coupled with the Walton recordings made in New York by André Kostelanetz, far more than a light-music specialist. These include the characteristically bustling showpiece that Walton dedicated to him, the *Capriccio burlesco*, given a performance of tremendous brio, and the ever-delectable *Façade* pieces, as well as the most lovable and exuberant of Walton's three witty overtures, the *Johannesburg Festival*, stunningly done. Forward, larger-than-life recording.

Façade (original version; complete).
(B) *** Sony SBK 62400; *SBT 62400* [id.]. Vera Zorina, Phd. O, Ormandy – Holst: *Planets*. **

Ormandy's version of 16 movements from Walton's entertainment comes as a refreshingly unexpected coupling for Bernstein's colourful reading of *The Planets* which is hardly a first choice for this much-recorded work. But at bargain price the Walton recording is thoroughly worthwhile in its own right. It is a pity that all 21 movements were not recorded, for Vera Zorina, who recorded *Façade* as a bravado solo act in 1961, is an infectious, pointedly rhythmic reciter, her words sharply and often wittily projected, while under Ormandy the chamber group from the Philadelphia Orchestra plays with a brilliance, clarity and precision rarely matched. Their narrator is no less seductive in the cooler evocations (*En famille*; *Through gilded trellises*; *By the lake*) than in the captivating *Country dance*, *Polka* and *Waltz*. The *Jodelling song* is delightfully crisp, and the *Popular song* has a light-hearted insouciance. The integration of the vocal line and accompaniment in these later numbers is remarkable, while the closing *Sir Beelzebub* has striking panache from all concerned. Admirably vivid recording. It is a pity that the coupling is not more imaginative, but this is a real collector's item.

Façade: suites 1 & 2.
500♪ *** Hyperion Dig. CDA 66436 [id.]. E. N. Philh. O, Lloyd-Jones – BLISS: *Checkmate* ***; LAMBERT: *Horoscope*. *** ✿

Brilliantly witty and humorous performances of the two orchestral suites which Walton himself fashioned from his 'Entertainment'. This is music which, with its outrageous quotations, can make one chuckle out loud. Moreover it offers, to quote Constant Lambert, 'one good tune after another', all scored with wonderful felicity. The playing here could hardly be bettered, and the recording is in the demonstration bracket with its natural presence and bloom.

Scenes from Shakespeare (compiled Christopher Palmer): *As You Like It; Hamlet; Henry V; Richard III.*
(M) **(*) Chandos Dig. CHAN 7041 [id.]. Sir John Gielgud, Christopher Plummer, ASMF, Marriner.

This makes an apt and attractive compilation, putting together well-chosen selections from the recordings of Walton's Shakespeare film-music, first issued in the complete Chandos edition, not just the three masterly films directed by Laurence Olivier, but also the pre-war *As You Like It*. Roughly two-thirds of the *Henry V* music is included here, and about half of each of the other three. However, many collectors will opt to have more music and will prefer to hear the Shakespearean text in the theatre or cinema.

Symphony No. 1 in B flat min.; Overture Scapino; Siesta.
(BB) *** BMG Arte Nova Dig. 74321 39124-2 [id.]. Gran Canaria PO, Adrian Leaper.

Leaper's disc of Walton's *First* may be on a super-budget label and the orchestra may not be familiar, but it competes very well with almost any version in the catalogue. With finely disciplined playing, the reading is fresh and alert, idiomatic in its rhythmic pointing and with intense poetry in such key moments as the distant trumpet-call in the final coda. Starting almost inaudibly at the very start, Leaper seems intent on making the music emerge from mists, then he quickly builds up tension and momentum, even if in the first movement his reading is not as weighty as many. The clarity of the recording compensates and there is no lack of weight in the heavy brass, which has impressive bite. The slow movement brings inspired wind solos, and the Scherzo and finale are crisp and resilient, with busy ensembles made unusually clear, even transparent, a point that also marks Leaper's witty and sparkling account of the *Scapino overture*, in which the cello solo is most beautifully done. *Siesta* is aptly dreamy, not literal or chilly, as it can be, making this a disc to recommend to Waltonians and newcomers alike.

(i) *Symphony No. 1 in B flat min.;* (ii) *Variations on a theme by Hindemith.*
(B) *(*) BBC Radio Classics 15656 91782 [id.]. (i) BBC SO, Boult; (ii) RPO, composer.

Walton himself conducts a tense and purposeful performance of the *Hindemith variations*, one of the most enjoyable on disc; and the sound of the live broadcast, made in 1963 in the Royal Festival Hall, has remarkable depth and clarity for its period, with good presence. By contrast, Boult is a restrained interpreter of the *First Symphony*, a work which here loses much of its bite in the first two movements and much of its passion in the slow movement, taken far faster than usual. It is not helped by the rather cloudy 1973 recording, made in the same hall.

Symphony No. 2; Partita for orchestra; Variations on a theme by Hindemith.
500♪ ❁ (B) *** Sony SBK 62753; *SBT 62753* [id.]. Cleveland O, Szell.

In a letter to the conductor, Walton expressed himself greatly pleased with Szell's performance of the *Second Symphony*: 'It is a quite fantastic and stupendous performance from every point of view. Firstly it is absolutely right musically speaking, and the virtuosity is quite staggering, especially the Fugato; but everything is phrased and balanced in an unbelievable way. 'Szell's performance of the *Hindemith variations* is no less praiseworthy. Finally comes the *Partita*, which was commissioned by the Cleveland Orchestra and given its première a year before the recording was made. The recordings are bright, in the CBS manner, but the ambience of Severance Hall brings a backing warmth and depth, and these are technically among the finest of Szell's recordings in this venue.

The Wise virgins (ballet suite arr. from Bach).
(M) *** EMI CDM5 65911-2. Concert Arts O, Robert Irving – GLAZUNOV: *The Seasons;* SCARLATTI/TOMMASINI: *Good humoured ladies.* ***

Walton's orchestral arrangements of Bach created a score for the Sadler's Wells ballet in 1940. All the music except the second piece, a chorale-prelude, is extracted from cantatas, and the delightful '*Sheep may safely graze*' (richly presented here) is a highlight, alongside the tranquil '*See what His love can do*' from Cantata No. 85. However, some of the flamboyant brass writing and Walton's unashamedly anachronistic treatment brought the score into critical disfavour in the 1960s; and only recently has public opinion (after acknowledging the very real pleasures of Stokowski's Bach transcriptions) taken Walton's ballet excursion back into favour. It could not be better presented than it is here, and the resonant recording emphasizes the ebullience of the uninhibited moments, especially the robust finale.

CHAMBER MUSIC

(i–ii) *Piano quartet;* (i; iii) *Violin sonata;* (iv) *5 Bagatelles* (for guitar).
*** EMI Dig. CDC5 55404-2 [id.]. (i) Graham; (ii) Silverthorne, Welsh, Margalit; (iii) Alley; (iv) Kerstens.

This is a splendid addition to EMI's Anglo-American chamber music series. The two major works are also coupled together in the Chandos Walton Edition, but here you get a worthwhile bonus in the *Bagatelles* for guitar, with Tom Kerstens even lighter and more volatile than Julian Bream, for whom they were written. With Israela Margalit injecting fire, the performance of the *Piano quartet* is also lighter and more volatile than that in the Chandos edition, though the extra weight of that rival adds up increasingly in the last two movements. Janice Graham is also the soloist in the *Violin sonata*, again fanciful and light, while bringing warmth and purposefulness to a work that can easily seem wayward. Though the three pieces were recorded in different venues, the sound is consistent, excellent in each.

Violin sonata.
(BB) *** ASV Quicksilva CDQS 6191 [id.]. McAslan, Blakely – ELGAR: *Violin sonata.* ***
(M) (**) EMI mono CDM5 66122-2. Yehudi Menuhin, Louis Kentner – ELGAR; WALTON: *Sonatas.* **(*)

Lorraine McAslan gives a warmly committed performance of Walton's often wayward *Sonata*, coping well with the sharp and difficult changes of mood in both of the two long movements. The romantic melancholy of the piece suits her well and, though the recording does not make her tone as rounded as it should be, she produces some exquisite pianissimo playing, making this a very impressive début recording. John Blakely is a most sympathetic partner, particularly impressive in crisply articulated scherzando passages. At its modest cost this is very highly recommendable.

The Menuhins commissioned this sonata to be premièred by the present performers, and it was dedicated jointly to their wives. It was completed in 1940 but the composer withdrew it, and the present two-movement version was recorded in 1950. First recordings are always special, and this one is no exception; but it is a pity that the very forward recording tends to treble emphasis, which is unflattering to Menuhin's upper register in its CD transfer.

(i) *Belshazzar's Feast. Henry V* (film score): *suite.*
(M) *** Carlton Dig. 30367 01862 [id.]. (i) Luxon, Brighton Festival Ch., L. Coll. Mus., RPO, Previn.

(i) *Belshazzar's Feast;* (ii) *Henry V: Passacaglia; The Death of Falstaff; Touch her soft lips and part. Siesta; The Wise Virgins* (ballet): suite.
(B) ** BBC Classics 15656 9161-2. (i) Stephen Roberts, BBC Singers, LPO Ch., BBC SO & Ch., Pritchard; (ii) ECO, Mackerras.

(i) *Belshazzar's Feast. In honour of the City of London.*
500♪ (M) *** EMI Dig. CD-EMX 2225; *TC-EMX 2225* [id.]. (i) David Wilson-Johnson; L. Symphony Ch., LSO, Hickox.

Richard Hickox not only conducts one of the most sharply dramatic accounts of *Belshazzar's Feast* currently available, even crisper and keener (if less jazzy) than Previn's superb (1971) EMI version; but he couples it with the one major work of Walton left unrecorded: his cantata, *In honour of the City of London.* With forces almost as lavish as those in the oratorio, its vitality and atmospheric colour come over on this record to a degree generally impossible in live performance.

André Previn's RPO digital version of Walton's oratorio brings a performance in some ways even sharper and more urgent than his fine earlier version for EMI with the LSO. The chorus, singing with biting intensity, is set realistically behind the orchestra, and though that gives the impression of a smaller group than is ideal, clarity and definition are enhanced. Benjamin Luxon – who earlier sang in Solti's Decca version – is a characterful soloist, but his heavy vibrato is exaggerated by too close a balance. The five-movement suite from Walton's film-music for *Henry V* makes an attractive coupling. Previn was the first conductor on record since Walton himself to capture the full dramatic bite and colour of this music, with the cavalry charge at Agincourt particularly vivid.

Sir John Pritchard's radio broadcast from the opening night of the Proms in 1984 brings an expansive performance, particularly so at the start. Tension is not helped with the choral sound focused rather vaguely, but the excitement of the occasion, as the piece builds towards its triumphant conclusion, is very well caught. The soloist, Stephen Roberts, is in slightly gritty voice. The Barbican performances of the shorter Walton pieces, with the ECO conducted by Sir Charles Mackerras, come in clearer, rather mellow sound. The brass is beautifully caught in the Bach arrangements, even if the fast movements are not as biting as they can be.

Warlock, Peter (1894–1930)

'Centenary collection': (i) *Capriol suite;* (ii) *Serenade to Frederick Delius on his 60th birthday*. Songs: (iii) *Adam lay ybounden;* (iv) *Autumn twilight;* (v) *Balulalow;* (vi) *Bethlehem Down;* (vii) *Captain Stratton's fancy;* (viii) *The Curlew* (song-cycle); (ix) *I saw a fair maiden;* (x) *The Lady's birthday* (arrangement); (v) *Pretty ring time;* (x) *The shrouding of the Duchess of Malfi;* (xi) *Where riches is everlasting;* (xii) *Yarmouth Fair.*

500♪ (M) *** EMI CDM5 65101-2 [id.]. (i) E. Sinf., Neville Dilkes; (ii) Bournemouth Sinf., Norman Del Mar; (iii) Robert Hammersley, Gavin Williams; (iv) Frederick Harvey, Gerald Moore; (v) Janet Baker, Philip Ledger; (vi) Guildford Cathedral Ch., Barry Rose; (vii) Robert Lloyd, Nina Walker; (viii) Ian Partridge, Music Group of London; (ix) Westminster Abbey Ch., Douglas Guest; (x) Baccholian Singers, Jennifer Partridge; (xi) King's College, Cambridge, Ch., Willcocks; (xii) Owen Brannigan, Ernest Lush.

A splendid anthology of Warlock. Opening with one of our favourite versions of the *Capriol suite* from the English Sinfonia under Neville Dilkes, brightly coloured and full of vigour, followed by Warlock's touchingly tender tribute to Delius, the selection ranges over a well-chosen selection of favourite songs, solo and choral. The other key item is *The Curlew*. Ian Partridge, with the subtlest shading of tone-colour and the most sensitive response to word-meanings, gives an intensely poetic performance, beautifully recorded. Among other performances those of Dame Janet Baker stand out, but many of the songs here are persuasively beautiful. At the very close of the recital Owen Brannigan restores our high spirits with his characteristically ebullient delivery of *Yarmouth Fair*. The transfers are consistently well managed.

Weber, Carl Maria von (1786–1826)

(i) *Andante and Hungarian rondo for bassoon and orchestra;* (ii; v) *Andante and Hungarian rondo for viola and orchestra;* (i) *Bassoon concerto in F, Op. 75;* (iii; v) *Horn concertino in E min., Op. 45;* (iv; v) *Romanza Siciliana for flute and orchestra in G min.*

(B) ** Carlton Turnabout 30371 0066-2. (i) George Zukerman, Württemberg CO, Jörg Faerber; (ii) Ulrich Koch; (iii) Francis Orval; (iv) Peter Thalheimer, (v) Hamburg SO, Günter Neidlinger – MOZART: *Bassoon concerto in B flat, K.191.* **(*)

The interest here, besides George Zukerman's account of the *Bassoon concerto* (which is somewhat insubstantial and without much orchestral interest) is the *Andante and Hungarian rondo*. This is more characteristic of Weber's usual instrumental and melodic facility and was originally written for viola; it was rescored for bassoon by the composer. Both versions are offered. But whereas Zukerman's account, alongside that of the *Concerto*, is excellent, the viola version as played by Ulrich Koch (who is not given a credit on the documentation) sounds somewhat lugubrious. The *Romanza siciliana* is much more persuasive, and the *Horn concertino* is played with impressive assurance by Francis Orval. It is written to encompass the horn's extreme limits of bravura; but the horn chords which are its special feature (the soloist sings one note, plays another and sets the instrument's natural harmonics resounding) sound rather comic. A useful collection, nevertheless.

Clarinet concertos Nos. (i) *1 in F min., Op. 73;* (ii) *2 in E flat, Op. 74;* (iii) *Clarinet concertino, Op. 26.* (iv) *Grand duo concertante for clarinet and piano, Op. 48.*

❁ *** ASV CDDCA 747 [id.]. Emma Johnson, (i–iii) ECO, cond. (i) Yan Pascal Tortelier; (ii) Gerard Schwarz; (iii) Sir Charles Groves; (iv) with Gordon Black.

With Paul Meyer's fine performances on Denon no longer available in the UK, we haved moved our Rosette over to ASV's judicious re-assembling of Emma Johnson's equally scintillating accounts of these three Weberian showpieces, made at different times and with different conductors, all of whom prove to be highly sympathetic to their young soloist. In her fine, inspired version of the *First Concerto* the subtlety of expression, even in relation to most of her older rivals, is remarkable, with pianissimos more daringly extreme and with distinctly persuasive phrasing in the slow movement, treated warmly and spaciously. In the sparkling finale she is wittier than almost any, plainly enjoying herself to the full.

The opening ritornello of the *Second Concerto* is expounded most promisingly by Schwarz, and her first entry shows the soloist as precocious as ever, her use of light and shade ever imaginative. The serene cantilena of the slow movement is raptly sustained, then she makes the listener smile with pleasure at her very perky first entry in the vivacious finale. The *Concertino*, in some ways the most delightful work of the three, especially its delicious finale, is hardly less beguiling; and as a bonus we are offered a brilliant and individually expressive account of the *Grand duo concertante* for clarinet and piano, which is comparable in length with the concertos and technically is equally ambitious. Here she finds an admirable partner in Gordon Black, who accompanies with equal flair.

Clarinet concerto No. 1 in F min., Op. 73.
*** EMI Dig. CDC5 55155-2 [id.]. Sabine Meyer, Dresden State O, Blomstedt – MOZART: *Clarinet concerto* etc.; STAMITZ: *Clarinet concerto No. 10.* ***

Sabine Meyer gives a lusciously seductive account of the Weber *Concerto*, tickling the ear with her passage-work, yet gently songful in the romantic slow movement. The finale chortles with glee, and the work's dramatic contrasts are emphasized by the large-scale accompaniment from the Dresden orchestra which she directs herself with aplomb. Warm, resonant recording, admirably balanced.

(i) *Clarinet concerto No. 1 in F min., Op. 73;* (ii) *Clarinet concertino in E flat, Op. 26;* (iii) *Clarinet quintet in B flat, Op. 34.*
(M) ** Carlton/Turnabout 30371 00222. David Glazer; (i) Württemberg CO, Faerber; (ii) Innsbruck SO, Robert Wagner; (iii) Kohon Qt – STAMITZ: *Clarinet concerto.* **(*)

A useful Turnabout anthology, reasonably priced and now given an attractive additional Stamitz coupling. The performances of both the concertante works are on the dry side (the recording is partly at fault, not flattering to David Glazer's timbre, which is made a trifle hard); the *Quintet* is agreeably warmer, if at the expense of clarity of texture. Here Glazer's timbre is flattered and this is distinctly enjoyable.

(i) *Piano concerto Nos. 1 in C, Op. 11;* (ii) *2 in E flat, Op. 32;* (i) *Konzertstück in F min., Op. 79; Polacca brillante (L'Hilarité), Op. 72.*
(M) **(*) Carlton/Turnabout 30371 00452. Hamburg SO, with (i) Maria Littauer, cond. Siegfried Köhler; (ii) Akiko Sakara, cond. Günter Neidlinger.

There are better, more modern CDs of almost all these works, but this pioneering Turnabout collection (extended to 70 minutes on CD) is full of personality and remains distinctly enjoyable for those willing to make some allowances for the early stereo recordings. Yet they sound far fuller and more vivid than they ever did on LP, especially the *Konzertstück* and the sparkling *L'Hilarité*. Maria Littauer's playing has plenty of life and bounce, and here the piano-tone is fully acceptable; in the *Second Concerto* it is harder. But Akiko Sakara's performance is not without charm and, while the orchestral playing brings less finesse, there is still a pleasing, unsophisticated vitality here.

Grand pot-pourri for cello and orchestra, Op. 20.
(B) **(*) Carlton Turnabout 30371 0023-2 [id.]. Thomas Blees, Berlin SO, Carl-August Bünte – DANZI: *Cello concerto in E min.;* STAMITZ: *Cello concerto in A.* **(*)

Weber's *Grand pot-pourri* (strange title) is in fact an attractive cello concerto in all but name, not so vital a work as the fine Danzi and Stamitz concertos with which it is coupled, but an interesting addition to the Weber catalogue. The four comparatively brief sections display the cello well, and Thomas Blees confirms the good opinions inspired by the Danzi work. Warm, committed playing from the orchestra, and a vivid balance; only the comparative lack of amplitude in the orchestral sound inhibits a full three-star recommendation. But this triptych is a genuine bargain.

Overtures: *Der Freischütz; Oberon.*
*** DG Dig. 449 216-2 [id.]. Dresden State O, Sinopoli – R. STRAUSS: *Feuersnot* etc. ***

The odd choice of Weber as coupling for Sinopoli's sumptuous Strauss may reflect the associations of both composers with Dresden. It is good to have fine, modern, digital recordings of these two masterly overtures. With finely moulded slow introductions leading to exhilarating allegros, the results are equally warm and refined.

Symphonies Nos. 1 in C; 2 in C, J.50/51. Die Drei Pintos: Entr'acte. Silvana: Dance of the young nobles; Torch dance. Turandot: Overture; Act II: *March;* Act V: *Funeral march.*
500♪ ❁ (BB) *** Naxos Dig. 8.550928 [id.]. Queensland PO, John Georgiadis.

Weber wrote his two symphonies in the same year (1807) and, though both are in C major, each has its own individuality. The witty orchestration and operatic character of the writing are splendidly caught in these sparkling Queensland performances, while in the slow movements the orchestral soloists (notably the languishing viola in the *Adagio* of No. 2) relish their solos, for all the world like vocal cantilenas. Weber's writing is often unpredictable, not least in the surprising closing bars of No. 2; and Georgiadis and his players present both works with striking freshness and spontaneity. The Naxos recording is in the demonstration class.

Clarinet quintet in B flat, Op. 34.
(M) **(*) EMI CDM5 65995-2 [id.]. Gervase de Peyer, Melos Ens. – BERWALD: *Septet* ***; SPOHR: *Double quartet.* **

The Melos performance, with its extrovert dotted rhythms in the first movement and almost bucolic Scherzo, is very assured, and Gervase de Peyer's bravura playing in the finale is memorable. However, there is a slight lack of warmth here, caused partly by the recording acoustic, which is vivid but slightly dry.

Abu Hassan (opera; complete).
(M) *** RCA 74321 40577-2. Schreier, Hallstein, Adam, Dresden State Op. Ch., Dresden State O, Heinz Rogner.

Abu Hassan has long been known for its sparkling little overture, but the comic opera which it introduces is just as compact, a one-Act piece, the product of Weber's early maturity (1810–11), which tells of an artful poet and his wife who fool all around them in approved Arabian Nights fashion. The numbers have a Mozartian wit, and the one snag of the original LP version has now disappeared on CD, for the extensive narrative and dialogue in German is cued separately and can therefore be omitted at will. The libretto with translation leaves out this dialogue, assuming that the non-German listener will dispense with it. The 1971 recording is transferred smoothly and pleasingly; it lacks something in sparkle, but that is no real deterrent to an otherwise suitably light-hearted presentation, with the chorus and solo voices naturally caught.

Der Freischütz (complete).
*** Teldec/Warner Dig. 4509 97758-2 (2) [id.]. Orgonasova, Schäfer, Wottrich, Salminen, Berlin R. Ch., BPO, Harnoncourt.
500♪ (M) *** EMI CMS7 69342-2 (2). Grümmer, Otto, Schock, Prey, Wiemann, Kohn, Frick, German Op. Ch., Berlin, BPO, Keilberth.

Harnoncourt's electrifying and refreshing version of this operatic warhorse was recorded live at concert performances in the Philharmonie in Berlin in 1995. That adds to the dramatic impact, and the engineers have done wonders in conveying the atmosphere of a stage performance rather than a concert one, not least in the Wolf's glen scene, helped by recording of a very wide dynamic range. Harnoncourt, with his background of period performances, clarifies textures and paces the drama well, making it sound fresh and new. The cast is first rate, with Orgonasova singing radiantly as Agathe, not just pure but sensuous of tone, floating high pianissimos ravishingly. Christine Schäfer, sweet and expressive, makes Aennchen into far more than just a soubrette character, and Erich Wottrich as Max is clear and firm, aptly heroic and unstrained, if hardly beautiful. The line-up of baritones and basses is impressive too, all firm and clear, contrasting sharply with one another, a team unlikely to be bettered today. A clear first choice among modern, digital recordings.

Keilberth's is a warm, exciting account of Weber's masterpiece which makes all the dated conventions of the work seem fresh and new. In particular the Wolf's glen scene on CD acquires something of the genuine terror that must have struck the earliest audiences. Elisabeth Grümmer sings more sweetly and sensitively than one ever remembers before, with Agathe's prayer exquisitely done. Lisa Otto is really in character, with genuine coquettishness. Schock is not an ideal tenor, but he sings ably enough. The Kaspar of Karl Kohn is generally well focused, and the playing of the Berlin Philharmonic has plenty of polish. The overall effect is immensely atmospheric and enjoyable.

Webern, Anton (1883–1945)

5 Movements, Op. 5; Passacaglia, Op. 1; 6 Pieces for orchestra, Op. 6; Symphony, Op. 21.
500♪ (M) *** DG 423 254-2 [id.]. BPO, Karajan.

Karajan's expressive refinement reveals the emotional undertones behind this seemingly austere music, and the results are riveting. Karajan secures a highly sensitive response from the Berlin Philharmonic, who produce sonorities as seductive as Debussy. A strong recommendation, with excellent sound.

Weill, Kurt (1900-1950)

Concerto for violin and winds, Op. 12.
** Decca 452 481-2 [id.]. Chantal Juillet, Berlin RSO, Mauceri – KORNGOLD: *Violin concerto*; KRENEK: *Violin concerto.* ***

Written in 1924, at about the same time as Stravinsky was writing his piano concerto, also with wind accompaniment, this concerto asks for rather tougher, less soft-grained treatment than it receives from the expressive, poetic Juillet, whose style is better attuned to the more openly romantic works with which it is coupled. Though this is an early work, the wind writing clearly points forward to the mature Weill, a point rather blurred over by the players here. Nevertheless a valuable companion-piece for the other two concertos, also written by Central Europeans who found refuge in America.

Kleine Dreigroschenmusik.
(M) *** DG 439 488-2 [id.]. L. Sinf., David Atherton – BUSONI: *Doktor Faust:* excerpt; HINDEMITH: *Mathis der Maler (Symphony)*; PFITZNER: *Palestrina: 3 Preludes.* **

The London Sinfonietta and David Atherton give a lively and idiomatic account of this popular score. This is thoroughly recommendable, and the 1975 recording sounds very good indeed. The interesting couplings undoubtedly enhance the value of this CD.

'Kurt Weill on Broadway': excerpts from: The Firebrand of Florence; Johnny Johnson (Johnny's song); Knickerbocker Holiday; Love Life; One Touch of Venus (Westwind).
*** EMI Dig. CDC5 55563-2 [id.]. Thomas Hampson, Elizabeth Futral, Jerry Hadley, Jeanne Lehman, L. Sinf. Ch., L. Sinf., John McGlinn.

Thomas Hampson's magical collection of Weill numbers is a revelation. It was bold of him and John McGlinn to concentrate on the least-known of Weill's Broadway scores, but it reveals what richness there is there, even while one can usually understand why the original shows often failed. So a full 40 minutes are devoted to Weill's biggest flop, *The Firebrand of Florence*, an offbeat biography of Benvenuto Cellini. It was simply that the timing was wrong for such a subject, in the closing months of the Second World War, and the selection here is a delight. It starts with the *Song of the Hangman*, which has more overtones of Gilbert and Sullivan in black mood than of earlier Weill. The very start of the disc on *One touch of Venus* establishes instantly that poetry is the keynote of the American Weill, in total contrast with his previous work with Brecht in Germany. One of the numbers in the 20-minute selection from *Love Life* (lyrics by Alan Jay Lerner) is a duet, *I remember it well*. Only later did Lerner adapt it for Gingold and Chevalier in *Gigi*, for here it is a dreamy slow waltz, with the lovers blissfully unaware of their contradictions. The only well-known number is *It never was you* from *Knickerbocker Holiday*, and even that comes as a duet, not a solo. Hampson sings superbly, with just a hint of roughness under pressure, regularly heightening emotions by taking a direct approach. McGlinn draws deeply sympathetic performances from the London Sinfonietta and the other soloists. Scholarly and informative notes add greatly to enjoyment, as well as the texts. The wonder is that Weill, previously so different a character, completely and imaginatively acclimatized himself to the demands of Broadway.

Widor, Charles-Marie (1844–1937)

Symphony No. 5 in F minor, Op. 42/1: Toccata.
(B) **(*) EMI forte CZS5 69328-2 (2). Fernando Germani – BACH: *Concertos* etc. **; FRANCK: *Chorales* etc. *(*)

The kind of tonal opulence obtained from the Selby Abbey organ suits the Widor showpiece better than Franck, and the delightful *Toccata* fairly bounces along. Those wanting the complete symphony from which the *Toccata* is extracted should turn to David Sanger on Saga (EG 3361-2 – see our main volume).

Wieniawski, Henryk (1835–80)

Violin concertos Nos. 1 in F sharp min., Op. 14; 2 in D min., Op. 22; Fantaisie brillante on themes from Gounod's Faust, Op. 20.
(BB) ** Naxos 8.553517 [id.]. Marat Bisengaliev, Polish Nat. RSO, Wit.

(i) *Violin concertos Nos. 1–2;* (ii) *Caprice in A min.* (arr. Kreisler); *Obertass-Mazurka, Op. 19/1; Polonaise de concert No. 1 in D, Op. 4; Polonaise brillante No. 2, Op. 21; Scherzo tarantelle, Op. 16.*
(M) *** EMI CDM5 66059-2 [id.]. Itzhak Perlman; (i) LPO, Ozawa; (ii) Samuel Sanders.

Those who have enjoyed the relatively well-known *Second Concerto* of this contemporary of Tchaikovsky should investigate this coupling of his two concertos. The *First* may not be as consistently memorable as the *Second*, but the central *Preghiera* is darkly intense, and the finale is full of the showmanship that was the mark of the composer's own virtuosity on the violin. Perlman gives scintillating performances, full of flair, and is excellently accompanied. The recording, from 1973, has similar admirable qualities to the companion remastered CD, from the same period, of Paganini's *First Concerto*. The sound is warm, vivid and well balanced, and all the clearer and more realistic in its compact disc format. It is preferable to Perlman's digital re-make of the *Second Concerto*. The mid-priced reissue includes a mini-recital of shorter pieces. The *Caprice* and *Scherzo-tarantelle* are both dazzling, but lose some of their appeal from Perlman's insistence on a microphone spotlight. There is both charm and panache in the account of the *Obertass-Mazurka*, and Samuel Sanders comes more into the picture in the introductions for the two *Polonaises*, although the violin still remains far too near the microphone.

Though Bisengaliev's initial entry in the *First Concerto* on high double stopping is dauntingly edgy and abrasive, that is happily not typical of the performances as a whole. Born in Kazakhstan in 1962 and a Leipzig prizewinner in 1988, he may not be quite as imaginative or individual as rivals like Perlman or Shaham, and he is less bold in bravura, but the security of his technique is formidable, with a fine tonal range. His gentle half-tones in the slow movements of both works are strikingly beautiful, magically caught in the full and vivid Polish recording. The *Faust Fantaisie brillante*, like most such pot-pourris, is charming but rather outstays its welcome. The shuffling of themes, not usually the obvious ones, is most skilful, prompting deftly pointed playing from Bisengaliev. Wit and the Katowice orchestra provide most sympathetic support. Good value, but with Perlman now available at mid-price this is very much a bargain choice.

Williams, Grace (1906–1977)

(i) *Symphony No. 2; Ballads for orchestra;* (ii) *Fairest of stars* (for soprano and orchestra).
*** Lyrita SRCS 327 [id.]. (i) BBC Welsh SO, Handley; (ii) Janet Price, LSO, Groves.

Grace Williams is best known for colourful, atmospheric works like the *Fantasia on Welsh nursery rhymes* – see below – and much of her early music reflects the folk-based approach instilled in her by her principal teacher, Ralph Vaughan Williams. But in this *Second Symphony*, her most ambitious orchestral work, written in 1956 when she was fifty, she aimed at greater astringency, just as Vaughan Williams himself had done in his *Fourth Symphony*. The writing is sharp and purposeful from the start, relaxing more towards lyricism in the slow movement (which produces an endearing pastoral oboe theme) and the finale with its darkly Mahlerian overtones. The *Ballades* of 1968, characteristically based on Welsh ballad and 'penillion' forms, also reveal the darker side of Grace Williams's writing, notably in the stark contrasts of the third ballad. The performances, originally recorded for radio, are expressive and convincing, and the recording good. *Fairest of stars* is later, written in 1973, specifically for this recording. It is a relatively tough setting of Milton, and is strongly sung by Janet Price. The recording is first class.

(i) *Carillons for oboe and orchestra;* (ii) *Trumpet concerto. Fantasia on Welsh nursery rhymes;* (iii) *Penillion;* (iv) *Sea sketches* (for string orchestra).
*** Lyrita SRCS 323 [id.]. (i) Anthony Camden: (ii) Howard Blake; both with LSO; (iii) RPO; all cond. Groves; (iv) ECO, David Atherton.

It is good to have this attractive programme of works restored to the catalogue, all by a woman composer who (rarely among twentieth-century feminist musicians) glowingly shows that she believes in pleasing the listener's ear. No barbed wire here, and no lack of imaginative resource either, particularly in the memorably individual *Sea sketches*, a masterly suite of five contrasted movements which catch the sea's unpredictability as well as its formidable energy. Grace Williams focuses her scene-painting more acutely than is common, while the two slow sections, the seductive *Channel sirens* and the *Calm sea in summer*, are balmily, sensuously impressionistic, the former taking a somewhat unpromising idea and turning it into true poetry. The other works here range attractively from the simple – and at one time quite well-known – *Nursery-rhyme Fantasia* (which is a good deal more than a colourfully orchestrated pot-pourri) through two crisply conceived concertante pieces, to *Penillion*, written for the National Youth Orchestra of Wales. 'Penillion' is the Welsh word for stanza, and this is a set of four colourful, resourceful pieces, easy on the ear but full of individual touches; although Grace Williams does not use any folk material, she retains the idea of a central melodic line (on the trumpet in the first two pieces) in stanza form. The trumpet and oboe concertante pieces – superbly played by soloists from the LSO of the early 1970s – both show the affection and understanding of individual instrumental timbre which mark the composer's work. Excellent performances throughout (especially the vivid sea music) and very good analogue sound. This CD is surely an ideal representation of the composer at her most appealing.

Williamson, Malcolm (born 1931)

Violin concerto.
(M) *** EMI CDM5 66121-2. Yehudi Menuhin, LPO, Adrian Boult – L. BERKELEY: *Concerto;* PANUFNIK: *Concerto.* ***

An eloquent work with much greater expressive power and depth than one usually associates with this sometimes facile Australian composer. Menuhin plays it beautifully and the LPO under Boult give generous support. The 1971 Abbey Road recording is admirably full, yet clear and detailed. A satisfying and thoughtful concerto, completing a triptych which is well worth exploring.

Wirén, Dag (1905–1986)

(i–ii) *Miniature suite* (for cello & piano), *Op. 8b;* (ii) (Piano) *Improvisations; Little suite; Sonatina, Op. 25; Theme and variations, Op. 5;* (iii) *3 Sea poems;* (iv; ii) *2 Songs from Hösthorn, Op. 13.*
*** BIS Dig. CD 797 [id.]. (i) Torleif Thedéen; (ii) Stefan Bojsten; (iii) Jubilate Ch., Riska; (iv) Christina Högman.

Dag Wirén was a miniaturist *par excellence* and few of the individual movements recorded here detain the listener for more than two or three minutes. The early (and inventive) *Theme and variations*, Op. 5, is the longest work. Although it is slight, the *Sonatina for piano* often touches a deeper vein of feeling than one might expect to encounter. Good performances from all concerned, and the usual truthful BIS recording.

Wolf, Hugo (1860–1903)

Spanisches Liederbuch (complete).
500♪ (M) *** DG 423 934-2 (2) [id.]. Schwarzkopf, Fischer-Dieskau, Moore.

In this superb CD reissue the sacred songs provide a dark, intense prelude, with Fischer-Dieskau at his very finest, sustaining slow tempi impeccably. Schwarzkopf's dedication comes out in the three songs suitable for a woman's voice; but it is in the secular songs, particularly those which contain laughter in the music, where she is at her most memorable. Gerald Moore is balanced rather too backwardly – something the transfer cannot correct – but gives superb support. In all other respects the 1968 recording sounds first rate, the voices beautifully caught. A classic set.

Ysaÿe, Eugène (1858–1931)

Sonatas for solo violin, Op. 27: Nos. 1 in G min.; 2 in A min.; 3 in D min. (Ballade); 4 in E min.; 5 in G; 6 in E.
*** Nimbus Dig. NI 7715 [id.]. Oscar Shumsky.
(M) *** Turnabout/Carlton 30371 00242. Ruggiero Ricci.

Oscar Shumsky is a player of the old school whose concerns are far removed from the hard-nosed virtuosity of some of today's players. His artistry is everywhere in evidence in this 1982 recording, in the authority and naturalness of his phrasing, the sweetness of his tone and the security of his technique. True, there are one or two moments of imperfect intonation, but there are very few performances (as opposed to recordings) where every note in these impossibly demanding pieces is in perfect place. It is all wonderfully musical and splendidly free as if Shumsky is improvising these pieces.

Ruggiero Ricci's recording on Turnabout is much earlier. No date is given, but it probably derives from the early 1960s. He was in excellent form and clearly enjoys Ysaÿe's allusions to – and indeed quotations from – the Bach *Sonatas* and *Partitas*, and the effective use of the *Dies irae*. He also conveys not only a sense of fantasy (especially in the second and final sonatas) but also the imaginative individuality of Ysaÿe's violin writing for the instrument of which he was a supreme virtuoso. Ricci's playing is technically impressive too, and although he is not flattered by the close balance the recording projects his playing vividly into the listener's room. Most enjoyable and a stimulating alternative to Shumsky, who remains first choice.

Zemlinsky, Alexander von (1871–1942)

Die Seejungfrau; Sinfonietta, Op. 23.
*** EMI Dig. CDC5 55515-2 [id.]. Cologne PO, Conlon.

James Conlon, a devotee of Zemlinsky's music, here conducts a tender and poetic reading of Zemlinsky's ripely sensuous symphonic poem based on Hans Christian Andersen's fairy-tale about the mermaid. At speeds rather more expansive than those in Chailly's brilliant and finely detailed Concertgebouw version, he brings out the atmospheric beauty with a more affectionate manner. The recording is atmospheric rather than sharply focused, giving warmth to the less sensuous writing in the much later *Sinfonietta* of 1934, with neo-classicism framing what is still essentially a late-Romantic work.

Die Seejungfrau (The Mermaid); (i) *Psalms 13, 23.*
*** Decca 444 969-2 [id.]. (i) Ernst Senff Chamber Ch.; Berlin RSO, Chailly.

Zemlinsky's three-movement symphonic fantasy, based on the Hans Andersen story of the mermaid, is comparable with Schoenberg's high-romantic *Pelleas und Melisande*, written at the same period, an exotic piece full of sumptuous orchestral writing. It is beautifully performed here, with ample recording to match. *Psalm 23* is warm in expression, airy and beautiful. But do not expect a religious atmosphere: this is sensuous music, beautifully played and sung, which uses the much-loved words of the Psalm as an excuse for musical argument rather than illumination. *Psalm 13*, presented first on the disc (following after the main work) but composed 25 years later, still reveals the urgency of Zemlinsky's inspiration – never a revolutionary in the way Schoenberg was, but always inventive and imaginative. The choral sound is not as full as that of the orchestra, but this remains an excellent introduction to the composer, now reissued as part of Decca's 'Entartete' series – music suppressed during the 1930s and 1940s.

Lyrische Symphonie, Op. 18.
**(*) DG Dig. 449 179-2 [id.]. Voigt, Terfel, VPO, Sinopoli.

(i) *Lyrische Symphonie, Op. 18;* (ii) Lieder: *Entbietung; Im Lenz; Letzte Bitte; Selige Stunde; Stromüber; Unter blühenden Bäumen.*
**(*) RCA Dig. 09026 68111-2 [id.]. (i) Orgonasova, Skovhus, N. German RSO, Flor; (ii) Bo Skovhus, Helmut Deutsch.

(i) *Lyrische Symphonie, Op. 18;* (ii) *Sinfonische Gesänge, Op. 20.*
*** Decca Dig. 443 569-2 [id.]. Concg. O, Chailly, with (i) Alessandra Marc, Håkan Hagegård; (ii) Willard White.

With the help of opulent and finely detailed recording of vivid immediacy, Chailly conducts a performance which on balance is the most powerful yet, moving and passionate on the one hand, rapt and poetic on the other. He may not be quite as sensuous as Sinopoli, but the thrust of argument is even more telling, with the Concertgebouw producing ravishing sounds in playing marked by pinpoint ensemble. Håkan Hagegård is an outstanding baritone soloist, as illuminating in his pointing of words as Fischer-Dieskau was on the much earlier Maazel version. Alessandra Marc may not have quite such clear diction, but she combines warmth and power with an ability to produce the most beautiful pianissimos. The generous fill-up confirms the recommendation, Zemlinsky's setting of the words from the anthology of black poets in German translation, *Afrika singt*. Written some 30 years after the symphony, it brings a much more astringent style which yet conveys powerful emotions, helped by the fine, intense singing of Willard White.

Sinopoli's is a sensuous, expansive reading of the *Lyric Symphony*, bringing out its links with Mahler's *Lied von der Erde*, and he follows the composer's instructions over having weighty soloists. Bryn Terfel is excellent, even if the darkness of the voice is not always an advantage in bringing out the meaning of the text by Rabindranath Tagore. The dramatic soprano, Deborah Voigt, rides easily over the richest textures, but she misses the beauty of the gentler moments, with the top of the voice spreading. One snag of this version, longer than its rivals, is that no coupling is provided.

Flor's reading of the *Lyric Symphony* is relatively lightweight and understated, but with much subtle detail, beautifully reproduced in this recording. Skovhus is a thoughtful baritone soloist, also restrained, while the subtlety and precision of Orgonasova's singing emphasizes the qualities which her rival on DG lacks, above all the most beautiful range of pianissimo. Skovhus is equally sensitive in the songs with piano which come as fill-up.

Der Zwerg (Der Geburtstag der Infantin).
(M) *** EMI CDM5 66247-2 (2) [id.]. Isokoski, Martinez, Kuebler, Collis, Cologne PO, Conlon.

Der Zwerg, 'The Dwarf', is the preferred title for the definitive edition of this most striking yet most disturbing of Zemlinsky's operas. The text here was prepared for Conlon from the autograph score, revised in detail by the composer, which he presented to the Library of Congress in Washington. The version recorded previously, following the successful production of the opera, first in Hamburg, later at Covent Garden and other opera houses, was seriously cut, which means that this one-Acter, at 85 minutes, is too long for a single CD. Hence the two-disc format at mid-price. It is well worth it, for this live recording of the first performance of the definitive score offers a most moving and intense experience. The libretto, based on the Oscar Wilde fairy-story, has its sinister side, with the Princess left totally unmoved at the end by the tragic death of the dwarf, the result of a broken heart on finding out how ugly he is. Zemlinsky himself, very short of stature, was cruelly rejected by Alma Mahler, which first prompted Zemlinsky to write the symphonic poem, *Der Seejungfrau*, and 20 years later this opera, each reflecting intense personal emotions. Deeply moving as Kenneth Riegel's performance is on the earlier recording, David Kuebler here has the advantage of a more beautiful, younger-sounding voice, making the portrait more tenderly moving, bringing out the character's vulnerability. Nor is passion lacking, and Soile Isokoski makes a an excellent Princess, with Iride Martinez also singing beautifully as her favourite maid. Live recording on the dry side, but still vivid and full.

Art of conducting

'The Art of conducting': Video: '*Great conductors of the past*' (Barbirolli, Beecham, Bernstein, Busch, Furtwängler, Karajan, Klemperer, Koussevitzky, Nikisch, Stokowski, Richard Strauss, Szell, Toscanini, Walter, Weingartner): BRUCKNER: *Symphony No. 7:* Rehearsal (Hallé O, Barbirolli). GOUNOD: *Faust: ballet music* (with rehearsal) (RPO, Beecham). Silent film (BPO, Nikisch). Richard STRAUSS: *Till Eulenspiegel* (VPO, Richard Strauss). WEBER: *Der Freischütz overture* (Paris SO, Felix Weingartner). WAGNER: *Tannhäuser overture* (Dresden State O, Fritz Busch). MOZART: *Symphony No. 40* (BPO, Bruno Walter). BRAHMS: *Symphony No. 2* (rehearsal) (Vancouver Festival O, Bruno Walter). BEETHOVEN: *Egmont overture; Symphony No. 9* (Philh. O, Klemperer). WAGNER: *Die Meistersinger overture*. SCHUBERT: *Symphony No. 8 (Unfinished)*. BRAHMS: *Symphony No. 4* (both rehearsals) (BPO, Furtwängler). VERDI: *La forza del destino overture; La Traviata: Coro di zingarelle*. RESPIGHI: *The Pines of Rome* (NBC SO, Toscanini). PURCELL (arr. STOKOWSKI): *Dido and Aeneas: Dido's lament*. RESPIGHI: *The Pines of Rome* (BBC SO). TCHAIKOVSKY: *Symphony No. 5* (NYPO) (both cond. Stokowski). BEETHOVEN: *Egmont overture* (Boston SO, Koussevitzky). TCHAIKOVSKY: *Violin concerto* (Heifetz, NYPO, Reiner). BEETHOVEN: *Symphony No. 7* (Chicago SO, Reiner). BRAHMS: *Academic festival overture*. BEETHOVEN: *Symphony No. 5* (Cleveland O, Szell). BEETHOVEN: *Symphony No. 5*. DEBUSSY: *La Mer* (BPO, Karajan). SHOSTAKOVICH: *Symphony No. 5* (rehearsal and performance) (LSO). MAHLER: *Symphony No. 4* (VPO; both cond. Bernstein). BEETHOVEN: *Symphony No. 9* (Philh. O, Klemperer). (Commentary by John Eliot Gardiner; Isaac Stern, Jack Brymer, Beecham, Menuhin, Oliver Knussen, Suvi Raj Grubb, Szell, Walter, Klemperer, Hugh Bean, Werner Tháruchen, Richard Mohr, Stokowski, Julius Baker, Karajan).
❀ *** Teldec/Warner VHS 4509 95038-3 [id.].

This extraordinary video offers a series of electrifying performances by the great conductors of our century, all seen and heard at their very finest. Enormous care has been taken over the sound, even in the earliest recordings, for it is remarkably full-bodied and believable. But most of all it is to watch conductors weaving their magic spell over the orchestra which is so fascinating. And sometimes they do it imperceptibly, like Richard Strauss conducting *Till Eulenspiegel* with apparent nonchalance, yet making music with the utmost aural vividness; Fritz Busch creating great tension in Wagner; Bruno Walter wonderfully mellow in Brahms; Klemperer in Beethoven hardly moving his baton and yet completely in control; Furtwängler rehearsing the finale of Brahms's *Fourth Symphony* with a tremendous flow of adrenalin; Toscanini the martinet in Verdi; Stokowski moulding gloriously beautiful sound with flowing movements of his hands and arms; and, most riveting of all, Bernstein creating enormous passion with the LSO in Shostakovich's *Fifth Symphony*. Of the many commentaries from other artists and various musicians, the experience of Werner Thäringen stands out. He was participating in a Berlin performance when he suddenly realized that the sound around him had changed: it had become uncannily more beautiful. Not understanding why, he looked to the back of the hall . . . and saw that Furtwängler had just walked in. The great Nikisch is seen conducting (on silent film) but not heard – and no one knows what the music was!

EMI Centenary Edition (1897–1997)

Disc 1: SCHUBERT: *Ave Maria* (Edith Clegg with piano; 1898). AUBER: *Manon Lescaut: C'est l'histoire amoureuse* (Ellen Beach with piano; 1899). MENDELSSOHN: *Violin concerto in E min.: Finale* (excerpt) (Jacques Jacobs with piano; 1899). DELIBES: *Les filles de Cadiz* (Marie Tempest with piano; 1901). TCHAIKOVSKY: *The Queen of Spades: It is nearly midnight now* (Medea Mei-Figner with piano; 1901). LEONCAVALLO: Pagliacci: *Vesti la giubba* (Enrico Caruso with Salvatore Cottone; 1902). GOUNOD: *Faust: Vous qui faites l'endormie* (Pol Plançon with Landon Ronald; 1902). BIZET: *Carmen: Habanera* (Emma Calvé with Landon Ronald; 1902). WAGNER: *Die Walküre: Leb' wohl, dukühnes, herrliches Kind* (Anton van Rooy with piano; 1902). SCHUBERT: *Heidenröslein, D.257* (Minnie Nast with piano; 1902); *Die Forelle, D.550* (Leopold Demuth with piano; 1902). SULLIVAN: *The Mikado: A more humane Mikado* (Richard Temple with piano; 1902). BRAHMS: *Hungarian dance No. 2* (Joseph Joachim with piano; 1903).

VERDI: *Otello: Esultate!* (Francesco Tamagno with piano; 1903). GRIEG: *Lyric pieces: To the spring, Op. 43/6* (composer; 1903). HATTON: *Simon the cellarer* (Sir Charles Santley with piano; 1903). SARASATE: *Caprice Basque, Op. 24* (composer with piano; 1903). DEBUSSY: *Pelléas et Melisande: Mes longs cheveux* (Mary Garden with composer; 1903). DONIZETTI: *Lucia di Lammermoor: Del ciel clemente* (Dame Nellie Melba with Philippe Gaubert, flute, and Landon Ronald; 1904). VERDI: *Otello: Era la notte* (Victor Maurel with piano; 1904). ROSSINI: *Il barbiere di Siviglia: Ecco ridente in cielo* (Fernando di Luca with Carlo Sabajno; 1904). GOLDMARK: *Die Königin von Saba: Magische Töne* (Leo Slezak with piano; 1905). MOZART: *Don Giovanni: Or sai chi l'onore* (Lilli Lehmann with piano; 1906). ROSSINI: *Il barbiere di Siviglia: Largo al factotum* (Titta Ruffo with O, Carlo Sabajno; 1906). BELLINI: *La Sonnambula: Ah, non credea mirarti* (Adelina Patti with Alfredo Barili; 1906). GOUNOD: *Roméo et Juliette: Je veux vivre dans ce rêve* (Geraldine Farrar with O; 1906). DONIZETTI: *Don Pasquale: Cheti, cheti, immantinente* (Giuseppe di Luca, Ferruccio Corradetti with piano; 1907).

Disc 2: BACH: *Partita No. 3: Prelude in E* (Joseph Szigeti, violin; 1908). ROSSINI: *Il barbiere di Siviglia: Una voce poco fa* (Elvira de Hidalgo with O; 1908). SMETANA: *Dalibor: Jac je mí* (Emmy Destinn with O; 1908). VERDI: *Aida: O patria mia* (Celestina Boninsegna with O, Carlo Sabajno; 1909). GOUNOD: *Mireille: O d'amor messagera* (Luisa Tetrazzini with O, Percy Pitt; 1909). VERDI: *Otello: Si, pel ciel marmoreo giuro!* (Giovanni Zenatello, Pasquale Amato with O, Edoardo Vitale; 1909). MOZART: *Die Zauberflöte: Infelice, sconsolata* (Frieda Hempel with O; 1911). SCHUBERT: *An die Musik, D.547* (Elena Gerhardt with Arthur Nikisch; 1911). TOSTI: *La serenata* (Mattia Battistini with Carlo Sabajno; 1911). WIENIAWSKI: *Mazurka in D, Op. 19/2* (Jan Kubelik, violin, with piano; 1911). VERDI: *Rigoletto: Questa o quella* (Ippolito Lazaro with O; 1911); *Un ballo in maschera: Saper vorreste* (Selma Kurz with O; 1911). RUBINSTEIN: *The Demon: Do not weep, child* (Feodor Chaliapin with O; 1911). CHOPIN: *Etude in F min., Op. 25/2* (Ignacy Jan Paderewski, piano; 1912). GIORDANO: *Andrea Chénier: Un dì all'azzurro spazio* (Bernardo de Muro with O, 1912). ROSSINI: *Il barbiere di Siviglia: Se il mio nome* (Dmitri Smirnov with piano; 1913). R. STRAUSS: *Ariadne auf Naxos: Es gibt ein Reich* (Maria Jeritza with O; 1913). DONIZETTI: *Lucia di Lammermoor: Tu che a Dio spiegasti l'ali* (Tito Schipa with O, Carlo Sabajno; 1913). BEETHOVEN: *Symphony No. 5: first movement* (BPO, Arthur Nikisch; 1913). SCHUBERT: *Die schöne müllerin: Das Wandern* (Sir George Henschel accompanying himself on the piano; 1914). ELGAR: *Land of hope and glory* (Dame Clara Butt with O, Arthur Godfrey; 1915).

Disc 3: MOZART: *Die Entführung aus dem Serail: Martern aller Arten* (Maria Ivogün with O, Manfred Gurlitt; 1919). SAINT-SAENS: *Marche militaire française* (composer, piano; 1919). CHARPENTIER: *Louise: Depuis le jour* (Marie-Louise Edvina with O; 1919). DVORAK (arr. KREISLER): *Slavonic dance No. 1* (Jacques Thibaud, violin, with Harold Craxton; 1922). MEYERBEER: *L'Africaine: O paradis* (Fernand Ansseau with O; 1922). VERDI: *Rigoletto: La donna è mobile* (Miguel Fleta with O, Carlo Sabajno; 1923); *Falstaff: L'onore! Ladri!* (Mariano Stabile with O; 1924). LISZT: *Liebestraum No. 3 in A flat* (Wilhelm Backhaus, piano; 1925). CHOPIN: *Waltz in D flat, Op. 64/1* (Vladimir de Pachmann, piano; 1926); *Prelude in G sharp min., Op. 28/12* (Alfred Cortot; 1926). R. STRAUSS: *Der Rosenkavalier film music* (excerpt) (L. Tivoli O, composer; 1926). PUCCINI: *La bohème: Donde lieta uscì* (Dame Nellie Melba with ROHCG O, Vincenzo Bellezza; 1926). HOLST: *The Planets: Mercury* (LSO, composer; 1926). BIZET: *Carmen: La fleur que tu m'avais jetée* (Georges Thill with O, Philippe Gaubert; 1927). MENDELSSOHN: *Oh for the wings of a dove* (Ernest Lough, Temple Church Ch., Sir George Thalben-Ball; 1927). TARREGA: *Tremolo study* (Andrés Segovia, guitar; 1927). QUILTER: *Now sleeps the crimson petal* (John McCormack with Edwin Schneider; 1927). WAGNER: *Die Walküre: Hojotoho!* (Frieda Leider, Friedrich Schorr with Berlin State Op. O, Leo Blech; 1927). VERDI: *Aida: Ritorna vincitor* (Florence Austral with O, Carlo Sabajno; 1927); *Il Trovatore: Ah! si, ben mio* (Aureliano Pertile with La Scala, Milan O, Carlo Sabajno; 1927). WAGNER: *Lohengrin: Einsam in trüben Tagen* (Elisabeth Rethberg with Berlin State Op. O, Fritz Zweig; 1927). VERDI: *Rigoletto: Bella figlia dell'amore* (Beniamino Gigli, Amelita Galli-Curci, Louise Homer, Giuseppe de Luca, NY Met. Op. O, Giulio Setti; 1927).

Disc 4: PUCCINI: *Turandot: In questa reggia* (Eva Turner with O, Stanford Robinson; 1928). J. STRAUSS, Jr: *Casanova: Nuns' chorus* (Anni Frind, Berlin Theatre Ch. and O, Ernest Hauke; 1928). BEETHOVEN: *Piano trio in B flat (Archduke): Scherzo* (Alfred Cortot, Jacques Thibaud, Pablo Casals; 1928). LEHAR: *Das Land des Lächelns: Dein ist mein ganzes Herz* (Richard Tauber, Berlin State O, composer; 1929). SULLIVAN: *HMS Pinafore: Never mind the why and wherefore* (Henry Lytton, George Baker, Elsie Griffin with O, Dr Malcolm Sargent; 1930). GRETCHANINOV: *Second Liturgy of St John Chrysostom: The Creed* (G. Pavlenko, Met. Paris Russian Church Ch., Nicolai Afonsky; 1931). VALVERDE: *Clavelitos* (Conchita Supervia with O; 1931). MUSSORGSKY: *Boris Godunov: Monologue* (Feodor Chaliapin, LSO, Max Steinmann; 1931). ELGAR: *Violin concerto in B min., Op. 61:* excerpt (Yehudi Menuhin, LSO, composer; 1932). BEETHOVEN: *Piano sonata No. 14 in C sharp min. (Moonlight): first movement* (Artur Schnabel;

1934). SCHUBERT: *Heidenröslein, D.257* (Elisabeth Schumann with Karl Alwin). HANDEL: *Solomon: The Arrival of the Queen of Sheba* (LPO, Sir Thomas Beecham; 1933). BACH: *Prelude and fugue in C min., BWV 847* (Edwin Fischer, piano; 1933). MOSS: *The Floral dance* (Peter Dawson with O, Clifford Greenwood; 1934). MASCAGNI: *Cavalleria rusticana: Voi lo sapete, o mamma* (Claudia Muzio with O, Lorenzo Molajoli; 1935). CHOPIN: *Etude in G flat, Op. 10/5* (Vladimir Horowitz, piano; 1935). WAGNER: *Die Walküre: Winterstürme . . . Du bist der Lenz* (Lauritz Melchior, Lotte Lehmann, VPO, Bruno Walter; 1935). BACH: *Toccata in D min. from BWV 565* (Albert Schweitzer, organ; 1935); *Goldberg variations, BWV 988: Aria* (Wanda Landowska, harpsichord; 1934). DINICU (arr. HEIFETZ): *Hora staccato* (Jascha Heifetz, violin, with Emanuel Bay; 1937). MOZART: *Don Giovanni: Questo è il fin di chi fa mal* (Ina Souez, Luise Helletsgruber, Audrey Mildmay, Koloman von Pataky, Salvatore Baccaloni, Roy Henderson, Glyndebourne O, Fritz Busch; 1936).

Disc 5: ROSSINI: *Overture La scala di seta* (BBC SO, Arturo Toscanini; 1938). BACH: *Cello suite No. 1, BWV 1007: Prelude* (Pablo Casals; 1938). CHOPIN: *Mazurka in B flat, Op. 7/1* (Artur Rubinstein; 1938). KREISLER: *Schön Rosmarin* (composer with Franz Rupp; 1938). MENDELSSOHN (arr. RACHMANINOV): *A Midsummer Night's Dream: Scherzo* (Benno Moiseiwitsch; 1939). YRADIER: *La Paloma* (Beniamino Gigli, Milan O da Camera, Ruggiero Ricci; 1939). BACH (arr. HESS): *Jesu, joy of man's desiring* (Dame Myra Hess; 1940). VERDI: *Otello: Esultate!* (Giacomo Lauri-Volpi, La Scala, Milan, O, Gino Marinuzzi; c. 1940). BEETHOVEN: *Overture The Ruins of Athens* (LSO, Felix Weingartner; 1940). BERLIOZ: *Les nuits d'été: Absence* (Maggie Teyte, LSO, Leslie Heward; 1940). PUCCINI: *Gianni Schicchi: O my beloved father* (Joan Hammond, Hallé, Leslie Heward; 1940). J. STRAUSS, Jr: *Pizzicato polka* (with Josef Strauss) (VPO, Hans Knappertsbusch; 1942). HANDEL: *Messiah: Rejoice greatly* (Isobel Baillie, Liverpool PO, Sir Malcolm Sargent; 1944). PUCCINI: *Turandot: Nessun dorma* (Jussi Björling with O, Nils Grevillius; 1944). BRAHMS: *Violin concerto in D: third movement* (Ginette Neveu, Philh. O, Issay Dobrowen; 1946). SAINT-SAENS: *The Swan* from *Carnival of the animals* (Pierre Fournier with Gerald Moore; 1946). MOZART: *Overture Le nozze di Figaro* (VPO, Herbert von Karajan; 1946). BRITTEN (arr.): *The Plough boy* (Peter Pears, Benjamin Britten; 1947). VERDI: *Aida: Ritorna vincitor* (Ljuba Welitsch, Philh. O, Josef Krips; 1947). THOMAS: *Mignon: Addio Mignon, fa core!* (Giuseppe di Stefano with O, Alberto Erede; 1947). MOZART: *Le nozze di Figaro: Non più andrai* (Erich Kunz, VPO, Herbert von Karajan; 1947).

Disc 6: PROKOFIEV: *Symphony No. 1 (Classical): Gavotte* (BPO, Sergiu Celibidache; 1948). VERDI: *Otello: Era la notte* (Tito Gobbi, RPO, Alberto Erede; 1948). MAHLER: *Kindertotenlieder: Oft denk' ich, sie sind nur ausgegangen* (Kathleen Ferrier, VPO, Bruno Walter; 1949). CHOPIN: *Waltz in A flat, Op. 42* (Dinu Lipatti; 1950). SCHUBERT: *Die schöne Müllerin: Ungeduld* (Dietrich Fischer-Dieskau, Gerald Moore; 1951). WAGNER: *Tristan und Isolde: Liebestod* (Kirsten Flagstad, Philh. O, Wilhelm Furtwängler; 1952). DEBUSSY: *Préludes, Book I: La cathédrale engloutie* (Walter Gieseking; 1953). PUCCINI: *Tosca: Vissi d'arte* (Maria Callas, La Scala, Milan, O, Victor de Sabata; 1953). MOZART: *Horn concerto in E flat, K.495: Rondo* (Dennis Brain, Philh. O, Herbert von Karajan; 1953). KHACHATURIAN: *Gayaneh: Sabre Dance* (Philh. O, composer; 1954). J. STRAUSS, Jr: *Die Fledermaus: Klänge der Heimat* (Elisabeth Schwarzkopf, Philh. O, Herbert von Karajan; 1955). WALTON: *Façade: Popular song* (Philh. O, composer; 1955). NOVACEK: *Perpetuum mobile* (Yehudi Menuhin with Gerald Moore; 1956). MOZART: *Le nozze di Figaro: Voi signor, che giusto siete* (Sena Jurinac, Graziella Sciutti, Monica Sinclair, Hugues Cuénod, Sesto Bruscantini, Franco Calabrese, Ian Wallace, Glyndebourne O, Vittorio Gui; 1955). BEETHOVEN: *Symphony No. 5 in C min.: first movement* (Philh O, Otto Klemperer; 1955). RAVEL: *Daphnis et Chloé, Suite No. 2: Danse générale* (Philh. O, Guido Cantelli; 1955/6). PUCCINI: *La Bohème: O soave fanciulla* (Victoria de los Angeles, Jussi Björling, Robert Merrill, RCA Victor O, Sir Thomas Beecham; 1956). GRIEG: *Piano concerto in A min.: opening* (Solomon, Philh. O, Herbert Menges; 1956). BRAHMS: *Ständchen* (Hans Hotter, Gerald Moore; 1956). RAVEL: *Piano concerto in G: Presto* (Arturo Benedetti Michelangeli, Philh. O, Ettore Gracis; 1957).

Disc 7: GLINKA: *Overture Ruslan and Ludmilla* (Philh. O, Constantin Silvestri; 1959). GOUNOD: *Faust: Et voïci le jardin charmant* (Victoria de los Angeles, Nicolai Gedda, Boris Christoff, O du Théâtre National de l'Opéra, André Cluytens; 1958). BEETHOVEN: *Piano sonata in E flat (Les Adieux), Op. 81a: Le Retour* (Claudio Arrau; 1959). MENDELSSOHN: *Violin concerto in E min.: Andante* (Yehudi Menuhin, Philh. O, Efrem Kurtz; 1958). MOZART: *Don Giovanni: Signor, guardate un poco* (Joan Sutherland, Elisabeth Schwarzkopf, Luigi Alva, Eberhard Wächter, Giuseppe Taddei, Philh. O, Carlo Maria Giulini; 1959). BACH: *Cello suite No. 3, BWV 1009: Sarabande* (Paul Tortelier; 1960). SMETANA: *The Bartered bride: Dance of the comedians* (RPO, Rudolf Kempe; 1961). MOZART: *Così fan tutte: Un'aura amorosa* (Alfredo Kraus, Philh. O, Karl Boehm; 1962). TCHAIKOVSKY: *Piano concerto No. 1 in B flat min.: opening* (John Ogdon, Philh. O, Sir John Barbirolli; 1962). PUCCINI: *La Bohème: Donde lieta usci* (Mirella Freni, Rome Op. O, Thomas Schippers; 1963). SATIE: *Gymnopédie No. 1* (Aldo Ciccolini; 1964). BIZET: *Carmen:*

Habanera (Maria Callas, René Duclos Ch., O du Théâtre National de l'Opéra, Georges Prêtre; 1964). PUCCINI: *Turandot: Principessa di morte* (Birgit Nilsson, Franco Corelli, Rome Op. O, Francesco Molinari-Pradelli; 1965). ELGAR: *Cello concerto in E min.: Adagio* (Jacqueline du Pré, LSO, Sir John Barbirolli; 1965). ELGAR: *Sea pictures: In haven (Capri)* (Janet Baker, LSO, Sir John Barbirolli; 1965). R. STRAUSS: *Vier letzte Lieder: Frühling* (Elisabeth Schwarzkopf, Berlin RSO, George Szell; 1965). PUCCINI: *Madama Butterfly: Bimba dagli occhi pieni di malia* (Renata Scotto, Carlo Bergonzi, Rome Op. O, Sir John Barbirolli; 1966). BEETHOVEN: *Piano sonata in C min. (Pathétique): Rondo* (Daniel Barenboim; 1966).

Disc 8: CHOPIN: *Polonaise in A flat (Heroic), Op. 53* (Maurizio Pollini; 1968). MASCAGNI: *L'Amico Fritz: O amore, o bella luce del core* (Luciano Pavarotti, ROHCG, Gianandrea Gavazzeni; 1968). CANTELOUBE: *Chants d'Auvergne: Baïlèro* (Victoria de los Angeles, Lamoureux O, Jean-Pierre Jacquillat; 1969). TRAD. (arr. WILLCOCKS): *Sussex carol* (King's College, Cambridge, Ch., Sir David Willcocks; 1969). BEETHOVEN *Triple concerto for violin, piano and cello in C: Largo* (David Oistrakh, Sviatoslav Richter, Mstislav Rostropovich, BPO, Herbert von Karajan; 1969). PUCCINI: *Turandot: Signore, ascolta* (Montserrat Caballé, LSO, Mackerras; 1970). ELGAR: *Enigma variations, Op. 36: Nimrod* (LSO, Sir Adrian Boult; 1970). SUSATO: *La Mourisque* (Early Music Consort of London, David Munrow; 1971). J. STRAUSS, Sr: *Radetzky march* (J. Strauss O, Vienna, Willi Boskovsky; 1971). GERSHWIN: *Rhapsody in blue: opening* (Gervase de Peyer, clarinet, LSO, André Previn, piano and cond.; 1971). PAGANINI: *Caprice in A min., Op. 1/24* (Itzhak Perlman; 1972). VERDI: *Aida: Celeste Aida* (Plácido Domingo, Philh. O, Riccardo Muti; 1974). HUMMEL: *Trumpet concerto in E flat: Rondo* (Maurice André, BPO, Herbert von Karajan; 1974). DVORAK: *Piano concerto in G min., Op. 33: third movement* (Sviatoslav Richter, Bav. State O, Carlos Kleiber; 1976). MOZART: *Eine kleine Nachtmusik, K.525: Allegro* (ASMF, Neville Marriner; 1976). BERLIOZ: *Symphonie fantastique: Marche au supplice* (O Nat. de France, Leonard Bernstein; 1976). YOUMANS (arr. HARRIS): *Tea for two* (Yehudi Menuhin and Stéphane Grappelli with rhythm; 1977).

Disc 9: BARBER: *Adagio for strings* (Phd. O, Eugene Ormandy; 1978). LEONCAVALLO: *Pagliacci: Vesti la giubba* (José Carreras, Philh. O, Riccardo Muti; 1979). GREGORIAN CHANT: *Veni sancte spiritus sequence (Mode 1)* (Benedictine Abbey of Silos Ch., Francisco Lara; 1980). BEETHOVEN: *String quartet in B flat, Op. 130: Cavatina* (Alban Berg Qt; 1982). MOZART: *Così fan tutte: Soave sia il vento* (Margaret Marshall, Agnes Baltsa, José van Dam, VPO, Riccardo Muti; 1982). C. P. E. BACH: *Harpsichord concerto in D: Allegretto* (Bob van Asperen, Melante Amsterdam; 1981/2). JOSQUIN DES PRES: *El grillo* (Hilliard Ens.; 1983). WILLAERT: *Vecchie letrose* (Montserrat Figueras, Hespèrion XX, Jordi Savall; 1983). MONTEVERDI: *Vespers (1610):* excerpt (Taverner Consort, Ch. and Players, Andrew Parrott; 1983/4). VIVALDI: *The Four Seasons: Spring (Allegro)* (Anne-Sophie Mutter, VPO, Herbert von Karajan; 1984). MOZART: *Requiem in D min.: Dies irae* (Paris Ch. and O, Daniel Barenboim; 1984). OFFENBACH: *La Belle Hélène: Amours divins* (Jessye Norman, Capitole de Toulouse Ch. and O, Michel Plasson; 1984). WEBER: *Clarinet concertino in E flat, Op. 26: Allegro* (Sabine Meyer, Dresden State O, Herbert Blomstedt; 1985). GERSHWIN: *Porgy and Bess: Summertime* (Dame Kiri Te Kanawa, NY Ch., New Princess Theatre O, John McGlinn; 1986). BEETHOVEN: *Symphony No. 8 in F: last movement* (L. Classical Players, Roger Norrington; 1986). VERDI: *Requiem: Sanctus* (La Scala, Milan, Ch. and O, Riccardo Muti; 1987). KERN: *Show Boat: Make believe* (Frederica von Stade, Jerry Hadley, L. Sinf., John McGlinn; 1987). BEETHOVEN: *Romance for violin and orchestra No. 2* (Frank Peter Zimmermann, ECO, Jeffrey Tate; 1987). MAHLER: *Symphony No. 8: conclusion* (LPO and Ch., Klaus Tennstedt; 1986).

Disc 10: GERSHWIN: *Porgy and Bess: Bess, you is my woman now* (Willard White, Cynthia Hayman, LPO, Sir Simon Rattle; 1988). WAGNER: *Die Walküre: Loge, hör! Lausche hieher!* (James Morris, Bav. RSO, Bernard Haitink; 1988). MEYERBEER: *L'Africaine: O paradis* (Plácido Domingo, ROHCG O, John Barker; 1988). SCHUBERT: *Winterreise: Der Lindenbaum* (Olaf Bär, Geoffrey Parsons; 1988). HUMPERDINCK: *Hansel und Gretel: Der kleine Sandmann bin ich . . . Abends, will ich schlafen geh'n* (Barbara Hendricks, Barbara Bonney, Anne Sofie von Otter, Bav. RSO, Jeffrey Tate; 1989). ORFF: *Carmina Burana: Ecce gratum* (LPO and Ch., Franz Welser-Möst; 1989). BRUCH: *Violin concerto No. 1 in G min., Op. 26: Finale* (Kyung-Wha Chung, LPO, Klaus Tennstedt; 1990). MOZART: *Don Giovanni: Or sai chi l'onore* (Cheryl Studer, VPO, Riccardo Muti; 1990). MEYERBEER: *Chant des moissonneurs vendéens* (Thomas Hampson, Geoffrey Parsons; 1991). IVES: *Set No. 1: Calcium light music* (Ens. Modern, Ingo Metzmacher; 1991). BACH: *Cello suite No. 6, BWV 1012: Gigue* (Mstislav Rostropovich; 1992). BRAHMS: *Hungarian dance No. 2* (Sarah Chang, violin, with Jonathan Feldman; 1993). SCARLATTI: *Sonata in G, K.55* (Christian Zacharias, piano; 1993). RACHMANINOV: *Symphony No. 2 in E min.: Adagio* (opening) (St Petersburg PO, Mariss Jansons; 1993). SCHUBERT: *Piano sonata in A, D.959: Andantino* (Stephen Kovacevich; 1994). SCHUMANN: *Piano quintet in E flat, Op. 44: Scherzo* (Martha Argerich, Dora Schwarzberg, Lucy Hall, Nobuko Imai, Mischa Maisky; 1994). MASSENET: *Werther: Toute mon âme est là! . . . Pourquoi me réveiller?* (Roberto Alagna, LPO, Richard Armstrong; 1995). WAGNER: *Die Meistersinger: Verachtet mir die Meister nicht* (Bav. State Op. Ch. and O, Wolfgang Sawallisch; 1993).

Disc 11: A Documentary History of EMI Classics narrated by Thomas Hampson.
❁ (M) *** EMI CMS5 66182-2 (10 bonus disc) [id.].

It is impossible to comment in detail on an anthology as fascinatingly wide-ranging as this EMI centenary celebration, opening with the very first Schubert song to be recorded (*Ave Maria*) in Maiden Lane, London, in 1898 and ending with the closing scene from a modern, digital, stereo recording of Wagner's *Die Meistersinger*, conducted by Sawallisch, recorded in Munich 95 years later. The year-by-year history of the company, detailing its achievements, is admirably narrated by Thomas Hampson on the bonus CD (which is very well selected indeed). Initially, one might pick out one of Caruso's very first records (*Vesti la giubba* from *Pagliacci*), made in 1902, while the accompanying booklet is sprinkled with other celebrated names from the gramophone's early years – the violinist Joachim, friend of Brahms, Edvard Grieg and Pablo de Sarasate, and countless famous singers from the 'golden age'. Arthur Nikisch conducts the first movement from Beethoven's *Fifth* (the first symphony to be recorded complete in 1913), and we hear Kreisler play his own music, the young Menuhin in Elgar and making the first ever recording of Bach's solo *Sonatas and Partitas* in 1936. There is the illustrious soprano, Isobel Baillie, Peter Dawson's unforgettable *Floral dance*, Flagstad, Christoff, Melchior, Gigli, Cortot, Gieseking, Heifetz, Horowitz, Lipatti, Schnabel, Solomon, Toscanini, and so on. Most remarkable of all is an excerpt (on the Hampson commentary disc) of Sir Thomas Beecham's experimental stereo recording – of Mozart's *Jupiter Symphony* – in 1934, and Bruno Walter conducting Mahler before he fled Nazi Germany; and, of course, Furtwängler, who stayed behind. Later on we come to Kathleen Ferrier, Callas, Schwarzkopf, De los Angeles, Fischer-Dieskau, the horn player, Dennis Brain, in Mozart, Perlman, Domingo, Cantelli conducting Tchaikovsky's *Fifth Symphony* for one of the first EMI mono LPs, Ormandy in Philadelphia, Marriner and his Academy. More composers appear: Bartók at the piano, Walton and Khachaturian conducting their own works. The first symphony to be recorded in stereo was Prokofiev's *Seventh*, directed by Nicolai Malko in 1955. As we come nearer our own time, names become more and more familiar, if no less legendary: Barbirolli, Janet Baker, Kiri te Kanawa, Thomas Hampson, Jacqueline du Pré, Boult, Karajan, Klemperer, Kempe, Pavarotti, Previn, Kyung Wha Chung, Bernstein, Rostropovich, Kovacevich, Alagna. This is an extraordinarily rich treasury to be dipped into. It is well documented and very beautifully packaged indeed in a strong box in which each sleeved disc has its own slot. A remarkable achievement.

'The Originals: Legendary performances from the DG Catalogue', Volume II

'The Originals' (complete).
(M) **(*) DG mono/stereo 449 710 (20) [id.].

BACH: *Cello suites Nos. 1–6.*
Pierre Fournier (449 711-2).

BRAHMS: *Symphonies Nos. 1–4.*
BPO, Eugen Jochum ((mono) 449 715-2 (2)).

(i) BRUCKNER: *Symphony No. 4 in E flat.* (ii) SIBELIUS: *Night ride and sunrise.*
(i) BPO; (ii) Bav. RSO; Eugen Jochum ((stereo/ mono) 449 718-2).

CHOPIN: *Piano concerto No. 1 in E min., Op. 11.* LISZT: *Piano concerto No. 1 in E flat.*
Martha Argerich, LSO, Abbado (449 719-2).

(i) FRANCK: *Symphony in D min.* (ii) MENDELSSOHN: *Symphony No 5 in D (Reformation), Op. 107.*
(i) Berlin RSO; (ii) BPO; Maazel (449 720-2).

GRIEG: *Lyric pieces: Op. 12/1; Op. 38/1; Op. 43/1–2; Op. 47/2–4; Op. 54/4–5; Op. 57/6; Op. 62/4 and 6; Op. 65/5; Op. 68/2–3 and 5; Op. 71/1, 3, 6–7.*
Emil Gilels (449 721-2).

MAHLER: *Symphony No. 1;* (i) *Lieder eines fahrenden Gesellen.*
(i) Dietrich Fischer-Dieskau; Bav. RSO, Kubelik (449 735-2).

MOZART: *Piano concertos Nos.* (i) *19 in F, K.459;* (ii) *27 in B flat, K.595. Piano sonata No. 2 in F, K.280.*
Clara Haskil; (i) BPO; (ii) Bav. State O; (i–ii) Ferenc Fricsay ((mono/stereo) 449 722-2).

MOZART: Concert arias: *Ah! lo previdi . . . Ah t'invola, K.272; A questo seno . . . Or che il cielo, K.374; Alma grande e nobil core, K.578; Betracht dies Herz und frage mich, K.42; Vado, ma dove? o Dei!, K.583; Bella mia fiamma . . . Resta, o cara, K.528; Misera, dove son! . . . Ah! non son io che parlo, K.369.*
Gundula Janowitz, VSO, Wilfried Boettcher (449 723-2).

RESPIGHI: *The Fountains of Rome; The Pines of Rome; Ancient airs and dances: suite No. 3 for strings.* BOCCHERINI: *Quintettino.* ALBINONI: *Adagio in G min.* (arr. GIAZOTTO).
BPO, Karajan (449 724-2).

R. STRAUSS: *Ein Heldenleben, Op. 40.* WAGNER: *Siegfried idyll.*
BPO, Karajan (449 725-2).

TCHAIKOVSKY: *Swan Lake: suite; Sleeping Beauty: suite; Nutcracker suite.*
BPO, Rostropovich (449 726-2).

LEONCAVALLO: *I Pagliacci* (complete).
Carlyle, Bergonzi, Taddei, Panerai, La Scala, Milan, Ch. & O, Karajan (449 727-2).

MOZART: *Le nozze di Figaro* (complete).
Janowitz, Mathis, Troyanos, Janowitz, Fischer-Dieskau, Prey, German Op. Ch. & O, Boehm (449 728-2 (3)).

VERDI: *Macbeth* (complete).
Cappuccilli, Verrett, Ghiaurov, Domingo, La Scala, Milan, Ch. & O, Abbado (449 732-2 (2)).

As before, the second batch (20 discs instead of 29) of 'Originals' comes packaged in a stiff cardboard container and for anyone purchasing the complete set there is a reduction in price. Once again each CD looks like a miniature reproduction of the original vinyl LP, and again the transfers show a distinct improvement over earlier issues of the same music on CD. While many of these discs are self-recommending, there are some controversial inclusions, notably Jochum's mono set of the Brahms symphonies, undoubtedly fascinating and in many ways compelling but wayward enough to cause irritation for some listeners. The remastering of the mono recordings from the 1950s, however, here quite transforms the impact of the orchestra, compared with the original LPs. All these reissues are considered separately under their composer entries, and this is the most sensible way to approach them.

'The Originals: Legendary performances from the DG Catalogue', Volume III

'The Originals' (complete).
(B) **(*) DG 449 736-2 (14) [id.].

As with previous volumes, this series of Originals comes packaged in a box, with a considerable saving if the whole set is purchased. However, even more than with the earliest collection, the reader is best advised to make individual choices, for not everything here is of equal appeal. Each recording is discussed in detail under its relevant composer entry or entries. Karajan's Mendelssohn disc and Abbado's superb *Simon Boccanegra* stand out, and should not be missed.

(i) BEETHOVEN: *Missa solemnis in D, Op. 123.* REGER: *Variations and fugue on a theme by Mozart, Op. 132.*
BPO, Boehm, with (i) Stader, Radev, Dermota, Greindl, St Hedwig's Cathedral Ch. (449 737-2) (2).

BEETHOVEN: *Piano sonatas Nos. 28 in A, Op. 101; 29 in B flat (Hammerklavier), Op. 106; 30 in E, Op. 109; 31 in A flat, Op. 110; 32 in C min., Op. 111.*
Maurizio Pollini (449 740-2) (2).

MENDELSSOHN: *Symphonies Nos. 3 in min. (Scottish), Op. 56; 4 in A (Italian), Op. 90; Overture: The Hebrides (Fingal's Cave).*
BPO, Karajan (449 743-2).

(i) MILHAUD: *Les Choéphores.* HONEGGER: *Symphony No. 5 (Di tre re).* ROUSSEL: *Bacchus et Ariane* (ballet): *suite No. 2, Op. 43.*
LOP, Markevitch, with (i) Moizan, Bouvier, Rehfuss, Nollier, University Ch. (449 748-2).

MOZART: *Die Zauberflöte* (complete).
Lear, Peters, Wunderlich, Fischer-Dieskau, Crass, Hotter, BPO, Boehm (449 749-2) (2).

PROKOFIEV: (i) *Piano concerto No. 5 in G, Op. 55. Piano sonata No. 8 in B flat, Op. 84; Visions fugitives, Op. 22/3, 6 & 9.*
Sviatoslav Richter, with (i) Warsaw PO, Rowicki (449 744-2).

SCHUBERT: *Symphonies Nos. 3 in D, D.200; 8 in B min. (Unfinished), D.759.*
VPO, Carlos Kleiber (449 745-2).

SCHUBERT: (i) *Piano quintet in A (Trout), D.667. String quartet No. 14 in D min. (Death and the Maiden), D.810.*
Amadeus Qt, (i) with Gilels, Zepperitz (449 746-2).

SCHUMANN: *Dichterliebe, Op. 48.* BEETHOVEN: *Zärtliche Liebe; Adelaide; Resignation; Der Kuss.* SCHUBERT: *An Silvia; Lied eines Schiffers an die Dioskurern; Liebhaber in allen Gestalten; Der Einsame; Im Abendrot; Ständchen (Leise flehen meine Lieder); An die Laute; Der Musensohn; An die Musik.*
Fritz Wunderlich, Hubert Giesen (449 747-2).

VERDI: *Simon Boccanegra* (complete).
Freni, Cappuccilli, Carreras, Ghiaurov, Van Dam, Foiani, La Scala, Milan, Ch. and O, Abbado (449 752-2) (2).

Heifetz, Jascha (violin)

'The Heifetz Collection'

RCA's '*Heifetz collection*' celebrates an extraordinary legacy of recordings, extending to 65 CDs in 46 volumes, representing a supreme artist who, by common consent among his peers, was the most gifted violinist of the twentieth century, and probably of all time. His recorded repertoire was remarkably wide and quite adventurous, although he did not seek to interpret experimental, avant-garde works. He made many first recordings and always had something fresh to contribute to established masterpieces. Often his unmatched technical facility encouraged him to choose tempi faster than usual, but never simply for the sake of display: he always put the composer first. This collection was originally issued as an unwieldy if reasonably priced complete set, but the discs are currently being reissued separately, or in groups, at mid-price. The whole series should be available during the lifetime of this book, but we have listed only the CDs we have been able to lisen to. John Pfeifer has obviously done his best with sometimes recalcitrant originals, often unflatteringly closely balanced, while some background noise remains on the 78 transfers.

Volume 3: GLAZUNOV: *Méditation.* PAGANINI: *Caprice No. 20* (both with Arpád Sándor). VIEUXTEMPS: *Violin concerto No. 4 in D min., Op. 314.* WIENIAWSKI: *Violin concerto No. 2 in D min., Op. 22* (both with LPO, Barbirolli); *Polonaise brillante No. 1 in D, Op. 4.* CYRIL SCOTT: *Tallahassee suite.* FALLA: *Danza española No. 1.* GRIEG: *Violin sonata No. 2 in G, Op. 13* (all with Emanuel Bay). POULENC: *Mouvement perpétuel.* DINICU: *Hora staccato.* SZYMANOWSKI: *Roxana's song.* BAZZINI: *La ronde des lutins.* BACH: (Unaccompanied) *Violin sonatas Nos. 1, BWV 1001; 3, BWV 1005.*
(M) (**) RCA mono 09026 61734-2 (2) [id.].

The very first item here (persuasively recorded in 1934) offers a tenderly romantic performance of the Glazunov *Méditation* and establishes not only the sophistication of detail but also the warmth and beauty of Heifetz's lyricism, and this is borne out in the Wieniawski and Vieuxtemps *Concertos*, recorded a year later. The Wieniawski *Andante* is ravishing and the first violin entry in the Vieuxtemps quite magical. Although the solo instrument is far too close, it is caught fairly truthfully, if sounding a bit scratchy at times (notably in the Vieuxtemps dashing Scherzo), and it is a pity that Barbirolli's fine accompaniments are made to sound so papery, except in the slow movements. Among the other encores, Poulenc's *Mouvement perpétuel* has charm but is a shade too schmaltzy; the brilliant *Hora staccato* (1935) and the transcribed Szymanowski song both sound as if the microphone was inside the solo instrument! Bazzini's *La ronde des lutins* is also right up front, but the sound is cleaner (1937). Cyril Scott's *Tallahassee suite* is a novelty these days, with only the *Danse nègre* remembered. Heifetz makes both the last two movements memorable by playing the tune lyrically in harmonics. The two Bach unaccompanied *Violin sonatas* are remarkably consistent with the later versions (in Volume 17), but the sound is understandably rougher. The Grieg *G major Sonata* is a delightful performance but suffers from a degree of wow; otherwise the sound is good, apart from the exaggerated violin balance.

Volume 4: FAURE: *Violin sonata No. 1 in A, Op. 13*. BRAHMS: *Violin sonata No. 2 in A, Op. 100* (both with Emanuel Bay); *Violin concerto in D, Op. 77*. PROKOFIEV: *Violin concerto No. 2 in G min., Op. 63* (both with Boston SO, Koussevitzky). SAINT-SAENS: *Introduction and rondo capriccioso, Op. 28* (with LPO, Barbirolli); *Havanaise, Op. 83*. SARASATE: *Zigeunerweisen, Op. 20* (both with LSO, Barbirolli).
(M) (**) RCA mono 09026 61735-2 (2) [id.].

The piano introduces the Fauré *Sonata* with timbre which is dry and uningratiating, then almost immediately Emanuel Bay becomes subservient to the very bright, forward violin-sound and the overall effect robs the work of much of its charm, although the lyrical finale comes off well. The Brahms *Sonata* (also from 1936) is ill-focused at the opening, but the warmth of the performance means one is willing to make allowances for the technical disabilities. The *Introduction and rondo capriccioso* of Saint-Säens (1935), the *Havanaise* and Sarasate's *Zigeunerweisen* (both 1937) were recorded at Abbey Road. They are all ravishingly played (Heifetz at his finest), with scintillating finales (especially the Sarasate) and, provided one accepts an orchestra which makes less impact than the violin, the sound is quite acceptable. Again the solo violin dominates the Prokofiev (1937) and Brahms (1937) *Concertos* (with Koussevitzky), and in the former the close microphones negate the Symphony Hall ambience, so it is the slow movement which makes the strongest impression. The Brahms *Concerto* is sonically very much more successful, with the Boston Symphony shrill-sounding but effectively in the picture, and one can respond to what is undoubtedly an outstanding performance, with a thrilling finale.

Volume 5: BRAHMS: *Double concerto for violin, cello and orchestra, Op. 102* (with Feuermann, Phd. O, Ormandy). BEETHOVEN: *Violin concerto in D, Op. 61* (with NBC SO, Toscanini). WALTON: *Violin concerto in B min.* (with Cincinnati SO, Goossens). CHAUSSON: *Concert for violin, piano and string quartet, Op. 21* (with Sanromá, Musical Art Qt). PROKOFIEV: *Gavotte, Op. 32/3; March, Op. 12/1*. RACHMANINOV: *Etude-tableau, Op. 39/2; Daisies; Oriental sketch* (all with Emanuel Bay).
(M) (***) RCA mono 09026 61736-2 (2) [id.].

The Heifetz–Feuermann partnership was justly celebrated in their 1939 recording of the Brahms *Double concerto*, especially for the eloquence of the *Andante*. Ormandy, already proving himself a natural accompanist, provides passionately committed support, and the acoustic of the Philadelphia Academy helps the orchestra to sound relatively expansive. The overall balance is surprisingly well managed. The 1940 set of the Beethoven *Violin concerto* used the notorious NBC Studio 8-H but, although dry, the sound is not thin, and again the balance is very convincing for this is a partnership of equals (the only time these two great musicians recorded together) and Toscanini makes sure the orchestra is well in the picture. The slow movement is Elysian and the finale sparkles, the pacing just about perfect. It was Heifetz who commissioned the Walton *Concerto* and who gave the first performance, as well as making this inspirational wartime recording of the original score, which has never been surpassed, in 1941. Heifetz's contribution is glorious and the partnership with Goossens (one of the most underrated of conductors) produces the feeling of total spontaneity. The Scherzo is dazzling, but it is the work's bitter-sweet lyricism that the soloist captures so seductively. The sound, using the Music Hall in Cincinnati, is worthy of the playing, by the standards of those days. The atmospheric Chausson *Concert* is well chosen to make a foil for the Walton, the delicacy of the central movements well observed. The latter recording, made in the appropriately named Lotus Club (in New York), is confined but suitably intimate. The encores are agreeable, with the song-transcription, *Daisies*, the most striking. But altogether this compilation is indispensable.

Volume 6: Transcriptions/arrangements: BACH: *Concerto for two violins, BWV 1043* (with RCA Victor CO, Waxman); *English suite No. 6: Gavottes*. CASTELNUOVO-TEDESCO: *Sea Murmurs; Tango*. RAVEL: *Valses nobles et sentimentales, Nos. 6, 7*. MEDTNER: *Fairy tale, Op. 20/1*. DEBUSSY: *La chevelure; La fille aux cheveux de lin; Il pleure dans mon coeur*. FALLA: *Jota; Pantomime*. NIN: *Cantilène asturienne*. MILHAUD: *Corcovado*. BAX: *Mediterranean*. HALFFTER: *Danza de la gitana*. POLDOWSKI: *Tango*. BEETHOVEN: *German dance No. 6*. MENDELSSOHN: *Piano trio in D min., Op. 49: Scherzo. Song without words, Op. 19/1*. CHOPIN: *Nocturne, Op. 72/1*. ARENSKY: *Concerto in A min.: Tempo di valse* (with Emanuel Bay). RIMSKY-KORSAKOV: *Flight of the bumblebee*. MOZART: *Divertimento No. 17, K.334: Minuet*. KORNGOLD: *Much Ado About Nothing: Garden scene; Holzapfel und Schlehwein (March)* (all with Emanuel Bay). SARASATE: *Romanza andaluza*. SCHUBERT: *Piano sonata, D.850: Rondo*. TANSMAN: *Mouvement perpétuel* (all with Emanuel Bay). BRUCH: *Scottish fantasy* (with RCA Victor SO, Steinberg). VIEUXTEMPS: *Violin concerto No. 5, Op. 37* (with LSO, Sargent).
(M) (***) RCA mono 09026 61737-2 (2) [id.].

The outer movements of the Bach *Double concerto* are pretty fast. Heifetz plays both solo parts, and to have him twice in the slow movement, so to speak, singing his cantabile line with an equally ravishing response, forestalls any criticism about lack of contrast. This was achieved by recording the principal solo part on film and adding the second part to the recording with the soloist using earphones (Heifetz never repeated the exercise). Franz Waxman, the Hollywood composer, conducts the accompaniments with real zest. Castelnuovo-Tedesco's *Tango* falls less easily on the ear than it might when it follows so closely on the heels of the Bach finale but, once one has adjusted, the following series of sweetmeats will surely titillate even the most jaded palate, especially Debussy's haunting *Il pleure dans mon coeur* and the seductive *Pantomime* from Falla's *El amor brujo* (later, the same composer's glittering *Jota* ends the programme). Mendelssohn's *Scherzo* from the *D minor Piano trio* and the Arensky *Tempo di valse* bring delightful contrasting insouciance, while Rimsky's *Bumblebee* has seldom buzzed so vociferously or flown at such velocity. All these items were recorded with the faithful Emmanuel Bay in October 1946, and the sound is generally quite sophisticated. The second disc opens with a further batch of encores. Heifetz is equally charismatic and elegant when playing the familiar *Minuet* from Mozart's *Divertimento*, K.334, as in the lesser-known but no less catchy *Rondo* from Schubert's *D major Piano sonata*, D.850. Debussy's *La fille aux cheveux de lin* brings a bewitching interlude, and Heifetz demonstrates his fondness for Korngold by including two utterly different but equally characteristic transcriptions from *Much Ado About Nothing*. Again the 1946–7 sound is a great improvement on comparable earlier recordings. This applies equally to the pair of concertante works which end the programme, Bruch's *Scottish fantasia* and Vieuxtemps's *Concerto No. 5 in A minor*, where the 1947 orchestral accompaniment is at last beginning to sound full-bodied and realistic. Needless to say, Heifetz's presentation of Bruch's endearing Scottish melodies is a special delight, while the finale is joyously rhythmic. The brief *Adagio* of the Vieuxtemps is also played superbly, with the reprise quite magical. This may be a lightweight programme but it could surely not be better presented.

Volume 7: ELGAR: *Violin concerto in B min., Op. 61* (with LSO, Sargent). SAINT-SAENS: *Violin sonata No. 1 in D min., Op. 75* (with Emanuel Bay). TCHAIKOVSKY: *Violin concerto in D, Op. 35* (with Philh. O, Susskind). BEETHOVEN: *Violin sonata No. 9 in A (Kreutzer), Op. 47* (with Moiseiwitsch).
(M) (***) RCA mono 09026 61738-2 (2) [id.].

These were all works that Heifetz was to record again, but not with greater freshness, and by the 1950s he was being given recording of excellent quality. With Sargent in top form underpinning the performance, he provides an inspirational reading of the Elgar *Concerto*, notable for its natural volatility; yet the tenderness and warmth are never in doubt and the slow movement is deeply felt. The finale has an impulsive freedom and sense of fantasy which make the long cadenza sound completely spontaneous, especially as earlier themes are recalled. Heifetz had a soft spot for the lighthearted Saint-Saëns *Sonata* which follows and makes it seem to be a minor masterpiece. How elegantly he plays the delicious *Allegretto moderato*, almost a waltz, which takes the place of the Scherzo, and the finale, a fizzing *moto perpetuo*, is played with breathtaking agility. The 1950 recording of the Tchaikovsky *Concerto* is first class in every way and Susskind makes an ideal partner – his springing of the polacca tutti of the first movement is a joy. The work's opening is beautifully managed and Heifetz's entry and his presentation of the main themes are wonderfully warm and affectionate. The finale has great dash and sparkle. In the *Kreutzer Sonata* Moiseiwitsch is immediately commanding, and this is a superbly authoritative and alive account – as fine as any ever recorded. The slow-movement variations are glorious and full of imaginative touches from both artists; in every way this is preferable to Heifetz's stereo remake with Brooks Smith (see below), and certainly the mono recording (made at Abbey Road) is in the demonstration bracket.

Volume 8: BRAHMS: *Violin sonata No. 3 in D min., Op. 108* (with William Kapell). BEETHOVEN: *Romances Nos. 1, 2* (with RCA Victor SO, Steinberg). BRUCH: *Violin concerto No. 1 in G min., Op. 26* (with LSO, Sargent). WIENIAWSKI: *Polonaise brillante No. 1, Op. 4*. HANDEL: *Sonata in D, Op. 1/13*. SCHUBERT: *Violin sonatina in G min., D.408* (all three with Emanuel Bay). BLOCH: *Sonatas Nos. 1* (with Emanuel Bay); *2 (Poème mystique)* (with Brooks Smith). RAVEL: *Tzigane* (with LAPO, Wallenstein).
(M) (**(*)) RCA mono 09026 61739-2 (2) [id.].

William Kapell rather takes a back seat in the opening Brahms *Sonata*, which is nevertheless given a warmly passionate reading. But the 1950 recording (made in Hollywood) has returned to the up-front sound-balance which makes the violin's upper range somewhat fierce. Heifetz's first version of the Max Bruch *Concerto* (1951) is also a bit top-heavy, although the glowing warmth of the slow movement is impossible to resist and the finale has great zest. Sargent again proves a fine partner. So does William Steinberg in the two *Romances*, which are presented with appealing simplicity. Heifetz's Handel is stylishly dignified, with a nobly shaped *Larghetto*. He treats the Schubert *Sonatina* very classically and is perhaps too emphatic for so innocent a piece. But the veiled tone at the opening of Bloch's *First Sonata* and his subtle changes of colour demonstrate his natural affinity with this composer, and although later fortissimos register rather fiercely the music's special atmosphere is sensitively caught. The *Second Sonata* (*Poème mystique*) is in essence a series of eight brief vignettes with connecting material; its diversity of mood is imaginatively explored, with the *Più lento* ('*Gloria in excelsis Deo*') particularly touching. The finale is marked *Molto quieto* yet produces a final outburst of extraordinary passion. The Ravel *Tzigane* (Heifetz's only recording) is pretty intense, too. The solo playing becomes dazzling at the close but is let down by the thin, brash orchestral tuttis.

Volume 9: MOZART: *Violin sonatas in B flat, K.378; K.454* (with Emanuel Bay); *Duo in B flat, K.424; Divertimento in E flat, K.563* (with Emanuel Feuermann). HANDEL: *Harpsichord suite No. 7 in G min.: Passacaglia* (trans. Johan Halvorsen) (all three with William Primrose); *Sonata in E, Op. 1/15* (with Emanuel Bay). GRIEG: *Violin sonata No. 2 in G, Op. 13* (with Brooks Smith). SINDING: *Suite in A min., Op. 10* (with LAPO, Wallenstein).
(M) (**) RCA mono 09026 61740-2 (2) [id.].

These Mozart performances (from 1941), in which Heifetz is joined by William Primrose and (in the *E flat Divertimento* for string trio) also by Feuermann, are at times curiously stiff rhythmically, almost as if regulated by clockwork. Felicitous playing, of course, and immaculate ensemble, but the bright forward sound does not help to give the feeling that these artists are relaxing and enjoying themselves. The two *Violin sonatas* (1936) are more communicative and lively but still a bit literal. However, the Handel *Passacaglia* (1941), very effectively arranged as a *Duo*, is splendidly done and is most diverting. The *Sonata* from Op. 1, recorded a decade later, is even more spontaneous; Heifetz clearly relishes the noble *Largo* and perhaps overdoes the intensity here. But the result, if distinctly out of period style, is persuasive when the tune itself is so appealing. The early Grieg *Sonata* is the highlight of the set. It is both played and recorded beautifully (1955). The interpretation is very little different from his 78-r.p.m. version of 1936, but the sound is vastly superior and the result is sheer delight. The first movement of the Sinding *Suite* brings another dazzling *moto perpetuo* at which Heifetz was so adept, and he follows it with a G-string soliloquy to open the slow movement. The finale is inconsequential but with a folksy flavour. Good (1953) recording; but this is not one of the more memorable programmes, and it is a pity that the Grieg *Sonata* was included here instead of within one of the more enticing compilations.

Volume 10: BEETHOVEN: *String trios Opp. 3; 9/1, 3* (with Primrose, Piatigorsky); *Violin sonatas Nos. 3 in E flat; 8 in G*. MOZART: *Violin sonata in C, K.296* (all three with Emanuel Bay); *Violin concerto No. 5 in A (Turkish), K.219* (with LSO, Sargent).
(M) (**) RCA mono 09026 61741-2 (2) [id.].

The two Beethoven *Violin sonatas* which open Volume 10 bring consistently felicitous playing from Heifetz, especially the two closing movements of Op. 10/3. But Emanuel Bay is backwardly placed and his personality fails to come through. These performances are no match for the later, stereo set with Brooks Smith. The last of Mozart's five *Violin concertos* was a favourite with Heifetz and he recorded it three times. This is the second version, with Sargent making a strong partner. The first movement has great verve, the *Adagio* much intensity – perhaps a shade too much – but the finale has lots of character. The three Beethoven *String trios* are together on the second disc. The (1957) recording is rather dry and studio-bound but faithful enough, and this is real chamber-music playing, the music intimately shared among three musicians of the highest calibre. There is shared virtuosity, too, of course, notably in the *Presto* finale of Op. 9/1, but no ostentatious self-seeking. The Op. 3 *Trio in E flat*, with its two slow movements, is presented with disarming simplicity.

Volumes 11–15: BEETHOVEN: *Violin concerto in D, Op. 61*. MENDELSSOHN: *Violin concerto in E min., Op. 64*. PROKOFIEV: *Violin concerto No. 2 in G min., Op. 63* (all three with Boston SO, Munch). BRAHMS: *Double concerto for violin, cello and orchestra, Op. 102* (with Piatigorsky, RCA Victor SO, Wallenstein); *Violin concerto in D, Op. 77*. TCHAIKOVSKY: *Violin concerto in D, Op. 35* (both with Chicago SO, Reiner); *Sérénade mélancolique, Op. 26; Serenade in C, Op. 48: Waltz* (with CO). SIBELIUS: *Violin concerto in D min., Op. 47* (with Chicago SO, Hendl). GLAZUNOV: *Violin concerto in A min., Op. 82* (with RCA Victor SO, Hendl). BRUCH: *Violin concerto No. 1 in G min., Op. 26; Scottish fantasy, Op. 46* (with Osian Ellis). VIEUXTEMPS: *Violin concerto No. 5 in A min., Op. 37* (all with New SO of London, Sargent). MOZART: *Sinfonia concertante, K.364* (with William Primrose, RCA Victor SO, I. Solomon). BACH: *Double violin concerto* (with Erick Friedman, Thornton Lofthouse, New SO of London, Sargent).
(M) *** RCA 09026 61779-2 (5) [id.].

With Volumes 11–15 we at last come to the stereo recordings, and it is a great pity that the five discs are packaged together in this way, rather than being offered separately. The remastering for CD is consistently impressive, but many collectors could already have one or more of the recordings included in what is undoubtedly a very impressive first collection.

RCA's digital transfer of the early (1955) Beethoven recording has a remarkable sense of realism and presence, with the soloist only a little closer than is natural. The performance may adopt fast speeds but it never sounds rushed, finding time for individuality and imagination in every phrase. For some listeners the comparative lack of serenity in the first movement (though not in the *Larghetto*) will be a drawback, but the drama of the reading is unforgettable. Heifetz's unique timbre is captured marvellously; the assured aristocracy of the playing confounds criticism.

As with the Beethoven, so the transfer of the Brahms *Violin concerto* (recorded ten months earlier) makes vivid and fresh what was originally a rather harsh Chicago recording, more aggressive than the Boston sound. The speeds for all three movements may be fast, but Heifetz's ease and detailed imagination make them more than just dazzling, while the central *Andante*, at a flowing speed, is delectably songful.

The stereo remake of the Tchaikovsky *Concerto*, fine though it is, has not quite the simplicity and glow of the earlier, mono set with Susskind (see above). But with the upper range of the 1957 recording smoothed and the orchestral presence enhanced, the magic of Heifetz can now be enjoyed more fully. There is some gorgeous lyrical playing and the slow movement marries deep feeling and tenderness in ideal proportions, while the finale scintillates. Reiner accompanies positively, producing fierily positive tuttis. A fine performance of the *Sérénade mélancolique* and an arrangement of the *Waltz* make attractive encores.

As one might expect, Heifetz then gives a fabulous performance of the Mendelssohn *Concerto*. His speeds are consistently fast, yet in the slow movement his flexible phrasing sounds so inevitable and easy that it is hard not to be convinced. The finale is a *tour de force*, light and sparkling, with every note in place. The recording remains brightly vivid, but the sound is smoother than before.

Heifetz's 1959 stereo performance of the Sibelius *Concerto* with the Chicago Symphony Orchestra under Walter Hendl set the standard by which all other versions have come to be judged. It is also one of his finest recordings; in remastered form the sound is vivid, with the Chicago ambience making an apt setting for the finely focused violin-line. The purity and luminous beauty of the violin-tone at the opening put the seal on this as an interpretation of unusual depth, consummate technique and supreme artistry.

In the *arioso*-like slow movement of the Prokofiev No. 2, Heifetz chooses a faster speed than is usual, but there is nothing unresponsive about his playing, for his expressive rubato has an unfailing inevitability. In the spiky finale he is superb, and indeed his playing is glorious throughout. The 1959 recording has been further improved by the current remastering, which is smoother and richer than ever before, with a fine glow of resonance and plenty of bloom in the slow movement.

Heifetz is incomparable in the Glazunov *Violin concerto*. His account is the strongest and most passionate (as well as the most perfectly played) in the catalogue. In his hands, the work's sweetness is tempered with strength. The RCA Orchestra under Hendl gives splendid support and again the current remastering of the (1963) sound has added lustre to the quality.

In the Bruch *Violin concerto*, Heifetz plays with supreme assurance. The slow movement shows him in top romantic form. He then follows on with the *Scottish fantasia*, and the panache and subtlety of his bowing and control of colour bring a wonderful freshness to Bruch's charming Scottish whimsy. Sargent accompanies sympathetically and it is noticeable that, though the soloist is balanced much too closely, there is never any doubt that Heifetz can still produce a true pianissimo.

The quicksilver of Heifetz is just as well suited to the modest but attractive *Fifth Concerto* of Vieuxtemps, and Sir Malcolm provides a musical and well-recorded accompaniment. The balance of the soloist is rather close, but the digital remastering is again very successful in adding to the warmth and bloom of the 1961 sound.

The last three performances are new to CD. Although Wallenstein is not as fine an accompanist as Ormandy, he provides a sympathetic backcloth for the Heifetz–Piatigorsky partnership in the Brahms *Double concerto* which, if it does not quite match Heifetz's earlier version with Feuermann, is still a strong, warm-hearted account with a strikingly brilliant finale. The 1960 recording has been improved out of all recognition upon the harsh quality of the LP, and there is certainly no lack of warmth here.

The Mozart *Sinfonia concertante* dates from 1956 and brings a quite fruitful partnership between Heifetz and Primrose. If other performances are fresher and more inspirational in the slow movement, this is still warmly enjoyable, although the brisk pace for the finale is not entirely convincing. The recording is remarkably successful, with a freshly detailed orchestral backcloth.

For his second recording of the Bach *Double concerto*, recorded in Walthamstow Town Hall in 1961, Heifetz is joined by his pupil, Erick Friedman, a fine soloist in his own right. Once again outer movements are brisk, but in the slow movement the interchange, although warmly musical, does not match Heifetz's earlier, mono version, where he played both solo parts so memorably.

Volume 16: BEETHOVEN: *Violin sonatas Nos. 1–10.*
(M) (**(*)) RCA mono/stereo 09026 61747-2 (3) [id.]. with Emanuel Bay, Brooks Smith.

Although recorded in unflatteringly dry sound with the violin balanced very close, and despite the fact that Heifetz sometimes takes his preference for fast speeds to extremes, his flair and imagination shine through in the whole cycle. The bold assurance of the playing tends to work against any deeper, darker qualities emerging, but nevertheless these performances consistently give the lie to the idea that Heifetz was a cold player. Even when he chooses a fast tempo and sticks firmly to it, the individuality of phrasing and expression is magnetic. Each movement becomes a refreshing voyage of discovery. Not that Emanuel Bay (Brooks Smith in the *Kreutzer*) is allowed to be an equal partner. Deft and responsive, he simply follows and supports the great virtuoso. The *Kreutzer*, one of the last works to be recorded, is offered in stereo.

Volume 17. BACH: (Unaccompanied) *Violin sonatas Nos. 1–3, BWV 1001, 1003 & 1005; Violin partitas Nos. 1–3, BWV 1002, 1004 & 1006.*
(M) (***) RCA mono 09026 61748-2 (2) [id.].

The dry and limited mono sound of Heifetz's classic set, dating from the 1950s, does not prevent one being thrilled by the astonishing bravura of his playing. Speeds are often extremely fast – phenomenally so in the fugues – yet rhythms are controlled superbly. Though the power of the performances is overwhelming, the closeness and dryness of the acoustic give a kind of drawing-room intimacy, as if the master-violinist was in your own room. With slow movements as well as fast taken faster than usual, these are not meditative readings – but nor are they cold, for Heifetz's creative imagination in his phrasing has one consistently registering the music afresh.

Volume 20: BRUCH: *Violin concerto No. 2 in D min., Op. 44.* CONUS: *Violin concerto in E min.* WIENIAWSKI: *Violin concerto No. 2 in D min., Op. 22* (all three with RCA Victor SO, I. Solomon). TCHAIKOVSKY: *Sérénade mélancolique, Op. 26* (with LAPO, Wallenstein).
(M) (***) RCA mono 09026 61751-2 [id.].

Bruch's *Second Concerto* has always been under-rated because of the fame of the first, but, as Heifetz demonstrates here, in the work's first (1954) recording, it has no lack of fine ideas and the finale is very jolly. Both this and the Conus *Concerto* have since been taken up by Perlman. But Heifetz's 1952 account was the first to reveal the latter's appealingly simple brand of lyricism. However, Wieniawski's *Second D minor Concerto* is the highlight of the collection, with its winsome central *Romanze* and twinkling *moto perpetuo* finale (*à la* zingara), where Heifetz is in his element. Tchaikovsky's *Sérénade mélancolique* makes a touching encore. The mono sound is very good throughout, apart from the usual very forward balance for the soloist.

Volume 21: KORNGOLD: *Violin concerto in D, Op. 35* (with LAPO, Wallenstein). ROZSA: *Violin concerto, Op. 24* (with Dallas SO, Hendl); *Sinfonia concertante, Op. 29 (Theme with variations)* (with Piatigorsky, CO). WAXMAN: *Carmen fantasy* (with RCA Victor SO, Voorhees).
(M) **(*) RCA mono/stereo 09026 61752-2 [id.].

It was Heifetz who established the Korngold *Violin concerto* in the recorded repertoire. It is quite familiar now from more recent versions, but the playing in this 1953 mono recording is dazzling: the lyrical music sounds gorgeous and the material, drawn from film scores, is always appealing – and especially when presented like this. The Rózsa *Concerto*, which has the advantage of stereo, is slightly less memorable but is still worth hearing in such a performance. The *Theme with variations* is inventive but not melodically memorable. Here Heifetz is joined by Piatigorsky, also in very good form, and they work very hard to make something of this relatively intractable piece. Waxman's *Carmen fantasy* (mono, 1946) is simply a string of Bizet's hit tunes, and they are presented with a panache that is little short of astonishing. Few reservations have to be made about the recording.

Volume 22: CHAUSSON: *Poème, Op. 25* (with RCA Victor SO, cond. Izler Solomon). LALO: *Symphonie espagnole, Op. 21.* SAINT-SAENS: *Havanaise; Introduction and Rondo capriccioso* (with RCA Victor SO, Steinberg). SARASATE: *Zigeunerweisen* (all cond. Steinberg).
(M) (***) RCA mono 09026 61753-2 [id.].

In the Chausson *Poème*, Heifetz, as usual, is much too close to the microphone, which affects this subtle piece more than most. But the playing is masterly. The performances of the Saint-Saëns *morceaux de concert* have extraordinary charisma: Heifetz's chimerical bowing in the coda of the *Havanaise* is captivating. Similarly the 1951 account of the Lalo *Symphonie espagnole* has superb panache, and there are no complaints about the mono recording, except that it omitted the *Intermezzo* (a practice curiously common at that time); the playing is dazzling. The Sarasate *Zigeunerweisen* scintillates in the fireworks, while the lyrical melody brings the most luscious tone and sophisticated colouring. Apart from the balance, this collection has satisfactory sound and makes a marvellous sampler for Heifetz's great artistry and supreme command of his instrument.

Volume 23: WALTON: *Violin concerto in B min.* (with Philh. O, composer). GRUENBERG: *Violin concerto, Op. 47* (with San Francisco SO, Monteux).
(M) (**(*)) RCA mono 09026 61754-2 [id.].

This is the later version of the Walton *Violin concerto*, first issued in 1951, which Heifetz made with the composer conducting, using the revised score. Speeds are often hair-raisingly fast, but few Heifetz records convey as much passion as this, in music which he inspired and helped to edit, as Joachim did with Brahms. The mono recording is dry, but it seems warmer with more bloom in this new transfer, and the high-voltage electricity has never been matched in this radiant music. However, the earlier mono recording of the original score has an inspirational quality not quite equalled by this later recording. Moreover the coupled Gruenberg *Concerto*, also commissioned by Heifetz, is not a work of any great individuality, even if its songful slow movement (based on fragments from spirituals) is well sustained by the Heifetz bow, and the lively dance finale invites and receives much brilliance from the soloist.

Volume 24: BACH: *Violin concertos Nos. 1–2* (with LAPO, Wallenstein). MOZART: *Violin sonata in B flat, K.454.* PAGANINI: *Caprices Nos. 13, 20* (arr. KREISLER) (with Brooks Smith). VITALI: *Chaconne in G min.* (with Ellsasser (organ)).
(M) (**) RCA mono 09026 61755-2 [id.].

Wallenstein is hardly a Bach stylist, although he uses a reduced-size orchestra; but outer movements are quite lively and Heifetz invests each slow movement, and especially that from the *A minor Concerto*, with his own special charisma, and there is no denying the lyrical beauty of the playing. The Mozart *Sonata* is crisp and clean; again the slow movement is not entirely in style but is still enjoyable. The two Kreisler-arranged Paganini *Caprices* are slow and luscious, while the once-famous Vitali *Chaconne* is heard in Respighi's arrangement with a superfluous organ part which undermines the effect of the violin variants. This is one of the least rewarding issues in the Heifetz Edition.

Volume 25: SPOHR: *Violin concerto No. 8 in A min., Op. 47* (with RCA Victor SO, I. Solomon); *Double quartet, Op. 65* (with Baker, Thomas, Piatigorsky, Amoyal, Rosenthal, Harshman, Lesser). BEETHOVEN: *Serenade, Op. 8* (with Primrose, Piatigorsky).
(M) (***) RCA mono/stereo 09026 61756-2 [id.].

Spohr's *Gesangszenekonsert* is in mono and dates from 1954. A dazzling performance which, in sheer beauty and refinement of tone, remains unsurpassed. Although the recording acoustic could with advantage have been more ample, this is still good sound for its period, and in some ways it is more appealing than the dryish (1968) stereo recording of the *D minor Double quartet*. The first violin dominates the texture, a reminder both of Spohr's prowess as a violinist and – certainly – of Heifetz's. His distinctive timbre and glorious tone shine through. The Beethoven *String serenade* is neatly played by this illustrious trio, but the confining effect of the studio acoustic make the music sound dry in both senses of the word. The result is often spirited but curiously uningratiating.

Volume 26: MOZART: *Violin concerto No. 5 in A (Turkish), K.219* (with CO). *Violin sonata in B flat, K.378* (with Brooks Smith). *String quintet in G min., K.516* (with Baker, Primrose, Majewski, Piatigorsky).
(M) (**(*)) RCA mono/stereo 09026 61757-2 [id.].

A marvellously exhilarating account of the *A Major Concerto* from Heifetz, while his actual entry in the first movement is quite ethereal. He directs the accompanying group himself. The early-1960s stereo is fully acceptable and the performance memorable, with the crystalline clarity of articulation matched by warmth of timbre and aristocratic phrasing. The *String quintet* suffers from an over-stressed urgency in the first movement, which is surely too fast and which robs the music of much of its underlying melancholy. There is nevertheless much to admire in the rest of the work, for the playing itself is very fine. The studio recording is pleasing, the stereo natural although closely balanced. The *Sonata* is a 1954 mono recording of good quality, and the performance comes off rather well.

Volume 27: ARENSKY: *Piano trio No. 1 in D min., Op. 32.* TURINA: *Piano trio No. 1, Op. 35* (both with Pennario). KODALY: *Duo, Op. 7* (all three with Piatigorsky).
(M) (**) RCA 09026 61758-2 [id.].

The Arensky *Trio* is a fine work in the Russian romantic chamber tradition, music which can verge on the Palm Court if it is played in a simpering way but which is richly rewarding if played full-bloodedly. It has a splendid lollipop Scherzo with a virtuoso part for the pianist. This Pennario throws off with aplomb, and his companions are fully equal to the surge of emotionalism elsewhere. After a strong opening, the Turina *Trio* turns out to be quite lightweight and not strikingly Spanish in atmosphere. Unfortunately, in both works the dry recording militates against the music's effect, and this also applies to the Kodály *Duo*, which nevertheless brings some ethereal playing in the central *Adagio*. A picture on the leaflet shows the bare studio in which these recordings were made: no wonder the effect lacks ambience and warmth.

Volume 28: BRAHMS: *String quintet No. 2 in G, Op. 111* (with Baker, Thomas, Rosenthal). BEETHOVEN: *Piano trio in E flat, Op. 70/2* (with Pennario). BOCCHERINI: *Violin sonata in D* (all three with Piatigorsky). MOZART: *Serenade No. 7 in D (Haffner): Rondo* (with Brooks Smith).
(M) (**) RCA 09026 61759-2 [id.].

Although there is not the richness of string blend one might expect in the first movement of the Brahms *Quintet*, the inner movements bring a compensating transparency of texture and the sound itself is quite acceptable. It is a fine performance, as is the lively account of the Beethoven *Piano trio*. The Boccherini *Sonata*, a duo for violin and cello, is an inventive work, and the interplay between Heifetz and Piatigorsky is appealing. The *Rondo* from the Mozart *Haffner Serenade* is then played by Heifetz with great brilliance as a breathtaking encore. But overall this does not gel as a particularly distinctive concert.

Volume 29: BEETHOVEN: *Piano trio No. 7 in B flat (Archduke), Op. 97*. SCHUBERT: *Piano trio in B flat, D.898* (both with Rubinstein, Feuermann)
(M) (***) RCA mono 09026 61760-2 [id.].

These two glorious performances were studio recordings made in 1941. The sound is remarkably good and, although there are a few tiny clicks, otherwise the background noise is not too intrusive. The balance is forward, but the three instruments are more sonorously captured here than in some of the later Heifetz–Piatigorsky stereo records. The playing in the *Archduke* has tremendous life and warmth, while the *Andante* of the Schubert *Trio* is wonderfully simple in its lyrical flow, with Feuermann and Heifetz opening the movement with a magical dialogue. The Scherzo sparkles, without being taken too fast, and the finale has a splendid, natural impetus; here it is Rubinstein who catches the ear, even though he is placed more backwardly. This is one of the finest CDs of the series.

Volume 30: MOZART: *Violin concerto No. 4 in D, K.218* (with New SO of London, Sargent). BEETHOVEN: *Piano trio in E flat, Op. 1/1* (with Lateiner). VIVALDI: *Double concerto for violin and cello in B flat, RV 547* (with CO). HANDEL: *Passacaglia* from *Harpsichord suite No. 7* (trans. Halvorsen) (all three with Piatigorsky).
(M) (**) RCA 09026 61761-2 [id.].

Heifetz takes a brisk view of the first movement of the Mozart *D major Concerto* but plays his runs with crystal clarity and typical verve. This is very much Mozart *à la* Heifetz, and this is a distinct gain in the *Finale*, though something lyrical is lost in the slow movement. Sargent's accompaniment matches the solo line perfectly. The Beethoven *Piano trio* is crisp and neat; the recording is a little dry, but the players convey their pleasure in the music and the finale is winningly spirited. Although a chamber orchestra is used in the Vivaldi *Concerto*, the effect is heavy and a bit gruff in the outer movements and the ear craves more transparency. The *Andante*, however, brings a winning interplay between the two illustrious soloists. The *Passacaglia* from the *G minor Harpsichord suite* of Handel sits uneasily on the instrumental combination of violin and cello; although the playing is of high quality, the end result is ineffective.

Volume 31: A. BENJAMIN: *Romantic fantasy* (with Primrose, RCA Victor O, I. Solomon). STRAVINSKY: *Suite italienne*. GLIERE: *Prelude, Op. 39/1* (both with Piatigorsky). WIENIAWSKI: *Capriccio-valse, Op. 7*. FALLA: *Jota; Nana (Berceuse)*. SGAMBATI: *Serenata napoletana* (all three with Brooks Smith). CASTELNUOVO-TEDESCO: *The Lark* (with Emanuel Bay). BRAHMS: *Hungarian dance No. 7* (with LAPO, Wallenstein).
(M) (***) RCA mono/stereo 09026 61762-2 [id.].

Heifetz didn't like Bartók, and Arthur Benjamin was his idea of a modern composer who wrote music which was enjoyable to play. He wasn't far wrong (about Benjamin) and the *Romantic fantasy* is a very winning triptych, with a horn soloist (Joseph Eger) to catch the ear as the first-movement *Nocturne* opens. Heifetz and Piatigorsky are a bit rough and angular with the opening of Stravinsky's *Suite italienne* (arranged as a duo for violin and cello), but after that they titillate the ear, both spikily and tenderly. The rest of the programme is a series of utterly seductive encores, played with a brilliance and panache that are justly legendary. The sound is good, and the closing *Hungarian dance* is irresistible in its quixotic rubato.

Volume 32: BRAHMS: *Piano trio No. 1 in B, Op. 8* (with Feuermann and Rubinstein). DOHNANYI: *Serenade in C for string trio, Op. 10* (with Primrose and Feuermann). R. STRAUSS: *Violin sonata in E flat, Op. 18* (with Brooks Smith).
(M) (***) RCA mono 09026 61763-2 [id.].

Another of the very finest records of the series, so much so that each performance has been listed and discussed under its composer. The performance of the Richard Strauss *Sonata* has never been surpassed.

Volume 33: FRANCK: *Piano quintet in F min.* (with Pennario, Baker, Primrose and Piatigorsky). DVORAK: *Piano trio (Dumky), Op. 90* (with Lateiner and Piatigorsky). SIBELIUS: *Nocturne* (with Brooks Smith).
(M) *(**) RCA 09026 61764-2 [id.].

Leonard Pennario leads a dramatic and intelligent reading of the Franck *Piano quintet*, excelling in fine phrasing and a sensitive use of timbre. But the one who steals the show time and time again is Heifetz: his way of playing those many wistful and passionate sentences is irresistible. Indeed, although the piano is well in the picture, the violin dominates throughout and Israel Baker and William Primrose are quite outbalanced. The stereo is two-dimensional. The internal balance is much better in the *Dumky Trio*, and Piatigorsky's singing line often dominates. Not surprisingly, it is a sparkling performance, but Heifetz plays with wonderful tenderness too. It is a pity that the artists are placed so forwardly; one might relish the presence, but it reduces the dynamic range and tends to make Heifetz sound shrill when he is being forceful. But this is magnificent music-making, and the Sibelius *Nocturne* makes a charismatic encore.

Volume 34: MOZART: *String quintet (No. 5) in C, K.515* (with Baker, Primrose, Majewski, Piatigorsky). BACH: *Partita No. 2, BWV 1004: Chaconne*. MENDELSSOHN: *Piano trio No. 2 in C min., Op. 66* (with Pennario, Piatigorsky).
(M) (**(*)) RCA 09026 61765-2 [id.].

The Mendelssohn and Mozart recordings were part of the Heifetz–Piatigorsky concerts series of recordings, dating from 1963 and 1964 respectively. Both recordings are dry and closely balanced, but the Mozart performance, although its technical efficiency is somehow emphasized by the acoustic, is strongly projected and has an underlying warmth. The finale sparkles and there is less of the feeling of intense pressure which adversely affected the opening movement of this group's earlier recording of the *G minor Quintet*. The two-dimensional studio recording of the Mendelssohn *Trio* does not help its intimacy, but it remains a fine performance, especially the *Andante* and dazzling Scherzo. The compelling account of the Bach *Chaconne* was recorded for a Heifetz TV special.

Volume 35: MENDELSSOHN: *Octet, Op. 20* (with Baker, Belnick, Stepansky, Primrose, Majewski, Rejto). TOCH: *Divertimento, Op. 37/2* (both with Piatigorsky). RACHMANINOV: *Daisies*. Robert Russell BENNETT: *A Song sonata*. SHULMAN: *Cod liver 'ile*. GERSHWIN: *It ain't necessarily so* (all with Brooks Smith). STRAVINSKY: *Berceuse*. SHOSTAKOVICH: *Danse fantastique, Op. 5/2* (both with Emanuel Bay). Heifetz on music (talk).
(M) (**(*)) RCA mono/stereo 09026 61766-2 [id.].

The Mendelssohn *Octet*, like the Franck *Quintet* above, was recorded in conjunction with a series of Pilgrimage Theatre Concerts, given at Hollywood in the autumn of 1961 by a star cast of musicians, most of them resident in California. With Heifetz and Piatigorsky as the twin props of this enterprise excitement was guaranteed, but the playing brings reservations too. The *Octet* of Mendelssohn certainly responds to this galaxy of virtuoso string-players. Heifetz, leading the ensemble, is very much in evidence, but if now and then the work sounds like a violin concerto, this is due not only to the vigour of Heifetz's playing but also to the way this brilliant piece is scored. The lightness and grace of the famous *Scherzo* is unforgettable. But the close balance prevents full enjoyment. The Toch *Divertimento* (a duo) is a fine piece, and the bravura of these virtuosi is extraordinary in the closing *Vivace molto*. The sound improves considerably in the Rachmaninov song and the other novelty, an engaging *Song sonata* by Robert Russell Bennett, a radio recording from 1955 sounding unexpectedly good. Its three movements are marked *Belligerent*, *Slow and lonely* – with haunting, veiled tone from Heifetz – and *Madly dancing*, which is rhythmically catchy and a chance for the letting down of hair, which is well taken. Stravinsky's *Berceuse* (wonderfully warm-toned) makes a good foil for the vibrant Shostakovich miniature. Before the final *It ain't necessarily so*, Heifetz offers some homely advice – to students on practising, about his purchase of an electric car as a symbol of the need to fight against Californian smog, and some homespun philosophy too. (Self-) Discipline, he suggests, is important for enjoying life, while he is sure that 'We have too many comforts – actually they are not conducive for dreaming.'

Volume 36: TCHAIKOVSKY: *Piano trio in A min., Op. 50*. MENDELSSOHN: *Piano trio in D min., Op. 49* (both with Rubinstein, Piatigorsky).
(M) (**) RCA mono 09026 61767-2 [id.].

These recordings date from 1950. They were made in a very dry acoustic and allowances have to be made for their two-dimensional quality and lack of range, particularly so far as the piano timbre is concerned. The playing is high-powered and at times a bit hard-driven, particularly the *Scherzo* of the Mendelssohn. Nevertheless the golden tone of Heifetz and Piatigorsky is a joy in itself (as is the digital dexterity of Rubinstein); the playing is marvellously authoritative and much of it is *con amore*, but it is public, 'big-time' playing, not chamber-music-making. There is a substantial cut in the finale of the Tchaikovsky.

Concerts of Orchestral and Concertante Music

Academy of St Martin-in-the-Fields, Sir Neville Marriner

Italian concertos: GABRIELI: *Canzona noni toni.* CORELLI: *Concerti grossi in D; in G min., Op. 6/7, 8.* GEMINIANI: *Concerto grosso in E min., Op. 3/3.* MANFREDINI: *Concerto grosso in G min., Op. 3/10.* ALBINONI: *Concerto a 5 in A min., Op. 5/5.* TORELLI: *Concerto musicale in D min., Op. 6/10.* LOCATELLI: *Concerto grosso in D min., Op. 1/9.*
(M) *** Decca 436 224-2 [id.].

Although it opens with the noble, antiphonally conceived Gabrieli *Canzona* – how strongly this composer's musical personality comes through, even in a short piece – which derives from a slightly later source, in essence this 72-minute CD combines much of the contents of the two LPs which at the beginning of the 1960s launched the Academy of St Martin-in-the-Fields. This particular field of small chamber ensembles specializing in performances of baroque music had previously been cornered by Italian groups like I Musici, often restricting themselves very much to the home product. From the very beginning, Marriner and the St Martin's group showed themselves willing to offer a repertoire covering the widest possible range; furthermore the standard of playing and care for style and detail were to set and maintain a new international standard of excellence which even now, three decades later, has not been surpassed. However, the collection assembled for the reissue omits the non-Italian repertoire (the Avison and the excerpts from Handel's Op. 6, for instance) and lets the Academy upstage the Italian groups on their own ground. The playing is wonderfully alive and spirited, and the works by Manfredini and Locatelli, instead of sounding anonymous, as they so often do, emerge with as strong an expressive individuality as those by their more celebrated compatriots, Corelli and Albinoni. The recording is admirably remastered; its slight touch of astringency in the violins seems properly authentic and there is plenty of body and warmth.

SUPPE: Overture: *Light cavalry.* GRIEG: *2 Elegiac melodies, Op. 34; Holberg suite, Op. 40: Prelude.* TCHAIKOVSKY: *Andante cantabile* (from *String quartet No. 1).* DVORAK: *Nocturne in B, Op. 40.* PONCHIELLI: *La Gioconda: Dance of the hours.* NICOLAI: *The Merry Wives of Windsor* (overture). FAURE: *Pavane, Op. 50.* BOCCHERINI: *String quintet in E, Op. 13/5: Minuet.* WAGNER: *Siegfried idyll.* HANDEL: *Solomon: Arrival of the Queen of Sheba.* J. S. BACH: *Cantata No. 208: Sheep may safely graze; Cantata No. 147: Jesu, joy of man's desiring; Christmas oratorio: Pastoral symphony.* HANDEL: *Berenice: Minuet. Messiah: Pastoral symphony.* SCHUBERT: *Rosamunde: Entr'acte No. 3 in B flat.* GLUCK: *Orfeo ed Euridice: Dance of the blessed spirits.* BORODIN: *String quartet No. 2 in D: Nocturne.* SHOSTAKOVICH: *The Gadfly: Romance.* MUSSORGSKY/RIMSKY-KORSAKOV: *Khovanshchina: Dance of the Persian slaves.* RIMSKY-KORSAKOV: *Tsar Saltan: The Flight of the bumble bee. The Snow Maiden: Dance of the tumblers.*
(BB) *** CfP Silver Double Dig. CD-CFPSD 4811 (2).

This CfP Silver Double draws on the contents of three different (HMV) digital collections, recorded between 1980 and 1987. The first included the *Siegfried idyll*, in which Marriner uses solo strings for the gentler passages, a fuller ensemble for the climaxes, here passionately convincing. Delicately introduced by the harp and the gentle striking of the morning hour, the account of the *Dance of the hours* has characteristic finesse and colour, while there is comparably gracious phrasing in *The Merry Wives of Windsor overture*. The other, mainly gentle, pieces by Tchaikovsky, Fauré, Boccherini and Grieg are given radiant performances. To open the second disc, Handel's *Queen of Sheba* trots in very briskly and here the noble contour of Handel's famous *Berenice* melody is the first thing to strike the ear; but it is the Schubert *Entr'acte* from *Rosamunde* and the passionately expressive Borodin *Nocturne* that resonate in the memory. With the Shostakovich *Barrel organ waltz* providing a touch of piquancy and Mussorgsky's *Persian slaves* suitably sinuous and sentient, this makes a most agreeable entertainment, ending with gusto with Rimsky's *Tumblers*. The digital sound is excellent throughout.

'Fantasia on Greensleeves': VAUGHAN WILLIAMS: *Fantasia on Greensleeves; The Lark ascending* (with Iona Brown); *English folksong suite.* WARLOCK: *Serenade; Capriol suite.* BUTTERWORTH: *A Shropshire lad; Two English idylls; The Banks of green willow.* DELIUS: *A Village Romeo and Juliet: The walk to the Paradise Garden. Hassan: Intermezzo and serenade. A song before sunrise; On hearing the first cukoo in spring; Summer night on the river; La Calinda.* ELGAR: *Serenade for strings, Op. 20; Sospiri for strings, harp and organ; Elegy for strings, Op. 58; The Spanish Lady (suite); Introduction and Allegro, Op. 47.*
(B) *** Decca Double 452 707-2 (2) [id.].

This exceptionally generous programme, mainly of English pastoral evocations but including Iona Brown's Elysian account of *The Lark ascending* and Elgar's two string masterpieces in not wholly idiomatic but very characterful performances, is self-recommending, for the Academy are thoroughly at home here and play with consistent warmth and finesse, while the vintage Decca sound never disappoints. Marvellous value for money.

Alain, Marie-Claire (organ)

'A Celebration'.
(M) *** Erato/Warner Analogue/Dig. 0630 15343-2 (6) [id.].

CD1: *J. S. Bach and his predecessors:* LEBEGUE: *Magnificat du premier ton; Noël: Où s'en vont ces gais bergers; Pour l'amour de Marie.* TUNDER: *Choral-fantasia: Jesu Christus, wahr' Gottes Sohn.* BRUHNS: *Prelude and fugue in E min.* BUXTEHUDE: *Chorales: In dulci jubilo, BuxWV 197; Der Tag, der ist so freudenreich, BuxWV 182; Magnificat primi toni, BuxWV 203.* BOHM: *Chorale: Gelobet seist du, Jesu Christ.* BACH: *Fuga sopra il Magnificat, BWV 733; Canonic variations on Vom Himmel hoch, BWV 769; Prelude and fugue in C, BWV 547*

CD2: *The late baroque:* BACH: *Toccata and fugue in D min., BWV 565; Trio sonata in C, BWV 529; Fugue in G min., BWV 578; Trio (Adagio) (after BWV 1027); (Allegro) BWV 1027a; Concerto in D min. (after Vivaldi), BWV 596.* HANDEL: *Concerto in B flat, Op. 4/6.* C. P. E. BACH: *Concerto in E flat, Wq. 35* (both with Paillard CO).

CD3: *The 19th century:* BOELY: *Fantasia and fugue in B flat, Op. 18.* MENDELSSOHN: *Prelude and fugue in C min.* LISZT: *Prelude and fugue on B-A-C-H.* BOELLMAN: *Gothic suite, Op. 25.* WIDOR: *Symphony No. 5: Allegro cantabile; Toccata.* FRANCK: *Prélude, fugue et variation, Op. 18.* GUILMANT: *Sonata in D min. (Allegro assai).*

CD4: *The 20th century:* VIERNE: *Suite No. 2, Op. 53: Toccata in B flat.* A. ALAIN: *Scherzo in E min.; Toccata on l'Antienne 'Cantemus Domino'.* J. ALAIN: *2 Danses à Agni Yavishta; Intermezzo; Litanies; Aria.* POULENC: *Concerto in G min. for organ, strings and timpani* (with ORTF, Martinon). MESSIAEN: *La Nativité du Seigneur: Les bergers; Dieu parmi nous*

CD5: *Rare recordings: from Pachelbel to Mozart:* BACH: *Cantata No. 35: Sinfonia No. 2* (with Paillard CO); *14 Canons on the Goldberg bass* (with O. Alain). PACHELBEL: *Toccata in C; Prelude in D min.; Chorals: Vom Himmel hoch; Chaconne in F min.* BACH: *10 Canons from The Musical offering, BWV 1079.* VIVALDI: *Concerto in D min. for violin, organ and strings, RV 541* (with Toso, Sol. Ven., Scimone). MOZART: *Fantasia for mechanical organ in F min., K.608; Sonata in C, K.336 (Allegro).*

Bonus disc: BACH: *Prelude and fugue in G, BWV 541; Chorale, BWV 721; Aria, BWV 587; Canzona, BWV 588.* C. P. E. BACH: *Sonata No. 6 in G min., Wq.70/6.*

Marie-Claire Alain's recording career is justly celebrated here by Erato, for she has been making recordings for this label since 1953. The sixth (bonus) CD offered here includes four works which were on that first Bach LP, plus a sampler of her latest recording of organ sonatas by Bach's son, Carl Philipp Emanuel, made in 1996. The other five discs survey her achievement over the intervening 40 or so years. There is very little here that is not of high calibre and the range is remarkable, always using organs suitable for the repertoire. The five recitals are arranged in historical order, beginning with Johann Sebastian and his predecessors, followed by a second disc of Bach but with concertos by Carl Philipp Emanuel and Handel. Then comes the nineteenth century, ranging from Boëly, Mendelssohn and Liszt to the French School – Boëllman, Widor, Franck and Guilmant. Compact disc 4 moves on to the twentieth century but stays in France, and all of it is real music, by Vierne, Poulenc, Alain and – of course – Messiaen. The fifth CD purports to be 'rare recordings', but they are not really so very rare, including Bach *Canons* and a Vivaldi *Concerto for violin, organ and strings* which is not one of the plums. But overall this set is well worth considering, especially by those who want some basic organ repertoire for a modest-sized collection. The reproduction is of a high standard.

American Carnegie Hall Youth Orchestra, Sir Georg Solti

'Carnegie Hall project': WAGNER: *Die Meistersinger: Overture*. BRAHMS: *Variations on a theme of Haydn (St Antoni chorale), Op. 56a*. SHOSTAKOVICH: *Symphony No. 9 in E flat, Op. 70*. R. STRAUSS: *Don Juan, Op. 20*. SMETANA: *Overture: The Bartered Bride*.
**(*) Decca Dig. 444 458-2 [id.].

This disc is the impressive result of a project undertaken by Sir Georg Solti at Carnegie Hall in New York over 16 days in June 1994. A series of rehearsals and study-sessions involved 15 musicians from five top American orchestras, acting not only as leading players but coaching their respective sections of budding young professionals. Solti comments in his explanatory note for this disc that 'the results are beautiful', and this is winningly demonstrated in these live recordings made at the two concerts which crowned the whole project. *Don Juan* is undoubtedly thrilling, but the most remarkable performance here is of the Shostakovich symphony, for it would be hard to imagine a more exhilarating account of this equivocal work, witty and pointed and with enormous vigour demonstrated in the Scherzo and finale. It is remarkable too what natural flexibility marks the playing in such a work as the *Meistersinger Prelude*, with free rubato in the big melodies coupled with perfect ensemble. The clarity of texture allows some magic solo playing to be fully appreciated in all the works, notably from the principal oboe and horn. Solti's energetic brilliance also makes *The Bartered Bride overture* fizz, but some ears might prefer the Brahms *St Antoni variations* to relax a bit more.

(i) **American Symphony Orchestra Wind Group** or (ii) **Orchestra, Leopold Stokowski**

(i) MOZART: *Serenade No. 10 for 13 wind instruments in B flat, K.361*. (ii) VIVALDI: *L'Estro armonico: Concerto grosso in D min., Op. 3/11*. BACH: *Jesu, joy of man's desiring* (arr. SCHICKELE); *Sheep may safely graze* (arr. STOKOWSKI). CORELLI: *Concerto grosso in G min. (Christmas), Op. 6/8*.
(M) *** Van. 08 8009 71 [id.].

Stokowski's expressive exaggerations – inevitable even in Mozart – are never extreme, so that they do not get in the way of enjoyment of this highly characterful performance of the *Wind serenade*. The solo work in the lovely *Adagio* third movement is exceptionally sensitive in its flexibility, and the sprung rhythms of the fast movements are infectiously controlled. The Bach transcriptions, too, are warmly enjoyable, but it is the baroque *concerti grossi* that show the Stokowski magnetism at its most telling. In the Corelli, Igor Kipnis provides the continuo and he is nicely balanced. Allegros sparkle and the famous *Pastorale* is expressively beautiful. In the Vivaldi, the continuo is almost inaudible, but again the string playing is buoyant and joyful in allegros, while the third-movement *Largo* is quite ravishing. The 1966–7 recordings are excellent and the transfers first rate.

Amsterdam Loeki Stardust Quartet, Academy of Ancient Music, Christopher Hogwood

'Concerti di flauti': HEINICHEN: *Concerto a 8 in C*. SCHICKHARDT: *Concerto No. 2 in D min. for 4 recorders & continuo; Concerto No. 3 in G for 4 recorders & continuo*. TELEMANN: *Concertos for 2 recorders & strings: in A min.; in B flat*. MARCELLO: *Concerti di flauti in G*. VIVALDI: *Concerto in A in due cori, con flauti obbligati, RV 585*.
*** O-L Dig. 436 905-2 [id.].

The Heinichen *Concerto a 8* (which doesn't mean there are eight soloists!) is a charmer, with a barely scored drone effect in the *Pastorel* followed by a graceful minute-long *Adagio* to counter the chortling in the outer movements. The Schickhardt D minor work opens equally invitingly (with the effect of a carol) and is elegantly tuneful throughout. In its companion in G major, the solo style is very chordal, with moments almost like a piquant harmonium. Both the Telemann works are predictably inventive and enjoyable; perhaps the first, in A minor, wins by a short head, while in the happy Marcello piece one can feel the Italian sunshine. But the most masterly concerto here is the splendid Vivaldi antiphonal *Concerto in A major* which uses violin soloists as well as the recorders (used sparingly as an obbligato) and even brings in a brief solo organ contribution. The slow movement is dominated by the violin duo. Needless to say, the whole programme is expertly and authentically presented. The recording, made in London's Henry Wood Hall, has a nice ambience, though the balance is a trifle close (particularly in the Vivaldi). A very stimulating concert just the same.

Anderson, John (oboe), Philharmonia Orchestra, Simon Wright

'Venetian oboe concertos': ALBINONI: *Concertos in B flat, Op. 7/3; in D, Op. 7/6.* MARCELLO: *Concerto in D min.* VIVALDI: *Concertos in D, RV 453; in F, RV 455; in A min., RV 461.* CIMAROSA/BENJAMIN: *Concerto in C min.*
(M) **(*) Nimbus Dig. NI 7027 [id.].

John Anderson is principal oboist of the Philharmonia and he plays these concertos with warmth, elegance and grace. The one slight drawback is the rather plushy tuttis from the resonantly recorded Philharmonia Orchestra. Although they give delicate support in the Marcello *Adagio*, the orchestral touch is heavier in the *Larghetto* of the Vivaldi *A minor*, RV 461. The concerto arranged by Arthur Benjamin from the music of Cimarosa is a highlight, the *Introduction* delicately tender and the second movement deliciously pointed.

André, Maurice (trumpet)

Trumpet concertos and arrangements: (with (i) Munich CO; (ii) Stadlmair; (iii) Richter. (iv) Hedwig Bilgram (organ); (v) ECO, Mackerras; (vi) Zurich Coll. Music O, Sacher). (i; ii) Joseph HAYDN: *Concerto in E flat.* (i; iii) TELEMANN: *Concertos in C min.; E min.* (from *Oboe concerto*); *Sonata for trumpet and strings in D.* (i; ii) Franz Xaver RICHTER: *Concerto in D.* (i; iii) HANDEL: *Concertos Nos 1–3* (arr. from *Oboe concertos*). (iv) VIVIANI: *Sonata No. 1 for trumpet and organ in C.* (v) VIVALDI: *Double trumpet concerto in C, P. 75.* TORELLI: *Concerto in D.* Gottfried Heinrich STOELZEL: *Concerto in D.* (i; ii) Michael HAYDN: *Concerto in D.* (vi) A. SCARLATTI: *Sinfonia No. 2 in D for flute, trumpet and strings.*
(B) **(*) DG Double DG 413 853-2 (2) [id.].

Maurice André's concert opens with the greatest trumpet concerto of all, by Haydn, and here André takes the *Andante* in a rather leisurely fashion; but he is gracious and serene, and most listeners will respond to his elegance. Often the baroque concertos, too, temper the virtuosity in outer movements with very agreeable central *Andantes*, of which the Torelli is a fine example. The *Sonata for trumpet and organ* by Giovanni Bonaventura Viviani (1683–*c.* 1692) is a very attractive piece, comprising five brief but striking miniatures, each only a minute or so in length. Alessandro Scarlatti's engaging *Sinfonia* is also in five movements and incorporates a solo flute. The latter is all but drowned out in the *Spiritoso* first movement but takes the solo role in the two brief *Adagios* (the second quite touching); the trumpet returns to echo the flute in the central *Allegro* and they share the *Presto* finale. Michael Haydn's concerto, a two-movement concertante section of a seven-movement *Serenade*, has incredibly high tessitura but, characteristically, Maurice André reaches up for it with consummate ease. In the Vivaldi *Double concerto* he plays both solo parts. The three Telemann works are all characteristcally inventive, and one can understand why André wanted to play the transcribed oboe concerto which ends the concert. The solo trumpet is generally well caught, but the Munich recordings date from the late 1960s and the strings as recorded are a bit thin and husky, the focus not improved by the digital remastering. Not that there is any lack of warmth or ambience overall, but the later recordings with Mackerras and the ECO, made a decade later, are smoother and obviously more modern.

Argerich, Martha (piano)

'Duo Piano Extravaganza': MOZART: *Andante with 5 variations, K.501.* DEBUSSY: *En blanc et noir* (both with Stephen Kovacevich). BARTOK: *Sonata for 2 pianos and percussion* (with Kovacevich, Goudswaard, De Roo). RACHMANINOV: *Suite No. 2 for 2 pianos, Op. 17.* LUTOSLAWSKI: *Variations on a theme of Paganini.* RAVEL: *La valse* (all with Nelson Freire). BARTOK: *Concerto for 2 pianos and percussion* (with Freire, Labordus, Pustjens, Concg. O, Zinman). SAINT-SAENS: *Carnival of the animals* (with Freire, Kremer, Van Keulen, T. Zimmermann, Maisky, Hörtnagel, Grafenauer, Brunner, Steckeler & Salmen-Weber).
(B) *** Ph. Duo Dig./Analogue 446 557-2 (2).

Mozart's charming *Andante and variations* is here taken at a rather brisker tempo than usual, but the playing of Argerich and Kovacevich is unfailingly sensitive and vital, and they are equally imaginative in Debussy's *En blanc et noir*, which comes from the last years of his life and is full of unexpected touches. Then, joined by Willy Goudswaard and Michel de Roo, they give a strongly atmospheric and finely characterized performance of Bartók's *Sonata for two pianos and percussion*. At that point Argerich changes keyboard partners and, with Nelson Freire, two more percussionists and the Concertgebouw Orchestra under Zinman, offers us the *Concerto* which Bartók drew from his sonata. Comparing the two, one might wonder why a full orchestra was necessary, to add relatively little. Argerich and Freire continue with a dazzling virtuoso account of Rachmaninov's *Second Suite*, rushing the waltzes off their feet (the movement is marked *presto*, but they play it *prestissimo*). Their virtuosity is further tested by Lutoslawski's *Variations* for piano duo (based wittily on that famous Paganini tune), dating from 1941, and they are not found wanting: the result is exhilarating. Their contribution concludes charismatically with Ravel's own transcription of *La valse*. The recital ends with an affectionate but distinctly eccentric account of Saint-Saëns's *Carnival des animaux* presented in the composer's own original chamber version. From the very beginning, pacing is deliberately slow, the approach essentially refined (but with the instrumentalists adding a few jocular individual comments), and the *Tortoises* nearly grind to a halt. The *Kangaroos*, however, are very light on their feet, the *Aquarium* ethereally transparent, the *Cuckoo in the woods* mistily atmospheric, and the *Birds* flit about daintily. The self-consciously clumsy *Pianists* bring us back to the human world, and after the *Fossils* have had their witty gamble the *Swan* glides in very gently and gracefully on Mischa Maisky's elegant cello. The finale springs to life with sparkling rhythmic pointing and dashing roulades from the piano duo. This is perhaps not a *Carnival* for all seasons, but it is refreshingly different and, like the rest of this superb collection, it is very well recorded.

Baltimore Symphony Orchestra, David Zinman

'Russian sketches': GLINKA: *Overture: Ruslan and Ludmilla*. IPPOLITOV-IVANOV: *Caucasian sketches*. RIMSKY-KORSAKOV: *Russian Easter Festival overture*. TCHAIKOVSKY: *Francesca da Rimini, Op. 32. Eugene Onegin: Polonaise.*
**(*) Telarc Dig. CD 80378 [id.].

Opening with a fizzingly zestful performance of Glinka's *Overture Ruslan and Ludmilla*, with impressively clean articulation from the violins, this remarkably well-recorded concert of Russian music readily demonstrates the excellence of the Baltimore Symphony in every department. The *Caucasian sketches* are a disappointment, but only because Zinman's conception of the evocative first three movements (*In the Mountain Pass*, *In the Village* and *In the Mosque*) is too refined, not Russian enough in feeling; but the famous *Procession of the Sardar* has plenty of piquant colour and impetus. *Francesca da Rimini* brings the most brilliant playing and the middle section, with its rich, Tchaikovskian woodwind palette, is glowingly beautiful. However, the impact of the closing pages here depends more on the spectacular Telarc engineering than on the conductor, who does not generate the necessary degree of passionate despair in the work's great climax. Rimsky-Korsakov's *Russian Easter Festival overture* is a different matter, generating considerable excitement. It is superbly done, with lustrous colours from every section of the orchestra and a memorable solo contribution from the trombones (who are also very impressive in *Francesca*). The recording here is very much in the demonstration bracket and shows Telarc engineering at its most realistic, thrilling in its breadth and body of orchestral tone, with excellent detail and a convincing presence in a natural concert-hall acoustic.

Bamberg Symphony Orchestra, Rudolf Kempe

'In memoriam': BRAHMS: *Symphony No. 2 in D, Op. 73; Variations on a theme of Haydn, Op. 56a*. SCHUBERT: *Symphony No. 8 (Unfinished)*. SMETANA: *Má Vlast: From Bohemia's woods and fields*. MOZART: *Serenade No. 13 (Eine kleine Nachtmusik), K.525*. BIZET: *L'Arlésienne: suites 1–2*.
(B) *** RCA 74321 32771-2 (2) [id.].

A first-class tribute to a fine conductor, with the single proviso that the Bamberg violins in this 1963 recording are made to seem a bit emaciated above the stave; otherwise the sound is full and nicely resonant. The Brahms *Second* is a splendidly alive reading with a strong lyrical impetus, and the *Variations* are comparably successful. But it is the electrifying account of Schubert's *Unfinished* that resonates in the memory, immensely dramatic, yet with the opening and close of the second movement radiantly beautiful in its contrasting repose. The shorter works all go well, the Bizet the least individual, but still played with affection and style.

Baroque Music

'Music of the Baroque' (played by: (i) Orpheus CO; (ii) Simon Standage; (iii) David Reichenberg; (iv) Trevor Pinnock (harpsichord); (v) English Concert Ch.; (vi) English Concert, Trevor Pinnock; (vii) Söllscher (guitar), Camerata Bern, Füri; (viii) Hannes, Wolfgang & Bernhard Läubin, Simon Preston, Norbert Schmitt): (i) HANDEL: *Solomon: Arrival of the Queen of Sheba.* (vi) *Water Music: Allegro – Andante; Air; Bourrée; Hornpipe.* (i) *Xerxes: Largo.* (v, vi) *Messiah: Hallelujah chorus.* (vi) *Music for the royal fireworks: La Réjouissance.* (iii; iv; vi) *Oboe concerto No. 1 (Adagio; Allegro).* (vi) *Concerto grosso, Op. 6/12 in B min. (Aria; Larghetto e piano).* (i) PACHELBEL: *Canon in D.* (viii) MOURET: *Rondeau.* J. S. BACH: (i) *Jesu, joy of man's desiring.* (vi) *Brandenburg concerto No. 3 in G (Allegro).* PURCELL: *Sound the trumpet, sound.* (ii; vi) VIVALDI: *The Four seasons: Winter (Largo).* (vii) *Lute concerto in D (Largo).* (i) ALBINONI (arr. GIAZOTTO): *Adagio in G min.* CORELLI: *Christmas concerto, Op. 6/8 (Allegro; Pastorale; Largo).* (iv) DAQUIN: *Le Coucou.*
(B) *** DG Dig. 449 842-2 [id.].

This 75-minute concert draws on various digital recordings made during the 1980s to make a most agreeable entertainment. The various items have all been issued previously, and their performance pedigrees, on either modern or original instruments, cannot be gainsaid. The opening *Arrival of the Queen of Sheba* and the elegantly played Pachelbel *Canon* feature the Orpheus Chamber Orchestra, but Pinnock's suite from the Handel *Water music* is equally persuasive in demonstrating the advantages of period instruments in baroque repertoire. Such contrasts are aurally stimulating and, with plenty of favourite items included, this makes a very successful bargain sampler, when all the music is consistently well played and recorded. However, the lack of proper documentation is a drawback: the two excellent vocal soloists in Purcell's *Sound the trumpet* are unnamed.

BBC Symphony Orchestra

'BBC Proms Centenary 1895–1995': BERLIOZ: *Symphonie funèbre et triomphale:* 3rd movt: *Apothéose* (cond. Sir John Pritchard). TCHAIKOVSKY: *Nutcracker suite* (cond. Sir Malcolm Sargent). ELGAR: *Symphony No. 1 in A flat* (cond. Sir Adrian Boult). GLUCK: *Orfeo ed Euridice: Che disse? ch'ascolto . . . Addio, addio, o miei sospiri* (J. Baker; cond. Raymond Leppard). WAGNER: *Tannhäuser: Overture & Venusberg music* (with BBC Women's Chorus; cond. Sir Thomas Beecham). JANACEK: *Sinfonietta* (cond. Rudolf Kempe). SHOSTAKOVICH: *Tahiti trot* (arr. of YOUMANS: *Tea for two*; cond. Gennady Rozhdestvensky). R. STRAUSS: *Der Rosenkavalier: suite* (Hallé O, Sir John Barbirolli).
(M) *(**) Carlton Classics DMCD 98 (2) [id.].

Though this collection of broadcast performances from the Proms on two generously filled CDs has a number of recordings to cherish, the choice of items is unrepresentative to the point of being bizarre. Why no recordings of Sir Henry Wood, when Beecham – hardly a conductor much associated with the Proms – is included with the *Tannhäuser overture* and *Venusburg music*? Dating from 1954, it comes with atmospheric chorus. Surely Sir Colin Davis and Basil Cameron, for long Prom associates of Wood, should also be here? Yet there is much to enjoy, even if the upper-mid-price (£19.99 suggested price) is rather high for such a mixed bag.

The gem of the collection is Boult's 1976 Prom performance of Elgar's *First Symphony*. The tape-hiss may be high, but it is not enough to get in the way of one of the most passionate performances of Elgar on disc, with the weight of brass vividly caught. The great melodies of the slow movement are warmly flexible, moulded with more loving rubato than Boult ever allowed himself in the studio, while the finale surges to a thrilling close that brings a gulp to the throat, fully justifying the wild Prom cheer at the end. The Pritchard Berlioz, dating from 1983, is most atmospheric, and though Sargent's 1966 account of Tchaikovsky's *Nutcracker suite* (surely inappropriate representation) is winningly fresh, the audience is maddeningly intrusive and noisy. The '*Addio*' aria from Gluck's *Orfeo* draws from Dame Janet Baker not just her characteristic intensity but a dazzling display of crisply defined coloratura. The Beecham *Tannhäuser* item (with offstage women's chorus included in the *Venusberg music*) has obvious magic, and is aptly set against Barbirolli's ripely flamboyant account with the Hallé of Strauss's *Rosenkavalier suite*. Rudolf Kempe in Janáček's *Sinfonietta* is welcome too, a most sympathetic reading, even if this music needs sharper focus. The selection ends with a gem, Rozhdestvensky's scintillating account – allegedly the first British performance – of Shostakovich's arrangement of *Tea for two*, a vintage Prom event. Recordings are of good BBC quality.

BBC Symphony Orchestra, Sir Adrian Boult

'Boult's BBC years': BEETHOVEN: *Symphony No. 8 in F, Op. 93.* HUMPERDINCK: *Overture Hansel and Gretel.* TCHAIKOVSKY: *Capriccio italien, Op. 45; Serenade for strings, Op. 48.*
(***) Beulah mono 1PD12 [id.].

These recordings return to the catalogue for the first time since the days of shellac and will almost certainly be new to the majority of younger collectors. The Beethoven is a strong, sturdy performance which gives a good idea of the excellence of the BBC Symphony Orchestra in the early days of its existence. It comes from 1932 and the strings produce an opulent, weighty sound without having the opaque quality they developed in the post-war years. The sound is not at all bad for the period, and the transfer does it justice. The Tchaikovsky *Serenade* was recorded five years later in the same Abbey Road studio but with the acoustic sounding much drier. A patrician account with no nonsense about it that may since have been surpassed by many other great partnerships but which will give pleasure to those old enough to remember Sir Adrian's pre-war and wartime broadcasts. The Colston Hall, Bristol, in which the orchestra recorded the *Capriccio italien* in 1940, has the richer acoustic, and the performance combines dignity and freshness.

BBC Symphony Orchestra, or (i) Light Symphony Orchestra, Sir Adrian Boult

'English gramophone premières': BLISS: *Music for strings.* VAUGHAN WILLIAMS: *Job: A Masque for dancing.* (i) Ethel SMYTH: *2 Interlinked French folk melodies; Interlude from Entente Cordiale.*
(M) (***) Dutton Lab. mono CDAX 8016 [id.].

Here are two key works in the Boult discography: the Bliss *Music for strings* and Vaughan Williams's *Job*, sounding better than they have ever done before. The Bliss was premièred at the Salzburg Festival in 1935, and Boult and the strings of the BBC Symphony Orchestra recorded it two years later at the Abbey Road Studios. While later stereo recordings have improved on the sound of Bliss's string sonorities, no one has surpassed the intensity of the playing here. Doubtless the war held up the recording of *Job*, written in 1930, which Vaughan Williams had dedicated to Sir Adrian, for it was not committed to disc until 1946, the first of four recordings Boult made of it, and in some ways the freshest. A self-recommending issue for all admirers of this fine British conductor.

BBC Symphony Orchestra, Sir Charles Groves

English music: ELGAR: *Cello concerto* (with Zara Nelsova, cello). VAUGHAN WILLIAMS: *In the fen country.* PURCELL: *Abdelazer: suite* (with Royal Liverpool PO, Sir Malcolm Sargent). BRITTEN: *Young person's guide to the orchestra (Variations on a theme of Purcell).*
(B) **(*) BBC Radio Classics BBCRD 9111 [id.].

Outstanding among these Proms performances, recorded by the BBC between 1969 and 1977, is Zara Nelsova's warm and intense reading of the Elgar *Cello concerto*, with Sir Charles Groves adding to the electricity. This is a performance of touching simplicity by a fine soloist who has been too little recorded. Groves is similarly purposeful in the Britten *Variations*, where the biting tension in the statement of the Purcell theme contrasts with the easy-going manners in the same theme, as heard in the last movement of the Purcell suite from which it derives, as conducted by Sir Malcolm Sargent. The rare Vaughan Williams piece, a 'symphonic impression' first heard in 1909, makes a warmly attractive fill-up. Atmospheric if not very clearly defined sound. A 71-minute collection that is more than the sum of its parts.

Belgian Radio & TV Philharmonic Orchestra, Brussels, Alexander Rahbari

Romantic symphonic music from Antwerp: MORTELMANS: *Spring idyll.* ALPAERTS: *Pallieter: Wedding feast.* VAN HOOF: *1st Symphonic suite.* BLOCKX: *Milenka: Flemish Fair.* STERNFIELD: *Song and dance at the court of Mary from Burgundy.*
(BB) ** Discover Dig. DICD 920100 [id.].

Flemish rhapsodies: BRUSSELMANS: *Flemish rhapsody*. SCHOEMAKER: *Flemish rhapsody*. DE JONG: *Flemish rhapsody*. ABSILL: *Flemish rhapsody*. ROUSSEL: *Flemish rhapsody*. DE BOECK: *Flemish rhapsody*.
(BB) **(*) Discover DICD 920101 [id.].

This is all unknown repertoire – easy-going late nineteenth- or twentieth-century music from Belgium. On the first CD, Mortelmans' *Spring idyll* is lyrically appealing but perhaps a shade extended for its thematic content, the Jef Van Hoof and Jan Blockx suites agreeably inventive but innocuous. By far the most attractive music comes in the suite of *Song and dance from Burgundy*, nicely scored and piquantly harmonized dances by Susato and his sixteenth-century contemporaries, somewhat comparable with Respighi's *Ancient airs and dances*.

The Flemish rhapsodies all use folk material very effectively, although Brusselmans employs themes of his own invention, written in folk style. All these works are colourfully orchestrated and make agreeable listening, using jolly tunes which in flavour are often like Christmas carols. By far the most striking is the work by the Frenchman, Albert Roussel, which has a characteristic touch of harmonic astringency to tickle the ear. The playing of the Brussels orchestra under Rahbari is enthusiastic yet does not lack finesse, and the recording has an attractive concert-hall ambience and balance. It is not always too sharply defined in some of the more elaborately scored climaxes of the rhapsodies, but the effect is natural. The documentation is excellent.

Berlin Philharmonic Orchestra, Herbert von Karajan

LISZT: *Les Préludes, G.97*. SIBELIUS: *Finlandia, Op. 26; Pélleas et Mélisande: suite*. SMETANA: *Má vlast: Vltava*.
(M) *** DG Dig. 445 550-2 [id.].

This is an outstanding concert, showing Karajan at his most charismatic; and the orchestral playing is certainly in a class of its own. In the performance of *Pelléas et Mélisande* we have a version of Sibelius's subtle and atmospheric score that can compare with the classic Beecham version, originally dating from 1957. Indeed in certain movements, *Spring in the park* and the *Pastorale*, it not only matches Sir Thomas but almost surpasses him. The *Pastorale* is altogether magical, and there is plenty of mystery in the third movement, *At the seashore*, omitted from the Beecham version. Some may find the opening movement, *At the castle gate*, a little too imposing, but the fervour and eloquence of the playing should win over most listeners. The recording is very striking, with great clarity and presence. Karajan is also at his finest in this performance of *Vltava*, and there is some radiant playing from the Berlin orchestra in the moonlit stillness before the river approaches the St John's Rapids. *Les Préludes* is vibrant but a little brash. *Finlandia* reinforces the feeling that this Berlin Philharmonic/Karajan partnership has never been equalled, not even by Toscanini and the NBC Symphony Orchestra.

Boskovsky Ensemble, Willi Boskovsky

'Viennese bonbons': J. STRAUSS, Sr: *Chinese galop; Kettenbrücke Waltz; Eisele und Beisele Sprünge. Cachucha galop*. J. STRAUSS, Jr: *Weine Gemüths waltz; Champagne galop; Salon polka*. LANNER: *Styrian dances; Die Werber & Marien waltzes; Bruder halt galop*. MOZART: *3 Contredanses, K.462; 4 German dances, K.600/1 & 3; K.605/1; K.611*. SCHUBERT: *8 Waltzes & Ländler*.
(M) *** Van. 8.8015.71 [OVC 8015].

This is a captivating selection of the most delightful musical confectionery imaginable. The ensemble is a small chamber group, similar to that led by the Strausses, and the playing has an appropriately intimate Viennese atmosphere. The transfer is impeccable and the recording from the early 1960s, made in the Baumgarten Hall, Vienna, is fresh, smooth and clear, with a nice bloom on sound which is never too inflated.

'Rare old Vienna dances, Vol. 2: *The charm of old Vienna'*: Johann STRAUSS Sr: *Gitana galop; Annen polka; Hofball-Tänze; Seufzer galop*. MAYER: *Schnofler-Tanz'*. HAYDN: *Zingarese Nos. 1, 6 & 8; Katherinen Tänze Nos. 4, 6, 8 & 12*. SCHUBERT: *Tänze from Opp. 9, 18, 67, 77 & 127; Ecossaisen, Op. 49*. LANNER: *Abendsterner waltz; Cerrito polka; Neue Wiener Ländler, Op. 1*. STELZMÜLLER: *Stelzmüller Tanz'*.
(M) **(*) Van. 08 8016.71 [OVC 8016].

Boskovsky's series of recordings of Viennese light music continues to intoxicate with their lightness of touch and transparency of texture. The style is not so far removed from a Schrammeln orchestra, and the recording is warm and lively throughout. However, the present disc is a little below the very high standard of Volumes 1 and 3, containing a certain amount of wallpaper music, while the CD transfers are not always too smooth, occasionally bringing a touch of edge to Boskovsky's violin, with textures not cleanly focused in the Schubert *Ecossaisen* and Haydn *Katherinen Tänze*. Even so, there are some delectable lollipops here, notably the opening *Gitana galop* of Johann Strauss Senior with its horn obbligato, and his very catchy *Annen polka* (not to be confused with his son's piece of the same name). Lanner's *Cerrito polka*, too, is most engaging, and Mayer's *Schnofler-Tanz'* have an almost decadent touch of schmalz.

'Rare old Vienna dances, Vol. 3: *Greetings from old Vienna':* SCHUBERT: *Gratzer galop; Ecossaisen; Galop.* LANNER: *2 Mazurkas; Malapou galop. Hansjörgel polka.* Johann STRAUSS Sr: *Badjaderen Waltz, Op. 53.* Johann STRAUSS Jr: *Scherz polka, Op. 72.* Josef STRAUSS: *Marien-Klänge waltz, Op. 214.* PAYER: *Galanterie Waltz.* BEETHOVEN: *6 Contredanses. Four 'Dances of old Vienna'* by STELZMULLER, GRUBER and ANON.
(M) *** Van. 08.8017.71 [OVC 8017].

This is just as delightful as the first issue in Boskovsky's delectable series. The opening Schubert *Gratzer galop* will entice anyone, played as lightly as this, and Lanner's pieces are equally sparkling. Hieronymus Payer's *Galanterie waltz* is aptly named and quite charming, as are the four brief '*Dances of old Vienna*', with two included from the composer of the carol, *Silent night*. Even with this intimate group of strings, Boskovsky manages the authentically silky Viennese lilt, notably in the *Marien-Klänge waltz* of Josef Strauss, but father Johann's *Badjaderen* is hardly less winning. Wonderfully natural and transparent sound, immaculately transferred to CD.

Boston Pops Orchestra, Arthur Fiedler

'Classics for children': SAINT-SAENS: *Carnival of the animals* (with verses by Ogden Nash, spoken by Hugh Downs; Leo Litwin & Samuel Lipman, pianos). BRITTEN: *Young person's guide to the orchestra* (with commentary by Eric Crozier, spoken by Hugh Downs). GRIEG: *Peer Gynt suite No. 1, Op. 46; Suite No. 2: Solveig's song* (with Eileen Farrell). LOESSER: *Hans Christian Andersen* (film music): Medley, arr. HAYMAN: *Kid stuff* (suite).
(M) **(*) RCA 09026 68131-2 [id.].

A very successful collection, well designed to appeal to quite young children. Hugh Downs, speaking directly and with no suggestion of precociousness, makes Ogden Nash's witticisms concerning the Saint-Saëns menagerie seem less contrived than usual and occasionally raises a smile. He is also excellent with Crozier's description of Britten's orchestra. Both works are very well played, the Saint-Saëns with vigour and enthusiasm and bringing a fine cello solo in *Le Cygne* from Martin Hoherman. The only reservation is the resonant empty-hall sound, which is flattering at modest levels but becomes a bit harsh in fortissimos, with the famous Boston acoustics not always tamed. But children are unlikely to mind, and we enjoyed the programme throughout, not least the string of good tunes at the end (Hayman's suite includes the *Children's marching song* from Rodgers' *The King and I*, *Mary had a little lamb* and *Alouette*). The only orchestral blot is the playing of the solo horn in *Morning* from *Peer Gynt*, which sounds nervous and wobbly: clearly a sub-principal had taken over for the recording. Otherwise almost full marks.

'Pops Caviar': BORODIN: *In the Steppes of Central Asia; Prince Igor: Overture; Polovtsian dances.* RIMSKY-KORSAKOV: *Russian Easter Festival overture; Flight of the bumble bee.* KHACHATURIAN: *Gayaneh: suite. Masquerade: galop.* TCHAIKOVSKY: *Eugene Onegin: Polonaise. Sleeping Beauty: waltz.*
(M) **(*) RCA 09026 68132-2 [id.].

Vibrant performances, with the Khachaturian *Gayaneh suite* (Fiedler at his most ebullient) and Tchaikovsky items standing out. The Borodin pieces could be more romantic, but they are certainly alive and very well played. The 'Living stereo' from the late 1950s is extremely vivid.

'Pops Christmas party': Leroy ANDERSON: *A Christmas festival; Sleigh ride.* TCHAIKOVSKY: *Nutcracker* (ballet): extended excerpts. SCOTT: *Toy trumpet.* HUMPERDINCK: *Hänsel und Gretel: Dream pantomime.* MOZART: *Sleigh ride.* MARKS: *Rudolph the red-nosed reindeer.* COOTS: *Santa Claus is coming to town.*
(M) ** RCA 09026 61685-2 [id.].

Introduced with Leroy Anderson's brightly scored Christmas pot-pourri, this 72-minute selection centres on Fiedler's extremely vivid 1956 set of highlights from the *Nutcracker*, as seasonal an offering as you could wish. The early stereo lacks something in opulence, but the zest and character of the playing compensates. Some of the other items are less repeatable, but they are presented with plenty of spirit.

'Fiedler encores': SIBELIUS: *Finlandia*. GRIEG: *Peer Gynt suite No. 1; Suite No. 2: Solveig's song*. DVORAK: *Slavonic Dance, Op. 46/1*. SMETANA: *Má vlast: Vltava*. VAUGHAN WILLIAMS: *English folk song suite*. IVES: *Variations on 'America'*.
(M) **(*) Decca Phase Four 448 952-2 [id.].

These recordings derive from a pair of LPs originally published in 1975 and 1978. The 1975 performance of the *Peer Gynt* excerpts is direct, alive and spontaneous. It is recorded with exceptional life and vividness and is very enjoyable indeed. There are more tender accounts of *Solveig's song* available, but that is the only reservation. The other items make a characteristically lively concert. Fiedler always keeps the pot boiling, even if his balance of various ingredients lacks subtlety at times. The outer movements of the *English folksongs suite* come off with robust vigour, and he gives a splendidly rumbustious account of Ives's *Variations on 'America'*. The overall balance is forward, which precludes wide dynamic contrasts but ensures good projection and detail if not the last degree of refinement.

Bournemouth Sinfonietta, Richard Studt

English string music: BRITTEN: *Variations on a theme of Frank Bridge, Op. 10*. HOLST: *St Paul's suite, Op. 29/1*. DELIUS: *2 Aquarelles*. VAUGHAN WILLIAMS: *5 Variants of Dives and Lazarus*. WARLOCK: *Capriol suite*.
(BB) *** Naxos Dig. 8.550823 [id.].

This is the finest of the concerts of string music recorded for Naxos by Richard Studt and the excellent Bournemouth Sinfonietta. The Britten *Frank Bridge variations* is particularly memorable, showing easy virtuosity yet often achieving the lightest touch, so that the *Vienna waltz* movement sparkles in its delicacy. The *Funeral march* may not be so desperately intense as Karajan's famous mono version with the Philharmonia, but it is still very touching; and the following *Chant* is ethereal in its bleakly refined atmosphere. The sprightly Holst *St Paul's suite* and Warlock's *Capriol*, agreeably robust, could hardly be better played, while Vaughan Williams's *Dives and Lazarus* is especially fresh and conveys the famous biblical story of the rich man and the beggar most evocatively, especially in the very beautiful closing section, when Lazarus finds himself in heaven. The recording, made in St Peter's Church, Parkstone, is full-bodied, immediate and real – very much in the demonstration bracket.

20th Century string music. BARTÓK: *Divertimento*. BRITTEN: *Simple symphony, Op. 4*. WALTON: *2 Pieces from Henry V: Death of Falstaff (Passacaglia); Touch her soft lips and part*. STRAVINSKY: *Concerto in D*.
(BB) ** Naxos Dig. 8.550979 [id.].

This is the least successful of the three concerts of string music recorded by Naxos in Bournemouth. The Sinfonietta players do not sound completely at ease in the shifting moods of the Bartók *Divertimento* and their ensemble could be crisper in the Stravinsky *Concerto*. The *Simple Symphony* comes off brightly, with a gently nostalgic *Sentimental sarabande* and a brisk, alert finale, but the *Playful pizzicato* could be more exuberant, especially in its famous trio which the composer did so joyously. The two Walton pieces are warmly atmospheric, and there are no complaints about the sound.

Bournemouth Sinfonietta or Symphony Orchestra, Norman Del Mar

English music: HOLST: *Brook Green suite; A Somerset rhapsody*. DELIUS: *Air and dance*. VAUGHAN WILLIAMS: *Concerto grosso; Aristophanic suite: The Wasps*. ELGAR: *Serenade for strings*.
(M) *** EMI CDM5 65130-2 [id.].

This CD generously combines the contents of two previously issued LPs of English music, substituting Elgar's *Serenade* for Warlock's. Holst's *Brook Green suite* was originally written for the St Paul's School for Girls, where Holst was in charge of music. It emerged as far more than an exercise for students, as Del Mar's dedicated performance demonstrates, most strikingly in the vigorous final dance. The *Concerto grosso* of Vaughan Williams on the other hand was written for a jamboree at the Royal Albert Hall with hundreds of string players of the Rural Music Schools Association. Here (in its début recording) it is given as a straight work for double string orchestra. The enchanting Delius miniatures and the evocative Holst *Somerset rhapsody* make an excellent contrast, while the *Wasps overture* – here dashingly performed – and the other items in the suite are delightful, too. Del Mar brings out the wit in the *March of the kitchen utensils* with his mock pomposity. The recording throughout is splendid.

(i) **British Symphony Orchestra,** (ii) **London Symphony Orchestra,** (iii) **Symphony Orchestra,** (iv) **Queen's Hall Orchestra,** (v) **London Philharmonic Orchestra; Sir Henry Wood**

'The Best of Sir Henry J. Wood': (i) BACH: *Brandenburg concerto No. 3.* (ii) HAYDN: *Symphony No. 45 in F sharp min. (Farewell).* (ii) SCHUBERT: *Symphony No. 8 in B min. (Unfinished).* (ii) LITOLFF: *Concerto No. 4: Scherzo* (with Irene Scharrer). (iii) RACHMANINOV (arr. WOOD): *Prelude in C sharp min.* (iv) DVORAK: *Symphonic variations* (with rehearsal sequence). (iv) BRUCKNER: *Overture in C min.* (iv) BEETHOVEN: *Symphony No. 5 in C min., Op. 67.* (iv) BRAHMS: *Variations on a theme of Haydn.*
(M) (***) Dutton Lab. mono 2CDAX 2002 (2) [id.].

This collection is aptly named. During the great days of the Proms, this annual summer musical jamboree, so essentially British, was the source of a musical education for many devotees, long before the coming of LPs, tapes and CDs, and when a Beethoven symphony on four or five 78 shellac discs could cost a substantial part of a week's wages. There were no frills (except perhaps in a Tchaikovsky symphony, where Wood was inclined to allow himself a fair amount of freedom), and he delivered strong, direct readings of uncommon freshness – as these recordings illustrate. The Bach *Third Brandenburg* is a joy. It uses a large group of strings but with plenty of light and shade and possesses an invigorating vitality. Haydn's *Farewell Symphony* – played here with remarkable finesse – was recorded at a time when only the late *London Symphonies* were heard at concerts – and that almost solely due to Sir Thomas Beecham. Beethoven's *Fifth* is without the histrionics of a Toscanini, a sound reading which is surprisingly satisfying even today. We also hear Wood rehearsing (the words remarkably clear) in his direct, no-nonsense manner (he had only limited rehearsal time at his disposal, but British musicians could always sight-read with incredible dexterity – even at a performance, if they had to!). The transfers are typical of Dutton expertise and are remarkably full and vivid. Everything here sounds alive; only the Dvořák *Symphonic variations* is disappointing, but that is at least partly because the Decca recording is so lacklustre – made in 1937, just before the arrival of Arthur Haddy who was to transform the company's technical prowess with the coming of wartime FFRR 78s. But that is another story.

(i) **Brymer, Jack** (clarinet), **Vienna State Opera Orchestra, Felix Prohaska;** (ii) **David Glazer** (clarinet), **Würtemberg CO, Faerber;** (iii) **Joza Ostrack** (clarinet), **Mozart Festival Orchestra, Lizzio**

Clarinet concertos: (i) KROMMER: *Concerto in E flat.* WAGNER (BAERMANN): *Adagio for clarinet and strings.* DEBUSSY: *Première rapsodie.* (ii) WEBER: *Clarinet concerto No. 1 in F min.; Clarinet concertino, Op. 26;* STAMITZ: *Concerto No. 3.* (iii) MOZART: *Concerto in A, K.622.*
(M) *** Van. 08.9176.72 (2).

Jack Brymer's performance of the Krommer *Concerto* with its melting *Adagio* and delightful, chortling finale is a joy, while the Baermann *Adagio* (once attributed to Wagner) and the Debussy *Rapsodie* are also superbly poised. David Glazer's Weber (the *First concerto* and the engaging *Concertino*) is most elegant, with the slow movement of the concerto beautifully phrased and both finales winningly jocular – the close of the *Concertino* chirrups just as it should. The Stamitz is plainer but still very agreeable. Joza Ostrack's performance of the greatest work of all, by Mozart, agreeably combines warmth and finesse; so altogether this makes a worthwhile anthology. Accompaniments are well managed and the recordings are all fully acceptable, if not absolutely refined; but the interest of the repertoire – so conveniently gathered together – more than compensates. No recording dates are given.

Camden, Anthony (oboe), **City of London Sinfonia, Nicholas Ward**

Italian oboe concertos: CIMAROSA, arr. Arthur BENJAMIN: *Concerto in C.* BELLINI: *Concerto in E flat.* RIGHINI: *Concerto in C.* FIORILLO: *Sinfonia concertante in F* (with Julia Girdwood). CORELLI, arr. BARBIROLLI: *Concerto in A.* PERGOLESI/BARBIROLLI: *Concerto in C min.*
(BB) **(*) Naxos Dig. 8.553433 [id.].

This collection recalls the series of outstanding recordings made by Evelyn Rothwell for Pye/PRT with her husband, Sir John Barbirolli, conducting. He specially arranged the highly engaging pastiche works of Corelli and Pergolesi for her to play and put his signature firmly on the *Sarabanda* of the Corelli *Concerto*, which he scored as a duet for oboe and cello, his own instrument. We hope Lady Barbirolli's recordings will be restored to the catalogue before too long. Meanwhile these sympathetic and stylishly played performances from Anthony Camden will suffice admirably, particularly at Naxos price. He has a most attractive timbre, and Nicholas Ward's accompaniments are impeccable. There are two very small reservations. The Fiorillo *Sinfonia concertante*, which features a pair of oboes (the second part is neatly managed by Julia Girdwood), although nicely written for the two soloists, is very conventional in its material and the first movement is a shade too long. The other point concerns the delightful five-note opening phrase of Arthur Benjamin's delicious Cimarosa confection, which Camden plays curiously lethargically, echoed by Ward. It is a small point, but Lady Barbirolli's account still lingers in the memory. The Naxos recording is excellently balanced and truthful.

Casals, Pablo (cellist, conductor)

Casals Edition

(with (i) Paul Baumgartner; (ii) John Wummer, Bernard Goldberg, Prades Festival O): BACH: (i) *Viola da gamba sonatas Nos. 1–3, BWV 1027–9;* (ii) *Brandenburg concerto No. 4 in G, BWV 1049.*
(M) ** Sony mono SMK 66572 [id.].

(with (i) Dame Myra Hess, Joseph Szigeti; (ii) Mieczyslaw Horszowski, Alexander Schneider): (i) BRAHMS: *Piano trio in C, Op. 87.* (ii) MENDELSSOHN: *Piano trio in D min., Op. 49.*
(M) ** Sony mono/stereo SMK 66571 [id.].

(cond. Perpignan Festival O; with (i) Yvonne Lefebure; (ii) Rudolf Serkin): MOZART: *Piano concertos Nos.* (i) *20 in D min., K.466;* (ii) *22 in E flat, K.482.*
(M) ** Sony mono SMK 66570 [id.].

(cond. Perpignan Festival O; with (i) Marcel Tabuteau, Alexander Schneider): MOZART: *Symphony No. 29 in A, K201; Eine kleine Nachtmusik;* (i) *Divertimento No. 11 in D, K251.*
(M) ** Sony mono SMK 66569 [id.].

Casals was a great musician, so that nothing he touched is without interest to musicians or music-lovers alike. These four discs give a glimpse of the breadth and depth of his musicianship – not that all of them are likely to win (or necessarily deserve) universal favour. CBS documented all these Prades and Perpignan performances in a handsome LP set, some of whose contents are reproduced here. The Bach sonatas with Paul Baumgartner as pianist were recorded in 1950 at the inaugural Prades Festival and, flawed though they may be in some respects (grunts and other extraneous noises), they are performances of great humanity, as indeed was the *Fourth Brandenburg* with two fine flautists, John Wummer and Bernard Goldberg, with the Prades Festival Orchestra. Needless to say, the orchestral forces are fairly large, and the continuo is a piano (as was common at this time) – think of the Boston set under Koussevitzky with its wonderfully light accents – but good style is related to musical truth and sensitive phrasing more than it is to the correct size or composition of ensembles. The 1950 recordings naturally call for some tolerance but are still more than just acceptable.

The Brahms *C major Trio*, Op. 87, with Joseph Szigeti and Myra Hess, comes from 1952 and has appeared previously, in harness with the Szigeti and Ormandy account of the *Violin concerto*, with the Philadelphia Orchestra, when we described it as perhaps low on 'fi' but high on musicianship and humanity: 'a richly rewarding account that soon rises above the inevitable sonic limitations, Szigeti's moments of rough tone and Casals's groans'. The Mendelssohn *Trio*, recorded in 1961 (with Alexander Schneider and Mieczyslaw Horszowski) in the White House, at the request of President Kennedy, is in stereo and finds Casals inspired but not in the fullest command of his instrument. The ghost of the celebrated 1929 recording with Thibaud and Cortot is not wholly exorcized.

The Mozart concertos also come from the 1952 Perpignan Festival and are again mono. The *D minor*, K.466, with Yvonne Lefebure, has not appeared before, and it shows elegance and taste, though Serkin's *E flat*, K.482, has the greater character. Neither is a 'library' choice, but there are lessons to be learnt from both performances. Serkin is still the responsive and sensitive artist he was in pre-war days, before the mannerisms that disfigured his Mozart playing in the 1960s afflicted him. The *Symphony No. 29 in A* and the remaining pieces on the same disc also derive from Perpignan in 1952 and have that vitality and dedication we associate with Casals as a great musician. The *Divertimento* also affords an opportunity to hear the legendary Marcel Tabuteau, a player of unfailing eloquence and artistry.

Chicago Symphony Orchestra, Fritz Reiner

'The Reiner sound': RAVEL: *Rapsodie espagnole; Pavane pour une enfante défunte.* LISZT: *Totentanz* (with Byron Janis). WEBER/BERLIOZ: *Invitation to the dance.* RACHMANINOV: *The Isle of the dead, Op. 29.*
(M) *** BMG/RCA 09026 61250-2.

'*The Reiner sound*', a combination of marvellous orchestral playing and the glorious acoustics of Chicago's Orchestra Hall, recorded with the simplest stereo microphone techniques, is heard at its finest and most distinctive in the superb Ravel items. The Liszt *Totentanz* brings an exciting bravura contribution from Byron Janis, and the Weber is agreeably polished and spirited. The microphone balance in *The Isle of the dead* is a shade close, but this, too, is one of the finest of Reiner's Chicago recordings.

'Russian showpieces': MUSSORGSKY: *Pictures at an exhibition* (orch. Ravel); *Night on a bare mountain* (arr. RIMSKY-KORSAKOV). TCHAIKOVSKY: *Marche slave; Suite No. 1: Marche miniature.* BORODIN: *Polovtsian march.* KABALEVSKY: *Colas Breugnon overture.* GLINKA: *Ruslan and Ludmilla overture.*
(M) *** BMG/RCA 09026 61958-2 [id.].

Reiner's famous (1957) recording of the *Pictures* (discussed in the composer section) is linked with a powerful *Night on a bare mountain* within a 1959 concert of shorter Russian pieces, all brilliantly played and spectacularly recorded. Reiner's account of the *Ruslan and Ludmilla overture* is not quite as taut as Solti's famous LSO version, but its racy geniality is very attractive. *Colas Breugnon* with its syncopated cross-rhythms has plenty of gusto; the *Polovtsian march* is robustly rhythmic and Tchaikovsky's *Marche slave* suitably sombre, yet with an exciting coda.

Chicago Symphony Orchestra, Frederick Stock

WAGNER: *Die Meistersinger Overture.* BRAHMS: *Hungarian dances Nos. 17–21.* GOLDMARK: *In the springtime Overture.* SUK: *Fairy tales: Folkdance (polka).* GLAZUNOV: *Les ruses d'amour: Introduction and waltz.* TCHAIKOVSKY: *Symphony No. 5 in E min.* PAGANINI: *Moto perpetuo, Op. 11* (orch. Stock). WALTON: *Scapino: comedy overture.* DOHNANYI: *Suite for orchestra, Op. 19.* R. STRAUSS: *Also sprach Zarathustra.* STOCK: *Symphonic waltz. Op. 8.*
✿ (M) (***) Biddulph mono WHL 021/22 [id.].

Frederick Stock, born in Germany in 1872, studied composition and violin at the Cologne Conservatoire; among his teachers was Humperdinck, and Mengelberg was a fellow student. He began his career as an orchestral violinist, and in 1895 he emigrated to America to join the ranks of the Chicago Symphony as a viola player. The orchestra was then four years old. In 1905 he was hired on a temporary basis as its musical director; but he stayed on for nearly 40 years until he died in October 1942. He built the orchestra into the splendid ensemble which Fritz Reiner was eventually to inherit and established its world reputation, especially for its brass playing, although (on the evidence of these recordings) the strings were equally impressive. Like Reiner, he had the advantage of the marvellous acoustics of Chicago's Symphony Hall in which to make his records which, alongside Stokowski's Philadelphia recordings, are technically among the finest to come out of America in the late 1920s. Indeed the sound in Tchaikovsky's *Fifth* (1927) is so warm and full-bodied that in no time at all one forgets one is listening to an old recording and simply revels in the rich string patina and fine woodwind colours (heard at their finest in the elegantly played waltz movement). The brass come fully into their own in the finale. Stock's interpretation is endearingly wilful, very like Mengelberg's more famous reading, which was made only six months later. Stock pulls back at the entry of the secondary group in the first movement. The effect is emphasized because of a side change but is consistent in the recapitulation. The slow movement is very much *con alcuna licenza* (Tchaikovsky's marking) and the horn soloist must have needed great nerve to sustain his great solo at the chosen spacious tempo. But Stock has that supreme gift of being able to create the feeling of a live performance while making a recording, and this *Fifth*, for all its eccentricities, is very enjoyable. The finale has the traditional cut which was so often observed at that time, but the effect is seamless and the final brass peroration has only ever been topped by Stokowski's 78-r.p.m. Philadelphia set. The programme opens with a thrillingly sonorous account of *Die Meistersinger overture* (1926), with the tension held right to the end, in spite of the big rallentando at the majestic reprise of the introductory 'fanfare'. The Brahms dances, played with virtuosity and considerable panache, were recorded in 1925 but never issued, and both the Suk *Polka* (1926) and the charming Glazunov *Waltz* (1929) show the colourful palette of Stock's Chicago woodwind section, while Goldmark's *In the springtime overture* sounds uncommonly fresh in this early (1925) performance. The Dohnányi suite too (1928) is stylishly and pleasingly done, with nice touches of wit and plenty of lilt in the waltz featured in the closing movement, where Stock handles the tempo changes with affectionate sophistication. But here for some reason the recording is very closely miked and dry; was it actually recorded in Symphony Hall, one wonders, for there is little ambient effect?

Stock's most famous record is of Walton's *Scapino overture*, which he commissioned for the orchestra's fiftieth anniversary celebrations. It is played here with fizzing virtuosity and much élan and is particularly valuable in being the only existing recording of Walton's original score before the composer made his revisions. This and an equally brilliant account of Paganini's *Moto perpetuo*, deftly played in unison by the orchestral violins, were recorded in 1941, the sound brightly lit (the violins are closely miked in the Paganini) but retaining underlying warmth. The set ends appropriately with a work indelibly associated with Chicago because of Reiner's superb, later, stereo version: Strauss's *Also sprach Zarathustra*. But Stock's account certainly does not come under its shadow. The spectacular opening is remarkably well caught and the passion of the violins is thrilling. This was made in 1940, and here the Columbia engineers made a compromise between brilliance and richness of timbre, with the hall ambience adding a natural breadth. The range of dynamic is striking, and Stock's reading must be placed among the finest, for it is seemingly completely spontaneous, yet splendidly controlled and shaped. The orchestral concentration is held at the highest level throughout, and particularly so during the darkly dormant section of the score on the lower strings associated with 'Science' and the later passage on the high violins; Stock then follows with an exciting accelerando to reach the spectacular climax in 'The Convalescent'. He maintains this thrust through to the closing pages, with the tolling bell coming through plangently, and the coda very touching. Then for an encore the conductor provides a charmingly tuneful *Symphonic waltz* of his own composition, endearingly inflated but not boring when presented with such zest, and sumptuously recorded in 1930. Yet there is nothing 'historic' about live music-making of this calibre, and this fascinating set is very highly recommended. It certainly does Stock's reputation full justice.

Chung, Kyung Wha (violin)

'The Great violin concertos': MENDELSSOHN: *Concerto in E min., Op. 64* (with Montreal SO, Dutoit). BEETHOVEN: *Concerto in D, Op. 61* (with VPO, Kondrashin). TCHAIKOVSKY: *Concerto in D, Op. 35*. SIBELIUS: *Concerto in D min., Op. 47* (both with LSO, Previn).
(B) **(*) Decca Double Analogue/Dig. 452 325-2 (2) [id.].

This Double Decca begs comparison with Grumiaux's Philips Duo called, more sensibly, '*Favourite violin concertos*' (see below). But Grumiaux offers Brahms instead of Sibelius and concentrates on repertoire in which his refined, poetic style produces satisfying results in all four works. Chung only scores three out of four. Her collection is let down by the 1979 account of the Beethoven which, measured and thoughtful, lacks the compulsion one would have predicted, due largely to the often prosaic conducting of Kondrashin. There is poetry in individual movements – the minor-key episode of the finale, for example, which alone justifies the unusually slow tempo – but, with too little of the soloist's natural electricity conveyed and none of her volatile imagination, it must be counted a disappointment, despite the first-class digital sound.

The Mendelssohn, made two years later, could not be more different. Chung favours speeds faster than usual in all three movements and the result is sparkling and happy, with the lovely slow movement fresh and songful, not at all sentimental. With warmly sympathetic accompaniment from Dutoit and the Montreal orchestra, amply recorded, the result was one of her happiest recordings.

The Sibelius/Tchaikovsky pairing (from 1970) has already been successfully reissued at mid-price as part of Decca's Classic Sound series (425 080-2) and is highly praised in our main volume. She brings an equally sympathetic and idiomatic response to both concertos, and Previn's accompaniments are of the highest order. The latter is a much better investment than the latest format, unless the Mendelssohn is essential.

Cincinnati Pops Orchestra, Erich Kunzel

'Favourite overtures': SUPPE: *Light cavalry; Poet and peasant*. AUBER: *Fra Diavolo*. HEROLD: *Zampa*. REZNICEK: *Donna Diana*. OFFENBACH: *Orpheus in the Underworld*. ROSSINI: *William Tell*.
*** Telarc Dig. CD 80116 [id.].

In this spectacularly recorded (1985) collection of favourite bandstand overtures the playing has fine exuberance and gusto (only the galop from *William Tell* could perhaps have had greater impetus) and the resonant ambience of Cincinnati's Music Hall lends itself to Telarc's wide-ranging engineering, with the bass drum nicely caught. Perhaps the opening of *Fra Diavolo* would have benefited from a more transparent sound, but for the most part the opulence suits the vigorous style of the music-making, with *Zampa* and the Suppé overtures particularly successful.

Cleveland Symphonic Winds, Fennell

'Stars and stripes': ARNAUD: *3 Fanfares.* BARBER: *Commando march.* LEEMANS: *Belgian Paratroopers.* FUCIK: *Florentine march, Op. 214.* KING: Barnum and Bailey's favourite. ZIMMERMAN: *Anchors aweigh.* J. STRAUSS Sr: *Radetzky march.* VAUGHAN WILLIAMS: *Sea songs; Folk songs suite.* SOUSA: *The Stars and stripes forever.* GRAINGER: *Lincolnshire posy.*
*** Telarc Dig. CD 80099 [id.].

This vintage collection from Frederick Fennell and his superb Cleveland wind and brass group is one of the finest of its kind ever made. Severance Hall, Cleveland, has ideal acoustics for this programme and the playing has wonderful virtuosity and panache. Add to all this digital engineering of Telarc's highest calibre, and you have a very special issue.

Concertgebouw Orchestra

'Early years' (cond. (i) Eduard van Beinum; (ii) Kiril Kondrashin; (iii) Karl Boehm; (iv) George Szell; (v) Paul van Kempen; (vi) Pierre Monteux): (i) BEETHOVEN: *Symphony No. 2 in D;* (ii) *Symphony No. 3 in E flat (Eroica).* (iii) R. STRAUSS: *Death and transfiguration.* MOZART: *Symphony No. 26 in E flat, K.184;* (iv) *Symphony No. 34 in C, K.338.* (v) TCHAIKOVSKY: *Symphony No. 6 in B min. (Pathétique).* (vi) SCHUBERT: *Symphony No. 8 (Unfinished).*
(M) *** Ph. mono 438 524-2 (3) [id.].

This is one of the most successful sets in Philips's *'Early years'* series. Some of the performances here come close to greatness and nearly all are touched by distinction. They represent quite a time-span: Paul van Kempen's *Pathétique*, made in 1951, is very impressive indeed, and so for that matter is the Kondrashin *Eroica* from 1979. Eduard van Beinum was always respected, but this account of Beethoven's *Second Symphony* prompts one to feel that he is actually underrated. A useful and worthwhile compilation, despite variable sound-quality.

(i) Concertgebouw Orchestra; (ii) LSO, Pierre Monteux

(i) BEETHOVEN: *Symphony No. 3 in E flat (Eroica).* SCHUBERT: *Symphony No. 8 (Unfinished).* (ii) TCHAIKOVSKY: *Swan Lake* (ballet): *highlights.* BRAHMS: *Symphony No. 2 in D, Op. 73; Tragic overture, Op. 81; Academic festival overture, Op. 80.* RAVEL: *Boléro; La valse; Ma Mère l'Oye.* DEBUSSY: *Images; Le martyre de Saint Sébastien.*
(M) ** Ph. 442 544-2 (5) [id.].

This Philips box, celebrating Monteux's recordings in London and Amsterdam during the early 1960s, is rather a mixed offering. Monteux's 1962 Concertgebouw *Eroica* is better played (though not better recorded) than his Vienna Philharmonic version for Decca of five years earlier (see above, under its composer entry). But in any case that Vienna performance is much more satisfying interpretatively; the Philips version is let down by the absence of real weight in the *Funeral march*. Monteux's *Unfinished* is also disappointing. In the first movement there is an unashamed speed-change between the first and second subjects, while Monteux believes in treating the second movement in leisurely fashion and obtaining the maximum contrast. This is not among his more alert performances, although the recording is full and well balanced. The Concertgebouw Orchestra seemed to inspire him less than the LSO. However, much the same comments must be made about his London account of Brahms's *Second Symphony*, which offers relaxed idiomatic playing and an eminently sound reading; yet the performance fails to resound in the memory in quite the way of his earlier Decca records of the Beethoven symphonies. Incidentally, the *Tragic overture*, recorded at the same time, which has rather more drama, has not been issued before.

Monteux's complete 1964 version of Ravel's *Ma Mère l'Oye* is a poetic, unforced reading given characteristically refined and naturally balanced sound by the Philips engineers, though the effect is not as translucent as Paray's Mercury version (434 343-2 – see under the composer). *La Valse* goes well too, but *Boléro* brings a slight quickening of tempo in the closing pages.

The 59-minute selection from Tchaikovsky's *Swan Lake*, often reissued in the days of LP, was one of Monteux's Philips successes. The spacious acoustic means that the 1962 recording hardly sounds dated, and it suits the conductor's approach to the finale, which he takes slowly – some might feel too slowly – and grandly, supported by rich-toned brass. Throughout, the LSO playing is beautifully turned. Hugh Maguire is the only individual to be named (for his violin solo in the Dance of Odette and the Prince), but the comparably fine contribution of the principal oboe is also worth noting.

Undoubtedly the best of the five discs included here is the classic Monteux coupling of *Images* and the orchestral version of *Le martyre de Saint Sébastien*, and this needs restoring to the catalogue as an individual issue. Monteux's performance of *Images* was notable for its freshness and impetus (although this is achieved by the concentration of the playing rather than by fast tempi). The 1963 recording is another tribute to the Philips engineering of the time, for there is a fine sheen of warmth and sensuousness to the strings (especially in *Les parfums de la nuit*), while the woodwind is delicately hued. This vivid yet refined feeling for colour is carried through into the orchestral sections from *Le martyre*. The fragility of texture of Debussy's exquisite scoring is marvellously balanced by Monteux, and he never lets the music become static.

Concertgebouw Orchestra, Georg Szell

'The Concertgebouw recordings': SCHUBERT: *Rosamunde: Overture; Ballet music No. 2; Entr'actes Nos. 1 & 3.* MENDELSSOHN: *A Midsummer Night's Dream: Overture; Scherzo; Nocturne; Wedding march.* MOZART: *Symphony No. 34 in C, K.338.* BEETHOVEN: *Symphony No. 5 in C min., Op. 67.* SIBELIUS: *Symphony No. 2 in D, Op. 43.*
(M) *** Ph. 442 727-2 (2) [id.].

George Szell was musical director of the Cleveland Orchestra from 1946 until his death in 1970, and he turned his players into an ensemble of the most remarkable virtuosity. But he also occasionally guest-conducted other orchestras with great success, and the present anthology spans the decade from 1957 to 1966. Probably the most striking performance here is the Sibelius *D major Symphony*. Szell's reading is marvellously taut and well held together, and its merits are well known: great tension and power. The remastered sound is a great improvement on the earlier CD reissue. Beethoven's *Fifth* is hardly less thrilling; if not quite as intense as his Cleveland version, that is not necessarily a drawback, with such fine playing. The Schubert and Mendelssohn incidental music is hardly less impressive. The *Rosamunde overture* has a strikingly resilient spring and the *Ballet music* and *Entr'actes* match polish and charm. Particularly attractive is the way Szell quickens the pace of the middle section of the *B flat Entr'acte* so that the effect of the reprise of the famous principal melody is heightened. The lightness and clean, sweet articulation of the violins in the Mendelssohn *Midsummer Night's Dream overture* are a delight: the wonderfully nimble wind-playing in the *Scherzo* is no less engaging, and there is a fine horn solo in the *Nocturne*. Szell, as usual, offers big-band Mozart, but the playing in the *Andante* has refinement as well as warmth, and the finale brings a bustle achieved from articulation of great precision.

Czech Philharmonic Orchestra, Gerd Albrecht

HAAS: *Studies for string orchestra.* SCHULHOF: *Symphony No. 2.* ULLMANN: *Symphony No. 2.* KLEIN: *Partita for strings.*
*** Orfeo Dig. C 337941 A [id.].

Like the issues in Decca's *Entartete Musik* series, this Orfeo disc features music dismissed by the Nazis as decadent, all here by Jewish composers from Czechoslovakia slaughtered in the Holocaust. Pavel Haas, often counted as Janáček's most important pupil, wrote his *Studies* in Theresienstadt, the prison camp where the Nazis assembled Jewish intellectuals, later to be killed in death camps. Tautly argued in four sections lasting eight minutes, it was given its first performance in the camp under one of the then inmates who happily managed to survive, Karel Ančerl, later the conductor of the Czech Philharmonic. Albrecht and today's Czech Philharmonic bring out the vitality of the writing, with no hint in it of self-indulgence or self-pity. This is a composer writing in sight of death simply because he has to, relishing a last opportunity. The *Symphony No. 2* of Erwin Schulhof was written in 1932, long before the Nazis invaded Czechoslovakia, a work very much of its period with a charming *Scherzo alla Jazz* influenced by Stravinsky's *Soldier's tale*. The *Symphony No. 2* of Viktor Ullmann, also in four crisp movements, was one of no fewer than 25 works that he wrote in Theresienstadt, including the opera, *The Emperor of Atlantis*, also on disc. Though he was a pupil of Schoenberg, he here returned to tonality, communicating directly. The youngest of the four, Gideon Klein from Moravia, more specifically drew inspiration from folk roots, very much in the way that Bartók did in Hungary. His *Partita for strings*, like the Pavel Haas *Studies*, has darkness in it, notably in the central variation movement, but here too the piece culminates in a mood of energetic optimism, a heart-warming expression of defiance. Very well played and recorded, the four works are the more moving for giving only momentary hints of what the composers were going through. First-rate sound.

Cziffra, György (piano)

Cziffra Edition, Volume 2: CHOPIN: *Piano concerto No. 1 in E min., Op. 11* (with O de Paris, György Cziffra, Jr). *Ballade No. 4 in F min., Op. 52; Etudes: in E; in A flat, Op. 10/3 & 10; in A flat & F min., Op. 25/1–2; Impromptu No. 1 in A flat, Op. 29; Nocturne No. 2 in E flat, Op. 9/2; Polonaise in A (Military), Op. 40/1.*
(M) ** EMI CDM5 65251-2 [id.].

The Cziffra Edition comes from EMI France and was prompted by the pianist's death in 1994. He was a pianist of prodigious technical gifts and a wide stylistic range. His playing always has great personality, but its impulse is at times exasperatingly wayward. When he kept his emotional responses in check (as in early French keyboard music), his performances could be very impressive and, if you accept the unrestricted flamboyance, his Liszt could also be pretty staggering. Cziffra's account of the Chopin *E minor Concerto* has plenty of life, helped by a robust orchestral contribution from his son, who yet opens the central *Romance* very persuasively. There are moments of genuine poetry but the reading as a whole is characteristically extrovert. The solo performances are less attractive and too often sound calculated. Fair recording, using the Paris Salle Wagram. The concerto dates from 1968 and the rest from over the next decade.

Cziffra Edition, Volume 3 (with Philh. O, André Vandernoot): LISZT: *Piano concertos Nos. 1 in E flat; 2 in A.* TCHAIKOVSKY: *Piano concerto No. 1 in B flat min., Op. 23.*
(M) **(*) EMI CDM5 65252-2 [id.].

The two Liszt concertos suit Cziffra's bold, volatile manner very well indeed and the glittering solo playing has enormous panache, while there is no lack of lyrical warmth. The *Second Concerto* is even finer than the *First*. There is much of the grand manner in his performance and he has clearly persuaded Vandernoot to back him up in his interpretation. The work's quicksilver moods bring a true feeling of spontaneity. Surprisingly, the Tchaikovsky *B flat minor* comes off very much less successfully. Cziffra, as always, displays a prodigious technique but, during the first movement, conductor and soloist seem not wholly agreed on the degree of forward thrust the music needs. In spite of the use of the Kingsway Hall, the recordings (made in 1958 and 1961) are comparatively two-dimensional and the strings tend to shrillness in the Tchaikovsky.

Detroit Symphony Orchestra, Neeme Järvi

'Encore!': CHABRIER: *Fête polonaise.* GLINKA: *Kamarinskaya; Valse fantaisie.* SIBELIUS: *Andante festivo for strings.* BOLZONI: *Minuet.* DVORAK: *Humoresque.* DARZINS: *Valse mélancolique.* ELLINGTON: *Solitude* (trans. for strings). SHOSTAKOVICH: *The Gadfly: Romance.* MUSSORGSKY: *Gopak.* DEBUSSY: *Suite bergamasque: Clair de lune.* SCHUMANN: *Abendlied, Op. 107/6.* MEDINS: *Aria.* GERSHWIN: *Promenade: walking the dog.* SOUSA: *The Stars and Stripes forever.*
**(*) Chandos Dig. CHAN 9227 [id.].

The acoustics of Detroit's Orchestra Hall, made famous by the Mercury engineers at the end of the 1950s, remain impressive and the Detroit orchestra is flattered here by opulently glowing sound, which especially suits the Glinka pieces and the lovely Sibelius *Andante festivo*. The rest of the programme is rather slight, consisting entirely of lollipops, some well-known, plus a few engaging novelties. All are presented with Järvi's customary flair and are very well played. If you enjoy this kind of concert, there is no need to hesitate for the programme is generous: 73 minutes.

Detroit Symphony Orchestra, Paul Paray

'French opera highlights': HEROLD: *Overture: Zampa.* AUBER: *Overture: The Crown diamonds.* GOUNOD: *Faust: ballet suite; Waltz* (from Act II). SAINT-SAENS: *Samson et Dalila: Bacchanale.* BIZET: *Carmen: Danse bohème.* BERLIOZ: *Les Troyens: Royal hunt and storm.* MASSENET: *Phèdre overture.* THOMAS: *Mignon: Gavotte.*
(M) *** Mercury 432 014-2 [id.].

Paul Paray's reign at Detroit tempted the Mercury producers to record a good deal of French music under his baton, and here is a good example of the Gallic verve and sparkle that were achieved. The only disappointment is the unslurred horn phrasing at the magical opening and close of the *Royal hunt and storm*.

'Marches and overtures à la Française': MEYERBEER: *Le Prophète: Coronation march.* GOUNOD: *Funeral march for a marionette.* SAINT-SAENS: *Marche militaire française; Marche héroïque.* DE LISLE: *La Marseillaise.* Overtures: ADAM: *Si j'étais roi.* BOIELDIEU: *La Dame blanche.* ROSSINI: *William Tell.* OFFENBACH: *La belle Hélène; Orpheus in the Underworld. Contes d'Hoffmann: Barcarolle* etc.
(M) **(*) Mercury 434 332-2 [id.].

A generous and flavourful Gallic concert, recorded in three different Detroit venues, with acoustics not entirely flattering to the orchestra, who nevertheless always play splendidly. The Adam and Boieldieu overtures need the glow of Kingsway Hall: here the resonance of Cass Technical High School slightly clouds detail. The marches and the Offenbach items were recorded in 1959 in Old Orchestral Hall, and the sound is more expansive. The most memorable pieces are the wittily engaging Gounod (always to be remembered as Alfred Hitchcock's TV signature-tune) and the spirited *Belle Hélène overture*, not put together by the composer, but none the worse for that. Throughout, the élan of the playing always brings enjoyment, and the virtuosity of the fiddles in the *William Tell galop* is exhilarating.

Du Pré, Jacqueline (cello)

'A Lasting inspiration' (with Daniel Barenboim, cond. or piano): BOCCHERINI: *Cello concerto in B flat* (arr. GRUTZMACHER). DVORAK: *Cello concerto (Adagio); Silent woods, Op. 68/5.* HAYDN: *Cello concerto in C.* BEETHOVEN: *Piano trio No. 5 in D (Ghost), Op. 70/1; 7 Variations on 'Bei Männern'* (both with Pinchas Zukerman). BRAHMS: *Cello sonata No. 1 in E min., Op. 38.* FRANCK: *Sonata in A* (arr. DELSART) *(Allegro ben moderato).*
(M) **(*) EMI PRD CD 9 [id.].

A medium-priced anthology that is self-recommending if the mixed programme is of appeal. The chamber-music performances have the same qualities of spontaneity and inspiration that have made Du Pré's account with Barbirolli of Elgar's *Cello concerto* come to be treasured above all others. Any tendency to self-indulgence, plus a certain leaning towards romantic expressiveness, is counterbalanced by the urgency and intensity of the playing. In the Brahms *Sonata* it is hard to accept the blatant change of tempo between first and second subjects, but here too there is warmth and flair. If some find Du Pré's approach to Haydn too romantic, it is nevertheless difficult to resist in its ready warmth. The Beethoven *Ghost Trio* is comparably individual and inspirational. The sound-quality is fairly consistent, for all the remastered transfers are successful.

Eastman-Rochester Orchestra, Howard Hanson

American orchestral music: BARBER: *Capricorn concerto, Op. 21* (with Joseph Mariano (flute), Robert Sprenkle (oboe), Sidney Mear (trumpet)). PISTON: *The Incredible flutist* (ballet suite). GRIFFES: *Poem for flute and orchestra.* KENNAN: *3 Pieces.* MCCAULEY: *5 Miniatures for flute and strings* (all with Joseph Mariano (flute)). BERGSMA: *Gold and the Señor Commandante* (ballet suite).
(M) *** Mercury 434 307-2 [id.].

A first-rate concert of pioneering recordings, made between 1957 and 1963. The collection is worth having for Barber's *Capricorn concerto* alone, a less characteristic work than, say, any of the *Essays for orchestra*, or the solo concertos. Walter Piston's ballet *The Incredible flutist* comes from 1938 and the suite is one of the most refreshing and imaginative of all American scores. Griffes' *Poem* with its gentle, shimmering textures is French in feeling but is thoroughly worthwhile in its own right. Joseph Mariano is an excellent soloist as he is in the more simplistic but engaging *Miniatures* of the Canadian, William McCauley (born 1917). Kent Kennan's *Three Pieces* are clearly influenced by the ballet music of Stravinsky. Bergsma's ballet is rather noisy at times, and fails to be memorable, though brightly scored. Excellent performances throughout and typically vivid Eastman-Rochester sound.

American orchestral music II: MCPHEE: *Tabuh-Tabuhan (Toccata for orchestra).* SESSIONS: *The Black maskers (suite).* Virgil THOMSON: *Symphony on a hymn tune; The Feast of love* (with David Clatworthy).
(M) *** Mercury 434 310-2 [id.].

McPhee's *Tabuh-Tabuhan*, written in 1936, uses Balinese music for its main colouring and rhythmic background. Roger Sessions' *Black maskers suite* was written as incidental music for a play by Andreyev about devil worship and the Black Mass, but it is not in the same class as, say, Prokofiev's *Scythian suite*. This is no fault of the performance or recording. The Virgil Thomson *Symphony*, although based on hymn-like material, is attractively quirky (reflecting the composer's Parisian years, the influence of Les Six, and Satie in particular). The cantata could hardly be more contrasted in its warmly flowing lyricism, a heady setting of an anonymous Latin love poem. The poet revels in the erotic joys of love, and the composer and his excellent soloist are obviously delighted by the voluptuous feeling of the words. As always the vintage Mercury sound is vivid with colour.

American music: MOORE: *Pageant of P. T. Barnum*. CARPENTER: *Adventures in a perambulator*. Bernard ROGERS: *Once upon a time (5 Fairy tales)*. Burrill PHILLIPS: *Selection from McGuffey's Reader*.
(M) *** Mercury 434 319-2 [id.].

John Alden Carpenter's suite was a favourite of American audiences before the Second World War and is diverting and often charming. The idiom is amiably innocuous but surprisingly seductive, not least the closing number, *Dreams*. Douglas Moore's *Pageant of P. T. Barnum* is hardly less accessible, with its engaging portraits of *Jenny Lind*, *General and Mrs Tom Thumb* and *Joice Heth*, a negress who was supposedly 160 years old! Bernard Rogers's set of *Five Fairy tales* is scored with whimsical charm. William Holmes McGuffey's *Readers* formed the staple textbook diet of schoolchildren in mid-nineteenth-century America. The gently nostalgic second movement pictures *John Alden and Priscilla* (who sailed on the *Mayflower*), and the noisy finale depicts *Paul Revere's midnight ride*. If this is perhaps the least memorable of the four works included here, its composer sums up rather succinctly the ethos of the whole programme. The performances are affectionate and committed throughout and the early stereo (1956–8) remarkably truthful.

Eastman Wind Ensemble, Frederick Fennell

'Hands across the sea – Marches from around the world': SOUSA: *Hands across the sea; The US Field Artillery; The Thunderer; Washington Post; King Cotton; El Capitan; The Stars and Stripes forever*. GANNE: *Father of victory (Père de la victoire)*. Mariano SAN MIGUEL: *The golden ear*. TIEKE: *Old comrades*. PROKOFIEV: *March, Op. 99*. HANSSEN: *Valdres march*. Davide DELLE CESE: *Inglesina*. COATES: *Knightsbridge*. MEACHAM: *American patrol*. GOLDMAN: *On the Mall*. MCCOY: *Lights out*. KING: *Barnum and Bailey's favourite*. ALFORD: *Colonel Bogey*. KLOHR: *The Billboard*.
(M) *** Mercury 434 334-2 [id.].

March records don't come any better than this, and nor does military/concert-band recording. The sparkling transients at the opening of *Hands across the sea* and the peppy spirit of the playing (as with all the Sousa items, and especially *The Stars and Stripes forever*) give the listener a real lift, while the French *Father of victory* and German *Old comrades* are just as full of character. The Prokofiev is as witty as you like, and Fennell shows he understands the more relaxed swagger of the British way in *Colonel Bogey*. First rate – but, with a 65-minute programme, this needs to be taken a march or two at a time, unless you want to fall out with the neighbours – this is not a CD to reproduce gently!

American wind band music: Morton GOULD: *West Point (Symphony for band)*. GIANNINI: *Symphony No. 3*. HOVHANESS: *Symphony No. 4, Op. 165* (cond. A. Clyde Roller).
(M) ** Mercury 434 320-2 [id.].

Fine playing, but the music here is often too inflated to give pleasure on repetition. Gould's *West Point Symphony* is in two movements, *Epitaphs* (which at 11 minutes 55 seconds is far too long) and *Marches*. The *Symphony No. 3* of Vittorio Giannini improves as it proceeds: the Scherzo and finale are the most interesting movements and the most attractively scored. Best by far is the Hovhaness *Symphony No. 4* (admirably directed by A.Clyde Roller) with its bold, rich, brass sonorities in the slower outer movements contrasting with marimba, vibraphone and other tuned percussion instruments in the central *Allegro*. Splendid sound, too.

Music from ballet and opera: SULLIVAN/MACKERRAS: *Pineapple Poll: suite* (arr. DUTHOIT). ROSSINI/ RESPIGHI: *La boutique fantasque: suite* (arr. Dan GODFREY). GOUNOD: *Faust: ballet suite* (arr. WINTERBOTTOM). WAGNER: *Lohengrin: Prelude to Act III; Bridal chorus* (arr. WINTERBOTTOM); *Elsa's procession* (arr. CAILLIET). *Das Rheingold* (arr. Dan GODFREY).
(M) ** Mercury 434 322-2 [id.].

Although played with characteristic Eastman verve, this is essentially a programme for admirers of wind band transcriptions – here mostly traditional scorings by prominent British military band arrangers. Little of this music gains from its loss of string textures, and the famous Rossini/Respighi *Boutique fantasque* lacks sumptuousness. All this would be entertaining on the bandstand, but at home the ear craves the full orchestra.

Elizabethan Serenade

'Elizabethan Serenade' (played by (i) Slovak RSO, Andrew Penny; (ii) Czecho-Slovak RSO, Adrian Leaper; (iii) RTE Concert O or Czecho-Slovak or Slovak RSO, Ernest Tomlinson; (iv) Slovak RSO, Gary Carpenter): (i) COATES: *By the sleepy lagoon;* (ii) *London suite: Knightsbridge march. Dam busters march.* CURZON: *Robin Hood suite: March of the bowmen.* KETELBEY: *Bells across the meadows; In a monastery garden; In a Persian market* (both with chorus). (iii) ELLIS: *Coronation Scot.* (ii) HAYDN WOOD: *Sketch of a dandy;* (iii) *Roses of Picardy.* (ii) FARNON: *Westminster waltz.* (i) DUNCAN: *Little suite: March.* (iii) BINGE: *Sailing by; Elizabethan serenade.* BENJAMIN: *Jamaican rumba.* TOMLINSON: *Little serenade.* WHITE: *Puffin' Billy.* (ii) GERMAN: *Tom Jones: Waltz.* (iii) COLLINS: *Vanity Fair.* (iv) MAYERL: *Marigold.*
(BB) *** Naxos Dig. 8.553515 [id.].

The Naxos collection is in effect a super-bargain sampler for a worthwhile (full-priced) Marco Polo Light Music composer series, and it inexpensively duplicates a great deal of the repertoire included on the two Hyperion CDs below. Our allegiance to their excellence remains, but the strong appeal of the present collection is obvious. The performances are a little more variable but are always very good, and those conducted by Ernest Tomlinson, who includes his own delightful *Little serenade*, are excellent, notably Edward White's *Puffin' Billy*, Arthur Benjamin's *Jamaican rumba* and the morceau by Anthony Collins. There are no complaints about the recording either. Excellent value, but the Hyperion discs, played by the New London Orchestra under Ronald Corp (see below), are worth their extra cost.

English Chamber Orchestra, Daniel Barenboim

English music (with (i) Neil Black; (ii) Pinchas Zukerman): DELIUS: *On hearing the first cuckoo in spring; Summer night on the river; 2 Aquarelles; Fennimore and Gerda: Intermezzo.* VAUGHAN WILLIAMS: *Fantasia on Greensleeves;* (i) *Oboe concerto;* (ii) *The Lark ascending.* WALTON: *Henry V* (film incidental music): *Passacaglia: The death of Falstaff; Touch her soft lips and part.*
(M) *** DG 439 529-2 [id.].

We have always had a soft spot for Barenboim's warmly evocative ECO collection of atmospheric English music. Even if the effect is not always totally idiomatic, the recordings have a warmth and allure that are wholly seductive.

English Chamber Orchestra, Benjamin Britten

'English music for strings': PURCELL (ed. Britten): *Chacony in G min.* ELGAR: *Introduction and allegro, Op. 47.* BRITTEN: *Prelude and fugue for strings, Op. 47; Simple Symphony, Op. 4.* DELIUS: *2 Aquarelles.* BRIDGE: *Sir Roger de Coverley for string orchestra.*
❁ (M) *** Decca 448 569-2 [id.].

This rich-toned recording, still sounding extraordinarily real and vivid, was surely a prime candidate for reissue in Decca's 'Classic Sound' series. It was one of the first made at The Maltings, Snape, in 1968 (although the *Prelude and fugue*, which has been added to fill out the CD, dates from three years later). The warm acoustic gives the strings of the English Chamber Orchestra far greater weight than you would expect from their numbers. Britten drew comparably red-blooded playing from his band, whether in his own *Simple Symphony* (a performance unsurpassed on disc), the engaging Bridge dance or the magnificent Purcell *Chacony*, which has never sounded more imposing. It is good to find him treating his own music so expressively. In the Delius the delicacy of evocation is delightful, while the Elgar is in some ways the most interesting performance of all, moving in its ardour yet with the structure of the piece brought out far more clearly than is common. An indispensable reissue to set alongside Barbirolli's coupling of the string music of Elgar and Vaughan Williams.

English Northern Philharmonia, David Lloyd-Jones

'Victorian concert overtures': MACFARREN: *Chevy Chase.* PIERSON: *Romeo and Juliet, Op. 86.* SULLIVAN: *Macbeth.* CORDER: *Prospero.* ELGAR: *Froissart, Op. 19.* PARRY: *Overture to an unwritten tragedy.* MACKENZIE: *Britannia, a nautical overture, Op. 52.*
*** Hyperion Dig. CDA 66515 [id.].

Sir George (Alexander) Macfarren (1813–87) was an English composer of Scottish descent who taught at and eventually became Principal of the Royal Academy of Music. His music was very successful in its day; he was a distinguished early editor of Purcell's *Dido and Aeneas* and of major stage works of Handel; many of his own operas were produced in London, including one based on the story of Robin Hood. A CD showing us a wider range of his music is overdue; meanwhile he makes a strong contribution to this collection of Victorian concert overtures with *Chevy Chase*, a spirited, tuneful piece that was admired by Mendelssohn. Pierson's *Romeo and Juliet* hardly explores its theme with any substance but Frederick Corder's *Prospero* has a certain flamboyant gravitas. Mackenzie's *Britannia* is a pot-boiler featuring a borrowed tune now famous at the Proms. Against all this and more, Elgar's *Froissart* stands out as the early masterpiece it was. The whole concert is persuasively performed by the excellent Northern Philharmonia under the versatile David Lloyd-Jones.

English Sinfonia, Sir Charles Groves

'Entente cordiale': FAURE: *Masques et bergamasques, Op. 112; Pavane, Op. 50.* ELGAR: *Chanson de nuit; Chanson de matin, Op. 15/1 – 2.* DELIUS: *On hearing the first cuckoo in spring.* RAVEL: *Pavane pour une infante défunte.* WARLOCK: *Capriol suite.* BUTTERWORTH: *The Banks of green willow.* SATIE: *Gymnopédies Nos. 1 & 3* (orch. Debussy).
(B) *** Carlton Dig. PCD 2017.

Having given us some attractive Haydn and Schubert recordings with the English Sinfonia, Sir Charles Groves then offered a happy juxtaposition of French and British music. He opens with a performance of Fauré's *Masques et bergamasques* which is sheer delight in its airy grace, and later he finds passion as well as delicacy in the Butterworth rhapsody, very effectively followed by Debussy's languorous orchestrations of the Satie *Gymnopédies*. Groves's approach to Warlock's *Capriol* dances is essentially genial (Marriner's version has more zest); but all this music-making is easy to enjoy. The playing is polished and spontaneous and the recording, made at Abbey Road, quite splendid.

English String Orchestra or English Symphony Orchestra, William Boughton

'The spirit of England': ELGAR: *Overture Cockaigne; Introduction and allegro, Op. 47; Sospiri, Op. 70.* DELIUS: *Summer evening.* BUTTERWORTH: *The banks of green willow; A Shropshire lad.* FINZI: *Suite from Love's Labour's Lost; Clarinet concerto* (with Alan Hacker). VAUGHAN WILLIAMS: *The lark ascending* (with Michael Bochmann); *Oboe concerto* (with Maurice Bourgue); *Fantasia on a theme of Thomas Tallis; Fantasia on Greensleeves.* PARRY: *Lady Radnor's suite.* BRIDGE: *Suite for string orchestra.* HOLST: *St Paul's suite.* WARLOCK: *Capriol suite.* BRITTEN: *Variations on a theme of Frank Bridge, Op. 10.*
✿ (B) *** Nimbus Dig. NI 5210/3 [id.].

The Birmingham-based English String and Symphony Orchestras under William Boughton are completely at home in this repertoire. One has only to sample the excitingly animated account of Holst's *St Paul's suite* (which also has much delicacy of feeling), the ideally paced Warlock *Capriol suite*, or the vibrant account of Britten's *Frank Bridge variations*, to discover the calibre of this music-making. The recordings were made in the Great Hall of Birmingham University which, with its warm reverberation, gives the strings a gloriously rich body of tone, supported by sumptuous cello and bass sonorities. The Elgar *Introduction and allegro* expands wonderfully at its climax (yet the fugue is not blurred) and in Vaughan Williams's *Lark ascending*, where the violin solo is exquisitely played with wonderful purity of tone by Michael Bochmann, the closing pianissimo seems to float in the still air. The work most suited to such an expansive acoustic is Vaughan Williams's *Tallis fantasia*, a deeply expressive performance which gives the listener the impression of sitting in a cathedral, with the solo string group, perfectly matched and blended in timbre, evoking a distant, ethereal organ. The lovely Butterworth pieces are tenderly sympathetic, and Alan Hacker's rhapsodically improvisatory account of Finzi's *Clarinet concerto* is full of colour and warmth. Perhaps Maurice Bourgue's oboe is balanced a little too closely in Vaughan Williams's *Oboe concerto* but the ear adjusts. On the other hand, the flutes melt magically into the strings in the famous *Greensleeves fantasia*. Delius's *Summer evening*, an early work, is quite memorable, and the suites of Parry and Finzi are full of colourful invention. The Bridge *Suite for strings* brings a lively response, with sumptuous textures. Only the opening *Cockaigne overture* of Elgar is a little lacking in profile and drama – and even here Boughton's relaxed, lyrical approach is enjoyable, for he broadens the final climax very satisfyingly. Very inexpensively priced indeed, this box makes an outstanding bargain.

English Symphony Orchestra; English String Orchestra; Philharmonia Orchestra, William Boughton

'The Spirit of England' Volume II: HOLST: *The Planets, Op. 32; The Perfect Fool* (ballet music), *Op. 39.* ELGAR: *Enigma variations, Op. 36. The Wand of Youth suite No. 2, Op. 1b.* PARRY: *An English suite.* FINZI: *Eclogue* (with Martin Jones, piano). BRIDGE: *There is a willow grows aslant a brook.* DELIUS: *Florida suite.* VAUGHAN WILLIAMS: *The Wasps: Overture.* IRELAND: *Downland suite: Minuet.* BERKELEY: *Serenade for strings.* BRITTEN: *Peter Grimes: 4 Sea interludes. Young person's guide to the orchestra.*
(B) **(*) Nimbus Dig. NI 5450/3 [id.].

An enjoyable enough bargain collection, warmly and often vividly played and given characteristically spacious and resonant sound which is always pleasing to the ear. However, it is much too richly upholstered for Elgar's *Wand of Youth* (and why offer the second suite and not the first?), although it suits Boughton's enjoyably expansive account of *Enigma*, even if *Nimrod*, paced very slowly, lacks something in ultimate tension. *The Planets* is well played by the Philharmonia Orchestra, but *Mars* fails the malignancy test and Boughton's reading overall is somewhat undercharacterized (except in the strikingly poignant *Saturn*); the use of the Royal Albert Hall for this recording has meant close microphones, which have produced a surprisingly small-scale effect for such a spectacular venue. The Finzi *Eclogue* (with Martin Jones the sympathetic soloist), the Delius *Florida suite*, Parry's *English suite* and the Berkeley *String serenade* are very successful, as are the shorter pieces, by Bridge, Ireland and Walton; but the Britten performances, though evocative (notably the first *Sea interlude*), are lacking something in dramatic profile and bite, and the *Young person's guide to the orchestra* ideally needs a sharper definition.

Ensemble Wien

'Lanner and Strauss Waltzes, Polkas, Galops': LANNER: *Jubel waltz; Eisens und Katinkens Vereinigung galop; Die Werber waltz; Hans Jörgel polka; Abendsterne waltz; Vermählungs waltz.* Johann STRAUSS Sr: *Tivoli-Rutsch waltz; Eisle- und Beisele-Sprünge polka; Cachucha galop; Kettenbrücke Waltz; Gitana galop.* Josef STRAUSS: *Die guten, alten Zeiten waltz.*
**(*) Sony Dig. SK 52485 [id.].

It is good to have a modern, digital collection of this early Viennese dance repertoire, even if the recording is too immediate and unglamorous and the playing, though immaculate, too often a bit stiff and unsmiling. Much of Lanner's music is instantly forgettable and needs a coaxing charm of the kind Boskovsky could so easily manage. Paul Guggenberger, the leader, understands the Viennese lilt and often plays rather nicely (as in *Die Werber* and the *Abendsterne waltz* which charmingly recalls a famous folk-tune); but almost all the pieces seem to open rather gruffly, partly the effect of the close microphones. Once we reach the group of four pieces by Johann Strauss Senior at the end of the programme, the players seem to relax more, and the Josef Strauss waltz which comes at their centre is the highlight of the programme. But even here the rhythm seems too calculated.

European Community Chamber Orchestra, Eivind Aadland

HINDEMITH: *5 Pieces for strings, Op. 11.* BARBER: *Adagio, Op. 11.* BRITTEN: *Simple symphony, Op. 4.* WARLOCK: *Capriol suite.* BARTOK: *Romanian folk dances.*
(B) ** Carlton IMP Dig. PCD 2044 [id.].

Excellent playing from this fine group of European musicians. However, they cannot make Hindemith's rather austere set of string pieces (written for student performance) sound much more than utility music, and they miss the final degree of passion at the climax of Barber's *Adagio*, which is otherwise eloquently played. Some of the tempi in the *Capriol suite* seem slightly eccentric, but the Bartók dances are vibrant and, apart from a lack of a nursery-rhyme exuberance in the *Playful pizzicato*, the account of the Britten *Simple symphony* has comparable liveliness and crispness of ensemble.

Fleisher, Leon (piano), Boston Symphony Orchestra, Seiji Ozawa

Left-hand Piano concertos: BRITTEN: *Diversions for piano and orchestra.* PROKOFIEV: *Piano Concerto No. 4.* RAVEL: *Piano concerto in D for the left hand.*
*** Sony Dig. SK 47188 [id.].

These superb concertante works, originally written for the one-armed Austrian pianist, Paul Wittgenstein, but rejected by him, make the perfect vehicle for one of the finest of all American pianists, Leon Fleisher. Unable to play with his right hand any longer, Fleisher here shows that his power and artistry are undiminished from the days when he was the favourite recording pianist of George Szell, with the vintage Cleveland orchestra. Though the Ravel and Prokofiev concertos have been recorded many times, these accounts are a match for any of them, while Britten's highly original set of variations is a rarity on disc, very welcome indeed in Fleisher's masterly performance.

Fournier, Pierre (cello)

'Homage to Pierre Fournier': DVORAK: *Cello concerto* (with BPO, Szell). BLOCH: *Schelomo* (with BPO, Wallenstein). BRUCH: *Kol Nidrei* (with LAP, Martinon). SCHUBERT: *Arpeggione sonata, D.821* (arr. for cello; with Jean Fonda, piano). Recital (with Lamar Crowson, piano): FRANCOEUR: *Sonata in E: Adagio cantabile; Allegro vivo.* HAYDN: *Sonata in C: Minuet.* WEBER: *Violin sonata No. 3: Larghetto; Rondo.* CHOPIN: *Nocturne, Op. 9/2.* RIMSKY-KORSAKOV: *Le Coq d'or: Hymn to the sun. Tsar Sultan: Flight of the bumble bee.* SCHUMANN: *Adagio and Allegro, Op. 70.* GOUNOD: *Ave Maria.* BRAHMS: *Feldeinsamkeit, Op. 86/2.* POPPER: *Elfentanz, Op. 39.* DVORAK: *Rondo, Op. 94.* SAINT-SAENS: *Carnival of the animals: The Swan.* PAGANINI: *Variations on a theme from 'Moses' by Rossini.*
(B) *** DG Double 447 349-2 (2) [id.].

A fine tribute to the great French cellist. The highlight is the Dvořák *Concerto* in partnership with Szell (discussed under its composer listing), but the *Arpeggione sonata* also shows Fournier at his finest. In the shorter pieces Fournier's sense of line is matched by his phenominal technique: witness the remarkable display of fireworks in Popper's *Elfentanz*, or the controlled virtuosity in the Dvořák *Rondo*. The little Weber *Sonata* is also impressive, and Saint-Saëns's famous Swan glides in with suave elegance. Excellent, truthful recording from the 1960s.

(i) French National Radio Orchestra; (ii) London Symphony Orchestra, Leopold Stokowski

DEBUSSY: (i) *Images:* (ii) *Ibéria. Nocturnes* (with BBC Women's Chorus). RAVEL: *Rapsodie espagnole.* (i) IBERT: *Escales.*
(M) *** EMI CDM5 65422-2 [id.].

This brings together two separate LPs, with the *Nocturnes* and the Ravel *Rapsodie*, brilliantly done by the LSO, representing one of the very finest of Stokowski's Capitol records, made at Abbey Road in 1957. Here is 'full dimensional sound' with the microphones less close than in most of the American recordings on this label, and there is atmosphere as well as brilliance. The second of the *Nocturnes*, *Fêtes*, is taken fast, giving it electric intensity. *Sirènes* is then sensuously evocative, leading on to the thrillingly high-powered reading of the Ravel. In the French recordings, made in the Salle Wagram in 1958, the sound is brightly lit, but there is still plenty of ambience. The playing of the French National Radio Orchestra is warmly persuasive but with ensemble less crisp. Stokowski's panache and his feeling for colour are consistently persuasive, with the opening evocation of *Palermo* in *Escales* bringing some unforgettably languorous playing from the strings, while the combination of Mediterranean warmth and passion in *Valencia* is even more highly charged. Though the 1957/8 recordings do not convey a true pianissimo, the dynamic range is still impressive and the sound is wonderfully vivid and immediate.

Gallois, Patrick (flute)

'Une flûte à l'opéra' (with L. Festival O, Ross Pople): Opera arias for flute and orchestra from VERDI: *La Traviata* (arr. GENIN; orch. GUIOT); *Un ballo in maschera* (arr. GENIN; orch. PIERRE). ROSSINI: *William Tell* (arr. DEMERSSEMAN/BERTHELEMY; orch. GALLOIS). GODARD: *Berceuse de Jocelyn.* MASSE: *Les noces de Jeanette: Air du rossignol* (both arr. & orch. PIERRE). MASSENET: *Thaïs: Méditation* (arr. PREZMAN). BIZET: *Carmen fantasia* (arr. BORNE; orch. PIERRE).
*** DG Dig. 445 822-2 [id.].

Patrick Gallois is clearly a new international star in the flautists' firmament. His tone is uniquely recognizable and beautiful, his playing naturally stylish, his musicianship impeccable and, as this light-hearted and entertaining collection demonstrates, his technique is dazzling. He plays a modern wooden flute which he suggests is particularly suitable for the present repertoire as it has 'more colour and juster intonation than a traditional wooden flute . . . and its timbre is closer to that of the human voice than a metal instrument'. He certainly makes it tell in the scintillating coloratura with which he surrounds the selection from Verdi's *La Traviata* and the excerpts from *William Tell,* which feature a brief but witty morsel of the famous *Galop* with the most engaging additional embroidery. Ross Pople opens the famous *Berceuse de Jocelyn* with lovely, gentle playing from the orchestral strings, and the charm of the flute solo here is very seductive, while in the equally popular *Méditation* from *Thaïs* the melodic line is richly expressive without any feeling of sentimentality. Finally we are offered all those hits from *Carmen* which Sarasate arranged so effectively for the violin. Gallois' claim as to the vocal possibilities of his instrument is readily apparent here in the quite beautiful performance of the *Flower song*; he is hardly less bewitching in the 'Habanera' and then decorates it with great panache, finally frolicking nimbly through the *Danse bohème* and genially introducing the *Toreador song* as a surprise just before a breathtaking final burst of bravura.

'Flute concertos from Sans-Souci' (with C. P. E. Bach CO, Peter Schreier): C. P. E. BACH: *Concerto in G, Wq. 169.* BENDA: *Concerto in E min.* FREDERICK THE GREAT: *Concerto No. 3 in C.* QUANTZ: *Concerto in G.*
*** DG Dig. 439 895-2 [id.].

C. P. E. Bach (fairly briefly), Benda and Quantz were all musicians in the employ of Frederick the Great, whose own *Flute concerto* included here is rather impressive, notably its *Grave* slow movement. The Bach concerto is well known and the chamber orchestra carrying his name makes the very most of its sprightly outer movements while Gallois' contribution throughout the programme is impeccably stylish and elegant and his decoration always imaginative. The *Adagio un poco Andante* of the Benda *Concerto* shows his luminous line, as does the rather lovely *Arioso* which is the centrepoint of the Quantz work; it is played most delectably, followed by a lively moto perpetuo finale of equal charm. Here the neat string articulation and the soloist's finesse mirror each other equitably, as they do in the catchy last movement of the Benda work. Fresh, clean recording and a bright string-sound demonstrate that modern instruments can present this repertoire with the same lightness and transparency as original instruments. There are few collections of baroque flute concertos in this bracket and none more generous (77 minutes) – but this is not a concert to be played all at once.

Galway, James (flute)

'Pachelbel's Canon and other Baroque favourites' (with various orchestras & conductors): VIVALDI: *Concerto in D (Il Gardellino), Op. 10/3:* 1st & 2nd movts. *Four Seasons: Spring* (arr. GALWAY). TELEMANN: *Suite for strings in A min.: Réjouissance; Polonaise.* PACHELBEL: *Canon.* HANDEL: *Sonatas: in A min., Op. 1/4:* 4th movt; *in F, Op. 1/11: Siciliana; Allegro* (both with Sarah Cunningham, Philip Moll). *Solomon: Arrival of the Queen of Sheba* (arr. GERHARDT). *Messiah: Pifa (Pastoral Symphony). Xerxes: Largo.* BACH: *Suite Nos. 2 in B min., BWV 1067: Minuet & Badinerie; 3 in D, BWV 1068: Air. Trio sonata Nos. 2 in G, BWV 1039:* 4th movt (with Kyung Wha Chung, Moll, Welsh); *Flute sonatas: Nos. 2 in E flat, BWV 1031: Siciliano* (with Maria Graf, harp); *4 in C, BWV 1033:* 2nd movt (arr. GERHARDT for flute & O). *Concerto in E min., BWV 1059/35* (ed. Radeke): 3rd movt. ALBINONI: *Adagio.* QUANTZ: *Concerto in C:* Finale. MARAIS: *Le Basque* (arr. GALWAY/GERHARDT).
*** BMG/RCA Dig./Analogue 09026 61928-2 [id.].

If the famous Bach *Air* from BWV 1068 is spun out somewhat romantically and the *Siciliano* from BWV 1031 (with harp accompaniment) is too solemn, Handel's famous *Largo* is gloriously managed, completely vocal in feeling. Galway certainly dominates Pachelbel's *Canon* in a way not intended by the composer, but his elegant line and simple divisions on the lovely theme are very agreeable. Any of the composers included here would surely have been amazed at the beauty of his tone and the amazing technical facility, always turned to musical effect. He is a wonderful goldfinch in Vivaldi's Op. 10/3, while Gerhardt's arrangement of Handel's *Arrival of the Queen of Sheba*, which exchanges oboes for flutes, is ear-tickling. The engaging Quantz concerto movement is as sprightly in the strings (of the Württemberg Chamber Orchestra) as it is in the felicitously decorated solo part. The Bach and Handel sonata excerpts are refreshing and the (Handel) *Siciliana* from Op. 1/11 is matched in pastoral charm by the beautiful account of the *Pifa* from *Messiah*, but is not more engaging than the lollipop of the whole concert: the delicious *Le Basque* of Marais, one of Galway's most endearing arrangements. The recording naturally balances the soloist forward, but the sound is first class throughout. This is a full-price record but it includes 68 minutes of entertainment, perfect for a fine summer evening.

'Dances for flute' (with Nat. PO, Gerhardt or Mancini; I Solisti di Zagreb, Scimone; The Chieftains; RPO, Myung-Whun Chung; and other artists): GODARD: *Waltz.* CHOPIN: *Minute waltz in D flat, Op. 64/1.* DEBUSSY: *La plus que lente; Petite suite: Ballet.* J. S. BACH: *Suite No. 2, BWV 1067: Polonaise; Menuet; Badinerie.* TRAD.: *Crowley's reel; Brian Boru's march; Belfast hornpipe.* KHACHATURIAN: *Waltz; Sabre dance.* MERCADANTE: *Concerto in D: Polacca.* MANCINI: *Pie in the face polka; Pennywhistle jig.* RODRIGO: *Fantasia para un gentilhombre: Canario.* BENJAMIN: *Jamaican rhumba.* MOZART: *Divertimento in D, K.334: Menuetto.* VIVALDI: *Concerto in D (Il Gardellino): Cantabile.* DINICU: *Hora staccato.* GOSSEC: *Tambourin.* KREISLER: *Schön Rosmarin.*
*** BMG/RCA 09026 50917-2 [id.].

Galway can certainly make his flute dance – often in scintillating fashion. This collection is essentially for the sweet-toothed, but its consummate artistry is remarkable: just sample the delicious opening Godard *Waltz*. The traditional pieces are especially enjoyable, and two real lollipops are the Mercadante *Polacca* (from a virtually forgotten concerto) and the (Beechamesque) Gossec *Tambourin*. We also have a soft spot for Mancini's *Pennywhistle Jig*. Good sound and 64 minutes of music.

Gilels, Emil (piano)

'Gilels Edition'
(M) (**) BMG/ Melodiya 74321 40116-2 (5) [id.].

BEETHOVEN: *Piano sonatas Nos. 8 (Pathétique), Op. 13; 14 (Moonlight), Op. 27/2.* SCHUBERT: *Impromptu, D.935/1.* RAVEL: *Pavane pour une infante défunte; Jeux d'eau.* MEDTNER: *Sonata-reminiscenza, Op. 38/1.* CHOPIN: *Etude, Op. 25/2.* PROKOFIEV: *The Love for 3 oranges: Scherzo; March* (74321 40117-2).

CHOPIN: *Piano concerto No. 1.* POULENC: *Concert champêtre in D* (with Moscow PO, Kondrashin) (74321 40118-2).

MOZART: *Piano sonatas, K.281 & K.310; Fantasia, K.397; 6 Variations, K.398; 10 Variations, K.455* (74321 40119-2).

SCHUBERT: *Moments musicaux, D. 780.* SHOSTAKOVICH: *Sonata No. 2, Op. 64.* SCHUMANN: *Arabeske.* CHOPIN: *Ballade No. 1* (74321 40120-2).

SCRIABIN: *Piano sonata No. 3; 5 Preludes, Op. 74.* BEETHOVEN: *Sonata No. 29 (Hammerklavier), Op. 106* (74321 40121-2).

These five CDs are available both as a boxed set and separately; wisely so, since it puts the collector in a position to pick and choose. Nothing by Gilels is less than distinguished. As one American critic wrote at about the time of this recital, 'With the very first notes anyone with half an ear must realize he is in the presence of one of the greatest of pianists.' But the quality of sound of these recordings is so variable as to justify detailed comment and grading.

The first disc (74321 40117-2) comes from a recital Gilels gave in the Grand Hall of the Moscow Conservatoire just before Christmas 1968, in front of a very attentive audience. The programme is close to a Carnegie recital which HMV recorded in February 1969, including the *Moonlight Sonata* and an incomparable performance of the Medtner *Sonata-reminiscenza*. The present recital includes some particularly beautiful Ravel and a no less eloquent account of the Medtner sonata. The short Prokofiev excerpts from *Love for three oranges* are much to be relished. The recording calls for tolerance: it is shallow and in no way does justice to the sheer beauty of sound one recalls Gilels making in the flesh. Three stars for the playing, one for the sound.

The next CD (74321 40118-2) couples the Chopin *Piano concerto No. 1* with the Poulenc *Concert champêtre*, played on the piano, not the harpsichord, with Kondrashin and the Moscow Philharmonic. Here the recordings, which are from 1962, present more serious problems. The Chopin is pretty rough and climaxes are distinctly coarse. Gilels makes the *Concert champêtre* sound convincing enough, such is the extraordinary range of colour he commanded.

The Mozart disc (74321 40119-2) comes from a live recital given in January 1970 in the Grand Hall of the Moscow Conservatoire. According to BMG/Melodiya's documentation, none of the performances have been available before. From the early *B flat sonata*, K.281, whose finale is delivered with such wit, through to the marvellously characterized *A minor*, K.310, this finds Gilels at his most individual and sublime, exquisite in every detail, without the slightest trace of preciosity. The sound is not as distinguished as the playing but is perfectly acceptable. The performances are certainly three-star and Rosette-worthy, but the sound rates two stars.

The Schubert *Moments musicaux*, D.780, and Shostakovich *Sonata No. 2* (74321 40120-2) together with the Schumann and Chopin pieces come from a recital given in March 1965. Gilels recorded the Schubert and the Shostakovich for HMV and RCA respectively in the West not long afterwards, both in marginally better sound. The present performances are every bit as fine, and the recording is perfectly acceptable. Gilels's account of the Shostakovich *Sonata* has never been surpassed on disc.

The Scriabin *Sonata No. 3* and the *Preludes*, Op. 74, and Beethoven's *Hammerklavier Sonata* (74321 40121-2) are the highlights of the set. Recorded at a 1984 recital, only a fortnight before he gave much the same programme at London's Festival Hall, they offer eminently satisfactory sound – though again it does not do full justice to the range of colour or delicacy of touch Gilels commanded in real life. But then, nor does his DG *Hammerklavier* (410 527-2), which has great presence and clarity but is marred by a certain glare. This live recording comes closer to capturing what those who attended his London recital will recall. One of the most impressive *Hammerklavier*s now available.

Glennie, Evelyn (percussion)

'Light in darkness': Music by GLENNIE; ABE; MCLEOD; EDWARDS; MIKI; TANAKA.
**(*) RCA Dig. RD 60557.

'Dancin'' (with Nat. PO, Barry Wordsworth): Music by RODGERS; HEROLD; SAINT-SAENS; J. STRAUSS Jr; arr. by Gordon LANGFORD.
*** RCA Dig. RD 60870; *RK 60870*.

Evelyn Glennie's remarkable artistic skills have caught the fancy of the wider public, fascinated with the idea of her apparently insuperable affliction – for a musician. But she tells us that, such is the ingenuity of nature, she can sense everything directly, through her body. Included on the first collection is her own imaginative piece, *Light in darkness*, using tuned percussion instruments and highlighting the exotic marimba. Here she explores music from a wide geographical range for which the percussion condiment is essential. However, for most listeners the more obviously popular alternative collection called '*Dancin*' will be an easy first choice. Here she receives splendid back-up from Barry Wordsworth and the National Philharmonic in the widest range of music for the dance, which surely does make one's feet tap, whether it be a clever arrangement by Gordon Jacob, pieces by Johann Strauss, a ballet by Richard Rodgers, a medley associated with the Broadway team of Ginger and Fred, or the irresistible *Clog dance* from *La fille mal gardée*. The recording is first rate and makes one recall the title of an early RCA stereo demonstration LP dominated by percussion, called '*Music for Band, Brrroom and harp*' (which RCA should dig out of their vaults and reissue).

'Rebounds' (with Scottish CO, Paul Daniel): MILHAUD: *Concerto pour batterie et petite orchestre*. Richard Rodney BENNETT: *Concerto for solo percussion and chamber orchestra*. ROSAURO: *Concierto para marimba e orquestra de cordas*. MIYOSHI: *Concerto for marimba and strings*.
*** BMG/RCA Dig. 09026 61277-2; *09026 61277-4* [id.].

Here is a chance for Glennie to show what she can do with more ambitious concert music – although, of course, there are popular influences and jazz rhythms in the works by both Richard Rodney Bennett and Rosauro. Bennett even offers an aleatory element for the percussionist. But his concerto is imaginatively thought out and has plenty of atmosphere and colour. The Milhaud concerto (its title sounds so much more inviting in French) is a most spontaneous piece, without fireworks but very effectively written. Other than that, the most enjoyable work here is the tuneful four-movement concerto by the Brazilian, Ney Rosauro, with a haunting *Lament* for slow movement, an engaging *Dança*, followed by an imaginative finale. The Miyoshi *Marimba concerto* is in a kaleidoscopic single movement. All these works are brilliantly played and the collection is much more diverse and entertaining than one might expect. The recording engineers have a field day yet they do not try to create exaggerated effects.

Gutman, Michael (violin), Royal Philharmonic Orchestra, José Serebrier

'Four seasons': MILHAUD: *Spring concertino.* RODRIGO: *Concierto d'estio (Summer concerto).* CHAMINADE (orch. Paul Ut): *Autumn.* SEREBRIER: *Winter concerto.*
**(*) ASV Dig. CDDCA 855 [id.].

This is a well-conceived anthology that went a bit awry. Milhaud's *Spring concertino* is a fresh one-movement piece with a whiff of jazz *à la français*, and Rodrigo's *Concierto de estio*, conceived in the manner of Vivaldi, is the composer's own favourite among his many concertos; the central movement is an engaging *Sicilienne* with variations. Chaminade's *Autumn* is the composer's arrangement for violin and piano of her most successful lollipop, which another hand has subsequently orchestrated. The snag is that the conductor here, José Serebrier, has produced an undistinguished and rather wild concerto for *Winter*, even quoting themes associated with that season from Haydn, Glazunov and Tchaikovsky: the result is a bit of a hotch-potch. Performances and recording do not let the side down, but ASV need to reissue this with a further winter appendix – there is plenty of room, for the CD plays for only around 54 minutes.

Hälsingborg Symphony Orchestra, Okko Kamu

'Swedish orchestral favourites': SODERMAN: *Swedish festival music.* STENHAMMAR: *The Song* (cantata): *Interlude.* LARSSON: *Pastoral suite; A Winter's Tale: Epilogue.* PETERSON-BERGER: *Frösöblomster: 4 Pieces.* ALFVEN: *Roslagspolka; Midsummer vigil; Gustavus Adolphus II suite.* WIREN: *Serenade for strings: Marcia.*
(BB) *** Naxos Dig. 8.553115 [id.].

A useful anthology of popular favourites from the Swedish repertory, nicely played by the Hälsingborg orchestra and Okko Kamu, which should have wide appeal, not only in but outside Sweden. The playing is lively, the performances of the Alfvén and Lars-Erik Larsson pieces are as good as any in the catalogue, the recording is excellent and the price is right.

Hardenberger, Håkan (trumpet)

Trumpet concertos (with LPO, Elgar Howarth): M. HAYDN: *Concerto No. 2 in C.* HERTEL: *Concerto No. 1 in E flat.* MOLTER: *Concerto No. 1 in D.* L. MOZART: *Concerto in D.* F. RICHTER: *Concerto in D.*
*** Ph. Dig. 426 311-2 [id.].

Håkan Hardenberger makes everything sound completely effortless and, although none of these pieces is an imperishable masterpiece, he plays them all as if they were. Hugely enjoyable and beautifully recorded, with just the right amount of resonance, presence and bloom. Strongly recommended.

Twentieth-century trumpet concertos (with BBC PO, Elgar Howarth): HARRISON BIRTWISTLE: *Endless parade.* MAXWELL DAVIES: *Trumpet concerto.* BLAKE WATKINS: *Trumpet concerto.*
*** Ph. 432 075-2 [id.].

All three works here offer considerable difficulties for the everyday music-lover to approach, but the performances are of a superlative standard, and a record of this calibre gives one the chance to explore their musical intricacies at leisure. In Harrison Birtwistle's aptly named *Endless parade*, textures and ideas, dynamics and colour all continually vary, as in a kaleidoscope. Maxwell Davies uses a plainsong, *Franciscus pauper et humilis*, as a basis, centrally evoking the idea of St Francis preaching to the birds. There is no question as to the evocative power of this work, in spite of its cryptic format. Michael Blake Watkins's *Concerto* may have an apparently more conventional layout, but its argument is complex; at one point the soloist has a heated dialogue with the three orchestral trumpets. The recording is outstandingly vivid.

Hardenberger, Håkan (trumpet), I Musici

Baroque trumpet concertos (with I Musici): VIVALDI: *Concerto for 2 trumpets in C, RV 537.* CORELLI: *Sonata in D for trumpet and 2 violins.* ALBINONI: *Trumpet concerto in B flat, Op. 7/3.* TORELLI: *Sonata for trumpet and strings in D.* MARCELLO: *Trumpet concerto in D min.* VIVIANI: *Trumpet sonata prima.* FRANCESCHINI: *Sonata in D for 2 trumpets and strings.* BALDASSARE: *Sonata in F for trumpet and strings.*
*** Ph. Dig. 442 131-2 [id.].

Having given us a superb coupling of the two finest trumpet concertos – by Haydn and Hummel – with lesser works by Stamitz and Hertel thrown in for good measure (Ph. 420 203-2), Hardenberger now turns his attention to baroque repertoire. He plays with similar flair and gleaming tone, and he is a dab hand at embellishment, without overdoing things. However, apart from the fine Torelli concerto and works by Vivaldi and Corelli, there is little of note from this era written in this form, and he has had to turn his attention to works originally intended for oboe; so we have here two attractive concertos of this kind from Albinoni and Marcello, played with engaging flexibility and skill. The other three concertos, by Viviani, Franceschini and Baldassare, are agreeable but hardly memorable.

Harp concertos

Harp concertos (played by: (i) Marisa Robles; (ii) ASMF, Iona Brown; (iii) Osian Ellis, LSO, Bonynge; (iv) Werner Tripp, Hubert Jellinek, VPO, Münchinger; (v) Philh. O, Dutoit): (i; ii) BOIELDIEU: *Harp concerto in C.* DITTERSDORF: *Harp concerto in A* (arr. PILLEY). (iii) GLIERE: *Harp concerto, Op. 74.* (i; ii) HANDEL: *Harp concerto, Op. 4/6.* (iv) MOZART: *Flute and harp concerto in C, K.299.* (i; v) RODRIGO: *Concierto de Aranjuez.*
(B) *** Decca Double 452 585-2 (2) [id.].

Boieldieu's *Harp concerto* has been recorded elsewhere but never more attractively. The (originally Argo) recording is still in the demonstration class and very sweet on the ear. Dittersdorf's *Harp concerto* is a transcription of an unfinished keyboard concerto with additional wind parts. It is an elegant piece, thematically not quite as memorable as Boieldieu's, but captivating when played with such style. Glière's is an unpretentious and tuneful work, with Osian Ellis performing brilliantly. Excellent (1968) Kingsway Hall recording. Handel's Op. 4/6 is well known in both organ and harp versions. Marisa Robles and Iona Brown make an unforgettable case for the latter by creating the most delightful textures while never letting the work sound insubstantial. The ASMF accompaniment, so stylish and beautifully balanced, is a treat in itself, and the recording is well-nigh perfect. The much earlier Vienna recording of Mozart's *Flute and harp concerto* is played stylishly and has stood the test of time, the recording smooth, full, nicely reverberant and with good detail. Refinement and beauty of tone and phrase are a hallmark throughout, and Münchinger provides most sensitive accompaniments. The glowing acoustic of St Barnabas Church, London, creates an attractively romantic aura for Marisa Robles's magnetic and highly atmospheric account of the composer's own arrangement for harp of his *Concierto de Aranjuez*. Robles is so convincing an advocate that for the moment the guitar original is all but forgotten, particularly when, with inspirational freedom, she makes the beautful slow movement sound like a rhapsodic improvisation. It is a haunting performance, and the digital sound is first rate. Altogether an excellent anthology; however, the Boieldieu, Dittersdorf and Handel concertos on the first disc are also available separately at mid-price, and we gave a Rosette to this disc in our main volume (Decca 425 723-2; *425 723-4*).

Haskil, Clara (piano)

Clara Haskil: The Legacy: Volume II: Concertos

(for Volumes I & III, see below, under Instrumental recitals)

BEETHOVEN: *Piano concerto No. 3 in C min., Op. 37.* CHOPIN: *Piano concerto No. 2 in F min., Op. 21.* FALLA: *Nights in the gardens of Spain* (all with LOP, Markevitch). MOZART: *Piano concertos Nos. 9 in E flat (Jeunehomme), K.271; 23 in A, K.488; Concert rondo in A, K.386* (with VSO, Sacher or Paumgartner); *20 in D min., K.466* (two versions, with VSO, Paumgartner or LOP, Markevitch); *24 in C min., K.491* (with LOP, Markevitch). SCHUMANN: *Piano concerto in A min., Op. 54* (with Hague PO, van Otterloo).
(M) **(*) Ph. mono/stereo 442 631-2 (4) [id.].

This second box of recordings, issued in the Philips 12-disc 'Clara Haskil Legacy', is of concertante works. The earliest of Haskil's concerto records is the Schumann (1951) and is not quite as poetic as that of her compatriot, Lipatti (Haskil was born in Bucharest), though there are some wonderful things, such as the reposeful development section of the first movement and the slow movement. The Hague orchestra's oboe has a surprisingly wide vibrato. Haskil's refinement and grace are to be heard at their best in the Mozart concertos (K.466 and K.491 were recorded in the month before her death), and her fire and temperament, albeit beautifully controlled, in the Falla *Nights in the gardens of Spain*. Her family had originally come from Spain. One snag about the set is that the Beethoven is split over two CDs.

Heath, Edward (conductor)

'80th birthday celebration': ELGAR: *Cockaigne overture* (with LSO). ROSSINI: *La Cenerentola overture*. HANDEL: *Organ concerto in F, Op. 4/4* (with John Birch); *Solomon: Arrival of the Queen of Sheba*. DANKWORTH: *Tom Sawyer's birthday* (with Richard Baker, nar.) (all with BBC Academy O). BRAHMS: *Academic festival overture* (with European Community Youth O).
(M) *** EMI Analogue/Dig. CDTED 80.

It was bold of Edward Heath as Prime Minister to conduct the LSO in Elgar's *Cockaigne* in November 1971, and the warmth and brilliance of his reading, recorded live, put it among the most cherishable versions on disc. As an eightieth-birthday tribute it is here coupled with recordings he made later with orchestras of young people. With the Academy of the BBC Rossini's *Cenerentola overture* is full of fun, while a Handel *Organ concerto* and the *Arrival of the Queen of Sheba* have fine bounce and energy, as has *Tom Sawyer's Saturday* by John Dankworth, with Richard Baker as narrator. Finally Brahms's *Academic festival overture* with the ECYO exuberantly brings together causes that Heath has long cherished: Europe, youth and music. The audience in enthusiasm even jumps the gun with its applause. Good warm sound.

Hungarian State Orchestra, Mátyás Antal

'Hungarian festival': KODALY: *Háry János: suite*. LISZT: *Hungarian rhapsodies for orchestra Nos. 1, 2 & 6* (arr. DOEPPLER). HUBAY: *Hejre Kati* (with Ferenc Balogh). BERLIOZ: *Damnation de Faust: Rákóczy march*.
(BB) *** Naxos Dig. 8.550142; *4550142* [id.].

The Hungarian State Orchestra are in their element in this programme of colourful music for which they have a natural affinity. There is no more characterful version of the *Háry János suite* (we have already mentioned it in the Composer index) and Hubay's concertante violin piece, with its gypsy flair, is similarly successful, even if the violin soloist is not a particularly strong personality. The special interest of the Liszt *Hungarian rhapsodies* lies in the use of the Doeppler orchestrations, which are comparatively earthy, with greater use of brass solos than the more sophisticated scoring most often used in the West. The performances are suitably robust and certainly have plenty of charisma. The brilliant digital recording is strong on primary colours but has atmosphere too, and produces plenty of spectacle in the Berlioz *Rákóczy march*.

Karajan Edition (EMI)

The Berlin years, Vol. 1

BEETHOVEN: *Piano concertos Nos. 1 in C, Op. 15; 2 in B flat, Op. 19*.
Alexis Weissenberg, BPO (CDM5 66090-2).

BEETHOVEN: *Piano concertos Nos. 3 in C min., Op. 37; 5 in E flat (Emperor), Op. 73*.
Alexis Weissenberg, BPO (CDM5 66091-2).

BEETHOVEN: (i) *Piano concerto No. 4 in G, Op. 58;* (ii) *Triple concerto in C, Op. 56*.
(i) Alexis Weissenberg; (ii) David Oistrakh, Rostropovich, Richter; BPO (CDM5 66092-2).

BRAHMS: *Variations on a theme of Haydn, Op. 56a;* (i) *Piano concerto No. 2 in B flat, Op. 83*.
BPO, (i) with Hans Richter-Haaser (CDM5 66093-2).

BRUCKNER: *Symphony No. 4 in E flat (Romantic)*.
BPO (CDM5 66094-2).

BRUCKNER: *Symphony No. 7 in E.*
BPO (CDM5 66095-2).

HAYDN: *Symphonies Nos. 83 in G min. (The Hen); 101 in D (Clock); 104 in D (London).*
BPO (CDM5 66097-2).

MOZART: *Symphonies Nos. 29; 35 (Haffner); 36 (Linz); 38 (Prague); 39; 40; 41 (Jupiter). Rehearsal extracts.*
BPO (CMS5 66113-2 (3)). Also available separately: *Nos. 29, 35 & 36* (CDM5 66098-2); *Nos. 38 & 39* (with rehearsal extracts) (CDM5 66099-2); *Nos. 40 & 41* (with rehearsal extracts) (CDM5 66100-2).

MOZART: (i) *Sinfonia concertante in E flat, K.297b.* BRAHMS: (ii) *Violin concerto in D, Op. 77.*
(i) Steins, Stähr, Hauptmann, Braun; (ii) Kremer; (i–ii) BPO (CDM5 66101-2).

SCHUBERT: *Symphonies Nos. 1–6, 8–9; Rosamunde ballet music, D.797; Overture (Die Zauberharfe), D.644.* WEBER: *Der Freischütz: overture.*
BPO (CMS5 66114-2 (4)). Also available separately: *Nos. 1–2* (with WEBER) (CDM5 66102-2); *Nos. 3–4; Rosamunde ballet* (CDM5 66103-2); *Nos. 5–6; Overture, D.644* (CDM5 66104-2); *Nos. 8–9* (CDM5 66105-2).

R. STRAUSS: *Don Quixote, Op. 35.* WAGNER: *Tannhäuser:* (i) *Overture and Venusberg music. Die Meistersinger: Overture.*
BPO, (i) with German Op. Ch. (CDM5 66106-2).

R. STRAUSS: *Sinfonia domestica, Op. 53.* WAGNER: *Tristan und Isolde: Prelude & Liebestod; Lohengrin: Preludes to Acts I & III.*
BPO (CDM5 66107-2).

R. STRAUSS: *Ein Heldenleben, Op. 40.* WAGNER: *Der fliegende Holländer: Overture; Parsifal: Preludes to Acts I & III.*
BPO (CDM5 66108-2).

BRAHMS: *Tragic Overture, Op. 81.* HINDEMITH: *Mathis der Maler* (symphony). BRUCKNER: *Symphony No. 8 in C min.*
BPO (CMS5 66109-2 (2)).

Karajan's period with EMI, after he had left Decca, was less consistently successful than his later, DG era, when he probably reached the peak of his recording career. Some collectors will resist the sumptuous orchestral sound he was given in the works of Haydn and Mozart and also perhaps in Schubert too, where we are now accustomed to more transparent textures. In the Beethoven concertos he was not well partnered by Weissenberg, but in the Brahms *B flat Concerto* it was surely Karajan, rather than his soloist, Hans Richter-Haaser, who was responsible for the waywardness of the interpretation. Not surprisingly, he is heard at his finest in the music of Bruckner, Richard Strauss, Wagner and Hindemith. All these recordings are separate issues.

King, Thea (clarinet)

'The clarinet in concert': BRUCH: *Double concerto in E min., for clarinet, viola and orchestra, Op. 88* (with Nobuko Imai). MENDELSSOHN: *2 Concert pieces for clarinet and basset horn: in F min., Op. 113; in D min., Op. 114* (with Georgina Dobrée). CRUSELL: *Introduction and variations on a Swedish air, Op. 12* (all 4 works with LSO, Alun Francis). SPOHR: *Variations in B flat for clarinet and orchestra in a theme from Alruna.* RIETZ: *Clarinet concerto in G min., Op. 29.* SOLERE: *Sinfonie concertante in F for 2 clarinets* (with Georgina Dobrée). HEINZE: *Konzertstück in F* (all with ECO, James Judd or Andrew Litton).
(B) *** Hyperion Dyad Dig. CDD 22017 (2) [id.].

A thoroughly engaging programme of forgotten music (the Bruch is not even listed in the *New Grove*), all played with skill and real charm, and excellently recorded. The Bruch *Double concerto* is particularly individual, but the two attractive Mendelssohn concert pieces (each in three brief movements) and the quixotic Crusell *Variations* are by no means insubstantial. They are discussed more fully under their composer entries. The novelties on the second disc are slighter but no less entertaining: the jaunty Spohr *Variations* followed by the *galant* concerto by Julius Rietz (1812–77) with its engaging lyrical flow. One cannot help but smile at the garrulous chatter between the two solo instruments, which evokes the clinking of tea-cups, in Etienne Solère's *Sinfonie concertante*, while Gustav Heinz's warmly tuneful *Konzertstück* has a jocular, Hummelian finale to match the bouncing closing Rondeau of the Solère. The playing brings many chortling roulades and a seductive timbre from the ever-stylish Thea King, and Georgina Dobrée is a nimble partner in the *Sinfonie concertante*. The accompaniments are excellent too, while the recording has fine range and presence.

Lawson, Colin (clarinet, basset horn), Parley of Instruments, Peter Holman

'English classical clarinet concertos': John MAHON: *Concerto No. 2 in F; Duets Nos. 1 & 4 in B flat for 2 basset horns* (with Michael Harris). J. C. BACH: *Concerted symphony in E flat*. James HOOK: *Concerto in E flat*.
** Hyperion Dig. CDA 66869 [id.].

The clarinet (invented around 1700) did not achieve a strong solo profile until well into the eighteenth century, and even then it was not favoured by amateurs. Mozart remains the only composer of that period to have written really great music for it. Thus, even more than in his companion disc of violin concertos, Peter Holman has had to scrape the barrel a bit and even include a *Concerted symphony* by J. C. Bach, which in the event is the most enterprising work here, but featuring (besides a pair of clarinets) two oboes, bassoon and two horns. It has a very striking first movement and a touching *Larghetto*, which opens with a bassoon solo; the flute then takes over, and the clarinets enter much later. The most unusual scoring is in the closing Minuet, where in the Trio the woodwind take over entirely. James Mahon's *Duos* for basset horns are agreeable but sub-Mozart. His *Concerto*, however, goes even further than the contemporary violin concertos (see below), by using a complete Scottish folksong for his ingenious *Andante* and another popular tune (*The wanton God*) for the Rondo finale. James Hook's *Concerto* has little that is individual to say in its conventional and rather long opening movement, yet it includes the prettiest roulades for the clarinet soloist. However, the composer reserves the real fireworks for the final Rondo, especially in the spectacular closing episode, introduced by the horns, where the clarinet ripples hectically up and down its register in a quite abandoned manner. Colin Lawson is fully equal to such bravura and he plays with fine style throughout. Holman provides excellent accompaniments, but it is a pity that the music itself is so uneven.

Leningrad Philharmonic Orchestra, Yevgeni Mravinsky

The Mravinsky Edition (complete)

() **(*) RCA 74321 25189-2 (10) [id.].

Volume 1: BRAHMS: *Symphony No. 2 in D, Op. 73*. SCHUBERT: *Symphony No. 8 in B min. (Unfinished), D.759*. WEBER: *Oberon: Overture*.
(M) **(*) RCA 74321 25190-2 [id.].

Volume 2: MOZART: *Overture: The Marriage of Figaro; Symphony No. 39 in E flat, K.543*. MUSSORGSKY: *Khovanshchina: Prelude to Act I*. SIBELIUS: *Legend: The Swan of Tuonela, Op. 22/2; Symphony No. 7 in C, Op. 105*.
(M) **(*) RCA 74321 25191-2 [id.].

Volume 3: STRAVINSKY: *Agon* (complete). SHOSTAKOVICH: *Symphony No. 15 in A, Op. 141*.
(M) **(*) RCA 74321 25192-2 [id.].

Volume 4: BRUCKNER: *Symphony No. 9 in D min*.
(M) ** RCA 74321 25193-2 [id.].

Volume 5: TCHAIKOVSKY: *The Nutcracker:* excerpts. PROKOFIEV: *Romeo and Juliet: suite No. 2*.
(M) *** RCA 74321 25194-2 [id.].

Volume 6: HINDEMITH: *Symphony, Die Harmonie der Welt*. HONEGGER: *Symphony No. 3 (Symphonie liturgique)*.
(M) *** RCA 74321 25195-2 [id.].

Volume 7: BEETHOVEN: *Symphony No. 4 in B flat, Op. 60*. TCHAIKOVSKY: *Symphony No. 5 in E min*.
(M) **(*) RCA 74321 25196-2 [id.].

Volume 8: BARTOK: *Music for strings, percussion and celeste*. DEBUSSY: *Prélude à l'après-midi d'un faune*. STRAVINSKY: *Apollo* (ballet; complete).
(M) **(*) RCA 74321 25197-2 [id.].

Volume 9: SHOSTAKOVICH: *Symphonies Nos. 6 in B min., Op. 54; 10 in E min., Op. 93.*
(M) **(*) RCA 74321 25198-2 [id.].

Volume 10: WAGNER: *Götterdämmerung: Siegfried's Funeral march. Lohengrin: Preludes to Acts I & III. Die Meistersinger: Overture. Tannhäuser: Overture. Tristan und Isolde: Prelude & Liebestod. Die Walküre: Ride of the Valkyries.*
(M) **(*) RCA 74321 25199-2 [id.].

Yevgeni Mravinsky's stature has gained increasing recognition among the wider musical public outside his native country since his death in 1988. Mravinsky did not make many commercial records: the derisory terms offered to the Leningrad orchestra during the days of the Soviet Union were not conducive to recording. Moreover Mravinsky did not like recording under studio conditions, and so the bulk of his legacy derives from the concert hall. The discs are available both separately and as a ten-CD set.

(Volume 1: 74321 25190-2) Mravinsky's accounts of the Brahms *Second Symphony* and the Schubert *Unfinished Symphony*, together with the Weber *Oberon Overture*, come from concerts given at the end of April 1978. They should not be confused with the performances he gave at the Vienna *Festwochen* later that summer (for which they were obviously preparation) and which appeared briefly on a four-LP EMI/ Melodiya set in the early 1980s, including also the *Fifth Symphonies* of Tchaikovsky and Shostakovich. (Then the Vienna *Oberon*, at under 9 minutes, occupied a whole LP side!) Generally speaking these performances are, if anything, finer, with a moving *Unfinished* and a lyrical but vital Brahms.

(Volume 2: 74321 25191-2) The Mozart pieces, the *Figaro overture* and the *Symphony No. 39 in E flat*, come from the same 1965 concert as the two Sibelius works, *The Swan of Tuonela* and the *Seventh Symphony*. The Mussorgsky *Dawn on the Moscow river*, the evocative *Prelude* to the first Act of *Khovanshchina*, was given two days earlier. The *Seventh* is a performance of stature. Even if Mravinsky rushes the very opening ascent in the cellos and the trombone does have a wide vibrato, it has that intensity this score must have. Although the characterful account of the *Figaro overture* has been available before on Olympia, the Mozart symphony has not; it is a performance of the old school, with great power and again much lyrical intensity. There is a slight drop in pitch at 5 minutes 15 seconds into the slow movement.

(Volume 3: 74321 25192-2) That same intensity is to be found in the 1965 performance of Stravinsky's *Agon*, even if it is evident that the players are not completely inside this particular score; some of the jewelled, hard-edged sound-world Stravinsky evokes is missing. The sound is perfectly acceptable without being in the first flight. Shostakovich's *Fifteenth Symphony* comes from May 1976. Authenticity of feeling and dramatic power compensate for imperfections of execution – and generally rough recording – and the darkness and intensity of the slow movement come over superbly in Mravinsky's hands. There is no doubting the special insights he brings to the work. The new transfer has perhaps a fractionally sharper image.

(Volume 4: 74321 25193-2) Bruckner's *Ninth Symphony* comes from a public performance in 1980, though, for all the skill of the RCA team, the sound still remains fairly coarse and rough-grained. The performance has tremendous grip and strong personality, though Mravinsky moves things on sometimes where greater breadth might be better, and there are some idiosyncratic touches (excessive slowness at letter R in the Novak Edition, track 1, 15 minutes 50 seconds), but sonic limitations do inhibit a strong recommendation.

(Volume 5: 74321 25194-2) The excerpts from Tchaikovsky's *Nutcracker* and the *Second suite* from Prokofiev's *Romeo and Juliet* are identical with the performances that previously appeared on Philips in 1988. The Tchaikovsky is quite magical, possessing all the warmth and enchantment one could wish for, and the sound is every bit as good as the Philips transfer. The Prokofiev, too, is music-making of real stature. As we said first time round, 'phrases breathe and textures glow; detail stands in the proper relation to the whole. There is drama and poetry, and wonderfully rapt *pianissimi*.' However, the fourth movement, the *Dance* in the printed score, is omitted from this recording.

(Volume 6: 74321 25195-2) Both the Hindemith *Symphony*, *Die Harmonie der Welt*, and Honegger's masterly *Symphonie liturgique* come from 1965. Both are performances of stature and few allowances need to be made for the sonic limitations of either work. Sonically this is infinitely superior to the 1980 Bruckner *Ninth* or the 1976 Shostakovich *Tenth*. In fact the CD is among the most desirable of the present set. Mravinsky maintains a tremendous grip on the Hindemith and his *Liturgique* is a very distinguished and imaginative performance.

(Volume 7: 74321 25196-2) The Beethoven *Fourth Symphony* dates from 29 April 1973. It is a performance that calls only the most exalted comparisons to mind – Weingartner, Toscanini's pre-war

BBC performances. The Tchaikovsky *Fifth Symphony* comes from the same concert – and what a concert it must have been! The performance is even more electrifying than either of the earlier DG versions, though climaxes are somewhat rough. RCA's advanced technology has managed to tame them a little, and this account can certainly be recommended alongside the DG versions – and the coupling certainly makes it highly recommendable.

(Volume 8: 74321 25197-2) The performance of Bartók's *Music for strings, percussion and celeste*, the Debussy *Prélude à l'après-midi d'un faune* and Stravinsky's *Apollo* all come from 1965, which would seem to be a good vintage for Leningrad recordings and, in the Bartók at least, an unbronchial time for audiences. Even the pianissimo introduction to the Bartók is relatively (though not completely) undisturbed. The Stravinsky, which is new to UK catalogues, finds the Leningrad strings in splendid form, although Mravinsky rather favours a more heavily accented articulation and less seductive tone-quality than we find in Markevitch's 1963 LSO recording. The balance is closer than in the Bartók. There are some extraneous audience noises here, too, which will irritate some listeners.

(Volume 9: 74321 25198-2) Mravinsky's account of the Shostakovich *Sixth* comes from 1972. Though its first movement is not in fact slower than his 1965, it is not quite as intense in feeling. The *Tenth Symphony* was among the symphonies Mravinsky conducted in 1976 to mark what would have been the composer's seventieth birthday. The opening bars suffer from an intrusively restive audience (and the microphones do not capture the very first note). The performance (31 March 1976) is tremendously intense and of great documentary interest. The recording is mono; though this is not stated on the disc, it certainly sounds as if it is. Generally speaking, the recording is not as good as its 1972 companion.

(Volume 10: 74321 25199-2) Mravinsky's Wagner is of stature and breadth, and the anthology of pieces collected here ranges from 1965 to 1982, the year of his retirement. Variable quality but invariably fine playing from the Leningrad orchestra, and decent transfers. Incidentally, the complete set comes in a very flimsy cardboard slipcase – ours came unstuck within the first few minutes' use!

Lindberg, Christian (trombone), BBC National Orchestra of Wales, Grant Llewellyn

American trombone concertos: CHAVEZ: *Concerto.* ROUSE: *Concerto in memory of Leonard Bernstein.* Augusta Read THOMAS: *Meditation.*
(***) BIS Dig. CD 788 [id.].

By the time he started writing his concerto, Chavez was already in the terminal stages of cancer and his wife had just died. The work opens with an extended morose soliloquy in which the orchestra provides dissonantly pungent support; at times the pacing quickens, but the disconsolate atmosphere remains and, though some percussive intrusions towards the end provide more lively contrast, this music undoubtedly brings longueurs and is essentially depressing. The *Meditation* by Augusta Read Thomas opens much more positively, with the soloist proceeding over a series of lively orchestral interjections. Bell effects (echoed by the strings) and a percussive spicing add variety, and there is a final eruption of energy. But the meagre musical invention is unenticing. Easily the finest work here is the concerto by Rouse which, though darkly atmospheric, readily holds the listener most compellingly. The music climbs up from the lower depths (the opening evocation rather like that at the beginning of the Ravel *Left-hand Piano concerto*). After an exciting climax the soloist has a ruminative cadenza before dashing off in a dazzling scherzo (superb bravura from Lindberg), with the orchestra just about managing to keep up, yet doing so with some panache. There is a series of hair-raising orchestral explosions, followed by a mêlée of urgently volatile brass figurations which then die away slowly, leading to the touching finale marked *Elegiaco, lugubre*. This is designated by Rouse as a memorial to Leonard Bernstein and quotes what is described as the 'Credo' theme from Bernstein's *Third (Kaddish) Symphony*. The movement has an unrelenting thrust and the central orchestral declamation of grief makes a powerful statement, before the soloist steals in with his own gentle and moving valedictory lament. Then, Orpheus-like, he returns into the depths. Superb solo playing throughout this disc, and very fine recording. But the Rouse is the only piece here of real memorability, and it badly needs new couplings.

Lipatti, Dinu (piano)

(with Nadia Boulanger; Philh. O, Zürich Tonhalle O, Lucerne Festival O; Galliera, Ackermann, Karajan): BACH: *Chorale, Jesu, joy of man's desiring* (arr. HESS, from BWV 147); *Chorale preludes, BWV 599 & 639* (both arr. BUSONI); *Partita No. 1, BWV 825; Siciliana* (arr. KEMPFF, from BWV 1031). D. SCARLATTI: *Sonatas, Kk. 9 & 380.* MOZART: *Piano concerto No. 21 in C, K.467; Piano sonata No. 8 in A min., K.310.* SCHUBERT: *Impromptus Nos. 2–3, D.899/2 & 3.* SCHUMANN: *Piano concerto in A min., Op. 54.* GRIEG: *Piano concerto in A min., Op. 16.* CHOPIN: *Piano concerto No. 1 in E min., Op. 11; Barcarolle, Op. 60; Etudes, Op. 10/5 & 25/5; Mazurka No. 32, Op. 50/3; Nocturne No. 8, Op. 27/2; Piano sonata No. 3 in B min., Op. 58; Waltzes Nos. 1–14.* LISZT: *Années de pèlerinage, 2nd Year: Sonnetto 104 del Petrarca.* RAVEL: *Alborada del gracioso.* BRAHMS: *Waltzes* (4 hands), *Op. 39/1–2, 5–6, 10, 14–15.* ENESCU: *Piano sonata No. 3 in D, Op. 25.*
✿ (M) (***) EMI CZS7 67163-2 (5).

This set represents Lipatti's major recording achievements. Whether in Bach (*Jesu, joy of man's desiring* is unforgettable) or Chopin – his *Waltzes* seem to have grown in wisdom and subtlety over the years – Scarlatti or Mozart, these performances are very special indeed. The remastering is done well, and this is a must for anyone with an interest in the piano.

Lloyd Webber, Julian (cello)

'English idyll' (with ASMF, Neville Marriner): VAUGHAN WILLIAMS: *Romanza.* ELGAR: *Romance in D min., Op. 62; Une idylle, Op. 4/1.* DELIUS: *2 Pieces for cello and chamber orchestra.* GRAINGER: *Youthful rapture. Brigg Fair* (arrangement). DYSON: *Fantasy.* IRELAND: *The holy boy.* WALFORD DAVIES: *Solemn melody.* HOLST: *Invocation, Op. 19/2.* Cyril SCOTT: *Pastoral and reel.*
**(*) Ph. 442 530-2 [id.].

The highlights of Julian Lloyd Webber's programme of English concertante miniatures are the Holst *Invocation*, with its nocturnal mood sensitively caught, and George Dyson's *Fantasy*, where the playing readily captures Christopher Palmer's description: 'exquisitely summery and sunny – its chattering moto perpetuo evokes images of bees and butterflies'. Grainger's passionate *Youthful rapture* is given just the right degree of ardent espressivo, as are Delius's warmly flowing *Caprice* and *Elegy*, written (during the composer's last Fenby period) for Beatrice Harrison. The two transcriptions, Vaughan Williams's *Romanza* (originally part of the *Tuba concerto*) and the Elgar *Romance*, conceived with bassoon in mind, were both arranged for cello by their respective composers and are effective enough in their string formats, although by no means superseding the originals. However, Lloyd Webber gives the full romantic treatment both to John Ireland's simple tone-picture, *The holy boy*, and to Grainger's arrangement of *Brigg Fair*, to which not all will respond; for the closing Cyril Scott *Pastoral and reel* (with its telling drone effect) he returns to a more direct style, with pleasing results. Sympathetic accompaniments and warm, atmospheric recording.

'The Julian Lloyd Webber collection' (with ECO or RPO, (i) Barry Wordsworth; (ii) Nicholas Cleobury): Andrew LLOYD WEBBER: *Theme and Variations 1–4.* (i) *Aspects of Love: Love changes everything. Phantom of the Opera: Music of the night.* (ii) SAINT-SAENS: *The Swan.* MOZART: *Rondo alla Turca.* DEBUSSY: *Clair de lune.* BACH/GOUNOD: *Ave Maria.* VANGELIS: *Un après-midi* (with Vangelis & synthesizers). LENNON/MCCARTNEY: *When I'm sixty-four.* TRAD.: *Skye boat song; Londonderry air.* ALBINONI: *Adagio* (arr. GIAZOTTO). BERNSTEIN: *West Side Story: Somewhere.* BACH: *Jesu, joy of man's desiring.* LEHAR: *You are my heart's delight.* RIMSKY-KORSAKOV: *Flight of the bumble bee.* Johann & Josef STRAUSS: *Pizzicato polka.* SCHUMANN: *Träumerei.* ELGAR: *Cello concerto:* 1st movt (cond. Y. Menuhin).
** Ph. Dig. 446 050-2 [id.].

Seventy-five minutes of cello lollipops may be too much of a good thing for some tastes. J. L. W. describes the content as being 'drawn – with one important exception – from [his] less ''serious'' recordings', and the programme establishes its popular credentials by opening with the Andrew Lloyd Webber *Paganini variations*, used as signature tune for ITV's South Bank Show. There are many good tunes here, but mostly romantic ones; a few more bumble-bees would have been advantageous. However, this fine British cellist knows how to shape a good tune: Schumann's *Träumerei*, for instance, is presented very persuasively. The 'exception' ends the programme: the first movement of Elgar's *Cello concerto*, tempting enough, but ending rather abruptly: the slow movement would surely have been a better choice. Pleasant recording.

London Gabrieli Brass Ensemble

'The splendour of baroque brass': SUSATO: *La Danserye: suite*. G. GABRIELI: *Canzona per sonare a 4: La Spiritata*. SCHEIDT: *Suite*. PEZEL: *Ceremonial brass music*. BACH: *The Art of fugue: Contrapunctus IX*. CHARPENTIER: *Te Deum: Prelude in D*. arr. JAMES: *An Elizabethan suite*. CLARKE: *The Prince of Denmark's march*. HOLBORNE: *5 Dances*. STANLEY: *Trumpet tune*. LOCKE: *Music for His Majesty's sackbutts and cornetts*. PURCELL: *Trumpet tune and ayre*. *Music for the funeral of Queen Mary* (with Chorus).
❁ (BB) *** ASV CDQS 6013.

This is one of the really outstanding brass anthologies, and the digitally remastered analogue recording is very realistic. The brass group is comparatively small: two trumpets, two trombones, horn and tuba; and that brings internal clarity, while the ambience adds fine sonority. This makes a superb entertainment to be dipped into at will. The closing *Music for the funeral of Queen Mary* brings an eloquent choral contribution. Introduced by solemn drum-beats, it is one of Purcell's finest short works and the performance here is very moving. The arrangements throughout the concert (usually made by Crispian Steele-Perkins, who leads the group both sensitively and resplendently) are felicitous and the documentation is excellent. This is a very real bargain.

London Gabrieli Brass Ensemble, Christopher Larkin

Original 19th-century music for brass: BEETHOVEN: *3 Equales for 4 trombones*. CHERUBINI: *Trois pas redoublés et la première marche; Trois pas redoublés et la seconde marche*. DAVID: *Nonetto in C min*. DVORAK: *Fanfare*. LACHNER: *Nonet in F*. RIMSKY-KORSAKOV: *Notturno for 4 horns*. SIBELIUS: *Overture in F min; Allegro; Andantino; Menuetto; Praeludium*.
*** Hyperion Dig. CDA 66470 [id.].

'From the steeples and the mountains': IVES: *From the steeples and the mountains; Let there be light*. BARBER: *Mutations for brass*. HARRIS: *Chorale for organ and brass*. Virgil THOMSON: *Family portrait*. COWELL: *Grinnell fanfare; Tall tale; Hymn and fuguing tune No. 12*. GLASS: *Brass sextet*. RUGGLES: *Angels*. CARTER: *A Fantasy upon Purcell's Fantasia upon one note*.
*** Hyperion Dig. CDA 66517 [id.].

It is difficult to decide which of these two programmes is the more enterprising and the more rewarding. If you are responsive to brass sonorities and you acquire one of them, you will surely want its companion. Beethoven's *Equales* were used at the composer's funeral. They are brief, but noble and dignified. The Sibelius suite is folksy, uncharacteristic writing, but has genuine charm.

The second concert opens and closes with the always stimulating music of Charles Ives. *From the steeples and the mountains* is scored for four sets of bells, trumpet and trombones, and its effect is clanguorously wild! Elliot Carter's Purcell arrangement also has tolling bells, and is quite haunting. Of the other pieces the most striking is the Barber *Mutations*, which draws on the chorale, *Christe du Lamm Gottes* with highly individual effect. Most passionate of all is Ruggles' pungently compressed, muted brass *Angels*, yet the piece is marked 'Serene'! The brass playing throughout the two discs is as communicative as it is expert and the recording is splendidly realistic and present.

London Philharmonic Orchestra, Sir Thomas Beecham

'Favourite overtures': MENDELSSOHN: *The Hebrides (Fingal's Cave); Ruy Blas*. SUPPE: *Morning, noon and night in Vienna*. NICOLAI: *The Merry Wives of Windsor*. ROSSINI: *La scala di seta; William Tell; La gazza ladra; Semiramide*.
(M) (**(*)) Dutton Lab. mono CDLX 7001 [id.].

These are all very famous performances, recorded at Abbey Road in the 1930s and admirably balanced by Walter Legge, and the Mendelssohn *Fingal's Cave overture* is uniquely evocative and poetic, one of the finest performances ever recorded. The transfers are expert (the brass in *Ruy Blas* sounds tangibly robust) with only one exception – but unfortunately that was one of Sir Thomas's most famous records. In May 1933 (originally issued on Columbia LX 255) he recorded a delectable but slightly cut version of Rossini's *La scala di seta* overture, making room on side two for an encore, Handel's *Arrival of the Queen of Sheba*. This piece instantly became a favourite lollipop and it has remained so until the present day. For some reason it is omitted here; also the transfer of the opening of the overture is fuzzy in focus, which certainly was not the case with the original 78 disc as we knew it. The other Rossini items are splendid.

La gazza ladra was also slightly cut (to fit on two 78 sides) but has characteristic panache, and one can see Sir Thomas's whiskers bristling at the opening flourish of *Morning, noon and night*.

'The Beecham touch': DVORAK: *Slavonic rhapsody No. 3*. DEBUSSY: *Prélude à l'après-midi d'un faune*. ROSSINI (arr. RESPIGHI): *Rossiniana*. BIZET: *La Jolie fille de Perth* (suite). BERLIOZ: *La damnation de Faust: Dance of the Sylphes*.
(M) (***) Dutton Lab. mono CDLX 7002 [id.].

The Beecham touch was one of utter magic, especially in French music which he so loved. Bizet's *Fair maid of Perth* suite is uniquely cultivated and special, and what is so remarkable here is the warmth and fullness of the sound and the Abbey Road glow on the woodwind: the famous *Sérénade* is wonderfully refined. The Berlioz *Dance of the Sylphes* is sheer gossamer (only Stokowski among other conductors could create this kind of luminous delicacy), while the *Prélude à l'après-midi d'un faune*, both refined and sensuous, immediately casts a spell over the listener. (Incidentally, here as elsewhere the playing dates itself by occasional subtle portamenti in the string phrasing.) Dvořák's *Slavonic rhapsody* has great rhythmic flair – one can imagine Beecham's eyes twinkling as the music surges forward exuberantly. These are among the very finest of Michael Dutton's transfers, and no Beecham admirer should miss them.

London Philharmonic Orchestra, Sir Hamilton Harty

'The art of Sir Hamilton Harty' (recordings from 1933 and 1935): BAX: *Overture to a picaresque comedy*. BERLIOZ: *Roméo et Juliette, Op. 7: Romeo's reverie and Feast of the Capulets. Funeral march for the last scene of Hamlet, Op. 18/3*. HANDEL, arr. HARTY: *Royal Fireworks music: suite; Water music: suite*. SCHUBERT: *Marche militaire*. SIBELIUS: *Valse triste*. SMETANA: *Overture: The Bartered Bride*.
(M) (***) Dutton Lab. mono CDLX 7016 [id.].

These early recordings Sir Hamilton Harty made for Columbia come up sounding better than ever. No later recording has come anywhere near Harty's pioneering account of Bax's *Overture to a picaresque comedy*, which has great character and sparkle. It is a marvellous piece, and this alone would be worth the price of the record. But Harty's Berlioz was unsurpassed in its day. His *Romeo's reverie and Feast of the Capulets*, which featured in Percy Scholes's 'Columbia History of Music' on two 10-inch 78s (which RL still treasures) combines atmosphere and magic, and not even Colin Davis's *Funeral march for the last scene of Hamlet* erases the memory of this 1937 version. All the other items give unalloyed pleasure, and the Dutton transfers are of the highest quality.

London Symphony Orchestra, Ataulfo Argenta

'España': CHABRIER: *España*. RIMSKY-KORSAKOV: *Capriccio espagnol, Op. 34*. GRANADOS: *Spanish dance No. 5 (Andaluza), Op. 37*. MOSZKOWSKI: *5 Spanish dances, Book I, Op. 12*. DEBUSSY: *Images*.
(M) *** Decca 443 580-2 [id.].

Ataulfo Argenta (about whom the documentation of this reissue in Decca's 'Classic Sound' series says nothing) was one of the more promising stars on the Decca roster in the late 1950s, but sadly he died before the promise could fully be realized. Nevertheless this brightly recorded mixture of Spanishry, mostly from the pens of non-Spaniards, readily displays his flair, not least in the sparkling account of Chabrier's title-piece. The slight but endearingly dated Moszkowski dances are beautifully played, and the last three are especially successful. But the highlight of the disc is Rimsky's *Capriccio* which (alongside Maazel's DG Berlin Philharmonic version from the same period) has never been surpassed for its brilliance and Mediterranean colour, with superb virtuosity from the LSO. The 1957 Kingsway Hall recording with its glittering percussion is dazzling in this CD transfer and only a slight tightness in the upper range of the violins prevents the highest technical accolade. The fullness and range are astonishing for their time, and the Decca recording team can well be proud of the early stereo. The Debussy *Images* (recorded in Victoria Hall, Geneva, the same year) show the conductor's fine ear for intricate detail, so well etched by the recording, but the response of the Suisse Romande Orchestra (used to playing this work under Ansermet) has less allure and body of tone than that produced by the LSO. A fascinating collector's CD, just the same.

London Symphony Orchestra, Albert Coates

'Russian favourites': GLINKA: *Ruslan and Ludmilla: Overture; Kamarinskaya.* BORODIN: *In the Steppes of Central Asia; Prince Igor: Polovtsian march.* LIADOV: *8 Russian folksongs, Op. 58.* MUSSORGSKY: *Sorochinsky Fair: Gopak.* TCHAIKOVSKY: *Marche slave.* RIMSKY-KORSAKOV: *May night overture. Dubinushka; Maid of Pskov: Storm music; Mlada: Procession of the Nobles; Snow Maiden: Danse des bouffons.* STRAVINSKY: *The Firebird: The princesses' game; Infernal dance.*
(***) Koch mono 37700-2 [id.].

On the Koch Historic label comes a collection of Coates's recordings with the LSO of Russian lollipops, vividly transferred by H. Ward Marston. Made between 1928 and 1930, they sound astonishingly fresh, with brass bright and forward. The *Procession of the Nobles* from Rimsky-Korsakov's *Mlada* has never been recorded with such flair and excitement, and consistently these performances reflect the natural understanding of a musician of British parentage born in Russia. As well as four other Rimsky items, the disc also has nine favourite pieces by Glinka, Borodin (a famous version of *In the Steppes of Central Asia*), Liadov, Mussorgsky, Tchaikovsky and Stravinsky.

London Symphony Orchestra, Antal Dorati

ENESCU: *Romanian rhapsody No. 2.* BRAHMS: *Hungarian dances Nos. 1–7; 10–12; 15; 17–21; Variations on a theme of Haydn, Op. 56a.*
(M) ** Mercury 434 326-2 [id.].

Dorati is completely at home in the Enescu *Second Rhapsody* (played passionately – but, as music, not nearly as memorable as No. 1) and the Brahms *Hungarian dances*, where he captures a true Hungarian spirit. When he takes a piece faster than expected, one does not feel he is being wilful or intent on showing off, but simply that he and his players are enjoying themselves. If the delicious rubato in No. 7 does not spell enjoyment, one would be very surprised. The recording, made at either Watford or Wembley, sounds firmer and cleaner than on LP. The *Variations* are enjoyable but not distinctive.

London Symphony Orchestra, Sir Charles Mackerras

'Kaleidoscope – An orchestral extravaganza': SMETANA: *The Bartered Bride: Dance of the comedians.* NICOLAI: *Overture: The Merry Wives of Windsor.* Johann STRAUSS Sr: *Radetzky march.* WEBER: *Overture: Abu Hassan.* MEYERBEER: *Le Prophète: Coronation march.* BRAHMS: *Hungarian dance No. 1.* THOMAS: *Overture: Mignon.* TCHAIKOVSKY: *Mazeppa: Cossack dance.* SUPPE: *Overture: The Jolly robbers.* OFFENBACH: *Overture: Orpheus in the Underworld.* WEBER, arr. BERLIOZ: *Invitation to the dance.* GLINKA: *Jota aragonesa.*
(M) *** Mercury 434 352-2 [id.].

The insert-note for this zestful concert is illustrated with a picture of Mackerras taken 35 years ago, before he became Sir Charles, for – almost unbelievably – these recordings were made at Walthamstow in July 1961. The performances sparkle with life and vivacity: the opening *Dance of the comedians* is matched in exhilaration by the highlight of the concert, the fizzingly crisp *Cossack dance* from Tchaikovsky's *Mazeppa*. The orchestra is obviously enjoying itself in the series of bandstand overtures, with responsive playing in all departments, and the lollipops are hardly less effervescent. The one snag is that the violin timbre above the stave is thin, at times to the point of shrillness; but many will readily adjust to this when otherwise the sound approaches demonstration bracket in its colour, sonority and presence, so that Glinka's glittering *Jota aragonesa* makes a spectacular final item. Containing the contents of a pair of LPs (originally published in the UK on the Philips label) the playing time is enticingly generous (75 minutes).

London Symphony Orchestra, Leopold Stokowski

'Orchestral transcriptions': BYRD: *The Earl of Salisbury and Galliard pavan.* CLARKE: *Trumpet voluntary.* SCHUBERT: *Moment musical No. 3 in F min.* CHOPIN: *Mazurka in A min., Op. 17/4.* TCHAIKOVSKY: *Chant sans paroles.* DUPARC: *Extase.* RACHMANINOV: *Prelude in C sharp min., Op. 3/2* (with Czech PO: BACH arrangements: *Chorale prelude: Wir glauben all' an einen Gott ('Giant fugue'), BWV 680; Easter cantata, BWV 4: Chorale; Geistliches Lied No. 51: Mein Jesu, BWV 487; Passacaglia and fugue in C min., BWV 582; Toccata and fugue in D min., BWV 565; Well-tempered Clavier, Book 1: Prelude No. 8 in E flat min., BWV 853*).
(M) *** Decca Phase Four 448 946-2 [id.].

Sumptuously recorded, with the LSO on top form in 1974, these lollipops are often flagrantly far removed from their composer's original conceptions, becoming virtually newly composed in their vivid, Stokowskian orchestral flamboyance. The *Trumpet voluntary* is surely a collectors' item, with its sweetly anachronistic violins in the middle section, and the Chopin *Mazurka* is hardly less extraordinary in its transformation, opening mysteriously with *sul ponticello* strings, and turning into a dreamy rhapsody with its indulgent flute solo. The Byrd *Pavan* is treated as romantically and seductively as the *Song without words* of Tchaikovsky, yet the Schubert *Moment musical* has a bouncing charm. There are plenty of bold histrionics in the scoring of Rachmaninov's most famous *Prelude*, but imaginative touches too, and the LSO respond passionately. With its collection of Bach transcriptions, recorded two years earlier in Czechoslovakia, this is a treasurably unique stereo sampler of Stokowski's orchestral magic – his persistent search for the warmest *espressivo* and sonorously rich beauty of texture, irrespective of any other considerations. The CD transfers are highly successful.

Ma, Yo-Yo (cello)

'Great cello concertos': HAYDN: *Concerto in D, Hob VIIb/2* (with ECO, Garcia). SAINT-SAENS: *Concerto No. 1, Op. 33* (with O Nat. de France, Maazel). SCHUMANN: *Concerto in A min., Op. 129* (with Bav. RSO, C. Davis). DVORAK: *Concerto in B min., Op. 104* (with BPO, Maazel). ELGAR: *Concerto in E min., Op. 85* (with LSO, Previn).
(M) *** Sony Dig./Analogue M2K 44562 (2) [id.].

An enticing mid-priced package, offering at least two of the greatest of all cello concertos, in Yo-Yo Ma's characteristic and imaginatively refined manner. Only the performance of the Haydn gives cause for reservations and these are slight; many will enjoy Ma's elegance here. He is also lucky in his accompanists, and the CBS sound gives no reasons for complaint.

Marsalis, Wynton (trumpet), ECO, Leppard

'The London concert': HAYDN: *Concerto in E flat.* L. MOZART: *Concerto in D.* FASCH: *Concerto in D.* HUMMEL: *Concerto in E.*
*** Sony Dig. SK 57497 [id.].

The title of this collection suggests a live occasion, but in fact these four concertos were recorded over a period of a week in 1993, at St Giles's Church, Cripplegate. The playing is as expert and stylish as we have come to expect from this remarkable American player. His approach, as we have noticed before, is just a little cool but none the worse for that for there is also admirable poise, and in the finale of the Hummel he lets himself go with the most infectious bravura. Incidentally there is no improvising in cadenzas: 'I don't feel comfortable enough to improvise in music of this period,' Marsalis tells us candidly in the notes. The recording gives him a striking but not exaggerated presence in relation to the orchestra.

(Eduard) Melkus Ensemble – see under **Ulsamer Collegium**

Meyer, Sabine (clarinet), Zurich Opera Orchestra, Franz Welser-Möst

'A night at the opera': VERDI: *Fantasia de concerto on themes from Rigoletto* (arr. HERRLINGER/GIAMPIERI). MOZART: *Die Zauberflöte: Die Bildnis.* DANZI: *Konzertstück: Variations on 'La ci darem la mano' from Mozart's Don Giovanni.* WEBER: *Der Freischütz: Leise, leise; Theme and variations concertante in B flat, Op. 33.* ROSSINI: *Il barbiere di Siviglia: Una voce poco fa* (arr. SCHOTTSTADT); *Introduction, theme and variations in E flat.*
** EMI Dig. CDC5 56137-2 [id.].

Sabine Meyer is a clarinettist of luscious tone and impeccable technique, but she is inclined to languish too much in this operatic programme, most strikingly so in Agathe's *Leise, leise* from *Der Freischütz*, and the long selection from *Rigoletto* tends to outstay its welcome. She is at her best in the cabaletta of *Una voce poco fa*, where there is even a touch of wit, and she manages the jocular final variation of Weber's *Variations* (which is very like the *Clarinet concertino*) very winningly. Not surprisingly she is at her finest in Rossini's spectacular display piece, which closes the concert with an infectious combination of flair and technical brilliance. Welser-Möst accompanies attentively, and the recording is agreeable if a bit resonant.

Milstein, Nathan (violin)

'The art of Nathan Milstein' (with (i) Pittsburgh SO, Steinberg; (ii) New Philh. O, Frühbeck de Burgos; (iii) Philh. O, Fistoulari, or (iv) Leinsdorf; (v) Erica Morini & CO; (vi) O, Robert Irving; (vii) Leon Pommers; (viii) Artur Balsam; (ix) Rudolf Firkušný): (i) GLAZUNOV: *Violin concerto in A min., Op. 90.* (ii) PROKOFIEV: *Violin concerto No. 2, Op. 63.* (iii) SAINT-SAËNS: *Violin concerto No. 3, Op. 61.* (i) TCHAIKOVSKY: *Violin concerto in D, Op. 35.* (iii) BRAHMS: *Violin concerto in D, Op. 77.* (iv) BEETHOVEN: *Violin concerto in D, Op. 61.* (i) DVORÁK: *Violin concerto in A min., Op. 53.* (v) VIVALDI: *Double violin concerto in D min., Op. 3/11.* (vi) RACHMANINOV: *Vocalise, Op. 34/14.* MUSSORGSKY: *Sorochintsky Fair: Gopak.* GLAZUNOV: *Meditation, Op. 32.* TCHAIKOVSKY: *Waltz-scherzo, Op. 34; Souvenir d'un lieu cher, Op. 42.* RIMSKY-KORSAKOV: *Fantasia on Russian themes, Op. 33* (arr. KREISLER). (vii) VIVALDI: *Violin sonata No. 2 in A.* HANDEL (arr. HUBAY): *Larghetto.* CORELLI: *La Follia, Op. 5/12.* TARTINI: *Violin sonata in G min. (Devil's trill).* BACH: *Air from Suite No. 3, BWV 1068.* MOZART: *Violin sonatas: in C, K.296; in E min., K.304.* RIMSKY-KORSAKOV: *Tsar Saltan: Flight of the bumble bee.* GLUCK: *Orfeo: Dance of the Blessed spirits.* BRAHMS: *Hungarian dance No. 2.* MASSENET: *Thaïs: Méditation.* CHOPIN: *Nocturne No. 20 in C min.* FALLA: *Jota.* WIENIAWSKI: *Scherzo-Tarantelle, Op. 16.* DEBUSSY: *Minstrels.* SARASATE: *Introduction and tarantella, Op. 43.* KREISLER: *Prelude and allegro in the style of Pugnani.* (viii) HANDEL: *Violin sonata in D, Op. 1/4.* VITALI: *Chaconne.* PROKOFIEV: *Violin sonata No. 2 in D.* (ix) BEETHOVEN: *Violin sonata No. 5 in F (Spring).*
(M) **(*) EMI stereo/mono ZDMF7 64830-2 (6).

BACH: (Unaccompanied) *Violin sonatas and partitas, BWV 1001/6* (complete).
❀ (M) (***) EMI mono ZDS7 64793-2 (2) [id.].

Milstein recorded for companies other than EMI, and his career went on long after the mid-1960s, when this survey ends. But certainly the recordings here often show him at his freshest and in fine technical form. In 1960 he played the Tchaikovsky *Concerto* with glitter and panache, with Steinberg absolutely on the ball with the matching accompaniment. He also found the warmth to do justice to the romanticism of the Glazunov and the scintillating technique to bring off the fireworks in the finale; he was pretty impressive, too, in the Saint-Saëns No. 3. His Dvořák, however, was efficient and clean rather than particularly beguiling, and the Prokofiev No. 2 does not find him at his best either. The Brahms *Concerto* was a straightforwardly lyrical reading, with the slow movement particularly beautiful. It is most satisfying; but he treated the Beethoven *Concerto* at that time as a relatively lightweight and intimate tonal edifice and played his own cadenzas to prove he had an individual view. The set also includes an impressive *Spring Sonata* with Firkušný, but why no Kreutzer? Many of the shorter pieces come off with the flair we associate with Perlman, and in the classical chamber works Milstein is always impressive. With generally excellent transfers, admirers of this artist should find much to relish here, even if he was to go on to record finer versions of some of the key works later.

As an appendix, EMI have reissued Milstein's superb early mono set of the Bach *Sonatas and partitas* for solo violin. With brisker tempi than in his later, DG, stereo recording (see under the composer), the result is exhilaratingly fresh and spontaneous, and the vivid recording has remarkable presence.

Minneapolis Symphony Orchestra, Antal Dorati

Concert: GERSHWIN: *An American in Paris*. COPLAND: *Rodeo (4 Dance episodes)*. SCHULLER: *7 Studies on themes of Paul Klee*. BLOCH: *Sinfonia breve*.
(M) ** Mercury 434 329-2 [id.].

This is a disappointing collection, a rare occurrence for this label, but you can't win them all! Dorati's *Rodeo* lacks the incandescent vitality of Bernstein's electrifying New York version, and Gershwin's *American in Paris* doesn't suit the Hungarian conductor too well either (try the big blues tune at its trumpet entry). The almost over-detailed recording does not help, either here or in Bloch's rather dry *Sinfonia breve*, which needs richer string textures. It is highly suitable for Schuller's sharply etched *Seven studies on themes of Paul Klee* but, brilliantly though this is played, the music itself does not live up to the promise of titles like *The twittering machine* and *Little blue devil*.

Montreal Symphony Orchestra, Charles Dutoit

'Fête à la française': CHABRIER: *Joyeuse marche; España* (rhapsody). DUKAS: *L'apprenti sorcier*. SATIE: *Gymnopédies 1 and 2*. SAINT-SAENS: *Samson et Dalila: Air and Danse bacchanale*. BIZET: *Jeux d'enfants*. THOMAS: *Overture: Raymond*. IBERT: *Divertissement*.
*** Decca Dig. 421 527-2 [id.].

A nicely organized programme, opening vivaciously with Chabrier's *Joyeuse marche* and closing with a gloriously uninhibited account of the finale of Ibert's *Divertissement*, police-whistle and all. The *Gymnopédies* have a wistfully gentle melancholy, and Bizet's *Jeux d'enfants* a fine sense of style; while Thomas's *Raymond Overture* has all the gusto of the bandstand. First-class Decca sound, brightly vivid to suit the music.

'Rhapsody': LISZT: *Hungarian rhapsody No. 2* (arr. MULLER-BERGHAUS). DVORAK: *Slavonic rhapsody No. 3, Op. 45/3*. ALFVEN: *Swedish rhapsody No. 1 (Midsummer watch), Op. 19*. ENESCU: *Romanian rhapsody No. 1, Op. 11*. GLAZUNOV: *Oriental rhapsody, Op. 29*.
*** Decca Dig. 452 482-2 [id.].

Bringing together four popular favourites among nationalistic rhapsodies, this is a superb showpiece disc, not only offering Montreal sound of the most sumptuous kind, but also ripely satisfying performances, full of panache. The masterstroke, confirming that this is a most cherishable issue, is the inclusion of the very rare *Oriental rhapsody* of Glazunov. Like a cross between the *Polovtsian dances* and *Scheherazade*, with plentiful echoes of both, it is just as colourful and attractive as the better-known pieces. In five evocative, well-contrasted movements following a clearly defined programme, it was written in 1889, the year after Rimsky wrote *Scheherazade*, when Glazunov in his mid-twenties had been spending much of his time completing Borodin's *Prince Igor*. This might easily be guessed when the very first melody, illustrating the sleeping city, brings obvious echoes of Borodin's 'Stranger in paradise' theme. At the very end, at the height of the final orgy it returns in glory; and one's only surprise is that such a lollipop as this has been allowed to languish. At least here Dutoit and the Montreal orchestra give it sumptuous treatment, both warmly expressive and brilliant, with richly resonant string tone.

Mravinsky, Yevgeni – see under Leningrad Philharmonic Orchestra

Musica ad Rheinum, Jed Wentz (flute)

'Baroque concerti from the Netherlands': SCHICKHARDT: *Concerto in G min. for flute, 2 oboes and strings*. SOLNITZ: *Sinfonia in A for strings, Op. 3/4*. DE FESCH: *Concerto in B flat for 2 violins and strings, Op. 10/2*. GRONNEMAN: *Concerto in G for flute, 2 violins and continuo*. HURLEBUSCH: *Concerto in A min. for 2 oboes, violin and strings*.
❁ *** 8NM Classics Dig. 92037 [id.].

The only Dutch-born composer represented in this programme is Willem de Fesch (1687–1757). His *Double violin concerto* is an attractive piece but it cannot be said that it exerts a strong individuality, and that applies to his colleagues here. Their music, while not showing personal hallmarks, is wonderfully diverse and inventive, especially in the use of instrumental colour. As the leader of Musica ad Rhenum is a flautist, many of the concertos here are dominated by this instrument but, because of the delightfully graceful and spirited solo playing, none outstays its welcome. Gronneman's *Concerto for solo flute in G major* felicitously uses the two other flutes in the ripieno to play trios; on the other hand, Schickhardt's six-movement *Concerto in G minor* makes use of his oboes orchestrally in the outer movements, varying the textures internally: the second opens with the two solo oboes, the third and fourth are scored for flute and bass continuo alone. It is a beautifully conceived work, while the more robust *Concerto grosso in A minor* of Hurlebusch, with its sombre slow movement for strings alone, integrates the oboes and solo violin within the ripieno, although the oboes get a chance to shine in the finale. The performances here are wonderfully spirited and cultivated, authentic in texture yet captivatingly so. The recording is full, transparent and real. Well worth seeking out – it is distributed by Impetus in the UK.

Musica da Camera, Robert King

Baroque chamber works: BACH: *Cantata No. 42: Sinfonia*. CORELLI: *Concerto grosso in G min. (Christmas), Op. 6/8*. PACHELBEL: *Canon and Gigue*. HANDEL: *Concerto grosso in B flat, Op. 3/2*. VIVALDI: *L'Estro armonico: Concerto in D min., Op. 3/11*. ALBINONI, arr. GIAZOTTO: *Adagio for organ and strings*.
*** Linn Dig. CKD 012 [id.].

An exceptionally successful concert of baroque music, with a very well-chosen programme, presented on an authentic scale, with what appears to be one instrument to a part. Phrasing is thoroughly musical and the intimacy and transparency of sound are achieved without loss of sonority or disagreeable squeezing of phrases. The familiar *Largo* of the Corelli *Christmas concerto* is particularly fresh, and the opening of the famous Pachelbel *Canon* on a sombre solo bass-line is very telling. The colour of the lively Bach and Handel works (using wind as well as strings) is attractively realized. Excellent, realistic recording.

I Musici

ALBINONI: *Adagio in G min.* (arr. GIAZOTTO). BEETHOVEN: *Minuet in G, WoO 10/2*. BOCCHERINI: *Quintet in E, Op. 11/5: Minuet*. HAYDN (attrib.): *Quartet, Op. 3/5; Serenade*. MOZART: *Serenade No. 13 in G (Eine kleine Nachtmusik), K.525*. PACHELBEL: *Canon*.
*** Ph. Dig. 410 606-2 [id.].

A very enjoyable concert, recorded with remarkable naturalness and realism. The effect is very believable indeed. The playing combines warmth and freshness, and the oft-played Mozart *Night music* has no suggestion whatsoever of routine: it combines elegance, warmth and sparkle. The Boccherini *Minuet* and (especially) the Hoffstetter (attrib. Haydn) *Serenade* have an engaging lightness of touch.

Mutter, Anne-Sophie (violin)

'Modern': STRAVINSKY: *Violin concerto in D* (with Philh. O, Sacher). LUTOSLAWSKI: *Partita for Anne-Sophie Mutter* (with Philip Moll, piano); *Chain II* (with BBC SO, composer). BARTOK: *Violin concerto No. 2*. MORET: *En rêve* (with Boston SO, Ozawa). BERG: *Violin concerto*. RIHM: *Time chant* (with Chicago SO, Levine).
(M) *** DG Dig. 445 487-2 (3) [id.].

Here is an unexpected portrait of an outstanding young artist linked with the attractions of inexpensively cutting one's teeth on twentieth-century violin repertoire, offered in brilliant, modern, digital recordings. The Stravinsky *Concerto* makes a splendid opener: there is no more recommendable version, with wit and feeling nicely balanced and excellent, sharply defined sound. The Berg is hardly less successful. Mutter opens with the most delicate pianissimo and her reading is intensely passionate. Her Bartók is more controversial, played with stunning virtuosity and brilliance but at times overcharacterized, even glossy in its brilliance, and in the scherzando section of the second movement she is much faster than the metronome marking; indeed the performance tends to sensationalize the concerto, although the playing is not unfelt and the bravura is astonishing. The Lutoslawski pieces are among the best of his recent compositions and evoke a powerful response from their dedicatee. The Moret is a slight but enticing piece with plenty of shimmering sonorities and a dazzling solo part. The finale erupts suddenly but the introspective musing of the earlier writing returns with sporadic bursts of energy from the soloist which bring the piece to a lively conclusion. The Rihm concerto is a rhapsodical, meditative piece, its effect heightened by the orchestral backing. It is played with superb concentration.

Mutter, Anne-Sophie (violin), Vienna Philharmonic Orchestra, James Levine

'Carmen-fantasie': SARASATE: *Zigeunerweisen; Carmen fantasy.* WIENIAWSKI: *Légende.* TARTINI: *Sonata in G min. (Devil's trill).* RAVEL: *Tzigane.* MASSENET: *Thaïs: Méditation.* FAURE: *Berceuse.*
*** DG Dig. 437 544-2 [id.].

This is an unashamedly fun record, with Mutter playing with freedom and warmth and obviously enjoying herself. Comparing the *Carmen fantasy* of Sarasate with Perlman shows Mutter as equally sharp in characterization, yet Perlman's easy style is in the end the more beguiling. But Mutter's Ravel *Tzigane* is made stunningly Hungarian in its fiery accelerando at the end, while Tartini's famous *Devil's Trill Sonata* is played as a virtuoso piece, rather than placed back in the eighteenth century – no harm in that in the present context. The recording is vividly close.

Nakariakov, Sergei (trumpet), Lausanne Chamber Orchestra, López-Cobos

JOLIVET: *Concertino for trumpet, piano and strings* (with Alexander Markovich, piano). HUMMEL, TOMASI, HAYDN: *Trumpet concertos.*
*** Teldec/Warner Dig. 4509 90846-2 [id.].

The very gifted teenage Russian trumpeter makes a brilliant contribution to the Jolivet *Double concerto*. His partner, the pianist Alexander Markovich, plays very well too, but the balance is less than ideal. Yet, at under ten minutes, the work does not outstay its welcome and it has a catchy, angular main theme. The Tomasi solo concerto is more kaleidoscopic, with lyrical and rhythmic elements alternating and a whiff of jazz in the melodic style. In the Haydn and Hummel *Concertos* Nakariakov does not quite match the famous Hardenberger performances, and the orchestral playing in Lausanne is serviceable rather than outstanding. Nakariakov plays the Hummel in the key of E flat, rather than the brighter E major favoured by Hardenberger, but both this and the Haydn bring a superb solo contribution from the young Russian virtuoso, and the lovely *Andante* of the latter work is memorably warm and graceful before a sparkling finale which matches that of the Hummel in high spirits.

National Symphony Orchestra

'This is full frequency range recording' (cond. (i) Sydney Beer; (ii) Anatole Fistoulari; (iii) Boyd Neel; (iv) Victor Olof): (i) BIZET: *L'Arlésienne: suite No. 1.* (ii) BERLIOZ: *Damnation de Faust: Hungarian march.* GLIERE: *The Red Poppy: Russian sailors' dance.* TCHAIKOVSKY: *Marche slave; The Oprichnik: Overture.* (i) WAGNER: *Gotterdämmerung: Siegfried's Rhine Journey.* (iii) SAINT-SAENS: *Danse macabre.* WOLF-FERRARI: *The Jewels of the Madonna: Intermezzos, Acts I and II.* (i) DELIUS: *Irmelin prelude.* (iv) CHABRIER: *España.*
(M) (***) Dutton mono CDK 1200 [id.].

Made by the National Symphony Orchestra between June and November 1944, these recordings represented the full emergence of Decca's newly developed recording process with an extended range. The founder of the orchestra, using his wealth benevolently, was Sidney Beer, who persuaded many star players to join him. Particularly impressive are his readings of the Bizet suite and the Wagner, with wind and brass superbly caught. Boyd Neel steps away from his usual image as a chamber conductor in a crisp, flamboyant account of *Danse macabre* with Leonard Hirsch, the NSO leader, a prominent and firm soloist. The Wolf-Ferrari interludes are less successful, with higher hiss and violins less sweet. Fistoulari's bright, rhythmically alert contributions inspire recordings of such vividness one can hardly believe they are over 50 years old; the rare *Oprichnik Overture* is specially welcome. Most spectacular of all is the final item, Chabrier's *España*, with Victor Olof, best known as recording producer for both EMI and Decca, here whizzing the players thrillingly through the showpiece. The occasion prompted his engineering colleague, Arthur Haddy, to produce sound that is so vivid, with a remarkably wide dynamic range, one could almost swear it is in stereo. Malcolm Walker provides a model note, not just outlining the background of *ffrr* but giving an impressively detailed history of the Decca company from 1929 onwards

New London Consort, Philip Pickett

'The Feast of Fools': 1st Vespers; Music from the Office; The drinking bout in the cathedral porch; Mass of the asses, drunkards and gamblers; 2nd Vespers; Ceremony of the Baculus; The banquet; Processional.
*** O-L Dig. 433 194-2 [id.].

Philip Pickett and the New London Consort, inspired in their treatment of early music, present an invigorating, ear-catching sequence drawn from the roistering parodies of church practice that in medieval times were celebrated between Christmas and Epiphany. In modern terms the jokes may be heavy-handed, whether involving vestry humour, drunken cavortings or animal-imitations (as in the *Kyrie* of the *Asses, 'Hinhan Eleison'*), but the wildness of much of the music is infectious, performed here with uninhibited joy. Carl Orff's *Carmina Burana* (inspired from similar Latin sources) hardly outshines these originals.

New London Orchestra, Ronald Corp

'British light music classics': Vol. 1: COATES: *Calling all workers.* TOYE: *The haunted ballroom.* COLLINS: *Vanity Fair.* FARNON: *Jumping bean.* BAYNES: *Destiny.* CURZON: *The Boulevardier.* LUTZ: *Pas de quatre.* BINGE: *The Watermill; Elizabethan serenade.* WILLIAMS: *The Devil's galop.* GIBBS: *Dusk.* WHITE: *Puffin' Billy.* KETELBEY: *Bells across the meadows.* Charles WILLIAMS: *The old clockmaker.* JOYCE: *Dreaming.* ELLIS: *Coronation Scot.* ANCLIFFE: *Nights of gladness.*
*** Hyperion Dig. CDA 66868 [id.].

Almost as soon as it was issued, Ronald Corp's stylish and beautifully played collection of inconsequential but engaging English miniatures rose up and held its place in the bestseller lists. This was the kind of music that used to be heard on seaside piers and which was played by spa orchestras in the years between the two World Wars – orchestras that have long since disappeared. The robust *Nights of gladness* (1912) was composed by Charles Ancliffe on return from service as a bandmaster in India, while Sydney Baynes's *Destiny waltz*, from the same year, has a cello solo which, years later, was played by Sir John Barbirolli at Hallé balls; Archibald Joyce's *Dreaming* dates from the previous year, while two other hauntingly atmospheric pieces, *Dusk* by Armstrong Gibbs and Geoffrey Toye's *Haunted ballroom*, were both written in 1935. Vivian Ellis's *Coronation Scot*, a catchy sound-picture of a steam locomotive, dates from 1939 and became famous when it was used as the signature tune for BBC radio's 'Paul Temple' detective series. More recently, Ronald Binge has added his engaging *Elizabethan serenade* (1951) and a delicate portrait of *The Watermill* (1958). It was the famous Sibelius conductor, Anthony Collins, who wrote the delectable morsel, *Vanity Fair*, and he once said in a radio interview that he valued its composition above all his other achievements 'because it will keep my name alive long after my records have been forgotten'. The affectionate, polished performances here will certainly help to do that: they give much pleasure, and Tony Faulkner's recording balance is beautifully judged.

'British Light Music Classics': Vol. 2: COATES: *London suite: Knightsbridge.* FLETCHER: *Bal masqué.* BUCALOSSI: *Grasshopper's dance.* WOOD: *'The Archers' theme': Barwick Green.* HARTLEY: *Rouge et Noir.* FARNON: *Peanut polka; Westminster waltz.* FRANKEL: *Carriage and pair.* HAYDN WOOD: *The Horse Guards, Whitehall* (*Down your way* theme). DUNCAN: *Little suite: March* (*Dr Finlay's Casebook* theme). BINGE: *Sailing by.* VINTER: *Portuguese party.* RICHARDSON: *Beachcomber.* FINCK: *In the shadows.* DOCKER: *Tabarinage.* KETELBEY: *Sanctuary of the heart.* ELGAR: *Carissima.* Charles WILLIAMS: *Girls in grey.* WHITE: *The runaway rocking horse.* CURZON: *Robin Hood suite: March of the Bowmen.*
*** Hyperion Dig. CDA 66968 [id.].

Ronald Corp's first collection of popular evergreens has been one of Hyperion's biggest successes (see above) and this 76-minute collection is just as delightful, for the supply of catchy and popular numbers shows no sign of drying up. Radio and television signature-tunes provide the cornerstones, with *Barwick Green* (*The Archers*) by Arthur Wood pointing the way, a piece inspired not by the West Country or the fictional world of Ambridge, but by a village near Leeds. From Eric Coates's *Knightsbridge March* onwards, chosen in the early 1930s to introduce the pioneering radio magazine programme, *In Town Tonight*, here is a rich source of nostalgia, including Haydn Woods's *Horseguards March* ('Down your Way'), Ronald Binge's *Sailing By* (Radio 4 signing off) and Trevor Duncan's catchy *March* (for *Dr Finlay's Casebook*) which reminds one a little of the *Marcia* of Dag Wirén and is here played most delicately. What comes out from every one of these 20 pieces is not just their catchy memorability and tunefulness, but the brilliance and subtlety of the instrumentations. They are full of the sort of effects that only a really practical musician, close to players, could think up; and they are here made the more enjoyable by the warmth and clarity of the sound. It is welcome that Elgar is this time included with one of his lesser-known pieces, *Carissima*, not to mention Ben Frankel with the jaunty *Carriage and pair*, with its clip-clopping rhythm vividly evoking the period Parisian atmosphere of the film *So Long at the Fair*. A must for anyone at all given to nostalgia.

Oistrakh, David (violin)

'The Originals' (with (i) VSO; (ii) Igor Oistrakh; (iii) RPO, Goossens; (iv) Dresden State O, Konwitschny): (i) BACH: (i) *Violin concertos Nos. 1 in E; 2 in A min;* (ii–iii) *Double violin concerto in D min., BWV 1041–3.* BEETHOVEN: (iii) *Romances Nos. 1 in G, 2 in F, Opp. 40 & 50.* BRAHMS: (iv) *Violin concerto, Op. 77.* TCHAIKOVSKY: *Violin concerto, Op. 35.*
(M) (***) DG stereo/mono 447 427-2 (2) [id.].

In 'The Originals' series at mid-price, DG here offers reissues of classic Oistrakh recordings unavailable for years in any format. Rarest are the 1954 mono recordings of the Brahms and Tchaikovsky *Concertos*, more relaxed, more volatile readings than those Oistrakh recorded later in stereo. Oistrakh moves effortlessly from dashing bravura to the sweetest lyricism, the complete master. The Bach and Beethoven offerings are hardly less welcome. Allowing for the practice of the time, these Bach performances are all strong and resilient, consistently bringing out the sweetness and purity of Oistrakh's playing, not least in the rapt accounts of the slow movements. Directing the Vienna Symphoniker from the violin, Oistrakh may make the tuttis in the two Bach solo concertos rather heavy, but he then transforms everything the moment he starts playing. The Bach *Double concerto* with Oistrakh father and son, accompanied by Goossens and the RPO, is more magnetic still, and they accompany him no less sympathetically in the warm, poised readings of the two Beethoven *Romances*.

(with (i) Moscow RSO, Aram Khachaturian; (ii) Moscow RSO, Gennady Rozhdestvensky; (iii) Sviatoslav Richter): (i) KHACHATURIAN: *Violin concerto in D min.* (ii) SIBELIUS: *Violin concerto in D min., Op. 47.* (iii) FRANCK: *Violin sonata in A.* SHOSTAKOVICH: *Violin sonata, Op. 134.*
(B) *** Carlton VoxBox CDX 5120 (2) [id.].

These performances have previously been in circulation under various logos: on HMV/Melodiya during the 1970s, and later on Chant du Monde and other labels. The Khachaturian dates from 1940. Oistrakh recorded it during the war, as he did the Miaskovsky *Concerto*. Unfortunately he did not re-record the latter, but this 1965 account of the Khachaturian (made with the composer conducting) is a fine one; strangely enough, this is not superior – even as a recording – to the 1954 EMI version with the Philharmonia (CDC5 55035-2 – see our main volume). Likewise the Sibelius is wonderfully noble and lyrical (as indeed was his fine Stockholm performance with Sixten Ehrling, recorded in mono in 1953). The Franck *Sonata* with Richter remains in a class of its own, as does (even more so) the Shostakovich of which Oistrakh was the dedicatee. The transfers are decent rather than exceptional. There is not that much difference between the CD version of the Shostakovich *Sonata* and the original LP. But what music-making!

Osipov State Russian Folk Orchestra, Vitaly Gnutov

'Balalaika favourites': BUDASHIN: *Fantasy on two folk songs.* arr. GORODOVSKAYA: *At sunrise.* KULIKOV: *The Linden tree.* OSIPOV: *Kamarinskaya.* MIKHAILOV/SHALAYEV: *Fantasy on Volga melodies.* ANDREYEV: *In the moonlight; Under the apple tree; Waltz of the faun.* SOLOVIEV/SEDOY: *Midnight in Moscow.* TCHAIKOVSKY: *Dance of the comedians.* SHISHAKOV: *The living room.* arr. MOSSOLOV: *Evening bells.* arr. POPONOV: *My dear friend, please visit me.* RIMSKY-KORSAKOV: *Flight of the bumble bee.*
✿ (M) *** Mercury 432 000-2 [id.].

The Mercury recording team visited Moscow in 1962 in order to make the first recordings produced in the Soviet Union by Western engineers since the Revolution. The spirit of that unique occasion is captured wonderfully here – analogue atmosphere at its best. The rippling waves of balalaika sound, the accordion solos, the exhilarating accelerandos and crescendos that mark the style of this music-making: all are recorded with wonderful immediacy. Whether in the shimmering web of sound of *The Linden tree* or *Evening bells*, the sparkle of the folksongs or the sheer bravura of items like *In the moonlight*, which gets steadily faster and louder, or in Rimsky's famous piece (sounding like a hive full of bumble bees), this is irresistible, and the recording is superbly real in its CD format.

Jean-François Paillard Chamber Orchestra, Paillard

'Baroque melodies': ALBINONI: *Adagio* (arr. GIAZOTTO). PACHELBEL: *Canon*. BACH: *Suite No. 2, BWV 1067: Minuet and Badinerie. Cantata No. 140: Wachet auf. Cantata No. 147: Jesus bleibet meine Freude. Suite No. 3, BWV 1068*. HANDEL: *Concerti grossi* (excerpts): *Op. 6/6: Musette. Op. 6/10: Gavotte*. VIVALDI: *Piccolo concerto in A min, P. 83: Larghetto*. MARCELLO: *Oboe concerto in C min.: Adagio*. CORELLI: *Badinerie & Gigue*. VIVALDI: *Violin concerto in A min., Op. 3/6: Allegro*. ZIPOLI: *Adagio for oboe, cello and strings*. RAMEAU: *Tambourins*. MOLTER: *Trumpet concerto in D: Andante for strings*. CLARKE: *Trumpet voluntary*.
(M) **(*) BMG/RCA Dig. 09026 65468-2 [id.].

There seems to be an unlimited market for baroque collections including the Albinoni *Adagio* and Pachelbel *Canon*, and this one is as good as most. The various individual concertante movements are well chosen and expertly played on modern instruments by soloists of the calibre of Christian Larde (flute/piccolo) and Pierre Pierlot (oboe). The orchestral playing does not lack warmth and style, and the recording is excellent, but this group sounds blander than the Academy of St-Martin-in-the-Fields in this repertoire. Nevertheless, with 73 minutes' music, this is a very agreeable late-evening collection.

Perlman, Itzhak (violin)

'Great Romantic Violin Concertos' (with (i) Chicago SO or (ii) Philh. O, Giulini; (iii) Concg. O, Haitink; (iv) RPO, Lawrence Foster; (v) Phd. O, Ormandy): (i) BRAHMS: *Concerto in D, Op. 77*. (iii) BRUCH: *Concerto No. 1 in G min., Op. 26*. (ii) BEETHOVEN: *Concerto in D, Op. 61*. (iv) PAGANINI: *Concerto No. 1 in D, Op. 6*. (iii) MENDELSSOHN: *Concerto in E min., Op. 64*. (v) TCHAIKOVSKY: *Concerto in D, Op. 35*.
(M) **(*) EMI Analogue/ Dig. CMS7 64922-2 (3).

These major Perlman recordings include his earlier (1980) studio recording of the Beethoven *Concerto*; it is among the most commanding of his readings and the element of slight understatement, the refusal to adopt too romantically expressive a style, makes for a compelling strength, perfectly matched by Giulini's thoughtful, direct accompaniment. The (1976) Brahms is also a distinguished performance, again finely supported by Giulini, this time with the Chicago orchestra, a reading of darker hue than is customary, with a thoughtful and searching slow movement rather than the autumnal rhapsody which it so often becomes. The (1983) Bruch *G minor concerto* must be counted a disappointment, however, not helped by the harsh, early digital recording which gives an edge to the solo timbre. The performance is heavily expressive and, like the Mendelssohn (recorded at the same time), is not nearly as spontaneous as Perlman's earlier, analogue recording with Previn. The Paganini (1971) is one of Perlman's very finest records and, although the traditional cuts are observed, the performance has irresistible panache and has been transferred to CD very well. In the Tchaikovsky (1978) the soloist is placed less aggressively forward than is usual. Perlman's expressive warmth goes with a very bold orchestral texture from Ormandy and the Philadelphia Orchestra. However, admirers of these artists are unlikely to be disappointed.

'The Art of Itzhak Perlman' (with Israel PO, Mehta; Pittsburgh SO, Previn; LPO, Ozawa; RPO, Foster; also Ashkenazy, Bruno Canino, Samuel Sanders, Previn (piano) and other artists): BACH: *Concerto, BWV 1056; Partita No. 3, BWV 1006*. VIVALDI: *Concerto, RV 199*. MOZART: *Oboe quartet, K.370*. BRAHMS: *Sonata No. 3; Hungarian dances 1–2, 7 & 9*. SINDING: *Suite, Op. 10*. WIENIAWSKI: *Concerto No. 1*. SIBELIUS: *Concerto*. KHACHATURIAN: *Concerto*. KORNGOLD: *Concerto*. STRAVINSKY: *Suite italienne*. ANON.: *Doyna*. YELLEN/POLLACK: *My Yiddishe Momma*. FOSTER (arr. HEIFETZ): *The Old folks at home*. PONCE (arr. HEIFETZ): *Estrellita*. JOPLIN: *The Rag-time dance; Pineapple rag*. SMETANA: *Z domoviny*. KREISLER: *Liebesfreud; Liebesleid*. RACHMANINOV (arr. PRESS/GINGOLD): *Vocalise*. GRAINGER: *Molly on the shore*. PREVIN: *Look at him; Bowing and scraping*. TRAD. (arr. KREISLER): *Londonderry air*. SARASATE: *Carmen fantasy*.
(M) *** EMI Analogue/Dig. CMS7 64617-2 (4) [ZDMD 64617].

This box contains a feast of this great violinist's recordings. He made the choice himself and, while the concertos, particularly the Wieniawski, Sibelius, Khachaturian, and Korngold (and not forgetting the dazzling concertante *Carmen fantasy* of Sarasate or the *Suite* of Sinding) are all indispensable, the shorter pieces on the last disc just as readily display the Perlman magic. They include the delectable jazz collaboration with Previn, the beautifully played Kreisler encores, and many popular items which are readily turned into lollipops. The stylish account of the Stravinsky *Suite italienne* which ends disc three is also one of the highlights of the set. For the most part the recordings have the violin very forwardly balanced, but that was Perlman's own choice; the sound is otherwise generally excellent.

Philadelphia Orchestra, Leopold Stokowski

'Philadelphia rarities' (1928–1937): arr. STOKOWSKI: *2 Ancient liturgical melodies: Veni, Creator Spiritus; Veni, Emmanuel*. FALLA: *La vida breve: Spanish dance*. TURINA: *Gypsy dance, Op. 55/5*. DUBENSKY: *Edgar Allan Poe's 'The Raven'* (narr. Benjamin DE LOACHE). arr. ONOYE: *Etenraku: Ceremonial Japanese prelude*. MCDONALD: *The legend of the Arkansas traveller; The Festival of the workers (suite): Dance of the workers. Double piano concerto* (with Jeanne Behrend & Alexander Kelberine). EICHHEIM: *Oriental impressions: Japanese nocturne. Symphonic variations: Bali*. SOUSA: *Manhattan Beach; El Capitan*.
(M) (***) Cala mono CACD 0501 [id.].

All these recordings show what splendid recorded sound Stokowski was achieving in Philadelphia as early as 1929. The opening Stokowski liturgical arrangements show how that master of orchestral sonority could make liturgical chants his very own, with a discreet tolling bell to indicate their source. Falla's *Spanish dance* shows him at his most sparklingly chimerical. Dubensky's music does not add a great deal to Edgar Allan Poe, but the narrator, Benjamin de Loache, certainly does, presenting the narrative with the essentially genial, melodramatic lubricity of Vincent Price. Hidemaro Konoye and Stokowski and his players conspire between them to provide an extraordinarily authentic Japanese sound in *Etenraku*, and then in *The legend of the Arkansas traveller* we have a complete change of local colour for Alexander Hilsberg's folksy, sub-country-and-western violin solo. Henry Eichheim's Japanese and Balinese impressions are suitably exotic, but not music one would wish to return to. As for Harl McDonald's *Double piano concerto*, the piano writing is splashy and the finale is spectacularly based on the *Juarezca*, a jazzy Mexican dance. The two soloists provide convincing, extrovert dash, and Stokowski obviously revels in what Noël Coward might have described as 'potent cheap music' if with nothing like the melodic appeal of Coward's own work. The two Sousa marches have both poise and élan, but here the sound is barely adequate – not the fault of the CD transfer. The programme lasts for 78 minutes and Stokowksi aficionados need not hesitate.

Philharmonia Orchestra, Nicolai Malko

BORODIN: *Prince Igor: Overture; Polovtsian Dances; Polovtsian March. Symphony No. 2 in A min.* RIMSKY-KORSAKOV: *Maid of Pskov (Ivan the Terrible) Overture*. LIADOV: *8 Russian folksongs*. GLAZUNOV (with Sokolov and Liadov): *Les vendredis: Polka*.
(**) Testament mono/stereo SBT1062 [id.].

Nicolai Malko, from 1926 the chief conductor of the Leningrad Philharmonic and the first interpreter of Shostakovich's *First Symphony*, made all too few recordings; though some of these with the Philharmonia lack tautness, his feeling for the Slavonic idiom is unerring. This reading of the *Prince Igor overture* is light and transparent (in newly unearthed stereo) but lacks dramatic bite, and so do the *Polovtsian dances*, polished but not involving. The *Polovtsian March* is quite different: a tense, swaggering performance which reveals the true Malko. Then after an amiable, low-key account of the first movement of the Borodin symphony, the Scherzo second movement brings a virtuoso performance. Best of all is the Rimsky-Korsakov overture, in full-bodied stereo. After a relaxed, colourful account of the Liadov *Folksongs*, the corporately written *Polka* makes a charming encore, an Elgar-like salon piece.

Philharmonia Orchestra, Igor Markevitch

Orchestral portrait: BARTOK: *Dance suite*. RAVEL: *La valse*. SATIE: *Parade*. BUSONI: *Tänzwalzer*. LIADOV: *Kikimora*. CHABRIER: *Le roi malgré lui: Fête polonaise*. LISZT: *Mephisto waltz*.
(***) Testament (mono) SBT 1060 [id.].

The seven varied items here make an illuminating portrait of a conductor who at the time seemed destined to be more central in the world of recording than he became. With immaculate transfers the 1950s mono recordings have astonishing vividness and presence. In the effervescent account of Satie's *Parade* (sadly cut in the last movement) the brass and percussion (including the celebrated typewriter) have wonderful bite, and so have the joyful brass fanfares at the start of the Chabrier *Polonaise*, done in Viennese style. Perhaps most vivid of all is the virtuoso performance of the *Mephisto waltz*.

Pierlot, Pierre (oboe)

'The magic of the oboe' (with Sol. Ven., Scimone; or Paillard CO, Jean-François Paillard): VIVALDI: *Concertos in C, RV 452; F, RV 455.* ALBINONI: *Concerto a cinque in D min., Op. 9/2.* CIMAROSA: *Concerto* (arr. BENJAMIN). ZIPOLI: *Adagio for oboe, cello, organ and strings* (arr. GIOVANNINI). MARCELLO: *Concerto in C min.* BELLINI: *Concerto.*
(M) *** Erato/Warner 4509 92130 [id.].

For once, a record company's sobriquet for a collection does not disappoint: this is indeed a magical and very generous (74 minutes) collection, well recorded. One might say the cream of baroque oboe concertos are included here, and Benjamin's arrangement of movements by Cimarosa with its delightful central *Siciliano* and spiccato finale is as engaging as any. The Albinoni and Marcello concertos have memorable slow movements, too, and the Bellini a catchy Polacca finale. The novelty is Zipoli's *Adagio*, sumptuously arranged by Francesco Giovannini after the manner of Giazotto's 'Albinoni *Adagio*'. It doesn't quite come off, but it is a very near miss. Throughout, Pierlot's sweet, finely focused timbre and graceful phrasing are a constant pleasure.

Radio Television Eireann Concert Orchestra, Dublin, Ernest Tomlinson

'British light music – Miniatures': Anthony COLLINS: *Vanity Fair.* Mark LUBBOCK: *Polka dots.* Armstrong GIBBS: *Dusk.* Benjamin FRANKEL: *Carriage and pair.* Vivian ELLIS: *Coronation Scot.* Arthur BENJAMIN: *Jamaican song; Jamaican rumba.* Robert DOCKER: *Tabarinage.* ELGAR: *Beau Brummel.* Harry DEXTER: *Siciliano.* Ken WARNER: *Scrub, brothers scrub!* Gordon JACOB: *Cradle song.* Thomas ARNE, arr. TOMLINSON: *Georgian suite: Gavotte.* Gilbert VINTER: *Portuguese party.* Geoffrey TOYE: *The Haunted ballroom* (concert waltz). Edward WHITE: *Puffin' Billy.* George MELACHRINO: *Starlight Roof waltz.* Clive RICHARDSON: *Beachcomber.*
**(*) Marco Polo Dig. 8.223522 [id.].

Anthony Collins was right to be proud of his delightful vignette, 'Vanity Fair', for its theme is indelible, and it comes up very freshly here in a programme of unassuming orchestral lollipops, including many items with almost equally catchy musical ideas, even a *Gavotte* by Thomas Arne, arranged by the conductor to sound just a little like a caricature. The tunes are usually pithy and short, like Harry Dexter's daintily wispy *Siciliano*, but sometimes the writing is gently evocative, like the two romantic waltzes, *Dusk* of Armstrong Gibbs, and Geoffrey Toye's *Haunted ballroom*, and Gordon Jacob's delicate *Cradle song*. Novelties like Benjamin Frankel's clip-clopping *Carriage and pair*, Edward White's *Puffin' Billy*, and Ken Warner's moto perpetuo, *Scrub, brothers scrub!* readily evoke the world of Leroy Anderson, while Clive Richardson's quirky *Beachcomber* makes one want to smile. The conductor, Ernest Tomlinson, understands that their very slightness is part of the charm of nearly all these pieces, and he presents them with a simplicity that is wholly endearing. The only relative disappointment is Vivian Ellis's wittily evoked *Coronation Scot*, which needs much more verve than it receives here. Good playing and good recording, although the acoustic effect noticeably becomes more brash for the second item, Mark Lubbock's breezy *Polka dots*.

Rampal, Jean-Pierre (flute)

'20th century flute masterpieces' (with (i) LOP, Froment; (ii) O de l'ORTF, Martinon; (iii) LOP, Jolivet; (iv) Robert Veyron-Lacroix): (i) IBERT: *Concerto.* (ii) KHACHATURIAN: *Concerto* (arr. from *Violin concerto*). (ii) JOLIVET: *Concerto.* (iii) MARTINU: *Sonata.* HINDEMITH: *Sonata.* PROKOFIEV: *Sonata in D.* POULENC: *Sonata.*
(M) **(*) Erato/Warner 2292 45839-2 (2) [id.].

The concertos on the first CD have less than perfectly focused orchestral strings, and the Khachaturian arrangement is dispensable. But the Ibert *Concerto* is winning and the more plangent Jolivet not inconsiderable. The highlights of the collection are all on the second disc, three out of four of them inspired works delightfully written for the instrument and marvellously played. Only the first movement of the Hindemith is a bit below par in its utilitarian austerity; the cool slow movement and more vigorous finale have something approaching charm. The Prokofiev *Sonata* (also heard in a version for violin – but the flute is the original) is a masterpiece, and Rampal makes the very most of it. Then comes the delightful Poulenc piece with its disarmingly easy-flowing opening, delicious central cantilena and scintillating finale with hints of *Les Biches*. The recording of the sonatas, made in 1978, is vividly firm and realistic. If this set is reissued later on a Bonsai Duo, it will be well worth seeking out.

(i) **RCA Victor Symphony Orchestra** (ii) **Symphony of the Air, Leopold Stokowski**

'Rhapsodies': (i) LISZT: *Hungarian rhapsody No. 2*. ENESCU: *Romanian rhapsody No. 1*. SMETANA: *Má Vlast: Vltava. The Bartered Bride overture*. (ii) WAGNER: *Tannhäuser: Overture and Venusberg music* (with chorus). *Tristan und Isolde: Prelude to Act III*.
(M) *** BMG/RCA 09026 61503-2 [id.].

Recorded in 1960 and 1961, this collection shows the great orchestral magician at his most uninhibitedly voluptuous. The opening tutti of the Liszt *Hungarian rhapsody* with full-throated horns and richly sonorous double basses makes a huge impact, and the Enescu is comparably sumptuous in its glowing colours. *Vltava* is romanticized, with an expansive treatment of the main lyrical theme, but *The Bartered Bride Overture* is bursting with energy, with the stereo clearly defining the emphatic string entries of the opening fugato. The *Overture and Venusberg music* from *Tannhäuser* combines sensuousness with frenetic excitement, and then a sentient relaxation appears in the *Tristan Prelude* to Act III. This is over-the-top Stokowski at his most compulsive, but is not for musical puritans. The CD transfers encompass the breadth of amplitude of the forwardly balanced recordings without problems.

Reilly, Tommy (harmonica)

Harmonica concertos (with (i) Munich RSO, Gerhardt; (ii) Basel RSO, Dumont; (iii) SW German RO, Smola; (iv) Munich RSO, Farnon; (v) O, Farnon): (i) SPIVAKOVSKY: *Harmonica concerto*. (ii) ARNOLD: *Harmonica concerto, Op. 46*. (iii) VILLA-LOBOS: *Harmonica concerto*. (iv) MOODY: *Toledo (Spanish fantasy)*. (v) FARNON: *Prelude and dance*.
*** Chandos Dig. CHAN 9218 [id.].

This is definitely the most attractive of Tommy Reilly's three concertante collections. The Spivakovsky is a particularly winning piece, with a catchy tune in the first movement, rather like a Leroy Anderson encore, a popular, romantic central interlude, marked *Dolce*, and a delicious *moto perpetuo* finale. Not surprisingly, the Malcolm Arnold is very appealing too, one of this composer's best miniature concertos, written in 1954 for the BBC Proms. The Villa-Lobos, written in 1955, should be much better known. Scored for a small orchestra of strings, single wind, harp, celesta and percussion, it has a neo-classical character. It produces a quite lovely melody for the *Andante*; only the finale, which moves along at a genial pace, has piquant hints of the composer's usual Brazilian preoccupation. James Moody's *Spanish fantasy* might be described as good cheap music, and it offers the soloist a glittering chance to demonstrate his bravura with infectious panache. Farnon's hauntingly nostalgic *Prelude and dance* (a charmingly inconsequential little waltz) brings a felicitous interleaving of both themes. The recording balance is surely as near perfect as one could wish.

Rostropovich, Mstislav (cello)

'Rostropovich live' (with Moscow PO or USSR R. & TV O, Rozhdestvensky): ELGAR: *Cello concerto in E min., Op. 68*. RESPIGHI: *Adagio with variations for cello and orchestra*. MILHAUD: *Cello concerto No. 1, Op. 136*.
*(**) Russian Disc RDCD 11 104 [id.].

A larger-than-life account of the Elgar *Concerto* from Rostropovich, a performance of contrasts with great dash in the Scherzo, yet an *Adagio* of deep inner feeling and a gentle, heart-touching reprise at the close of the finale. The Respighi *Variations* are beautifully played and made almost to seem as inspired as the Tchaikovsky *Rococo* set, while the diverse moods of the Milhaud concerto – *Nonchalant, Grave and Joyeux* – are winningly characterized. The 1964 analogue recording is fully acceptable, not as flattering to Rostropovich's tone as Western recordings and with the orchestra noticeably thin in the tuttis of the Milhaud. With only 52 minutes' playing time, this CD, for all its attractions, is overpriced.

(i) **Royal Opera House Orchestra, Covent Garden,** (ii) **Philharmonia Orchestra,** (iii) **Sadler's Wells Orchestra,** (iv) **London Philharmonic Orchestra, Constant Lambert**

'Ballet Conductor Supreme': (i) Gavin GORDON: *The Rake's Progress ballet music.* (ii) JACOB (arr. of LISZT): *Apparitions: Cave scene (Mephisto Waltz No. 3); Galop.* (ii) WALDTEUFEL: Waltz: *Sur la plage, Op. 234.* (iii) LAMBERT (arr. of BOYCE): *The Prospect before us.* (iv) WEINBERGER: *Variations on 'Under the spreading chestnut tree'.*
(**) Time Machine mono TM 0099-2 [id.].

No doubt Constant Lambert was the greatest ballet conductor of his day. Collectors of the older generation will recall these performances from the days of 78s and the BBC Home Service on which they were frequently broadcast. Even then Gavin Gordon's score, *The Rake's Progress*, sounded pretty nondescript and empty, and its companions included here are of slender musical interest. The transfers are decent but this is a period piece for ballet aficionados.

Royal Philharmonic Orchestra, Sir Thomas Beecham

'French favourites': CHABRIER: *Overture Gwendoline* (with O Nat. de l'ORTF); *España* (rhapsody) (with LPO). GOUNOD: *Faust: ballet music.* GRETRY: *Zémir et Azor: ballet music.* MASSENET: *Cendrillon: Waltz. La Vierge: The last sleep of the Virgin.* BIZET: *Roma: Carnaval à Roma. Patrie overture.*
(M) (***) EMI mono CDM7 63401-2 [id.].

A programme of French music which Sir Thomas loved so well and played incomparably, derives from a number of (mainly late-1950s) sources, with the supercharged *Gwendoline Overture* recorded in Paris, the seven numbers of the elegantly vivacious *Faust ballet music* in Walthamstow, along with most of the other pieces, except the two most famous items, the delectably fragile *Last sleep of the Virgin* of Massenet (Abbey Road) and the incomparably effervescent *España* in Kingsway Hall. These latter two items derive from 78s, and Michael Dutton's transfers have remarkable realism and brilliance; the upper range of *España* only slightly pinched and the percussive condiment glittering.

'Lollipops': TCHAIKOVSKY: *Eugene Onegin: Waltz.* SIBELIUS: *Kuolema: Valse triste.* BERLIOZ: *Damnation of Faust: Menuet des follets; Danses des sylphes. Les Troyens: Marche.* DVORAK: *Legend in G min., Op. 59/3.* DEBUSSY: *L'enfant prodigue: Cortège et Air de danse.* CHABRIER: *Marche joyeuse.* GOUNOD: *Roméo et Juliette: Le sommeil de Juliette.* VIDAL: *Zino-Zina: Gavotte.* GRIEG: *Symphonic dance No. 2 in A, Op. 64/2.* DELIUS: *Summer evening.* SAINT-SAENS: *Samson et Dalila: Danse des prêtresses de Dagon; Bacchanale.* MOZART: *Thamos, King of Egypt: Entr'acte. Divertimento in D, K.131: Minuet. March in D (Haffner), K.249.*
(M) **(*) EMI CDM7 63412-2 [id.].

It was Beecham who first used the word 'lollipop' to describe his brand of succulent encore pieces. In this selection of 17 examples, Beecham's devotion to French music shines out, with over half of the items by French composers; but the account of the *Waltz* from Tchaikovsky's *Eugene Onegin* chosen to start the disc is totally untypical of Beecham, with its metrical, unlilting rhythms. The transfers generally convey a good sense of presence but tend to emphasize an edge on top, which is an unfortunate addition to previous incarnations of this music on disc.

Royal Philharmonic Orchestra, Per Dreier

'Norwegian rhapsody': GRIEG: *Peer Gynt suite No. 1. Elegiac melody: The last spring. Norwegian dance No. 2.* SVENDSEN: *Polonaise; Variations on a Norwegian folk tune; Norwegian artists' carnival.* KJERULF: *The Wedding in Hardanger.* BULL: *Solitude.* NORDRAAK: *Maria Stuart: Purpose; Valse caprice. Olav Trygvason; National anthem.* HALVORSEN: *Entry of the Boyars; Danse visionnaire.*
(M) *** Carlton Dig. 30367 0117-2 [id.].

A cheap and cheerful CD of popular Scandinavian repertoire, presented with character and charm by the late Per Dreier and the RPO. The novelties by Kjerulf and Nordraak are just as appealing as the better-known items. Thoroughly recommendable performances, and good recording.

(i) **Royal Philharmonic Orchestra** or (ii) **Philharmonia Orchestra, Vladimir Ashkenazy**

'Russian delights': (i) TCHAIKOVSKY: *Capriccio italien, Op. 45; Francesca da Rimini, Op. 32.* (ii) RIMSKY-KORSAKOV: *The Tale of Tsar Saltan: suite, Op. 57; Flight of the bumblebee.* BORODIN: *Prince Igor: Polovtsian dances* (with Matthew Best, L. Opera Ch.).
(B) *** Decca Eclipse Dig. 448 989-2; *448 989-4* [id.].

This Ashkenazy compilation is first class in every respect, and the recordings (made between 1983 and 1988) are of Decca's finest vintage. *Capriccio italien* is superb, spectacular, elegant and possessed of exhilarating impetus. *Francesca da Rimini* is very exciting too, with much fine wind-playing from the RPO in the lyrical central section. Ashkenazy is also in his element in the dazzlingly scored *Tsar Saltan suite*, and the Philharmonia players obviously relish the good tunes, sonorous brass writing and glittering effects. In the *Polovtsian dances* the singing of the London Opera Chorus has striking fervour, with solo interjections from Matthew Best (normally not included) to bring an added edge of excitement, although it is a pity that the percussion-led opening dance is omitted.

Royal Stockholm Philharmonic Orchestra, Andrew Davis

'Nobel Prize ceremony music': ALFVEN: *Swedish festival music, Op. 25.* BERWALD: *Overture Estrella de Soria.* ROMAN: *Drottningholms-Musique No. 1.* BERNSTEIN: *Overture Candide.* BARBER: *Adagio for strings, Op. 11.* DVORAK: *Slavonic dance No. 9, Op. 72/1.* BRAHMS: *Academic festival overture, Op. 80.* GLINKA: *Overture Ruslan and Ludmilla.* GRIEG: *Peer Gynt: Morning.* ROSENBERG: *Orfeus in Town: Tango and finale.* SIBELIUS: *Karelia: Alla marcia.* NIELSEN: *Aladdin: Oriental march.*
*** Finlandia/Warner Dig. 0630 14913-2 [id.].

The prizes, awarded annually since 1900 from the legacy of Alfred Nobel, are presented in Stockholm on 10 December each year, and the 1996 ceremony marked the centenary of Nobel's death. Since its inception the prize-giving has been accompanied by an orchestral concert, the choice of music for which has traditionally been unadventurous. However, few will complain about the collection on this memento CD, especially as (apart from Davis's valedictory performance of the Barber *Adagio*) it is all presented with vigour, and the orchestral playing has elegance (especially in the Berwald overture) as well as plenty of energy and sparkle (notably in the Bernstein, Brahms and Glinka). Roman's *Drottningholms-Musique No. 1* makes a personable baroque interlude. Alfvén's occasional piece (a polacca with a good tune in the middle) opens the programme spiritedly, but the rather solemn Nielsen march brings a rather low-key ending. Bright, slightly over-resonant sound, which nevertheless suits the occasion.

St Louis Symphony Orchestra, Leonard Slatkin

'Encore': SOUSA: *The Stars and Stripes forever.* GLIERE: *The Red Poppy: Russian sailors' dance.* LIADOV: *Musical snuffbox.* RIMSKY-KORSAKOV: *The Snow Maiden: Dance of the tumblers.* TCHAIKOVSKY: *Eugene Onegin: Polonaise.* GLINKA: *Overture: Ruslan and Ludmilla.* DVORAK: *Slavonic dance No. 8, Op. 46/8.* SMETANA: *The Bartered Bride: Dance of the comedians.* FAURE: *Pavane.* CHABRIER: *España.* FALLA: *El amor brujo: Ritual fire dance.* PAGANINI: *Moto perpetuo.* BARBER: *Adagio for strings, Op. 11.* Johann STRAUSS Jr: *Unter Donner und Blitz (Thunder and lightning) polka.* GERSHWIN: *Promenade.* COPLAND: *Rodeo: Hoedown.* GRAINGER: *Irish tune from County Derry.*
**(*) RCA Dig. 09026 68511-2 [id.].

An enjoyable, brightly played and very well-recorded concert, if not quite in the demonstration bracket. Among the early highlights are Rimsky's vivacious *Dance of the tumblers* and Liadov's winningly scored *Musical snuffbox*, but Chabrier's *España* could use rather more unbuttoned zest, while Paganini's *Moto perpetuo*, although it has the violins producing brilliant bravura ensemble, rather jogs along and lacks the kind of show-off panache which makes one sit up. But then comes a deeply moving account of Barber's *Adagio*, opening with rapt, elegiac feeling and building towards a splendidly intense climax (the violin-sound quite glorious) and then closing gently and very touchingly. The only snag is that if you do not have a remote control, you have to leap up after the piece has ended, as the following Strauss *Thunder and lightning polka* zestfully lights up the heavens. It is followed by the second highlight of the concert (which also could not be further removed from Barber): Gershwin's *Promenade*, with a delectably jazzy clarinet solo from George Silfies, as smartly sophisticated as it is lilting. Copland's *Hoedown* is rousingly energetic; then the concert ends with a warmly beautifully account of Grainger's arrangement of the *Londonderry air*, given both spaciousness and grace. But what a pity the Barber *Adagio* was not left to close the concert.

St Paul Chamber Orchestra, Bobby McFerrin

'Paper music': MOZART: *Le nozze di Figaro overture; Serenade No. 13 in G (Eine kleine Nachtmusik).* BOCCHERINI: *String quintet in E: Minuet.* FAURE: *Pavane.* STRAVINSKY: *Pulcinella: Minuet and Finale.* VIVALDI: *Double cello concerto in G min., RV 531* (with Peter Howard). MENDELSSOHN: *A Midsummer Night's Dream: Scherzo.* BACH: *Violin concerto in A min., BWV 1041: 1st movt.* TCHAIKOVSKY: *Andante cantabile, Op. 11.*
**(*) Sony Dig. SK 63600 [id.].

Bobby McFerrin began his musical career in the world of pop music, and in 1988 had a hit single which reached No. 1. His background, however, included a father who was the first black singer at the Met. and a mother who was both a singer and a teacher. So it was not surprising that he found himself being drawn back to the classical sound-world. He made his début with the San Francisco Symphony in 1990 and went on to conduct most of America's top orchestras. Now he is director of the Saint Paul Chamber Orchestra and spends much of his time as a musical evangelist in schools. He is already a famous figure in the USA. 'Paper music' is an American jazz musician's term for music that is written down rather than improvised. If one hears McFerrin play this kind of popular repertoire at a concert, the effect of his personality is highly communicative; but here, although the music-making is alive, elegantly turned and aptly paced (especially *Eine kleine Nachtmusik*), there is nothing specially individual about it until he introduces his wordless vocal melismas in a voice a little like that of a counter-tenor. His feeling for dynamic nuance is remarkable, as is his range. In the present concert he sweetly vocalizes the Boccherini *Minuet* and Fauré's *Pavane* in this way, then he replaces the solo violin line in the Bach concerto and follows up by taking over the second cello part in Vivaldi's *Double concerto*. He does this with such skill that one is almost convinced that it is a viable approach, especially if for the musical novice the result is often both magnetic and appealing. The highlight of his vocalizing here is Tchaikovsky's *Andante cantabile*, which he intones while conducting a refined accompaniment. This is obviously not a CD for general recommendation, but it speaks well for McFerrin's musicianship; if he can bring a new audience into the concert hall, then he has our full support.

Sakonov, Josef (violin), London Festival Orchestra

'Violin encores': HUBAY: *Hejre Kati.* GODARD: *Berceuse de Jocelyn.* TCHAIKOVSKY: *Valse sentimentale; None but the lonely heart.* STERNHOLD: *Fêtes tziganes.* MASSENET: *Thaïs: Méditation.* HEUBERGER: *Opernball: Im chambre séparée.* KORNGOLD: *Garden scene.* MONTI: *Czárdás*
(M) *** Decca Phase Four 444 786-2 [id.] (with miscellaneous works by KETELBEY ***).

This collection makes an admirable coupling for Decca's Ketèlby collection. Josef Sakonov is a specialist in Hungarian fireworks and Zigeuner melodies. He plays on one of a pair of Guarnerius violins dating from 1735 and he certainly produces a sumptuous tone, helped by the very forward balance of the Phase Four recording. Heuberger's *Im chambre séparée* is used to show off the luscious effects possible on the lower strings of this superb instrument, while there are some dazzling fireworks in the bravura items (Sternhold's *Fêtes tziganes* a real highlight). There is taste as well as flamboyance here, and the opening melody and Tchaikovsky's *Valse* are very nicely done. With vivid sound, this is most enjoyable when presented with such flair.

Scottish Chamber Orchestra, Laredo

'String masterpieces': ALBINONI: *Adagio in G min.* (arr. GIAZOTTO). HANDEL: *Berenice: Overture. Solomon: Arrival of the Queen of Sheba.* BACH: *Suite No. 3, BWV 1068: Air. Violin concerto No. 1 in A min., BWV 1041: Finale.* PACHELBEL: *Canon.* PURCELL: *Abdelazar: Rondo. Chacony in G min.*
(B) *** Carlton Dig. PCD 2001.

An excellent issue. The playing is alive, alert, stylish and committed without being overly expressive, yet the Bach *Air* has warmth and Pachelbel's *Canon* is fresh and unconventional in approach. The sound is first class, especially spacious and convincing on CD, well detailed without any clinical feeling. The Purcell *Rondo* is the tune made familiar by Britten's orchestral guide; the *Chaconne* is played with telling simplicity.

Serenades: 'Favourite Serenades'

'Favourite Serenades' (played by (i) Netherlands CO, Zinman; (ii) ECO, Leppard; (iii) I Musici; (iv) ASMF, Marriner; (v) Accardo, Leipzig GO, Masur; (vi) Netherlands Wind Ens., Edo de Waart; (vii) Catherine Michel, Monte Carlo Op. O, Almeida): (i) TCHAIKOVSKY: *String serenade, Op. 48.* (ii) DVORAK: *Serenade for strings, Op. 22.* (iii) MOZART: *Eine kleine Nachtmusik.* (iv) HOFFSTETTER/HAYDN: *Serenade from String quartet in F, Op. 3/5.* (v) BRUCH: *Serenade for violin and orchestra, Op. 75.* (iii) WOLF: *Italian serenade in G.* (vi) R. STRAUSS: *Serenade for wind, Op. 7.* (vii) RODRIGO: *Concierto serenade for harp and orchestra.*
(B) **(*) Ph. 438 748-2 (2) [id.].

A generous 156-minute anthology about which there are few reservations. Zinman's account of the Tchaikovsky *Serenade* has not the very strongest profile, but it is polished and warmly recorded. I Musici play Wolf's infectiously gay little masterpiece extremely well, even if perhaps they do not do full justice to its effervescent spirit and sheer *joie de vivre*. Everything else here will certainly give pleasure, especially the rare Max Bruch concertante serenade, so enticingly tuneful with Accardo in ravishing form. Catherine Michel's account of Rodrigo's *Serenade concerto* for harp is not quite as enticing as Zabaleta's famous DG version, but the spicy harmonies are made to catch the ear with piquant abrasiveness. Excellent sound (mostly from the 1970s) and smooth remastering ensure aural pleasure throughout.

Serenata of London, Barry Wilde

SIBELIUS: *Suite champêtre, Op. 98b; Canzonetta, Op. 62a.* TCHAIKOVSKY: *Elegy in G.* DVORAK: *2 Waltzes, Op. 54/1–2; Nocturne in B, Op. 40; Humoresque in G flat, Op. 101.* ELGAR: *Salut d'amour, Op. 12; Sospiri, Op. 70.* GRIEG: *2 Melodies, Op. 53; Nordic melodies, Op. 63; 2 Elegiac pieces, Op. 34.*
(B) *** Carlton Dig. PCD 1108 [id.].

The Serenata of London under Barry Wilde here provides a very well-balanced concert of comparatively lightweight repertoire, played with such agreeable finesse and warmth that it makes a highly enjoyable hour-long entertainment. Whether in little-known Sibelius, the lovely Tchaikovsky *Elegy*, the delectable Dvořák *Waltzes* or the Grieg *Melodies*, the spontaneity of the playing brings the music to life, and the size of the orchestra seems just right when they are so well recorded.

Silvestri, Constantin

'Artist profile' (with (i) Philh. O; (ii) VPO; (iii) Bournemouth SO; (iv) LPO; (v) Paris Conservatoire O): (i) RIMSKY-KORSAKOV: *May night overture.* (ii) RAVEL: *Rapsodie espagnole.* (iii) ELGAR: *Overture: In the South (Alassio), Op. 50.* (iv) DVORAK: *Symphony No. 8 in G, Op. 88.* (v) GLINKA: *Overture Ruslan and Ludmilla.* (i) BORODIN: *Prince Igor: Overture; Polovtsian dances.* TCHAIKOVSKY: *Symphony No. 5 in E min., Op.64.*
(B) **(*) EMI CZS5 68229-2 (2) [id.].

Undoubtedly the highlight of this concert is the electrifying account of Elgar's *In the South overture*, recorded with the Bournemouth Symphony Orchestra in 1967, only two years before Silvestri's death, a performance which has never been surpassed in its ongoing intensity. The introspective temperament of Tchaikovsky's *Fifth Symphony* also suits Silvestri and, in spite of the characteristic eccentricities of rubato (which are not always quite spontaneous), he builds up the climaxes in the first two movements with great excitement. The *Andante* is very telling, and the horn solo is quite lovely; the waltz, too, is given real elegance. The finale opens with dignity and then the *Allegro vivace* goes with the wind, with brilliant Philharmonia virtuosity carrying the day. Here the early-1957 Kingsway Hall recording, though full-bodied, has a degree of harshness. The Borodin *Prince Igor overture* generates similar romantic feeling (with another superb horn solo) and thrust, and the *Polovtsian dances* glow with colour and sweep to their close with explosive energy. Silvestri's LPO recording of Dvořák's *Eighth* is also enjoyable: at times wilful, at others warm and genial, full of verve, but never eccentric. Rimsky-Korsakov's *May night* has a particularly enticing blend of rich colours and vivid detail while the Glinka *Ruslan and Ludmilla* generates exciting bravura from the Philharmonia strings, without being pressed too hard. The glitteringly extrovert account by the VPO of Ravel's *Rapsodie espagnole*, if not particularly subtle, brings plenty of excitement.

Slovak Philharmonic Orchestra

'Russian Fireworks' (cond. (i) Richard Hayman; (ii) Kenneth Jean; (iii) Stephen Gunzenhauser; (iv) Michael Halász): (i) IPPOLITOV-IVANOV: *Caucasian sketches: Procession of the Sardar*. (ii) LIADOV: *8 Russian folksongs*. KABALEVSKY: *Comedian's galop*. MUSSORGSKY: *Sorochinski Fair: Gopak. Khovanshchina: Dance of the Persian slaves*. (iii) LIADOV: *Baba Yaga; The enchanted lake; Kikimora*. (iv) RUBINSTEIN: *Feramor: Dance of the Bayaderes; Bridal procession. The Demon: Lesginka*. (ii) HALVORSEN: *Entry of the Boyars*.
(BB) *** Naxos Dig. 8.550328 [id.].

A vividly sparkling concert with spectacular digital sound, more than making up in vigour and spontaneity for any lack of finesse. The Liadov tone-poems are especially attractive and, besides the very familiar pieces by Ippolitov-Ivanov, Halvorsen and Mussorgsky, it is good to have the Rubinstein items, especially the *Lesginka* which has a rather attractive tune.

Slovak State Philharmonic Orchestra (Košice), Mika Eichenholz

'Locomotive music (A musical train ride)' Vol. 1: LANNER: *Ankunfts waltz*. Johann STRAUSS Sr: *Reise Galop; Souvenir de Carneval 1847 (quadrille); Eisenbahn-Lust (waltz)*. HOYER: *Jernban galop*. Johann STRAUSS Jr: *Reiseabenteuer waltz*. MEYER: *Jernvägs-Galop*. Eduard STRAUSS: *Glockensignale waltz; Mit Dampf polka; Lustfahrten waltz; Tour und Retour polka*. Josef STRAUSS: *Gruss an München polka*. GRAHL: *Sveas helsning till Nore waltz*. LUMBYE: *Copenhagen Steam Railway galop*.
**(*) Marco Polo Dig. 8.223470 [id.].

'Locomotive music' Vol. 2: LANNER: *Dampf Waltz*. FAHRBACH: *Locomotiv-Galop*. Johann STRAUSS Jr: *Wilde Rosen waltz; Vergnügungszug polka; Spiralen waltz; Accelerationen waltz*. GUNGL: *Eisenbahn-Dampf galop*. Eduard STRAUSS: *Polkas: Reiselust; Ohne Aufenthalt; Treuliebchen; Ohne Bremse; Von Land zu Land; Bahn frei; Feuerfunken waltz*. ZIEHRER: *Nachtschwalbe polka*.
**(*) Marco Polo Dig. 8.223471 [id.].

This seems a happy idea on which to base a two-CD collection of Viennese-style dance music, but in the event the only piece which celebrates the effect of a train journey really successfully is the *Copenhagen Steam Railway galop*. The Slovak performance has rather a good whistle but seems more concerned with rhythm than with charm and cannot compare with the account included in the splendid Unicorn collection of Lumbye's dance music so beautifully played by the Odense Symphony Orchestra under Peter Guth, which carries a Rosette. The first Marco Polo disc opens with Lanner's *Ankunfts* ('Arrival') *waltz*, which ironically dates from before the railway had even arrived in Vienna. It is enjoyable for itself; the other highlights are more descriptive. Frans Hoyer's *Jernban-Galop* makes a fair shot of a train starting up and has a rather engaging main theme, while Jean Meyer's *Jernvägs-Galop* follows Lumbye's pattern of an elegant opening and a whistle start, with the side-drum snares giving a modest railway simulation. This too is attractive melodically, but the coda is too abrupt. Eduard Strauss's *Mit Dampf* has a rather half-hearted whistle but plenty of energy, and his *Lustfahrten waltz* is lyrically appealing.

The second disc opens with Lanner again, but the *Dampf* refers to the steam of a coffee house! It is followed by Fahrbach's jolly *Locomotiv-Galop*, where the effects are minimal and primitive. However, Joseph Gungl does better, with an opening whistle which returns on a regular basis against supporting bass-drum beats. Johann Strauss's *Vergnügungszug polka* concentrates on the exhilaration of a day out on an excursion train, but Eduard Strauss's *Bahn frei*, comparably zestful, manages a cleverly brief introductory train imitation, and *Ohne Aufenthalt* has a gentle bell to set off. If most of this repertoire is unadventurous in terms of evocation, it is all tuneful and brightly presented; the playing is not without finesse and has plenty of zest, and the orchestra is very well recorded – and not in a train shed either. But these are full-priced CDs and one is plainly not travelling in a first-class carriage with the VPO.

South West German Radio Orchestra, Baden-Baden, Ernest Bour

'L'Œuvre du XX siècle' Vol. 1: DEBUSSY: *La Mer; Khamma; Jeux*. RAVEL: *Rapsodie espagnole; Ma Mère l'Oye (suite); Valses nobles et sentimentales; Le tombeau de Couperin*. STRAVINSKY: *The Rite of spring; Le chant du rossignol*. ROUSSEL: *Suite in F, Op. 33; Symphonies Nos. 3 in G min., Op. 42; 4 in A, Op. 53*.
❀ (B) **(*) Astrée Audivis E 7800 (4) [id.].

Ernest Bour was a champion of the new music both of the French and Viennese schools, though his sympathies were wide. He even conducted the première outside Denmark of Holmboe's *Seventh Symphony*. He is probably best known for the miraculously stylish première mono recording of Ravel's *L'Enfant et les sortilèges* – given a Rosette in our main edition and re-listed above, under the composer (Testament SBT 1044). He was a true musician wholly unconcerned with building a career or hype. The bulk of his career was spent in Strasbourg, Hilversum and Baden-Baden. Four bargain CDs, each nicely packaged with a splendid booklet. The recordings derive from the archives of the Südwestfunk, Baden-Baden, and vary in quality – not surprisingly, given the fact that they range from 1965 to 1987. They are all made in the Hans Rosbaud Studio and a few of them sound studio-bound and insufficiently transparent. Roussel's marvellously spirited *Suite en F* (1965) is a case in point, but fortunately the two symphonies, recorded in 1967 (No. 3) and 1977 (No. 4) are very good indeed without being in the demonstration bracket. There is an atmospheric *Le sacre* (1969) and, on the same disc, *Le chant du rossignol* (1972) offers splendid sound; the performance, while it does not quite match the Chicago version under Reiner (see under Stravinsky in our composer index), runs it pretty close.

The Debussy performances have a very idiomatic and natural feel to them. There is a finely paced account of *La Mer* (1968) with good sound, a very persuasive version of *Khamma* (1987) with excellent sound, and an outstanding *Jeux* (1984), worthy to rank alongside the finest now before the public. The Ravel performances are all recorded between 1967 and 1974 and show Bour's natural affinity for this composer. The *Fería* from *Rapsodie espagnole* may not be as intoxicating as the Reiner but it comes a close second; the *Ma Mère l'Oye* suite (1972) shows great tenderness and panache, and there is much tenderness and real style in the *Valses nobles*, though the 1967 recording is less transparent than the *Jeux* or, for that matter, *Le tombeau de Couperin*. This set cannot be a three-star recommendation as it is uneven, but it really deserves a Rosette for the special interpretative qualities Bour brings to much of this music. Like Fricsay now (though not in his lifetime), Bour was underrated and deserves some long-overdue recognition.

'L'OEuvre du XX siècle' Vol. 2: SCHOENBERG: *5 Orchestral pieces, Op. 16; Variations for orchestra, Op. 31; Accompaniment to a motion picture scene, Op. 34; Theme and variations for orchestra, Op. 43b.* BERG: *3 Orchestral pieces, Op. 6; Altenberg Lieder, Op. 4* (with Halina Lukomska); *Violin concerto* (with Salvatore Accardo). WEBERN: *6 Pieces for orchestra, Op. 6; 5 Pieces for orchestra, Op. 15; 4 Lieder, Op. 13* (with Halina Lukomska); *Symphony, Op. 21; Variations, Op. 30.* BARTOK: *The Wooden prince (suite); Dance suite; Divertimento.*
(B) **(*) Astrée Audivis E 7805 (4) [id.].

Ernest Bour was a champion of the Second Viennese School and, judging by these discs, one of its outstanding exponents. These performances have much greater warmth than Boulez or Gielen bring to this repertoire. The Webern items speak far more naturally than in Boulez's hands, for all the latter's clarity and refinement. As with the French music listed above, the recordings derive from the archives of the Südwestfunk, Baden-Baden, and were all made in the Hans Rosbaud Studio. The *Five Orchestral pieces*, Op. 16, of Schoenberg are among the earliest (1962) and the Berg *Violin concerto* and Webern *5 Pieces*, Op. 10, among the latest (1976). Two of the highlights here are the Berg *Concerto* with Salvatore Accardo as soloist and the Webern, Op. 10, as well as the Schoenberg five *Orchestral pieces* and *Variations*, Op. 31, but the Bartók is no less idiomatic. Those who find Karajan's Schoenberg and Berg too beautified, and Boulez's too clinical, will welcome this highly persuasive music-making. Recordings are not quite three-star but the performances are. Bour was obviously a selfless and dedicated music-maker, and readers wanting a suitable entry point into this world need look no further.

Starker, János (cello), Philharmonia Orchestra, (i) Carlo Maria Giulini; (ii) Walter Susskind

(i) BOCCHERINI: *Concerto in B flat.* (ii) FAURE: *Elegie.* DVORAK: *Concerto in B min.* DOHNANYI: *Konzertstück, Op. 12.* PROKOFIEV: *Concerto in E min., Op. 58.* MILHAUD: *Concerto No. 1.*
(B) EMI forte CZS5 68745-2 (2).

The *Elegie* is played rather straightforwardly, always with beautiful tone and a firm line but lacking the quiet reflection which is part of its character. A similar approach is taken with the Dvořák *Concerto*, but there is plenty of vitality and warmth and often sensitive playing. The tunes are played beautifully with a firm line and a lovely tone, nicely caught by the recording.

Steele-Perkins, Crispian (trumpet)

Six Trumpet concertos (with ECO, Anthony Halstead): J. HAYDN: *Concerto in E flat.* TORELLI: *Concerto in D.* M. HAYDN: *Concerto No. 2 in C.* TELEMANN: *Concerto for trumpet, two oboes and strings.* NERUDA: *Concerto in E flat.* HUMPHRIES: *Concerto in D, Op. 10/12.*
(M) *** Carlton 30366 0066-2 [id.].

Collectors who have relished Håkan Hardenberger's famous full-price collection of trumpet concertos might well go on to this equally admirable concert, which duplicates only the Haydn – and that in a performance hardly less distinguished. Crispian Steele-Perkins has a bright, gleaming, beautifully focused timbre and crisp articulation, with easy command of the high tessitura of the Michael Haydn work and all the bravura necessary for the sprightly finales of all these concertos. His phrasing in the slow movement of Joseph Haydn's shapely *Andante* is matched by his playing of the *Largo* of the Neruda and the *Adagio–Presto–Adagio* of the Torelli, another fine work. Anthony Halstead with the ECO gives him warmly sympathetic support. The recording balance gives the soloist plenty of presence, but the orchestra is recorded rather reverberantly, an effect similar to that on the Hardenberger record.

Steele-Perkins, Crispian (trumpet), Tafelmusik, Jeanne Lamon

STRADELLA: *Sonata for 8 strings and trumpet.* BIBER: *Sonatas Nos. 1 & 4 for trumpet, strings & continuo; Trumpet duets Nos. 1, 5, 11 & 13.* VIVALDI: *Concerto for 2 trumpets.* ALBINONI: *Trumpet concerto.* TELEMANN: *Trumpet concerto.* HANDEL: Arias from: *Serse: Caro voi siete all'alma; Admeto: Se L'arco avessi.* Marches from: *Scipone; Judas Maccabaeus; Atalanta* (overture).
*** Sony Dig. SK 53365 [id.].

The Stradella and Biber *Sonatas* are in essence trumpet-led miniature suites, interspersing slow and fast movements appealingly; while Biber's four brief duets are also full of character. The Vivaldi *Double concerto* is comparatively well known, and the Albinoni work which combines solo trumpet with three oboes is divertingly colourful, especially with baroque oboes. The Telemann *Concerto* is a splendid piece, and in the *Aria* Steele-Perkins plays with exquisitely fined-down tone against the equally subtle continuo. He is a superb soloist and uses a natural baroque trumpet with almost unbelievable refinement, yet is appropriately robust when the music calls for it. In the works involving two instruments he has a fine partner in John Thiessen. What makes this collection special is the beauty of the accompaniments from the superb Tafelmusik, playing their original instruments under the direction of Jeanne Lamon – although in the Stradella and Biber *Sonatas* the partnership between trumpet and ripieno is more equal. The recording is of the highest quality.

Stern, Isaac (violin)

'A Life in Music': Boxes I–II (for Boxes III–IV, see under Instrumental Recitals)
'A Life in music': Box I
(M) *** Sony Analogue/Dig. SX11K 67193 (11) [id.].

Volume 1: VIVALDI: *The Four Seasons, Op. 8/1–4* (with Jerusalem Music Centre CO); *Concertos for 2 violins, RV 516, 524* (arr. RAMPAL) (with Jean-Pierre Rampal (flute), Franz Liszt CO); *Concerto for 3 violins, RV 551* (with Pinchas Zukerman, Itzhak Perlman, NYPO, Mehta); *L'estro armonico: Double concerto in A min., Op. 3/8* (arr. FRANKO); *Concertos for 2 violins, RV 514, 517, 509, 512* (with David Oistrakh, Phd. O, Ormandy). Carl STAMITZ: *Sinfonia concertante in D* (with Pinchas Zukerman (viola), ECO, Barenboim) (SM2K 66472 (2)) [id.].

Volume 2: BACH: *Violin concertos 1–2, BWV 1041–2* (with ECO, Schneider); *Concerto for 2 violins, BWV 1043* (with Itzhak Perlman, NYPO, Mehta); *Concerto for oboe & violin in C min., BWV 1060* (with Harold Gomberg, NYPO, Bernstein) (SMK 66471) [id.].

Volume 3: MOZART: (i) *Violin concertos No. 1, K.207;* (ii) *No. 2, K.211;* (iii) *No. 3, K.216;* (ii) *No. 4, K.218;* (i) *No. 5, K.219;* (ii) *Adagio in E, K.261; Rondo in C, K.373.* (iv) *Concertone for 2 violins in C, K.190;* (v) *Sinfonia concertante for violin & viola, K.364.* (i) Columbia SO, Szell; (ii) ECO, Schneider; (iii) Cleveland O (members), Szell; (iv; v) Pinchas Zukerman, ECO; (iv) Schneider; (v) Barenboim (SM3K 66475 (3)) [id.].

Volume 4: BEETHOVEN: *Violin concerto in D, Op. 61* (with NYPO, Barenboim); (i) *Triple concerto in C,*

Op. 56 (with Eugene Istomin (piano)); BRAHMS: *Double concerto in A min., Op. 102* (i) (with Leonard Rose (cello), Phd. O, Ormandy); *Violin concerto in D, Op. 77* (with NYPO, Mehta) (SM2K 66941 (2)) [id.].

Volume 5: MENDELSSOHN: *Violin concerto in E min., Op. 64.* DVORAK: *Violin concerto in A min., Op. 53; Romance in F min., Op. 11* (with Phd. O, Ormandy) (SMK 66827) [id.].

Volume 6: TCHAIKOVSKY: *Violin concerto in D, Op. 35.* SIBELIUS: *Violin concerto in D min., Op. 47* (with Phd. O, Ormandy) (SMK 66829) [id.].

Volume 7: WIENIAWSKI: *Violin concerto No. 2 in D min., Op. 22.* BRUCH: *Violin concerto No. 1 in G min., Op. 26* (with Phd. O, Ormandy). TCHAIKOVSKY: *Méditation, Op. 42/1* (orch. Glazunov) (with Nat. SO, Rostropovich); *Sérénade mélancolique, Op. 26* (with Columbia SO, Brieff) (SMK 66830) [id.].

There is a feast of superb playing here. It is a pity that the choice of the Beethoven and Brahms *Concertos* features Stern's recent versions instead of his more inspired, earlier accounts (with Bernstein and Ormandy respectively) and the Dvořák *Concerto*, too, is something of a disappointment. But the Bruch, Mendelssohn, Sibelius and Tchaikovsky are glorious, and both the Bach *Double concerto* and Mozart *Sinfonia concertante* bring comparably inspirational music-making. The solo Mozart *Concertos* also give much pleasure, while in the Vivaldi collection, where Stern's partner is David Oistrakh, there are some more marvellous performances of baroque double concertos, and the results are very compelling indeed. Although too often recordings are balanced very forwardly, the remastered sound is a very great and consistent improvement on the old LPs.

'A Life in music': Box II
(M) **(*) Sony SX9K 67194 (9) [id.].

Volume 8: LALO: *Symphonie espagnole.* SAINT-SAENS: *Introduction & Rondo capriccioso.* RAVEL: *Tzigane* (with Phd. O, Ormandy). SAINT-SAENS: *Violin concerto No. 3* (with O de Paris, Barenboim). SARASATE: *Zigeunerweisen.* WAXMAN: *Carmen-Fantasie* (with O, Waxman). FAURE: *Berceuse, Op. 16.* CHAUSSON: *Poème, Op. 25* (with O de Paris, Barenboim). DEBUSSY: (i) *La fille aux cheveux de lin;* (ii) *Clair de lune* (with Columbia SO, (i) Brieff; (ii) Katims) (SM2K 64501 (2)) [id.].

Volume 9: BARTOK: *Violin concertos Nos.* (i) *1;* (ii) *2* ((i) with Phd. O, Ormandy; (ii) with NYPO, Bernstein) (SMK 64502) [id.].

Volume 10: PROKOFIEV: *Violin concertos Nos. 1–2* (with NYPO, Mehta). BARTOK: *2 Rhapsodies for violin and orchestra* (with NYPO, Bernstein) (SMK 64503) [id.].

Volume 11: BERG: *Violin concerto* (with NYPO, Bernstein); *Chamber concerto for piano, violin & 13 wind* (with Peter Serkin, LSO (members), Abbado) (SMK 64504) [id.].

Volume 12: STRAVINSKY: *Violin concerto in D* (with Columbia SO, cond. composer). ROCHBERG: *Violin concerto* (with Pittsburgh SO, Previn) (SMK 64505) [id.].

Volume 13: BARBER: *Violin concerto, Op. 14* (with NYPO, Bernstein). MAXWELL DAVIES: *Violin concerto* (with RPO, Previn) (SMK 64506) [id.].

Volume 14: HINDEMITH: *Violin concerto* (with NYPO, Bernstein). PENDERECKI: *Violin concerto* (with Minnesota O, Skrowaczewski) (SMK 64507) [id.].

Volume 15: BERNSTEIN: *Serenade for violin, strings, harp and percussion, after Plato's Symposium* (with Symphony of the Air, cond. composer). DUTILLEUX: *Violin concerto 'L'Arbre des songes'* (with O Nat. de France, Maazel) (SMK 64508) [id.].

Although there are a few more reservations here than with Box I, there are some unforgettable performances too. The Barber *Concerto* remains unsurpassed and unsurpassable, as does the Stravinsky, recorded in mono with the composer, while the Dutilleux and Hindemith works are almost as fine. In the Stravinsky, no apology need be made for the sound and the performance is electrifying. The two-disc set which includes music of Lalo, Saint-Saëns, Chausson and others is particularly enticing and makes a good sample of the sheer calibre and remarkable charisma of Stern's playing.

Stinton, Jennifer (flute)

'20th-century flute concertos' ((i) with Geoffrey Browne; SCO, Steuart Bedford): HONEGGER: (i) *Concerto da camera for flute, cor anglais and strings.* IBERT: *Flute concerto.* NIELSEN: *Flute concerto.* POULENC, arr. BERKELEY: *Flute sonata.*
*** Collins Dig. 1210-2.

Honegger's *Concerto da camera for flute, cor anglais and strings* is a duo concertante piece, and the Poulenc is a transcription by Lennox Berkeley of the *Sonata for flute and piano* (1957). The Nielsen is a fine performance although its contrasts could be more strongly made. But Ibert's charming and effervescent piece comes off very well, though the orchestral playing is not particularly subtle. Honegger's *Concerto da camera* is very nicely played, as is the Poulenc, and beautifully recorded; though the orchestral contribution falls short of real distinction, this remains a very enjoyable recital, which deserves its third star.

Stockholm Sinfonietta, Esa-Pekka Salonen

'A Swedish serenade': WIREN: *Serenade for strings, Op. 11.* LARSSON: *Little serenade for strings, Op. 12.* SODERLUNDH: *Oboe concertino* (with A. Nilsson). LIDHOLM: *Music for strings.*
**(*) BIS Dig. CD 285 [id.].

The most familiar piece here is the Dag Wirén *Serenade for strings.* Söderlundh's *Concertino for oboe and orchestra* has a lovely *Andante* whose melancholy is winning and with a distinctly Gallic feel to it. It is certainly played with splendid artistry by Alf Nilsson and the Stockholm Sinfonietta. The Lidholm *Music for strings* is somewhat grey and anonymous though it is expertly wrought. Esa-Pekka Salonen gets good results from this ensemble and the recording lives up to the high standards of the BIS label. It is forwardly balanced but has splendid body and realism.

Stockholm Sinfonietta, Jan-Olav Wedin

'Swedish pastorale': ALFVEN: *The Mountain King, Op. 37: Dance of the Cow-girl.* ATTERBERG: *Suite No. 3 for violin, viola and string orchestra.* BLOMDAHL: *Theatre Music: Adagio.* LARSSON: *Pastoral suite, Op. 19; The Winter's Tale: Four vignettes.* ROMAN: *Concerto in D, for oboe d'amore, string orchestra and harpsichord, BeRI 53.* ROSENBERG: *Small piece for cello and string orchestra.*
*** BIS Dig. CD 165 [id.].

In addition to affectionate accounts of the *Pastoral suite* and the charming vignettes for *The Winter's Tale*, the Stockholm Sinfonietta include Atterberg's *Suite No. 3*, which has something of the modal dignity of the Vaughan Williams *Tallis fantasy*. It has real eloquence and an attractive melancholy, to which the two soloists, Nils-Erik Sparf and Jouko Mansnerus, do ample justice. The Blomdahl and Roman works are also given alert and sensitive performances; they make one think how delightful they are. Hilding Rosenberg's piece is very short but is rather beautiful. A delightful anthology and excellent (if a trifle closely balanced) recording. Confidently recommended.

(Leopold) Stokowski Symphony Orchestra, Leopold Stokowski

'Music for strings': PURCELL: *King Arthur suite: Hornpipe.* J. S. BACH: *Suite No. 3: Air; Mein Jesu, was für Seelenweh befällt dich in Gethsemane; Partita in E: Preludio.* HANDEL: *Alcina: Tamburino.* GLUCK: *Orpheus and Eurydice: Dance of the blessed spirits. Iphigenia in Aulis: Lento. Armide: Musette.* BOCCHERINI: *Minuet.* PAGANINI: *Moto perpetuo.* BORODIN: *Quartet No. 2: Nocturne.* TCHAIKOVSKY: *Quartet No. 1: Andante cantabile.* RACHMANINOV: *Vocalise.* TURINA: *La Oracion del Torero.* T. BERGER: *Rondino giocoso.*
(M) ** EMI CDM5 65912-2 [id.].

These recordings, which date from 1957–8 and which appeared originally on the Capitol label, have never before sounded so full and lustrous, and together make a most pleasant compilation of string arrangements. Tempi are generally leisured, and Stokowski's Bach has seldom sounded more indulgent, especially the famous *Air* from the *Third Orchestral Suite*. The violin *Preludio*, however, has plenty of dash, brilliantly played after the fashion of the equally successful Paganini display-piece. However, the Borodin and Tchaikovsky *Quartet* slow movements are again slow and sumptuous almost to the point of lethargy, and it is in the Turina *Oracion* that the Stokowskian magic ravishes the senses by its sheer sonic radiance.

Stokowski, Leopold

'Stokowski Stereo Collection'.
(M) *** RCA [09026 62599-2] (13).

Disc 1: (i) BACH: *Transcriptions.* (ii) HANDEL: *Music for the Royal Fireworks* – with (i) LSO; (ii) RCA Victor SO (09026 62605-2).

Disc 2: (i) BEETHOVEN: *Symphony No. 3 in E flat (Eroica), Op. 55; Overture Coriolan.* (ii) BRAHMS: *Academic festival overture* – with (i) LSO; (ii) New Philh. O (09026 62514-2).

Disc 3: CANTELOUBE: *Songs of the Auvergne.* VILLA-LOBOS: *Bachianas Brasileiras No. 5.* RACHMANINOV: *Vocalise* – all with Anna Moffo, American SO (09026 62600-2).

Disc 4: (i) DVORAK: *Symphony No 9 in E min. (From the New World), Op. 95.* (ii) SMETANA: *Vltava; Overture: The Bartered bride* – with (i) New Philh. O; (ii) RCA Victor SO (09026 62601-2).

Disc 5: MAHLER: *Symphony No. 2 in C min. (Resurrection).* BRAHMS: *Symphony No. 4 in E min., Op. 98* – with (i) Brigitte Fassbaender, Margaret Price, LSO and Ch.; (ii) New Philh. O (09026 62606-2 (2)).

Disc 6: RIMSKY-KORSAKOV: (i) *Scheherazade;* (ii) *Russian Easter Festival overture* – with (i) RPO; (ii) Chicago SO (09026 62604-2).

Disc 7: SHOSTAKOVICH: *Symphony No. 6 in B min., Op. 54; The age of gold: suite.* KHACHATURIAN: *Symphony No. 3 (Symphonic poem)* – all with Chicago SO (09026 62516-2).

Disc 8: PROKOFIEV: *Romeo and Juliet* (excerpts). MENOTTI: *Sebastian: suite* – both with members of NBC SO (09026 62517-2).

Disc 9: (i) TCHAIKOVSKY: *Symphony No. 6 in B min. (Pathétique), Op. 74.* (ii) ENESCU: *Roumanian rhapsody No. 1.* LISZT: *Hungarian rhapsody No. 2* – with (i) LSO; (ii) RCA Victor SO (09026 62602-2).

Disc 10: WAGNER: Volume 1: excerpts from *Das Rheingold; Die Walküre; Rienzi; Tannhaüser; Tristan und Isolde* – with Symphony of the Air; soloists, RPO (09026 62597-2).

Disc 11. WAGNER: Volume 2: orchestral excerpts from: *Tristan und Isolde; Die Meistersinger; Götterdämmerung* – with RPO, LSO (09026 62598-2).

Disc 12: *'Inspiration':* BACH, BEETHOVEN, HANDEL, GLUCK, TCHAIKOVSKY, WAGNER, RACHMANINOV, etc., with Norman Luboff Ch., N. SO of L., RCA SO (09026 62599-2).

Disc 13: *'The Final Bach Toccata and fugue; rehearsals and sessions':* BACH, BEETHOVEN, MAHLER, WAGNER, LSO, RPO, NBC SO (members) (09026 68643-2).

This impressive set, including the contents of all the stereo LPs Stokowski made for RCA, has been issued in a boxed set in the USA as we go to press. We do not have the full details but we felt that it must be listed *faute de mieux.* It will surely be irresistible when it arrives, as a report from a leading authority on Stokowski, Edward Johnson, tells us that RCA 'have done wonders with the original masters, and everything has come up far better than on the original LPs'. Hopefully they will soon appear in the UK.

Stuttgart Chamber Orchestra, Münchinger

'Baroque concert': PACHELBEL: *Canon.* GLUCK: *Orfeo: Dance of the Blessed Spirits.* HANDEL: *Water music: suite No. 3; Organ concerto in F* (*Cuckoo and the nightingale;* with M. Haselböck); *Oboe concerto No. 3 in G min.* (with L. Koch). L. MOZART: *Toy Symphony.* ALBINONI: *Adagio in G min.* (arr. GIAZOTTO). BACH: *Suite No. 3, BMV 1068: Air.* BOCCHERINI: *Minuet* (from *String quintet in E. Op. 13/5*).
(B) **(*) Decca Dig. 448 239-2; *448 239-4* [id.].

Beautifully recorded – the CD is particularly fine – this is an attractive concert with a very well-played suite from Handel's *Water music*, and the engaging *Cuckoo and the nightingale Organ concerto* (with Martin Haselböck an excellent soloist) to give a little ballast. The performance of Pachelbel's *Canon* is a little heavy-handed, but the strongly expressive account of Albinoni's *Adagio* is convincing. The *Toy Symphony* has some piquant special effects, and the shorter lollipops are played quite elegantly. The overall mood is a trifle serious, but that is Münchinger's way. For the Eclipse reissue, an elegant performance of a Handel *Oboe concerto* has been added.

Symphony of the Air, Leopold Stokowski

RESPIGHI: *The Pines of Rome*. KHACHATURIAN: *Symphony No. 2 (The Bell)*. SHOSTAKOVICH: *Symphony No. 1 in F min., Op. 10; Prelude in E flat* (orch. Stokowski); *Lady Macbeth of Mtsensk: Entr'acte*. BLOCH: *Schelomo (Hebrew rhapsody)* (with Georg Neikrug, cello). FRESCOBALDI: *Gagliarda*. PALESTRINA: *Adoramus te*. CESTI: *Tu mancavi a tormentarmi, crudelussima speranza* (all 3 orch. Stokowski). GABRIELI: *Sonata pian' e forte*
(M) *** EMI ZDMB5 65427-2 (2) [id.].

This brings together a varied group of recordings made by Stokowski with the Symphony of the Air (formerly NBC Symphony Orchestra) on the United Artists label. Nearly all were made at Carnegie Hall in 1958/9 and, if the playing is variable, Stokowski's readings are all characterful and compelling. He conducts the Respighi with characteristic flair and intensity so that, quite apart from the panache of the outer movements, the clarinet solo in the third movement leading up to the nightingale sounds has rarely been more evocative. He plays the bombastic Khachaturian symphony, inspired by the Second World War, for all it is worth and a lot more besides. In these two works the sound is less full and open than on the Capitol recordings that Stokowski made in London and Paris during the same period. But the Shostakovich *First Symphony* has a convincing concert-hall balance and is pointedly done, an outstanding performance even if the first movement is relatively relaxed, slacker than the rest. *Schelomo* (forwardly but not too dryly recorded in the Manhattan Towers Hotel, New York City) has Neikrug as a satisfyingly firm and expressive cello soloist, even if he hardly matches Feuermann on Stokowski's classic Philadelphia recording. The maestro's own arrangements of sixteenth- and seventeenth-century Italian pieces may be as unauthentic as could be, but the performances are magnetic, especially the accounts of the richly scored Palestrina piece and the infinitely touching *Aria* of Pietro Cesti, played most beautifully. The brass in the solemn Gabrieli *Sonata* is thrilling, with the Carnegie Hall acoustic adding to the sonority.

Thames Chamber Orchestra, Michael Dobson

'The baroque concerto in England' (with Black, Bennett): ANON. (probably HANDEL): *Concerto grosso in F*. BOYCE: *Concerti grossi: in E min. for strings; in B min. for 2 solo violins, cello and strings*. WOODCOCK: *Oboe concerto in E flat; Flute concerto in D*.
*** CRD CRD 3331; *CRDC 4031* [id.].

A wholly desirable collection, beautifully played and recorded. Indeed the recording has splendid life and presence and often offers demonstration quality – try the opening of the Woodcock *Flute concerto*, for instance. The music is all highly rewarding. The opening concerto was included in Walsh's first edition of Handel's Op. 3 (as No. 4) but was subsequently replaced by another work. Whether or not it is by Handel, it is an uncommonly good piece, and it is given a superbly alert and sympathetic performance here. Neil Black and William Bennett are soloists of the highest calibre, and it is sufficient to say that they are on top form throughout this most enjoyable concert.

Tortelier, Paul (cello)

'The early HMV Recordings' (1947–8) (with (i) Gerald Moore; (ii) RPO, Del Mar, or (iii) Beecham): (i) DEBUSSY: *Sonata*; (ii) FAURE: *Elégie;* (iii) R. STRAUSS: *Don Quixote, Op. 35*. (ii) TCHAIKOVSKY: *Variations on a Rococo theme, Op. 33*. (i) TORTELIER: *Le pitre*.
(M) (***) EMI mono CDH5 65502-2 [id.].

Tortelier's first record of *Don Quixote* comes from 1947 and was recorded in the presence of Strauss himself. It was reissued some years ago with Beecham's account of the suite from *Le bourgeois gentilhomme*. When this *Don Quixote* first appeared, the authors of *The Record Guide* (1951) called it 'one of the finest orchestral recordings ever made; the performance is noble in proportions and full of exquisite detail'; and it still sounds pretty impressive, nearly half a century later. The emphasis in the present issue is on the young Tortelier, and his eloquent Tchaikovsky *Rococo variations* with Norman Del Mar conducting the RPO is first class. The Fauré *Elégie* was never issued (there is a rather sour orchestral chord at the beginning), but Tortelier's contribution is as splendid here as it is in the Debussy *Sonata*. Admirers of the great French cellist – and those interested in *Don Quixote* – should not miss these splendid transfers.

Toulouse Capitole Orchestra, Michel Plasson

French Symphonic poems: DUKAS: *L'apprenti sorcier*. DUPARC: *Lénore; Aux étoiles*. FRANCK : *La chasseur maudit*. LAZZARI: *Effet de nuit*. SAINT-SAENS: *Danse macabre*.
*** EMI Dig. CDC5 55385-2 [id.].

An interesting and (on the whole) successful programme, let down by the brilliant but unbeguiling account of *The Sorcerer's apprentice*. There is more fun in this piece than Plasson finds. Similarly, the humour of *Danse macabre* is not within Plasson's perceptions, although he gives an excitingly dramatic account of the piece and there is a seductive violin solo from Malcolm Stewart. There is plenty of gusto in *Le chasseur maudit*, where the opening horn-call is arresting, the chase is properly demonic and the malignant middle section masterful, when Christian stalwarts are sinisterly warned of the Satanic welcome waiting for those choosing the hunt rather than the church for their Sunday morning occupation. Hardly less telling is Duparc's *Lénore*, an equally melodramatic scenario (also espoused by Liszt, with narrative included – see above under the composer). This concerns a ghoulish midnight embrace with a skeleton after the eager heroine has been carried off on horseback by her dead lover. But the two most memorable pieces here are the radiantly serene *Aux étoiles* ('The astral light of dawn'), also by Duparc, and – most haunting of all – Sylvio Lazzari's impressionistic *Effet de nuit*, with its bleakly sinuous evocation on the bass clarinet of the scaffold silhouetted in the rain against the darkening evening sky. Its climax depicts 'three ghastly prisoners marching dejectedly' in the pitiless downpour, urged on by 225 halberdiers. The recording is excellent: spacious, yet vivid; it is a shame about *L'apprenti sorcier*.

Tuckwell, Barry (horn), Academy of St Martin-in-the-Fields, Sir Neville Marriner or (i) with English Chamber Orchestra

Horn concertos: TELEMANN: *Concerto in D*. CHERUBINI: *Sonata No. 2 in F for horn and strings*. Christoph FORSTER: *Concerto in E flat*. WEBER: *Concertino in E min., Op. 45*. Leopold MOZART: *Concerto in D*. Giovanni PUNTO: *Concertos Nos. 5 in F; 6 in E flat; 10 in F; 11 in E*. (i) Michael HAYDN: *Concertino in D* (arr. SHERMAN). Joseph HAYDN: *Concerto No. 1 in D*.
❁ (B) *** EMI forte CZS5 69395-2 (2).

Barry Tuckwell readily inherited Dennis Brain's mantle and held his place as Britain's pre-eminent horn player for several decades before finally retiring in 1997. This EMI forte double-CD celebrates his supreme achievement in nearly a dozen of the finest concertos for his instrument; the Tuckwell recordings of the key works by Wolfgang Amadeus and Richard Strauss are of course available elsewhere. His supreme mastery and ease of execution, his natural musicality and warm lyricism of line – to say nothing of his consistent beauty of tone – make every performance here memorable, and he has the advantage of polished, graceful accompaniments from the ASMF under Marriner, except in the works by Michael and Joseph Haydn in which he directs the ECO himself with comparable elegance. The concerto of Telemann opens with a catchy *moto perpetuo*, despatched with aplomb; then comes a fine *Adagio* which often moves to the very top of the horn's upper range before the tension is released in the buoyant finale. The Cherubini *Sonata* opens with a melancholy *Largo*, then erupts into joyous high spirits, while the racing opening arpeggios of the concerto by Leopold Mozart and the tight trills in the finale (with harpsichord echoes) are managed with comparable exuberance. The Weber is an attractively diverse and extensive (17 minutes) set of variations and includes a good example of horn 'chords', where the soloist plays one note and hums another; it also has an exceptionally joyful finale. One of the novelties is a delightful concerto by the virtually unknown Christoph Forster (1693 – 1745) with its amiably jogging first movement marked *Con discrezione* and its brief, disconsolate *Adagio* followed by a closing Rondo in which, though the clouds clear away, the lyrical feeling remains. In some ways most striking of all is the collection of four concertos by the Bohemian virtuoso, Giovanni Punto, a successful and highly cultivated composer whose music is enjoyably distinctive, a mixture of Mozartian influences and Hummelian *galanterie*. The individual CD of these four works was issued to celebrate Barry Tuckwell's fiftieth birthday, and the performances show him at his finest. The recording throughout is of EMI's finest analogue quality, and the remastering retains the warmth and beauty of the originals.

Udagawa, Hideko (violin)

Concertante works (with LPO, Klein): GLAZUNOV: *Violin concerto in A min., Op. 82.* TCHAIKOVSKY: *Souvenir d'un lieu cher, Op. 42.* CHAUSSON: *Poème, Op. 25.* SARASATE: *Romanze andaluza, Op. 22/1.* SAINT-SAENS: *Caprice, Op. 52.*
(B) *** Carlton Dig. 30367 0031-2 [id.].

With the violin balanced forward, the Glazunov receives a heartfelt performance which rivals almost any, even if the finale does not offer quite such bravura fireworks as Itzhak Perlman (at full price). It is valuable to have all three of the haunting pieces which Tchaikovsky called *Souvenirs d'un lieu cher* – the *Méditation* and *Mélodie*, much better known than the central *Scherzo*. They are here done in Glazunov's orchestral arrangements. The Chausson *Poème* is warmly convincing if a little heavy-handed, the Sarasate Andalusian *Romanze* dances delightfully, and only in the final Saint-Saëns *Caprice* does Udagawa's playing sound a little effortful in its virtuosity. Warm, full recording to match.

Ulsamer Collegium, Josef Ulsamer with Konrad Ragossnig (lute) and Eduard Melkus Ensemble

'Dance music through the ages'

I: Renaissance dance music: ANON.: *Lamento di Tristano; Trotto; Istampita Ghaetta; Instampita Cominciamento di gioia; Saltarello; Bassa danza à 2; Bassa danza à 3.* GULIELMUS: *Bassa danza à 2.* DE LA TORRE: *Alta danza à 3.* ATTAIGNANT: *Basse danses: La brosse – Tripla – Tourdion; La gatta; La Magdelena.* DALZA: *Calata ala Spagnola.* NEUSIEDLER: *Der Judentanz; Welscher Tanz.* MILAN: *Pavana I/II.* MUDARRA: *nesca guarda me las vacas.* PHALESE: *Passamezzo – Saltarello; Passamezzo d'Italye – Reprise – Gallarde.* LE ROY: *Branle de Bourgogne.* B. SCHMIDT: *Englischer Tanz; Tanz: Du hast mich wollen nemmen.* PAIX: *Schiarazula Marazula; Ungaresca – Saltarello.* SUSATO: *Ronde.* GERVAISE: *Branle de Bourgogne; Branle de Champagne.*

II: Early Baroque dance music: MAINERIO: *Schiarazula Marazula; Tedesca – Saltarella; Ungaresca – Saltarella.* BESARDO: *Branle – Branle gay.* MOLINARO: *Saltarello; Ballo detto Il Conte Orlando: Saltarello.* GESUALDO: *Gagliarda del Princippe di Venosa.* CAROSO: *Barriera (Balletto in lode della Serenissima D. Verginia Medici d'Este, Duchessa di Modena); Celeste Giglio (Balletto in lode delli Serenissimi Signori Don Ranuccio Farnese, e Donna Margarita Aldobrandina Duca, e Duchessa di Parma e idi Piacenza etc.).* CAROUBEL: *Pavana de Spaigne; 2 Courantes; 2 Voltes.* HOLBORNE: *Pavane: The Funerals; Noel's galliard; Coranto: Heigh ho holiday.* ANON.: *Kempe's jig.* DOWLAND: *Queen Elizabeth her galliard; Mrs Winter's jump.* SIMPSON: *Alman.* GIBBONS: *Galliard.* PRAETORIUS: *Galliarde de la guerre; Reprise.* HAUSSMANN: *Tanz; Paduan; Galliard; Catkanei.*

III: High Baroque dance music: ANON.: *Country dances: Running footman; Greensleeves and Pudding eyes; Cobler's jigg; How can I keep my maiden head.* SANZ: *Canarios.* CORRETTE: *Menuet I/II.* HOTTETERRE: *Bourrée.* BOUIN: *La Montauban.* SANZ: *Pasacalle de la Cavalleria de Napoles; Españoletas; Gallarda y Villano.* CHEDEVILLE: *Musette.* REUSNER: *Suite Paduan (Allemande; Courantel Sarabande; Gavotte; Gigue).* POGLIETTI: *Balletto (Allemande; Amener; Gavotte; Sarabande; Gavotte).* DESMARETS: *Menuet; Passe-pied.* FISCHER: *Bourrée; Gigue.* ANON.: *Gavotte.* LOEILLET II DE GANT: *Corente; Sarabande; Gigue.* LULLY: *L'Amour malade* (opéra ballet): Conclusion; *Une Noce de Village* (dance suite).

IV Rococo dance music (Eduard Melkus Ensemble): C. P. E. BACH: *5 Polonaises, Wq.190; 2 Menuets with 3 Trios, Wq.189.* RAMEAU: *Zoroastre: Dances (Air tendre en Rondeau; Loure; Tambourin en Rondeau; Sarabande; Gavotte gaye avec Trio; Premier Rigaudon; Air en Chaconne.* STARZER: *Contredanse; Gavotte mit Trio; Pas de deux; Menuet; Gavotte mit Trio; Moderato; Gavotte; Menuet mit Trio; Gavotte mit Trio; Passe-pied mit Trio.*

V: Viennese classical dance music: EYBLER: *Polonaise.* HAYDN: *2 Menuets, Hob IX/11:4 & IX/16:12.* GLUCK: *Orfeo ed Euridice: Ballet: Don Juan (Allegretto).* MOZART: *6 Landerische, K.606; 5 Kontretänze, K.609.* ZEHN: *Deutsche.* BEETHOVEN: *4 Kontretänze, WoO 14/4, 5, 7 & 12.* SALIERI: *Menuetto.* WRANITZKY: *Quodlibet.*

VI: Viennese dance music from the Biedermeier period (1815–48): PALMER: *Waltz in E*. BEETHOVEN: *Mödlinger Tänze Nos. 1–8, WoO 17*. MOSCHELES: *German dances with trios and coda*. SCHUBERT: *5 Minuets with Trios, D.89; 4 komische Ländler, D.354*. ANON.: *Linzer Tanz; Vienna polka*. LANNER: *Hungarian galop in F*.
❁ (B) *** DG 439 964-2 (4) [id.].

This collection, on four well-filled CDs (recorded between 1972 and 1974), explores the history of European dance music from the beginning of the fifteenth century right through to the first three decades of the nineteenth century, just about the time when Johann Strauss Senior was making his début. The members of the Ulsamer Collegium play an extraordinary range of authentic period instruments. Keyboards, strings, wind and plucked vihuela, as well as guitar, lute and hurdy-gurdy, are used with the greatest imagination, always to seduce the ear with variety of colour. There is not a whiff of pedantry or of abrasiveness of the kind that too often accompanies 'authentic' performances, yet the documentation is characteristically and fascinatingly thorough. The consistent tunefulness of the music is a constant source of pleasure and surprise. Among the composers of early baroque dance music, Pierre Francisque Caroubel and Mario Fabrizio Caroso stand out: the suite of dances by the former, played variously on gambas and recorder consort, is most diverting. On the second CD, the keyboard, gamba and lute pieces from the English Elizabethan school hardly need advocacy, but they are beautifully played (the lute and guitar solos of Konrad Ragossnig are most distinguished throughout the set) as is the jolly suite of dances by Valentin Haussman – another unfamiliar name to turn up trumps. Among the high baroque composers Esaias Reusner (1636–79) provides another diverting dance suite which, like the ballet music of Alessandro Poglietti, proves as elegant and finished as the ballet suite of Lully. In the Rococo era, Carl Philipp Emanuel Bach contributes five spirited *Polonaises*, and after a gracious interlude from Rameau there is a set of more robust and extrovert dances from Josef Starzer (1726–87). We enter the Viennese classical period with a clash of cymbals enlivening a *Polonaise* by Joseph Eybler (1764–1846), who sounds ahead of his time; but the two *Minuets* of Haydn stay well in period. As this stage of the proceedings the excellent Eduard Melkus Ensemble take over. The first of the Mozart *Contredanses*, K.609, which opens the fourth CD makes reference to a famous tune from *Figaro*, and Paul Wranitzky quotes from the same opera in his *Quodlibet*. Beethoven produced irresistible music. Moscheles and Schubert follow his example, the latter providing some deliciously flimsy *Ländler*, while the delicate *E major Waltz* of Michael Palmer (1782–1827), the two anonymous dances from Linz and Vienna and the *Hungarian galop* of Joseph Lanner (which ends the programme) point onwards to the heyday of Viennese dance music, when Johann Strauss Junior was to reign supreme. Overall, this is a most stimulating and rewarding survey.

Vienna Philharmonic Orchestra, Hans Knappertsbusch

'Orchestral favourites': J. STRAUSS Sr: *Radetzky march*. KAREL KOMZAK: Waltz: *Bad'ner Mad'ln*. J. STRAUSS Jr: Polkas: *Annen polka; Tritsch-Tratsch polka; Leichtes Blut*. Waltzes: *Accelerationen. G'schichten aus dem Wienerwald*. ZIEHRER: Waltz: *Wiener Bürger*. WEBER/BERLIOZ: *Invitation to the dance*. NICOLAI: Overture *The Merry wives of Windsor*. TCHAIKOVSKY: *Nutcracker suite*. BRAHMS: *Variations on a theme of Haydn; Academic festival overture*. SCHUBERT: *Marche militaire, Op. 51/1*.
(B) ** Decca Double 440 624-2 (2) [id.].

Hans Knappertsbusch has earned a gramophone reputation for rather slow and sometimes lethargic tempi, but the Strauss performances are lively enough, if without real magic. However, the *Nutcracker suite* is given rather a po-faced account. The Weber/Berlioz *Invitation to the dance*, although a little stiff, has something of a swing, and the overture goes quite well. The recordings are fair for their day: the Strauss items (1957) sound a bit dated, but the later part of the programme (1960) is quite vividly focused. However, this set does not show the conductor in his very best light.

Virtuosi di Praga, Oldřich Vlček

Music for strings: GRIEG: *Holberg suite*. RESPIGHI: *Ancient airs and dances: Suite No. 3*. ELGAR: *Serenade in E min., Op. 20*. ROUSSEL: *Sinfonietta, Op. 52*.
(BB) **(*) Discover Dig. DICD 920236 [id.].

The Prague Virtuosi are an expert body of soloists who command an impressive sonority in spite of their modest size (here eleven players). Some ears might feel that the Elgar *Serenade* lacks ripeness of Elgarian feeling, yet the *Larghetto* is tenderly affecting. Equally, the Respighi suite of *Ancient airs* sounds fresher, less anachronistically voluptuous than usual. The chamber scale suits the *Holberg suite* admirably, with plenty of energy and bite. But undoubtedly the most effective performance here is the Roussel *Sinfonietta*, bracingly astringent and grippingly vital.

Wallfisch, Elizabeth (violin), Parley of Instruments, Peter Holman

'English classical violin concertos': James BROOKS: *Concerto No. 1 in D*. Thomas LINLEY Jr: *Concerto in F*. Thomas SHAW: *Concerto in G*. Samuel WESLEY: *Concerto No. 2 in D*.
**(*) Hyperion Dig. CDA 66865 [id.].

Peter Holman and his Parley of Instruments expend much energy and Elizabeth Wallfisch considerable musical sensibility to bring these concertos from the late eighteenth century fully to life. They succeed admirably in that, working hard over music which is usually felicitous and always well crafted but too often predictable. In first movements one keeps getting the impression of second-rate Haydn. However, the opening movement of the James Brooks *Concerto* is amiably pleasing in its melodic contours and offers the soloist plenty of lively bravura. Its brief *Largo affettuoso* is agreeable too, and the dancing finale sparkles on the Wallfisch bow, and she produces a neat cadenza. Thomas Linley offers a *galant* Moderato first movement, another all-too-brief but graceful slow movement with a nice rhythmic snap; the finale is a charming gavotte. But Thomas Shaw goes one better in his *Adagio*, creating the best tune on the disc, for his slow movement, again with a Scottish snap, is most winning, very like a folksong. The finale bounces and the horns hunt boisterously. Wesley's first movement is vigorous and assured, if too long; and in the slow movement a pair of the orchestral violins join the soloist in a trio. The finale is very jolly and buoyant. The recording is excellent and, dipped into, this collection will give pleasure, providing you do not expect too much.

Williams, John (guitar)

Guitar concertos (with ECO, (i) Sir Charles Groves; (ii) Daniel Barenboim): (i) GIULIANI: *Concerto No. 1 in A, Op. 30*. VIVALDI: *Concertos in A and D*. RODRIGO: *Fantasia para un gentilhombre;* (ii) *Concierto de Aranjuez*. VILLA-LOBOS: *Concerto*. (i) CASTELNUOVO-TEDESCO: *Concerto No. 1 in D, Op. 99*.
(M) *** Sony M2YK 45610 (2) [id.].

This bouquet of seven concertante works for guitar from John Williams could hardly be better chosen, and the performances are most appealing. Moreover the transfers are very well managed and, if the guitar is very forward and larger than life, the playing is so expert and spontaneous that one hardly objects. All these performances are among the finest ever recorded, and Groves and Barenboim provide admirably polished accompaniments, matching the eager spontaneity of their soloist.

'The Seville concert' ((i) with Orquesta Sinfónica de Sevilla, José Buenagu): ALBENIZ: *Suite españolas: Sevilla; Asturias*. BACH: *Lute suite No. 4, BWV 1006a: Prelude*. D. SCARLATTI: *Keyboard sonata in D min., Kk 13* (arr. WILLIAMS). (i) VIVALDI: *Concerto in D, RV 93*. YOCUH: *Sakura variations*. KOSHKIN: *Usher waltz, Op. 29*. BARRIOS: *Sueño en la Floresta*. (i) RODRIGO: *Concierto de Aranjuez: Adagio*.
*** Sony Dig. SK 53359 [id.].

With so much reappearing from the Julian Bream archive, it is good to have a first-rate, modern recital from the estimable John Williams. It was recorded in Spain (in the Royal Alcázar Palace) as part of a TV programme, which accounts for its hour-long duration and the inclusion of the ubiquitous Rodrigo *Adagio* as the closing item. The recording is very realistic and present, yet the balance is natural and the effect not jumbo-sized. John Williams's intellectual concentration is as formidable as his extraordinary technique. This playing comes as much from the head as from the heart. He is first rate in Bach and brings a sense of keyboard articulation to the engaging *D minor Sonata* of Scarlatti (who was Bach's almost exact contemporary). His strength is felt in the flamenco accents of Albéniz's *Asturias*, a sense of the darkly dramatic is powerfully conveyed in Koshkin's *Usher waltz* (after Edgar Allan Poe). Yet his playing can be charmingly poetic, as in the delicate account of the *Largo* of the Vivaldi concerto; touchingly gentle, as in Yocuh's charming pentatonic evocation of cherry blossoms; or thoughtfully improvisational, as in the Barrios *Sueño en la Floresta*.

Yepes, Narciso (guitar)

'Guitarra española' (with Spanish R. & TV O, Odón Alonso; LSO, Rafael Frühbeck de Burgos): SANZ: *Suite española.* MUDARRA: *Fantasia que contrahaza la harpa en la manera de Ludovico.* NARVAEZ: *Diferencias sobre 'Guárdame las vacas'.* SOLER: *Sonata in E.* SOR: *10 Etudes; Theme and variations, Op. 9.* ALBENIZ: *Suite española: Asturias (Leyenda). Recuerdos de viaje: Rumores de la caleta. Piezas caracteristicas: Torre bermeja (Serenata). Malagueña, Op. 165.* GRANADOS: *Danza española No. 4 (Villanesca).* TARREGA: *Alborada (Capriccio); Danza mora; Sueño; Recuerdos de la Alhambra; Marieta (Mazurka); Capricho árabe (Serenata); Tango.* FALLA: *El amor brujo: El círculo mágico; Canción del fuego fatuo. Three-cornered hat: Danza del molinaro (Farruca). Homenaje: Le tombeau de Claude Debussy.* TURINA: *Sonata, Op. 61. Fandanguillo, Op. 36; Garrotín y soleares; Ráfaga.* BACARISSE: *Passapie; Concertino in A min. for guitar and orchestra, Op. 72.* YEPES: *Catarina d'Alió.* RODRIGO: *En los trigales; Concierto de Aranjuez; Fantasia para un gentilhombre; Concierto madrigal for 2 guitars and orchestra* (with Godelieve Monden, Phil. O, Garcia Navarro). PUJOL: *El abejorro; Estudios.* TORROBA: *Madroños.* MONTSALVATGE: *Habanera.* OHANA: *Tiento; Concierto tres gráficos for guitar and orchestra.* RUIZ-PIPO: *Canción y danza No. 1; Tablas para guitarra y orquestra.* ANON:. *Jeux interdits (Romance); Canciones populares catalanes: La filla del marxant; La filadora; El mestre; La cançó del lladre.*
(M) *** DG 435 841-2 (5).

Narciso Yepes died just as we were going to print, and this collection celebrates his long-lived and distinguished recording achievement in music from his own country. It was inevitable that the three most famous concertante works of Rodrigo would be included, which will involve duplication for many collectors, but the other concertante works, by Barcarisse, Ruiz-Pipó and Ohana are less familiar and very welcome. Among the more ambitious solo pieces are the *Suite* of Sanz and Soler *Sonatas*, plus the *Studies* of Sor. But many of the miniatures are equally memorable in their atmospheric potency (not least the Falla transcriptions), when Yepes's performances – with their vivid palette and high level of concentration – constantly remind us of Beethoven's assertion that a guitar is an orchestra all by itself. Generally excellent sound.

Zabaleta, Nicanor (harp)

'Great concertante works for harp': MOZART: *Flute and harp concerto, K.299* (with Karlheinz Zöller, BPO). BOIELDIEU: *Harp concerto.* RODRIGO: *Concierto serenata* (with Berlin RSO, Märzendorfer). HANDEL: *Harp concerto, Op. 4/6.* ALBRECHTSBERGER: *Harp concerto in C.* DITTERSDORF: *Harp concerto in A.* DEBUSSY: *Danse sacrée et danse profane.* RAVEL: *Introduction and allegro for harp, string quartet, flute and clarinet* (all with members of Paul Kuentz CO).
(B) *** DG Double 439 693-2 (2) [id.].

Zabaleta was an absolute master of his instrument and all these performances are touched with distinction. Johann Albrechtsberger taught Hummel and Beethoven, and his lightweight concerto is very pleasing when played with such flair and delicacy. The same might be said of the charming Boieldieu and Dittersdorf works, both of which display invention of some character, while the Handel and Mozart concertos are acknowledged masterpieces. In the latter, Karlheinz Zöller makes a distinguished partner. When it was first issued on LP, we gave Zabaleta's version of Rodrigo's delectable *Concierto serenata* a Rosette. In the outer movements especially, the delicate yet colourful orchestration tickles the ear in contrast to the beautifully focused harp timbre. Zabaleta is marvellous too in Ravel's *Introduction and allegro*, with sensitive support from members of the Paul Kuentz Chamber Orchestra, and warmly atmospheric sound. The Mozart and Boieldieu works come from the early 1960s; the others are later and, with excellent transfers, this 145 minutes of concertante harp music will surely offer much refreshment, though these are obviously not CDs to be played all at once.

Amsterdam Loeki Stardust Quartet: Daniel Brüggen, Bertho Driever, Paul Leenhouts, Karel van Steenhoven (recorders)

'Capriccio di flauti': MERULA: *Canzon: La Lusignuola.* JOHNSON: *The Temporiser.* BYRD: *Sermone blando.* ANON.: *Istampa: Tre fontane; Prince Edward's pavan; The Queen of Ingland's pavan.* J. S. BACH: *Contrapunctus I. Fuge alla breve e staccato, BWV 550; Brandenburg concerto No. 3, BWV 1048:* Finale. SWEELINCK: *Mein juges Leben hat ein end.* FRESCOBALDI: *Capriccio V sopra la Bassa Fiamenga; Canzon prima.* CONFORTI: *Ricercar del quarto tono.* PALESTRINA: *Lamentationes Hieremiae.* TRABACI: *Canzon Franzesa terza.* ASTON: *Hugh Ashton's maske.* TAVERNER: *In nomine.* SHOTT: *Aan de Amsterdamse Grachten.*
(M) *** O-L 440 207-2 [id.].

The Amsterdam Loeki Stardust Quartet are superbly expert players: their blend is rich in colour and their ensemble wonderfully blended and polished. They can also be heard in an outstanding collection of concertos for recorders in consort with the Academy of Ancient Music – see above – but here they are in holiday mood, presenting an enticing series of lollipops. Not that everything is frivolous. There are moments of solemnity, and the pieces by Conforti and Palestrina (among others) bring an appropriate touch of gravitas, while the *Sermone blande* of Byrd is aptly named. But it is the piquant bravura one returns to most readily. *The Temporiser* of Johnson is a delicious *tour de force* and Bach's *Fuga alla breve e staccato* and the sparkling finale of the *Third Brandenburg concerto* are a joy. After a remarkable variety of mood and colour, the concert ends with the winningly florid *Aan de Amsterdamse Grachten*, which readily conjures up a picture of a Dutch carousel. The recording has striking presence and realism.

Anderson, John (oboe), Gordon Back (piano)

'Capriccio': PONCHIELLI: *Capriccio.* HUE: *Petite pièce.* PALADILHE: *Solo.* KALLIWODA: *Morceau de salon, Op. 228.* PASCULLI: *Concerto sopra motivi dell'opera 'La Favorita' di Donizetti.* FAURE: *Pièce.* DONIZETTI: *Solo.* SCHUMANN: *3 Romances, Op. 94.* FRANCK: *Pièce No. 5.* SINIGAGLIA: *Variations on a theme of Schubert, Op. 19.*
(M) **(*) ASV Dig. CDWHL 2100 [id.].

The three *Romances* by Schumann are the highlight of the programme: they have more substance than the rest and are beautifully played, while Sinigaglia's ingenuous variations on one of Schubert's most charming melodies makes for an engaging finale. The decoratively florid *Capriccio* of Ponchielli which opens the recital receives the most stylish bravura from the soloist; but it is completely inconsequential. The *Petite pièce* of Georges Hue is more distinctive and Paladilhe's *Solo* (in fact a duo with piano) is amiable too, as is the Kalliwoda *Morceau*, although it is rather longer than a morceau. When we come to Pasculli's cleverly contrived fantasia on Donizetti's *La favorita*, the tunes are more indelible, and the resulting virtuosity is impressive. Donizetti's own *Solo* is another attractive miniature, as is the lilting Franck *Pièce*. John Anderson is a first-rate oboist and he is persuasively supported throughout by Gordon Back. The recording is very real and immediate. But this lightweight 75-minute concert needs to be dipped into rather than taken all at once.

Argerich, Martha (piano)

CHOPIN: *Scherzo No. 3 in C sharp min., Op. 39; Barcarolle in F sharp min., Op. 60.* BRAHMS: *2 Rhapsodies, Op. 79.* PROKOFIEV: *Toccata, Op. 11.* RAVEL: *Jeux d'eau.* LISZT: *Hungarian rhapsody No. 6; Piano sonata in B min.*
(M) (**) DG 447 430-2 [id.].

Argerich's phenomenal technique (she was twenty-one at the time of this début recital) is as astonishing as the performances are musically exasperating. This artist's charismatic impulsiveness is well known, but in presenting the opening Chopin *Scherzo* she seems not to want to show any musical control whatsoever and is carried away by her own glittering roulades; the *Barcarolle* is also very volatile, but here she does not ride roughshod over the lyrical flow. The Brahms *First Rhapsody* is explosively fast; then suddenly she puts the brakes on and provides most poetic playing in the central section. Such a barnstorming approach is more readily at home in the Prokofiev *Toccata*, and she goes over the top in the Liszt *Hungarian rhapsody* with a certain panache. *Jeux d'eau* brings a certain Ravelian magic. The Liszt *Sonata* has been added on; it dates from a decade later and yet again, although the bravura is breathtaking and there is no lack of spontaneity, the work's lyrical feeling and indeed its breadth are to some extent sacrificed to the insistent forward impulse of the playing. Good but not exceptional recording, a bit hard in the Liszt, though that may well reflect faithfully the percussive attack of Argerich's powerful hands.

Ashkenazy, Vladimir (piano)

'Piano favourites': BEETHOVEN: *Für Elise; Piano sonata No. 14 (Moonlight), Op. 27/2.* SCHUMANN: *Kinderszenen: Träumerei. Arabeske.* CHOPIN: *Mazurka in B flat, Op. 7/1; Nocturnes: in E flat, Op. 9/2; in B, Op. 32/1; Waltzes: in E flat (Grand valse brillante), Op. 18; in B min., Op. 69/2; Polonaise in A flat, Op. 53.* LIADOV: *Musical snuffbox, Op. 32.* MUSSORGSKY: *Pictures: The hut on hen's legs; The great gate of Kiev.* RAVEL: *Pavane pour une infante défunte.*
(M) **(*) Decca Dig. 430 759-2 [id.].

A well-selected and generous (71 minutes) recital. All the recordings are digital – but, even so, there are slight differences in piano timbre (and level) between items, most noticeable when Chopin's *Mazurka in B flat* closely follows the mellower (and rather deliberate) account of Schumann's *Träumerei*. It might have been better to end with the Mussorgsky *Great gate of Kiev* but, as it is, the fine performance of Beethoven's *Moonlight sonata* is far from an anticlimax.

Barere, Simon (piano)

'The complete HMV recordings, 1934–6': LISZT: *Etude de concert, G.144/2. Années de pèlerinage, 2nd Year (Italy): Sonnetto 104 del Petrarca, G.161/5. Gnomenreigen, G.145/2; Réminiscences de Don Juan, G.418* (2 versions); *Rapsodie espagnole, G.254; Valse oubliée No. 1, G.215.* CHOPIN: *Scherzo No. 3 in C sharp min., Op. 39; Mazurka No. 38 in F sharp min., Op. 59/3; Waltz No. 5 in A flat, Op. 42.* BALAKIREV: *Islamey* (2 versions). BLUMENFELD: *Etude for the left hand.* GLAZUNOV: *Etude in C, Op. 31/1.* SCRIABIN: *Etudes: in C sharp min., Op. 2/1; in D sharp min., Op. 8/12* (2 versions). LULLY/GODOWSKI: *Gigue in E.* RAMEAU/GODOWSKI: *Tambourin in E min.* SCHUMANN: *Toccata in C, Op. 7* (2 versions).
❀ (***) Appian mono CDAPR 7001 (2) [id.].

This two-CD set offers all of Barere's HMV recordings, made in the mid-1930s, including the alternative takes he made in the studio. What can one say of his playing without exhausting one's stock of superlatives? His fingerwork is quite astonishing and his virtuosity almost in a class on its own. The set contains an absolutely stunning account of the *Réminiscences de Don Juan*, and his *Islamey* knocks spots off any successor in sheer virtuosity and excitement; it is altogether breathtaking, and much the same might be said of his *Rapsodie espagnole*. Nor is there any want of poetry – witness the delicacy of the Scriabin *C sharp minor Etude* or Liszt's *La leggierezza*. Readers wanting to investigate this legendary artist should start here. One of the most important functions of the gramophone is to chart performance traditions that would otherwise disappear from view, and this set is one to celebrate.

Bashmet, Yuri (viola), Mikhail Muntian (piano)

GLINKA: *Viola sonata in D min.* ROSLAVETS: *Viola sonata.* SHOSTAKOVICH: *Viola sonata, Op. 147.*
**(*) BMG/RCA Dig. 09026 61273 [id.].

Bashmet makes a powerful response to Shostakovich's bleak, desperately felt *Viola sonata*; he balances it with Glinka's guilelessly youthful piece and another work by Nikolai Roslavets which not all listeners will welcome with open arms, its apparent emotional force seeming something of an illusion if one returns to it very often.

Bate, Jennifer (various organs)

Eighteenth-century organ music on period instruments from Adlington Hall, the Dolmetsch Collection, St Michael's Mount, Kenwood House, Killerton House, Everingham chapel.

Vol. 1: John READING: *Airs for French horns & flutes*. STANLEY: *Voluntaries, Op. 5/7 & 10; Op. 6/5; Op. 7/3*. HANDEL: *Fugue in B flat*. ROSEINGRAVE: *Voluntary in G min*. TRAVERS: *Voluntary in D min. & major*. WALOND: *Voluntary in A min*. RUSSELL: *Voluntary in E min*. Samuel WESLEY: *Short pieces Nos. 7 & 12; Voluntary, Op.6/1*.
*** Unicorn Dig. DKPCD 9096 [id.].

Vol. 2: GREENE: *Voluntary in C min*. STANLEY: *Voluntaries, Op. 5/6 & 9; Op. 6/7; Op. 7/2*. HANDEL: *Fugue in A min*. LONG: *Voluntary in D min*. WALOND: *Voluntary in B min*. NARES: *Introduction and fugue in F*. RUSSELL: *Voluntary in A min*. Samuel WESLEY: *Short piece No. 9; Voluntary, Op. 6/3*.
**(*) Unicorn Dig. DKPCD 9099 [id.].

Vol. 3: GREENE: *Voluntary in B min*. STANLEY: *Voluntaries, Op. 6/1 & 10; Op. 7/1 & 6*. WALOND: *Voluntary in G*. HANDEL: *Fugue in B min.; Voluntary in C*. BURNEY: *Cornet piece in E min*. RUSSELL: *Voluntary in A*. WESLEY: *Short pieces Nos 6 & 8. Voluntary, Op. 6/6*.
*** Unicorn Dig. DKPCD 9101 [id.].

Vol. 4: GREENE: *Voluntary in E flat*. STANLEY: *Voluntaries, Op. 5/8; Op. 6/6, 8 & 9; Op. 7/7*. HANDEL: *Voluntary in C; Fugue in G min*. ROSEINGRAVE: *Fugue No. 13*. DUPUIS: *Voluntary in B flat*. WESLEY: *Voluntary, Op. 6/9*.
**(*) Unicorn Dig. DKPCD 9104 [id.].

Jennifer Bate is making a survey of eighteenth-century English organ music, using five different English organs from stately homes to secure maximum variety of presentation. But these instruments are all relatively light-textured and sound bright and sweet. Each programme is made up in the same way: opening with an agreeable *Voluntary* of Maurice Greene, then offering a clutch of *Voluntaries* by John Stanley, followed by music of Walond and Handel, and usually ending with *Short pieces* by Samuel Wesley. None of these are great composers, save Handel, and his chosen examples are relatively minor works. Jennifer Bate plays all this music in impeccable style and she is beautifully recorded; so the attractions of each disc depend on the items included. Easily the most engaging are the works which use cornet or trumpet stops, which are colourful and jolly, while the Vox humana stop, as in the finale of Stanley's Op. 6/5 on the first disc, is also ear-tickling. Indeed the first volume is a good place to start, with Op. 5/7 by the same composer also quite engaging. The voluntaries are usually in two sections, but William Russell's E minor piece is in three with an imposing opening and the fugue used as a centrepiece. Samuel Wesley's *Short piece No. 12* is a contrapuntal moto perpetuo. The second disc also offers more examples of Stanley's ready facility, notably Op. 7/2 and Op. 5/6, but on the whole this is a less interesting programme than Volume 3 which again shows Stanley at his more inventive in Op. 7/1; Op. 6/1 begins with a pleasing *Siciliano*. Handel's *Voluntary in C* brings some attractive interplay of parts in its second movement and it is followed by Burney's *Cornet piece*, which has a whiff of the *Halleluia chorus*. In Volume 4 Jennifer Bate registers Stanley's Op. 5/8 with piquant skill: this is a three-part work, while the trumpet theme in Op. 6/6 might almost have been written by Purcell. Volume 1, however, is the disc to try first, then, if you enjoy this, go on to Volume 3. But only the real enthusiast will want all four CDs, for much of the writing here is fairly conventional.

British organ music: ELGAR: *Sonata No. 1 in G, Op. 28* (Royal Albert Hall organ). Samuel WESLEY: *Air with variations (composed for Holsworthy church bells); Introduction and fugue in C sharp min*. STANFORD: *Prelude and postlude on a theme of Orlando Gibbons, Op. 105/2; 2 Short preludes and postludes, Op. 101/2 & 4*. PARRY: *Fantasia and fugue in G min*. (organ of St James's Church, Muswell Hill). WALFORD DAVIES: *Solemn melody*. VAUGHAN WILLIAMS: *Prelude on a Welsh hymn tune No. 2: Rhosymedre*. ELGAR: *Imperial march, Op. 32* (arr. MARTIN) (organ of St Andrew's Church, Plymouth).
(BB) **(*) ASV Dig./Analogue CDQS 6160 [id.].

As can be seen from the organs used, this 75-minute recital draws on three different sources. The Elgar *Sonata* features the Royal Albert Hall organ, used impressively and flamboyantly, although quieter passages recede. The recordings made at Muswell Hill draw on a recital originally published on the Hyperion label which we greeted enthusiastically with the comment that the offered programme could stand alongside many more fashionable French compilations for quality and variety of invention. Samuel Sebastian Wesley's rather gentle *Variations* on *Holsworthy church bells* have charm, and his *Introduction and fugue* is strongly argued and well structured, but less flamboyant than the comparable piece by Parry. Other items in the original programme (by Wesley's father, Samuel, and by Russell, Stanley and Charles Wood) have been replaced by three more obviously popular pieces, by Walford Davies and Vaughan Williams, and by Elgar's *Imperial march*, which could use more uninhibited panache than is offered here. However, generally speaking Jennifer Bate's choice of tempi and registration is admirable, and the organs seem well chosen for the repertoire.

Belgian Wind Quintet

'Summer music': BEETHOVEN: *Wind quintet in E flat.* HOLST: *Wind quintet in A flat, Op. 14.* BARBER: *Summer music, Op. 31.* ARRIEU: *Quintet in C.*
(BB) *** Discovery Dig. DICD 920322 [id.].

A delightful collection, well worth its modest price. The many felicities of the Barber *Summer music* are matched by those of the much less familiar work of Holst, contemporary with the *Military band suites*. Claude Arrieu (born 1903) also writes very engagingly: her *Quintet* is both elegant and witty. The playing of the Belgian group is polished and spontaneous, and they are very well recorded.

Bergen Wind Quintet

BARBER: *Summer music, Op. 31.* SAEVERUD: *Tunes and dances from Siljustøl, Op. 21a.* JOLIVET: *Serenade for wind quintet with principal oboe.* HINDEMITH: *Kleine Kammermusik, Op. 24/2.*
*** BIS CD 291 [id.].

Barber's *Summer music* is a glorious piece dating from the mid-1950s; it is in a single movement. Saeverud's *Tunes and dances from Siljustøl* derive from piano pieces of great charm and sound refreshing in their transcribed format. Jolivet's *Serenade* is hardly less engaging, while Hindemith's *Kleine Kammermusik*, when played with such character and finesse, is no less welcome. Throughout, the fine blend and vivacious ensemble give consistent pleasure.

Berman, Lazar (piano)

Live recital – 27th June 1992: SCHUBERT: *Piano sonata No. 21 in B flat, D960.* LISZT: *Concert paraphrases of Schubert Lieder: Der Leiermann; Täuschung, Gretchen am Spinnrade; Die junge Nonne; Ave Maria; Erlkönig. Mephisto waltz; Années de pèlerinage, 1st Year: Chapelle de Guillaume Tell.* BEETHOVEN/RACHMANINOV: *Extract from The Ruins of Athens.*
(BB) ** Discovery DICD 920164/5 (2) [id.].

Berman's 1992 recital is uncommonly well recorded for a live occasion and the presence of the artist is in no doubt; indeed we have to wait a full half-minute for him to start after the introductory applause. His account of Schubert's last, greatest sonata is obviously both felt and considered. It is certainly dramatic but also wayward, and not all will respond to Berman's agogic distortions of the flow, particularly in the first movement. The Liszt items provide repertoire for which he is famous and the *Mephisto waltz* shows him at his most commanding. Some of the Schubert song transcriptions may be felt to be over-dramatized, though no one could complain about the *Erl-King*. The Beethoven/Rachmaninov encore is properly piquant.

Bowyer, Kevin (organ)

Blackburn Cathedral organ: *'A feast of organ exuberance'*: WOLF–G. LEIDEL: *Toccata Delectatione, Op. 5/35.* SWAYNE: *Riff-Raff.* BERVEILLER: *Suite; Cadence.*
(M) *** Priory Dig. 001 [id.].

The spectacular sound made by the magnificent 1969 Walker organ in Blackburn Cathedral is well demonstrated by this first-rate recital. Leidel is from the former East Germany, and his acknowledged influences from Messiaen and Scriabin are well absorbed into his own style. The *Toccata for pleasure* is titillating in its colouring and certainly exuberant in its extravagant treatment of its basic idea, which goes far beyond the minimalism achieved by many of his contemporaries. Giles Swayne is Liverpool-born and his quirky *Riff-Raff*, in the words of the performer, suggest 'isolated flashes of light of varying intensity'. Berveiller comes from the traditional French school of Dupré. His *Suite* is eminently approachable music, with a whimsical second-movement *Intermezzo* to remain in the memory, and a smoothly rich *Adagio*, before the Widorian finale. His *Cadence* provides a lightweight but by no means trivial encore. What one remembers most of all from this concert is the magnificent sonority of the organ, beautifully captured within its natural ambience, and that in itself shows how well composers and performer have combined their talents.

Bream, Julian

❀ *'The Julian Bream Edition'*

The Julian Bream Edition runs to some 30 CDs (available as a boxed set in the USA: 09026 61583-2), representing three decades of a remarkably distinguished recording career. Bream has now moved over to EMI, so this edition is essentially retrospective. The miscellaneous recitals are considered below, although the concertante collections are listed as composer entries in our main volume, and the Elizabethan lute songs are listed under Peter Pears among Vocal Recitals. The whole is an astonishing achievement overall, but we especially recommend Volumes 1–2, 13 and 26–27.

Bream, Julian (lute)

Volume 1. '*The golden age of English lute music*': Robert JOHNSON: *2 Almaines; Carman's whistle*. John JOHNSON: *Fantasia*. CUTTING: *Walsingham; Almaine; Greensleeves*. DOWLAND: *Mignarda; Galliard upon a galliard of Daniel Bachelar; Batell galliard; Captain Piper's galliard; Queen Elizabeth's galliard; Sir John Langton's pavan; Tarleton's resurrection; Lady Clifton's spirit*. ROSSETER: *Galliard*. MORLEY: *Pavan*. BULMAN: *Pavan*. BACHELAR: *Monsieur's almaine*. HOLBORNE: *Pavan; Galliard*. BYRD: *Pavana Bray; Galliard; Pavan; My Lord Willoughby's welcome home*.
(M) *** BMG/RCA 09026 61584-2 [id.].

Bream is a natural lutenist and a marvellously sensitive artist in this repertoire, and here he conjures up a wide range of colour, matched by expressive feeling. Here Dowland is shown in more extrovert mood than in many of his lute songs, and overall the programme has plenty of variety. The CD combines two recitals, the first 15 items recorded by Decca in London in September 1963, and the rest of the programme in New York City 2½ years later. The recording is exemplary and hiss is minimal.

Volume 2. '*Lute music from the Royal Courts of Europe*': LANDGRAVE OF HESSE: *Pavan*. MOLINARO: *2 Saltarelli; Ballet detto Il Conte Orlando; Fantasia*. PHILLIPS: *Chromatic pavan and galliard*. DOWLAND: *Fantasia; Queen Elizabeth's galliard*. HOWLETT: *Fantasia*. DLUGORAJ: *Fantasia; Finale; Villanellas Nos. 1–2; Finale*. FERRABOSCO II: *Pavan*. NEUSIDLER: *Mein Herz hat sich mit Lieb' verpflicht; Hie' folget ein welscher Tanz; Ich klag' den Tag; Der Juden Tanz*. BAKFARK: *Fantasia*. BESARD: *Air de cour; Branle; Guillemette; Volte*. DOWLAND: *Forlorn hope fancy; My Lord Willoughby's welcome home* (for 2 lutes).
(M) *** BMG/RCA 09026 61585-2.

Molinaro's music has a disconsolate, nostalgic quality: its atmosphere attracted Respighi, who included *Il Conte Orlando* when he orchestrated his suite of *Ancient airs and dances*. Wojciech Dlugoraj's two *Villanella* are equally touching and his busy *Finale* (which we hear in two versions) gives Bream a chance to display some crisply articulated bravura. Hans Neusidler, a leading German lutenist of the period, offers an equally varied group, with each piece curiously titled, ending with an exotic so-called 'Jewish dance'. The Burgundian Jean-Baptiste Besard's music is hardly less characterful, again bringing contrast between the doleful *Air de cour* and *Guillemette* and the two lively dances. Phillips's *Chromatic pavan and galliard* is strongly written, and the Dowland *Fantasia* and his splendidly regal *Galliard* for Queen Elizabeth are at the end of the programme with *Forlorn hope fancy*, before Lord Willoughby rides in vigorously in an arrangement for two lutes, both, of course, played by Bream.

Bream, Julian (guitar)

Volume 8. *'Popular classics for the Spanish guitar'*: VILLA-LOBOS: *Chôros No. 1; Etudes in E min. & C sharp min.; Prelude in E min.; Suite popolar brasileira: Schottische-chôro.* TORROBA: *Madraños.* FALLA: *Homenaje pour le tombeau de Debussy. Three-cornered Hat: Miller's dance* (arr. BREAM). TURINA: *Fandanguillo.* arr. LLOBET: *El testament d'Amelia.* SANZ: *Canarios.* M. ALBENIZ: *Sonata* (arr. PUJOL). RODRIGO: *En los trigales.* MOZART: *Larghetto and Allegro, K.229.* GIULIANI: *Sonata in C, Op. 15: Allegro. Rossiniana No. 1, Op. 119* (both ed. Bream).
(M) *** BMG/RCA Analogue/Dig. 09026 61591-2.

This collection in itself admirably scans Bream's RCA recording career, opening with material from an outstanding early recital made at Kenwood House in 1962, to which other items have been judiciously added from as early as 1959, and from 1965–8 and 1971, plus the two digital Falla pieces which are as late as 1983. Not surprisingly, the tension is a little variable, though the recital makes a very satisfactory whole. The highest voltage comes in the Villa-Lobos pieces which, though often thoughtful and ruminative, sound wonderfully spontaneous, and the Turina *Fandanguillo* is also very fine. The Mozart and Giuliani excerpts are appropriately mellow. Very real recording, with the various acoustics always well managed.

Volume 9. *'Baroque guitar'*: SANZ: *Pavanas; Galliardas; Passacalles; Canarios.* GUERAU: *Villano; Canario.* J. S. BACH: *Prelude in D min., BWV 999; Fugue in A min., BWV 1000.* WEISS: *Passacaille; Fantasie; Tombeau sur la mort de M. Comte de Logy.* VISEE: *Suite in D min.* FRESCOBALDI: *Aria con variazione detta la Frescobalda* (arr. SEGOVIA). D. SCARLATTI: *Sonata in E min., K.11* (arr. BREAM); *Sonata in E min., K.87* (arr. SEGOVIA). CIMAROSA: *Sonata in C min., Sonata in A* (both arr. BREAM).
(M) *** BMG/RCA 09026 61592-2.

The four Sanz pieces are strong in colour and atmosphere, and Sylvius Weiss also emerges with an individual voice. The eight-movement *Suite* by Robert Visée, a French court lutenist who lived from about 1650 until 1725, has the most attractive invention. The famous 'La Folia' emerges seductively as the *Sarabande* (it is beautifully played); and the *Gavotte*, two *Minuets*, *Bourrée* and *Gigue* which follow are all loosely based on its melodic contour. Frescobaldi's *Aria con variazione* is another memorable work. Scarlatti's keyboard sonatas transcribe well enough for guitar and the two sonatas of Cimarosa, though not strictly baroque music, are very personable.

Volume 11. *'Romantic guitar'*. PAGANINI: *Grand sonata in A.* SCHUBERT: *Sonata in G, D.894: Menuetto.* MENDELSSOHN: *Venetian boating song; Canzonetta* (all 3 ed. Bream). FALLA: *Homenaje pour le tombeau de Debussy.* RAVEL: *Pavane pour une infante défunte.* ALBENIZ: *Suite española: Granada; Leyenda (Asturias)* (arr. BREAM). TARREGA: *Lagrima (Prelude); 3 Mazurkas.*
(M) ** BMG/RCA 09026 61594-2.

A pleasant but uneven recital. The opening Paganini *Grand sonata* (21 minutes) is a trifle inflated and the Schubert arrangement is not a great success, while the Mendelssohn *Song without words* comes off much better than the *Canzonetta* (arranged from the *String quartet*, Op. 72). Of the other items, the Tarrega pieces have the greatest memorability. The recordings come from three different sources and there is an uncomfortably awkward tape-join between the very relaxed account of the Ravel *Pavane* and the first of the Albéniz pieces.

Volume 12. *'Twentieth-century guitar I'*: BERKELEY: *Sonatina, Op. 52/1; Theme and variations.* ROUSSEL: *Segovia, Op. 29.* SMITH BRINDLE: *El polifemo de oro (4 Fragments).* MARTIN: *4 Pièces brèves.* HENZE: *Kammermusik: 3 Tentos.* RAWSTHORNE: *Elegy.* WALTON: *5 Bagatelles.*
(M) *** BMG/RCA 09026 61595-2.

The finest works here are the Walton *Bagatelles* – dedicated to Bream – and Henze's *Drei Tentos*, interludes from a larger work, which are very attractive in their picturesque impressionism. Lennox Berkeley's *Sonatina*, too, is an enjoyably amiable piece; the *Theme and variations* is more ambiguous thematically and harmonically. Roussel's *Segovia* has a characteristic touch of acerbity. Reginald Smith Brindle's *Fragments* provides four musical invocations of the poetry of Lorca, while in his *Four Pièces* Frank Martin re-creates for the guitar with characteristic finesse the world of the eighteenth-century lute suite. Bream makes the most of all his opportunities and where the music can charm the ear he does not miss a trick. He concludes the Rawsthorne *Elegy*, which the composer did not live to complete, by reprising the restrained opening section. Overall, however, the work remains emotionally uncompromising. Excellent recording.

Volume 13. *'Twentieth-century guitar II'*: MOMPOU: *Suite compostellana*. OHANA: *Tiento*. TORROBA: *Sonatina*. GERHARD: *Fantasía*. VILLA-LOBOS: *Suite populaire brésilienne; Etudes Nos. 5 in C; 7 in E*.
(M) *** Dig./Analogue BMG/RCA 09026 61596-2.

This is an exceptionally rewarding recital of one of the very finest of the many reissues in the Julian Bream Edition. Mompou's six-movement *Suite compostellana* is sheer delight with its muted flamenco feeling and air of wistful melancholy. Ohana's *Tiento*, a considerable piece which looks back to the sixteenth century, opens by musing over the famous *La Folia*, and Gerhard's almost equally striking *Fantasía* is similarly improvisational in feeling. Bream plays both pieces marvellously and is quite melting in the *Andante* of Torroba's *Sonatina* – a more ambitious piece than the name would suggest and the composer's finest work for guitar. To this digital collection the attractive, lighter Villa-Lobos suite is added, recorded two decades earlier, but impressively real and present.

Volume 26. Music of Spain: *'La guitarra romántica'*: TARREGA: *Mazurka in G; Etude in A; Marieta; Capricho árabe; Prelude in A min.; Recuerdos de la Alhambra*. MALATS: *Serenata*. PUJOL: *Tango Espagñol; Guajira*. LLOBET: *Canciones populares catalanas*. TURINA: *Fandanguillo, Op. 36; Sevillana, Op. 29; Homenaje a Tárrega*.
(M) *** BMG/RCA Dig./Analogue 09026 61609-2.

A mainly digital recital of Spanish music opens with an attractive, lightweight Tárrega group including the *Capricho árabe* and his most famous evocation, the *Recuerdos de la Alhambra*, which in Bream's hands is curiously muted and withdrawn. Then after works by Malats and Pujol (his *Guajira* has some fine special effects) there follows the delightful Llobet suite of nine *Canciones populares catalanas*. The programme ends with vibrant flamenco-inspired music of Turina, including the composer's last (two-part) guitar work, the *Homenaje a Tárrega*. Bream's dynamism in these performances makes one almost believe he was Spanish-born. The final work (consisting of a *Garrotín* and *Soleares*) was recorded at Kenwood House in 1962 and is exceptional in that here the resonance inflates the guitar image; for the rest of the recital the recording is ideal in all respects.

Volume 27. *'Guitarra'* (Music of Spain): MUDARRA: *Fantasias X & XIV*. Luis DE MILAN: *Fantasia XXII*. Luis DE NARVÁEZ: *La canción del Emperador; Conde claros*. Santiago DE MURCIA: *Prelude & Allegro*. BOCCHERINI: *Guitar quintet in D, G. 448* (arr. for 2 guitars): *Fandango*. SOR: *Grand solo, Op. 14; Variations on a theme of Mozart, Op. 9; Fantasie, Op. 7; Sonata, Op. 25: Minuet*. AGUADO: *Rondo in A min., Op. 2/3*. TARREGA: *Study in A; Prelude in A min.; Recuerdos de la Alhambra*.
(M) *** BMG/RCA Dig./Analogue 09026 61610-2 [id.].

An admirable survey covering 400 years and featuring several different instruments, all especially built by José Ramanillos and including a Renaissance guitar and a modern classical guitar. Bream's natural dexterity is matched by a remarkable control of colour and unerring sense of style. Many of the earlier pieces are quite simple but have considerable magnetism. The basic recital was recorded digitally in 1983 at Bream's favourite venue, Wardour Chapel, Windsor, and is laid out chronologically. Two additional Sor items, the *Fantasie*, Op. 7, and the *Minuet* from Op. 25, were made 18 years earlier in New York and, as they are analogue, have sensibly been added at the end.

'Homage to Segovia': TURINA: *Fandanguillo, Op. 36; Sevillana, Op. 29*. MOMPOU: *Suite compostelana*. TORROBA: *Sonatina*. GERHARD: *Fantasia*. FALLA: *Homenaje pour le tombeau de Claude Debussy; Three cornered hat* (ballet): *3 Dances*. OHANA: *Tiento*.
(M) *** BMG/RCA Dig. 09026 61353-2 [id.].

Readers who have already acquired Bream's earlier digital recital concentrating on the music of Albéniz and Granados will find this hardly less impressive, both musically and technically. The programme here is even more diverse, with the Gerhard *Fantasia* adding a twentieth-century dimension, while Ohana's *Tiento* has a comparable imaginative approach to texture. Throughout, Bream plays with his usual flair and spontaneity, constantly imaginative in his use of a wide dynamic range and every possible colouristic effect. The set of six miniatures by Federico Mompou is particularly diverting.

'Nocturnal': MARTIN: *4 pièces brèves*. BRITTEN: *Nocturnal after John Dowland*. BROUWER: *Sonata*. TAKEMITSU: *All in Twilight*. LUTOSLAWSKI: *Folk melodies* (trans. Bream).
*** EMI Dig. CDC7 54901-2 [id.].

After his remarkable achievement on the RCA label, Julian Bream has now changed recording companies and seems to be starting all over again. However, this recital of twentieth-century guitar music is – in parts at least – a tough nut to crack. This is not a CD to play all at once. The Martin *Pièces* and the ingenious extended *Nocturne* of Britten, concentrated as the playing is, need to be taken one at a time, and the Brouwer *Sonata* (for all its quotations – notably from Beethoven's *Pastoral Symphony*) does not make friends immediately. The Takemitsu is shameless guitar impressionism and not especially tangible. Finally we have some readily inviting folk tunes, aptly harmonized by Lutoslawski, and charm makes its entry for the first time in a 72-minute programme. Vividly immediate recording, but don't set the volume level too high.

Sonatas: Antonio JOSE: *Sonata* (ed. Bream). PAGANINI: *Grand sonata, Op. 9* (ed. Bream). CASTELNUOVO-TEDESCO: *Sonata (Omaggio a Boccherini), Op. 77*.
*** EMI Dig. CDC5 55362-2 [id.].

The most striking movement of the work by Antonio José is the vibrant finale, but the pensive *Pavana triste* is also quite haunting. Paganini's *Grand sonata* was written as an unequal duo with violin, but Bream has effectively incorporated the relatively flimsy violin part into the guitar texture. It is an amiable work with a delicate second-movement *Romance* in siciliano style and a set of variations on an agreeably innocent theme for its finale. Castelnuovo-Tedesco's *Sonata* has bright outer movements framing another siciliano slow movement (*dolce malinconico*) and an elegant *grazioso* Minuet. The performances could hardly be more persuasive, subtle in nuance and colour. The recording, too, is naturally present without being over-projected.

'Baroque guitar': SANZ: *Pavanos; Canarios*. J. S. BACH: *Prelude in D min., BWV 999; Fugue in A min., BWV 1000; Lute suite in E min., BWV 996*. SOR: *Fantasy and Minuet*. WEISS: *Passacaille; Fantaisie; Tombeau sur la morte de M. Comte de Logy*. VISEE: *Suite in D min*.
(BB) *** RCA Navigator 74321 24195-2.

This is a shorter version of the baroque recital which forms Volume 9 of the Julian Bream Edition. It still includes well over an hour of music as Bream's superb account of Bach's *E minor Lute suite* has been added. The recording is very natural, and this makes a fine recital in its own right, realistically recorded. A very real bargain in RCA's bargain-basement Navigator series.

SOR: *Sonata, Op. 22: Minuetto & Rondo Allegretto. Andante Largo, Op. 5/5; Estudios Nos. 5, 19 & 12; Largo from Fantasie*. TURINA: *Homanaje a Tarrega, Op. 69: Garrotin; Soleares. Fandanguillo, Op. 36; Rafaga, Op. 53*. FALLA: *Le tombeau de Claude Debussy*. VILLA-LOBOS: *Preludes Nos. 1–5*. TORROBA: *Preludio in E. Sonatina in A: Andante & Allegro. Burgalesa*.
(B) *** Millenium MCD 80113 [id.].

This early recital by Julian Bream dates from 1956, but it shows him with an already prodigious technique, a musician-interpreter of the highest calibre. Indeed, following after the last of the Sor items, the lively neo-classical *Rondo Allegretto* (played with crisp flair), the four highly evocative Turina pieces show Bream's characteristically inspirational way with Spanish repertoire, which he plays as colloquially and spontaneously as any Mediterranean-born guitarist. The middle section of the *Fandanguillo* is haunting and the piece ends magically. Bream was to record the Villa-Lobos *Preludes* again, for RCA, but the playing here is already freely inspirational, especially the evocative *E minor Prelude*, made to sound like distant bells tolling. Everything here springs vividly to life: how engaging is the Torroba *Preludio in E major*, while the subtle atmosphere of the closing *Burgalesa* is beautifully caught. We are not sure whether the recording is stereo or mono (the guitar is central and very realistically projected), but there is a most convincing ambience.

Bream, Julian (guitar and lute)

'The ultimate guitar collection' ((i) with Monteverdi O, Gardiner): (i) VIVALDI: *Lute concerto in D, RV 93* (ed. Bream). Lute pieces: CUTTING: *Packington's round; Greensleeves*. DOWLAND: *A Fancy (Fantasia)*. Guitar pieces: SANZ: *Canarios*. Matéo ALBENIZ: *Sonata in D* (arr. PUJOL). Isaac ALBENIZ: *Suite española, Op. 47: Cataluna; Granada; Sevilla; Cádiz; Leyenda (Asturias). Mallorca, Op. 202. Cantos de España: Cordoba, Op. 232/4*. FALLA: *Three-cornered Hat: Miller's dance*. TARREGA: *Recuerdos de la Alhambra*. VILLA-LOBOS: *Chôros No. 1; Preludes Nos. 1 in E min.; 2 in D*. RODRIGO: *En los trigales;* (i) *Concierto de Aranjuez. Tres piezas espanolas*. GRANADOS: *Cuentos para la juventud: Dedicatoria. Tonadilla: La Maja de Goya. Danzas españolas Nos. 4 (Villanesca); 5 (Valses poéticos)*.
✿ (B) *** RCA Dig./Analogue 74321 33705-2 (2) [id.].

The extraordinary achievement of RCA's 'Juliam Bream Edition' is admirably summed up by this inexpensive pair of CDs which include two and a half hours of the most popular repertoire for guitar, plus a small group of lute pieces for good measure. There is not a single item here that is not strong in musical personality, and every performance springs vividly and spontaneously to life. John Eliot Gardiner provides highly distinguished accompaniments for the two justly famous concertos, by Vivaldi (for lute) and

Rodrigo (for guitar). The first of the two CDs provides a well-planned historical survey, opening with Elizabethan lute music and progressing through to include three magnetic pieces by Villa-Lobos. Highlights include an electrifying performance of Falla's *Miller's dance* from *The Three-cornered Hat* and, of course the most famous guitar piece of all, the *Recuerdos de la Alhambra* of Tárrega. The second collection, which is entirely digital (from 1982–3), concentrates mainly on Isaac Albéniz and Granados (not forgetting the superb accounts of the *Cordoba* by the former and the *Danza espanola No. 5* by the latter, which are highly praised in our composer section). It ends appropriately with Rodrigo's *Tres piezas españolas*, with its remarkable central *Passacaglia*. The recordings are of the highest quality and are excellently transferred to CD.

Bream, Julian and **John Williams** (guitar duo)

'Together': Disc 1: CARULLI: *Serenade in A, Op. 96.* GRANADOS: *Danzas españolas: Rodella aragonesa; Zambra, Op. 37/6 & 11.* ALBENIZ: *Cantos de España: Bajo la palmera, Op. 232/3. Ibéria: Evocación.* GIULIANI: *Variazioni concertanti, Op. 130.* JOHNSON: *Pavan & Galliard* (arr. BREAM). TELEMANN: *Partie polonaise.* DEBUSSY: *Rêverie; Children's corner: Golliwog's cakewalk. Suite bergamasque: Clair de lune.*

Disc 2: LAWES: *Suite for 2 guitars* (arr. BREAM). CARULLI: *Duo in G, Op. 34.* SOR: *L'encouragement, Op. 34.* ALBENIZ: *Cantos de España: Córdoba, Op. 232/4; Suite española: Castilla (Seguidillas).* GRANADOS: *Goyescas: Intermezzo* (arr. PUJOL). *Danzas españolas: Oriental, Op. 37/2.* FALLA: *La vida breve: Spanish dance No. 1.* RAVEL: *Pavane pour une infante défunte.* FAURE: *Dolly* (suite), *Op. 56* (both arr. BREAM).
(B) *** RCA 74321 20134-2 (2) [id.].

The rare combination of Julian Bream and John Williams was achieved by RCA in the studio on two separate occasions, in 1971 and 1973, providing the basic contents of these two recitals. Further recordings were made live in Boston and New York in 1978, during a North American concert tour. Curiously, it is the studio programmes which seem the more spontaneous, and Fauré's *Dolly suite*, which sounds a little cosy, is the only disappointment (it also brings some audience noises). Highlights are the music of Albéniz and Granados (notably the former's haunting *Evocación* from *Iberia*, and *Cordoba*, which Bream also included on a very successful solo recital). The transcription of the *Goyescas Intermezzo* is also very successful, as is Debussy's *Golliwog's cakewalk* in a quite different way. Giuliani's *Variazioni concertanti*, actually written for guitar duo, brings some intimately gentle playing, as does the *Theme and variations* which forms the second movement of Sor's *L'encouragement*; while the *Cantabile* which begins this triptych is delightful in its simple lyricism. The Carulli *Serenade* opens the second recital very strikingly, while on the first disc the performance of Ravel's *Pavane*, very slow and stately, is memorable. The Elizabethan lute music by Johnson and Lawes and the Telemann *Partie polonaise* (written for a pair of lutes) bring a refreshing change of style in what is predominantly a programme of Spanish music. The concert ends with Albéniz's *Seguidillas*, and an appropriately enthusiatic response from the audience. With the overall timing at a very generous 149 minutes, the pair of discs comes for the cost of a single premium-priced CD and can be recommended very strongly indeed. This is music-making of the very highest order, and the CD transfers bring fine presence and a natural balance.

Brendel, Alfred (piano)

Vanguard 'Alfred Brendel Collection'

Volume 1: MOZART: *Piano concertos Nos. 9 in E flat, K.271; 14 in E flat, K.449* (with I Solisti di Zagreb, Janigro). *Piano sonata No. 8 in A min., K.310; Fantasia in C min., K.396; Rondo in A min., K.511; 9 Variations on a Minuet by Duport, K.573.*
(M) *** Van. 08 9161 71 (2).

Volume 2: CHOPIN: *Andante spianato et Grande polonaise brillante, Op. 22; Polonaises Nos. 4 in C min., Op. 40/2; 5 in F sharp min., Op. 44; 6 in A flat, Op. 53; 7 (Polonaise-fantasie), Op. 61.* LISZT: *Hungarian rhapsodies Nos. 2–3, 8, 13, 15 (Rákóczy march); Csárdás obstinée.*
(M) **(*) Van. 08 9163 72 (2) .

Volume 3: SCHUBERT: *Piano sonatas Nos. 15 in C (Unfinished), D.840; 19 in C min., D.958; 16 German dances, D. 783.* SCHUMANN: *Etudes symphoniques; Fantasia in C.*
(M) *** Van. 08 9165 72 (2).

Vanguard have now produced their own 'Alfred Brendel collection' from recordings made in the 1960s.

Each set of two CDs is offered in a slip-case but with no price saving. The separate discs are discussed above, under their composer headings.

Brüggen, Frans (recorder)

'The Frans Brüggen Edition' (complete)
(M) *** Teldec/Warner 4509 97475-2 (12) [id.].

Volume 1: TELEMANN (with Anner Bylsma, Gustav Leonhardt): *Essercizii musici: Sonata in C, TWV 41:C5; in D min, TWV 41:d4. Fantasias: in C, TWV 40:2; in D min., TWV 40:4; in F, TWV 40:8; in G min., TWV 40:9; in A min., TWV 40:11; in B flat, TWV 40:12. Der getreue Music-Meister: Canonic sonata in B flat, TWV 41:B3; Sonatas in C, TWV 41:C2; in F, TWV 41:F2; in F min., TWV 41:f1* (4509 93688-2).

Volume 2: *Italian recorder sonatas* (with Anner Bylsma, Gustav Leonhardt): CORELLI: *Sonatas: in F, Op. 5/4; La Follia (Variations in G min.), Op. 5/12.* BARSANTI: *Sonata in C.* VERACINI: *Sonatas in G; in A min.* (1716). BIGAGLIA: *Sonata in A min.* CHEDEVILLE: *Sonata in G min., Op. 13/6.* MARCELLO: *Sonata in D min., Op. 2/11* (4509 93669-2).

Volume 3: *English ensemble music* (with Kees Boeke, Walter van Hauwe, Anner Bylsma, Gustav Leonhardt, Brüggen Consort): HOLBORNE: *Dances and airs.* TAVERNER: *In nomine.* TYE: *In nomine (Crye).* BYRD: *In nomine; The leaves be green.* Thomas SIMPSON: *Bonny sweet Robin.* MORLEY: *La Girandola; Il Lamento; La Caccia.* JEFFREYS: *Fantasia.* PARCHAM: *Solo in G.* Robert CARR: *Divisions upon an Italian ground.* William BABELL: *Concerto in D.* PEPUSCH: *Sonata in F.* PURCELL: *Chaconne in F* (4509 97465-2).

Volume 4: *Early baroque recorder music* (with Kees Boeke, Walter van Hauwe, Anner Bylsma, Wouter Möller, Bob van Asperen, Gustav Leonhardt): Jacob VAN EYCK: *Batali; Doen Daphne d'over schoonne Maeght; Pavane Lachryme; Engels Nachtegaeltje.* FRESCOBALDI: *Canzon: La Bernadina.* Giovani Paolo CIMA: *Sonatas in D & G.* Giovanni Battista RICCIO: *Canzon in A; Canzon in A (La Rosignola).* SCHEIDT: *Paduan a 4 in D.* ANON.: *Sonata in G* (4509 97466-2).

Volume 5: *Late baroque recorder music* (with Jeanette van Wingerden, Kees Boeke, Walter van Hauwe, Franz Vester, Joost Tromp, Brian Pollard, Anner Bylsma, Wouter Möller, Gustav Leonhardt, Bob van Asperen): TELEMANN: *Quartet in D min., TWV 43:d1.* FASCH: *Quartet in G.* LOEILLET: *Quintet in B min.* QUANTZ: *Trio sonata in C.* Alessandro SCARLATTI: *Sonata in F.* Johann MATTHESON: *Sonata No. 4 in G min.* (4509 97467-2).

Volume 6: *French recorder suites* (with Kees Boeke, Nikolaus Harnoncourt, Anner Bylsma, Gustav Leonhardt): Charles DIEUPART: *Suites in G min. & A.* HOTTETERRE: *Suite No. 1* (4509 97468-2).

Volume 7: *French recorder sonatas* (with Kees Boeke, Walter van Hauwe, Anner Bylsma, Gustav Leonhardt): Philibert DE LAVIGNE: *Sonata in C (La Barssan).* BOISMORTIER: *Sonata in F.* PHILIDOR: *Sonata in D min.* Louis-Antoine DORNEL: *Sonata (a 3 Dessus) in B flat.* François COUPERIN: *Le rossignol-en-amour* (4509 97469-2).

Volume 8: VIVALDI: *Chamber concertos* (with Jürg Schaefleit, Otto Fleischmann, Alice Harnoncourt, Walter Pfeiffer, Nikolaus Harnoncourt, Gustav Leonhardt): *in C, RV 87; in D, RV 92 & RV 94; in G min., RV 105; in A min., RV 108; in C min., RV 441; in F, RV 442* (4509 97470-2).

Volume 9: HANDEL: *Recorder sonatas* (with Alice Harnoncourt, Anner Bylsma, Nikolaus Harnoncourt, Gustav Leonhardt, Herbert Tachezi): *in G min., HWV 360; in A min., HWV 362; in C, HWV 365; in F, HWV 369, Op. 1/2, 4, 7 & 11; in F, HWV 389, Op. 2/4. Fitzwilliam sonatas Nos. 1 in B flat, HWV 377; 3 in D min., HWV 367a* (4509 97471-2).

Volume 10: TELEMANN: *Concertos and orchestral music* (with VCM, Harnoncourt): *Concertos: in C; à 6 in F; Suite (Overture) in A min., TWV 55:a2* (4509 97472-2).

Volume 11: J. S. BACH: *Chamber and orchestral music* (with Jeanette van Wingerden, Leopold Stastny, Marie Leonhardt, Nikolaus Harnoncourt, Gustav Leonhardt, Herbert Tachezi): *Concertos: in A min., BWV 1044; in F, BWV 1057; Sonata concerto from Cantata No. 182; Sonatina from Cantata No. 106; Trio sonata in G, BWV 1039* (4509 97473-2).

Volume 12: *Recorder sonatas and concertos* (with Frans Vester, Alice Harnoncourt, Nikolaus Harnoncourt, Anner Bylsma, Gustav Leonhardt, Herbert Tachezi, VCM; Amsterdam CO): LOEILLET: *Sonata in C min.; Sonata in G.* SAMMARTINI: *Concerto in F.* HANDEL: *Trio sonata in B min.* NAUDOT: *Concerto in G.* TELEMANN: *Double concerto in E min.* (4509 97474-2).

Frans Brüggen is perhaps the greatest master of the recorder of the post-war era. In his hands phrases are turned with the utmost sophistication, intonation is unbelievably accurate and matters of style exact. There is spontaneity too and, with such superb musicianship and the high standard of recording we have come to expect from the Teldec Das Alte Werk series, these reissues in Brüggen's own special edition can almost all be recommended without reservation. He is equally at home in early or late baroque music. Throughout the collection, Frans Brüggen and his estimable colleagues demonstrate various period instruments; Anner Bylsma, Gustav Leonhardt and Bob van Asperen are present to provide a distinguished continuo, while Harnoncourt and the Vienna Concentus Musicus and Schröder's Amsterdam Chamber Orchestra are available for authentic concerto accompaniments.

Volume 1 is a single-disc anthology of Telemann's chamber music. Brüggen plays with his usual mastery and, as one would expect from Gustav Leonhardt's ensemble, the performances have polish and authority, and they are excellently recorded.

Volume 2 with its collection of Italian recorder sonatas is surely a perfect sampler for the whole edition, for it gives the opportunity for this king of recorder players to demonstrate his expertise and musicianship to maximum effect, admirably partnered by Anner Bylsma and Gustav Leonhardt. Corelli puts the famous 'Follia' melody through all possible hoops and Brüggen obliges with nimble virtuosity. The Veracini works are also primarily for violin, though the recorder is an optional alternative for the *G major Sonata*. All this music is played with exemplary skill, and no recorder enthusiast will want to be without this splendid example of Brüggen's art.

The collection of English ensemble music which constitutes Volume 3 is particularly diverting, opening with Holborne's *Suite of dances and airs* which alternates recorder and viols. The several *In nomines* are all differently scored and are very different in character too, while the folksong arrangements by Byrd and Simpson are touching. The *Solo* (Suite) by Andrew Parcham, the *Divisions* of Robert Carr and Pepusch's *Sonata* are all engaging and are played with characteristic skill and musicianship so that only occasionally does the ear detect the limitations of early instruments.

Volume 4 introduces works by Jacob Van Eyck, which are unaccompanied but are aurally titillating, particularly the primitive *Batali* with its 'bugle' calls, while the florid upper tessitura of *Engels Nachtegaeltje* really takes wing. The Frescobaldi *Canzon* and the works by Cima and Riccio use an organ and cello continuo, and the delightful *La Rosignola* is for recorder trio with cello and harpsichord.

Later baroque chamber music is represented on Volume 5, with works by Alessandro Scarlatti, Telemann and Johann Mattheson standing out, while Volume 6 brings entertainingly elegant and tuneful *Suites* by Dieupart (a French-born musician who taught in London around 1700 and whose harpsichord music influenced Bach) and Hotteterre (known as Le Romain). These suites are very much cast in the style favoured by Telemann, with an *Overture* and a collection of dances.

Volume 7 concentrates on French recorder sonatas and brings another vivid nightingale evocation – *Le rossignol-en-amour*, by François Couperin.

Volumes 8 – 10 are composer collections of music by Vivaldi, Handel and more Telemann, all discussed in detail under their composer entries, above. Volume 11, offering a Bach collection, is the only relative disappointment. Two of the major works here are transcribed, and BWV 1044 comes off more effectively than BWV 1057. Best is the *Trio sonata in G*, BWV 1039, although the two cantata excerpts are pleasing.

A final excellent sampler is provided by the collection of *Recorder sonatas* and *concertos* which makes up Volume 12, featuring a chamber ensemble and both the Amsterdam Chamber Orchestra and the Vienna Concentus Musicus. The Telemann *Double concerto in E minor for recorder and flute* is a particularly fine one, and the dulcet duet in the slow movement begins rather like Handel's *Where'er you walk*. The Sammartini *Concerto* has an unexpectedly solemn *Siciliano* for its slow movement. The Handel *Trio sonata* is a splendid work, and the two Loeillet *Sonatas* are light and airy and full of charm, while even the less striking Naudot piece emerges as music of character. All these performances are outstandingly successful.

The recordings were nearly all made during the 1960s, with a few dating from the following decade, and they are of the highest quality, as are the vivid CD transfers. Documentation is very good. As we go to press, the individual issues have been deleted.

Cann, Claire and Antoinette (piano duo)

'Romantic favourites on 2 pianos': SAINT-SAENS: *Danse macabre*. DEBUSSY: *Petite suite*. TCHAIKOVSKY (arr. CANN): *Nutcracker suite:* excerpts. BRAHMS: *Variations on a theme of Haydn (St Antoni chorale), Op. 56b; Waltzes, Op. 39/1–2, 5–6, 9–11 & 15*. MACDOWELL (arr. NIEMANN): *Hexentanz*. LISZT (arr. BRENDEL): *Hungarian rhapsody No. 2*.
❀ (M) *** Apollo Recordings Dig. ARCD 961 [id.].

We are glad to welcome the début recital of the Cann duo back to the catalogue. With the demise of the Pianissimo label it was unavailable for some time but now returns on the Apollo label, distributed in the UK by Canterbury Classics. It is difficult to imagine a more scintillating piano duet record than this. Saint-Saëns's skeletons – summoned by an evocative midnight bell – dance as vigorously as do MacDowell's witches in the brilliant *Hexameron*, while Debussy's delightful *Petite suite* – played here very effectively on two pianos, rather than with four hands on one – is full of charm. The Cann sisters then produce a rich-textured fullness of tone for the Brahms *Haydn variations*, which are every bit as enjoyable here as in their orchestral dress. Most remarkable of all are the excerpts from the *Nutcracker suite*, conceived entirely pianistically and glittering with colour. Indeed the *Sugar plum fairy* has a much stronger profile than usual and the *Chinese dance* an irresistible oriental glitter. The *Hungarian dances* bring beguiling variety of mood and texture and display an easy bravura, ending with a lovely performance of the famous *Cradle song* (*No. 15 in A flat*), while the dazzling Liszt *Hungarian rhapsody* ends the recital with great exuberance and much digital panache. The recording, made in Rosslyn Hill Chapel, is exceptionally real and vivid and is ideally balanced.

Center City Brass Quintet

Brass quintets: Malcolm ARNOLD: *Quintet*. Viktor EWALD: *Quintet No. 1 in B flat min*. Eugene BOZZA: *Sonatine*. Ludwig MAURER: *3 Pieces*. Ingolf DAHL: *Music for six brass instruments*. CALVERT: *Suite from the Monteregian Hills*.
*** Collins Dig. 1489-2 [id.].

The Center City Brass Quintet takes its name from the downtown district of Chicago where it was formed by five brass players studying at the Curtis Institute. The individual musicians went on to become principals in major American orchestras but have continued to keep their quintet performances active. The present admirably chosen concert demonstrates the group's easy virtuosity and fine blending of sonority. The irrepressible Arnold *Quintet* with its characteristically dark central *Chaconne* and jazzy finale is the highlight of the programme, but if Ewald's *Quintet* is less audacious it is agreeably melodic and sonorously scored. Bozza's *Sonatine* is sprightly occasional music, with the melancholy of the slow movement nicely offset by the exuberant, unbuttoned Scherzo. The finale is a bizarre march which quotes from Shostakovich and Ravel. Maurer's three pieces are brief but strikingly rich in sonorous colouring. Dahl opens by extravagantly recalling a Bach chorale and then, in his plangently expressive yet lively third movement, he introduces an ingeniously interwoven fugato, leading to a thrillingly expansive coda. Calvert's *Suite from the Monteregian Hills* is engagingly based on French-Canadian folksongs and ends with a disrespectful finale which at its close celebrates a French Christmas carol. Not a single item here lacks freshness of ideas, and the players clearly relish this attractive repertoire, playing with sparkling bravura and creating an often lusciously expansive richness of sound. The recording is in the demonstration bracket. A most enjoyable concert.

Clarion Ensemble

'Trumpet collection': FANTINI: *Sonata; Brando; Balletteo; Corrente*. MONTEVERDI: *Et e pur dunque vero*. FRESCOBALDI: *Canzona a canto solo*. PURCELL: *To arms, heroic prince*. A. SCARLATTI: *Si suoni la tromba*. BISHOP: *Arietta and Waltz; Thine forever*. DONIZETTI: *Lo L'udia*. KOENIG: *Post horn galop*. ARBAN: *Fantasia on Verdi's Rigoletto*. CLARKE: *Cousins*. ENESCU: *Legende*.
❀ *** Amon Ra CD-SAR 30 [id.].

The simple title '*Trumpet collection*' covers a fascinating recital of music for trumpet written over three centuries and played with great skill and musicianship by Jonathan Impett, using a variety of original instruments, from a keyed bugle and clapper shake-key cornopean to an English slide trumpet and a posthorn. Impett is a complete master of all these instruments, never producing a throttled tone; indeed in the Purcell and Scarlatti arias he matches the soaring soprano line of Deborah Roberts with uncanny mirror-image precision. Accompaniments are provided by other members of the Clarion Ensemble. The

Frescobaldi *Canzona* brings a duet for trumpet and trombone, with a background harpsichord filigree, which is most effective. With demonstration-worthy recording, this is as enjoyable as it is interesting, with the *Posthorn galop* and Arban's *Rigoletto variations* producing exhilarating bravura.

Cohler, Jonathan (clarinet)

'Cohler on clarinet' (with Judith Gordon, piano): BRAHMS: *Sonata No. 1 in F min., Op. 120/1.* WEBER: *Grand duo concertante, Op. 48.* BAERMANN: *Quintet No. 3, Op. 23: Adagio* (arr. for clarinet & piano). SARGON: *Deep Ellum nights* (3 Sketches).
*** Ongaku Dig. 024-101 [id.].

This fine collection marks the recording début of an outstanding, Boston-born, American clarinettist. He has a splendid technique and a lovely tone, and he is already master of an extraordinarily wide range of repertoire. The opening Brahms *F minor Sonata* is a supreme test, and he passes with distinction. The Weber *Grand duo concertante* is suitably good-natured, with a songful central cantilena and plenty of wit in the finale. The Baermann *Adagio* shows how ravishingly Cohler can shape a melting legato line with a breath-catching pianissimo at its peak. He then throws his hat in the air in the three exuberant *Sketches* of Simon Sargon, where sultry melodic lines are interrupted by all kinds of jazzy glissandos and uninhibited syncopations, notably an explosive burst of energy intruding into the *Quiet and easy* central section. The finale is like a flashy cakewalk. The recording is truthful, but the piano is placed behind in a too resonant acoustic (the empty Paine Concert Hall at Harvard University), which is a tiresome misjudgement. Even so, Judith Gordon provides sympathetic support and the playing more than compensates.

'More Cohler on clarinet' (with Randall Hodgkinson, piano): BRAHMS: *Sonata No. 2 in E flat, Op. 120/2.* POULENC: *Sonata.* SCHUMANN: *Fantaisiestücke, Op. 73.* MILHAUD: *Sonatina, Op. 100.* STRAVINSKY: *3 Pieces* (for solo clarinet).
*** Ongaku Dig. 024-102 [id.].

Cohler's second disc is much more satisfactorily balanced. His excellent partner, Randall Hodgkinson, is fully in the picture. The opening of the Brahms *E flat Sonata* is agreeably warm and relaxed, and the theme-and-variations finale brings a pleasing interplay between the two artists. Poulenc's *Sonata* is beautifully done, the lovely *Romanza* (*Très calme*) is cool in the way only a player who knows about jazz can manage, while the fizzing finale also brings a hint of rapture in its contrasting lyrical theme. The warmth of the Schumann pieces, for which Cohler imaginatively modifies his timbre, contrasts with the outrageous Milhaud sonatina, with both outer movements marked *Très rude* but the *Lent* centrepiece quite magical. The three dry Stravinsky fragments make a perfect close to a disc which is outstanding in every way.

Composers at the piano

Famous composers playing their own works on the Welte Mignon piano (1905–6): Richard STRAUSS: *Salome: Salome's dance. Feuersnot: Love scene. Rêverie, Op. 9/4; Ein Heldenleben: Liebesszene.* SAINT-SAENS: *Samson et Dalila: Dance of the Priestesses of Dagon; Delilah's air.* D'ALBERT: *Tiefland: Pedro's arrival at the Mill; Nuri's song; Spanish dancing song.* HUMPERDINCK: *Hänsel und Gretel: Pantomime.* KIENZL: *Der Evangeligmann: Selig sind, die Verflogung leiden.* LEONCAVALLO: *Pagliacci: Intermezzo. Romance in A min.* GRIEG: *Pictures from life in the country: The bridal procession passes, Op. 19/2.* MAHLER: *Ich ging mit Lust durch einen grünen Wald. Lieder eines fahrenden Gesellen; Symphony No. 4: 4th movement.*
(M) ** Teldec/Warner 4509 95354-2 [id.].

We are convinced that the Welte Mignon system, whereby the player cuts a piano roll direct from the keyboard, can be uncannily accurate, and the best example of this early method of recording lies with Rachmaninov's recordings of his own repertoire. But here the results, if fascinating, are also very disappointing. With one exception, none of these composers seems able to project his own music and usually demonstrates clumsy technique. The exception is Edvard Grieg, and his fresh presentation of a simple country scene has remarkable presence and charm. The sound itself is very good, as the Welte Mignon playbacks were recorded in excellent stereo in 1969/70.

Crabb, James, and **Geir Draugsvoll** (accordions)

Début recital: STRAVINSKY: *Petrushka* (ballet; complete). MUSSORGSKY: *Pictures at an exhibition* (both arr. CRABB/DRAUGSVOLL).
(B) **(*) EMI Debut CDZ5 69705-2 [id.].

It seems impossible to believe that Stravinsky's brilliantly scored ballet, played on a pair of piano accordions, could sound remarkably like the orchestral version; but this phenomenal transcription brings all the colours of the Stravinskian palette vividly before the listener. Only the bold sound of unison horns and the bite of massed strings eludes these virtuosi, and they bring the ballet's drama and pathos fully to life. This is an extraordinary listening experience. Mussorsky's *Pictures from an exhibition* is equally ingenious but is far less consistently effective, for one's ear is used to bold brass sonorities and spectacle. *Catacombes* and the big finale do not really come off, although the grotesque *Baba-Yaga* certainly does, played with proper rhythmic venom; otherwise the most effective pictures are those in which we normally expect woodwind chattering: *Tuileries*, *Limoges* and the cheeping chicks. Nevertheless it's a good try, and the playing itself has astonishing bravura. Well worth sampling on EMI's bargain Debut label. The recording cannot be faulted.

Cziffra, György (piano)

Cziffra Edition, Volume 1: LISZT: *Piano sonata in B min.; Concert paraphrase of Mendelssohn's Wedding march from A Midsummer Night's Dream; Concert study No. 1: Waldesrauschen. Harmonies poétiques et religieuses: Funérailles. Etudes d'éxécution transcendante d'après Paganini: La Campanella; La Chasse*
(M) *(**) EMI CDM5 65250-2 [id.].

Cziffra plays with extraordinary virtuosity and temperament, but he can also be exasperatingly wilful and self-aware. There are moments of exquisite poetry but also a feeling of calculation, alternating with wild bursts of bravura. The two *Paganini studies* show him at his most spontaneously volatile. The Paris studio recordings, made over a period between 1958 and 1975, are variable, and often unflatteringly hard.

Cziffra Edition, Volume 4: DAQUIN: *Le coucou; L'hirondelle.* LULLY: *Gavotte & Rondeau.* RAMEAU: *Le rappel des oiseaux; Tambourin; L'Egyptien; La Poule; Dardanus: Rigaudon.* F. COUPERIN: *Les Papillons, Les Moissonneurs; Les Folies françaises ou les Dominos; Les Barricades mystérieuses; L'Anguille; La Bandoline; Les petits moulins à vent; Le Tic-toc ou les maillotins.* RAVEL: *Le tombeau de Couperin: Toccata. Sonatine; Jeux d'eau.*
(M) **(*) EMI CDM5 65253-2 [id.].

Cziffra liked to play seventeenth- and eighteenth-century keyboard music. Lully's *Gavotte and Rondo* and Rameau's *Tambourin* are most strongly characterized and *L'Egyptien* is quite as immediate as *La Poule*, which clucks very positively indeed. It is, however, the Couperin group which is the most successful of all, with the divisions of *Les Folies françaises ou les Dominos* full of charm and character, and *Les Moissonneurs* very rhythmic and positive. *L'Anguille* is delightful and in *Les petits moulins à vent* one can sense the gusting of the wind. *Le Tic-toc ou les maillotins* is hardly less engaging. The Ravel performances are of the very highest calibre, showing profound delicacy of feeling. The account of the *Sonata* is quite incandescent, abounding in character and colour; and *Jeux d'eau* glitters iridescently and is technically a *tour de force*. Recordings are forwardly balanced but reasonably faithful, again using the Paris Salle Wagram, mostly in 1980–81.

Cziffra Edition, Volume 5: MOZART: *Piano sonata No. 8 in A min., K.310.* BEETHOVEN: *Piano sonata No. 22 in F, Op. 54.* SCHUMANN: *Etudes symphoniques, Op. 13; Novelette in F sharp min., Op. 21.*
(M) **(*) EMI mono/stereo CDM5 65254-2 [id.].

In Mozart, Cziffra assumes a much less flamboyant keyboard personality. His playing is alive, precisely articulated and, with its own kind of reserve, quite stylish. Cziffra's choice of a Beethoven sonata is not an obvious one and his reading is strong and penetrating. The Schumann *Etudes symphoniques* open gravely, then the first variation sets off with an impulse which is never to flag throughout. This is playing of ready virtuosity and considerable variety from a keyboard lion whose impulsiveness bursts out in the bravura studies but which can be reined back poetically in an instant and hold the listener by its very poise. The *Novelette* is even more chimerical in its wide-ranging mood and dynamic. The recordings were made in the Salle Wagram, Paris, between 1957 (the Mozart is mono, and acoustically rather dead, although otherwise faithful) and 1968.

Cziffra Edition, Volume 6: Encores and Arrangements: BACH/BUSONI: *Chorales: Wachet auf, BWV 645; In dir ist Freude, BWV 615; Erschienen ist der herrliche Tag, BWV 629*. Domenico SCARLATTI: *Sonatas: in C, Kk 159; in A, Kk 113; in D, Kk 96*. François COUPERIN: *Les Moissonneurs*. LULLY: *Gavotte in D min*. RAMEAU: *Dardanus: Rigaudon*. MOZART: *Sonata, K.331: Alla turca*. MENDELSSOHN: *A Midsummer Night's Dream: Scherzo*. BIZET: *L'Arlésienne: Minuet* (both arr. RACHMANINOV). FRANCK: *Prélude, choral et fugue*. DEBUSSY: *La plus que lente*. DOHNANYI: *Capriccio, Op. 28*. KHACHATURIAN: *Gayaneh: Sabre dance* (arr. CZIFFRA).
(M) *** EMI CDM5 65255-2 [id.].

If you want a single disc to remember the sheer individuality and character of Cziffra's playing – and indeed his fabulous digital dexterity – this collection of encores and transcriptions is the one to go for. The opening Bach/Busoni arrangements are most impressive. *Wachet auf* is gentle yet very clear and positive, and the staccato articulation in the third (*Erschienen ist der herrliche Tag*), against which the chorale is purposefully projected, brings masterly pianism, as does the gracefully light presentation of the first of the three Scarlatti *Sonatas* (Kk 159) while the second (Kk 113) brings some astonishing runs. The Couperin, Lully and Rameau encores are also included in Volume 4, but here they have even more charm, while the famous Mozart *Alla turca* is bracingly clear, almost suggesting a fortepiano. Like the elaborate paraphrase of Bizet's engaging *Minuet* from *L'Arlésienne*, Rachmaninov's famous arrangement of the Mendelssohn *Scherzo* from *A Midsummer Night's Dream* is just a little mannered, and the César Franck *Prélude, chorale and fugue* is very romantic indeed, but Debussy's *La plus que lente* is appealingly rhapsodic. The Dohnányi *Capriccio* brings almost unbelievable, quicksilver brilliance, and the exhilarating *Sabre dance* is even more breathtaking in its glittering profusion of notes. The recordings cover two decades of Cziffra's performing career, the earliest in 1956, the last in 1975, and generally the sound is very believable and present.

Duo Reine Elisabeth (Wolfgang Manz and *Rolf Plagge)*

Russian music for two pianos: STRAVINSKY: *Petrushka*. SCRIABIN: *Romance in A min*. SHOSTAKOVICH: *Concertino, Op. 94*. RACHMANINOV: *6 Morceaux, Op. 11*.
(BB) *** Discover Dig. DICD 920150 [id.].

Petrushka has plenty of colour and a surprising degree of charm; the finale swings along infectiously. The melodically lavish, early Scriabin *Romance* then contrasts aptly with the wittily audacious Shostakovich *Concertino*, which has the temerity to open with an echo of the slow movement of Beethoven's *G major Piano concerto*. The six Rachmaninov *Morceaux* are strongly and colourfully characterized, and their diversity gives much pleasure. In short, Wolfgang Manz and Rolf Plagge create an impressive artistic symbiosis, playing with spontaneity as well as commanding impressive technical resource. Very good recording too – not too reverberant. A bargain.

Du Pré, Jacqueline (cello)

Early BBC recordings, Vol. 1 (with Stephen Kovacevich, Ernest Lush): BACH: (Unaccompanied) *Cello suites Nos. 1 in G; 2 in D min., BWV 1007/8*. BRITTEN: *Cello sonata in C, Op. 65; Scherzo; Marcia*. FALLA: *Suite populaire espagnole* (arr. MARECHAL).
(M) (***) EMI mono CDM7 63165-2.

Early BBC recordings, Vol. 2 (with Ernest Lush, (i) William Pleeth): BRAHMS: *Cello sonata No. 2 in F, Op. 99*. F. COUPERIN: (i) *13th Concert à 2 instruments* (*Les Goûts-réunis*). HANDEL: *Cello sonata in G min*. (arr. SLATTER).
(M) (***) EMI mono CDM7 63166-2.

These two discs gather together some of the radio performances which Jacqueline du Pré gave in her inspired teens. Her 1962 recordings of the first two Bach *Cello suites* may not be immaculate, but her impulsive vitality makes phrase after phrase at once totally individual and seemingly inevitable. In two movements from Britten's *Cello sonata in C*, with Stephen Kovacevich as her partner, the sheer wit is deliciously infectious, fruit of youthful exuberance in both players. The first of the two discs is completed by Falla's *Suite populaire espagnole*, with the cello matching any singer in expressive range and rhythmic flair. The second has fascinating Couperin duets played with her teacher, William Pleeth; the Handel *Sonata* is equally warm and giving. Best of all is the Brahms *Cello sonata No. 2*, recorded at the 1962 Edinburgh Festival.

Recital (with (i) Gerald Moore (piano); (ii) Roy Jesson (organ); (iii) Osian Ellis (harp); (iv) John Williams (guitar)): (i) PARADIS: *Sicilienne*. SCHUMANN: *3 Fantasy pieces, Op. 73*. MENDELSSOHN: *Song without words in D, Op. 109*. FAURE: *Elégie in C min., Op. 24*. BRUCH: *Kol nidrei, Op. 47*. (ii) BACH: *Adagio from BWV 564*. (iii) SAINT-SAENS: *The swan*. (iv) FALLA: *Suite populaire espagnole: Jota*.
*** EMI CDC5 55529-2 [id.] – DELIUS: *Cello concerto*. ***

This heart-warming recital collects together more recordings Jacqueline du Pré made in her teens for EMI, plus the beautiful performance of Fauré's *Elégie* she recorded in 1969 with Gerald Moore for his seventieth-birthday record. There have been few performances of *The Swan* to match this in natural unforced expressiveness (beautifully accompanied on the harp by Osian Ellis), and the other items all have one marvelling afresh at the maturity of so young a virtuoso. Excellent transfers.

Fergus-Thompson, Gordon (piano)

'Reverie': DEBUSSY: *Rêverie; Arabesque No. 1; Suite bergamasque: Clair de lune*. SCRIABIN: *Etude, Op. 42/4*. BACH: *Chorales: Wachet auf* (trans. Busoni); *Jesu, joy of man's desiring* (trans. Hess). GLINKA: *The Lark* (trans. Balakirev). GODOWSKY: *Alt Wien*. SAINT-SAENS: *The Swan* (arr. GODOWSKY). SCHUMANN: *Arabeske in C, Op. 18; Kinderszenen: Träumerei*. BRAHMS: *Intermezzo in A, Op. 118*. GRIEG: *Lyric pieces: Butterfly, Op. 43/1; Nocturne, Op. 54/4*. RAVEL: *Le tombeau de Couperin: Forlane. Pavane pour une infante défunte*.
(M) *** ASV Dig. CDWHL 2066.

This 76-minute recital fills a real need for a high-quality recital of piano music for the late evening, where the mood of reverie is sustained without blandness. Gordon Fergus-Thompson's performances are of high sensibility throughout, from the atmospheric opening Debussy items to the closing Ravel *Pavane*. Perhaps his Bach is a little studied but the rest is admirably paced, and the two favourite Grieg *Lyric pieces* are particularly fresh. Excellent recording.

Fernández, Eduardo (guitar)

'The World of the Spanish guitar'. ALBENIZ: *Sevilla; Tango; Asturias*. LLOBET: *6 Catalan folksongs*. GRANADOS: *Andaluza; Danza triste*. TARREGA: *Estudio brillante; 5 Preludes, Minuetto, 3 Mazurkas; Recuerdos de la Alhambra*. SEGOVIA: *Estudio sin luz; Neblina; Estudio*. TURINA: *Fandanguillo; Ráfaga*.
(M) *** Decca Dig 433 820-2; *433 820-4* [id.].

Fernández is most naturally recorded in the Henry Wood Hall. His programme is essentially an intimate one and centres on the highly rewarding music of Tárrega, although opening colourfully with items from Albéniz's *Suite española*. The Llobet group of *Folksongs*, and Segovia's hauntingly atmospheric *Neblina* ('Mist') make further highlights. Later there is bravura from Turina, notably the spectacular *Ráfaga* ('Gust of wind') but even here, though the playing is vibrant, there is no flashiness. With an hour of music and digital sound, this well-chosen programme is excellent value.

Fierens, Guillermo (guitar)

'Spanish guitar music': VILLA-LOBOS: *Preludes Nos. 1–3*. PONCE: *Preludio, Balletto & Giga*. CASTELNUOVO-TEDESCO: *Capriccio diabolico; Sonata*. ALBENIZ: *Asturias*. TURINA: *Fandanguillo*. SOR: *Introduction and allegro (Gran solo), Op. 14*.
(B) *** ASV Quicksilva Dig. CDQS 6190 [id.].

Argentinian-born Guillermo Fierens studied under Segovia and has won several international prizes, including a First at Rio de Janeiro's Villa-Lobos competition. He is thoroughly sympathetic to that composer's music, and he presents this whole programme brightly and sympathetically, with plenty of personality and character. His technique is commandingly immaculate, his rubato nicely judged. He is very personable in the lively Ponce triptych (pastiche pieces of some charm) and the attractively spontaneous *Sonata* by Castelnuovo-Tedesco, particularly the two engaging central movements, and he finds plenty of bravura for the same composer's *Capriccio diabolico*. (Although it hardly matches Paganini in diabolism, it still makes a strong impression.) The *Gran solo* of Sor is equally appealing, but the highlight of a well-balanced programme is a magically evocative account of the famous *Asturias* of Albéniz. The recording has a vivid presence without being on top of the listener. Excellent value on all counts.

Freeman-Attwood, Jonathan (trumpet), Iain Simcock (organ)

Sonatas for trumpet and organ: ALBINONI: *Sonatas in A, Op. 1/3 & Op. 6/11; in C.* FRESCOBALDI: *Canzona seconda detta la Bernardina; Canzona terza detta la Lucchesina.* FASCH: *Concerto in D for clarino.* MUFFAT: *Suite in F from Indissolubilis Amicitia.* VIVIANI: *Sonata No. 1 in C.* TELEMANN: *Concerto in C min.* MOURET: *Symphonies de Fanfares.*
*** Proudsound Dig. PROUCD 135 [id.].

The combination of trumpet and organ has recently become fashionable as a way of playing baroque music, and the present collection is justified by the sheer excellence of the trumpet playing and the appealing musicianship of Jonathan Freeman-Attwood, who essays a wide dynamic and expressive range. He is tastefully accompanied on the organ of Bromley Parish Church by Iain Simcock. The recording, too, is first class, well balanced and pleasingly set back so that the trumpet has a gleaming presence without overwhelming the listener. Virtually the entire programme consists of arrangements (and how effective are the two Frescobaldi *Canzonas*). One piece actually conceived for trumpet with 'organo o gravicembalo' is the five-movement *Sonata* of Viviani, a pleasingly simple work, while in the third movement (*Les Gendarmes*) from Muffat's engaging suite from *Indissolubilis Amicitia*, the trumpeter is required to stamp his foot vehemently to imitate pistol-shots. All the music here is agreeable, but this is strictly a record to be dipped into rather than played throughout: 66 minutes of trumpet and organ can be too much of a good thing.

Fretwork

'In nomine': 16th-century English music for viols: TALLIS: *In nomine a 4, Nos. 1 & 2; Solfaing song a 5; Fantasia a 5; In nomine a 4, No. 2; Libera nos, salva nos a 5.* TYE: *In nomine a 5 (Crye); In nomine a 5 (Trust).* CORNYSH: *Fa la sol a 3.* BALDWIN: *In nomine a 4.* BULL: *In nomine a 5.* BYRD: *In nomine a 4, No. 2. Fantasia a 3, No. 3.* TAVERNER: *In nomine; In nomine a 4.* PRESTON: *O lux beata Trinitas a 3.* JOHNSON: *In nomine a 4.* PARSONS: *In nomine a 5; Ut re mi fa sol la a 4.* FERRABOSCO: *In nomine a 5; Lute fantasia No. 5; Fantasia a 4.*
*** Amon Ra CD-SAR 29 [id.].

This was Fretwork's début CD. The collection is not so obviously of strong popular appeal as the later collection for Virgin but is nevertheless very rewarding and distinguished, and it includes the complete consort music of Thomas Tallis. The sound is naturally pleasing in a fairly rich acoustic and readers can be assured that there is no vinegar in the string-timbre here; indeed, the sound itself is quite lovely in its gentle, austere atmosphere.

'Heart's ease': HOLBORNE: *The Honiesuckle; Countess of Pembroke's paradise; The Fairie round.* BYRD: *Fantasia a 5 (Two in one); Fancy in C.* DOWLAND: *Mr Bucton, his galliard; Captaine Digorie Piper, his galliard; Lachrimae antiquae pavan; Mr Nicholas Gryffith, his galliard.* BULL: *Fantasia a 4.* FERRABOSCO: *In nomine a 5.* GIBBONS: *In nomine a 5; Fantasia a 4 for the great dooble base.* LAWES: *Airs for 2 division viols in C: Pavan of Alfonso; Almain of Alfonso. Consort sett a 5 in C: Fantasia; Pavan; Almain.*
*** Virgin Dig. VC7 59667-2 [CDC 59667].

An outstanding collection of viol consort music from the late Tudor and early Stuart periods; the playing is both stylish and vivacious, with a fine sense of the most suitable tempo for each piece. The more lyrical music is equally sensitive. This is a tuneful entertainment, not just for the specialist collector, and Fretwork convey their pleasure in all this music. The William Byrd *Fancy* (from *My Ladye Nevells Booke*) is played exuberantly on the organ by Paul Nicholson, to bring some contrast before the closing Lawes *Consort set*. The recording is agreeably warm, yet transparent too.

Galway, James (flute)

'The French recital' (with Christopher Riley, piano): FAURE: *Sonata, Op. 13.* WIDOR: *Suite for flute and piano, Op. 34.* DEBUSSY, arr. GALWAY: *Prélude à l'après-midi d'un faune; La plus que lente; Prélude: La fille aux cheveux de lin. Petite suite: En bateau.*
**(*) RCA Dig. O9026 68351-2 [id.].

Galway's silvery timbre is well suited to Fauré. He does not miss the work's simplicity of line, and he makes his own special colouring tell in the soaring *Andante*, while the Scherzo is deliciously vivacious, although here the resonant recording refuses to separate flute and piano completely. Fortunately Galway is sympathetically partnered by Christopher Riley, and they are very well balanced. Both play the tripping theme of the finale with an engaging insouciance. The surprise here is the Widor *Suite*, a wonderful quiz item – for who would guess that this was the composer of the Famous Organ '*Toccata*'? The delightful, flowing opening movement has much in common with Fauré (although it was written 23 years earlier), and the skippity-jig Scherzo is most winning. Then comes a lovely, innocuous, slightly sentimental (and very French) 'Romance' with a swirling cadenza before the winning reprise. The finale sets off gaily, then produces yet another pleasing lyrical idea, before giving the soloist plenty of opportunity for bravura roulades in its scintillating closing section. Most enjoyable and a real find.

But why, instead of offering another of the countless French flute sonatas readily available, did Galway choose to offer transcriptions? It can only be said that to offer the *Prélude à l'après-midi d'un faune* as a flute solo is almost unbelievably self-regarding. How can this artist think that after the introduction, which is his by rights, the sensuous allure of the glowing middle section for strings can sound anything but inadequate on flute and piano? The two-piano transcriptions are rather more effective and perfectly acceptable, but the lovely '*En bateau*' also needs to rock gently on orchestral waters.

Gendron, Maurice (cello)

'The early years (1960–67)' (with (i) Jean Françaix; (ii) Peter Gallion, piano): (i) SCHUBERT: *Arpeggione sonata, D.821.* BEETHOVEN: *Variations: on Mozart's 'Ein Mädchen', Op. 66; 'Bei Männern', WoO 46* (both from *Die Zauberflöte*); *Variations on Handel's 'See the conqu'ring hero comes' from Judas Maccabaeus, WoO 45.* DEBUSSY: *Sonata in D min.* FAURE: *Sonata No. 2 in D min., Op. 117.* FRANCAIX: *Berceuse; Rondino staccato; Nocturne; Sérénade* (all arr. GENDRON); *Mouvement perpétuel.* MESSIAEN: *Quatuor pour la fin du temps: Louange à l'éternité de Jésus.* (ii) POPPER: *Serenade, Op. 54/2.* HANDEL: *Xerxes: Largo* (arr. GENDRON). SAINT-SAENS: *Carnival of the animals: Le cygne.* SCHUMANN: *Kinderszenen: Träumerei.* RIMSKY-KORSAKOV: *Flight of the bumble bee.* PAGANINI: *Variations on a theme of Rossini* (*Moses fantasy*, arr. GENDRON). MOSZKOWSKI: *Guitare, Op. 45/2* (arr. GENDRON). KREISLER: *Liebesleid.* FALLA: *La vida breve: Spanish dance No. 1.* BACH: *Chorale: Ich ruf' zu dir, Herr Jesu Christ, BWV 639* (arr. GENDRON). CHOPIN: *Introduction and Polonaise brillante in C, Op. 3.* FITZENHAGEN: *Moto perpetuo* (arr. GENDRON). GRANADOS: *Andaluza, Op. 37/5.* DVORAK: *Humoresque, Op. 101/7.*
(M) *** Ph. 438 960-2 (3) [id.].

The elegant French cellist, Maurice Gendron, has always been well served by the Philips recording engineers who consistently catch his urbane, polished timbre in perfect focus. He does not readily wear his heart on his sleeve, yet while he shows himself a naturally debonair Schubertian in the *Arpeggione sonata* he can also rise with ardour to the expressive feeling of the Debussy and Fauré sonatas which are played with discerning eloquence. His slightly recessive solo personality is surely ideal for the engaging Françaix miniatures, and it is this composer himself who provides a remarkably sympathetic partnership for the diverse programme on the first two CDs – just sample the cultivated way the pair of them introduce Handel's fine melody in Beethoven's *Judas Maccabaeus variations*. The second CD ends with a characteristically intimate account of the famous cello soliloquy from Messiaen's *Quartet for the end of time*. The immaculately played lollipops on the third disc are given a slightly more forward balance. Yet perhaps one needs a more extrovert approach to some of these items. Rimsky's bumble bee buzzes comparatively gently and the neat bravura of Fitzenhagen's *Moto perpetuo* is a more suitable example of Gendron's virtuosity, though he readily demonstrates his easy command in the high tessitura of the Paganini variations, where his timbre is always sweet. Perhaps overall this collection is a rather lightweight representation of a great artist, but the polish of Gendron's playing is always a pleasure in itself.

Gilels, Emil (piano)

MEDTNER: *Sonata reminiscenza, Op. 38.* PROKOFIEV: *Sonata No. 3 in A min., Op. 28.* SCRIABIN: *Sonata No. 4 in F sharp, Op. 30.* STRAVINSKY: *Petrushka suite* (arr Gilels). VAINBERG: *Sonata No. 4 in B min.*
*** Russian Disc. MK 417702.

This is piano playing in a class of its own. It communicates that special authority which only great pianists have, together with that sense of dash and élan given to very few. The recordings, made in the Grand Hall of the Moscow Conservatory in 1957 and (in the case of the Medtner) 1968, are emphatically not three-star but the artistry of this playing transcends all sonic limitations, and the *Petrushka*, one of his most celebrated performances, has a dazzling brilliance and extraordinary powers of characterization. Any very occasional slip is more musical than many a dry virtuoso's right notes.

Grumiaux, Arthur (violin), Riccdardo Castagnone (piano)

'The early years': DEBUSSY: *Sonata in G min.* LEKEU: *Sonata in G.* SCHUBERT: *3 Sonatinas; Duo sonata in A.* KREISLER: *Liebesleid; Liebesfreud; Schön Rosmarin; Caprice viennois; Tambourin chinoise.* TARTINI: *Sonata in G min. (Devil's trill), Op. 1/4.* CORELLI: *Sonata in D min., Op. 5/12.* VITALI: *Ciaccona.* VERACINI: *Sonata in A, Op. 1/7.* PAGANINI: *I Palpiti, Op. 13; La Treghe, Op. 8.*
(M) *** Ph. 438 516-2 (3) [id.].

Here are three CDs of beautifully natural and unaffected music-making. The Debussy and Lekeu sonatas occupy the first CD and come from 1956, as does the Tartini *Devil's Trill sonata* and its companions. The Schubert *Sonatinas* and *Duo* were made two years later but the sound is amazingly fresh. These performances have an aristocratic finesse that will delight all connoisseurs of violin playing. Not to be missed.

Grumiaux, Arthur (violin), István Hajdu (piano)

'Favourite violin encores': PARADIS: *Sicilienne.* MOZART: *Rondo, K.250; Divertimento in D, K.334: Minuet.* GLUCK: *Mélodie.* GRANADOS: *Danza española No. 5.* KREISLER: *Schön Rosmarin; Liebesleid; Liebesfreud; Rondino on a theme of Beethoven; Andantino in the style of Padre Martini.* VERACINI: *Allegro; Largo* (arr. CORTI). VIVALDI: *Siciliano* (arr. from *Op. 3/11*). LECLAIR: *Tambourin.* BEETHOVEN: *Minuet in G.* SCHUBERT: *Ave Maria; Ständchen.* DVORAK: *Humoresque in G flat, Op. 101/7; Songs my mother taught me, Op. 55/4; Sonatine in G, Op. 100: Larghetto.* MASSENET: *Thaïs: Méditation.* TCHAIKOVSKY: *Valse sentimentale, Op. 51/6.* ELGAR: *La Capricieuse.* FAURE: *Après un rêve, Op. 7/1; Les berceaux, Op. 23/1.* ALBENIZ: *Tango, Op. 165/2.* PONCE: *Estrellita.* SIBELIUS: *Nocturne, Op. 51/3.* PERGOLESI: *Andantino.* SCHUMANN: *Kinderszenen: Träumerei.* BACH/GOUNOD: *Ave Maria.* PAGANINI: *Sonata No. 12 in E min., Op. 3/6.* WIENIAWSKI: *Souvenir de Moscou, Op. 6.* RAVEL: *Pièce en forme de habanera; Tzigane.* SARASATE: *Zigeunerweisen, Op. 20/1.* FIOCCO: *Allegro.* BLOCH: *Baal Shem: Nigun.* KODALY: *Adagio.*
(B) *** Ph. Duo 446 560-2 (2).

Marvellous fiddler as he is, Grumiaux is not an extrovert in the manner of a Perlman who likes to dazzle and be right on top of the microphones; instead, these are essentially intimate performances. Yet when fire is needed it is certainly forthcoming, as in the superb account of Ravel's *Tzigane*. But Grumiaux is completely at home in what are mostly elegant *morceaux de concert*, and especially the Kreisler encores. He brings a particularly nice touch of rubato to *Schön Rosmarin* and produces a ravishingly stylish *Liebesleid*, while the *Andantino in the style of Martini* is engagingly ingenuous. Schumann's *Träumerei* is made to sound as if originally conceived as a violin solo. The *Méditation* from *Thaïs* is delectably romantic without being oversweet, and the following *Valse sentimentale* of Tchaikovsky has just the right degree of restraint. But Grumiaux's simplicity of style is heard at its most appealing in Wieniawski's *Souvenir de Moscou*, with its warm melody elegantly decorated and then let loose in a burst of Paganinian fireworks. István Hajdu accompanies with comparable taste, notably in Bach's unwitting contribution to Gounod's *Ave Maria*, while his simple introduction to Elgar's *La Capricieuse* is a model of how to set the scene for a salon piece of this kind. He is equally helpful in echoing Grumiaux in Schubert's lovely *Serenade* and in his discreet backing for Ponce's gently voluptuous *Estrellita*. The recording is most natural, without any edginess on the violin-tone, and the piano is pleasingly balanced within a warm acoustic.

Hall, Nicola (guitar)

'The art of the guitar': WALTON: *5 Bagatelles.* BACH: (Unaccompanied) *Violin sonata No. 2 in A min., BWV 1003* (arr. HALL). TORROBA: *Sonatina.* RODRIGO: *Invocación y danza (Hommage à Manuel de Falla).* MERTZ: *Hungarian fantasy, Op. 65/1.*
**(*) Decca Dig. 440 678-2 [id.].

Nicola Hall, a pupil of John Williams, gives an astonishing display of her virtually flawless technique in a well-chosen programme in which the highlight is the set of *Five Bagatelles* of Walton, played with warmth, some subtlety and considerable panache. She is disappointing in her Bach transcription, however, far too literal and studied: the third-movement *Andante* plods along heavily. But the Torroba *Sonatina* sparkles with Spanish sunshine and the opening of the Rodrigo *Invocación* is quite haunting. The Mertz *Hungarian fantasia*, not in itself an especially inspired piece, brings a chance for glittering virtuosity and a very exciting coda. The recording has a vivid yet natural presence and enough – but not too much – resonance, so that the guitar sounds real and life-sized.

Haskil, Clara (piano)

Clara Haskil: The Legacy: Volume 1: Chamber music (with Arthur Grumiaux): BEETHOVEN: *Violin sonatas Nos. 1–10*. MOZART: *Violin sonatas Nos. 18; 21; 24; 26; 32; 34*.
(M) (***) Ph. mono 442 625-2 (5) [id.].

Volume 3: Solo piano music: BEETHOVEN: *Sonatas Nos. 17 in D min. (Tempest), Op. 31/2; 18 in E flat Op. 31/3* (two versions). MOZART: *Sonata in C, K.330; 9 Variations on a minuet by Jean-Pierre Duport, K.573*. RAVEL: *Sonatine*. Domenico SCARLATTI: *Sonatas in E flat, Kk.193; B min., Kk.87; F min., Kk.386*. SCHUBERT: *Sonata No. 21 in B flat, D.960*. SCHUMANN: *Abegg variations, Op. 1; Bunte Blätter, Op. 99; Kinderszenen, Op. 15; Waldszenen, Op. 82*.
(M) **(*) Ph. mono/stereo 442 635-2 (3) [id.].

Clara Haskil is a much-venerated pianist, as the very appearance of this 12-CD set shows. Each of the three volumes is available separately but single discs from the collection are not. The first volume (five CDs) is devoted to the Beethoven and Mozart sonatas with her long-standing partner, Arthur Grumiaux; the second (see above), of four CDs, is devoted to her various concerto recordings, including two of the Mozart *D minor*, K.466, one with the Wiener Symfoniker and Paul Sacher in mono (1954), the second with the Lamoureux Orchestra and Markevitch (1960); the third volume (three CDs) collects her solo repertoire, including two different accounts of the Beethoven sonatas (1955 and 1960).

The earliest recordings, the three Scarlatti sonatas, Ravel's *Sonatine* and the Schumann *Abegg variations* and the *Piano concerto in A minor* (with Willem van Otterloo conducting the Hague Orchestra) come from 1951, and the last, the Mozart *Piano concertos in D minor*, K.466, and *C minor*, K.491, and the Beethoven *C minor concerto*, from 1960, the year of her death. Although it is doubtless a truism, her playing is more private than public; hers is a reflective, inward-looking sensibility with nothing of the virtuoso or showman. Her musical dedication is total. Her Schumann is particularly searching and penetrating. And there is an innocence about her Mozart which makes it wonderfully fresh and immediate.

Perhaps part of the success of her partnership with Arthur Grumiaux in the cycle of Beethoven and Mozart sonatas may spring from the understanding she gained of the violin as well as the experience of her earlier partnerships with Enescu, Szigeti and Francescatti. Philips are reticent in disclosing whether they are mono or stereo: they are in fact mono. Notwithstanding, the sound is very pleasing indeed and the playing is beautifully natural yet innately aristocratic.

The solo recordings are equally self-recommending and her Schumann in particular is of exceptional insight. The set is accompanied by very perceptive notes by Max Harrison.

Hill-Wiltschinsky Guitar Duo

Recital: D. SCARLATTI: *Sonata, Kk 141*. SOR: *Fantaisie, Op. 54*. ANON.: *Jota*. HILL: *Rondo for 2 guitars; Canzone*. arr. *The lark in the morning*. MENDELSSOHN: *Song without words, Op. 19/1*. DOWLAND: *2 Elizabethan lute duets: Le rossignol; My Lord Chamberlaine, his galliard*. WILTSCHINSKY: *Nocturne*. PETIT: *Toccata*. KOMPTER: *Milan suite*. CASTELNUOVO-TEDESCO: *Prelude and fugue in F sharp min*. GIULIANI: *Variazioni concertanti, Op. 130*. FAMPAS: *Fantasie*. FALLA: *Three-cornered hat: Ritual fire dance*.
(M) *** Carlton IMP Dig. 30367 00612 [id.].

Here is an attractively intimate, late-evening recital of music for guitar duo that could too easily be passed by. The only item which does not suit the laid-back evening mood of this well-matched pair (Robin Hill and Peter Wiltschinsky) is the vibrant *Ritual fire dance* of Manuel de Falla, which is far more electrifying in Bream's solo performance. But this still leaves an enticing hour-long programme in which every number has a distinct appeal. The Sor 'Introduction, theme and variations' which make up his *Fantaisie*, Op. 54 (wrongly attributed here to Scarlatti) and the equally agreeable Giuliani *Variazioni concertante* are well matched by Hill's own *Rondo*, and his *Canzone* is charming, as is his colleague's *Nocturne*. The Mendelssohn *Song without words* flows winningly and the novelties by Petit and Fampas are very striking. Then the amateur Jan Marten Kompter (the managing director of a Dutch chemical firm) provides four beguiling pastiches which look backward in time. The playing is spontaneously immaculate, and the duo is beautifully recorded.

Horowitz, Vladimir (piano)

'Encores': BIZET/HOROWITZ: *Variations on a theme from Carmen*. SAINT-SAENS/LISZT/HOROWITZ: *Danse macabre*. MOZART: *Sonata No. 11, K.331: Rondo alla turca*. MENDELSSOHN/LISZT/HOROWITZ: *Wedding march and variations*. MENDELSSOHN: *Elégie, Op. 85/4; Spring song, Op. 62/6; The shepherd's complaint, Op. 67/5; Scherzo a capriccio: Presto*. DEBUSSY: *Children's corner: Serenade of a doll*. MOSZKOWSKI: *Etudes, Op. 72/6 & 11; Etincelles, Op. 36/6*. CHOPIN: *Polonaise in A flat, Op. 53*. SCHUMANN: *Kinderszenen: Träumerei*. LISZT: *Hungarian rhapsody No. 15; Valse oubliée No. 1*. RACHMANINOV: *Prelude in G min., Op. 23/5*. SOUSA/HOROWITZ: *The Stars and Stripes forever*.
(M) (***) BMG/RCA mono GD 87755 [7755-2-RG].

These encore pieces have been around for some time and, apart from the Rachmaninov *Prelude* and the Mendelssohn, derive from the days of the 78-r.p.m. record and the mono LP. Allowances have to be made for the quality which, as one would expect in this kind of compilation, is variable. So in its different way is the playing, which varies from dazzling to stunning!

Hurford, Peter (organ)

'Organ favourites': Sydney Opera House organ: BACH: *Toccata and fugue in D min., BWV 565; Jesu, joy of man's desiring*. ALBINONI: *Adagio* (arr. GIAZOTTO). PURCELL: *Trumpet tune in D*. MENDELSSOHN: *A Midsummer Night's Dream: Wedding march*. FRANCK: *Chorale No. 2 in B min*. MURRILL: *Carillon*. WALFORD DAVIES: *Solemn melody*. WIDOR: *Organ symphony No. 5: Toccata*. Royal Festival Hall organ: FRANCK: *Pièce héroïque*. Ratzeburg Cathedral organ: BOELLMANN: *Suite gothique*.
(B) **(*) Decca Eclipse Dig. 452 166-2; *452 166-4* [id.].

Superb sound here, wonderfully free and never oppressive, even in the most spectacular moments. The Widor is spiritedly genial when played within the somewhat mellower registration of the magnificent Sydney instrument (as contrasted with the Ratzeburg Cathedral organ), and the pedals have great sonority and power. The Murrill *Carillon* is equally engaging alongside the Purcell *Trumpet tune*, while Mendelssohn's wedding music has never sounded more resplendent. The Bach is less memorable, and the Albinoni *Adagio*, without the strings, is not an asset to the collection either. The *Pièce héroïque* and the *Suite gothique* have been added for the Eclipse reissue.

Isoir, André (Koenig organ at Bon Pasteur, Angers)

French Renaissance organ music: Bransles; Galliards and other dances by GERVAIS; FRANCISQUE; ATTAIGNANT. JANEQUIN: *Allez my fault*. SANDRIN: *Quand ien congneu*. Eustache du CAURROY: *Fantaisie sur une jeune fillette*. ATTAIGNANT: *3 Versets du Te Deum; Prélude aux treize motets; Kyrie cunctipotens. Fantaisies* by GUILLET; LE JEUNE; RACQUET. RICHARD: *Prélude in D min*. THOMELIN: *Duo*. LA BARRE: *Sarabande*. Henri du MONT: *Prélude No. 10 in D min.; Pavane in D min*. ANON.: *Fantaisie; Ave Maris Stella*. ROBERDAY: *Fugue et caprice No. 3 in C; Fugues Nos. 10 in G min.; 12 in D*.
(M) *** Cal. CAL 6901 [id.].

The Angers organ has a spicy régale stop which is used tellingly in several of the dance movements included in the programme, notably Gervaise's *Bransle de Bourgogne* and a *Basse dance*, *Bransle* and *Gaillarde* of Attaignant and also in Sandrin's *Quand ien congneu*. A warmer palette is found for Eustache du Caurroy's agreeable *Fantaisie sur une jeune fillette*. This is a French equivalent to the divisions found in Elizabethan music, whereas the piquant *Fantaisie sur orgue ou espinette* of Guillaume Costeley is very succinct. Attaignant's *Kyrie cunctipotens* and the *Third Fantaisie* of Charles Guillet are essentially chorale preludes, as is the more elaborate *Fantaisie* of Charles Racquet, but the *Second Fantaisie* of Claude le Jeune, a remarkable piece, anticipates the chorale variations of Bach, but using two different fugal subjects. Joseph Thomelin's (two-part) *Duo* is a winning miniature and Joseph de la Barre's *Sarabande* also has a gentle charm, while the three *Fugues* of François Roberday show impressive craftsmanship. No. 12, which ends the recital resplendently, is a good example of Isoir's imaginative registrations, which find ear-tickling contrasts between the plangent and mellow timbres that this organ offers, while the music is kept very much alive. A generous (76 minutes) and stimulating recital, although not to be played all at one sitting.

(i) Jackson, Francis (organ of York Minster); (ii) Michael Austin (organ of Birmingham Town Hall)

'Pipes of splendour': (i) COCKER: *Tuba tune*. PURCELL: *Trumpet tune and almand*. JACKSON: *Division on 'Nun Danket'*. LEIGHTON: *Paean*. DUBOIS: *Toccata in G*. GUILMANT: *Allegretto in B min., Op. 19*. GIGOUT: *Scherzo in E*. MULET: *Carillon-Sortie*. (ii) REGER: *Toccata and fugue in D min./major, Op. 59/5–6*. DUPRE: *Prelude and fugue in B, Op. 7*. FRANCK: *Final in B flat*.
(M) *** Chandos CHAN 6602 [id.].

It was Francis Jackson who made Cocker's *Tuba tune* (with its boisterous, brassy, principal tune) justly famous, and it makes a splendid opener. But the entire programme shows that it is possible to play and record an English organ without the result sounding flabby. The *Toccata* of Dubois is very winning and, in its quieter central section, detail is beautifully clear, as it is in the charming Guilmant *Allegretto* and the lightly articulated Gigout *Scherzo*. Mulet's *Carillon-Sortie* rings out gloriously and Leighton's *Paean* brings a blaze of tone. The items played in Birmingham by Michael Austin are no less stimulating, especially the two French pieces which have a fine piquant bite, while the Reger isn't in the least dull. Superb transfers of demonstration-standard analogue recording from the early 1970s.

John, Keith (organ)

'Great European organs No. 10': Tonhalle, Zurich: MUSSORGSKY (trans. John): *Pictures at an exhibition*. ALAIN: *3 Danses (Joies; Deuils; Luttes)*.
*** Priory Dig. PRCD 262 [id.].

Keith John has made his own transcription of Mussorgsky's *Pictures* – and pretty remarkable it sounds. Only the pieces like *Tuileries* that require pointed articulation come off less well than on orchestra or piano, but *Gnomus* and *Bydlo* and, especially, the picture of the two Polish Jews are all remarkably powerful, while the closing sequence of *Catacombs*, *The Hut on fowl's legs* and *The Great gate of Kiev* are superb. The three Alain pieces make a substantial encore. This is as much a demonstration CD as an orchestral version of the Mussorgsky.

'Great European organs No. 26': Gloucester Cathedral: STANFORD: *Fantasia and toccata in D min., Op. 57*. REGER: *Prelude and fugue in E, Op. 56/1*. SHOSTAKOVICH: *Lady Macbeth of Mtsensk: Passacaglia*. SCHMIDT: *Chaconne in C min*. RAVANELLO: *Theme and variations in B min*.
*** Priory Dig. PRCD 370 [id.].

Keith John, having shown what he can do with Mussorgsky, turns his attention here to little-known nineteenth- and twentieth-century organ pieces. The programme is imaginatively chosen and splendidly played – indeed the bravura is often thrilling – and most realistically recorded on the superb Gloucester organ. Both the Schmidt *Chaconne* and Ravanello *Theme and variations* are fine works, and the Shostakovich *Passacaglia*, an opera entr'acte, was originally conceived as a work for organ.

Organ of St Mary's, Woodford: *'Toccata!'*: BACH/BUSONI: *Partita No. 2 in D min., BWV 1004: Chaconne* (trans. K. John). BACH/RACHMANINOV: *Partita No. 3 in E, BWV 1006: suite* (trans. K. John). GUILLOU: *Sinfonietta*. HEILLER: *Tanz-Toccata*.
(M) *** Priory Dig. PRCD 002 [id.].

It was a most imaginative idea to use Busoni's arrangement of Bach's famous *D minor Partita for unaccompanied violin* as a basis for an organ transcription, and the result is like nothing you have ever heard before – especially when Keith John gets cracking on the pedals. The three excerpts from the *E major Partita* (as originally transcribed by Rachmaninov) are hardly less successful: how well the opening *Prelude* sounds on the organ, and one can forgive Keith John's affectionately mannered touch on the famous *Gavotte*. We then have a dramatic, almost bizarre change of mood and colour from Jean Guillou's 'neoclassical' (more 'neo' than 'classical') *Sinfonietta*. Even though it opens with a Bachian flourish, its colouring and atmosphere are highly exotic, the austere central *Allegretto* leading to a somewhat jazzy but naggingly insistent, partly contrapuntal and plangent *Gigue*. Heiller's *Tanz-Toccata*, with its complex rhythms and chimerical changes of time-signature, finally brings a positive link with Stravinsky's *Rite of spring* during the insistent motoric final pages. After his remarkable Bach performances, Keith John's kaleidoscopic registration here shows how adaptable and versatile is the modern (1972) organ at St Mary's, Woodford.

Johnson, Emma (clarinet)

'A clarinet celebration' (with Gordon Back, piano): WEBER: *Grand duo concertante; Variations concertantes.* BURGMULLER: *Duo.* GIAMPIERI: *Carnival of Venice.* SCHUMANN: *Fantasy pieces, Op. 73.* LOVREGLIO: *Fantasia de concerto, La Traviata.*
*** ASV Dig. CDDCA 732 [id.].

ASV have reissued and repackaged Emma Johnson's outstanding 72-minute collection, dating from 1990. It is still at full price but is worth it. These are party pieces rather than encores, all of them drawing electric sparks of inspiration from this winning young soloist. Even in such virtuoso nonsense as the Giampieri *Carnival of Venice* and the Lovreglio *Fantasia* Johnson draws out musical magic, while the expressiveness of Weber and Schumann brings heartfelt playing, with phrasing creatively individual. Gordon Back accompanies brilliantly, and the sound is first rate.

'British clarinet music' (with Malcolm Martineau (piano); (i) Judith Howard (soprano)): IRELAND: *Fantasy sonata in E flat.* VAUGHAN WILLIAMS: *6 Studies in English folk song;* (i) *3 Vocalises for soprano voice and clarinet.* BAX: *Clarinet sonata.* BLISS: *Pastoral;* (i) *2 Nursery rhymes.* STANFORD: *Clarinet sonata.*
*** ASV Dig. CDDCA 891 [id.].

Stanford's *Sonata* has the usual Brahmsian flavour but uses an Irish lament for the expressive central *Adagio*; then the finale has the best of both worlds by combining both influences. Vaughan Williams's *Six Studies in English folk song* (1927) are beguilingly evocative, while the *Vocalises* for soprano voice and clarinet are brief but rather touching; they were written in the last year of the composer's life. Both the Bax two-movement *Sonata* and the Ireland *Fantasy Sonata* are fine works, and Bliss's *Pastoral* is wartime nostalgia written while the composer was in France during World War One. Needless to say, Emma Johnson plays everything with her usual spontaneity and musicianship, and she has a fine partner in Malcolm Martineau, while Judith Howard's contribution is pleasingly melismatic. Excellent, atmospheric recording, made in the London Henry Wood Hall.

Kang, Dong-Suk (violin), **Pascal Devoyon** (piano)

French violin sonatas: DEBUSSY: *Sonata in G min.* RAVEL: *Sonata in G.* POULENC: *Violin sonata.* SAINT-SAENS: *Sonata No. 1 in D min.*
(BB) *** Naxos Dig. 8.550276; *4550276* [id.].

One of the jewels of the Naxos catalogue, this collection of four of the finest violin sonatas in the French repertoire is self-recommending. The stylistic range of this partnership is evident throughout: they seem equally attuned to all four composers. This is warm, freshly spontaneous playing, given vivid and realistic digital recording in a spacious acoustic. A very real bargain.

Kayath, Marcelo (guitar)

'Guitar classics from Latin America': PONCE: *Valse.* PIAZZOLA: *La muerte del angel.* BARRIOS: *Vals, Op. 8/3; Choro de saudade; Julia florida.* LAURO: *Vals venezolanos No. 2; El negrito; El marabino.* BROUWER: *Canción de cuna; Ojos brujos.* PERNAMBUCO: *Sons de carrilhões; Interrogando; Sono de maghia.* REIS: *Si ela perguntar.* VILLA-LOBOS: *5 Preludes.*
(B) *** Carlton Dig. PCD 2012 [id.].

Marcelo Kayath's inspirational accounts of the Villa-Lobos *Preludes* can stand comparison with the finest performances on record. He plays everything here with consummate technical ease and the most appealing spontaneity. His rubato in the Barrios *Vals* is particularly effective, and he is a fine advocate too of the engaging Lauro pieces and the picaresque writing of João Pernambuco, a friend of Villa-Lobos. The recording, made in a warm but not too resonant acoustic, is first class.

'Guitar classics from Spain': TARREGA: *Prelude in A min.; Capricho arabe; Recuerdos de la Alhambra.* GRANADOS: *La Maja de Goya.* ALBENIZ: *Granada; Zambra; Grandina; Sevilla; Mallorca.* TORROBA: *Prelude in E; Sonatina; Nocturno.* RODRIGO: *Zapateado.* TRAD.: *El Noy de la mare.*
(B) *** Carlton IMP Dig. PCD 2037 [id.].

Following the success of his first, Latin-American recital, Marcelo Kayath gives us an equally enjoyable Spanish collection, full of colour and spontaneity. By grouping music by several major composers, he provides a particularly revealing mix. The two opening Tarrega pieces are predominantly lyrical, to bring an effective contrast with the famous fluttering *Recuerdos de la Alhambra*, played strongly. Then after the

Granados come five of Albéniz's most colourful and tuneful geographical evocations, while the Torroba group includes the *Sonatina*, a splendid piece. After Rodrigo he closes with the hauntingly memorable *El Noy de la mare*. There is over an hour of music and the recording has a most realistic presence; but take care not to set the volume level too high.

King, Thea (clarinet), Britten Quartet

Clarinet music: HOWELLS: *Rhapsodic quintet*. COOKE: *Clarinet quintet*. MACONCHY: *Clarinet quintet*. FRANKEL: *Clarinet quintet, Op. 28*. HOLBROOKE: *Eilean shona*.
*** Hyperion Dig. CDA 66428 [id.].

Five strongly characterized works for clarinet quintet by British composers make up a most attractive disc, beautifully played by Thea King and the outstanding Britten Quartet. The masterpiece which sets the pattern for the sequence is the beautiful *Rhapsodic quintet* of Howells, one of the finest of his early works, dating from 1917. The Holbrooke rounds the group off, a brief, song-like soliloquy for clarinet and strings inspired by a Celtic story. The recording is clear and forward with a fine bloom on all the instruments.

Kissin, Evgeni (piano)

'Carnegie Hall Début' (30 September 1990) *Highlights*: LISZT: *Etude d'exécution transcendante No. 10; Liebestraum No. 3; Rhapsodie espagnole*. SCHUMANN: *Abegg Variations, Op. 1; Etudes symphoniques, Op. 13; Widmung* (arr. LISZT).
*** BMG/RCA Dig. 09026 61202-2 [61202-2].

Evgeni Kissin has phenomenal pianistic powers; not only is this a *tour de force* in terms of technical prowess but also in sheer artistry. Both sets of Schumann *Variations* are remarkable. The Liszt *Rhapsodie espagnole* is played with superb bravura. Kissin's range of colour and keyboard command throughout is dazzling. The Carnegie Hall was packed and the recording balance, while a bit close, is perfectly acceptable. The excitement of the occasion is conveyed vividly.

'In Tokyo' (12 May 1987): CHOPIN: *Nocturne in A flat, Op. 32/2; Polonaise in F sharp min., Op. 44*. LISZT: *Concert studies Nos. 1 in D flat (Waldesrauschen); 2 in F min. (La Leggierezza)*. PROKOFIEV: *Sonata No. 6 in A, Op. 82*. RACHMANINOV: *Etudes tableaux, Op. 39/1 & 5; Lilacs*. SCRIABIN: *Etude in C sharp min., Op. 42/5; Mazurka in E min., Op. 25/3*.
*** Sony Dig. SK 45931 [id.].

Kissin was only fifteen at the time of his Tokyo début, but he sounds fully mature throughout this recital. He plays Prokofiev's *Sixth Sonata* for all it is worth with no holds barred, and the effect is altogether electrifying – one finds oneself on the edge of one's chair. He is no less at home in the Rachmaninov *Etudes tableaux* and the Liszt *La Leggierezza*, which he delivers with marvellous assurance and poetic feeling. His Scriabin, too, is pretty impressive. The microphone placing is too close – but no matter, this is breathtaking piano playing.

Klien, Walter and Beatriz (piano duo)

MILHAUD: *Scaramouche, Op. 165*. CHABRIER: *Cortège Burlesque; Souvenirs de Munich; 3 Valses Romantiques*. FAURE: *Dolly Suite, Op. 56*. RAVEL: *Ma Mère L'Oye*. BRAHMS: *16 Waltzes, Op. 39*.
(B) *** Carlton/Turnabout 30371 00142.

An irresistible collection of French piano-duet music with the delightful Brahms *Waltzes* thrown in for good measure, taken from an earlier LP. Mr and Mrs Walter Klien give *Scaramouche* a buoyant, brilliant performance that ultimately gains from the pianists' refusal to jazz the rhythms up too freely. The lilt is just enough and no more; similarly in Fauré's charming *Dolly suite* the degree of restraint puts the music in scale without sentimentality. In the Ravel one hardly misses the orchestral tones one is used to, and the extrovert gem of the collection comes among the Chabrier items, when (outrageously) the composer uses themes from *Tristan* for a quadrille – so outrageously that even Wagner is said to have laughed at it. The new timing is 78 minutes and, even with recordings of different vintages, the sound on CD is acceptably consistent and certainly it never detracts from the sparkling playing.

Kynaston, Nicholas (organ)

'Great organ music' (played on organ of (i) Clifton Cathedral; (ii) Royal Albert Hall): (i) J. S. BACH: *Fantasia and fugue in G min., BWV 542; Fugue in G (Alla gigue), BWV 577; Prelude and fugue in B min, BWV 544; Toccata and fugue in F, BWV 540; Concerto No. 2 in A min., BWV 593* (after Vivaldi); (ii) *Toccata and fugue in D min., BWV 565.* SCHUMANN: *Canon in B min., Op. 56/5.* MENDELSSOHN (arr. BEST): *Athalie: War march of the priests.* SAINT-SAENS: *Fantasie in E flat; Fantasie II in D flat, Op. 101.* GIGOUT: *Grand choeur dialogue; Toccata in B min.* WIDOR: *Symphonies: Nos. 1 in C min., Op. 13/1: Marche pontificale. 4 in F min., Op. 13/4: Andante cantabile. 5 in F min., Op. 42/1: Toccata. 6 in C min, Op. 42/2: Allegro. 9 in C min. (Gothique), Op. 70: Andante sostenuto.* BONNET: *Etude de concert.* MULET: *Carillon-sortie.*
(BB) **(*) CfP Silver Double CDCFPSD 4760 (2).

Nicholas Kynaston's recital (drawing on three LPs, recorded between 1970 and 1975) uses two organs. The opening *Toccata and fugue in D minor* is played on the Royal Albert Hall organ, with its resonant sonority and wide dynamic range effectively demonstrated but not exaggerated. The change of timbre with the second Bach piece, the *Fantasia and fugue in G minor*, is disconcerting, for this, like the rest of the Bach items, is played on the organ of Clifton Cathedral, beautifully recorded with clean, brilliant treble and a clear yet ample bass response sounding very like a baroque organ. Kynaston's performance is buoyant, as is the lively *Fugue à la gigue* (which may not be authentic but is most enjoyable when registered so piquantly). The other works are more considered and didactic, while in the attractively registered Vivaldi transcription (derived from the eighth concerto in *L'Estro armonico*) the central *Adagio* is rather subdued. Using the Royal Albert Hall organ for the French repertoire is perhaps more controversial but the two Gigout pieces are very colourful and effective, and the movements from the Widor symphonies come off well too, with the grandiose opening of the *Allegro* of the *Sixth Symphony* matched by the climaxes of the *Marche pontificale* of the *First*, while the swirling figurations of famous *Toccata* from the *Fifth* are balanced by the massive effects from the pedals. In the Saint-Saëns and Liszt pieces, the exaggeratedly wide dynamic contrasts characteristic of this instrument are at the very heart of Kynaston's interpretations, and some might find the gentler music seems too recessed. But overall this is an impressive achievement.

Labèque, Katia and Marielle (piano duo)

'Encore!': Adolfo BERIO: *Polka; Maria Isabella (Waltz); La Primavera (Mazurka).* BACH: *Jesu, joy of man's desiring* (arr. HESS). GERSHWIN: *Preludes Nos. 1–3; Promenade (Walking the dog).* STRAVINSKY: *Tango; Waltz.* Luciano BERIO: *Wasserklavier.* BRAHMS: *Waltz in A flat.* TCHAIKOVSKY: *The Seasons: June.* BERNSTEIN: *West Side story: Jet song; America.* JOPLIN: *Bethena (Ragtime waltz); The Entertainer.* JAELL: *Valse.* BARTOK: *New Hungarian folksong.* SCHUMANN: *Abendlied.*
*** Sony Dig. SK 48381 [id.].

The Labèque sisters have never made a better record than this, and the playing scintillates, especially the Bernstein and Stravinsky items, while the Labèques' Scott Joplin is admirably cool and the account of Myra Hess's arrangement of the famous Bach *Chorale* is gentle and quite beautiful. Luciano Berio's evocative *Wasserklavier* is a real lollipop, but the surprise is the selection of four catchy and often boisterous pieces by his grandfather, Adolfo, a church organist 'of doubtful faith' (according to his grandson); Luciano gives his imprimatur to the lively Labèque performances, even while he feels that their 'modern and uninhibited pianism' might not have suited his more conventional grandfather.

LaSalle Quartet

Chamber music of the Second Viennese School: BERG: *Lyric suite; String quartet, Op. 3.* SCHOENBERG: *String quartets: in D; No. 1 in D min., Op. 7; No. 2 in F sharp min., Op. 10/3* (with Margaret Price); *No. 3, Op. 30; No. 4, Op. 37.* WEBERN: *5 Movements, Op. 5; String quartet* (1905); *6 Bagatelles, Op. 9; String quartet, Op. 28.*
(M) *** DG 419 994-2 (4) [id.].

DG have compressed their 1971 five-LP set on to four CDs, offering them at a reduced and competitive price. They have also retained the invaluable and excellent documentary study edited by Ursula Rauchhaupt – which runs to 340 pages! It is almost worth having this set for the documentation alone. The LaSalle Quartet give splendidly expert performances, even if at times their playing seems a little cool; and they are very well recorded. An invaluable issue for all who care about twentieth-century music.

Lawson, Peter (piano)

'The American piano sonata, Vol. 1': COPLAND: *Piano sonata*. IVES: *Three page sonata*. CARTER: *Piano sonata*. BARBER: *Piano sonata, Op. 26*.
*** Virgin Dig. VC7 59008-2 [VC 59008].

Peter Lawson plays the Copland *Sonata* with an understanding that is persuasive and an enthusiasm that is refreshing. Elliott Carter's *Sonata* is thoroughly accessible as well as convincing. Lawson can hold his own with such earlier recordings as the Charles Rosen, and he certainly has the advantage of fresher recording quality. In the 1950s and 1960s, the Barber *Sonata*, Op. 26, like that of Ginastera, had a far stronger profile than any other American sonata, and the catalogue has recently been enriched by the return of Horowitz's and Van Cliburn's recordings. Lawson comfortably takes its various hurdles in his stride, and he also gives us the Charles Ives *Three page Sonata*. For what it is worth, in playing the Ives *Three page sonata* Lawson uses the Cowell edition, rather than the later Kirkpatrick. A generous and valuable recital.

'The American piano sonata, Vol. 2': GRIFFES: *Sonata*. SESSIONS: *Sonata No. 2*. IVES: *Sonata No. 1*.
*** Virgin/EMI Dig. VC7 59316-2 [CDC 59316].

The Griffes and Sessions *Sonatas* are American classics and Peter Lawson has their measure. Ives is Ives, and that means a real original, even if some of his writing is little short of exasperating – but stimulating, too. The piano recording is nothing if not boldly vivid. An important disc and a generous one: 76 minutes.

Lawson, Peter and Alan MacLean (piano duet)

English music for piano duet: BERNERS: *Valses bourgeoises; Fantasie espagnole; 3 Morceaux*. Constant LAMBERT: *Overture* (ed. Lane), *3 Pièces nègres pour les touches blanches*. RAWSTHORNE: *The Creel*. WALTON: *Duets for children*. Philip LANE: *Badinages*.
*** Troy Dig. TROY 142 [id.].

The collection centres on Lord Berners, who had a recurring twinkle in the eye and loved to parody; moreover his inspiration regularly casts a glance in the direction of Satie and Poulenc, as the *Trois morceaux* readily demonstrate. Both Walton and Constant Lambert were his friends, admired his individuality and came under his influence. Lambert's *Trois pièces nègres* have a Satiesque title, yet they are all the composer's own work: the *Siesta* is quite haunting and the catchy *Nocturne* brings sparkling Latin-American rhythmic connotations, far removed from Chopin. The four engaging Rawsthorne miniatures, inspired by Izaak Walton's *Compleat Angler*, fit equally well into the programme. The Walton *Duets for children* have a disarming simplicity and often a nursery rhyme bounce, *Hop scotch* is particularly delightful, and vignettes like *The silent lake* and *Ghosts* will surely communicate very directly to young performers. Walton's final *Galop* was arranged by Philip Lane, who also provides four of his own pieces to close the concert with a strongly Gallic atmosphere. Performances by Peter Lawson and Alan MacLean are strong on style yet also convey affection. Excellent recording in a nicely resonant but not muddy acoustic.

Leach, Joanna (piano)

'Four square': SOLER: *Sonata No. 90 in F sharp*. HAYDN: *Sonata in C, Hob XVI/1*. J. S. BACH: *Partita No. 1 in B flat: Prelude; Minuets I & II; Gigue*. MOZART: *Fantasie in D min., K.397; Sonata No. 11 in A, K.331*. SCHUBERT: *Impromptu in A flat, D.899/4*. MENDELSSOHN: *Songs without words, Op. 19/1*.
*** Athene Dig. CD 3 [id.].

There is no more convincing fortepiano recital than this. Joanna Leach uses an 1823 Stodart with its effectively dark lower register for the Soler *Sonata*, then plays the same instrument later to show its attractive upper range in an almost romantic performance of Mozart's *Fantasia in D minor*; she ends the recital with the *A major Sonata*, K.331, with the introductory variations particularly inviting. For the Haydn, she chooses a 1789 Broadwood, a more brittle sound, and for the Bach a very effective 1787 instrument made by Longman & Broderip. In the Schubert and Mendelssohn pieces an 1835 D'Almaine brings us that bit nearer a modern piano. Fine performances throughout, and excellent recording. A fascinating way of discovering what the piano's ancestors could do best.

Lipatti, Dinu (piano)

CHOPIN: *Sonata No. 3 in B min., Op. 58*. LISZT: *Années de pèlerinage: Sonetto del Petrarca, No. 104*. RAVEL: *Miroirs: Alborada del gracioso*. BRAHMS: *Waltzes, Op. 39/1, 2, 5, 6, 10, 14 & 15* (with Nadia Boulanger). ENESCU: *Sonata No. 3 in D, Op. 25*.
(M) (***) EMI mono CDH7 63038-2.

The Chopin is one of the classics of the gramophone, and it is good to have it on CD in this excellent-sounding transfer. The Brahms *Waltzes* are played deliciously with tremendous sparkle and tenderness; they sound every bit as realistic as the post-war records. The Enescu *Sonata* is an accessible piece, with an exuberant first movement and a rather atmospheric *Andantino*, but the sound is not as fresh as the rest of the music on this valuable CD. A must for all with an interest in the piano.

'Last recital – Besançon, 16 November 1950': J. S. BACH: *Partita No. 1 in B flat min., BWV 825*. MOZART: *Sonata No. 8 in A min., K.310*. SCHUBERT: *Impromptus in E flat; in G flat, D.899/2–3*. CHOPIN: *Waltzes Nos. 1, 3–14*.
(M) (***) EMI mono CDH5 65166-2 [id.].

No collector should overlook this excellent 73-minute recital, originally issued on a pair of LPs. Most of these performances have scarcely been out of circulation since their first appearance: the haunting account of the Mozart *A minor Sonata* and the Bach *B flat Partita* have had more than one incarnation: the collection of Chopin *Waltzes* is perhaps most famous of all, and its legendary reputation is well earned. The remastering is expertly done, and the ear notices that among his other subtleties Lipatti creates a different timbre for the music of each composer.

Little, Tasmin (violin), **Piers Lane** (piano)

'Virtuoso violin': KREISLER: *Prelude and allegro in the style of Pugnani; Caprice viennois*. BRAHMS: *Hungarian dance Nos. 1 & 5*. SHOSTAKOVICH: *The Gadfly: Romance*. DRIGO: *Valse bluette*. FIBICH: *Poème*. FALLA: *La vida breve: Spanish dance*. WIENIAWSKI: *Légende, Op. 17*. SARASATE: *Introduction and Tarantelle, Op. 43*. BLOCH: *Baal Sheem: Nigum*. DEBUSSY: *Beau soir*. RIMSKY-KORSAKOV: *Flight of the bumblebee* (both arr. HEIFETZ). DELIUS: *Hassan: Serenade* (arr. TERTIS). KROLL: *Banjo and fiddle*. RAVEL: *Tzigane*.
(B) *** CfP Dig. CD-CFP 4675; *TC-CFP 4675* [id.].

A pretty dazzling display of violin fireworks from a brilliant young fiddler who conveys her delight in her own easy virtuosity The opening Kreisler pastiche, *Prelude and allegro*, is presented with real style, and later the *Caprice viennois* has comparable panache and relaxed charm. The schmaltzy daintiness of Drigo's *Valse bluette* is followed by an unexaggerated but full-timbred warmth in Fibich's *Poème*. The gypsy temperament of the Falla and the ready sparkle of Sarasate's *Tarantella* and Kroll's *Banjo and fiddle* are offset by the lyrical appeal of the more atmospheric piece. The violin is very present – perhaps the microphones are a fraction too close, but the balance with the piano is satisfactory and there is not the exaggerated spotlight here which virtually ruins Perlman's comparable 1994 collection with Samuel Sanders called '*Bits and Pieces*' (EMI CDC7 54882-2), where immediately in the opening Corelli Op. 5 *La Folia* chaconne, as arranged by Kreisler, the violin-timbre is made to sound aggressive, even harsh.

Ma, Yo-Yo (cello), **Lynn Chang, Ronan Lefkowitz** (violins), **Jeffrey Kahane, Gilbert Kalish** (pianos)

IVES: *Trio for violin, clarinet and piano*. BERNSTEIN: *Clarinet sonata* (arr. MA). KIRCHNER: *Triptych*. GERSHWIN: *3 Preludes* (arr. HEIFETZ/MA).
*** Sony Dig. SK 53126 [id.].

An unexpectedly rewarding and beguiling mix which is more than the sum of its component parts. The whole 65-minute recital is just the thing for late-evening stimulation. The early Bernstein sonata transcription is full of that ready melodic and rhythmic appeal which makes the composer's concert music so individual, and the Gershwin encore, equally felicitously transcribed, is hardly less appealing. The meat of the programme is in the Kirchner *Triptych,* while jokesy Ives provides a *Trio* (quoting corny 'folk' tunes with relish), bringing the usual audacious 'remembering', this time picturing '*Sunday evening on the campus*', thus concluding the entertainment with much spirit and aplomb.

Malcolm, George (harpsichord)

'The world of the harpsichord': BACH: *Italian concerto, BWV 971; Chromatic fantasia and fugue in D min., BWV 903; French suite No. 5 in G, BWV 816; Toccata in D, BWV 912.* PARADIES: *Toccata.* DAQUIN: *The cuckoo.* RIMSKY-KORSAKOV: *Flight of the bumble bee* (arr. MALCOLM). RAMEAU: *Pièces de clavecin: La Poule; Le rappel des oiseaux; Tambourin.* François COUPERIN: *Pièces de clavecin: Le rossignol-en-amour; Le carillon de Cithère.* TEMPLETON: *Bach goes to town.* MALCOLM: *Bach before the mast.*
❀ (M) *** Decca 444 390-2 [id.].

This is a delectable collection, a CD of harpsichord music that should be in even the smallest collection, spanning as it does the gamut of the late George Malcolm's wide repertory. His Bach performances are very considerable indeed; the *Chromatic fantasia* has an appropriate improvisatory element, the *Italian concerto* is full of vitality, and the best known of the *French suites* has a genial, lyrical intimacy to offset the buoyant *Toccata in D.* The comparative gravitas of Bach goes well with the charm of Rameau and Couperin, with their descriptive pieces realized with flair, notably *Le rappel des oiseaux* and *Le carillon de Cithère.* The two witty Bach imitations make a tempting hors d'oeuvre and the Rimsky-Korsakov is similarly a fun piece, played with great bravura; but no one should dismiss the mixture, for there is plenty of real substance here and playing of great distinction. The 1960s recording of the harpsichord (unnamed, but almost certainly a modern copy of a fine baroque instrument) is in the demonstration class, beautifully balanced – not too close – and natural within an airy but not over-resonant acoustic.

Marsalis, Wynton (trumpet), Judith Lynn Stillman (piano)

'On the 20th century': RAVEL: *Pièce en forme de Habanera.* HONEGGER: *Intrada.* TOMASI: *Triptyque.* STEVENS: *Sonata.* POULENC: *Eiffel Tower polka.* ENESCU: *Légende.* BERNSTEIN: *Rondo for Lifey.* BOZZA: *Rustiques.* HINDEMITH: *Sonata.*
*** Sony Dig. SK 47193 [id.].

What a wonderful player Wynton Marsalis is! His instrumental profile is so strong and stylish, his basic timbre unforgettably full of character, as at the very opening with the quiet, stately presentation of Ravel's *Pièce en forme de Habanera.* The Enescu *Légende* is hardly less distinctive, while the melodic line of Bozza's *Rustiques* (not in the Ravel class) yet sounds remarkably special, and the jolly roulades of the finale bring the easy manner of true virtuosity. Yet for fizzing bravura turn to the witty Poulenc polka (*Discours du général* from *Les Mariés de la Tour Eiffel* – like a silent movie speeded up – transcribed by Don Stewart for two trumpets in which Wynton takes both parts, with a little electronic help). The Halsey Stevens *Sonata* is a first-class piece and Marsalis makes the Hindemith, which has an effectively dry slow movement and a *Trauermusik* finale, sound almost like a masterpiece, helped by the fine piano contribution of Judith Stillman. The recording has an uncanny presence and realism: it is as if this superb artist was just out beyond the speakers.

McLachlan, Murray (piano)

Piano music from Scotland: SCOTT: *8 Songs* (trans. Stevenson): *Since all thy vows, false maid; Wha is that at my bower-door?; O were my love yon lilac fare; Wee Willie Gray; Milkwort and bog-cotton; Crowdieknowe; Ay waukin, O; There's news, lasses, news.* CENTER: *Piano sonata; 6 Bagatelles, Op. 3.; Children at play.* STEVENSON: *Beltane bonfire. 2 Scottish ballads: The Dowie Dens O Yarrow; Newhaven fishwife's cry.*
❀ *** Olympia Dig. OCD 264 [id.].

Francis George Scott (1880–1958) was a prolific and striking composer of songs and Ronald Stevenson's very free transcriptions, somewhat after the fashion of Liszt's concert paraphrases, are imaginatively creative in their own right. Ronald Center's *Piano sonata* is restless and mercurial, lacking much in the way of repose, but the joyous syncopations of the first movement are infectious and the work is a major contribution to the repertory and not in the least difficult to approach. The *Six Bagatelles* are even more strikingly diverse in mood. *Children at play* is an enchanting piece, with a musical-box miniaturism of texture at times, yet the writing is by no means inconsequential. All this music is played with commitment and considerable bravura by Murray McLachlan, who is clearly a sympathetic exponent, and the recording is extremely vivid and real. Our Rosette is awarded not just for enterprise, but equally from admiration and pleasure.

Meyers, Anne Akiko (violin), **Sandra Rivers** (piano)

'Salut d'amour': ELGAR: *Salut d'amour*. RENTARO: *Kojyo no Tsuki*. FALLA: *Suite populaire espagnole* (trans. Kochánski). DEBUSSY: *La plus que lente; La fille aux cheveux de lin*. KREISLER: *Recitativo and Scherzo, Op. 6* (for solo violin); *Liebesleid; Liebesfreud*. RACHMANINOV: *Vocalise, Op. 34/14*. VON PARADIS: *Sicilienne*. Flausino Rodrigues do VALE: *Prelude No. 15: Ao pé da fogueira* (arr. HEIFETZ). KOSAKU: *Aka-Tonbo* (arr. SIGEAKI). GERSHWIN: *Porgy and Bess: It ain't necessarily so* (arr. HEIFETZ). RAVEL: *Pièce en forme de habanera*.
*** RCA Dig. 09026 62546-2 [id.].

Anne Akiko Meyers, born in California in 1970 (who has already given us a highly individual account of the Mendelssohn concerto), is essentially a thoughtful and poetic artist and, though there is no lack of dash or bravura here when called for, this is primarily an intimate recital. The familiar Elgar salon piece which gives the disc its title is appealingly fresh, providing an immediate example, of which there are many here, of the sweet yet never cloying lyricism which is a true mark of the Meyers style. The two haunting Japanese melodies (both arranged by Saegusa Sigeaki especially for the recording) shows her natural simplicity of line, while the Falla *Suite populaire espagnole* has plenty of sparkle and temperament, although it is the gently whispered *Asturiana* and the delightful *Nana*, played on the half-tone, that are especially memorable, alongside her delicate performances of the Debussy *La plus que lente* and the charming portrait of *La fille aux cheveux de lin*. The restrained romanticism of Kreisler's *Liebesleid* then contrasts with the more flamboyant *Liebesfreud*, while the Gershwin number is as seductive as the closing Ravel *Habanera*, although in quite a different way. Sandra Rivers accompanies with great sympathy throughout. A delightful recital, unsurpassed of its kind, and most naturally balanced and recorded. But if you are looking for self-conscious fiddlistic fireworks, this is not the place where you will find them.

Moiseiwitsch, Benno (piano)

1938–1950 recordings: MUSSORGSKY: *Pictures at an exhibition*. BEETHOVEN: *Andanti favori, WoO 57; Rondo in C, Op. 51/1*. WEBER: *Sonata No. 1: Presto; Invitation to the dance* (arr. TAUSIG). MENDELSSOHN: *Scherzo in E min., Op. 16*. SCHUMANN: *Romanzen: No. 2, Op. 28/2*. CHOPIN: *Nocturne in E flat, Op. 9/2; Polonaise in B flat, Op. 71/2; Barcarolle, Op. 60*. LISZT: *Liebestraume No. 3; Etude de concert: La leggierezza. Hungarian rhapsody No. 2 in C sharp min. Concert paraphrase of Wagner's Tannhäuser overture*. DEBUSSY: *Pour le piano: Toccata. Suite bergamasque: Clair de lune. Estampes: Jardins sous la pluie*. RAVEL: *Le tombeau de Couperin: Toccata*.
(**(*)) APR mono CDAPR 7005 (2) [id.].

Moiseiwitsch never enjoyed quite the exposure on records to which his gifts entitled him, though in the earlier part of his career he made a great many. Later, in the electrical era he was a 'plum-label' artist and was not issued on the more prestigious and expensive 'red-label'. In this he was in pretty good company, for Solomon and Myra Hess were similarly relegated. This anthology gives a good picture of the great pianist in a wide variety of repertory: his *Pictures at an exhibition*, made in 1945, was for some time the only piano version; and those who identify him solely with the Russians will find his Chopin *Barcarolle* and Debussy *Jardins sous la pluie* totally idiomatic. The transfers are variable – all are made from commercial copies, some in better condition than others.

Nakariakov, Sergei (trumpet), **Alexander Markovich** (piano)

'Trumpet works': GERSHWIN: *Rhapsody in blue* (arr. DOKSHITSER). ARENSKY: *Concert waltz*. ARBAN: *Carnival of Venice*. RAVEL: *Pavane pour une infante défunte*. BERNSTEIN: *Rondo for Lifey*. GLAZUNOV: *Albumblatt*. STOLTE: *Burleske*. HARTMANN: *Arbucklenian polka*. FIBICH: *Poème*. RIMSKY-KORSAKOV: *Flight of the bumblebee*. DINICU: *Hora staccato*. GLIÈRE: *Valse*. RUEFF: *Sonatina*.
*** Teldec/Warner Dig. 9031 77705-2 [id.].

An astonishing CD début by a brilliant Russian schoolboy virtuoso, barely fifteen at the time. Nakariakov's supreme command of the instrument is matched by instinctive musicality and taste. He manages to sound suitably transatlantic in an incredible full-length arrangement of Gershwin's *Rhapsody in blue*, and is even better in Bernstein's entertainingly ebullient *Rondo for Lifey*. Lovely tone and simplicity of line make Fibich's *Poème* sound appealingly restrained, and in the bandstand variations by Arban and Hartmann the playing is stylishly infectious. Highlights are Stolte's witty *Burlesque* and the very considerable *Sonatina* by Jeanine Rueff in which trumpeter and pianist, as elsewhere, make a genuine partnership. But for ear-tickling bravura try Dinicu's *Hora staccato*, which surely would have impressed Heifetz. Excellently balanced and realistic recording.

ARBAN: *Variations on a theme from Bellini's 'Norma'; Variations on a Tyrolean song.* BIZET, arr. WAXMAN: *Carmen fantasy.* BRANDT: *Concert piece No. 2.* FALLA: *Spanish dance.* FAURE: *Le réveil.* PAGANINI: *Caprice, Op. 1/17; Moto perpetuo, Op. 11.* SARASATE: *Zigeunerweisen, Op. 20/1.* SAINT-SAENS: *Le cygne.*
**(*) Teldec/Warner Dig. 4509 94554-2 [id.].

Sergei Nakariakov exhibits some stunning technique in his second Teldec recital, coupling various trifles including Franz Waxman's *Carmen fantasy* and Paganini's *Moto perpetuo*, as well as the remainder of his programme. He was only seventeen when this recording was made and, although not many will want to hear more than a few of these pieces at a time, there is much to enjoy. He is a veritable Russian Håkan Hardenberger, save for the fact that, on the evidence of this disc, he does not always command the latter's extraordinary variety of tonal colour or his impeccable taste.

Navarra, André (cello), Erika Kilcher (piano)

Recital: *Sonatas* by: LOCATELLI; VALENTINI; BOCCHERINI: *in A & G.* GRANADOS: *Goyescas: Intermezzo.* FALLA: *Suite populaire espagnole* (arr. Maurice MARECHAL). NIN: *Chants d'Espagne: Saeta; Andalousie.*
(M) *** Cal. CAL 6673 [id.].

Navarra's recital dates from 1981 and shows this fine cellist in top form. He is splendidly partnered by Erika Kilcher who, although she is backwardly balanced in relation to the up-front cello (recorded somewhat dryly), makes a highly artistic contribution with her sympathetic accompaniments. This is immediately noticeable in the splendid opening sonata of Locatelli. But it is the four-movement work by Giuseppe Valentini which is the highlight of the Italian repertoire, a most engaging piece with an elegant *Gavotte* and an aria-like *Largo*, framed by two energetic outer movements in which Navarra's spiccato-like articulation of *moto perpeptuo* allegros is most infectious. He is equally at home in the Spanish half of the programme, and Kilcher joins him in providing colourful characterization of the five miniatures which make up the Falla suite. In the second of the two Nin pieces, *Andalousie*, Navarra sounds like a larger-than-life Spanish guitar. However, it is a pity that the documentation does not identify the Italian sonatas more positively.

Nettle and Markham (two-piano duo)

'In England': CARMICHAEL: *Puppet overture.* GRAINGER: *Country gardens; Lisbon; The brisk young sailor; The lost lady found; Handel in the Strand; English waltz.* VAUGHAN WILLIAMS: *Fantasia on Greensleeves.* WALTON: *Façade: Popular song; Tango pasodoble; Old Sir Faulk; Swiss yodelling song; Polka.* NICHOLAS: *Quiet peace No. 1.* DRING: *Fantastic variations on Lillibulero.* BRIDGE: *Sally in our alley.* COATES: *By the sleepy lagoon.* BLAKE: *Slow ragtime; Folk ballad.* GAY: *Lambeth Walk.* SCOTT: *Lotus Land.* LAMBERT: *3 Pièces nègres: Siesta.* WARLOCK: *Capriol suite: Pavane.* BRITTEN: *Mazurka elegiaca, Op. 23/2.* HOLST: *The Planets: Jupiter.*
(M) *** Carlton 30367 0017-2 [id.].

A recital of mostly brief lollipops lasting nearly 78 minutes might seem too much of a good thing, but Nettle and Markham play with such spirit that the result is almost always diverting. Perhaps they languish a bit in some of the slower pieces, *Greensleeves* and Warlock's *Pavane*, for instance; but for the most part the effect is highly spontaneous, and especially so in the Grainger items which are nicely sprinkled around the programme. *Lisbon, The brisk young sailor* and *The lost lady found* all come together, following neatly after Cyril Scott's *Lotus Land*, to make a winning triptych. The recording is excellent.

New Century Saxophone Quartet

'Main Street USA': GOULD: *Pavane. Main Street waltz; Main Street march.* GERSHWIN: *Promenade; Three quartet blues; Merry Andrew. Porgy and Bess: Clara, Clara; Oh, I got plenty o' nuttin'; Bess, you is my woman now; Oh, I can't sit down; It ain't necessarily so; Summertime; There's a boat dat's leavin' for New York; Oh Lawd, I'm on my way.* BERNSTEIN: *West Side Story: I feel pretty; Balcony scene; Tonight; Cha-cha/Meeting scene; Jump; One hand, one heart; Gee, officer Krupke; Scherzo; Somewhere.*
*** Channel Classics Dig. CCS 9896 [id.].

Uncommonly fine playing, with superbly blended timbres and a subtly appealing melodic lead from Michael Stephenson on the soprano saxophone, means that this collection of famous show melodies is very appealing. Gould's delightful *Pavane* is presented with a neat degree of whimsy and the three Gershwin instrumental numbers have a pleasing sophistication. Stephenson's line in the songs is quite remarkably vocal in feeling. '*It ain't necessarily so*' recalls Fats Waller, and the Balcony scene from *West Side Story* is really touching. Steven Kirkman gives admirably restrained support on percussion, when needed, and the balance and recording could hardly be bettered.

Ogdon, John and Brenda Lucas (pianos)

RACHMANINOV: *Suites for 2 pianos Nos. 1 (Fantasy), Op. 5; 2 in C, Op. 17; Six pieces for piano duet, Op. 11; Polka italienne.* ARENSKY: *Suite for 2 pianos, Op. 15.* KHACHATURIAN: *Sabre dance.* SHOSTAKOVICH: *Concertino, Op. 94.* DEBUSSY: *Petite suite; Fêtes.* BIZET: *Jeux d'enfants.*
(B) **(*) EMI forte CZS5 69386-2 (2).

John Ogdon and Brenda Lucas's readings of the two Rachmaninov *Suites*, not ideally imaginative but enjoyable nevertheless, are aptly coupled with other duet recordings made by them, including the delightful Arensky *Suite* which includes the famous waltz. It is good too to have the long-neglected *Concertino* of Shostakovich and the anything-but-neglected *Sabre dance*, which is rather heavy-going here. However, the Debussy *Petite suite* is very engaging, and most valuable of all is the complete recording of Bizet's *Jeux d'enfants* – all twelve movements. Only the five included by the composer in his orchestral suite are at all well known, and many of the others are equally charming, not least the opening *Rêverie* (*L'Escarpolette*), the Scherzo (*Les chevaux de bois*) and the *Nocturne* (*Colin-Mainard* – 'Blind man's buff'). Fine ensemble and sparkling fingerwork, but just occasionally a touch of rhythmic inflexibility. Good, mid-1970s recording.

Oslo Wind Ensemble

Scandinavian wind quintets: FERNSTROM: *Wind quintet, Op. 59.* KVANDAL: *Wind quintet, Op. 34; 3 Sacred Folktunes.* NIELSEN: *Wind quintet, Op. 43.*
(BB) *** Naxos Dig. 8.553050 [id.].

A super-bargain account of the Nielsen *Quintet*, more relaxed in its tempi and measured in approach than the account by the Scandinavian Quintet on Marco Polo. Very decently recorded, too. The Swedish musician, John Fernström, was a prolific composer whose output runs to twelve symphonies and much else besides. (He was for years solely represented in the catalogue by a *Concertino for flute, women's choir and small orchestra*). This *Wind quintet* is not quite so charming, but is well worth hearing – as, for that matter, is the *Wind quintet* by the Norwegian, Johan Kvandal, a thoughtful figure who is a composer of imagination and substance.

Parker-Smith, Jane (organ)

Organ of Coventry Cathedral: *'Popular French Romantics':* WIDOR: *Symphony No. 1: March pontifical. Symphony No 9 (Gothique), Op. 70; Andante sostenuto.* GUILMANT: *Sonata No. 5 in C min., Op. 80; Scherzo.* GIGOUT: *Toccata in B min.* BONNET: *Elfes, Op. 7.* LEFEBURE-WELY: *Sortie in B flat.* VIERNE: *Pièces de fantaisie: Clair de lune, Op. 53/5; Carillon de Westminster, Op. 54/6.*
*** ASV Dig. CDDCA 539 [id.].

The modern organ in Coventry Cathedral adds a nice bite to Jane Parker-Smith's very pontifical performance of the opening Widor *March* and creates a blaze of splendour at the close of the famous Vierne *Carillon de Westminster*, the finest performance on record. The detail of the fast, nimble articulation in the engagingly Mendelssohnian *Elfes* of Joseph Bonnet is not clouded; yet here, as in the splendid Guilmant *Scherzo* with its wider dynamic range, there is also a nice atmospheric effect. Overall, a most entertaining recital.

Organ of Beauvais Cathedral: *'Popular French Romantics' Vol. 2:* FRANCK: *Prélude, fugue et variation, Op. 18.* GUILMANT: *Grand choeur in D* (after Handel). MULET: *Carillon-sortie.* RENAUD: *Toccata in D min.* SAINT-SAENS: *Prelude and fugue.* VIERNE: *Symphony No. 1: Finale. Stèle pour un enfant défunt.* WIDOR: *Symphony No. 4: Andante and Scherzo.*
*** ASV Dig. CDDCA 610 [id.].

With his *Prélude and fugue*, Saint-Saëns is in more serious mood than usual but showing characteristic facility in fugal construction; Widor is first mellow and then quixotic – his *Scherzo* demands the lightest articulation and receives it. High drama and great bravura are provided by the Vierne *Finale* and later by Albert Renaud's *Toccata* and Henri Mulet's *Carillon-sortie*, while Franck's *Prélude, fugue et variation* and the poignant Vierne *Stèle pour un enfant défunt* bring attractive lyrical contrast: here Jane Parker-Smith's registration shows particular subtlety. The organ is splendidly recorded.

Payne, Joseph (organ of Vermont University)

Early French organ music: MARCHAND: *11 Pièces d'orgue, Livre II.* COMPERE: *Ave Maria gratia plena; Paranimphus salutat virginem.* JAPART: *Fortuna d'un grand tempo.* CORRETTE: *Messe du huitième ton* (complete). DE GRIGNY: *Hymns: Ave maris stella; A solis ortus (Crudelis Herodes); Fugue à 5.*
(BB) ** Naxos 8.553214 [id.].

This is an enterprising and generous (77 minutes) programme covering a wide range of music. Loyset Compère and Jean Japart lived in the latter half of the fifteenth century and their organ works must be among the earliest to have survived. Both the Marchand *Pièces* and the Corrette *Messe* bring plenty of colour and variety, and Joseph Payne registers everything effectively with a reedy tang which makes it sound French. The sound is full and clearly focused. The snag is the lack of an ecclesiastical ambience, something which is surely essential in a record of this kind, while less important at a live recital. André Isoir's recital on the organ at Bon Pasteur, Angers, is a far better choice for this repertoire (see above).

Perlman, Itzhak (violin)

'A la carte' (with Abbey Road Ens., Lawrence Foster): MASSENET: *Thaïs: Méditation.* GLAZUNOV: *Mazurka Obéreque; Méditation, Op. 32.* RACHMANINOV: *Vocalise, Op. 34/14.* SARASATE: *Zigeunerweisen, Op. 20; Introduction and Tarantelle, Op. 43.* RIMSKY-KORSAKOV: *Russian fantasy* (arr. KREISLER). TCHAIKOVSKY: *Scherzo, Op. 42/2* (orch. Glazunov). WIENIAWSKI: *Légende, Op. 17.* KREISLER: *The old refrain; Schön Rosmarin.*
**(*) EMI Dig. CDC5 55475-2 [id.].

Perlman is in his element in this luscious concert of mostly Russian lollipops – although, as it happens, the most delectable playing of all comes in the Sarasate *Zigeunerweisen*. But the pieces by Glazunov, Tchaikovsky's sparkling *Scherzo* and the Rimsky-Korsakov *Fantasy* also show the extraordinary range of colour and sheer charisma of this fiddling. Alas, as always, the violin is too closely balanced, and this is most disadvantageous in the Wieniawski *Légende*, which loses much of its romantic atmosphere. Perlman's closing solo encore, Kreisler's *Schön Rosmarin*, ends the programme with extraordinary panache. Otherwise Lawrence Foster accompanies discreetly.

Petri, Michala (recorder or flute)

'Greensleeves' (with Hanne Petri, harpsichord, David Petri, cello): ANON.: *Greensleeves to a grounde; Divisions on an Italian ground.* Jacob VAN EYCK: *Prins Robberts Masco; Philis Schoon Herderinne; Wat Zal Men op den Avond Doen; Engels Nachtegaeltje.* CORELLI: *Sonata, Op. 15/5: La Folia.* HANDEL: *Andante.* LECLAIR: *Tambourin.* F. COUPERIN: *Le rossignol vainqueur; Le rossignol en amour.* J. S. BACH: *Siciliano.* TELEMANN: *Rondino.* GOSSEC: *Tambourin.* PAGANINI: *Moto perpetuo, Op. 11.* BRUGGEN: *2 Studies.* CHRISTIANSEN: *Satie auf hoher See.* HENRIQUES: *Dance of the midges.* SCHUBERT: *The Bee.* MONTI: *Czárdás.* HERBERLE: *Rondo presto.* RIMSKY-KORSAKOV: *Flight of the bumblebee.*
(M) *** Ph. Dig. 420 897-2.

Marvellously nimble playing from Michala Petri, and 71 minutes, digitally recorded at mid-price, so one can afford to pick and choose. Some of the music opening the recital is less than distinctive, but the Couperin transcriptions are a delight and Paganini's *Moto perpetuo* vies with Henriques' *Dance of the midges* for sparkling bravura. There are some attractively familiar melodies by Bach and Handel, among others, to provide contrast, and Henning Christiansen's *Satie auf hoher See* is an unexpected treat. Monti's *Czárdás* ends the programme infectiously.

Pollini, Maurizio (piano)

STRAVINSKY: *3 movements from Petrushka.* PROKOFIEV: *Piano sonata No. 7 in B flat, Op. 83.* WEBERN: *Variations for piano, Op. 27.* BOULEZ: *Piano sonata No. 2.*
(M) *** DG 447 431-2 [id.].

The Prokofiev is a great performance, one of the finest ever committed to disc; and the Stravinsky *Petrushka* is electrifying. Not all those responding to this music will do so quite so readily to the Boulez, fine though the playing is; but the Webern also makes a very strong impression. This is the equivalent of two LPs and is outstanding value. It is a natural candidate for reissue in DG's set of 'Originals' of legendary performances.

Preston, Simon (organ)

'The world of the organ' (organ of Westminster Abbey): WIDOR: *Symphony No. 5: Toccata.* BACH: *Chorale prelude, Wachet auf, BWV 645.* MOZART: *Fantasia in F min., K.608.* WALTON: *Crown imperial* (arr. MURRILL). CLARKE: *Prince of Denmark's march* (arr. PRESTON). HANDEL: *Saul: Dead march.* PURCELL: *Trumpet tune* (arr. TREVOR). ELGAR: *Imperial march* (arr. MARTIN). VIERNE: *Symphony No. 1: Finale.* WAGNER: *Tannhäuser: Pilgrims' chorus.* GUILMANT: *March on a theme of Handel.* SCHUMANN: *Study No. 5* (arr. WEST). KARG-ELERT: *Marche triomphale (Now thank we all our God).*
(M) *** Decca 430 091-2; *430 091-4.*

A splendid compilation from the Argo catalogue of the early to mid-1960s, spectacularly recorded, which offers 69 minutes of music and is in every sense a resounding success. Simon Preston's account of the Widor *Toccata* is second to none, and both the Vierne *Finale* and the Karg-Elert *March triomphale* lend themselves admirably to Preston's unashamed flamboyance and the tonal splendour afforded by the Westminster acoustics. Walton's *Crown imperial*, too, brings a panoply of sound which compares very favourably with an orchestral recording. The organ has a splendid trumpet stop which makes both the Purcell piece and Clarke's *Prince of Denmark's march*, better known as the '*Trumpet voluntary*', sound crisply regal.

Prometheus Ensemble

'French impressions': RAVEL: *Introduction & allegro for harp, flute, clarinet and string quartet.* DEBUSSY: *Danses sacrée et profane; Sonata for flute, viola and harp.* ROUSSEL: *Serenade.*
*** ASV Dig. CDDCA 664 [id.].

This young group gives eminently well-prepared and thoughtful accounts of all these pieces. The *Danses sacrée et profane* sound particularly atmospheric and the Debussy *Sonata* is played with great feeling and sounds appropriately ethereal. The Roussel, too, is done with great style and, even if the *Introduction and allegro* does not supersede the celebrated Melos account, the Prometheus do it well.

Puyana, Rafael (harpsichord)

'The Golden Age of harpsichord music': ANON.: *My Lady Carey's Dompe.* BULL: *Les Buffons; The King's hunt.* PEERSON: *The Primerose; The fall of the leafe.* BYRD: *La Volta.* PHILIPS: *Pavana dolorosa; Galliard dolorosa.* BESARD: *Branle gay.* Louis COUPERIN: *Tombeau de M. de Blancrocher; Pavane.* Antoine FRANCISQUE: *Branle de Montiradé.* BACH: *Keyboard concerto in D min., after Marcello.* FREIXANET: *Sonata in A.* Mateo ALBENIZ: *Sonata in D.* CHAMBONNIERS: *Le Moutier* (after Louis Couperin). RAMEAU: *Gavotte et Doubles.* DIEUPART: *Passepied.* François COUPERIN: *La Pantomime.*
❀ (M) *** Mercury 434 364-2 [id.].

If you think you don't enjoy listening to the harpsichord, Rafael Puyana, who was a pupil of Landowska, will surely persuade you otherwise in this remarkably diverse, 75-minute recital, for he is a supreme master of his instrument. He plays a large, modern, double-keyboard Pleyel harpsichord (replicating one of Landowska's own instruments). In his bravura hands it produces an astonishingly wide range of dynamic, colour and sonority, no better demonstrated than in the *Gavotte et Doubles* of Rameau, which is a continuously inventive set of variations, running on for about ten minutes. Puyana effectively uses every possible device to divert his listeners, to say nothing of demonstrating his own dexterity, which he does again more simply in the engagingly brief *Passepied* of Charles Dieupart (who died in 1740). Martin Peerson's modest variations on a popular song of the period, *The Primerose*, and the more dolorous evocation of *The fall of the leafe* both feature the highly effective dynamic contrasts which this instrument can provide.

The programme opens with the piquant *My Lady Carey's Dompe*, a lollipop if ever there was one, presented with great panache. John Bull's divisions on *Les Buffons* and *The King's Hunt* have never sounded more vital, while Puyana's account of the charming *La Volta* of William Byrd makes one appreciate why it was reputedly a favourite dance of Queen Elizabeth I. Perhaps Puyana goes over the top a bit in his robust presentation of the pieces by Peter Philips, and he plays Bach's *Concerto in D minor* (supposedly after Alessandro Marcello, but sounding more like Vivaldi) in such a robust manner that it is almost if he were sitting at the keyboard of an organ. But the crisply articulated *Sonata* of Freixanet is very effective indeed, and the *Sonata* of Mateo Albéniz is a *tour de force*. The instrument's resonant lower octave is really made to tell in Louis Couperin's *Tombeau*; while the elegant *Le Moutier* of Jacques Champion de Chambonnières brings a nice sonic contrast on three different levels, within a time period of just over two minutes. The Mercury recording is real and vivid, but please don't set the volume level too high. This is one of two harpsichord compilations that deserve a place in every collection: the other is George Malcolm's Decca anthology, '*The World of the harpsichord*', utterly different but equally rewarding – see above.

Rachmaninov, Sergei (piano)

'The Ampico piano-roll recordings 1919–33': BACH: *Partita No. 4: Sarabande.* BEETHOVEN: *Ruins of Athens: Turkish march.* GLUCK, arr. SGAMBASTI: *Melodie d'Orfeo.* MENDELSSOHN: *Song without words (Spinning song), Op. 67/4.* HENSELT: *Si oiseau j'étais, Op. 2/6.* LISZT: *Concert paraphrases on: Schubert's Das Wandern; Mädchens Wunsch of Chopin, Op. 74/1.* SCHUBERT: *Impromptu No. 4 in A flat, Op. 90.* CHOPIN: *Scherzo in B flat min., Op. 31; Nocturne in F, Op. 15/1; Waltzes: in E flat, Op. 18; in F, Op. 34/1.* BIZET arr. RACHMANINOV: *L'Arlésienne: Minuet.* PADEREWSKI: *Minuet in G, Op. 14/1.* RUBINSTEIN: *Barcarolle.* TCHAIKOVSKY: *Troika in E, Op. 37/11; Valse in A flat, Op. 40/8.*
(M) ** Decca 440 066-2 [id.].

After Rachmaninov's splendid Ampico-roll recordings of his own music (Decca 425 964-2 – see our main volume) this is curiously disappointing. The playing often seems unrelaxed, even stiff (the Bach, for instance, or Liszt's paraphrase of Schubert's *Das Wandern*). The Chopin pieces seem to come off best (although the effect is not entirely spontaneous) and, while this is very accomplished and often characterful music-making (as in the closing Tchaikovsky items), the great pianist seems at times to be inhibited by the recording conditions. The sound (the player-piano was reproduced in Kingsway Hall in 1978/9) is real and vivid, if a trifle hard-edged.

Ragossnig, Konrad (Renaissance lute)

'Renaissance lute music': Disc 1: England: DOWLAND: *King of Denmark's Galliard; Lachrimae antiquae pavan; Fantasia; My Lady Hunsdon's puffe; Melancholy galliard; Mrs Winter's jump; Semper Dowland, semper dolens; Earl of Essex his galliard; Forlorne hope fancy.* BATCHELAR: *Mounsiers almaine.* BULMAN: *Pavan.* CUTTING: *Almain; Greensleeves; Walsingham; The squirrel's toy.* ANON.: *Sir John Smith his Almain.* MORLEY: *Pavan.* JOHNSON: *Alman.* HOLBORNE: *Galliard.* Italy: CAPIROLA: *Ricercars 1, 2, 10 & 13.* SPINACINO: *Ricercar.* Francesco da MILANO: *Fantasia.*

Disc 2: Italy (continued): MOLINARO: *Fantasias 1, 9 & 10. Saltarello – Ballo detto Il Conte Orlando – Saltarello.* BARBETTA: *Moresca detta le Canarie.* TERZI: *Ballo tedesco e francese – Tre parti di gagliarde.* NEGRI: *La spagnoletto – Il bianco fiore.* Santino Garsi de PALMA: *Aria del Gran Duca – La Cesarina – La Mutia – La ne mente per la gola – Gagliarda Manfredina – Ballo del Serenissimo Duca di Parma – Corenta.* Spain: MILAN: *Pavanas 1–6; Fantasias 10–12 & 16.* MUDARRA: *Pavana de Alexandre; Gallarda; Romanesca: O guárdame las vacas; Diferencias sobre Conde claros; Fantasia que contrahaze la harpa en la manera de Luduvico.* Luis de NARVAEZ: *Diferencias sobre Guádame las vacas; Milles regres. La canción des Emperador del quarto tono de Jusquin; Fantasia; Baxa de contrapunto.*

Disc 3: Poland & Hungary: CEDA: *Praeludium; Galliarda 1 & 2; Favorito*. ANON.: *Balletto Polacho*. POLAK: *Praeludium*. DLUGORAJ: *Chorea polonica*. BAKFARK: *Fantasia; Finale; Villanella; Finale; Kowaly; Finale; 4 Fantasies*. Germany: JUDENKUNIG: *Hoff dantz*. NEWSIDLER: *Ellend bringt peyn; Der Juden Tantz; Preambel; Welscher tantz Wascha mesa*. Landgraf Moritz von HESSEN: *Pavane*. ANON.: *Der gestraifft Danntz – Der Gassenhauer darauff*. WAISSEL: *Fantasia; Deutscher Tantz*. OCHSENKHUN: *Innsbruck, ich muss dich lassen*.

Disc 4: Netherlands: ADRIAENSSEN: *Fantasia; Courante; Branle simple de Poictou*. HOWET: *Fantasie*. SWEELINCK: *Psalms 5 & 23*. Joachim van den HOVE: *Galliarde*. VALLET: *Prelude; Galliarde; Slaep, soete, slaep*. France: ATTAIGNANT: *Chansons: Tant que vivray; Destre amoureux. Basse dances: Sansserre; La Magdelena. Branle gay: C'est mon amy; Haulberroys*. Adrien le ROY: *Passemeze*. BALLARD: *Entrée de luth; Corante; Branle de village*. BESARD: *Branle; Gagliarda; Branle gay; Gagliarda vulgo dolorata; Allemande; Air de cour: J'ai trouvé sur l'herbe assise; Volte; Branle – Branle gay; Guillemette; Ballet; Pass' e mezo; Chorea rustica*.
❁ (B) *** DG 447 727-2 (4) [id.].

This admirable four-disc Archiv set gives us a comprehensive survey of the development of lute music throughout Europe in the fifteenth, sixteenth and the first half of the seventeenth century. English lute music came to its peak at the end of the Elizabethan and beginning of the Jacobean eras and is well represented by that master of melancholy, John Dowland – although he could also be spirited, witness *My Lady Hunsdon's Puffe*. But the oldest-known (written-down) lute music came from Italy and the remarkably flexible *Ricercars* of Vincenzo Capirola (born in 1474) make an ideal example of music which is essentially improvisational in feeling yet settling down into formal shape. The equivalent of the lute in Spain was the vihuela de mano (an ancestor of the guitar) and it was in Spain that the variation form was born, using the term 'diferencias'. Here besides the solemn music and dances we have fine examples of *Diferencias* by Mudarra and Narvaéz.

Polish and Hungarian lute music is comparatively little known, but, as the four late-sixteenth-century pieces by Diomedes Cato demonstrate, its manner closely reflects the Renaissance style in the rest of Europe. The Hungarian, Valentin Bakfark, however, is revealed as a composer of considerable individuality and his two *Villanellas* are particularly haunting. The German repertoire, too, is particularly strong in character and it brings some novelties, like Newsidler's extraordinarily exotic *Juden Tanz*. In the Netherlands programme, Sweelinck's music (two beautiful Psalm evocations) catches the ear, while the *Galliarde* and the touching *Slaepe, sote slaep* draw the listener's attention to his little-known contemporary, Nicolas Vallet. The programme of French music which concludes the survey is hardly less rich in fine invention and this is obviously because Pierre Attaignant and Robert Ballard were publishers first and foremost, and they both obviously had an ear for a hit number. Thus all the anonymous pieces listed under their names are full of character: sample the *Branle gay: C'est mon amy*, the charming *La Magdalena* or the rustic *Branles de village* with its drone imitation suggesting a hurdy-gurdy. Jean-Baptiste Besard, however, was an outstanding French lutenist (also a doctor of law and a physician) and his music is of the highest quality: the *Gagliarda vulgo dolorata*, *Air de cour, J'ai trouvé sur l'herbe assise*, *Branle gay* and sad little *Guillemette* can be spoken of in the same breath as the best Dowland pieces. Throughout his long programme, recorded between 1973 and 1975, Konrad Ragossnig plays with impeccable style. His spontaneous feeling brings all this music vividly to life and his variety of timbre and subtle use of echo dynamics always intrigue the ear. The recording is very fine indeed, giving his period lute a natural presence and very slightly more body than RCA provide for Julian Bream, who nevertheless can continue to be recommended alongside the present set: he is especially at home in the English repertoire.

Rév, Lívia (piano)

'For children': BACH: *Preludes in E, BWV 939; in G min., BWV 930*. DAQUIN: *Le coucou*. MOZART: *Variations on Ah vous dirai-je maman, K.265*. BEETHOVEN: *Für Elise*. SCHUMANN: *Album for the young Op. 63:* excerpts. CHOPIN: *Nocturne in C min., Op. posth*. LISZT: *Etudes G. 136/1 & 2*. BIZET: *Jeux d'enfants: La Toupie*. FAURE: *Dolly: Berceuse*. TCHAIKOVSKY: *Album for the young, Op. 39: Maman; Waltz*. VILLA-LOBOS: *Prole do bebê:* excerpts. JOLIVET: *Chansons naïve 1 & 2*. PROKOFIEV: *Waltz, Op. 65*. BARTOK: *Evening in the country; For Children:* excerpts. DEBUSSY: *Children's corner:* excerpts. MAGIN: *3 Pieces*. MATACIC: *Miniature variations*.
*** Hyperion CDA 66185.

A wholly delectable recital, and not just for children either. The whole is more than the sum of its many parts, and the layout provides excellent variety, with the programme stimulating in mixing familiar with unfamiliar. The recording is first class. Highly recommended for late evening listening.

Reykjavik Wind Quintet

Jean-Michel DAMASE: *17 Variations*. DEBUSSY (arr. BOZZA): *Le petit nègre*. FAURE (arr. WILLIAMS): *Dolly suite: Berceuse, Op. 56/1*. FRANCAIX: *Quintet No. 1*. IBERT: *3 Pièces brèves*. MILHAUD: *La cheminée du roi René, Op. 205*. PIERNE: *Pastorale, Op. 14/1*. POULENC (arr. EMERSON): *Novelette No. 1*.
*** Chandos Dig. CHAN 9362 [id.].

A delightful recital for late-night listening. Elegant, crisp playing from this accomplished Icelandic ensemble. The Damase *Variations* are delightful, as indeed are the Françaix and Milhaud pieces, and the Chandos recording is in the best traditions of the house.

Robles, Marisa (harp)

'The world of the harp': FALLA: *Three-cornered Hat: Danza del corregidor*. ALBENIZ: *Rumores de Caleta; Torre bermeja*. BIDAOLA: *Viejo zortzico*. EBERL (attrib. Mozart): *Theme, variations and rondo pastorale*. BEETHOVEN: *Variations on a Swiss song*. BRITTEN: *Ceremony of carols: Interlude*. FAURE: *Impromptu, Op. 86*. PIERNE: *Impromptu-caprice, Op. 9*. SALZEDO: *Chanson de la nuit*. BRAHMS: *Lullaby*. BACH: *Well-tempered Clavier: Prelude No. 1*. CHOPIN: *Mazurka, Op. 7/1; Prelude, Op. 28/15 (Raindrop)*. HASSELMANS: *La source*.
(M) *** Decca 433 869-2 [id.].

The artistry of Marisa Robles ensures that this is a highly attractive anthology and the programme is as well chosen as it is beautifully played. As ex-Professor of the harp at the Madrid Conservatory, Miss Robles has a natural affinity for the Spanish music that opens her programme, and other highlights include a magnetic account of the Britten *Interlude* and the Salzedo *Chanson de la nuit* with its bell-like evocations. The Eberl *Variations* are highly engaging. The excellent recordings derive from the Argo catalogue of the 1960s and '70s, except for the Chopin, Brahms, Bach and Hasselmans pieces, which have been added to fill out the present reissue (75 minutes). The delicious Hasselmans roulades are the epitome of nineteenth-century harp writing. The CD has a most realistic presence.

Romero, Pepe (guitar)

Spanish music (with (i) Celín Romero): ANON.: *Jeux interdits*. ALBENIZ: *Suite española, Op. 47: Sevilla; Granada. Recuerdos de viaje, Op. 71: Rumores de la caleta. Mallorca* (barcarolle), *Op. 202. España (6 hojas de álbum), Op. 165: Asturias;* (i) *Tango*. GRANADOS: (i) *Danzas españolas, Op. 37: Andaluza; Goyescas: Intermezzo*. Celedonio ROMERO: *Malagueña; Romantico*. TARREGA: *Capricho arabe; Pavana*. SOR: *Introduction & variations on a theme by Mozart, Op. 9*.
(M) **(*) Ph. Dig. 434 727-2 [id.].

A thoroughly professional and immaculately played collection of favourites. The effect is intimate, pleasing rather than electrifying – the virtuoso showing his paces in familiar pieces. The flamenco-based pieces by the performer's father, Celedonio, bring a sudden hint of fire. For the reissue Celín Romero joins his brother for three duets, and this brings added spontaneity, although the intimate mood remains – witness the Granados *Spanish dance* which does not have the electricity of Julian Bream's solo version. The recording is very natural, but no information is provided about the music (except titles).

Los Romeros

Spanish guitar favourites (with Pepe Romero, Celín Romero, Celedonio Romero, Celino Romero): GIMENEZ: *La boda de Luis Alonso: Malagueña – Zapateado; El baile de Luis Alonso: Intermedio*. BOCCHERINI: *Guitar quintet No. 4 in D, G.448: Grave – Fandango*. Celedonio ROMERO: *Fantasia Cubana; Malagueñas*. FALLA: *El amor brujo: Ritual fire dance*. SOR: *L'encouragement, Op. 34*. PRAETORIUS: *Bransle de la torche; Ballet; Volta*. TARREGA: *Capricho árabe*. TURINA: *La oración del torero*. TORROBA: *Estampas*.
❁ *** Ph. Dig. 442 781-2 [id.].

Opening with a compelling *Malagueña – Zapateado* of Jerónimo Giménez and closing with an engaging and lighter *Intermedio* encore by the same composer, both from zarzuelas, this 74-minute collection of mainly Spanish music grips and entertains the listener as at a live concert. Celedonio contributes two pieces of his own, a charming solo lightweight *Fantasia Cubana*, and the others join him for his glittering flamenco *Malagueñas*, which has an improvisatory central section before the dashing coda with castanets.

Among the more famous pieces arranged for the four players are the very effective Falla *Ritual fire dance* and Turina's *La oración del torero* (full of evocation), while Sor's *L'encouragement*, with its ingenuous lilting *Cantabile*, a simple but artful *Theme and variations* and elegant closing *Valse*, is played as a duet by Pepe and Celino. Tárrega's haunting *Capricho árabe* is exquisitely phrased by Celino. The arrangement of the three Praetorius dances, with an added condiment of percussion, is colourfully in period. Torroba's *Estampas* brings a highly imaginative response from the group, making this a highlight of the concert. The recording gives the guitars splendid presence against the attractively warm ambience, which in no way blurs the sharpness or focus of the players' attack.

Rubinstein, Artur (piano)

'The last recital for Israel': BEETHOVEN: *Piano sonata No. 23 (Appassionata), Op. 57.* SCHUMANN: *Fantasiestücke, Op. 12.* DEBUSSY: *La plus que lente; Pour le piano: Prélude.* CHOPIN: *Etudes, Op. 25/5; Op. 10/4. Nocturne, Op. 15/2; Polonaise, Op. 53.*
** RCA 09026 61160-2 [id.].

When this disc first appeared, four years ago, it was to great acclaim. One of our finest judges of piano playing and recording called the *Appassionata* 'sensational'. It is amazing in its way, given the fact that the great pianist was eighty-eight when he gave this recital. But to be perfectly honest, this enthusiasm is difficult to share. Indeed the *Appassionata* left R.L. comparatively uninvolved. Perhaps the poor sound-quality contributes to the monochrome impression; the keyboard colour and dynamic range are not as wide as we are used to from this artist, though the sound is better on the CD than on the video-tape (RCA 09026 61160-3). Of course there are some good things during the programme, but on the whole it proves a disappointment.

'Carnegie Hall highlights': DEBUSSY: *Préludes, Book I: La cathédral engloutie; Book II: Ondine. Images, Book I: Hommage à Rameau; Book II: Poissons d'or.* SZYMANOWSKI: *Mazurkas, Op. 50/1–4.* PROKOFIEV: *12 Visions fugitives from Op 22.* VILLA-LOBOS: *Prole do bebê.* SCHUMANN: *Arabesque, Op. 18.* ALBENIZ: *Navarra.*
(M) *** BMG/RCA 09026 61445-2 [id.].

Rubinstein was still at his technical peak when these recordings were made during a series of recitals at Carnegie Hall in October, November and December 1961. The performances are wonderfully poised and spontaneous, and the technical accuracy is little short of amazing when one realizes there were no tape splices here. The Debussy pieces are musically outstanding (Rubinstein announces *Ondine* himself, so it must have been an encore, and he plays it beautifully). The Szymanowski *Mazurkas* have wonderful style and the Prokofiev miniatures show an amazing range of colour and sharp characterization. The titles (*Con eleganza – Pittoresco*; *Ridicolosamente*; *Con vivacità*; *Con una dolce lentezza*; *Dolente*; *Feroce* and the slightly misleading *Allegretto tranquillo*) all speak for themselves. The Villa-Lobos suite of dolls is delightful and the closing *Clown doll* (*Polichinelle*) brings fabulous articulation. After the Schumann *Arabesque*, Rubinstein finds a closing burst of passion for Albéniz's *Navarra*, and the audience's response confirms that this was a closing item. But apart from the applause, the audience is remarkably unobtrusive.

'The music of France': (a) RAVEL: *Valses nobles et sentimentales; Le tombeau de Couperin: Forlane. Miroirs: La vallée des cloches.* POULENC: *3 Mouvements perpétuels; Intermezzi: in A flat; in D flat.* FAURE: *Nocturne in A flat, Op. 33/3.* CHABRIER: *Pièce pittoresque No. 10: Scherzo-valse.* (b) DEBUSSY: *Estampes: La soirée dans Grenade; Jardins sous la pluie; Images, Book I: Hommage à Rameau; Reflets dans l'eau; Book 2: Poissons d'or. La plus que lente; Préludes, Book I: Minstrels.*
(M) *** BMG/RCA (a) stereo / (b) mono 09026 61446-2 [id.].

The main part of this recital dates from 1963. The playing is eminently aristocratic and full of insights. The Ravel pieces and the Poulenc could hardly be bettered. The recording has been further enhanced in the present transfer and has both sonority and presence – it is finer than the Carnegie Hall recordings listed above. The Debussy programme derives from 78s made in 1945 and a 1952 mono LP (*Minstrels* is a very striking account). Indeed all the performances are well worth having, especially *Reflets dans l'eau* where the sound is remarkably open.

Russian Piano School

Russian Piano School: '*The great pianists*' Volumes 11–20.
(M) **(*) BMG/Melodiya 74321 33230-2 (10) [id.].

We covered the first ten CDs of the *Russian Piano School* in our last main edition, and now RCA have followed it up with another set of ten. As with the first, they have wisely made them available separately and have also priced them competitively. The artists represented in this second set are less well known (some of them are barely even names outside Russia), but the same astonishing standards of pianistic wizardry and poetic insight prevail. There are some splendid things in this box; but this is another case where the collector is best advised to pick and choose among the separate issues. Yelena Bekman-Shcherbina is hardly known in the West, yet her recital is unforgettable, and there are other little-known but not less distinguished pianists to be discovered here, notably Edvard Syomin and, the youngest artist on the present roster (at the time of making the recordings), Yekaterina Ervy-Novitskaya. Readers will observe that we have given Grigory Ginsburg's remarkable collection of Liszt's *Concert paraphrases* a Rosette (BMG/Melodiya mono 64321 33210-2 – see below).

Bekman-Shcherbina, Yelena

Volume 11: GLINKA/BALAKIREV: *The Lark*. BALAKIREV: *Au jardin (Etude-idylle in D flat)*. GLINKA: *Souvenir de mazurka*. TITOV: *Waltzes: in F min.; G; E min*. LISZT: *Concert paraphrase of Alyabiev's 'The Nightingale'*. RUBINSTEIN: *Waltzes: in A flat, Op. 14/1; in F, Op. 82/5; Barcarolle in A min., Op. 93/3*. TCHAIKOVSKY: *Scherzo humoristique in D, Op. 19/2*. LIADOV: *Mazurkas: in D min., Op. 15/2; in G (Rustique), Op. 31/1*. GLAZUNOV: *Etude in E (Night), Op. 31/3*. ARENSKY: *Le ruisseau dans la forêt, Op. 36/15; Etude in F sharp, Op. 36/13*. SCRIABIN: *Preludes: in A; in F sharp min., Op. 15/1–2; Waltz in A flat, Op. 38*. RACHMANINOV: *Prelude in G, Op. 32/5; Etudes-tableaux: in E flat min.; E flat, Op. 33/6–7*.
(M) (***) BMG/Melodiya mono 74321 33209-2 [id.].

Yelena Bekman-Shcherbina is one of the least familiar names and, in the words of Christoph Rueger, her playing 'breathed the elegant, sentimental and patriotic atmosphere of the Russian salon at the turn of the century'. The Balakirev transcription of Glinka's *The Lark*, a transcription of one of the songs from *Farewell to St Petersburg*, is an ideal example of this, and so are the Arensky *Le ruisseau dans la forêt* and Balakirev's *Au jardin* (*Etude-idylle in D flat*). Born in 1882, the same year as Stravinsky, Bekman-Shcherbina studied with Paul Pabst, a teacher of Goldenweiser and Vasily Safonov. She gave the first performances of a number of Scriabin pieces and championed the music of Debussy, Roger-Ducasse and Sibelius. She possessed a wonderful cantabile touch and a melting lyricism. Listen to her Rachmaninov *G major Prelude*! These recordings were all made in 1948 and 1950, not long before her death, and few allowances need to be made for their quality (we have heard worse recordings from the 1970s!). A find!

Ginsburg, Grigory

Volume 12: LISZT: Concert paraphrases: *Fantasia on two themes from Mozart's Nozze di Figaro'* (completed Busoni); *Reminiscences from: Mozart's 'Don Giovanni'; Bellini's 'Norma'; Verdi's 'Rigoletto'; Gounod's 'Faust'*. GINSBURG: *Transcription of 'Largo al factotum' from Rossini's 'Barbiere di Siviglia'*.
❁ (M) (***) BMG/Melodiya mono 64321 33210-2 [id.].

Grigory Ginsburg featured in the earlier ten-CD collection in partnership with his teacher, Alexander Goldenweiser, but his solo recordings are quite dazzling. He was a celebrated Liszt performer and this disc is one of the highlights of a set that is itself all highlights! The *Fantasia on two themes from Mozart's 'Nozze di Figaro'* completed by Busoni beggars description for its lightness of touch and sheer virtuosity. Ginsburg's own transcription of the *Largo al factotum* from Rossini's *Barbiere di Siviglia* has enormous sparkle and humour – not to mention virtuosity. Ginsburg died in 1961 and these recordings, which are of varying quality, come from 1948–58 (the earliest are by no means the most frail). In any event, such is the magnetism of the playing that any sonic limitations are forgotten.

Oborin, Lev

Volume 13: BEETHOVEN: *Sonata No. 31 in A flat, Op. 110*. CHOPIN: *Sonata No. 3 in B min., Op. 58*. BRAHMS: *4 Pieces, Op. 119*. SCRIABIN: *Sonata No. 2 in G sharp min. (Sonata-fantaisie), Op. 19*.
(M) (**) BMG/Melodiya mono 74321 33211-2 [id.].

Lev Oborin belongs to the same generation as Ginsburg and is best remembered in the West as a marvellous chamber-music partner who recorded with Oistrakh and Knushevitzky, though he made relatively few solo appearances. He won the Chopin Competition in 1927, where he won the special accolade of Szymanowski, who is reported to have said, 'It is no shame to bow before him. He creates beauty.' The Beethoven *Sonata in A flat*, Op. 110, recorded in 1952, is an immaculately classical and selfless account, handicapped by an instrument which needs the ministrations of a technician. It is nevertheless a distinguished performance, more so than the Chopin *B minor Sonata*, recorded the previous year. Both the Brahms *Pieces*, Op. 119, and the Scriabin *Second Sonata*, recorded in 1953 and 1955 respectively, are refined and musicianly without perhaps being outstanding.

Grinberg, Maria

Volume 14: SEIXAS: *Minuet in F min.; Toccata in F min.* SOLER: *Sonatas Nos. 2 in C sharp min.; 11 in G min.; 12 in F sharp min.* Domentico SCARLATTI: *Sonatas, Kk.11, 22, 69 & 113.* MOZART: *Fantasia in C min., K.396* (completed Stadler). SCHUMANN: *Bunte Blätter, Op. 99*, excerpts: *Nos. 1–8; 10 & 13.* BRAHMS: *Variations on a theme of Schumann in F sharp min., Op. 11; Waltzes Op. 39/1, 3, 6–7, 15–16.*
(M) **(*) BMG/Melodiya stereo/mono 74321 33212-2 [id.].

Maria Grinberg was born in Odessa in 1908 (the birthplace of so many Russian musicians from Horowitz to Oistrakh) and made some appearances outside the then Soviet Union, including Holland, but did not make a lasting impression. She is obviously an artist of remarkable quality and the pieces by Seixas, Soler and Domenico Scarlatti, recorded in 1967, show an astonishing elegance and style. These are marvellous and subtle performances, alone worth the price of the disc. The Schumann *Bunte Blätter*, Op. 99, are played superbly but the 1947 recording is clangorous and messy. The Brahms *Variations on a theme of Schumann*, recorded in 1964 in decent sound, are quite masterly – among the best accounts of the piece to have been put on record.

Nikolayeva, Tatiana Petrovna

Volume 15: SCHUMANN: *3 Romances, Op. 28; Variations on an original theme in E flat.* PROKOFIEV: *Sonata No. 8 in B flat, Op. 84; Peter and the wolf, Op. 69* (music only; freely transribed Nikolayeva).
(M) **(*) BMG/Melodiya 74321 33213-2 [id.].

Tatiana Nikolayeva has enjoyed celebrity in the West, thanks to her recordings of the Shostakovich *Preludes and fugues*, which were dedicated to her. The Schumann was recorded in 1983 (the sound is airless and close), the Prokofiev in the early 1960s. She certainly makes the Prokofiev *Eighth Sonata* very much her own and holds the listener in thrall in much the same ways as did Gilels and Richter. Her own transcription of *Peter and the wolf* is as imaginative as its execution. Performances of stature.

Zhukov, Igor

Volume 16: BACH: *Passacaglia in C min., BWV 582* (arr. ZHUKOV). SCHUMANN: *Waldszenen, Op. 82.* TCHAIKOVSKY: *Souvenir de Hapsal, Op. 2.* RACHMANINOV: *Barcarolle in G min., Op. 10/3.* PROKOFIEV: *Children's music (12 easy pieces), Op. 65.*
(M) ** BMG/Melodiya stereo/mono 74321 33214 [id.].

Ashkenazy, Vladimir

Volume 17: CHOPIN: *24 Etudes, Op. 10/1–12; Op. 25/1–12.* LISZT: *Mephisto waltz No. 1.*
(M) (***) BMG/Melodiya mono 74321 33215 [id.].

The two pianists featured in the pair of CDs listed above are familiar in the West, Igor Zhukov less so than Vladimir Ashkenazy. Zhukov has recorded concertos by, among others, Medtner (No. 1), Rimsky-Korsakov and Balakirev, which have been in and out of the catalogue here. In them his virtuosity is pretty electrifying. By the exalted standards of this set as a whole, however, he is, relatively speaking, average – but that is no mean compliment in this context! If you are collecting individual discs rather than the whole box, this is not one to which you need give the highest priority. The Schumann *Waldszenen* and the Tchaikovsky and Rachmaninov items come off well, and the Prokofiev *Children's music*, Op. 65, is a rarity. The Ashkenazy recital is the familiar set of the *Etudes*, Opp. 10 and 25, from 1959–60, once available on Chant du Monde, and is one of the classics of the piano discography; the *Mephisto waltz No. 1* makes an admirable bonus. The sound is quite respectable.

Virsaladze, Eliso

Volume 18: CHOPIN: *Sonata No. 3 in B min., Op. 58; Ballade No. 3 in A flat, Op. 47; Mazurkas Nos. 21 in C sharp min., Op. 30/4;; 23 in D, Op. 33/2; Waltzes Nos. 2 in A flat, Op. 34/1; 9 in A flat, Op. 69/1; Nocturne No. 8 in D flat, Op. 27/2; Polonaises Nos. 6 in A flat (Heroic), Op. 53; 7 (Polonaise-fantaisie), Op. 61.*
(M) ** BMG/Melodiya 74321 33216-2 [id.].

Syomin, Edvard

Volume 19: GODOWSKY: *Renaissance* (free arrangements after Rameau), *Nos. 1, 3 & 6.* CHOPIN: *Souvenir de Paganini; Berceuse in D flat, Op. 57.* STANCHINSKY: *3 Preludes* (1907); *5 Preludes* (1907–12). MEDTNER: *Fairy-tales, Op. 20.* EIGES: *Sonata-Toccata No. 4, Op. 15.* ALBENIZ: *Navarra; Tango in D, Op. 165/2.* BUSONI: *Chamber fantasia on Bizet's opera 'Carmen'.* GODOWSKY: *Künsterleben (symphonic metamorphoses on Johann Strauss's waltz).*
(M) *** BMG/Melodiya stereo/mono 74321 33217-2 [id.].

Eliso Virsaladze's Chopin is admirable but not special, certainly not as extraordinary as Edvard Syomin's recital. Nikolayeva spoke of Syomin's 'profound musical culture, virtuosity and freedom of self-expression'. Born in Moscow in 1945, he remains virtually unknown outside his native country, and the development of his career was, so Christoph Rueger's notes tell us, handicapped by a family tragedy and hindered by the Soviet regime. Fortunately he enjoyed the patronage of Melodiya and the Soviet Radio, and it is from their archives that the present recordings come. The recordings range from 1969 through to 1985 and are of variable quality, but the playing in the Busoni *Carmen fantasy* is astonishing. The *Preludes* by Alexei Stanchinsky (1888–1914) are quite touching and, apart from Daniel Blumenthal's record of the *Piano sonatas* for Marco Polo, his only current representation in the catalogue.

Ervy-Novitskaya, Yekaterina

Volume 20: PROKOFIEV: *Sarcasms, Op. 17; Visions fugitives, Op. 22; Romeo and Juliet: 10 Pieces, Op. 75.*
(M) *** BMG/Melodiya 74321 33218-2 [id.].

The youngest of the pianists in this collection (at the time of making her recordings) is Yekaterina Ervy-Novitskaya, who was born in 1951. She received much encouragement from Lev Oborin, whose post-graduate assistant she became. When she was seventeen she won the first prize at the *Concours Musicale Reine Elisabeth* in Brussels. But the acclaim of such keyboard luminaries as Neuhaus and Rubinstein did not prevent her from retiring from the platform to settle in Brussels and devote herself to bringing up a family and to teaching. She made a comeback in Moscow in 1995; but these recordings come from 1969, when she was eighteen, save for the *Romeo and Juliet Pieces*, Op. 75, recorded in 1975. In any event she obviously has great affinity for the composer, and her account both of the *Fifth Sonata* (in its post-war, revised version) and of the *Visions fugitives* are impressively characterized.

Salomon Quartet

'The string quartet in 18th-century England': ABEL: *Quartet in A, Op. 8/5.* SHIELD: *Quartet in C min., Op. 3/6.* MARSH: *Quartet in B flat.* WEBBE: *Variations in A on 'Adeste fidelis'.* Samuel WESLEY: *Quartet in E flat.*
** Hyperion Dig. CDA 66780 [id.].

A good idea, let down by the indifferent invention of much of the music itself. The amateur, John Marsh, stands up very well alongside his professional companions, and his five-movement *Quartet in B flat* (modelled on Haydn's Op. 1/1 and almost as pleasing) is the first piece to catch the listener's attention, for Abel is a very dull dog indeed. Samuel Webbe's *Variations on 'O come all ye faithful'* do little but repeat the melody with decorations. Samuel Wesley begins conventionally and agreeably, then produces a real lollipop as the Trio of the Minuet and a similarly winning finale. No complaints about the performances: the Salomon Quartet play everything freshly and with total commitment, using original instruments stylishly and in the sweetest possible manner. They are very realistically recorded, too. Three stars for the performers but not the programme.

Satoh, Toyohiko (lute)

'Gaultier and the French lute school': Ennemond GAULTIER: *Tombeau de Mezangeau; Courante; Carillon; Rossignol; Testament de Mezangeau; Canarie.* Dennis GAULTIER: *Tombeau de Madamoiselle Gaultier; Cleopâtre amante (Double).* Jacques GALLOT: *Prélude; Le bout de l'An de M. Gaultier; Courante la cigogne; Sarabande la pièce de huit heures. Volte la Brugeoise.* DUFAUT: *Prélude; Tombeau de M. Blanrocher; Dourante; Sarabande (Double); Gigue.* MOUTON: *Prélude. Tombeau de Gogo (Allemande); La belle homicide/Courante de M. Gaultier (Double de la belle homicide); Gavotte; La Princesse sarabande; Canarie.* Robert de VISEE: *Tombeau de M.Mouton (Allemande).*
*** Channel Classics Dig. CCS 8795 [id.].

Toyohiko Satoh has already given us a collection of the music of Robert de Visée (CCS 7795) whose *Tombeau de M. Mouton* provides one of the most affecting pieces here, to close a recital which is in essence a survey of French lute music of the seventeenth century. Satoh is clearly an expert in this field, and he plays an original lute made by Laurentius Grieff of Ingolstadt in 1613, which was modified into an 11-course French baroque instrument around 1670. It took four years for the Dutch lute-maker, Van der Waals, to restore it to playing condition, and its gut strings create a pleasingly warm sonority. Satoh's playing is robust yet thoughtful and it has an improvisatory freedom which extends even to the dance movements. (Dufaut's *Gigue*, for instance, is jolly enough but would be difficult to dance to.) This is apparently possible because, around 1630, a new French tuning was developed within the lute school centring round Le vieux Gaultier (Ennemond Gaultier of Lyon, 1575–1651). This allowed more freedom for the fingers of the left hand, enabling lutenists to write their music in a *style brisé* (broken style), which was later to spread across Europe. Gaultier and his cousin Denis (Gaultier le jeune) were important innovators in their time and they also introduced the idea of the dignified 'tombeau' mementos, as well as vignettes with sobriquets like *Le rossignol* and *Carillon*, yet which are in no way imitative. The two versions of the *Canarie* (by Ennemond Gaultier and Mouton respectively) are based on the same melody and dance form, with a dotted rhythm, and both are among the more striking items here, alongside the expressive *Sarabande* of Dufaut and Mouton's *La Princesse*, which features the famous *La Folia*. Rather unexpectedly, the same composer's *La belle homicide* is a cheerful piece.

Scandinavian Wind Quintet

Danish concert: NIELSEN: *Wind quintet, Op. 43.* HOLMBOE: *Notturno, Op. 19.* NORGARD: *Whirl's world.* ABRAHAMSEN: *Walden.*
*** Marco Polo Dacapo Dig. 8.224001 [id.].

The Scandinavian Wind Quintet give an eminently acceptable account of the Nielsen which can stand up to most of the competition. The Holmboe *Notturno* is a beautiful piece from 1940 whose language blends the freshness of Nielsen with the neo-classicism of Hindemith yet remains totally distinctive. The Nørgård is less substantial but is not otherwise available; Hans Abrahamsen's *Walden* is thin but atmospheric. Very present and lifelike recording.

Schiller, Allan (piano)

'Für Elise': Popular piano pieces: BEETHOVEN: *Für Elise.* FIELD: *Nocturne in E (Noontide).* CHOPIN: *Mazurka in B flat, Op. 7/1; Waltz in A, Op. 34/2. 3 Ecossaisen, Op. 72/3; Fantaisie-impromptu, Op. 66.* MENDELSSOHN: *Songs without words: Venetian gondola song, Op. 19; Bees' wedding, Op. 67.* LISZT: *Consolation No. 3 in D flat.* DE SEVERAC: *The music box.* DEBUSSY: *Suite bergamasque: Clair de lune. Arabesques Nos. 1 and 2. Prélude: The girl with the flaxen hair.* GRIEG: *Wedding day at Troldhaugen; March of the dwarfs.* ALBENIZ: *Granada; Tango; Asturias.*
(BB) *** ASV CDQS 6032.

A particularly attractive recital, diverse in mood, spontaneous in feeling and very well recorded. The acoustic is resonant, but the effect is highly realistic. There are many favourites here, with Allan Schiller at his most personable in the engaging Field *Nocturne*, De Severac's piquant *Music box* and the closing *Asturias* of Albéniz, played with fine bravura. The Chopin group, too, is most successful, with the Scottish rhythmic snap of the *Ecossaisen* neatly articulated and the famous *B flat Mazurka* presented most persuasively.

Scott Whiteley, John (organ)

Organ of York Minster: *'Great Romantic organ music'*: TOURNEMIRE: *Improvisation on the Te Deum.* JONGEN: *Minuet-Scherzo, Op. 53.* MULET: *Tu es Petra.* DUPRE: *Prelude and fugue in G min., Op. 3/7.* R. STRAUSS: *Wedding prelude.* KARG-ELERT: *Pastel in B, Op. 92/1.* BRAHMS: *Chorale prelude: O Gott, du frommer Gott, Op. 122/7.* LISZT: *Prelude and fugue on BACH, G.260.*
*** York CD 101.

A superb organ recital, with the huge dynamic range of the York Minster organ spectacularly captured on CD and pianissimo detail registering naturally. John Scott Whiteley's playing is full of flair: the attractively complex and sparklingly florid *Prelude and fugue* of Marcel Dupré is exhilarating and reaches a high climax, while the grand Liszt piece is hardly less overwhelming. The opening Tournemire *Improvisation* is very arresting indeed, while Jongen's *Minuet-Scherzo* displays Scott Whiteley's splendidly clear articulation.

Steele-Perkins, Crispian (trumpet), Stephen Cleobury (organ)

'The King's trumpeter': MATHIAS: *Processional.* L. MOZART: *Concerto in E flat.* BOYCE: *Voluntaries in D.* ANON.: *3 16th Century dances.* TELEMANN: *Concerto da caccia in D.* GOUNOD: *Meditation: Ave Maria.* STEELE: *6 Pieces, Op. 33.*
**(*) Priory Dig. PRCD 189 [id.].

Crispian Steele-Perkins is here given a chance to show his paces on a modern trumpet. The programme opens with Mathias's distinctly catchy *Processional* and covers a fairly wide range of repertoire, ending with the six characterful pieces by Christopher Steele. The disc is relatively short measure (53 minutes), but the playing is first class and the balance most convincing.

Stern, Isaac (violin)

'A Life in Music': Boxes III–IV (for Boxes I–II, see under Orchestral and Concertante Music)

'A Life in music': Box III
(M) **(*) Sony Analogue/Dig. SX12K 67195 (12) [id.].

Volume 16: (i) BACH: *Trio sonatas in G, BWV 1038; in C min., BWV 1079.* W. F. BACH: *Trio sonata in A min.* (ii) J. C. BACH: *Trio sonata in C.* (iii) *Sonata in C.* (ii) TELEMANN: *Quartet (Trio sonata) in E min.* (with (i; ii; iii) Jean-Pierre Rampal (flute); (i) Leslie Parnas (cello); (ii) Mstislav Rostropovich (cello); (i; iii) John Steele Ritter ((i) harpsichord; (iii) fortepiano); (ii) Matthias Spaeter (lute)) (Dig. SMK 64509) [id.].

Volume 17: BEETHOVEN: *Piano trios Nos. 1–3, Op. 1/1–3; 8, WoO 38; 10 (Variations in E flat), Op. 44;* (with Leonard Rose (cello), Eugene Istomin (piano)) (SM2K 64510) [id.].

Volume 18: BEETHOVEN: *Piano trios Nos. 4 in B flat, Op. 11; 5 in D (Ghost), Op. 70/1; 6 in E flat, Op. 70/2; 7 in B flat (Archduke), Op. 97; 9 in B flat, WoO 39; 11 (Variations on 'Ich bin der Schneider Kakadu'), Op. 121a* (with Leonard Rose (cello), Eugene Istomin (piano)) (SM2K 64513) [id.].

Volume 19: (i) SCHUBERT: *Piano trios Nos. 1–2, Op. 99, 100.* (ii) MOZART: *Piano quartet No. 2 in E flat, K.493.* (i) HAYDN: *Piano trio in E flat, Hob XV/10* ((i) with Leonard Rose (cello); (ii) with Milton Katims (viola), Mischa Schneider (cello); (i; ii) with Eugene Istomin (piano)) (SM2K 64516 (2)) [id.].

Volume 20: MENDELSSOHN: *Piano trios Nos. 1 in D min., Op. 49; 2 in C min., Op. 66* (with Leonard Rose (cello), Eugene Istomin (piano)) (SMK 64519) [id.].

Volume 21: BRAHMS: *Piano trios Nos. 1 in B, Op. 8; 2 in C, Op. 87; 3 in C min., Op. 101* (with Leonard Rose (cello), Eugene Istomin (piano)); *Piano quartets Nos. 1 in G min., Op. 25; 2 in A, Op. 26; 3 in C min., Op. 60* (with Jaime Laredo (viola), Yo-Yo Ma (cello), Emanuel Ax (piano)) (SM3K 64520 (3)) [id.].

Volume 22: (i) ANON.: *Greensleeves*. FOSTER: *I dream of Jeannie with the light brown hair*. KREISLER: *Liebesleid*. SCHUBERT: *Ave Maria*. (ii) MENDELSSOHN: *On wings of song*. (i) BRAHMS: *Hungarian Dance No. 5*. DVORAK: *Humoresque*. RIMSKY-KORSAKOV: *Flight of the bumblebee*. (ii) RACHMANINOV: *Vocalise*. (i) TCHAIKOVSKY: *None but the lonely heart*. (ii) BORODIN: *Nocturne*. (i) BENJAMIN: *Jamaican Rumba*. (ii) SATIE: *Gymnopédie No. 3*. (i) GERSHWIN: *Bess, you is my woman now*. COPLAND: *Hoedown* (with (i, ii) Columbia SO; (i) Milton Katims; (ii) Frank Brieff) (SMK 64537) [id.].

With Box III it is perhaps better to pick and choose rather than to go for the complete box. The *Trio sonatas* by Bach and his sons plus an attractive work of Telemann offer some very distinguished playing (especially in the performances featuring Rostropovich) and one can adjust to the up-front balance. The Beethoven and Brahms *Piano trios* and *Quartets* are indispensable, but the Schubert and Mendelssohn are not. Many will enjoy the final selection of lollipops, sumptuously recorded, although the effect is a bit schmaltzy and they are best taken in small doses. Superb playing, of course, as throughout all three Boxes. All the records (or smaller compilations) are available separately and most are discussed in detail under their composer entries. Overall this is a remarkable achievement.

'A Life in music': Box IV: Chamber and instrumental music
(M) **(*) Sony Analogue/Dig. SX12K 67196 (12) [id.].

Box IV completes Sony's Isaac Stern Edition and in many ways it is one of the most attractive collections in the survey. Each issue is available separately.

Volume 23: C. P. E. BACH or J. S. BACH: *Sonata in G min., BWV 1020*. J. S. BACH: *Violin sonata* (for violin and harpsichord) *No. 3, BWV 1016; Sonata for violin and continuo, BWV 1023*. HANDEL: *Sonata in D, Op. 1/3*. TARTINI: *Sonata in G min. (Dido Abbandonata), Op. 1/10* (with Alexander Zakin) (mono SMK 68361) [id.].

These recordings come from 1952–3 and, although the violin is balanced rather forwardly, in all other respects the mono recording is first class. Stern shows himself thoroughly at home in baroque repertoire; even though he uses a minimum of embellishments, the style is impeccable. The *Adagio* of the *G minor Sonata*, now thought to be by C. P. E. Bach, is glorious. Alexander Zakin is a splendid partner, playing simply and directly and making one feel for the moment that these works were intended to be heard in a violin/piano partnership, even the continuo sonata, BWV 1023. Similarly in Handel, Stern plays the noble line of the *D major Sonata* with natural sympathy and unexaggerated warmth. The (originally three-movement) Tartini *Sonata* is heard in an arrangement by Leopold Auer, who added a *Largo* taken from the fifth sonata of the same opus, which makes a suitably dramatic interlude to lead into the lively finale. The connection of the work with Metastasio's libretto about Dido (set to music by at least four composers) is obscure, but it served to keep the sonata in the repertoire.

Volume 24: BEETHOVEN: *Violin sonatas Nos. 1–10* (with Eugene Istomin) (Dig./Analogue SM3K 64524 (3)) [id.].

Stern and Istomin make an inspirational partnership, obviously striking sparks off each other in performances that are brimming with zest and vitality. The performances have striking rhythmic strengths as well as lyrical appeal and are discussed more fully under their composer entry.

Volume 25: SCHUBERT: *Violin sonatinas Nos. 1–3; Rondo in B min. (Rondeau brillant), D.895; Duo in A (Grand duo), D.574; Fantaisie in C, D.934* (all with Daniel Barenboim). HAYDN: *Violin concerto in C, Hob VIIa/1* (with Columbia CO) (Dig./Analogue (mono) SM2K 64528 (2)) [id.].

Stern and Barenboim find an ideal partnership: the performances have a natural warmth and plenty of character, yet there is an unaffected simplicity and directness of style which especially suits the three early *Sonatinas*. The Haydn *Concerto*, excellently recorded in mono in 1947, is a very acceptable bonus.

Volume 26: BRAHMS: *Violin sonatas Nos. 1–3* (with Alexander Zakin) (SMK 64531) [id.].

Stern and Zakin give splendidly vital and characterful performances of the Brahms *Sonatas*. They have genuine power and conviction, but the 1960 recording brings the usual CBS problem of that period: Stern was far too close to the microphones. The original LP produced far from comfortable tone-quality, but the improvement in the CD remastering is very striking; his tone now emerges, closely scrutinized but unscathed and despite the balance Alexander Zakin's contribution is not submerged. Admirers of these artists will still consider this disc worth its cost.

Volume 27: FRANCK: *Violin sonata in A.* DEBUSSY: *Violin sonata.* ENESCU: *Violin sonata No 3 in A min., Op. 25* (all with Alexander Zakin) (SMK 64532) [id.].

Stern recorded the Franck *Sonata* in 1959. It is a work which suits him especially well and he gives a performance of heartfelt, extrovert feeling, especially in the slow movement, although some might not care for the portamento in its closing bars. Throughout there is much subtlety of detail too. As ever in that period, he was too closely recorded, but the projection suits the intensity of the finale. In some way the Debussy *Sonata* suits him less well; but this is still a commanding performance, impossible not to enjoy, even if one which rather wears its heart on its sleeve. The Enescu *Third Sonata* (1926) is a remarkable work of great vitality and interest, strongly influenced by Romanian folklore, but through its harmonic flavours and rhythmic influences and styles rather than by quoting folksong. The exotic *Andante sostenuto e misterio* even suggests oriental influences from further east and has an improvisatory quality which Stern captures superbly, while the dashing finale throws off sparks of every kind. Its upper tessitura harmonics and histrionics are flawlessly managed, the glissando lyrical spurts given a gypsy passion. In this instance the very close microphones add to the bite, even though, at those times when Stern is pressing hard on the strings, the sound is not quite comfortable.

Volume 28: HINDEMITH: *Violin sonata.* BLOCH: *Violin sonata; Baal shem: Three pictures of Chassidic life* (all with Alexander Zakin). COPLAND: *Violin sonata* (with composer) (mono/stereo SMK 64533) [id.].

The Hindemith *Sonata* (1939) is neither intimidating nor dull. It begins with a friendly if busy melodic flow, and there is a touching melody for the opening and close of the central movement. Stern obviously relishes its engaging *moto perpetuo* central section, and his dainty, light, bravura articulation is spellbinding as the introductory material is reintroduced. The fugal finale again opens simply and, even if its harmonic progressions seem devious at first hearing, their Hindemithian logic soon falls into place. The mono recording, from 1946, is just a little confined but is otherwise very good. Bloch has to be presented with whole-hearted conviction if his music is to make any contact at all, and this performance has just that quality. Stern's playing could hardly be more committed or full of passion and, despite a somewhat forward balance, we would recommend these most persuasive performances of both works, which have never been surpassed.

The Copland recording, which is new to us, is the highlight of the disc. It was made in 1967, with the composer at the piano, and is clearly definitive, for although Stern is still very forward the piano is very much in the picture. The lively central section of the first movement is framed by an *Andante semplice* in which the piano coolly repeats a chordal duplet whose harmonic flavour is instantly identifiable by anyone who has heard the famous Copland ballets. The haunting central *Lento* has a comparable simplicity, and Stern's G-string re-statement of the main theme near the close is particularly telling. The sharply rhythmic finale with its dancing syncopations introduces material we have heard before, notably the coda (which recalls the opening), yet, with the piano chords transformed, the effect is much more upbeat. A marvellously compelling performance, and if Stern is again too near the microphones as Klemperer once said about something entirely different – 'You will get used to it!'

Volume 29: PROKOFIEV: *Violin sonatas Nos. 1–2* (with Alexander Zakin) (SMK 64534) [id.].

Stern's performances with Zakin are of high quality, the *Andante* of the *F minor* memorably atmospheric, especially after the extrovert bravura of the *Allegro brusco*. But here, more than in most of these reissues, the close balance makes Stern's fortissimo timbre sound unnecessarily acerbic.

Volume 30: BARTOK: *Violin sonatas Nos. 1–2* (with Alexander Zakin). WEBERN: *4 Pieces for violin and piano, Op. 7* (with Charles Rosen) (SMK 64535) [id.].

Stern and Zakin are completely involved in the Bartók *Sonatas*, and the cantabile melisma which opens the *Adagio* of the *First Sonata* can never have sounded more lyrically beautiful on record, while the gutsy bravura of the finale is equally compelling. The rapt opening of the *Second Sonata* is comparably concentrated. The four brief, sharply focused Webern *Pieces* are presented with comparable intensity and authority. Once again one must complain about the too-close balance of the recordings, made in 1967 and 1971 respectively, but the effect is not destructive.

Volume 31: 'Encores with piano': SARASATE: *Caprice basque*. PUGNANI: *Sonata in D: Largo espressivo*. NOVACEK: *Perpetuum mobile*. BLOCH: *Baal shem: Nigun (Improvisation)*. LECLAIR: *Sarabande et tambourin*. MOZART: *Haffner Serenade: Rondo allegro*. GLUCK: *Orpheus and Euridyce: Mélodie*. TCHAIKOVSKY: *Valse sentimentale*. SCHUMANN: *Waldszenen: Bird as prophet*. KREISLER: *Schön Rosmarin*. DVORAK: *Slavonic dance, Op. 46/2*. SZYMANOWSKI: *Chant de Roxane; La Fontaine d'Arethuse*. STRAVINSKY: *Firebird: Berceuse*. DINICU: *Hora staccato*. MILHAUD: *Saudades do Brasil: Tijuca*. PROKOFIEV: *Romeo and Juliet: Danse des jeunes filles des Antilles; Masques*. FALLA: *Suite after 7 Spanish popular songs* (with Alexander Zakin) (mono SMK 64536) [id.].

Marvellous playing from Stern throughout: he is quite dazzling in the arrangement of the Rondo from Mozart's *Haffner Serenade*, while the Kreisler transcription of Gluck's most famous *Mélodie* from *Orféo et Euridice* is played with ravishing delicacy. Tchaikovsky's *Valse sentimentale* and Schumann's *Prophet bird* (from *Waldszenen*), arranged by Leopold Auer, are presented with comparable exquisite grace. If elegant flair is what you are looking for, try Kreisler's *Schön Rosmarin*, while Szymanowski's *Chant de Roxane* and *La fontaine d'Arethuse* are ethereally sensuous, helped by Zakin's atmospheric backing. The *Berceuse* from Stravinsky's *Firebird* is infinitely gentle and touching, while for sparkling, easy bravura the Dinicu *Hora staccato* takes some beating. The two excerpts from Prokofiev's *Romeo and Juliet* are indelibly characterized, although they are not less seductive than the exotic closing Falla suite. The recordings are all mono, made in either 1947 or 1952, but the effect is faithful, if a little dry: the opening Sarasate *Caprice basque* ideally needs a more flatteringly sumptuous acoustic.

Tal, Yaara, and Andreas Groethuysen (piano duo)

DVORAK: *From the Bohemian forest, Op. 68*. RUBINSTEIN: *6 Characteristic pictures, Op. 50*. RACHMANINOV: *6 Pieces, Op. 11*.
*** Sony Dig. SK47199 [id.].

Anything that this remarkably musical and sensitive partnership has recorded is special, and this programme – and in particular the Rachmaninov Op. 11 pieces – proves no exception. They make every phrase breathe naturally and freshly.

Thurston Clarinet Quartet

'Clarinet masquerade': FARKAS: *Ancient Hungarian dances from the 17th century*. MOZART (arr. WHEWELL): *Divertimento No. 2*. TOMASI: *3 Divertissements*. GARNER (arr. BLAND): *Misty*. JOBIM (arr. BLAND): *The Girl from Ipanema*. DESPORTES: *French suite*. ALBINONI (arr. THILDE): *Sonata in G min*. STARK: *Serenade*. GERSHWIN (arr. BLAND): *Rhapsody: Summertime*. PHILLIPS (arr. HARVEY): *Cadenza*; (arr. FERNANDEZ): *Muskrat Sousa*.
(M) *** ASV Dig. CDWHL 2076 [id.].

A light-hearted concert, but an entertaining one which will especially appeal to those who like the clarinet's sonority, reedier than the flute's and with more character. The opening suite of Hungarian folk dances (with the chirps and cheeps in the finale very engaging) leads on to a Mozart *Divertimento* for basset horns. The other pieces, the insouciant Tomasi and the Desportes suite (full of Ravelian elegance) are all amiable, and the arrangement of Gershwin's *Summertime* has the famous opening swerve of *Rhapsody in blue* as its introduction. Finally there is the exuberant *Muskrat Sousa* which features a combination of *12th Street Rag* and *South Rampart Street Parade*. The recording is immaculately vivid.

Tureck, Rosalyn (piano)

'Live at the Teatro Colón': BACH: *Adagio in G, BWV 968; Chromatic fantasia and fugue, BWV 903; Partita No. 1, BWV 825: Gigue. Goldberg variation No. 29, BWV 988; Clavierbüchlein for Anna Magdelena Bach: Musette in D*. MENDELSSOHN: *Songs without words, Op. 19/1*. SCHUBERT: *Moments musicaux Nos. 2 in A flat; 3 in F min*. BACH/BUSONI: *Chaconne (from BWV 1004)*. BRAHMS: *Variations and fugue on a theme by Handel, Op. 24*.
**(*) VAI Audio Dig. VIAI 1024-2 (2) [id.].

Rosalyn Tureck has lost none of her magic, as this Buenos Aires (1992) live recital demonstrates, and it is good to find her so sympathetic in Schubert and Mendelssohn, as well as in Bach. Her articulation in the Brahms *Handel variations* suggests she is thinking as much of Handel as of Brahms, but that is a comment, not a criticism. The Bach/Busoni *Chaconne* is splendid. Excellent recording, but there are two snags: the almost hysterical applause which bursts in as soon as a piece has ended and the fact that this recital would almost have fitted on one CD. These two play for just 83 minutes 31 seconds.

Vieaux, Jason (guitar)

Recital: MERLIN: *Suite del recuerdo*. PUJOL: *Preludios Nos. 2, 3 , & 5*. ORBON (de SOTO): *Preludio y Danza*. KROUSE: *Variations on a Moldavian hora*. BARRIOS: *Valses, Op. 8/3 & 4; Julia Florida: Barcarola*. MOREL: *Chôro; Danza Brasileira; Danza in E min*. BUSTAMENTE: *Misionera*.
✿ (BB) *** Naxos Dig. 8.553449 [id.].

This is the finest début guitar recital we have heard for some years. Jason Vieaux is a young American musician, already a prize-winner – and no wonder. This Latin-American repertoire is unfailingly diverting in his hands: there are no familiar names here except that of Barrios, yet almost every item is either memorably evocative or it makes the pulse quicken. Vieaux's completely natural rubato at the opening *Evocación* of José Luis Merlin's *Suite del recuerdo* is quite masterly and the slow crescendos in the final *Carnavalito* are thrilling; then there is a complete change of mood and the *Evocación* makes a haunting return before the final *Joropo*. The *Preludios* of Pujol are quite magical; Vieaux then lets his hair down for the *Candombe*. The two *Valses* of Barrios are deliciously fragile, with the central *Barcarola* hardly less subtle, while the more robust Brazilian dances of Jorge Morel have real panache. The Naxos recording has good ambience and is present yet not too closely balanced. Unforgettable.

Wagler, Dietrich (organ)

'Great European organs, No. 24': Freiberg Dom, Silbermann organ: SCHEIDT: *Magnificat Noni toni*. CLERAMBAULT: *Suite de premier ton*. BUXTEHUDE: *Prelude and fugue in D min*. KREBS: *Choral preludes: Mein Gott, das Herze bring ich dir; Herr Jesus Christ, dich zu uns wend; Herzlich tut mich verlangen; O Ewigkeit du Donnerwort*. J. S. BACH: *Fantasie in G; Prelude and fugue in C*.
**(*) Priory Dig. PRCD 332 [id.].

The organ, rather than the player, is the star of this record; the latter's performances are sound but very much in the traditional German style. But he knows his instrument and the opening *Magnificat Noni toni* of Scheidt sounds resplendent, with the following Clerambault *Suite* also very effectively registered. A well-balanced programme, lacking only the last degree of flair in presentation.

Wild, Earl (piano)

'The virtuoso piano': HERZ: *Variations on 'Non più mesta' from Rossini's La Cenerentola*. THALBERG: *Don Pasquale fantasy, Op. 67*. GODOWSKY: *Symphonic metamorphosis on themes from Johann Strauss's Künsterleben (Artist's life)*. RUBINSTEIN: *Etude (Staccato), Op. 23/2*. HUMMEL: *Rondo in E flat, Op. 11*. PADEREWSKI: *Theme and variations, Op. 16/3*.
(M) *** Van. 08.4033.71 [OVC 4033].

Earl Wild's famous performances from the late 1960s re-emerge on CD with their scintillating brilliance given even greater projection by the digital remastering. Wild's technique is prodigious and his glittering bravura in the engaging Herz *Rossini variations* and Thalberg's equally entertaining *Don Pasquale fantasy* is among the finest modern examples of the grand tradition of virtuoso pianism. Godowsky's piece may have a heavy title, but in Earl Wild's hands, for all the decorative complexities, the lilting waltz-rhythms are still paramount.

Williams, John (guitar)

'Spanish guitar music': I. ALBENIZ: *Asturias; Tango; Cordoba; Sevilla*. SANZ: *Canarios*. TORROBA: *Nocturno; Madroños*. SAGRERAS: *El Colibri*. M. ALBENIZ: *Sonata in D*. FALLA: *Homenaje; Three-cornered hat: Corregidor's dance; Miller's dance. El amor brujo: Fisherman's song*. CATALAN FOLKSONGS: *La Nit de Nadal; El noy de la mare; El testamen de Amelia*. GRANADOS: *La maja de Goya. Spanish dance No. 5*. TARREGA: *Recuerdos de la Alhambra*. VILLA-LOBOS: *Prelude No. 4 in E min*. MUDARRA: *Fantasia*. TURINA: *Fandanguillo, Op. 36*.
(M) *** Sony SBK 46347; *SBT 46347* [id.].

John Williams can show strong Latin feeling, as in the vibrant *Farruca* of the *Miller's dance* from Falla's

Three-cornered hat, or create a magically atmospheric mood, as in the hauntingly registered transcription of the *Fisherman's song* from *El amor brujo*. He can play with thoughtful improvisatory freedom, as in the Villa-Lobos *Prelude*, with its pianissimo evocation, or be dramatically spontaneous, as in the memorable performance of Turina's *Fandanguillo*, which ends the recital magnetically. The instinctive control of atmosphere and dynamic is constantly rewarding throughout a varied programme, and the technique is phenomenal, yet never flashy, always at the service of the music. The remastering brings a clean and truthful, if very immediate, image. Background is minimal and never intrusive.

Wilson, Christopher (lute)

'La Magdalena' (Lute music in Renaissance France): BLONDEAU (publ. ATTAIGNANT): *La brosse (Recoupe et Tourdion); La Magdalena (Recoupe et Tourdion).* ANON., publ. ATTAIGNANT: *Bransle de Poictou; Tant que vivray; Pavane; Gaillarde; Prelude; Une bergerotte.* FRANCESCO DE PARIGI: *2 Recercars.* BERLIN: *Fantaisie No. 3; Trio No. 2.* PALADIN: *Anchor che col partir; Fantaisie.* MORLAYE: *Bransle d'Ecosse No. 1; Bransle gay; Fantaisie; Sans liberté; Pavane; Gaillarde piemontoise.* ALBERT DE RIPPE: *Pleurés mes yeux; 2 Fantaisies; Galliarde.* Adrian LE ROY: *Passemeze; La souris.* BAKFARK: *Si grand è la pietà.*
*** Virgin Veritas/EMI Dig. VC5 45140-2.

An agreeable, unassertive, hour-long programme for the late evening, although perhaps a few more lively dances would have made the recital even more attractive. Certain items stand out, like the anonymous portrayal of *Une bergerotte*, the title-piece and the two works of Jean Paul Paladin (although *Anchor che col partir* is a transcription of a famous madrigal of the period – by Cipriano da Rore). Valentin Bakfark's *Si grand è la pietà* brings yet another madrigal arrangement (by Jacques Arcadelt). Most of this music has a character of gentle melancholy, so the exceptions, like the *Bransle gay* and the *Gaillarde piemontoise* (both by Morlaye), make a welcome diversion. The two pieces by Adrian Le Roy are also rather more extrovert, but the pervading atmosphere is doleful. Christopher Wilson plays with much sensitivity and he is beautifully recorded, provided one accepts the rather misty, ecclesiastical acoustic.

Yates, Sophie (virginals)

English virginals music: BYRD: *Praeludium – Fantasia; The barley breake; The Tennthe pavan (Sir William Petre); Galliard to the Tennthe pavan; The woods so wild; Hugh Aston's ground; The Bells.* DOWLAND: *Lachrymae pavan* (arr. BYRD). James HARDING: *Galliard* (arr. BYRD). GIBBONS: *Fantasia.* ANON.: *My Lady Careys dompe.* TOMKINS: *Barafostus's dreame.* Hugh ASTON: *Hornepype.* BULL: *In nomine.*
** Chandos Dig. CHAN 0574 [id.].

Sophie Yates is a thoughtful and accomplished player and she uses a modern copy by Peter Bavington of an Italian instrument made at the very beginning of the seventeenth century. Her programme is well thought out and, even though it is dominated by the music of Byrd, it is musically well balanced. The snag is the resonant recording, which gives a larger-than-life impression of the instrument which even the lowering of the volume control does not entirely diminish.

Zabaleta, Nicanor (harp)

'Arpa española': ALBENIZ: *Managueña, Op. 165/3; Suite española: Granada (Serenata); Zaragoza (Capricho); Asturias (Leyenda). Mallorca, Op. 202; Tango español.* FALLA: *Serenata andaluza.* TURINA: *Ciclo pianistico No. 1: Tocata y fuga.* GOMBAU: *Apunte bético.* GRANADOS: *Danza española No. 5.* HALFFTER: *Sonatina* (ballet): *Danza de la pastora.* LOPEZ-CHAVARRI: *El viejo castillo moro.*
❁ (M) *** DG 435 847-2 [id.].

A good deal of the music here belongs to the guitar (or piano) rather than the harp, but Nicanor Zabaleta, with his superb artistry and sense of atmosphere, makes it all his own. Throughout this delightful programme, Zabaleta gives each piece strong individuality of character. In the Granados *Spanish dance No. 5* he matches the magnetism of Julian Bream's famous recording, and Manuel de Falla's *Serenata andaluza* is hardly less captivating. DG's sound balance is near perfection, as is the choice of acoustic, and the magic distilled by Zabaleta's concentration, often at the gentlest levels of dynamic, is unforgettable.

Vocal Recitals and Choral Collections

Art of singing

'The Art of singing': Video: *'Golden voices of the century'* (Björling, Callas, Caruso, Chaliapin, Christoff, Corelli, De los Angeles, De Luca, Di Stefano, Flagstad, Gigli, Martinelli, Melchior, Olivero, Pinza, Ponselle, Leontyne Price, Schipa, Stevens, Supervia, Sutherland, Tauber, Tebaldi, Tetrazzini, Tibbett, Vickers, Wunderlich): Excerpts: PUCCINI: *La Bohème*. SAINT-SAENS: *Samson et Dalila*. VERDI: *Rigoletto*. LEONCAVALLO: *I Pagliacci* (all silent film excerpts with Caruso). DONIZETTI: *Lucia di Lammermoor:* sextet with Caruso, mimed. DE CURTIS: song *Torna a Surriento* (Giovanni Martinelli). HANDEL: *Xerxes: Ombra mai fu* (Beniamino Gigli). FLOTOW: *Martha: M'appari* (Tito Schipa). ROSSINI: *Il Barbiere di Siviglia: Largo al factotum* (Giuseppe de Luca). FLOTOW: *Martha: M'appari* (Luisa Tetrazzini). PUCCINI: *La Bohème: Quando me'n vo* (Conchita Supervia). BIZET: *Carmen: Chanson Bohème; Habanera* (Rosa Ponselle). SCHUBERT: *Ständchen* (Richard Tauber). RIMSKY-KORSAKOV: *The Maid of Pskov*. IBERT: *Chanson du duc* (both with Fyodor Chaliapin). WAGNER: *Die Walküre: Hojotoho!* (Kirsten Flagstad). BIZET: *Carmen: Chanson du toréador* (Lawrence Tibbett). SAINT-SAENS: *Samson et Dalila: Mon coeur s'ouvre* (Risë Stevens). WAGNER: *Die Walküre: Winterstürme* (Lauritz Melchior). MUSSORGSKY: *Boris Godunov: Coronation scene* (Ezio Pinza). PUCCINI: *La Bohème: Che gelida manina; Mi chiamano Mimi; O soave fanciulla* (Jussi Björling, Renata Tebaldi). FALLA: *La vida breve: Vivan los que rien* (Victoria de los Angeles). MEYERBEER: *Les Huguenots: O beau pays* (Joan Sutherland). VERDI: *Aida: O patria mia* (Leontyne Price). MUSSORGSKY: *Boris Godunov: Death scene* (Boris Christoff). PUCCINI: *Tosca: Vissi d'arte;* (i) *Act III duet* (Magda Olivero, (i) with Alvinio Misciano). MOZART: *Die Zauberflöte: Dies Bildnis ist bezaubernd schön* (Fritz Wunderlich). BEETHOVEN: *Fidelio: In des Lebens* (Jon Vickers). PUCCINI: *Turandot: Non Piangere, Liù* (Franco Corelli). LEONCAVALLO: *I Pagliacci: Vesti la giubba* (Giuseppe di Stefano). (i) VERDI: *La Traviata: Parigi, o cara;* (ii) PUCCINI: *Tosca: Duet and Vissi d'arte* (both Maria Callas, with (i) Alfredo Kraus, (ii) Tito Gobbi). (Commentary by Magda Olivero, Thomas Hampson, Schuyler Chapin, Kirk Browning, Nicola Rescigno.)
*** Teldec/Warner VHS 0630 15893-3 [id.].

This is Teldec's vocal equivalent of the *Art of Conducting*. While almost all the film excerpts included here are fascinating, this comparable vocal survey proves less uniformly compulsive than its orchestral equivalent. Moreover, while almost all the comments on the earlier video concerning the conductors themselves and their various idosyncrasies proved very perceptive, the commentaries here, especially the contributions by the singers themselves, seem much less illuminating. Thomas Hampson's definition of the meaning of *legato*, a term which almost explains itself, is perversely over-complicated. But now to the singing.

Two performances stand out above the rest in magnetism. A live telecast, with good sound, from the Met. in 1956 brought Renata Tebaldi and Jussi Bjoerling together in virtually the whole of the great Act I love scene in *La Bohème*, from *Che gelida manina* to their final exit, with their glorious voices ending the Act from offstage. They are dressed in a curiously formal way – one might even say overdressed – and Tebaldi is not shown to be the greatest actress in the world, but their voices match superbly. The other scene is even more electrifying – a live telecast made in December of the same year for which obviously no expense was spared, and the set and production were fully worthy. Boris Christoff's Death scene from *Boris Godunov* is deeply moving; Nicola Moscona is a hardly less resonant Pimen, and an unnamed boy is very touching as Boris's young son. Hardly less impressive is the great Kirsten Flagstad (at her vocal peak), introduced by Bob Hope, who manages to keep a straight face, in a Paramount movie, *The Big Broadcast of 1938*. She sings *Hojohtoho* thrillingly from *Die Walküre*, waving her spear with remarkable conviction.

Risë Stevens, Lauritz Melchior, Victoria de los Angeles in Falla and Joan Sutherland in Meyerbeer coloratura add to the vocal pleasures, and Leontyne Price's gloriously full-voiced *O patria mia* from *Aida* is engulfing. What a stage presence she has! Another highlight is Magda Olivero's charismatically seductive *Vissi d'arte* from *Tosca*. The great Callas ends the programme by singing the same aria (in 1964) but, although her presence is commanding, the actual singing, with its wobbling vibrato, is no match for Olivero.

The early recordings are interesting, but the sound is such that they are usually less than overwhelming vocally, with Gigli and Tito Schipa possible exceptions. A hilarious interlude is provided by a 1908 silent film with professional actors hopelessly overacting and miming the words of the Sextet (*Chi mi frena*) from *Lucia di Lammermoor*, designed to accompany the famous 1911 RCA recording by Caruso, Daddi, Journet, Scotti, Sembrich and Severina. Another smile comes when Rosa Ponselle is shown singing *Carmen* for an MGM screen test in 1936 and her fan gets in the way of the camera! All in all, this is a considerable entertainment, but one hoped, unrealistically perhaps, for more items like *Boris* and *Bohème*.

Alagna, Roberto (tenor)

'Sanctus': Sacred songs (with Toulouse Ch. and O, Plasson): BACH/GOUNOD: *Ave Maria*. GOUNOD: *Repentance (O divine Redeemer); St Cecilia Mass: Sanctus; Angelic greeting (Ave Maria)*. FRANCK: *Panis angelicus; The Procession*. ADAM: *Midnight, Christians*. FAURE: *O salutaris hostia; Crucifix*. BERLIOZ: *Requiem: Sanctus*. SAINT-SAENS: *Panis angelicus*. BIZET: *Agnus dei*. CAPLET: *Panis angelicus*. L. BOULANGER: *Piè Jesu*.
* EMI Dig. CDC5 56206-2 [id.].

This sumptuously over-produced record has already been a big hit in France. After the opening *Ave Maria*, however, Alagna's singing gets buried in an over-resonantly unclear chorus until the Caplet *Panis Angelicus* near the end. The Gounod items are unbelievably mushy.

American Boychoir, Atlantic Brass Quintet, James Litton

'Trumpets sound, voices ring: A joyous Christmas': arr. WILLCOCKS: *O come all ye faithful; Once in Royal David's city*. RUTTER: *Angel tidings; Star carol; The Lord bless you and keep you*. BRAHMS: *Regina coeli*. ELGAR: *The snow*. GAWTHROP: *Mary speaks*. MENDELSSOHN, arr. WILLCOCKS: *Hark! the herald angels sing*. VAUGHAN WILLIAMS: *Hodie; Lullaby*. FRASER: *This Christmastide (Jessye's carol)*. CORELLI: *Concerto grosso in G min. (Christmas), Op. 6/8*. MANZ: *E'en so, Lord Jesus, quickly come*. TELEMANN: *Lobet den Herrn, alle Heiden; Meine Seele, erhebt den Herrn*. CASALS: *Nigra sum*. Spiritual: *Go tell it to the mountain*.
*** MusicMasters Dig. 01612 67076-2 [id.].

Gleaming brass fanfares introduce this lively and attractively diverse American collection featuring a gleaming treble line against full brass sonorities. The Americans follow the English King's College tradition at the opening of *Once in Royal David's city* but cap its climax resplendently. The three Rutter carols are ideal for boy trebles and the infectious *Star carol* brings an engagingly light rhythmic touch. Elgar's much less well-known portrayal of *The snow* is very touching, while *Jessye's carol* has one of those gentle but haunting melodies that persist in the memory: its descant is particularly apt, and it builds to an expansive climax. Both *Mary speaks* and Paul Manz's *E'en so, Lord Jesus* are modern carols with an appealing simplicity, matched by Pablo Casals's better-known *Nigra sum*. The two Telemann items featuring famous chorales are both floridly testing of the boys' resources, and here the faster passages are not always completely secure. But they provide a nice baroque contrast, and it was a happy idea to include a brass transcription of Corelli's famous *Christmas concerto grosso* which, if sounding comparatively robust, is still highly effective when played so well. The choral singing is generally of a high calibre and the recording has a natural, warm ambience and is admirably clear.

Angeles, Victoria de los (soprano)

'The fabulous Victoria de Los Angeles'

Disc 1: RAVEL: *Shéhérazade; 5 Mélodies populaires grecques; 2 Mélodies hébraïques*. DUPARC: *L'invitation au voyage; Phidylé*. DEBUSSY: *L'Enfant prodigue: L'année en vain chasse l'année*. CHAUSSON: *Poème de l'amour et de la mer*.

Disc 2: MONTSALVATGE: *5 canciones negras*. GRANADOS: *Colección se canciones amatorias; Llorad corazón; Iban al pinar*. RODRIGO: *4 madrigales amatorios; Triptic de Mossèn Cinto*. ESPLÁ: *5 canciones playeras españolas*. TOLDRA: *4 cançons*. TRAD.: *La Dama d'Aragó; El cant dels ocells; Canço de Sega*. MOMPOU: *El Combat del Somni*.

Disc 3: DEBUSSY: *Chansons de Bilitis; Fêtes galantes; Noël des enfants qui n'ont plus de maisons.* RAVEL: *Chants populaires.* HAHN: *3 jours de vendage; Le rossignol de lilas.* FAURE: *Tristesse; Au bord de l'eau; Les Roses d'Ispahan; Toujours.* FALLA: *7 canciones populares españolas. Psyché; Soneto a Córdoba.* TOLDRA: *12 canciones gallegas: As floriñas dos toxos.* TURINA: *Farruca.* RODRIGO: *Villancicos: Pastorcito santo.*

Disc 4: SACRATI: *Prosperina: E dove t'aggiri.* A. SCARLATTI: *Le violette.* HANDEL: *Joshua: Oh! had I Jubal's lyre.* SCHUBERT: *Der Tod und das Mädchen. Die schöne Müllerin: Wohin?; An die Musik; Mignon und der Harfner.* BRAHMS: *Dein blaue Auge; Vergebliches Ständchen; Sapphische Ode.* FAURE: *Chansons d'amour; Clair de lune; Pleurs d'or.* PURCELL: *Let us wander; Lost is my quiet.* HAYDN: *Schlaf in deiner engen Kammer.* J. C. BACH: *Ah! lamenta, oh bella Irene.* BEETHOVEN: *Irish songs: Oh! would I were but that sweet linnet; He promised me at parting; They bid me slight my Dermot dear. Welsh song: The dream.* BERLIOZ: *Les fleurs des landes: Le Trébuchet.* DVORAK: *Möglichkeit; Der Apfel.* TCHAIKOVSKY: *Scottish ballad.* SAINT-SAENS: *Pastorale.* MOZART: *La Pertenza.*
(M) *** EMI CMS5 65061-2 (4) [ZDMD 65061].

A seventy-fifth-birthday celebration, this well-documented set subdivides into a pair of CDs of French and Spanish repertoire with orchestra, and two more with piano. While the French classics give special delight, it is good that room was made for the two separate Rodrigo song selections, as this composer prized his vocal music above all else and it is too little known. Apart from the mélodies, the third disc includes some especially delightful folk-inspired repertoire from both countries, where de los Angeles was in her element; on the fourth, a wide-ranging programme (in which she has the estimable support of Gerald Moore) shows her remarkable versatility. The recordings were made in the 1960s when the voice was at its freshest. If you are an admirer of this lovely voice, snap the set up quickly, for it is unlikely to be around for very long.

'Diva': Arias from ROSSINI: *Il barbiere di Siviglia.* GOUNOD: *Faust.* VERDI: *La Traviata; Otello.* PUCCINI: *La Bohème; Madama Butterfly; Suor Angelica; Gianni Schicchi.* MASCAGNI: *Cavalleria ruricana.* LEONCAVALLO: *Pagliacci.* CATALANI: *La Wally.* MASSENET: *Manon.* BIZET: *Carmen.* GIMENEZ: *La Tempranica.* CABALLERO: *Gigantes y Cabezudos.* BARBIERI: *Il barberillo de Lavaplés.*
(M) *** EMI mono/stereo CDM5 65579-2 [id.].

This splendid compilation brings it home how many of the classic sets of the 1950s and 1960s have Victoria de los Angeles as a golden-toned heroine, responding with heartfelt expressiveness. These include the two incomparable Beecham sets of Puccini's *La Bohème* and Bizet's *Carmen*, Gui's Glyndebourne-based set of Rossini's *Barbiere*, Monteux's magical set of Massenet's *Manon*, Cluytens's recording of *Faust*, Serafin in Puccini's *Il trittico*, not to mention the RCA New York recording in 1953 of *I Pagliacci*, in which de los Angeles sings charmingly as Nedda communing with the birds – not the role one expects from her. These are well supplemented by two items from her superb (1954) opera recital, including a tenderly beautiful *Ave Maria* from *Otello* and three final numbers from Spanish zarzuelas, making a winning collection overall.

Anonymous 4

'The Lily and the lamb' (Chant and polyphony from medieval England): *Conducti, Hymns, Motets, Sequences*; Antiphon: *Ave regina coelorum.*
*** HM Dig. HMU 907125 [id.].

The Anonymous Four (Ruth Cunningham, Marsha Genensky, Susan Hellauer and Johanna Rose) are an American vocal quartet whose voices merge into a particularly pleasing blend. They came together in 1986, bringing with them a variety of musical skills, including instrumental proficiency and a musicological background. The group focuses on medieval music, mainly sacred, spanning 500 years, from the eleventh to the fourteenth century. It is perhaps appropriate that this first collection should be devoted to hymns, sequences and motets dedicated to the Virgin Mary.

Women in medieval times identified with Mary and in particular her suffering as she saw her son dying on the cross. The second item in this programme, a monodic hymn, begins with the words 'The gentle lamb spread on the cross, hung all bathed with blood'. For women of those times, death was an everyday event, especially since only a proportion of their many children survived into adulthood and they saw their young loved ones succumb to disease and other causes. The singers here blend their voices into one, whether singing monody or in simple polyphony, as in the Sequence, *Stillat in stelam radium*, or the beautiful motet, *Veni mater gracie*. The voices are heard floating in an ecclesiastic acoustic and the effect is mesmeric.

'Miracles of Sant'Iago' (Medieval chant and polyphony for St James from the Codex Calixtinus): *Agnus dei trope, Benedicamus tropes, Kyrie trope, Antiphon, Conducti, Hymns, Invitatory, Offertory, Prosae, Responsories.*
*** HM Dig. HMU 907156 [id.].

The Cathedral of Santiago in Compostela is the home of a manuscript of five books called collectively Jacobus, and its music was designed to be sung by groups of young French boy-trebles. It proves ideal material for the Anonymous Four and its musical interest is immediately demonstrated by the brilliantly decorated Benedicamus trope, *Vox nostra resonet*. Much of the music is plainchant, but the early examples of two-part polyphony are very striking. Again the singing here is magnetic and the warm resonance of the recording very flattering.

'An English Ladymass' (13th- and 14th-century chant and polyphony in honour of the Virgin Mary): *Alleluias, Gradual, Hymn, Introit, Kyrie, Motets, Offertory, Rondellus, Sequences, Songs.*
**(*) HM Dig. HMU 907080 [id.]

In medieval times most large churches and cathedrals had a lady chapel, where a Ladymass could be sung regularly to the Virgin Mary. And these still exist today in larger Catholic cathedrals, like Chartres in France. They usually have an extraordinary atmosphere and one watches with respect as young mothers not only attend alone but also bring their children to present to the statue of the Virgin. Here the Anonymous Four have arranged their own Mass sequence with the Propers interspersed with appropriate motets, hymns, a Gradual and Alleluia, finally concluding with the hymn, *Ave Maris stella*. In doing so they make their own homage to the Virgin Mother which is well planned. The music is beautifully sung, although this is perhaps not one of their most potent collections.

'Love's illusion' (French motets on courtly love texts from the 13th-century Montpellier Codex): *Plus bele que flor / Quant revient / L'autrier joer; Puisque bele dame m'eime; Amours mi font souffrir / En mai; Ne sai, que je die; Si je chante / Bien doi amer; Or ne sai je que devenir / puisque d'amer; Hé Dieus, de si haut si bas / Maubatus; Celui en qui / La bele estoile / La bele, en qui; Qui d'amours se plaint; Amours, dont je sui / L'autrier, au douz mois / Chose Tassin; Au cuer ai un mal / Ja ne m'en repentirai / Jolietement; Quant voi la fleur; Quant se depart / Onques ne sai amer; Joliement / Quant voi la florete / Je sui joliete; Amor potest conqueri / Adamorem sequitur; Ce que je tieng / Certes mout / Bone compaignie; J'ai si bien mon cuer assiz / Aucun m'ont; Ne m'oubliez mie; J'ai mis toute ma pensee / Je n'en puis; Blanchete / Quant je pens; Dame, que je n'os noumer / Amis donc est / Lonc tans a; Li savours de mon desir / Li grant desir / Non veul mari; Entre Copin / Je me cuidoie / Bele Ysabelos; S'on me regarde / Prennés i garde / Hé, mi enfant; Quant yver la bise ameine; Ne m'a pas oublié; On doit fin[e] Amor / La biauté; Ja n'amerai autre que cele; Quant je parti de m'amie.*
*** HM Dig. HMU 907109 [id.].

For this programme the Anonymous Four have moved away from liturgical music and chosen 29 thirteenth-century motets from the Montpellier Codex, setting courtly love texts with simple and affecting polyphony. It is remarkable how the atmosphere of this music brings a more secular, plaintive quality. The means are the same but the expressive result is different, for the words are about the joys and regrets and the feelings of love. Many of these songs are dolorous but *Ne se, que je die* (about pride, hypocrisy and avarice) and *Qui l'amours se plaint* are both dance songs. This is one of the most attractive of this fine group's collections. They are obviously moved, as women, by the words they sing, and they find remarkable variety of expressive feeling here. Occasionally a drone is added under the melodic line to telling effect, and one never misses an instrumental backing. The recording is well up to standard. A splendid disc.

'On Yoolis Night' (Medieval carols and motets): *Antiphons, Carols, Hymns, Motets, Responsory, Rondella, Songs.*
*** HM Dig. HMU 907099 [id.].

This is a delightful collection. The carol, *Alleluia, A new work*, and the anonymous setting of *Ave Maria* are both enchanting discoveries, and many of these items have that curious, Christmassy colouring. The dance song *Gabriel from heaven-king* and the lovely *Lullay: I saw a sweet seemly sight* are matched by *As I lay on Yoolis night*, while the closing *Nowel* is wonderfully joyful. The simple medieval implied harmonies in no way inhibit the character but increase the special colour of these carols, which are sung tenderly or with great spirit by this excellent group. Here is a record to lay in store for next Christmas, but to play at other times too.

'A Star in the East' (Medieval Hungarian Christmas music): *Alleluias, Antiphons, Communion, Evangelium, Gradual, Hymns, Introit, Lectio, Motet, Offertory, Sanctus, Songs, Te Deum.*
*** HM Dig. HMU 907139 [id.].

The repertoire here is comparatively unsophisticated but full of charm, and the singing has the right kind of innocence. The programme came about by accident. While one of the group was researching the music of Hildegard of Bingen at Columbia University Library, a book of Hungarian Christmas music fell off the shelf at the researcher's feet, inviting its performance. There is not a great deal of polyphony here, but that is not a feature of many of our own favourite Christmas carols either. There is no lack of melody. Excellent recording and splendid documentation.

'A Portrait': excerpts from *'Miracles of Sant'Iago'; 'The Lily and the lamb'; 'A Star in the East'; 'Love's illusion'; 'An English Ladymass'; 'On Yoolis night'.*
(B) *** HM Dig. HMX 2907210 [id.].

Here is a carefully chosen selection of highlights from the six CDs listed above. It's well worth sampling to find out whether the pure yet richly expressive vocal style of this remarkable female group will tempt you to explore further in one direction or another.

Ars Nova, Bo Holten

Portuguese polyphony: CARDOSO: *Lamentatio; Magnificat secundi toni.* LOBO: *Audivi vocem de caelo; Pater peccavi.* MAGALHAES: *Vidi aquam; Missa O Soberana luz; Commissa mea pavesco.* Manuel da FONSECA: *Beata viscera.* Bartolomeo TROSYLHO: *Circumdederunt.* Pedro de ESCOBAR: *Clamabat autem mulier.*
(BB) *** Naxos Dig. 8.553310 [id.].

In every respect this is an outstanding anthology. Apart from the major items from the Portuguese 'famous three' contemporaries, Cardoso, Lôbo and (the least-known) Filippe de Magalhães, which are discussed above under their respective composer entries, the motets by the earlier figures, Pedro de Escobar (*c.* 1465–1535), Bartolomeo Trosylho (*c.* 1500–*c.* 1567) and Manuel da Fonseca (*maestre da capela* at Braga Cathedral in the mid sixteenth century), are all touchingly, serenely beautiful, if perhaps less individual. The singing of this Danish Choir is superb and so is the Naxos recording. Texts and translations are provided, although for some reason they are printed separately. A unique bargain of the highest quality.

Augér, Arleen (soprano)

'Love songs' (with Dalton Baldwin, piano): COPLAND: *Pastorale; Heart, we will forget him.* OBRADORS: *Del Cabello más sutil.* OVALLE: *Azulao.* R. STRAUSS: *Ständchen; Das Rosenband.* MARX: *Selige Nacht.* POULENC: *Fleurs.* CIMARA: *Stornello.* QUILTER: *Music, when soft voices die; Love's philosophy.* O. STRAUS: *Je t'aime.* SCHUMANN: *Widmung; Du bist wie eine Blume.* MAHLER: *Liebst du um Schönheit.* TURINA: *Cantares.* LIPPE: *How do I love thee?* COWARD: *Conversation Piece: I'll follow my secret heart.* GOUNOD: *Serenade.* SCHUBERT: *Liebe schwärmt auf allen Wegen.* BRIDGE: *Love went a-riding.* FOSTER: *Why, no one to love.* DONAUDY: *O del mio amato ben.* BRITTEN (arr.): *The Salley Gardens.* LOEWE: *Camelot: Before I gaze at you again.*
✿ *** Delos Dig. D/CD 3029 [id.].

This extraordinarily wide-ranging recital is a delight from the first song to the last. Arleen Augér opens with Copland and closes with *Camelot*, and she is equally at home in the music by Roger Quilter (*Love's philosophy* is superbly done), Noël Coward and the *Rückert* song of Mahler. Britten's arrangement of *The Salley Gardens*, ravishingly slow, is another highlight. The layout of the recital could hardly have been managed better: each song creates its new atmosphere readily, but seems to be enhanced by coming after the previous choice. Dalton Baldwin's accompaniments are very much a partnership with the singing, while the playing itself is spontaneously perceptive throughout. With a good balance and a very realistic recording, this projects vividly like a live recital.

'Grandi Voci': Arias from: MOZART: *Le nozze di Figaro; Don Giovanni* (with Drottningholm Court Theatre O, Ostman). *Mass No. 18 in C min. (Great), K.427: Et incarnatus est* (with AAM, Hogwood). HAYDN: *Scena di Berenice: Berenice, che fai? La Circe: Son pietosa, son bonina. Arianna a Naxos; Il canzoniere: Solo e pensoso. Miseri noi, misera patria* (with Handel & Haydn Society, Hogwood).
(M) *** Decca Dig. 440 414-2 [id.].

Arleen Augér is a pure-toned Countess in Ostman's period-instrument performance of *Le nozze di Figaro* and a radiant Donna Anna in his rather more successful Drottningholm *Don Giovanni*. Neither of these complete recordings could be counted a first choice (or anything like it), so to preserve the key arias is very worthwhile, while Hogwood's recording of Mozart's *Mass in C minor* includes a filled-out orchestration for *Et incarnatus est*, which suits Augér's voice to perfection. However, the main interest of this fine recital is the series of arias and cantatas by Haydn (lasting nearly an hour) which she recorded with the Handel and Haydn Society of Boston in 1988. She personifies the lamenting Ariadne and Berenice to perfection and is equally touching in *Son pietosa, son bonina*, which the composer himself extracted from his opera, *La Circe*, for concert performance. Perhaps finest of all is the lovely *Miseri noi, misera patria*, only recently rediscovered, a lament for a desecrated city pillaged by marauding troops, which certainly has something to say to our own generation.

(i) **Bach Choir, Sir David Willcocks**; (ii) **Philip Jones Brass Ensemble, Philip Jones**

'In dulci jubilo – A Festival of Christmas': (i; ii) arr. WILLCOCKS: *Fanfare – O come all ye faithful. Gabriel's message; Angelus ad Virginem; Ding dong! merrily on high; God rest you merry, gentlemen; Unto us a son is born; Once in Royal David's city; Hush my dear, lie still and remember; Away in a manger; Sussex carol.* TRAD.: *A virgin most pure; In dulci jubilo.* RUTTER: *Shepherd's pipe carol; Star carol.* GRUBER: *Stille Nacht.* MENDELSSOHN: *Hark the herald angels sing.* (ii) BACH: *Christmas oratorio: chorales: Nun seid Ihr wohl gerochen; Ach, mein herzliebes Jesulein.* TRAD.: *Lord Jesus hath a garden; Come all ye shepherds; Il est né.* arr. IVESON: *We three kings; Jingle bells – Deck the hall; The holly and the ivy.* arr. RUTTER: *Wassail song. We wish you a merry Christmas.*
(B) **(*) Decca Eclipse Dig. 448 980-2; *448 980-4* [id.].

The titling and documentation of this otherwise admirable Eclipse collection is misleading. It is basically an early (1980) digital concert by the Bach Choir, colourfully accompanied by the Philip Jones Brass Ensemble, conducted by Sir David Willcocks. Fresh simplicity is the keynote: the brass fanfares bring a touch of splendour, but the accompaniments are not over-scored. *Silent night* has never sounded more serene, and the other carols bring a wide variety of mood, while the two engaging Rutter pieces make a further refreshing contrast. However, as a central interlude there is a selection of ten items taken from a separate collection of Christmas music by Philip Jones and his Brass Ensemble without the choir, recorded two years later, also in the Kingsway Hall. Once again sound and playing are of very high quality. Appropriately framed by two chorales from Bach's *Christmas oratorio*, these arrangements are again effectively varied, with *Jingle bells* and *We wish you a merry Christmas* making a sparkling contrast with the gentler and more solemn music. But it must be said that carols are meant to include the words!

Baillie, Dame Isobel (soprano)

'The unforgettable Isobel Baillie': HANDEL: *Samson: Let the bright Seraphim. Rodelinda: Art thou troubled. Messiah: I know that my Redeemer liveth; If God be with us. Theodora: Angels ever bright and fair. Joshua: Oh! Had I Jubal's lyre.* BACH: *Cantata No. 68: My heart ever faithful; Cantata No. 201: Ah yes, just so* (arr. MOTTL). MOZART: *La finta giardiniera: A maiden's is an evil plight. The marriage of Figaro: O come, do not delay.* HAYDN: *The Creation: With verdure clad.* MENDELSSOHN: *Elijah: Hear ye, Israel.* OFFENBACH: *Tales of Hoffmann: Doll's song.* SCHUBERT: *The shepherd on the rock* (with Charles Draper, clarinet); *To music.* ARNE: *Where the bee sucks.*
❁ (M) *** Dutton Lab. mono CDLX 7013 [id.].

It must be unique for a soprano's recording career to span over half a century, yet over all that time Isobel Baillie rarely if ever let down her maxim which provided the title of her autobiography: 'Never sing louder than lovely'. Handel's *I know that my Redeemer liveth* was certainly her most popular record during the war years. Alan Blyth describes this famous 1941 performance in the accompanying insert leaflet: 'Notes are hit fully and truly in the middle, and they are joined together in a seamless line. At the same time Baillie was able to swell and diminish her tone with total ease.' Like the rest of the programme, it is flawlessly transferred by the miraculous Dutton/CEDAR process, and one can enjoy Leslie Heward's warm Hallé accompaniment alongside the voice. In her duet with the trumpet (Arthur Lockwood) which opens the disc, *Let the bright Seraphim*, her bright, gleaming tone wins out every time, and elsewhere there are dazzling displays of agility (as in the 1930 *Doll's song* and the delightful Arne *Where the bee sucks* from 1943) as well as purity and loveliness (as in the 1941 *Art thou troubled* or Susanna's aria from *The marriage of Figaro*, recorded in 1927). Her simplicity of style was just right for Schubert, and her account of *The Shepherd on the rock*, recorded a year later, shows the bright, fresh timbre, which was uniquely hers, under perfect control. The timbre of Charles Draper, the distinguished clarinettist who plays the obbligato, by comparison seems dry and lustreless. A record to treasure on all counts.

Baker, Dame Janet (mezzo-soprano)

'An Anthology of English song' (with Martin Isepp): VAUGHAN WILLIAMS: *The Call; Youth and Love*. IRELAND: *A Thanksgiving; Her Song*. M. HEAD: *Piper*. C. ARMSTRONG GIBBS: *This is a sacred city; Love is a sickness*. DUNHILL: *The Cloths of Heaven; To the Queen of Heaven*. WARLOCK: *Balulalow; Youth*. HOWELLS: *King David; Come sing and dance*. I. GURNEY: *Sleep; I will go with my father a-ploughing*. FINZI: *Come away, come away, Death; It was a lover and his lass*.
(M) *** Saga EC 3340-2 [id.].

A glorious collection superbly sung. Janet Baker's artistry on one of her earliest records reveals moments of pure enchantment in these unpretentious settings of English lyrics. She herself chose them and, though the majority have not immediate popular appeal, they grow more and more attractive on repetition – the melismatic Alleluias in Howells's *Come sing and dance*, the golden simplicity of Gurney's *I will go with my father a-ploughing*. Martin Isepp is an outstanding accompanist, always sympathetic, and the recording is completely natural and very well balanced. The CD transfer brings an astonishing sense of presence and realism. There are good notes, and if the playing time is merely 45 minutes every one of them is treasurable.

'Arie amarose' (with ASMF, Marriner): GIORDANO: *Caro mio ben*. CACCINI: *Amarilli mia bella*. STRADELLA: *Ragion sempra addita*. SARRI: *Sen corre l'agnelletta*. CESTI: *Intorno all'idol mio*. LOTTI: *Pur dicesti, o bocca bella*. Alessandro SCARLATTI: *Spesso vibra per suo gioco; Già il sole dal gange; Sento nel core*. CALDARA: *Come raggio del Sol; Sebben crudele me fai languir'; Selve amiche*. BONONCINI: *Del più a me non v'ascondete*. DURANTE: *Danza fanciulla gentile*. PERGOLESI: *Ogni pena più spietata*. MARTINI: *Plaisir d'amour*. PICCINI: *O notte o dea del mistero*. PAISIELLO: *Nel cor più non mi sento*.
(M) *** Ph. 434 173-2 [id.].

A delightful recital of classical arias, marred only by the absence of libretti. However, unlike the original (1978) LP, the CD has good supporting notes by Lionel Salter, which are essential for proper enjoyment of this repertoire. The programme is cleverly arranged to contrast expressive with sprightly music and the wide range of tonal graduation and beautiful phrasing is matched by an artless lightness of touch in the slighter numbers. The accompaniments are intimate and tasteful; there is no more fetching example than Pergolesi's *Ogni pena più spietata*, with its deft bassoon obbligato (which Stravinsky used for *Pulcinella*) or the short closing song with harpsichord, Paisiello's *Nel cor più non mi sento*. Caldara's *Come raggio del Sol* and *Selve amiche* are most touching, while Scarlatti is there to lighten the mood with *Già il sole dal gange*. The recording has a warm acoustic and the resonance is kind to the voice without loss of orchestral detail. The CD transfer is pleasingly vivid and natural.

'Janet Baker sings' (with Gerald Moore, piano): FAURE: *Automne; Prison; Soir; Fleur jetée; En sourdine; Notre amour; Mai; Chanson du pêcheur; Clair de lune*. STANFORD: *La belle dame sans merci*. PARRY: *Proud Masie; O mistress mine*. William BUSCH: *Rest*. WARLOCK: *Pretty ringtime*. VAUGHAN WILLIAMS: *Linden Lea*. GURNEY: *Fields are full*. BRITTEN: *Corpus Christi carol*. IRELAND: *Sally Gardens*. QUILTER: *Love's Philosophy*. SCHUBERT: *Am Grabe; Anselmos; Abendstern; Die Vogel; Strophe aus Die Götte; Griechenlands; Gondelfahrer; Auflösung*. Richard STRAUSS: *Morgen!; Befreit*.
✿ (M) *** EMI CDM5 65009-2 [id.].

Just after he had officially retired, in the late 1960s Gerald Moore returned to the recording studio to accompany Janet Baker, an artist whom he counted high among the many great singers he had accompanied in his career. This recital brings together a sequence of magical perfomances of songs especially dear to Dame Janet, with the voice consistently golden in tone. The Fauré group brings out her intense love of singing in French, and her devotion to the German Lied shines out equally in Schubert and Strauss. The group of ten English songs demonstrates that this neglected genre has comparable claims in beauty and intensity, with such favourite items as Vaughan Williams's *Linden Lea* and Quilter's *Love's philosophy* given heartfelt performances. Even this singer rarely sang with more beauty than here.

Bär, Olaf (baritone), Helmut Deutsch (piano)

'Christmas Lieder': CORNELIUS: *6 Weihnachtslieder, Op. 8. Simeon; Christus der Kinderfreud; Christkind.* HUMPERDINCK: *Der Stern von Bethlehem; Altdeutsches Weihnachtslied; Das Licht der Welt; Christkindleins Wiegenlied; Weihnachten.* Richard TRUNK: *7 Christmas Lieder, Op. 71.* Joseph HAAS: *Krippenlieder (6 Songs of the Crib), Op. 49.* REGER: *Morgengesang; Uns ist geboren ein Kindelein; Christkindleins Wiegenlied; Maria am Rosenstrauch; Ehre sei Gott in der Höhe!.*
✿ *** EMI Dig. CDC5 56204-2 [id.].

Olaf Bär has never made a finer or more rewarding record than this superb collection of German Christmas songs, introducing two unfamiliar composers among the more famous names. Peter Cornelius was born on Christmas Eve so perhaps it is not surprising that his set of *Weihnachtslieder* so readily captures the seasonal mood with such spontaneity, while Humperdinck's Christmas settings have all the character and charm one would expect from the composer of *Hänsel und Gretel*. The delightful contribution from Richard Trunk is one of the two surprises here. Trunk's remarkable feeling for words and easy melodic lyricism are very much in the mainstream of German Lieder and, even if the style of the music is more eclectic, its invention is engagingly individual. The highlight is the masterly *Idyll*, picturing Mary beneath a lime tree rocking her son to sleep with four angels on guard overhead. The setting is magically evocative and should be far better known. The other unfamiliar name is that of Joseph Haas. His strophic songs bring a romantic melodic style which also features a strong folk element, and Haas winningly favours a repeated refrain at the end of each verse of all six examples included here. Max Reger's contribution sustains a more serious mood, but it is lightened by the easy spontaneity of Olaf Bär's singing and his consistent variety of colour and dynamic. Indeed, throughout he gives inspired performances, relishing the countless subtleties in the marriage of text and vocal line, while Helmut Deutsch's accompaniments are equally imaginative. This is by no means just a seasonal collection, but one to be enjoyed throughout the year. The Abbey Road recording is completely natural – very much in the demonstration bracket.

Bartoli, Cecilia (soprano)

Italian songs (with András Schiff): BEETHOVEN: *Ecco quel fiero istante!; Che fa il mio bene?* (2 versions); *T'intendo, si, mio cor; Dimmi, ben mio; In questa tomba oscura.* MOZART: *Ridente la calma.* HAYDN: *Arianna a Naxos.* SCHUBERT: *Vedi quanto adoro ancora ingrato!; Io vuo'cantar di Cadmo; La pastorella; Non t'accostar all'urna; Guarda, che bianca luna; Se dall'Etra; Da quel sembiante appresi; Mio ben ricordati; Pensa, che questo istante; Mi batte'l cor!.*
*** Decca Dig. 440 297-2 [id.].

Bartoli and Schiff make a magical partnership, each challenging the other in imagination. These 17 Italian songs and one cantata by the great Viennese masters make a fascinating collection, not just Haydn and Mozart but Beethoven and Schubert as well. Beethoven's darkly intense *In questa tomba* is well enough known but, as sung by Bartoli, with András Schiff adding sparkle, the lighter songs are just as magnetic, with Beethoven showing his versatility in two astonishingly contrasted settings of the same love-poem.

'Chant d'amour': BIZET: Mélodies: *Adieux de l'hôtesse arabe; Chant d'amour; La coccinelle; Ouvre ton coeur; Tarantelle.* BERLIOZ: *La Mort d'Ophélie; Zaïde.* DELIBES: *Les filles de Cadiz.* VIARDOT: *Les filles de Cadiz; Hai Luli!; Havanaise.* RAVEL: *4 Chansons populaires; 2 Mélodies Hébraïques; Tripatos; Vocalise-etude en forme de Habanera.*
*** Decca Dig. 452 667-2; *452 667-4*. [id.].

This is a delectable disc, a winning collection of French songs, many of them unexpected, which inspire Bartoli to the most seductive singing. One would have predicted that Delibes's sparkling setting of Musset's poem, *Les filles de Cadiz*, would draw out Carmen-like fire from her, but here that charming song is set alongside the setting of the same poem made by the great prima donna, Pauline Viardot, giving a refreshingly different view. The other Viardot items too come as a delightful surprise, as do the Bizet songs, including *La coccinelle*, 'The Ladybird', a sparkling waltz, superbly characterized here. The better-known Berlioz and Ravel songs are beautifully done too, with Myung-Whun Chung revealing himself just as inspired in the role of pianist as of conductor. Excellent sound.

Battle, Kathleen (soprano), Plácido Domingo (tenor)

'Battle and Domingo Live' (with Metropolitan Opera O, Levine): Arias & duets from: VERDI: *La traviata.* DONIZETTI: *Don Pasquale; Lucia di Lammermoor; L'elisir d'amore.* GOUNOD: *Roméo et Juliette.* MOZART: *Don Giovanni.* LEHAR: *Die lustige Witwe.* Overtures to: VERDI: *La forza del destino.* ROSSINI: *L'Italiana in Algeri.*
(M) *** DG Dig. 445 552-2 [id.].

These gala occasions can often be very stimulating for the audience, but only very occasionally do they produce an outstanding record. The present recital is surely the exception that proves the rule. From Levine's vibrant *La forza del destino overture* onwards, the 'live' communication of these performances comes across readily. The *La Traviata* duet has great charm, with Domingo obviously matching his voice to the smaller but lovely sound which Battle naturally commands. The lesser-known duet from *Romeo and Juliet* is hardly less delightful, and *Là ci darem la mano* is engagingly relaxed and elegant: who wouldn't be seduced by this Don? No complaints about the solo arias either, but the unforgettable charmer is the final ravishing Waltz duet from *The Merry widow* which is (quite rightly) sung in English. The ringing final cadence is breathtaking. Few hours of operatic excepts are as magical as this one, and the recording is splendid.

Behrens, Hildegard (soprano)

'Grandi voci' Song-cycles: BERLIOZ: *Nuits d'été.* RAVEL: *Shéhérazade.* Arias from: WAGNER: *Der fliegende Höllander.* WEBER: *Der Freischütz.* BEETHOVEN: *Fidelio.*
*(*) Decca Dig./Analogue 448 250-2 [id.].

This recital in Decca's Grandi Voci series does little to advocate Hildegard Behrens's vocal and interpretative powers. Her voice is too often made to sound cumbersome, especially in the opening *Villanelle* of the Berlioz cycle, although she is more evocative and certainly rich-toned in *Shéhérazade*. In the same way she sounds ungainly in the great *Abscheulicher* from *Fidelio*, the voice sounding less beautiful than it can, and Agathe's lovely scene from *Der Freischütz* also seems awkward in its phrasing. Easily the best thing here is the memorable excerpt from *The Flying Dutchman* in which she is strikingly dramatic, and lyrical too. Throughout she is recorded most vividly.

Berganza, Teresa (mezzo-soprano)

'Canciones españolas' (with Narciso Yepes, guitar, Félix Lavilla, piano): SABIO: *Rosa das rosas; Santa Maria.* FUENLLANA: *Pérdida de Antequera.* ANON.: *Dindirindin; Nuaves te traygo, carillo; Los hombres con gran plazer.* MUDARRA: *Triste estava el rey David; Si me llaman a mí; Claros y frescos rios; Ysabel, perdiste la tu faxa.* TORRE: *Dime, triste corazón, Púmpano verde.* VALDERRABANO: *De dónde venis, amore?* MILAN: *Toda mi vida os amé; Aquel caballero, madre.* TRIANA: *Dínos, madre del donsel.* ENCINA: *Romerico.* VAZQUEZ: *Vos me matastes; En la fuente del rosel.* NARVAEZ: *Con qué la lavaré?* ANCHIETA: *Con amores, la mi madre.* ESTEVE: *Alma sintamos.* GRANADOS: *La maja dolorosa: Oh, muerte cruel!; Ay, majo de mi vida!; De aquel majo amante. El majo discreto; El tra la lá y el punteado; El majo timido.* GURIDI: *Canciones castellanas: Llámale con el pañuelo; No quiero tus avellanas; Cómo quieres que adivine!* FALLA: *7 Canciones populares españolas.* LORCA: *13 Canciones españolas antiquas.* TURINA: *Saeta en forma de Salve a la Virgen de la Esperanza; Canto a Sevilla: El fantasma. Poema en forma de canciones: Cantares.* MONTSALVATGE: *5 Canciones negras.*
(M) *** DG 435 848-2 (2).

This collection dates from the mid-1970s when Berganza was at her peak, the voice fresh, her artistry mature. In essence she provides here a history of Spanish song, opening with two pieces taken from the *Cantigas de Santa Maria*, dating from the thirteenth century, and moving on through Renaissance repertory and, with only one song from the eighteenth century, to the nineteenth and twentieth, traditional settings by Lorca, Falla's *7 Spanish popular songs* and the engaging *Canciones negras* of Montsalvatge. The collaboration with Narciso Yepes seems ideal, for he is an inspirational artist, while her husband, Félix Lavilla, provides the later piano accompaniments. This is not a specialist recital: the music communicates readily in the most direct way, and excellent notes and translations are provided. The balance is very natural and the CD transfers are immaculately managed. This is repertoire one first associates with Victoria de los Angeles, but Berganza makes it her own and there are not many more attractive Spanish song-recitals than this.

'Grandi voci': MOZART: Concert arias: *Ombra felice! . . . lo ti lascio, K.255; Misero me! . . . Misero pargoletto, K.77; Se ardire e speranza, K.82; Conserati fedel, K.23. Nozze di Figaro:* (alternative aria): *Giunse alfin il momento . . . Al desio do chi t'adora, K.577* (all with VCO, György Fischer); *Ch'io mi scordi di te? . . . None temer, amato bene, K.505* (with Geoffrey Parsons, piano, LSO, Pritchard). HAYDN: *Arianna a Naxos* (cantata; with Félix Lavilla, piano.)
(M) *** Decca 448 246-2 [id.].

These Mozart arias were originally issued in the early 1980s within a Decca set gathering together all the arias for soprano, in which Berganza was joined by a number of other singers. It is good to hear her voice still remarkably fresh in 1981 and the singing as stylish as ever (notably so in the opening *Ombra felice! . . . lo ti lascio* and the long alternative aria for Susanna in Act IV of *Figaro*, which was to be replaced by the less taxing *Deh vieni*) and then make a comparison with the superb account of *Ch'io mi scordi di te?* which she recorded with Pritchard (with Geoffrey Parsons playing the piano solo) 19 years earlier in 1962, when the voice had a ravishing youthful bloom. The recital concludes with a highly dramatic and lyrically persuasive account of the ambitious Haydn cantata, *Arianna a Naxos*, made in 1977 with her husband at the piano.

Bergonzi, Carlo (tenor)

'Grandi voci' (arias from): VERDI: *Aida; Luisa Miller; La forza del destino; Il trovatore; Un ballo in maschera; Don Carlo; La Traviata.* MEYERBEER: *L'africana.* GIORDANO: *Andrea Chénier.* CILEA: *Adriana Lecouvreur.* PUCCINI: *Tosca; Manon Lescaut; La Bohème.* PONCHIELLI: *La Gioconda.*
(M) **(*) Decca 440 417-2 [id.].

This recital, consisting mainly of Bergonzi's early stereo recordings, a dozen arias recorded with the Orchestra of the Santa Cecilia Academy, Rome, under Gavazenni in 1957, shows him on consistently peak form. He does not attempt the rare pianissimo at the end of *Celeste Aida*; but here among Italian tenors is a thinking musical artist who never resorts to vulgarity. The lovely account of *Che gelida manina* (with Serafin) comes from two years later. The early stereo has transferred well and retains a bloom on the voice. The other recordings also derive from sets: *La Traviata* (1962), *Un ballo* (1960–61), *Don Carlo* (1965), both with Solti, while the stirring *Cielo e mar* from *La Gioconda* (1967) shows that Bergonzi's tone retained its quality. These added items help to make up a generous playing time of 71 minutes, besides adding variety to what was originally essentially a collection of favourites. Everything sounds fresh.

Bjoerling, Jussi (tenor)

Operatic recital: Arias from: PONCHIELLI: *La Gioconda.* PUCCINI: *La Fanciulla del West; Manon Lescaut.* GIORDANO: *Fedora.* CILEA: *L'Arlesiana.* VERDI: *Un ballo in maschera; Requiem.* MASCAGNI: *Cavalleria Rusticana* (with Tebaldi). LEHAR: *Das Land des Lächelns.*
(M) *** Decca 443 930-2.

Jussi Bjoerling provides here a flow of headily beautiful, finely focused tenor tone. These may not be the most characterful renderings of each aria, but they are all among the most compellingly musical. The recordings are excellent for their period (1959–60). The Lehár was the last solo recording he made before he died in 1960. The transfers to CD are admirably lively and present.

Bjoerling, Jussi, Enrico Caruso, Beniamino Gigli (tenors)

'The three original tenors'

Disc 1, Caruso: Arias from: FRANCHETTI: *Germania.* VERDI: *Rigoletto; Aida.* MASSENET: *Manon.* DONIZETTI: *L'elisir d'amore.* BOITO: *Mefistofele.* PUCCINI: *Tosca.* MASCANI: *Iris.* GIORDANO: *Fedora.* PONCHIELLI: *La Gioconda.* LEONCAVALLO: *Pagliacci.* CILEA: *Adriana Lecouvreur.* BIZET: *Les pêcheurs de perles.* MEYERBEER: *Les Huguenots.* Songs by DENZA; TOSTI; ZARDO; TRIMARCHI; LEONCAVALLO; PINI-CORSI (CDH7 61046-2).

Disc 2, Gigli: Arias from: GOUNOD: *Faust.* BIZET: *Carmen; Les pêcheurs de perles.* MASSENET: *Manon.* HANDEL: *Serse.* DONIZETTI: *Luci di Lammermoor; L'elisir d'amore.* VERDI: *Rigoletto; Aida.* LEONCAVALLO: *Pagliacci.* MASCAGNI: *Cavalleria rusticana.* PUCCINI: *La Bohème; Tosca.* GIORDANO: *Andrea Chénier.* Song: MARISTELLA: *Io conosco un giardino* (CDH7 61051-2).

Disc 3, Bjoerling: Arias from: DONIZETTI: *L'elisir d'amore*. VERDI: *Il Trovatore; Un ballo in maschera; Aida*. LEONCAVALLO: *Pagliacci*. PUCCINI: *La Bohème; Tosca; La Fanciulla del West; Turandot*. GIORDANO: *Fedora*. CILEA: *L'Arlésiana*. MEYERBEER: *L'Africaine*. GOUNOD: *Faust*. MASSENET: *Manon*. FLOTOW: *Martha*. ROSSINI: *Stabat mater* (CDH7 61053-2).
(B) *** EMI CZS5 69535-2 (3) [id.].

This bargain box brings together three of the discs already issued in EMI's Références series, demonstrating that these three tenors can easily survive any comparison with later generations. The Caruso selection is devoted exclusively to his earliest recordings, including the very first ten items, recorded in 1902 in the Grand Hotel, Milan, in April 1902, with piano accompaniment, starting with an aria from Franchetti's *Germania*. Other items include not just arias but Neapolitan songs, recorded in the two years following. The Gigli disc covers recordings made between 1927 and 1941 and includes such ensemble items as the Quartet from *Rigoletto* and the Sextet from *Lucia di Lammermoor* (each with Galli-Curci, Homer and De Luca), and the Act I duet from *La Bohème* with Maria Caniglia. The Bjoerling disc has recordings made in his golden period between 1936 and 1947, mostly from the Italian repertory, revealing him to be a stylist with few rivals among native Italians.

'Three legendary tenors in opera and song'

Caruso: Arias from: BIZET: *Carmen*. MASSENET: *Manon*. VERDI: *Otello; La forza del destino; Aida*. GIORDANO: *Andrea Chénier*. PUCCINI: *Tosca*.

Gigli: Arias from: LEONCAVALLO: *I Pagliacci* (also Song: *Mattinata*) BIZET: *Les pêcheurs de perles* (also Duet: *Del tempo al limitar;* with Giuseppe de Luca). VERDI: *La Traviata*. PUCCINI: *Tosca*. Song: DI CAPUA: *O sole mio*.

Bjoerling: Arias from VERDI: *Rigoletto*. PUCCINI: *La Bohème; Turandot*. RIMSKY-KORSAKOV: *Sadko*. MEYERBEER: *L'Africana*. MASSENET: *Manon*. Song: TOSTI: *Ideale*.
(M) (***) Nimbus mono NI 1434 [id.].

Nimbus also caught on to the idea of promoting a selection from three legendary tenors from their archives at about the same time as EMI, but they decided that a single disc (75 minutes) would be the best proposition. Their system of playing back 78-r.p.m. originals through a big fibre horn and re-recording them works very well here with the three voices naturally caught, but the orchestral backing more variable. The documentation is poor and no recording dates are given, but the excerpts are obviously hand-picked and recorded over a fairly wide time-span. Items which obviously stand out are: Caruso's *Un dì, all'azzurro spazio* from *Andrea Chénier* and of course *Celeste Aida* (with a remarkably believable brass fanfare); Gigli's honeyed *E lucevan le stelle* from *Tosca* and his thrilling *O sole mio*; and Bjoerling's *Che gelida manina* from *Bohème*, the seductive *Sadko* 'Song of India' and his glorious *Nessun dorma*. The collection ends splendidly with Caruso and De Luca matching their voices sensationally in the frisson-creating *Pearl fishers* duet.

Bott, Catherine (soprano)

'Sweeter than roses' (with Pamela Thorby, Anthony Robson, Pavlo Beznosiuk, Rachel Podger, Paula Chateauneuf, Richard Egarr, Mark Levy): PURCELL: *Bonduca: O lead me to some peaceful gloom. The Fairy Queen: Thrice happy lovers; O let me weep. Henry II, King of England: In vain 'gainst love I strove. The History of King Richard III: Retir'd from any mortal's sight. King Arthur: Fairest isle. The Married Beau: See where repenting Celia lies. Oedipus: Music for a while. Pausanias: Sweeter than roses. Rule a Wife and have a Wife: There's not a swain. Sir Anthony Love: Pursuing beauty. The Tempest: Dear pretty youth. Timon of Athens: The cares of lovers. Tyranic love: Ah! how sweet it is to love*. LOCKE: *My lodging it is on the cold ground*. BLOW: *Lovely Selina*. DRAGHI: *Where are thou, God of dreams?* COURTEVILLE: *Creep, creep, softly creep*. ECCLES: *The Villain: Find me a lonely cave*. WELDON: *The Tempest: Dry those eyes; Halcyon days*.
*** O-L Dig. 443 699-2 [id.].

Catherine Bott is just as much at home in the world of English Restoration songs from the theatre as she is in the seductive Mediterranean atmosphere of Barbara Strozzi (see above). As we know from that collection, she has totally mastered the art of making embellishments seem part of the vocal line, and the freshness of her approach is ever delightful. Most of the programme is Purcellian, with quite a few touching favourites like *Fairest isle* (a winner if ever there was one), *Music for a while*, *The Plaint* (the subtitle of *O let me weep*) and of course the title-song. *There's not a swain*, from *Rule a Wife and have a Wife* (a title that wouldn't go down too well these days) is a charmer. The songs by other contemporaries have been well selected, notably Draghi's moving *Where art thou, God of dreams?*. The instrumental accompaniments (which feature recorder, oboe, violins and continuo) are tasteful rather than strong. A fine recital, just the same.

Bott, Catherine (soprano), New London Consort, Philip Pickett

'Music from the time of Columbus': VERARDI: *Viva El Gran Re Don Fernando.* ANON.: *A los Maytines era; Propinan de Melyor; Como no le andare yo; Nina y viña; Calabaza, no sé, buen amor; Perdí la mi rueca; Al alva venid buen amigo; Dale si la das.* URREDA: *Muy triste.* J. PONCE: *Como esta sola mi vida.* ANCHIETA: *Con amores mi madre.* ENCINA: *Triste españa; Mortal tristura; Mas vale trocar; Ay triste que vengo; Quedate carillo.* MEDINA: *No ay plazer en esta vida.* DE LA TORRE: *Danza alta.* DE MONDEJAR: *Un solo fin des mis males.*
*** Linn Dig. CKD 007 [id.].

The songs offered here are broadly divided into two groups, the romantic ballads, usually of a melancholy disposition (the word 'triste' occurs frequently), and the usually jollier *villancio* form, which brings a repeated refrain. Catherine Bott is the most delightful soloist, singing freshly and simply, often with ravishing tone, and there is much to give pleasure. In the anonymous songs it is fascinating to discover just how international medieval folk music was, for more than once the listener is reminded of the Auvergne songs collected later in France by Canteloube. The two most delightful items are saved until the end, first a truly beautiful love song, *Al alva venid buen amigo* ('Come at dawn my friend') in which a young woman reflects on her lover's visits, and then lets her thoughts change to consider the birth of 'him who made the world' from the Virgin Mary. In complete contrast is the robust and charmingly naughty villancio, *Dale si la das* ('Come on, wench of Carasa'). The recording is first class, naturally balanced in a pleasing acoustic, and full documentation is provided.

'Mad songs': PURCELL: *From silent shades; From rosy bow'rs; Not all my torments can your pity move. Don Quixote: Let the dreadful engines. A Fool's Preferment: I'll sail upon the dog star.* ECCLES: *The Mad Lover: Must them a faithful lover go?; Let all be gay; Cease of Cupid to complain; She ventures and He wins: Restless in thought. Don Quixote: I burn, my brain consumes to ashes. Cyrus the Great: Oh! take him gently from the pile. The Way of the World: Love's but the frailty of the mind.* WELDON: *Reason, what art thou?; While I with wounding grief.* D. PURCELL: *Achilles: Morpheus, thou gentle god.* BLOW: *Lysander I pursue in vain.* ANON.: *Mad Maudlin; Tom of Bedlam.*
*** O-L Dig. 433 187-2 [id.].

Purcell and his contemporaries, including his brother Daniel, John Eccles, John Blow and others, in such mad-songs as these, devised a whole baroque genre. The best-known song here is Purcell's *I'll sail upon the dog star*, but mostly these are miniature cantatas in contrasted sections of recitative and aria, displaying a refreshingly unclassical wildness, often set against pathos. They make a marvellous vehicle for the soprano Catherine Bott, who in this and other discs emerges as an outstanding star among early-music performers, with voice fresh, lively and sensuously beautiful.

Bowman, James (counter-tenor)

'The James Bowman collection' (with The King's Consort, Robert King): BACH: *Erbarme dich; Stirb in mir.* HANDEL: *Almighty power; Crueltà nè lontananza; Impious mortal; Tune your harps; Welcome as the dawn of day; Thou shalt bring them in; Or la tromba; Eternal source of light.* PURCELL: *Britain, thou now art great; O solitude; By beauteous softness mixed; An Evening hymn; On the brow of Richmond Hill; Vouchsafe, O Lord.* ANON.: *Come tread the paths.* GABRIELI: *O magnum mysterium.* FORD: *Since I saw your face.* COUPERIN: *Jerusalem, convertere.*
(B) *** Hyperion Dig. KING 3 [id.].

Apart from the opening Bach item, which has not previously been published and which is not entirely flattering, this admirable 78-minute sampler will delight fans of James Bowman as it shows his art and fine vocal control over a wide range of repertoire at which he excelled. Robert King and his Consort provide admirable support.

Caballé, Montserrat (soprano)

'Rossini, Donizetti and Verdi rarities' (with RCA Italiana Ch. & O, (i) Cillario; (ii) Guadagno; (iii) Amb. Op. Ch., LSO Cillario): Arias & excerpts from: (i) ROSSINI: *La Donna del lago; Otello; Stabat Mater; Armida; Tancredi; L'assedio di Corinto.* (ii) DONIZETTI: *Belisario; Parisina d'este* (with M. Elkins, T. McDonnell). *Torquato Tasso; Gemma di Vergy.* (iii) VERDI: *Un giorno di regno; I Lombardi; I due Foscari* (with M. Sunara); *Alzira; Attila; Il Corsaro; Aroldo* (with. L. Kozma).
(M) *** BMG/RCA GD 60941 (2) [09026 60941-2].

Caballé's conviction as well as her technical assurance make for highly dramatic results in scenas that not many years ago would have been laughed out of court. It makes these rarities more attractively convincing that the arias are presented with surrounding detail from a group of well-chosen supporting artists. The Rossini selection is no less rewarding, though the aria from the *Stabat Mater* hardly qualifies as a rarity. The Verdi arias, taken from operas of the early years when the composer was working 'in the galleys', make a further commandingly brilliant recital when sung with such assurance. Caballé is again at her finest, challenged by the technical difficulties as well as by the need to convey the drama. She makes one forget that between the big, memorable tunes there are often less-than-inspired passages. Fine accompaniments throughout and splendidly smooth and vivid CD transfers ensure the success of these two discs, between them offering 144 minutes of music.

Operatic excerpts (with Pavarotti, Milnes, Baltsa) from VERDI: *Luisa Miller.* BELLINI: *Norma.* BOITO: *Mefistofele.* PUCCINI: *Turandot.* GIORDANO: *Andrea Chénier.* PONCHIELLI: *La Gioconda.*
(M) *** Decca 443 928-2 [id.].

Although the disc centres on Caballé and is described as 'Operatic arias', there are in fact plenty of duets, and ensembles too. All the excerpts come from highly recommended complete sets, and Pavarotti figures often and strongly. In Bellini, Giordano or Boito, and especially as Liù in *Turandot*, Caballé is often vocally ravishing and she finds plenty of drama and power for Verdi and Ponchielli. There are at least two and sometimes three or four items from each opera, admirably chosen to make consistently involving entertainment. Alas, the back-up notes are inadequate, concentrating on Caballé's association with each of the operas included.

'Diva': Arias from: PUCCINI: *Madama Butterfly; Tosca; Manon Lescaut; La Bohème; Turandot; La Rondine.* ROSSINI: *William Tell.* BELLINI: *Il Pirata, I Puritani.* VERDI: *Giovanna d'Arco; Macbeth; Don Carlo; Aida.* BOITO: *Mefistofele.* MASCAGNI: *Cavalleria rusticana.*
(M) *** EMI CDM5 65575-2 [id.].

This fine compilation is framed by items from Caballé's 1970 Puccini recital in which she impersonates Mimì, Tosca and Butterfly, singing more impressively than she characterizes. Otherwise these are items from complete sets made between 1970 (Giulini's *Don Carlo*) and 1980 (Muti's *I Puritani*). The items are not always the obvious choices from each opera but from first to last they demonstrate the consistent beauty of her singing at that period, responding to a wide range of conductors.

Callas, Maria (soprano)

'Mad scenes and Bel canto arias' (with Philh. O, Rescigno): DONIZETTI: *Anna Bolena: Piangete voi; Al dolce guidami. La figlia del reggimento: Convien partir. Lucrezia Borgia: Tranquillo ei possa . . . Come è bello. L'elisir d'amore: Prendi, per me sei libero.* THOMAS: *Hamlet: A vos jeux; Partagez-vous mes fleurs; Et maintenant écoutez ma chanson.* BELLINI: *Il Pirata: Oh! s'io potessi . . . Col sorriso d'innocenza; Sorgete, Lo sognai ferito esangue.*
*** EMI CDC7 47283-2 [id.].

If, as ever, the rawness of exposed top-notes mars the sheer beauty of Callas's singing, few recital records ever made can match, let alone outshine, her collection of mad scenes in vocal and dramatic imagination. This is Callas at her very peak; Desmond Shawe-Taylor suggested this as the collection which, more than any other, summed up the essence of Callas's genius. For the CD reissue further arias have been added, notably excerpts from Donizetti's *La figlia del reggimento*, *L'elisir d'amore* and *Lucrezia Borgia* (from the mid-1960s), a fair example of the latter-day Callas, never very sweet-toned, yet displaying the usual Callas fire. However, the singing here is less imaginative and there are few phrases that stick in the memory by their sheer individuality. Nevertheless, the main part of the recital is indispensable; the digital remastering has enhanced the originally excellent recordings and given the voice striking presence.

'La Divina I': Arias from: PUCCINI: *Madama Butterfly; La Bohème; Gianni Schicchi; Turandot; Tosca.* BIZET: *Carmen.* CATALANI: *La Wally.* ROSSINI: *Il barbiere di Siviglia.* BELLINI: *Norma.* SAINT-SAENS: *Samson et Dalila.* VERDI: *Rigoletto; La Traviata.* GOUNOD: *Roméo et Juliette.* MOZART: *Don Giovanni.* MASCAGNI: *Cavalleria rusticana.* PONCHIELLI: *La Gioconda.*
**(*) EMI stereo/mono CDC7 54702-2 [id.].

'La Divina II': Arias from: GLUCK: *Alceste; Orphée et Eurydice.* BIZET: *Carmen.* VERDI: *Ernani; Aida; I vespri siciliani; La Traviata; Don Carlo.* PUCCINI: *Manon Lescaut; La Bohème.* CHARPENTIER: *Louise.* THOMAS: *Mignon.* SAINT-SAENS: *Samson et Dalila.* BELLINI: *La sonnambula.* CILEA: *Adriana Lecouvreur.* DONIZETTI: *Lucia di Lammermoor.*
*(*) EMI stereo/mono CDC5 55016-2 [id.].

'La Divina III': Arias and duets from: GIORDANO: *Andrea Chénier.* SPONTINI: *La vestale.* MASSENET: *Manon.* PUCCINI: *Manon Lescaut; La Bohème* (with Giuseppe di Stefano); *Madama Butterfly* (with Nicolai Gedda); *Turandot.* BIZET: *Carmen* (with Nicolai Gedda). ROSSINI: *Il barbiere di Siviglia* (with Tito Gobbi). DELIBES: *Lakmé.* VERDI: *Aida; Il Trovatore.* LEONCAVALLO: *Pagliacci.* MEYERBEER: *Dinorah.*
*** EMI stereo/mono CDC5 55216-2 [id.].

'La Divina' I–III; Maria Callas in conversation with Edward Downes'
(M) **(*) EMI CMS5 65746-2 (4) [id.].

This handsome (limited-edition) box is clearly aimed primarily at the Callas aficionado, as the back-up documentation includes three separate photographs as well as a liberally illustrated booklet giving a year-by-year biography, beginning with her birth in December 1923. It details her career and personal life through to her tragic final three years as a disillusioned recluse in her Paris apartment, where she died in 1977. The three recital discs (with nearly four hours of music) cover her recording career pretty thoroughly, although the first two are inadequately documented, giving only the date each recording was *published.* '*Divina III*', however, provides both the actual dates and venues of the recordings and details of the other artists involved. A fourth CD offers a conversation between Callas and Edward Downes as broadcast in the USA in two parts – in the intervals of Metropolitan Opera performances in December 1967 and in January 1968. Throughout the three programmes, results are inevitably uneven and if at times the rawness of exposed top-notes mars the lyrical beauty of her singing, equally often her dramatic magnetism is such that many phrases stay indelibly in the memory. Each disc has its share of highlights, with the earlier recordings usually the more memorable. What is perhaps surprising are the omissions: nothing, for instance, from the collection of 'Mad scenes' she recorded with Rescigno. However, many of the choices are apt. '*La Divina I*', for instance, includes her sharply characterful, early 1954 recording of *Una voce poco fa* from Rossini's *Barbiere*, yet '*La Divina III*' draws on the later, complete set for the duet *Dunque io son*, with Tito Gobbi. All three recital discs are available separately, with the third certainly the place to start, as it centres on early recordings, including the excerpt from *La Vestale*, and opens with the movingly intense *La mamma morta* from *Andrea Chénier*. However, it is astonishing that, having provided so much information about the singer, EMI chose not to include any translations, resting content with a brief synopsis of each aria.

Cambridge Singers, John Rutter

'Portrait': BYRD: *Sing joyfully; Non vos relinquam.* FAURE: *Cantique de Jean Racine; Requiem: Sanctus.* RUTTER: *O be joyful in the Lord; All things bright and beautiful; Shepherd's pipe carol; Open thou mine eyes; Requiem: Out of the deep.* PURCELL: *Hear my prayer, O Lord.* STANFORD: *Beati quorum via; The Bluebird.* TRAD.: *This joyful Eastertide; In dulci jubilo.* HANDEL: *Messiah: For unto us a child is born.* FARMER: *A pretty bonny lass.* MORLEY: *Now is the month of maying.* DELIUS: *To be sung of a summer night on the water.* VICTORIA: *O magnum mysterium.* TERRY: *Myn lyking.*
(M) *** Coll. Dig./Analogue CSCD 500; *CSCC 500* [id.].

John Rutter has arranged the items here with great skill so that serene music always makes a contrast with the many exuberant expressions of joy, his own engaging hymn-settings among them. Thus the bright-eyed hey-nonny songs of John Farmer and Thomas Morley are aptly followed by the lovely wordless *To be sung of a summer night on the water* of Delius, and Stanford's beautiful evocation of *The Bluebird* (one of Rutter's own special favourites). The sound, vivid and atmospheric, suits the colour and mood of the music quite admirably. Not to be missed!

'The Cambridge Singers Collection' (with Wayne Marshall, City of L. Sinf.): DEBUSSY: *3 Chansons d'Orléans.* Folksongs (arr. RUTTER): *The Keel row; The Willow tree.* Gregorian Chant: *Regina caeli laetare.* BRUCKNER: *Ave Maria.* VERDI: *Laudi alla Vergine Maria.* STANFORD: *Magnificat in D; Te Deum in C.* PURCELL: *Remember not, Lord, our offences.* TAVERNER: *Christe Jesu, pastor bone.* PHILIPS: *O Beatum et sacrosanctum diem.* PEARSALL: *Lay a garland.* RUTTER: *Riddle song; Waltz; Magnificat* (1st movement); *The Wind in the Willows* (excerpt, with The King's Singers, Richard Baker, Richard Hickox). TRAD. (arr. RUTTER): *Sing a song of sixpence.*
(M) **(*) Coll. Dig. CSCD 501 [id.].

Here is an attractively chosen, 64-minute sampler, including a wide range of tempting repertoire from arrangements of folksongs to Stanford and Verdi. The Taverner and Philips items are particularly welcome. Rutter includes a fair proportion of his own music, but the opening (only) from his setting of *The Wind in the Willows* will not be something one would want to return to very often.

'Christmas day in the morning' (with City of London Sinfonia; (i) Stephen Varcoe): TRAD., arr. RUTTER: *I saw three ships; Sans day carol; Un flambeau, Jeannette, Isabelle; Wexford carol; Quittes pasteurs; Go tell it on the mountain; Deck the hall; We wish you a merry Christmas;* (i) *Riu, riu, chiu.* RUTTER: *Mary's lullaby; Star carol; Jesus child; Donkey carol; Wild wood carol; The very best time of year; Shepherd's pipe carol; Christmas lullaby.* WILLAN: *What is this lovely fragrance?* WARLOCK: *Balulalow; I saw a fair maiden.* TAVENER: *The Lamb.* VAUGHAN WILLIAMS: (i) *Fantasia on Christmas carols.* TRAD., arr. WILLCOCKS: *Blessed be that maid Mary.*
**(*) Collegium Dig. COLCD 121 [id.].

Admirers of Rutter's own carols will certainly be drawn to his latest Christmas collection, for alongside the favourites there are several new ventures in his inimitably lively rhythmic style. The *Donkey carol*, too, becomes more passionate than in previous accounts. But in general, although the whole programme is enjoyable, beautifully sung and smoothly recorded, the feeling of spontaneous freshness, so enticing on his earliest Decca collection, made with the choir from Clare College, is less apparent here, and at times there is a hint of blandness (noticeable with the ritardando at the close of Tavener's *The Lamb*). *Go tell it on the mountain* does not sound entirely idiomatic, and while *We wish you a merry Christmas* ends the concert spiritedly, the Vaughan Williams *Fantasia*, even though it has a fine climax, does not quite match the King's version (see below) in robust, earthy vigour.

Caruso, Enrico (tenor)

'Verismo arias (1906–1916)' from PUCCINI: *La Bohème* (with Melba, Farrar, Viafora, Scotti); *Tosca; Madama Butterfly* (with Farrar, Scotti). PONCHIELLI: *La Gioconda.* MASCAGNI: *Cavalleria rusticana.* LEONCAVALLO: *La Bohème; Pagliacci.* FRANCETTI: *Germania.* GIORDANO: *Andrea Chénier.* PUCCINI: *Manon Lescaut.*
(M) *** BMG/RCA 09026 61243-2.

French opera (1906–1916): Highlights from GOUNOD: *Faust* (with Farrar, Scotti, Journet). Arias from: MASSENET: *Le Cid; Manon.* BIZET: *Carmen; Les pêcheurs de perles.* SAINT-SAENS: *Samson et Dalila.* HALEVY: *La juive.*
(M) *** BMG/RCA 09026 61244-2.

These two discs, alongside a Verdi collection (see our main volume), are phenomenally well transferred with the aid of special digital techniques that seek to eliminate the unwanted resonances of the acoustic horn used in the original recording process. This restoration was achieved in the early 1980s using a Soundstream programme, master-minded by Thomas Stockham. The results are uncannily successful: the voice emerges with remarkable freshness and purity (sample the *Flower song* from *Carmen*) and only the accompaniments, heavily laden with wind and brass, give the game away; otherwise one might think the recordings much more modern. The two selections include many famous records, covering the decade of 1906–16, and it is good to hear such singers as Melba, who joins Caruso in the duet, *O soave fanciulla*, and Farrar, Viafora and Scotti in the Act III *Bohème Quartet*. Farrar, Journet and Scotti are also present in the seven items from *Faust* included on the French recital. There are obviously more issues to come; they will be most welcome.

Chanticleer

'Sing we Christmas': PRAETORIUS: *Es ist ein Ros entsprungen*. VICTORIA: *O magnum mysterium*. TRAD.: *In dulci jubilo* (with verse 2 arr. M. PRAETORIUS; verse 3 arr. H. PRAETORIUS; verse 4 arr. BACH). *O Jesuslein süss, O Jesuslein mild* (verse 1 arr. SCHEIDT; verse 2 arr. BACH). JOSQUIN DES PRES: *O virgo virginum*. HANDL: *Hodie Christus natus est; Mirabile mysterium*. ANON.: *Verbo caro factum est: Y la Virgen le dezia*. GUERRERO: *A un niño llorando*. HOWELLS: *Here is the little door*. SAMETZ: *Noel canon*. arr. WILLCOCKS: *Quelle est cette odeur agréable*. arr. RIBO: *El Noi de la mare*. IVES: *A Christmas carol*. BILLINGS: *A virgin unspotted*. HOLST: *In the bleak midwinter*. arr. JENNINGS: *Glory to the newborn king* (fantasia on four spirituals). GRUBER: *Stille Nacht*.
**(*) Teldec/Warner Dig. 4509 94563-2 [id.].

The rich sonority of the very familiar opening Praetorius carol immediately demonstrates the body and homogeneity of the singing of this fine choral group of a dozen perfectly matched male voices; but while the choir's dynamic contrasts are not in question, the close balance prevents an absolute pianissimo, and the resonance brings a degree of clouding when lines interweave swiftly, as in Jacob Handl's *Hodie Christus natus est*. The lush blend of the slowly flowing *Mirabile mysterium*, with its haunting momentary stabs of dissonance, shows the choir at its finest, as does Victoria's contemplatively gentle setting (*O magnum mysterium*) and the rapt interweaving polyphony of Josquin's *O virgo virginum*, where the depth of sonority is extraordinary. If Herbert Howells's *Here is the little door* and Holst's *In the bleak midwinter* are made to seem too static, the Ives *Christmas carol* suits the sustained style, while Sametz's ingenious *Noel canon* is admirably vigorous, as is William Billings's *A virgin unspotted*. The extended sequence of four traditional gospel songs, arranged by Joseph Jennings, is perhaps the highlight of the concert, sung colloquially with some fine solo contributions, especially from the bass; and the closing *Stille Nacht* brings an unforgettably expansive resonance, with the voices blending like a brass chorale.

Christ Church Cathedral Choir, Oxford, Francis Grier

'Carols from Christchurch' (with Harry Bicket, organ): GARDNER: *Tomorrow shall be my dancing day*. TRAD.: *O thou man; In dulci jubilo*. HADLEY: *I sing of a maiden*. HOWELLS: *Sing lullaby; Here is the little door*. WARLOCK: *Bethlehem Down*. MATHIAS: *Sir Christèmas*. arr. BACH: *O little one sweet*. TCHAIKOVSKY: *The crown of roses*. HOWELLS: *A spotless rose*. WISHART: *Alleluya, a new work is come on hand*. BRITTEN: *A ceremony of carols* (with Frances Kelly harp): *Shepherd's carol; A Boy was born: Jesu, as Thou art our Saviour*.
(M) *** ASV CDWHL 2097 [id.].

This is among the most attractive of recent mid-priced reissues of carol collections, the more particularly as it includes not only a first-class account of Britten's *Ceremony of carols*, plus *Jesu, as Thou art our Saviour*, with its piercing momentary dissonances, but also the dialogue *Shepherd's carol*, so effectively featuring four soloists. The dozen other carols also bring some radiantly expressive singing, particularly in the three inspired Howells works; the Hadley carol, too, is delightful. They are framed by the admirably lively items by Gardner and Wishart, with Mathias's buoyant *Sir Christèmas* as a centrepiece. Generally good, analogue sound from the early 1980s.

Christofellis, Aris (sopraniste)

'Farinelli et son temps' (with Ensemble Seicentonovecento, Flavio Colusso): arias from: DUNI: *Demofoonte*. GIACOMELLI: *Merope*. METASTASIO: *La Partenza*. HANDEL: *Ariodante; Serse*. BROSCHI: *Artaserse*. HASSE: *Artaserse; Orfeo*. ARIOSTI: *Artaserse*. PERGOLESI: *Adriano in Siria*.
*** EMI Dig. CDC5 55250-2 [id.].

What did operatic castratos sound like in the eighteenth century? The only recording of a genuine castrato, made at the turn of the century, is a travesty, merely the squawking of an old man. By any reckoning, here is a much closer answer, a finely trained high falsettist who, in the beauty and evenness of the sound, with a minimum of ugly hooting, suggests that this may well approximate to the sound of a castrato. A recording may exaggerate the size of Christofellis's voice – by report the singing of the great castratos was exceptionally powerful – but he is artist enough, with a formidable technique, to make a splendid show in this dazzling series of arias originally written for the great castrato, Farinelli. Some of his cadenzas are breathtaking. One brief song is by Farinelli's greatest friend, the librettist Metastasio, and Farinelli's own setting of the same words is also included. The items from Handel's *Ariodante* and *Serse*, better known than the rest, come in performances which stand up well against those we have had from female singers, and Christofellis in his note pays tribute to the pioneering work of Marilyn Horne. The performances are all lively and alert, and the recording of the voice is full and vivid, though the instrumental accompaniment is backwardly placed.

Christoff, Boris (bass)

'Russian songs' (with LOP, Tzipine; Paris Conservatoire O, Cluytens; Alexandre Labinsky, Alexandre Tcherepnine, Janine Reiss, Serge Zapolsky, or Nadia Gedda-Nova (piano); Gaston Marchesini, Maud-Martin Tortelier (cello)): GLINKA: *The Midnight review; Cradle song; What, young beauty; Where is our rose?; The Lark; Ah, you darling, lovely girl; Doubt; Grandpa, the girls once told me; How sweet to be with thee; Do not say the heart is sick; Hebrew song; Elegy; I remember the wonderful moment.* BORODIN: *Those folk; Song of the dark forest; From my tears; The Sea princess; The Pretty girl no longer loves me; The Magic garden; Arabian melody; The false note; The fishermaiden. Listen to my song, little friend; The Sleeping princess; Pride; For the shores of thy far native land; The sea; Why art thou so early, dawn?; My songs are poisoned.* CUI: *Songs, Op. 44: Le Hun; Berceuse; Le ciel est transi; Les songeants. Ici-bas; The tomb and the rose; The Love of a departed one; A Recent dream; Pardon!; Desire; Conspiracy; Song of Mary; The Imprisoned knight; Album leaf; The Prophet; The Statue of Tsarskoïe; In Memory of V. S. Stassov.* BALAKIREV: *Prologue; Song of Selim; Song: The Yellow leaf trembles; The Pine tree; Nocturne; Starless midnight, coldly breathed; The Putting-right; November the 7th; Dawn; Hebrew melody; The Wilderness; The Knight; The Dream; Look, my friend.* RIMSKY-KORSAKOV: *The Pine and the palm; On the hills of Georgia; The Messenger; Quietly evening falls; Hebrew song; Zuleika's song; Across the midnight sky; I waited for thee in the grotto at the appointed hour; The sea is tossing; The Upas tree; The Prophet; Quiet is the blue sea; Slowly drag my days; Withered flower; The rainy day has waned.* TCHAIKOVSKY: *Don Juan's serenade; The Mild stars shone for us; Child's song; Cradle song; Night; Do not ask; As they kept on saying, 'Fool'; To sleep; Disappointment; the canary; None but the weary heart; Again, as before, alone; A Legend.* RACHMANINOV: *Fate; How fair is this spot; When yesterday we met; All once I gladly owned; Morning; All things depart; Thy pity I implore; Christ is risen; Loneliness; O never sing to me again; The dream; The soldier's wife; The Harvest of sorrow; Oh stay, my love; The world would see thee smile; Night is mournful.* Folksongs: arr. SEROV: *The Evil power.* TRAD.: *Doubinouchka. Song of the Volga; The Bandore; Down Peterskaya Street; Going down the Volga; Notchenka* (Folksongs with Russian Ch., Potorjinsky).
(B) *** EMI mono CZS7 67496-2 (5) [CDZE 67496].

This survey covers recordings by the great Bulgarian bass made between 1954 and 1969. The great majority come from the 1960s, the earliest are the Russian folksongs recorded in 1954 and the Rachmaninov and Rimsky-Korsakov (1959). But throughout this remarkably extensive programme, the magnificent voice is in perfect shape and the recordings are faithfully transferred. Some might think a big voice like Christoff's would be unsuitable for art songs, but his sensitivity is never in question and, whenever necessary, he scales it down, especially (for instance) in several of the Glinka songs where he has a cello obbligato. This repertoire is enormously rich in melody and, just as in the opera house, Christoff's art demonstrates the widest emotional range. Characterization is always strong and his feeling for words is just as striking here as in his performances of the stage repertory. Most of the songs are piano accompanied (with a whole range of excellent accompanists) but occasionally orchestral versions are used, as in Rimsky-Korsakov's *The prophet* or Balakirev's *Prologue*, when the orchestra is vividly balanced. The collection ends with an exhilarating half-dozen traditional Russian folksongs in which Christoff is joined by an enthusiastic (if backwardly balanced) Russian chorus and balalaika ensemble. The result is irresistible, with melancholy and joy side by side in a wonderfully Slavonic way. These five well-filled discs not only demonstrate some of the riches hitherto hidden in EMI's international vaults; they also give us unique performances of repertoire most of which is otherwise totally inaccessible. The snag lies in the documentation. As this derives from EMI's French stable, even the song-titles are given in French. (It was a major task identifying and translating them!) No texts are provided, simply a 2½-page biographical note.

The City Waites

'The Musicians of Grope Lane': Music of brothels and bawdy houses of Purcell's England: *Diddle diddle or The kind country lovers; The fair maid of Islington; Green stockings; The jovial lass or Dol and Roger; Mundanga was; Lady of pleasure; The old wife; The beehive; Blue petticoats or green garters; The Gelding of the Devil; The maid's complaint for want of a dil doul; Oyster Nan; The frolic; The husband who met his match; The jovial broom man; The disappointment; The lusty young smith; Greensleeves and yellow lace; The jolly brown turd;* Two rounds: *Tom making a manteau; When Celia was learning. Lady lie near me; Oh how you protest; A ditty delightful of Mother Watkin's ale; Miss Nelly*
(M) *** Musica Oscura Dig. 070969 [id.].

There really was a Grope Lane, which meant exactly what it says. Apart from a lubricious woodcut at the front of the booklet, illustrating the gelding of the Devil (taken from a broadsheet in the Samual Pepys Library), it is the words that count here rather than the music, for it is no good having lewd words that one cannot hear, even if they are all included in the booklet. And ballads like *The jovial lass* and *The lusty young smith* are unequivocally lewd; others use metaphor more tastefully and also have a touch of wit, like the 'Ditty delightful', in which the young maid tells her lover, 'I am afraid to die a maid'. He promises to give her Watson's ale and when, after her first draught, she innocently asks for a second, she is disconcerted when she has to wait a little. 'Let us talk a little while,' he suggests. So full marks for the diction of the City Waites and also their swinging dialect style with ballads that usually fall far short of being art songs. The items here are sometimes accompanied, sometimes not, but they are made into a lively entertainment by being interwoven with instrumental pieces from Playford's *Dancing Master*.

Codex

Codex: 'Treasures from the DG Archiv Catalogue'.
(M) **(*) DG mono/stereo 453 161-2 (10) [id.].

The word 'Codex' originally described a quire of manuscript pages held together by stitching – the earliest format of a book; it went on to mean a collection of rare and valuable documents. So the term is used here, appropriately enough, to encapsulate what DG suggest are 'rare documents in sound from 50 years of pioneering recording, ranging from the serene counterpoint of a Machaut, the intensely spiritual polyphony of a Victoria to the imposing state music of a Handel'. The majority of these recordings have never before appeared on CD, and the only snag from the collector's point of view is that authentic styles of performance have changed greatly during the last half-century, as scholarship has re-researched its sources and re-determined the stylistic parameters. The highlight of the collection is Emilio De'Cavaleri's *Rappresentatione di Anima, et di Corpo*, which is well worth seeking out independently. All the discs are currently available separately.

Disc 1 (with Brussels Pro Musica Antiqua, Safford Cape): LEONIN: *Judaea et Jerusalem*. PEROTINUS: *Sederunt principes*. MACHAUT: *Messe de Nostre Dame*. DU FAY: *Vergine bella. Vexilla Regis. Flos florum. Veni creator spiritus. Alma redemtoris mater* (DG mono 453 162-2).

The first disc here opens with an organum duplum, *Judaea et Jerusalem*, of Léonin, and an organum quadruplum, *Sederunt principes* of Pérotinus. The singers of Safford Cape's Pro Musica Antiqua are expertly matched and balanced, and their austere style, slow and deliberate, is not inappropriate. But one would have expected rather more vitality conveyed in Machaut's *Messe de Nostre Dame* (the first known complete polyphonic setting of the Ordinary of the Mass); here the approach is very pure and literal, and the accompaniment (for recorder, fiddles and lute) highly conjectural. All three alternative performances, listed above under the composer, are more stimulating. When one moves on to the selection of hymns, motets and antiphons by Du Fay, the singing suddenly springs to expressive life. The opening accompanied alto solo, *Vergine bella* (a setting of the first verse of an Italian canzona by Petrarch), is justly famous, while *Flos florum*, for mixed voices and fiddles, is both complex and beautiful, as is the account of the (unaccompanied) three-voiced setting of the ninth-century Pentecostal hymn, *Veni creator spiritus*; while the glorious *Alma redemptoris mater* (for accompanied alto, tenor and bass), which paraphrases an eleventh-century Marian antiphon, caps the collection eloquently.

Disc 2 (with Schola Cantorum, Francesco Coradini, Fosco Corti; (i) with Arnoldo Foà): ANON.: Marian Antiphons: *Alma redemptoris mater; Ave regina caelorum; Regina caeli laetare; Salve regina*. Francesco CORTECCIA: (i) *Passione secondo Giovanni (St John Passion)* (453 163-2).

The Florentine composer, Francesco Corteccia (1502–71), took holy orders in 1526 and became organist at the Church of San Lorenzo in 1531; he ended his career as chapel master at Florence Cathedral and he also supervised the music at the Medici Court. His *St John Passion* dates from 1527. The choral writing is simple and touchingly serene. The snag here is that the commentary of the Evangelist is not sung but spoken, and the cueing does not separate the spoken part of the performance, which will be frustrating for non-Italian-speaking listeners, seeking to hear the music without the narrative. Nevetheless the various uninterrupted set-pieces for the choir, including *Tristis est anima mea unsque ad mortem*, the exquisite *Tenebrae factae sunt* and notably *Caligaverunt oculi mei* (which we hear again, below, in Victoria's setting), are very moving, none more so than the desolate closing Evangelicum: *Post haec autem rogavit Pilatum Joseph ab Arimathea*, which is sung here very gently, with a superbly sustained closing pianissimo dying away in the closing fall. Arnoldo Foà speaks the part of the Evangelist with admirable simplicity, and the singing and recording could hardly be bettered. The disc opens with four Marian antiphons, which are also beautifully presented.

Disc 3: Thomás Luis de VICTORIA (with Regensburger Domchor, Hans Schrems): *Missa Vidi speciosam*. Motets and Responsories: *Vidi speciosam; Tamquam ad latronen; O Domine Jesu Christe; Amicus meus; Unus ex discipulis meis; Caligaverunt oculi mei; Dum complerentur; Surrexit Pastor Bonus. Lamentations of Jeremiah: Aleph. Ego vir didens paupertam meam* (453 164-2).

Victoria's *Missa Vidi speciosam* is a parody Mass based on a *Canticum canticorum* motet, also included here, whose words have a distinctly pantheistic character ('I have seen what was like a beautiful dove, rising above the rivers of water, whose fragrance was beyond value in its vestments; and, like spring days, flowers of roses and lilies of the valley surrounded it'). The perfumed symbolism of these words invaded the Mass and, although Victoria modified his musical style somewhat for his ecclesiastical setting, it gives the work an expressive richness which makes it suitable for performance by the mixed voices of Regensburg Choir, even though their expressive manner and their use of vibrato are somewhat anachronistic. The recording brings a limited dynamic range and the plangent Latin ardour of Victoria's writing is elusive, although the closing *Agnus Dei* is heartfelt. The choir are happier in the motets and responsories: the motet on which the Mass is based is beautifully sung, as is the deeply expressive *Caligaverunt occuli mei* ('My eyes have been stitched shut from my weeping'), and the excerpt from the *Lamentations of Jeremiah* is appealingly serene. The choir blends well, but the resonance prevents the clearest focus of inner detail and occasionally intonation is slightly suspect.

Disc 4: Emilio DE'CAVALIERI: *Rappresentatione di Anima, et di Corpo* (with Tatiana Troyanos, Hermann Prey, Kurt Equiluz, Herbert Lackner, Theo Adam, Teresa Zylis-Gara, Edda Moser, V. Chamber Ch., V. Capella Academica, Ens. Wolfgang von Karajan, Mackerras) (453 165-2).

We have not previously encountered this fine (1970) recording of Cavalieri's *The Dialogue of Soul and Body*, not an opera, but much more theatrical than an oratorio. It was not produced for Lent but, more appropriately, at carnival time in February 1600. Cavalieri was in charge of music at the Court of Grand Duke Ferdinand I of Tuscany, and he developed a novel kind of pastoral play in which dialogue, songs and choruses were all sung. The libretto philosophizes on the conflicting demands of hedonistic pleasures and the necessity of spiritual preparation for life's inevitable end. Act I opens with the prudent consideration that time flies, and Time (the excellent Theo Adam) suggests that the audience had better make every moment count, before the sounding of the Last Trump. Good Counsel (the dry-voiced Herbert Lackner) opens Act II with the warning that 'Life is nothing but a battle', and at its close Earthly Life is disrobed and found to be death in disguise; Act III counts the blessings of Heaven and offers a dramatically explicit warning of Hell. At its close, all take the righteous path and glorify the Lord and virtue's victory. With fine, animated choral singing as a backcloth – their first entry, *Questa vita mortale, per fuggir presto ha l'ale* ('This mortal life has wings to fly so fast'), is delightful – the principals bring the piece vividly to life. Tatiana Troyanos is in splendid voice as Anima, Soul. 'I did not fashion myself', she sings, 'And how can I calm these desires of mine'; and Hermann Prey is appropriately dark-voiced and commanding, even gruff, as Corpo (Body). In the small parts, Paul Esswood represents Pleasure, and Kurt Equiluz proves an ardently light-hearted Intellect when he points out in scene iii that 'Every heart loves happiness' (*Ogni cor ama il bene*), while in Act II Teresa Zylis-Gara is a fine Guardian Angel. Anima has an engaging echo dialogue with heaven when she asks if the world should shun all pleasures, and receives an unequivocal reply. Later, the same echo device is used even more effectively when the four-part chorus are echoed in reply by a two-part chorus as they seek to confirm mankind's ultimate destiny in heaven. All in all, this is a most attractive entertainment, with the most uplifting moral purpose to set against its hedonsitic celebrations of human enjoyment. Mackerras was just the man for it: the performance swings along vivaciously, and it is excellently recorded. A real find.

Disc 5: Orlando GIBBONS: *Fantasias for viols Nos. I & II a 3; II a 4; In nomine a 5. O Lord I lift my heart to Thee; Thus Angels sung; Almighty and everlasting God; O my love, how comely now; O Lord, increase my faith; This is the record of John; What is our life? The silver swan. The Cries of London: God give you good morrow; A good sausage* (with Alfred Deller, Deller Consort, Consort of Viols of Schola Cantorum Basiliensis, Wenzinger). MORLEY: *Good love, then fly thou to her. Farewell disdainful; Hark, jolly shepherds, hark; Now is the gentle season; My lovely wanton pearl; Sweet nymph, come to thy lover; Stay heart, run not so fast; O grief, even on the bud* (with Ambrosian Singers, Denis Stevens) (mono/stereo 453 166-2).

The Gibbons programme (from the mid-1950s) provides variety by effectively interspersing the vocal numbers with Fantasias for viols which are played impeccably by Wenzinger and his Schola Cantorum Basiliensis. Deller leads his well-matched vocal group in a series of anthems and hymns that are expressively sung but, with consistently leisured tempi and a limited dynamic range, lack variety. The highlight is the fine verse anthem, *This is the record of John. The Cries of London* are more lively, but they come off even more effectively when the style is more vernacular. The mono recording is full but closely balanced. The Denis Stevens collection of songs and madrigals of Thomas Morley dates from a decade later and is sung by small groups of soloists with great charm and and impeccable style. *Farewell disdainful* and *O grief, even on the bud* are particularly touching. The original collection from which these items are drawn had added variety from the inclusion of harpsichord pieces, admirably played by Valda Aveling. Unaccountably, they are here omitted and are a great loss, especially when there was plenty of room for them, for the overall playing time here is 63 minutes.

Disc 6: HANDEL: *Utrecht Te Deum and Jubilate; Coronation anthem: Zadok the Priest* (with Ilse Wolf, Helen Watts, Wilfred Brown, Edgar Fleet, Thomas Hemsley, Geraint Jones Singers & O, Jones) (453 167-2).

Handel's *Utrecht Te Deum and Jubilate*, first performed in 1713, shows how rapidly he absorbed the style of English cathedral music, improving on it, yet suggesting by his use of soloists and chorus the verse anthem style that goes back to Purcell and Gibbons. As a writer of occasional music Handel had few equals, and these works show him at his best and most brilliant. Nobody now, apart from the historians, cares about the Peace of Utrecht, but the music Handel wrote for the happy year is still vividly before us in this lively performance by Geraint Jones. Ilse Wolf, Edgar Fleet and Thomas Hemsley sing with excellent tone and style; Helen Watts brings her artistry to bear on what is really music for a counter-tenor. Wilfred Brown is a little below his usual high standard. There is adequate depth, even though small resources are used and, though the most famous coronation anthem is not as overwhelming as some like it to be, the 1959 sound remains very impressive and hardly dated.

Disc 7: Carl Philipp Emanuel BACH: *Keyboard fantasias: in C Wq 61/6; in C min. (Probestücke), Wq 63/6* (with Colin Tilney); Lieder: *Uber die Finsternis kurz vor dem Tod, Jesu; Der Frühling; Prüfung am Abend; Morgengesang; Bitten; Trost der Erlösung; Passionslied; Die Güte Gottes; Abendlied; Wider den Ubermut; Demut; Weihnachtslied; Jesus in Gethsemane; Der Tag des Weltgerichts. Psalms: 19, 130 & 148* (with Dietrich Fischer-Diekau, Joerg Demus) (453 168-2).

On the evidence of this collection, Carl Philipp Emanuel was not a true songsmith. Fischer-Dieskau makes the very most of these mainly brief items, but few are melodically memorable. The most attractive are *Trost der Erlösung* and *Die Güte Gottes*, although *Abendlied* and *Wider den Unbermut* are quite pleasing. The Psalms are altogether more striking, all three quite memorable, No. 19 surprisingly lively, and the minuscule No. 148 most engagingly light-hearted. The Christmas Lied is also very attractive. Fisher-Dieskau's voice was at its warmest and freshest at the beginning of the 1970s, and Demus accompanies him sensitively, if rather distantly on a Tangentenflügel (a somewhat advanced fortepiano). The two rhythmically quirky *Fantasias* are attributed to Colin Tilney's clavichord, but it is recorded much too closely and the result is ugly: indeed the instrument is difficult to recognize.

Disc 8: Michel-Richard DELALANDE: *Simphonies pour les souper du roi: Quatrième suite; Sixième suite – Premier Caprice*. Jean-Joseph MOURET: *Fanfares: Première suite. Simphonies: Seconde suite*. PHILIDOR: *Marche à quatre timbales*. LULLY: *Airs de trompettes, timbales et hautbois*. Marc-Antoine CHARPENTIER: *Te Deum: Prélude* (with soloists, Paul Kuentz CO, Kuentz) (453 169-2).

The composer Lalande (or Delalande, all in one word, like Debussy) provided table music of considerable charm for the formal dinners of two French monarchs, Louis XIV and Louis XV, and in 1745 a definitive edition appeared in Paris. It is this score that Paul Kuentz uses as a basis for the two *Suites* recorded here. Mouret, a contemporary of Delalande, captivated the Parisian public for many years with his stage and symphonic music, but his last years were clouded by insanity, due largely to a rapid loss of reputation which coincided with the ascendancy of Rameau. As a musical servant of the French court and nobility, Mouret earned his title of '*le musicien des graces*', and the urbane charm of his symphonies evokes the spirit of the age in an inimitable and even forceful manner. His two attractive suites, the first featuring a solo trumpet and the second a pair of horns, both give their soloists attractive music to play while providing plenty of interest in the overall texture. The Lully set of *Airs* is consistently heavily scored and becomes a bit wearing to the ear, while Philidor uses drums alone; the Charpentier *Prélude* to the celebrated *Te Deum* makes a brief coda, playing for only a minute and a half. Paul Kuentz and his chamber orchestra, topped by the clear, high roulades of Adolf Scherbaum's trumpet, strive manfully to reproduce the spacious ambience at Versailles. If they fall short of their mark, it is due to acoustical rather than musical deficiences, for a Paris studio was used for the sessions and as a result the sound is a little tight and unresponsive. Nevertheless there is much to enjoy here, and the one vocal item in Delalande's fourth suite (*Quitte ici tes ailes*) is well sung by Edith Selig.

Disc 9: TARTINI: *Violin concertos: in D; in G*. NARDINI: *Violin concerto in E flat* (with Eduard Melkus, violin, Vienna Capella Academica, Wenzinger); *Violin sonata in G* (with Lionel Salter, harpsichord) (453 170-2).

Perhaps surprisingly, the DG Archivists have been unable to identify these two Tartini concertos very clearly, and the notes merely tell us that the *G major* dates from the middle period of the composer's creative career and may have been first heard in Prague in 1724, while the *D major* is most probably a late work. Like the Nardini with which they are coupled, both concertos are typical of their composer; because Tartini was a more individual musical personality, they come alive fully as individual works. With their Italianate melodic warmth, in some ways this pair of concertos looks forward to the nineteenth century, but if the florid virtuoso writing in the outer movements holds a balance between the classical style and the grander manner of the future, the slow movements are embroidered with an ornamentation that is essentially baroque in implication. Both concertos are played with sensitivity and musical confidence, and in every respect the music-making here (both solo and orchestral) has more warmth and charm than the Olympia series listed under the composer (above). But to come off in the spirit in which they were written, they need more of the Heifetz and less of the scholar. They were primarily meant to entertain and perhaps astonish, and to do this they need to be thrown off like quicksilver. Nardini's concerto is more conventional, with long cadenza-like interpolations like those in Locatelli's *Art of the Violin*. Edward Melkus plays the fireworks confidently. Yet somehow, as with Tartini, the result fails to convey the excitement – the *raison d'être* of the music – which was obviously generated for listeners of 200 years ago. The *Sonata*, an agreeable little three-movement duo, is again devised to display the soloist, and here the backwardly balanced Lionel Salter makes the most of an indifferent supporting keyboard part. Excellent recording throughout.

Disc 10: SOLER: *Concertos for 2 keyboard instruments Nos. 1–6* (with Kenneth Gilbert and Trevor Pinnock (harpsichords or fortepianos)) (453 171-2).

These Soler concertos are described in the surviving autograph as intended for two organs, but Kenneth Gilbert and Trevor Pinnock use either two harpsichords (copies of Florentine instruments after Vincenzio Sodi, 1782) or two fortepianos (copies by Adlam Burnett of Heilmann, *c*. 1785) – and very attractive they sound too. The music itself is not very substantial and does not possess the character of some of Soler's solo harpsichord music. Most of the concertos are in two movements, the second being minuets plus variations. These are highly skilful performances, well recorded; if the music is not of outsize personality, it is far from unpleasing.

Columbus Consort

'Christmas in early America' (18th-century carols and anthems): BELCHER: *How beauteous are their feet.* HOLYOKE: *How beauteous are their feet; Th'Almighty spake and Gabriel sped; Comfort ye my people.* CARR: *Anthem for Christmas.* STEPHENSON: *If angel's sung a Saviour's birth.* HUSBAND: *Hark! The glad sound.* HEIGHINGTON: *While shepherds watched their flocks by night.* FRENCH: *While shepherds watched their flocks by night.* BILLINGS: *While shepherds watched their flocks by night.* PETER: *Unto us a child is born.* ANTES: *Prince of Peace, Immanuel.* MICHAEL: *Hail Infant newborn.* HERBST: *To us a Child is born.* SCHULZ: *Thou Child divine.* DENCKE: *Meine Seele erhebet den Herrn.* GREGOR: *Hosanna! Blessed he that comes in the name of the Lord.* Charles PACHELBEL: *Magnificat anima mea Dominum.*
*** Channel Classics Dig. CC 5693 [id.].

A fascinating look back to the celebration of Christmas in the New World in the late eighteenth century, both by the British colonial settlers in New England and by their Moravian counterparts in Pennsylvania and North Carolina, where the inheritance was essentially in the European tradition. The English style is usually fairly simple and hymn-like, but with overlapping part-writing and occasional solo dialogues (as in the rhythmically interesting *Th'Almighty spake*). Samuel Holyoke shows himself to be a strikingly fresh melodist while, of the three settings of *While shepherds watched* to different tunes, William Billings emerges as the most striking and imaginative. Benjamin Carr's *Anthem for Christmas* is a musical pastiche (indeed a kind of 'musical switch' with brief quotations from Corelli's *Christmas concerto* and Handel's *Messiah* among other works). The Moravian/German music is usually more elaborate. Johann Peter's delightful motet-like carol, *Unto us a Child is born*, has characteristically resourceful accompanimental string-writing and those who follow him – David Moritz Michael, Johannes Herbst, J. A. P. Schulz and Jeremiah Dencke – all write in a tradition descended from the great German composers, capped by Charles Pachelbel (son of the Johann Pachelbel of *Canon* fame). He played the organ in Boston, New York and Charleston in the 1730s and 1740s, and his *Magnificat* for double chorus celebrates a much more florid style, utterly different from the music which opens this programme. The surprise is that this concert is performed not by American singers but by a Dutch group of expert vocal soloists, with a choral and string ensemble who sing and play with convincing authenticity and an agreeably stylish spontaneity. The recording is realistic and clear and made within a perfectly judged acoustic.

Crespin, Régine (soprano)

'Grandi voci' (with Ch. of the Grand Théâtre, Suisse Romande O, Alain Lombard, or Vienna Volksoper O, Georges Sebastian): Arias from: GLUCK: *Iphigénie en Tauride.* BERLIOZ: *La Damnation de Faust.* GOUNOD: *Sapho.* BIZET: *Carmen.* OFFENBACH: *La Grande Duchesse de Gérolstein; La belle Hélène; La Périchole.* HAHN: *Ciboulette.* CHRISTINE: *Phi-Phi.* MESSAGER: *J'ai deux amants.* O. STRAUSS: *Les Trois valses.*
(M) *** Decca 440 416-2 [id.].

More than any other of her many recordings, this presents the complete Crespin, a commanding personality with a ringing, vibrant voice, but also an artist with a keen sense of fun. Marvellous as the opera rarities are, ranging wide, the operetta items are what most listeners will remember with most affection – the Duchess reviewing her troops, the heroine tipsy in *La Périchole* – vulgarity skirted by the naughtiest and most tantalizing of margins. Fine 1970/71 recording, and this reissue now has an overall timing of 73 minutes. Not to be missed.

Danish National Radio Choir, Stefan Parkman

'Scandinavian contemporary a cappella': TORMIS: *Raua needmine.* NORGARD: *And time shall be no more.* RAUTAVAARA: *Suite de Lorca, Op. 72.* SANDSTROM: *A cradle song.* JERSILD: *3 Romantike korsange.*
*** Chandos Dig. CHAN 9264 [id.].

Tormis is an honorary Scandinavian: he hails from Estonia. Jørgen Jersild and Per Nørgård are both Danish, Sven-David Sandström Swedish (and mightily overrated in his homeland), and Einojuhani Rautavaara comes from Finland. Stefan Parkman has brought the Danish National Radio Choir to considerable heights and now it almost (but not quite) rivals the Swedish Radio Choir in its heyday under Eric Ericsson. None of the music is quite good enough to enter the permanent repertory in the way that the sublime motets of Holmboe's *Liber canticorum* should and doubtless will. By their side, this is all pretty small beer, but the Jersild and Rautavaara are worth investigating.

Robert DeCormier Singers and Ensemble, Robert DeCormier

'Children go where I send thee' (A Christmas celebration around the world) (with soloists from the Choir): Traditional songs and carols from: Sweden (arr. DECORMIER): *Ritsch, Ratsch, filibon*. Italy: *Dormi, dormi, O bel bambin*. Austria: *Da Droben vom Berge*. Nigeria: *Betelehemu*. Spain: *A la nanita, nanita;* (Catalonia): *El noi de la mare*. USA: *Children go where I send thee; Poor little Jesus;* (Appalachian): *In the valley*. Puerto Rico: *La Trulla*. Germany: *Es is ein' Ros' entsprungen*. France: *Ecoutons donc les aubades*. India: *Lína avatárá*. Canada: *Huron carol*. Syria: *Miladuka*. Argentina: *La peregrinacion*. West Indies: *The Virgin Mary had a baby boy*.
*** Arabesque Dig. Z 6684 [id.].

The excellent Robert DeCormier Singers have already recorded a number of fine collections, including a John Dowland anthology (*'Awake sweet love'*: Z 6622) and two previous Christmas collections (*'A Victorian Christmas'*: Z 6525 and *'The first nowell'*: Z 6526) but none has been more attractive than this geographically wide-ranging programme of Christmas songs with children in mind. The arrangements are simple, for every number has great character and needs no embellishment. The programme opens enticingly with a tick-tock (*Ritsch, ratsch*) Swedish carol which is immediately captivating; it is followed with an exquisite Italian lullaby. The oldest item is a Syrian Christmas hymn, *Miladuka* ('The Nativity') which, based on plainchant, is thought to be more than 1,000 years old. It is presented here in harmonized form and is quite haunting, as is the example from Northern India, *Lína avatárá* ('He chose to be among us'), which is introduced softly on flute and chiming percussion. When the voices enter, the harmonies are bare, whereas the Nigerian song about Bethlehem has rich upper intervals above the sonorous repeated bass and soon becomes exultant. The Argentinian carol, *The Pilgrimage*, is lusciously Latin, while the Spanish examples are simpler but lilting. The only really familiar carol is from Germany and it is beautifully and serenely presented. The concert ends swingingly with the more familiar West Indian *The Virgin Mary had a baby boy* which is given the lightest, most infectious rhythmic touch. Altogether this splendidly recorded anthology, with its nicely judged instrumental accompaniments, will give great pleasure – to grown-ups as well as to children.

Deller, Alfred (counter tenor)

Alfred Deller Edition

'Western wind and other English folksongs and ballads' (with Desmond Dupré, lute & guitar, John Southcott, recorder): *Western wind; Early one morning; Black is the colour; All the pretty little horses; Lowlands; The Sally gardens; Bendemeer's Stream; Annie Laurie; The Miller of the Dee; Cockles and mussels; Drink to me only; The foggy, foggy dew; The frog went a-courtin'; The turtle dove; Pretty Polly Oliver; The carrion crow; The wife of Usher's Well; Henry Martin; I am a poor wayfaring stranger; Cold blows the wind; Skye boat song; Every night the sun goes down; Song of a wedding.*
(M) *** Van. 08.5032.71 [id.].

A ravishing collection of folksongs, recorded in 1958 when the great counter-tenor was at the very peak of his form. The early stereo gives a lovely bloom to his voice, and here, as throughout this fine series, the CD transfers are of a high calibre. The opening *Western wind* is justly another of Deller's 'hits', but *Lowlands* is hardly less beautiful, and many other items here show the magic of his tonal nuancing and his natural, spontaneous musicianship. *Annie Laurie* is wonderfully fresh and brings a frisson as he soars up to the top of his range, while the irrepressible *Miller of Dee*, the petite *Pretty Polly Oliver*, and jaunty *Foggy dew* show him well able to lighten his presentation in the most sparkling manner. *Every night when the sun goes down* brings an almost Gershwinesque, bluesy feeling. In the charming *All the pretty little horses*, *The Frog went a'courtin'* and the *Skye boat song*, John Southcott touches in discreet obbligati on the recorder, and throughout Desmond Dupré provides persuasive lute accompaniments. The last four songs listed appear on record for the very first time in any format.

Tavern songs: *'Catches, glees and other divers entertainments'* (with the Deller Consort): PURCELL: *Man is for woman made; Sir Walter; To thee and to the maid; Chiding catch; Once, twice, thrice; When the cock begins to crow; Epitaph, Under this stone; An ape, a lion, a fox, and an ass; True Englishmen; Young Collin; If all be true.* Earl of MORNINGTON: *'Twas you, sir.* SAVILE: *Had she not care enough.* TURNER: *Young Anthony.* TRAD.: *Amo amas, I love a lass.* CORNYSHE: *Ah, Robin; Hoyda, jolly Rutherkin.* LAWES: *Bess Black; Sing fair Clorinda; The captive lover.* ANON.: *I am athirst; Troll the bowl; We be soldiers three; He that will an alehouse keep; Inigo Jones; Summer is icumen in.* ECCLES: *Wine does wonders.* TRAVERS: *Fair and ugly, false and true.* BENNET: *Lure, falconers lure.* ROGERS: *In the merry month of May.* SPOFFORTH: *L'ape e la serpe.* HILTON: *Call George again.* ATTERBURY: *As t'other day.* ARNE: *The street intrigue; Which is the properest way to drink.* BLOW: *Bartholomew Fair; The self banished; Galloping Joan.* BOYCE: *John Cooper.* BARNABY: *Sweet and low.*
(M) **(*) Van. 08.5039.71 [id.].

In this extraordinarily generous 78-minute collection from 1956, 40 items in all, the Deller Consort consisted of Gerald English, Wilfred Brown, Maurice Bevan, Edgar Fleet and Owen Grundy, and they sing, unaccompanied, various catches and glees, part-songs, rounds (of which *Summer is icumen in* is a prime example) and semi-madrigals from both Elizabethan and Restoration England, right up to the pre-Victorian period. The opening 'Choice collection of the most diverting catches', attributed to Purcell, are mainly bawdy, explicitly about the joys of love-making in an age of frankness. The Elizabethan romantic lute-songs had an essential finesse and delicacy of feeling, so the more robust dialogue pieces acted as a healthy counter-balance. The popular ballads could also be restrained, and this opening group ends with a touching glee, *Under this stone*, about the late-lamented Gabriel John. There are many other part-songs intended to charm with their vivacity, and *Young Anthony peeping through the keyhole*, by William Turner (1651–1740) becomes more complex as its hero eagerly joins the two ladies he has overheard discussing their probity. *Ah, Robin*, a lovely glee by William Cornyshe, is better known today, slightly altered in rhythm, as *Sing we Nowell*, while the music for the glee/madrigal *Amo, amas, I love a lass*, with its naughty Latin parody text, could have come straight out of *HMS Pinafore*. Purcell's 'patter' trio, *True Englishmen*, also shows how much Sullivan borrowed from this fertile source. *We be soldiers three* even quotes doggerel French in the way of British soldiers who, in this instance, have returned from the Flemish wars, while *L'ape e la serpe*, a late-eighteenth-century glee by Reginald Spofforth, is sung in Italian. The performances are suitably direct, never prissy, and this especially applies to the robust drinking songs, although occasionally one would have welcomed a more spontaneously earthy bite. The recording is clear and immediate, the ambience dry but pleasing.

PURCELL (with the Deller Consort, (i) Oriana Concert Choir & O; (ii) L. Kalmar O, Walter Bermann, harpsichord)): (i) *Come ye sons of art (Ode on Queen Mary's birthday, 1694); Rejoice in the Lord alway (Bell anthem);* (ii) *My beloved spake; Welcome to all pleasures (Ode on St Cecilia's Day, 1683).*
(M) **(*) Van. 08.5060.71 [id.].

These Purcell performances convey much joy in the music-making, even if for some ears the warmly upholstered (and tonally beautiful) overtures may sound slightly anachronistic. It is good to hear Deller in the famous solos, notably *Strike the viol*, with its intertwining flute obbligato (in *Come ye sons of art*), and *Here the Deities approve* in *Welcome to all the pleasures*, while in the former he is joined by his son, Mark – who sounds more like a treble – for the 'counter-tenor' duet, *Sound the trumpet*. The Deller Consort almost turns *My beloved spake* into a series of madrigals. Pleasingly full sound from 1962.

'Madrigal masterpieces': The Renaissance in France, Italy and England (with Eileen Pouler, Mary Thomas, Wilfred Brown, Gerald English, Maurice Bevan, Geoffrey Coleby, Deller Consort): JANEQUIN: *Ce moys de may; La bataille de Marignan; Au joly boys.* LASSUS: *Mon coeur se recommande à vous; Matona mia cara.* MARENZIA: *Scaldava il sol.* MONTEVERDI: *Baci, soavi, e cari; Ecco mormorar l'onde; A'un giro sol bell'occhi; Non piu guerra!; Sfogava con le stelle.* BYRD: *My sweet little baby* (lullaby). MORLEY: *Now is the month of maying.* GESUALDO: *Ecco moriro dunque/Hai gia mi disco loro.* TOMKINS: *When David heard that Absolom was slain.*
(M) ** Van. 08.5061.71 [id.].

We have moved on in the style of performance of Italian madrigals since this collection was (excellently, if closely) recorded in 1959. The Deller Consort are entirely happy in the English repertoire. Morley's *Now is the month of maying* almost explodes with spring-like vitality, and the Byrd and Tomkins items are beautiful. The Lassus *Mon coeur se recommande à vous* is touchingly serene in the same way, and *Matona mia cara* is freshly presented, but the Janequin and Monteverdi items are less successful, although *Baci, soavi, e cari* has an appealing simplicity.

TALLIS (with Wilfred Brown, Gerald English, Eileen McLoughlin, Maurice Bevan, Deller Consort): *Lamentations of Jeremiah the Prophet*. 5 hymns alternating plainchant and polyphony: *Deus tuorum militum; Jam Christus astra ascenderat; Jesu Salvator Saeculi; O nata lux de lumine; Salvator mundi Domine.*
(M) ** Van. 08.5062.71 [id.].

Alfred Deller pioneered so much repertoire on LP, and even today Tallis's settings of the *Lamentations of Jeremiah* are not generously represented on disc. They are given poised, expressive performances and the motets are presented with their alternating plainsong, but the close recording robs the music-making of atmosphere and the dynamic range is very limited.

MONTEVERDI: *Il ballo delle Ingrate* (with Eileen McLoughlin, David Ward, April Cantelo, Amb. S., L. Chamber Players, Denis Stevens); *Lamento d'Arianna* (with Honor Sheppard, Sally le Sage, Max Worthley, Philip Todd, Maurice Bevan, Deller Consort).
(M)**(*) Van. 08.5063.71 [id.].

Deller's pioneering 1956 stereo recording of Monteverdi's *Il ballo delle Ingrate* would not, perhaps, be a first choice today, but at the time he had the advantage of Denis Stevens's scholarly assistance, and the performance has remarkable authenticity as well as considerable dramatic life. The famous *Lamento d'Arianna* is slightly less successful.

'The three ravens': Elizabethan folk and minstrel songs (with Desmond Dupré, guitar & lute): *The three ravens; Cuckoo; How should I your true love know; Sweet nightingale; I will give my love an apple; The oak and the ash;* (Lute) *Go from my window; King Henry; Coventry carol; Barbara Allen; Heigh ho, the wind and the rain; Waly, waly; Down in yon forest; Matthew, Mark, Luke and John;* (Lute) *A Toye; The Tailor and the mouse; Greensleeves; The Wraggle Taggle Gipsies; Lord Rendall; Sweet Jane; The frog and the mouse; The seeds of love; Near London town; Who's going to shoe your pretty little foot?; Blow away the morning dew; Searching for lambs; Sweet England; Dabbling in the dew; Just as the tide was flowing.*
(M) **(*) Van. 08.5064.71 [id.].

Opening charismatically with *The three ravens*, this very early (1956) recital contains some outstanding performances, notably of *Barbara Allen*, the delightful *Tailor and the mouse*, *The frog and the mouse*, and the captivating *Who's going to shoe your pretty little foot?*. *Searching for lambs* brings another favourite melody, and Deller's inimitable *Greensleeves* is certainly memorable. As before, Desmond Dupré provides highly sympathetic accompaniments, and here he also has a couple of solo opportunities in which to shine. But although the mono recording is admirably truthful, this collection is not quite so spontaneously appealing as the stereo recital listed above, even if it is comparably generous (73 minutes).

'The holly and the ivy': Christmas carols of old England (with April Cantelo, Gerald English, Maurice Bevan, Deller Consort, Stanley Taylor, recorder, Desmond Dupré, lute): *Patapan; We three kings of orient are; I saw three ships; The Coventry carol; It came upon the midnight clear; Good King Wenceslas; Once in Royal David's city; Rocking; The first nowell; God rest you merry gentlemen; Wither's Rocking hymn; Silent night; Wassail song; Dormi Jesus; Boar's head carol; Past three o'clock; Lullay my liking; Adam lay ybounden; Herrick's carol; Angelus ad Virginem; The holly and the ivy; O little one sweet; Song of the Nuns of Chester; Winter-Rose; In dulci jubilo.*
(M) **(*) Van. 08.5065.71 [id.].

Opening vivaciously with *Patapan*, this Christmas collection, simulating a visit from a village group of waits, often has a pleasing simplicity, although at times its madrigalesque style may strike some ears as lacking robustness. The Consort is heard at its best in *I saw three ships*, *Good King Wenceslas* and *The holly and the ivy*. But the highlights are all from Deller himself, and he is in magical form in the *Angelus ad Virginem*, *Winter-Rose* (with a delicate recorder obbligato from Stanley Taylor) and *O little one sweet*, more robust in *Adam lay ybounden*, but again displaying his unique nuancing of colour and dynamic. His serene account of the *Coventry carol* is heard here on disc for the first time.

François COUPERIN: *Leçons de ténèbres I–III* (excerpts) (with Wifred Brown, Desmond Dupré, viola da gamba, Harry Gabb, organ).
(M) *(*) Van. 08.5066.71 [id.].

Although there is some remarkable singing here, Deller cannot compare with Gérard Lesne in this repertoire – his manner is curiously histrionic and self-aware, unusually so for this artist. Harry Gabb's discreet organ accompaniment is to be commended, but Dupré's viola da gamba is too backwardly balanced.

'Duets for counter-tenors' (with Mark Deller & Bar. Ens.): MORLEY: *Sweet nymph, come to thy lover; Miraculous love's wounding; I go before my darling.* PURCELL: *Sweetness of nature.* SCHUTZ: *Erhöre mich wenn ich; Der Herr ist gross.* JONES: *Sweet Kate.* ANON.: *Ah, my dear son.* MONTEVERDI: *Currite populi; Angelus ad pastores ait; Fugge, fugge, anima mea; Salve Regina.* BLOW: *If my Celia could persuade; Ah, heaven, what is't I hear.* DEERING: *O bone Jesu; In coelis.*
(M) *(*) Van. 08.5067.71 [id.].

Deller's style needs no advocacy, and he has trained his son well to follow faithfully in his footsteps. But although Mark has a fine (treble rather than alto) voice, he does not have his father's subtle instinct for light and shade. So in this case a succession of duets for counter-tenors proves far from ideal planning for a whole recital. Moreover the voices are placed very forwardly, somewhat edgily recorded, and robbed of a convincing dynamic range; there are no possibilities for pianissimo singing here.

William BYRD: *'Byrd and his age'* (with Wenzinger Consort of Viols of Schola Cantorum Basiliensis, August Wenzinger): *My sweet little darling; Lullaby, my sweet little baby* (both arr. FELLOWES); *Fantasia for viols in G min.; Ye sacred muses (Elegy on the death of Thomas Tallis); Come pretty babe* (arr. Peter LE HURAY & Thurston DART). ANON.: *Guishardo; Ah, silly poor Joas; O Death, rock me asleep.* WHYTHORNE: *Buy new broom.* Richard NICHOLSON: *In a merry May morn.* Robert PARSONS: *Pandolpho* (all six arr. Peter WARLOCK). William CORKINE: *What booteth love?* (arr. Thurston DART). FERRABOSCO: *Fantasias for viols: in F & G.*
(M) ** Van. 08.5068.71 [id.].

The advantage of accompaniments from the excellent Schola Cantorum Basiliensis under Wenzinger is reduced by the rather forward balance of the voice in relation to the string group, and when the viols play alone the effect is rather dry. It is on the whole a melancholy programme, although *Buy new brooms* comes centrally as a bright diversion. But it is *Ah, silly poor Joas*, the Byrd *Lullaby*, and especially the very touching *Pandolpho* that are memorable, while the closing *O Death, rock me asleep* shows Deller at his most moving.

BACH and HANDEL: BACH: *Cantata No. 170: Vergnügte Ruh', beliebte Seelenlust* (with Leonhardt Bar. Ens.); *Cantata No. 54: Widerstehe doch: Aria: Widerstehe doch; Recitative: Die Art verruchter Sünden; Aria: Wer Sünde tut, der ust vom Teufel. Mass in B min.: Agnus Dei.* HANDEL: Arias: *Orlando: Ah! stigie larve* (Mad scene). *Jepthe: Tis heav'ns all ruling power. Theodora: Kind heaven; Sweet rose and lily.*
(M) ** Van. 08.5069.71 [id.].

These are among Deller's earliest recordings for Vanguard, dating from 1954. In the Bach cantatas Leonhardt provides dull, plodding accompaniments, and his ensemble of original instruments is uninspiringly meagre. The interest of this collection then centres on Deller himself, and he rises to the occasion, especially in the *Agnus Dei* from the *Mass in B minor*, which is most beautifully sung. The Handel accompaniments are more robust and it is good to hear Deller in these operatic excerpts, especially in Orlando's mad scene, but he is also at his finest in both the excerpts from *Theodora*.

'The Cries of London and English Ballads and folksongs': The Cries of London (with April Cantelo, Wilfred Brown, Amb. S., Deller Consort, L. Chamber Players): John COBB: *These are the cries of London.* RAVENSCROFT: *New oysters; Bellman's song; The painter's song; Brooms for old shoes.* DERING: *The cries of London* (all ed. Stevens); *Country cries* (ed. Revell). ANON.: *A quart a penny; I can mend your tubs and pails.* NELHAM: *Have you any work for the tinker?* (all ed. Stevens). WEELKES: *The cries of London* (ed. Noble). English ballads and folksongs (with Deller Consort; Desmond Dupré, lute): *When cockleshells turn silver bells; An Eriskay love lilt; Peggy Ramsay* (arr. Gerard WILLIAMS); *Bushes and briars; Brigg Fair; The cruel mother; A sweet country life* (arr. Imogen HOLST); *The bitter withy; Lang a-growing; The lover's ghost; Lovely Joan; She moved through the fair; A brisk young lad he courted me* (arr. Norman STONE); *Geordie.*
(M) **(*) Van. 08.5072.71 [id.].

Richard Dering's *Fantasia* is sophisticated and creates a continuous ten-minute musical kaleidoscope, ingeniously linking the airs in a seemingly natural sequence, ending with a melodious apotheosis on the words 'and so good night'. Weelkes's selection is little more than half as long, using one soloist, here the fresh-voiced April Cantelo. Even so, she gets through a great many lyrical exhortations to buy, ending with a gentle *Alleluia*. The second half of the recital brings Deller back (in 1959) to the world of ballads and folksongs, opening with a bewitchingly gentle account of *When cockleshells turn silver bells*. Both *The lover's ghost* and the *Eriskay love lilt* take him soaringly upwards, rapturously comparable with *Annie Laurie* on an earlier recital. He is effectively joined by the Consort in *Peggy Ramsay* and they bring variety to the collection with characteristic accounts of *A sweet country life* and *A brisk young lad*. Dupré and his lute set the scene for the lovely *Bushes and briars*. *The cruel mother*, which tells a dreadful story of infanticide, also shows him imaginatively stretched, while *Lang a-growing* with its neat Scottish snap is most effectively done.

VAUGHAN WILLIAMS: Arrangements of folksongs (with Deller Consort, Desmond Dupré, lute): *An acre of land; Bushes and briars; Ca' the yowes; The cuckoo and the nightingale; The dark-eyed sailor; Down by the riverside; A farmer's son so sweet; Greensleeves; John Dory; Just as the tide was flowing; The jolly ploughboy; Loch Lomond; The lover's ghost; My boy Billy; The painful plough; The spring time of the year; The turtle dove; Ward the Pirate; Wassail song.*
(M) ** Van. 08.5073.71 [id.].

These highly artistic folksong settings can be effectively performed either by choir or by soloists, and here Deller often alternates his own estimable solo contributions with choral versions. The recording is a little dry, but the stereo adds to the sense of atmosphere. An enjoyable collection, but not one of the finest of the series. It is discussed more fully under its composer listing, above.

'Grandi voci': CAMPION: *Never weatherbeaten sail; Most sweet and pleasing are thy ways, O God; Author of light; To music bent.* ANON.: *Miserere my maker* (all with Desmond Dupré, lute). BUXTEHUDE: *Jubilate domino* (with Instrumental Ens.). BACH: *Magnificat in D: Et misericordia. Esureintes implevit bonis* (with Wilfred Brown, Kalmar Orchestra, Colombo). PURCELL: *Come ye sons of art* (excerpts; with John Whitworth, St Anthony Singers). HANDEL: *Sosarme*: extended excerpts (with Ritchie, St Cecilia Orchestra; both cond. Lewis) .
(M) (***) Decca mono 448 247-2 [id.].

Compiled from Oiseau-Lyre mono recordings of the 1950s, which followed his earliest HMV records, this fine 75-minute collection of favourites and rarities explains how Alfred Deller, distinctive in timbre and style, established the counter-tenor voice with a wider public than ever before. His voice is youthfully fresh and has probably not been caught more beautifully on record than here in a nicely laid-out recital, ending with a half-hour of music from Handel's *Sosarme*, in which he is heard in duet with Margaret Ritchie as Emilia, who makes a delightful partner. This has been well transferred and both voices are given a realistic presence, while the accompaniment sounds agreeably full. However, in the other set of excerpts (9 minutes 26 seconds) from *Come ye sons of art* the chorus and orchestra are much more restricted.

Domingo, Plácido (tenor)

'Great voice': Excerpts from: BIZET: *Carmen* (with Berganza). PUCCINI: *Manon Lescaut* (with Caballé); *Fanciulla del West*. VERDI: *La Traviata* (with Cotrubas); *Macbeth*. WAGNER: *Tannhäuser*. Songs: CATARI: *Core 'ngrato*. LARA: *Granada*. LEONCAVALLO: *Mattinata*. FREIRE: *Ay, ay, ay*. CURTIS: *Non ti scordar di me*.
(B) **(*) DG 431 104-2 [id.].

Opening with the *Flower song* from *Carmen* (noble in line rather than melting), it includes also the vibrant 'live' *Manon Lescaut* duet which is also featured on the companion Caballé recital (only this time, curiously, the applause is cut off at the end). Stylish in Verdi and warmly moving in Walther's *Prize song* from *Die Meistersinger*, with resonant choral backing, the disc ends with a few top Italian pops, over-recorded but certainly making an impact. But the selection (59 minutes) is not as generous as other CDs in this series and, as usual, there is no documentation other than titles. At bargain price, however, many will be tempted.

'Domingo sings Caruso': Arias from LEONCAVALLO: *La Bohème; Pagliacci*. DONIZETTI: *L'elisir d'amore*. MASSENET: *Manon; Le Cid*. CILEA: *L'Arlesiana*. FLOTOW: *Martha*. PUCCINI: *La Fanciulla del West; La Bohème*. VERDI: *Rigoletto; Aida*. MEYERBEER: *L'Africana*. GOUNOD: *Faust*. HALEVY: *La juive*. MASCAGNI: *Cavalleria rusticana*.
(M) **(*) BMG/RCA 09026 61356-2 [id.].

Domingo's heroic stage presence comes over well, the ringing tone able to impress in a lyrical phrase, even though more fining down of the tone and a willingness to sing really softly more often would enhance the listener's pleasure. But in the theatre this is obviously a voice to thrill, and the engineers have captured it directly and realistically, from the sobbing verismo of *Pagliacci* to the crisp aristocracy in *Rigoletto*. The selection is an interesting one – the opening aria from Leoncavallo's *Bohème* suggests that this opera is worth reviving.

'Grandi voci' (arias from): BIZET: *Carmen*. WAGNER: *Lohengrin*. R. STRAUSS: *Die Frau ohne Schatten* (with LPO or VPO, Solti). OFFENBACH: *Les Contes d'Hoffmann* (with SRO, Bonynge). MEYERBEER: *L'Africaine*.
(M) *** Decca Analogue/Dig. 440 410-2 [id.].

All but one of these recordings come from distinguished complete sets in which Domingo played a major part in ensuring their excellence. Whether as a superb Lohengrin or as the Emperor in Solti's more recent *Die Frau ohne Schatten*, there is no mistaking the nobility of this singing, and the great tenor readily shows his range in the excerpts from *Carmen* and the sparkling *Legend of Kleinzach* from *Contes d'Hoffmann*, all given vintage Decca sound. *O paradis* was recorded live in Rome in 1990.

Early Music Consort of London, David Munrow

The David Munrow Edition

'The Art of courtly love' (with James Bowman, Charles Brett, Martyn Hill, Geoffrey Shaw): I: 'Guillaume de Machaut and his age': Jehan de LESCUREL: *A vous douce debonaire* (chanson). MACHAUT: *Amours me fait desirer; Dame se vous m'estés lointeinne; De Bon Espoir – Puis que la douce rousee; De toutes flours; Douce dame jolie; Hareu! hareu! le feu; Ma fin est mon commencement; Mes esperis se combat; Phyton le mervilleus serpent; Quant j'ay l'espart; Quant je suis mis au retour; Quant Theseus – Ne quier veoir; Se ma dame m'a guerpy; Se je souspir; Trop plus est belle – Biauté paree – Je ne sui mie certeins*. P. des MOLINS: *Amis tout dous vis*. ANON.: *La Septime estampie real*. F. ANDRIEU: *Armes amours – O flour des flours*. II: *'Late 14th century avant-garde'*: GRIMACE: *A l'arme a l'arme*. FRANCISCUS: *Phiton Phiton*. BORLET: *2 Variants on the tenor 'Roussignoulet du bois'; Ma tedol rosignol*. SOLAGE: *Fumeux fume; Helas! je voy mon cuer*. Johannes de MERUCO: *De home vray*. ANON.: *Istampitta Tre fontane; Tribum quem; Contre le temps; Restoés restoés*. HASPROIS: *Ma douce amour*. VAILLANT: *Trés doulz amis – Ma dame – Cent mille fois*. PYKINI: *Plasanche or tost*. Anthonello de CASERTA: *Amour m'a le cuer mis*. Matteo da PERUGIA: *Andray soulet; Le greygnour bien*. III: *'The Court of Burgundy'*: DU FAY: *Ce moys de may; La belle se siet; Navré ju sui d'un dart penetratif; Lamention Sanctae Matris Ecclesiae Constantinopolitaine (O tres piteulx – Omnes amici); Par droit je puis bien complaindre. Donnés l'assault; Helas mon dueil; Vergine bella*. BINCHOIS: *Je ne fai tousjours que penser; Files a marier; Amoreux suy et me vient toute joye; Je loe Amours et ma dame mercye; Vostre très doulx regart; Bien puist*. ANON.: *La Spagna* (bass danse) *Variants I & II*.
(M) *** Virgin Veritas/EMI VED5 61284-2 (2) [ZDMB 61284].

David Munrow's two-disc set *'The art of courtly love'* spans the period 1300–1475 in some depth. The survey is divided into three sections: *'Gaullaume de Machaut and his age'*, *'Late fourteenth-century avant-garde'* and *'The Court of Burgundy'*. The first section is introduced arrestingly by two cornetts and an alto shawm, who accompany a striking chanson of Jehan de Lescurel (died 1304) which must have had 'hit' status in its time (*A vous douce debonaire*). The bare harmonies give a real tang to the tune. Then comes the first of many numbers by the justly famous Guillaume de Machaut (*Hareu! hareu! le feu . . . le feu d'ardant desir*) which one hardly needs to translate, and it is certainly ardent! But it is the expressive romantic chansons of Du Fay that make one appreciate how readily the composer came to dominate the combination of lyric poetry and music in fourteenth-century France and to epitomize the title, *'The art of courtly love'*. The virelais, *Se ma dame m'a guerpy* ('If my lady has left me') and *Quant je suis mis au retour*, for solo tenor and chorus, with its sad introductory bass rebec solo, surely anticipate the melancholy eloquence of Dowland, while Machaut could also be attractively lighthearted as in *Se je souspir* ('If I sigh'), or robustly jolly and spiritedly extrovert (*Douce dame jolie*). The second CD opens with a particularly lovely vocal trio by Jehan Vaillant (?1360–90) which anticipates *The first nowell* in its vocal line, and a following ballade, *Amour m'a la cuer mis*, by Anthonello de Caserta (whose career spanned the turn of the century) demonstrates how forward-looking were other composers of 'the late fourteenth-century avante-garde', while Solage is no less enterprising (flourished 1370–90) in providing lugubrious humour with his baritone solo *Fumeux fume* ('He who fumes and lets off steam provokes hot air') with its unlikely melodic line. (Not surprisingly, Munrow gives this rondeau an appropriately bizarre instrumental backing.) 'A man's true worth' (*De home vray*), a ballade by the late-fourteenth-century Johannes de Meruco, also brings lively melodic twists and turns. Gilles Binchois (*c*. 1400–1460) was another leading figure of the time, well represented here, and, like Machaut, he had a wide range. But it is the lovely rondeau duet, *Amoreux suy et me vient toute joye* ('Filled with love, I am overjoyed, hoping that your kindness might bring sweet comfort'), that one specially remembers. With its expressive pleading so direct in its appeal, it is one of the set's highlights and is ravishingly sung here. With the music from

'The Court of Burgundy' we meet the remarkable Guillaume Du Fay with his exhilarating rondeau, *Ce moys de may*, so different in mood from his Masses, followed by an engagingly melancholy echoing duet for two counter-tenors, *La belle se siet au piet de la tour* ('The maiden sits . . . weeping, sighing and venting her grief'), while the virelai, *Helas mon dueil*, a rejected lover's lament, is infinitely touching. However, the collection ends in lively fashion with the anonymous basse danse, *La Spagna*, and here (as in the other instrumental items) Munrow's choice of colour brings an extra dimension to what is basically a very simple dance. All the soloists are distinguished and at their finest. Incidentally, although the translations are not affected, the documentation for this set has the list of titles for the second disc mixed up, starting with bands 12–15, then following with 1–11, but they are all there.

'Monteverdi's contemporaries' (with James Bowman, Martyn Hill and Paul Elliott): MAINERIO: *Il primo libro di balli: 10 Dances*. GUAMI: *Canzoni per sonar: Canzona a 8*. LAPPI: *Canzoni per sonar: La negrona*. PRIULI: *Sacrorum Concentuum: Canzona prima a 12*. PORTA: *Sacro convito musicale: Corda Deo dabimus*. BUSATTI: *Compago ecclesiastico: Surrexit Pastor bonus*. DONATI: *Concerti ecclesiastici, Op. 4: In te Domine speravi*. D'INDIA: *Novi concentus ecclesiastici; Isti sunt duae olivae*. GRANDI: *Motetti con sinfonie, Libro I: O vos omnes; Libro III: O beate Benedicte*.
❁ (M) *** Virgin Veritas/EMI VER5 61288-2 [CDM 61288].

Munrow's art is shown to even greater advantage in his collection of music by Monteverdi's contemporaries which has a comparatively short time-span (1535–1644). Opening with five dances from Giorgio Mainerio's *Il primo libro di balli*, vividly scored, mainly for wind and brass, but unexpectedly bringing a xylophone solo in the *Ballo francese*, the programme continues with other impressive instrumental pieces by Gioseffo Guami, Pietro Lappi and Giovanni Priuli. Then come five more of the Mainerio dances, two of which are solos for the cittern, notably the brilliant and catchy *Schiarazula marazula*, which is as intricately titillating as its title suggests. But this all serves to act as a prelude to a superb collection of vocal music, nearly all of which is entirely unknown. Ercole Porta's sonorous setting of *Corda Deo dabimus* has the counter-tenor (James Bowman) and tenor (Martyn Hill) sonorously underpinned by sackbutts; Cherubino Busatti's *Surrexit Pastor bonus* which follows (James Bowman at his most inspired) is unforgettable. The setting of this short but deeply poignant motet dramatically alternates moods: bright and lighthearted for '*The good shepherd is risen – Alleluia*' and then (with a sudden change) movingly eloquent in telling of the crucifixion, with a despairing downward scale for the word '*mori*' (die) which is infinitely touching. Ignazio Donati's tenor duet, *In te Domine speravi* (Martyn Hill and Paul Elliott) is almost equally eloquent. There is a fine motet from Sigismondo d'India, then comes the other highlight, Alessandro Grandi's tragically beautiful *O vos omnes*, gloriously sung by Bowman. This is unforgettable. The concert ends happily in celebration with Grandi's *O beate Benedicte*, with counter-tenor and tenor duetting happily, sometimes in harmony, at others in felicitous imitation with the accompaniment for cornett, tenor sackbutt, organ and bass violin adding to the simple polyphony. Here as elsewhere Munrow's instrumentation has an imaginative flair matched by no other exponent of this repertoire. The recording is superb and this collection, including several out-and-out masterpieces among much else that is rewarding, is on no account to be missed

East London Chorus, Locke Brass Consort, Michael Kibblewhite

'Essentially Christmas' (with Jane Lister, harp): BLISS: *Royal fanfares I–II*. Arr. EDWARDS: *Wassail! (Sussex carol; Lute-book lullaby; Gloucestershire wassail)*. WALTON: *Coronation Te Deum* (arr. PALMER). KELLY: *6 Abingdon carols (King Herod and the cock; Dark the night; The carnal and the crane; Jesu, son most sweet and dear; Spanish carol; Sweet dreams, form a shade)*. RUTTER: *Te Deum*. VAUGHAN WILLIAMS: *Blessed Son of God; O clap your hands*. ARNELL: *Ceremonial and Flourish*. GRAINGER: *English Gothic music: Angelus ad virginem; Puellare gremium; The matchless maiden*. GREGSON: *Make a joyful noise*.
*** Koch Dig. 3-7202-2 [id.].

In fact this collection is hardly 'essentially Christmas', for the programme includes regal fanfares and various spectacular pieces for other occasions, all in highly effective arrangements so that the accompaniments can be given over to brass. Apart from the Walton and Rutter works, and Vaughan Williams's splendid *O clap your hands* (all otherwise available), there is also Edward Gregson's appropriately named *Make a joyful noise*, which receives its cheerful première recording here. Bryan Kelly's *Abingdon carols* are essentially austere, often with a certain medieval flavour, so they make a good foil, as does Percy Grainger's *English Gothic music*, also recorded here for the first time. These eccentric arrangements with their 'elastic scoring' seem determinedly inauthentic and all the more enjoyable for that. With excellent support from the Locke Brass Consort, Michael Kibblewhite and his East London

Singers give vigorous yet finished performances in which exuberance often erupts, though they catch the darker mood of the six *Abingdon carols* equally impressively. The expansive digital recording has plenty of brilliance and breadth of sonority to make this a Christmas record that can be used at other times during the year.

Emmanuel College, Cambridge, Chapel Choir, Timothy Prosser

'Carols from Cambridge': TRAD.: *Veni, veni Emmanuel; The Angel Gabriel; In dulci jubilo.* RUTTER: *What sweeter music.* GAUNTLETT: *Once in Royal David's city.* arr. WILLCOCKS: *Ding dong! merrily upon high; O come all ye faithful.* BRITTEN: *A Hymn to the virgin; Friday afternoons, Op. 7: New year carol.* arr. JACKSON: *Noël nouvelet.* arr. VAUGHAN WILLIAMS: *This is the truth sent from above; Wither's Rocking hymn.* MATHIAS: *Sir Christèmas.* WARLOCK: *Bethlehem Down; Benedicamus Domino.* arr. HAMMOND: *Swete was the song the Virgin Soong.* GARDNER: *Tomorrow shall be my dancing day.* BERLIOZ: *L'enfance du Christ: Shepherds' farewell.* LEIGHTON: *Lully, lulla, thou tiny Child.* RAVENSCROFT: *Remember, O thou man.* HOPKINS: *We three kings.* ORD: *Adam lay y-bounden.* GRUBER: *Stille Nacht.* arr. RUTTER: *Wexford carol.*
(M) *** ASV Dig. CDWHL 2104 [id.].

Opening with the famous melodic chant, *Veni, veni Emmanuel* which turns out to be medieval in origin and not a Victorian hymn, this is a particularly appealing mid-priced collection, beautifully recorded. Although it includes (as the third item) *Once in Royal David's city*, sung in crescendo in the Willcocks arrangement, a strongly expressed *O come all ye faithful*, and Mathias's jovial *Sir Christèmas*, as outgoing and vigorous as one could wish, the style of performance, as befits a smaller chapel choir, is for the most part a pleasingly intimate one. Unlike King's College, Emmanuel uses women's voices, but they are as sweet and pure as any boy trebles, the overall blending and ensemble are nigh perfect and the effect is disarmingly simple, notably so in the lovely *Shepherds' farewell* from Berlioz's *L'Enfance du Christ.* Anna Dennis is a pleasingly fragile soloist in Vaughan Williams's setting of *Wither's rocking hymn*; Rutter's *What sweeter music* and Warlock's *Bethlehem down* are especially touching. Enterprisingly, the famous *Stille Nacht* is presented in its charming original version for two solo voices (Julia Caddick and Sarah Fisher) and guitar. Grüber hastily scored it in this fashion when the organ broke down just before its first performance on Christmas Eve 1818 – in the appropriately named Church of St Nicholas (Oberndorf, Austria). Not all the choices are obvious, and Britten's *New Year carol*, taken from *Friday afternoons*, is an engaging novelty. Prosser and his splendid singers are equally impressive in the livelier carols: the rhythmic syncopations of Gardner's *Tomorrow shall be my dancing day* are as sparkling as the bounce of *We three kings*, and the choir's lightness of touch is equally appealing in Warlock's *Benedicamus Domino* which ends the concert joyfully.

Evans, Rebecca (soprano), Michael Pollock (piano)

'Debut': BELLINI: *6 Ariette da camera.* VERDI: *Stornella.* RESPIGHI: *Notturno; Storia breve; Tanto bella; Lagrime; L'ultima ebbrezza; Luce.* ROSSINI: *Serate musicale, Vol. 1: L'invito; La pastorella delle Alpi; La promessa.* DONIZETTI: *Ah! rammenta, o bella Irene; A mazzanotte; La ninn-nanna.* WOLF-FERRARI: *4 Rispetti, Op. 11.*
(B) **(*) EMI Dig. CDZ5 69706-2 [id.].

The young Welsh soprano, Rebecca Evans, makes an excellent choice of artist for the EMI Debut series. This programme, devised by the excellent accompanist, Michael Pollock, a specialist in this area, consists almost entirely of miniatures, chips off the workbenches of great opera-composers, which consistently flaunt the Italian love of lyricism. It is striking how, after the opening Bellini group, Verdi immediately has one listening with new attention, when his two lively songs make the singer sparkle. The three Rossini items too – from the *Serate musicale* – bring extra vigour and striking tunes. Two of the Donizetti songs are longer and much closer to operatic models, but the Wolf-Ferrari group brings a charming conclusion, ending with a tiny squib of a tarantella. The recording is bright and forward, even if it does not quite catch the full beauty of Rebecca Evans's voice.

Flagstad, Kirsten (soprano)

'Prima voce' (with Edwin McArthur, piano): GRIEG: *Haugtussa* (song-cycle). Songs by ALNAES; BEETHOVEN; BRIDGE; CHARLES; DVORAK; GRIEG; ROGERS; SCOTT; R. STRAUSS.
(M) (**) Nimbus mono NI 7871 [id.].

Flagstad recorded Grieg's masterpiece, *Haugtussa* ('The Troll maiden'), no fewer than three times, and each time with the same pianist, Edwin McArthur. The first was in 1940; then she recorded it again ten years later – though it is the 1956 LP, when the voice was past its prime, that is the best known. The 1940 version is included here, along with a number of 78s she made in the mid-1930s when her voice was at its glorious best. The Nimbus transfer gives it an added ambience, as if one is picking up another, added acoustic. This proves a little tiring on the ear.

Songs (with Edwin McArthur) by ALNAES; BEETHOVEN; BRAHMS; CHARLES; DVORAK; GRIEG; GRONDAHL; HURUM; RONALD; SCHUBERT; SCOTT; R. STRAUSS.
(*(*)) Pearl mono GEMMCD 9092 [id.].

The Pearl set includes many of the same (1936) recordings as do Nimbus and Simax. In the Pearl, no attempt is made to tame the background noise, and at times the surfaces are distinctly rough and obtrusive; perhaps they did not have access to such good copies. The Flagstad sound was unique and her voice flawless. Pearl offer straight transfers without filtering, which is all right if copies are perfect. They do not include the 1940 *Haugtussa* and in terms of playing time offer less value for money.

'Great sacred songs' (with LPO, Boult) (sung in English): MENDELSSOHN: *Hear my prayer – O for the wings of a dove. St Paul: Jerusalem.* GRUBER: *Silent night.* GOUNOD: *Ah, turn me not away . . . O divine Redeemer.* PARRY: *Jerusalem.* BORTNYANSKY: *Jubilate.* TRAD.: *O come, all ye faithful.* LIDDLE: *Abide with me.* BACH: *St Matthew Passion: Break in grief; Cantata No. 147: Jesu, joy of man's desiring; If thou be near.* HANDEL: *Messiah: He shall feed His flock; I know that my Redeemer liveth; Praise ye the Lord.*
(M) ** Decca 452 066-2 [id.].

In recording *Abide with me* Flagstad was following famous footsteps and this whole 1957 collection of what might be called 'sacred pops' has had deserved popularity over the years. It is very well recorded, with a particularly vivid projection of the voice. Flagstad sings with great majesty and weight, but her swoops and slides are quite out of keeping with what we now expect in such repertoire. Maybe those who will buy this CD will not be troubled by the stylistic considerations – but why, oh why, did Madame Flagstad have to give us that switch-back ride in *Hear my prayer*? Leslie Woodgate's arrangements are sugary – but here again popular demand will have its say. This is at least preferable to the latest manifestation of over-arranging on the comparable CD from Alagna (see above).

Freni, Mirella (soprano)

'Grandi voci' (arias from): PUCCINI: *La Bohème; Tosca; Madama Butterfly.* ROSSINI: *Guglielmo Tell.* VERDI: *Falstaff.* LEONCAVALLO: *Pagliacci.* BOITO: *Mefistofele.* BELLINI: *Bianca e Fernando.* Folksongs, arr. BALILA PRATELLA: *Ninnananna di Modigliana; Ninnananna romagnola.*
(M) *** Decca Analogue/Dig. 440 412-2 [id.].

Since making most of these recordings – many of them taken from complete Decca sets made between 1963 and 1980, including her superb Mimi and Butterfly with Karajan – Freni has expanded to even more dramatic roles, but her purity, clarity and sweetness in these mainly lyric roles are a constant delight, nicely varied. The recital ends with two delightful lullabies, essentially folksongs, arranged by Francesco Balila Pratella. The sound is consistently fresh.

Fretwork, with **Jeremy Budd** (treble), **Michael Chance** (counter-tenor)

'A Play of passion': ANON.: *In paradise; The Dark is my delight; What meat eats the Spaniard; Come tread the paths; Allemande and galliard; Ah, silly poor Joas.* HOLBORNE: *Infernum and galliard; Pavan and galliard* (3 versions). ALBARTI: *Pavan and galliard.* FARRANT: *Ah, alas, you salt sea gods.* FERRABOSCO: *Alman a 5; Pavan and alman a 5.* JOHNSON: *Eliza is the fairest Queen; Come again.* COBBOLD: *Ye mortal weights.* BYRD: *Fair Britain Isle.* GIBBONS: *The Silver swan; Pavan and galliard; What is our life?.*
**(*) Virgin/EMI Dig. VCS5 45007-2.

The title of this new compilation from Fretwork may be confusing. The words are Sir Walter Raleigh's:

'What is our life? a play of passion', and Gibbons's setting of Raleigh's verse is the closing item here. Much of the repertoire here has a feeling of Elizabethan melancholy and, although there are some more robust songs, the mood of the instrumental interludes is also very restrained; although the atmosphere is sustained well, one would like the clouds to lift rather more often. The recording is very refined and true.

Gabrieli Consort & Players, Paul McCreesh

'A Venetian coronation (1595)': Giovanni GABRIELI: *Canzonas Nos. XIII a 12; IX a 10; XVI a 15; Deus qui beatum Marcum a 10 Intonazione ottavo toni; Intonazione terzo e quarto toni; Intonazioni quinto tono alla quarta bassa; Omnes gentes a 16; Sonata No. VI a 8 pian e forte*. Andrea GABRIELI: *Intonazione primo tono; Intonazione settino tono;* Mass excerpts: *Kyrie a 5–12; Gloria a 16; Sanctus a 12; Benedictus a 12; O sacrum convivium a 5; Benedictus dominus Deus sabbaoth*. BENDINELLI: *Sonata CCCXXXIII; Sarasinetta*. THOMSEN: *Toccata No. 1*.
*** Virgin/EMI Dig. VC7 59006-2 [CDC 59006].

This recording and its DG successor below won *Gramophone* Early Music Awards in two consecutive years. '*A Venetian coronation*' is a highly imaginative if conjectural reconstruction of the Mass and its accompanying music as performed at St Mark's for the ceremonial installation of Doge Marino Grimaldi in 1595. The evocation begins with sounding bells (Betjeman would have approved) and the choice of music is extraordinarily rich, using processional effects to simulate the actual scene, like a great Renaissance painting. The climax comes with the Mass itself; and the sounds here, choral and instrumental, are quite glorious. The spontaneity of the whole affair is remarkable and the recording superb.

'Venetian Vespers' including: MONTEVERDI: *Laudate pueri; Laudate dominum; Deus qui mundum; Laetatus sum*. Giovanni GABRIELI: *Intonazione* (for organ). RIGATTI: *Dixit dominus; Nisi dominus; Magnificat; Salve regina*. GRANDI: *O intemerata; O quam tu pulchra es*. FASALO: *Intonazione* (for organ). BANCHIERI: *Suonata prima; Dialogo secondo* (for organ). FINETTI: *O Maria, quae rapis corda hominum*. CAVALLI: *Lauda Jerusalem*. MARINI: *Sonata con tre violini in eco*. ANON.: *Praeambulum*.
*** DG Dig. 437 552-2 (2) [id.].

Sequels can sometimes fall flat (as Hollywood so often demonstrates), but this one certainly doesn't, for the musical intensity of the performance is no less vivid here, and the spatial effects and polychoral interplay are equally impressive in this hypothetical re-creation of a Vespers at St Mark's. Grandiose effects alternate with more intimate sonorities, but the feeling of drama which was part and parcel of the Venetian Renaissance tradition is fully conveyed. Once again all the participants are on their toes, and playing and singing (soloists as well as chorus) are transcendent with detail in the accompaniment always effective and stylish. The recording is splendidly opulent, yet never loses its definition.

Ghiaurov, Nicolai (bass)

'Russian songs' (with (i) Zlatina Ghiaurov (piano), or (ii) Kaval Ch. & O): (i) TCHAIKOVSKY: *None but the lonely heart; Not a word, O my love; Don Juan's serenade; It was in the early spring; Mid the noisy stir of the ball; I bless you, woods*. BORODIN: *For the shores of your far-off native land*. GLINKA: *Midnight review*. RUBINSTEIN: *Melody*. DARGOMIZHSKY: *The worm; Nocturnal breeze; The old corporal*. (ii) Folksongs: *The cliff; the Volga boatmen; The little oak cudgel; Bandura; Stenka Razin; Along Petersburg Street; In the dark forest; Dark eyes; Dear little night; The Twelve brigands; Farewell, joy*.
(B) *** Decca Double 443 024-2 (2) [id.].

One of the problems of producing a record of Russian songs is the inherent danger of monotony of dark colouring and Slavic melancholy. This difficulty is not entirely avoided in Ghiaurov's 1971 recital, as the Tchaikovsky songs have (understandably) been grouped together and have a recognizably similar idiom. Even so, there is some splendid music, and *It was in early spring* and *I bless you, woods* are particularly memorable for their characteristically yearning melodic lines. With the appearance of Glinka's colourful *Midnight review* the mood lightens (even though this is a descriptive piece about old soldiers rising from their graves for a ghostly parade). The three Dargomizhsky songs are notably fine.

For the reissue, the solo recital has been paired with a vibrantly authentic collection of folksongs with the Kaval Chorus and Orchestra – plentifully spiced with balalaikas. Favourite items like the *Volga Boatmen* and *Dubinushka* ('The little oak cudgel'), *Dark eyes* ('Ochi chorni') cannot fail when sung so vividly and presented so atmospherically.

'Grandi voci': Russian and Italian arias (with LSO Ch., LSO, Edward Downes) from: RIMSKY-KORSAKOV: *Sadko*. MUSSORGSKY: *Boris Godunov*. TCHAIKOVSKY: *Eugene Onegin; Iolanta*. RACHMANINOV: *Aleko*. GLINKA: *A Life for the Tsar*. RUBINSTEIN: *The Demon*. BORODIN: *Prince Igor*. BIZET: *Carmen*. VERDI: *Don Carlo; Nabucco. I vespri siciliani* (the latter cond. Abbado).
(M) **(*) Decca 448 248-2 [id.].

Nicolai Ghiaurov's 76-minute recital in Decca's *Grandi voci* is in the main compiled from two previous collections, recorded in 1962 and 1964, although it has now been extended to include Procida's aria from Verdi's *I vespri siciliani*, taken from a Verdi collection of 'Great scenes', admirably directed by Claudio Abbado. In the Russian repertoire Ghiaurov has to yield to his fellow Bulgarian, Boris Christoff, in sheer artistry, particularly on detail. He is best in the comparatively straightforward arias but the vocal quality is what matters, and this is all magnificent singing. The recording too is of Decca's most vivid and flatters Ghiaurov's lyrical line.

Glyndebourne Opera

'Glyndebourne Festival Opera' (1934–1994): Excerpts from MOZART: *Le nozze di Figaro* (Audrey Mildmay, Aulikki Rautawaara; Monica Sinclair; Sesto Bruscantini; Ian Wallace; Daniel McCoshan; Franco Calabrese; Graziella Sciutti; Claudio Desderi; Gianna Rolandi; Glyndebourne Festival Ch.); *Così fan tutte* (Heddle Nash; Erich Kunz; Delores Ziegler; Claudio Desderi; Carol Vaness); *Don Giovanni* (Luise Helletsgruber, Audrey Mildmay; Koloman von Pataky; Roy Henderson, Ina Souez; Salvatore Bassaloni; Thomas Allen; Elizabeth Gale); *Idomeneo* (Richard Lewis; Sena Jurinac; Léopold Simoneau); *Die Entführung aus dem Serail* (Margaret Price). GAY: *The Beggar's opera* (Constance Willis; Michael Redgrave; Audrey Mildmay). ROSSINI: *La Cenerentola* (Juan Oncina), *Le Comte Ory* (Cora Canne-Meijer; Juan Oncina; Sari Barabas); *Il barbiere di Siviglia* (Victoria de los Angeles; Lugi Alva; Sesto Bruscantini). MONTEVERDI: *L'Incoronazione di Poppea* (Magda László; Richard Lewis). GERSHWIN: *Porgy and Bess* (Willard White; Cynthia Haymon).
(M) (***) EMI stereo/mono; Analogue/Dig. CDH5 65072-2 [id.].

Issued to celebrate the opening of the new opera house at Glyndebourne in May 1994, exactly 50 years after the original theatre, this delightful compilation of 20 items ranges wide, starting with the original *Figaro* recording of 1934 conducted by Fritz Busch and concluding with Gershwin's *Porgy and Bess* conducted by Simon Rattle. In his choice of items Paul Campion has opted for some less predictable numbers, even from the obvious classic recordings, like the pre-war Busch sets or the Haitink recordings of recent years. Even more welcome are the rarities. The 1940 recording of *The Beggar's Opera* is a period piece, with Audrey Mildmay, wife of John Christie, the founder, opposite Michael Redgrave as singer. The recordings from the immediate post-war period were of excerpts only and have had very limited currency over the years. The samples here come out very freshly, with Busch conducting for Erich Kunz and Blanche Thebom in *Così fan tutte* and for Richard Lewis in *Idomeneo*. The Vittorio Gui period is well represented in Rossini as well as in Mozart, even if Victoria de los Angeles never actually sang Rosina at Glyndebourne but only recorded it with the company. It is good too to have the sensuously beautiful final duet from Monteverdi's *Poppea* in the Raymond Leppard version, and a rare CfP recording of *Entführung* with the young Margaret Price as Constanze. A treasury of singing to capture the unique flavour of opera at Glyndebourne.

Gomez, Jill (soprano)

'A recital of French songs': BIZET: *Chanson d'Avril; Adieux de l'hôtesse arabe; Vous ne priez pas; La chanson de la rose*. BERLIOZ: *Irlande, Op. 2*, excerpts: *Le coucher du soleil; L'origine de la harpe; La belle voyageuse*. DEBUSSY: *Proses lyriques: De rêve; De grève; De fleurs; De soir. Noël des enfants qui n'ont plus de maisons*.
(M) *** Saga EC 3333-2 [id.].

As in her companion Saga recital of Spanish songs (which still awaits reissue), Jill Gomez consistently captivates the ear in this perceptively chosen collection of French mélodies. Her vividly understanding characterization of the music from the three composers represented means that each emerges with complete individuality. The simple charm of Bizet is conveyed without bringing the slightest suggestion of triviality. The close of his most famous song, *Adieux de l'hôtesse arabe*, is managed very adroitly, and *Vous ne priez pas* is given just the right degree of ardour; she then brings the lightest touch to *La chanson de la rose*. Her soaring line in Berlioz evokes plenty of atmosphere and there is a nicely judged hint of ecstasy, while the languor of Debussy's four *Proses lyriques* brings an instant change of mood and evocation, reflected by John Constable's highly sensitive accompaniments. The passion of *De grève* is matched by the rich colouring of *De fleurs*, and the ardent vigour of *De soir*. Perhaps most memorable of all is the closing song, which Debussy wrote during the First World War, vividly and touchingly depicting a homeless child's plea to Santa Claus. The recording is generally faithful and the playing time (50 minutes) more generous than with most of the companion Saga reissues. However, although Felix Aprahamian's notes are indispensable, it ought to have been possible to include translations on a mid-priced reissue.

Gomez, Jill (soprano), John Constable (piano)

'Cabaret classics' (with John Constable, piano): WEILL: *Marie Galante: 4 Songs. Lady in the Dark: My ship. Street scene: Lonely house. Knickerbocker holiday: It never was you.* ZEMLINSKY: *3 Songs from Op. 27.* SCHOENBERG: *4 Brettl Lieder.* SATIE: *3 Caf é-concert songs: La Diva de l'Empire; Allons-y, Chochotte; Je te veux.*
❀ *** Unicorn Dig. DKPCD 9055 [id.].

Jill Gomez's delicious Schoenberg performances make clear that writing these innocently diatonic numbers can have been no chore to the future ogre of the avant-garde. The same is true of the two Kurt Weill groups, strikingly contrasted at the beginning and end of the recital. The French-text songs from *Marie Galante* use material adapted from *Happy End*. Weill's mastery is even more strikingly illustrated in the three Broadway songs, ravishing numbers all three: *My ship*, *Lonely house* and *It never was you*. It is worth getting the record just for Gomez's ecstatic pianissimo top A at the end of that last item. The other groups, as delightful as they are revealing, are from Alexander von Zemlinsky (not quite so light-handed), and the Parisian joker, Satie, in three café-concert songs, including the famous celebration of English music-hall, *La Diva de l'Empire*. John Constable is the idiomatic accompanist. Gomez's sensuously lovely soprano is caught beautifully.

Gothic Voices, Christopher Page

'The Guardian of Zephirus' (Courtly songs of the 15th century, with Imogen Barford, medieval harp): DU FAY: *J'atendray tant qu'il vous playra; Adieu ces bons vins de Lannoys; Mon cuer me fait tous dis penser.* BRIQUET: *Ma seul amour et ma belle maistresse.* DE CASERTA: *Amour ma' le cuer mis.* LANDINI: *Nessun ponga speranza; Giunta vaga bilta.* REYNEAU: *Va t'en mon cuer, avent mes yeux.* MATHEUS DE SANCTO JOHANNE: *Fortune, faulce, parverse.* DE INSULA: *Amours n'ont cure le tristesse.* BROLLO: *Qui le sien vuelt bien maintenir.* ANON.: *N'a pas long temps que trouvay Zephirus; Je la remire, la belle.*
*** Hyperion CDA 66144 [id.].

In 1986 The Gothic Voices began what was to become a large-scale survey of medieval music, secular and sacred – for the two are inevitably intermingled. From the beginning, the project was an adventure in exploration, as much for the artists as for the listener, for comparatively little is known about how this music sounded on voices of the time. The songs of the troubadours and trouvères – outside the church – sometimes drew on ecclesiastical chant, but other such chansons had a modal character of their own. They were essentially monophonic, i.e. a single line of music, perhaps with an instrumental accompaniment, but the rhythmic patterns were unrecorded and, like much else in this repertoire, are inevitably conjectural in modern re-creative performance. Much of the repertoire on the first disc (and indeed elsewhere) is unfamiliar, with Du Fay the only famous name; but everything here is of interest, and the listener inexperienced in medieval music will be surprised at the strength of its character. The performances are naturally eloquent and, although the range of colour is limited compared with later writing, it still has immediacy of appeal, especially if taken in short bursts. The recording balance is faultless and the sound first rate. With complete security of intonation and a chamber-music vocal blend, the presentation is wholly admirable. There is full back-up documentation.

'The Castle of Fair Welcome' ('Courtly songs of the latter 15th Century', with Christopher Wilson, lute): ANON.: *Las je ne puis; En amours n'a si non bien; Mi ut re ut.* MORTON: *Le souvenir de vous me tue; Que pourroit plus; Plus j'ay le monde regardé.* REGIS: *Puisque ma dame.* BEDYNGHAM: *Myn hertis lust.* BINCHOIS: *Deuil angoisseux.* VINCENET: *La pena sin ser sabida.* FRYE: *So ys emprinted.* ENRIQUE: *Pues servićio vos desplaze.* CHARLES THE BOLD: *Ma dame, trop vous mesprenés.* DU FAY: *Ne je ne dors.*
*** Hyperion Dig. CDA 66194 [id.].

Christopher Page has by now established a basic procedure for his presentation of this early vocal repertoire: he has decided that it will be unaccompanied and usually performed by a modest-sized vocal group. So, in the present collection, further variety is provided with four instrumental pieces (played on harp and lute). Not surprisingly, the two most striking works here are by Du Fay (remarkably compelling) and Binchois; but the programme overall has been carefully chosen and it is given a boldly spontaneous presentation which cannot but intrigue the ear. As always, the recording is first class.

'The Service of Venus and Mars': DE VITRY: *Gratissima virginis; Vos quie admiramini; Gaude gloriosa; Contratenor.* DES MOLINS: *De ce que fol pense.* PYCARD: *Gloria.* POWER: *Sanctus.* LEBERTOUL: *Las, que me demanderoye.* PYRAMOUR: *Quam pulchra es.* DUNSTABLE: *Speciosa facta es.* SOURSBY: *Sanctus.* LOQUEVILLE: *Je vous pri que j'aye un baysier.* ANON.: *Singularis laudis digna; De ce fol, pense. Lullay, lullay; There is no rose; Le gay playsir; Le grant pleyser; Agincourt carol.*
*** Hyperion Dig. CDA 66283 [id.].

The subtitle of this collection is '*Music for the Knights of the Garter, 1340–1440* '; few readers will recognize many of the names in the list of composers above. But the music itself is fascinating and the performances bring it to life with extraordinary projection and vitality. The recording too is first class, and this imaginatively chosen programme deservedly won the 1988 *Gramophone* award for Early Music. Readers interested in trying medieval repertoire could hardly do better than to start here.

'A song for Francesca': ANDREAS DE FLORENTINA: *Astio non mori mai. Per la ver'onesta.* JOHANNES DE FLORENTINA: *Quando la stella.* LANDINI: *Ochi dolenti mie. Per seguir la speranca.* ANON.: *Quando i oselli canta; Constantia; Amor mi fa cantar a la Francesca; Non na el so amante.* DU FAY: *Quel fronte signorille in paradiso.* RICHARD DE LOQUEVILLE: *Puisquie je suy amoureux; Pour mesdisans ne pour leur faulx parler; Qui ne veroit que vos deulx yeulx.* HUGO DE LATINS: *Plaindre m'estuet.* HAUCOURT: *Je demande ma bienvenue.* GROSSIN: *Va t'ent souspir.* ANON.: *O regina seculi; Reparatrix Maria; Confort d'amours.*
*** Hyperion Dig. CDA 66286 [id.].

The title, '*A Song for Francesca*', refers not only to the fourteenth-century French items here, but to the fact that the Italians too tended to be influenced by French style. More specifically, the collection is a well-deserved tribute to Francesca MacManus, selfless worker on behalf of many musicians, not least as manager of Gothic Voices. The variety of expression and mood in these songs, ballatas and madrigals is astonishing, some of them amazingly complex. The Hyperion recording is a model of its kind, presenting this long-neglected music most seductively in a warm but clear setting.

'The marriage of Heaven & Hell' (Anonymous motets, songs and polyphony from 13th-century France). Also: BLONDEL DE NESLE: *En tous tans que vente bise.* MUSET: *Trop volontiers chanteroie.* BERNART DE VENTADORN: *Can vei la lauzeta mover.* GAUTIER DE DARGIES: *Autre que je laureta mover.*
*** Hyperion Dig. CDA 66423 [id.].

The title of this collection dramatically overstates the problem of the medieval Church with its conflicting secular influences. Music was universal and the repertoire of the *trouvère* had a considerable melodic influence on the polyphonic motets used by the Church, though actual quotation was very rare. Nevertheless, on occasion, vulgar associations in a vocal line could ensue and the clergy tore their hair. It all eventually led to the Council of Trent when, the story goes, the purity of Palestrina's contrapuntal serenity saved the day. Certainly medieval church music was robust and full of character, but here one is also struck by its complexity and intensity. The performances have a remarkable feeling of authenticity, and the background is admirably documented.

'Music for the Lion-hearted King' (Music to mark the 800th anniversary of the coronation of Richard I): ANON.: *Mundus vergens; Noves miles sequitur; Anglia planctus itera; In occasu sideris.* BRULE: *A la douçour de la bele saison; Etas auri reditu; Pange melos lacrimosum; Vetus abit littera; Hac in anni ianua.* LI CHASTELAIN DE COUCI: *Li nouviauz tanz; Soi sub nube latuit.* BLONDEL DE NESLE: *L'amours dont sui espris; Ma joie me semont; Purgator criminum; Ver pacis apperit; Latex silice.*
*** Hyperion Dig. CDA 66336 [id.].

Partly because of the intensity, partly because of the imaginative variety of the choral response, all this twelfth-century music communicates readily, even though its comparatively primitive style could easily lead to boredom. The performances are polished but vital, and there is excellent documentation to lead the listener on. This may be a specialist record, but it could hardly be better presented.

'The Medieval romantics' (French songs and motets, 1340–1440): ANON: *Quiconques veut; Je languis d'amere mort; Quant voi le douz tanz; Plus bele que flors; Degentis vita; Mais qu'ilvous viegne.* SOLAGE: *Joieux de cuer.* DE PORTA: *Alma polis religio.* MACHAUT: *C'est force; Tant doucement; Comment qu'a moy lonteinne.* TENORISTA: *Sofrir m'estuet.* SENLECHES: *En ce gracieux temps.* DU FAY: *Je requier a tous; Las, que feray.* VELUT: *Je voel servir.* LYMBURGIA: *Tota pulchra es.*
*** Hyperion Dig. CDA 66463 [id.].

Machaut (fourteenth century) and Du Fay (fifteenth) are names which have now become individually established. Du Fay was master of the secular song-form called the 'virelais' (opening with a refrain, which then followed each verse) and Machaut was one of the first (if not *the* first) composers to set the Ordinary of the Mass; he too wrote chansons and virelais. But of course there is also much music here by other (unknown) composers and our old friend, Anon. The virelais are sung unaccompanied. Sometimes there are vocal melismas (extra parts without words) set against the textual line. So this collection represents the medieval blossoming of songs and part-songs alongside the motets, for secular and sacred never really grew apart. As usual, the Gothic Voices perform this repertoire with skill and confidence and lots of character, and the splendid documentation puts the listener fully in the historical picture.

'Lancaster and Valois' (French and English music, 1350–1420): MACHAUT: *Donnez, signeurs; Quand je ne voy; Riches d'amour; Pas de tor en thies pais.* SOLAGE: *Tres gentil cuer.* PYCARD: *Credo.* STURGEON: *Salve mater domini.* FONTEYNS: *Regail ex progenie.* CESARIS: *Mon seul voloir; Se vous scaviez, ma tres douce maistresse.* BAUDE CORDIER: *Ce jour de l'an.* ANON.: *Sanctus; Soit tart, tempre, main ou soir; Je vueil vivre au plaisir d'amours; Puis qu'autrement ne puis avoir; Le ior; Avrai je ja de ma dame confort?.*
*** Hyperion Dig. CDA 66588 [id.].

This stimulating series has always been essentially experimental, for we do not know just how unaccompanied medieval voices were balanced or how many were used. In the documentation with this record, Christopher Page suggests that on this disc he feels he has the internal balance just about right, and the vocal mix varies, sometimes led by a female voice, sometimes by a male. More Machaut here, some slightly later French settings, and the usual balance between sacred and secular. Everything sounds vital and alive.

'The study of love' (French songs and motets of the 14th century): ANON.: *Pour vous servir; Puis que l'aloe ne fine; Jour a jour la vie; Combien que j'aye; Marticius qui fu; Renouveler me feist; Fist on dame; Il me convient guerpir; Le ior; En la maison Dedalus; Combien que j'aye; Le grant biauté; En esperant; Ay las! quant je pans.* MACHAUT: *Dame, je suis cilz – Fin cuers; Trop plus – Biauté paree – Je ne suis; Tres bonne et belle; Se mesdisans; Dame, je vueil endurer.* SOLAGE: *Le basile.* PYCARD: *Gloria.*
*** Hyperion Dig. CDA 66619 [id.].

The Gothic Voices' exploration is moving sideways rather than forward, for Machaut is still with us. The present collection of settings demonstrates the medieval literary and poetic understanding of 'love' – romantic and spiritual. The anonymous examples are often as stimulating as any of the songs and motets here, and the Pycard *Gloria* is obviously included to remind us again that church music is about the love of God. This and the previous three CDs should be approached with some caution, starting perhaps with '*The Medieval romantics*'.

'The voice in the garden' (Spanish songs and motets, 1480–1530): JUAN DEL ENCINA: *Mi libertad; Los sospiros no sosiegan; Triste España sin ventura.* LUIS DE NARVAEZ: *Fantasias;* (after) *Paseávase el rey Moro.* FRANCISCO DE PENALOSA: *Precor te, Domine; Ne reminiscaris, Domine; Por las sierras de Madrid; Sancta Maria.* JULIUS DE MODENA: *Tiento.* PALERO (after): *Paseávase el rey Moro.* ENRIQUE: *Mi querer tanto vos quiere.* LUIS MILAN: *Fantasias Nos. 10; 12; 18.* GABRIEL: *La Bella Malmaridada; Yo creo que n'os dió Dios.* ANON.: *Dentro en el vergel; Harto de tanta porfía; Entra Mayo y sale Abril; Dindirin; Ave, Virgo, gratia plena; A la villa voy; Pasa el agoa.*
*** Hyperion Dig. CDA 66653 [id.].

Here the Gothic Voices travel to Spain and take with them Christopher Wilson (vihuela) and Andrew-Lawrence King (harp). Their earlier concerts have included instrumental items (kept separate from the vocal music) and here the same policy is followed, but the mix of sacred, secular and instrumental is more exotic than usual. As throughout this series, the recording is of the highest quality.

'The Spirits of England and France': (Binchois and his contemporaries, with Shirley Rumsey, Christopher Wilson, Christopher Page, lute): BINCHOIS: *Qui veut mesdire; Amoreux suy; Adieu mon amoreuse joye; Ay! doloureux; Magnificat secundi toni; Se la belle.* CARDOT: *Pour une fois.* VELUT: *Un petit oyselet; Laissiés ester.* ANON.: *Abide, I hope; Exultavit cor in Domino.* LE GRANT: *Se liesse.* DE LYMBURGIA: *Descendi in ortum meum.* POWER: *Gloria.* DUNSTABLE: *Beata Dei genitrix.* FONTAINE: *J'ayme bien celui.* MACHAUT: *Il m'est avis.* BITTERING: *En Katerina solennia.*
*** Hyperion Dig. CDA 66783 [id.].

Christopher Page and his group have been exploring early English and French repertoire in a number of earlier Hyperion anthologies. Here they turn to the early decades of the fifteenth century and to the music of Binchois (who died in 1460) and his contemporaries. Binchois is represented by a series of medieval love songs, all in three parts, very word-sensitive, even poignant in feeling, climaxed by the remarkably expressive *Ay! doloureux*, the most expansive and the most memorable. Then we turn to religious music and, besides a fine Binchois *Magnificat*, there is also Power's eloquent *Gloria* in five voices and fine examples of the music of Dunstable and even of Machaut. It is a heady mix, and it is the contrast here that makes this finely sung and recorded collection so stimulating.

'The Spirits of England and France': (with Shirley Rumsey, Christopher Wilson, Christopher Page, lute): ANON.: *The Missa Caput:* an English Mass setting from *c.* 1440 interspersed with the story of the *Salve regina.* Carols: *Jesu for thy mercy; Jesu fili Dei; Make us merry; Nowell, nowell, nowell; Clangat tuba; Alma redemptoris mater; Agnus Dei* (Old Hall Manuscript).
*** Hyperion Dig. CDA 66857 [id.].

The inclusion here of the anonymous English *Missa Caput* gives a special interest to this collection. Composed around 1440, it survived in seven different manuscripts, and it is credited with having had a strong influence on the Masses of Ockeghem. The quality of the music is sure, for it has long been attributed to Du Fay. Indeed it is a remarkable and powerful setting, well worth discovering, and it is given added impact by the urgency of Christopher Page's direction. The performance intersperses the Mass Propers with verses from a recently discovered Latin song narrating the origins of the Marian antiphon, *Salve Regina*, with a view to alternating monody and polyphony, and this works remarkably well. The rest of the concert, a collection of early carols, makes an attractively lightweight pendant to the major work. The Gothic Voices sing with great eloquence throughout this 66-minute programme and this is one of their most attractively conceived collections. The recording, as ever with this series, is first class.

'The Spirits of England and France': ANON.: *Missa Veterum hominem; Jesu, fili virginis; Doleo super te; Gaude Maria virgo; Deus creator omnium; Jesu salvator; A solis ortuas; Salvator mundi; Christe, Qui lux es; To many a well; Sancta Maria virgo; Mater ora filium; Ave maris stella; Pange lingua.* DUNSTABLE: *Beata mater.*
*** Hyperion Dig. CDA 66919 [id.].

The *Missa Veterum hominem* might be considered as complementary to the *Missa Caput*, offered on the previous CD from the Gothic Voices, and the present compilation is equally successful. Both Masses were composed at about the same time, in the late 1440s; both were written for four voices. Once again in performing this work (with comparable urgency) Christopher Page seeks to vary the vocal texture by alternating the Mass polyphony with monodic plainchant hymns and opening with an early, three-part carol, *Jesu, fili Virgini*; there are three of these, the last of which, *Deus creator omnium*, uses the same liturgical text as is employed in the *Kyrie* of the *Mass*.

'Gramophone Greats'

'20 Gramophone All-time Greats' (original mono recordings from 1907 – 1935): LEONCAVALLO: *Pagliacci: Vesti la giubba* (Caruso); *Mattinata* (Gigli). BISHOP: *Lo here the gentle lark* (Galli-Curci with flute obbligato by Manuel Beringuer). PURCELL: *Nymphs and shepherds* (Manchester Schools Children's Choir (Choir Mistress: Gertrude Riall), Hallé O, Harty). MENDELSSOHN: *Hear my prayer – O for the wings of a dove* (Ernest Lough, Temple Church Ch., Thalben Ball). MARSHALL: *I hear you calling me* (John McCormack). ELGAR: *Salut d'amour* (New SO, composer). J. STRAUSS: *Casanova: Nuns' Chorus* (Ch. & O of Grossen Schauspielhauses, Berlin, Ernst Hauke). RACHMANINOV: *Prelude in C sharp min., Op. 3/2* (composer). TRAD.: *Song of the Volga Boatmen* (Chaliapin). KREISLER: *Liebesfreud* (composer, Carl Lamson). MOSS: *The floral dance* (Peter Dawson, Gerald Moore). BACH: *Chorale: Jesu, joy of man's desiring* (arr. & played Dame Myra Hess). HANDEL: *Messiah: Come unto Him* (Dora Labette, O, Beecham). SAINT-SAENS: *Samson and Delilah: Softly awakes my heart* (Marian Anderson). BIZET: *Fair Maid of Perth: Serenade* (Heddle Nash). CHOPIN: *Waltz in C sharp min., Op. 64/2* (Cortot). LEHAR: *Land of Smiles: You are my heart's delight* (Richard Tauber). KERN: *Showboat: Ol' man river* (Paul Robeson). SULLIVAN: *The lost chord* (Dame Clara Butt).
(M) (***) ASV mono CDAJA 5112 [id.].

It seems strange and somewhat sad that this marvellous collection of classical 78-r.p.m. hit records, covering a period of three decades, should be coming from ASV rather than HMV (EMI), who are responsible for so many of the actual recordings. Their amazing technical excellence means that they can be enjoyed today as they were then, with occasional clicks and generally not too intrusive background 'surface' noise to create the right ambience. Caruso still projects vividly from a 1907 acoustic master and Amelita Galli-Curci's soprano is as clear and sweet as the day it was made (1919). Other highlights (for us) include the Manchester School Children's choir of 250 voices, electrically recorded in Manchester's Free Trade Hall in 1929. The story goes that, just before the record was made, Sir Hamilton Harty bought cream buns and pop for every child, and that accounts for the warm smile in the singing. Master Ernest Lough's *O for the wings of a dove* is another miracle of perfection from a young boy treble, and Peter Dawson's exuberant *Floral dance* has astonishing diction – you can hear every word – and here Gerald Moore's bravura accompaniment is a key part of the sheer pleasure this performance still gives. Finally, Dame Clara Butt with her deep masculine contralto, clanging like a bell in its lowest register, delivers the sacred piece so beloved by Victorians: Sullivan's *Lost chord*. The transfers are all good (except perhaps for Dame Myra Hess's *Jesu, joy of man's desiring*, where the background surely could have been cut back a bit more).

Gruberová, Edita (soprano)

'French and Italian opera arias' (with Munich R. O, Kuhn): DELIBES: *Lakmé: Bell song*. MEYERBEER: *Les Huguenots: Nobles seigneurs, salut!* GOUNOD: *Roméo et Juliette: Waltz song*. THOMAS: *Hamlet: Mad scene*. DONIZETTI: *Lucia di Lammermoor: Mad scene*. ROSSINI: *Semiramide: Bel raggio lusinghier. Il barbiere di Siviglia: Una voce poco fa*.
(M) *** EMI Dig. CD-EMX 2234 [CDM5 65557-2].

Gruberová, for long type-cast in the roles of Queen of the Night and Zerbinetta, here formidably extends her range of repertory in a dazzling display of coloratura, impressive not only in the Italian repertory but in the French too, notably the *Hamlet* mad scene. The agility is astonishing, but the tone as recorded often hardens on top, although the CD provides extra fullness and clarity.

Hagegård, Håkan (baritone), Thomas Schuback (piano)

'Dedication': BRAHMS: *An die Nachtigall; An ein Veilchen; An die Mond*. FOERSTER: *An die Laute*. GOUNOD: *A toi mon coeur*. HAHN: *A Chloris*. MOZART: *An Chloë, K.524; Ich würd' auf meinem Pfad (An die Hoffnung), K.390*. SCHUBERT: *An Mignon; An den Tod; An den Mond; An den Leier; An die Musik; Am mein Herz*. STRAUSS: *Zueignung*. WOLF: *An eine Aeolsharfe*.
**(*) BIS CD 54 [id.].

This recital is called *'Dedication'* and it begins with the Strauss song of that name. The collection first appeared in LP form in 1976 but was in circulation only intermittently in this country. The record was made at the outset of the distinguished Swedish baritone's career when he was in his mid-twenties and in wonderfully fresh voice. He sounds very much like a youthful Fischer-Dieskau but is at times a trace too studied, colouring the voice rather too expressively and adopting rather self-consciously deliberate tempi.

There are times when one longs for him to be a little more unbuttoned. However, there is far more to admire and relish than to criticize, in particular the gloriously fresh vocal tone, and the sensitive playing of Thomas Schuback. Admirers of this artist will probably have this on LP; others need not hesitate.

Hampson, Thomas (baritone)

'German opera arias' from: KORNGOLD: *Die tote Stadt*. LORTZING: *Zar und Zimmermann; Der Wildschütz*. MARSCHNER: *Hans Heiling; Der Vampyr*. WEBER: *Euryanthe*. SPOHR: *Faust*. KREUTZER: *Das Nachtlager in Granada*. SCHREKER: *Der ferne Klang*. HUMPERDINCK: *Königskinder*. WAGNER: *Tannhäuser; Die Walküre*.
*** EMI Dig. CDC5 55233-2 [id.].

Hampson here presents a fascinating collection of rarities, many of them otherwise unavailable on disc, making one wonder, while listening to his red-blooded performances, why most of these items are so neglected. Anyone wanting to investigate the byways of German opera in the nineteenth and early twentieth century will find much treasure here, starting with a charming Korngold waltz-song from *Die tote Stadt*. Returning to familiar repertory, giving perspective, he rounds the recital off with two Wagner items, *O star of Eve* from *Tannhäuser* and then – invading what is officially the Heldentenor repertory – Siegmund's 'Spring greeting' from *Walküre*. A recital to treasure, beautifully recorded.

'Thomas Hampson Collection' Vol. 1 (with (i) David Lutz; (ii) Geoffrey Parsons; (iii) Philh. O, Berio): MAHLER: (i) *Lieder eines fahrenden Gesellen* (excerpts): *Ging heut' Morgen über's Feld; Die zwei blauen Augen*. Lieder: *Aus! Aus!; Selbstgefühl;* (ii) *Revelge; Des Antonius von Padua Fischpredigt; Der Tamboursg'sell; Das irdisch Leben; Das himmlische Leben; Urlicht; Es sungen drei Engel; Absösung im Sommer; Ich ging mit Lust; Um schlimme Kinder artig zu machen;* (iii) *Scheiden und Meiden:* orch. BERIO: *Nicht wiedersehen!; Hans und Grete; Scheiden und Meiden*.
*** Teldec/Warner Dig. 4509 98822-2 [id.].

This compilation of various Mahler performances recorded by Hampson is an attractively mixed bag, with nine of the songs he recorded (with piano) from the *Des Knaben Wunderhorn* cycle. Also two of the *Fahrenden gesellen* songs and two early *Wunderhorn* settings, all of them chosen (as Hampson explains) because Mahler's piano accompaniments are not just piano reductions but individual compositions. Conversely, he has four of the five discreet orchestrations of early Mahler songs made by Berio, with every item revealing the warmth of Hampson's understanding of this composer, rich, varied and firm.

'Thomas Hampson Collection' Vol. 2 (with Geoffrey Parsons): Lieder: MENDELSSOHN: *Jaglied; Altdeutsches Frühlingslied*. SCHUMANN: *Sehnsucht nach der Waldgegend; Stille Tränen; Alte Laute; Stirb, Lieb' und Freud; An Anna I; Sängers Trost; Muttertraum; Der Soldat; Der Spielmann*. LOEWE: *Herr Oluf*. MAHLER: *Der Schwildwache Nachtlied; Zu Strassburg auf der Schanz'*. WEBER: *Abendsegen*. Richard STRAUSS: *Himmelsboten*. BRAHMS: *Der Uberläufer; Wiegenlied*.
*** Teldec/Warner Dig. 4509 98823-2 [id.].

An attractively varied selection of Hampson's Teldec recordings of Lieder, dedicated to the memory of Geoffrey Parsons, including rarities alongside better-known songs and pointedly leaving Schubert on one side; the interplay of singer and pianist is a consistent delight.

'Thomas Hampson Collection' Vol. 3 (with (i) Jerry Hadley, Welsh Nat. Op. O, Rizzi; (ii) Concg. O, Harnoncourt): Operatic scenes from: (i) PUCCINI: *La Bohème*. BIZET: *Les pêcheurs de perles*. DONIZETTI: *L'elisire d'amore*. VERDI: *I vespri siciliani; Don Carlos*. (ii) MOZART: *Don Giovanni* (with László Polgár & Robert Holl); *Così fan tutte* (with Charlotte Margiono & Delores Ziegler); *Le nozze di Figaro* (with Barbara Bonney).
**(*) Teldec/Warner Dig. 4509 98824-2 [id.].

Described as 'Operatic Scenes', this collection opens with five celebrated baritone – tenor duets (with Jerry Hadley), the last two from Verdi's operas in French, *Don Carlos* and *Vêpres siciliennes*, before ranging over numbers from Mozart operas, including Giovanni's champagne aria, taken from Harnoncourt's recordings. A nicely varied selection, even if the lovely *Così fan tutte* trio, *O soave sia il vento*, loses all magic at Harnoncourt's rushed speed.

'Thomas Hampson Collection' Vol. 4: *'Songs by American composers'* (with (i) St Paul CO., Hugh Wolff; (ii) Armen Guzelimian, piano): (i) COPLAND: *Old American songs*. (ii) IVES: *Gruss; Frülingslieder; Du bist wie eine Blume; Ein Ton; Ich grolle nicht; Wiegenlied; Feldeinsamkeit; Ilmenau (Wanderer's Nachtlied)*. (ii) MACDOWELL: *Das Rosenband; Mein liebschen, wir sassen beisammen; Nachtlied*. (ii) GRIFFES: *Wohl lag ich einst in Gram und Schmerz; Der träumende See; An den wind; Mit schwarzen Segeln; Das ist ein Brausen und Heuln; Meens Stille; Zwei Könige sassen auf Orkadal; Nachtlied*.
*** Teldec/Warner Dig. 4509 98825-2 [id.].

This splendid collection of songs by American composers not only offers an outstanding version of Copland's colourful *Old American songs* but a generous grouping of the German Lieder settings that even the most distinctive and characterful American composers, including Ives, felt they had to write before American music established a fully distinctive voice in the world of serious music. Macdowell here is tunefully Victorian, while Ives in particular seems intent on challenging some of the greatest German song-composers in rival settings of their most celebrated songs. If he never matches such models, the results are fresh and attractive in Hampson's warm and expressive performances. Griffes touches an extra vein of poetry in his settings, with Hampson equally responsive.

'Leading man (Best of Broadway)': KERN: *All the things you are*. KRETZMER: *Les Misérables: Bring him home*. LLOYD WEBBER: *Phantom of the Opera: Music of the night*. RODGERS: *Carousel: Soliloquy*. LOEWE: *Gigi. Camelot: If ever I would leave you*. ADLER: *The Pajama Game: Hey there*. SONDHEIM: *Unusual way; Not a day goes by*. NORMAN: *The Secret Garden: How could I ever know?*. MENKEN: *Beauty and the Beast: If I can't love he*.
*** EMI Dig. CDC5 55249-2 [id.].

Starting with a classic number by Jerome Kern, *All the things you are*, Hampson's Broadway selection ranges on up to *The Phantom of the Opera* and *Les Misérables*, when atmosphere and evocation seem to weigh more heavily than good tunes. The *Soliloquy* from *Carousel* – one of the few numbers from that great musical without a big tune – here can be seen to point forward, but one number (among the most recent here, dating from 1991) unashamedly returns to older standards of tunefulness, *How could I ever know?* from *The Secret Garden* by Marsha Norman and Lucy Simon. Hampson with his rich, dark voice seems totally at home in each number, finding no problems in adapting to this idiom, switching easily and aptly to half-speech in such a patter-number as the title-song from *Gigi*. Paul Gemignani conducts what is called the American Theater Orchestra, though you have to look through the small print to learn that information. Full, immediate recording.

Hespèrion XX

'Llibre Vermell de Montserrat' (A fourteenth-century pilgrimage): *O Virgo splendens; Stella splendens in monte; Laudemus Virginem Mater est; Los set goyts recomptarem; Splendens ceptigera; Polorum regina omnium nostra; Cincti simus concanentes: Ave Maria; Mariam Matrem Virginem; Imperayritz de la ciutat joyosa; Ad mortem festinamus; O Virgo splendens hic in monte celso*.
(M) *** Virgin Veritas/EMI VER5 61174-2.

In the Middle Ages the Spanish monastery of Montserrat was an important place of pilgrimage and, although a great deal of the music held in the library there was lost in a fire at the beginning of the nineteenth century, one early manuscript, the Llibre Vermell (Red Book), has survived to remind us of the music of that period. It dates from 1400 and is especially fascinating in including ten anonymous choral songs for the use of the pilgrims 'while holding night vigil' who may 'sometimes desire to sing and dance in the Church Square (where only respectable and pious songs may be sung)'. The music is extraordinarily jolly and robust, often written in the style of the French virelais (featuring alternating musical lines, with the first framing a central repeated tune). Canonic devices are also used and the effect is often quite sophisticated. There is no better example of this spirited music than *Los set goyts*, an infectious round dance complete with refrain. Various instrumental groupings add lively colour and support to the vocal line; the performances are full of joy, though at times emotionally respectful too. The analogue recording was made in France, but the resonant acoustic seems perfectly judged. This is a life-enhancing collection to cheer one up, and it shows that life in the Middle Ages was not always grim.

Hilliard Ensemble

'A Hilliard Songbook': New music for voices: GUY: *Un coup de dès*. FELDMAN: *Only*. MOODY: *Endechas y Canciones; Canticum Canticorum I*. HELLAWELL: *True Beautie* (cycle of 8 songs). ROBINSON: *Incantation*. TORMIS: *Kullervo's message*. ANON.: *Adoro te devote*. MACMILLAN: *... here in hiding ...* PART: *And one of the Pharisees ...; Summa*. LIDDLE: *Whale rant*. METCALF: *Music for The Star of the Sea*. FINNISSY: *Stabant autem iuxta cruceme*. CASKEN: *Sharp Thorne*.
*** ECM Dig. 453 259-2 (2) [id.].

The Hilliard Ensemble are best known for exploring the world of early music. In this CD, however, they survey modern trends and at times they find a surprising affinity with the repertoire with which they are more familiar. The opening number here is avant garde with a vengeance. Extraordinary instrumental noises (contrived from an amplified double-bass) act as a prelude to *Un coup de dès*, and the performance appears to turn into a fight among the participants, with animal noises thrown in. Then we turn to real music, Morty Feldman's touching, unaccompanied solo soliloquy, *Only*, about flight (Rogers Covey-Crump). Ivan Moody's set of four *Endechas y Canciones* chime with the current trend towards medievalism, very bare in their part-writing but spiced with dissonances. Piers Hellawell's melodic lines are unpredictable, but his eight vignettes are all very brief and concentrated: the music fits the Elizabethan texts, which are about colours. The set is held together effectively by four different settings of *True Beautie* which are quite haunting, and it is made the more effective by alternating baritone, tenor and counter-tenor soloists. The closing concerted number, *By falsehood*, is genuinely poignant. Paul Robinson's *Incantation* (the text is Byron's) is an ambitious (15-minute) dialogue between lead singer (a bit like a cantor) and the main group, usually moving chordally using a spiced modal harmony. *Kullervo's message* is a lively ballad, setting an English translation from *The Kalevala*. The second disc opens with Gregorian chant, then shocks the listener with the pungent fortissimo dissonance at the opening of James MacMillan's ingeniously woven motet. After the more familiar style of Arvo Pärt we move on to Elizabeth Riddle's mournful *Whale Rant* in which two texts are presented in bravura juxtaposition, one set to a famous hymn with the harmony touched up, the other a plangent soliloquy. The result is something of a *tour de force*. John Casken's *Sharp Thorne* brings exuberant bursts of sound, and we finally return to Ivan Moody setting texts from *The Song of Songs* which emphasize the link modern composers have found with the past. The whole programme is sung with great eloquence and is beautifully recorded, and no one could accuse any of the composers here of writing in a routine manner.

Holm, Renate (soprano), Werner Krenn (tenor), Vienna Volksoper Orchestra, Walter Weller

'Operetta gala' (with (i) Pilar Lorengar): Arias and duets from J. STRAUSS Jr: (i) *Der Zigeunerbaron; Eine Nach in Venedig*. MILLOCKER: *Der Bettelstudent*. SUPPE: *Boccaccio*. KALMAN: *Die Zirkusprinzessin*. DOSTAL: *Clivia; Die ungarische Hochzeit; Die Csárdásfürstin*. KUNNEKE: *Der Vetter aus Dingsda*. KATTNIGG: *Bel Ami; Mädels vom Rhein*. ZELLER: *Der Vogelhändler*. CZERNIK: *Chi sa?*.
(M) **(*) Decca 436 898-2 [id.].

This recital is taken from a two-LP collection, recorded in the Sofiensaal in 1970. The Lehár items have been reissued separately (see above under the composer) and, to make up the playing time, Pilar Lorengar contributes three additional numbers. Renate Holm and Werner Krenn have very fresh and pleasing voices, and their lyrical singing is most beguiling. The programme opens delectably with the number made famous by Hollywood as '*One day when we were young*', and there are plenty of other attractive contributions from both these artists, not least Werner Krenn's *Ich bin nur ein armer Wandergesell'* (more familiar as '*Good night, pretty maiden, good night*') from Künneke's *Cousin from nowhere* and the charming duet, *Bel ami*, of Kattnigg. Pilar Lorengar's contributions offer more fluttery and forceful soprano tone, but she sings her Hungarian-style numbers with much character. The real snag is that overall there is too much lyrical music of a similar style. What a pity Decca did not add a chorus and have more lively numbers to offer contrast. No complaints about Walter Weller's stylish accompaniments, and the vintage Decca recording is first rate.

Horne, Marilyn (mezzo-soprano)

'Grandi voci' Arias from: HANDEL: *Semele; Rodelinda.* MOZART: *La clemenza di Tito.* GLUCK: *Alceste.* BIZET: *Carmen.* SAINT-SAENS: *Samson et Dalila.* GOUNOD: *Sapho.* ROSSINI: *L'Italiana in Algeri; La donna del lago.* Song: ARDITI: *Boléro.*
(M) *** Decca Analogue/Dig. 440 415-2 [id.].

The dramatic opening aria, *Iris hence away*, from Handel's *Semele*, sets the scene on this as a recital from an artist who surely personifies the generic title of this fine Decca series. Most of the other items come from a trio of LP recitals which Marilyn Horne made with her husband, Henry Lewis (who had guided her career), between 1964 and 1967. Her performance of Handel's *Dove sei* is as powerful as it is moving, and these widely varied excerpts show her as having a really big, firm mezzo voice, yet finding no difficulty whatever in coping with the most tricky florid passages. The range is astounding, and the vibrancy of the *Carmen* excerpts make a foil for the Delilah characterization. The famous *Mon coeur s'ouvre à ta voix* is taken in a long-breathed, spacious manner to bring out the music's richly sensuous potential. When every single item brings wonderment, it is impossible to single out one above the rest. The 76-minute collection ends with a live recording of *Mura felici* from *La donna del lago*, made much later, in 1981, but the vocal flexibility is as amazing as ever and the chest register still seemingly as powerful.

Huddersfield Choral Society, Brian Kay; Phillip McCann; Simon Lindley

'A Christmas celebration' (with Sellers Engineering Band): TRAD.: *Ding dong merrily on high; Kwmbaya; Joys seven; Away in a manger; Deck the hall; O Christmas tree (Tannenbaum); Coventry carol.* JAMES: *An Australian Christmas.* GRUBER: *Silent night.* BACH: *Cantata No. 140: Zion hears the watchmen's voices.* GARDNER: *The holly and the ivy.* arr. RICHARDS: *A merry little Christmas.* HOLST: *In the bleak mid-winter.* arr. WILLCOCKS: *Tomorrow shall be my dancing day.* BRAHMS: *Lullaby.* arr. SMITH: *Santa Claus-Trophobia.* MATHIAS: *Sir Christèmas.* LANGFORD: *A Christmas fantasy.*
(M) *** Chandos Dig. CHAN 4530.

Sumptuously recorded in the generous acoustic of Huddersfield Town Hall, opening with a spectacular arrangement of *Ding dong merrily* and closing with Gordon Langford's colourful pot-pourri *Fantasy*, this CD offers rich choral tone, well laced with opulent brass. There are simple choral arrangements too, beautifully sung by the Huddersfield choir, like Stephen Cleobury's *Joys seven*, Langford's *Deck the hall* and David Willcocks's slightly more elaborate *Tomorrow shall be my dancing day*, while Grüber's *Silent night* remains the loveliest of all serene carols. In other favourites the brass is nicely intertwined, as in *Away in a manger* and the *Coventry carol*, or it provides a sonorous introduction, as in Holst's *In the bleak mid-winter*. Mathias's rhythmically energetic *Sir Christèmas* provides a little spice. The brass are given their head in a solo spot, an effective novelty number, *Santa Claus-Trophobia*, arranged by Sandy Smith, which brings an impressive contribution from the solo tuba. Undoubtedly the brass contribution adds much to the entertainment value of this superbly recorded and well-presented 70-minute concert.

Hvorostovsky, Dmitri (bass)

'Songs and dances of death' (Russian songs and arias; with Kirov O, St Petersburg, Gergiev): MUSSORGSKY: *Songs and dances of death.* Arias from: RIMSKY-KORSAKOV: *Sadko; Kashei the Immortal; The Snow Maiden; The Tsar's Bride.* BORODIN: *Prince Igor.* RUBINSTEIN: *The Demon; Nero.* RACHMANINOV: *Aleko.*
*** Ph. Dig. 438 872-2 [id.].

This magnificent collection, which displays the dark, tangy baritone of Hvorostovsky superbly, takes its title from the culminating items, Mussorgsky's *Songs and dances of death*, here given in their orchestral form. Only occasionally is thc firm projection of the beautiful voice marred by a roughening under pressure. Otherwise this is among the finest recital discs of its kind, with fascinating rarities like the Demon's arias from Rubinstein's opera, *The Demon*, and arias from four Rimsky-Korsakov operas, as well as the Prince's magnificent aria from Borodin's *Prince Igor*. Excellent sound and warm, intense accompaniments.

Kanawa, Dame Kiri Te (soprano)

'Classics': Arias from: MOZART: *Die Entführung aus dem Serail; Idomeneo; Don Giovanni; Vesperae solennes de Confessore; Die Zauberflöte; Exsultate, jubilate.* HANDEL: *Samson.* GOUNOD: *Messe solennelle de Saint Cécile; Faust.* SCHUBERT: *Ave Maria.* J. STRAUSS Jnr: *Die Fledermaus.*
(M) *** Ph. Dig. 434 725-2 [id.].

Admirers of Dame Kiri will find this a pretty good sampler of her diverse talents, including as it does Mozart's *Exsultate, jubilate* with its famous *Alleluia* and the similarly beautiful *Laudate dominum* from the *Solemn Vespers*, plus Handel's brilliant *Let the bright seraphim*. An excellent 74-minute selection from recordings made over two decades from the early 1970s onwards. The notes, however, concentrate on the singer rather than the music.

'Diva': Arias from: CHARPENTIER: *Louise.* MASSENET: *Manon; Hérodiade.* BERLIOZ: *La Damnation de Faust.* GLUCK: *Iphigénie en Tauride.* PUCCINI: *Suor Angelica.* LEONCAVALLO: *Pagliacci.* GIORDANO: *Andrea Chénier.* CILEA: *Adriana Lecouvreur.* Richard STRAUSS: *Der Rosenkavalier.* TCHAIKOVSKY: *Eugene Onegin.*
(M) *** EMI Dig. CDM 65578-2 [id.].

Like others in EMI's Diva series of compilations, this selection has been shrewdly drawn from the limited number of recordings Dame Kiri has made for that company, principally a recital of French opera arias recorded in 1988 and an Italian opera recital made in 1989. These provide a fruitful source for the first nine items, but they are crowned by excerpts from two complete opera sets, the Marschallin's monologue and final solo from Act I of *Der Rosenkavalier* and (in English) *Tatiana's Letter scene* from *Eugene Onegin*, a recording made with Welsh National Opera forces. The creamy beauty of the voice is beautifully caught.

Kansas City Chorale, Charles Bruffy

'American Christmas carols': SUSA: *3 Mystical carols: The shepherds sing; This endless night; Let us gather hand in hand.* John CARTER: *In time of softest snow.* ROREM: *Shout the glad tidings.* arr. Mark JOHNSON: *Silent night.* BELMONT: *Nativitas* (cycle of 8 carols). SOWERBY: *Love came down at Christmas.* IVES: *A Christmas carol.* FREED: *3 Shepherd carols: Shepherds! Shake off your drowsy sleep; O come to Bethlehem; Angels we have heard on high.* DELLO JOIO: *The Holy Infant's lullaby.* MARTINSON: *There is no rose.* arr. FISSINGER: *I saw three ships.* COWELL: *Sweet was the song the Virgin sang.* arr. OLDHAM: *3 Carols, Op. 20: Silent night.*
*** Nimbus Dig. NI 5413 [id.].

Very little here is familiar, and the ear is constantly being tweaked by the freshness of the harmonic progressions, with the choral writing of John Tavener occasionally springing to mind. Indeed, the affinity between the bare intervals of the earliest harmonized church music and the poignant dissonance so effectively used by these twentieth-century American composers is often very striking, notably so in the works which give the collection its title. *Nativitas* is a cycle of eight choral carols by Jean Belmont, born in California but now living in Kansas City. In setting two early chants, and other texts from the fifteenth, sixteenth and seventeenth centuries, she creates a flowing series of mystical and haunting evocations celebrating the Virgin Mary and the pastoral circumstances of the birth of her son, ending with a celebratory '*Noe, psallite, noe*'. The Pennsylvanian Conrad Susa's *Three mystical carols* which open the programme are no less individual, the first picturing the joyous shepherds with a certain pungency, the second (*This endless night*) offering a comparatively restrained dialogue between solo soprano and tenor and the fuller chorus, and the last in energetic medieval dance style. The triptych of Arnold Freed (of New York City) also features two lively, joyful carols to frame a dream-like picture of the sleeping child. John Carter's gentle *In time of softest snow* is more romantic but no less touching, while the burst of choral energy in Ned Rorem's *Shout the glad tidings* expends itself like a shooting star in 47 seconds. The contribution from Charles Ives is surprisingly traditional, a richly glowing pastoral siciliano, while Henry Cowell's *Sweet was the song* is comparably ear-catching in its sensuous simplicity. Dello Joio's *Holy Infant's lullaby* has a delicate 'shepherd's pipe' organ introduction, and Joel Martinson's beautiful *There is no rose* is easily lyrical, with a hauntingly delicate refrain at the end of each verse. Both the so-called 'arrangements' of *Silent night* are re-composed variants. In the first, by Mark Johnson, the full carol finally emerges out of the mists, but austerely harmonized; in the second, ravishingly sung by Pamela Williamson in duet with solo flute (with harp), the original tune emerges only on the closing '*Alleluia*'. Edward Fissinger's *I saw three ships* keeps close to the original, though his delightful dancing rhythm is most infectious. A stimulating and unusually rewarding collection, superbly sung and recorded.

King's College, Cambridge, Choir, Stephen Cleobury

'Ikos': Alma Redemptoris mater (Marian antiphon). GORECKI: *Totus tuus; Amen. Ave Maria* (Offertory antiphon); *Regina coeli laetare* (Marian antiphon); *Alleluia – Venite ad me.* PART: *Magnificat; The Beatitudes. Beati mondo corde* (Communion antiphon). TAVENER: *Magnificat and Nunc dimittis (Collegium Regale). Funeral Ikos. Requiem aeternam* (Introit antiphon with verse); *Ego sum resurrectio et vita; In paradisum – Chorus angelorum* (Funeral antiphons).
(M) *** EMI CDC5 55096-2 [id.].

In the notes for this admirable collection of modern liturgical settings, John Milsom suggests that their connecting link is 'ritual detachment'. He continues: 'Everything inclines to modesty, to mystery, to meditation, to musical refinement – and to the model of the past.' And that final comment is surely the key to this remarkably communicative *a cappella* music of our time which, for all its modernity, constantly seeks to identify with a medieval atmosphere of unquestioning faith. Each of the composers here occupies ecclesiastical space with floating threnodies. Pärt's comparatively static *Magnificat* relies on intensity of sonority rather than movement; his better-known *Beatitudes*, gentle and rippling, is regularly pierced by dissonance, with the organ entering briefly and unexpectedly at the close to add a florid postlude and then disappear into infinity. Górecki's *Amen* is vocally much more dramatic and, although only having one word of text, continually explores its emotional potential, moving from serenity to sudden bursts of passion. Tavener's undulating *Magnificat* is given its special character by flitting references to Byzantine chant. His simple and beautiful *Funeral Ikos* brings a haunting mixture of monody and chordal progressions on the word 'Alleluia', just occasionally touched with dissonance, and recalling his famous carol, *The Lamb*. Górecki's masterly *Totus tuus* opens stirringly and is a superbly concentrated example of his minimalist choral progression. The music constantly redefines the intensity of the repetitions of the text, ending with a haunting diminuendo on *Mater mundi . . . Totus sum Maria!*, then with the constantly recurring name 'Maria' fading gently into silence. The conductor, Stephen Cleobury, directs glorious, deeply felt performances of all this music and emphasizes the medieval associations by placing Latin chants before and after each piece, ending with two touching *Funeral antiphons*, the first sung by the men alone, the second, *In paradisum*, soaring radiantly with the trebles. The recording is superb: the famous King's acoustic adds much to the music.

King's College, Cambridge, Choir, Sir David Willcocks

'A Festival of Lessons and carols' (recorded live in the Chapel, Christmas Eve 1958, with Simon Preston, organ): *Once in Royal David's City*. BACH: *Christmas Oratorio: Invitatory*. Lesson I. *Adam lay ybounden*. Lesson II. *I saw three ships*. Lesson III. *Gabriel's message. God rest you merry, gentlemen; Sussex carol*. Lesson IV. *In dulci jubilo*. Lesson V. *Away in a manger; While shepherds watched*. Lesson. VI. *O come, all ye faithful*. Lesson VII. *Hark! the herald angels sing*.
(B) *** Decca 436 646-2; *436 646-4*.

It was the early mono recording of the King's Christmas Eve service of lessons and carols which – together with the BBC recording of Dylan Thomas's *Under Milk Wood* – brought initial success to the Argo label before it became part of the Decca group. With the coming of stereo the Festival was re-recorded to provide what only stereo can provide: an imaginary seat in the Chapel. The present CD offers that early stereo venture and shows the remarkable success with which the Argo engineers captured the magic of the chapel acoustic – the opening processional remains demonstration-worthy today. Seven of the nine lessons are interspersed with the favourite carols to remind us indelibly what Christmas is really about.

'Carols from King's': TRAD., arr. WILLCOCKS: *On Christmas night; Tomorrow shall be my dancing day; Cherry tree carol; The Lord at first; A Child is born in Bethlehem; While shepherds watched*. TRAD., arr. VAUGHAN WILLIAMS: *And all in the morning*. CORNELIUS: *Three Kings*. EBERLING: *All my heart this night rejoices*. GRUBER: *Silent night* (arr. WILLCOCKS). Trad. Italian, arr. WOOD: *Hail, blessed Mary*. TRAD., arr. SULLIVAN: *It came upon the midnight clear*. Trad. French, arr. WILLCOCKS: *Ding dong! merrily*. Trad. Basque, arr. PETTMAN: *I saw a maiden*. DARKE: *In the bleak midwinter*. Trad. German: *Mary walked through a wood of thorn*. BAINTON: *A Babe is born I wys*. PRAETORIUS: *Psallite unigenito*.
(B) *** CfP CD-CFP 4586; *TC-CFP 4586* [CDB 67356].

This recital was planned and recorded as a whole in 1969. The programme has an attractive lyrical flavour, with plenty of delightful, unfamiliar carols to add spice to favourites like *Tomorrow shall be my dancing day* and *In the bleak midwinter*, which sound memorably fresh. The arrangements are for the most part straightforward, with added imaginative touches to charm the ear, like the decorative organ 'descant' which embroiders *Ding dong! merrily on high*. The King's intimacy gives much pleasure here, yet the disc ends with a fine, robust version of *While shepherds watched*. Most rewarding and a real bargain.

'Noël': Disc 1: MENDELSSOHN: *Hark the herald angels sing*. TRAD.: *The first Nowell; While shepherds watched; I saw three ships; Ding dong! merrily on high; King Jesus hath a garden; Unto us a son is born; O come all ye faithful; Away in a manger; The holly and the ivy; God rest ye merry, gentlemen; See amid the winter's snow; Past three o'clock*. arr. BACH: *In dulci jubilo*. arr. VAUGHAN WILLIAMS: *O little town of Bethlehem*.

Disc 2: TRAD.: *Once in Royal David's city; Sussex carol; Rocking; Rejoice and be merry; Joseph was an old man; As with gladness men of old; The infant King; Christ was born on Christmas day; Blessed be that maid Mary; Lute-book lullaby; Personent hodie; In the bleak midwinter; Coventry carol; Shepherds, in the field abiding*. CORNELIUS: *The three kings; A great and mighty wonder*. WARLOCK: *Balulalow*. TCHAIKOVSKY: *The crown of roses*. TERRY: *Myn lyking*. JOUBERT: *Torches*. VAUGHAN WILLIAMS: *Fantasia on Christmas carols* (with Hervey Alan & LSO).
(B) **(*) Decca Double 444 848-2 (2) [id.].

This Double Decca is essentially a combined reissue of a pair of bargain-priced LP collections, made over a span of eight years at the end of the 1950s and the beginning of the 1960s. They were counted excellent value when they first appeared in Decca's 'World of' series. The 50-minute programme on the first disc concentrates on established King's favourites; the second is not only more generous (66 minutes), but also includes novelties which are designed to get the listener inquiring further, such as Warlock's *Balulalow*, the engaging *Lute-book lullaby* and Joubert's *Torches*. This collection opens with the famous processional version of *Once in Royal David's city* and closes with a superbly joyful performance of Vaughan Williams's *Fantasia on Christmas carols*, very well recorded, with Hervey Alan the excellent soloist. Otherwise the sound is always pleasingly full and atmospheric, but with some of the earlier recordings from the late 1950s not quite as clean in focus as those made in the mid-1960s.

King's College, Cambridge, Choir, Willcocks or Philip Ledger

'The King's Christmas collection': *'Favourite carols'*; *'Festival of lessons and carols'*; *'Procession with carols on Advent Sunday'*; *'Christmas music from King's'* (as detailed below).
(M) *** EMI CMS5 66245-2 (4) [CDMD 66245]

These four King's Christmas records, which have stood the test of time, are here gathered in a tempting slip-case, an attractive addition to any carol-lover's stocking.

'Favourite carols from Kings': GAUNTLETT: *Once in Royal David's city*. TRAD., arr. VAUGHAN WILLIAMS: *O little town of Bethlehem*. TRAD., arr. STAINER: *The first nowell*. TRAD., arr. LEDGER: *I saw three ships*. TRAD. German, arr. HOLST: *Personent hodie*. TERRY: *Myn Lyking*. HOWELLS: *A spotless rose*. KIRKPATRICK: *Away in a manger*. HADLEY: *I sing of a maiden*. TRAD. French, arr. WILLCOCKS: *O come, o come Emmanuel*. TRAD., arr. WILLCOCKS: *While shepherds watched; On Christmas night*. arr. WOODWARD: *Up! Good Christian folk and listen*. DARKE: *In the bleak midwinter*. GRUBER: *Silent night*. TRAD., arr. WALFORD DAVIES: *The holly and the ivy*. TRAD., arr. SULLIVAN: *It came upon the midnight clear*. CORNELIUS: *Three kings*. SCHEIDT: *A Child is born in Bethlehem*. TRAD. German, arr. PEARSALL: *In dulci jubilo*. WADE: *O come, all ye faithful*. MENDELSSOHN: *Hark! the herald angels sing*.
(M) *** EMI CDM5 66241-2 [id.].

With 71 minutes of music and 22 carols included, this collection, covering the regimes of both Sir David Willcocks and Philip Ledger, could hardly be bettered as a representative sampler of the King's tradition. Opening with the famous processional of *Once in Royal David's city*, to which Willcocks contributes a descant (as he also does in *While shepherds watched*), the programme is wide-ranging in its historical sources, from the fourteenth century to the present day, while the arrangements feature many famous musicians. The recordings were made between 1969 and 1976, and the CD transfers are first class. The two closing carols, featuring the Philip Jones Brass Ensemble, are made particularly resplendent.

'A Festival of Lessons and Carols from King's' (1979) includes: TRAD.: *Once in Royal David's city; Sussex carol; Joseph and Mary; A maiden most gentle; Chester carol; Angels, from the realms of glory*. HANDEL: *Resonet in laudibus*. ORD: *Adam lay ybounden*. GRUBER: *Stille Nacht*. MATHIAS: *A babe is born*. WADE: *O come all ye faithful*. MENDELSSOHN: *Hark! the herald angels sing*.
(M) *** EMI CDM5 66242-2 [id.].

This 1979version of the annual King's College ceremony has the benefit of fine analogue stereo, even more atmospheric than before. Under Philip Ledger the famous choir keeps its beauty of tone and incisive attack. The opening processional, *Once in Royal David's city*, is even more effective heard against the background quiet of CD, and this remains a unique blend of liturgy and music.

'Procession with carols on Advent Sunday' includes: PALESTRINA (arr. from): *I look from afar; Judah and Jerusalem, fear not.* PRAETORIUS: *Come, thou Redeemer of the earth.* TRAD.: *O come, o come, Emmanuel!; Up, awake and away!; 'Twas in the year; Cherry tree carol; King Jesus hath a garden; On Jordan's bank the Baptist's cry; Gabriel's message; I wonder as I wander; My dancing day; Lo! he comes with clouds descending.* BYRT: *All and some.* P. NICOLAI, arr. BACH: *Wake, o wake! with tidings thrilling.* BACH: *Nun komm' der Heiden Heiland.*
(M) *** EMI CDM5 66243-2 [id.].

This makes an attractive variant to the specifically Christmas-based service, though the carols themselves are not quite so memorable. Beautiful singing and richly atmospheric recording; the wide dynamic range is demonstrated equally effectively by the atmospheric opening and processional and the sumptuous closing hymn.

'Christmas music from King's' (with Andrew Davis, organ, D. Whittaker, flute, Christopher van Kampen, cello and Robert Spencer, lute): SWEELINCK: *Hodie Christus natus est.* PALESTRINA: *Hodie Christus natus est.* VICTORIA: *O magnum mysterium; Senex puerum portabat.* BYRD: *Senex puerum portabat; Hodie beata virgo.* GIBBONS: *Hosanna to the Son of David.* WEELKES: *Hosanna to the Son of David; Gloria in excelsis Deo.* ECCARD: *When to the temple Mary went.* MACONCHY: *Nowell! Nowell!.* arr. BRITTEN: *The holly and the ivy.* PHILIP (The Chancellor): *Angelus ad virginem.* arr. POSTON: *Angelus ad virginem; My dancing day.* POSTON: *Jesus Christ the apple tree.* BERKELEY: *I sing of a maiden.* TAYLOR: *Watts's cradle song.* CAMPION: *Sing a song of joy.* PEERSON: *Most glorious Lord of life.* Imogen HOLST: *That Lord that lay in Assë stall.* WARLOCK: *Where riches is everlastingly.*
(M) *** EMI CDM5 66244-2 [id.].

A happily chosen survey of music (63 minutes), inspired by the Nativity, from the fifteenth century to the present day. As might be expected, the King's choir confidently encompasses the wide variety of styles from the spiritual serenity of the music of Victoria to the attractive arrangements of traditional carols by modern composers, in which an instrumental accompaniment is added. These items are quite delightful and they are beautifully recorded (in 1965). The motets, from a year earlier, were among the first recording sessions made by the EMI engineers in King's College Chapel, and at the time they had not solved all the problems associated with the long reverberation period, so the focus is less than sharp. Even so, this group demonstrates the unique virtuosity of the Cambridge choir, exploiting its subtlety of tone and flexibility of phrase.

Kirkby, Emma (soprano)

'Madrigals and wedding songs for Diana' (with David Thomas, bass, Consort of Musicke, Rooley): BENNET: *All creatures now are merry-minded.* CAMPION: *Now hath Flora robbed her bowers; Move now measured sound; Woo her and win her.* LUPO: *Shows and nightly revels; Time that leads the fatal round.* GILES: *Triumph now with joy and mirth.* CAVENDISH: *Come, gentle swains.* DOWLAND: *Welcome, black night . . . Cease these false sports.* WEELKES: *Hark! all ye lovely saints; As Vesta was.* WILBYE: *Lady Oriana.* EAST: *Hence stars! too dim of light; You meaner beauties.* LANIER: *Bring away this sacred tree; The Marigold; Mark how the blushful morn.* COPERARIO: *Go, happy man; While dancing rests; Come ashore, merry mates.* E. GIBBONS: *Long live fair Oriana.*
*** Hyperion CDA 66019 [id.].

This wholly delightful anthology celebrates early royal occasions, aristocratic weddings, and in its choice of Elizabethan madrigals skilfully balances praise of the Virgin Queen with a less ambivalent attitude to nuptial delights. Emma Kirkby is at her freshest and most captivating, and David Thomas, if not quite her match, makes an admirable contribution. Accompaniments are stylish and well balanced, and the recording is altogether first rate.

'O tuneful voice' (with Rufus Müller, Timothy Roberts (fortepiano or harpsichord), Frances Kelley (harp)): HAYDN: *O tuneful voice; She never told her love; Sailor's song.* Samuel ARNOLD: *Elegy.* PINTO: *Invocation to Nature; A Shepherd lov'd a nymph so fair; From thee, Eliza, I must go; Eloisa to Abelard; Minuet in A.* STORACE: *The curfew.* LINLEY THE ELDER: *The lark sings high in the cornfield; Think not, my love.* JACKSON: *The day that saw thy beauty rise; Time has not thinn'd my flowing hair.* SHIELD: *Ye balmy breezes, gently blow; Hope and love; 'Tis only no harm to know it, you know.* CARDON: *Variations on 'Ah vous dirai-je, maman'.* HOOK: *The emigrant.* SALOMON: *Go, lovely rose; Why still before these streaming eyes; O tuneful voice.*
*** Hyperion Dig. CDA 66497.

This programme is centred in eighteenth-century England, although Haydn could be included because of his London visits. Indeed Salomon, his impresario, is featured here as a composer, and a very able one, too; but it is Haydn's comparatively rare song which gives the CD its title and shows Emma Kirkby on top form, just as charming but with greater depth of expression than in her companion Hyperion and Oiseau-Lyre collections, the latter having the same geographical basis but offering repertoire from an earlier period. Kirkby sings like a lark in the cornfield, and Rufus Müller joins her in some duets by William Jackson and also shares the solo numbers. There are innocently rustic songs from William Shield in which each artist participates, and much else besides: this 74-minute programme has a wide range of mood and style.

'A Portrait' (with AAM, Hogwood): HANDEL: *Disseratevi, o porte d'Averno; Gentle Morpheus, son of night.* PURCELL: *Bess of Bedlam; From rosie bow'rs.* ARNE: *Where the bee sucks there lurk I; Rise, Glory, rise.* DOWLAND: *I saw the lady weepe.* D'INDIA: *Odi quel rosignuolo.* TROMBONCINO: *Se ben hor non scopro il foco.* VIVALDI: *Passo di pena in pena.* J. S. BACH: *Ei! wie schmeckt der Coffee süsse.* HAYDN: *With verdure clad.* MOZART: *Laudate Dominum; Exsultate, jubilate, K.165.*
(M) *** O-L Dig. 443 200-2 [id.].

Admirers of Emma Kirkby's style in early and baroque music will delight in this well-chosen 76-minute sampler of her work. L'Oiseau-Lyre have altered and expanded the orginal issue and the excerpt from Handel's *Messiah* has been replaced by the remarkable Angel's aria, *Disseratevi, o porte d'Averno*, from Part I of *La Resurrezione* (calling on the gates of the Underworld to be unbarred to yield to God's glory). It opens with joyous baroque trumpets and oboes, and Emma Kirkby shows with her florid vocal line that anything they can do, she can do better. This is rather effectively followed by Purcell's melancholy mad song, *Bess of Bedlam*, and the equally touching *From rosie bow'rs*. Music by Arne lightens the mood and later there are excerpts from Bach's *Coffee cantata* and popular solos by Haydn and Mozart. This recital is as well planned as it is enjoyable, and Hogwood ensures that accompaniments are consistently fresh and stylish. First-class sound.

Larin, Sergej (tenor), Bekova Eleonora (piano)

'Songs by the Mighty Handful': RIMSKY-KORSAKOV: *It was not the wind blowing from above; The octave; The nymph; Clearer than the singing of the lark; The scurrying bank of clouds disperses; On the hills of Georgia; Of what in the silence of the night; Captivated by the rose, the nightingale; Silence descends on the yellow cornfields; A pressed flower.* CUI: *A statue at Tsarskoye Selo; The burnt letter.* BORODIN: *The fair maid has stopped loving me; For the shores of the distant homeland.* BALAKIREV: *You are full of captivating bliss; Barcarolle; Look, my friend.* MUSSORGSKY: *Songs and dances of Death.*
*** Chandos Dig. CHAN 9547 [id.].

Sergej Larin with his outstandingly beautiful and expressive tenor presents vivid portraits of the five Russian composers grouped as 'The Mighty Handful', all but Mussorgsky here represented in miniatures. The ten Rimsky-Korsakov songs are totally unpretentious, simple ballads that he wrote in joyful relaxation, a mood which is reflected in the music. The two Cui songs are far more intense, as are the two by Borodin, one of them, *The fair maid has stopped loving me*, with cello obbligato played by Alfia Bekova. The three Balakirev songs are tiny chips from the workbench, beautifully crafted. Only Mussorgsky is presented at full stretch with the greatest and best-known of the items here, the *Songs and dances of Death*. Larin, having for the earlier songs used his most honeyed tones and velvety, seamless production, including a wonderful head-voice on top, here darkens his tone thrillingly, ending with a searing account of *The Field Marshal Death*. A superb disc, revealing a great new artist.

Larmore, Jennifer (mezzo-soprano)

'A Portrait': excerpts from MONTEVERDI: *L'incoronazione di Poppea; L'Orfeo*. HANDEL: *Giulio Cesare*. MOZART: *Mass in C min.*
(B) *** HM Dig. HMT 7901575 [id.].

An excellent reminder of the art of an outstandingly fine mezzo. Five excerpts are offered from her recording of Handel's *Giulio Cesare*, in which she took the principal role with distinction. But she is heard to equal effect as Monteverdi's *Ottavio*, especially in her very touching *Addio Roma*. Her contribution to the Mozart *C minor Mass* is hardly less impressive. This is in essence a sampler, but a well-planned and enjoyable one.

Lemper, Ute, Matrix Ensemble, Robert Ziegler

'Berlin cabaret songs' (sung in German) by SPOLIANSKY; HOLLAENDER; GOLDSCHMIDT; BILLING; NELSON.
*** Decca Dig 452 601-2 [id.].

The tangy, sexy voice of Ute Lemper is here caught at its most provocative in a colourful sequence of cabaret songs reflecting the sleazy, decadent atmosphere of Berlin under the Weimar Republic, as observed in the popular cabarets of the city. With Lemper characterizing delectably, with German consonants adding extra bite, often 'over the top' as in the delightful *Ich bin ein Vamp*, the authentic flavour is here presented in music with new vividness. The conductor, Robert Ziegler, has restored the original orchestrations as closely as he can (no scores survive, only piano reductions), and the result is a delight, a valuable addition to the 'Entartete Musik' series. Not only is the music fascinating and characterful, so are the words, including even a gay anthem, with oompah bass, *Das lila Lied*, written by Mischa Spoliansky under a pseudonym. It is good too to have included a song by Berthold Goldschmidt which he wrote for his wife in 1930.

'Berlin cabaret songs' (sung in English): SPOLIANSKY: *It's all a swindle; The smart set; When the special girlfriend; I am a vamp; L'heure bleue; Maskulinum*. HOLLAENDER: *Sex appeal; Take it off Petronella!; Chuck out the men! Oh just suppose; I don't know who I belong to; A little yearning; Oh, how we wish that we were kids again; Munchausen*. NELSON: *Peter, Peter; A little Attila*. GOLDSCHMIDT: *The washed-up lover*. BILLING: *The Lavender song*.
*** Decca Dig 452 849-2 [id.].

This offers the same programme as the disc above, but in English translation. Inevitably some of the bite is lost with softer English consonants, but it is amazing how much of the original tang and snarl Lemper manages to inject, and there is much to be said for having the words instantly identifiable to the English speaker, with diction crystal clear.

Lontano, Odaline de la Martinez

'British women composers, Vol. 1': WALLEN: *It all depends on you*. COOPER: *The Road is wider than long*. MACONCHY: *My dark heart*. LEFANU: *The Old woman of Beare*.
**(*) Lorelt Dig. LNT 101 [id.].

This *avant-garde* music will perhaps suit some tastes; little that happens here is predictable. *It all depends on you* brings a rather curious setting of poems by Philip Larkin, presented in a very colloquial style by Fiona Baines with instrumental support. There are moments of jazz, and the last song is an almost unaccompanied setting of *Lift through the breaking day*. Then comes a much more popularly styled work, *The Road is wider than long*, in no way difficult and quite ear-catching. Elizabeth Maconchy provides a more complex setting of Synge poems, *My dark heart*, which is certainly imaginative in its instrumentation. Jane Manning is the confident soloist here and also in a partly sung, partly spoken, version of an Irish poem by Nicola LeFanu. Excellent recording, but this record is not for general consumption.

'British women composers, Vol. 2': DE LA MARTINEZ: *Canciones*. WEIR: *Airs from another planet*. MAXWELL: *Pibroch*. TANN: *Winter sun, summer rain*. ALBERGA: *Dancing with the shadow* (suite).
**(*) Lorelt Dig. LNT 103 [id.].

The programme here is more tangible than on Volume 1, and also rather more accessible. The most striking works are Judith Weir's *Airs from another planet* for piano and wind quintet, where four Scottish dances are heard through a musical distorting prism. The last is a bagpipe air, and that prepares the way for

Melinda Maxwell's *Pibroch*, evoked rather hauntingly on oboe and cello. The programme opens with four vibrant and very free Lorca settings by Odaline de la Martinez, accompanied by percussion, except for the third, a love song, in which the piano adds to the atmosphere. Hilary Tann's *Winter sun, summer rain*, where the closing section pictures 'that very special light which illuminates the Welsh countryside in the aftermath of a rainfall', is a piece for viola, cello, flute, clarinet and celeste. Finally *Dancing with the shadow* by Eleanor Alberga is a not too thorny three-movement piece for flute, clarinet, violin, cello and percussion, with a very lively finale. Fine performances and clear recording, but only for the adventurous.

Lorengar, Pilar (soprano)

'Grandi voci': Arias from: PUCCINI: *La Bohème; La rondine; Madama Butterfly; Turandot; Gianni Schicchi.* DVORAK: *Rusalka.* CHARPENTIER: *Louise.* BIZET: *Carmen; Les Pêcheurs de perles.* MASSENET: *Manon* (with St Cecilia Ac. O, Patanè). MOZART: *Le nozze di Figaro.* BEETHOVEN: *Fidelio.* WEBER: *Der Freischütz.* WAGNER: *Tannhäuser.* KORNGOLD: *Die tote Stadt* (with Vienna Op. O, Walter Weller).
(M) *(*) Decca 443 931-2 [id.].

It was a mistake for Pilar Lorengar to open this collection – compiled from two separate, earlier recitals, recorded in 1966 and 1970 – with *They call me Mimi*. Hers is a vocal personality of strong character and temperament, but the style of her singing fails to convince here, and a surer legato is needed in this aria. She is much better as Butterfly and is impressive in Liù's aria. In the German repertoire her vibrato is troublesome in almost every item, with the trills in *Dove sono* barely distinguishable from sustained notes and the throat occasionally constricting to produce something not far from a yodel. The highlight of the collection is the famous *Invocation to the moon* from Dvořák's *Rusalka*.

Lott, Felicity (soprano), Graham Johnson (piano)

Mélodies on Victor Hugo poems: GOUNOD: *Sérénade.* BIZET: *Feuilles d'album: Guitare. Adieux de l'hôtesse arabe.* LALO: *Guitare.* DELIBES: *Eclogue.* FRANCK: *S'il est un charmant gazon.* FAURE: *L'absent; Le papillon et la fleur; Puisqu'ici bas.* WAGNER: *L'attente.* LISZT: *O quand je dors; Comment, disaint-ils.* SAINT-SAENS: *Soirée en mer; La fiancée du timbalier.* M. V. WHITE: *Chantez, chantez jeune inspirée.* HAHN: *Si mes vers avaient des ailes; Rêverie.*
(B) *** HM HMA 901138 [id.].

Felicity Lott's collection of Hugo settings relies mainly on sweet and charming songs, freshly and unsentimentally done, with Graham Johnson an ideally sympathetic accompanist. The recital is then given welcome stiffening with fine songs by Wagner and Liszt, as well as two by Saint-Saëns that have a bite worthy of Berlioz. It makes a headily enjoyable cocktail. Now reissued in the Musique d'Abord series, this is a bargain not to be missed.

Ludwig, Christa (mezzo-soprano)

'The Art of Christa Ludwig' (with Gerald Moore or Geoffrey Parsons (piano) & (i) Herbert Downes (viola); (ii) Philh. O, Klemperer; (iii) Berlin SO, Stein or Forster): BRAHMS: *Sapphische Ode; Liebestreu; Der Schmied; Die Mainacht. 8 Zigeunerlieder. 4 Deutsche Volkslieder: Och mod'r ich well en Ding han!; We kumm ich dann de Pooz erenn?; In stiller Nacht; Schwesterlein.* Lieder: *Dein blaues Auge; Von ewiger Liebe; Das Mädchen spricht; O wüsst ich doch; Wie Melodien zieht es mir; Mädchenlied; Vergebliches Ständchen; Der Tod, das ist die kühle Nacht; Auf dem See; Waldeinsamkeit; Immer leiser word mein Schlummer; Ständchen; Gestillte Sehnsucht;* (i) *Geistliches Wiegenlied.* MAHLER: *Hans und Grete; Frühlingsmorgen; Des Knaben Wunderhorn: Ich ging mit Lust durch einen grünen Wald; Wo die schönen Trompeten blasen; Der Schildwache Nachtlied; Um schlimme Kinder; Das irdische Leben; Wer hat dies Liedlein erdacht; Lob des hohen Verstandes;Des Antonius von Padua Fischpredigt; Rheinlegendchen.* Rückert Lieder: *Ich atmet' einen linden Duft; Liebst du um Schönheit; Um Mitternacht; Ich bin der Welt abhanden gekommen.* SCHUMANN: *Frauenliebe und -Leben, Op. 42.* REGER: *Der Brief; Waldeinsamkeit.* SCHUBERT: *Die Allmacht; Fischerweise; An die Musik; Der Musensohn; Ganymed; Auf dem Wasser zu singen; Ave Maria; Die Forelle; Gretchen am Spinnrade; Frühlingsglaube; Der Tod und das Mädchen; Lachen und Weinen; Litanei auf das Fest Aller Seelen; Erlkönig; Der Hirt auf dem Felsen.* WOLF: *Gesang Weylas; Auf einer Wanderung.* R. STRAUSS: *Die Nacht; Allerseelen; Schlechtes Wetter.* RAVEL: *3 Chansons madécasses.* SAINT-SAENS: *Une flûte invisible.* RACHMANINOV: *Chanson géorgienne; Moisson de tristesse.* ROSSINI: *La regata veneziana* (3 canzonettas). (ii) WAGNER: *Wesendonk Lieder.* (iii) HANDEL: *Giulio*

Cesare: Cleopatra's aria. BACH: *St John Passion: Aria: Es ist vollbracht!.* (ii) WAGNER: *Tristan und Isolde: Mild und leise.*
(M) *** EMI CMS7 64074-2 (4).

Christa Ludwig is an extraordinarily versatile artist with a ravishing voice, readily matched by fine intelligence and natural musical sensitivity to place her among the special singers of our time, including De los Angeles and Schwarzkopf (to name two from the same EMI stable). She was as impressive in Schubert as she was in Strauss and Brahms, and her Mahler is very special indeed. This compensates for the below-par Schumann song-cycle. Her voice took naturally to the microphone, so this four-disc set is another source of infinite musical pleasure to be snapped up quickly before it disappears. The recordings come from the 1950s and 1960s and are very well transferred indeed.

'Farewell to Salzburg' (with Charles Spencer (piano)): SCHUMANN: *Stille Tränen; Der Nussbaum; Märzveilchen; Aus den hebräischen Gesängen; Der Himmel hat eine Träne geweint; Die Stille; Mondnacht.* MAHLER: *Rheinlegendchen; Das irdische Leben; Ich bin der Welt abhanden gekommen; Um Mitternacht.* BRAHMS: *Dein blaues Auge; An eine Aolsharfe; Immer leiser wird mein Schlummer; Mädchenlied; Der Schmied; Ständchen; Vergebliches Ständchen.* R. STRAUSS: *Gefunden; Begegnung; Du meines Herzens Krönelein; Nacht; Ruhe, meine Seele; Morgen!.*
*** BMG/RCA Dig. 09026 61547-2 [id.].

This was the programme, representing four central Lieder composers, which Christa Ludwig chose for her final appearance at the Salzburg Festival in August 1993, a sentimental occasion. Rather than recording that recital live, she made this recording earlier in the year in a friendly venue and, though the voice is less velvety than it was earlier, with more of an edge, the artistry is just as intense. She may take Brahms's *Vergebliches Ständchen* more cautiously than before, but – with Charles Spencer an ever-attentive accompanist – the humour is just as delightful, and such taxing songs as Mahler's *Ich bin der Welt*, Brahms's *Immer leiser* and Strauss's *Morgen* show that her poise, her ability to spin a fine legato line were undiminished.

Luxon, Benjamin (baritone), **David Willison** (piano)

'The world of favourite ballads': HARRISON: *Give me a ticket to heaven.* TOSTI: *Parted.* HUHN: *Invictus.* SANDERSON: *Friend o'mine.* QUILTER: *Now sleeps the crimson petal.* MOSS: *The floral dance.* MURRAY: *I'll walk beside you.* STERNDALE-BENNETT: *The carol singers.* RASBACH: *Trees.* WATSON: *Anchored.* ANON., arr. KAYE: *Mr Shadowman.* TOURS: *Mother o' mine.* ADAMS: *The holy city.* JACOBS/BOND: *A perfect day.* GLOVER: *Rose of Tralee.* LAMB: *The volunteer organist.* MASCAGNI: *Ave Maria.* CLARKE: *The blind ploughman.* BRAHE: *Bless this house.* DAVIS: *God will watch over you.*
(M) *** Decca 443 391-2; *443 391-4* [id.].

Here Benjamin Luxon provides a solo collection of some 20 ballads, recorded in 1975. The bluff hints of characterization never step into the area of outright send-up, although just occasionally he goes over the top. A touch more restraint in *The floral dance*, where the final verse is very histrionic, would have been welcome, although David Willison's piano accompaniment conjures up the 'fiddle, cello, big bass drum, cornet, flute and euphonium' rather effectively. Yet Peter Dawson showed how a more direct manner could be so telling in this famous number (see above, in '*Gramophone Greats*'). The sentimental ballads like *I'll walk beside you*, *A perfect day* and the *Rose of Tralee* are very pleasingly done, while Roger Quilter's *Now sleeps the crimson petal* is sung beautifully. But it is the dialogue songs that come off especially well, notably *Mr Shadowman*, which is most engaging, and, best of all, the opening number, '*Give me a ticket to heaven please, before the last train is gone*', which is a real show-stopper. David Willison accompanies most sympathetically and the recording is suitably vivid. However, there are a few strenuous fortissimos where the voice seems to catch the microphone and the tone is harshened.

McCormack, John (tenor)

'Songs of my heart': TRAD.: *The garden where the praties grow; Terence's farewell to Kathleen; Believe me if all those endearing young charms; The star of the County Down; Oft in the stilly night; The meeting of the waters; The Bard of Armagh; Down by the Salley Gardens; She moved thro' the fair; The green bushes.* BALFE: *The harp that once through Tara's halls.* ROECKEL: *The green isle of Erin.* SCHNEIDER: *O Mary dear.* LAMBERT: *She is far from the land.* HAYNES: *Off to Philadelphia.* MOLLOY: *The Kerry dance; Bantry Bay.* MARSHALL: *I hear you calling me.* E. PURCELL: *Passing by.* WOODFORD-FINDEN: *Kashmiri song.* CLUTSAM: *I know of two bright eyes.* FOSTER: *Jeannie with the light brown hair; Sweetly she sleeps, my Alice fair.*
(M) (***) EMI mono CDM7 64654-2 [id.].

In Irish repertoire like *The star of the County Down* McCormack is irresistible, but in lighter concert songs he could also spin the utmost magic. *Down by the Salley Gardens* and Stephen Foster's *Jeannie with the light brown hair* are superb examples, while in a ballad like *I hear you calling me* (an early pre-electric recording from 1908) the golden bloom of the vocal timbre combining with an artless line brings a ravishing frisson on the closing pianissimo. Many of the accompaniments are by Gerald Moore, who proves a splendid partner. Occasionally there is a hint of unsteadiness in the sustained *piano* tone, but otherwise no apology need be made for the recorded sound which is first class, while the lack of 78-r.p.m. background noise is remarkable.

Metropolitan Opera (artists from)

'Metropolitan Opera Gala': Arias from BIZET: *Pêcheurs de Perles* (Robert Alagna; Bryn Terfel). CHARPENTIER: *Louise* (Renée Fleming). GOUNOD: *Faust* (Samuel Ramey; Plácido Domingo); *Roméo et Juliette* (Ruth Ann Swenson). LEHAR: *Giuditta* (Ileana Cotrubas). VERDI: *Don Carlo* (Dolora Zajick). MOZART: *Don Giovanni* (Fleming, Terfel, Jerry Hadley, Kiri Te Kanawa, Hei-Kyung Hong, Julien Robbins). Johann STRAUSS Jr: *Die Fledermaus* (Håkan Hagegård; Karita Mattila). MASSENET: *Werther* (Alfredo Kraus). SAINT-SAENS: *Samson et Dalila* (Grace Bumbry). WAGNER: *Tannhäuser* (Deborah Voight). OFFENBACH: *La Périchole* (Frederica von Stade). Richard STRAUSS: *Der Rosenkavalier* (Fleming, Anne Sofie Von Otter, Heidi Grant Murphy). Tribute to James Levine (Birgit Nilsson)
**(*) DG Dig. 449 177-2; Video VHS 072 451-3 [id.].

Recorded live at James Levine's 25th anniversary gala in April 1996, this offers an extraordinary galaxy of stars, often teamed up in unexpected ways – as, for example, Alagna and Terfel in the first item, the *Pearl fishers* duet. The singers represented a range from such relative newcomers as those rising stars to veterans like Alfredo Kraus and Grace Bumbry. Few of the voices are heard at their very finest, not helped by a rather hard acoustic, but the variety of party pieces here is enough of a delight. The video re-creates the occasion the more satisfactorily, but it is worth hearing the disc for the end of Birgit Nilsson's speech, involving a shattering cry of '*Hojotoho!*'.

'RCA Met. 100 Singing Years'

Disc 1: Excerpts from: DONIZETTI: *Lucia di Lammermoor* (Marcella Sembrich); *L'elisir d'amore* (Antonio Scotto). PUCCINI: *Tosca* (Emma Eames); *La bohème* (Marcel Journet). BERLIOZ: *Damnation de Faust* (Pol Plançon). BIZET: *Carmen* (Emma Calvé). THOMAS: *Hamlet* (Nellie Melba). MEYERBEER: *L'africana* (Giuseppe Campanari); *Le prophète* (Ernestine Schumann-Heink). WAGNER: *Der fliegende Holländer* (Johanna Gadski); *Parsifal* (Clarence Whitehill). PONCHIELLI: *La Gioconda* (Louise Homer). HALEVY: *La juive* (Enrico Caruso). WOLF-FERRARI: *Le donne curiose* (Geraldine Farrar, Hermann Jadlowker). TCHAIKOVSKY: *Pique dame* (Emmy Destinn). VERDI: *Un ballo in maschera* (Pasquale Amato). GIORDANO: *La cena delle beffe* (Frances Alda).

Disc 2: Excerpts from: LEONCAVALLO: *I Pagliacci* (Alma Gluck). VERDI: *La traviata* (John McCormack; Giuseppe de Luca); *Rigoletto* (Luisa Tetrazzini); *La forza del destino* (Rosa Ponselle). MASCAGNI: *L'amico Fritz* (Miguel Fleta, Lucrezia Bori). TCHAIKOVSKY: *Eugene Onegin* (Giovanni Martelli). MUSSORGSKY: *Boris Godunov* (Paul Althouse, Margarete Ober). MEYERBEER: *L'africana* (Beniamino Gigli); *Dinorah* (Amelita Galli-Curci). KORNGOLD: *Die tote Stadt* (Maria Jeritza). ROSSINI: *Il barbiere di Siviglia* (Tito Ruffo). PUCCINI: *La fanciulla del West* (Edward Johnson). WAGNER: *Die Meistersinger* (Friedrich Schorr, Elisabeth Rethberg).

Disc 3: Excerpts from: BELLINI: *Norma* (Giacomo Lauri-Volpi). TAYLOR: *The King's henchman* (Lawrence Tibbett). DONIZETTI: *Lucia di Lammermoor* (Toti dal Monte); *L'elisir d'amore* (Tito Schipa). WAGNER: *Tannhäuser* (Lauritz Melchior); *Tristan und Isolde* (Kirsten Flagstad); *Die Walküre* (Kerstin Thorborg); *Lohengrin* (Helen Traubel). MOZART: *Don Giovanni* (Ezio Pinza). CHARPENTIER: *Louise* (Grace Moore). GOUNOD: *Roméo et Juliette* (Gladys Swarthout). RIMSKY-KORSAKOV: *Le coq d'or* (Lily Pons). GLUCK: *Alceste* (Rose Bampton). MASSENET: *Manon* (Richard Crooks). HAGEMAN: *Caponsacchi* (Helen Jepson). BIZET: *Carmen* (Bruna Castagna). MOZART: *Le nozze di Figaro* (Bidú Sayão).

Disc 4: Excerpts from: GIORDANO: *Andrea Chénier* (Zinka Milanov). PUCCINI: *Manon Lescaut* (Jussi Bjoerling, Enrico Caruso; Dorothy Kirsten); *Madama Butterfly* (Licia Albanese). R. STRAUSS: *Der Rosenkavalier* (Risë Stevens, Erna Berber). GOUNOD: *Faust* (Leonard Warren). MUSSORGSKY: *Boris Godunov* (Alexander Kipnis). OFFENBACH: *Les contes d'Hoffmann* (Jarmila Novotna). BARBER: *Vanessa* (Steber, Elias, Resnik, Gedda, Tozzi, Cehanovsky). DONIZETTI: *Lucia di Lammermoor* (Jan Peerce). THOMAS: *Mignon* (Patrice Munsel). VERDI: *Aida* (Richard Tucker); *Don Carlo* (Robert Merrill); *Otello* (Ramón Vinay, Giuseppe Valdengo).

Disc 5: Excerpts from: WAGNER: *Die Meistersinger* (Set Svanholm). VERDI: *Macbeth* (Jerome Hines); *Un ballo in maschera* (Marian Anderson); *Otello* (Tito Gobbi); *Macbeth* (Carlo Bergonzi); *La traviata* (Anna Moffo). PUCCINI: *La bohème* (Giuseppe di Stefano); *Turandot* (Birgit Nilsson, Jussi Bjoerling). BELLINI: *La sonnambula* (Roberta Peters). ROSSINI: *Il barbiere di Siviglia* (Cesare Valletti). LEONCAVALLO: *I Pagliacci* (Jon Vickers). BARBER: *Antony and Cleopatra* (Leontyne Price).

Disc 6: BIZET: *Carmen* (Franco Corelli, Mirella Freni). WAGNER: *Lohengrin* (Sándor Kónya). VERDI: *Aida* (Grace Bumbry, Plácido Domingo); *Otello* (Renata Scotto, Katia Ricciarelli); *Rigoletto* (Alfredo Kraus); *Il Trovatore* (Fiorenza Cossotto). LEVY: *Mourning becomes Electra* (Sherrill Milnes). PUCCINI: *La bohème* (Montserrat Caballé). DONIZETTI: *La favorita* (Shirley Verrett). CILEA: *Adriana Lecouvreur* (Domingo). MOZART: *Die Zauberflöte* (Martti Talvela); *Così fan tutte* (Kiri te Kanawa). ROSSINI: *L'italiana in Algeri* (Marilyn Horne).
(M) (***) BMG/RCA mono/stereo 09026 61580-2 (6).

With all the singers represented in roles they appeared in at the Met., this lavishly presented collection offers a rich storehouse of fine singing, as well as a fascinating account of that opera house's history over 100 years. Starting with Marcella Sembrich in part of the mad scene from Donizetti's *Lucia di Lammermoor*, each singer is represented only once, with no duplication of items. Even Caruso is represented with only one item, an aria from Halévy's *La Juive*, his last role at the Met. It also means that such a singer as Nicolai Gedda is represented only in an ensemble number from Barber's *Vanessa*. Even so, the variety and unexpectedness of some of the choices is refreshing, as for example having Sherrill Milnes in an aria from Marvin David Levy's *Mourning becomes Electra*. With such a wide coverage it is impossible to comment on more than a fraction of the content but for lovers of fine singing there is little here to disappoint.

Milnes, Sherrill (baritone)

Arias from: ROSSINI: *Il barbiere di Siviglia*. BELLINI: *I puritani*. DONIZETTI: *La Favorita*. VERDI: *Ernani; Don Carlos; Otello; Rigoletto; Luisa Miller*. PONCHIELLI: *La Gioconda*. PUCCINI: *La Fanciulla del West; Tosca*. ROSSINI: *Guglielmo Tell*.
(M) *** Decca 443 929-2 [id.].

Opening with a fizzing account of Figaro's famous *Largo al factotum* from *Il barbiere*, most of these items come from a 1972 studio recital, conducted by Silvio Varviso, in which Decca provided the other singers and the Ambrosian Opera Chorus in the excerpts from *Ernani*, *La Gioconda* amd *Otello*, where the *Brindisi* is another sparkling highlight and Iago's creed very powerful indeed. The remaining excerpts come from various complete sets which usually bring an added flow of adrenalin, especially the splendid excerpts from *Guillaume Tell* and the *Te Deum* scene from *Tosca*. But everything here is enjoyably vivid.

Monteverdi Choir, English Baroque Soloists, Gardiner

Gardiner Collection

CAMPRA: *Requiem Mass.*

(M) *** Erato/Warner 4509 99714-2 [id.]. Nelson, Harris, Orliac, Evans, Roberts, Monteverdi Ch., E. Bar. Soloists, Gardiner.

CARISSIMI: (i) *Jephte;* (ii) *Jonas;* (iii) *Judicium Salomonis (The Judgement of Solomon)* (oratorios).

(M) *** Erato/Warner Dig. 4509 99715-2 [id.]. (i–iii) Ruth Holton; (i) Nigel Robson, Ashley Stafford; (ii) Mark Tucker, Stephen Varcoe; (iii) Stephen Varcoe, Stephen Charlesworth, Susan Hemmington; His Majesties Sagbutts & Cornetts; Monteverdi Ch., E. Bar. Soloists, Gardiner.

MONTEVERDI: Ballet e balletti: *Tirsi e Clori* (complete). *Il ballo delle ingrate: ballet. Orfeo:* excerpts: *Lasciate i monti; Vieni imeneo; Ecco pur ch'a voi ritorno; Moresca. Madrigali guerrieri e amorosi: Volgendo il ciel* (ballet); *Scherzi musicali: De la Belleza* (ballet).

(M) **(*) Erato/Warner Dig. 4509 99716-2 [id.]. Kwella, Rolfe Johnson, Dale Woodrow, Monteverdi Ch., E. Bar. Soloists, Gardiner.

'Sacred choral music': D. SCARLATTI: *Stabat Mater.* CAVALLI: *Salve regina.* GESUALDO: *Ave, dulcissima Maria.* CLEMENT: *O Maria vernana rosa.*

(M) *** Erato/Warner Dig. 4509 99717-2 [id.].

'Music of the Chapels Royal of England': PURCELL: Motet: *Jehova, quam multi sunt hostes mei;* Verse anthem: *My beloved spake;* Full anthems: *O God, Thou has cast us out and scatter'd us abroad; Hear my prayer.* LOCKE: *How doth the city sit solitary.* BLOW: Motet: *Salvator Mundi.* Pelham HUMFREY: *Verse anthem: O Lord my God.*

(M) *** Erato/Warner 4509 99718-2 [id.].

Gardiner Collection, as above: Music by CAMPRA; CARISSIMI; MONTEVERDI; D. SCARLATTI; HUMFREY; PURCELL etc.

(B) *** Erato/Warner Analogue/Dig. 4509 99713-2 (5) [id.].

The present batch of five CDs includes music ranging from Monteverdi's opera-ballets and three attractively individual chamber cantatas by Carissimi to André Campra's glorious *Requiem Mass*, all of which are discussed under their composer entries. Of the two remaining collections the first is centred on Domenico Scarlatti's *Stabat Mater*. The shorter works which fill out this collection are no less worthwhile, notably the rewarding Gesualdo motet from the *Sacrae cantiones*, whose remarkably expressive opening has few precedents in its harmonic eloquence, and another Marian motet by Jacques Clément, better known as Clemens non Papa. The recording is very good indeed without being in the demonstration bracket.

The fine concert centred round the Chapel Royal of England offers Pelham Humfrey's complex and ambitious 13-minute verse anthem, *O Lord my God*, as its masterly highlight. Its passionate supplication for God's help has the kind of pathos Purcell expressed in Dido's famous lament. The Purcell anthems are splendid, of course (notably the succinct *Hear my prayer*, which is wonderfully powerful and concentrated), but are comparatively well known. What is also valuable in this impressive collection is the glorious anthem of Matthew Locke, *How doth the city sit solitary*, and John Blow's very moving motet, *Salvator Mundi*, in which he, too, married Italian and English expressive styles and conveyed great depth of feeling. John Eliot Gardiner paces all this music unerringly, and the singing of the English Baroque Soloists – whether as a choral group or individually – is well up to standard. The expansive recording, made in the London Henry Wood Hall, is spacious and full. Overall the music on these five CDs makes a highly stimulating anthology.

'Christmas in Venice': Giovanni GABRIELI: *Canzona: Sol sol la sol; Audite principes; Angelus ad pastores; Quem vidistis, pastores?; Salvator noster; Sonata pian' e forte; O magnum mysterium.* BASSANO: *Hodie Christus natus est.* MONTEVERDI: *Exultent caeli. Vespers: Magnificat.*

(M) *** Decca 436 285-2 [id.].

A welcome for the reissue of this famous collection, first published in 1972; on the CD, the *Magnificat* from Monteverdi's *Vespers* has been added. Although one could not imagine a more welcome Christmas present, it would be a pity if this concert were relegated to a purely seasonal category, for the record is one to be enjoyed the year through. The insert-note draws a picture of Christmas being celebrated in St Mark's in Venice at the beginning of the seventeenth century, with the church ablaze with the light of more than a thousand candles, plus sixty huge torches and silver lamps. The acoustic chosen for this recording has been beautifully managed. The rich, sonorous dignity of Gabrieli's *Sonata pian' e forte* sounds resplendent, and in the choral numbers the vocal and instrumental blend is expert. The most impressive work here (apart from the *Magnificat*) is Gabrieli's glorious *Quem vidistis, pastores?*; Monteverdi's *Exultent caeli* is shorter, but one is again amazed by the range of expressive contrast, from the exultant opening *Let the heavens rejoice* to the magically simple setting of the phrase *O Maria*, a moment of great beauty each time it recurs. Then there is Gabrieli's fine *Salvator noster*, a motet for three five-part choirs, jubilantly rejoicing at the birth of Christ. One especially attractive feature of Gabrieli's writing is his setting of the word *Alleluia* used to close each of his pieces; the jauntiness of the style is fresh and exhilarating. The CD transfer is admirable.

Nash, Heddle (tenor)

'The incomparable Heddle Nash': PUCCINI: *La Bohème, Act IV* (complete; with Lisa Perli, Brownlee, Alva, Andreva, LPO, Beecham). Arias from: MOZART: *Così fan tutte* (with Ina Souez); *Don Giovanni* (all in Italian). ROSSINI: *The Barber of Seville*. VERDI: *Rigoletto*. BIZET: *The Fair Maid of Perth*. Johann STRAUSS Jr: *Die Fledermaus* (with Denis Noble) (all in English).
(M) (***) Dutton Lab. mono CDLX 7012 [id.].

Once again Dutton Laboratories provide incomparable transfers from 78s – of such quality that Beecham's extraordinarily theatrical (1935) Act IV of *La Bohème*, sung in Italian, communicates like a modern recording. Heddle Nash sings ardently, but Lisa Perli (Dora Labette) as Mimi is equally touching and, if the rest of the cast are less distinctive, Beecham's direction carries the day. Nash's four Mozart recordings (also sung in Italian) are included, notably the 1929 *Il mio tesoro*. Most cherishable of all is the *Serenade* from *The Fair Maid of Perth* from 1932, but there is some very striking Verdi in English, full of flair (in spite of awkward words) and a sparkling Johann Strauss duet with Dennis Noble. It seems carping to criticize that, with only 69 minutes, there would have been room for more. But what there is is technically state of the art.

New College, Oxford, Choir, Higginbottom

'Carols from New College': O come all ye faithful; The angel Gabriel; Ding dong merrily on high; The holly and the ivy; I wonder as I wander; Sussex carol; This is the truth; A Virgin most pure; Rocking carol; Once in Royal David's city. ORD: *Adam lay y-bounden.* BENNETT: *Out of your sleep.* HOWELLS: *A spotless rose; Here is the litle door.* DARKE: *In the bleak midwinter.* MATHIAS: *A babe is born; Wassail carol.* WISHART: *Alleluya, a new work is come on hand.* LEIGHTON: *Lully, lulla, thou little tiny child.* JOUBERT: *There is no rose of such virtue.*
*** CRD CRD 3443; *CRDC 4443* [id.].

A beautiful Christmas record, the mood essentially serene and reflective. Both the Mathias settings are memorable and spark a lively response from the choir; Howells' *Here is the little door* is matched by Wishart's *Alleluya* and Kenneth Leighton's *Lully, lulla, thou little tiny child* in memorability. Fifteen of the twenty-one items here are sung unaccompanied, to maximum effect. The recording acoustic seems ideal and the balance is first class. The documentation, however, consists of just a list of titles and sources – and the CD (using the unedited artwork from the LP) lists them as being divided on to side one and side two!

New London Consort, Philip Pickett

'The Pilgrimage to Santiago' (21 cantigas from the collection of King Alfonso el Sabio).
*** O-L Dig. 433 148-2 (2) [id.].

Philip Pickett and his brilliant team of singers and players present what is described as 'a musical journey along thc mcdicval pilgrim road to the shrine of St James at Santiago de Compostela'. The 21 pieces, lasting over two hours, together provide a mosaic of astonishing richness and vigour, directly related to the four main pilgrim routes to the shrine, via Navarre, Castile, Leon and Galicia. Pickett argues the importance of the Islamic influence in Spain, with bells and percussion often added to the fiddles, lutes, tabors and other early instruments. So the long opening cantiga, *Quen a virgen ben servira*, begins with an instrumental introduction, where (echoing Islamic examples) the players attract attention with tuning-up and flourishes, before the singing begins. The main cantiga then punctuates the 12 narrative stanzas sung by the solo soprano with a catchy refrain, *Those who serve the virgin well will go to paradise*. Standing out among the singers is the soprano, Catherine Bott, the soloist in most of the big cantigas, warm as well as pure-toned, negotiating the weird sliding portamentos that, following Islamic examples, decorate some of the vocal lines. Vivid sound, though the stereo spread of the chorus is limited.

'The Feast of Fools': 1st Vespers; Music from the Office; The drinking bout in the cathedral porch; Mass of the asses, drunkards and gamblers; 2nd Vespers; Ceremony of the Baculus; The banquet; Processional.
*** O-L Dig. 433 194-2 [id.].

Philip Pickett and the New London Consort, inspired in their treatment of early music, present an invigorating, ear-catching sequence drawn from the roistering parodies of church practice that in medieval times were celebrated between Christmas and Epiphany. In modern terms the jokes may be heavy-handed, whether involving vestry humour, drunken cavortings or animal-imitations (as in the *Kyrie* of the *Asses*, *'Hinhan Eleison'*), but the wildness of much of the music is infectious, performed here with uninhibited joy. Carl Orff's *Carmina Burana* (inspired from similar Latin sources) hardly outshines these originals.

Norman, Jessye (soprano)

'Great moments of Jessye Norman'.
Disc 1: WAGNER: *Tristan: Prelude and Liebestod. Tannhäuser: Dich, teure Halle; Allmächt'ge Jungfrau. Der fliegende Holländer: Johohoe! Götterdämmerung: Brünnhilde's immolation scene.*
Disc 2: WAGNER: *Wesendonk Lieder.* SCHUBERT: *Dem Unendlichen; Der Winterabend; Auflosung.* POULENC: *Tu vois le feu du soir; La fraîcheur et le feu* (1–7). RAVEL: *Chansons madécasses* (1–3); *Chanson du rouet; Si morne.*
Disc 3: BRAHMS: *German Requiem: Ihr habt nun Traurigkeit.* BERLIOZ: *Roméo et Juliette: Premiers transports que nu n'oublie.* OFFENBACH: *Les Contes d'Hoffmann:* excerpts. *La belle Hélène*: excerpts.
(M) **(*) EMI Analogue/Dig. CMS5 65526-2 (3) [id.].

One snag for the EMI compilers is having only a limited range of recordings to draw from, which means that each issue overlaps with the others. This three-disc collection is the most comprehensive, with the complete Wagner recital with Tennstedt on the first disc, the second including Wagner's *Wesendonklieder* (with piano) and songs by Schubert, Poulenc and Ravel, and the third a curious mixture of Brahms (from Tennstedt's version of the *German Requiem*), Berlioz (the usual Juliet aria) and Offenbach, a more generous selection from *Contes d'Hoffmann* (five items, including more material unearthed in the Oeser Edition) and *La belle Hélène* (six) than on the *Diva* disc. There are many treasures here, but the mixture is hardly more widely representative than the *Diva* compilation, and here too no texts are given.

'Diva' (from above): Arias from WAGNER: *Tannhäuser; Der fliegende Holländer; Tristan und Isolde.* OFFENBACH: *Contes d'Hoffmann; La belle Hélene.* BERLIOZ: *Roméo et Juliette.*
(M) *** EMI CDM5 65576-2 [id.].

This is a magnificent compilation, framed by four items from Jessye Norman's Wagner recital of 1987 with Klaus Tennstedt: Elisabeth's two arias from *Tannhäuser*, *Senta's Ballad* from *Der fliegende Holländer* and *Isolde's Liebestod*, all superb. Her formidable powers of characterization in tragedy and comedy alike are illustrated in the sequence of excerpts from Offenbach's *Contes d'Hoffmann* (four, including long-buried material from the Oeser Edition) and *La belle Hélène* (three), vocally flawless too. It is also good to have her Juliet represented, taken from Muti's otherwise flawed version of Berlioz's *Roméo et Juliette*. More than with most issues in this well-planned series, it is a snag to have no texts provided.

'L'incomparable Jessy Norman': Arias from: OFFENBACH: *La belle Hélène.* WEBER: *Euryanthe.* BERLIOZ: *Roméo et Juliette.* BRAHMS: *German Requiem.* WAGNER: *Wesendonk Lieder.* RAVEL: *Chansons madécasses 1–3.*
(M) *** EMI Dig. CDM7 69256-2 [id.].

This Jessye Norman compilation from EMI France also overlaps with the other EMI issues, with only one item exclusive to this CD, the *Cavatina* from Weber's *Euryanthe*. Over half the disc is devoted to the German repertory, with the *Wesendonklieder* and the aria from the Brahms *Requiem* again included, and with Juliet's aria, the *Invocation to Venus* from *La belle Hélène* and Ravel's *Chansons madécasses* representing the French repertory. Take your pick, for here too there is much magnificent singing, with the glorious voice used commandingly.

Oberlin, Russell (counter-tenor)

'Las Cantigas de Santa Maria' (with Joseph Iadone, lute): *Prologo. Cantigas Nos. 7, 36, 97, 111, 118, 160, 205, 261, 330, 340 & 364.*
❀ *** Lyrichord LEMS 8003 [id.].

The 400 *Cantigas de Santa Maria*, all of which have music, come from the time of Alfonso El Sabio, king of Spain (1221–84). He is credited with being their composer, but that seems unlikely since they are very diverse. The texts are in Galician, a language in general use in medieval Spain for literary and artistic purposes. They are all concerned with miracles associated with the Virgin Mary, but the music itself has considerable variety and, while the basic style may come from European monodic chant, the melisma has a distinctly Spanish colouring, which in itself has Arab influences. The selection of a dozen items is very well made, for these simple strophic songs have an instant appeal when sung with such lyrical ease by the incomparable Russell Oberlin. The character of the *Cantigas* seems to suit his special timbre especially well, and he has made no finer record than this.

The recital opens with a Prologue in which the singer relates the qualities necessary to be a good troubadour and invokes the Virgin's acceptance of his skills with some confidence. Two of the settings are lively dance songs, *Cantiga* 36 telling how Mary appeared in the night on the mast of a ship journeying to Brittany and saved it from danger, and *Cantiga* 205 about the rescue of a Moorish woman with her child who were sitting on top of a tower which collapsed – yet neither she nor the child came to any harm. But it is the beauty of the lyrical music which is so striking, notably so in *Cantigas* 118 and 330, which are concerned with the restoration of a dead child to life and a simple song of praise for the Virgin herself. The recording is natural and vivid and, as with the other discs in this series, the CD remastering by Nick Fritsch is first class. The content of this reissue is not generous in playing time, but it is of the very highest musical quality and interest.

Oberlin, Russell (counter-tenor), **Seymour Barab** (viol)

Troubadour and trouvère songs, Volume 1: BRULE: *Cil qui d'amor me conseille.* DE BORNEIL: *Reis glorios, verais lums e clartatz.* DANIEL: *Chanson do – Ih mot son plan e prim.* D'EPINAL: *Commensmens de dolce saison bele.* RIQUIER: *Ples de tristor, marritz e doloires*; DE VENTADOUR: *Can vei la lauzeta mover.*
*** Lyrichord LEMS 8001 [id.].

It is good to see the legendary Russell Oberlin return to the catalogue. Older readers will recall his Covent Garden appearance as Oberon in Britten's *Midsummer Night's Dream*. Unfortunately his concert career was cut short and he has since pursued a distinguished career as a scholar. This 1958 recital of *Troubadour and trouvère songs* first appeared on the Experiences Anonymes label and, like so many of his all-too-few recordings (including an incredible Handel aria disc), has long been sought after. This voice was quite unique, a *real* counter-tenor of exquisite quality and, above all, artistry. The disc is expertly annotated and is of quite exceptional interest. LEMS stands for Lyrichord Early Music Series, and the discs we have heard so far are artistically impressive.

'Troubadour and trouvère songs', Volume 5: *English medieval songs: The St Godric songs. Worldes blis ne last no throwe. Bryd one breve; Man mei longe him liues wene; Stond wel moder under rode.*
*** Lyrichord LEMS 8005 [id.].

The *St Godric Songs* are the earliest known in the English language. St Godric died in 1170, so they date from halfway through the twelfth century. The other items here belong to the latter part of the century. As with his first disc, above, Russell Oberlin is completely convincing in this repertoire, the purity of line and beauty of timbre consistently appealing. The accompanying viol is discreet and the sound is remarkably clear and vivid.

Opera: 'Essential Opera'

'Essential opera I': BIZET: *Carmen: Prelude* (LPO, Solti); *Flower song* (Domingo). PUCCINI: *Tosca: Vissi d'arte* (Kiri Te Kanawa). *La Bohème: Che gelida manina. Turandot: Nessun dorma* (both Pavarotti); *Non piangere Liù . . . Ah! per l'ultima volta!* (Pavarotti, Montserrat Caballé, Nicolai Ghiaurov, Tom Krause). *Gianni Schicchi: O mio babbino caro* (Tebaldi). *Madama Butterfly: Un bel dì vedremo* (Mirella Freni). VERDI: *Il Trovatore: Anvil chorus. Nabucco: Va pensiero (Chorus of Hebrew slaves)* (Chicago Symphony Ch. & O, Solti). *Rigoletto:* Quartet: *Bella figlia dell'amore* (Sutherland, Tourangeau, Pavarotti, Milnes). *Aida: Grand march and ballet* (La Scala, Milan, Ch. & O, Maazel). MOZART: *Nozze di Figaro: Voi che sapete* (Frederica von Stade). *Don Giovanni: Finch'han dal vino* (Bernd Weikl). CATALANI: *La Wally: Ebben? Ne andrò lontana* (Tebaldi). ROSSINI: *Il barbiere di Siviglia: Largo al factotum* (Leo Nucci). OFFENBACH: *Contes d'Hoffmann: Barcarolle: Belle nuit, o nuit d'amour* (Sutherland and Huguette Tourangeau). MASCAGNI: *Cavalleria rusticana: Intermezzo* (Nat. PO, Gavazzeni).
**(*) Decca Analogue/Dig. 433 822-2 [id.].

'Essential opera II': WAGNER: *Die Walküre: The ride of the Valkyries* (VPO, Solti). BIZET: *Carmen: Habanera* (Tatiana Troyanos). MOZART: *Le nozze di Figaro: Non più andrai* (Samuel Ramey); *Dove sono* (Kiri Te Kanawa). *Così fan tutte:* Trio: *Soave sia il vento* (Lucia Popp, Brigitte Fassbaender; Tom Krause). *Don Giovanni:* Duet: *Là ci darem la mano* (Popp; Krause). *Die Zauberflöte: Der Vogelfänger bin ich ja* (Michael Kraus). PUCCINI: *Madama Butterfly: Humming chorus* (Vienna State Op. Ch., Karajan). *Turandot: Signore ascolta!* (Montserrat Caballé). *Tosca: E lucevan le stelle* (Domingo). *La Bohème: Sì, mi chiamano Mimì . . . O soave fanciulla* (Freni; Pavarotti). VERDI: *La Traviata: Un dì felice* (Joan Sutherland; Luciano Pavarotti). *Rigoletto: La donna è mobile* (Pavarotti). LEONCAVALLO: *Pagliacci: Vesti la giubba* (Pavarotti). ROSSINI: *Il barbiere di Siviglia: Una voce poco fa* (Cecilia Bartoli). BIZET: *Les pêcheurs de perles:* Duet: *Au fond du temple saint* (Gregory Cross; Gino Quilico). CILEA: *L'Arlesiana: Lamento di Federico* (José Carreras). DELIBES: *Lakmé:* Duet: *Sous le dôme épais* (Sutherland; Jane Berbié). GOUNOD: *Faust: Soldiers' chorus* (Ambrosian Opera Ch., LSO, Bonynge).
**(*) Decca Analogue/Dig. 440 947-2 [id.].

With a great deal of hype, Decca's first (full-priced) 'Essential opera' compilation became a chart-topper and sold in large quantities. It includes many favourites, offering 77 minutes of music and some obvious star performances, mostly from Pavarotti and Freni, and Domingo's *Flower song* from *Carmen*. Although generally the excerpts are vividly presented, Solti opens the programme with a *Carmen Prélude* that offers less brilliant sound than usual from Decca. The Tebaldi excerpt from Catalani's *La Wally* is most welcome, but is it 'essential opera'? Not everything is quite on this artist's level and it is easy to find similar and, in certain cases, preferable selections from the same source, costing less.

The second selection (78 minutes) follows a similar formula. Solti again opens the proceedings with an exciting *Ride of the Valkyries* (though, curiously, an orchestral version without the vocal parts) and there is plenty to enjoy. But one of the most memorable excerpts, the great love scene from Act I of *La Bohème* (*Sì, mi chiamano Mimì . . . O soave fanciulla*) with Freni and Pavarotti, is also available on other, less expensive anthologies.

Oxford Pro Musica Singers, Michael Smedley

'Follow that star' (with Timothy Bennett). *Carols in close harmony*: BLANE: *Have yourself a merry little Christmas.* BERNARD: *Winter wonderland.* GRITTON: *Follow that star; On olde rhyme; Deck the hall.* COOT: *Santa Claus is coming to town.* HAIRSTON: *Mary's boy child.* BARRATT: *Just another star.* WELLS: *The Christmas song.* TRAD.: *Ding dong merrily on high; The angel Gabriel; Gaudete; Riu, riu chiu!; Coventry carol; In dulci jubilo.* GRUBER: *Silent night.* HOWELLS: *A spotless rose.* arr. RUTTER: *I wonder as I wander.* TAVENER: *The Lamb; Nativity; Today the Virgin.* CORNELIUS: *Three Kings.* arr. David BLACKWELL: *The Virgin Mary had a baby boy; Mary had a baby; Jingle bells.*
**(*) Proudsound Dig. PROUCD 134 [id.].

The first nine carols here are arranged by Peter Gritton in the American close-harmony style – and, provided you can enjoy the sentimentality of Judy Garland's number from *Meet Me in St Louis, Have yourself a merry little Christmas*, and the even more famous *Winter wonderland*, you can ignore the brackets round the third star. The excellent Oxford Pro Musica Singers seem as much at home here as they are in David Blackwell's arrangements of *The Virgin Mary had a baby boy* and *Mary had a baby* in the rhythmic style of spirituals, and the somewhat over-elaborate but effective *Jingle bells.* In between come some splendid traditional carols, including the folksy *Riu, riu chiu!*, all beautifully sung, and –

perhaps the highlight of the concert – three glorious modern carols by John Tavener. The digital recording is first class.

Patti, Adelina (soprano)

'The Era of Adelina Patti' ((i) Adelina Patti, (ii) Victor Maurel; (iii) Pol Plançon; (iv) Mattia Battistini; (v) Mario Ancona; (vi) Lucien Fugère; (vii) Francisco Vignas; (viii) Emma Calvé; (ix) Maurice Renaud; (x) Fernando de Lucia; (xi) Francesco Tamagno; (xii) Nellie Melba; (xiii) Félia Litvinne; (xiv) Wilhelm Hesch; (xv) Lillian Nordica; (xvi) Mario Ancona; (xvii) Edouard de Reszke; (xviii) Marcella Sembrich; (xix) Francesco Marconi; (xx) Mattia Battistini; (xxi) Lilli Lehmann; (xxii) Sir Charles Santley): Arias from: VERDI: (ii) *Falstaff;* (i, iii) *Don Carlos;* (iv, xx) *Ernani;* (v, xiv) *Otello.* ADAM: (iii) *Le Chalet.* GLUCK: (vi) *Les Pèlerins de la Mecque.* MOZART: (i, ii, xx) *Don Giovanni;* (i, vii, xxi) *Le nozze di Figaro.* MEYERBEER: (vii) *Le Prophète.* BIZET: (viii) *Carmen.* MASSENET: (ix, xi) *Hérodiade;* (x) *Manon.* THOMAS: (xii) *Hamlet.* WAGNER: (xiii) *Lohengrin;* (xiv) *Die Meistersinger von Nürnberg.* ERKEL: (xv) *Hunyadi László.* DONIZETTI: (xvi) *La favorita;* (xix) *Lucrezia Borgia;* (xii) *Lucia.* BELLINI: (i) *La Sonnambula;* (xviii) *I Puritani.* FLOTOW: (xvii) *Martha.* ROSSINI: (x) *Il barbiere di Siviglia.* GOMES: (xx) *Il Guarany.* Songs by TOSTI; (vi) RAMEAU; (i, vi) YRADIER; (i) HOOK; (i) BISHOP; (ix) GOUNOD; (xv) R. STRAUSS; (xxii) HATTON.
(M) (***) Nimbus mono NI 7840/41 [id.].

The very first item on this wide-ranging collection of historic recordings has one sitting up at once. The voice ringing out from the loudspeakers prompts cheering from the singer's little audience. The clear-toned baritone is singing *Quand'ero paggio* from Verdi's *Falstaff* and, encouraged, he repeats it. More cheering and a third performance, this time in French, to cap the occasion. The singer is Victor Maurel, the baritone whom Verdi chose as his first Falstaff in 1893 and, before that, his first Iago in *Otello*. The recording dates from 1907, and many lovers of historic vocal issues will remember it well. Yet hearing it on the Nimbus transfer to CD brings a sense of presence as never before.

That company's controversial technique of playing an ancient 78 disc with a thorn needle on the best possible acoustic horn gramophone is at its most effective here, with exceptionally vivid results on these acoustic recordings. They not only convey astonishing presence but also a sense of how beautiful the voices were, getting behind the tinny and squawky sounds often heard on old 78s. This is an ideal set for anyone not already committed to historic vocals who simply wants to investigate how great singing could be 90 years ago, providing such an unexpected mix of well-known items and rarities, to delight specialists and newcomers alike.

The first of the two discs offers recordings that Nimbus regards as technically the finest of their day, including Patti in 1906, not just singing but shouting enthusiastically in a Spanish folksong, *La Calesera*, '*Vivan los españoles!*' Recorded much later in 1928 comes the French baritone, Lucien Fugère, eighty at the time but singing with a firm focus that you might not find today in a baritone in his twenties.

The second of the two discs has just as fascinating a mixture, but the recordings 'have not survived the decades so well'. Even so, it is thrilling to hear Sir Charles Santley, born in 1834, the year after Brahms, singing *Simon the Cellarer* with tremendous flair at the age of seventy-nine, and the coloratura, Marcella Sembrich, sounding even sweeter in Bellini than on previous transfers.

Pavarotti, Luciano (tenor)

'Pavarotti's greatest hits': PUCCINI: *Turandot: Nessun dorma. Tosca: Recondita armonia; E lucevan le stelle. La Bohème: Che gelida manina.* DONIZETTI: *La fille du régiment: O mes amis . . . Pour mon âme. La Favorita: Spirito gentil. L'elisir d'amore: Una furtiva lagrima.* R. STRAUSS: *Der Rosenkavalier: Di rigori armato.* LEONCAVALLO: *Mattinata.* ROSSINI: *La danza.* DE CURTIS: *Torna a Surriento.* BIZET: *Carmen: Flower song.* BELLINI: *I Puritani: A te o cara. Vanne, O rose fortunata.* VERDI: *Il Trovatore: Di qual tetra . . . Ah, si ben mio; Di quella pira. Rigoletto: La donna è mobile; Questa o quella. Requiem: Ingemisco. Aida: Celeste Aida.* FRANCK: *Panis angelicus.* GOUNOD: *Faust: Salut! Demeure.* SCHUBERT: *Ave Maria.* LEONCAVALLO: *I Pagliacci: Vesti la giubba.* PONCHIELLI: *La Gioconda: Cielo e mar.* DENZA: *Funiculi, funicula.*
*** Decca 417 011-2 (2) [id.].

This collection of 'greatest hits' can safely be recommended to all who have admired the golden beauty of Pavarotti's voice. Including as it does a fair proportion of earlier recordings, the two discs demonstrate the splendid consistency of his singing. Songs are included as well as excerpts from opera, including

Torna a Surriento, *Funiculi, funicula*, Leoncavallo's *Mattinata* and Rossini's *La Danza*. The sound is especially vibrant on CD.

'Tutto Pavarotti': VERDI: *Aida: Celeste Aida. Luisa Miller: Quando le sere al placido. La Traviata: De' miei bollenti spiriti. Il Trovatore: Ah si ben mio; Di quella pira. Rigoletto: La donna è mobile. Un ballo in maschera: La rivedrà nell'estasi.* DONIZETTI: *L'elisir d'amore: Una furtiva lagrima. Don Pasquale: Com'è gentil.* PONCHIELLI: *La Gioconda: Cielo e mar.* FLOTOW: *Martha: M'appari.* BIZET: *Carmen: Flower song.* MASSENET: *Werther: Pourquoi me réveiller.* MEYERBEER: *L'Africana: O paradiso.* BOITO: *Mefistofele: Dai campi dai prati.* LEONCAVALLO: *Pagliacci: Vesti la giubba.* MASCAGNI: *Cavalleria Rusticana: Addio alla madre.* GIORDANO: *Fedora: Amor ti vieta.* PUCCINI: *La Fanciulla del West: Ch'ella mi creda. Tosca: E lucevan le stelle. Manon Lescaut: Donna non vidi mai. La Bohème: Che gelida manina. Turandot: Nessun dorma.* ROSSINI: *Stabat Mater: Cuius animam.* BIZET: *Agnus Dei.* ADAM: *O holy night.* DI PAPUA: *O sole mio.* TOSTI: *A vucchella.* CARDILLO: *Core 'ngrato.* TAGLIAFERRI: *Passione.* CHERUBINI: *Mamma.* DALLA: *Caruso.*
(M) *** Decca 425 681-2 (2) [id.].

Opening with Dalla's *Caruso*, a popular song in the Neapolitan tradition, certainly effective, and no more vulgar than many earlier examples of the genre, this selection goes on through favourites like *O sole mio* and *Core 'ngrato* and one or two religious items, notably Adam's *Cantique de Noël*, to the hard core of operatic repertoire. Beginning with *Celeste Aida*, recorded in 1972, the selection of some 22 arias from complete sets covers Pavarotti's distinguished recording career with Decca from 1969 (*Cielo e mar* and the *Il Trovatore* excerpts) to 1985, although the opening song was, of course, recorded digitally in 1988. The rest is a mixture of brilliantly transferred analogue originals and a smaller number of digital masters, all or nearly all showing the great tenor in sparkling form. The records are at mid-price, but there are no translations or musical notes.

'King of the high Cs': Arias from: DONIZETTI: *La fille du régiment; La Favorita.* VERDI: *Il Trovatore.* R. STRAUSS: *Der Rosenkavalier.* ROSSINI: *Guglielmo Tell.* BELLINI: *I Puritani.* PUCCINI: *La Bohème.*
(M) *** Decca 433 437-2 [id.].

A superb display of Pavarotti's vocal command as well as his projection of personality. Though the selections come from various sources, the recording quality is remarkably consistent, the voice vibrant and clear, the accompanying detail and the contributions of the chorus are also well managed. The Donizetti and Puccini items are particularly attractive. The opening number – Tonio's aria from the Act I finale of *La fille du régiment* – ending with a whole series of 'pinging' top Cs, is thrillingly hair-raising. The recordings were made between 1967 and 1972 when the voice was at its freshest.

'The essential Pavarotti' (with various orchestras and conductors): Arias from: VERDI: *Rigoletto; Il Trovatore; La Traviata; Aida.* PUCCINI: *La Bohème; Turandot; Tosca; Fanciulla del West; Manon Lescaut.* DONIZETTI: *L'elisir d'amore.* FLOTOW: *Martha.* BIZET: *Carmen.* LEONCAVALLO: *I Pagliacci.* GIORDANO: *Fedora.* MEYERBEER: *L'Africana.* MASSENET: *Werther.* Songs: DALLA: *Caruso.* LEONCAVALLO: *Mattinata.* TOSTI: *Aprile; Marechiare; La Serenata.* CARDILLO: *Core 'ngrato.* ROSSINI: *La Danza.* MODUGNO: *Volare.* DENZA: *Funiculì, funiculà.* DI CURTIS: *Torna a Surriento.* DI CAPUA: *O sole mio!* SCHUBERT: *Ave Maria.* FRANCK: *Panis angelicus.* MANCINI: *In un palco della Scala* (with apologies to Pink Panther). GIORDANO: *Caro mio ben.* BIXIO: *Mamma.*
(M) *** Decca Analogue/Dig. 436 173-2 (2) [id.].

Such a collection as this is self-recommending and scarcely needs a review from us, merely a listing. The first disc opens with *La donna è mobile* (*Rigoletto*), *Che gelida manina* (*La Bohème*), *Nessun dorma* (*Tosca*), all taken from outstandingly successful complete recordings, and the rest of the programme, with many favourite lighter songs also given the golden touch, is hardly less appealing. The second CD includes Pavarotti's tribute to the Pink Panther and ends with a tingling live version of *Nessun dorma*, to compare with the studio version on disc one. Vivid, vintage Decca recording throughout.

'Grandi voci' (with Nat. PO, Chailly or Fabrittis): GIORDANO: *Fedora: Amor ti vieta. Andrea Chénier: Colpito qui m'avete . . . Un di all'azzuro spazio; Come un bel dì di maggio; Si, fui soldata.* BOITO: *Mefistofele: Dai campi, dai prati; Ogni mortal . . . Giunto sul passo estremo.* CILEA: *Adriana Lecouvreur: La dolcissima effigie; L'anima ho stanca.* MASCAGNI: *Iris: Apri la tua finestra!* MEYERBEER: *L'Africana: Mi batti il cor . . . O Paradiso.* MASSENET: *Werther: Pourquoi me réveiller.* PUCCINI: *La Fanciulla del West: Ch'ella mi creda. Manon Lescaut: Tra voi belle; Donna non vidi mai; Ah! non v'avvicinate! . . . No! No! pazzo son!* (with Howlett).
(M) **(*) Decca Dig. 440 400-2 [id.].

This first digital recital record from Pavarotti had the voice more resplendent than ever. The passion with which he tackles Des Grieux's Act III plea from *Manon Lescaut* is devastating, and the big breast-beating numbers are all splendid, imaginative as well as heroic. But the slight pieces, Des Grieux's *Tra voi belle* and the *Iris Serenade*, could be lighter and more charming. The CD gives the voice even greater projection, with its full resonance and brilliance admirably caught, but it does also make the listener more aware of the occasional lack of subtlety of the presentation.

'Live': Recital 1: Arias and duets from: VERDI: *La Traviata; I vespri siciliani; Aida*. MASSENET: *Werther*. PONCHIELLI: *La Gioconda*. DONIZETTI: *La figlia del reggimento; L'elisir d'amore*. MEYERBEER: *L'Africana*. BOITO: *Mefistofele*. MASCAGNI: *L'amico Fritz*. PUCCINI: *Tosca*. Recital 2: Arias from VERDI: *La Traviata; Aida; Macbeth; La forza del destino; I Lombardi; Il Corsaro; Falstaff; Un ballo in maschera;* Duet from *Otello (Già nella notte densa)*. Arias from PUCCINI: *Turandot*.
(B) **(*) Double Decca 443 018-2 (2) [id.].

Here are two Pavarotti recitals for the price of one, although in the second, mainly a Verdi collection, Katia Ricciarelli, in splendid voice, gets the lion's share of the arias and she and Pavarotti join for only a single duet – from *Otello*. Pavarotti rounds off the programme as usual with *Nessun dorma*, to tumultuous applause. However, applause is not really a problem on the second disc, whereas it is often intrusive on the first. Artistically, however, the partnership of Pavarotti and Freni works well (as we know from their complete recordings). The *Werther* and *Africana* items were new to Pavarotti's repertory at the time; sweet singing from Freni, too, though her delivery at times could be more characterful. Vividly robust recording.

Pears, Peter (tenor)

'Elizabethan lute songs' (with Julian Bream): FORD: *Fair, sweet, cruel; Come, Phyllis, come*. MORLEY: *Come, sorrow, come; It was a lover and his lass; Mistress mine, well may you fare; Thyrsis and Mila; I saw my lady weeping; With my Love my life was nestled; What if my mistress now*. ROSSETER: *When Laura smiles; What then is love but mourning; Sweet, come again; What is a day? Whether men do laugh or weep*. DOWLAND: *I saw my lady weep; Awake, sweet love; In darkness let me dwell; Fine knacks for ladies; Sorrow, stay; If my complaints; What if I never speed*. PILKINGTON: *Rest, sweet nymphs*. ANON.: *Have you seen but a whyte lillie grow? Miserere, my maker*. CAMPION: *Come, let us sound; Fair, if you expect admiring; Shall I come, sweet love*
(M) *** Decca mono/stereo 444 524-2 [id.].

The first nine songs on this CD were recorded in mono in 1956; the rest come from a delightfully spontaneous stereo recital of two years later. The early songs stand up well by comparison, and the mono sound is excellent. Pears's very individual timbre readily identifies with the underlying melancholy which characterizes so many Elizabethan songs. While the stereo brings an extra atmosphere, the earlier items are still very welcome.

Pears, Peter (tenor), Julian Bream (lute)

Julian Bream Edition, Volume 19. *Elizabethan lute songs*: MORLEY: *Absence; It was a lover and his lass; Who is is?*. ROSSETER: *What then is love?; If she forsake me; When Laura smiles*. DOWLAND: *I saw my lady weep; Dear, if you change; Stay, Time; Weep you no more; Shall I sue?; Sweet, stay awhile; Can she excuse?; Come, heavy sleep; Wilt thou unkind, thus leave me?; Sorrow stay; The lowest trees have tops; Time's eldest son, Old Age; In darkness let me dwell; Say, love, if ever thou didst find*. FORD: *Come Phyllis; Fair, sweet, cruel*.
(M) *** BMG/RCA 09026 61609-2 [id.].

This vintage collection was recorded between 1963 and 1969 when Pears was at the peak of his form. The Dowland songs are particularly fine, sung with Pears's usual blend of intelligence and lyrical feeling, their nostalgic melancholy tenderly caught. Excellent, vivid, well-balanced recording, with Bream's expert accompaniments well in the picture. Most refreshing.

Polyphony, Stephen Layton

'O magnum mysterium' (A sequence of twentieth-century carols and Sarum chant): Plainchant: *O radix Iesse; A magnum mysterium; Puer natus est nobis; Reges Tharsis; Verbum caro factum est.* WISHART: *3 Carols, Op. 17, No. 3: Alleluya, A new work is come on hand.* HOWELLS: *3 Carol-anthems: Here is the little door; A spotless rose; Sing lullaby.* Richard Rodney BENNETT: *5 Carols: There is no rose; Out of your sleep; That younge child; Sweet was the song; Susanni.* Kenneth LEIGHTON: *Of a rose is my song; A Hymn of the Nativity; 3 Carols, Op. 25: The Star song; Lully lulla, thou little tiny child; An Ode on the birth of our Saviour.* WARLOCK: *As dew in Aprylle; Bethlehem Down; I saw a fair maiden; Benedicamus Domino; A Cornish Christmas carol.* BYRT: *All and some.* WALTON: *What cheer?.*
*** Hyperion Dig. CDA 66925 [id.].

A gloriously sung collection in which (what Meurig Bowen's extensive notes describe as) 'the magnificent corpus of British carols' is alive and still impressively expanding in the twentieth century. The atmosphere is readily set by the opening plainchant, which frames and punctuates the concert with appropriate liturgical texts. Peter Wishart's exuberant *Alleluya* and the poignant *A spotless rose* immediately catch up the listener. This is the first of Howells's *Three carol-anthems*, of which the others are equally lovely (especially the rocking *Sing Lullaby*). The five Richard Rodney Bennett carols have their own particular brand of cool dissonance, with *There is no rose* and *Sweet was the song* particularly haunting. But perhaps it is the series of beautiful Peter Warlock settings one remembers most for their ready melodic and harmonic memorability (notably *As dew in Aprylle*, the lovely *Bethlehem Down*, and the serene *Lullaby my Jesus*) alongside the soaring music of Kenneth Leighton, helped in the ambitious *Nativity hymn* and the *Ode on the birth of our Saviour* by the rich, pure line of the soloist, Libby Crabtree, and in *Lully, lulla* by the equally ravishing contribution of Emma Preston-Dunlop. Walton's *What cheer?* brings an exuberant rhythmic spicing, but for the most part this programme captures the tranquil pastoral mood of Christmas Eve. The recording could hardly be bettered, clear yet with the most evocative ambience.

Price, Leontyne (soprano)

'The Prima Donna Collection' (with RCA Italiana Op. O, Molinari-Pradelli, New Philh. O, Santi; LSO, Downes; or Philh. O, Henry Lewis): Disc 1: Arias from: PURCELL: *Dido and Aeneas.* MOZART: *Le nozze di Figaro.* VERDI: *La Traviata; Otello* (with C.Vozza). MEYERBEER: *L'Africaine.* MASSENET: *Manon.* CILEA: *Adriana Lecouvreur.* Gustave CHARPENTIER: *Louise.* PUCCINI: *Turandot* (with D. Barioni, Amb. Op. Ch.). KORNGOLD: *Die tote Stadt.* BARBER: *Vanessa.*

Disc 2: HANDEL: *Atalanta.* MOZART: *Don Giovanni.* WEBER: *Der Freischütz.* WAGNER: *Tannhäuser.* VERDI: *Macbeth* (with C. Vozza, E.El Hage). BOITO: *Mefistofele.* DVORAK: *Rusalka.* DEBUSSY: *L'enfant prodigue.* GIORDANO: *Andrea Chénier.* ZANDONAI: *Francesca da Rimini.* PUCCINI: *Suor Angelica.* MENOTTI: *Amelia goes to the ball.*

Disc 3: GLUCK: *Alceste.* MOZART: *Don Giovanni.* VERDI: *I Lombardi; Simon Boccanegra.* FLOTOW: *Martha.* OFFENBACH: *La Périchole.* WAGNER: *Die Walküre.* Johann STRAUSS Jr: *Die Fledermaus.* BIZET: *Carmen.* MASCAGNI: *Cavalleria rusticana.* MASSENET: *Thaïs.* PUCCINI: *Gianni Schicchi.* POULENC: *Les dialogues des Carmélites.*

Disc 4: HANDEL: *Semele.* MOZART: *Idomeneo.* BERLIOZ: *La Damnation de Faust.* WEBER: *Oberon.* BELLINI: *Norma* (with B. Martinovich, Amb. Op. Ch.). VERDI: *Rigoletto.* WAGNER: *Tristan und Isolde.* LEONCAVALLO: *I Pagliacci.* CILEA: *Adriana Lecouvreur.* BRITTEN: *Gloriana.*
(M) *** BMG/RCA 09026 61236-2 (4).

This anthology is drawn from a series of recitals which Leontyne Price recorded for RCA in London and Rome between 1965 and 1979, including many items made when she was at the very peak of her form. Some of the very finest performances come on Disc 1. The famous *Lament* from Purcell's *Dido and Aeneas* makes a moving opener, the voice is wonderfully fresh; and the following performances are all gloriously sung – clearly these early sessions with Molinari-Pradelli in Rome were highly productive. But there are many fine things elsewhere. The Sleep-walking scene from Verdi's *Macbeth* on Disc 2 is a disappointment (Lady Macbeth is plainly not one of her best parts), but her *Come in quest' ora bruna* from *Simon Boccanegra* is very fine, and she finds unusual expressive depth in Offenbach's Act III Prison aria from *La Périchole*. She is, not unexpectedly, superb in *Voi lo sapete* from *Cavalleria rusticana* (disc 3), and a highlight from the final disc is the passionately felt *D'amour l'ardente flamme* from Berlioz's *Damnation de Faust*. The languorously played cor anglais solo here is characteristic of the consistent excellence of the accompaniments and, like the voice, they are beautifully recorded. Care has been taken with detail, so that in the long scene from Act I of *Norma* (with *Casta diva* at its centre) there is support from the Ambrosian Chorus, recorded in fine perspective. As she has already recorded a complete *Carmen*, it is good to hear Miss Price singing richly in the subsidiary role of Micaëla, and the programme includes a fair sprinkling of novelties, not least a rare excerpt from Britten's *Gloriana*. In a programme as long as this (approaching five hours of music) there are bound to be minor vocal flaws, but they are surprisingly few, and vocally the performances are amazingly consistent. A feast of opera, very well ordered – each disc makes a satisfying solo recital.

'The essential Leontyne Price'

Discs 1–2: *'Her greatest opera roles'*: Arias from: VERDI: *Aida; Il trovatore; Ernani; La forza del destino*. MOZART: *Così fan tutte Don Giovanni*. PUCCINI: *Madama Butterfly; Tosca; Manon Lescaut; Turandot*. POULENC: *Dialogue des Carmélites*. R. STRAUSS: *Ariadne auf Naxos*. BARBER: *Antony and Cleopatra*.

Discs 3–4: *'Great opera scenes'* from: VERDI: *Otello; Macbeth; Don Carlo*. BEETHOVEN: *Fidelio*. PUCCINI: *Suor Angelica; La Rondine; La Bohème*. BIZET: *Carmen*. VERDI: *La Traviata*. MOZART: *Le nozze di Figaro*. R. STRAUSS: *Die ägyptische Helena; Salome; Die Frau ohne Schatten*. TCHAIKOVSKY: *Eugene Onegin*. BARBER: *Vanessa*. MASSENET: *Manon*. PURCELL: *Dido and Aeneas*.

Discs 5–6: *'Leontyne Price and Friends'*: Excerpts from: VERDI: *Otello; Aida* (with Plácido Domingo; Sherrill Milnes; Marilyn Horne); *Un ballo in maschera; Ernani* (both with Carlo Bergonzi); *Requiem* (with Janet Baker); *Il Trovatore* (with Milnes). MOZART: *Così fan tutte* (with Horne; Tatiana Troyanos). BELLINI: *Norma*. PUCCINI: *Madama Butterfly* (both with Horne). GERSHWIN: *Porgy and Bess* (with William Warfield). BIZET: *Carmen* (with Franco Corelli).

Discs 7–8: *'Leontyne Price in song'*: BERLIOZ: *Nuits d'été*. R. STRAUSS: *Vier letzte Lieder*. FAURE: *Clair de lune; Notre amour; Au cimetière; Au bord de l'eau; Mandoline*. POULENC: *Main dominée par le coeur. Miroirs brûlants: Je nommerai ton front; Tu vois le feu du soir. Ce doux petit visage*. BARBER: *Knoxville, Summer of 1915*. SCHUMANN: *Frauenliebe und -leben, Op. 42; Widmung (Myrthen); Mignon; Volksliedchen; Schöne Wiege meiner Leiden; Er ist's; Heiss mich nicht reden; Lust der Sturmnacht*. R. STRAUSS: *Allerseelen; Schlagendes Herzen; Freundliche Vision; Wie sollten wir geheim*. WOLF: *Der Gärtner; Lebe wohl; Morgentau; Geh, Geliebter, geh jetzt*.

Discs 9–10: *'Spirituals, hymns, & Sacred songs'*: *Ev'ry time I feel the spirit; Let us break bread together; His name so sweet; 'Round about de mountain; Swing low, sweet chariot; Sit down, servant; He's got the whole world in his hands; Deep river; My soul's been anchored in de Lord; On ma journey; A city called Heaven; Ride on, King Jesus; I wish I knew how it would feel to be free; Sinner, please don't let this harvest pass; Sweet little Jesus boy; There is a Balm in Gilead; Let us cheer the weary traveller; Ev'ry time I feel the spirit; My way is cloudy; Nobody knows the trouble I've seen; I couldn't hear nobody pray*. DYKES: *Holy, holy, holy; Lead kindly light*. KNAPP: *Blessed assurance*. SCHUBERT: *Ave Maria*. CONVERSE: *What a friend we have in Jesus*. TRAD.: *Amazing grace; Fairest Lord Jesus; I wonder as I wander*. MALOTTE: *The Lord's prayer*. DOANE: *Pass me not, O gentle Saviour*. Samuel S. WESLEY: *The Church's one foundation*. BRAHE: *Bless this house*. LOWRY: *I need Thee every hour*. BACH/GOUNOD: *Ave Maria*. GERSHWIN: *Porgy and Bess: Summertime*. WARD: *America the beautiful*. JOHNSON: *Lift ev'ry voice and sing*. LUTHER: *A mighty fortress is our God*. HOWE: *Battle hymn of the Republic*.

Disc 11: *'In recital and Interview'*: BRAHMS: *Zigeunerlieder, Op. 103*. CILEA: *Adriana Lecouvreur: Io son l'umile ancella*. TRAD.: *This little light of mine*. Interview with John Pfeiffer (recorded in April 1995).
(M) *** RCA 09026 68153-2 (11) [id.].

'The essential Leontyne Price': Arias and excerpts from: VERDI: *La forza del destino; Il Trovatore; Otello* (with Plácido Domingo). PUCCINI: *Madama Butterfly; La Rondine*. BIZET: *Carmen*. MOZART: *Così fan tutte* (with Marilyn Horne). Songs: BERLIOZ: *Nuits d'été: Absence*. R. STRAUSS: *Vier Letzte Lieder: Beim Schlafengehen*. MALOTTE: *The Lord's prayer*. GERSHWIN: *Porgy and Bess: Summertime. Spiritual: Swing low sweet chariot; Ride on King Jesus*.
(M) *** RCA 09026 68152-2 [id.].

To celebrate the seventieth birthday in February 1997 of this commanding American soprano, RCA have compiled this formidable collection of 11 discs, presenting them in the most extravagant format, with a fully bound, well-illustrated book – including full texts – to match a substantial album in similar format containing the discs. The presentation is among the most impressive we have seen since the coming of CD, and the choice of items lives up to its lavishness, with the first two discs devoted to Price's 'Greatest opera roles', mainly of Mozart, Verdi, Puccini and Strauss, but also including the role of the heroine in Barber's *Antony and Cleopatra*, specially written for her. The next two discs containing 'Great opera scenes' range wider still, concentrating on the same composers but also including unexpected items from Purcell's *Dido and Aeneas* and Tchaikovsky's *Eugene Onegin*. The two discs, 'Price and friends', have her in duet with such artists as Carlo Bergonzi, Franco Corelli, Plácido Domingo, Dame Janet Baker and her one-time husband, William Warfield. The two discs of song then include such substantial items as Barber's *Knoxville* – one of her most magical recordings – Schumann's *Frauenliebe*, Strauss's *Four Last songs* and Berlioz's *Les nuits d'été*. Spirituals, hymns and sacred songs make up the next two discs, leaving a final one of miscellaneous items, Brahms's *Zigeunerlieder*, and the heroine's artistic credo from Cilea's *Adriana Lecouvreur*, all rounded off with an interview conducted by the late John Pfeiffer who master-minded the whole presentation just before he died.

What this rich collection repeatedly brings home is the glorious consistency of Price in her singing over the longest period, with barely any signs of wear in the voice even in the later recordings, and with every note firmly and surely in place, with golden tone pouring forth. There may be some operatic roles which she personally did not enjoy – Verdi's Lady Macbeth for one, as she makes clear in her interview – but the quality of her singing was never impaired. It is good too to have it brought home how wide her sympathies have been, readily encompassing such genres as German Lieder. A timely summary of a great career, with a well-chosen sampler disc for those not wanting to stretch to the whole survey. This single CD, however, does not include translations.

'Grandi voci': Arias from: MOZART: *Don Giovanni*. VERDI: *Aida; Requiem*. PUCCINI: *Tosca*. R. STRAUSS: *Ariadne auf Naxos*. GERSHWIN: *Porgy and Bess*. Songs: SCHUBERT: *Ave Maria*. MOZART: *Exsultate jubilate: Alleluja*. TRAD.: *Sweet little Jesus boy*.
(M) *** Decca 440 402-2 [id.].

Leontyne Price can be heard at her finest here: the Verdi and Puccini arias central to her repertory are superbly done. It is good too to have her represented in Mozart (in Donna Elvira's three key arias) and Strauss, recorded at the peak of her career, though style there is less positive and individual. Nevertheless this very enjoyable recital is more than the sum of its parts, and the programme ends appropriately with an affecting performance of *Summertime* from *Porgy and Bess*. Excellent sound throughout.

Pro Cantione Antiqua, Bruno Turner

'Ars Britannica': Old Hall Manuscript: COOKE: *Alma proles*. DUNSTABLE: *Crux fidelis; O crux gloriosa; Gaude virgo*. FOREST: *Qualis est dilectus; Albanus roseo rutilat*. PYCARD: *Gloria*. DAMETT: *Salve porta paradisi*. POWER: *Credo*. CHIRBURY: *Agnus dei*. Madrigals: WEELKES: *Those sweet delightful lillies; Some men desire spouses; Come sirrah Jack ho!; Come, let's begin to revel't*. WARD: *Retire, my troubled soul; O my thoughts surcease*. MORLEY: *Hark, jolly shepherds; Die now, my heart; You black bright stars*. BYRD: *Come, woeful Orpheus*. TOMKINS: *O let me dye for true love; O yes, has any found a lad?*. WILBYE: *Lady, when I behold; As matchless beauty; Weep, o mine eyes*. PILKINGTON: *Care for my soul*. Lute songs: PILKINGTON: *Down-a-down*. DOWLAND: *A shepherd in a shade; Fine knacks for ladies; Where sin sore wounding; I must complain; Sweet, stay awhile; Mr Dowland's midnight; Now, oh now I needs must part*. CAMPION: *Never weather-beaten sail; Jack and Jone; A secret love*. FORD: *Since first I saw; There is a lady*.
(M) *** Teldec/Warner 2292 46004-2 (2) [id.].

On two mid-price CDs Bruno Turner directs his superb all-male vocal team (with the tenor, Ian Partridge, prominent) in one of the richest and most enjoyable collections available of Elizabethan madrigals and lute songs. As a prelude comes church music from the fifteenth-century Old Hall manuscript, covering such remarkable pre-Tudor composers as Pycard and Lionel Powers, as well as John Dunstable. The Elizabethan collection also covers the widest range of composers, including Byrd, Wilbye, Weelkes, Pilkington and the still-underappreciated John Ward. Recorded between 1977 and 1979, the sound is exceptionally full and well focused.

Psalmody, Parley of Instruments, Peter Holman

'While shepherds watched' (Christmas music from English parish churches and chapels 1740–1830): BEESLY: *While shepherds watched.* ANON.: *Let an anthem of praise; Hark! how all the welkin rings.* J. C. SMITH: *While shepherds watched.* HELLENDAAL: *Concerto in E flat for strings, Op. 3/4: Pastorale.* KEY: *As shepherds watched their fleecy care.* ARNOLD: *Hark the herald angels sing.* CLARK: *While shepherds watched.* HANDEL: *Hark! the herald angels sing.* JARMAN: *There were shepherds abiding in the field.* S. WESLEY: (Piano) *Rondo on 'God rest you merry, gentleman'* (Timothy Roberts). MATTHEWS: *Angels from the realms of glory.* HANDEL: *Hymning seraphs wake the morning.* FOSTER: *While shepherds watched.*
*** Hyperion Dig. CDA 66924 [id.].

This is a Christmas collection of genuine novelty. None of the settings of *While shepherds watched* uses the familiar tune (the regal closing version from John Foster of Yorkshire is remarkably lively, as is the lighter variation from Joseph Key of Northampton, *As shepherds watched their fleecy care* with woodwind accompaniment). There are other surprises too. Handel's *Hark the herald angels* is neatly fitted to *See the conqu'ring hero comes*, and *Hymning seraphs* (presented as a tenor solo with fortepiano) turns out to be our old keyboard friend, '*The harmonious blacksmith*'. Peiter Hellendaals's *Pastorale for strings* is in the best *concerto grosso* tradition, although Samuel Wesley's variations on *God rest you merry* are merely ingenious. Nevertheless the whole programme is presented with pleasing freshness and is very well sung, played and recorded.

Ramey, Samuel (bass)

Arias from: MOZART: *Le nozze di Figaro.* HANDEL: *Rodelinda.* DONIZETTI: *Anna Bolena.* VERDI: *I masnadieri; Macbeth.* BELLINI: *Norma.* STRAVINSKY: *The Rake's progress.* WEILL: *Street scene.* arr. COPLAND: *Old American songs – Set No. 1.*
(M)*** Decca Grandi Voci Dig. 448 251-2 [id.].

Instead of centring on a studio recital, Decca's Grandi Voci collection celebrating the achievement of Samuel Ramey selects excerpts from various complete recordings in which he has participated with distinction during the 1980s, beginning with excerpts from Solti's sparkling *Nozze di Figaro* (in which he took the name-role with distinction, making Figaro a more romantic figure than usual) and ending with his fine set of Copland's *Old American songs*, recorded with Warren Jones in 1990. With consistently vivid Decca sound, this gives a rounded picture of one of the finest basses of our time, whose range was remarkable.

Rolfe Johnson, Anthony (tenor), David Willison (piano)

English songs: VAUGHAN WILLIAMS: *Songs of travel.* BUTTERWORTH: *A Shropshire Lad.* IRELAND: *The land of lost content.* GURNEY: *Down by the Salley Gardens; An Epitaph; Desire in spring; Black Stitchel.* WARLOCK: *My own country; Passing by; Pretty ring time.*
(B) *** PCD Carlton 1065.

It would be hard to design a better programme of twentieth-century English songs than this, providing one accepts the omission of Britten, and it is a surprise to discover that this nearly-70-minutes-long programme derives from two (Polygram) Polydor LPs from the mid-1970s. At that time this label was not exactly famous for this kind of repertoire but there is hidden treasure here. The performances of the Vaughan Williams and Butterworth cycles are full of life and colour (and are splendidly accompanied), and it is especially good to have the far lesser-known Gurney songs. The recordings have transferred well. A bargain.

Russian Liturgical Music

St Petersburg Litany – Night Vigil.
*** DG Dig. 445 653-2 [id.]. Priests & Ch. of the Cathedral of the Transfiguration, St Petersburg, Boris Glebov.

Anyone who has attended a Russian Orthodox service will know how impressive an experience it is. With the collapse of the Soviet Union interest in this Church's repertoire has burgeoned, witness the proliferation of recordings of Rachmaninov's *Vespers* as well as the music of Bortniansky and Kastalsky. In the days of LP, DG recorded the Easter services at Mount Athos, and they have now repeated the process in

St Petersburg. The Palm Sunday Vigil lasts some three hours – the present disc runs for 72 minutes. This is a rich panoply of sound, ranging from the ringing of bells, large and small, to the service itself, which is sung throughout without spoken interludes or instrumental accompaniments. It is atmospherically recorded and offers quite an experience.

St George's Canzona, John Sothcott

Medieval songs and dances: *Lamento di Tristano; L'autrier m'iere levaz. 4 Estampies real; Edi beo thu hevene quene; Eyns ne soy ke plente fu; Tre fontane.* PERRIN D'AGINCOURT: *Quant voi en la fin d'este.* Cantigas de Santa Maria: *Se ome fezer; Nas mentes semper teer; Como poden per sas culpas; Maravillosos et piadosos.*
*** CRD CRD 3421; *CRDC 4121* [id.].

As so often when early music is imaginatively re-created, one is astonished at the individuality of many of the ideas. This applies particularly to the second item in this collection, *Quant voi en la fin d'este,* attributed to the mid-thirteenth-century trouvère, Perrin d'Agincourt, but no less to the four Cantigas de Santa Maria. The instrumentation is at times suitably robust but does not eschew good intonation and subtle effects. The group is recorded vividly and the acoustics of St James, Clerkenwell, are never allowed to cloud detail. The sound is admirably firm and real in its CD format.

Schmidt, Joseph (tenor)

Complete EMI recordings: Arias (sung in German) from: MEYERBEER: *L'africaine.* FLOTOW: *Martha; Alessandro Stradella.* KIENZL: *Der Evangelimann.* KORNGOLD: *Die tote Stadt.* ADAM: *Der Postillon von Longjumeau.* MASSENET: *Manon; Der Cid.* TCHAIKOVSKY: *Eugene Onegin.* MORY: *La Vallière.* GOTZE: *Der Page des Königs.* Johann STRAUSS Jr: *1001 Nacht; Der Zigeunerbaron; Simplicus.* LEHAR: *Zigeunerliebe.* TAUBER: *Der Singende Traume.* DONIZETTI: *Der Liebestrank (L'elisir d'amore).* VERDI: *Rigoletto; Der Troubadour (Il trovatore).* LEONCAVALLO: *Der Bajazzo (Pagliacci).* PUCCINI: *La Bohème; Tosca; Das Mädchen aus dem Goldenen Westen (Fanciulla del West); Turandot.* SERRANO: *El Trust do Los Tenorios.* SPOLIANSKY: *Das Lied einer Nacht* (film). Lieder & Songs: SCHUBERT: *Ständchen; Ungeduld.* BENATZKY: *Wenn du treulos bist.* NIEDERBERGER: *Buona notte, schöne Signorina.* LEONCAVALLO: *Morgenständchen.* LABRIOLA: *Serenata.* BISCARDI: *L'ariatella.* DENZA: *Funiculi, funicula.* BUZZI-PECCIA: *Lolita.* DI CAPUA: *O sole mio.*
(M) (***) EMI mono CHS7 64673-2 (2) [id.].

Joseph Schmidt, born in 1904 in what is now Romania, studied in Berlin, and developed what by any standards is one of the most beautiful German tenor voices ever recorded, less distinctive than that of Richard Tauber, but even more consistently honeyed and velvety in the upper registers, exceptionally free on top, so that the stratospheric top notes in *Le Postillon de Longjumeau* have never sounded so beautiful and unstrained. This is the ideal lyric tenor voice, not just for the German repertory, including operetta, but for the Italian; it was tragic that, standing less than five foot high, he was precluded from having an operatic career. Nevertheless, he was most successful in his concert work as well as in his recording career, as this glowing collection demonstrates. He even had a brilliantly successful American tour in 1937; but sadly, as a Jew, he got caught up in Europe during the Second World War, and died from a chest complaint in a Swiss refugee camp in 1942. The records – with informative notes – make a superb memorial, here at last given full prominence in excellent transfers.

Schwarzkopf, Dame Elisabeth (soprano)

'Elisabeth Schwarzkopf sings operetta' (with Philharmonia Ch. and O, Ackermann): Excerpts from: HEUBERGER: *Der Opernball.* ZELLER: *Der Vogelhändler.* LEHAR: *Der Zarewitsch; Der Graf von Luxembourg; Giuditta.* J. STRAUSS, Jr: *Casanova.* MILLOCKER: *Die Dubarry.* SUPPE: *Boccaccio.* SIECZYNSKY: *Wien, du Stadt meiner Träume.*
✿ *** EMI CDC7 47284-2 [id.].

This is one of the most delectable recordings of operetta arias ever made, and it is here presented with excellent sound. Schwarzkopf's 'whoopsing' manner (as Philip Hope-Wallace called it) is irresistible, authentically catching the Viennese style, languor and sparkle combined. Try for sample the exquisite *Im chambre séparée* or *Sei nicht bös*; but the whole programme is performed with supreme artistic command and ravishing tonal beauty. This outstanding example of the art of Elisabeth Schwarzkopf at its most enchanting is a disc which ought to be in every collection. The CD transfer enhances the superbly balanced recording even further; it manages to cut out nearly all the background, gives the voice a natural presence and retains the orchestral bloom.

'Encores' (with Gerald Moore or Geoffrey Parsons): BACH: *Bist du bei mir*. GLUCK: *Einem Bach der fliesst*. BEETHOVEN: *Wonne der Wehmut*. LOEWE: *Kleiner Haushalt*. WAGNER: *Träume*. BRAHMS: *Ständchen; 3 Deutsche Volkslieder*. MAHLER: *Um schlimme Kinder artig zu machen; Ich atmet' einen linden Duft; Des Antonius von Padua Fischpredigt*. TCHAIKOVSKY: *Pimpernella*. arr. WOLF-FERRARI: *7 Italian songs*. MARTINI: *Plaisir d'amour*. HAHN: *Si mes vers avaient des ailes*. DEBUSSY: *Mandoline*. arr. QUILTER: *Drink to me only with thine eyes*. ARNE: *When daisies pied; Where the bee sucks*. arr. GUND: *3 Swiss folk songs*. arr. WEATHERLY: *Danny Boy*. J. STRAUSS, Jnr: *Frühlingsstimmen* (with VPO, Joseph Krips).
(M) *** EMI stereo/mono CDM7 63654-2.

Schwarzkopf herself has on occasion nominated this charming account of *Danny Boy* as her own favourite recording of her singing, but it is only one of a whole sequence of lightweight songs which vividly capture the charm and intensity that made her recitals so memorable, particularly in the extra items at the end. As a rule she would announce and explain each beforehand, adding to the magic. The range here is wide, from Bach's heavenly *Bist du bei mir* to the innocent lilt of the Swiss folksong, *Gsätzli*, and Strauss's *Voices of spring*.

'Unpublished recordings' (with (i) Philh. O, Thurston Dart; (ii) Kathleen Ferrier, VPO, Karajan; (iii) Philh. O, Galliera; (iv) Walter Gieseking, Philh. O, Karajan): J. S. BACH: (i) *Cantata No. 199: Mein Herze schwimmt im Blut: Auf diese Schmerzens Reu; Doch Gott muss mir genädig sein; Mein Herze schwimmt im Blut*. (ii) *Mass in B min.: Christe eleison; Et in unum Dominum; Laudamus te*. (iii) MOZART: *Nehmt meinen Dank, K.383*. (iv) GIESEKING: *Kinderlieder*. R. STRAUSS: *4 Last songs*.
(M) (**(*)) EMI CDM7 63655-2.

Long-buried treasure here includes Bach duets with Kathleen Ferrier conducted by Karajan, a collection of charming children's songs by Gieseking, recorded almost impromptu, and, best of all, a live performance of Strauss's *Four Last songs* given under Karajan at the Festival Hall in 1956, a vintage year for Schwarzkopf. Sound quality varies, but the voice is gloriously caught.

'Lieder recital' (with Gerald Moore, piano): BACH: *Bist du bei mir*. PERGOLESI: *Se tu m'ami, se tu sospiri*. HANDEL: *Atalanta: Care selve*. GLUCK: *Die Pilger von Mekka: Einam Bach der fliesst*. BEETHOVEN: *Wonne de Wehmut*. SCHUBERT: *An Sylvia; Romanze aus Rosamunde; Die Vögel; Der Einsame; Vedi quanto adoro*. WOLF: *Kennst du das Land; Philine; Nachtzauber; Die Zigeunerin*. Richard STRAUSS: *Ruhe meine Seele; Wiegenlied; Schlechters Wetter; Hat's gesang, bleibt's nicht dabei*. Encores: MOZART: *Warnung*. SCHUMANN: *Der Nüssbaum*. SCHUBERT: *Ungeduld*.
(M) (**(*)) EMI mono CDH5 66084-2 [id.].

Schwarzkopf's 1956 Salzburg recital with Gerald Moore is the third to have appeared on CD, more varied than the earlier two, another great occasion caught on the wing. It ranges from Bach and Handel arias, expansive and poised, through a Schubert-like Gluck song and rare Beethoven to Schwarzkopf's regular repertory of Schubert, Wolf and Strauss, delectably done. Wolf's *Kennst du das Land*, greatest of all Lieder for a woman, here comes not as a climax but at the start of a group, building up with biting intensity. No texts are provided.

Sciutti, Graziella (soprano)

'The early years' (with (i) VSO, Moralt; (ii) LOP, Dervaux; (iii) Jaqueline Bonneau, piano): Excerpts from (i) MOZART: *Così fan tutte; Don Giovanni*. (ii) BELLINI: *La Sonnambula; I Puritani*. DONIZETTI: *Don Pasquale; Linda di Chamounix*. ROSSINI: *Semiramide*. (iii) FAURE: *Rencontre; Toujours; Adieu*. RAVEL: *5 Mélodies populaires grecques*. DEBUSSY: *Ariettes oubliées*.
(M) (**) Ph. mono 442 750-2 [id.].

Graziella Sciutti, a singer of great charm, made a later, Decca stereo recital, which showed off her vocal talents much more effectively than this Philips collection. Easily the most impressive items here are the Mozart arias, taken from Moralt's 1956 mono set of *Così fan tutte* in which her Despina shone out from the rest of the cast. She proves a no less charming Zerlina in *Don Giovanni*, recorded the previous year, when, apart from her two solos, she joins with George London in *Là ci darem la mano*. The other arias come from an earlier (1953) mono recital, where she proves not well suited to the Bellini arias but sounds nearer her best as *Linda di Chamounix* and (especially) *Semiramide*, where the touch of flutter in her timbre adds to the vocal character. The French song-recital is transferred from an LP pressing, as the master tape has become lost or degraded, and here the highlight is the *Cinq mélodies populaires grecques*, in which she sings with great charm.

Shirley-Quirk, John (baritone)

'A Recital of English songs' (with Martin Isepp (harpsichord and piano), Nona Liddell and Ivor McMahon (violins), Ambrose Gauntlett (viola da gamba)): PURCELL: *Man is for woman made; Music for a while; 'Twas within a furlong of Edinborough Town; Cantata: When night her purple veil* (arr. BRITTEN). HUMFREY: *A hymne to God the Father.* BUTTERWORTH: *A Shropshire lad* (song-cycle). MOERAN: *Three songs from Ludlow Town.*
(M) *** Saga EC 3336-2 [id.].

A splendid collection of seventeenth- and twentieth-century English songs, with John Shirley-Quirk at his finest. The Housman settings by Butterworth and Moeran are particularly affecting in their lyrical directness. The Purcell and Humfrey items too are very well done, with stylish accompaniment. The recording is not as clean as it might be, but it is acceptable at the price. There is little hint of its age in the presentation, the only date mentioned being 1996.

'Songs of travel' (with Viola Tunnard): VAUGHAN WILLIAMS: *Songs of travel; Linden Lea; Silent noon.* IRELAND: *Sea fever.* STANFORD: *Drake's drum; The Old Superb.* KEEL: *Trade winds.* WARLOCK: *Captain Stratton's fancy.*
(M) **(*) Saga EC 3338-2 [id.].

With really sensitive singing, John Shirley-Quirk makes it abundantly clear how completely the best of British songs stand comparison with the mainstream of German Lieder. Some of the Vaughan Williams cycle (like *The Roadside Fire*) have a freshness and simplicity that put them close to Schubert, and this complete recording includes an epilogue written with the other songs in the early years of the century but kept in a drawer for years and published only after the composer's death. The other items are among the best known of all British songs. Some of them might be described as school songs, but Shirley-Quirk's singing turns a simple but beautifully wrought song like Keel's *Trade winds* into something extraordinarily moving, while Stanford's *The Old Superb* is unforgettable in its rumbustious vigour. The recording, over 30 years old, is marginally a little restricted in the treble, but the overall effect is most convincing. The name of the accompanist is mis-spelt on the CD and in the notes, which include such gems as '. . . the cycle, full of music as youthfull, frech and beautifull as on the day it was written . . .' Only the year 1996 is mentioned as a date of publication.

Simionato, Giulietta (mezzo-soprano)

'Grandi voci': Arias and excerpts from: ROSSINI: *Il barbiere di Siviglia; La Cenerentola.* VERDI: *Don Carlos; Il Trovatore* (with Mario del Monaco); *Un ballo in maschera* (with Carlo Bergonzi); *La forza del destino.* BELLINI: *I Capuleti e i Montecchi; Norma.* SAINT-SAENS: *Samson et Dalila.* THOMAS: *Mignon.* MASSENET: *Werther.* BIZET: *Carmen.* DONIZETTI: *La Favorita.*
(M) *** Decca 440 406-2 [id.].

This provides a superb 77-minute sampler of a singer who bids fair to achieve legendary status, an Italian mezzo with a firm, finely projected voice who could snort fire to order. The recital begins with four excerpts (from *Il barbiere*, *La Cenerentola*, *I Capuleti e i Montecchi* and *Don Carlos*) recorded in mono in 1954, showing the voice at its freshest – the cabaletta from *Una voce poco fa* is sheer delight – and then covers most of her other favourite roles, with recordings made up until 1961, including a richly sustained *Casta diva* from that year. Her rich middle range and sense of line are eloquently demonstrated in *Printemps qui commence* from *Samson et Dalila* and Mignon's lovely *Connais-tu le pays?*, while the ardour of the *Air de la lettre* from Massenet's *Manon* is very moving, helped by a passionate accompaniment from Previtale. The collection ends with Preziosilla's *Rataplan* from *La forza del destino*, sung with a thrilling military precision seldom encountered on record. Molinari-Pradelli and the Santa Cecilia Chorus and Orchestra add to the *vivo*, and the spectacle is well laced with a splendid side-drum. Here (in early 1955 stereo) as elsewhere the Decca engineers do her proud.

Sinfonye, Stewart Wishart

'Gabriel's greeting' (Medieval carols) including: *Gabriel framevene king; Salva Virgo virginium; Ave Maria virgo virginium; Ther is no rose of swych vertu; Lolay, lolay; Nowell, nowell.*
**(*) Hyperion Dig. CDA 66685 [id.].

Unlike the Taverner Consort who range over many centuries of music, Sinfonye concentrate on vocal and instrumental music from the thirteenth, fourteenth and fifteenth centuries, which usually consists of simple ostinato-like rhythmic ideas with a very distinct melodic and harmonic character. These five singers and instrumentalists present their programme with spirit and vitality, but the range of the music is necessarily limited. Those who take to the repetitive medieval style will undoubtedly find this refreshing, and the recording is pleasingly live and atmospheric.

The Sixteen, Harry Christophers

Music from the Eton Choirbook

Volume I: *'The Rose and the ostrich feather'*: FAYRFAX: *Magnificat (Regale).* HYGONS: *Salve regina.* TURGES: *From stormy wyndis.* BROWNE: *Stabat iuxta Christi Crucem.* ANON.: *This day dawnes.* CORNYSH: *Salve regina.*
*** Collins Dig. 1314-2 [id.].

Volume II: *'Crown of thorns'*: DAVY: *Stabat mater.* BROWNE: *Jesu, mercy, how may this be?; Stabat mater.* CORNYSH: *Stabat mater.* SHERYNGHAM: *Ah, gentle Jesus.*
*** Collins Dig. 1316-2 [id.].

Volume III: *'The Pillars of Eternity'*: CORNYSH: *Ave Maria, mater Dei.* DAVY: *O Domine caeli terraeque; A myn hart remembir the well; A blessed Jheso.* LAMBE: *Stella caeli.* WILKINSON: *Credo in Deum – Jesus autem; Salve regina.*
*** Collins Dig. 1342-2 [id.].

Volume IV: *'The Flower of all Virginity'*: Hugh KELLYK: *Gaude flore virginali.* ANON.: *Ah, my dear, ah, my dear Son!; Afraid, alas, and why so suddenly?* NESBETT: *Magnificat.* FAYRFAX: *Most clear of colour.* BROWNE: *Salve regina; O Maria salvatoris mater.*
*** Collins Dig. 1395-2 [id.].

This is a glorious anthology, gloriously sung. The music in the Eton Choirbook was not restricted to local performance and the emblems which give the first volume its sobriquet demonstrate the link with the Chapel Royal. What the chosen music also demonstrates (as with other anthologies of early church music) is the close links between secular music and music for worship. Throughout the rich textures with soaring trebles are thrilling. The settings of Cornysh and John Browne are particularly memorable: the latter's *O Maria salvatoris mater* which closes the fourth volume is breathtakingly beautiful. Volume IV is devoted to Marian antiphons but includes also the Nesbett *Magnificat* and three songs which have associations with the Marian theme and which certainly do not lack intensity. The second volume, '*Crown of Thorns*', centres on settings of the *Stabat Mater* and adds to the two composers mentioned the music of Richard Davy; the third explores Davy's output further in the ambitious and profound *O Domine caeli*. Two new names also appear in this tribute to musical eternity, Robert Wilkinson's complex canon, *Credo in Deum – Jesus autem*, and Lambe's impressive *Stella caeli*. But perhaps the best place to start exploring this remarkable series is Volume 4, '*The Flower of all Virginity*', which opens with Hugh Kellyk's glowing appraisal of the Virgin: *Gaude flore virginali* ('Rejoice in the flower of your maidenhood, and in the special honour due to you, surpass all the shining hosts of angels'). Christophers seems to have an instinct for the right tempo for these tonally abundant works with their flowing lines, and the expansive beauty of the choral sound never interferes with one's ability to hear the detail. The Sixteen constantly produce radiant tone and their performances match warm, expressive feeling with commendable accuracy of intonation.

American choral music: BARBER: *Agnus Dei; Reincarnations, Op. 16.* FINE: *The hour glass.* REICH: *Clapping music.* BERNSTEIN: *The Lark* (choruses). COPLAND: *4 Motets.* DEL TREDICI: *Final Alice* (acrostic song).
**(*) Collins Dig. 1287-2 [id.].

The Sixteen now make a big jump from the early sixteenth century to the mid-twentieth. They begin with our old friend, Barber's *Adagio*, but in choral form as an *Agnus Dei*, and here the choral climax compares well with the intensity of the better string versions. Reich's *Clapping* literally welcomes the Bernstein choruses (incidental music for a Hellman play) but Copland's *Four Motets* – a 1921 student work – is not typical, and the rest of the programme has a more limited appeal, though very well sung and recorded.

'An early English Christmas collection': Plainchant: *Verbum caro. Salutation carol* (15th century). *Nowell sing we, both all and some* (c. 1450). *Piae Cantiones: Gaudete* (1582); *Hail Mary, full of grace* (c. 1420); *There is no rose* (c. 1420); *Nowell, nowell: Out of your sleep* (c. 1450); *Sweet was the song the virgin sang* (c. 1600); *Ave rex angelorum* (c. 1450); *Drive the cold winter away* (c. 1600); *Nowell, nowell: the boares head* (c. 1500); *Greensleeves* (c. 1600); *Angelus ad virginem* (14th century, Dublin); *Nowell, nowell; Dieu vous garde* (c. 1500); *Make we joy* (c. 1450). SHEPPARD: *Gloria in excelsis; Verbum caro.* RAVENSCROFT: *Remember, O thou man.* PYGOTT: *Quid petis, O fili?*. BYRD: *Lullaby my sweet little babe.*
*** Collins Dig. 1492-2 [id.].

Early medieval carols were often joyous song-dances, with the vigour of the dance more important to the participants than the melody. The *Salutation carol* is a fine monodic example, while the north European *Gaudete*, with its infectious cross-rhythms, and the rousing *Nowell, nowell: Out of your sleep* are hardly less enthusiastic. *Nowell sing we, both all and some* is also lively, but its richness of harmony gives it a mellower character, while *Hail Mary, full of grace* and *There is no rose*, both more plainly harmonized, are other beautiful examples of a more lyrical style. The works of John Sheppard, Richard Pygott and the spaciously floating *Lullaby my sweet little babe* of William Byrd are spiritually serene. The lovely *Remember, O thou man* of Ravenscroft sounds much more like a recognizably traditional carol, as does the beautiful *Sweet was the song the virgin sang*. *Greensleeves* provides a robust contrast, presented like a tavern song, and the Irish *Angelus ad virginem* has a distinctly folksy flavour. The performances here could hardly be bettered, rich in sonority and feeling, and always aptly paced. The recording, too, is of the highest quality to provide a Christmas collection with a difference and a highly rewarding and well-planned concert.

Souliotis, Elena (soprano)

'Grandi voce': Arias and scenes from: VERDI: *Nabucco; Macbeth; Luisa Miller; Un ballo in maschera; Anna Bolena* (final scene); *La forza del destino.* MASCAGNI: *Cavalleria rusticana.* PONCHIELLI: *La Gioconda.*
(M) *** Decca 440 405-2 [id.].

The charismatic Greek diva Elena Souliotis had a sadly brief (if at times sensational) recording career, and all the excerpts here come from between 1965 and 1967. Rightly, the selection opens with Abigail's venomous scena from *Nabucco*, her finest recording role. The thrilling wildness as she spits fire with extraordinary passion is unforgettable. The same reckless ardour and the vocal power in the chest register make *Voi lo sapete* from *Cavalleria rusticana* equally arresting. (She made her final appearance as Santuzza at Covent Garden in 1973.) As a fiery stage personality she had much in common with Callas, but in these carefully chosen excerpts her upper tessitura is shown as more reliable. *Pace, pace mio Dio* (1967) is finely spun, and the group of Verdi items (a riveting Lady Macbeth, a dominant Luisa Miller, Amelia in *Un ballo*), taken from a 1966 recital, are all most impressive, while the final scene (20 minutes) from Donizetti's *Anna Bolena* is very touching – *Al dolce guidami castel natio* quite lovely. The recital ends with an electrifyingly uninhibited *Suicido!* from *La Gioconda*, again from 1967, showing the sheer power of the voice over the widest range. Some of the singing in this recital may be uneven (though the standard is surprisingly consistent) but the tension never abates. No wonder Alan Blyth comments in his perceptive note: 'She resembled a comet that flashed brightly across the operatic scene and was too soon extinguished.' The Decca recording certainly lights up the sky.

Stefano, Giuseppe di (tenor)

'Grandi voci': Arias and excerpts from: GIORDANO: *Andrea Chénier.* PUCCINI: *Tosca; Turandot.* MASSENET: *Werther; Manon.* BIZET: *Carmen; Les Pêcheurs de perles.* GOUNOD: *Faust.* DONIZETTI: *L'elisir d'amore.* PONCHIELLI: *La Gioconda.* VERDI: *La forza del destino.* BOITO: *Mefistofele* (with Cesare Siepi).
(M) *** Decca 440 403-2 [id.].

Flamboyance rarely goes with keen discipline. As Rudolf Bing (among others) has said, if those qualities had been matched in di Stefano, we should have had a tenor to rival Caruso. As it is, a cross-section taken from Decca recordings made between 1955 and 1959 gives a splendid idea not just of his beauty of voice but of his power to project character and feelings. But do not look for stylish restraint in *Una furtiva lagrima* – the tear is anything but furtive – and do not seek a French tenorissimo in *En fermant les yeux* from Massenet's *Manon* but ardour and full timbre. The Puccini excerpts, notably Calaf's *Nessun dorma* and the ringing *Recondita armonia* from *Tosca*, demonstrate there was life before Pavarotti, while the tender opening of *E lucevan le stelle* from the same opera shows that di Stefano could fine his tone down in the most ravishing manner when he needed to. The Decca recordings offer early examples of stereo, but the transfers are remarkably full and vivid.

Streich, Rita (soprano)

Lieder: (with (i) Erich Werba; (ii) Günther Weissenborn): (a) (i) MOZART: *An Chloe; Die kleine Spinnerin; Das Lied der Trennung; Das Veilchen; Der Zauberer; Sehnsucht nach dem Frühling; Un moto di gioia; Oiseaux, si tous les ans; Dans un bois solitaire; Das Kinderspiel; An die Einsamkeit; Die Verschweigung. Warnung*. SCHUBERT: *Die Forelle; Auf dem Wasser zu singen; Seligkeit*. WOLF: *Wohin mit der Freud?; Wiegenlied; Die Kleine; Nachtgruss*. R. STRAUSS: *Der Stern; Einerlei; Schlechtes Wetter*. MILHAUD: *Au clair de la lune. 4 Chansons de Ronsard, Op. 223; Folksongs: Canto delle risaiole; Gsätzli; Z'Lauterbach*. (b) (i) SCHUBERT: *Heidenröslein; Arietta der Claudine; Lied der Mignon II; Nähe des Geliebten; Liebhabner in allen Gestalten; Der Hirt auf dem Felsen* (with Heinrich Geuser); *An den Mond; Die Vögel; Das Lied im Grünen*. (b) SCHUMANN: *Der Nussbaum; Die Stille; Schneeglöcken; Die Lotusblume; Intermezzo; Aufträge*. BRAHMS: *Ständchen; Mädchenlied; Vergebliches Ständchen; Wiegenlied*. (a) WOLF: *Verschwiegene Liebe; Die Spröde; Die Bekehrte; Der Gärtner*. (b) R. STRAUSS: *Schlagende Herzen; Wiegenlied; Amor; An die Nacht*.
(M) ** DG (a) mono; (b) stereo 437 680-2 (2) [id.].

Rita Streich's voice was naturally suited to Mozart, and on the first of these two discs, recorded in mono, these simple songs cannot fail to touch the listener. When it comes to the first group of Schubert Lieder, however, charm is not enough; one needs to feel more involvement with the words, and the same applies to Wolf, although the *Wiegenlied* suits her style admirably. The radiant vocalism cannot fail to add a rich colouring in a song like Richard Strauss's *Der Stern*, while *Schlechtes Wetter* has an attractive lightness of touch. But the outstanding highlight of the first of these two CDs is the songs of Milhaud. Her easy coloratura encompasses the leaps and vocal bravura of the *Chansons de Ronsard* quite spectacularly. These songs need to be extracted for separate issue. On technical grounds there need be no qualms, so vivid is the sound-picture that this might almost be stereo.

The second disc offers stereo recordings made between 1959 and 1961 while the voice was still as fresh as ever. She sings throughout with ease and purity of tone. There is also much evidence of a keenly sensitive mind, not perhaps that of a born Lieder singer, but certainly that of a born musician. In the famous 'Shepherd on the rock' (*Der Hirt auf dem Felsen*) she forms an almost instrumental partnership with the fine clarinet soloist, Heinrich Geuser, and there is no doubt of the appeal of *Die Vögel* when the vocalism is without any kind of blemish. She is certainly sympathetic to the more withdrawn mood of many of the Schumann songs and finds an affinity with Brahms too, especially in *Vergebliches Ständchen* and the lovely *Wiegenlied*. Her directness of manner can be very effective in a song like Wolf's *Der Gärtner*, and she has her own way with the closing Richard Strauss group. Throughout, she is accompanied most sympathetically, and the recording is very real and natural.

Sutherland, Dame Joan (soprano)

'The art of the prima donna' (with ROHCG Ch. & O, Francesco Molinari-Pradelli): ARNE: *Artaxerxes: The soldier tir'd*. HANDEL: *Samson: Let the bright seraphim*. BELLINI: *Norma: Casta diva. I Puritani: Son vergin vezzosa; Qui la voce. La Sonnambula: Come per me sereno*. ROSSINI: *Semiramide: Bel raggio lusinghier*. GOUNOD: *Faust: Jewel song. Roméo et Juliette: Waltz song*. VERDI: *Otello: Willow song. Rigoletto: Caro nome. La Traviata: Ah fors' è lui; Sempre libera*. MOZART: *Die Entführung aus dem Serail: Marten aller Arten*. THOMAS: *Hamlet: Mad scene*. DELIBES: *Lakmé: Bell song*. MEYERBEER: *Les Huguenots: O beau pays*.
✿ (M) *** Decca 452 298-2 (2) [id.].

This ambitious early two-disc recital (from 1960) has now, rather appropriately, been reissued in Decca's Classic Sound series, for the recording on CD is amazingly full and realistic, far more believable than many new digital recordings. It remains one of Dame Joan Sutherland's outstanding gramophone achievements, and it is a matter of speculation whether even Melba or Tetrazzini in their heyday managed to provide sixteen consecutive recordings quite as dazzling as these performances. Indeed, it is the Golden Age that one naturally turns to rather than to current singers when making any comparisons. Sutherland herself, by electing to sing each one of these fabulously difficult arias in tribute to a particular soprano of the past, from Mrs Billington in the eighteenth century, through Grisi, Malibran, Pasta and Jenny Lind in the nineteenth century, to Lilli Lehmann, Melba, Tetrazzini and Galli-Curci in this, is asking to be judged by the standards of the Golden Age. On the basis of recorded reminders she comes out with flying colours, showing a greater consistency and certainly a wider range of sympathy than even the greatest Golden Agers possessed. The sparkle and delicacy of the *Puritani Polonaise*, the freshness and lightness of the Mad scene from Thomas's *Hamlet*, the commanding power of the *Entführung* aria and the breathtaking brilliance of the Queen's aria from *Les Huguenots* are all among the high spots here, while the arias which Sutherland later recorded in her complete opera sets regularly bring performances just as fine – and often finer – than the later versions.

'The age of Bel canto' (with Marilyn Horne (mezzo-soprano), Richard Conrad (tenor), New SO of London, LSO and Chorus, Bonynge): PICCINNI: *La buona figliuola: Furia di donna irata.* HANDEL: *Atalanta: Care selve. Samson: With plaintive notes. Semele: Iris, hence away.* LAMPUGNANI: *Meraspe: Superbo di me stesso.* BONONCINI: *Astarto: Mio caro ben.* ARNE: *Artaxerxes: Oh! too lovely!* SHIELD: *Rosina: Light as thistledown; When William at eve.* MOZART: *Il rè pastore: Voi che fausti ognor donate. Die Zauberflöte: O zittre nicht. Die Entführung aus dem Serail: Ich baue ganz auf deine Stärke.* BOIELDIEU: *Angéla: Ma Fanchette est charmante.* ROSSINI: *Semiramide: Serbami ognor sì fido. Il barbiere di Siviglia: Ecco, ridente.* AUBER: *La Muette de Portici: Ferme tes yeux.* WEBER: *Der Freischütz: Und ob die Wolke sie verhülle.* BELLINI: *Beatrice di Tenda: Angiol di pace. La straniera: Un ritratto? . . . Sventurato il cor che fida.* DONIZETTI: *Don Pasquale: Tornami a dir che m'ami. Lucrezia Borgia: Il segreto per esser felici.* VERDI: *Attila: Santo di patria . . . Allor che i forti corrono.* ARDITI: *Bolero.*
(M) *** Decca 448 594-2(2) [id.].

For some reason this 1963 set has never been issued on CD before in its original complete form. Now it also reappears in Decca's Classic Sound series. In this famous early recital Sutherland generously shared the honours with other singers who, like herself, have a deep concern for restoring the Bel canto tradition. The tenor, Richard Conrad, sings far more tastefully than most of his tenor colleagues, with a pleasing lightness, but it is Marilyn Horne who firmly establishes her claim to stand beside Sutherland as a singer, often outshining her. It is enormously to Sutherland's credit that she welcomes such competition instead of trying to exaggerate her own merits by picking nonentities. Sutherland can easily afford such generosity, and the style of singing throughout the recital has a consistency obviously guided by Richard Bonynge. One may sometimes object to his insistence on a basically mannered style, but in this recital it is generally less obtrusive than hitherto. It is good to be reminded what a fine Mozartian Sutherland is, in the Queen of the Night's aria, and the delightful point of Shield's *Light as thistledown* is irresistible. Her *Semiramide* duet brings a performance of equal mastery. An essential set for all lovers of the art of singing. Full texts and translations are included.

'Grandi voci': BELLINI: *Norma: Sediziose voci . . . Casta diva . . . Ah! bello a me ritorna. I Puritani: Qui la voce sua soave . . . Vien, diletto* (with ROHCG O, Molinari-Pradelli). VERDI: *Attila: Santo di patria . . . Allor che i forti corrono . . . Da te questo or m'è concesso* (with LSO, Bonynge). DONIZETTI: *Lucia di Lammermoor: Ancor non giunse! . . . Regnava nel silenzio; Il dolce suono mi colpi di sua voce! . . . Ardon gl'incensi* (Mad scene). *Linda di Chamounix: Ah! tardai troppo . . . O luce di quest'anima.* VERDI: *Ernani: Surta è la notte . . . Ernani! Ernani, involami. I vespri siciliani: Mercè, dilette amiche* (*Boléro*).
❀ (M) *** Decca 440 404-2 [id.].

Sutherland's 'Grandi voci' disc is one of the most cherishable of all operatic recital records, bringing together the glorious, exuberant items from her very first recital disc, made within weeks of her first Covent Garden success in 1959, and – as a valuable supplement – the poised accounts of *Casta diva* and *Vien, diletto* she recorded the following year as part of the 'Art of the Prima Donna'. It was this 1959 recital which at once put Sutherland firmly on the map among the great recording artists of all time. Even she has never surpassed the freshness of these versions of the two big arias from *Lucia di Lammermoor*, sparkling in immaculate coloratura, while the lightness and point of the jaunty *Linda di Chamounix* aria and the *Boléro* from *I vespri siciliani* are just as winning. The aria from *Attila* comes from 'The age of bel canto' (1963). The sound is exceptionally vivid and immediate, though the accompaniments under Nello Santi are sometimes rough in ensemble.

Tallis Scholars, Peter Phillips

'Christmas carols and motets': Ave Maria settings by JOSQUIN DES PRES; VERDELOT; VICTORIA. *Coventry carol* (2 settings). BYRD: *Lullaby*. PRAETORIUS: *Es ist ein Ros'entsprungen; Joseph lieber, Joseph mein; In dulci jubilo; Wachet auf.* BACH: *Wachet auf.* Medieval carols: *Angelus ad virginem; There is no rose; Nowell sing we.*
*** Ph. Dig. 454 910-2 [id.].

There is something unique about a carol, and even the very early music here has that special intensity of inspiration which brings memorability. There are some familiar melodies too, notably those set by Praetorius; but much of this repertoire will come as refreshingly new to most ears. The singing has a purity of spirit. The CD is very much in the demonstration class for the clear choral image, heard against the ideal acoustics of St Pierre et St Paul, Salle, Norfolk.

'Western Wind Masses': SHEPPARD: *Mass, The Western wynde.* TAVERNER: *Mass, Western Wynde.* TYE: *Mass, Western wind.*
*** Ph. Dig. 454 927-2 [id.].

It was a splendid idea for Gimell to gather together the three key Mass settings which use the well-known source theme, the *Western Wynde*. The performances are as eloquent as we can expect from this source and they are beautifully recorded. Taverner's setting emerges as the most imaginative, but Tye comes pretty close. A most enterprising issue which deserves support.

Tauber, Richard (tenor)

'Opera arias and duos' (with (i) Elisabeth Rethberg; (ii) Lotte Lehmann) from: MOZART: *Don Giovanni.* MEHUL: *Joseph.* OFFENBACH: *Contes d'Hoffmann.* THOMAS: *Mignon.* TCHAIKOVSKY: *Eugene Onegin.* SMETANA: (i) *The Bartered Bride.* WAGNER: *Die Meistersinger.* PUCCINI: *Turandot;* (i) *Madama Butterfly.* KORNGOLD: (ii) *Die tote Stadt.*
(M)(***) EMI mono CDH7 64029-2 [id.].

Starting as early as 1922 with Mozart's *Dalla sua pace* from *Don Giovanni*, then immediately following with the 1939 *Il mio tesoro*, this recital charts Tauber's recording career as far as 1945 with the Méhul *Champs paternels* from *Joseph*. Elisabeth Rethberg joins him now and then, notably in the *Butterfly* excerpt, sung in German. The voice is well caught by the transfers, but there are occasionally some noises off. Yet the standard of singing here is so consistently high that one can readily make allowances. For a sampler, try the glorious *Hoffmann* excerpts (1929) or *Lensky's aria* from *Eugene Onegin* (1923).

Taverner Consort, Choir and Players, Andrew Parrott

'Venetian church music': GABRIELI: *Intonazione del non tono; In ecclesiis; Canzon VIII; Fuga del nono tono; Magnificat.* MONTEVERDI: *Adoramus te, Christ; Currite populi; Christe, adoramus te.* GRANDI: *O quam tu pulchra es.* CASTELLO: *Sonata seconda.* LEGRENZI: *Sonata da chiesa.* LOTTI: *Crucifixus.*
*** EMI Dig. CDC7 54117-2 [id.].

This superb collection brings home what inspired music was written for St Mark's, Venice, in addition to what we know by Monteverdi and the Gabrielis. The tradition persisted and developed over the century which followed, thanks to such composers as Giovanni Legrenzi and Antonio Lotti, a contemporary of Vivaldi. The choral items are aptly punctuated by such fine instrumental pieces as Dario Castello's *Sonata secunda* (with John Holloway the expressive violinist), heightening the impact of such magnificent motets as *In ecclesiis* by Giovanni Gabrieli, in Andrew Parrott's skilled hands expansive as well as brilliant.

'The Carol album': ANON.: *Veni, veni Emmanuel; Stille Nacht; Il est né, le divin enfant; Nova! Nova!; Marche des rois; The Babe of Bethlehem; Verbum caro; Y la Virgen; Glory to God on high; This endere nyghth; O Jesulein süss; God rest you merry, gentlemen; Swete was the song the Virgine soong; Quem pastores laudavere; Quanno nascete ninno; Riu, riu, chiu; Gabriel fram heven-king; Christum wir sollen loben schon; Coventry carol; Gaudete! Verbum caro; In hac anni circulo; Alleluya; A nywe werk is come on hondde; The old year now away is fled; Ding! dong! merrily on high (Branle de l'Officiel).*
*** EMI Dig. CDC7 49809-2 [id.].

'The Carol album' 2: TYE: *While shepherds watched.* HOPKINS: *Three Kings of Orient.* NILES: *I wonder as I wander; Lullay, thou tiny little child; Procedenti Puero-Eya! novus annus est.* ANON.: *Qui crevit celum (Song of the Nunns of Chester); There is no rose of swych Vertu. Quelle est cette odeur agréable?* arr. JOUBERT: *There is no rose of such virtue.* BENDINELLI: *Sonata for 3 trumpets on Joseph, lieber, Joseph mein.* English TRAD.: *All hayle to the dayes; The Lord at first did Adam make.* French TRAD.: *O du fröhliche! O du selige!; Lullay, lullay: Als I lay on Yoolis Night.* Sarum Plainchant: *Letabundus.* THOMSEN: *Sonata for 5 trumpets based upon In dulci jubilo.* MENDELSSOHN: *Hark! the Herald Angels sing* (with WESLEY: organ interlude).
*** EMI Dig. CDC7 54902-2 [id.].

The Taverner group's much-praised first Christmas record was initially missed by us. Now the balance is redressed and we include also the even more successful second collection, which has perhaps greater general appeal. In Volume I Andrew Parrott sought to go back to the originals of these Christmas songs, from early medieval times through almost to the present day, and the result is unusually refreshing, with simplicity the keynote, yet with great variety inherent in the programme itself. The performances are sometimes robust, sometimes tenderly gentle, but always vivid and appealing, and the recording is first class.

The second disc is even more stimulating. It opens and closes with favourites, but in between comes the widest range of styles, with some delightful solo performances: *I wonder as I wander, Lullay, thou little tiny child* and *Lullay, lullay: Als I lay on Yoolis night. The Song of the Chester Nunns* is particularly beautiful, as is the fifteenth-century English version of the famous *There is no rose of swych vertu*, which makes a contrast with Joubert's adaptation of an even barer medieval setting of the same carol. The Sarum Plainchant, *Letabundus*, is made the more telling by a tolling bell, and the two traditional English carols are presented in a robust, colloquial manner. The recording is most realistically balanced, with the ecclesiastical acoustic perfectly managed. It need hardly be said that on both CDs documentation is excellent.

'The Christmas Album' (Festive music from Europe and America): BILLINGS: *Methinks I see an heav'nly host; A virgin unspotted.* FOSTER: *While shepherds watched their flocks.* CEREROLS: *Serafin, quin con dulce harmonia.* Francisco de VIDALES: *Los que fueren de buen gusto.* PRAETORIUS: *Magnificat super Angelus ad pastores.* Marc-Antoine CHARPENTIER: *In nativitatem Domini nostri Jesu Christi canticum.* PASCHA: *Gloria.* arr. GREATOREX: *Adeste fidelis.*
(M) *** Virgin Veritas/EMI Dig. VC5 45155-2 [CDC 54529].

A refreshing new Christmas collection which treads much unfamiliar territory. Opening and closing with jolly carols that sound almost like rustic drinking songs, from the New England composer William Billings – with the chorus giving their pronunciation an appropriate transatlantic twang – the concert moves from a bright baroque setting of *While shepherds watched their flocks*, a new tune, with Bachian trumpets, by John Foster (1762–1822) to a haunting *Gloria* by Edmund Pascha. This represents Slovakia; from France there is a charming Christmas sequence by Marc-Antoine Charpentier. In between comes a gloriously sonorous *Magnificat* by Michael Praetorius and, at last something familiar, *Adeste fidelis*, arranged by Thomas Greatorex in a choral *concerto grosso* style. Best of all are the *Villancicos*, one by Joan Cererols from Catalonia, one even jollier by the seventeenth-century Mexican, Francisco de Vidales, which in their colour and vitality reflect the popular dance music of the time. Performances are as lively as they are stylish and the soloists are excellent. The 1991 recording, made at St John at Hackney, London, has plenty of atmosphere and presence.

Tebaldi, Renata (soprano)

Italian songs (with Richard Bonynge): DONIZETTI: *Me voglio fa'na casa.* MASCAGNI: *La tua stella; Serenata.* TOSTI: *Sogno.* ROSSINI: *L'invito.* ZANDONAI: *L'assiuolo.* CIMARA: *Stornello.* PONCHIELLI: *Noi leggevamo insieme.* PAISOTTI (attrib. PERGOLESI): *Se tu m'ami.* PARADISI: *M'ha presa alla sua ragna.* A. SCARLATTI: *O cessate di piagarmi.* GLUCK: *O, del mio dolce ardor.* RICCI: *Il carrettiere del Vomero.* MERCADANTE: *Lo sposa del marinaro.* BELLINI: *Malinconia, ninfa gentile.* PUCCINI: *E l'uccellino.*
(M) ** Decca 436 202-2 [id.].

With the famous voice still in fine fettle in 1972, Tebaldi here turns to a selection of mostly little-known songs, almost all from famous composers. As the rather gusty, if lilting, opening Donizetti number shows, the performances are earthy and direct and have little of the subtlety one usually associates with art singing. She gives a winningly robust portrayal of the carter trying to get his mule to take the wagon up the steep road home to see his girlfriend (Ricci's *Il carettiere del Vomero*), and she obviously has sympathy with the music of Gluck and Alessandro Scarlatti. Indeed the songs that come off best are the lyrical ones, like

Mascagni's *Serenata*, most beautifully sung, and the gentle lullaby, *E l'uccellino*, of Puccini which ends the recital memorably. Cimara's fruity *Stornello* is done in appropriate ultra-romantic style, but otherwise the highlight is Zandonai's *L'assiuolo* ('The owl') with its reminder of Verdi's *Willow song* from *Otello*. This has a charming postlude for the piano, which Richard Bonynge plays with graceful sensitivity: most of the other accompaniments are simply a vocal support.

'Grandi voci': Arias and excerpts from: PUCCINI: *Madama Butterfly; La Bohème* (with Carlo Bergonzi); *Turandot* (with Mario del Monaco); *Tosca; Gianni Schicchi; Suor Angelica; La Fanciulla del West* (with Cornell MacNeil); *Manon Lescaut*. VERDI: *Aida; Otello* (with Luisa Ribacci); *La forza del destino*. CILEA: *Adriana Lecouvreur*. GIORDANO: *Andrea Chénier*. BOITO: *Mefistofele*. CATALANI: *La Wally*.
(M) *** Decca 440 408-2 [id.].

Those wanting a single-disc, stereo representation of Tebaldi's vocal art could hardly do better than this. It is good that her early mono complete sets of *La Bohème* and *Madama Butterfly* are now again available, and the selection here rightly concentrates on her stereo remakes of the key Puccini operas in the late 1950s, when the voice was still creamily fresh. *Vissi d'arte* (1959) is particularly beautiful. She could be thrilling in Verdi too, as the splendid *Ritorna vincitor!* vibrantly demonstrates, taken from Karajan's complete *Aida*, made in the same year. With a playing time of 75 minutes, this recital should disappoint no one, for the Decca recordings come up as vividly as ever.

'A Tebaldi festival' (with (i) New Philh. O, cond. (ii) Anton Guadago; or (iii) Richard Bonynge; (iv) Monte Carlo Op. O, Fausto Cleva): (i; ii) WAGNER: *Tannhäuser: Salve d'amor, recinto eletto! (Dich teure Halle); Elisabeth's prayer. Lohengrin: Elsa's dream. Tristan und Isolde: Liebestod*. BIZET: *Carmen: Habanera* (with Ambrosian Ch.); *Card scene* (all sung in Italian). SAINT-SAENS: *Samson et Dalila: Amor! i mieie fini proteggi (Amor, viens m'aider); S'apre per te il mio cor (Mon coeur s'ouvre à ta voix)*. MASSENET: *Manon: Addio, o nostro piccolo desco (Adieu, notre petite table); La tua non è mano che mi tocca? (N'est-ce plus ma main?)*. (i; iii) VERDI: *Aida: Ritorna vincitor!*. PUCCINI: *La Bohème: Musetta's waltz song*. (iv) BELLINI: *Norma: Sediziose voci . . . Casta diva* (with Alfredo Mariotti & Turin Ch.); *I Puritani: Qui la voce . . . Vien, diletto. La Sonnambula: Ah! non credea mirarti*. VERDI: *Nabucco: Ben io t'invenni . . . Salgo già del trono. Don Carlo: O don fatale*. Songs: ROSSINI: *Péchés de vieillesse: La regata veneziana* (3 songs in Venetian dialect). LARA: *Granada*. PONCE: *Estrellita*. CARDILLO: *Catari, Catari*. TOSTI: *'A vucchella*. DE CURTIS: *Non ti scordar di me*. RODGERS: *Carousel: If I loved you*.
(M) **(*) Decca 452 456-2 (2) [id.].

What, Wagner in Italian! Tebaldi, for so long a favourite diva, could apparently get away with almost anything during her vintage years with Decca in a collection which ranges into unexpected corners. She amply justifies her choice of language in the rich lyricism of her Wagner, and it is good to hear such a ravishing account of *Musetta's waltz song*, a role she never assumed in the opera house. *Ritorna vincitor!*, too, is unforgettable, both commanding and richly secure – finer than her performance in her complete stereo set (under Karajan). Plainly she has also chosen many of the other items out of sheer affection – the little songs of Lara, Ponce and Tosti – although the dialect songs of Rossini suit her less well. In those lighter items Douglas Gamley's lush arrangements and Bonynge's indulgent accompaniments add to the glamour of the presentation in the warm acoustics of Kingsway Hall. Though all this opening group was recorded as recently as 1969, the voice was still in fine condition, and anyone who has ever responded to the ripe, rich tone of this generous artist should revel in the sweetmeats presented here, not least the lovely melody from Rodgers's *Carousel*. The closing group of Bellini and Verdi excerpts dates from the previous year and was produced by Christopher Raeburn in Monte Carlo. These items have never been issued before and presumably were not passed by Tebaldi herself. Although the two Verdi excerpts (from *Nabucco* and *Don Carlo*) are thrillingly dramatic and in Bellini the singing brings some glorious legato, cabalettas have moments of wildness and intonation is not always secure. Indeed *Ah! non credea mirarti* should not have been issued, for it does the singer no justice. However, for the most part this is an endearing recital, and she is given consistently supportive accompaniments, while the voice never loses its bloom.

Songs and arias (with Giorgio Favaretto, piano): Recital I: Songs: ANON.: *Leggiadri occhi bello*. A. SCARLATTI: *Le violette*. ROSSINI: *Soirées musicales: La promessa*. BELLINI: *Dolente immagine di fille mia; Vanne, o rosa Fortunata*. MARTUCCI: *La canzone dei recordi (Al folto bosco; Cavanta il ruscello; Sul mar la navicella)*. TRAD., arr. FAVARA: *A la barcillunisa*. MASETTI: *Passo e non ti vedo*. TURINA: *Poema en forma de canciones: Cantares*. Arias: HANDEL: *Giulio Cesare: Piangerò la sorte mia*. SARTI: *Giulio Sabino: Lungi dal caro bene*.

Recital II: Songs: A. SCARLATTI: *Chi vuole innamorarsi.* ROSSINI: *Péchés de vieillesse: 3 Songs in Venetian dialect (Anzoleta avanti La Regata; Anzoleta co passa la Regata; Anzoleta dopo la Regata).* Arias: A. SCARLATTI: *Il Seddecia, Re di Gerusalemme: Caldo sangue.* HANDEL: *Armadigi de Gaula: Ah! spietato.* MOZART: *Ridente la calma, K.152; Un moto di gioia, K.579.* BELLINI: *Vaga luna che inargenti; Per pietà, bell'idol mio.* MASCAGNI: *M'ama . . . non m'ama.* RESPIGHI: *Notte.* TOSTI: *'A vucchella.* DAVICO: *O luna che fa lum.*
(B) ** Decca Double 452 472-2 (2) [id.].

Here combined on a Double Decca are a pair of song recitals which Tebaldi recorded fairly early in her career, in 1956 and 1957 respectively, and which have been out of the catalogue for 40 years, although four items – by Scarlatti, Rossini, Mozart and the charming Favara folksong arrangement – were put out on a stereo '45' disc at the beginning of the 1960s. The voice sounds young and fresh but, like many another Italian opera singer, Tebaldi proved hardly a stylist in eighteenth-century music, and the lighter songs do not always suit her big voice. But when she comes to the arias it is a different matter. Cleopatra's lament from the third Act of Handel's *Giulio Cesare* brings a natural, flowing legato, and Sarti's *Lungi dal caro bene* is gently ravishing. The two Bellini ariettas are also appealingly sung, and Verdi's *Stornella* makes a light-hearted contrast, while the three excerpts from Martucci's seven-part mini-cycle about another forsaken maiden, sadly and affectionately remembering past times with her lover, produces a charming and touching response. The following Sicilian folksong, *A la barcillunisa*, soars like a Puccini aria, and the first disc ends seductively with Turina's *Cantares*.

The second recital opens with a vivacious canzonetta, nicely articulated, warning of the dangers of falling in love, and the following Scarlatti and Handel arias do not disappoint. Tebaldi obviously had a soft spot for Rossini's songs in Venetian dialect (which come from his 'Sins of my old age') and she sings them with a lighter touch here than in her later recording (see above). Tebaldi's Mozart singing is freely peppered with intrusive aitches and occasional swerves, but she is back on form in the two Bellini songs and, after a rich-voiced if a very operatic version of Respighi's *Notte*, she finishes in lighter vein with a lilting Tosti favourite – another song she included in her later recital – and a meltingly affectionate account of a colloquial Tuscan song, arranged by Vincenzo Davico. Throughout, Giorgio Favaretto accompanies quite supportively, if without producing a distinctive personality, but the recording balance does not flatter him and the piano sounds rather withdrawn at times.

Terfel, Bryn (bass-baritone), **Malcolm Martineau** (piano)

'The Vagabond and other English songs': VAUGHAN WILLIAMS: *Songs of travel (The vagabond; Let beauty awake; The roadside fire; Youth and love; In dreams; The infinite shining heavens, Whither must I wander; Bright in the ring of words; I have trod the upward and the downward slope).* BUTTERWORTH: *Bredon hill (Bredon hill; Oh fair enough; When the lad for longing sighs; On the idle hill of summer; With rue my heart is laden); The Shropshire lad* (6 songs): *Loveliest of trees; When I was one-and-twenty; Look not in my eyes; Think no more, lad; The lads in their hundreds; Is my team ploughing?* FINZI: *Let us garlands bring (Come away, death; Who is Silvia?; Fear no more the heat of the sun; O mistress mine; It was a lover and his lass).* IRELAND: *Sea fever; The vagabond; The bells of San Marie.*
✿ *** DG Dig. 445 946-2 [id.].

No other collection of English songs has ever quite matched this one in its depth, intensity and sheer beauty. Terfel, the great Welsh singer of his generation, here shows his deep affinity with the English repertory, demonstrating triumphantly in each of the 28 songs that this neglected genre deserves to be treated in terms similar to those of the German *Lied* and the French *mélodie*. The Vaughan Williams songs are perhaps the best known, nine sharply characterized settings of Robert Louis Stevenson which, thanks to Terfel's searching expressiveness and matched by Martineau's inspired accompaniments, reveal depths of emotion hardly suspected.

The five Shakespeare settings by Finzi are just as memorable in their contrasted ways, five of the best-known lyrics from the plays that have been set countless times but which here are given new perspectives, thanks both to the composer and to the singer. The eleven Butterworth settings of Housman are among the finest inspirations of this short-lived composer, and it is good to have three sterling Ireland settings of Masefield, including the ever-popular *Sea fever*, which with Terfel emerges fresh and new. The singer's extreme range of tone and dynamic, down to the most delicate, firmly supported half-tones, is astonishing, adding intensity to one of the most felicitous song-recital records in years. The warm acoustic of Henry Wood Hall gives a glow both to the voice and to the piano.

Operatic arias (with Metropolitan Op. O, James Levine) from: MOZART: *Le nozze di Figaro; Così fan tutte; Don Giovanni; Die Zauberflöte.* WAGNER: *Tannhäuser; Der fliegende Holländer.* OFFENBACH: *Contes d'Hoffmann.* GOUNOD: *Faust.* BORODIN: *Prince Igor.* DONIZETTI: *Don Pasquale.* ROSSINI: *La Cenerentola.* VERDI: *Macbeth; Falstaff.*
✿ *** DG Dig. 445 866-2 [id.].

Not many operatic recital discs match this formidable, keenly enjoyable one offering, in Terfel's own words, 'a future diary of my opera plans' and demonstrating not just the warmth and musical imagination of this brilliant young singer but his range and power too. This account of *Non più andrai* is weightier, marginally broader and even more characterful than the one he recorded as part of John Eliot Gardiner's complete set, and that is typical of his development. Though Mozart remains central to his repertory, it is striking that the most thrilling items of all are those which test him most severely, such as Igor's aria from Borodin's *Prince Igor* and the Dutchman's monologue. The Falstaff monologue from Act I of Verdi's comic masterpiece similarly finds him presenting a larger-than-life portrait with no holds barred over the widest dynamic range. This is singing that is not just strong, varied and imaginative but consistently beautiful too.

Toronto Children's Chorus, Toronto Symphony Orchestra (members), Jean Ashworth Bartle

'Adeste fidelis' (with Louis & Gino Quilico, baritones, Judy Loman, harp): TRAD.: *La cloche de Noël; Un flambeau, Jeannette, Isabella; Pat-a-pan; Fum-fum-fum; Coventry carol; Huron carol; I wonder as I wander.* ADAM: *Cantique de Noël.* BERLIOZ: *L'enfance du Christ; Trio des Ismailites.* BACH/GOUNOD: *Ave Maria.* FRANCK: *Panis angelicus.* SALZEDO: *Concert variations on 'Adeste fidelis'; Concert variations on 'O Tannenbaum'* (both for harp). YON: *Gesù bambino.* ZIMARINO: *Ninna Nanna a Gesù bambino.* BACH: *Cantata No. 208: Chorale: Sheep may safely graze.* PRAETORIUS: *Es ist ein Ros' entsprungen.* REGER: *Mariä Wiegenlied.* GRUBER: *Stille nacht.* LEONTOVITCH: *Carol of the bells.* KOUNTZ: *The sleigh.* arr. CABLE: Christmas medley: *Christmas song; White Christmas; Have yourself a merry little Christmas.*
**(*) CBS Records Dig. SMCD 5119 [id.].

Although coming from Toronto, this programme of Christmas music has a recurring French flavour. The two baritone soloists sing strongly in their various solos and ripely together in duet, as in Franck's *Panis angelicus*. The programme opens with a nicely rustic woodwind introduction for *La cloche de Noël*, while *Pat-a-pan* has a charming flute accompaniment. The children's voices are pristinely fresh here, as in Praetorius's lovely *Est ist ein Ros' entsprungen* and in Reger's use of another familar German melody in *Mariä Wiegenlied*. Their innocence of approach and clean ensemble ensure that the *Carol of the bells*, *Coventry carol* and Kountz's sparkling *Sleigh* evocation are very appealing. There are harp interludes to provide further variety. However, some listeners might find that the sleek sophistication of the modern pop carols at the close of the programme makes an uneasy transition, although they are well presented, and Irving Berlin's *White Christmas* certainly suits children's voices.

Vienna State Opera Chorus and Orchestra

Vienna State Opera Live Edition

Volume I (1933–1936) (with Viorica Ursuleac, Richard Mayr, Eva Hadrabova, Maria Gerhart, Koloman von Pataky, Charles Kullmann, Toti dal Monte, Luigi Montesanto, Aldo Sinnone, Giacomo Lauri-Volpi, Josef Kalenberg, Rudolf Bockelmann, Gertrude Rünger, Kerstin Thorborg, Julius Pölzer, Ezio Pinza, Lauritz Melchior, Anny Konetzni, Josef von Manowarda, Kirsten Flagstad, Torsten Ralf, Luise Helletsgruber, Ludwig Hofmann, Richard Tauber, Jarmila Novotna): excerpts from: R. STRAUSS: *Der Rosenkavalier* (cond. Clemens Krauss). TCHAIKOVSKY: *Eugene Onegin.* VERDI: *Aida* (both cond. Hugo Reichenberger). *Otello* (cond. Victor de Sabata). ROSSINI: *Il barbiere di Siviglia.* BELLINI: *La Sonnambula* (both cond. Giuseppe del Campo). WAGNER: *Tannhäuser* (cond. Robert Heger); *Die Meistersinger; Parsifal; Götterdämmerung* (all cond. Felix Weingartner); *Lohengrin* (cond. Hans Knappertsbusch & Josef Krips). D'ALBERT: *Tiefland.* GOUNOD: *Faust* (both cond. Karl Alwin). LEHAR: *Giuditta* (cond. composer).
(M) (**) Koch Schwann mono 3-1451-2 (2) [id.].

Volume II (1938–39) WAGNER: *Parsifal:* excerpts (with Hans Grahl, Herbert Alsen, Anny Konetzni, Hermann Wiedemann, Luise Helletsgruber, Elisabeth Rutgers, Maria Schober, Esther Réthy, Dora Komarek, Dora With; cond. Hans Knappertsbusch). *Die Meistersinger:* excerpts (with Rudolf Bockelmann, Josef von Manowarda, Eugen Fuchs, Erich Zimmermann, Tiana Lemnitz, Rut Berglund, Nürnberger Opernchor; cond. Furtwängler).
(M) (**(*)) Koch mono 3-1452-2 (2) [id.].

Volume III (1933–42) (with Josef Witt, Else Schürhoff, Else Schulz, Paul Schöffler, Anton Dermota, Herbert Alsen, Hans Hotter, Joachim Sattler, Mela Bulgarinovic, Jakob Sabel, Anny Konetzni, Else Böttcher, Franz Völker, Elisabeth Rethberg, Josef von Manowarda, Jaro Prohaska, Josef Kalenberg, Hermann Wiedemann, Max Lorenz, Rosette Anday, William Wernigk, Luise Helletsgruber, Henny Trundt, Emil Schipper, Marit Angerer; cond. Richard Strauss; Josef Krips): excerpts from: R. STRAUSS: *Salome*. MOZART: *Idomeneo* (new version by Richard Strauss & Lothar Wallerstein). WEBER: *Der Freischütz*. WAGNER: *Die Meistersinger; Siegfried; Götterdämmerung.*
(M) (**(*)) Koch Schwann mono 3-1453-2 (2) [id.].

Volume IV (1933–42) (with Jussi Bjoerling, Maria Nemeth, Rosette Anday, Todor Mazaroff, Alexander Swed, Sigurd Bjoerling, Kerstin Thorborg, Ludwig Hofmann, Piero Pierotic, Maria Reining, Piroska Tutsek, Herbert Alsen, Margit Bokor, Friedrich Ginrod, Alexander Kipnis, Esther Réthy, Karl Norbert, Josef Kalenberg, Koloman von Pataky, Nikolaus Zec, Aenne Michalski, René Maison): excerpts from: VERDI: *Aida* (cond. Victor de Sabata); *Don Carlo* (cond. Bruno Walter). LEONCAVALLO: *I Pagliacci* (cond. Karl Alwin & Wilhelm Loibner). GOUNOD: *Faust* (cond. Josef Krips). WAGNER: *Tannhäuser* (cond. Wilhelm Furtwängler); *Der fliegende Holländer* (cond. Robert Heger). PUCCINI: *Tosca* (cond. Leopold Reichwein); *Turandot* (cond. Rudolf Moralt). SAINT-SAENS: *Samson et Dalila* (cond. Hugo Reichenberger).
(M) (**) Koch Schwann mono 3-1454-2 (2) [id.].

Volume V (1933–43) R. STRAUSS: *Die Aegyptische Helena:* excerpts (with Viorica Ursuleac, Franz Völker, Margit Bokor, Alfred Jerger, Helge Roswaenge; cond. Clemens Krauss); *Die Frau ohne Schatten*: excerpts (with Torsten Ralf, Hilde Konetzni, Elisabeth Höngen, Josef Herrmann, Else Schulz, Herbert Alsen, Emmy Loose, Wenko Wenkoff; cond. Karl Boehm); *Daphne* (with Maria Reining, Alf Rauch, Anton Dermota; cond. Rudolf Moralt).
(M) (***) Koch Schwann mono 3 1455-2 (2) [id.].

Volume VI (1933–42) (with Anny Konetzni, Max Lorenz, Margarete Klose, Helena Braun, Sigmund Roth, Paul Schoeffler, Daniza Ilitsch, Elena Nikolaidi, Mathieu Ahlersmeyer, Herbert Alsen, Ludwig Hofmann, Josef Kalenberg, Alfred Jerger, Viorica Ursuleac, Erich Zimmermann): excerpts from: WAGNER: *Tristan und Isolde* (cond. Furtwängler); *Parsifal; Die Walküre; Siegfried* (cond. Hans Knappertsbusch); *Götterdämmerung* (cond. Leopold Reichwin); *Die Meistersinger* (cond. Clemens Krauss). VERDI: *Aida* (cond. Leopold Ludwig).
(M) (**) Koch Schwann mono 3-1456-2 (2) [id.].

Volume VII (1937–44) (with Todor Mazaroff, Ester Réthy, Elsa Brems, Josef Witt, Alfred Jeger, Margit Bokor, Enid Szantho, Anton Dermota, Alois Pernerstorfer, Karl Friedrich, Else Schulz, Maria Nemeth, Kerstin Thorborg, Alexander Sved) excerpts from: BIZET: *Carmen*. PFITZNER: *Palestrina*. VERDI: *Aida* (all cond. Bruno Walter). SMETANA: *The Bartered bride*. SCHMIDT: *Notre Dame* (cond. Rudolf Moralt).
(M) (**) Koch Schwann mono 3-1457-2 (2) [id.].

Volume VIII (1941–2) VERDI: *Un ballo in maschera:* excerpts (with Max Lorenz, Mathieu Ahlersmeyer, Hilde Konetzni, Elena Nikolaidi, Alda Noni, Sigmund Roth; cond. Karl Boehm); *Aida* excerpts (with Set Svanholm, Daniza Ilitsch, Hans Hotter, Elena Nikolaidi, Josef von Manowarda; cond. Vittorio Gui); *Falstaff* (with Georg Hann, Karl Kronenberg, Esther Réthy, Adele Kern, Anton Dermota, Josef Wit, Mela Mugarinovic, Elena Nikolaidi, William Wernigk; cond. Clemens Krauss).
(M) (*(**)) Koch Schwann mono 3-1458-2 (2) [id.].

Volume IX (1933–37) WAGNER: *Der Ring des Nibelungen*: excerpts from: *Das Rheingold* (with Jaro Prohaska, Nikolaus Zec, Herbert Alsen, Anny Konetzni; cond. Josef Krips); *Die Walküre* (with Ludwig Hofmann, Frank Völker, Hilde Konetzni, Rose Merker, Herbert Alsen, Kerstin Thorborg, Dora With; cond. Bruno Walter); *Siegfried* (with Richard Schubert, Gertrude Kappel, Erich Zimmermann; cond. Robert Heger); *Götterdämmerung* (with Gertrude Kappel, Josef Kalenberg, Emil Schipper, Wanda Achsel, Rosette Anday; cond. Robert Heger).
(M) (**) Koch Schwann mono 3-1459-2 (2) [id.].

Volume X (1934–41) (with Jan Kiepura, Esther Réthy, Alfred Jerger, Alexander Kipnis, Ludwig Hofmann, Mathieu Ahlersmeyer, Maria Reining, Maria Cebotari, Martha Rohs, Viorica Ursuleac, Franz Völker, Maria Nemeth, Hilde Konetzni, Elena Nikolaidi, Herbert Alsen, Vera Mansinger, Max Lorenz, Enid Szantho, Georg Monthy, Dora Komarek): excerpts from: MOZART: *Le nozze di Figaro* (cond. Karl Boehm). WAGNER: *Die Meistersinger* (cond. Clemens Kraus). BIZET: *Carmen* (cond. Karl Alwin). PUCCINI: *Turandot* (cond. Hugo Reichenberger). VERDI: *Don Carlo* (cond. Bruno Walter); *Falstaff* (cond. Wilhelm Loibner). NICOLAI: *Das lustigen Weiber von Windsor* (cond. Felix Weingartner). WAGNER: *Die Meistersinger; Siegfried; Götterdämmerung* (cond. Hans Knappertsbusch); *Tannhäuser* (cond. Wilhelm Furtwängler).
(M) (**) Koch Schwann 3-1460-2 (2) [id.].

Volume XI (1941–1943) WAGNER: *Tristan und Isolde:* highlights (with Max Lorenz, Anny Konetzni, Herbert Alsen, Paul Schoeffler, Margarete Klose, Georg Monthy, Karl Ettl, Willy Franter, Hermann Gallos, cond. Wilhelm Furtwängler)
(M) (**(*)) Koch Schwann 3-1461-2 (2) [id.].

Volume XII (1933–6) (with Lotte Lehmann, Maria Jeritza, Helge Roswaenge, Eva Hadrabova, Elisabeth Schumann, Berthold Sterneck, Richard Mayr, Josef Kalenberg, Friedrich Schorr, Eyvind Laholm, Kerstin Thorborg, Ludwig Hofmann, Joel Berglund, Alexander Svéd, Gunnar Graarud, Emil Schipper): excerpts from: R. STRAUSS: *Der Rosenkavalier* (cond. Hans Knappertsbusch); *Salome*. MASCAGNI: *Cavalleria rusticana* (both cond. Hugo Reichenberger). WAGNER: *Tannhäuser* (cond. Robert Heger); *Die Meistersinger* (cond. Felix Weingartner); *Die Walküre* (cond. Clemens Krauss). GOUNOD: *Faust* (cond. Josef Krips). GIORDANO: *Andrea Chénier* (cond. Robert Heger). LEONCAVALLO: *I Pagliacci* (conductor unknown).
(M) (**) Koch Schwann mono 3-1462-2 [id.].

Volume XIII (1937–9) (with Maria Reining, Julius Pölzer, Herbert Alsen, Wilhelm Rode, Josef von Manowarda, Set Svanholm, Wilhelm Schirp, Beniamino Gigli, Maria Nemeth, Rosette Anday, Alexander Svéd, Alfred Jerger, Paul Schoeffler, Margherita Perras, Alfred Piccaver, Elisabeth Schumann, Emil Schipper, Anny Konetzni, Todor Mazaroff, Elena Nikolaidi): excerpts from: MOZART: *Le nozze di Figaro*. SALMHOFER: *Ivan Sergejewitsch Tarassenko*. SCHMIDT: *Notre Dame* (all cond. Wilhelm Loibner). PUCCINI: *La Fanciulla del West* (cond. Hans Duhan). LEONCAVALLO: *I Pagliacci*. MASCAGNI: *Cavalleria rusticana*. VERDI: *Aida* (all cond. Karl Alwin). WAGNER: *Parsifal* (cond. Hans Knappertsbusch); *Der fliegende Holländer; Tannhäuser* (cond. Leopold Reichwein). WEBER: *Der Freischütz* (cond. Rudolf Moralt).
(M) (**) Koch Schwann 3-1463-2 (2) [id.].

Volume XIV (1933) Clemens Krauss conducts WAGNER: *Das Rheingold* (with Josef von Manowarda, Bella Paalen, Hermann Wiedemann, Viorica Ursuleac, Gunnar Graarud, Viktor Madin, Josef Kalenberg, Erich Zimmermann, Franz Markhoff, Luise Helletsgruber); *Die Walküre* (with Friedrich Schorr, Maria Jeritza, Felice Hüni-Mihacsek, Franz Völker, Richard Mayr, Rosette Anday, Aenne Michalski); *Götterdämmerung* (Henny Trundt, Josef Kalenberg, Rosette Anday, Josef von Manowarda, Emil Schipper); *Die Meistersinger* (Rudolf Bockelmann, Nikolaus Zec, Hermann Wiedemann, Viorica Ursuleac, Erich Zimmermann, Karl Ettl, Gertrude Rünger); *Parsifal* (Gunnar Graarud, Josef von Manowarda, Emil Schipper, Gertrude Rünger, Hermann Wiedemann).
(M) (**) Koch Schwann mono 3-1464-2 (2) [id.].

Volume XV (1933–41) R. STRAUSS: *Arabella:* excerpts (with Viorica Ursuleac, Margit Bokor, Alfred Jerger, Adele Kern, Gertrude Rünger, Richard Mayr); *Friedenstag:* complete (with Hans Hotter, Viorica Ursuleac, Herbert Alsen, Josef Wit, Hermann Wiedemann, Mela Bugarinovic; both cond. Clemens Krauss); *Ariadne auf Naxos* (with Anny Konetzni), Sev Svanholm, Adele Kern, Else Schulz, Alfred Jerger, Alexander Pichler, Alfred Muzzarelli; cond. Rudolf Moralt).
(M) (**(*)) Koch Schwann mono 3-1465-2 (2) [id.].

Volume XVI (1933–41) (with Viorica Ursuleac, Franz Völker, Gertrude Rünger, Josef von Manowarda, Rosette Anday, Zdenka Zika, Emil Schipper, Richard Mayr, Hilde Konetzni, Anny Konetzni, Wanda Achsel, Karl Hammes, Julius Pölzer, Alfred Jerger): excerpts from: WAGNER: *Rienzi; Götterdämmerung* (cond. Josef Krips & Clemens Krauss); *Lohengrin* (cond. François Rühlmann); *Die Walküre* (cond. Clemens Krauss & Hans Knappertsbusch). LEONCAVALLO: *I Pagliacci* (cond. Karl Alwin). VERDI: *Don Carlo; Otello*. R. STRAUSS: *Die Frau ohne Schatten* (all cond. Clemens Krauss); *Elektra* (cond. Hans Knappertsbusch).
(M) (**) Koch Schwann mono 3-1466-2 (2) [id.].

Volume XVII (1936–1943): Hans Knappertsbusch conducts (with Erna Berger, Maria Reining, Josef von Manowarda, Tiana Lemnitz, Michael Bohnen, Franz Völker, Paul Kötter, Herbert Alsen, Margarethe Teschemacher, Anny Konetzni, Hilde Konetzni, Rose Pauly, Set Svanholm, Max Lorenz, Norbert Ardelli, Margit Bokor, Elisabeth Schumann, Ella Flesch): excerpts from: MOZART: *Die Zauberflöte*. WEBER: *Der Freischütz*. WAGNER: *Lohengrin; Götterdämmerung; Tannhäuser*. R. STRAUSS: *Elektra; Der Rosenkavalier*. WOLF-FERRARI: *Jewels of the Madonna*.
(M) (**) Koch Schwann mono 3-1467-2 (2) [id.].

Volume XVIII (1944): WAGNER: *Die Meistersinger:* highlights (with Josef Herrmann, Kurt Böhme, Erich Kunz, Peter Klein, Maria Reining, Martha Rohs; cond. Karl Boehm); *Lohengrin:* highlights (with Franz Völker, Joseph von Manowarda, Maria Müller, Jaro Prohaska, Margarete Klose; cond. Heinz Teitjen).
(M) (**(*)) Koch Schwann mono 3-1468-2 [id.].

Volume XIX (1941–3) (with Set Svanholm, Hilde Konetzni, Helena Braun, Paul Schoeffler, Alfred Poell, Piroshka Tutsek, Julius Pölzer, Kurt Böhme, Maria Reining, Max Lorenz, Joel Berglund, Maria Nemeth, Todor Mazaroff, Esther Réthy): excerpts from: GLUCK: *Iphigénie in Aulis*. SMETANA: *Dalibor* (both cond. Leopold Ludwig). WAGNER: *Tannhäuser* (cond. Leopold Reichwein); *Die Meistersinger* (cond. Karl Boehm); *Die fliegende Holländer* (cond. Leopold Reichwein); *Die Walküre* (cond. Hans Knappertsbusch & Wolfgang Martin); *Götterdämmerung*. WEBER: *Der Freischütz* (both cond. Hans Knappertsbusch).
(M) (**) Koch Schwann mono 3-1469-2 (2) [id.].

Volume XX (1935–7): Wilhelm Furtwängler conducts WAGNER: excerpts from *Die Walküre* (with Franz Völker, Maria Müller, Walter Grossman, Anny Konetzki, Alfred Jerger, Rosette Andray); *Die Meistersinger* (with Karl Kamann, Herbert Alsen, Max Lorenz, Erich Zimmermann, Maria Reining, Enid Szantho); *Tannhäuser* (with Max Lorenz & Maria Müller, Anna Báthy).
(M) (**(*)) Koch Schwann mono 3-1470-2 (2) [id.].

Volume XXI (1941–4) (with Karl Kronenberg, Paul Schoeffler, Maria Cebotari, Anton Dermota, Alfred Jerger, Erich Kunz, Josef Witt, Hans Hotter, Else Schürhoff, Esther Réthy, Helena Braun, Elena Nikolaidi, Herbert Alsen, Danica Ilitsch): excerpts from: MOZART: *Così fan tutte* (cond. Clemens Krauss). R. STRAUSS: *Capriccio* (cond. Karl Boehm). PFITZNER: *Palestrina* (cond. Rudolf Moralt). ORFF: *Carmina Burana*. BORODIN: *Prince Igor*. EGK: *Columbus* (1st version) (all cond. Leopold Ludwig); *Joan von Zarissa* (ballet; cond. composer).
(M) (*(*)) Koch Schwann mono 3-1471-2 (2) [id.].

Volume XXII (1940–41) (with Hans Hotter, Helena Braun, Josef von Manowarda, Daga Söderqvist, Joachim Sattler, William Wernigk, Mela Bugarinovic, Irma Beilke, Erich Kunz): excerpts from: LEONCAVALLO: *Der Bajazzo* (cond. Anton Paulik). WAGNER: *Der fliegende Holländer; Die Walküre* (cond. Rudolf Moralt); *Parsifal; Siegfried* (cond. Hans Knappertsbusch); *Götterdämmerung* (cond. Leopold Reichwein). MOZART: *Le nozze di Figaro* (cond. Clemens Krauss).
(M) (**) Koch Schwann mono 3-1472-2 (2) [id.].

Volume XXIII (1943): Karl Boehm conducts Wagner & Richard Strauss: WAGNER: *Die Meistersinger:* excerpts (with Josef Herrmann, Erich Kunz, Max Lorenz, Peter Klein, Maria Reining). R. STRAUSS: *Ariadne auf Naxos:* complete (with Maria Reining, Max Lorenz, Alda Noni, Irmgard Seefried, Paul Schoeffler, Josef Witt, Alfred Muzzarelli, Friedrich Jelinek, Hermann Baier, Hans Scheiger, Emmy Loose, Melanie Frutschnigg, Elisabeth Rutgers, Erich Kunz, Richard Sallaba, Marjan Rus, Peter Klein).
(M) (**(*)) Koch Schwann mono 3-1473-2 (2) [id.].

Volume XXIV (1937–1943): Hans Knappertsbusch conducts excerpts from *Der Ring des Nibelungen:* (with Ludwig Hofmann, Enid Szantho, Hans Hotter, Helena Braun, Max Lorenz, Hilde Konetzni, Set Svanholm, Paul Schoeffler, Mela Bugarinovic, Adele Kern, Erich Zimmermann, Josef Kalenberg, Emil Schipper, Elisabeth Schumann, Nikolaus Zec, Anny Konetzni, Fred Destal, Alexander Kipnis).
(M) (**) Koch Schwann mono 3-1474-2 (2) [id.].

This astonishing collection of historic recordings, covering an enormous range of performances at the Vienna State Opera between 1933 and 1943, owes its existence to the fact that a certain Herr May set up primitive recording equipment backstage in the opera house and simply recorded what he could. The excerpts were usually short, but in two instances they cover complete Strauss operas: *Friedenstag* from 1938 in Volume 15 and *Ariadne auf Naxos* from 1943 in Volume 23. Volume 5 is another one to investigate, bringing together highlights from three Strauss operas, all discussed separately, above, under their composer entries. More problematically, the quality of recording varies enormously too, with many of them no better than the primitive cylinder recordings being made at the turn of the last century. The problem was the equipment, which involved recording direct on to a disc, which for best results had to be warmed to a certain temperature. That was often not possible, but the editors of this collection have sifted out the best and most interesting material and have used modern technology to eliminate the worst problems.

Even so, in most instances a 'creative ear' has to be used for full enjoyment, and the series will mainly attract vocal specialists for, not surprisingly, the voices are caught better than the orchestra. Sometimes, as in two brief excerpts from the Woodbird's music in *Siegfried* (Volume 3), the singer, Luise Helletsgruber, standing in the wings is very much on-stage for the recording machine. Another hazard is that sometimes there is the noise of scene-shifting or stagehands chattering, oblivious to what is otherwise going on. One of the least enjoyable sets of excerpts is of a 1942 performance of Carl Orff's *Carmina Burana* (Volume 21), constantly interrupted by chattering and with any sharpness in the performance under Leopold Ludwig completely blunted by the dim sound. Yet the baritone in that is Karl Kronenberg, one of the little-known singers represented here, who emerges as a fine artist. In the same volume he sings Guglielmo in *Così fan tutte* opposite Anton Dermota (in German), but the rest of the volume is very variable, even if it is good to hear Maria Cebotari in part of the Countess's final monologue from Strauss's *Capriccio* in the Vienna première (March 1944).

More than any other composer, Wagner is well represented in this vast archive of recordings. Quite apart from these seven volumes devoted entirely to Wagner, the composer is represented in a high proportion of the rest, often with the most valuable recordings of all. One big snag is that Wagner, more than any other major opera composer, depends on the orchestra, and these recordings convey only a sketchy idea of what orchestral sounds were emerging into the theatre from the pit. The voices on stage are different, and there are many incidental passages which one cherishes, particularly with such Heldentenoren as Franz Volker and Josef Kalenberg hardly known on commercial recordings. Max Lorenz too, the leading Heldentenor of his day, was too little recorded, and he is well represented here, as is the dramatic soprano, Maria Müller. But such conductors as Furtwängler, Walter and Boehm are already represented in the catalogues with recordings covering much of the same material, either complete or in much more consistent excerpts, recorded in far more vivid sound, both in the studio and from live performances. Even so, any Wagnerian curious about the singing tradition of the 1930s – dramatically good but vocally living up to legendary status only occasionally – will find much fascinating material here. For all the horrors of crumbly sound, it is still a compelling experience to listen in on a great opera-house.

Italian operas are almost invariably sung in German, with Volume 8 offering excerpts from Verdi's *Ballo*, *Aida* and *Falstaff* all in German. One fleeting delight comes in Volume 13 when by some improbable casting Elisabeth Schumann as Nedda communes with the birds in an excerpt from *I Pagliacci* under Karl Alwin in May 1937. The magic of the moment is vividly caught. Also in that volume are three examples of Alfred Piccaver's singing, for long a favourite in Vienna but too little recorded. From *Pagliacci* he sings firmly and resonantly in *Vesti la giubba* (in German) but very slowly, while his Turiddu from *Cavalleria rusticana* is most disappointing, and so is Dick Johnson's big aria from Puccini's *Fanciulla del West*, taken very slowly and sentimentally. There are excerpts from Mozart's *Nozze di* (or *Hochzeit von*) *Figaro* in that volume too, but the only really enjoyable performance is from Paul Schoeffler as *Figaro*.

Among the outstanding tenors in the Italian and French repertory is the Bulgarian, Todor Mazarov, always a favourite in Vienna, who had a long career but curiously remained neglected in the world of recording. In *Don Carlo* (Volume 4) he sings in his native language, only later using German. He also appears as Radames in *Aida* and as Don José in *Carmen*, both with Bruno Walter conducting (Volume 7). Yet, fine as he is, he yields before Jussi Bjoerling, who is also heard as Radames, singing in Swedish with Victor de Sabata conducting (Volume 4). The physical thrill of Bjoerling's singing, as well as the expressive variety compared with other tenors, comes over vividly. Other valuable items include the only available recordings made on stage by the legendary Maria Jeritza (Volume 12), all taken from performances in 1933 – Santuzza in *Cavalleria rusticana*, as well as Brünnhilde in *Walküre* and Salome. Far more clearly than her few studio recordings, they explain her extraordinary magnetism. Another unique item, giving an idea of stage presence, is of Toti dal Monte singing a snatch of Bellini's *La Sonnambula* in Italian (Volume 1). As a sampler there is much to be said for Volume 1, which ranges wide over the whole repertory, with many of the most celebrated names represented, a longer list than in other volumes, both of singers and of conductors.

The examples of Mozart are generally disappointing, but in Volume 3 it is interesting to hear Richard Strauss's heavyweight treatment of *Idomeneo* in his own much-edited edition for, though the singing is largely indifferent and the strings lumber along, the woodwind playing is often stylish. In that volume the *Idomeneo* excerpts complete a whole disc of Strauss conducting. The rest is taken from two performances of *Salome*, given in 1942, both with Else Schulz rather raw in the title-role, but with Paul Schoeffler in one and the young Hans Hotter in the other both tellingly characterful and clean-focused as Jokanaan. The other disc in Volume 3 has Josef Krips conducting Weber's *Der Freischütz* (1933) as well as three

Wagner operas, *Meistersinger* (1937), *Siegfried* (1937) and *Götterdämmerung* (1933). Max in *Der Freischütz* is sung superbly by Franz Volker, another fine artist too little-known, thanks to his sparse recordings. Max Lorenz, the leading Heldentenor of his day, is predictably a fine Siegfried, but also impressive is Josef Kalenberg both as Siegfried in *Götterdämmerung* and as Walther in an all-too-sketchy excerpt from the *Prize Song* rehearsal in Act III of *Meistersinger*.

Provided one is prepared to use a creative ear and to sift out the good from the bad, there is much to enjoy in eavesdropping on a great opera-house at a period, often regarded as legendary but which turns out to be more variable than expected in quality of performance.

Vishnevskaya, Galina (soprano)

Russian songs (with (i) Mstislav Rostropovich, piano; (ii) Russian State SO, Igor Markevitch): (i) TCHAIKOVSKY: *None but the lonely heart; Not a word, beloved; Heed not, my love*. PROKOFIEV: *5 Poems of Anna Akhmatova*. MUSSORGSKY: *Songs and dances of death;* (ii) orch. Markevitch: *Cradle song; The dazzling lassie; Night; Where are you, dear star?; Scallywag; The Dnieper*.
(M) *** Ph. 446 212-2 [id.].

The young Vishnevskaya sang many of these songs when she came to the Aldeburgh Festival in 1961 and there is the same intensity here as there was in the Jubilee Hall for that suddenly arranged and most exciting concert. Vishnevskaya even overcomes what one would have imagined were impossible difficulties of transferring the Mussorgsky *Songs and dances of death* from bass to soprano. The result is not always what one imagines the composer intended – but no one could miss how compelling it is. Only occasionally under pressure does the voice grow hard. The singer's mastery of vocal characterization comes out repeatedly. *None but the lonely heart* shows Vishnevskaya at her most impressive, recognizably Russian in her timbre but steadier than most. Her sensitive singing of the Prokofiev songs shows how completely they follow the broad Russian tradition. The recording is rather reverberant, with the piano sounding unusually close for a song recital. Rostropovich, as at Aldeburgh, seems just as much at home accompanying his wife on the piano as playing his cello, and certainly there is the same consummate artistry. The other Mussorgsky songs, including the composer's very first, *Where are you, dear star?*, and the *Cradle song*, a lullaby sung to a dying child, were recorded in Russia a year later with orchestrations by Markevitch, who accompanies with the Russian State Symphony Orchestra. They are hardly less compulsive.

Von Otter, Anne Sofie (soprano)

'*Wings in the night*' (Swedish songs; with Bengt Forsberg, piano): PETERSON-BERGER: *Aspåkers-polska (Aspåker's polka); Återkomst (Return); Böljeby-vals (Böljeby waltz); Som stjärnorna på himmeln (Like the stars in the sky); Marits visor (3 songs, Op. 12); Intet är som väntanstider (Nothing is like the time of waiting); När jag går för mig själv (When I walk by myself)*. SJOGREN: *6 Songs from Julius Wolff's Tannhäuser*. Sigurd von KOCH: *I månaden Tjaitra (In the month of Tjaitra); Af Lotusdoft och månens sken (Of lotus scent and moonshine); De vilda svanarna (The wild swans) (3 songs)*. STENHAMMAR: *Jungfru blond och jungfru brunett (Miss Blond and Miss Brunette); I lönnens skymning (In the maple's shade); Jutta kommer till Folkungarna (Jutta comes to the Volkungs); En strandvisa (A seaside song); Det far ett skepp (A ship is sailing); Vandraren (The wanderer)*. RANGSTROM: *Afskedet (The farewell); Gammalsvenskt (Old Swedish); Melodi; Pan; Bön till natten (Supplication to night); Vingar i natten (Wings in the night)*. ALFVEN: *Skogen sover (The forest is asleep); Jag kysser din vita hand (I kiss your white hand)*.
✿ *** DG Dig. 449 189-2 [id.].

So often Swedish singers, once they have made a name for themselves in the world, neglect their native repertoire in favour of Schumann, Brahms, Strauss and Wolf. Anne Sofie von Otter is an exception and, fresh from her recent successes in Scandinavian repertoire, above all her Grieg *Haugtussa* and her Sibelius recitals on BIS, she gives us a splendid anthology of Swedish songs. The disc takes its name from one of Ture Rangström's most haunting songs, *Vingar i natten* (*Wings in the night*), and, indeed, his are some of the loveliest songs in the Swedish *romans* repertoire. (*Romans* is the Nordic equivalent of *Lied*.) *Bön till natten* (*Prayer to the night*) is arguably the most beautiful of all Swedish songs and has the innocence and freshness of Grieg combined with a melancholy and purity that are totally individual. Von Otter also includes songs by the composer-critic, Wilhelm Peterson-Berger, whose criticism was much admired in his native Sweden and who was compared with Bernard Shaw (he is in fact an opinionated windbag) but whose songs have a certain wistful charm. The Stenhammar songs are among his finest, and she adds some familiar Alfvén and less familiar repertoire by Emil Sjögren and Sigurd (not to be confused with Erland) von Koch. A disc to be treasured.

Walker, Norman (bass)

'A portrait of Norman Walker': HANDEL: *Acis and Galatea: I rage, I melt, I burn . . . O ruddier than the cherry. Judas Maccabeaus: I feel the deity within . . . Arm, arm ye brave. Messiah: Why do the nations; The trumpet shall sound.* HAYDN: *The Creation: And God said; Now heav'n in fullest glory.* ELGAR: *Dream of Gerontius: Jesu by that shuddering dread.* HOLBROOKE: *Dylan: Sea King's song; The Children of Don: Noden's song.* GOUNOD: *Faust: Then leave her* (final trio; with Joan Cross, Webster Booth). MARCELLO: *Le quattro Stagioni: Dalle cime del'Api . . . Venti olà.* LANDI: *La morte d'Orfeo: Bevi, bevi.* PURCELL: *What can be done* (trio; with Aldred Deller, Richard Lewis). STORACE: *The pretty creature.* LANE WILSON: *False Phyllis.* HAYNES: *Off to Philadelphia.* CAPEL: *Love could I only tell thee!* MOZART: *The Magic Flute: O Isis and Osiris; The Abduction from the Seraglio: Ah, my pretty brace of fellows.*
✿ (M) (***) Dutton mono CDLX 7021 [id.].

Born in 1907, Norman Walker was by training one of the last of the great pre-war British basses, but his sense of style, his clean focus and his technical finesse gave him in many ways a linking role, ushering in a new generation of British singers. This splendid compilation, prepared in collaboration with Walker's record-archivist son, Malcolm, gives a vivid idea of a singer whose career was sadly cut short when he was still in his forties. The earliest recording, never previously published, is of *O Isis and Osiris* from *The Magic Flute*, made when he was only 21, with the voice already fully formed, but in an old-fashioned, rallentando style. Three of the recordings date from the 1930s – two excerpts from rare Holbrooke operas and the glorious *Trio* from Gounod's *Faust* with Joan Cross and Webster Booth – but most are from the early post-war period, when Walker contributed to such classic recordings as Sargent's pioneering version of Elgar's *Dream of Gerontius* (thrillingly represented here in one of the most vivid transfers) and both of his *Messiah* recordings, as well as the HMV 'History of Music in Sound'. Full and dark as the voice is, Walker's agility in ornaments and rapid divisions is phenomenal, not least in another, previously unpublished recording, a witty account of Osmin's aria from *The Seraglio*, done in English with Gerald Moore accompanying. What is remarkable is not only the charisma and vocal richness but also the clarity of the diction. The splendid Dutton transfers are among his finest yet, with plenty of body in the sound and the voice often given an extraordinarily real presence.

Walker, Sarah (mezzo-soprano), Roger Vignoles (piano)

'Dreams and fancies' (Favourite English songs): IRELAND: *If there were dreams to sell.* DELIUS: *Twilight fancies.* ARMSTRONG GIBBS: *Silver; Five eyes.* VAUGHAN WILLIAMS: *Silent noon; The water mill.* WARLOCK: *The fox; Jillian of Berry; The first mercy; The night.* SULLIVAN: *Orpheus with his lute.* HOWELLS: *King David; Gavotte; Come sing and dance; The little road to Bethlehem.* STANFORD: *The monkey's carol.* BRIDGE: *Isobel.* CLARKE: *The seal man; The aspidistra.* HAVELOCK NELSON: *Dirty work.* HOIBY: *Jabberwocky.* QUILTER: *Now sleeps the crimson petal.* GURNEY: *Sleep.* DUNHILL: *The cloths of heaven.*
*** CRD Dig. CRD 3473; *CRDC 4173* [id.].

A well-designed and delightful programme, and it is good to see the Roger Quilter favourite, *Now sleeps the crimson petal*, back in favour alongside both the familiar and unfamilar items included here. Dunhill's *The cloths of heaven*, too, leaves the listener wanting more. The secret of a miscellaneous (72 minutes) recital like this is for each song to lead naturally into the next, and that is what happens here, while the listener relaxes and enjoys each contrasted setting as it flows by. Sarah Walker is in inspired form and is very well accompanied.

Way, Anthony (treble), St Paul's Cathedral Choir, ECO, John Scott

'The choirboy's Christmas': arr. WILCOCKS: *O come all ye faithful; Sussex carol; Once in Royal David's city; Away in a manger; Ding dong merrily on high; See amid the winter's snow.* GRUBER: *Silent night.* GARDNER: *Tomorrow shall be my dancing day.* BRITTEN: *Ceremony of carols: Balulalow* (with Lucy Wakeford, harp). HANDEL, arr. RUTTER: *Joy to the world.* arr. WALFORD DAVIES: *The holly and the ivy.* DARKE: *In the bleak midwinter.* arr. LLOYD: *What Child is this?.* arr. CARTER: *A maiden most gentle.* COOKE: *O men from the fields.* CORNELIUS: *The three kings.* arr. HAZEL: *Past three o'clock.* SCHEIDT: *O little one sweet.* arr. ALEXANDER: *Do you hear what I hear?.* MENDELSSOHN, arr. WILLCOCKS: *Hark! the herald angels sing.*
**(*) Decca Dig. 455 050-2; *455 050-4* [id.].

Though not likely to repeat the success of '*The Choir*', this traditional carol collection, led agreeably by the pure, slightly wan treble of Anthony Way, has a direct sincerity and absence of sentimentality which will rightly please this remarkable treble's many admirers. It is beautifully recorded (in the summer of 1996) in the Temple Church, where Ernest Lough's famous record of *O for the wings of a dove* was made some seven decades earlier. Way's voice remains as fresh as ever. The programme opens and closes resplendently with *O come all ye faithful* and *Hark! the herald angels sing* and, among the other Willcocks arrangements, *Ding dong merrily on high* stands out; of those made by John Rutter, *Joy to the world* and *The twelve days of Christmas* are characteristically memorable. One notices also how beautifully the singers bring out the meaning of the words in the Walford Davies version of *The holly and the ivy*. But for the most part this is a fairly intimate programme. Anthony Way is at his best in the radiant Britten *Balulalow* and *What child is this?*, a delightful setting of *Greensleeves*, with lute accompaniment (Tom Finucaine), and in the very effective and more elaborate *Do you hear what I hear?*.

Westminster Cathedral Choir, David Hill

'Treasures of the Spanish Renaissance': GUERRERO: *Surge propera amica mea; O altitudo divitiarum; O Domine Jesu Christe; O sacrum convivium; Ave, Virgo sanctissima; Regina coeli laetare.* LOBO: *Versa est in luctum; Ave Maria; O quam suavis es, Domine.* VIVANCO: *Magnificat octavi toni.*
*** Hyperion CDA 66168 [id.].

This immensely valuable collection reminds us vividly that Tomas Luis de Victoria was not the only master of church music in Renaissance Spain. Francisco Guerrero is generously represented here, and the spacious serenity of his polyphonic writing (for four, six and, in *Regina coeli laetare*, eight parts) creates the most beautiful sounds. A criticism might be made that tempi throughout this collection, which also includes fine music by Alonso Lobo and a superb eight-part *Magnificat* by Sebastian de Vivanco, are too measured, but the tension is held well, and David Hill is obviously concerned to convey the breadth of the writing. The singing is gloriously firm, with the long melismatic lines admirably controlled. Discreet accompaniments (using Renaissance double harp, bass dulcian and organ) do not affect the essentially a cappella nature of the performances. The Westminster Cathedral acoustic means the choral tone is richly upholstered, but the focus is always firm and clear.

Westminster Cathedral Choir, James O'Donnell

'Masterpieces of Mexican polyphony': FRANCO: *Salve regina.* PADILLA: *Deus in adiutorium; Mirabilia testimonium; Lamentation for Maundy Thursday; Salve regina.* CAPILLAS: *Dis nobis, Maria; Magnificat.* SALAZAR: *O sacrum convivium.*
*** Hyperion Dig. CDA 66330 [id.].

The Westminster Choir under James O'Donnell are finding their way into hitherto unexplored Latin vocal repertoire – and what vocal impact it has! These musicians were employed in the new cathedrals when Spain colonized Mexico; only Capillas was native-born (though of Spanish descent). Padilla shows he had brought over a powerful Renaissance inheritance with him and uses double choir interplay to spectacularly resonant effect. Not all the other music is as ambitious as this, but there is a devotional concentration of feeling which illuminates even the simpler settings. The singing has the body and fervour this music needs, and the choir is splendidly recorded.

'Masterpieces of Portuguese polyphony': CARDOSO: *Lamentations for Maundy Thursday; Non mortui; Sitvit anima mea; Mulier quae erat; Tulerunt lapides; Nos autem gloriosi.* REBELO: *Panis angelicus.* DE CRISTO: *3 Christmas responsories; Magnificat a 8; Ave Maria a 8; Alma redemptoris mater; Ave maris stella; O crux venerabilis; Sanctissima quinque martires; Lachrimans sitivit; De profundis.*
*** Hyperion Dig. CDA 66512 [id.].

With the help of the Tallis Scholars we have already discovered Manuel Cardoso and the unique character of Portuguese Renaissance music. The present collection duplicates four of the motets on the Tallis Scholars' CD, but the Westminster performances are slightly more robust and add to their character. The *Lamentations for Maundy Thursday* show the composer at his most imaginatively expressive, 'a resplendent example of his chromatic serenity', as Ivan Moody, the writer of the excellent notes on this CD, aptly puts it. The music of Cardoso's contemporary, Pedro de Cristo (*c.* 1550–1618) is hardly less individual. His *Magnificat a 8* for two choirs is particularly arresting, as is the much simpler *O magnum mysterium*, while the *Sanctissimi quinque martires* (celebrating five Franciscans who were killed in 1220 while attempting to convert Moroccan Moslems) has a radiant, flowing intensity. Rebelo's *Panis angelicus* is rich in its harmonic feeling, and Fernandez's *Alma redemptoris mater* ends the programme in a mood of quiet contemplation.

'Adeste fidelis' (with Ian Simcock): WADE: *O come all ye faithful.* TRAD.: *Gabriel's message; O come, O come Emanuel; Ding dong merrily on high; A maiden most gentle; I wonder as I wander; O little town of Bethlehem; In dulci jubilo; The holly and the ivy.* GAUNTLETT: *Once in Royal David's city.* DARKE: *In the bleak mid-winter.* CORNELIUS: *The three kings.* PETRUS: *Of the Father's love begotten.* KIRKPATRICK: *Away in a manger.* WARLOCK: *Bethlehem down.* HADLEY: *I sing of a maiden.* GRUBER: *Silent night.* HOWELLS: *Sing lullaby.* TAVENER: *The Lamb.* PARRY: *Welcome yule.* MENDELSSOHN: *Hark the Herald Angels sing.*
*** Hyperion Dig. CDA 66668 [id.].

An extremely well-sung traditional carol collection. Although many of the arrangers are distinguished names, the arrangements of traditional carols are essentially simple, and the concert makes a great appeal by the quality of the singing and the beautiful digital recording, with the choir perfectly focused and realistically set back just at the right distance within the cathedral acoustic. The programme is spiced with one or two attractive modern settings, notably Patrick Hadley's ravishing *I sing of a maiden* and John Tavener's highly individual carol, *The Lamb.*

'Favourite motets from Westminster Cathedral': MENDELSSOHN: *Ave Maria; Hymn of Praise: I waited for the Lord.* BACH: *Cantata No. 147: Jesu, joy of man's desiring.* FRANCK: *Panis angelicus.* MAWBY: *Ave verum corpus.* ROSSINI: *O salutaris hostia.* HARRIS: *Faire is the heaven.* HOLST: *Ave Maria; Nunc dimittis.* GOUNOD: *Ave Maria.* FAURE: *Maria Mater gratiae.* ELGAR: *Ave verum corpus.* MOZART: *Ave verum.* GRIEG: *Ave maris stella.* DE SEVERAC: *Tantum ergo.* VILLETTE: *Hymne à la Vierge.* SCHUBERT: *The Lord is my Shepherd.*
*** Hyperion Dig. CDA 66669 [id.].

The Westminster Cathedral Choir is a traditional men and boys choir of the highest calibre. The treble line is particularly rich, and this is essentially a satisfyingly full-throated concert, although there is no lack of dynamic nuance, and phrasing always flows naturally and musically. Franck's *Panis angelicus*, which gives the collection its sobriquet, is splendidly ripe, and other favourites like Bach's *Jesu, joy of man's desiring* and Mozart's *Ave verum* are most satisfyingly done. Elgar's *Ave verum* too is a highlight, and Schubert's lovely setting of *The Lord is my Shepherd* is very successful in its English version. Among the novelties, De Séverac's *Tantum ergo* and the touching *Hymne à la Vierge* of Pierre Villette stand out, and the concert ends with a memorable account of Holst's setting of *Nunc dimittis*, which opens ethereally and then soars into the heavens: the trebles are superbly ardent at the climax. The recording is outstandingly full and the cathedral ambience is caught without too much blurring.

Winchester Cathedral Choir, Waynflete Singers, Bournemouth Symphony Orchestra, David Hill

'Christmas fantasy': VAUGHAN WILLIAMS: *Fantasy on Christmas carols* (with Donald Sweeney). *Wassail song; The blessed son of God.* FINZI: *In terra pax* (with Libby Crabtree, D. Sweeney). HOWELLS: *A spotless rose; Sing lullaby.* WARLOCK: *Lullaby my Jesus; Benedicamus Domino; Balulalow; Bethlehem down.* IRELAND (arr. HAZELL; BROWN): *The holy boy.* HOLST: *Christmas song: Personent hodie.* DELIUS: *Sleigh ride.*
*** Decca Dig. 444 130-2 [id.].

It is good to have a fine, modern version of Vaughan Williams's *Fantasia on Christmas carols* and a passionate account of Finzi's *In terra pax*, coupled with a selection of some of the finest individual English carols. Those of Warlock are especially delightful, especially *Balulalow* (with its treble solo), while the trebles also contribute to the delightful arrangement of Ireland's *The holy boy*. First-class singing and playing throughout and a lovely warm recording – in the demonstration bracket.

Wunderlich, Fritz (tenor)

'Great voice': Arias and excerpts from: MOZART: *Die Zauberflöte; Die Entführung aus dem Serail.* VERDI: *La Traviata* (with Hilde Gueden); *Rigoletto* (with Erika Köth); *Don Carlos* (with Hermann Prey). TCHAIKOVSKY: *Eugene Onegin.* LORTZING: *Zar und Zimmermann; Der Waffenschmied.* ROSSINI: *Il barbiere di Siviglia.* PUCCINI: *La Bohème* (with Hermann Prey). *Tosca.* Lieder: SCHUBERT: *Heidenröslein.* BEETHOVEN: *Ich liebe dich.* TRAD.: *Funiculi-funicula; Ein Lied geht um die Welt* (with R. Lamy Ch.).
(B) *** DG 431 110-2 [id.].

Here is 70 minutes of gloriously heady tenor singing from one of the golden voices of the 1960s. Mozart's *Dies Bildnis* makes a ravishing opener, and *Hier soll ich dich denn sehen* from *Die Entführung* is equally beautiful. Then come two sparkling excerpts from *La Traviata* with Hilde Gueden and some memorable Tchaikovsky, like all the Italian repertoire, sung in German. The Rossini excerpt is wonderfully crisp and stylish. Wunderlich is joined by the charming Erika Köth in *Rigoletto* and by Hermann Prey for the rousing *Don Carlos* duet (*Sie ist verloren . . . Er ist's! Carlos!*) and the excerpt from *Bohème*. Last in the operatic group comes the most famous *Tosca* aria, *Und es blitzen die Sterne* (not too difficult to identify in Italian) sung without excessive histrionics. The Schubert and Beethoven Lieder are lovely and, if the two final popular songs (with chorus) bring more fervour than they deserve, one can revel in everything else. Excellent recording throughout. It is a pity there are no translations or notes, but with singing like this one can manage without them. A splendid bargain.